Poets
American and British

Poets
American and British

Ian Scott-Kilvert
(for the British Council)

George Stade
Leonard Unger
A. Walton Litz
Editors in Chief

VOLUME 3

CHARLES SCRIBNER'S SONS
An Imprint of Macmillan Library Reference
NEW YORK

Charles Scribner's Sons
An imprint of Macmillan Library Reference
1633 Broadway
New York, NY 10019

Library of Congress Cataloging-in-Publication Data

Poets : American and British / Ian Scott-Kilvert . . . [et al.], editors in chief.
p. cm.
Includes bibliographical references and index.
ISBN 0-684-80605-3 (set : alk. paper). — ISBN 0-684-80608-8 (v. 1 : alk. paper)
1. American poetry—Bio-bibliography—Dictionaries. 2. English poetry—Bio-bibliography—Dictionaries. 3. American poetry—Dictionaries. 4. English poetry—Dictionaries. I. Scott-Kilvert, Ian.
PS308.P64 1998
821.009'03—dc21 98-36811
CIP

3 5 7 9 11 13 15 17 19 20 18 16 14 12 10 8 6 4 2

PRINTED IN THE UNITED STATES OF AMERICA

The paper used in this publication meets the minimum requirements of American National Standard for Information Sciences—Permanence of Paper for Printed Library Materials. ANSI Z39.48-1992.

Edwin Arlington Robinson
(1869–1935)

LOUIS COXE

GRANTED A REAL talent and an access to experience, a poet deserves the name and earns it chiefly by his honesty. It is never enough that he be up with or beyond the times; who knows what those are? Technical feats rise, shine, evaporate, and fall, and there are unread poets who could have taught Shakespeare lessons in prosody. The sources from which poets "steal" metaphors and ideas often show the difference between knowing all about poetry and being a poet: it is not a matter of know-how, for if it were, Abraham Cowley would be greater than John Milton and Edward Young than Samuel Johnson. What is necessary is to see and to say with that direct honesty of vision that is apparently accessible only to genius and is therefore to the ordinary critic the least readily detectable of poetic qualities. A passion torn to tatters, a fit of the vapors, or a commitment to slogans of whatever degree of sophistication does not argue a true poetic vision; what counts supremely is the double commitment to the Muse and to the view of things the Muse inspires. In many cases, poets take years to find the vision, to see it for what it is, and that seeing may be only momentary and fleeting, but we know ultimately whether the poet has seen indeed or whether he has merely faked and trumped up. Larger or smaller, deeper or shallower, vision truly seen and honestly shown marks the poet, and it may be said fairly enough that in few instances have the contemporary critics shared enough of the visionary power or the honesty to see the poet's for what they are.

Edwin Arlington Robinson is a poet of true vision and unimpeachable honesty. Lest that sound forbidding—suggestive of something crabbed, angular, and inept—one should add that he had a consummate mastery of versification and rhetoric, that he could pile on the colors with the best of them, and that he had the inventiveness to tease the mind with symbol and intellectual puzzle. He indulged these capacities from time to time, the latter most frequently, but not until his later years did he allow them to assume the upper hand. All of Robinson's best work is the product of a sensibility that was on guard against fraud, that concerned itself with making into form what vision had discovered. The word "seeing" occurs frequently in Robinson, on various levels of seriousness and relevance; for this poet honesty is not so much what one has as what one tries to achieve after however much time spent among deceptions, lies, illusions. He knew a great many people, including members of his own family, who perished by such chimeras. He was born into, and grew to full maturity in, a time that is a kind of *locus classicus* for all lies on whatever scale. See Henry Adams, the later works of Mark Twain, and any history of the years just before the Great War and of that war itself. The era marked Robinson, for good and for ill. It disillusioned him with democracy and with the classic New England liberalism, and it "dated" him hopelessly in the eyes of the later generation of poets and literary folk.

To an older friend he wrote from his deathbed in the New York Hospital: "I doubt if you would care much for Auden and Spender. They are for the youngsters." It is not untypical of the man that he should have read these poets and be in a position to speak of them, yet give the impression of being the old fogy; ironically he puts himself in the position of his correspondent, who was twenty years his senior, and sees perfectly the faults of that rigidity of taste and habit likely to come with age. The diffidence, the hesitancy, with which he always expressed and qualified opinions stayed with him all his life, even in the era of his apparent preeminence after achieving both fame and something like fortune. His fine poem "Hillcrest," written at the artists' summer colony in Peterborough, New Hampshire, which was founded and maintained by the widow of the musician Edward MacDowell, expresses his acute sense of the insignificance of human achievement and the ephemeral nature of any one man's claim to rightness. He was a considerable "lion" at the MacDowell Colony during his latter years and he enjoyed being lionized, yet he never forgot that " . . . great oaks return / To acorns out of which they grew." In 1925, with a Pulitzer prize and other awards to his credit (if that is the phrase!), he wrote thus to a friend asking for a *Blue Guide* to London: "I'm not going to London, but sometimes I like to take up that book. It is almost as exciting as an illustrated seed catalogue, and far more reliable."

Small wonder that the generation of Pound and Eliot did not find Robinson's work and aesthetic congenial, chiefly because they never took the trouble to read him, but also, and understandably, because the era of which Robinson was inevitably part had finally ended in the hitherto unknown destructiveness of World War I. The period between the American Civil War and the War to End War may seem to us in retrospect not to lack appeal; to those who lived in it, like Henry Adams and Mark Twain, it seemed the shabbiest, most degrading of times. We can read their separate records of it: *The Education of Henry Adams* and *The Gilded Age*; in the latter. Twain created the most memorable of all fictional persons representative of the promoter in that raucous era, Colonel Beriah Sellers, the immortal speculator and harebrained proponent of get-rich-quick. He might well have been the spiritual godfather of Robinson and of his entire generation.

Robinson's youth and young manhood, the years leading up to *The Torrent and the Night Before* (1896), seem to have been lived in a barren time indeed. He was born in the tiny village of Head Tide, Maine, in 1869, at the very dawn of the Gilded Age, and though the family moved very shortly thereafter to the larger town of Gardiner, Maine, on the Kennebec River, we today can see both the provinciality on the one hand and the national craze for speculation and wealth on the other which equally marked the Robinson family and many others of the period. Despite all that might be said of Maine's natural beauty, its classical New England heritage, its abiding interest in learning and literature, and its tough moral legacy of Puritanism (rather less severe in Maine than elsewhere in New England), the fact remains that the Gardiner of 1870–1900 was a typical American boom town with its trade in lumber, ice, and shipping as well as certain manufactures. The more substantial capitalists of the town had interests in western properties and speculative enterprises: lumber, land, railroads, mines. And just as the depredation of the land of Maine and other parts of the country typified the attitude of the exploiters, so did their driving, piratical Philistinism in the arts and culture generally set the tone of public and private taste. Poetry, real poetry, had to go underground. From the death of Emily Dickinson (and who had ever heard of her?) in 1886, and of Whitman in 1892, until the renascence at the time of World War I, there is almost literally nothing in the poetry of America. Stephen Crane died young and inchoate; all the early promise of Vachel Lindsay and Edgar Lee Masters turned to little or nothing much, and the one truly impressive, salient figure of this lonely time is that of the lonely, dedicated, self-deprecating man for whom, if ever for any poet, the time was out of joint.

Robinson's father had moved to Gardiner in anticipation of a boom in his business; he was concerned in the lumber trade and had ventured into speculation in western property. He was a man of a not insensitive nature and in different circumstances might have shown his oldest and youngest boys more sympathy. The poet's mother was a woman of some literary taste, though perhaps we may feel free to be skeptical of the quality of such taste as it impinged upon the sensibility of her son. It should be said that in Robinson's early years he read as poets usually do: widely, omnivorously, wholly without discrimination, and it may be that much that was bad had as strong an effect upon him as the good. Be that as it may, the good was not entirely lacking, in literature, education, and recreation. There was a literary set in Gardiner and notable among its members was Dr. Alanson Tucker Schumann, a physician and poet whose infatuation with poetry led him to Robinson when the latter was a boy in high school. Perhaps Robinson may have had him partly in mind when he spoke in "The Wandering Jew" of a "fealty that presents / The tribute of a tempered ear / To an untempered eloquence." But the boy learned a great deal from Schumann, particularly verse forms and a respect for them. Under that kindly tutelage Robinson wrote ballades, villanelles, rondeaus, and other forms so dear to the post-Pre-Raphaelite heart. Nor was the regimen anything but beneficial: Schumann was a taskmaster and Robinson learned a respect for scrupulous workmanship the results of which may be seen not only all through his work, but more directly in such early poems as the villanelle "The House on the Hill," which exhibits the typically Robinsonian merging of the old, traditional form with the laconic, sinewy plain diction that was both new and typical of the region, and "The Ballade of Broken Flutes," Robinson's statement of his mission as the bringer of a new kind of poetry. Is it mere coincidence that the poet's mother was descended from the family of America's first poet, Anne Bradstreet?

And of course Gardiner was the home of Laura E. Richards, the daughter of Julia Ward Howe who wrote "The Battle Hymn of the Republic." Mrs. Richards was an author and the friend of authors; whatever one may think of her taste and her own literary work, one must acknowledge both her great humanity and her insight. She practically dragged the young, shy poet out of hiding and into her ebullient, charming family, where Robinson found another home after his own had disintegrated. Here he found stimulation of various kinds: the companionship of Mrs. Richards, her architect husband, and their sons and daughters, and simple recognition as a poet. True, we may see in the influence of the family certain limiting factors, of taste and of ideas, but Mrs. Richards was certainly on sure ground in preferring and encouraging the lyrical rather than the philosophical Robinson. It would seem that Robinson himself took little advice from anyone throughout his career, but he took from the Richardses affection and a sense of identity as poet. Perhaps Miss Rosalind Richards is the woman of Hagedorn's hints (in his biography) and perhaps we shall know one day when the documents pertaining to the poet deposited in the Houghton Library at Harvard are made available.

Love and marriage were not to be for Robinson. Gardiner, the Tilbury Town of the poems, left a mark on him, in part because of its very nature as a town of its time and place and in part because of the personal tragedies and wounds he knew there. So many of the portraits of his early volumes seem drawn from life, his own or another's, that the reader never forgets what Gardiner meant to him always. For years the young man was to all intents and purposes an idler and a failure; the consciousness that he was so considered embittered him far beyond anything the actual opinion of his fellow townsmen seems to have warranted. Many admired and liked him, but it was not a merely parochial matter with Robinson: his response to the realization that he was indeed a poet is characteristically American. If art is considered trivial and idle in America, he might have said, then I can justify my life and work only by success. And success means publication and profits, money and position. After all, Gardiner, along with all America, strove mightily with Roscoe Conkling, the Stalwart Republican from New York, and President U. S. Grant for the power and the money that are success, and when in their turn Robinson's father and both brothers failed in the scramble, the young man might well have felt in his heart that he was doomed with the rest of his kin. He saw, in any event, a vision of American life that marked him permanently. The moral collapse of his brothers, on top of the horrible death by diphtheria of his mother and the disintegration of his father, could scarcely be accounted for by the philosophies and theologies of a century of New England storekeepers. After all, Puritanism no longer worked as a creed; Unitarianism had given way to Mrs. Eddy's gospel of Christian Science, and the sages of Concord provided pretty thin gruel to the hungry poet of the Grant-McKinley dispensation.

The young Robinson, classically, was a sensitive youth—he was born with his skin inside out, as he said himself—and though he had friends (friends were his passion) and loved his years at the Gardiner High School, he was always an enigma to his associates and to his family, who let him go his dreamy way, but scarcely thought that he would ever outshine the brilliant, handsome Dean, the oldest, or the driving, vital Herman, next in order. To a Freudian, all things are Oedipal and there is indeed a case for seeing in Robinson's life the familiar pattern of the unwanted third son, rejected, kindly enough, by the father and kept at a distance by a too-beloved mother. In his later years, Robinson seems to have gained help from a psychiatrist who was also a poet, Dr. Merrill Moore. Gardiner in the eighties and nineties knew no such amenities, and one may perhaps be permitted to feel a callous relief since if Robinson had the anguish, we have the poetry. Yet we must feel pity as well, for the years following Robinson's graduation from high school, with the exception of two at Harvard, must have been an almost unrelieved agony of soul. Dean, the star of the family, was breaking up under the influence of drugs; he contracted the habit while trying to force himself into the exhausting routine of a country doctor. The father, Edward Robinson, decayed physically while his investments vanished; Herman, now married and with two small daughters, somehow seemed to have lost his way. Colonel Beriah Sellers like a proper godfather had vowed things in Herman's name. Yet before the smash became total, E.A.R. had his two years as a special student at Harvard. Following a period of isolation and near-despair after his graduation from high school, Cambridge, Boston, and Harvard came as deliverers and saviors. The young poet learned something of languages and literatures, of taverns and aesthetics, of the theater and above all of opera, particularly Wagner. When the money gave out and he had to leave, he even then knew he had been saved, though Barrett Wendell, the critic and Harvard professor, years later, when Robinson told him he had to leave Harvard after two years, growled, "You were damn lucky." Perhaps he was.

Try as one will, one cannot help the conviction that throughout his life Robinson was the victim of the classic strategy of America with its artists, poets in particular, perhaps. It would seem that the formative years provide a diet too thin, too miserly and deficient in nutriment, the last years a regimen of indigestible fats: success, when and if it comes, comes with a vengeance, frequently confirming the artist in his worst faults and conferring on him both an authority of opinion beyond his competence and opportunities to sell not just his work but himself to commercial interests. But before Robinson could have reached any such position, he knew fully what neglect and unsuccess could be. His was for a time the world of the down-and-out, the panhandlers and outcasts. Abject poverty and slavery to alcohol went hand in hand. In later years he himself said that the only thing that saved him was that he never took a drink before six in the evening.

Yet the worst was isolation, isolation from the best minds of his time and from those whose work and thought might have been useful and encouraging to him. Kind, understanding, and helpful as Robinson's friends were (and indeed they kept him alive and in health for years with simple charity), they do not seem to us today men and women who could have helped him in his struggle to learn and to grow as a poet; in all humility, we must call them second-rate. Of the poets with whom he was well acquainted, three names stand out: William Vaughn Moody, Josephine Preston Peabody, and Ridgely Torrence, of whom the first two were far better known in their time than Robinson. There were literary figures of various shades of distinction among his friends and associates, notably Mrs. Richards, yet again there was none who seemed to have the insight into the true quality of his best work that would have helped the poet to grow. For all the voluminous correspondence with the literary and near literary which carried Robinson on through many years, there can be no escaping the conclusion that time, place, and circumstance conspired to deprive him of incentives toward development, growth, and change. His first book sets a pattern which will not be broken, and in his beginning is his end.

Robinson is a nineteenth-century product, a Romantic, and a scion of the New England stock. Did he not say himself that had he lived in the time of Brook Farm he would have been strongly tempted to go along? One can see in him the qualities that made a Jones Very, and although he repudiated both Thoreau and Emerson, as philosophers or thinkers, he admired Emerson's poetry, saturated himself in nineteenth-century prose and poetry, and generally conformed to the canons of taste of the sensitive, provincial, cultivated New Englander. It was some old atavistic urge that led him to Poe and to Hawthorne, to the darker side. He seems to have known nothing of Melville, though he liked Whitman and Twain, particularly the former, but it should be said that like most New Englanders of the age, his eyes were on England rather than his own country—for literature at least—and surely his love of Cowper and Crabbe shows how much more comfortable he was with traditional English verse than with that of the Decadents. He dismissed the *Yellow Book* as mere sensation. He seemed to feel kinship among poets of the nineties only with Kipling and Hardy. And all his tastes, like his ideas and convictions, came early and came to stay. In this as in so much else he is typical of his race and milieu, the New England eccentric with the eccentricity raised to genius and the right to his crotchets confirmed and made great by virtue of his earning and living that right to the end and with the utmost rigor. It is not too much to say that Robinson worked out to its conclusion and at large what Emily Dickinson, tentatively, found and named in the decay of the New England sensibility. The tradition still lives, and strongly, in the work of Robert Lowell, in whose dramatic soliloquies or monologues one may find the plain, vital influence of Robinson and his peculiar, involute syntax. *The Mills of the Kavanaughs* is Lowell's obeisance—and perhaps farewell—to his master.

After the destruction of family ties, for the most part, with Gardiner, Robinson went to live in New York, where he stayed almost without intermission, except for long summers at the MacDowell Colony, until his death in 1935. He knew poverty so great that he was often without proper food and clothing and lived on the charity of his friends. His first books made no impression on the "little sonnet men" who reviewed for magazines, nor did any periodicals think it worthwhile to publish this unknown when after all Clinton Scollard and George Edward Woodberry and many another sweetsinger were the acknowledged masters. Robinson's first two books were published at his own expense and that of friends, and the manuscript of *Captain Craig* (1902) languished in a brothel until the editor who had left it there came back, not presumably for the manuscript. He turned it down in any case. In 1905, President Theodore Roosevelt, who had heard of Robinson's work through his son Kermit, found a place, a sinecure, in the New York Custom House for the poet, and for four years Robinson knew financial independence. He also knew bondage to drink. At any rate, he did not write much in these years at the Custom House; it was an extended period of frustration which finally disappeared, and in 1910 he published *The Town Down the River.*

In this volume we may see the typically Robinsonian themes and approaches, but with possibly three exceptions, none of the poems represents the finest he could do. "For a Dead Lady" surely shows him at his best in one of his veins, and to a lesser extent and in a less formidable vein, "Two Gardens in Linndale." And "Momus" has a terse, bitter strength that characterizes the epigrammatic strain that is one of his most pungent. It would appear that in these years Robinson was looking for a stance, a position from which to view his own experience and his ideas. As he grew older and took to writing the long narrative poems, his tendency to become oracular, cryptic, and philosophical by turns overcame the achieved starkness of his view; moreover in his letters one may find evidence that Robinson, when he was at his best as poet, had no thoroughgoing idea of his own best qualities. At one time a young lady who was writing a graduate thesis on the philosophy in his work wrote to ask him certain questions. In his reply he told her that he wished she could concern herself less with the philosophy and more with the poetry, a recommendation we may properly wish the poet himself had adopted. For the fatal New England fascination with cloudy abstractions miscalled thought or profundity overcame Robinson and he never broke the spell, except as it would seem almost inadvertently. Even in as interesting a long narrative as *Amaranth* (1934) the nightmare atmosphere, the very real subject, the grim humor, and the subdued lyricism frequently get lost in the interminable rehashing of Favorite Transcendentalisms: what is Truth? or Reality? In the Arthurian trilogy of a few years before we can see much the same tendency.

Robinson is a late Romantic, a Victorian, a transcendentalist whose lust after the abstract was inveterate and nearly always, when indulged, destructive. The moment of stasis, of balance, when he treats the Vast with steady eye and nerve, is to be found in "The Man against the Sky" in the volume of that title (1916); he met the subject with all its imponderables and impalpables head on in that poem, and never fully recovered. Although "The Man against the Sky" solves nothing—and it is of course unfashionable to do other than dismiss it—it nonetheless seems to be almost the last time in literature (Western) when a poet singlehanded calls down the Eternal Verities and Cosmic Powers and asks them to declare themselves. It is an altogether remarkable performance and would have been wholly impossible for a more "sophisticated" poet; one knows why Mr. Eliot characterized Robinson as "negligible"; the direct attack is hardly the Eliot strategy.

Yet there are times and poems that put real questions and often imply real answers. Essentially, like any good poet, Robinson is less the philosopher than the metaphysician, and the question for him is the old ontological one. "The Man against the Sky" sums up the essence of Robinson's thought and feeling on the subject, thought and feeling which when they are working poetically prompt most of his best work, in both shorter lyrics and the poems of middle length. How does a man reconcile the idea of a beneficent, omnipotent God with the naked and frightening facts of existence? "What inexorable cause / Makes time so vicious in his reaping"? God or no God, for Robinson the true question is this: Is there a life after this one? If so, then it is all worth it, the suffering and the terror. If not, then why live? Yet in fact men do not often commit suicide, a phenomenon which Robinson seizes upon as a kind of proof that man does not end with the grave. Again and again, he will assert his belief in immortality and the ultimate importance of this life, while he utterly rejects materialism. Everywhere, in the poems, letters, and reported comment, such a deliberate choice of belief crops up, implied or stated. For all their polarities of style and rhetoric, "The Man against the Sky" and Wallace Stevens' "Sunday Morning" are complementary and classical views of the single question, and clearly emerge less from differing philosophies than from opposed temperaments. There is a will to doubt as well as to belief, and the existentialists' answer is not the only possible one. If truly philosophical influence on Robinson's views can be found, it seems clear, from Mr. Stevick's essay mentioned in the bibliography at the end of this essay, that William James played the leading part in such influence. Yet even here it should be noted that James himself emphasizes that in dealing with such matters, he has entered the realm of metaphysics, and Robinson's discomfort under the rubric "philosopher" ought to be taken at least as seriously as any quasi-philosophical propositions he may seem to enunciate.

Robinson was a poet and poems are made with words, yet as a man so conspicuously of his century and heritage he was often at war with mere language and all unknowingly. By his own testimony it was words that fascinated him, that made and kept him a poet and a fine one, though the New Englander and the Victorian in him insisted that he must be the Seer, the Prophet, the Unacknowledged Legislator. Small wonder that in the direct conflict of these tendencies poetry is sometimes annihilated, and grist to the Ph.D. mill accumulates. This is not to say that Robinson had no mind and no ideas; it is simply that he mistook speculation in verse for poetic thought, as did unnumbered nineteenth-century writers before him. Still, each time he got a long poem out of his system and had as it were satisfied the Transcendental Philosopher in him, he could turn to real poetry again, and in *The Three Taverns* (1920) and *Avon's Harvest* (1921) he published some half-dozen of his best poems; even in the volume *Dionysius in Doubt* (1925), the last of his books containing short lyrics, there are two of his best sonnets, "New England" and "The Sheaves," and one or two others of real quality. But after that, there are only the long narratives, for the most part one each year up to his death. Of these, only *Amaranth* would seem to bear repeated reading, and that in part for reasons not wholly artistic.

He had in a sense become a Man of Letters in the solid nineteenth-century sense of the term and the punctual appearance of a new volume seemed necessary to him—not, one supposes, because he needed the money as he himself claimed, but because publication, so long denied him, was both compensatory and reassuring. It made him as poet real to himself; when there was no book, there was no poet and no man, for rarely has an American poet lived in and for his work as did Robinson. One might say that apart from it, he had no life at all, at least after he went to New York to live. "If only they had said something about me! It would not have mattered what. They could have called me stupid or crazy if they liked. But they said nothing. Nobody devoted as much as an inch to me. I did not exist." If this, Robinson's own statement, is not absolutely true, it is near enough to full accuracy to convey the near-despair the poet must have felt during the years of total neglect. Friends helped, as did alcohol until it interfered with the poetry and then it was alcohol that had to go. But the lean years made a permanent and damaging mark on Robinson as poet, though they seem to have deepened his capacity as a man for the understanding of suffering, loneliness, and despair, as many of his letters testify. Deliberately reticent for fear of damaging self-exposure, he seems to have become more and more committed to one of his less attractive poetic characteristics, that of overqualification. Even in his letters, as apparently in conversation, his statements are frequently qualified by a deprecatory admission that the exact opposite may well be the case. Eventually this not unattractive personal quality is to become a stylistic tic and finally almost a major poetic device. In "Eros Turannos" we can note the modifying, qualifying lines and phrases. By the time of the long narratives, the tendency has solidified and we observe the not uncommon phenomenon of a poet's self-parody: his complication of the simple and his propensity for giving to us for complex what is merely complicated and obscured, in other words, over-qualified. These lines for *Cavender's House* (1929) illustrate the point:

He knew there was a woman with two
  hands
Watching him, but he saw no more of her
Than would assure him she was there. He
  feared
To see her face, and he feared not to see it;
And then he found it as it was before,
Languid and unrevealing. Her eyes closed,
And her lips moved as if repeating words
That had no meaning. . . .

Robinson tried, over a period of years, to write drama and fiction that would make some money—to no avail—and one suspects that in this case failure derived from a shortcoming he himself pointed out: he had no real subject. He later destroyed all his manuscripts of fiction, but two Ibsenite plays were published which leave no doubt that what is a bore in the poems is equally so in the plays. The truth is that the lack of a real subject in his later years, coupled with a growing inaptitude for straightforward storytelling, finally rendered narrative for the most part unavailable to him. The lines just quoted show how far he has come from the concrete and the sensuous and he will go even farther. Yet up until the last ten years of his life he was capable of first-rate work in various stanza forms, notably the sonnet.

Neglect, near-despair, and poverty had formed him and they worked themselves out to the bitter end even in the days of success. "Why don't they *read* me?" he would ask in mock despair. It was, and is, a good question and one surely that many a poet would like a fit answer to. They didn't read him because they did not like his tone of voice. For all that has been written of Robinson's originality, one is hard put to it to say precisely where the innovations lie. He is simple. Yet his vocabulary is frequently polysyllabic and his metric jingly and derived. He seems rarely to be aware of the natural world or of the city, or if he does use the city as locale it is only in the vaguest, most perfunctory way as a stylized background. None of the qualities we associate with the Imagists, with Pound or Eliot, or with the ferment of the period is here, nor is there a trace of Frost's feeling for and against nature and rural New England. Even as serenely autumnal and lovely a poem as "Isaac and Archibald" lacks the specific and the minutely noted detail we think of as central to "nature poetry," whatever that may be. It is far closer to Wordsworth than to Frost and perhaps to Cowper than to either of the others in feeling. But one cannot read Robinson expecting certain things and find what he has to tell. If in his own time editors and others dismissed him because they thought his work grim and "pessimistic" they were at least nearer the right track than those who, enamored of the Great Rebellion, thought of him as a stuffy, mindless Yankee who had failed to get the word. The fact is, of course, that Robinson, between two movements and two worlds, could not be accepted by either. When triumph and commercial success came, they came late and for the most part in response to relatively inferior work.

Robinson loved words. Shy and almost wholly inarticulate in company, he wrote with great labor and with total absorption; not unexpectedly, therefore, he frequently confused best and worst in his work and failed to see where the logic of his own poetic intelligence took him. In his love of the involute and the tangential, he is kin to Henry James; in his fascination with language and metric, to Tennyson. But in his penetrating, naked vision of the reality that underlies human predicaments he seems close to the French novelists of the late nineteenth century and to Ibsen. He professed dislike of Flaubert and he sometimes inveighed against the sexual concern of many of the naturalists, yet Zola and Whitman cast a spell on him, however briefly. Kipling's capacity to make poetry out of the commonplace interested and excited him, but more than all of these there was a Yankee eclecticism of language that made him go anywhere for words that would when pressed together make something hard, curious, and impenetrable. Milton, Shakespeare, Browning, Crabbe, Tennyson, Cowper, and a host of Romantics supply part of the vocabulary and the subject matter a vocabulary discovers for itself.

And what is the subject? the temper of it and the tone in which it comes to us? "When the stars are shining blue / There will yet be left a few / Themes availing— / And these failing, / Momus, there'll be you." Here is one of the faces of his Muse, and another was Pity; not tenderness or really what we would call sympathy, but pity for poor souls caught in the trap that their own weakness and fate have combined to spring. Viewed from the modern point of view, many of the best poems lack what is called compassion, as witness the destruction of Pink, Miss Watchman, and Atlas in *Amaranth.* We somehow demand that the poet express a feeling for the fates of his doomed victims. Robinson will not gratify the common expectations, for he is concerned to show the plight and to imply the terror and the rigor of the doom—a doom, one sees, both merited and gratuitous. When this fate is a secretion from the poem and not its nominal subject, the poem is likely to be terse, packed, and utterly objective: the poet presents certain people in certain predicaments and tells what happened. In nearly every case we can see that the issue is one of illusion overcoming the sense of reality. At times illusion is shown as something a character wills and achieves; a state which the person deliberately chooses as preferable to actuality or as providing the only alternative to suicide. Job's wife, Robinson implies, is the stern realist and recommends to Job that he "curse God and die." She has seized "the swift logic of a woman." But though many of Robinson's fated creatures do indeed doom themselves by failing to "see," as he puts it, there are occasionally those who, staking their lives and honors on "illusions," come through triumphantly.

Conrad might have understood these poems had he known them. For Robinson as for Conrad, illusion is the very stuff of living and the naked realist is either the complete and successful Romantic, or a suicide. Illusion is willed and forced into some kind of reality, or it is escape. And in the latter case, it will eventually destroy its slave. The mother in "The Gift of God" forces her wholly inaccurate dream of her son's worth into what is for her the realm of fact which nothing can violate because it rests on limitless unselfish love. The wife in "Eros Turannos" has chosen to deceive herself but has reached a point at which the extent of the deception and its origins are about to reveal themselves—with destruction inevitable. In "Veteran Sirens" the women who "cry out for time to end his levity" have discovered that the joke is on them and not on anyone else; the wife of "The Mill" needs only to know what she knows and to have heard her husband say "There are no millers any more." After that, what else can happen than does?

In creating his effects of fate and of "levity," Robinson relies heavily on a hard surface of objective statement, an intermittent current of humor—from gentle to sardonic—and a metric that seems frequently at odds with the subject matter, as though a pastoral elegy should be set to the tune of "Jingle Bells." The tripping, sometimes metronomic, measure alternates with sonorities, as the language alternates between the homely phrase and the "grand manner." In "Mr. Flood's Party" we see a similar technique in imagery: the juxtaposition of the grand and the ordinary, Eben Flood with his jug of hard cider to his lips "like Roland's ghost, winding a silent horn." The image and the language are at once evocative, original, and straight out of the tradition. And they are meant to be, for the "larger humor of the thing," as Robinson says in another place. The very objectivity with which Robinson views his destroyed and self-destroying characters allows him to forgo compassion and to present their plights with humor while he never shirks the rigor and the pity of the particular destiny. It is an appeal to us, as readers, to apply the same technique to our own capacities for self-deception, to see ourselves as "the clerks of time" or to watch "great oaks return / To acorns out of which they grew." The humor and levity arise from Robinson's refusal, when he is at his best, to consider human error as necessarily cosmically tragic. His Captain Craig, indomitable in defeat and death, is in fact a failure not only in the world's eyes, but in the eyes of the perceptive beholder and perhaps in his own too. And of course Robinson implies that all men are failures in this sense; "poets and kings are but the clerks of time." Hence "the larger humor," the levity, can be felt only by sensibilities realistic enough to understand their own plights and to relate those plights to the whole human condition.

Of course, there are occasions and poems when this sort of humor will not do, will not answer the call of a spirit too appalled at the workings of fate to achieve the right tone. In much of Robinson's work there is another face to the god of reality and understanding. Some facts are too horrible to face and too gratuitously violent for understanding. Poems like "For a Dead Lady" and "The Mill" belong to this category. In the former there is no attempt whatever at mitigating the horror or at achieving acceptance or understanding. Such things are simply *there.* To understand would be to play God; to accept would be demonic. On the whole, this side of the Robinsonian subject is less common than the former; it is not, for example, commonly to be seen at all in the longer poems, where frequently violent acts, often perverted acts, create denouement or tragic conflict almost as though violence has for Robinson taken the place of what might be termed the irrational principle in life. In *Lancelot* and *Amaranth,* to cite two of Robinson's best long narratives, understanding, acceptance, and the promise of a new life form the very basis of the subject and the theme, but it must be confessed that some of Robinson's finest work moves in the direction of stating or implying that at the center of our existence is something implacable, irrational, and not to be propitiated. The old cliché often used of Robinson that he celebrated the success of failure and the failure of success has only a limited application, notable in such a poem as "Old Trails"; actually, he found little reward in failure as such, nor do his failures like Captain Craig and Eben Flood in any sense "triumph"; they are as deluded as the man who congratulates himself on his success. Men fall short of essential humanity and it is here that Robinson's irony usually comes into play, in poems which treat of people in particular situations which show them as inadequate to the human demands made upon them. These poems have plot, action, place, and time; they nearly always involve a man or a woman who is confronted with a situation, involving others, which demands a radical reappraisal of the self and one's conduct. The character is called upon to discard a cherished image of himself, plights to the whole human condition. and nearly always, in refusing or failing to do so, the character suffers disaster.

In order to see how Robinson works out the fates of such people in such poems, it might be well to look closely at two or three of the best examples and try to see what goes on. The best poems of the sort described have a dense, deceptive surface, organized in a seemingly careful, orderly way and proceeding quietly, baldly almost, while the narrator subtly assumes the point of view of the reader and imperceptibly helps him to assess and understand, finally leaving with him the realization that the ending is both inevitable and wholly human. The following analyses, then, attempt to show how certain of Robinson's best poems, each representative of a different aspect of the Robinsonian subject, achieve the desired effect.

"Eros Turannos" unfolds as narrative, compressed and suggestive yet without the trickery that occasionally irritates us, as in the case of "The Whip" or "How Annandale Went Out." Most noticeably, the language is general, the tone expository, the purpose of the poem communication rather than expression. Adumbrated in the first stanza, certain images, whose latent power and meanings are reserved until the final lines, have the function of motifs, repeated constantly and expanded as the poem opens out into suggestion. There are three such images or symbols: waves, tree, stairs leading down. Throughout, these symbols control and provide a center for the meanings possible to the poem, and from the mention of "downward years" and "foamless weirs" in the first stanza to the triple vision of the last four lines these elements recur, the same but altered. As is the case with so many Robinson poems, the reader must supply, from the general materials provided, his own construction, yet the poet has seen to it that there can be only one possible final product. The poem contains two complementary parts: the abstract, generalized statement and the symbolic counterpart of that statement, each constituting a kind of gloss upon the other; each moves through the poem parallel to the other, until at the end they become fused in the concrete images. In addition to the three symbols mentioned, we find also that of blindness and dimness, summed up in the single word "veil" yet continually present in the words "mask," "blurred," "dimmed," "fades," "illusion." All this culminates in the sweeping final image: "Or like a stairway to the sea / Where down the blind are driven." Yet such inner order, such tight articulation as these examples may indicate, derives no more from the concrete than from the generalized; contrary to Marianne Moore's professed belief, not all imaginary gardens need have actual toads in them, nor, conversely, do we have to bother with the toad at all if our garden is imagined truly enough. What we must have is room—for toads or non-toads, but room anyhow, and Robinson seems to say that there will be more room if we don't clutter the garden with too many particular sorts of fauna and flora. For in "Eros Turannos" we are not told the where or the wherefore; only, and it is everything, the how and the just so. In the hinted-at complexity of the woman's emotion, in the suggested vagueness of the man's worthlessness, lies the whole history of human trust and self-deception: none shall see this incident for what it really is, and the woman who hides her trouble has as much of the truth as "we" who guess and guess yet, the poem implies, without coming nearer to the truth than men usually do.

"Eros Turannos" is the Robinsonian archetype, for in it we can find the basic elements, the structural pattern, that he was to use frequently and with large success. The most cursory reading affords a glimpse into the potential power as well as the dangers of such a form; Robinson's use of it provides examples of both. In the poem in question he reaches an ultimate kind of equipoise of statement and suggestion, generalization and concretion. The first three words of the poem set the tone, provide the key to a "plot" which the rest will set before us. "She fears him": simple statement; what follows will explore the statement, and we shall try to observe the method and evaluate its effect.

> She fears him, and will always ask
>   What fated her to choose him;
> She meets in his engaging mask
>   All reasons to refuse him;
> But what she meets and what she fears
> Are less than are the downward years,
> Drawn slowly to the foamless weirs
>   Of age, were she to lose him.

The epigrammatic tone of the verse strikes one immediately; we are aware that here is a kind of expository writing, capable in its generality of evoking a good deal more than the words state. Important though unobtrusive imagery not only reinforces and enriches the exposition but by calculated ambiguity as well sets a tone of suspense and fatality. The man wears a mask: he conceals something that at once repels and attracts her; notice the play on "engaging" and the implications that involves. The motif is an important one for the poem, as is that contained in the metaphor of "weirs," since these two suggestions of deception, distrust, entrapment, blindness, and decline will be continually alluded to throughout the poem, to find an ultimate range of meaning in the final lines.

The second stanza will in such expressions as "blurred" and "to sound" keep us in mind of the motifs mentioned, without actually requiring new imagistic material or forcing us to re-imagine the earlier metaphors. The intent here is not to be vague but to retain in the reader's consciousness what has gone before as that consciousness acquires new impressions. Hence, in stanza three, Robinson can now introduce a suggestive sketch of the man's nature while he reminds of the woman's and continues to explore it:

A sense of ocean and old trees
  Envelops and allures him;
Tradition, touching all he sees,
  Beguiles and reassures him;

That engaging mask of his becomes apparent to us here in this man who finds a solace and security in the love of his wife and in her solid place in the community, and yet the inister note first sounded in the image of "weirs" is lightly alluded to in the phrase "a sense of ocean." Moreover, that he too is "beguiled" presents a possibility of irony beyond what has yet been exploited.

And all her doubts of what he says
Are dimmed with what she knows of days—
Till even prejudice delays
  And fades, and she secures him.

The possibilities are many. We grasp readily enough the pathos of her situation: a woman with a worthless husband, proud and sensitive to what the town is whispering yet ready to submit to any indignity, to close her eyes and ears, rather than live alone. Surely a common enough theme in American writing and one that allows the poet to suggest rather than dramatize. Again, in "dimmed" we catch an echo of what has gone before, and in the last two lines the abstract noun "prejudice" with its deliberately general verbs "delays" and "fades" presents no image but rather provokes the imagination to a vision of domestic unhappiness familiar to us all, either in fiction or empirically. And of course the finality of "secures," ironic neither in itself nor in its position in the stanza, takes on irony when we see what such security must be: the woman finds peace only by blinding herself and by seeing the man as she wishes to see him.

Stanza four once again recapitulates and explores. Statement alternates with image, the inner suffering with the world's vision of it:

And home, where passion lived and died,
Becomes a place where she can hide,
While all the town and harbor side
  Vibrate with her seclusion.

If this stanza forms the climax of the plot, so to speak, the next comes to a kind of stasis, the complication of events and motives and themes we see so often in Henry James. The outside world of critical townspeople, hinted at before, now comes to the foreground, and we get a complication of attitudes and views—the world's, the woman's, the man's, our own—and the poet's is ours too. Yet even in a passage as seemingly prosaic and bare as this, Robinson keeps us mindful of what has gone before. In stanza four such words as "falling," "wave," "illusion," "hide," and "harbor" have served to keep us in mind of the various themes as well as to advance the plot, and in the fifth stanza Robinson presents us with a series of possible views of the matter, tells us twice that this is a "story," reiterates that deception and hiding are the main themes, as in the metaphorical expression "veil" and in the simple statement "As if the story of a house / Were told, or ever could be." And at last, in the final lines, thematic, narrative, and symbolic materials merge in the three images that accumulate power as they move from the simple to the complex, from the active to the passive, from the less to the more terrible:

Though like waves breaking it may be,
Or like a changed familiar tree,
Or like a stairway to the sea
  Where down the blind are driven.

For the attentive reader the narrative cannot fail; Robinson has given us the suggestive outline we need and told us how, in general, to think about this story. He has kept us constantly aware of place, time, actors, and action even though such awareness is only lightly provoked and not insisted on. In the last stanza the curious downward flow of the poem, the flow of the speculation, reaches an ultimate debouchment—"where down the blind are driven." Apart from the metrical power, the movement of the poem is significant; Robinson has packed it with words that suggest descent, depth, and removal from sight, so that the terrible acceptance of the notion that we must "take what the god has given" becomes more terrible, more final as it issues out in the logic of statement and imagery and in the logic of the plot.

If much of the poem's power depends upon the interaction of statement and suggestion, still another source of energy is the metric. Robinson here uses a favorite device of his, feminine rhymes, in alternating tetrameter and trimeter lines, and gives to soft-sounding, polysyllabic words important metrical functions; as a result, when he does invert a foot or wrench the rhythm or use a monosyllable, the effect is striking out of all proportion to its apparent surface value. Surely the plucking, sounding quality of the word "vibrate" in the last line of the fourth stanza is proof of this, though equally effective is the position of "down" and "blind" in the final line of the poem.

Contemporary verse has experimented with meters, rhyme, and rhythm to such an extent that one has to attune the ear to Robinson's verse; at first it sounds jingly and mechanical, perhaps inept, but after we make a trial of them, the skill, the calculation, have their way and the occasional deviations from the set pattern take on the greater power because they are deviations:

> Pity, I learned, was not the least
> Of time's offending benefits
> That had now for so long impugned
> The conservation of his wits:
> Rather it was that I should yield,
> Alone, the fealty that presents
> The tribute of a tempered ear
> To an untempered eloquence.

This stanza from "The Wandering Jew" shows the style. This is mastery of prosody—old-fashioned command of the medium. The reversing of feet, use of alternately polysyllabic and monosyllabic words of syncopation ("To an untempered eloquence") are devices subtly and sparingly used. The last stanza of the same poem gives another instance, and here the running on of the sense through three and a half lines adds to the effect:

> Whether he still defies or not
> The failure of an angry task
> That relegates him out of time
> To chaos, I can only ask.
> But as I knew him, so he was;
> And somewhere among men to-day
> Those old, unyielding eyes may flash,
> And flinch—and look the other way.

Deviation implies a basic pattern, and although in many cases, particularly in the blank-verse narratives, syllable counting mars the prosody, nonetheless the best poems subtly attune themselves to the "tempered ear," syncopate on occasion, and jingle to good effect.

This analysis is technical and only partial; it seems to presuppose that we must lapse into Cleanth Brooks's "heresy of paraphrase." Granted. Yet this but begs a question, inasmuch as all of Robinson's poetry assumes that one will want to find the paraphrasable element the poet has carefully provided. These are poems *about* something, and what the something is we must discover. That is why we should consider Robinson as a poet with a prose in view; to read "Eros Turannos" or "For a Dead Lady" or "The Gift of God" is to feel that the scope of a long naturalistic novel has emerged from a few stanzas. Yet Allen Tate, in a brief essay, says that Robinson's lyrics are "dramatic" and that T. S. Eliot observes this to be a characteristic of the best modern verse. One is really at a loss to know what the word "dramatic" means in this regard; Robinson's poetry is not dramatic in any sense of the word commonly accepted, unless it be that Robinson, like Henry James, frequently unfolds a scene. To look for anything like drama in the poems is idle, in that the excitement they convey is of a muted sort, akin to that which James himself generates. This poet wears no masks; he is simply at a distance from his poem, unfolding the "plot," letting us see and letting us make what applications we will. This directness, this prose element, in Robinson's verse is easy enough to find, less so to define or characterize. One can say this, however: just as Pope was at his best in a poetry that had morality and man in society as its subject matter and its criterion, so Robinson is happiest as a poet when he starts with a specific human situation or relationship, with a "story." "Eros Turannos" is *about* the marriage of untrue minds, but specifically it is not about just untrueness and minds; it is about untrue man A and suffering, self-deluding woman B, as well as about those worldly wisemen who conjecture and have all the "dope." Usually unsuccessful in speculative verse, Robinson excels in just this naturalistic case history, this story of a Maine Emma Bovary. If the theme is still failure, Robinson rings a peculiar change upon it, since at last the poem forces us to accept the implication that there *is* and must be a "kindly veil between / Her visions and those we have seen"; that all of us must "take what the god has given," for failure is, in Robinson's world, the condition of man and human life. We do the best we can. In "Old Trails," the best one can is not often good, and what is indeed success in the world's eyes has a very shoddy look to those who recognize the success as merely "a safer way / Than growing old alone among the ghosts." It is the success of Chad in James's *The Ambassadors*, who will go home to the prosperous mills and Mamie and Mom, not that of Strether, who could have had the money and the ease but took the way of "growing old among the ghosts."

A briefer, more compact poem than "Old Trails," one that deals with another aspect of the theme, is the sonnet "The Clerks," which for all its seeming spareness is a very rich, very deft performance. The octave opens colloquially, gives us a general location and an unspecified number of clerks; the speaker is the poet, as poet and as man. Robinson draws an evocative, generalized sketch of the clerks' past, of their prime as well as of the slow attrition of time and labor, and affirms that despite the wear they have sustained these men are still good and human. It is in the sestet that the poem moves out into suggestion, that it implies a conceit by which we can see how all men are clerks, time-servers, who are subject to fears and visions, who are high and low, and who as they tier up also cut down and trim away. To call the poem a conceit is no mere exercise of wit, for Robinson has clearly punned on many unobtrusive words in the sonnet. What is the clerks' "ancient air"? Does it mean simply that the men are old and tired? or that their manner is one of recalling grand old times of companionship that never really existed? or that one must take "air" literally to mean their musty smell of the store? These possibilities are rendered the more complex by the phrase "shopworn brotherhood" immediately following, for then the visual element is reinforced, the atmosphere of shoddiness and shabbiness, of Rotary club good-fellowship, and the simple language has invested itself with imagistic material that is both olfactory and visual. And of course, one may well suspect sarcasm in the assertion that "the men were just as good, / And just as human as they ever were." How good were they? Yet lest anyone feel this is too cynical, Robinson carefully equates the clerks with "poets and kings."

As is the case with "Eros Turannos," this poem proceeds from the general to the specific and back to the general again, a generality now enlarged to include comment on and a kind of definition of the human condition. Throughout there have been ironic overtones, ironic according to the irony we have seen as peculiarly Robinsonian in that it forms one quadrant of the total view. It has to do here with the discrepancy between the vision men have of their lives and the actuality they have lived. The poet here implies that such discrepancy, such imperfection of vision is immutably "human" and perhaps therefore, and ironically, "good." That the clerks (and we are all clerks) see themselves as at once changed and the same, "fair" yet only called so, serves as the kind of lie men exist by, a lie that becomes an "ache" on the one hand and the very nutriment that supports life on the other. You, all you who secretly cherish some irrational hope or comfort, merely "feed yourselves with your descent," your ancestry, your career, your abject position miscalled a progress. For all of us there can be only the wastage, the building up to the point of dissatisfaction, the clipping away to the point of despair.

Despite the almost insupportable rigor of Robinson's attitude, we can hardly accuse him of cynicism or of hopelessness. In every instance his view of people is warm and understanding, not as the patronizing seer but as the fellow sufferer. Such feeling informs the poems we have discussed and fills "The Gift of God" with humanity no cynic could imagine, no despair encompass. For in this poem the theme of failure turns once more, this time in an unexpected way so that we see Robinson affirming self-deception of this specific kind as more human, more the gauge of true love than all the snide fact-finding the rest of the world would recommend. The poem is about a mother's stubborn, blind love for a worthless (or perhaps merely ordinary) son, and this in the teeth of all the evidence her neighbors would be delighted to retail. Again, the poem is a compact narrative; again the irony exists outside the poem, not in its expression. As in so many of the best poems, Robinson says in effect: here is the reality, here is the illusion. *You* compare them and say which is which and if possible which is the correct moral choice.

The metaphorical material we can roughly classify as made up of imagery relating to royalty, apotheosis, sacrifice, and love. From the first few lines we are aware of a quality which, by allusion to the Annunciation and the anointing of kings, establishes the mother's cherished illusion and thereby makes acceptance of the emergent irony inescapably the reader's duty; he must compare the fact and the fiction for and by himself; Robinson will not say anything in such a way as to make the responsibility for choice his own rather than the reader's. He will simply render the situation and leave us to judge it, for all of Robinson's poems presuppose an outside world of critics and judges, of ourselves, people who see and observe more or less clearly. His irony is external; it lies in the always hinted-at conflict between the public life and the private, between the thing seen from the inside and from the outside, with the poet, the speaker, presenting a third vision, not one that reconciles or cancels the other two, but one which simply adds a dimension and shows us that "everything is true in a different sense."

If the dominant motifs in "The Gift of God" are as indicated above, the progression of the poem follows undeviatingly the pattern suggested. In the first stanza Annunciation; the second, Nativity; the third, vision; the fourth, a stasis in which the mother seems to accept her son's unusual merit and her own vision of him as real; the fifth, a further extension of vision beyond anything actual; the sixth, the culmination of this calculated vision in the apotheosis. More than a schematized structure, the poem depends not only on the articulation of motifs and a plot, but equally on symbolic material that interacts with the stated or implied events in the "plot." Thus, from the outset the poet has juxtaposed the illusory vision and the "firmness" of the mother's faith in it; the language has a flavor of vague association with kingship, biblical story, and legend, notably conveyed by such words as "shining," "degree," "anointed," "sacrilege," "transmutes," and "crowns." Yet in the careful arrangement of his poem Robinson has not oversimplified the mother's attitude. She maintains her "innocence unwrung" (and the irony of the allusion is not insisted on) despite the common knowledge of people who know, of course, better, and Robinson more than implies the innocence of her love in the elevated yet unmetaphorical diction he uses. Not until the final stanza does he open the poem out, and suddenly show the apotheosis in the image of "roses thrown on marble stairs," subtly compressing into the last three lines the total pathos of the poem, for the son ascending in the mother's dream is "clouded" by a "fall": the greatness his mother envisions is belied by what we see. And who is in the right? For in the final turn of the "plot," is it not the mother who gives the roses of love and the marble of enduring faith? Is the dream not as solid and as real as human love can make it? If we doubt this notion, we need only observe the value Robinson places on the verb "transmutes" in stanza five: "*Transmutes* him with her faith and praise." She has, by an absolute miracle of alchemy, transmuted base material into precious; by an act of faith, however misplaced, found the philosopher's stone, which is love wholly purged of self.

What we have come to realize is that in these poems we have been considering we are concerned with narrative—narrative of a peculiar kind in which the story is not just about the events, people, and relationships but about the very poetic devices which are the vehicle of the narration and its insights. In "The Gift of God" symbol and theme have a narrative function; they must do in brief and without obtrusiveness what long passages of dialogue, exposition, and description would effect in a novel. As a result, the reader is compelled to take the entire poem in at once; he either "understands" it or he does not. Naturally there are subtleties which emerge only after many readings; yet because these poems are narratives, Robinson must concentrate upon communication, upon giving us a surface that is at once dense yet readily available to the understanding.

> As one apart, immune, alone,
> Or featured for the shining ones,
> And like to none that she has known
> Of other women's other sons,—
> The firm fruition of her need,
> He shines anointed; and he blurs
> Her vision, till it seems indeed
> A sacrilege to call him hers.

This is on one hand simple telling of plot: the mother sees her son as unique and feels unworthy to be his mother. Simple enough. But the story is more than this, more than a cold telling of the facts about the mother's vision of her son. We see on the other hand that it is her need of the son, and of the vision of him, which complicates the story, while the suggestion of kingship, ritual, and sacrifice in the diction, with the implication of self-immolation and deception, further extends the possibilities of meaning.

All this we grasp more readily than we may realize, for Robinson prepares for his effects very early and while he extends meaning is careful to recapitulate, to restate and reemphasize the while he varies and complicates:

> She sees him rather at the goal,
> Still shining; and her dream foretells
> The proper shining of a soul
> Where nothing ordinary dwells.

In these lines Robinson affirms the mother's illusion—it is a "dream" that "foretells"—and recapitulates the theme of kingship, of near-divinity, in the repetition of "shining." The stanza that follows gives the poem its turn, states specifically that the son is merely ordinary, that the mother deludes herself, that her motive in so doing is "innocent," and in stanza five the poem, as we have seen, turns once more, pivots on the verb "transmute," turns away from the simple ironical comparison we have been experiencing and reveals a transmuted relationship: son to mother, vision to fact, and an ultimate apotheosis of the mother under the guise of a mistaken view of the son. The poem is about all these things and is equally about the means of their accomplishment within the poem. This is a poetry of surfaces, dense and deceptive surfaces to be sure but still a poetry that insists on the communication of a whole meaning, totally and at once:

> She crowns him with her gratefulness,
> And says again that life is good;
> And should the gift of God be less
> In him than in her motherhood,
> His fame, though vague, will not be small,
> As upward through her dream he fares,
> Half clouded with a crimson fall
> Of roses thrown on marble stairs.

The recapitulation, the tying together, of the symbolic and thematic materials serves in this, the last stanza, a narrative as well as an expressive purpose. The tone is epigrammatic rather than prosaic and must shift delicately, come to the edge of banality, then turn off and finally achieve a muted sublimity that runs every risk of sentimentality and rhetoric yet never falters. The verse requires of us what it requires of itself: a toughness that can encompass the trite and mawkish without on the one hand turning sentimental itself or on the other resorting to an easy irony. The technique is the opposite of dramatic in that Robinson leaves as much to the reader as he possibly can; he uses no persona; the conflict-in-action before our eyes, as it unfolds itself at once, passes through complications, and returns to the starting point, the same yet altered and, to some degree, understood. To this extent Robinson is ratiocinative rather than dramatic; what we and the characters themselves think about the "plot" is as important as the plot, becomes indeed the full meaning of the plot.

Here, again, Robinson is likely to seem behind the times to certain readers. The narrative mode is unpopular in contemporary verse, and even poems about people who are not legendary or at least historical seem to be out of fashion. But the form is an old and honorable one with practitioners as variously gifted as Crabbe, Chaucer, Skelton, Prior, Tennyson, Browning, Kipling, certain Pre-Raphaelites and Decadents, a not inconsiderable company. And Wordsworth made a form of his own of it. Nearly always, the temptation is to move to the long narrative, the viability of which in recent decades is a vexed question. Nonetheless, however strongly dramatic monologue persists in our own era, the narrative lyric has largely disappeared, largely because of the tendency of most modern poetry to be, on the one hand, abstract, philosophical, didactic, or, on the other, rhapsodic, quasi-mystical, symbolist. Certain of the best practitioners in each mode transcend boundaries and mingle the two; one thinks of Stevens and Yeats here. But a Hart Crane, a Dylan Thomas, a Pound: these poets have a particular country from which they rarely stray with success. Robinson had, of course, a historical and local advantage: the nineteenth century was still available to him as an influence and a source, and his upbringing served to keep him isolated, during his formative years, from a too-doctrinaire rejection of his heritage. There is a disadvantage in rebellion and experiment, as there is in indiscriminate acceptance. Robinson took over much Romantic feeling and practice because it suited him. What did not suit him in it was its diction, it remoteness from real experience, and its mere rhetoric. For him, the narrative lyric represented an eclectic form combining many sorts of Romantic poetry, but with the superaddition of a new vocabulary, a sense of real life in a particular time and place, and a zeal for solid truth. Hence his deliberate omission from *Tristram* of the love potion. That was too much to swallow!

For all that has been said of the shorter poems, we are still left with the vexed question of the blank-verse narratives, the longer and the shorter. Clearly, any attentive reader will single out for first place among the latter such poems as "Isaac and Archibald," "Aunt Imogen," "Rembrandt to Rembrandt," and "The Three Taverns." All are notable for the absence of that garrulity which grew on Robinson, particularly in the last decade of his life, as well as for their structure and genuine intellectual content: in them Robinson thinks as a poet doing a job of work should think. The first is a New England pastoral, muted yet rich in tone, gently ironic yet lyrical, and marked by the poet's characteristic humorous self-deprecation as well as his insight into both youth and age. The second poem, less ambitious perhaps, is a marvel of escape from a trap that seems to promise certain capture in sentimentality; it is the story of an old maid who finds her annual emotional release in a month's stay with her sister and her children. What saves the poem is its utter honesty of feeling and language; the poem is not about pathos—pathos simply leaks out of the plain account the poet gives. But "Rembrandt to

Rembrandt," a more ambitious piece, addresses itself to the problem of the solitary artist and in so doing is even more intimately autobiographical in feeling than the others. Again, the poem never makes the mistake of being about its own emotions; Robinson here concentrates on the artist's agonized yet sardonic assessment of his own plight. There is no solution, no dedication to the higher aims; only the realization that he moves among demons of self-doubt, self-delusion, and self-pity. Something of the same kind appears in "The Three Taverns," in which St. Paul seems to be analyzing for us the relative importance of faith and the Law. And here Robinson, abandoning a heritage of Calvinism and a more recent tradition of Puritan fideism, comes out strongly, in the persona of Paul, for a faith at once personal and based on authority, ruled finally by wisdom slowly and painstakingly acquired. There are to be few sudden visions and visitations and those only for the elect.

If the foregoing remarks indicate, as they should, that in these shorter narratives Robinson is doing the poet's work with economy, high intelligence, and skill, what is to follow must of necessity show the other side of the coin. One must say candidly that with the exception of parts of the Arthurian cycle and of *Amaranth,* all the later long narratives are arid, badly thought out, and, as it were, tired. The reasons for this decay appear earlier and there is no need to rehearse them. Briefly, however, here are some of the qualities which these long poems show.

Merlin (1917), *Lancelot* (1920), and *Tristram* (1927) make up the Arthurian cycle and for all their failings surely treat the epic Arthurian theme with greater meaning and importance than do any other works of modern times, T. H. White's possibly excepted. The poems are of course allegorical in conception, at least in the case of the first two, and *Lancelot* really comes close to maintaining a successful interplay of the actual and the symbolic on an extended scale. Yet we have to admit that Robinson's besetting sins, the overelaboration of the obvious and whimsical garrulity, always potential in his work, here begin to exert their fatal influence. Everything Robinson wrote in blank verse in the last fifteen or twenty years of his life is too long, too diffuse, too manneristic. One feels that, like James, Robinson began to enjoy his own work too much, the sound of his own voice tended to intoxicate him. But enough—there are superb passages in *Merlin* and the characters of Vivian and Merlin are real and believable; Lancelot, Arthur, and Guinevere are also powerfully imagined, particularly Lancelot in the poem of that name. If Gawain is hopelessly tedious with the tedious whimsy that grew on Robinson, the figure of Lancelot emerges as heroic, human yet larger than life, a great soldier and a man of noble nature.

Fundamentally, the weakness of the whole cycle derives from Robinson's uneasy poetic and structural compromise: here is myth, symbol, allegory, yet here equally are men and women of the twentieth century. Reconciliation of these disparate parts is, if not impossible, at least an immensely formidable task. Robinson comes close to success in *Lancelot* only because myth, symbol, and allegory disappear when the poem is at its best and we have the powerfully conveyed triangular affair of Arthur, Guinevere, and Lancelot. In *Tristram*—Robinson's great popular success—there is much lyric beauty but the poem is fatally flawed by a love affair at once sticky and verbose and by characters more reminiscent of routine historical novels than of men and women out of myth and legend. And the later narratives, though perhaps less embarrassing in their portrayals of love and lovers, do fatally remind one of *Redbook,* if only in the names of heroines: Laramie, Gabrielle, Natalie, Karen. Only *Amaranth,* in returning to the old subject of failure and self-delusion in artists, touches reality and by fits and starts finds life and meaning. Robinson's last poem, *King Jasper* (1935), is another raid on the abstract by way of allegory and shows the poet's exhaustion—he was on his deathbed when it was completed—as do perhaps to some extent all these late narratives. "A series of conversations terminated by an accident." This dismissal of Ibsen's *A Doll's House* quoted by Yeats might serve to characterize the general effect of these poems on the modern reader, and if it seems sweeping and harsh, any qualifications can serve only to mitigate the judgment, not revoke it.

Yet Robinson stands alone among American poets in his devotion to the long poem. *Captain Craig* remains unique in our annals, rivaled in England by one or two of John Masefield's. In the narrative poem of moderate length, like "Isaac and Archibald," there is no one to touch him; Wordsworth's "Michael" and Keats's "Lamia" would seem the sole competitors in the genre throughout modern times. Robinson of course precedes Frost, in both time and originality, as a writer of short narratives. Frost's "The Death of the Hired Man," for example, lacks both the verbal complexity and the metrical subtlety of Robinson; when Frost turns to such a poem as "Out, Out," however, he is on firm ground indeed where none can outdo him. Both poets clearly find the compressed, elliptically told story their "supreme fiction." It is entirely possible that certain readers can never bring themselves to enjoy verse of this sort—muted, ironic, understated. For some, Robinson is less exciting than, say, Wallace Stevens, born only ten years after Robinson, just as Coleridge seems to many readers more exciting than Wordsworth, Hopkins more daring and absorbing than Tennyson. One might put it this way: Robinson in his best work has no specific religious or philosophical position to recommend, as neither Keats nor Wordsworth has; Hopkins, Stevens, Pound—these are poets who want to sell us something, a theory, a set of ideas or principles. If we like the principles we will love the poetry. For some, Robinson has a defect which goes far, in their view, to cancel out most if not all of his great merit; there is a certain dryness and mechanicalness of tone and feeling which for certain readers will always be an insuperable obstacle, as the "egotistical-sublime" of Wordsworth will always limit his audience. The reader who likes "Michael" will probably like "Isaac and Archibald." Robinson writes about himself in a guise some of us can recognize and enjoy; he does not pose, he does not try to give opinions. Personality in a poet is of the essence. We must like him as he speaks to us or we had better not read him.

That his poetic personality included a strong lyrical element cannot be denied, though it is frequently overlooked, largely because the poet rarely indulged it. We have seen that it was at least once overindulged in *Tristram* and we know that Robinson often kept it in reserve that its appearance might have the greater effect. The language, the imagery, of this lyricism derive largely from nineteenth-century sources, as in the opening lines of "The Man against the Sky," in which poem, as in "The Dark Hills," a deliberate use of highly colored rhetoric is central to the purpose. Unlike many poets of recent years, Robinson was not afraid of lyricism, nor, unlike still others, did he try to overwhelm the reader with "original" and striking imagery. The image of Eben Flood like "Roland's ghost winding a silent horn" is a typical example of one kind of Robinsonian lyricism in that it is euphonious, nostalgic, traditional—and wittily ironic.

But not all Robinson's lyrical flights are of these two sorts, the rhetorical or the ironic. Many occur as climaxes to poems which have begun in a muted, somber tone, rise gradually, and reach a peak of grandeur and eloquence in the final lines. We can observe the technique in such poems as "The White Lights," "On the Night of a Friend's Wedding," "The Sheaves," and of course, "The Gift of God." But there are still those poems which are primarily, almost purely, lyrical, and though few critics think of Robinson as a lyricist, or even as a poet of great versatility, a thorough reading of his work discloses a number of fine poems of quiet but powerful lyric intensity. "Luke Havergal" is one, a poem of almost macabre symbolism. Others, like "Pasa Thalassa Thalassa" and "The Wilderness," with their overtones of Kipling and Swinburne, seem Pre-Raphaelite in quality, as does the "Villanelle of Change." There remains nonetheless the conviction that Robinson's greatest triumphs and happiest effects derive from the "mixed" lyric, the poem rooted in situation which combines narrative, lyrical and ironic, often humorous, qualities with the intent of creating a more complex emotional state in the reader than that effected by the "pure" lyric. "The House on the Hill," "Veteran Sirens," "John Evereldown," and "New England," all display in their differing accents and rhythms the possibilities of this "mixed" form. Wit, pathos, lyrical power, and understatement combine in varied ways to produce complex states of feeling. It is one of the truly Robinsonian characteristics which can be called both modern and highly personal, characteristic of the man and the manner.

Finally, it must be avowed that any writer with a marked manner—and Robinson's manner is strongly marked—offends certain sensibilities, and those often the most acute. The defects and virtues of a poet are so closely allied that frequently they go hand in hand and it takes many bad poems to generate one good one. Robinson's fault was of course to mistake the attempt for the achieved thing. Can anyone say Robinson is alone in such misapprehension? We have seen the damaging effects on Robinson of exile from the kind of give-and-take the knowledge of the better contemporary minds can provide. He had protected his one talent so long and under such stress that we cannot wonder that he took little advice and criticism when it came to him. He was not a Browning; his latter days were divided between the MacDowell Colony in the summers, New York, and visits to friends and to "Tilbury Town," whither he now came as her most famous son—and can we imagine what that must have done to his long-battered pride? But he was not spoiled. He did not surround himself with doting women, or go to tea-fights and give readings—he shrank from these with horror, and a touch of cynicism. He kept on writing, as we have seen, and writing increasingly to satisfy, perhaps to justify, a conception of himself as poet and as man. The great fault of the nineteenth-century men of letters was to publish everything, and Robinson was of his time in this as in so much else. But his successes are many and large—in the narrative poem, the sonnet, the reflective lyric, the narrative lyric, and the dramatic monologue. Limited by environment, tradition, and circumstance, he yet managed to write the finest poems written in America between 1900 and 1920. In England and Ireland were Hardy, Yeats, and Wilfrid Owen and there were Pound and Eliot to be heard. Yet if we consider calmly, apart from notions of "influence" and contemporaneity, we will be forced to admit that the latter two men's work had not by this time achieved the self-contained excellence here under discussion. For all the obvious repetitiousness and aridity of Robinson's later work, twenty years of productiveness, and productiveness of excellence, is an unusually long period for an American writer. Robinson is not Great as Dante and Shakespeare and Milton and Sophocles are Great, but he is in the very front rank of American writers.

Selected Bibliography

WORKS OF EDWARD ARLINGTON ROBINSON

The Torrent and the Night Before, (Cambridge, Mass.: Privately printed, 1896).
The Children of the Night, (Boston: Badger, 1897).
Captain Craig, (Boston and New York: Houghton Mifflin, 1902).
The Town Down the River, (New York: Scribners, 1910).
Van Zorn, (New York: Macmillan, 1914) Play. *The Porcupine,* (New York: Macmillan, 1915). (Play).
The Man against the Sky, (New York: Macmillan, 1916).
Merlin, (New York: Macmillan, 1917).
Lancelot, (New York: Seltzer, 1920).
The Three Taverns, (New York: Macmillan, 1920).
Avon's Harvest, (New York: Macmillan, 1921).
Collected Poems, (New York: Macmillan, 1921).
Roman Bartholow, (New York: Macmillan, 1923).
The Man Who Died Twice, (New York: Macmillan, 1924).
Dionysius in Doubt, (New York: Macmillan, 1925).
Tristram, (New York: Macmillan, 1927).
Sonnets 1889–1927, (New York: Gaige, 1928).
Cavender's House, (New York: Macmillan, 1929).
Collected Poems, (New York: Macmillan, 1929).

The Glory of the Nightingales (New York: Macmillan, 1930).
Selected Poems, (New York: Macmillan, 1931).
Matthias at the Door, (New York: Macmillan, 1931).
Nicodemus, (New York: Macmillan, 1932).
Talifer, (New York: Macmillan, 1933).
Amaranth, (New York: Macmillan, 1934).
King Jasper, (New York: Macmillan, 1935).
Collected Poems, (New York: Macmillan, 1937).
Selected Early Poems and Letters of E. A. Robinson, edited by Charles T. Davis (New York: Holt, 1960).
Selected Poems, edited by Morton Dauwen Zabel, with an Introduction by James Dickey (New York: Macmillan, 1965).

LETTERS

Letters of Edwin Arlington Robinson to Howard George Schmitt, edited by Carl J. Weber (Waterville, Maine: Colby College Library, 1943).
Selected Letters of Edwin Arlington Robinson, with an Introduction by Ridgely Torrence (New York: Macmillan, 1940).
Untriangulated Stars: Letters of Edwin Arlington Robinson to Harry de Forest Smith, edited by Denham Sutcliffe (Cambridge, Mass: Harvard University Press, 1947).

BIBLIOGRAPHIES

Hogan, Charles Beecher, *A Bibliography of Edwin Arlington Robinson,* (New Haven, Conn.: Yale University Press, 1936).
Lippincott, Lillian, *A Bibliography of the Writings and Criticism of Edwin Arlington Robinson,* (Boston: Faxton, 1937).

CRITICAL AND BIOGRAPHICAL STUDIES

Barnard, Ellsworth, Edwin Arlington Robinson: A Critical Study. (New York: Macmillan, 1952).
———. *Edwin Arlington Robinson: Centenary Essays,* (Athens: University of Georgia Press, 1969).
Coffin, R. P. T., *New Poetry of New England: Frost and Robinson,* (Baltimore, Md.: Johns Hopkins Press, 1938).
Coxe, Louis, *Edwin Arlington Robinson: The Life of Poetry,* (New York: Pegasus, 1969).
Fussell, Edwin S., *Edwin Arlington Robinson: The Literary Background of a Traditional Poet,* (Berkeley: University of California Press, 1954).
Hagedorn, Hermann, *Edwin Arlington Robinson,* (New York: Macmillan, 1938).
Neff, Emery, *Edwin Arlington Robinson,* American Men of Letters Series (New York: Sloane, 1948).
Robinson, W. R., *Edwin Arlington Robinson: A Poetry of the Act,* (Cleveland: Press of Case Western Reserve University, 1967).
Smith, Chard Powers, *Where the Light Falls: A Portrait of Edwin Arlington Robinson,* (New York: Macmillan, 1965).
Stevick, Robert D., "Robinson and William James," *University of Kansas City Review,* 25: 293–301 (June 1959).
Winters, Yvor, *Edwin Arlington Robinson,* The Makers of Modern Literature Series (Norfolk, Conn.: New Directions, 1946).

THEODORE ROETHKE
(1908–1963)

RALPH J. MILLS, JR.

It is sometimes said of modern poetry that its day is over, that the revolution which swept through all the arts from about 1910 until a decade after World War I died out in the political anxiety and commitment of the 1930's, and that while the great poets who created the modern idiom—Yeats, Eliot, and Pound, for example—pursued their own ways to artistic maturity, writers growing up after them could no longer find the stimulating atmosphere of participation in what Randall Jarrell so aptly called "an individual but irregularly cooperative experimentalism." To a certain extent that view is correct: there has been no concerted poetic movement of real consequence here or in England since the work of Auden, Spender, Day Lewis, and MacNeice in the thirties. Yet even if the excited collective activity inspired by radical and widespread creative ferment gradually dissipated in those years, there was no lack of purpose and talent among the American poets who began to publish notable work near the outset of World War II or the others who appeared soon afterwards.

In his essay "The End of the Line," from which I quoted above, Randall Jarrell acted as a brilliant self-appointed spokesman for his contemporaries, for Robert Lowell, John Frederick Nims, Karl Shapiro, Richard Eberhart, Richard Wilbur, and Theodore Roethke, as well as for himself, when he defined the situation of the younger poet in 1942. "Today, for the poet," he said, "there is an embarrassment of choices: young poets can choose—do choose—to write anything from surrealism to imitations of Robert Bridges; the only thing they have no choice about is making their own choice. The Muse, forsaking her sterner laws, says to everyone: 'Do what you will.' "

The American poets of that generation did exactly what they willed and have produced, without the impetus of any common enterprise other than devotion to their art, a remarkable body of poetry. Ironically enough, they are poets on whom the label of academicism has been fastened occasionally; yet outside of the fact that many of them like Roethke have taught for a living that word, with its pejorative overtones, would seem to have little application. We have academic verse when a poet, instead of learning from the poetic tradition by remaining alive and open to its possibilities in relation to his own gifts and aspirations, submits himself to it automatically or, to change the metaphor, polishes the surface of old conventions. The weakness of the academic writer lies in an acceptance of literature before personal experience and imagination as the source of his art. But the poets I have named, and some not mentioned, showed originality, concern for language, and an abiding honesty toward the facts of their experience. If comparisons with the pioneer writers of twentieth-century modernism do not offer these successors the historical advantage, there is still no doubt in my mind that two or three of the latter can already hold their own surprisingly well in such formidable company.

Of all these later poets Theodore Roethke appears the most considerable, in terms of imaginative daring, stylistic achievement, richness of diction, variety and fullness of music, and unity of vision. From his first book, published in 1941, to the posthumous volume *The Far Field* (1964) he consistently proved himself a poet discontented with the restrictions of a settled manner of composition. This is not to say, of course, that Roethke lacked steadiness or certitude, that he was frivolous or insubstantial; quite the reverse. His poetry grew in distinct stages, each one with its own peculiar qualities and aims, each one expanding and developing from its predecessor, each providing its own special means of furthering the poet's central themes and subjecting them to different modes of apprehension. We should not be surprised then in reading through Roethke's books to discover a wide range of moods and styles: tightly controlled formal lyrics, dramatic monologues and something like an interior monologue, nonsense verse, love lyrics, and meditative poems composed in a very free fashion. His experience reaches from the most extraordinary intuition of the life of nature to lightning flashes of mystical illumination.

To fit Roethke definitely within a given tradition or to link him finally with other poets, past or present, who share certain of his predilections is tempting but too easy. He expressed an affection for John Clare and borrowed the title for his third book from Wordsworth's *The Prelude,* yet he was not drawn to the natural world in quite the same way as either of them, though he maintained affinities with both. Again one might like to proclaim him an investigator of the irrational, a poet obsessed with the pure flow of inner experience, with the preconscious and the unconscious: a poet similar to the young Dylan Thomas or Paul Eluard. Or perhaps he should be classed with the visionary poets he so admired: Blake, Whitman, and Yeats. No doubt every one of these attempts at classification would tell us a partial truth about Roethke, but none would give us the whole of it. He was, in fact, equally at home with any of these other poets, though we will be defeated in the endeavor to read his poetry honestly if we settle for a particular category in which to lodge him and so avoid further thought. Roethke needs first to be seen through his own work.

Behind the profusion of experience we have noted in Roethke's writing one comes upon a preoccupation with the poet's own self as the primary matter of artistic exploration and knowledge, an interest which endows the poems with a sense of personal urgency, even necessity. What do we mean by this self? I think the self, as we shall want to use the word here, can best be called the main principle of the poet's individual life—or for that matter, of any human life—a principle of identity and of being which is generally spiritual in character but also reaches into the realm of the physical. It partakes of what Martin Buber includes in his definition of the "primary word *I-Thou,*" which is the speech of a person's entire being in relationship with the other creatures and things of the world, for Roethke viewed the self as continually seeking a harmonious dialogue with all that is. The bulk of Roethke's poetry derives its imaginative strength from the author's restless quest for that communion in which self and creation are joined. Though they take the self as theme we cannot look in these poems for the sort of personal element we associate with the later work of Robert Lowell. Yet they are in their way just as intimate, maybe even more intimate, since some penetrate the protective screen of conscious thought. Lowell focuses often on other personalities, the family, the world of historical time, while Roethke's concentration either is inward, almost untouched by public happenings or by history, or turns outward to the existence of things in nature. But in order to understand his fundamental attachment to this theme of the self we must now look closely at its development within a growing body of poetry.

By any standards *Open House* (1941) is a remarkable first collection of poetry. Roethke's sensitive use of language and his craftsmanship stand out on every page; and if one returns to this book after reading his other work it becomes plain that the author's main interests were already present here. The title poem is a frank announcement of his intention to use himself in some way as the material of his art, but we are not told how. The poem is sharp in its personal disclosure and might justifiably serve as a motto for all of Roethke's subsequent verse:

> My secrets cry aloud.
> I have no need for tongue.
> My heart keeps open house,
> My doors are widely swung.
> An epic of the eyes
> My love, with no disguise.
>
> My truths are all foreknown,
> This anguish self-revealed.
> I'm naked to the bone,
> With nakedness my shield.
> Myself is what I wear:
> I keep the spirit spare.

These sparse, carefully rhymed stanzas char acterize Roethke's earlier poetic technique, and their kind is visible everywhere in *Open House.* A certain economy and simplicity of diction, as well as insistent, forceful rhythms, more freely employed as he matured, are in fact lasting trademarks of his style, even though he abandoned some of them almost entirely on occasion in favor of experiments with considerably looser forms. Such departures are especially evident in the long sequence of interior monologues from *The Lost Son* and *Praise to the End,* in the "Meditations of an Old Woman" from *Words for the Wind,* and in the "North American Sequence" from *The Far Field.* But the experiments are always interspersed, even in later work, with returns to the simple lyric. Here, as an illustration, is a stanza from "Once More, the Round," which Roethke wrote for his 1962 New Year's greeting:

> Now I adore my life,
> With the Bird, the abiding Leaf,
> With the Fish, the questing Snail,
> And the Eye altering All;
> And I dance with William Blake
> For love, for Love's sake.

The two subjects on which Roethke's imagination most often fastens in *Open House* are the correspondence between the poet's inner life and the life of nature, and the strengths or weaknesses of the individual psyche. Frequently he tries to demonstrate hidden relationships in the processes of both, as in "The Light Comes Brighter," a poem which begins with a very direct account of winter's end and the arrival of spring to a particular landscape:

> The light comes brighter from the east; the
> caw
> Of restive crows is sharper on the ear.
> A walker at the river's edge may hear
> A cannon crack announce an early thaw.
>
> The sun cuts deep into the heavy drift,
> Though still the guarded snow is winter-
> sealed,
> At bridgeheads buckled ice begins to shift,
> The river overflows the level field.

The observation and description are quite accurate and undoubtedly derive from the poet's childhood experience of the Michigan countryside. But as in the poetry of Léonie Adams, which Roethke always admired, nature yields a secret analogy with human existence, though it does not appear until the closing lines:

> And soon a branch, part of a hidden scene,
> The leafy mind, that long was furled,
> Will turn its private substance into green,
> And young shoots spread upon our inner
> world.

Mind and nature are bound in these lines by certain laws and enjoy a common awakening. Still we are left to tease out most of the implications for ourselves because the poet merely hints at the possibilities of this comparison in the present poem. In many of the other poems in this volume Roethke offers further seasonal descriptions but never makes the implied correspondences with human life any more definite than what we have already seen in the lines quoted.

Elsewhere in the book he takes the durability of the mind by itself as artistic material; and in a few poems which show an indebtedness to W. H. Auden he portrays the opposition to this mental stability through the figures of those victimized by unconscious forces, inherited sicknesses that threaten to destroy psychic balance:

> Exhausted fathers thinned the blood,
> You curse the legacy of pain;
> Darling of an infected brood,
> You feel disaster climb the vein.

These last poems, though they are of little aesthetic interest so far as the bulk of Roethke's writing is concerned, possess some value in foreshadowing the motives behind the tremendous imaginative leap he took in the seven years between *Open House* and *The Lost Son.* For the powers of the unconscious had at last to be dealt with, and are dealt with in the astonishing sequence of interior monologues which record the poet's odyssey through subterranean regions of the psyche, a spiritual journey that remains one of the boldest experiments in modern American poetry. Taken altogether the poems in *Open House* are indicative of Roethke's major themes, but they hardly prepare the reader for the change to an intensely subjective vision in the next book or for the readjustment of his perceptions demanded by this shift. With *The Lost Son* (1948) he emerges as a poet of undeniable originality and stature, whose writing bears its own stylistic signature.

The section of poems with which *The Lost Son* opens may catch by complete surprise the reader who has seen nothing but Roethke's previous work. While emphasis on nature is still maintained, attention has now moved away from the earlier images of natural and seasonal activity in the larger sense to a reduced, microscopic scrutiny of plant life that seems almost scientific in its precision but is obviously prompted by the poet's intuition, passion, and sympathy. What in preceding poems would most likely have been a careful description of the outer appearance of a plant or flower becomes an attempt to seize imaginatively the essential life of the flower, as in the haunting "Orchids," where it overlaps ours:

> They lean over the path,
> Adder-mouthed,
> Swaying close to the face,
> Coming out, soft and deceptive,
> Limp and damp, delicate as a young bird's
> tongue;
> Their fluttery fledgling lips
> Move slowly,
> Drawing in the warm air.

The basis for this sudden alteration in distance and perspective must have been the poet's decision to utilize his close experience in childhood with plants and flowers as substantial matter for his art. However it came about the choice was fortunate because it marked out the route his poetic imagination was to take and, one likes to think, even urged him on his way by revealing the similarities existing between his human life and that of the inhabitants of the plant kingdom which had played so important a part in his youth. Through this new personal vision of the vegetable and mineral, insect and animal, knowledge of which he owed to his boyhood, Roethke found before him the difficult problems of spiritual evolution and the search for psychic identity.

The poet was born in Saginaw, Michigan, in 1908, received his education at the University of Michigan and Harvard, and subsequently taught at Lafayette College, Pennsylvania State University, Bennington College, and for some time at the University of Washington in Seattle, where he was professor of English and poet in residence at the time of his death on August 1, 1963. As a boy he grew up in and around the greenhouses that were the center of the Roethke family's floral establishment, one of the largest and most famous of its time. The business was both retail and wholesale; it was operated by Roethke's father and his Uncle Charlie, aided by a staff of trained florists and also by a working crew of eccentric figures which included the three marvelous old ladies Frau Bauman, Frau Schmidt, and Frau Schwartze, about whom the poet wrote a wonderful and moving elegy that captures the beauty and pleasure of these women at their task. I quote here only a few lines from the first stanza:

> Gone the three ancient ladies
> Who creaked on the greenhouse ladders,
> Reaching up white strings
> To wind, to wind
> The sweet-pea tendrils, the smilax,
> Nasturtiums, the climbing
> Roses, to straighten
> Carnations, red
> Chrysanthemums; the stiff
> Stems, jointed like corn,
> They tied and tucked,—
> These nurses of nobody else.

As a boy Roethke played and worked around these greenhouses. Many of his experiences he transformed elegantly, and often humorously, into poems: we need only look at "Big Wind," "Old Florist," "Child on Top of a Greenhouse," and the poem above to be conscious of that. But from the same intimate knowledge of his father's greenhouses he began those poetic ventures into the scarcely visible—except to the eye of a determined and fascinated observer—motions of plant life that we noticed in "Orchids." In another poem, appropriately entitled "The Minimal," Roethke renders himself in the act of watching:

> I study the lives on a leaf: the little
> Sleepers, numb nudgers in cold dimensions,
> Beetles in caves, newts, stone-deaf fishes,
> Lice tethered to long limp subterranean
>   weeds,
> Squirmers in bogs,
> And bacterial creepers
> Wriggling through wounds
> Like elvers in ponds,
> Their wan mouths kissing the warm
>   sutures,
> Cleaning and caressing,
> Creeping and healing.

In the poet's attentive gaze this tiny world increases its size and comes curiously near in its procedures to the one we would like to believe is exclusively man's. Something in the human psyche responds to these minute activities, discovers a mysterious, even terrifying, attraction to levels of existence to which reason or intelligence would quickly assign an inferior value. But an indispensable part of the imaginative breakthrough Roethke achieves in his second book is just this exposure of himself to subrational elements. Thus the disturbing quality in these poems results from the dramatic recreation of affinities with the lower orders of life, parallels we have banished from thought. And how startling it is for the scientific, technological mind of contemporary man to countenance such images of his origins, of archaic sources of life he shares with lesser forms than himself. If Roethke's endeavors start with a return to his own past experience, the poems surpass the barriers of privacy to delineate hidden patterns in creation; and they accomplish this with a freshness of language and imaginative energy unmatched by any other poet since Dylan Thomas. A poem like "Cuttings, later" brings poet—and thus reader—and the newly born plants into a correspondence so delicate and yet profound that there can be only one true conclusion: a kind of psychic rebirth for the poet through his sympathetic contemplation of propagating plants:

> This urge, wrestle, resurrection of dry
>   sticks,
> Cut stems struggling to put down feet,
> What saint strained so much,
> Rose on such lopped limbs to a new life?
>
> I can hear, underground, that sucking and
>   sobbing,
> In my veins, in my bones I feel it,—
> The small waters seeping upward,
> The tight grains parting at last.
> When sprouts break out,
> Slippery as fish,
> I quail, lean to beginnings, sheath-wet.

Roethke's inclination in these poems to reveal a deep and permanent tie between the "minimal" world of flowers, plants, and small creatures he so benevolently scrutinizes and the inner world of man prepares for the sequence of experimental monologues, the first of which appear in the last section of *The Lost Son* and which are continued in *Praise to the End* (1951). The sequence poems are, so far as I know, unique in modern literature. Undoubtedly they owe their inspiration to the poet's pursuit of the correspondences just mentioned and to the fact that his previous work keeps insisting on such an immersion in the prerational and unconscious areas of experience in the hope of bringing unity to the self and gaining a new harmony with creation.

The poems are grouped around an associational scheme, as Roethke once suggested, and seem closer perhaps to certain experimental tendencies in the modern novel, such as stream of consciousness, than they do to the efforts of most contemporary poets. "Each poem"—there are fourteen in all—"is complete in itself," Roethke says in his "Open Letter" from *Mid-Century American Poets*, "yet each in a sense is a stage in a kind of struggle out of the slime; part of a slow spiritual progress; an effort to be born, and later, to become something more." The poems treat portions of a spiritual journey undertaken by a child-protagonist, a journey the narrative of which does not develop in a direct, logical manner because it is viewed internally through the fluid movements and reactions of the protagonist's mind. This protagonist, through whom we comprehend whatever happens in the poems, plays a double role: he is both a mask for the poet and a universal type, any man, for Roethke is at pains to avoid the limitations of a totally personal significance in the experience created by this poetic sequence. The journey, while it is basically psychic and spiritual, also has similarities with quest myths: the hero's descent into the underworld of the self; a series of ordeals he must pass or an enemy to be vanquished; his victorious return to familiar reality, which is now changed by his efforts. This sort of parallel will make it clear at once that while Roethke's primary intention is the "struggle for spiritual identity" (his phrase) in the individual protagonist, that struggle symbolizes a more general body of human experience. This last dimension is, however, implied rather than heavily outlined through a detailed system of allusion.

In several of the poems we have seen from *The Lost Son,* as well as in a number of others that cannot be discussed here, Roethke presses back toward the very beginnings of existence in his concentration on the life process of plants. This practice by itself is sufficient to separate his interests from his contemporaries' and to display his genuine innovation. Roethke wishes in these poems to uncover through his imagination the laws of growth in a flower and relate them to the development of the human self, though it is done metaphorically rather than scientifically. But short lyric poems are ultimately unsatisfactory as vehicles for such ambitions because they are not flexible enough and do not readily permit the singular approach to experience the poet now envisages. What he is aiming at is a poetic "history of the psyche" (his phrase) which opens with the earliest stages of life and traces the evolution of the spirit in its ordeal of inner and outer conflicts, its desire for "unity of being," to borrow a term from Dante by way of Yeats, that final condition of grace which is a harmony of the self with all things. In Roethke's later work the love of man and woman is involved in this idea of unity and so is an awareness of the Divine. Yet the protagonist's route in the poems is anything but easy, for regressive instincts, desires to remain on the lowest plane of existence or to become a lump of inanimate matter, war upon the natural impulse to growth. The spirit tries to release the self from these destructive attractions and to rise toward the full embrace of life. Nature is the context in which the individual assumes at last his rightful identity, finds love, and engages the spirit in further encounters. Roethke depicted some of the terrors and humiliations attending this venture into buried regions in a poem entitled "The Return":

A cold key let me in
That self-infected lair;
And I lay down with my life,
With the rags and rotting clothes,
With a stump of scraggy fang
Bared for a hunter's boot.

The self-imposed, and no doubt personally necessary, journey on which the poet sets forth with the first poem of the sequence (as rearranged by Roethke in the order he wishes in *Words for the Wind*), "Where Knock Is Open Wide," immediately alters ordinary spatial and temporal dimensions. Spatial because the poems view a secret landscape of the inner self that resembles the external world only in fragmentary details supplied by memory or momentary perceptions, and these are heightened, distorted, or transfigured, as in a dream, by the various struggles of the spirit in its search for freedom and unity. Temporal because the poet, or the projection of himself which is the protagonist, needs to go back to his childhood experience so that he can relive this evolutionary process in writing about it. Thus we witness the activity of the poems from the standpoint of the poet-protagonist himself.

It has already been suggested that these poems carry echoes of archetypal patterns from other modes of experience, particularly mythical and religious. Because the protagonist travels into the regions of memory, the preconscious and the unconscious, he shows distinct similarity to the heroes of myth whom Jung saw as representative of the quest for psychic wholeness. Like those fabulous heroes or the lesser ones of fairy tales Roethke's lone protagonist must endure the trials and dangers of a mission into the darkness of personal history. The prize to be won is rebirth and illumination, what is called in one of the poems "a condition of joy."

The title of "Where Knock Is Open Wide" is taken from Christopher Smart's poem of praise and celebration, "Song to David," LXXVII, but Roethke's piece, which presents the sensations and thoughts of earliest childhood, seems to use the line from Smart to imply birth and entry into the world. From this aspect Roethke's poem somewhat resembles Dylan Thomas' "Before I Knocked," which describes experiences of a child (in this case, Jesus) in the womb. Indeed, Thomas is probably the only one of Roethke's immediate contemporaries who also investigates successfully the fluid exchange of past and present within the self. Roethke establishes his atmosphere with childish perceptions:

A kitten can
Bite with his feet;
Papa and Mamma
Have more teeth.

He goes on in a few lines to what appears to be an image of birth:

Once upon a tree
I came across a time . . .

The tree is a species of the common symbol of the Tree of Life, and the next line recalls the protagonist's introduction to time. A stanza further on we learn the nature of the journey and something of its method:

What's the time, papa-seed?
Everything has been twice.
My father is a fish.

This brief passage draws the protagonist back toward the instant of his conception and fixes our attention on the movement into his personal past, which is a reversal of the temporal order. The middle line makes plain the fact that the poet is not simply rendering the original stages of development in a fictional individual but reliving them in himself to interpret their meaning. We seem to hear the voices of the protagonist and the poet blending in this line. The identification of the father with a fish has again a double reference: first, in allusion to a fishing trip of the father and son, bits of which are given later; second, in hinting at the evolutionary scheme emphasized previously. This process of evolution we witness in the protagonist is universal and leads away, as Roethke writes in his "Open Letter," from "the mire," where "man is no more than a shape writhing from the old rock." In the third section of the poem he sounds the same theme by employing the word "fish" once again, but now as a verb instead of a substantive. This change marks a step forward from domination by an image of ancestry among the lower forms of life to an active desire on the protagonist's part for self-completion:

> A worm has a mouth.
> Who keeps me last?
> Fish me out.
> Please.

Since our point of observation is located within the protagonist's mind, though not at the level of reason or calculation, certain external facts such as his changing age are not always easily determined. We gather, however, that the poems extend over a period from early childhood into late adolescence. Roethke's associative technique allows him to shift back and forth freely in the history of his protagonist, and so he can bring his artistic weight to bear on the themes which matter to him without particular regard for the consistency of linear time. The present poem ranges from the first years of life with their scraps of nonsense verse and nursery songs, through a brief section touching on the small boy's religious emotions, then his fishing trip, and ending with the initial signs of anxiety and guilt which accompany the feeling of desolation caused by the father's death. The narrative progression of the poems, if we may thus speak of it, depends upon Roethke's concern for the advances and setbacks of the evolving spirit.

The loss of his father empties the protagonist's world of its paternal image of God as well:

> Kisses come back,
> I said to Papa;
> He was all whitey bones
> And skin like paper.
> God's somewhere else,
> I said to Mamma.
> The evening came
> A long long time.

The last two lines predict a period of deprivation and loneliness to come. And in the next poem, "I Need, I Need," with its title so sharply indicative of the child's terrible hunger for affection and stability, he alternates between a search for the mother:

> A deep dish. Lumps in it.
> I can't taste my mother.

solitude and melancholy:

> Went down cellar,
> Talked to a faucet;
> The drippy water
> Had nothing to say.

and a final resort to the diversion of children's habits, rhymes, and games:

> A one is a two is
> I know what you is:
> You're not very nice,—
> So touch my toes twice.

But, clearly enough, these diversions exhibit the inner divisions and turmoil of the protagonist, too. In later sections of the poem a gradual easing of tensions occurs, succeeded by intimations of human possibility and of an abiding kinship with physical creation: "Hear me, soft ears and roundy stones! / It's a dear life I can touch." The poem finally closes by emphasizing two of the traditional four elements thought to compose the universe, water and fire:

> I said to the gate,
> Who else knows
> What water does?
> Dew ate the fire.

Here the gate symbolizes all that prevents the protagonist from rebirth into the world, from the potential of his existence. Like beings, objects, and places in fairy tale and folklore, creatures and things in Roethke's poetic cosmos are invested with magical properties, can hinder or help the spirit in its growth. Thus the protagonist seeks the true way by asking questions in this subterranean and animistic kingdom from which he must obtain new life or sink back into the "dark pond"—as Roethke calls the deep unconscious—where obvlivion awaits him. The water mentioned in the passage above should not, however, be identified with that sinister place; rather it signifies a continuation of the journey into daylight, the constant will of the self to accomplish, in Robert Frost's words, this "serial ordeal."

Dew consumes one fire in this same stanza only to disclose another kind in the next. The first should probably be understood as the fever of discord in the protagonist, while the second, which appears momentarily in the poem's final lines—"I know another fire. / Has roots."—surely is meant to remind us of fire's ancient use as a symbol of spirit. So we realize that the entire movement of the first two poems in the sequence constitutes an ascent from origins, from the introduction to death, the experience of fear and isolation, to the recognition of freedom and possibility beyond present conditions, though such prospects are never mistaken for a guarantee of security. Life, as it is seen in Roethke's poetry, can best be defined as always becoming.

"Bring the Day!" fulfills the promise of spiritual progress implied before. It is a celebration of self and nature together in a newly won relation, and as such it marks the conversion of the haunted landscape of unknown terrors and hidden demons projected by the self into the radiant external world of insects and birds, grass and flowers. The poem begins with an exuberant burst of song which sounds as if Roethke might have had both John Lyly and Edward Lear in mind when he wrote it:

> Bees and lilies there were,
> Bees and lilies there were,
> Either to other,—
> Which would you rather?
> Bees and lilies were there.

This mood of celebration, of self-possession and joy, prevails throughout the poem. Nature guides the protagonist further along the path he must travel and hints in symbols which recall those of "I Need, I Need" at the pattern of his journey from confinement to fluidity: "The grass says what the wind says: / Begin with the rock; / End with water."

The third and concluding section shows the emergent self in the image of a tiny bird waking to existence, feeling a little its own possibilities, and facing a life that has cast off its ties with the past and only looks forward. The gentle lyricism of the stanza again points up Roethke's uncanny sensitiveness to the subtlest details of nature and their covert human meanings:

> O small bird wakening,
> Light as a hand among blossoms,
> Hardly any old angels are around any more.
> The air's quiet under the small leaves.
> The dust, the long dust, stays.
> The spiders sail into summer.
> It's time to begin!
> To begin!

Following this poem three others, "Give Way, Ye Gates," "Sensibility! O La!" and "O Lull Me, Lull Me," lead up to "The Lost Son," which is the key poem of the sequence and, as Roethke said himself, the one with the most obvious narrative construction. The poems preceding "The Lost Son" continue to test various lines of inner tension we have already noted in the protagonist. Sexual agony, lack of identity, and solitude are cast as barriers against the vital energy of the spirit in its evolution but with no lasting success. The closing portion of "O Lull Me, Lull Me" measures the spirit's achievement and attests once more to the protagonist's intuition of harmony with creation:

> I'm more than when I was born;
> I could say hello to things;
> I could talk to a snail;
> I see what sings!
> What sings!

Light, movements of air, flowing water, and the music of song supply Roethke with some favorite metaphors for these sudden revelations of increase and communion. And they are peculiarly appropriate and effective metaphors because their source is the great world of nature, which stands, as we have seen, as the foundation and setting for the poet's investigation of human reality. In Roethke's writing man is always viewed in the framework of nature, or at least is never far distant from it. Whether the immediate subject is the individual self, love between man and woman, or some kind of visionary experience, it partakes of that natural world in evident or indirect relationships, in the physical details of imagery. Finally, in some of his last poems such as "The Far Field," "Meditation at Oyster River," and "The Rose" Roethke sees the realm of the spiritual beginning in nature; yet he never denies the validity of the natural in favor of the transcendental. He tends rather to hold them in his vision simultaneously, for to his imagination they blend and interchange endlessly.

"The Lost Son," as Hilton Kramer wrote in his fine essay on Roethke, summarizes the main theme and the developments which appear loosely in the sequence as a whole. The first of the poems from this group we examined took the early phases of life as their point of departure, but here the reference to a cemetery in the opening line and the attraction to death which it signifies states at once the conflict with the evolving self whose pull is toward fulfillment and maturity. The remainder of this initial section, which is entitled "The Flight," treats the confused and often tormented condition of the child-protagonist as he tries to learn the direction he must take to escape those forces working solely for his anguish or destruction. In keeping with Roethke's preoccupation with the irrational and subliminal side of his protagonist's experience the poem assumes the strange aura of dream and fairy tale we have come to expect of the entire sequence. The protagonist undertakes his journey without certainty of his bearings or his goal. All he can do, it seems, is ask questions and go where chance or the guidance of the spirit may lead him. The environment through which he travels (again we should stress the subjective character of his perceptions) displays hostility, though he has obvious feelings of sympathy for the smallest creatures, whose size and innocence resemble his own:

At Woodlawn I heard the dead cry:
I was lulled by the slamming of iron,
A slow drip over stones,
Toads brooding in wells.
All the leaves stuck out their tongues;
I shook the softening chalk of my bones,
Saying,
Snail, snail, glister me forward,
Bird, soft-sigh me home.

As in previous poems from the sequence Roethke juxtaposes fragments of children's songs, nursery rhymes, and riddles with apparently factual descriptions; thus he keeps a balance between external and subjective reality. But even the fairly straightforward passages distillate a symbolic meaning in terms of the quest on which the protagonist is bound:

Hunting along the river,
Down among the rubbish, the bug-riddled
  foliage,
By the muddy pond-edge, by the bog-holes,
By the shrunken lake, bunting, in the heat
  of summer.

The river with its steady flow, suggesting progress, intensifies by contrast the image of frustrated and unrewarded searching by the protagonist near those places, holes and slippery mud patches, that spell out the dangers of regression and defeat to his odyssey.

In "The Pit," the second part of the poem which is only one stanza long, the seductiveness of a descent into the earth, a relinquishing of self to the dark body of the mother, becomes an active threat to the protagonist. But an inner warning, perhaps by the spirit, prevents him from succumbing to what I think we must call a strong death-wish or a refusal of any further hardships in the search for human completion:

Where do the roots go?
  Look down under the leaves.
Who put the moss there?
  These stones have been here too long.
Who stunned the dirt into noise?
  Ask the mole, he knows.
I feel the slime of a wet nest.
  Beware Mother Mildew.
Nibble again, fish nerves.

The section following treats sexual agonies and alienation. Roethke builds up to a terrifying climax the tension between the protagonist and his surroundings. The short, terse lines which he handles so deftly are essential to the poet's creation of this climactic atmosphere:

The weeds whined,
The snakes cried,
The cows and briars
Said to me: Die.

But the full weight of the poem up to this point, which is brought to bear on the word "Die," is released in the next stanzas, and we suddenly realize that the protagonist has survived the worst of his trials. He finds himself at the calm center of a storm and recognizes that he is poised on the threshold of a new spiritual phase, of transformation and rebirth: "Do the bones cast out their fire? / Is the seed leaving the old bed? These buds are live as birds." Still more lines of conflict succeed these indications of change, but they terminate at last in a gentle apprehension of natural things, which is, in its turn, broken by an unexpected, violent flash of interior illumination and a period of turbulence ending in the restoration of the protagonist to the familiar climate of daily life.

The two concluding portions of the poem bring the protagonist home to his father's greenhouse and to an interval of waiting. The boy's sensitive awareness of the existence of the roses he tends and watches there ("The roses kept breathing in the dark. / They had many mouths to breathe with.") should also be understood to connote the self-recognition earned through his troublesome journey. Like these flowers he enjoys a precarious and fragile state of being; his scrutiny of their gradual response to the coming light of day duplicates a perception of his own slow ascent from the abyss of inner tensions:

A fine haze moved off the leaves;
Frost melted on far panes;
The rose, the chrysanthemum turned
  toward the light.
Even the hushed forms, the bent yellowy
  weeds
Moved in a slow up-sway.

The stately, graceful quality of this stanza, contrasting sharply with the clipped style of previous parts, leads us without disruption into the meditative attitude of the final section, in which the winter landscape, bare yet enduring, mirrors in its stark forms and objects the present condition of the protagonist. From this symbolic notation with its imagery of the "bones of weeds" and of "light" moving "slowly over the frozen field, / Over the dry seedcrowns, / The beautiful surviving bones / Swinging in the wind" there comes a shift to the mind of the protagonist deeply immersed in what has been happening to him. His mind also moves, but "not alone, / Through the clear air, in the silence." The poem closes with two stanzas reflecting the spiritual questions raised by the boy's experience as recounted in the first three sections of the poem and, presumably, in the other poems of the sequence placed before "The Lost Son":

Was it light?
Was it light within?
Was it light within light?
Stillness becoming alive,
Yet still?

A lively understandable spirit
Once entertained you.
It will come again.
Be still.
Wait.

We can hardly fail to notice here a recollection of T. S. Eliot's *Four Quartets,* a series of poems which parallel Roethke's in some respects. Both works are explorations of the self, its past history and its developments, though Eliot has no intention of representing those prerational areas of the mind into which Roethke so daringly plunges. Both works seek realization in a spiritual order, but Roethke declines to step into religious orthodoxy and relies upon his own intuition, while Eliot integrates his mystical perceptions with the traditions and beliefs of Catholic Christianity. Yet Roethke's reference to the senior poet is too obvious to be merely an unconscious allusion. I think we should see it as a deliberate echo of *Four Quartets* but also as a statement of difference. The illumination which occurs in "The Lost Son" may be a divine visitation or a gift of grace; however, it lacks any explicit theological structure of the kind embodied in so many of the details in Eliot's poems. For Roethke this moment of light appears to be given as a matter of course and is accepted as completely natural. Certainly it is merited to a degree by the ordeal through which the protagonist has passed, but it surely is not achieved in the sense in which Eliot achieves those mystical experiences at the heart of *Four Quartets,* that is, by prayer, selflessness, and meditation. Roethke's is the more Protestant approach, one that bases itself firmly on personal knowledge and evidence, on the lone individual's apprehension of the transcendent. And such a description applies to mystical poems like "In a Dark Time," included in *The Far Field.*

The purpose of this visitation at the close of "The Lost Son" is clear all the same, for it displays the progress of the spirit over the longest and most difficult stage of evolution. In the seven remaining poems of the sequence Roethke continues to record the advances and lapses of his protagonist, though we are by now conscious of the latter's increasing maturity. But he has not yet escaped the pains of sexuality and of alienation: they have become the problems of a person who has left childhood behind and arrived at a more comprehensive vision of himself and of the world around him. The poet even tells us the protagonist's age in the third part of "Praise to the End!":

> The sun came out;
> The lake turned green;
> Romped upon the goldy grass,
> Aged thirteen.

In spite of persistent obstacles passages of lyrical exaltation occur with greater frequency than they do in the poems preceding "The Lost Son." Such superior moments, with their pleasure in the beauty and variety of nature, look forward to some of Roethke's last poetry. Stanzas like the following from "I Cry, Love! Love!" (which takes its title from William Blake's "Visions of the Daughters of Albion") prepare the way for the vision of life we find in "The Far Field" or "Meditations of an Old Woman":

> I hear the owls, the soft callers, coming
> down from the hemlocks.
> The bats weave in and out of the willows,
> Wing-crooked and sure,
> Downward and upward,
> Dipping and veering close to the motionless
> water.
>
> A fish jumps, shaking out flakes of
> moonlight.
> A single wave starts lightly and easily
> shoreward,
> Wrinkling between reeds in shallower
> water,
> Lifting a few twigs and floating leaves,
> Then washing up over small stones.
>
> The shine on the face of the lake
> Tilts, backward and forward.
> The water recedes slowly,
> Gently rocking.

After the unusual and striking techniques which he introduces for his special purposes in the sequence poems, Roethke turns back again to a more formal manner in the early 1950's. In some of this work, most notably in

"Four for Sir John Davies" and later in "The Dying Man," he makes use of cadences somewhat reminiscent of those in the poetry of Yeats, but these are intentional effects on Roethke's part and not, as some critics would have us believe, signs of weakness and of an unassimilated influence. Roethke ably defended himself against such charges in his essay "How to Write Like Somebody Else," pointing out that the poet needs to work forward consciously from his predecessors, that "the language itself is a compound . . ." And finally, he adds, "the very fact" that the poet "has the support of a tradition, or an older writer, will enable him to be more himself—or more than himself."

What Roethke says on this subject is profoundly true and is peculiarly applicable to himself. With his sequence finished he could no longer exercise the devices employed there: that vein was thoroughly mined and could only be kept open at the risk of repetition, boredom, and stultification. But he had learned a good deal from the sequence, and the themes which engaged his imagination were far from exhausted; in fact, one might venture to say that the exploration of the past, of personal history, served to make the present very available to him. The evolution of the self was not done, and the love poems begun during this period show that this evolution was entering a new, more expansive phase which related the self to the other, or the beloved. Technically speaking, Roethke tested the possibilities of a formal style, but with a daring, a liberty and passion that go beyond the urgencies of amorous feeling. His experiments in the sequence poems freed him to attempt an altered diction and looser syntax, more exclamatory, interrogative, and aphoristic lines:

> I'd say it to my horse: we live beyond
> Our outer skin. Who's whistling up my
>   sleeve?
> I see a heron prancing in his pond;
> I know a dance the elephants believe.
> The living all assemble! What's the cue?—
> Do what the clumsy partner wants to do!

To get a better impression of the distance Roethke has traveled thus far in his poetic style, let us set next to those lines above from "Four for Sir John Davies" a stanza from "The Heron" in *Open House* which will call to mind the more restricted, tense character of the poet's first work:

> The heron stands in water where the swamp
> Has deepened to the blackness of a pool,
> Or balances with one leg on a hump
> Of marsh grass heaped above a musk-rat
>   hole.

The piece which best prepares us for the considerable group of love poems now gathered into their own section of *Words for the Wind* is "Four for Sir John Davies," an ambitious poetic cycle that appeared among the last pages of Roethke's Pulitzer Prize volume of selected poems, *The Waking* (1953). As the title implies a little covertly, the basic metaphor of the poem is dancing. Roethke draws openly on two other poets to enlarge the dimensions of his poems: they are the sixteenth-century English poet to whom these four pieces are dedicated and William Butler Yeats. From Davies' *Orchestra* (1594), a long philosophical poem on the harmonious relations of the various spheres of being in the universe, Roethke gains support for the cosmic scheme he includes in the first poem, "The Dance." But since Orchestra is constructed about a supposed dispute between Penelope and her suitor Antinous, who tries to persuade her to dance, the sexual theme has also already been evoked, though as yet only indirectly. And it is to Yeats that Roethke looks for precedence in the treatment of sexual love through the figure of the dance, as well as for certain rhythms and qualities of tone and diction.

"The Dance" begins with the poet recalling the universal system to be found in Davies' poem, then questioning whether man any longer conceives of the world in terms of the dance within his own mind. Whatever the answer to that question may be, he affirms his own participation in such a cosmic dance and even humorously identifies himself with the shambling but pleasurable gait of bears:

> The great wheel turns its axle when it can;
> I need a place to sing, and dancing-room,
> And I have made a promise to my ears
> I'll sing and whistle romping with the bears.

But Roethke intends something more than mild self-mockery here, for the bears in their dance throw into relief the sheer physical aspect of existence—in the poet as well as in themselves: "O watch his body sway!— / This animal remembering to be gay." The poem carries this note into the third stanza with emphasis now placed on the poet's own isolated dancing. In spite of the elation accompanying this joyous, willed activity there is an incompleteness in what he does that can only be corrected by the appearance of the beloved. This beginning poem of the four closes with a stanza expressing Roethke's debt to Yeats:

> I take this cadence from a man named
> Yeats;
> I take it, and I give it back again:
> For other tunes and other wanton beats
> Have tossed my heart and fiddled through
> my brain.
> Yes, I was dancing-mad, and how
> That came to be the bears and Yeats would
> know.

The next poem, "The Partner," brings together the poet and his beloved in the dance. It becomes clear immediately that their relationship is more than sensual, more even than love between two persons, for overtly sexual gestures generate metaphysical overtones until we sense that Roethke attains a kind of visionary intuition of human possibility through his dancing lovers:

> Things loll and loiter. Who condones the
> lost?
> This joy outleaps the dog. Who cares? Who
> cares?
> I gave her kisses back, and woke a ghost.
> O what lewd music crept into our ears!
> The body and the soul know how to play
> In that dark world where gods have lost
> their way.

The "dark world" of which the poet speaks is undoubtedly the maze of love and bodily attraction. It may further imply the realm of the human, fully realized in the sexual and spiritual bond of the pair, as opposed to a supernatural plane of being altogether removed from life. We enter that world more completely in "The Wraith," where lover and beloved apparently exchange identities through their union. Though this poem aims specifically in its imagery and reference at the intense moment of completion in the sexual act, it extends past that in Roethke's speculations on the meaning of the act. Certainly we do not exaggerate in saying that he wishes to reveal the spiritual transcendence emerging from carnal love in the poem:

> There was a body, and it cast a spell,—
> God pity those but wanton to the knees,—
> The flesh can make the spirit visible . . .

The wraith, "a shape alone, / Impaled on light, and whirling slowly down," who is the poet's image of his beloved, is briefly associated with Dante's Beatrice in the first stanza of "The Vigil." In those lines Roethke asserts the purity of the lover's vision of the beloved. Created from his "longing" it may be contradicted but not destroyed by the reality of the loved one as a person. But the allusion to Dante and Beatrice goes further because it supports the transcendental experience recorded in the poem's last stanza, an experience which never denies the physical nature of the love relationship and yet presents it as the cause of a breakthrough in the spiritual order:

> The world is for the living. Who are they?
> We dared the dark to reach the white and
> warm.
> She was the wind when wind was in my
> way;
> Alive at noon, I perished in her form.

> Who rise from flesh to spirit know the fall:
> The word outleaps the world, and light is
> all.

Such a visionary climax is predicted by the similar but less comprehensive bursts of illumination in "The Lost Son" and other poems of that sequence. Even more important is the fact that moments of this kind recur throughout the love poems and again, of course, in the unmistakably visionary and meditative work that follows. It is necessary to understand first of all that Roethke's love poems are not just evocations of the beloved or descriptions of his aroused emotions with regard to her; these play their part in what he writes, but it is only one part. As I hinted earlier, this group of poems brings to a certain measure of fulfillment the evolution of the self begun with the childhood and adolescence poems. So Roethke tends to locate the loved woman at the center of the physical universe: through her he communes with that world and its elements, and has his vision transformed. Once more we think of the reference to Dante, of Beatrice's guidance which brings that poet to a revelation of the Divine. Surely the beloved in Roethke's poems, though she can change swiftly from a wraithlike to an earthy creature, functions in a manner closely resembling her predecessor.

A poem that is one of the most fully achieved as well as one of the most representative of the considerations discussed here is "Words for the Wind," which gives its title to Roethke's collected verse. Others of the love poems do take up various strands of the themes of death, spirit versus flesh, ultimate belief, and so forth, but they gain much more prominence in "The Dying Man," an elegy to Yeats, and "Meditations of an Old Woman." In a recent anthology, *Poet's Choice,* edited by Paul Engle and Joseph Langland, Roethke says that "Words for the Wind" was written as an epithalamion to his bride during their honeymoon visit at W. H. Auden's villa in Ischia, but these are merely the external circumstances of composition. The poem itself is literally a song of joy, a mood in the poet which arises from delight in his companion but overflows into the world outside. Perhaps it would be even more accurate to say that his love for this woman awakens and refines in him a knowledge of a participation in the life of creation, in the being of all things. His beloved merges with flowers, the wind, a stone, the moon, and so she appears to be present in almost every living thing, in objects or the elements. As the last line of the opening stanza intimates, he has the sensitive reverence for them we think of in a St. Francis of Assisi, who would make a particularly appropriate patron saint for Roethke's poetry:

> Love, love, a lily's my care,
> She's sweeter than a tree.
> Loving, I use the air
> Most lovingly: I breathe;
> Mad in the wind I wear
> Myself as I should be,
> All's even with the odd,
> My brother the vine is glad.

Not only does this love result in a harmony with the cosmos but it accomplishes an internal balance too. The self that was, so to speak, divided against itself in many previous poems arrives at unity through another person, a woman who is frankly physical and sexual but is furthermore a creature of spiritual and mythological proportions. In the intensified perception of the poem we see her continual metamorphosis, her changing roles, but at the same time she remains a constant image within the poet himself, the archetypal female principle dwelling in man which Jung called the *Anima*:

> The shallow stream runs slack;
> The wind creaks slowly by;
> Out of a nestling's beak
> Comes a tremulous cry
> I cannot answer back;
> A shape from deep in the eye—
> That woman I saw in a stone—
> Keeps pace when I walk alone.

In spite of this disclosure of a psychic image Roethke concentrates most of his imaginative powers on the external world and the forms of nature. The second section of the poem is devoted almost totally to natural imagery through which the course of love and the person of the beloved are traced. Here we find creation transfigured by the lovers who move within it and color it with their complex of emotions, "the burden of this joy":

> The sun declares the earth;
> The stones leap in the stream;
> On a wide plain, beyond
> The far stretch of a dream,
> A field breaks like the sea;
> The wind's white with her name,
> And I walk with the wind.

Love in the figure of this woman "wakes the ends of life," Roethke tells us, and I do not believe it is misleading to say that she and the poems about her suggested to the poet some of the approaches and devices of his later writing. "The Dying Man" and "Meditations of an Old Woman," the two poetic cycles which conclude *Words for the Wind,* are meditative and both employ the persona or mask to obtain a more objective dramatization of viewpoint.

At the start of "The Dying Man" the imagined voice of Yeats alternates and blends with Roethke's through the five lyrics composing it, and the style is itself a combination of the poetic speech of the two men. This adaptation of the Yeatsian manner and mood is not merely casual but quite intentional. In his late poems Yeats was, of course, paradoxical, outrageous, and extremely powerful, with a seemingly boundless reserve of energy to dispose to these ends. He brought together spiritual and sensual modes of experience in unexpected, even sensational, ways and under the harsh light of his irony. Roethke wished at times to use his poetry as Yeats did, to probe the extremes of perception and knowledge which the self may attain. "The Dying Man" is just such an imaginative effort; and the fact that it is both an elegy for Yeats and a utilization of some of his language and techniques should not prevent us from seeing how Roethke is really examining himself and his own situation.

The opening poem, "His Words," records the message of "a dying man / . . . to his gathered kin." This man is presumably Yeats, and what he says seems an amalgam of the thought of Blake and Yeats. Here the last stanza proves most influential in stirring the mind of the poem's narrator (Roethke himself) to his own observations:

> "A man sees, as he dies,
> Death's possibilities;
> My heart sways with the world.
> I am that final thing,
> A man learning to sing."

The second poem begins with the revaluation of his life and work which these last words and the death following them force upon the poet-narrator. In addition, he feels the potentialities of existence revived: "I thought myself reborn." The subsequent stanzas range back over past experience, the poet's love and its opposite, the darkest moments of the spirit when he "dared to question all." A knocking "at the gate" announces most probably the presence of death, but the poet puts that off in the concluding line.

Three other poems, "The Wall," "The Exulting," and "They Sing, They Sing," make up the rest of the cycle. All of them reach beyond the bounds of a reasoned arrangement of ideas and perceptions in favor of a terse but ecstatic and visionary utterance. Themes are intermingled, but they include the poet's psychic burdens:

> A ghost comes out of the unconscious mind
> To grope my sill: It moans to be reborn!
> The figure at my back is not my friend;
> The hand upon my shoulder turns to horn.

and the fusion of natural and transcendental knowledge:

> Though it reject dry borders of the seen,
> What sensual eye can keep an image pure,
> Leaning across a sill to greet the dawn?

These passages, taken from "The Wall," both use the image of the sill as the apparent threshold separating the conscious self from the unconscious and from external reality. The wall turns up in the third stanza as the limit of what can be known, and thus the poet can recognize his dilemma as that of "a spirit raging at the visible."

"The Exulting" begins with a statement of the childlike innocence and freedom which once satisfied the poet but which now have aroused further yearnings:

> I love the world; I want more than the
> world,
> Or after-image of the inner eye.

Yet the most explicit account of the object of his desires, if it can be so described, is withheld until the final stanzas of the last poem. There nature asserts itself as a means of revelation for Roethke, and he has a vision of reality corresponding to the words of the dying man in the initial section of the poem—"Eternity is Now"—a vision that calls to mind Blake's famous passage from "The Marriage of Heaven and Hell": "If the doors of perception were cleansed every thing would appear to man as it is, infinite." The world gives the poet intuitions of the eternal and the infinite through its temporal, finite creatures and things—if he has learned how to see or has been granted this frightening clairvoyance:

> I've the lark's word for it, who sings alone:
> What's seen recedes; Forever's what we
> know!—
> Eternity defined, and strewn with straw,
> The fury of the slug beneath the stone.
> The vision moves, and yet remains the
> same.
> In heaven's praise, I dread the thing I am.

The poem's ending lines, of great strength and beauty, set forth the loneliness and uncertainty but also the singular determination of the poet in his confrontation of the unknowable or the void where the Divine may be sought. Roethke furnishes no answers and, as he does elsewhere, keeps within the strict confines of his personal perceivings:

> Nor can imagination do it all
> In this last place of light: he dares to live
> Who stops being a bird, yet beats his wings
> Against the immense immeasurable
> emptiness of things.

"Meditations of an Old Woman," a longer and superior group of poems, consists of several dramatic monologues spoken by an aging lady, modeled on the poet's mother, who muses on her past, on the meanings of an individual's existence, as she faces the prospect of death. Over and above those poems included in *Words for the Wind* and in the volume of light verse (which also reprints the so-called greenhouse poems) *I Am! Says the Lamb* (1961) there are a considerable number of later poems. Roethke planned a book for them, completing it shortly before his death; it appeared as *The Far Field* the following year. It ought to be said that the "North American Sequence" poems take the manner and technique of the "Meditations" as their starting place; some of them become even looser in form; other poems are fragmentary, explosive, and epigrammatic; some turn to a taut lyricism. Many are shaped by that mixture of description and reflection so prominent in the "Meditations." Through these poems runs a continued fascination with ultimate questions of mortality, God, the final significance of human life. Of course these are questions about the self too, and they constantly bring Roethke's evolutionary theme to its highest level, that is, to occasions of visionary knowledge. But we should look at "Meditations of an Old Woman" both as the foundation of later work and as the last part of *Words for the Wind.*

The "First Meditation," which inaugurates the series of five poems, offers the reader opening stanzas that create a harsh mood of old age, winter, frailty, and severely restricted expectations. We can capture something of the ominous quality of this section from the initial lines:

On love's worst ugly day,
The weeds hiss at the edge of the field,
The small winds make their chilly
  indictments.

Thus the title and the beginning provide us with the personal situation from which the speaker's memories and thoughts are set in motion. As Roethke so frequently does, he expresses the condition of a person's life through happenings or objects in nature. The old woman's recognition of death is conveyed vividly by external events: "stones loosen on the obscure hillside, / And a tree tilts from its roots, / Toppling down an embankment." And here we must remember that it is *her mind* which entertains these images of sliding stones and falling trees.

In spite of the temporal erosion that has worn away the speaker as though she were a thing exposed to wind and dust and rain there is an essential life of the spirit preserved in her described by Roethke as "light as a seed." Small that life may be, but it has a toughness and resiliency which enables it to burst forth with a vigorous assertion of its own being. The effort of the spirit to be renewed is characteristically reflected in careful details of the actions of nonhuman creatures, a fish, for example:

So the spirit tries for another life,
Another way and place in which to
  continue;
Or a salmon, tired, moving up a shallow
  stream,
Nudges into a back-eddy, a sandy inlet,
Bumping against sticks and bottom-stones,
  then swinging
Around, back into the tiny maincurrent, the
  rush of brownish-white water,
Still swimming forward—
So, I suppose, the spirit journeys.

This passage could be seen as a paradigm of the five poems, for the old woman's meditation, which spans the period of time in the poetic cycle, is analogous to the rest enjoyed by the salmon before he renews his journey against the stream. For precisely this brief duration we are allowed to enter the speaker's mend and witness her thoughts.

Within her consciousness, as might be expected, there are alternating currents of imagery and ideas. Her attention may shift rather abruptly from past to present, from the actual to the speculative, from knowledge to dream, as we would naturally imagine it to do readily in a person of advanced age who has a lifetime to think upon and its termination to face. Yet whatever these fluctuations of consciousness might be and however random they might seem at first glance, all of them contribute to a pattern of repeated affirmations of life which reach a peak of lyrical strength at the end of "What Can I Tell My Bones?"

In contrast to this pattern the poems also contain the elements of despair, evil, and nothingness: all that thwarts the steady forward movement of the spirit. One could, in a more comprehensive study of Roethke's poetry, draw up two lists, of his positive and negative imagery, and not simply for the poems under discussion but for his work in general. We have already noticed some of the recurring metaphors and symbols in passing. Most of them will be familiar to the reader who has watched the texts with care. On the positive side we find spring and summer; the sun and moon; small creatures of the bird, insect, and fish variety; wind and flowing water; flowers, plants, and grass. On the negative side would appear winter; aridity; still and muddy waters; holes, pits, or caves; dust; desolate landscapes. The old lady in her reflections also must countenance the memory of negative experience, if only to defeat it. In the following lines we can see how she conceives the life-denying by bringing it together in her mind with the lifegiving and the sacramental:

I have gone into the waste lonely places
Behind the eye; the lost acres at the edge of
  smoky cities.
What's beyond never crumbles like an
  embankment,
Explodes like a rose, or thrusts wings over
  the Caribbean.

There are no pursuing forms, faces on walls:
Only the motes of dust in the immaculate
hallways,
The darkness of falling hair, the warnings
from lint and spiders,
The vines graying to a fine powder.
There is no riven tree, or lamb dropped by
an eagle.

Like D. H. Lawrence, with whom the critic Kenneth Burke once very interestingly compared him, Roethke locates a substantial moral vocabulary in the natural order. Perhaps these uses are not intentional in every case of such imagery, but certainly his images very often serve a purpose of the kind I have named.

The moments of ecstasy in these poems, as elsewhere in Roethke's previous work, tend to occur through the life of nature or within its boundaries. "I'm Here," the second of the "Meditations," is largely devoted to memories of the old woman's girlhood years: from them arise scenes of an innocence, an awakening of flesh and spirit in concord with the surrounding world:

I was queen of the vale—
For a short while,
Living all my heart's summer alone,
Ward of my spirit,
Running through high grasses,
My thighs brushing against flower-crowns;
Leaning, out of all breath,
Bracing my back against a sapling,
Making it quiver with my body . . .

And again:

The body, delighting in thresholds,
Rocks in and out of itself.
A bird, small as a leaf,
Sings in the first
Sunlight.

The closing poem compels the speaker once more to encounter the forbidding prospect of a slow crumbling away to death; yet it is at last her love for all things, especially the commonplace or simple things of which our everyday world is made, that urges her back from somber meditation to the flow of existence. The tired, aging lady with whom the cycle of poems began emerges from shelter as if life had just been given her by an "agency outside . . . Unprayed-for, / And final." But Roethke is not explicit about this agency as yet. Later poems such as "In a Dark Time" recount the poet's experience of God in trancelike visions. The emphasis in the "Meditations" falls upon earthly possibility, the self's embrace of the entire horizon of existence open to it:

The sun! The sun! And all we can become!
And the time ripe for running to the moon!
In the long fields, I leave my father's eye;
And shake the secrets from my deepest
bones;
My spirit rises with the rising wind;
I'm thick with leaves and tender as a dove,
I take the liberties a short life permits—
I seek my own meekness;
I recover my tenderness by long looking.
By midnight I love everything alive.
Who took the darkness from the air?
I'm wet with another life.
Yea, I have gone and stayed.

Though cut tragically short by his premature death, Roethke's career is brought to a magnificent conclusion in the poems of *The Far Field.* Here we find an extension of his amazing, always increasing versatility in formal arrangement and experiment, his ability to explore several avenues of poetic endeavor simultaneously without sacrificing the value of one to the interests of another. In these poems various thematic preoccupations—the identity of the self, its relation to the beloved, to nature, and to God—also achieve rewarding fulfillment.

The book is organized in four sections. The first and last, "North American Sequence" and "Sequence, Sometimes Metaphysical," though contrasting in manner, are concerned with a search for the Divine and with spiritual illumination. In between there is a sizable group of love poems and a section of miscellaneous pieces aptly called "Mixed Sequence." The love poems, written for his wife, Beatrice, even include, with humor and understanding, the moments of their discord; but these are far outnumbered by celebrations of the ecstasy and joy of their relationship. At the end of the section we discover the incredibly moving and prophetic "Wish for a Young Wife":

My lizard, my lovely writher,
May your limbs never wither,
May the eyes in your face
Survive the green ice
Of envy's mean gaze;
May you live out your life
Without hate, without grief,
And your hair ever blaze,
In the sun, in the sun,
When I am undone,
When I am no one.

Of this kind of short lyric Roethke is a master, as we have seen in his work from the beginning. Over the years he had tested its possibilities as thought and experience deepened, and in "Sequence, Sometimes Metaphysical" he brings this taut, economical form to a peak of accomplishment in the treatment of difficult material. The twelve-poem sequence starts with "In a Dark Time," which is a statement of harrowing mystical union, and continues with poems reflecting on this encounter, as well as with other instances of spiritual revelation. While these experiences are, in one sense, extremely personal, Roethke uses recurrent images and metaphors, frequently drawn from the natural world, to objectify his inner life. Many of the pieces appeared singly in journals and made impressive reading by themselves; but now, taken altogether, they compose a cycle of visionary lyrics which must surely count among the finest in our literature. Let me quote, as an example, the first stanza of "The Tree, the Bird":

Uprose, uprose, the stony fields uprose,
And every snail dipped toward me its pure
horn.
The sweet light met me as I walked toward
A small voice calling from a drifting cloud.
I was a finger pointing at the moon,
At ease with joy, a self-enchanted man.
Yet when I sighed, I stood outside my life,
A leaf unaltered by the midnight scene,
Part of a tree still dark, still, deathly still,
Riding the air, a willow with its kind,
Bearing its life and more, a double sound,
Kin to the wind, and the bleak whistling
rain.

And, as one further instance of Roethke's power and clairvoyance in these poems, here are some lines from "Infirmity":

Things without hands take hands: there is
no choice,—
Eternity's not easily come by.
When opposites come suddenly in place,
I teach my eyes to hear, my ears to see
How body from spirit slowly does unwind
Until we are pure spirit at the end.

The poems of "North American Sequence" stand in marked formal contrast to such lyrics and indicate a continuation of the reflective monologue of "Meditations of an Old Woman." Now, however, the poet dispenses with the dramatic mask, speaks in his own person, and records the movements of his spiritual consciousness, his quest for a final unity. Roethke wrote in his essay "Some Remarks on Rhythm" of the need for the catalogue poem, for the careful and prolonged descriptive passage; and in these pieces with their lengthy, irregular lines, deliberately placed in the Whitman tradition, he has answered his own requirements. Disclosing the progressions and setbacks of his inward states, the desire to escape from the self and its attachments, the sequence also renders in stunning detail the life of nature in profound correspondence with the poet's inward being. It is difficult to quote without taking very long sections, so I will make do with a few lines from "Meditation at Oyster River":

The self persists like a dying star,
In sleep, afraid. Death's face rises afresh,
Among the shy beasts, the deer at the salt-
lick,

The doe with its sloped shoulders loping
across the highway,
The young snake, poised in green leaves,
waiting for its fly,
The hummingbird, whirring from quince-
blossom to morning-glory—
With these I would be.

Roethke once said to me, a year before his death, that this might well be his last book, a judgment I found both depressing and hard to believe. It was painfully accurate though, and these late poems, preoccupied with death and the ultimate phases of spiritual quest, beautifully complete his life's work as if by intuition. Few contemporary poets can match the daring, the richness, and the freedom—which is really to say, in summary, the beauty—of the totality of his writing. Surely the intensity and clarity of Roethke's vision, in addition to his tremendous lyrical force and technical facility, place him, as John Crowe Ransom has said, in company with some of the finest modern American poets. His art shows the poet's will to extend himself, to try his skill and imagination at every turn, and his growth was organic and true. Roethke's sense of direction was bold and challenging yet unfailingly precise. The metamorphoses or transformations through which he and his poems passed are caught in the old lady's words near the end of "What Can I Tell My Bones?" What they reveal of that speaker, her aspirations and strength, they also disclose about Roethke and the magnitude of his poetic achievement:

The wind rocks with my wish; the rain
shields me;
I live in light's extreme; I stretch in all
directions;
Sometimes I think I'm several.

Selected Bibliography

WORKS OF THEODORE ROETHKE

POETRY

Open House, (New York: Knopf, 1941).

The Lost Son and Other Poems, (Garden City, N.Y.: Doubleday, 1948).

Praise to the End, (Garden City, N.Y.: Doubleday, 1951).

The Waking: Poems 1933–1953, (Garden City, N.Y.: Doubleday, 1953).

Words for the Wind: The Collected Verse of Theodore Roethke, (Garden City, N.Y.: Doubleday, 1958).

I Am! Says the Lamb, (Garden City, N.Y.: Doubleday, 1961).

Sequence, Sometimes Metaphysical, (Iowa City: Stonewall Press, 1963).

The Far Field, (Garden City, N.Y.: Doubleday, 1964).

The Collected Poems of Theodore Roethke, (Garden City, N.Y.: Doubleday, 1966).

PROSE

On the Poet and His Craft: Selected Prose of Theodore Roethke, Edited by Ralph J. Mills, Jr. (Seattle: University of Washington Press, 1965).

Selected Letters of Theodore Roethke, edited by Ralph J. Mills, Jr. (Seattle: University of Washington Press, 1968).

MISCELLANEOUS

Straw for the Fire: Selections from Theodore Roethke's Notebooks 1943–1963, edited by David Wagoner (Garden City, N.Y.: Doubleday, 1972).

BIBLIOGRAPHY

Matheson, John William, *Theodore Roethke: A Bibliography,* (University of Washington: Master of Librarianship thesis, 1958).

McLeod, James R., *Theodore Roethke: A Manuscript Checklist,* (Kent, Ohio: Kent State University Press, 1971).

McLeod, James R., *Theodore Roethke: A Bibliography,* (Kent, Ohio: Kent State University Press, 1972).

BIOGRAPHY

Seager, Allan, *The Glass House: The Life of Theodore Roethke,* (New York: McGraw-Hill, 1968).

CRITICAL STUDIES

Arnett, Carroll, "Minimal to Maximal: Theodore Roethke's Dialectic," *College English* 18: 414–16, (May, 1957).

Bogan, Louise, "Stitched in Bone," *Trial Balances,* edited by Ann Winslow (New York: Macmillan, 1935). pp. 138–39.

Burke, Kenneth, "The Vegetal Radicalism of Theodore Roethke," *Sewanee Review* 58: 68–108, (Winter 1950).

Dickey, James, "Theodore Roethke," in *Babel to Byzantium: Poets and Poetry Now* (New York: Noonday Press, 1968). pp. 147–52.

Gross, Harvey, *Sound and Form in Modern Poetry,* (Ann Arbor: University of Michigan Press, 1964).

Kramer, Hilton, "The Poetry of Theodore Roethke," *Western Review* 18: 131–46, (Winter 1954).

Kunitz, Stanley, "News of the Root," *Poetry* 73: 222–25, (January 1949).

———, Stanley, "Theodore Roethke," *New York Review of Books* 1: 22 (October 17, 1963).

———, Stanley, "Roethke: Poet of Transformations," *New Republic* 152: 23–29 (January 23, 1965).

Lee, Charlotte I., "The Line as a Rhythmic Unit in the Poetry of Theodore Roethke," *Speech Monographs* 30: 15–22, (March 1963).

Malkoff, Karl, *Theodore Roethke: An Introduction to the Poetry,* (New York: Columbia University Press, 1966).

Martz, William J., *The Achievement of Theodore Roethke,* (Glenview, Ill.: Scott, Foresman, 1966).

Mills, Ralph J., Jr., "Roethke's Garden," *Poetry* 100: 54–59, (April 1962).

———, "Theodore Roethke," *Contemporary American Poetry* (New York: Random House, 1965), pp. 48–71.

———, *Creation's Very Self: On the Personal Element in Recent American Poetry,* (Fort Worth: Texas Christian University Press, 1969).

Northwest Review, 11, (Summer, 1971). Special issue on Theodore Roethke.

Ostroff, Anthony, ed., *The Contemporary Poet as Artist and Critic,* (Boston: Little, Brown, 1964). This includes essays on Roethke's "In a Dark Time," by John Crowe Ransom, Babette Deutsch, Stanley Kunitz, with a reply by the poet.

Rosenthal, M. L., *The Modern Poets,* (New York: Oxford University Press, 1960). pp. 240–44.

Scott, Nathan A., *The Wild Prayer of Longing,* (New Haven, Conn.: Yale University Press, 1971).

Schwartz, Delmore, "The Cunning and Craft of the Unconscious and the Preconscious," *Poetry* 94: 203–05, (June 1959).

Southworth, James G., "The Poetry of Theodore Roethke," (*College English,* 21: 326–38, March 1960).

Spender, Stephen, "Words for the Wind," (*New Republic,* 141: 21–22, August 10, 1959).

Staples, Hugh B., "The Rose in the Sea-Wind: A Reading of Theodore Roethke's," and "North American Sequence," (*American Literature* 6: 189–203, May 1964).

Stein, Arnold, ed., *Theodore Roethke: Essays on the Poetry,* (Seattle: University of Washington Press, 1965).

Tate, Allen, "In Memoriam—Theodore Roethke, 1908–1963," (*Encounter,* 21: 68, October 1963).

"Theodore Roethke's *Praise to the End!* Poems," (*Iowa Review,* 2: 60–79, Fall 1971).

Waggoner, Hyatt H., *American Poets from the Puritans to the Present,* (Boston: Houghton Mifflin, 1968).

Winters, Yvor, "The Poems of Theodore Roethke," (*Kenyon Review,* 3: 514–16, Autumn 1941).

CARL SANDBURG
(1878–1967)

GAY WILSON ALLEN

Carl Sandburg never won the Nobel Prize, but some Americans thought that he should have, and when Hemingway received it in 1954 he told reporters that it should have gone to Sandburg. Later in the year at the National Book Awards program in New York when Harvey Breit, of the *New York Times Book Review* staff, asked Sandburg how he felt about Hemingway's friendly gesture, he replied: "Harvey Breit, I want to tell you that sometime thirty years from now when the Breit boys are sitting around, one boy will say, Did Carl Sandburg ever win the Nobel Prize?' and one Breit boy will say, 'Ernest Hemingway gave it to him in 1954."

Whether or not Sandburg deserved the Nobel Prize, he was at least as well known and widely read in his own country as Hemingway, though perhaps not as famous abroad, for he had not outrun General Patton's tanks in the World War II invasion of Germany or led the vanguard in "liberating" Paris, to mention only two of Hemingway's fabulous adventures. Yet in his own way Sandburg was also newsworthy. No other American writer was at the same time so widely read and heard: hundreds of audiences had been entertained by his baritone voice, reading his poems, singing American folk ballads which he had collected, accompanying himself on his ubiquitous guitar, the familiar lock of unruly hair drooping over one eye. Innumerable photographs in newspapers and magazines and animated images on television and motion picture screens had made his face as much of a popular icon as Mark Twain's a generation earlier.

Of course these comparisons only establish the fact that Carl Sandburg was a great celebrity and a superb professional entertainer. Was he a great poet? At the peak of his productivity—say from 1930 to the entry of the United States in World War II—there seemed little doubt that he was, though even then some dissenting critical voices could be heard. By the time of his death in the late 1960's his reputation seemed less secure, though as a biographer of Lincoln he had no contemporary rival, and as a symbolical "voice of America" he was rivaled only by the New England poet Robert Frost, who bitterly resented any comparison. Actually, the competition of poets is always a mitigating factor in their reputations, especially contemporary. Friends of Frost tended to downgrade the prosodically freewheeling Sandburg. Admirers of T. S. Eliot were not inclined to hold a high opinion of the folksy author of *The People, Yes.* Though Ezra Pound had some appreciation of the revolutionary modernity of Sandburg, he "put him down," as Ben Jonson did Shakespeare, for his "small Latin and less Greek," or in Pound's own words, as "a lumberjack who has taught himself all that he knows." Lumberjacking happened to be one of the few occupations Sandburg had never tried, but he was unquestionably self-taught.

Whatever Carl Sandburg's future rank in literature may be—and posthumous reputations are impossible to predict (witness Melville, Whitman, and Emily Dickinson)—he was, as Thomas Lask declared in the *New York Times* at the time of Sandburg's death on July 23, 1967, "the American bard. The sense of being American informed everything he wrote." Sandburg's success as the voice and conscience of his time and generation, to a degree Whitman would have envied, is sufficient justification for a critical study of his life and career. This is the most rewarding approach to this enormously productive writer. The question of his "minor" or "major" status can wait for time to answer.

The America Sandburg knew and wrote about—at least until after World War II—was "mid-America," life on the prairies of Illinois and the shores of Lake Michigan from Milwaukee to Chicago and Harbert, Michigan. His mind was still lively and his typewriter busy during most of his final twenty-two years at Flat Rock, North Carolina, but his formative years were spent in the Midwest of his contemporaries Theodore Dreiser, Sherwood Anderson, Sinclair Lewis, Edgar Lee Masters, and Ernest Hemingway—the Hemingway of the Nick Adams stories, which some critics think his best. It can hardly be accidental that these men who were some of the most innovative and influential authors in America from World War I to the beginning of World War II all had a similar background. By the end of World War II the spurt of midwestern literary energy had nearly spent itself and passed to the South. But the two decades between the wars were dominated by these mid-American poets and novelists.

In changing the course of American literature Sandburg and his western contemporaries were, to be sure, assisted by their equally western predecessors Mark Twain, Hamlin Garland, and William Dean Howells. All of these writers were largely self-taught, like Abraham Lincoln, who grew up in Indiana and Illinois. The first white settlers to arrive in this region in their covered wagons, like the later impoverished emigrants from northern Europe, had had little formal education, and the traditions they brought with them were severely tested and modified by the harsh life of the frontier and the crude towns built in reckless baste. Experience was their school. The world that Dreiser, Anderson, Sandburg, and Hemingway knew bore little resemblance to the cultured society of Henry James, Edith Wharton, and Edwin Arlington Robinson. Empiricism shaped both their ethics and their aesthetics. In this sense they were all "from Missouri," skeptical of authority, disdainful of conventions, and personally independent to the point of eccentricity. Consequently their attitude toward human experience was realistic, the subject of their fiction and verse the life of ordinary people, and their style shaped by the idiom and rhythms of mid-American speech.

These midwestern writers were acutely conscious of social inequalities and injustices, and several were professed Socialists, including Sandburg. In religion they were mainly agnostic, though tolerant of the religious experience of others, and they had a somewhat Emersonian attitude toward nature (Emerson was always one of Sandburg's favorite authors). Their life-style was stubbornly individualistic, in speech, manners, opinions, and artistic self-expression. Sandburg's clothes never seemed to fit properly, and his indifference to his appearance was so pronounced as finally to suggest a theatrical pose; but it was entirely in character with the role he played in lecturing and singing ballads, and in harmony, too, with his own personality, for clothes were never more than a practical necessity to him.

Sandburg's indifference to fashion began with his early life in Galesburg, Illinois, where he was born January 6, 1878, near the tracks of the Chicago, Burlington, and Quincy Railroad, for which his father worked as a blacksmith. Both parents were Swedish immigrants who had come to the United States separately. Clara Anderson was working as a hotel chambermaid in another small Illinois town when she met August Sandburg, member of a railroad gang passing through. They were married in 1874 and settled in Galesburg after August was transferred to the C.B.&Q. repair shop. He could read his Swedish Bible but never learned to write, having to sign his name with an X. Mrs. Sandburg could write personal letters in colloquial Swedish and phonetically spelled English. Neither was the least interested in books, except for the Bible, and Carl had to discover the world of literature without any encouragement at home.

In primary school Carl learned the alphabet and began reading in a "primer" which had puzzling sentences about a ladies' tea party. He had never tasted tea (the Swedes preferred coffee) and he thought the ladies' conversation very silly. But he soon became fascinated by words, spoken or written. Several years later he received a card from the public library and became an avid reader, especially of history and biographies of American Revolution heroes. He was disappointed to find the biographies of Civil War generals dull and unconvincing; strange, he thought, because he had talked with men who had fought in this more recent war and he found their stories absorbingly interesting. Many of the older people in Galesburg remembered Lincoln's debate with Judge Douglas at Knox College. A plaque on one of the buildings commemorated the historic spot, and Sandburg many times stopped to read it.

One of the subjects young Sandburg enjoyed most in school was geography; both the places and the people in other parts of the world stirred his imagination. Literature did not yet arouse much enthusiasm in him, especially the poetry of Longfellow and the novels of Dickens, his teachers' favorites. He read *Tom Sawyer* and *Huckleberry Finn,* but at the time preferred James Otis' *Toby Tyler: or, Ten Weeks with a Circus,* and Charles Coffin's *The Boys of '76.* He read detective stories, too, of course out of school, but found them less absorbing than Champlin's *Young Folks' Cyclopaedia of Persons and Places.* He was not bored by school, however, and liked most of his teachers, but after he finished the eighth grade he had to go to work to help his father support the family of five children (not counting two boys who died of diphtheria at an early age). But for a bright, observant, and gregarious boy with endless curiosity and a sympathetic nature, education really began after he quit school. In his own revealing account of his boyhood in *Always the Young Strangers* (1953) he could say, looking back from maturity:

"In those years as a boy in that prairie town I got education in scraps and pieces of many kinds, not knowing that they were part of my education. I met people in Galesburg who were puzzling to me, and later when I read Shakespeare I found those same people were puzzling him. I met little wonders of many kinds among animals and plants that never lost their wonder for me, and I found later that these same wonders had a deep interest for Emerson, Thoreau, and Walt Whitman. I met superstitions, folk tales, and folklore while I was a young spalpeen, 'a broth of a boy,' long before I read books about them. All had their part, small or large, in the education I got outside of books and schools."

Not surprisingly, it was also outside school that the "young spalpeen" learned "that crime and politics are tangled with each other, that law and justice sometimes can be a monkey business with a bad smell." He made this declaration in *Always the Young Strangers* regarding a particularly revolting murder in Chicago of a Dr. Cronin, "leader in a camp of the Clanna-Gael fighters for the freedom of Ireland." One of the accused was "handy at passing money to jurymen" and went free. Another man allegedly connected with the murder "went free in a hurry on 'habeas corpus,' later was put on trial for jury bribing, and wriggled out free."

"Of course," Sandburg continues, "we got education out of the Cronin murder and the first and second trials. We learned that in time of peace, and no war on, men can kill a man not for money but because the man stands for something they hate and they want him out of the way. We learned that juries can be fixed, that if a convicted man waits a few years and gets a second trial there may be important witnesses who have died or moved away or somehow can't be found. . . . We learned things we didn't hear about in the Seventh Ward school and we never read about them in the detective stories of those days. . . ."

After a great variety of short-term jobs, delivering milk, cutting ice on the lake, assisting carpenters, painters, plumbers, barbers, druggists, etc., Sandburg decided at eighteen to see the country by traveling as a hobo to the wheat fields of Kansas. He rode freight trains, stopping at towns along the way to earn a little money at dishwashing or other temporary employment. He met other hoboes and shared food with them in their "jungles" near the railroad tracks. After working with a threshing crew he "bummed" his way to the Rocky Mountains and back home.

Sandburg was trying to learn the house-painting trade when the American battleship *Maine* was sunk in Havana harbor on February 15, 1898. Believing with most other Americans that Spain was responsible (exactly who or what caused the explosion has never been definitely known), he enlisted in the Sixth Infantry Regiment of the Illinois Volunteers. With this regiment he drilled for two months in Virginia, saw the national capitol while on leave, was transported to Guantánamo Bay in Cuba, then hastily shipped to Guánica, Puerto Rico, because of an epidemic of yellow fever in Cuba. The short war was nearly over before the Illinois soldiers arrived, and they saw no fighting, though they suffered in the tropical heat from wearing heavy wool Civil War uniforms, from thousands of insect bites, from dysentery and spoiled food which war profiteers had sold to the United States government.

As a "war veteran" Sandburg was admitted to Lombard College—the "other" college in Galesburg—without a high school diploma or an entrance examination. He supported himself by serving with the local fire department, studying and sleeping at night in the firehouse. The most remarkable teacher at Lombard, a man who won distinction later as an economist in Washington, D.C., was Professor Philip Green Wright. He taught English, mathematics, astronomy, and economics—some indication of the kind of college Lombard was. He took a special interest in Carl and gave him his first competent instruction in writing.

In college Sandburg played basketball and baseball, acted in a musical comedy, contributed to a literary magazine, and edited the college yearbook, but left in the spring of his senior year without a degree—probably because he had failed to take some courses required for graduation. These courses may have been in mathematics, because this was one of the subjects which later prevented his passing the entrance examination to West Point after he had been nominated by his congressman. His other failure was in English grammar.

Though Sandburg left college without a definite goal in life, he had experienced the satisfaction of writing down his own thoughts and seeing them in print in the college publications. But he was restless and began wandering again, this time in the East. He spent ten days in a Pittsburgh jail (for "deadbeating" his way on a freight train) before returning to Galesburg. Home again and without employment, he completed a batch of poems. Professor Wright had a small printing press in his basement, and there Sandburg's first three slender volumes were set up and privately printed: *In Reckless Ecstasy* in 1904 and *The Plaint of a Rose* and *Incidentals* in 1905.

It might surprise readers of Sandburg's *Chicago Poems* to find that he derived the title of his first book from the popular, romantic, and third-rate contemporary Marie Corelli, who praised the "reckless ecstasies of language." At this stage in his development as a poet Sandburg believed simply that "there are depths of life that logic cannot sound. It takes feeling." To produce this *feeling* he used the galloping meter of a Kipling, or almost any other popular poet of the period, as in the embarrassingly trite "Pulse-Beats and Pen-Strokes":

> For the hovels shall pass and the shackles
>   drop,
> The gods shall tumble and the systems fall;
> And the things they will make, with their
>   loves at stake,
> Shall be the gladness of each and all.

However, *Incidentals,* a collection of aphorisms, was in a prose-poetry form suggestive of Sandburg's maturer style:

> What is shame?
> Shame is the feeling you have when you
> agree
> with the woman who loves you that you
> are the
> man she thinks you are . . .
>
> Truth consists of paradoxes and a paradox
> is two facts that stand on opposite hilltops
> and across the intervening valley call
> each other liars.

These juvenilia Sandburg was glad to forget, and they have never been reprinted, except for brief quotations in Harry Golden's *Carl Sandburg* and in an article I wrote for an academic magazine.

Chicago was the place that Sandburg later made famous in his poems, but he could have written a book on Galesburg, Illinois, similar to Sherwood Anderson's psychological study of people in *Winesburg, Ohio,* or epitaphs of tragic failure like those in Edgar Lee Masters *Spoon River Anthology.* In fact, sketches of such stories and biographies Sandburg did publish in *Always the Young Strangers,* with the difference that the outright failures he mentions were few. Collectively the subjects of his sketches were a cross section of the nation, or in Sandburg's own words: "This small town of Galesburg, as I look back on it, was a piece of the American Republic. Breeds and blood strains that figure in history were there for me, as a boy to see and hear in their faces and their ways of talking and acting."

From 1902 to 1906 Sandburg wandered away and returned to Galesburg, supporting himself mainly by peddling stereoptican pictures, but he also contributed to a Chicago magazine called *Tomorrow.* In 1906 he became associate editor of another magazine in Chicago called *Lyceumite,* and began giving lectures on Walt Whitman. It was in Chicago that he met Winfield R. Gaylord, an organizer of the Social Democratic party in Wisconsin. The doctrines of the party strongly appealed to him and he accepted an offer to join Mr. Gaylord in his work.

Sandburg continued to lecture on Whitman, but gave most of his time to traveling and addressing workingmen in Wisconsin. "Labor is beginning to realize its power," he told them. "We no longer beg, we demand old-age pensions; we demand a minimum wage; we demand industrial accident insurance; we demand unemployment insurance; and we demand the eight-hour day, which must become the basic law of the land." These demands which seemed so radical in 1907–9 would become "the basic law of the land," not under a Socialist president but under the administration of Franklin D. Roosevelt and be extended in subsequent Democratic and Republican administrations. Yet the pioneers for these laws were those Wisconsin Socialists La Follette and Gaylord, and party recruiters like Carl Sandburg.

One day in 1908 at the Milwaukee Socialist headquarters Sandburg met Lilian Steichen, a schoolteacher from Illinois, who was there because she had been employed by the party to translate Socialist classics from French and German into English. She and Sandburg were immediately attracted to each other and were married several months later, a happy marriage that lasted until Sandburg's death. Mrs. Sandburg was the sister of Edward Steichen, who became a world-famous photographer and one of the poet's staunchest friends.

From recruiting members for the Socialist party Sandburg made an easy transition to Milwaukee journalism. He did reporting and wrote feature articles and some editorials for the *News,* the *Sentinel,* and the *Journal.* Milwaukee elected a Socialist mayor, Emil Seidel, and he employed Sandburg as a private secretary. But newspaper work remained his chief vocation. In 1912 he joined the liberal *Milwaukee Leader,* then went to the *Chicago Daily World* and, several newspaper jobs later, to the *Chicago Daily News,* with which he remained until the success of his biography of Lincoln, *The Prairie Years,* made it possible for him to resign and buy a farm in Harbert, Michigan, where his wife raised goats and he could give his full time to poetry and biography, with intervals of lecturing.

Sandburg's fierce sympathy with poor people, the oppressed and the exploited, which was to find expression in all his writing—in fact, was often the main reason for his writing at all—became permanently imbedded in his conscience and consciousness during his few years of propagating socialism in Wisconsin. However, he was never a Marxist, though he had read *Das Kapital* at Lombard with Professor Wright. He was more of a Populist and social reformer, perhaps influenced somewhat by "Teddy" Roosevelt in the early years of the twentieth century, and certainly by the muckraking journalists: Ida Tarbell, who wrote about the greed of John D. Rockefeller; Lincoln Steffens, who uncovered political corruption in the cities; and Upton Sinclair, the Socialist novelist, who shocked the nation into beginning pure-food legislation after *The Jungle* (1906) revealed the incredibly unsanitary conditions of the packing industry in Chicago. (Sinclair's equally strong indictment of the exploitation of laboring men, especially the nearly illiterate newcomers from Europe, by factory employers, real-estate dealers, and merchants did not produce such prompt results.) Sandburg, like Sinclair, was more concerned with the actual condition of the workingmen's lives than with ideology.

In 1908 Sandburg campaigned for Eugene V. Debs for the presidency, and in 1915 he and Jack London often wrote the entire contents of the *International Socialist Review,* using a variety of pseudonyms. At the outbreak of World War I he shared the pacifist views of other Socialists (Social Democrats in Wisconsin, trade-union Socialists in New York City, Fabians in England, and Christian Socialists in Germany, France, and Italy). He expressed his horror of killing in a group of "War Poems" (1914–15), and in the *International Socialist Review* he argued that soldiers were actually exploited laborers:

"It's a workingman's world. Shovels and shovelling take more time of soldiers than guns and shooting. Twenty-one million men on the battlefields of Europe are shovelling more than shooting. Not only have they dug hundreds of miles of trenches, but around and under the trenches are tunnels and labyrinthian catacombs. All dug by shovels. Technically, in social science and economics, the soldier is a parasite and a curious louse of the master-class imposed on the working class. Yet strictly now the soldier is a worker, a toiler on and under the land. He's a sucker, a shovelman who gets board and clothes from the government that called him to the colors. A mucker-gunman—that's what a soldier is."

Yet when the United States finally entered World War I, Sandburg broke with the Social Democrats and supported President Wilson. As Harry Golden recalls, "Outside Milwaukee the Wisconsin Socialists never made great headway until 1918, when they got the votes of many people of German descent who opposed America's entry into World War I. It was the kind of success that helped kill [the party]."

Sandburg never returned to the Socialist party, but he remained personally loyal to Debs and invited him to his home in suburban Chicago after Debs was released from prison. In 1933 Sandburg lost the friendship of Robert Frost by supporting Roosevelt and the New Deal. Six years later President Roosevelt warmly thanked him for a radio broadcast endorsing his policies and candidacy for a second term. Sandburg also did some campaigning for John F. Kennedy in 1960. He could count Justice William O. Douglas and Adlai Stevenson as personal friends, but at the same time he admired Republican Earl Warren. Thus the Social Democrat of the early twentieth century was, by mid-century, securely in the mainstream of American politics.

While still extremely busy in newspaper work and writing articles and editorials for Socialist magazines, Sandburg somehow found time to compose the poems which began to create a literary reputation for him when *Chicago Poems* was published in 1916. Some of these poems had attracted attention when first published by Harriet Monroe in *Poetry,* a magazine she started in Chicago in 1912. In fact, his poetic fame might be said to have begun with the publication of "Chicago" in *Poetry* in 1914. This was the key poem in the collection Henry Holt and Company published, a volume declared by Amy Lowell in the *New York Times Book Review*, to be "one of the most original books this age has produced."

In "Chicago" Sandburg admits all the faults of the city familiar to the world as the "stormy, husky, brawling . . . crooked . . . brutal" place where painted women lure farm boys under the gas lamps, gunmen kill and go free to kill again, and factory workers and their families starve because of low wages or unemployment. But this is not a social-protest poem. It is a lyric tribute to the vibrant, proud, happy, and laughing "City of the Big Shoulders . . . a tall bold slugger set vivid against the little soft cities . . ." If Chicago lacks the culture and beauty of the older cities, its inhabitants can take pride in its youth, vitality, and joy in being alive. This is the Chicago myth created by Sandburg, and it gave a great stimulation to midwestern literature.

In "Skyscraper" the poet strives to give the building a "soul." The skyscraper, he says, acquired its soul from the men who built it, those who dug the foundation, erected the girders, carried the mortar, laid the brick and fitted the stone, strung miles of wires and pipes; and later the stenographers, scrubbing women, and watchmen who worked in it. He ignores the business executives, but perhaps they have no soul-power to spare. Anyway, this is the manner in which the poet humanizes inanimate steel and stone.

In his newspaper prose Sandburg continued to fight for the causes he had espoused since his first affiliation with the Social Democratic party, but in most of his poems he attacked social evils obliquely. One exception was "To a Contemporary Bunk Shooter" (previously printed in *New Masses* undisguised as "Billy Sunday"):

> You come along . . . tearing your shirt. . . .
> yelling about Jesus.
>
> . . .
>
> He never came near clean people or dirty
> people but they felt cleaner because he
> came along. It was your crowd of bankers
> and business men and lawyers hired the
> sluggers and murderers who put Jesus out
> of the running.

He calls Billy Sunday "a bug-house peddler of second-hand gospel," telling "people living in shanties" that they can live in "mansions in the skies after they're dead and the worms have eaten 'em." Doubtless Billy Sunday deserved this cuffing, but the poem was indeed propaganda for the *New Masses.*

A prominent theme in *Chicago Poems* is the longing of ordinary people for the beauty and happiness they have never known. This clutching at dreams was not a creation of Sandburg's fantasy, but a social phenomenon which he accurately observed. The fact is confirmed by the contemporary midwestern novelists, Dreiser especially, whose early novels are repositories of social history. For example, in *Sister Carrie* (1900) the heroine is an unsophisticated girl who leaves a small town in Wisconsin to go to Chicago in search of pleasure and excitement. She finds only poverty, drudgery, and monotony until, by instinctive self-preservation from cold and hunger, she becomes a "kept woman." Yet in spite of subsequent fame and wealth in the theater, she never finds self-fulfillment, and continues dreaming of the happiness she has somehow missed. Many of the people in Sandburg's poems are brothers and sisters of Sister Carrie, such as "Mamie":

> Mamie beat her head against the bars of a
> little Indiana town and dreamed of
> romance and big things off somewhere
> the way the railroad trains all ran.

She thought of suicide and then decided that, "if she was going to die she might as well die struggling for a clutch of romance among the streets of Chicago."

> She has a job now at six dollars a week in
> the basement of the Boston store And
> even now she beats her head against the
> bars in the same old way and wonders if

there is a bigger place the railroads run to
from Chicago where maybe there is
  romance
  and big things
  and real dreams
  that never go smash.

A more cheerful theme in *Chicago Poems* is the laughter and joy workmen manage to find in spite of their toil and poverty. The face of the Jewish fish crier on Maxwell Street is the face "of a man terribly glad to be selling fish, terribly glad that God made fish, and customers to whom he may call his wares from a pushcart." The poet searches for "Happiness" and finds it one Sunday afternoon on the banks of the Desplaines River in "a crowd of Hungarians under the trees with their women and children and a keg of beer and an accordion." In "Fellow Citizens" the poet is told by a millionaire, an advertising executive named Jim Kirch, and the mayor that they are happy, but he discovers a man on Gilpin Place, near Hull House, making accordions and guitars which he plays himself after he has finished them, and "he had it all over the butter millionaire, Jim Kirch and the mayor when it came to happiness."

In the use of slang and undignified language Sandburg achieved in actuality the theory which Wordsworth set forth in his Preface to *Lyrical Ballads*: to "present incidents and situations from common life . . . in a selection of language really used by men . . ." Sandburg's poems are also more realistic than Wordsworth's, or even naturalistic (in the Zola sense), as in "The Walking Man of Rodin," with "The skull found always crumbling neighbor of the ankles." Yet Sandburg is also just as definitely romantic in his ability to see beauty in the commonplace. "The Shovel Man," for example, is

A dago working for a dollar six bits a day
And a dark-eyed woman in the old country
  dreams of him for one of the world's
  ready men with a pair of fresh lips and a
  kiss better than all the wild grapes that
  ever grew in Tuscany.

Perhaps it is not surprising that Sandburg most often found this beauty in the lives of foreign-born workmen, people like his own Swedish parents; but these recent Americans also constituted a large segment of the Chicago population. Sandburg was indeed at this period the Chicago poet.

In his second volume of poetry, *Cornhuskers* (1918), Sandburg played less the role of the urban poet and wrote more about rural sights and sounds and his wider experiences during World War I. He was now traveling more, lecturing, reading his poems, collecting and singing the folk ballads which he published later in *The American Songbag* (1927). His three daughters (Margaret, born in 1911, Janet in 1914, and Helga in 1918) also began to have an emotional effect on his literary imagination as he entertained them with the kind of child-fantasy stories he published in 1922 in *Rootabaga Stories.*

Cornhuskers opens with "Prairie," a poem partly autobiographical, partly cosmic, partly prophetic:

I was born on the prairie and the milk of its
  wheat, the red of its clover, the eyes of its
  women, gave me a song and a slogan.

Here the water went down, the icebergs slid
  with gravel, the gaps and the valleys
  hissed, and the black loam came, and the
  yellow sandy loam.

. . .

O prairie mother, I am one of your boys.

. . .

I speak of new cities and new people.
I tell you the past is a bucket of ashes
I tell you yesterday is a wind gone down,
  a sun dropped in the west.
I tell you there is nothing in the world,
  only an ocean of tomorrows,
  a sky of tomorrows.

I am a brother of the cornhuskers who say
  at sundown:
    Tomorrow is a day.

In these poems Sandburg shows his fondness for elemental things: sky, moon, stars, wind, birds, and animals. He celebrates nature in all seasons, but especially late summer and autumn: the ripening corn, the yellow cornflower in autumn wind, the blue of larkspur and Canadian thistle, and red-ripe tomatoes. In "Wilderness" he feels kinship with a wolf, a fox, a hog, a fish, a baboon, an eagle, and a mockingbird, and exclaims, "O, I got a zoo, I got a menagerie, inside my ribs." But he is over-fond of baby metaphors. In "Baby Face" the "white moon comes in on a baby face." In "The Year" buds "open baby fists / Into hands of broad flowers," while the winds sing "lullabies." "Handfuls" narrowly escapes sentimentality:

> Blossoms of babies
> Blinking their stories
> Come soft
> On the dusk and the babble;
> Little red gamblers,
> Handfuls that slept in the dust.

This book is dedicated to Janet and Margaret, each of whom gets a poem. In "Sixteen Months" the adoring father sees on Janet's lips the blue mist of dreams, smoke, and haze on "ten miles of corn" in morning sunlight. This is stretching metaphors to their limit. As "Child Margaret" writes the Arabic symbols, 1 and 7 have a military stance, 6 and 9 dance, 2 is a trapeze actor, 3 is humpbacked, and 8 knock-kneed. "Each number is a bran-new rag doll." This whimsical side of the poet may have surprised some readers who had Sandburg tagged as "the Chicago poet."

But Sandburg was a poet of many moods. In "Sunset from Omaha Hotel Window" he finds "The gloaming is bitter / As in Chicago / or Kenosha." From the observation car of a train he enjoys the "Still Life" pictures of the rolling prairie, new-mown hay, Holstein cows, a signalman in a Kansas City tower. Sitting by a steam radiator on a winter day he thinks about "Horses and Men in Rain," delivering milk or coal, grocery boys, mail carriers. His memory and sympathy are panoramic, like Whitman's in "Song of Myself"; but also nostalgic; and his empathy is selective, not the all-embracing compassion of the Messianic Whitman. He empathizes with the Greeks he saw in Keokuk working on a railroad; a pawnshop operator on a back street; lonely men in oyster boats in the Chesapeake Bay. He writes elegies for Adelaide Crapsey, the Brooklyn girl who composed poems in Japanese forms while dying of an incurable illness; for Don Magregor, the Colorado miner accused of murder, who died with Pancho Villa in Mexico; Buffalo Bill, hero of prairie boys; and "Old Osawatomie," now "six feet of dust under the morning stars."

Sandburg has often been compared to Whitman, and he frequently wrote on the same themes, but always with his own handling of them. The long verses of "Prairie" look superficially like Whitman's form, but the music is different. A major distinction is in their treatment of the theme of death. To Whitman death was always beautiful, an old mother crooning a lullaby from the ocean of immortality, but to Sandburg death is the final irony of life—stillness, nothingness. In "Cool Tombs" Abraham Lincoln and his assassin, Ulysses Grant and the "con men" who brought shame to his administration, lovely Pocahontas and "a streetful of people" are all equalized "in the dust . . . in the cool tombs." This is one of Sandburg's most beautiful lyrics, and most devastatingly ironic. In "Grass" the scars of World War I will be covered by the perennial grass, not in a Pantheistic transmutation of men into vegetation, but as nature erases the scars of human violation of life. Instead of Whitman's consolation, one is reminded of Hemingway's *nada*—"it was all nada." In Shenandoah Valley lie "The blue nobody remembers, the gray nobody remembers . . ." But generalizing about the brevity of life and the sureness of death in "Loam" the poet does seem to find some consolation in the eternal cycle:

> In the loam we sleep,
> . . .
> We rise;
> To shape of rose leaf,
> Of face and shoulder.

We stand, then,
To a whiff of life,
Lifted to the silver of the sun
Over and out of the loam
A day.

And "In Tall Grass," seeing a honeycomb and bees buzzing "in the dried head of a horse in a pasture corner," he would "ask no better a winding sheet . . ."

Sandburg's first reaction to World War I was that of most Socialists throughout the world. In "A Million Young Workmen, 1915" he exclaims with the bitterness of Stephen Crane in *War Is Kind*:

And oh, it would have been a great job of killing and a new and beautiful thing under the sun if the million knew why they hacked and tore each other to death.

. . .

I dreamed a million ghosts of the young workmen rose in their shirts all soaked in crimson . . . and yelled:
God damn the grinning kings, God damn the kaiser and the czar.

However, in "The Four Brothers," subtitled "Notes for War Songs (November, 1917)," Sandburg's mood is that of Whitman in his recruiting "Beat! Beat! Drums!":

I say now, by God, only fighters today will save the world, nothing but fighters will keep alive the names of those who left red prints of bleeding feet at Valley Forge in Christmas snow.

In fact, this is Sandburg's "Battle Hymn of the Republic," in which he has an apocalyptic vision that

Out of it all a God who knows is sweeping clean,
Out of it all a God who sees and pierces through,
is breaking and cleaning out an old thousand years,
is making ready for a new thousand years.

In spite of its unevenness *Cornhuskers* is one of his finest volumes of poems. The unevenness probably reflects the turbulence of the period in which these poems were written, 1915–18.

Smoke and Steel (1920) also shows the excitement of the war period, and some of the disillusionment of the aftermath, but especially the former in the jazzy rhythms of "Honky Tonk in Cleveland, Ohio" and "Jazz Fantasia." The title of the book is misleading, for most of the poems are neither social protest nor depiction of industrial life. In the title poem the poet sees "smoke" not as pollution or factory ugliness but as a parallel to human blood:

And always dark in the heart and through it,
Smoke and the blood of a man.
Pittsburgh, Youngstown, Gary—they make their steel with men.

The last clause is not uttered in sarcasm, for the poet who had prayed in *Cornhuskers* to be beaten on an anvil into a crowbar or a rivet for a skyscraper saw inspiring strength and beauty in steel. In the blast furnaces he now sees "women dancing, / Dancing out of the flues and smokestacks . . ."

"The Sins of Kalamazoo," says Sandburg, are "neither scarlet nor crimson" but "a convict gray, a dishwater drab," and so is the place itself. Yet he has "loved the white dawn frost of early winter silver / And purple over your railroad tracks and lumber yards." Sandburg, one should remember, was a contemporary of the Ash Can School of painters, whom he had almost parodied in "Nocturne in a Deserted Brickyard" in *Chicago Poems.*

There are intimations, almost premonitions, of Eliot's *Waste Land* and *Hollow Men* in some passages in *Smoke and Steel.* In "Four Preludes on Playthings of the Wind" the cedar doors are broken and the golden girls vanished from the city which thought itself "the greatest city, / the greatest nation: / nothing like us ever was." Now the black crows caw and the rats scribble their hieroglyphic footprints on dusty doorsills. The squabbling of European nations at the peace table had disillusioned Sandburg as early as March 1919, the date he gave for "The Liars":

> Across their tables they fixed it up,
> Behind their doors away from the mob.
> And the guns did a job that nicked off millions.
>
> . . .
>
> And now
> Out of the butcher's job
> And the boneyard junk the maggots have cleaned,
> Where the jaws of skulls tell the jokes of war ghosts,
> Out of this they are calling now: Let's go back where we were.
>
> . . .
>
> So I hear The People tell each other:
>
> . . .
>
> To hell with 'em all,
> The liars who lie to nations,
> The liars who lie to The People.

The closest Sandburg himself got to the war was as a Scripps newspaper correspondent in Stockholm from October 1918 to May 1919. His assignment was not the war itself but interviews with people who had been in or near the war zone, or had escaped the turmoil in Russia. His dispatches were little more than human-interest stories for newspaper readers. But crossing the North Atlantic in late autumn provoked atavistic sensations in the descendant of that ancient seafaring nation. However, seeing the many statues of kings on the streets of Stockholm aroused his democratic antipathy. He admired the Riksdag bridge held up by massive stones, and took special interest, as he would have in Chicago, in the old women selling apples or cleaning windows, and fishermen casting their nets beneath the bridge. So he decided that he would rather have young men read "five lines of one of my poems" then have a bronze statue on the "king's street."

An important influence unconnected with the war which became obvious in *Smoke and Steel* was the Japanese haiku. Sandburg had already become more aware of images because of the Imagistic movement discussed and practiced by Ezra Pound and Amy Lowell in Harriet Monroe's *Poetry.* However, though his "Fog" in *Chicago Poems* has often been cited as an Imagistic poem, it seems to have been written without any influence from Pound or Lowell. But the haiku taught him to insinuate cryptic wisdom in an image. In the folksy "Put Off the Wedding Five Times and Nobody Comes to It" he throws off the remark, "It will always come back to me in the blur of that hokku: The heart of a woman of thirty is like the red ball of the sun seen through a mist." ("Blur" seems inaccurate here; perhaps he means ambiguity.) A final section of short poems in *Smoke and Steel* contains several excellent adaptations of the Japanese haiku. For example, "Thin Strips":

> Under a peach tree I saw petals scattered
> . . . torn strips of a bride's dress, I heard
> a woman laugh many years ago.

Or "Wistful":

> Wishes left on your lips
> The mark of their wings.
> Regrets fly kites in your eyes.

Sandburg's third volume of poetry was followed not by another book of poems but by *Rootabaga Stories* (1922), stories he had made up to amuse his three little daughters. These stories have a fairy-tale sense of unreality, with transformations, actions that defy gravity, and the reduction of winds, moons, landscapes, and human actions to child-fantasy dimensions. But much of the fun is in the names and places, with their absurd sounds, outrageous puns, and comic imagery. There is the family that named its first boy Gimme the Ax and its first girl Ax Me No Questions. Jason Squiff wears a popcorn hat, popcorn mittens, and popcorn shoes. Henry Hagglyhoagly plays the guitar with his mittens on. Another story tells how "The animals lost their tails and got them back again traveling from Philadelphia to Medicine Hat." These are not Aesop fables or miraculous stories with a moral.

The "morals" are themselves jokes, like "Never Kick a Slipper at the Moon" when the moon looks like the toe and heel of a dancer's foot, for the shoe will go on to the moon. The verbal humor is the strongest indication that these tales were written by a poet.

The year following the publication of *Rootabaga Stories* Sandburg discussed with Alfred Harcourt, a New York publisher then working for Henry Holt, what book to write next. He had been interested in Abraham Lincoln since his boyhood, and for some years had been collecting Lincoln material: books, newspaper clippings, anecdotes told by people he met, and subjective impressions. Mindful of the success of Sandburg's book of stories for children, Harcourt suggested a life of Lincoln for teenagers, and this was the book Sandburg intended to write when he began his first Lincoln biography. But the work grew in the writing until it became two hefty volumes, written in simple language, imaginative detail, and a fictional style acceptable in a juvenile book, but much too long and detailed for this genre. It was published as *Abraham Lincoln: The Prairie Years* (1926) for general readers.

The narrative of *Prairie Years* rests on the known facts of Lincoln's early life, but many basic facts were unknown, or had been blurred in oral transmission, or had become displaced by folklore. Thus Sandburg attempts to fill in missing information or to elaborate meager facts. Regarding Lincoln's legitimacy, he tells the rumors and mentions the ambiguities. He has no doubt that Lincoln himself was legitimate, but his grandmother, Lucy Hanks, was as a girl "too free and easy in her behavior," and had borne a child, Nancy, while living with a man she had not legally married. "What was clear in the years that had passed was that Lucy . . . had married a man she wanted, Henry Sparrow, and nine children had come and they were all learning to read and write under her teaching. Since she had married the talk about her running wild had let down."

Sandburg gives Nancy Hanks a husband, Thomas Lincoln, and imagines her home in May 1808, the year preceding Abraham Lincoln's birth:

> "The Lincolns had a cabin of their own to live in. It stood among wild crab-apple trees.
>
> "And the smell of wild crab-apple blossoms, and the low crying of all wild things, came keen that summer to the nostrils of Nancy Hanks.
>
> "The summer stars that year shook out pain and warning, strange laughters, for Nancy Hanks."

The crabapple blossoms may well have been real, but how did the biographer know that "summer stars that year shook out pain and warning" to Nancy Hanks, as an annunciation of her future son of historic destiny? At the age of seven this son, himself, experiences spells of deep wonder, loneliness, and mysterious premonitions in the Indiana wilderness. His heroic qualities also soon begin to manifest themselves. At eighteen he can "take an ax at the end of the handle and hold it out in a straight horiontal line, easy and steady . . ." One day he walks thirty-four miles just to hear a lawyer make a speech. He becomes a famous wrestler, seemingly invincible. But he never misuses his fabulous strength, and of course his mind and character acquire the toughness and resilience, as if by supernatural design, which he will later need as president of a nation divided by a tragic war. He is the Cinderella hero of folklore, epic, and romance. And yet, in view of the incredible courage, strength, and endurance which Lincoln, as historical fact, did exhibit in the presidency, these symbolical details do not seem exaggerated, but possible and convincing.

Edmund Wilson has bitterly denounced Sandburg's biography of Lincoln (without distinguishing the *Prairie Years* from the *War Years*) as "romantic and sentimental rubbish." In *Patriotic Gore* he says, "there are moments when one is tempted to feel that the cruellest thing that has happened to Lincoln since he was shot by Booth has been to fall into the hands of Carl Sandburg." As an example, Wilson cites Sandburg's handling of the Ann Rutledge "love story":

"After the first evening in which Lincoln had sat next to her and found that bashful words tumbling from his tongue's end really spelled themselves out into sensible talk, her face, as he went away, kept coming back. So often all else would fade out of his mind and there would be only this riddle of a pink-fair face, a mouth and eyes in a frame of light cornsilk hair. He could ask himself what it meant and search his heart for an answer and no answer would come. A trembling took his body and dark waves ran through him sometimes when she spoke so simple a thing as, 'The corn is getting high, isn't it?' "

"The corn is getting high, indeed!" says Wilson. But he fails to give Sandburg credit for honestly admitting later that he had been "taken in" by this legend. When he condensed *The Prairie Years* for his one-volume *Abraham Lincoln* (1954) he changed the famous love affair to hypothesis and left out the "corny" description of Lincoln's emotions: "She was 21 and Lincoln 25 and in the few visits he had time for in this year when surveying and politics pressed him hard, he may have gone no further than to be a comforter. He may have touched and stroked her auburn hair once or more as he looked deep into her blue eyes and said no slightest word as to what hopes lay deep in his heart. . . . They were both young, with hope endless, and it could have been he had moments when the sky was to him a sheaf of blue dreams. . . ."

As Lincoln grows up in *The Prairie Years* Sandburg has more historical documents to draw upon, and the Lincoln in the state legislature, in Congress, and in the Chicago convention which nominated him for the presidency is almost wholly believable. Of course for the Lincoln-Douglas debates there were the printed speeches themselves, and newspaper accounts of the campaign for the presidency. Though Sandburg consistently keeps his hero a man basically honest in spite of his driving ambition, he is shown making deals (or consenting to them after they are made by his supporters), compromising as any politician must, and following expediency rather than conscience when that is advantageous. Sandburg is especially effective in showing how circumstances often guided Lincoln's conduct. As the president-elect sets out for Washington to be inaugurated, he is still growing in stature, and in tragic foreboding, a hero in an epic which will end, as he himself half-suspects, in his own physical destruction.

The enormous financial success of *The Prairie Years* encouraged Sandburg to continue his biography through Lincoln's presidency. He now felt a heavy responsibility to tell the story completely and accurately, and he sought professional help from librarians, historians, and book dealers in assembling source material. For the first time in his life he had financial security, and he could concentrate on his one consuming ambition, a complete and reliable biography of Abraham Lincoln.

The great economic depression which began with the stock-market crash in 1929 did not seriously affect Sandburg's personal life or literary plans. Of course a man with the social conscience which all his works display could not be indifferent to the suffering and discouragement of the millions of unemployed or underemployed Americans. Though as a Socialist he had criticized the established economic system, he still believed in the soundness of American society and the ability of its people to make needed changes. To reassert his faith in the common people and to help them regain confidence in themselves, he wrote and published *The People, Yes* (1936). An amalgam of folk wisdom and wit, verbal clichés, tall tales, preaching, slangy conversation, "cracker-barrel" philosophy, and Carl Sandburg cheerfulness, the book served its purpose, as Steinbeck's *Grapes of Wrath* did in another manner. It was wildly praised by people who liked Sandburg, and mostly ignored by those who did not. Mark Van Doren in a lecture on Sandburg at the Library of Congress in 1969 said, "*The People, Yes* is talk, nothing but talk." Van Doren did not mean this in a derogatory sense, and he was right. In this long talky poem we hear the voices of hundreds of Americans, and by listening we learn what kind of people they are, their ambitions, prejudices, superstitions, sense of humor, optimism, generosity, and sense of identity. But *The People, Yes* now seems repetitious and tedious—at least to this reader.

Three years later Sandburg published his truly monumental *Abraham Lincoln: The War Years* in four thick volumes, nearly 2500 pages. The critics were enthusiastic, the sales excellent, and it was awarded a Pulitzer Prize in 1940. Sandburg's six volumes of Lincoln biography were a culmination of thirty years of collecting, pondering, and writing about Lincoln. *The War Years* remains his most ambitious work, and it may be his most lasting. In spite of some lapses which scholars have pointed out, it is well documented—factual, solid, meticulously detailed. At times it seems too detailed, as if the author had emptied his filing drawers, but as a consequence Lincoln's life can be seen, felt, and heard from day to day, often in a chaos of conflicting advice, contradictory responsibilities, and demands for decisions which cannot wait for needed information. Under these pressures Lincoln is seen manfully struggling to make the right decisions, and Sandburg does not blink his misjudgments, or sometimes failure to act at all. He is not seen as an idealist, a man of con science, but always as a shrewd pragmatist, who will save the Union any way he can, with or without slavery. Sandburg also quotes contemporary criticism of Lincoln's failures and imagined failures, so that he may be seen from within and from without. His notorious fondness for stories is copiously illustrated, as might be expected of the author of *The People, Yes.*

Lincoln believed slavery wrong, and he would abolish it if he could, and finally did—or thought he had-but the time must be right. Considering the circumstances so fully presented in *The War Years,* it seems almost miraculous that any man could have held the Union together and won the war in spite of the profusion of graft, incompetent generals and other officials, "Copperhead" subversion, and personal antagonisms within the government, even in the president's Cabinet. That Lincoln did hold on and win makes him seem like a superman, but Sandburg does not load the dice in his favor, as he had at times in *The Prairie Years.* This biography is not only an honest and revealing account of Lincoln's "war years," but also one of the most revealing books ever written on how the American government works—how it looks from the inside in time of great crisis, tragic failures, and creeping success.

Sandburg's enjoyment of his literary triumph was severely tempered by a new, stupendous national crisis which affected him deeply. His total commitment to America's entrance into World War II caused him to undertake the boldest literary experiment of his career, a "novel" covering the whole span of American experience, from the coming of the Pilgrims to the horrors of World War II and the possible consequences of dropping the atom bomb on Japanese cities. This long, complicated work he called *Remembrance Rock* (1948), not from Plymouth Rock, but a rock-shrine in the garden of a fictional Supreme Court justice who slightly resembles Justice Oliver Wendell Holmes. Under the rock the justice had deposited soil from all the places most crucial in American history, and at the end of the novel his grandchildren and their wives and wives-to-be bring the symbolical collection up to date:

"At Remembrance Rock at high noon they laid in metal-bottomed crevices the little prepared copper boxes—gravel from Sicily, sand from Utah Beach on the Normandy coast, rainbow-tinted sand from a coral atoll in the South Pacific, harsh black volcanic ash from Okinawa. They packed in soil at the base of the boulder, leaving no sign of the sacred receptacle underneath."

The whole structure of this novel, if it may be so classified, is as obviously symbolical (its chief fault) as the many kinds of sand under the rock. Some of the characters are historical and some are fictional, representing the earliest white settlers of America, the period of the American Revolution, the migrations into and across the Great Plains, the Civil War, and World War II.

As in all of his writings, Sandburg is facile with conversation in *Remembrance Rock,* but the reader is made too aware of what each speaker "stands for." The story has heroic people and epic action, yet the total effect is that of a patriotic pageant rather than a novel. One can applaud the author's lofty intentions and his great effort without enjoying his art. This literary experiment was a labor of love, and Sandburg was hurt by the failure of the critics to warm up to it. It is not likely to remain as permanently valuable as his one-volume *Abraham Lincoln* (1954), his "distillation" of *The Prairie Years* and *The War Years,* or his big *Complete Poems.*

When the *Complete Poems* appeared in 1950, it was widely reviewed, yet did not receive the high praise of Sandburg's Lincoln biographies. This may have been partly because the fashions in poetry had changed since the years of the depression when *The People, Yes* was so well received. Poetry was now cerebral, dense, and intricately allusive under the influence of Pound and Eliot. The objections to Sandburg's poems were not so much their sententiousness, for Pound and Eliot were as sententious in their own ways as any poet could be, but to his irreverent attitude toward the art of poetry. One of the reviewers of *Complete Poems* was William Carlos Williams, whose poems might appear to be as spontaneously improvised as Sandburg's, but Williams had taken to brooding on his art and concocting theories about how an American poet ought to write, and he thought Sandburg had not given enough thought to these matters. Of course the "New Critics" frowned upon all tendentious poetry, and regarded structure, imagery, tension, and irony as more important than message. They did not so much condemn Sandburg as ignore him, because, they thought, he structured his poems by intuition or whim, and gave these critics few subtleties or ambiguities to challenge their ingenuity. In brief, Sandburg did not need to be explicated.

Complete Poems contains in chronological order the six books of poems (not counting the three privately printed booklets) Sandburg had published before 1950. Its appearance should have given critics an excellent opportunity to evaluate Sandburg's whole career as a poet. But actually none of the reviewers for major publications undertook this task. In fact, their reviews gave the impression that Sandburg was still the "Chicago poet" of 1916, that he had not grown or changed significantly. Evidently it was easier to fall back on the old clichés and stereotypes than to read (or reread) these more than seven hundred poems—seventy-two in a "New Section," some published for the first time anywhere.

Sandburg *had* grown, *had* changed, and several of his finest poems were to be found in the "New Section." Probably the critics had not read the best of these new poems, though they had been published before, but in magazines regarded as nonliterary: "The Fireborn Are at Home in Fire" and "Mr. Longfellow and His Boy" in *Collier's Magazine*; "The Long Shadow of Lincoln: A Litany," in the *Saturday Evening Post*; and the elegy on President Roosevelt, "When Death Came April Twelve 1945," in *Woman's Home Companion.* Of course it is true that one would not expect poems of such high literary quality (or even poems at all) in these mass publications, but a work of art should not be judged by the place of its unveiling.

By 1950 Sandburg had, in the eyes of some critics, two counts against him: he was so famous that he could sell his poems at high prices, and his poems were read and enjoyed by a large public. Even Frost was beginning to suffer from his popularity, but he had several critics of considerable prestige to defend him. Also his life-style protected him to some extent from the curse of success. But Sandburg's folksy manners and his love affair with "the people" were a constant affront and irritant to academic minds, and most literary critics were, and are, either in or close to the academic world. This is not special pleading for Sandburg; it is one observer's explanation of the manner in which *Complete Poems* was reviewed. The fact that the book won the Pulitzer Prize in poetry for that year does not contradict this explanation, nor do the honorary degrees showered upon Sandburg by universities.

In a preface called modestly "Notes for a Preface" Sandburg quotes with approval theories of poetry from Yeats, Synge, Macaulay, and Oliver Wendell Holmes. For example, from Synge: "When men lose their poetic feeling for ordinary life, and cannot write poetry of ordinary things, their exalted poetry is likely to lose its strength of exaltation, in the way men Cease to build beautiful churches when they have lost happiness in building shops. Many of the older poets, such as Villon and Herrick and Burns, used the whole of their personal life as their material, and the verse written in this way was read by strong men, and thieves, and deacons, not by little cliques only." It is hardly necessary to add that Sandburg tried to be just such a poet.

In defense of his abandoning rhyme and meter Sandburg quotes a famous rhymester, Dr. Oliver Wendell Holmes: "Rhythm alone is a tether, and not a very long one. But rhymes are iron fetters . . ." Tethers and fetters had always been intolerable to Sandburg, as he discovered as early as 1905. Also as a reader and contributor to *Poetry* in its early years, he was aware of the arguments for and against "free verse," a form (or, as its opponents said, lack of form) in which the phrase is the prosodic unit and the words themselves create their own rhythms. More important than where Sandburg learned free-verse techniques is the fact that he had an excellent ear for the musical sequence of sounds, the balancing and counterpointing of phrase against phrase. Sandburg wrote for both the ear and the eye. His famous "Chicago" poem has an almost architectural structure, beginning with the short, pithy salutation epithets:

> Hog Butcher for the World,
> Tool Maker, Stacker of Wheat . . .

Then come the twelve factual statements modified by the poet's own affirmation blocked out in parallel form:

> They tell me you are wicked and I believe
>   them, for I have seen your painted
>   women under the gas lamps luring the
>   farm boys. . . .

The seventh statement emphasizes the series of participles by spacing them as single lines, or verses:

> Fierce as a dog with tongue lapping for
>   action, cunning as a savage pitted against
>   the wilderness,
>   Bareheaded,
>   Shoveling,
>   Wrecking,
>   Planning,
>   Building, breaking, rebuilding . . .

Both the line breaks and the accents in the phrases play variations on the tempo, slowing or speeding up the sounds to add emphasis. The difference between these long lines and ordinary prose is in the skillful paralleling and accumulating of grammatical units (phrases and clauses). The resulting rhythm is grammatical, or rhetorical, rather than metrical.

Though scarcely any two of Sandburg's poems look alike on the page, or sound alike when read aloud, his sense of form seldom faltered. Notice the pattern of the opening lines of "Pencils" (*Smoke and Steel*):

>   Pencils
> telling where the wind comes from
>   open a story.
>
>   Pencils
> telling where the wind goes
>   end a story.
>
>   These eager pencils
>   come to a stop
>   . . . only . . . when the stars high over
>   come to a stop.

"Canadians and Pottawatomies" (*Good Morning, America*) is almost as syllabic (i.e., equal number of syllables in each line) as a poem by Marianne Moore:

> I have seen a loneliness sit
> in the dark and nothing lit up.

I have seen a loneliness sit
in the dark lit up like a Christmas
tree, a Hallowe'en pumpkin.

One of the many ways in which Sandburg's sense of rhythm became more subtle and sensitive was in his handling of syllabic weight, timbre, and vowel tone. This development culminated in the marvelous tone poem "When Death Came April Twelve 1945," which opens:

Can a bell ring in the heart
telling the time, telling a moment,
telling off a stillness come,
in the afternoon a stillness come
and now never come morning?

The bell intones throughout the elegy, not mechanically as in Poe's "The Bells," but resonating the deep feelings of the nation grieving for its lost commander, and the sons lost in the South Pacific or on European soil, all now sleeping after toil and battle. The tones of the poem, reinforcing the images of stillness and silence, have the empathy of cleansing and calming the emotions of the readers (hearers). In every technical detail the elegy is almost perfectly ordered, timed, and developed from the opening "Can a bell ring in the heart" to

the somber consoles rolling sorrow,
the choirs in ancient laments—chanting:
"Dreamer, sleep deep,
Toiler, sleep long,
Fighter, be rested now,
Commander, sweet good night."

Though Sandburg's patriotism had never been aroused before as it was during World War II, when he was willing to use his talents in any way possible to aid the preservation of a "free world," he was no blind patriot or jingoist. For the poem he read at William and Mary College in 1944, "The Long Shadow of Lincoln: A Litany," he used for an epigraph a quotation from Lincoln's 1862 message to Congress: "We can succeed only by concert. . . . The dogmas of the quiet past are inadequate to the stormy present. The occasion is piled high with difficulty, and we must rise with the occasion. As our case is new so we must think anew and act anew. We must disenthrall ourselves. . . ."

Sandburg knew the importance of *disenthralling ourselves* in the aftermath of World War II. His "Litany" begins:

Be sad, be cool, be kind,
remembering those now dreamdust
hallowed in the ruts and gullies,
solemn bones under the smooth blue sea,
faces warblown in a falling rain.

Remember and weep, he says, but "Make your wit a guard and cover." Looking toward peace and the difficulties of maintaining it, "'We must disenthrall ourselves.'"

There is dust alive
with dreams of The Republic,
with dreams of the Family of Man
flung wide on a shrinking globe

. . .

The earth laughs, the sun laughs
over every wise harvest of man,
over man looking toward peace
by the light of the hard old teaching:
"We must disenthrall ourselves."

Few men were less warped by the war, better kept their wit, or remained as sane as Carl Sandburg. In a group of poems for the "Present Hour" there is "Jan, the Son of Thomas," who asks:

Was I not always a laughing man?
Did I ever fail of ready jests?
Have I added a final supreme jest?
They may write where my ashes quiver:
"He loved mankind for its very faults.
He knew how to forget all wars past.
He so acted
as to forget the next war."

Sandburg did not believe with a certain "handsome mournful galoot" (T. S. Eliot?) that "The human race is its own Enemy Number One."

For him the Family of Man stinks now
  and if you look back
  for him it always has stunk.

In "Many Handles" Sandburg warns against "abstractions" and rigid classifications:

In the Dark Ages many there and then
had fun and took love and made visions
and listened when Voices came.
Then as now were the Unafraid.
Then as now, "What if I am dropped into
  levels of ambiguous dust and covered
  over and forgotten? Have I in my time
  taken worse?"

. . .

Should it be the Dark Ages recur, will there
be again the Immeasurable Men, the
Incalculable Women?

Though the poem ends with a question, the implication is plain that there will be great men and women for a new Dark Age, if it comes. In spite of a terrible premonition of a future atomic war, Sandburg counsels in "The Unknown War,"

Be calm, collected, easy.
In the face of the next war to come, be
  calm.
In the faint light and smoke of the flash and
  the mushroom of the first bomb blast of
  the Third World War, keep your wits
  collected.

. . .

We shall do the necessary.
We shall meet the inevitable.

Thirteen years after the appearance of *Complete Poems,* Sandburg published still another volume of poetry called *Honey and Salt.* The title poem is skeptical, witty, and philosophical on the permanence of love.

Is there any way of measuring love?
Yes but not till long afterward
when the beat of your heart has gone
many miles, far into the big numbers.
Is the key to love in passion, knowledge,
  affection?
All three—along with moonlight, roses,
  groceries,
givings and forgivings, gettings and
  forgettings,
  keepsakes and room rent,
  pearls of memory along with ham and
    eggs.

If love is "locked away and kept," it "gathers dust and mildew." How long does it last? "As long as glass bubbles handled with care / or two hot-house orchids in a blizzard / or one solid immovable steel anvil . . ." But

There are sanctuaries
  holding honey and salt.
There are those who
  spill and spend.

Many of the poems in this volume are about love, which was never sweeter or more savory than now for this eighty-five-year-old lover. Several poems are affectionate devotions to his one and only wife, and "Out of the Rainbow End" is a fond compliment to his brother-in-law Edward Steichen, whose hobby was growing delphiniums. But Sandburg knows also that "Love Is a Deep and a Dark and a Lonely":

and you take it deep take it dark
and take it with a lonely winding
and when the winding gets too lonely
then may come the windflowers

. . .

like leaves of windflowers bending low
and bending to be never broken.

The longest and most ambitious poem in *Honey and Salt* is "Timesweep." The theme might be said to be the same as "Wilderness" (1918), in which the poet lyrically boasted of his kinship with foxes, wolves, and other wild animals. But "Timesweep" is both more genuinely lyrical and more philosophical, lyrical in the poet's empathy with the natural forces and creatures with which he feels a sympathetic kinship, and philosophical in his knowledge of his place in the cosmic scheme. Since Sandburg has so often been compared with Whitman by many critics, it is interesting to place this poem beside passages treating the same theme in "Song of Myself." In section 31 Whitman declares:

> I find I incorporate gneiss, coal, long-threaded moss, fruits, grains, esculent roots,
> And am stucco'd with quadrupeds and birds all over,
> And have distanced what is behind me for good reasons,
> But call any thing back again when I desire it.

Then in section 44 Whitman returns to his evolutionary transmigration:

> I am an acme of things accomplish'd, and I an encloser of things to be.
> My feet strike an apex of the apices of the stairs,
> On every step bunches of ages, and larger bunches between the steps,
> All below duly travel'd, and still I mount and mount.
>
> . . .
>
> Before I was born out of my mother generations guided me,
> My embryo has never been torpid, nothing could overlay it.
>
> For it the nebula cohered to an orb,
> The long slow strata piled to rest it on,
> Vast vegetables gave it sustenance,
> Monstrous sauroids transported it in their mouths and deposited it with care.

Sandburg's poem is more personal, less "prophetic" in tone, more aware of human limitations, but the lyrical utterance of a sensitive man who enjoys the sights and sounds of his physical existence:

> The pink nipples of the earth in springtime,
> The long black eyelashes of summer's look,
> The harvest laughter of tawny autumn,
> The winter silence of land in snow covers,
> Each speaks its own oaths of the cool and the flame of naked possessions clothed and come naked again:
> The sea knows it all.
> They crept out of the sea.

The poet wonders where he came from, and whether there is any going back:

> Is it told in my dreams and hankerings, looking
> back at what I was, seeing what I am?
> Like so a man talking to himself
> of the bitter, the sweet, the bittersweet:
> he had heard likenings of himself:
> Cock of the walk, brave as a lion, fierce as a tiger,
> Stubborn as a mule, mean as a louse, crazy as a bedbug,
> Soft as a kitten, slimy as an octopus, one poor fish.

Yes, man, "proud man, with a peacock strut" is "a beast out of the jungle," an animal related to all the other animals. Frank Norris and other American naturalists of the late nineteenth century had used this thought to demolish man's pretensions to a special creation in the image of God and his delusions of free will. Sandburg has no such intentions:

> What is this load I carry out of yesterday?
> What are these bygones of dreams, moans, shadows?
> What jargons, what gibberish, must I yet unlearn?

He knows that his origins are in a "dim plasm in the sea . . . a drop of jelly," and the countless swimmers and crawlers who preceded the creature called man:

> I have had a thousand fish faces, sea faces,
> sliding off into land faces, monkey faces—
> I began in a dim green mist
> of floating faces.

He acknowledges his kindred and feels a degree of identity with them, and wonders what right he has to feel wiser than they. To the elephant he says the "Ignorance we share and share alike is immeasurable."

I have been woven among meshes of long
  ropes
and fine filaments: older than the rocks and
fresh as the dawn of this morning today are
the everliving roots who begot me,
who poured me as one more seeker
one more swimmer in the gold and gray
  procession
of phantoms laughing, fighting, singing,
  moaning toward the great cool calm of
the fixed return to the filaments of dust.

But he also knows that he is "more than a traveler out of Nowhere":

Sea and land, sky and air, begot me
  Somewhere.
Where I go from here and now, or if I go at
  all again, the
Maker of sea and land, of sky and air, can tell.

Knowledge that some almost infinite (or perhaps infinite) chain of life begot him out of Nowhere to Somewhere gives Sandburg sufficient assurance of a *purpose* at work, however humanly unknowable. He will not worry about theology, or teleology. Yet "Timesweep" throws more light on Sandburg's philosophy than any other literary work of his. At the end of this last poem we find a summation of his humanism, rooted in his early socialism, and consolidated by a lifetime of effort to propagate the idea that the Family of Man is One Man:

There is only one man in the world
and his name is All men.

. . .

There is only one Maker in the world
and His children cover the earth
and they are named All God's Children.

The poet who wrote this poem had come a long way on the road of art since writing "Chicago." No one knows the range of Sandburg who has not read the "new" poems in his collected *Complete Poems* and observed the further enrichment of his canon in *Honey and Salt.* In his "Notes for a Preface" to *Complete Poems* he remarked: "I have written by different methods and in a wide miscellany of moods and have seldom been afraid to travel in lands and seas where I met fresh scenes and new songs. All my life I have been trying to learn to read, to see and hear, and to write. At sixty-five I began my first novel, and the five years lacking a month I took to finish it, I was still traveling, still a seeker. I should like to think that as I go on writing there will be sentences truly alive, with verbs quivering, with nouns giving color and echoes. It could be, in the grace of God, I shall live to be eighty-nine, as did Hokusai, and speaking my farewell to earthly scenes, I might paraphrase: 'If God had let me live five years longer I should have been a writer.' "

Carl Sandburg did live to be eighty-nine, and he did not need five additional years to become a writer; he had been a writer, a prolific one, and at times a masterful one, for many years. When he became a poet is a subject on which critics have disagreed, and will doubtless continue to do so, but we might paraphrase his quotation from the Japanese painter and say that God created Sandburg a writer, but by his own efforts he became a poet.

Selected Bibliography

WORKS OF CARL SANDBURG

The titles listed below include the published writings of Carl Sandburg with the exception of limited editions, prefaces and introductions to works by other authors, addresses, and recorded readings and talks.

ANTHOLOGIES

Whitman, Walt, *Leaves of Grass,* with an introduction by Carl Sandburg (New York: Boni and Liveright, 1921).

The American Songbag, (New York: Broadcast Music, 1927).

New American Songbag, (New York: Broadcast Music, 1950).

BIOGRAPHY AND AUTOBIOGRAPHY

Abraham Lincoln: The Prairie Years, 2 vols (New York: Harcourt, Brace, 1926).

Abe Lincoln Grows Up, with illustrations by James Daugherty (New York: Harcourt, Brace, 1928) From *Abraham Lincoln: The Prairie Years.*

Streichen the Photographer, (New York: Harcourt, Brace, 1929).

Mary Lincoln: Wife and Widow, with Paul M. Angle (New York: Harcourt, Brace, 1932).

Abraham Lincoln: The War Years, 4 vols (New York: Harcourt, Brace, 1939).

Storm over the Land, (New York: Harcourt, Brace, 1942). From *Abraham Lincoln: The War Years.*

Always the Young Strangers, (New York: Harcourt, Brace, 1953).

Abraham Lincoln: The Prairie Years and the War Years, (New York: Harcourt, Brace, 1954) A distillation.

FOR YOUNG READERS

Rootabaga Stories, (New York: Harcourt, Brace, 1922).

Rootabaga Pigeons, (New York: Harcourt, Brace, 1923).

Abe Lincoln Grows Up, (New York: Harcourt, Brace, 1928).

Early Moon, (New York: Harcourt, Brace, 1930).

Prairie-Town Boy, (New York: Harcourt, Brace, 1955). From *Always the Young Strangers.*

Wind Song, (New York: Harcourt, Brace, 1960).

The Wedding Procession of the Rag Doll and the Broom Handle and Who Was in It, (New York: Harcourt, Brace, 1967).

NOVEL AND STORIES

Potato Face, (New York: Harcourt, Brace, 1930). ("Rootabaga stories for adults").

Remembrance Rock, (New York: Harcourt, Brace, 1948).

POETRY

In Reckless Ecstasy, (Galesburg: Asgard Press, 1904). Private press.

The Plaint of a Rose, (Galesburg: Asgard Press, 1905).

Incidentals, (Galesburg: Asgard Press, 1905).

Chicago Poems, (New York: Henry Holt, 1916).

Cornhuskers, (New York: Henry Holt, 1918).

Smoke and Steel, (New York: Harcourt, Brace, 1920).

Slabs of the Sunburnt West, (New York: Harcourt, Brace, 1922).

Good Morning, America, (New York: Harcourt, Brace, 1928).

The People, Yes, (New York: Harcourt, Brace, 1936).

Complete Poems, (New York: Harcourt, Brace, 1950).

Honey and Salt, (New York: Harcourt, Brace, 1963).

SELECTED EDITIONS OF POETRY

Selected Poems of Carl Sandburg, edited by Rebecca West (New York: Harcourt, Brace, 1926).

Poems of the Midwest, (Cleveland and New York: World Publishing Company, 1946). (*Chicago Poems* and *Cornhuskers).*

The Sandburg Range, (New York: Harcourt, Brace, 1957). Selection of poetry and prose.

Harvest Poems: 1910–1960, (New York: Harcourt, Brace, 1960).

PROSE MISCELLANY

The Chicago Race Riots, July 1919 with an introduction by Walter Lippmann (New York: Harcourt, Brace and Howe, 1919). Reprinted from the *Chicago Daily News.*

Home Front Memo, (New York: Harcourt, Brace, 1943).

The Photographs of Abraham Lincoln, with Frederick H. Meserve (New York: Harcourt, Brace, 1944).

Lincoln Collector: The Story of Oliver R. Barrett's Great Private Collection, (New York: Harcourt, Brace, 1949).

Address before a Joint Session of Congress, February 12, 1959, (New York: Harcourt, Brace, 1959). Published also in Washington, D.C., Worcester, Mass., and Cedar Rapids, Iowa.

LETTERS

The Letters of Carl Sandburg, edited by Herbert Mitgang (New York: Harcourt, Brace and World, 1968). Contains a useful chronological table.

BIBLIOGRAPHIES

Golden, Harry, *Carl Sandburg,* (see Biographies below) has a check list of Sandburg's works and *Honey and Salt* (see Poetry above) has a classified checklist.

The Sandburg Range: An Exhibit of Materials from Carl Sandburg's Library Placed on Display in the University of Illinois Library on January 6, 1958, with an introduction by John T. Flanagan; bibliographical descriptions and notes by Leslie W. Dunlap. University of Illinois Library, Adah Patton Memorial Fund, Publication Number Six, (Urbana, 1958).

Van Doren, Mark, *Carl Sandburg,* with a bibliography of Sandburg materials in the collections of the Library of Congress (Washington, D.C.: Library of Congress, 1969). This is the most extensive bibliography of Sandburg, including translations, addresses, introductions and prefaces, articles, interviews and conversations, manuscripts, musical settings, phonograph records, motion pictures.

BIOGRAPHIES

Callahan, North, *Carl Sandburg: Lincoln of Our Time,* (New York: New York University Press, 1970).

Golden, Harry, *Carl Sandburg,* (Cleveland and New York: World Publishing Company, 1961).

CRITICAL STUDIES

Allen, Gay Wilson, "Carl Sandburg: Fire and Smoke," *South Atlantic Quarterly* 59: 315–31 (Summer 1960).

Basler, Roy P., "Your Friend the Poet—Carl Sandburg," *Midway* 10: 3–15 (Autumn 1969).

Cargill, Oscar, "Carl Sandburg: Crusader and Mystic," *College English* 11: 365–72 (April 1950).

Van Doren, Mark, *Carl Sandburg,* (Washington, D.C.: Library of Congress, 1969).

Williams, William Carlos, Review of Carl Sandburg's *Complete Poems,* in *Poetry,* 7–8: 345ff (September 1951).

Delmore Schwartz
(1913–1966)

PAUL BRESLIN

At present, Delmore Schwartz is probably better known through Saul Bellow's fictional portrait in *Humboldt's Gift* than through his own writing. Many who have not read Schwartz know of him as the brilliant poet acclaimed as a genius in his early twenties, but doomed to decline into madness and early death. He is remembered more for his life than for his writing. Nonetheless, during the 1970's there was a modest increase of interest in Schwartz's work. In 1974, Richard McDougall published a short critical study of Schwartz in Twayne's United States Authors series. The excellent biography by James Atlas came out in 1977; since then we have had a selection of the stories, edited by Atlas, and a selection of "last and late poems," edited by Robert Phillips.

There have been a number of articles, most of them by friends and contemporaries: William Barrett, Dwight Macdonald, Philip Rahv, Sidney Hook, Alfred Kazin, and Irving Howe. These essays contain some sharp insights that are informed by vivid firsthand memories of the man and the milieu behind the work. As the memory of Schwartz recedes into the past, his work will have to stand or fall on its own. Its revaluation, by a generation to whom he is "Schwartz" and not "Delmore," has barely begun. In tracing the course of his career, this essay will also attempt to contribute to such a revaluation.

One cannot discuss Schwartz's work without also discussing his life, for he was an obsessively autobiographical writer. When one recalls that he came to prominence in the 1930's and 1940's, and that some of his most ardent admirers were New Critics such as Allen Tate and John Crowe Ransom, this autobiographical emphasis seems a little surprising. It was fashionable at the time, among the poets Schwartz most valued, to insist on the impersonality of poetry. Although Ransom, Tate, and T. S. Eliot were sometimes more personal than they cared to admit, one must look ahead to the work of Robert Lowell, John Berryman, and Sylvia Plath in the 1960's to find poems that are personal to the same degree and in the same sense as many of Schwartz's. Whatever our conclusions about the artistic value of his poetry, Schwartz has a historical importance as the first confessional poet. In his autobiographical fiction he had the precedent of James Joyce and Marcel Proust.

It is significant that Lowell, in his famous *Paris Review* interview of 1961, credited Schwartz with some influence on his change of style. Like Schwartz, Lowell had come to value "experience" more than "polish," and he wanted to reclaim for poetry the narrative complexity it had ceded to the novel. One might say that Lowell's *Life Studies* (1959) accomplishes what Schwartz had attempted, less successfully, in *Genesis: Book One* (1943): an autobiographical poetry that revisits childhood, not to rekindle a Wordsworthian capacity for joy but to inquire into the historical and personal origins of present unhappiness.

Schwartz's unhappiness began, in a sense, even before he was born on December 8, 1913.

His parents both came from Rumania in the great wave of Jewish emigration from Eastern Europe. His father, Harry Schwartz, met Rose Nathanson on the Lower East Side of New York City in 1909, and married her after a brief and stormy courtship. Harry had prospered in real estate, so the couple was able to move to a more fashionable neighborhood in Brooklyn. For a few years they were childless, for Rose Schwartz had a congenital condition that prevented her from conceiving. When Harry began to take up with other women, she thought that perhaps the arrival of a child would restore his sense of domestic responsibility. While he was away on business, she sold a bond given to her by an uncle and had the operation needed to correct her infertility. Even in the circumstances of his conception, Schwartz was a pawn in the struggle between his parents.

Then there was the matter of his first name, about which Schwartz was so sensitive that he devoted an entire play, *Shenandoah* (1941), to a family's quarrel over the naming of a son. The name they finally choose, Shenandoah Fish, is obviously analogous to Delmore Schwartz; it was also assigned to the protagonists of the autobiographical stories "America! America!," "New Year's Eve," and "A Bitter Farce." Schwartz thought of his name as a telling reminder that he was caught between two cultures. He had a traditional Jewish middle name—David. But his first name, which his parents apparently thought of as something sophisticated and "American," was an outlandish concoction, anomalous in both the Jewish context and the American.

The marriage of Schwartz's parents continued to deteriorate. A second child, Kenneth, was born in 1916, but the Schwartzes were legally separated in 1923 and divorced in 1927. Despite his unhappy childhood, Schwartz at least had the consolation of looking ahead to a large inheritance. This hope was disappointed. Harry Schwartz was able to salvage much of his fortune during the crash of 1929, but he died less than a year later. An unscrupulous executor drained away most of the estate, and what remained was tied up in litigation for years. Schwartz later thought of his father's death and the stock market crash as fatally linked, the private and public manifestations of some complex, inscrutable force. Indeed, he thought of his life in general as the product of dark determinisms: the persecution that drove the Jews of Eastern Europe to the New World; the economic collapse that made the loss of his inheritance even more bitter; the unconscious compulsions that set his parents against each other. In his fiction and poetry he usually viewed his story as a representative tragedy. He scarcely dared to desire freedom from suffering, but sought instead the tragic hero's understanding of his own suffering.

The turmoil of his family may explain Schwartz's erratic performance in school; he did well in English and other classes that engaged his imagination, but very poorly in everything else. Nonetheless, he showed early signs of literary ambition, and some of his teachers recognized his brilliance. Some of his juvenilia is preserved in *The Poet's Pack of George Washington High School* (1932). These poems are awkward and overdone in the usual way of adolescent verse, but they show a complexity of language and an awareness of modern styles (especially those of T. S. Eliot and Hart Crane) that set them apart from the neighboring contributions.

Schwartz spent the academic year 1931–1932 at the University of Wisconsin. A temporary lack of money kept him out of school for the first half of the following academic year, but he was able to enroll at New York University in February 1933. By the time he graduated in June 1935, Schwartz was a published poet; a month later he wrote the short story "In Dreams Begin Responsibilities," which remains among his finest work. When it was published in December 1937, as the lead item in the first issue of the newly revived *Partisan Review*, it made his reputation. "In Dreams" gave him the title for his first book, and it touched upon themes, symbols, and techniques that were to become characteristic of his writing. Both for its own excellence and for its prophecy of things to come, the story deserves close attention.

Although "In Dreams Begin Responsibilities" takes its title from one of the two epigraphs to William Butler Yeats's *Responsibilities,* Schwartz's "dream" is no Yeatsian vision of a spiritual world, but a reenactment of the date on which his father proposed to his mother, shown as a silent movie in a theater. The metaphor of the movie eloquently expresses Schwartz's fatalism: what we see in a movie seems to be happening in the present, but it is in fact the record of actions already completed and, therefore, unalterable. The actions in the film are described in the present tense, and although the movie is silent, the narrator can infer his parents' feelings at every moment. The present tense and omniscient narration tend to shift our attention from the narrator to the parents; we experience the action as present, except when the narrator disrupts the events with his responses. One therefore begins to apply the metaphor of the movie not only to the past as the narrator reconstructs it in his mind, but also to the courtship itself at the time it actually occurred. The parents are not free; the marriage will be a disaster, but they cannot help choosing each other.

The handling of detail reinforces our sense that the present is a repetition of the past, that the pattern of life is futile recurrence. We follow the father's walk to the mother's house; then both parents "walk down the same quiet streets once more." During this sequence the movie is interrupted, and when it resumes, "the film has been returned to a portion just shown." In another scene the parents ride on a merry-go-round. To the narrator, "it seems that they will never get off the merry-go-round because it will never stop." If the present is a repetition of the past, it is also, by the same logic, an adumbration of the future. Toward the end of the story, the couple visits a portrait photographer and a fortune-teller. In these scenes the outcome of the marriage reveals itself as already contained in its beginning, for the portrait will not come out right; and the mother's insistence on a consultation with the fortune-teller provokes a violent quarrel, itself an ominous prediction of the strife to come.

At first the narrator manages to lose himself in the action of the movie. But as his parents stroll by the sea at Coney Island, with the inevitable proposal of marriage drawing uncomfortably close, he becomes uneasy and leaves the theater for a moment. He has been disturbed by "the terrible sun which breaks up sight, and the fatal, merciless, passionate ocean." His parents also look upon the sunlit water, but remain blind to its frightening symbolic implications. In this section the language of the story has shifted from deliberately flat, matter-of-fact narrative to lyrical evocation. The image of his parents, poised at the beginning of their lives, looking uncomprehendingly at the dazzling blankness of the sea, belongs to a class of images that recurs throughout Schwartz's work. It is, for that matter, parallel to the image of the narrator, at the end of the story, looking out at the snow on his twenty-first birthday.

The sea and the snow both stand in opposition to the darkness of the theater, and to the corresponding darkness of the photographer's studio and the fortune-teller's booth, theaters in which the parents try to look at themselves. The dark theater is regressive and womblike. Within it, one can only be the spectator of one's own dreams and memories. To some extent it simply represents the state of dreaming, but there are others watching the movie besides the narrator. To them the events are interesting but not charged with personal significance. This situation represents the plight of the autobiographical artist: What happens when one shows home movies in a public theater? It also represents the plight of anyone with a burdensome past: One can't possibly expect others to share one's own obsession with it; and in order to live in a world with others, one must win some measure of detachment from it.

The moment his mother accepts his father's proposal, the narrator loses all detachment, forgetting that the past is past. He stands up and cries to the figures on the screen: "Don't do it. It's not too late to change your minds, both of you. Nothing good will come of it, only remorse, hatred, scandal, and two children whose characters are monstrous." He is moved, at this point, by several motives: a real sympathy for his parents' suffering, but also the child's irrational, guilty sense that this suffering is all his fault, and with that guilt, the suicidal wish never to have been born. This outburst angers the rest of the audience, and the usher, a sort of superego figure, arrives, "flashing his searchlight" and threatening to evict the narrator.

When, upon witnessing his parents' quarrel, the narrator bursts forth again, the usher makes good his threat and drags him "through the lobby of the theatre into the cold light," where he wakes up "into the bleak winter morning of [his] 21st birthday, the windowsill shining with its lip of snow, and the morning already begun." While dragging him outside, the usher has warned him: "You can't act like this even if other people aren't around!"

Coming out of the dark theater into the lobby means waking from the dream, but also the coming of age traditionally associated with twenty-first birthdays. At the end of the story, the narrator must turn aside from his origins and begin his own life. The bright blankness of the snow, the morning with its prospect of unused time, and the inviting world glimpsed through the window are appropriate emblems of beginning. In later years, as he sank gradually into despair, Schwartz used his imagery of beginning more and more mechanically, with an increasingly strident and unconvincing optimism.

But what a beginning he made! Three and a half years after his graduation from NYU Schwartz was famous. In the fall of 1935, he began graduate study in philosophy at Harvard. As a first-year student he placed work in *Poetry* and *New Caravan,* and won the Bowdoin Prize for the best essay by a graduate student in the humanities. When, in his second year of study, his mother declared herself unable to support him further, he returned to New York. Turning his full attention to his writing, Schwartz quickly made a name for himself, publishing poems, essays, verse plays, and fiction in prestigious literary quarterlies. By the spring of 1938 he felt sufficiently established to marry Gertrude Buckman, an old high school acquaintance who caught his attention when she turned up as a fellow student at NYU. At the end of the year, just after his twenty-fifth birthday, New Directions published *In Dreams Begin Responsibilities.*

Even as a young man, Schwartz was fond of the scheming and plotting that would degenerate into paranoid manipulation toward the end of his life. He lined up influential friends to secure praise for his book, working himself into acute anxiety over its reception. But his fears proved totally unfounded. *In Dreams Begin Responsibilities* succeeded beyond his fondest hopes. Allen Tate called its style "the first real innovation that we've had since Eliot and Pound"; Mark Van Doren, writing in *Kenyon Review,* found it "as good as any poetry has been for a long while, say at least a literary generation." Other high compliments arrived from Wallace Stevens, F. W. Dupee, R. P. Blackmur, and John Crowe Ransom; W. H. Auden, though more restrained in his praise, admired the book also. In November 1939, Schwartz received a letter from T. S. Eliot, who was "much impressed by *In Dreams Begin Responsibilities.*"

The praise both thrilled and terrified Schwartz. When fame was a vague and distant goal, it had seemed wholly desirable, but no sooner was it achieved than he began to wonder whether he deserved it. To some extent we may attribute this reaction to his insecurity, but it also demonstrates an instinctive honesty in judging his own accomplishment. To be sure, *In Dreams Begin Responsibilities* is a remarkable book for a man of twenty-five, and a distinguished book by all but the most Olympian standards. But fine as it is, many of Schwartz's contemporaries overpraised it. None of its poems belongs in a class with the best of Eliot, Ezra Pound, Hart Crane, or Auden, the poets with whom Schwartz was most frequently compared.

Doubtless the extravagant acclaim for *In Dreams Begin Responsibilities* reflected the critical vogue of "the tragic view of life" and the bleak look of the world on the brink of war. In retrospect, Schwartz's unremitting gloom can seem monotonous, and some of his pronouncements on history and fate belong in a speech by Polonius. Nonetheless, in the title story, in parts of "Coriolanus and His Mother," and in perhaps seven or eight of the lyrics, he added something permanent to modern literature—no small accomplishment for any writer, young or old.

Schwartz's reputation must rest primarily on this book and the collection of stories, *The World Is a Wedding* (1948). These, with the best of the essays and a handful of later poems and stories, should secure him a place in American letters. His range was limited, and his early promise was never fulfilled, but he managed to produce a small body of minor masterworks—poems, stories, and essays that, despite their limitations, have a distinctive character of their own, not replaceable by the work of his greater contemporaries.

In Dreams Begin Responsibilities opens with the title story, which has already been discussed. The second part is a long narrative poem "Coriolanus and His Mother." As in the story, Schwartz employs the metaphor of spectatorship, although the relationship of the spectacle to the observer's own circumstances is in this case more oblique. The narrator is watching a performance of *Coriolanus*; in a blank verse that by turns imitates and parodies William Shakespeare's, he summarizes the action as it unfolds before him, interpreting the story as he retells it. He shares his theater box with four great men who aid him in his interpretations: Aristotle, Ludwig van Beethoven, Karl Marx, and Sigmund Freud (Freud, although still alive when the poem was published, ascends in Schwartz's treatment to the lofty remoteness of his dead colleagues). There is also a fifth ghost, masked and unnamed, who remains ominously silent throughout. Between the acts the narrator is transported to the stage, where he delivers prose monologues that meditate, half seriously and half ironically, on such themes as pleasure, justice, choice, and identity, with oblique reference to the play.

In deciding to recount the whole story of Coriolanus, Schwartz was exercising the narrative poet's prerogative of treating a traditional story in his own manner, just as Shakespeare had followed Plutarch. On the whole, Schwartz's account is fast-paced, and it achieves interesting effects at times by juxtaposing modern and Renaissance styles:

> "*Noli me tangere!* How large they shout,
> Each would partake of my world's
> championship,
> Each thinks himself myself and I am fucked
> By every craven knight vicarious there.
> —Yet what a sweetness is that roaring kiss
> Spreading in waves throughout the whorish
> air."

In this passage the Latin injunction recalls Sir Thomas Wyatt's "Whoso List to Hunt"; the inversions of word order in the fourth and fifth lines sound archaic. But these pentameters also find room for the psychiatrist's "vicarious," the baseball fan's "world's championship," and the physicist's "Spreading in waves." The word "fucked," planted emphatically at the end of a line, belongs to both the old idiom and the new.

In his essay "Ezra Pound's Very Useful Labors" (1938), Schwartz criticized the lack of narrative continuity in the *Cantos,* and in "The Isolation of Modern Poetry" (1941) he remarked on the absence of good narrative verse in the twentieth century, despite great accomplishment in lyric forms. "Coriolanus and His Mother" has many fine moments, but it finally confirms Schwartz's diagnosis of the problem: "Dramatic and narrative poetry require a grasp of the lives of other men, and it is precisely these lives . . . that are outside the orbit of poetic style and poetic sensibility." To the extent that Schwartz's Coriolanus remains one of those "other men," we find him dull, for his story has been better told in Plutarch and Shakespeare. To the extent that he becomes an autobiographical persona, we find him interesting, but for this we do not require the narrative structure. Allusions to the well-known incidents of his story would suffice, woven into a much shorter, primarily meditative poem.

It is not hard to see why Schwartz found the life of Coriolanus suggestive for his own art. To begin with, his inclusion of the hero's mother in the title hints at the autobiographical connection. William Barrett remarks on Schwartz's "constant closeness to his mother, who did everything she could to prolong his narcissism, exaggerate his ego with praise, and yet in her clever and poisonous way insinuate in the child, then the boy, and then the young man, that the love and trust of anybody was not to be believed." Every word of this description applies to Coriolanus as Schwartz interprets him. One can also see in Coriolanus' aristocratic contempt for his fellow Romans a parallel to the contempt of Eliot, Pound, and other writers for modern democratic culture, a contempt Schwartz partly shared and partly repudiated. The story also raises the question of whether one can reject one's origins and still retain one's identity. Schwartz encountered this question in several ways: as an "alienated" artist on the margin of society, as a second-generation American Jew on the brink of assimilation, and as a young man who owed his existence to a marriage that he could only regard as a terrible mistake.

To some extent Schwartz reinterprets the story of Coriolanus in the way he retells it. He places Marxist rhetoric in the mouths of Brutus and the other spokesmen for the plebeians; he repeatedly compares Coriolanus with Narcissus and gives a Freudian turn to his contempt for the people by seizing on such details as his dislike of their "smell":

"You stink!" he cries. "You scum!" he
  shouts, shocked by
Their protest, offended by their being,
Nursing in mind, older than any thought,
A hatred of all who issue sweat, urine,
Or excrement, the child's profound distaste
Once for all smitten, never, alas! outworn.

Schwartz also draws out the psychoanalytic implications of the hero's extreme need for his mother's approval. But most of the interpretation comes in the form of commentary by the four great men in the audience. Beethoven is present mainly to lend his *Coriolan* overture as background music. Aristotle speaks frequently, but too much of what he has to say sounds like a lecture to undergraduates on *The Poetics.* The most interesting part of the commentary comes from Marx and Freud, who engage in a running debate about the nature and causes of the hero's tragic flaw.

To Marx, the hero's mother, Volumnia, is nothing but a living metaphor for the state. The real mother of Coriolanus is Rome and, more particularly, the patrician class. Coriolanus commits his fatal mistake in believing that he, or anyone else, exists completely as an individual. And yet the class pride that makes him "noble" contains, dialectically, the seed of this error; individual pride is but class pride carried to the extreme. Freud interprets the problem as personal rather than social, stemming from a regressive desire to return to the womb, or to the primary narcissism of the infant:

"His mother's breast," intrudes the
  Viennese,
"Delighted him too much, fixed his disease.
The child misunderstood, blind animal:
Dark Id rules all, and though impersonal,
Fixed to the womb this individual:
'O Mutter, Mutter, it is cold outside':
So speaks his wish to die, such is his pride."

Coriolanus finds the entire world wanting because nowhere within it can he regain the absolute gratification he enjoyed in infancy.

It is curious that Coriolanus should be presented as an embodiment of the untamed id, for in his hatred of pleasure and of the body, he seems, on the contrary, a victim of a tyrannical superego. One recalls Freud's observation, in *The Ego and the Id,* that the moral demands of a harsh superego have the same unconscious, compelled quality as the libidinal demands of the id. Schwartz seems uncertain whether the denial of instinct is neurosis or nobility. More generally, he seems unable to decide whether his hero is reducible to Freudian and Marxist explanations, or whether there is an irreducible part that transcends explanation. He sometimes entertains the possibility that something—call it the soul, or what you will—can escape the determinisms that trouble him so deeply.

Schwartz was finally more interested in interpreting the story of Coriolanus than in telling it. Although his anxious sense of unseen forces working behind outward events is typical of a good deal of modern literature, he drove the passion for explanation to extremes, as if the explanation could somehow undo the events or drain them of their power to harm. "Coriolanus and His Mother" struggles ponderously toward a kind of knowledge that is by its nature unattainable, since explanations must stop somewhere or lose themselves in infinite regress.

Caught in his Sisyphean conception of his art, Schwartz produced poems more notable for their ambition, brilliance, and moral passion than for technical assurance or formal unity. Though he could produce felicitous lines, Schwartz was endowed but modestly with the auditory imagination. When he later turned away from the intellectualism of his early poetry to an art of lyrical celebration, he could not work the magic of a Dylan Thomas or a Theodore Roethke in that mode. But some of the short poems of *In Dreams Begin Responsibilities* show him at his best; only infrequently would he match their achievement afterward.

Schwartz divided the lyrics of *In Dreams Begin Responsibilities* into two groups, the first (and less impressive) of which he called "The Repetitive Heart: Eleven Poems in Imitation of the Fugue Form." With a sobriety unusual in proponents of "musical form," he added in a note: "This suite of poems might perhaps be more exactly called poems in a form suggested by the fugue, since the contrapuntal effect is of course impossible in language." Schwartz's method of suggesting counterpoint depends mainly on the repetition of key words and phrases several times during each poem; these "fugues" might uncharitably be described as sestinas or villanelles, though the pattern of repetition is less regular. Sometimes a rhythmic pattern is repeated in several consecutive phrases, and sometimes the predominantly tetrameter lines are broken with a strong medial caesura, so that one hears an "entrance," an implied lineation within the line. Schwartz does not exploit self-interruption and fragmentation, as the German poet Paul Celan was to do in his famous "Todesfuge." There is, in short, no great technical innovation here. Nor is there, except in a few of the poems, very much substance with which the form can engage.

The one poem of real distinction in "The Repetitive Heart" is the frequently anthologized "The Heavy Bear Who Goes with Me," a meditation on the dualism of body and soul. In "The Heavy Bear . . ." Schwartz's Freudian and Marxist explanations give way to a rhetoric of Platonic idealism. What looks in "Coriolanus and His Mother" like neurotic rejection of pleasure becomes a noble exaltation of the spirit over the senses. The "bear" of the title is the body itself, perceived not as the habitation of the soul but as an oafish doppelgänger who mimics the soul's gestures, coarsening them even as he makes them manifest. He is "A caricature, a swollen shadow, / A stupid clown of the spirit's motive. . . .

Although he is an encumbrance, the bear can be pitied in his vulnerability. Enslaved to his desires and fears, he "Howls in his sleep for a world of sugar, / A sweetness intimate as the water's clasp." He has "followed" the soul "since the black womb held," and remains perpetually dissatisfied (like Coriolanus) in the less obliging world outside, where he "Boxes his brother in the hate-ridden city" and competes in "The scrimmage of appetite everywhere." He fears death and "Trembles to think that his quivering meat / Must finally wince to nothing at all."

Even in lovemaking, where one might suppose him welcome, the bear can do nothing right; instead, he

Stretches to embrace the very dear
With whom I would walk without him near,
Touches her grossly, although a word
Would bare my heart and make me
clear. . . .

In refusing to be ruled by spiritual love, the body frustrates its own desires, for the spirit's "word" would gain the woman's assent, whereas the bear, touching her "grossly," drives her away. Finally, the body is the enemy of all true selfhood. The speaker complains that the bear is "Dragging me with him in his mouthing care, / Amid the hundred million of his kind. . . ." Souls are unique; bodies are interchangeable.

We encounter the Platonic Schwartz again in one of the best of the "Twenty-Four Poems" that follow "The Repetitive Heart." Its title, "In the Naked Bed, in Plato's Cave," refers to the famous parable in book 7 of Plato's *Republic,* in which prisoners, chained facing the rear wall of a cave, mistake their own shadows, and those of objects at the mouth of the cave, for the primary substance of reality. The poem reveals well the tension between Schwartz's interest in social causation and his desire to dismiss the entire time-bound world as inherently hopeless. The cave metaphor has been given a this-worldly twist, for, as Richard McDougall points out, "the world outside is the actual world and not a simile for a reality beyond it. According to this substitution of the literal for the symbolic, Schwartz's meaning seems to be the exact opposite of Plato's: the world in time (and of being in time) *is* reality itself." Yet the metaphor leads back toward its original significance as the poem progresses.

McDougall's remark applies quite well to the opening lines:

In the naked bed, in Plato's cave,
Reflected headlights slowly slid the wall,
Carpenters hammered under the shaded
window,
Wind troubled the window curtains all
night long,
A fleet of trucks strained uphill, grinding,
Their freights covered, as usual.
The ceiling lightened again, the slanting
diagram
Slid slowly forth.
Hearing the milkman's chop,
His striving up the stair, the bottle's chink,
I rose from bed, lit a cigarette,
And walked to the window.

As the narrator of "In Dreams Begin Responsibilities" must leave the darkened theater to face the world outside his bedroom window, so here the speaker must move from isolated selfhood to relation with the world. The noises he hears just before dawn suggest the difficulties of that world: the trucks "strained uphill," the milkman was "striving up the stair."

Like the unchained prisoner in Plato's allegory, the speaker turns to look at the world outside the cave. Imagery of change yields to imagery of stasis, though the objects remain very much of this world:

. . . The stony street
Displayed the stillness in which buildings
stand,
The street-lamp's vigil and the horse's
patience.

This passage is followed by two remarkable lines, in which the speaker does glimpse something beyond what McDougall calls "the world in time":

The winter sky's pure capital
Turned me back to bed with exhausted eyes.

Just as Schwartz adapts Plato's idealist allegory to express a materialist idea, so in these lines he takes Marx's "capital" and makes it stand for an ideal transcendence. Like Plato's newly emancipated cave dweller, the speaker is blinded by the light, and returns to the "cave" of his bedroom. The sky is "pure capital" in the sense that its pure spirit has not been invested in any particular embodiment; it has not descended into the world in time.

After the speaker's return from the window, the stillness is broken and the day begins. Although the world has not taken on the absolute purity of the sky, it has become more intelligible and substantial than it was in the opening lines:

> . . . Morning, softly
> Melting the air, lifted the half-covered chair
> From underseas, kindled the looking-glass,
> Distinguished the dresser and the white
> wall.

The poem broadens at its close toward a general statement about the human condition:

> . . . So, so,
> O son of man, the ignorant night, the travail
> Of early morning, the mystery of beginning
> Again and again,
> while History is unforgiven.

Despite this overblown ending, "In the Naked Bed, in Plato's Cave" is unforgettable. If one had to pick Schwartz's best poem, it would be among the three or four possibilities.

"The Ballad of the Children of the Czar" also belongs on this short list. The poem begins with an image of sheltered innocence: "The children of the Czar / Played with a bouncing ball" one "May morning" in the palace gardens. But they lost control of the ball: "It fell among the flowerbeds / Or fled to the north gate."

As Schwartz develops this metaphor, it comes to stand for the precariousness of life: sooner or later, someone is bound to make the fatal throwing error. In the second section the poet presents himself at the moment when the aristocratic game of catch was played:

> While I ate a baked potato,
> Six thousand miles apart,
>
> In Brooklyn, in 1916,
> Aged two, irrational.

Although the focus has shifted to the poet, the year 1916 revises our understanding of the first section. It is the year before the Russian Revolution, and the children of the czar will soon perish with their father. The presence of the poet in Brooklyn has something to do with the czar also: the oppression of the Jews under Nicholas II resulted in his grandfather's immigration to America.

The poet can hardly sympathize with Nicholas II, but he can pity the fate of the czar's children. The third section is a meditation on the transmission of guilt from generation to generation. As Aeneas carried his father from the ruins of Troy, so each child must carry the guilt of his parents in his own psyche. The poet, though he will not be killed for his father's crimes, will be burdened, perhaps even destroyed, by the suspicion and guilt his parents have inculcated in him. We can repudiate our parents, or revolt against the czar, but one's parents were once victims of their parents, and the czar was once a child playing in the palace garden. In some final sense the guilty may be innocent; revenge, therefore, only increases guilt. Seeing "that history has no ruth / For the individual," the poet declares, "Let anger be general: / I hate an abstract thing." The problem lies in defining this "abstract thing" and representing it in a poem.

Schwartz returns to the ball metaphor in the fourth section and generalizes it, in the fifth, to include the earth itself: "The ground on which the ball bounces / Is another bouncing ball." The world "makes no will glad"; it is "A pitiless, purposeless Thing. . . ." The section ends in a curiously obsessive, flat string of declarations:

> The innocent are overtaken,
> They are not innocent.
>
> They are their father's fathers,
> The past is inevitable.

This state of affairs, perhaps, is the "abstract thing" the poet hates.

From this lofty plane of generality, the sixth and final section returns to the poet in his second year:

> I eat my baked potato.
>
> It is my buttered world,
> But, poked by my unlearned hand,

It falls from the highchair down
And I begin to howl.

The infant, vulnerable and totally absorbed in the act of eating the potato (his "buttered world"), is in the same plight as the adult, absorbed in maintaining his fragile existence amid hostile forces. The poem closes with another string of defiantly flat assertions, as grim and heavy as the fate they announce:

Even a bouncing ball
Is uncontrollable,

And is under the garden wall.
I am overtaken by terror

Thinking of my father's fathers
And of my own will.

The succession of rhymes and near rhymes reinforces the bluntness: "terror" and "fathers"; "ball," "-ble," "wall," and "will." It is possible that Schwartz has belabored the significance of his materials unduly. But here, for once, his search for grand historical themes within his own experience justifies itself. He locates himself within history, rather than appropriating history as a backdrop for a private melodrama.

There are several more modest successes among the "Twenty-Four Poems." "Far Rockaway," in language reminiscent of Hart Crane's "Voyages" and the seaside passage of "In Dreams Begin Responsibilities," evokes the seductive brilliance of the ocean:

The radiant soda of the seashore fashions
Fun, foam, and freedom. The sea laves
The shaven sand. And the light sways
 forward
On the self-destroying waves.

Vacationers lie "with the passionate sun," escaping "the rigor of the weekday," but here too the note of doom intrudes. "Time unheard moves," and a novelist, like a "nervous conscience amid the concessions," regards the scene distrustfully, reconstructing the private histories the sunbathers must carry within them.

"Tired and Unhappy, You Think of Houses" presents a similar dichotomy of seductive comfort and harsh reality. The thought of "houses/Soft-carpeted and warm," where "servants bring the coffee" entices the "Tired and unhappy" speaker. There is even a young girl singing—but what is the piece? "That song of Gluck where Orpheus pleads with Death." Even in this "banal dream," mortality will out. Better to face the harshness of urban reality, with its "anger exact as a machine!"

A more ambitious poem that similarly plays illusion against disillusionment is the "Prothalamion" Schwartz wrote to celebrate, if that is the word, his engagement to Gertrude Buckman. "Now I must betray myself," the poem begins; marriage is a "unity" but also a "bondage." Marriage means betrayal in a number of ways. The husband must not "wear masks or enigmatic clothes" before his wife; he must "betray" or reveal to her his "shocking nakedness." He must also at times "betray" or be disloyal to his own impulses in order to accommodate his wife. And his conduct in marriage will "betray" or reveal to himself the essence of his own character.

As we have already seen, Schwartz feared that his character had been irrevocably ruined in his childhood. As if to arm himself against the danger that his past will undo his marriage, Schwartz invites Marx and Freud to the wedding; they can "mark out the masks that face us there" and free the lovers from "self-deception." In a flourish of extravagance, he invites "all / Who are our friends somehow," representatives of the various arts and professions, and, for good measure, Wolfgang Amadeus Mozart, Athena, Robinson Crusoe, and Charlie Chaplin. Then suddenly, in a poignant reversal, he says:

But this is fantastic and pitiful,
And no one comes, none will, we are alone,
And what is possible is my own voice,
Speaking its wish, despite its lasting fear. . . .

To marry is to take on the care of another's body and mysterious soul. "You are heavy," he tells his bride; "when I carry you / I lift upon my back time like a fate. . . ." One remembers the "heavy bear" of the body, or the child carrying the father in "The Ballad of the Children of the Czar." The poem ends on a forced note of optimism, but not before running a diapason of misgivings. Gertrude Buckman was to leave Schwartz after four years of marriage; no one can say she hadn't been warned.

At least three other poems from *In Dreams Begin Responsibilities* deserve mention. "Father and Son," though flagrantly derivative of Yeats and occasionally marred by clumsy prosody, is nonetheless an interesting confrontation between the irresponsibility of a youth who "would be sudden now and rash in joy," and his father's intimations of guilt and mortality. The father sounds much more like the twenty-five-year-old poet than the son does.

"A Young Child and His Pregnant Mother" might be considered a companion piece for "Father and Son," but it keeps the usual philosophizing in abeyance, aiming primarily at an evocation of the child's feelings:

> And now this newest of the mysteries,
> Confronts his honest and his studious
> eyes—
>
> His mother much too fat and absentminded,
> Gazing far past his face, careless of him,
>
> His fume, his charm, his bedtime, and
> warm milk,
> As soon the night will be too dark, the
> spring
>
> Too late, desire strange, and time too fast,
> This first estrangement is a gradual thing
>
> (His mother once so svelte, so often sick!
> Towering father did this: what a trick!)

It is significant that Louise Bogan, one of the few reviewers with strong reservations about *In Dreams Begin Responsibilities*, admired this poem as more direct, less attitudinizing, than most of the others. One might also have expected her to like "The Ballet of the Fifth Year," which, despite momentary poaching from Crane's "To Brooklyn Bridge," is similarly straightforward. This poem also moves more deftly than any other in the volume. It contains only two sentences, the second of which sweeps, without losing momentum, through fifteen lines. The closing image has a definite, externalized clarity unusual in Schwartz:

> . . . I skated, afraid of policemen, five years
> old,
> In the winter sunset, sorrowful and cold,
> Hardly attained to thought, but old enough
> to know
> Such grace, so self-contained, was the best
> escape to know.

"The Ballet of the Fifth Year" is not an ambitious poem, but it has a "grace, so self-contained" that most of the weightier pieces lack.

In Dreams Begin Responsibilities ends with "Dr. Bergen's Belief," a play in prose and verse that need not detain us long; even Schwartz's most admiring reviewers ignored it. Dr. Bergen has become the leader of a religious cult. He believes that the sky is the eye of God, and that problems may be solved "intuitively" by staring at the sky until illumination comes. His daughter, Eleanor, has recently committed suicide. Dr. Bergen has obtained "intuitive" assurance that the suicide was done in obedience to divine guidance; Eleanor is thus the first martyr to his cause. But Eleanor's psychiatrist produces a letter showing the cause to have been less ethereal: Eleanor killed herself because she was in love with a married man. Overcome with doubt, Dr. Bergen throws himself from the second-story balcony of his house, seeking in death the revelation that has eluded him in life. Written in Schwartz's worst grandiloquent manner, the play is interesting only for its theme: who has the truth, the psychiatrist who reduces all to mundane causes or the mystic who seeks transcendence in a world beyond this one?

The success Schwartz achieved with his first book brought him other kinds of success as well. He became poetry editor of *Partisan Review* in 1939 and, in the fall of 1940, Briggs-Copeland instructor at Harvard. He won a Guggenheim fellowship for the academic year 1940–1941, which was renewed for the following year. During these years, he turned out a number of excellent articles and book reviews for *Partisan Review, Poetry, Kenyon Review,* and other literary magazines. As Philip Rahv observed, "While it is well-known that many poets have produced their best work in their early twenties, it is only very rarely that a critic has contributed anything memorable at that age." Schwartz's career appeared to be as solidly established as a man of his age could wish. And yet, his next ventures in poetry—a translation of Arthur Rimbaud's *Une saison en enfer* (1939) and *Shenandoah* (1941)—do not show him at his best; and the ambitious *Genesis: Book One* (1943), envisioned as the first part of a major autobiographical epic in verse and prose, shows him struggling with difficulties he could not resolve.

The Rimbaud translation was badly received because of its numerous errors; Schwartz revised it for a second edition in 1940, but the damage had been done. Wallace Stevens defended it in a letter to Leonard C. van Geyzel, saying that "It might be sophomoric from the point of view of translating from one language into another and yet contain things that matter." But this defense requires us to regard the poem as a Lowellian "imitation" rather than a translation. Writing for the *New York Review of Books* in 1967, Roger Shattuck preferred Schwartz's version to those of Louise Varèse and Wallace Fowlie, though he added: "Is it sheer perverseness that makes me find Schwartz's out-of-print version best?" Maybe it was "perverseness," or the sentiments aroused by Schwartz's death the year before; one might also add that neither the Varèse nor the Fowlie is a really distinguished translation. Considered as an English poem, Schwartz's *A Season in Hell* is the liveliest of the three, but it does not have the memorable felicity that makes one forgive the liberties in Pound's translations.

Shenandoah appeared as the eighth offering in the New Directions "Poet of the Month" series for 1941. James Atlas describes the reviews as "mixed"; but F. O Matthiessen, in his sympathetic review of *Genesis,* remarks that when Schwartz's "short verse play, *Shenandoah,* seemed slight, it became the fashion to declare that he had been overpraised and had not deserved his reputation in the first place." *Shenandoah* was not a disaster like the Rimbaud translation, but it did not do Schwartz's reputation any good. It belongs among neither the best nor the worst of his writings.

As noted earlier, *Shenandoah* deals with the naming of the protagonist, Shenandoah Fish. The adult Shenandoah witnesses and interprets the commotion occurring around his eight-day-old self on the stage. The autobiographical source of the material, if it were not already obvious, would be given away when Shenandoah's mother slips "Delmore" into a list of names for consideration. Once again Schwartz has depicted himself as a spectator watching his own origins reenacted before him. Such drama as the play can muster is provided by the conflict between Shenandoah's father, Walter Fish, and his uncle, Nathan Harris. Nathan has just finished medical school and has acquired enough sophistication to recognize the name "Shenandoah" as inappropriate. The rabbi, present for the circumcision ceremony, refuses to intervene, saying to himself: "Forbearance and humility are best: what good will it do me to become angry? The modern world is what it is." Finally, Walter Fish telephones his Gentile attorney, Mr. Kelly, to confirm his decision. "*After all,*" says Walter, "*this child is going to live in a world of Kellys!*" At the end of the play, the circumcision is performed offstage, and "*There is an appalling screech, as of an infant in the greatest pain.*"

As one of his epigraphs to the play, Schwartz quotes the *Encyclopaedia Britannica*: "It is the historic nature of all particulars to try to prove that they are universal by nature. . . ." But he apparently could not trust the particulars to do so on their own. In his commentaries the adult Shenandoah extracts the last drop of significance from the proceedings. Ruminating on the argument between Walter and Nathan, he declares:

> This is hardly the last time, little boy,
> That conflict will engage the consciousness
> Of those who might admire Nature, pray to
>   God,
> Make love, make friends, make works of
>   art, make peace—
> O no! hardly the last time: in the end
> All men may seem essential boxers, hate
> May seem the energy which drives the stars
> (*L'amor che move il sole e l'altre stelle!*)
> And war as human as the beating heart:
> So Hegel and Empedocles have taught.

After going on to list the "world-wide causes" that have conspired to choose his name, Shenandoah embarks on a catalog of the great alienated modern writers who will "obsess this child when he can read," and perorates by saying:

> This child will learn of life from these great
>   men,
> He will participate in their solitude,
> And maybe in the end, on such a night
> As this, return to the starting-point, his
>   name,
> Showing himself as such among his friends.

The speech that closes the play is similarly overwrought, rehearsing the sufferings worse than circumcision that will follow when "the horrors of modern life are your sole place," and "the dying West performs unspeakable disgrace / Against the honor of man, before God's utter gaze. . . ."

The problem with *Shenandoah* is not that it makes abstract or general statements in verse, but that the abstractions are several sizes too large for the particulars concerned. The effort to ensure that the audience understands the significance of Shenandoah's name—which is to say, of Schwartz's own—is so hysterically frenzied that one infers behind it a fear that perhaps the name is nothing but an accident, not very significant to anyone but the man who must bear it. A similar criticism can be made of Schwartz's next volume, *Genesis: Book One.*

Genesis grew out of drafts for an autobiographical poem that go back as far as 1931, when the poem was to have been entitled "Having Snow." Later, Schwartz tried writing the piece as prose, settling finally on alternating passages of prose and verse. The stylized prose, set up typographically like biblical verses, is used for narration. The poetry, for the most part blank verse but sometimes freely rhymed or metrically irregular, is reserved for analysis and commentary. Schwartz appears under the name Hershey Green. One winter night, as Hershey is trying to sleep, he thinks he sees snow falling outside the window. Going to the window, he finds that the moonlight and his imagination have tricked him. But although there is no literal snow, the illusion is a portent: the ghosts of the dead appear to Hershey and ask him to tell the "endless story" of his life. The story, which might indeed have proved "endless" if continued at the same pace, takes us from the young adulthood of Schwartz's grandparents in the old country to the incident, earlier recounted in "Prothalamion," when his mother found her husband in a roadhouse, dining with another woman. This incident occurred in 1921, when Schwartz was seven. For Hershey Green, his persona in *Genesis,* it marks the loss of innocence: "Childhood was ended here!"

We wait sixty-six pages for Hershey Green to be born; sixty-nine pages after that, he enters first grade. This exhaustive (and, for the reader, exhausting) reconstruction of early childhood reflects Schwartz's Freudianism. Though it would be difficult under the best circumstances to make a two-hundred-page book from the memories of early childhood, stranger projects have succeeded. But Schwartz's language does not, for the most part, recreate the child's experience with much vividness or exactness. It tells us what happened, and gives the names of the emotions that the child experienced, but it does little more. Hershey does not tell his story in the first person; instead Schwartz tells it in the third person, a technical decision that contributes to the lack of immediacy.

One possible explanation for the inert language of *Genesis* is suggested in a long letter to Schwartz from W. H. Auden, whom New Directions had consulted as a reader for the manuscript. In this letter (quoted extensively in the Atlas biography), Auden criticizes the assumptions outlined in Schwartz's preface. In an age when "their beliefs and values are embodied in great institutions and in the way of life of many human beings," Schwartz tells the reader, authors "do not have to bring in their beliefs and values from the outside; they have only to examine their experience with love in order to find particular beings and actions which are significant of their beliefs and values." The most fortunate of all were the authors of the Gospels, "who, as authors, perhaps had only to look up or remember." Schwartz does not consider his own situation to be so fortunate; he is defending his own need to "bring in . . . beliefs and values from outside." Nonetheless, Auden tells him: "The central fault in your poem is . . . just this false hope that if you only look up and remember enough, significance and value and belief will appear of themselves." Indeed, one might easily conclude that the "significance and value" of the incidents in *Genesis* were so overwhelmingly present for Schwartz that he forgot how much art is needed to re-create that overwhelming presence for someone else.

All the same, Schwartz belabors the "significance and value" of each incident, great and small. The explanations are not explanations at all, but astonishingly pointless reifications of every emotion and institution into a "divinity" or cosmic force. When Mrs. Green sells a bond to finance the operation that enables her to conceive Hershey, it proves that "Capitalismus penetrates each heart." When Hershey, watching the funeral of a young woman, wishes to see the corpse naked, it means that "Love and Death have lain by each other in his mind, Eros and Thanatos, the beginning and the end, Romeo and Juliet forever composed!"

Does Hershey Green go to school? No; say, rather, that

> "The school divinity exerts its power,
> Much like the big city on a farm boy—"
> "Against the parenthood, against the life
> Made by the family divinity. . . ."

"Elucidate, go on, make lucid all, / For it will do him good!" interrupts still another ghost, but it is hard to see how such pseudo insights could do anyone any good. When an analysand indulges in such explanations, the analyst is professionally obliged to set him straight.

However sincerely Schwartz may have intended Genesis as a cathartic self-exploration, part of him seems to have resisted that intention. The result is a work of autobiography that evades rather than engages the hard questions that its content raises: What, as a morally responsible adult, can one do to surmount a destructive heritage? What, as a poet, can one do to make art of such intractable materials as infantile sexuality and the perils of kindergarten? Schwartz explains himself away, telling his story with a curious suppression of affect, veiling his motives in grandiose universals. The problem, then, may not be quite what Auden said it was. Schwartz may have believed that his life would interpret itself if he recorded it faithfully enough, but he shrank from the pain of reexperiencing it as well as from the pain of understanding it.

Genesis: Book One must be accounted a failure, and the excerpts from the manuscript of the unpublished *Book Two* that Atlas reprints in *New Directions 35* do not suggest that the sequel would have been much better. Nonetheless, as one might expect from a writer of Schwartz's gifts, there are interesting passages scattered through it. Not all the narration is flat; not all the insight is bogus. Details like the unexpected snowfall on Christmas Eve, and Hershey's delight at receiving a bicycle the following morning, are evocatively presented. More somber scenes also stick in the memory: Hershey, on vacation with his father, looking at his phosphorescent watch in the darkness, waiting for his father to return from one of his amours; Hershey witnessing his father's shame during the roadhouse confrontation. Even the tedious ghosts get a witty line now and then:

> Forgive strange God, maker of Heaven and Earth,
> Who made the spring and fall with a slight tilt
> Such as vain *beaux* will give their Sunday hats!

Above all, one can respect what Schwartz was trying to do in *Genesis.* He was trying, in a time that favored tightly controlled lyric poetry, to write a huge, sprawling work that would triumph by its sheer intensity, sincerity, and inclusiveness. He wanted to crowd everything from his first day in kindergarten to World War I, from the right fielder's throw home in a Giants game to the stock market crash, into a single work of art.

The reception given *Genesis* was not as harsh as it might have been. The book drew praise not only from R. P. Blackmur and F. O. Matthiessen, whom Schwartz knew personally, but also from Richard Eberhart, Dudley Fitts, and Northrop Frye. But Schwartz wanted to be told that he had produced a masterpiece on the order of William Wordsworth's *Prelude,* and no one was prepared to go that far. There were also dismissive reviews from William Rose Benét and Horace Gregory, among others; nor did Schwartz's friend Dwight Macdonald care for *Genesis,* though he refrained from saying so in print.

It was a difficult time for Schwartz personally as well. His marriage was breaking up. Also, although he had risen to the rank of associate professor at Harvard, he felt burdened by his increased teaching load and ill at ease with his colleagues. In these circumstances his thirtieth birthday seemed little cause for celebration. He missed New York, and it was to New York that he returned when he left Harvard, without giving notice, in the spring of 1947.

Despite his unhappiness, Schwartz continued to produce excellent critical essays and stories, though it was a lean time for his poetry. Indeed, his next book, *The World Is a Wedding* (1948), almost equals the achievement of his first. It contains six previously uncollected stories, along with a reprinting of "In Dreams Begin Responsibilities."

In some ways the six later stories resemble "In Dreams Begin Responsibilities." They continue to use autobiographical material, and they employ the same deliberately flat style. But "In Dreams" occasionally modulates from the flat style into a more poetic language, and it supplements autobiography with the surrealistic device of the dream theater. The later work is more insistently flat, but it has a wider range of observation and a more complex treatment of relations among the characters. The exception to this generalization is "The Statues," which adopts the conventions of parable rather than those of realism.

The title story, the longest in the volume, concerns a circle of young intellectuals gathered around the unpublished writer Rudyard Bell, whom they revere as a genius. Episodic rather than tightly plotted, the story examines each of several characters in turn, with Rudyard's overbearing presence always in the background. We perceive the characters through the eye of Jacob Cohen, "the conscience of the group," its most compassionate and imaginative member. To a lesser extent Rudyard's embittered sister Laura also serves as a surrogate author. Like Jacob, she sees through the pretensions of Rudyard and his admirers, although she judges more harshly.

On the most universal level, "The World Is a Wedding" is about the difficulties of friendship, but the atmosphere of the Great Depression permeates the lives of the characters. After brilliant careers in college, Rudyard and his friends find only dull jobs or no jobs at all. The circle provides the only release for their intellectual energies. This claustral mutual dependence and the lack of prospects for advancement intensify the brittle egocentricity common in ambitious young persons even under more favorable circumstances. The meetings of the circle are full of one-upmanship, of conscious and unconscious cruelty. Even Laura, detached and lucid as her sarcasms often are, has a personal motive: She had hoped to find a husband among her brother's friends, but none of them is interested. The Depression may contribute indirectly to their indifference to her, for "their lower middle class poverty kept them from seeking out girls and entertaining the idea of marriage."

Atlas has identified Rudyard Bell as Paul Goodman, who indeed had a circle of admirers about him in the mid-1930's. Schwartz himself is Jacob Cohen. But if we read the story as autobiography, we must also find part of Schwartz in Rudyard Bell. Rudyard has, like Schwartz, an unlikely given name yoked to a common, one-syllable surname. One of his plays centers on a poet who, like Schwartz at the time the story was written, is obsessed with his own decline from early brilliance. His conversation with his former teacher, Percival Davis, is taken from an actual exchange between Schwartz and David Prall of Harvard. We might interpret Rudyard and Jacob as "bad" and "good" versions of Schwartz's character. But to read "The World Is a Wedding" purely as autobiography is to slight its universality, its insights into the life of the 1930's and the problems of late adolescence.

The theme of the Great Depression is intertwined with those of generational conflict and coming of age. The parents of the young men in the circle, who have struggled toward assimilation and economic security, cannot understand their sons' rejection of conventional social manners and of moneymaking. Upon meeting Israel Brown, an idealistic young teacher admired by the circle, Edmund Kish's mother can only ask: "How much money does he make?" This question becomes an ironic leitmotiv in the discussions of the group.

Rudyard and his friends carry their refusal of convention and compromise to noble but self-destructive extremes. Francis French, the only member of the group to secure a teaching job in a university, is dismissed when he refuses to make a nominal denial of an accusation of homosexuality. As a result, he is reduced to "the drudgery of teaching in a high school"; he no longer has time for his intellectual interests, and spends his evenings solely in pursuit of sexual pleasure. Rudyard himself, when visited by a producer who admires his plays, feigns contempt for success so convincingly that the opportunity is lost. Among the members of the circle, *contemptus mundi* is an honorific name for sour grapes. Their social habits have been formed around the need to make failure bearable; when a chance to escape from failure presents itself, they cannot respond appropriately.

Toward the end of the story, Rudyard's group has begun to drift apart. Relations have been strained by the rivalry between Marcus Gross and Ferdinand Harrap for the affections of a girl identified only as "Irene" (as the lack of a second name suggests, Irene hardly matters in herself). Jealous of Ferdinand's victory in love, Marcus threatens to reveal Irene's previous affair with Algernon Nathan, whom Ferdinand detests. Jacob restrains him; but Laura, jealous of the attention lavished on Irene, blurts out the secret when Ferdinand arrives. Quite apart from the rancor produced by this incident (which, we surmise, is typical), the Great Depression is ending. Some members of the circle have found jobs and drifted away from the neighborhood. Rudyard, the central figure in the group, has accepted a teaching job in Cleveland, so the others must decide whether to disband or to continue without him.

At this point Jacob launches into a long eulogy for the circle. In his readings he has found the words "the world is a wedding" (which Schwartz got from the Talmud). Meditating on this oracular statement, Jacob thinks of Pieter Brueghel's *The Peasant Wedding* as an illustration of it. The wedding ceremony includes many guests who can have little portion in the joy of the bride and groom: the celibate nuns, an "unkempt and middle-aged" musician whose abstracted gaze suggests that he is "thinking of his faded hopes." Even "the suitor whom the bride refused" must be present, "perhaps among the crush that crowds the door." The parents of the couple are old: "Their time is passed and they have had their day." And yet, Jacob continues, "this too is a pleasure and a part for them to play.

Like the members of the circle, most of the wedding guests do not have what they want; only the bride and groom have happiness, and they perhaps only for a little while. But participation in the ceremony releases and transforms everyone present. In this sense "the world is a wedding," "the most important kind of party, full of joy, fear, hope, and ignorance. And at this party there are enough places and parts for everyone." The circle, for all its bickering, has been "a circle of friendship," the kind one must have "to be present at the wedding of this world."

Laura, though she speaks more briefly, speaks last. During all the self-important philosophical discussions, she has been in the kitchen cooking for her brother's friends, who repay her kindness with indifference or condescension. It is the income from her job that has supported Rudyard for so many years. She replies to Jacob: "You can't fool me . . . the world is a funeral."

As Richard McDougall remarks, "Jacob and Laura . . . define the familiar polarities of Schwartz's mind," though his definition of these polarities as "loving communion" and "analytical reason" is misleading: Jacob is at least as analytical as Laura, and far more self-conscious. Manic and depressive would be closer to the truth: an untenably complete affirmation and an insupportably dreary despair.

"New Year's Eve," the next story in the collection, treats the discontents of friendship on a smaller scale. Again the plot is slight: A group of intellectuals, including Shenandoah Fish, his girl friend Wilhelmina Gold, and his friend Nicholas O'Neil, attend a New Year's Eve party at the home of Grant Landis, an editor and co-owner of "Centaur Editions, a small publishing house" that has just printed Shenandoah's first book. Like the characters of "The World Is a Wedding," the guests at the party seek each other out in order to mitigate or forget their own unhappiness. But for the most part they spend the evening hurting each other's feelings, motivated by an insecurity that finds malice in the remarks of others and replies in kind. Although, as intellectuals and writers, they are committed to a high calling, they are at least as petty as other people.

The representative man at this gathering is Oliver Jones, a talented writer who has compromised himself by courting popularity in his fiction and flattering the powerful in his reviews. "And all this behavior," Schwartz observes, "would have been unnecessary to Oliver, had he only known that he was really a gifted author!" Unsure of his gifts, Oliver belittles all pretensions to an integrity greater than his own. He spoils the party's one brief "period of good feeling" by reading and then mocking Edmund Wilson's admiration, in *Axel's Castle,* for Marcel Proust's affirmation of "laws which we have obeyed because we have carried their precepts within us without knowing who inscribed them there. . . ." Shenandoah leaves the party thinking, with Proust, that such laws must come from "some other world," since they certainly cannot derive from the pettiness of ours, in which writers are implicated as much as everyone else.

Schwartz left in his notes a key identifying the characters of "New Year's Eve": Shenandoah Fish is of course Schwartz himself, Wilhelmina Gold is Gertrude Buckman, and Nicholas O'Neil is William Barrett. The host, Grant Landis, is Dwight Macdonald, and Oliver Jones is an unflattering rendition of F. W. Dupee. Barrett's complaint about "The World Is a Wedding"—that it is "dull, unless you happen to know the people"—applies with more justice to "New Year's Eve." Whereas the longer story develops fictionalized characters enough so that we need not refer to their originals, "New Year's Eve" reduces character to caricature, and caricature loses its point if one doesn't "happen to know the people."

"A Bitter Farce," which follows "New Year's Eve," is more sharply focused. It tells of the young Shenandoah's encounters with anti-Semitism in his wartime summer classes. Shenandoah teaches two sections of composition, one for navy students and one for women. Discouraged by the heat of the summer and the bad prose of the navy students, Shenandoah often wanders "from discussions of spelling and grammar to . . . matters which are sometimes referred to as topics of the day." On one such occasion, Shenandoah's navy class draws him into a discussion of "the Negro problem." Asked if he would marry a Negro woman, Shenandoah decides not to "lose face with his students" by answering yes. "I would not marry a Negro woman," he replies, "but there are many white women I would not marry for the same reasons. . . ." Most of the students interpret this answer to mean "that Mr. Fish would not marry many white women as well as Negro women because he was a Jew," although this inference is incorrect.

Not long after this incident, one of the young ladies brings in a journal entry on the question: "If you had to marry one of them, which of these three would you choose, a Chinaman, a Jew, or a Negro?" A Jew would seem to be the closest racially, but, as the girl's friends point out, "there is something about Jews that other races can't stand." The student concludes with a halfhearted attempt at liberality; if "placed in that horrible position," she would "choose the one who was fairest and most honest, the kindest, and he whose ideas most nearly coincided with mine." Shenandoah declines to discuss the content of the passage. By commenting only on the style, he once more avoids confrontation.

But when provoked a third time, by a Mr. Murphy in the navy class, he can be silent no longer. He launches into a passionate defense, most of which is lost on his students. "My ancestors," he declares, "in whom I take pride, but not personal pride, were scholars, poets, prophets and students of God when most of Europe worshipped sticks and stones. . . ." After the bell rings, Murphy stays to talk to him. "I have nothing against you," says Murphy; "you always give me a square deal." Shenandoah considers reporting Murphy to his commanding officer, for such "extraordinary lack of tact and discretion" ill becomes "an officer-to-be." But although he can find no reason for his decision, he lets the incident drop. We are left to wonder whether he does so from generosity or from cowardice. Unfortunately, James Atlas did not reprint this story in his selection.

In the next story, "America! America!," Schwartz for once succeeded in portraying a character much different from himself. The central figure, Mr. Baumann, is neither artist nor intellectual, but a modestly successful insurance salesman. Shenandoah listens to his mother's recollections of Mr. Baumann at a time when he has been feeling "a loss or lapse of identity." On this occasion "His mother's monologue began to interest him more and more, much more than ever before, although she spoke of human beings who, being of her own generation, did not really interest Shenandoah in themselves."

As he listens, he fidgets with a silver spoon, engraved with his initials, that the Baumanns gave him when he was born. This detail clearly foreshadows his climactic recognition of

> . . . how closely bound he was to these people. His separation was actual enough, but there existed also an unbreakable unity. As the air was full of the radio's unseen voices, so the life he breathed in was full of these lives and the age in which they had acted and suffered.

He comes to understand that "the contemptuous mood which had governed him as he listened was really self-contempt and ignorance."

It is certainly the "separation" between Shenandoah and Mr. Baumann that strikes us first. Shenandoah has assumed the role of cosmopolitan and alienated young poet; he has just come back from a trip to Paris. (This detail, by the way, is not autobiographical.) Mr. Baumann is not cosmopolitan, alienated, or poetic; his success as an insurance man stems from his geniality. To succeed at insurance, "it was necessary to become friendly with a great many people," and to "join the lodges, societies, and associations of your own class and people. This had been no hardship to Mr. Baumann who enjoyed groups, gatherings, and meetings of all kinds."

Mr. Baumann values moneymaking and the good opinion of the community above all else, though the second goal often gets in the way of the first. He lacks the ruthless business instinct of Shenandoah's father, who does not allow bonhomie to interfere with profits. In a moment of weakness, Shenandoah's father takes Mr. Baumann and young Dick Baumann into his business; but upon discovering their amiable inefficiency he abruptly dissolves the partnership the long friendship between the two families notwithstanding.

Dick Baumann inherits his father's geniality, but is unable to make a living from it. For that matter, after the stock market crash, Mr. Baumann himself has a hard time of it. His reduced circumstances are partly a result of the Great Depression, but also partly the result of his obsolete methods. As his other son, Sidney, cruelly tells him, "the old oil" no longer works in the increasingly assimilated and impersonal ambience of the community. Sidney, for his part, seems incapable of work; the daughter, Martha, makes a good marriage but becomes "more impatient with her family year by year," and eventually wishes to sever all ties with them, though her husband prevents her from doing so.

The old ways, which served well enough for Mr. Baumann, will not do for his children. They must choose between failure and a radical break with the previous generation. In either case the result is bitterness: "The lower middle-class of the generation of Shenandoah's parents had engendered perversions of its own nature, children full of contempt for every thing important to their parents."

Despite the "gulf" between Shenandoah and his mother's old friend, the two have some things in common. We learn that Mr. Baumann, like Shenandoah, enjoys sleeping late in the morning. He is "pleasure-loving," and thus an object of suspicion in the eyes of Shenandoah's father. Within his provincial world he is considered an intellectual, a more traveled and cultured man than his neighbors. And he doesn't just "sell" insurance policies, he "writes" them. Mr. Baumann's frustrated desire for high culture is typical of his generation; it finds fulfillment in the next generation, when Shenandoah and others like him become writers and scholars. But if Shenandoah completes Mr. Baumann, he has also cut his ties to family and community, and so becomes incomplete in another sense. In his isolation he has cause to envy Mr. Baumann's secure bond to a community.

"All I ever wanted," laments Shenandoah in "New Year's Eve," "was to have friends and go to parties." But by this criterion he is a failure and Mr. Baumann is a success. Thinking of his generation's "contempt" for its parents, Shenandoah

> . . . began to feel that he was wrong to suppose that the separation, the contempt, and the gulf had nothing to do with his work; perhaps, on the contrary, it was the center; or perhaps it was the starting-point and compelled the innermost motion of the work to be flight, or criticism, or denial, or rejection.

Shenandoah finds his complementary relationship to Mr. Baumann difficult to acknowledge, but the acknowledgment is necessary for self-understanding.

"The Statues" stands apart from the other stories in *The World Is a Wedding.* Whereas the others deal with friendships and families in a quotidian social setting, "The Statues" is a parable, taking as its premise a miraculous event. One winter, at five o'clock on December 8 (Schwartz's birthday, as it just so happens), an unusual snow begins to fall in New York. It forms "curious and unquestionable designs, some of which were very human"; it also has "the hardness of rocks," so that it "could not be removed from the pavement." At first the mayor vows to get rid of the snow "as quickly as possible," but the citizens protest. There is a lull in all everyday activities—work and crime slow almost to a halt. Attendance drops at art galleries and movie theaters, for no art form, elite or popular, can compete with the astonishing snow sculptures.

The modern rational temper cannot account for this miracle. Scientists attempt to explain it by the laws of statistical probability, and even the clergy carefully avoids ascribing it to any supernatural power. Understood or not, the snowfall brings about a temporary utopia. It brings the central character, Faber Gottschalk, to discover in himself a passion for the good, the true, and the beautiful, scarcely apparent hitherto in his prosaic career as a dentist. But suddenly "a tireless and foul rain descended and to everyone's surprise utterly destroyed the fine statues." Everything immediately returns to normal, as if nothing unusual had ever happened. This story, like "A Bitter Farce," remains out of print; again, one wishes room had been found for it in Atlas' selection.

The last of the stories in *The World Is a Wedding,* aside from "In Dreams Begin Responsibilities," is "The Child Is the Meaning of This Life." It draws its characters from the household of Schwartz's maternal grandmother, Hannah Nathanson, whose fictional name is Ruth Hart. Schwartz appears under the name Jasper, but his story is subordinated to that of his mother's family. As in "America! America!" the second generation has lost the tough adaptability of the first. Ruth Hart has a generous, loving disposition and is dearly loved by all her friends. One might think that, despite the early death of her husband, she would succeed in raising capable, affectionate children. But her daughter Sarah (Jasper's mother) becomes sharp-tongued and resentful after her marriage to the rich but philandering Michael; her son Seymour is too lazy to hold a job, and gambles away what little money he has. Rebecca, the one loyal child, has helped to spoil Seymour; she even rescues him when he takes money belonging to his employer and bets it on a baseball game. She manages to make a respectable marriage to a dentist, but it is not a great success. Sarah's husband, a far better catch, repeatedly abandons his family to chase other women.

The characters are interesting, but the story lacks the power of "America! America!," in which the confrontation between Shenandoah's values and those of the Baumanns provides a much needed dramatic tension. Though only half the length of "The Child Is the Meaning of This Life," "America! America!" has more richness of implication.

If Atlas disappoints us by omitting "A Bitter Farce" and "The Statues" from his selection of Schwartz's stories, he makes up for it by restoring two noteworthy pieces that Schwartz for some reason never included in any of his books. "Screeno" was not published in any form until *Partisan Review* printed it in 1977, more than a decade after Schwartz's death. It concerns a young writer, Cornelius Schmidt, who goes to the movies and wins a game of "Screeno," apparently a variation of bingo played in theaters during the 1930's. The master of ceremonies, attempting to make conversation, asks Cornelius: "What do you do?" Cornelius replies that he is a poet. When the master of ceremonies and the audience find this amusing, Cornelius increases their hostility by reciting a passage from Eliot's "Gerontion." Just as everyone has become suspicious of Cornelius, an old man calls out from the balcony, claiming that he also holds a winning card. The master of ceremonies tries to avoid paying the old man his prize money, although the card is indeed complete. Cornelius denounces the management as dishonest and miserly, and, in a sudden burst of generosity, gives his own prize money to the old man, though he had planned to invest it in books.

Less completely successful but also interesting is "The Commencement Day Address," which was published in the *New Directions* annual for 1937. It provides a minimal fictional scaffolding for the undecorously passionate speech of the historian Isaac

Duspenser, who upbraids his audience for its frivolous indifference to history and mortality. The rhetoric of the speech is melodramatic but often powerful; perhaps the best passages of all come in Schwartz's descriptions of the ambience of the event:

> An airplane gnawed overhead, bare, abstract and geometrical in the cloud-flowered sky; and its tone accented the passage of the afternoon. One listener had a firm sense of the narrow metropolitan city, its ribs bound by deep, narrow rivers, narrow on all sides, narrow in its tall towers, full of thousands of drugstores and apartment houses, full of thousands of narrow avenues, all of which stood in back of the idyllic campus scene and showed its falsity.

"The Commencement Day Address" is an odd combination of short story, essay, and prose poem; indeed, Dr. Duspenser's talk includes a prose rearrangement of "In the Naked Bed, in Plato's Cave."

After the publication of *The World Is a Wedding,* we approach the years in Schwartz's life that Saul Bellow used as material for *Humboldt's Gift:* the second marriage, to Elizabeth Pollett, in 1949; the purchase of the rural New Jersey farmhouse in 1951; the ill-fated appointment at Princeton in 1952; the deterioration of the marriage; and, finally, the psychotic outburst against Hilton Kramer that ended with Schwartz's commitment to Bellevue Hospital for a week in 1957. During this period Schwartz alienated most of his old friends and began to lose his sense of membership in the literary community. His last book appeared in 1961, and he stopped publishing work in magazines after 1962. He taught at Syracuse University from 1962 to January 1965; despite his erratic teaching, he attracted a loyal following among the students. He might have stayed at Syracuse for the rest of his life, but instead left abruptly to spend his last months in cheap hotels in midtown Manhattan. When he died, on July 11, 1966, he was so isolated that the literary world knew nothing of his death for two days. Eventually a reporter, checking the morgue lists, recognized his name.

Received opinion has it that as Schwartz deteriorated, so did his work. "I'd bleed to say his lovely work improved / but it is not so," wrote John Berryman in one of his commemorative Dream Songs. Recently some critics have begun to question this judgment. Robert Phillips, in his foreword to *Last and Lost Poems of Delmore Schwartz,* takes issue with James Atlas' description of the opening stanza of "Darkling Summer, Ominous Dusk, Rumorous Rain" (1958) as composed of "haphazard, euphonious, virtually incomprehensible effusions." To dismiss such poetry because of its euphony, replies Phillips, "would be to dismiss Gerard Manley Hopkins, Dame Edith Sitwell, and Dylan Thomas, to name three."

But Atlas does not mean to dismiss the late poems because of their euphony. The problem is, rather, that they lack the meaning and emotional depth that would make the euphony amount to more than a technical effect. Here is the stanza, so that the reader may judge:

> A tattering of rain and then the reign
> Of pour and pouring-down and down,
> Where in the westward gathered the filming gown
> Of grey and clouding weakness, and, in the mane
> Of the light's glory and the day's splendor, gold and vain,
> Vivid, more and more vivid, scarlet, lucid and more luminous,
> Then came a splatter, a prattle, a blowing rain!
> And soon the hour was musical and rumorous:
> A softness of a dripping lipped the isolated houses,
> A gaunt grey somber softness licked the glass of hours.

These lines, it should be added, are better than most in the later poems of this type.

A critic should not be afraid to overturn a received opinion; but sometimes a received opinion happens also to be just, and in such cases one has the dull duty of confirming it. Although the late poetry is not a total loss, it contains only two or three poems that will stand comparison with the best eight or ten of *In Dreams Begin Responsibilities.* The late fiction in *Successful Love and Other Stories* (1961) is also clearly inferior to the stories in *The World Is a Wedding.*

The nadir of Schwartz's career came in 1950, with the publication of *Vaudeville for a Princess.* This collection of poems, alternating with prose sketches in the first of its three sections, is a virtually unmitigated disaster. Schwartz tells us in a note that the title was "suggested by Princess Elizabeth's admiration of Danny Kaye." The poems aim at wit and playfulness, but the wit is leaden, the playfulness grim and willful. As noted earlier in connection with *Genesis,* Schwartz's style could become lazy, in a way that suggests an inertia born of despair. In *Vaudeville for a Princess,* this despair is sometimes expressed as technical negligence. Metrical and syntactic clumsiness abounds, and in one of the sonnets, Schwartz simply doesn't bother to rhyme the last line of the sestet:

> Churchill nudged Roosevelt. With
> handsome glee
> Roosevelt winked! Upon life's peak they
> played
> (Power is pleasure, though anxious. Power is
> free!)
> Mah-jong or pat-a-cake with history:
> They swayed like elephants in the gaiety
> And the enormity of their success!

These lines exemplify the carelessness of the poems in other respects as well. The parenthetical sentences in the third line are awkward; the superfluous "Power is free!" looks like metrical padding; and one might have difficulty transporting the "elephants" of the fifth line to the "peaks" of the second. The tone of *Vaudeville for a Princess* was well described, in a savage but perceptive review by Hugh Kenner, as "frenetic embarrassment." The irony is too ponderous to be funny, too flippant to be profound. Rolfe Humphries, though he found the poems "solemn, owlish, abstract, and . . . entirely earless," liked the prose interludes of the first section, which struck him as witty, though "at times a bit glib." But these pieces have not worn well, and it is mostly the glibness that remains. Ranging from a discussion of automobiles to deliberately banal retellings of *Hamlet* and *Othello,* these sketches have the ephemeral quality of stand-up comedy, albeit a stand-up comedy for intellectuals.

The one good poem in *Vaudeville for a Princess* is "Starlight Like Intuition Pierced the Twelve," in which Christ's disciples, far from rejoicing in their master's completed mission, are overcome with guilt for their own inability to match his "Unspeakable unnatural goodness." Instead of providing comfort and hope, Christ's life has exhausted the possibilities of goodness: "No one will ever fit / His measure's heights, all is inadequate: / No matter what I do, what good is it?" Christ's perfection "stares" accusingly at human imperfection, like Rainer Maria Rilke's archaic torso of Apollo. The poem makes a sad contrast with Schwartz's earlier remark, in the preface to *Genesis,* that the makers of the Gospels "had only to look up or remember" in order to find a sustaining faith.

The style of *Vaudeville for a Princess* is not yet the euphonious, rhapsodic manner that Phillips identifies as Schwartz's late style. For this we must turn to the previously uncollected work that Schwartz included in *Summer Knowledge,* the selection of his poems that he published in 1959. In this poetry, vague imagery of light and morning, and an exclamatory, occasionless affirmation, run rampant. Some of the poems continue using formal stanzas; others use a long free-verse line like that of Walt Whitman, or of Theodore Roethke in "The Lost Son" or "North American Sequence."

Without any prejudice against free verse or poetry of lyrical celebration, one must object when free verse is handled so ponderously or when celebration becomes so disembodied, so divorced from experience. The following example, which is far from the most damning that might have been chosen, will have to suffice. Here is the opening of "A Little Morning Music":

> The birds in the first light twitter and
> whistle,
> Chirp and seek, sipping and chortling—
> weakly, meekly, they speak and bubble,
> As cheerful as the cherry would, if it could
> speak when it is cherry ripe or cherry
> ripening.
> And all of them are melodious, erratic, and
> gratuitous,
> Singing solely to heighten the sense of
> morning's beginning.
> How soon the heart's cup overflows, how it
> is excited to delight and elation!
>
> And in the first light, the cock's chant,
> roaring,
> Bursts like rockets, rising and breaking into
> brief brilliance;
> As the fields arise, cock after cock catches
> on fire,
> And the pastures loom out of vague blue
> shadow,
> The red barn and the red sheds rise and
> redden, blocks and boxes of slowly
> blooming wet redness;
> Then the great awe and splendor of the sun
> comes nearer,
> Kindling all things, consuming the forest of
> blackness, lifting and lighting up
> All the darkling ones who slept and grew
> Beneath the petals, the frost, the mystery
> and the mockery of the stars.

Some of the phrases are pleasing and evocative, taken in isolation. But as one can already sense in this passage, which is only the first half of the poem, there is no movement, only a proliferation of grandiose variations on the single image of morning. A little of this sort of description, wedded to an emotional occasion, set into motion and developed, could make a whole poem. But the rest of "A Little Morning Music" continues in the same vein. By the end of the poem, one questions the sincerity of all this joy: it seems rhetorical and manic, unmotivated by any adequate occasion, less concerned with the delights of morning than with the desperate assertion that all is well.

A few of the late poems *are* anchored in a specific occasion, and on the whole they prove to be the best ones. " 'I Am Cherry Alive,' the Little Girl Sang" is spoken, as its title suggests, by a child. It has the breathless, run-on rhythms of a child's speech:

> "I am cherry alive," the little girl sang,
> "Each morning I am something new:
> I am apple, I am plum, I am just as excited
> As the boys who made the Hallowe'en bang:
> I am tree, I am cat, I am blossom too:
> When I like, if I like, I can be someone new,
> Someone very old, a witch in a zoo:
> I can be someone else whenever I think
> who. . . . ["]

The language may strike us as slightly too precious, but it is still effective, as are the insistent rhymes.

The poems that James Atlas and Richard McDougall single out for praise are also dramatic monologues. Atlas admires the biblical group: "Abraham," "Sarah," and "Jacob"; McDougall prefers the monologues spoken by writers: "Sterne," "Swift," and "Baudelaire." All of these poems have their moments, especially "Jacob," but at times they seem too slackly written. They borrow too passively from their sources and are content with presenting a static attitude. A good dramatic monologue must progress and unfold as one moves from beginning to end.

Schwartz's borrowing is anything but passive in the wonderful "Seurat's Sunday Afternoon Along the Seine," a long free-verse meditation on Georges Seurat's *Un dimanche à la Grande-Jatte.* The source for this poem would seem to be not only the painting itself, but also Meyer Schapiro's article, "New Light on Seurat," published in the April 1958 issue of *Art News.* (The poem is dedicated "To Meyer and Lillian Schapiro.") Schwartz appears to have drawn upon Schapiro's commentary, even to the extent of adapting its language. Schapiro wrote:

> With all its air of simplicity and stylization, Seurat's art is extremely complex. He painted large canvases not to assert himself nor to insist on the power of a single idea, but to develop an image emulating the fullness of nature. One can enjoy in the *Grande Jatte* many pictures each of which is a world in itself. . . .

Schwartz's words echo Schapiro's in these lines:

> His vision is simple: yet it is also ample,
> complex, vexed, and profound
> In emulation of the fullness of Nature. . . .
> . . .
> Within this Sunday afternoon upon the
> Seine
> Many pictures exist inside the Sunday
> scene:
> Each of them is a world itself, a world in
> itself. . . .

More generally, Schwartz appears to have elaborated on Schapiro's description of the figures in the painting as "a secular congregation, grave and ceremonious, in their holiday communion with the summer light and air."

Schwartz's poem, though indebted to Schapiro's essay, is not a merely passive appropriation of it. Schwartz finds a pathos in the scene that Schapiro does not. The painting becomes a symbol of precarious reconciliation, in which

> The Sunday summer sun shines equally and
> voluptuously
> Upon the rich and the free, the comfortable,
> the *rentier,* the poor, and those who are
> paralyzed by poverty.
> Seurat is at once painter, poet, architect, and
> alchemist:
> The alchemist points his magical wand to
> describe and hold the Sunday's gold,
> Mixing his small alloys for long and long
> Because he wants to hold the warm leisure
> and pleasure of the holiday
> Within the fiery blaze and passionate
> patience of his gaze and mind
> Now and forever: O happy, happy throng,
> It is forever Sunday, summer, free. . . .

The "happy, happy throng" should recall the "happy, happy boughs" of John Keats's "Ode on a Grecian Urn," for here, as in Keats, the permanence of art reminds us of the impermanence of life. Outside the painting, time presses on. Seurat died young, and in his brief span had little Sunday leisure. To create the apparent spontaneity of the painting,

> . . . it requires the labors of Hercules,
> Sisyphus, Flaubert, Roebling:
> The brilliance and spontaneity of Mozart,
> the patience of a pyramid,
> And requires all these of the painter who at
> twenty-five
> Hardly suspects that in six years he will no
> longer be alive!

Although the transient pleasures that the artist celebrates are not for him, the world within the painting is in a sense more "real" than his. In it people can sometimes lose their self-consciousness and fear of death in ordinary happiness. They find a summer's day by the river sufficient in itself, without any need to "describe and hold" it. The artist can pay homage to this simplicity, but he has no share in it. The poem ends wistfully:

> . . . Far and near, close and far away,
> Can we not hear, if we but listen to what
> Flaubert tried to say,
> Beholding a husband, wife and child on just
> such a day:
> *Ils sont dans le vrai!* They are with the
> truth, they have found the way
> The kingdom of heaven on earth on Sunday
> summer day.
> Is it not clear and clearer? Can we not also
> hear
> The voice of Kafka, forever sad, in despair's
> sickness trying to say:
> "Flaubert was right: *Ils sont dans le vrai!*
> Without forbears, without marriage,
> without heirs,
> Yet with a wild longing for forbears,
> marriage, and heirs:
> They all stretch out their hands to me: but
> they are too far away!"

We hear not only Gustave Flaubert and Franz Kafka, but also Schwartz in these closing lines. In them he has made clear, for once, his true relation to the celebratory rhetoric in the late poetry.

None of the poems that Robert Phillips recovered for his selection *Last and Lost Poems of Delmore Schwartz* (1979) approaches the power of "Seurat's Sunday Afternoon Along the Seine," but a few of them are better than most of the late work in *Summer Knowledge.* One might recommend "America, America!" (which has no connection with the story "America! America!"), "Poem; Remember Midsummer: The Fragrance of Box," "Spiders," and the somber "All Night, All Night," with its bleak cry:

> *O your life, your lonely life*
> *what have you ever done with it,*
> *And done with the great gift of*
> *consciousness?*

There are occasional striking images, of a sensuous intensity rare in Schwartz's work. Here, for instance, is the third of the "Phoenix Lyrics":

> Purple black cloud at sunset: it is late
> August
> and the light begins to look cold, and as we
> look,
> listen and look, we hear the first drums of
> autumn.

On the whole, though, the examples in Phillips' book will hardly support a higher estimation of Schwartz's late poetry. By turning away from the personal and historic determinisms that had burdened him for so long, he sometimes attained a measure of spontaneity and sensuous immediacy missing in most of the early poetry. But it is freedom in a vacuum, the volatilized fantasy of a man who has nearly withdrawn from all relation to the world. Only in those poems in which some source in externality kept him from severing that relation did he continue to produce work of any substance.

Schwartz's last book, *Successful Love* (1961), finds his prose style in tolerable repair, but the stories lack the emotional force and social detail of the earlier work. The characters are not drawn from autobiographical sources; they are neither Jewish immigrants like Mr. Baumann nor Jewish intellectuals like Shenandoah Fish. Schwartz's style always tended to ward abstractness, and when he tried to depict a milieu he did not know intimately, the texture became too thin. "A Colossal Fortune" and "The Hartford Innocents" are amusingly plotted but too long for their slight content. "An American Fairy Tale" wittily reverses the cliché of the philistine father and the idealistic son: an aspiring young composer sells out and writes advertising jingles, while the father retires from his business and becomes a noted abstract expressionist painter. It's a good joke, but little more than that.

James Atlas' selection contains only one story from *Successful Love,* and it is unquestionably the right one. "The Track Meet," with its savage irony and disturbing symbolism, stands apart from—and above—the other late stories. The narrator, Frank Lawrence, is awakened at dawn by an unexpected English visitor, Reginald Law. Law takes Lawrence to a track meet, at which Law is surprised to find his mother among the spectators and his brothers among the participants. The competition becomes a symbolic commentary on the cruelty of human nature, especially of human nature as influenced by a capitalist, mass-culture-dominated society. One of the athletes kisses the lips of a girl on a billboard as if she were real; the runners punch and kick each other to gain position in the race, while the audience eggs them on. The brothers, who at first cooperated against the other athletes, begin to fight among themselves. When the race ends, an official shoots the winner, and five cheerleaders shoot the narrator's five brothers.

During these alarming events, Lawrence protests to his English companion that such tactics are "against the rules of the game." But if, as his name suggests, the Englishman represents "law," he does not stand for old-fashioned British propriety. The "law" he represents is post-Darwinian: " 'Nature is unfair,' said Law, 'and existence is also unfair.' " "Law" is also the first part of "Lawrence," as we understand at the end of the story.

The narrator wants to escape from his nightmare by waking to "the little things and small actions of early morning" (the language echoes the celebratory rhetoric of *Summer Knowledge*). But waking is no escape, as Law brutally explains:

> You don't escape from nightmare by waking up, you know. And if what occurred on the field were merely imaginary and unreal and merely your own private hallucination, then the evil that has terrified you is rooted in your own mind and heart. Like the rest of us . . . you not only know more than you think you know but more than you are willing to admit.

The other stories in *Successful Love* seem negligible in comparison with this one.

Schwartz's essays, although they cannot be said to have improved, remained lucid and at least intermittently interesting until he stopped writing them altogether in 1962. As a critic, Schwartz was preoccupied with the same issues as most of his contemporaries: the relationship between poetic statement and literal belief, and the tension between the need to connect poetry with a social context and the need to defend its autonomy and transcendence. His formulations of these problems usually derive from other critics, and his essays do not quite add up to a coherent and original view of literature.

Schwartz's special gift was his ability to analyze, define, and qualify the assertions of more imperious critics like T. S. Eliot, Yvor Winters, and Allen Tate. His "Poetry and Belief in Thomas Hardy" (1940), for instance, derives its central idea from the discussion of poetry and belief in T. S. Eliot's essay on Dante. But Schwartz defines more exactly than Eliot had done the ways in which a poet's beliefs do and do not affect the artistic success of a poem.

The assessments Schwartz makes of other critics, such as R. P. Blackmur and Winters, and of major writers such as Yeats, Wallace Stevens, Ernest Hemingway, and William Faulkner, show a fine ability to go straight to the essentials in a body of work, and to balance generosity with the impersonal severity that necessarily accompanies high standards. Even in a late essay, "The Present State of Poetry" (1958), he writes with a penetration and sanity untouched by the chaos of his personal life.

Selected Essays of Delmore Schwartz, edited by Donald A. Dike and David H. Zucker (1970), preserves Schwartz's best critical writings. If anything, one might wish the selection had been a little narrower, whereas in Atlas' edition of the stories, one would like a longer book. But if one adds to these two volumes *Summer Knowledge* and Atlas' biography, one gets a fairly complete sense of Schwartz's career. In England, Carcanet New Press issued Douglas Dunn's selection of the poems, *What Is to Be Given* (1976). Dunn weeded out the later poetry, perhaps too ruthlessly, although he retained " 'I Am Cherry Alive,' the Little Girl Sang" and the Seurat poem. He also omitted "Coriolanus and His Mother." But for those who would rather have slightly too little than slightly too much, this volume makes a good alternative to Schwartz's own selection. McDougall's study, though uneven, is often quite perceptive; it deserves more attention than it has apparently received. A paperback selection of the best short pieces on Schwartz would also be welcome.

Schwartz deserves to be rescued from the oblivion for which he seemed destined at the end of the 1960's, but he cannot be regarded as a major poet or writer of fiction. Whether he ever possessed, as his friends believed, the potential to become a major poet, we cannot say, but it seems extremely doubtful. He had intelligence, emotional intensity, and devotion to the art, but lacked a subtle ear. Nor is Schwartz's poetry notable for visual suggestiveness. The wit that dazzled everyone in his conversation rarely informs his writing, especially his most ambitious writing. A great poet can do without a first-rate ear, without vivid evocation of the physical world, or without exceptional grace or wit. One thinks of Thomas Hardy, Alexander Pope, and Wordsworth, respectively. But can a great poet dispense with all three of these gifts?

Rather than lament Schwartz's failure to become a major poet, we may be glad that he overcame his limitations, both personal and artistic, to the extent that he did. Not to the extent that we might have hoped, but enough to make us grateful for what he has left us.

Selected Bibliography

WORKS OF DELMORE SCHWARTZ

In Dreams Begin Responsibilities, (Norfolk, Conn.) New Directions (1938).

A Season in Hell, (Norfolk, Conn.: New Directions, 1939; 2nd ed., 1940).

Shenandoah, (Norfolk, Conn.: New Directions, 1941). Reprinted in *New Directions 32,* edited by James Laughlin, Peter Glassgold, and Frederick R. Martin. (New York: New Directions, 1976) 24–25.

Genesis: Book One, (New York: New Directions, 1943). Selections from the manuscript of *Book Two,* introduced by James Atlas, appear in *New Directions 35,* edited by James Laughlin, Peter Glassgold, and Frederick R. Martin. (New York: New Directions, 1977) 34–37.

The World Is a Wedding, (Norfolk, Conn.: New Directions, 1948).

Vaudeville for a Princess and Other Poems, (New York: New Directions, 1950).

Summer Knowledge: New and Selected Poems, 1938–1958, (Garden City, N.Y.: Doubleday, 1959). Reprinted as *Selected Poems (1938–1958): Summer Knowledge* (New York: New Directions, 1967).

Successful Love and Other Stories, (New York: Corinth Books, 1961).

Selected Essays of Delmore Schwartz, edited and with an introduction by Donald A. Dike and David H. Zucker and an appreciation by Dwight Macdonald (Chicago: University of Chicago Press, 1970).

What Is to Be Given: Selected Poems, edited and with an introduction by Douglas Dunn (Manchester, England: Carcanet New Press, 1976).

In Dreams Begin Responsibilities and Other Stories, edited and with an introduction by James Atlas; foreword by Irving Howe (New York: New Directions, 1978).

"Selections from the Verse Journals," with an introduction by James Atlas, *New Directions 36,* edited by James Laughlin, Peter Glassgold, and Frederick R. Martin (New York: New Directions, 1978) 40–48.

Last and Lost Poems of Delmore Schwartz, edited and with an introduction by Robert Phillips (New York: Vanguard Press, 1979).

BIOGRAPHICAL AND CRITICAL STUDIES

BOOKS

Atlas, James, *Delmore Schwartz: The Life of an American Poet,* (New York: Farrar, Straus and Giroux, 1977) paperback edition, (New York: Avon Books, 1978).

McDougall, Richard, *Delmore Schwartz,* (New York: Twayne Publishers, 1974).

ARTICLES, MEMOIRS, AND REVIEWS

Barrett, William, "Delmore: A 30's Friendship and Beyond," *Commentary* 58, no. 3: 41–54 (September 1974).

Bogan, Louise, "Young Modern," *Nation* 148: 353–54 (March 25 1939). Review of *In Dreams Begin Responsibilities.*

Bonham, Sister M. Hilda, "Delmore Schwartz: An Idea of the World," *Renascence* 13: 132–35 (1961).

Deutsch, R. H., "Poetry and Belief in Delmore Schwartz," *Sewanee Review* 74: 915–24 (1966).

———, "Delmore Schwartz: Middle Poems," *Concerning Poetry* 2, no. 2: 19–29 (1969).

Dike, Donald A., "A Case for Judgment: The Literary Criticism of Delmore Schwartz," *Twentieth Century Literature* 24: 492–509 (1978).

Flint, Robert W., "The Stories of Delmore Schwartz," *Commentary* 33: 336–39 (April 1962).

Halio, Jay L., "Delmore Schwartz's Felt Abstractions," *Southern Review* 1: 802–19 (1965).

Hook, Sidney, "Imaginary Enemies, Real Terror," *American Scholar* 47: 406–12 (1978).

Howe, Irving, "Delmore Schwartz—a Personal Appreciation," *New Republic* 146: 25–27 (March 19 1962).

———, "Purity and Craftiness," *Times Literary Supplement* 28: 458–59 (April 1978).

Humphries, Rolfe, "A Verse Chronicle," *Nation* 171: 490 (November 25 1950). Review of *Vaudeville for a Princess.*

Kazin, Alfred, "Delmore Schwartz, 1913–1966," *World Journal Tribune Book Week* 1: 17–18 (October 9 1966).

Kenner, Hugh, "Bearded Ladies and the Abundant Goat," *Poetry* 79: 50–53 (October 1951). Review of *Vaudeville for a Princess.*

Kloss, Robert J., "An Ancient and Famous Capital: Delmore Schwartz's Dream," *Psychonalytic Review* 65: 475–90 (1978).

Knapp, James F., "Delmore Schwartz: Poet of the Orphic Journey," *Sewanee Review* 78: 506–16 (1970).

Lyons, Bonnie, "Delmore Schwartz and the Whole Truth," *Studies in Short Fiction* 14: 259–64 (1977).

Macdonald, Dwight, "Delmore Schwartz (1913–1966)," and *New York Review of Books* 7, no. 3: 14–16 (September 8 1966).

Matthiessen, F. O., "A New York Childhood," *Partisan Review* 10: 292–94 (1943). Review of *Genesis.*

Novak, Michael Paul, "The Dream as Film: Delmore Schwartz's 'In Dreams Begin Responsibilities'," *Kansas Quarterly* 9, no. 2: 87–91 (1977).

Politzer, Heinz, "The Two Worlds of Delmore Schwartz: Lucifer in Brooklyn," translated by Martin Greenberg *Commentary* 10: 561–68 (December 1950).

Rahv, Phillip, "Delmore Schwartz: The Paradox of Precocity," *New York Review of Books* 17, no. 9: 19–22 (May 20 1971).

Zucker, David, "Self and History in Delmore Schwartz's Poetry and Criticism," *Iowa Review* 8, no. 4: 95–103 (1977).

Anne Sexton
(1928–1974)

SUZANNE JUHASZ

Anne sexton wrote poetry in what she called "language," her term for discourse that bypasses rational thought to express repressed truths that are frequently socially unacceptable. Her first discovery of other users of "language" was in a mental institution to which she had been committed. "I found this girl (very crazy of course) (like me I guess) who talked language. What a relief! I mean, well . . . someone!" she wrote in a letter. But as a poet and not just a patient Sexton moved past the solipsism of the madhouse, "magic talking to itself, / noisy and alone" ("You, Doctor Martin"), to make "language" the source of a body of poetry that thrilled, outraged, charmed, and deeply affected a generation of readers in the 1960s and early 1970s.

Sexton's transformation from suburban housewife into famous poet occurred at a moment in history when American woman were beginning to question anew the gender definitions that the culture had neatly laid out for them. Her quest for identity through language helped inspire many women making similar journeys. Finding words to speak the self, words that did not necessarily parallel the ones the culture offered ready-made, seemed a way toward self-discovery, and was one reason why women's poetry flourished in the late 1960s and early 1970s. Discussions about the cultural construction of gender or of language were not common then; feminism, both academic and political, did not have such a sophisticated vocabulary. Nevertheless, the search for this language and the belief in its potential were very real.

Sexton's idea of a language that would "verbalize the non-verbal," that "has nothing to do with rational thought," was clearly a way to get at truths that the culture did not necessarily recognize. "Put your ear close down to your soul and listen hard," she advised. Her description of what happened when she first read W. D. Snodgrass's "Heart's Needle" emphasizes the power of poetry as a non-analytic, essentially physical experience: "It walked out at me and grew like a bone inside of my heart." This sort of poetry invoked a process of discovery for reader and poet alike. "I think a poem that can do that to people, make them see themselves through yourself, is valid, . . . not unseemly, not too personal, but worth it," she wrote in a letter.

When Anne Sexton killed herself in 1974, she left ten volumes of poetry and essays, as well as unpublished poems and an unpublished play. While many readers have admired her poetry's honesty and vulnerability, its shocking revelations of word as well as experience, there have been others who have found it vulgar, badly written, and tastelessly personal. Sexton remains as controversial as she was during her lifetime. But she has persisted in affecting and influencing readers. The critical and biographical work done since her death attests to that fact. Sexton continues to provoke and engage her readers, and scholars are still trying to define the nature of her contribution and thereby assess its value.

Sexton's status as a woman poet is particularly interesting because the exploration and representation of gender are at the heart of her writing. There is no question in her poetry about the gender of its author; that is what is so alluring and painful about reading it. Her writing, in its very repetitiveness and excess, reveals both the potential or repressed power of authentic female identity and another kind of power—that of a patriarchal system to define the female in its own terms, as something attractively and seductively impotent. The language that Sexton found to express the truth of her psychic reality as it tracks "primitive" or repressed phenomena tells the stories of these two versions of the female self, both incarnated in one woman, Anne Sexton. Particularly in her dual emblems of the poet's persona, the witch (the poet as mother) and the rat (the poet as naughty child), Sexton reveals contradictory functions for poetry itself: it is language in the service of life, or of death.

The "double" female self, as Sexton's poetry inscribes it, takes the following forms. On the one hand there is the woman as culture creates her. This woman seeks identity through the reflected power of others, specifically of males. Fathers, husbands, lovers, doctors, teachers, writers, and God himself—all offer such a woman a piece of their pie if she lets them take her, use her, love her. Her so-called power in these situations is to seduce them into wanting her; she then becomes privy to all that they have and are. In this scenario, other women are clearly peripheral, especially mothers. A girl learns to reject her mother in order to escape the lure of the woman who created her and to cleave in any way that presents itself to the father: one father, all fathers. Anne Sexton writes painfully of a self trapped in bonds such as these.

On the other hand, in another "world," or so it feels, there is a woman who eludes this paradigm. Her identity comes neither from thralldom nor from domination (neither traditionally "female" nor "male") but from and by means of her relationship to others, especially to women, and even more specifically, to her mother and her daughters. In this condition of relatedness she becomes both like and different, connected and individuated. Motherhood is the source and conduit of this version of identity, and of the power that comes from having an identity, because the pre-oedipal relationship between mother and child is the central experience in our culture that is organized in this way. Using "language" to arrive at this place, this knowledge, Sexton sometimes, especially in writing of mothers and daughters, describes a female identity that is nonpatriarchal.

Sexton's poetry bespeaks both kinds of identities because, as is perhaps only "natural," both were hers. Or to put it another way, when her language roots at the truths she knows, it discovers more than one kind. When we read Sexton today, we may find ourselves wanting to pick and choose among these truths. We may well recoil from the poems (and there are so many of them) in which the speaker begs for men's "love" and is rendered helpless by it. As the critic Alicia Ostriker notes: "We may easily find Sexton's addiction to love, her insistence on need, infantile and repellent. She clearly finds it repellent herself, thereby somewhat outflanking us. What must mitigate our judgment is the recognition that we, too, are such addicts, were truth told." And we may respond as powerfully today as when they were first published to the poems in which Sexton, as mother or as daughter, speaks what Ostriker calls a "mother-tongue"; these are poems that can cause us to weep in recognition. However, to talk of Sexton's poetry is to acknowledge both these voices and identities, their conflicting presence, as they inform and create her oeuvre.

Sexton's madness cannot be ignored in discussing her art. Although there is a real distinction between being mad and being sane, there is also a relation between these states. Sexton's excessive sensitivity to aspects of existence experienced by the mad and the sane alike provided her with the subject material for her art, sent her into therapy and mental institutions throughout her life, and caused her to kill herself.

Sexton's definition of the artist's role was based on the condition with which her madness was associated: "Creative people must not avoid the pain they get dealt. I say to myself, sometimes repeatedly, 'I've got to get the hell out of this hurt.' . . . But no. Hurt must be examined like the plague." However, the kind of vision that fuels the artist extends further in madness, where it includes as well the inability to protect oneself from what one sees.

Sexton's madness was integrally involved with her art in a particular way, for her writing was encouraged and shaped by psychoanalysis and the therapeutic process. She explicitly connects "language with madness. "Insanity," she says in a letter, "is surely the root of language. However, it was psychoanalysis that helped her to make use of her madness: as patient, speaking in therapy a specific discourse based in "language, and then as poet, crafting "language" into forms that others could understand.

"Language," however, articulating experience that is not socially sanctioned, is not so choosy about what manner of experience that might be. If "language" is, in Diane Middlebrook's words, "the primitive speech of the buried self," it does not specify *what* self. "Language" can bring to light the child's earliest responses to mother as well as father. Psychic stress has its source in these moments from infancy and childhood, and it is precisely the job of psychoanalysis to return to them and retrieve the spoils. Nonetheless, classic psychoanalysis has a particular perspective on the nature of the self—its proper configuration, what hampers and what aids its development—that reinforces patriarchal definitions of self-identity. That is, although "language may be impartial, psychoanalysis is not. Therapy works to help the patient develop a "self" that conforms to cultural expectations.

When, for example, Sexton told an interviewer that she had to come home from her trip abroad because "I had, as my psychiatrist said, a 'leaky ego,' "she was referring to the negative connotations her analyst placed on her needing "my husband and my therapist and my children to tell me who I am." Sexton does not question the analyst's interpretation of her experience: "I got sick over there. I lost my sense of self." Self-identity, according to classic psychoanalytic theory, comes from having achieved maximum separation and individuation. The proper self is the self that stands alone.

However, recent feminist psychology has countered this idea with the notion of the "self-in-relation": a self that is formed "by means of continuous psychological connection, in which the presence of the other forms a basic component of one's own experiences of self," in the words of the psychologists Judith Jordan and Janet Surrey. Stressing the necessity of connection, this idea of self locates the sources of self-development in the original, pre-oedipal relationship between mother and infant. Therefore, growth is understood not as a process of achieving autonomy and independence through the breaking of early emotional ties, but rather as an ongoing interaction within the mother-child relationship. Sexton's search for self through "language" brought her to a knowledge of this kind of identity, one that contradicted what she was learning in analysis.

Consequently the role of psychoanalysis in Sexton's art was a complicated one. It fostered her use of a "language" which enabled her to speak the truths of her life in poetry, truths which included important aspects of her female experience that were conventionally devalued and misinterpreted. At the same time psychoanalysis served to teach her an idea about selfhood that emphatically countered these discoveries about female identity. The tenets of psychoanalysis, reinforced by the transference it fostered to yet another powerful father figure, the analyst himself, encouraged her to become a woman according to traditional gender definitions.

It was this patriarchal definition and tradition that finally held sway. Poetry did not save Anne Sexton, as she kept asserting it would, because her poetry itself, more and more, was put in the service of reinforcing her sickness, her neediness, and her powerlessness as a woman.

Anne Sexton, born Anne Gray Harvey on 9 November 1928, grew up and lived her life in suburban Boston. Her mother, Mary Gray Staples Harvey, was the daughter of a newspaper editor in Lewiston, Maine; her father, Ralph Churchill Harvey, was the affluent owner of a woolen firm engaged in interational trade. Anne was the youngest of three sisters; she usually spoke of herself as an unwanted child. Her favorite family member was her unmarried great-aunt, Anna Ladd Dingley, who lived with the Harveys until she was sent to a nursing home when Anne was thirteen.

Sexton attended public and private schools, and the Garland School, a finishing school. She was never considered a good student, although she wrote poetry during this period. In 1948 she eloped with Alfred Muller Sexton II, nicknamed Kayo, who was to be her husband for twenty-five years until she divorced him in November 1973. She was the mother of two daughters, Linda Gray Sexton and Joyce Ladd Sexton. As a bride she put all her energy into becoming a good housewife, but even then madness intervened. "Until diagnosed as mentally ill," writes her biographer, Diane Middlebrook, "Sexton had been regarded by her exasperated family as childish, selfish, incompetent. Her mother-in-law remembered the shock with which she first watched Sexton throwing herself, pounding and screaming, on the floor because she was enraged at being asked to do an errand." Severe depression following the birth of her first child led to her psychiatric hospitalization in 1954. In 1956, on her birthday, she made the first of what were to be many attempts at suicide. For several years thereafter her children were cared for by their grandmothers.

Sexton began writing poetry in earnest in 1956, when she was home from the hospital and her children were not living with their grandparents. After seeing I. A. Richards discussing sonnets, on educational television, she tried to write one herself. Her psychiatrist, Dr. Sidney Martin, also encouraged her to write. "Don't kill yourself," he said. "Your poems might mean something to someone else someday." Thus her career as a poet began; as she later wrote, poetry "gave me a feeling of purpose, a little cause, something to *do* with my life, no matter how rotten I was."

Attending a poetry workshop taught by John Holmes at the Boston Center for Adult Education, starting in 1957, was a major impetus to Sexton's work. There she discovered other poets, notably Maxine Kumin, who was to become her lifelong friend and colleague; there she began to learn about poetry. Holmes himself was a mixed blessing; unintimidating and accessible as a teacher, he was often unenthusiastic about Sexton and her poetry—its uninhibited and personal quality made him cringe. Other classes and workshops—a summer Antioch Writers' Conference in 1958, where she worked with W. D. Snodgrass, whose "Heart's Needle" had inspired her to write of her own deeply personal truths, and Robert Lowell's graduate poetry seminar at Boston University—helped her enormously to strengthen her skills and confidence. "Workshopping" a poem—developing it in response to others' criticism and comments—was a procedure she used with Maxine Kumin all her life.

Sexton's first book, *To Bedlam and Part Way Back,* was published in 1960, a year after her mother and father died. It was followed by *All My Pretty Ones* (1962), *Live or Die* (1966), *Love Poems* (1969), *Transformations* (1971), *The Book of Folly* (1972), and *The Death Notebooks* (1974). Later works, published posthumously, include *The Awful Rowing Toward God* (1975), *45 Mercy Street* (1976), and *Words for Dr. Y: Uncollected Poems with Three Stories* (1978). *The Complete Poems* was published in 1981.

During Sexton's career her fame grew; she received many prizes and awards, beginning with her appointment as a scholar in poetry at the Radcliffe Institute for Independent Study in 1961. A traveling fellowship from the American Academy of Arts and Letters in 1963 took her to Europe with a neighbor as her companion; however, emotional disturbance caused her to return a month early. In 1967 she received the Pulitzer Prize for *Live or Die.* A Guggenheim Fellowship in 1969 enabled her to work on her unpublished play *Mercy Street* in New York. In 1969 she also began teaching a poetry seminar at Boston University, where she was made a full professor in 1972. On 4 October 1974 she committed suicide by carbon monoxide poisoning in the garage of her home.

Throughout her creative period Sexton continued to live the life of a housewife as well as of a poet. In a letter she described it thus:

> I do not live a poet's life. I look and act like a housewife. My daughter says to her friends: "a mother is someone who types all day." But still I cook. But still my desk is a mess of letters to be answered and poems that want to tear their way out of my soul and onto the typewriter keys. At that point I am a lousy cook, a lousy wife, a lousy mother, because I am too busy wrestling with the poem to remember that I am a normal (?) American housewife. (*Letters,* p. 270)

Even if Sexton had wanted to separate her roles, she could not imagine ways to do so. Role models in the form of women poets who were married mothers were not abundant. Several times she used grant money to pay for child care or cleaning help. But because she lived and worked in this fashion, she demonstrated both the ways in which writing is not distinct from the life of a traditional woman and the ways in which the two roles come into conflict. Writing both belongs to female identity and puts it into question, as Sexton's career as a poet consistently illustrated.

In 1977 Linda Gray Sexton and Lois Ames published *Anne Sexton: A Self-Portrait in Letters.* Sexton's letters, comprising a more informal self-presentation than her poetry, add much to our understanding of her. They reveal her intensity, need, extravagance, humor, charm, generosity, manipulativeness pain, and fear. Sometimes inspiring, sometimes embarrassing, they are always moving. It is not easy to be with Anne Sexton, for her best and her worst are equally disconcerting.

Sexton's mother-daughter poems are where we find most clearly the expression of the female self-in-relation. In some of these poems she is daughter; in some she is mother; in some she is both. These connections are essential and flexible: a mother is also a daughter; a daughter turns into a mother; a daughter will mother her mother, in time. As early poems like "The Double Image" and late poems like "The Death Baby" insist, all of these are variations on the central relationship between mother and child, and these variations include the connection between life and death. The life that mothers bequeath contains death within it: the death of the mother, the death of the daughter. But that death in turn fosters life, for daughters live on when mothers are dead, to give life to new daughters. Individuality, or differentiation, must always be poised against and understood in terms of this profound connectedness. In this way self-identity is formed.

Sexton's poems reveal these truths, even when she herself might not have recognized them so readily in everyday life. Toward her mother she felt a tangle of emotions—anger, guilt, competition, disappointment, and jealousy—that continued long after her mother's death. Her poems probe deeper to show the source of these feelings in love, yearning, and a sense of abandonment. "I want mother's milk," she wrote late in her life, in the poem "Food": "I want breasts singing like eggplants, / and a mouth above making kisses." But in response to her, "baby all wrapped up in its red howl," her mother "pour[s] salt into my mouth. / [Her] nipples are stitched up like sutures." Despite the fact that Mary Gray's own traditional female socialization made it difficult for her to nurture her child properly, with true empathy and recognition of the child's own self—despite, that is, the truth of Sexton's need and longing—in her poems Sexton discovers a source for her own identity in the very fact of her mother, whose love was real, even if her ability to use it was deficient. "You were mine / after all," she writes about her mother in "The Double Image."

In this important poem the portraits of the dead mother and her suicidal daughter mirror one another, creating nothing less than a "double woman" with "matching smile, matching contour." This sense of connection evokes rage, guilt, and love: rage at her mother for attributing her recently diagnosed cancer to her daughter's suicide attempt; guilt that it might be so.

> Only my mother grew ill.
> She turned from me, as if death were
> catching,
> as if death transferred,
> as if my dying had eaten inside of her.
> (p. 38)[1]

We could see this identification as a crippling thing—Sexton's doctors did—except that it sits at the very heart of this poem addressed not to the mother but to the daughter, Joyce, Sexton's tiny child who had been taken from her while she was recovering from her suicide attempt. Love for the child *and* love for the mother are the poem's cardinal emotions, around which guilt, suffering, and fear hover. Love is what finally enables the speaker to come to life in a very literal way—she recovers from her attempt to kill herself in order to nurture her daughter. The insights of the poem into her relationship with her mother are there to help her get her daughter back.

Thus, even though "The Double Image' ends with the wisdom of the doctors—"I, who was never quite sure / about being a girl, needed another / life, another image to remind me. / And this was my worst guilt; you could not cure / nor soothe it. I made you to find me"—we, as readers, are not so convinced that this is such a naughty thing to do. Not when the child is described as "already loved, already loud in the house / of herself"; not when the name is mother" because for the first three years of her life the child never knew her as such: "You learn my name, / wobbling up the sidewalk, calling and crying. / You call me *mother* and I remember my mother again, / somewhere in greater Boston, dying."

Motherhood gave to Anne Sexton an authenticity and authority that was not hers when she was daughter alone, perhaps because the knowledge of the frailties and failures of her first mother-daughter relationship (as daughter) gave her both the intense desire for and the means to improve her subsequent ones (as mother). Recognizing the child for who she is, someone who is both "me" and "not-me," is a far cry from maternal narcissism, which involves seeing the child as simply an extension of yourself. One does not know what the everyday reality of Sexton's mothering was like, what it felt like to her daughters, but in her poems we experience her as a mother who sees both difference and sameness.

"Darling, life is not in my hands; / life with its terrible changes / will take you, bombs or glands," she writes to her daughter Linda in "The Fortress," evoking difference, as her mother's response "she looked at me / and said I gave her cancer" ("The Double Image") does not. At the same time the sense of likeness in "The Fortress" is strong: "I press down my index finger— / . . . on the brown mole / under your left eye, inherited / from my right cheek." What, then, can a mother do for her child? "I cannot promise very much. II give you the images I know." The poem concludes: "We laugh and we touch. I promise you love. Time will not take away that."

That touch is all-important; it is precisely what Sexton as mother uses to bridge the gap between sameness and difference. Sexton recalls that her mother never touched her except to "examine" her. In Sexton's poems to her daughters, the sensual physicality of the imagery is especially memorable. "Little Girl, My String Bean, My Lovely Woman" is emblematic of this kind of poem, as its title alone suggests:

> *Oh, little girl,*
> *my stringbean,*
> *how do you grow?*
> *You grow this way.*
> *You are too many to eat.*

1. All quotations of Sexton's poetry, unless otherwise noted, can be found in *The Complete Poems* (Boston: Houghton Mifflin, 1951). All page references are to this edition.

I hear
as in a dream
the conversation of the old wives
speaking of *womanhood.*
I remember that I heard nothing myself.
was alone.
I waited like a target.
. . .
and someday they will come to you,
someday, men bare to the waist, young
Romans
at noon where they belong,
. . .
But before they enter
I will have said,
Your bones are lovely,
and before their strange hands
there was always this hand that formed.

Oh, darling, let your body in,
let it tie you in,
in comfort.
(pp. 146–147)

At the same time, Sexton's maternal understanding extends backward in memory to her own mother, who "died / unrocked, unrocked" ("The Death Baby"). When her mother was dying she could not act upon impulses that made the two roles (mother, daughter) versions of the same kind of love: "To place my head in her lap / or even to take her in my arms somehow / and fondle her twisted gray hair." But in the poem "The Death Baby," these feelings find expression in words, where Sexton's tenderness toward that one ancient antagonist gives her further insight into another relationship that has been with her from the start—"Death, / you lie in my arms like a cherub, / as heavy as bread dough":

I rock. I rock
You are my stone child with still eyes like
marbles.
There is a death baby for each of us.
We own him.
His smell is our smell.
(p. 358)

Sexton's sense of herself as a mother is of a person who nurtures with look, touch, care, and images"—that is, her words themselves, her stories. The poems that she writes are a major part of her maternal gifts; consequently, from her recognition of this role in relation to her own daughters and mother it is not a large step to the concept of the poet as mother, the poet as witch.

Sexton's identification with the figure of the witch had originally to do with her madness: "I have gone out, a possessed witch, / haunting the black air, braver at night" ("Her Kind," 1960). However, by the time she published "Live" in 1966, the association between witch, mother, and writer had been made and the witch's positive power recognized by the poet's daughters:

I wear an apron.
My typewriter writes.
It didn't break the way it warned.
Even crazy, I'm nice
as a chocolate bar.
Even with the witches' gymnastics
they trust my incalculable city,
my corruptible bed.
(p. 169)

In *Transformations* (1971), perhaps her finest book, Sexton has the witch emerge as her strongest poetic persona in a sequence of poems whose subject was suggested by her daughter Linda. The witch is the mother, telling her children stories (in this case, Grimm's fairy tales): "The speaker in this case / is a middle-aged witch, me— / . . . ready to tell you a story or two" ("The Gold Key"). Her children are all of us: "Alice, Samuel, Kurt, Eleanor, / Jane, Brian, Maryel, / all of you draw near. / Alice, / at fifty-six do you remember?" And her stories are profoundly maternal, offering to her children revisions of patriarchal myths to reveal the truths that women know.

Sexton's revisions of these tales juxtapose the contemporary with the traditional, the psychoanalytic with the mythic, not simply to create a modern take on an old story but rather to advance a different idea about it.

Here "language" serves the purpose of speaking female knowledge, both conscious and unconscious: "Living happily ever after— / a kind of coffin, / a kind of blue funk. / Is it not?" ("The White Snake"). "Happily ever after" is how the old stories end. The word "coffin," however, gives us the perspective of the subject of the story, the princess, suddenly given access to the telling. Her perspective defines the ending, and it is not happy but "living death." The colloquialism of "blue funk" is out of place in the traditional fairy-tale world. It lets us see how contemporary princess brides are still being told to live in the old stories, regardless of what kinds of lies they perpetrate.

All of Sexton's re-interpretations have surprises for us, whether in the startling imagery—"[Rumpelstiltskin] tore himself in two. / Somewhat like a split broiler"; "the virgin is a lovely number: / cheeks as fragile as cigarette paper"—or in the situations themselves. In "Rapunzel," our interest is diverted from the handsome prince to the witch who has locked the girl in a tower. Suddenly we see how that Johnny-come-lately may replace rather than inaugurate "true love," and that the witch had something to protect, something to lose:

> Many a girl
> had an old aunt
> who locked her in the study
> to keep the boys away.
> They would play rummy
> or lie on the couch
> and touch and touch.
> (p. 245)

"Briar Rose (Sleeping Beauty)" tells of a girl with unquiet dreams, dreams that Sexton could share with her princess heroine across the centuries:

> It's not the prince at all,
> but my father
> drunkenly bent over my bed,
> circling the abyss like a shark,
> my father thick upon me
> like some sleeping jellyfish.
> (p. 294)

The inappropriateness of the imagery to the situation, the way in which the father, conceived of as a deadly, circling shark, turns into a repulsive, comatose jellyfish—heavy, disgusting, and inescapable—makes this version of the incest scene particularly dreadful. And the way in which the sexual act itself is textually repressed, deleted from the discourse, becomes a comment on not only this particular girl's psychological repression of the event but the way in which the culture at large has been guilty of replacing one story with another, one that is deemed more acceptable.

Some critics of Sexton's earlier books had decried their personal, "confessional" nature. Sexton is correct when in a letter she says of the *Transformation* poems that "it would . . . be a lie to say that they weren't about me, because they are just as much about me as my other poetry." However, much of their strength comes from the way in which the personal gets expanded in them so that she comes to tell a tale of her tribe—women. This identity that is at once individual and collective seems a logical poetic extension of her mother-self, "a self-in-relation," formed, we remember, "by means of continuous psychological connection, in which the presence of the other forms a basic component of one's own experiences of self." The mother-witch-poet of *Transformations* is Sexton at her best, because she draws on the stuff of a powerful female identity to speak on behalf of us all. *Transformations* is scary, funny, shocking, clever, and devastating. Each time the cliché turns, we recognize the buried female truths in those patriarchal bedtime stories.

If only the witch had triumphed. She was a power for life as well as truth. But Sexton could not break so completely from the culture's "wisdom"—not when she was imbibing it regularly from the many male authorities in whom she persistently sought to believe: her father, her husband, the male poets who mentored her, her doctors (most of whom were men), and finally, God. As much as these men "loved" her, equally they denigrated her. The only way to teach her was for her to be someone who was ignorant; the only way to cure her was for her to be someone who was sick; the only way to love her was for her to be someone who was needy; and the only way to save her was for her to be someone who had sinned. Poised against the witch as emblem of herself as poet was another—the rat.

The rat is the child of a very bad mother indeed, Eve herself, its birth an "unnatural act" ("Rats Live on No Evil Star"). The rat is "evilest of creatures / with its bellyful of dirt / and . . . two eyes full of poison." The rat takes center stage late in Sexton's oeuvre, as if the witch, once personifying her identity, has been vanquished. Now it is the rat who represents her soul, something clearly to be vilified. In "Rowing," the title poem of *The Awful Rowing Toward God* (1975), salvation is imaged as a door:

> and I will open it
> and I will get rid of the rat inside of me,
> the gnawing pestilential rat.
> Cod will take it with his two hands
> and embrace it.
> (p. 418)

The rat cannot save herself; God must do it for her.

The rat's dilemma is traceable through all of the poems (and they are many) in which Sexton, the bad girl who wants love—as much for her badness as in spite of it—attempts to seduce her many fathers through a bravura that is nonetheless always aware of their power to grant or withhold approval of her naughty charm. "In the long pull, John," she wrote to John Holmes, her first poetry teacher, "where you might be proud of me, you are ashamed of me. I keep pretending not to notice. . . . But then, you remind me of my father."

The poems that Sexton addressed to father figures represent a second major category in her work, running all the way from "You, Doctor Martin" in her first book, *To Bedlam and Part Way Back* (1960), to the painful supplications to God in *The Awful Rowing Toward God* and other poems of the early 1970s. Ralph Churchill Harvey, teaching her to eat oysters, that "father-food," so "moist and plump," at the Union Oyster House in Boston ("The Death of the Fathers"), is the obvious source for her attraction to patriarchal power, but the father figure appears elsewhere in her work in the form of the male psychiatrist. It is useful to focus on these doctor images in order to illuminate more closely the relation between Sexton as daddy's girl and Sexton as poet.

The patient-doctor relationship is set up clearly and centrally in the very first poem of Sexton's very first book, "You, Doctor Martin." Of course she loves him: he is "god of our block, / prince of all the foxes"; his "third eye / moves among us and lights the separate boxes / where we sleep or cry." Of all the crazy women, she is the best, "queen of this summer hotel." She attempts to lure him with her badness, her deviance from conventional femaleness ("Once I was beautiful. Now I am myself") as it is revealed through her lunatic insight—"magic talking to itself." She will trade him the special vision that comes with her madness for just one thing: love and salvation. Other fathers of whom she has made this request have betrayed as well as indulged her: Ralph Harvey, fading "out of sight / like a lost signalman / wagging his lantern / for the train that comes no more" ("The Death of the Fathers"); John Holmes, his fear "like an invisible veil between us" ("For John, Who Begs Me Not to Enquire Further"). But perhaps not the doctor, who, because of his peculiar calling, prizes the very things that have ultimately appalled the others, as the poem "Cripples and Other Stories" reveals:

> Oh the enemas of childhood,
> reeking of outhouses and shame!
> Yet you rock me in your arms
> and whisper my nickname.
> (p. 161)

This poem is addressed to "father-doctor," and it explicitly contrasts the relationship she has with him to her other loves:

My father didn't know me
but you kiss me in my fever.
My mother knew me twice.
and then I had to leave her.

But those are just two stories
and I have more to tell
from the outhouse, the greenhouse
where you draw me out of hell.

Father, I'm thirty-six
yet I lie here in your crib.
I'm getting born again, Adam,
as you prod me with your rib.
(pp. 162–163)

The doctor wants her stories. They are of such interest to him, as manifestations of the "language" so valued in the therapeutic process, because they demonstrate how very sick and contemptible she is. The connection between madness, femaleness, infantilism, and pollution is explicitly made, as the poem's imagery yokes outhouse and crib, crazy lady and Eve. Adam, the first man, is not lover and companion to Eve but her father-doctor-savior, poking her with his rib as a doctor would prod a patient with his stethoscope. This doctor's love becomes a version of that first biblical relationship, a manifestation of the paternal power that makes him proud, since he (and only he) can cure her: "You hold me in your arms. / How strange that you're so tender! / Child-woman that I am, / you think that you can mend her." There is a catch to this kind of father-love, even as there was with Ralph Harvey, though his involved a different kind of bargain. The complicity he wrapped her in was sex, as she writes in "The Death of the Fathers":

You danced with me never saying a word.
Instead the serpent spoke as you held
meclose.
The serpent, that mocker, woke up and
pressed against me
like a great god and we bent together
like two lonely swans.
(p. 324)

Complicity with the doctor required her belief in her madness.

Consequently, Sexton's poetry has functions other than to create life. It can also be used to demonstrate impotent need so that the all-powerful doctor-father will want to keep her alive. But this contract has significant drawbacks. First, it is dependent upon his continued presence; second, it demands her sickness, not recovery—for she is attractive to him only if she is sick. Frequent visits to the doctor are requisite; also necessary, we might surmise, are frequent relapses: major depressions, and of course (the ultimate proof), suicide attempts.

In 1964, when Dr. Martin decided to move his practice to Philadelphia, a hysterical letter to Anne Clarke, a California psychiatrist and friend of Sexton, revealed the extent and nature of the psychiatric patient's dependence upon the doctor:

> Dr. Martin is leaving . . . Christ. I can't. I *mean* I can't . . . eight years of therapy . . . At start me nothing . . . *really* nothing . . . for two years me still nothing . . . and then I start to be something and then my mother dies, and then father . . . a large storm . . . then recovery and that slow and trying to both Martin and me . . . I mean "hell" and not just "trying" . . . and I'd come quite far but . . . now . . . if he goes next Sept . . . I have had it. I can't make it (the intense trust, *the* transference all over AGAIN) . . . Please! Help me! . . . I HAVE GOT TO HAVE SOMEONE. (*Anne Sexton: A Self-Portrait in Letters,* p. 229)

For doctors, like lovers, husbands, teachers, and fathers, *do* leave. In each departure there is betrayal, even if someone else can be seduced into taking his place. Until the next betrayal. In *Anne Sexton: A Self-Portrait in Letters* Linda Gray Sexton and Lois Ames write that in her last months

> her friends grew angry and frustrated with her midnight suicide threats, her inability to go to the dentist alone, enter a store alone, mail a letter alone. She required constant service

> and care, and those closest to her began to set limits in self-protection. Anne saw these limits as unreasonable fences erected by those she loved—the ultimate desertion. (p. 389)

The father to whom Sexton turns at last, in her final poems, is God himself. Surely *he* will not abandon her. The poems that became *The Awful Rowing Toward God* were written in two and a half weeks, taking only three days off during that time, as she told an interviewer:

> One for exhaustion and two for a mental hospital. Then out and back to the book. Staying up till three A.M., and getting up again at six. Writing in seizure, practically not stopping; maybe not even drinking; maybe just gobbling my meal and running back in there again. The poems were coming too fast to rewrite. (quoted in Coburn, *No Evil Star,* p. 189)

In these poems the rat seeks God. If there had been moments in her writing when she had imagined God as a mother—sometimes as Mary or even "some tribal female who is known but forbidden" ("Somewhere in Africa")—that fantasy no longer works. Rather, in the poem "Is It True?" and other works from her last years, God, the ultimate doctor-father, is pictured offering salvation to the poet, who declaims her essential evil in order to be an appropriate object for his love:

> But the priest understands
> when I tell him that I want to
> pour gasoline over my evil body
> and light it,
> He says, "That's more like it!
> *That* kind of evil!"
> (p. 448)

These poems are, of course, further versions of those stories that she told to the doctor to please him. "A story! a story!" she promises God, and offers him her manic vision of apocalypse. Poetry is again her lure, but it can never be her power, not in this scenario. Power belongs only to the father, never to the daughter. God's power is explicitly revealed in the final poem of the volume, "The Rowing Endeth," when, having moored her boat at the dock of the island called God, she plays a game of poker with him. With a royal straight flush, she thinks she has won; but she is wrong, for "a wild card had been announced / but I had not heard it / being in such a state of awe / when He took out the cards and dealt." That is the point, and the ultimate dilemma. She adores God for his very lack of fairness, his lack of interest in equality, his power over her:

> Dearest dealer,
> I with my royal straight flush,
> love you for your wild card,
> that untamable, eternal, gut-driven *ha-ha*
> and lucky love.
> (p. 474)

When the patriarchy co-opts the poet's gift, the gift of "language," her stories become agents in the perpetuation of the hegemony to which the poet has abased herself. No power here. And no salvation. This kind of poetry is a blueprint for the loss of identity, not for the attainment of it. On the other hand, the witch's stories, the poems of the mother-poet, are both life-affirming and life-enhancing. The mother's primal power to create life manifests itself in words as well as personal relationships, as the "images" she gave to her one daughter, to her many daughters, served and continue to serve as affirmations of our identity as well as her own. These "images," or stories, are ways of naming and of recognizing what they name. Here was power—the power of life and of self-identity—released by "language" into the light of day.

Psychoanalysis created Anne Sexton the poet out of Anne Sexton the madwoman and helped to destroy her. It gave her the tools for a trade—poetry—but at the same time it taught her to put those tools to work in the service of the father. One reason for the inequality of the struggle between the witch and the rat is that Sexton apparently never had an awareness of a real precedent for her role as a mother-poet and hence found insufficient support for her endeavors. Her own mother was associated with things literary in the family mythology, although she wrote nothing other than occasional verse; but her endeavors were the source of a peculiar rivalry between them, especially from her mother's point of view, so that Mary Gray was, in Diane Middlebrook's words, both "censor and precursor." Nevertheless, it was her mother, not her father, who bore the literary mantle in Harvey household; and it is the daughter, with her grandmother's name, Linda Gray Sexton, who has inherited it. It is also significant that Sexton's relationships with the few actual women writers she knew, such as Maxine Kumin, Carolyn Kizer, Tillie Olsen, and Lois Ames, appear to have been exceptionally important to her. But they were few in contrast to the male writers, both in person and on the page, who influenced her ideas about poetry and poets. Masculine authority was dominant if not absolute.

Sexton's lasting significance, however, lies in the fact that at least some of the time she did manage to speak as a mother—to daughter-readers and daughter-writers, including her daughter Linda, and to many other women as well, women who now understand in a more self-conscious fashion the need for a mother as source and model. Sexton's mother-daughter poems are an important legacy in American women's poetry.

Selected Bibliography

PRIMARY WORKS

POETRY

To Bedlam and Part Way Back, (Boston: Houghton Mifflin, 1960).

All My Pretty Ones, (Boston: Houghton Mifflin, 1962).

Selected Poems, (London: Oxford University Press, 1964).

Live or Die, (Boston: Houghton Mifflin, 1966).

For the Year of the Insane, (Boston: Impressions Workshop, 1967). Broadside illustrated by Barbara Swan.

Poems by Thomas Kinsella, Douglas Livingstone, and Anne Sexton, (London: Oxford University Press, 1968). Selection of previously unpublished poems.

Love Poems, (Boston: Houghton Mifflin, 1969).

Transformations, (Boston: Houghton Mifflin, 1971).

The Book of Folly, (Boston: Houghton Mifflin, 1972).

The Death Notebooks, (Boston: Houghton Mifflin, 1974).

The Awful Rowing Toward God, (Boston: Houghton Mifflin, 1975).

45 Mercy Street, Edited by Linda Gray Sexton (Boston: Houghton Mifflin, 1976).

Words for Dr. Y: Uncollected Poems with Three Stories, Edited by Linda Gray Sexton. (Boston: Houghton Mifflin, 1978).

The Complete Poems, (Boston: Houghton Mifflin, 1981).

Selected Poems of Anne Sexton, Edited by Diane Wood Middlebrook and Diane Hume George. (Boston: Houghton Mifflin, 1988).

PROSE

"Feeling the Grass," (*Christian Science Monitor,* June 4 1959).

Foreword to *The Real Tin Flower: Poems About the World at Nine* by Aliki Barnstone, (New York: Crowell-Collier, 1968). Reprinted in "Stories for Free Children," (*Ms,* March 1975).

"Writing Exercises," In *The Whole Word Catalogue 1.* Edited by Rosellen Brown et al. (New York: Teachers and Writers, 1972). Written with Robert Clawson.

"Anne Sexton," In *World Authors, 1950–1970.* Edited by John Wakeman. (New York: H. W. Wilson, 1975). Autobiographical statement.

Anne Sexton: A Self-Portrait in Letters, Edited by Linda Gray Sexton and Lois Ames. (Boston: Houghton Mifflin, 1977).

"Journal of a Living Experiment," In *Journal of a Living Experiment: A Documentary History of The First Ten years of Teachers and Writers Collaborative.* Edited by Phillip Lopate. (New York: Teachers and Writers, 1979).

No Evil Star: Selected Essays, Interviews, and Prose, Edited by Steven E. Colburn. (Ann Arbor: University of Michigan Press, 1985).

CHILDREN'S BOOKS (WRITTEN WITH MAXINE KUMIN)

Eggs of Things, (New York: Putnam, 1963).

More Eggs of Things, (New York: Putnam, 1964).

Joey and the Birthday Present, (New York: McGraw-Hill, 1971).

The Wizard's Tears, (New York: McGraw-Hill, 1975).

SECONDARY WORKS

BIOGRAPHICAL AND CRITICAL STUDIES

Colburn, Steven E., ed., *Anne Sexton: Telling the Tale* (Ann Arbor: University of Michigan Press, 1988).

George, Diana Hume, *Oedipus Anne: The Poetry of Anne Sexton,* (Urbana: University of Illinois Press, 1987).

———, ed., *Sexton: Selected Criticism* (Urbana: University of Illinois Press, 1988).

Hall, Caroline King Barnard, *Anne Sexton,* (Boston: Twayne, 1989).

McClatchy, J. D., ed., *Anne Sexton: The Artist and Her Critics*(Bloomington: Indiana University Press, 1978).

Middlebrook, Diane Wood, *Anne Sexton: A Biography,* (Boston: Houghton Mifflin, 1991).

Wagner-Martin, Linda W., ed., *Critical Essays on Anne Sexton*(Boston: G. K. Hall, 1989).

BIBLIOGRAPHY

Northouse, Cameron, and Walsh, Thomas P., *Sylvia Plath and Anne Sexton: A Reference Guide,* (Boston: G. K. Hall, 1974).

William Shakespeare

(1564–1616)

STANLEY WELLS

William shakespeare was baptized in the great church of Holy Trinity, Stratford-upon-Avon, on 26 April 1564. Probably he was born no more than two or three days previously; 23 April, St. George's Day, traditionally celebrated as the date of his birth, is as likely to be correct as any. At the time, his father was an up-and-coming young man who took a prominent part in administering the town's affairs. He had married Mary Arden, who came from a family of higher social standing, about 1552, the year in which he was fined 12d. for failing to remove a dunghill from outside his house. For years after this, as his children were born and as some of them grew up, his position among his fellow townsmen improved. He was a member of the glovers' guild, and also dealt in wool and probably other commodities. In 1556 he was appointed an ale taster, with responsibility for the price and quality of the bread and ale offered to the town's two thousand or so inhabitants. He moved upward in the hierarchy: as constable (1558), principal burgess (about 1559), chamberlain (1561), alderman (1565), and, in 1568, bailiff, or mayor, and justice of the peace.

At this high point in his career he was the father of two sons, William and Gilbert (1566–1612). Two daughters, Joan and Margaret, had died in infancy. Another Joan was born in 1569; a Richard born in 1574 lived, apparently in Stratford and as a bachelor, until 1613. A late child, Edmund, came in 1580; he became an actor in London and died early, aged twenty-seven.

When young William was four years old, he could have had the excitement of seeing his father, dressed in furred scarlet robes and wearing the aldermanic thumb ring, regularly attended by two mace-bearing sergeants in buff, presiding at fairs and markets. Perhaps a little later, he would have begun to attend a "petty school" to acquire the rudiments of an education that would be furthered at the King's New School. We have no lists of the pupils at this time, but his father's position would have qualified him to attend, and the education offered was such as lies behind the plays and poems. The school had a well-qualified master, with the relatively good salary of £20 a year, from which he had to spare £4 to pay an usher, or assistant, to teach the younger boys. At the age of about eight Shakespeare would have begun a regime that might well have sent him "unwillingly" on the quarter-of-a-mile walk from his father's Henley Street house to the schoolroom above the Guildhall and next to the Guild Chapel. Classes began in the early morning, and hours were long. The basic medium of instruction was Latin. A charming scene in *The Merry Wives of Windsor* (IV.i), hardly required by the plot, shows a schoolmaster instructing young boys in their grammar, and must be an amused recollection of the dramatist's own schooldays. From grammar the pupils progressed to rhetoric and logic, and to works of classical literature. They might read Aesop's *Fables* and the fairly easy plays of Terence and Plautus, on one of which Shakespeare was to base an early comedy. They might even act scenes from them. They would go on to Caesar, Cicero, Virgil, Horace, and Ovid, who was clearly a favorite with Shakespeare in both the original and Arthur Golding's translation published in 1567.

But there was a life beyond school. Shakespeare lived in a beautiful and fertile part of the country; the river and fields were at hand; he could enjoy country pursuits. He had younger brothers and sisters to play with. Each Sunday the family would go to church, where his father as bailiff and, later, deputy bailiff, sat in the front pew as his rank required. There he would hear the sonorous phrases of the Bible, in either the Bishops' or the Geneva version, the Homilies, and the Book of Common Prayer, all of which made a lasting impression on him, as well as lengthy sermons that may have been less memorable. Sometimes groups of traveling players came to Stratford. Shakespeare's father would have the duty of licensing them to perform, and probably the boy saw his first plays in the Guildhall immediately below his schoolroom.

As he grew into adolescence, his father's fortunes waned. John Shakespeare fell into debt, and after 1576 stopped attending council meetings. His fellows treated him leniently, but in 1586 felt obliged to replace him as alderman. In 1592 he was listed among those persistently failing to go to church, perhaps for fear of arrest for debt.

But by this time William was in London, already displaying the genius that would enable him to recoup the family fortune. How he kept himself after leaving school we do not know. In 1582, at the age of eighteen, he married Anne Hathaway of Shottery, a mile or so from his home. The marriage was hasty, the bride, eight years older than her husband, pregnant. The clerk of the Worcester court, to which application for a special license was made on 27 November, wrote her name, mistakenly, it seems, as Anne Whateley of Temple Grafton. A daughter, Susanna, was baptized in Holy Trinity on 26 May 1583, and twins, Hamnet and Judith, on 2 February 1585.

The seven years that follow are a blank in our knowledge. Shakespeare may, as Aubrey reported a century later, have become a "schoolmaster in the country." He may have followed one or more of the innumerable other avocations—lawyer, soldier, sailor, actor, printer—that have been foisted upon him. He may have traveled overseas. All we know is that at some point he left Stratford, joined a theatrical company, went to London, and began to write—not necessarily in that order. The first certain printed allusion to him shows that, as actor turned playwright, he had aroused the envy of the dying Robert Greene who, in 1592, wrote scornfully of an "upstart crow" who thought himself "the only Shake-scene in a country."

Parodying a line from *3 Henry VI,* Greene conveniently helps to establish a date by which that play was written. His malice provoked a defense of Shakespeare by a minor playwright, Henry Chettle, who wrote of him as one whose "demeanor" was "no less civil than he excellent in the quality he professes. Besides, divers of worship have reported his uprightness of dealing, which argues his honesty, and his facetious grace in writing, which approves his art." Evidently he was well established in London by this time. But apparently he lived always in lodgings there, setting up no household. He seems to have felt that his roots were in Stratford. His family stayed there. How often he visited them we cannot tell. He had no more children. Perhaps he was gradually able to help his father who, in 1596, applied successfully for a grant of arms, and so became a gentleman. In August of the same year, William's son, Hamnet, died. In October, William was lodging in Bishopsgate, London, but in the next year he showed that he looked on Stratford as his permanent home by buying a large house, New Place, next to the Guild Chapel and the grammar school.

Over the following years, his growing worldly success can be followed in both Stratford and London records. In 1598 a minor writer, Francis Meres, published a book called

Palladis Tamia: Wit's Treasury, which includes the passage:

> As Plautus and Seneca are accounted the best for comedy and tragedy among the Latins, so Shakespeare among the English is the most excellent in both kinds for the stage; for comedy, witness his *Gentlemen of Verona,* his *Errors,* his *Love Labour's Lost,* his *Love Labour's Won,* his *Midsummer's Night Dream* and his *Merchant of Venice:* for tragedy, his *Richard II, Richard III, Henry IV, King John, Titus Andronicus* and his *Romeo and Juliet.*

We do not know what he meant by *Love Labour's Won.* It may be a lost play or an alternative title for a surviving one. The main importance of the list is that it gives us a date by which all these plays had been written. Add to it the two narrative poems, the three parts of *Henry VI, The Taming of the Shrew,* and (perhaps) the sonnets, and it is a remarkable output for a man of thirty-four, especially one who is usually regarded as a late starter.

In October 1598 Richard Quiney, whose son was to marry Shakespeare's daughter Judith, went to London to plead with the Privy Council on behalf of Stratford Corporation, in difficulties because of fires and bad weather. He wrote a letter, never delivered, to Shakespeare asking for the loan of £30, a sum large enough to suggest confidence in his friend's prosperity. In 1601 Shakespeare's father died. In May of the following year he paid £327 for 127 acres of land in Old Stratford. In 1604 he was lodging in London with a Huguenot family called Mountjoy, and became mildly involved with their daughter's marital problems. In the same year, through a lawyer, he sued for recovery of a small debt in Stratford. In 1605 he paid £440 for an interest in the Stratford tithes. In June 1607 his daughter Susanna married a distinguished physician, John Hall, in Stratford; his only grandchild, Elizabeth, was christened the following February. In 1609 his mother died there.

About 1610, Shakespeare's increasing involvement with Stratford suggests that he was withdrawing from his London responsibilities and retiring to New Place. He was only forty-six years old, an age at which a healthy man was no more likely to retire then than now. Possibly he had a physical breakdown. If so, it was not totally disabling. He was in London in 1612 for the lawsuit from which we know of his involvement with the Mountjoys. In March 1613 he bought a house in the Blackfriars for £140; he seems to have regarded it rather as an investment than as a domicile. In the same year the last of his three brothers died. In late 1614 and 1615 he was involved in disputes about the enclosure of the land whose tithes he owned. In February 1616 his second daughter, Judith, married Thomas Quiney, causing William to make alterations to the draft of his will, which was signed on 25 March. By now, surely, he knew that he was mortally ill. He died, according to his monument, on 23 April, and was buried in a prominent position in the chancel of Holy Trinity Church.

This selection of historical records shows clearly that Shakespeare's life is at least as well documented as those of most of his contemporaries who did not belong to great families. The identification of the Stratford worthy with the world's playwright is confirmed, if any confirmation is necessary, by the inscription on the memorial in the parish church, erected by 1623, which links him with Socrates and Virgil, and by much in the far greater memorial of that year, the First Folio edition of his plays, in which his great contemporary and rival, Ben Jonson, calls him "Sweet Swan of Avon."

SHAKESPEARE'S INTELLECTUAL AND THEATRICAL BACKGROUND

For a poetic dramatist, Shakespeare was born at the right time. He grew up during a period of increasing stability and prosperity in England. Queen Elizabeth was unifying the nation. Patriotic sentiment was increasing. Continental influences were helping in the transmission of classical knowledge which we call the Renaissance. The arts in general were flourishing; those of literature and drama bounded forward far more rapidly than in the earlier part of the century. The years between Shakespeare's birth and his emergence in London saw the appearance of the first major translations of Ovid, Apuleius, Horace, Heliodorus, Plutarch, Homer, Seneca, and Virgil; Shakespeare seems to have known most of these, and those of Ovid and Plutarch, at least, had a profound influence on him. During the same period appeared William Painter's *Palace of Pleasure,* an important collection of tales including some by Boccaccio that Shakespeare used; Holinshed's *Chronicles*; Lyly's *Euphues*; Sidney's *Arcadia* and *Astrophil and Stella*; early books of Spenser's *Faerie Queene*; Lodge's *Rosalynde*; prose romances and other pamphlets of Robert Greene; the early writings of Thomas Nashe; and other books that Shakespeare either used or must have known. Indeed, it is no exaggeration to say that almost all Shakespeare's major sources are in books written or first translated into English during the first thirty years of his life, though of course he could have read the Latin works, and, probably, those in French and Italian, even if they had not been translated. The greatest earlier English author known to him was Chaucer, and he was considerably influenced by the publication in 1603 of Florio's translation of Montaigne's *Essays.*

English dramatic literature developed greatly in Shakespeare's early years. Four years before his birth, blank verse was introduced as a dramatic medium in Sackville and Norton's *Gorboduc.* When he was two years old, George Gascoigne's *Supposes,* a translation from Ariosto and the first play written entirely in English prose, was acted; he was to draw on it in *The Taming of the Shrew.* These are early landmarks. He was already a young man before the pace of development really accelerated. John Lyly's courtly comedies, mostly in prose, began to appear in 1584, the year in which George Peele's *The Arrangement of Paris* was presented to the queen. The pace increased in the later 1580's, with Kyd's *The Spanish Tragedy,* Greene's *James IV,* and, above all, the emergence of Christopher Marlowe. Shakespeare was finding his feet in the theater. Our knowledge of the exact ordering of events in this period is so uncertain that we cannot always say whether he was influenced by the writers of these plays or himself exerted influence on them. What is undeniable is that English drama was rapidly increasing in range, scope, and power. Prose was for the first time becoming a rich dramatic medium—all the more so for its intermingling with verse styles that were immeasurably enriched by the ever more flexible uses that writers were making of blank verse. Growth in the size of acting companies and in the popularity of theatrical entertainment encouraged the writing of more ambitious plays, interweaving plot with subplot, tragedy with comedy, diversified with songs, dances, masques, and spectacular effects in ways that were unknown only a few years before.

The rapid progress of dramatic literature was thus inextricably linked with equally important developments in the theatrical arts. Shakespeare was twelve when James Burbage, already the father of the boy who was to become the greatest actor of Shakespeare's company, erected the Theatre, the first building in England designed primarily for theatrical performances. Before this, acting companies had roamed the land, the better ones under noble protection, playing where they could—in halls of great houses, at the Inns of Court, in guildhalls, and in inn-yards. Now one company, at least, had a permanent building; it was followed by others. The companies grew in size. They had the facilities to perform increasingly ambitious plays. They were encouraged by enthusiastic audiences and by the pleasure taken in drama by the queen and her court, even though they had also to resist the opposition of Puritan forces. They were, at the least, highly competent. Some gained international reputations. Boy actors, progressing through a system of apprenticeship, played female roles in a fully professional manner.

The Elizabethan theater, with its open roof, thrust, uncurtained stage, absence of representational scenery, rear opening, and upper level, was a sophisticated, if fundamentally simple, instrument. Modern theater designers are returning with excitement to its basic principles. It could accommodate spectacle and machinery, yet many plays written for it could be performed also in the unequipped halls that companies had to use on tour. It was a nonrepresentational, emblematic medium, shaped by and shaping the poetic dramas that prevailed on its stages.

We do not know when Shakespeare joined a company of players. In 1587 the Queen's Men lost one of their actors through manslaughter in Oxfordshire. They visited Stratford soon afterward. That they there enlisted Shakespeare is no more than an intriguing speculation. Some evidence suggests that he may have belonged to Pembroke's Men, first heard of in 1592. Certainly he was one of the Lord Chamberlain's Men shortly after they were founded, in 1594, and remained with them throughout his career. Rapidly this became London's leading company, outshining its main rival, the Lord Admiral's Men, led by Edward Alleyn. With the Chamberlain's Men, Shakespeare became a complete man of the theater: actor, businessman, and dramatic poet. He is the only leading playwright of his time to have had so stable a relationship with a single company. He wrote with their actors specifically in mind, and the conditions in which they performed helped also to shape his plays. They flourished; built the Globe as their London base from 1599; survived the competition of the successful children's companies in the early years of the new century; acquired King James I as their patron in 1603, soon after his accession; increased in size while remaining relatively stable in membership; and by 1609 were using the Blackfriars as a winter house—a "private" theater, enclosed, smaller, more exclusive in its patronage than the Globe. Perhaps it affected Shakespeare's playwriting style; yet his plays continued to be performed at the Globe and elsewhere.

EARLY SHAKESPEARE

The beginnings of Shakespeare's career as a writer are obscure. We have no juvenilia, sketches, or drafts. Yet beginnings there must have been. Even his earliest plays demonstrate a verbal power that suggests a practiced writer. Problems of chronology bedevil attempts to study his development. Regrettably, the editors of the First Folio did not print the plays in order of composition but imposed on them an arrangement into kinds: comedies, histories, and tragedies. The divisions are imperfect. Some of the tragedies are historical; some of the histories are tragical; and Shakespeare's greatest comic character appears in one of the histories. Shakespeare was no neoclassical respecter of the limits of dramatic genres. By reference to external evidence, such as contemporary allusions, and internal evidence, mainly stylistic development, scholars have attempted to determine the order of the plays' composition. The chronology proposed by E. K. Chambers is still accepted, with slight modification, as orthodox; but it remains partially conjectural. To treat the works in the assumed order of their composition would suggest more certainty about this order than is justified. To adopt the Folio's grouping would risk losing all sense of Shakespeare's development. In these pages the works will be divided into four groups: those written by about 1594, then those written between about 1594 and 1600, 1600 and 1607, and 1607 and 1612. Within these divisions the plays will be grouped by genre.

EARLY HISTORIES

One of the earliest theatrical projects in which Shakespeare was engaged was also one of the most ambitious: to transfer to the stage Edward Hall's narrative, in the last part of *The Union of the Two Noble and Illustre Families of Lancaster and York* (1548), of events, spanning over fifty years, that led to the founding of the Tudor dynasty in the marriage of Henry

VII to Elizabeth of York. The resulting plays were printed in the First Folio as *1, 2,* and *3 Henry VI* and *Richard III.* The first three seem to have been written by 1592, when Greene alluded to a line from the third. Bad texts of the second and third appeared in 1594 and 1595 respectively, as *The First Part of the Contention Betwixt the Two Famous Houses of York and Lancaster* and *The True Tragedy of Richard, Duke of York.* It has often been doubted whether *1 Henry VI* is entirely by Shakespeare. He may have revised someone else's work in order to form a dramatic sequence, but the plays are so closely related to one another that they are easily conceived of as the product of a single mind.

The enormous cast lists of the *Henry VI* plays reflect the difficulty of concentrating and focusing the mass of historical material. Some of the exposition of dynastic issues is labored, some of the action sketchily represented. Shakespeare's powers of individual characterization through language were not yet fully developed, and in *Henry VI* he was saddled with the liability of a passive hero. Perhaps in deference to decorum, Parts One and Three are composed entirely in verse; it does not avoid monotony. And some of the theatrical conventions employed are very much of their time, as the direction "Enter the KING with a supplication, and the QUEEN with Suffolk's head" (Part Two, IV.iv) is enough to show.

Nevertheless, these plays have many merits. They examine England's past in the light of its present at a time of national self-consciousness, of pride in national unity, and of fear that it might be dissipated, as Henry V's had been. On the way, they entertain and teach. They also display a deeply serious concern with political problems: the responsibilities of a king, his relationship with his people, the need for national unity, the relationship between national welfare and self-interest, the suffering caused by dissension, whether between nations or opposing factions within a nation, often mirrored in the image of a family, royal or not.

These concerns are bodied forth with much artistic success in the dramatic form and style. Part One, for example, opens with masterly thematic appropriateness in its portrayal of the ritual of national and personal mourning over the body of Henry V, nobly expressed, but rapidly degenerating into a family squabble. The scene ends with Winchester's declaration of personal ambition, just as the play ends with similar sentiments from Suffolk:

> Margaret shall now be Queen, and rule the King;
> But I will rule both her, the King, and realm.

Though the poetic style of these plays is often formal and declamatory, with extended similes and frequent classical allusions, there are also vivid, deflationary moments of colloquialism, as when Joan of Arc answers the enumeration of Talbot's honors with:

> Him that thou magnifi'st with all these titles"
> Stinking and fly-blown lies here at our feet.
> (Part One, IV.vii. 75–76)[1]

Part Two has some excellent prose. The scenes of Cade's rebellion show at an early stage Shakespeare's capacity for serious comedy. The horrifying episode in which Cade comments on the severed heads of Say and Cromer (IV.iii) justifies this Senecan device, because it combines with situation and language to provide an entirely convincing representation of the savagery of mob rule.

At times Shakespeare withdraws from the hurly-burly of violent action into reflective scenes of great beauty. The pastoral idea is expressed as well as anywhere in the remarkable scene of the Battle of Towton (Part Three, II.v), which, for all its stylization, forms a perfect dramatic emblem of the personal consequences of war. Henry, dismissed from the battle as useless, envies the shepherd's life. To one side of him appears a son carrying the

1. All quotations are from Peter Alexander, ed., *The Complete Works* (London–Glasgow, 1951).

body of a man he has killed, whom he discovers to be his father; to the other, a father carrying the body of a man he has killed, whom he discovers to be his son. Henry joins in their grief, and adds his own:

> Was ever King so griev'd for subjects' woe?
> Much is your sorrow; mine ten times so
> much.

Many of the most powerful scenes in these plays are of mourning, especially of children and parents. Yet the plays are memorable also for their portrayal of energetic evil, sometimes in figures of amoral wit, even charm. Especially remarkable are the duke of York's sons: Edward, later King Edward IV; George, duke of Clarence; and Richard, duke of Gloucester. Richard grows rapidly in menace in Part Three, emerging as the complete antihero in the splendid soliloquy in which he declares his ambitions:

> I'll drown more sailors than the mermaid
> shall;
> I'll slay more gazers than the basilisk;
> I'll play the orator as well as Nestor,
> Deceive more slily than Ulysses could,
> And, like a Sinon, take another Troy.
> I can add colours to the chameleon,
> Change shapes with Protheus for
> advantages,
> And set the murderous Machiavel to school.
> Can I do this, and cannot get a crown?
> Tut, were it farther off, I'll pluck it down.
> (III.ii. 186–195)

The rhetorical patterning, the end-stopped lines, the classical allusions, often regarded as limitations of Shakespeare's early style, contribute to a wonderfully energetic portrayal of the flights of Richard's imagination, which leads naturally to his dominance in *Richard III.* This play, of which a bad quarto appeared in 1597, cannot have been written much later than its precursors; but in it Shakespeare creates from his chronicle sources an aesthetically and morally satisfying pattern that shows him as the complete master of his material, able to subdue the world of fact to that of art.

Again, family relationships are important. Richard's engineering of Clarence's murder is ironically contrasted with their elder brother Edward's deathbed efforts to reunite the family. Richard bustles his way to the throne, overcoming all obstacles in a gloriously entertaining display of cynical hypocrisy, intelligence, and wit. But the forces of retribution grow in strength and are especially associated with women's mourning for the victims of past crimes. Murders of innocent children are seen in these plays as ultimate crimes against humanity. Richard's downfall begins when he alienates his chief supporter, Buckingham, by asking him to arrange the murder of his young nephews, the princes in the Tower. Tyrrel's description of their deaths (IV.iii) is an emotional climax. Opposition to Richard is focused in the idealized figure of Richmond, and the grand climax to the ritual of this and all these plays comes as the ghosts of Richard's victims appear to him and to Richmond. Richard's waking soliloquy shows that his self-sufficiency has defeated itself:

> I shall despair. There is no creature loves
> me;
> And if I die no soul will pity me:
> And wherefore should they, since that I
> myself
> Find in myself no pity to myself?
> (V.iii. 200–203)

He dies fighting, and Richmond's closing speech restates the image of England as a family:

> England hath long been mad, and scarr'd
> herself;
> The brother blindly shed the brother's
> blood,
> The father rashly slaughter'd his own son,
> The son, compell'd, been butcher to the sire.

Now he, as Henry VII, and Elizabeth, heirs of the houses of Lancaster and York, will bring unity to the kingdom. This patriotic climax, spoken by Elizabeth's grandfather, must have been peculiarly satisfying to the plays' first audiences.

Shakespeare is also concerned with dynastic issues in *King John,* a play about an earlier period of English history, first printed in 1623 but apparently written in the early 1590's. It is based in part on *The Troublesome Reign of John, King of England,* printed anonymously in 1591. As in the *Henry VI* plays, there is a strong sense of the futility and wastefulness of war. Shakespeare portrays a conflict in which neither side is right. King John knows that his claim to the English throne is weak. The French king, Philip, withdraws his support of the rival claimant, Prince Arthur, when John offers to make an advantageous match between his niece and the French dauphin. On both sides, selfishness, scheming, and personal greed put "commodity"—self-interest—before the common good. Shakespeare treats the situation ironically in, for instance, the scene before Angiers (II.i). The French Herald calls on the citizens to admit Arthur,

> Who by the hand of France this day hath made
> Much work for tears in many an English mother,
> Whose sons lie scattered on the bleeding ground.
> (II.i. 302–304)

The English Herald immediately calls on them to admit John and his soldiers,

> all with purpled hands,
> Dy'd in the dying slaughter of their foes.
> (II.i. 322–323)

The blood of both sides is wasted, for neither has won. There is a farcical element in the impasse and in John's acquiescence in the suggestion that the opposing armies should unite to

> lay this Angiers even with the ground;
> Then after fight who shall be king of it.
> (II.i. 399–400)

The ironical attitude finds personal embodiment in the figure of the Bastard, Philip Faulconbridge, who serves for the first half of the play as an ironic commentator. But grief is important here, too. Prince Arthur's mother, Constance, gives powerful expression to suffering and loss, and Arthur's threatened blinding and his death form an emotional focus. The discovery of his body turns the Bastard from a commentator into a participant, committed to humanity and England's welfare; and he ends the play as his country's spokesman:

> This England never did, nor never shall,
> Lie at the proud foot of a conqueror,
> But when it first did help to wound itself. . . .
> Come the three corners of the world in arms,
> And we shall shock them. Nought shall make us rue,
> If England to itself do rest but true.

EARLY COMEDIES

The mode of the history play was new when Shakespeare began to work in it; he may even have originated it. Comedy, however, had a long ancestry; and his early plays in this kind draw heavily on traditional modes and conventions, as if he were consciously experimenting, learning his craft by a process that included both imitation and innovation.

The Two Gentlemen of Verona, not printed until 1623, is clearly an early play. It derives partly from the prose romances popular in the late sixteenth century. The simple plot comes, perhaps indirectly, from a Portuguese romance, *Diana,* by Jorge de Montemayor. Shakespeare's craftsmanship in shaping it for the stage often falters. The play reveals his limited capacity at this period to orchestrate dialogue. Thirteen of its twenty scenes rely exclusively upon soliloquy, duologue, and the aside as comment. Scenes requiring the ability to show a number of characters talking together are generally unsuccessful. Most of the characters are only two-dimensional; some are laughably unrealized.

But *The Two Gentlemen of Verona* is full of charm and promise. It uses many motifs that Shakespeare was to develop in later plays. Those episodes in which he works within his limitations are often entirely successful. An example is the delightful scene (IV.ii) in which Proteus serenades his new love with "Who is Silvia?", while his old love looks on in disguise. The ironic wordplay of Julia's dialogue with the Host suggests real depth of character. Valentine and Proteus, too, have some human substance; and Proteus' servant, Launce, is the first in the great line of Shakespearian clowns. His monologues are masterpieces of comic dramatic prose, constructed with an artistry consummate enough to give the impression of artlessness. Some of the verse, too, is masterly; witness the astonishing matching of sound to sense in Proteus, tribute to the power of poetry:

> For Orpheus' lute was strung with poets' sinews,
> Whose golden touch could soften steel and stones,
> Make tigers tame, and huge leviathans
> Forsake unsounded deeps to dance on sands.
> (III.ii. 78–81)

The Two Gentlemen of Verona shows Shakespeare as already a great writer, though not a great playwright.

The Comedy of Errors, also printed in 1623, was written by Christmas 1594, when it was played at Gray's Inn. Its dramatic economy is much superior to that of *The Two Gentlemen of Verona.* Here, Shakespeare draws heavily on the traditions of Roman comedy. The action takes place in Ephesus within a single day and is based on Plautus' farce *Menaechmi,* which tells of a man accompanied by his slave and in search of his long-lost twin brother. Shakespeare turns the slave into a servant, Dromio, and gives him, too, a twin, who serves his master Antipholus' brother. The identical twins have identical names, and the result is a great increase in the possible errors of identification. Shakespeare frames the classically derived main action within an episode based on the romantic story of the wanderings of Apollonius of Tyre, which he was to use again in *Pericles.* This gives the Antipholuses a father, Egeon, and the comic complexities of the main action are overshadowed by his being condemned to die at five o'clock unless he can find someone to redeem him. By this and other means Shakespeare interfuses what might have been a merely mechanical farce with pointers to the potentially serious consequences of the misunderstandings. The untying of the comic knot is preceded by a moving lament from Egeon, about to be executed, who is not recognized by the man he believes to be the son he has brought up from birth. The resolution is effected by an Abbess who turns out to be Egeon's wife, a surprise to the audience paralleled in Shakespeare's work only by the apparent resurrection of Hermione in *The Winter's Tale.*

The ending of *The Comedy of Errors* is not just a solution of an intellectual puzzle, it is charged with emotional power. This play is a kind of diploma piece. In it Shakespeare outdoes his classical progenitors. He adapts his style admirably to his material. He modifies the intellectual complexity of his plot by infusing romantic motifs into it, and by relaxing the pace of the action from time to time to allow for the inclusion of discursive set pieces such as Dromio of Syracuse's marvelous prose description of the kitchen wench who was "spherical, like a globe." There is no faltering here.

The Taming of the Shrew, printed in the Folio, has a problematic relative, a play printed in 1594 as *The Taming of a Shrew,* once looked on as Shakespeare's source, now more generally regarded as a corrupt text of his play. It includes a rounding off of the Christopher Sly framework, which corresponds with nothing in the Folio. Perhaps that text is damaged too. Editors and directors sometimes, justifiably, add these episodes to the Folio text on the grounds that they may derive from lost Shakespearian originals.

In *The Comedy of Errors* Shakespeare shows people losing their sense of identity when recognition is withheld from them and acquiring a sense of reaffirmed identity when normality returns. In the Induction to *The Taming of the Shrew* he suggests how changes in external circumstances may join with the power of rhetoric to create a sense of changed identity. This play draws partly on conventions of Roman comedy, partly on English folk tale and drama. It owes a distinct debt to *Supposes,* George Gascoigne's prose translation of Ariosto's *I Suppositi.* "Supposes" is as much a key word in *The Taming of the Shrew* as is "errors" in *The Comedy of Errors.* The Induction displays the trick by which Sly is made to suppose that he is not a tinker but "a mighty lord." In the play performed for Sly's amusement, Lucentio, wooing Bianca, employs various "counterfeit supposes", but they are superficial. He, the shallowly romantic lover, is opposed to the unromantic Petruchio, who comes

> to wive it wealthily in Padua;
> If wealthily, then happily in Padua.
> (I.ii.73–74)

Petruchio is offered Kate, the shrew, apparently a far less attractive match than Bianca. And the most vital part of the play demonstrates the "suppose" by which he transforms the shrew into the ideal wife. The process is partly physical, partly mental. But its effect is not to reduce Kate to a state of subjection. Rather it teaches her the importance in human relationships of the ability to participate imaginatively in other people's lives. The play's final scene derives warmth and joy from the fact that Kate, in her new relationship with Petruchio, feels a freedom and wholeness that were previously outside her grasp. The achievement of Petruchio the realist is a romantic one: he creates an illusion and turns it into reality.

The Taming of the Shrew is a robust play that acts splendidly. It shows Shakespeare experimenting with techniques of structure and language in order to integrate a variety of diverse materials. It is interesting in the critical attitude that it adopts to romantic conventions. It contains much fine verse and prose; but, in the surviving text, it lacks the subordination of all the parts to the whole, which causes a less ambitious play, such as *The Comedy of Errors,* to seem a more rounded work of art.

Love's Labour's Lost is so different as to remind us forcibly of the uncertainties in the chronology of the early plays. Here Shakespeare seems to be writing for a more sophisticated, even courtly audience. The influences of earlier comedy appear to have been filtered through the plays of John Lyly, the leading court dramatist. The play contains topical allusions, some no longer explicable, which may also suggest that it originally had a coterie audience. It was first published in 1598, "as it was presented before her Highness this last Christmas," when it was said to be "newly corrected and augmented." But it was also acted in the public theaters—according to the title page of the second quarto, of 1631, "at the Blackfriars and the Globe"—and a court performance of 1605 suggests that it was not purely topical in its appeal.

In this play Shakespeare employs an exceptionally wide range of verse and prose styles, demonstrating his command of verbal artifice. This is appropriate, for the play is much concerned with artificiality. The king and his three lords have imposed unnatural restrictions on themselves. Beside them Shakespeare places Holofernes, the pedant who stands as an awful warning of what they may become if they persist in their denial of nature, and Costard and Jaquenetta, unspoiled children of nature. The arrival of the Princess of France and her three ladies offers an immediate challenge to the lords' resolutions, and the play's patterned, dancelike progress charts their slow acceptance of their own natures, their acknowledgments of the demands of society, and of the need for a proper and courteous use of the intelligence. Artificial behavior is reflected in artificial language. Significantly, the most important communication in the play does not need to be put into words:

> *Marcade* . . . the news I bring
> Is heavy in my tongue. The King your father—
> *Princess* Dead, for my life!
> *Marcade* Even so; my tale is told.
> (V.ii.706–709)

Artifice gives way before the ultimate reality of death. The lovers are forced into new relationships with one another, and Shakespeare shows that the adjustment is not easy.

The subdued ending of *Love's Labour's Lost* represents one of Shakespeare's most daring experiments with comic form. Usually the comic climax brings happiness; this one brings grief. After it there comes a slow movement toward resignation and hope, but the happy ending lies in the future, at least twelve months away; and that, says Berowne, is "too long for a play." *Love's Labour's Lost* offers its audience full enjoyment of artifice but also invites a critical attitude toward it. The play grows from intellectual playfulness to a warm humanity that comes to full, disturbing flood at the close. It is a play of ideas, a brilliantly dramatized debate; though in some senses it is of its age, it can still reach out vividly to us.

Shakespeare's early experiments in comedy have their perfect outcome in *A Midsummer Night's Dream,* printed in 1600 but probably written by 1595. No single influence is dominant. The design of the play came from Shakespeare's imagination, as it had for *Love's Labour's Lost,* with which it has much in common. It too has a patterned structure, a wide range of prose and verse styles, comedy springing from the follies of young love, a play-within-the-play. It has a similar grace of language, less intricacy and self-conscious brilliance. The theory that it was written for an aristocratic marriage is unsupported by external evidence; but marriage is central to the play's design, linking each of the distinct groups of characters. Theseus is to be married; the lovers wish to be, and finally are; the fairies, who have marital problems, are to intervene in the human plans for marriage and to deliver the concluding epithalamium; the laborers are to provide the entertainment for the multiple marriages, and one of them is bemusedly to receive the amorous attention of the Fairy Queen.

Though marriages form the natural conclusion to the action, there are, in the usual way of comedy, obstacles to be overcome. Misunderstandings among the young lovers are exacerbated by Puck's mischief; dissension between the Fairy King and Queen must be settled before human happiness can be achieved. The supernatural world is lightly suggestive of inexplicable influences upon human behavior, especially in love—"reason and love keep little company together now-a-days." And Shakespeare is led to explore the relationship between reason and the imagination in a way that suggests an affinity between love and artistic responsiveness. The inexperienced lovers are bewildered by their own emotions. The laborers are hopelessly confused by the problem of distinguishing between appearance and reality. But the lovers, temporarily released from the bands of society, come out of the dream world of the wood wiser than they had gone into it. Bottom is taken out of himself by his encounter with the Fairy Queen and, though he regards it as a dream, acknowledges it as "a most rare vision." Theseus looks with the eye of reason, but Hippolyta knows that

> all the story of the night told over,
> And all their minds transfigur'd so together,
> More witnesseth than fancy's images,
> And grows to something of great constancy.
> (V.i. 23–26)

The last act is a glorious celebration, a dance in which the shifting relationships between the performers of the interlude, the images they try to present, and their audience mirror the conflicting claims of illusion and reality, the world of the imagination—in which openness to experience can lead to wisdom—and the need to acknowledge the hard facts of life. The performance ends in goodwill and courtesy, on which the fairies bestow their blessing; and Puck, in his closing lines, reminds us that we are at liberty to take what we have seen as either truth or illusion:

> If we shadows have offended,
> Think but this, and all is mended,
> That you have but slumb'red here
> While these visions did appear.

The goodwill of the audience can help the players to "mend." As Holofernes had shown, imaginative detachment is "not generous, not gentle, not humble"; and, as we had witnessed in *The Taming of the Shrew,* imagination can turn illusion into reality.

EARLY TRAGEDIES

Shakespeare was more tentative in his early explorations of tragic than of comic form. Tragedies were conventionally based on history, and *Titus Andronicus* is set in the fourth century A.D., but the story, like that of his other early tragedy, *Romeo and Juliet,* is fictitious. Shakespeare may have adapted it from an earlier version of *The History of Titus Andronicus,* which survives only as an eighteenth-century chap-book. Ovid, whose *Metamorphoses* appears on stage (IV.i), is an important influence, as is Seneca. Except for Act Three, Scene Two, which first appeared in print in 1623, the play was printed in 1594; and it may have been written several years earlier, perhaps in collaboration with George Peele, perhaps merely under his influence. Popular in its time, it can now be enjoyed only with an exercise of the historical imagination, for its presentation of physical horror can easily seem ludicrous. The disjunction between action and language can bewilder, as when Marcus, seeing his niece with "her hands cut off, and her tongue cut out, and ravish'd" (II.iv), delivers nearly fifty lines of beautifully modulated blank verse; or, still more surprisingly, when Titus, having persuaded Aaron to cut off his hand, betrays no more emotion in what he says than if he had taken off a glove. Nevertheless, it is in the portrayal of suffering that the play justifies itself, and more than one production has shown that, given the right kind of stylized presentation, its ritualistic tableaux of suffering and woe can be profoundly moving. As in the early histories, Shakespeare is most successful in the expression of grief and the portrayal of energetic evil. Titus' lament over his mutilated daughter is elemental in a way that looks forward to Lear:

> I am the sea; hark how her sighs do blow.
> She is the weeping welkin, I the earth;
> Then must my sea be moved with her sighs;
> Then must my earth with her continual
> tears
> Become a deluge, overflow'd and drown'd.
> (III.i. 226–230)

Aaron, the Moorish villain, displays an enjoyment of evil and a cynical intelligence that relate him to Richard III and Iago; he develops into the play's most complex character. The final horrifying bloodbath, in which Titus serves Tamora with her two sons' heads baked in a pie, kills his own daughter and Tamora, and is himself killed by the emperor, who is then killed by Titus' son, is skillfully engineered; but the events are efficiently rather than imaginatively presented, and tragic emotions are not stirred.

Shakespeare took the well-known story of Romeo and Juliet from Arthur Brooke's long poem *The Tragical History of Romeus and Juliet,* published in 1562 and reprinted in 1587. The play is more markedly experimental than *Titus Andronicus.* It is not set in antiquity but in the sixteenth century. It has affinities with romantic comedy, telling of wooing and marriage. Its poetical center is the balcony scene, perhaps the most celebrated expression of romantic love in our literature; the romance is offset by much witty and bawdy comedy. The tragic outcome of the lovers' passion is the result of external circumstances: the still timelessness of Romeo and Juliet's inward experience, perfectly conveyed at the end of the balcony scene, is threatened and finally destroyed by the time-tied processes of the public feud between their families. The play, first printed in 1597, seems from its verbal styles to have been written several years after *Titus Andronicus.* For the first time among the plays discussed so far, we feel, not merely that the design is ambitious, but that Shakespeare's fecundity overflows the measure. Every rift is laden with ore, and the finished work delights and astonishes by its inventiveness, variety, complexity, and generosity. But it is not undisciplined. Indeed, this play is "early" in the sense that it still relies partly on formal verse structures—the lovers' first conversation, a moment of private communion in the public bustle of the ball, is cast in the form of a sonnet—and on clearly patterned action. Public strife is counterbalanced by private communion; the Prince, the civic governor, has his counterpart in Friar Lawrence, the personal confessor; Romeo's confidant, Mercutio, is matched by Juliet's, her Nurse. Characterization is both brilliant and functional. Shakespeare's verbal virtuosity makes marvelous individuals out of Mercutio and the Nurse, but they too are part of the pattern, each failing one of the lovers in understanding, pushing them still further into isolation. In their bawdy physicality, too, they act as foils to the lovers, whose passion includes but transcends the physical. Romeo and Juliet are gradually destroyed by the world of external reality: the world of uncomprehending relatives and friends, in which the senseless family feud—a symbol of misunderstanding, of the failures in human communication—destroys the most precious representatives of the families. Romeo and Juliet had achieved understanding and union; they had risked—and, in a sense, lost—all for the values of personal love. In this sense comedy is banished from the end of the play. The Prince calls together the heads of the opposing families and speaks of general woe. But out of the suffering comes a hard-won reconciliation. As in some of Shakespeare's later comedies, the union of lovers accompanies the healing of breaches among members of the older generation; but here the lovers are dead.

THE POEMS

Because of plague, London's theaters were closed for almost two years between June 1592 and June 1594. Shakespeare turned to nondramatic writing, perhaps because he feared that he might need an alternative career. A new kind of narrative poem was coming into vogue: tales of love based on Ovidian stories and techniques. Thomas Lodge's *Scilla's Metamorphosis* (1589) is an early example. Another, perhaps the finest, is Christopher Marlowe's *Hero and Leander.* Marlowe died in 1593, but the poem was not published until 1598. *Venus and Adonis* was printed in 1593, with the author's dedication to Henry Wriothesley, earl of Southampton, calling the poem "the first heir of my invention"—presumably meaning either his first poem or his first work to be printed. It was extraordinarily popular; at least eleven editions appeared before 1620, and five more by 1640. Partly it had a succès de scandale; Shakespeare makes Venus the suitor, Adonis her reluctant victim, which adds a piquant eroticism to Ovid's story.

The poem's success has not been maintained. Like *Love's Labour's Lost,* it is a sophisticated work, drawing attention to its craftsmanship, demanding admiration rather than submission. It will not be enjoyed if it is read for its story alone: Shakespeare takes nearly 1,200 lines where Ovid took about 75. Yet the narrative is unfolded with such order, clarity, and ease of versification that the general impression is one of speed. The style, though artificial, is varied, ranging from metaphysical elaboration to pared simplicity. Adonis provides the main psychological interest. His innocence and idealism contrast with Venus' experience and paradoxically physical, materialist outlook. It is the goddess who represents lust, the human boy who stands up for love. The tension between his youthful withdrawal from sexual experience and her overmature anxiety to rush into it provides the poem's dramatic impetus. Adonis' immaturity, amusing and touching, is appropriate to the essentially nontragic nature of a story with a quasi-tragic ending.

The Rape of Lucrece, printed the following year and also dedicated, more warmly, to Southampton, is a contrasting companion piece. The earlier poem is mythological. *Lucrece,* composed in the seven-line rhyme royal, is historical, based not on the *Metamorphoses* but on the *Fasti* ("Chronicles"). It is about people in society; its tone is not that of high comedy, but of tragedy. Like *Venus and Adonis,* it opens with speed in a stanza that carries concentrated suggestions of the power of Tarquin's lust. A long poem could not be sustained at this pitch, nor would the slender story support it. Shakespeare ekes out his material with meditative soliloquies, discursive episodes, and long moralizing passages. The amplificatory technique is less successful here than in *Venus and Adonis.* There we could remain detached enough to enjoy the poet's verbal flights, his decorative ingenuity, his digressive skill. *Lucrece* seems to demand more engagement with the emotions of the characters. Even the least relevant passages are often fine in their own right, but the parts are greater than the whole. Most important from the point of view of Shakespeare's later development seem to be those passages describing how Tarquin against his better nature is drawn inexorably on toward the crime that will destroy him. Just as a basic theme of Shakespearian comedy, the search for and final achievement of self-knowledge, is adumbrated in *Venus and Adonis,* so a basic motif of his tragedies, the problem caused by an absence of self-knowledge so disastrous that it is finally destructive of self, emerges in *Lucrece.* Tarquin, we are told, as he moves toward Lucrece's chamber' "still pursues his fear" (1. 308). Macbeth, before he kills Duncan, imagines Murder moving "With Tarquin's ravishing strides, towards his design" (II.i.55).

It may have been about the time that Shakespeare was writing the essentially public narrative poems that he also wrote his most seemingly private compositions, his sonnets. When they were written is only one of the mysteries about them. In 1598 Francis Meres referred to Shakespeare's "sugared sonnets among his private friends." In 1599 William Jaggard published corrupt versions of two of them in *The Passionate Pilgrim,* a volume of poems that he attributed to Shakespeare and that also includes three extracts from *Love's Labour's Lost,* four poems known to be by other poets, and eleven of unknown authorship that few have ascribed to Shakespeare. The complete 154 sonnets did not appear until 1609, though the title-page declaration "Never before imprinted" implies that they were not new. The publication appears to be unauthorized. It has a dedication by the publisher, Thomas Thorpe: "To the only begetter of these ensuing sonnets Mr W.H. all happiness and that eternity promised by our ever-living poet wisheth the well-wishing adventurer in setting forth." This sentence has been endlessly discussed, but we still do not know who Mr W.H. is, nor in what sense he was the sonnets' "only begetter." The volume also includes "A Lover's Complaint," a narrative poem of doubtful authenticity.

Sonnet sequences were popular in the 1590's, and Shakespeare's interest in the sonnet form is reflected in some of his early plays, especially *Romeo and Juliet* and *Love's Labour's Lost.* The fact that he did not publish his sonnets may imply that he thought of them as personal poems, but this is not altogether borne out by their content. Some are generalized meditations; some are comparatively formal utterances, like the first seventeen, in which he urges a young man to marry and beget children. Some proclaim a public design in the attempt to eternize their addressee. Some hint at a personal drama. The relationship between the poet and his friend is so close that it is sometimes interpreted as homosexual, though this is explicitly denied (20). It is threatened by another poet who seeks to replace the author in his friend's affections; the poet's mistress, a "black" woman (as he calls her), or Dark Lady, seduces the friend: the poet is more concerned for the friend than for his own relationship with the woman, which he frequently deplores. Sonnets 127–152 are mainly about the woman. They include some of the most tortured and introverted of the poems; it is difficult to imagine the poet wishing to show them even to the woman, let alone make them public. This personal drama might be fictional; if so, it is inefficiently projected. The sonnets are partly "dramatic" in the sense that some of them are written as if from within a particular situation, like speeches from a lost play. Some can be related to classical poetry; some draw on poetic conventions of the time; some represent a deliberate reaction against convention: few if any other sonnets of the time are as bawdy or as insulting to their addressees as some of Shakespeare's. A dramatic poet as great as Shakespeare may have written sonnets on imaginary themes that sound personal, but we know of no reason why he should have done so without intending to publish them. Yet as an autobiographical document, the sonnets are most unsatisfactory. Innumerable attempts have been made to rearrange them into a more coherent sequence, to identify the persons involved, and to elucidate topical allusions. None has succeeded.

To read all the sonnets consecutively is difficult. Though almost all of them have, superficially, the same form, this obscures the fact that their wide range of modes, of tone, of variations within the basic form, of intensity, and of interrelationship imposes disparate demands upon the attention. Some, including many of the most popular, are lyrical, confident outpourings of love, conveyed largely through natural imagery; some express the lover's humility and abasement. Some are well-ordered meditations on eternal poetic themes of time, the transience of beauty and of love; on the power of art, the inevitability of death; some are more narrowly, even enigmatically, related to a particular situation. Some are intellectual, witty workings out of poetic conceits; some, no less intellectual, are tortured, introspective self-communings. Though some seem to belong to the world of *The Two Gentlemen of Verona* or *Romeo and Juliet,* others are closer to *Measure for Measure* or *Troilus and Cressida.* Shakespeare the man remains as fascinatingly enigmatic in the sonnets as in the plays.

LATER HISTORIES AND MAJOR COMEDIES

After his wide-ranging earlier experiments, Shakespeare narrowed his scope and, during several prolific years after about 1594, wrote only comedies and history plays, of which *Richard II* alone is in tragic form. Here Shakespeare steps backward in his dramatization of history to begin a tetralogy, which, by carrying the story up to the reign of Henry V, will complete an eight-play sequence. The plays are strongly linked, yet each has its own individuality. *Richard II,* written about 1595, was printed in 1597. It was of topical interest. Queen Elizabeth was aging. Anxiety about the succession was growing. The queen's indulgence of her favorites caused unrest; comparisons were drawn between her and Richard II. The absence from the play of the deposition scene (IV.i) in the three editions printed during her lifetime must be attributed to censorship, official or not; and the commissioning by Essex's supporters of a special performance on the eve of his rebellion, in 1601, shows that many drew the parallel.

Nevertheless, Shakespeare's play has no obvious topical allusions. He emphasizes the universal rather than the particular elements of Bolingbroke's usurpation. The play is full of moral ambiguity. Richard, a faulty human being and a weak king, has the unquestioned right to the throne. Bolingbroke has no hereditary right but is wronged by Richard and better fitted for kingship. Shakespeare skillfully manipulates the audience's sympathies. In the early scenes we can only condemn Richard's frivolity and irresponsibility, which culminate in his callous and unconstitutional treatment of his dying uncle, John of Gaunt, whose noble speech on England (II.i. 31–68) laments the lapsing values of the old order. But after Bolingbroke becomes king, and also abuses power in the executions of Bushy and

Bagot and the arrest of the Bishop of Carlisle—another spokesman for traditional values—and as Richard's expression of his sufferings grows in eloquence, Richard takes on the stature of a tragic hero. Through him Shakespeare orchestrates, in wonderfully melodious verse, all the resonances of the situation; and the play expands from a political drama into an exploration of the sources of power, of the hold that symbols, including words, can have over men's imaginations, of the tensions between the demands of office and the qualities of those who hold office, of private and public values, of the differences and similarities between a "large kingdom" and a "little grave."

Bolingbroke's guilt haunts him throughout the next two plays of the sequence. Carlisle's prophecy that civil war will follow usurpation is fulfilled. *1 Henry IV* (printed twice in 1598 and reprinted five times before 1623) shows the king, wishing to expiate his guilt by a pilgrimage to Jerusalem, anguished by both national and filial rebellion. Just as, in *A Midsummer Night's Dream,* Oberon and Titania must be reconciled before the mortals' course of love can run smooth, so the dissolute Hal must reform and be reconciled with his father before rebellion can be put down. The issue resolves into a personal conflict between Hotspur, the rebel leader, and Hal, who defeats expectation and becomes the victor. Shakespeare has adjusted the facts, chronicled by Holinshed, to create a basically simple foundation on which he builds a history play with a greater social and emotional range than he had so far attempted. Here his genius for character portrayal, achieved largely through an astonishing capacity to deploy and extend the full resources of the English language, is at its greatest. Dominant is Falstaff, Shakespeare's invention, though distantly related to the historical Sir John Oldcastle as portrayed in *The Famous Victories of Henry V,* a minor source play printed in 1598. The character is rich, as the soliloquies particularly demonstrate; but the profundity of the role derives also from its integration into the total design, most subtly in the first tavern scene (II.iv) when Falstaff and Hal in turn take on the role of the king. Behind the game lurks reality, a subconscious and premonitory acknowledgment on Falstaff's part that the "son of England" should not "prove a thief and take purses," and on Hal's that he is bound eventually to "banish plump Jack." The tavern world provides more fully realized representatives of the ordinary folk of England than we have seen before. It is part of Hal's achievement to link this world with the court and the battlefield.

At the beginning of *2 Henry IV,* Hal seems to have returned to his former ways. There is an uncharacteristic element of repetition in the pattern of paternal reproach, filial repentance, and reconciliation. This may result from an initial uncertainty about whether to treat Henry IV's reign in one play or two. But Part Two has its individual tone, darker and more disturbing than its predecessor's. It brings to the surface moral issues only latent in the earlier play. Even there Falstaff at his most contemptible, stabbing Hotspur's corpse, was juxtaposed with Hal at his most heroic. Here, though we may temporarily condone Falstaff's misuse of his powers of conscription and his exploitation of Shallow and his companions, his self-exculpations are less disarming. In the great tavern scene (II.iv) his amorous exchanges with the deplorable Doll Tearsheet are poignant rather than funny, overshadowed by impotence and the fear of death. But Shakespeare does not encourage us to be morally complacent. Mistress Quickly and even Doll are presented in ways that show his delight in normal human instincts, as well as an awareness that they may be dangerous when out of control. Prince John may have right on his side, but the trick by which he betrays the rebels is distasteful; we can warm to Falstaff's condemnation of "the sober-blooded boy." The darker side of tavern life is savagely evident in the tiny scene (V.iv) of Doll's carting—"the man is dead that you and Pistol beat amongst you." The scene is strategically placed just before Hal's entrance as king; we can see the need for his rejection of Falstaff, though we can see the sadness of it, too.

2 Henry IV was written about 1598. First printed in 1600, it was, unlike Part One, not reprinted until 1623. At this stage in his career, Shakespeare was using a higher proportion of prose over verse than at any other period and was achieving with it some of his most complex and truly poetical effects. The political scenes of this play use verse, much of it very fine. But the quintessentially Shakespearian parts are the tavern scene and the Justice Shallow episodes, in which prose is handled with a subtlety matched only in Chekhov for the dramatic expression of emotional complexity.

Shakespeare rounded off his second historical sequence with *Henry V.* An apparent allusion to Essex in the Chorus to Act V suggests that it was written in 1599. A corrupt text of the following year omits the Choruses, first printed in 1623. *Henry V,* composed at the zenith of Shakespeare's career as a comic dramatist, brings history close to comic form. It has a wooing scene and ends, as comedies conventionally do, with a marriage, one that will unite realms as well as hearts (V.ii. 351). Our reactions are guided by the Chorus—Shakespeare's most extended use of this device except in *Pericles*—who speaks some of the play's finest poetry. From the "civil broils" of the earlier plays Shakespeare turns to portray a country united in war against France. There is more glory in such a war, and the play is famous—or notorious—as an expression of patriotism. It has less inwardness than its predecessors. But the horrors of war are strongly presented; the goal of war is peace, and the play suggests that inward peace of conscience is necessary in one who would win national peace. Henry shows concern about the justification for his course of action. More than once, and from both sides of the Channel, we are reminded of his "wilder days." The transition from "madcap prince" to the "mirror of all Christian kings" involves loss. Falstaff is dying; "the king has killed his heart." But Henry has accepted the responsibilities of kingship and talks of them, and its hollow rewards, in a speech that recalls one by his father (*2 Henry IV,* III.i. 1–31) and anticipates (historically) one by his son (*3 Henry VI,* II.v. 1–54). "The King is but a man" (IV.i. 103), and this one moves among his men with an honesty unimaginable in Richard II and quite different from his father's "courtship to the common people" (*Richard II,* I.iv. 24). His success in battle removes the guilt of his inheritance. He has become the "star of England" (final Chorus, 6). If in the process he has made difficult decisions with harsh consequences, that, Shakespeare implies, is the price of political success.

MAJOR COMEDIES

Shakespeare wrote his later histories over the same period as his greatest comedies. *The Merchant of Venice,* dating from about 1596, was entered in the Stationers' Register in 1598 and printed in 1600. Much of the plot material is implausible, deriving from folktale and legend. The wooing story comes from a collection published in Italian in 1558 as *Il Pecorone,* by Ser Giovanni Fiorentino. The pound-of-flesh story was well known. A lost play, *The Jew,* mentioned in 1579, may have been a source, and Shakespeare must have known Marlowe's *The Jew of Malta.*

The plot's sharp conflict between romantic and antiromantic values leads Shakespeare to define, partly by contrast, his first great romantic heroine and his first great comic antagonist. The opposition of Portia and Shylock provides the chief dramatic impetus, culminating in the controlled excitement of the trial (IV.i). It is easy to think of the play in terms of contrasts: between the beautiful, generous, merciful Portia and the scheming, miserly, legalistic Shylock; between their religions, Christianity and Judaism; between their settings, the idealized Belmont and the money markets of Venice; between the heights of lyrical poetry to which Portia can rise and Shylock's harsh prose. There are other tensions, too: the familiar conflict, in Bassanio, between love and friendship; the opposition, in the episodes of the caskets, between attractive but hollow superficiality and the rewards given to those "that choose not by the view" (III.ii. 131).

The oppositions in the play, though strong, are not entirely simple. The world of Belmont is idealized but flawed. The generous Bassanio has been prodigal. Antonio, noble in friendship, admits to treating Shylock with contempt. Gratiano, though ebullient, is vindictive. Even Portia has to adopt Shylock's legalism to achieve her good ends. Shylock, though villainous, has dignity, eloquence, and pathos. We may deplore his values yet respect his tenacity. Despite its lyricism, grace, drama, and high comedy, many people find *The Merchant of Venice* disturbing and express unease with it. Shakespeare portrays here a clash of values rather like that between Henry V and Falstaff. We know which side is right. We have no doubt that Portia should defeat Shylock as King Henry has to reject Falstaff. But in both plays there is pain in the defeat as well as joy in the victory.

Much Ado About Nothing, usually dated about 1598—it is not mentioned by Meres and was published in quarto in 1600—is also based on a traditional tale. It places less emphasis on poetry and romance, more on prose and wit. The young lovers of the main plot, Claudio and Hero, are unconvincing advocates for romantic values. Admittedly, Claudio expresses his love for Hero eloquently in the play's first verse passage, but only after he has assured himself that she is an heiress. We never see him alone with her, and their relationship seems as insubstantial as that of Lucentio and Bianca in *The Taming of the Shrew.* Claudio falls remarkably easily into the deception that Don John engineers, and gives Hero no opportunity to defend herself before launching into his bitter denunciations at the altar where they were to have been married. Her apparent death leads him to no real soul searchings, and her forgiveness and their subsequent reconciliation are sketchily presented. Questions are raised that might have been answered if we had more knowledge of Shakespeare's intentions. If Claudio is played as a callow adolescent, we may pity his succumbing to Don John's evil trickery. If he is more maturely presented, we may look on him rather as an illustration of the hollowness of attitudes to love that are based on illusion instead of knowledge and understanding.

Certainly the lovers of the main plot are less convincing than those of the subplot. There is more true poetry in single prose sentences of Beatrice's—"There was a star danc'd, and under that was I born"—than in many lines of Claudio's verse. This overturning of expectations is one of the ways in which romantic values are questioned. Beatrice and Benedick's "merry war," for all its wrangling, suggests a true engagement of personalities. The brief passage in which they declare their love (IV.i. 255-end) is perhaps the best prose love scene in the language, and we believe in them as complex and developing individuals.

In *Much Ado About Nothing* recurrent overhearings become a structural principle. "Nothing" in the title has been taken as a pun on "noting," and certainly the "misprisions" arising from the overhearings create the complications of the action. Almost all are tricked. Yet a fruitful counterpoint arises from the relationships of the different sets of characters. Dogberry and his companions of the watch have already overheard Borachio's confession when Claudio denounces Hero. The presence of Beatrice and Benedick during the scene of the thwarted wedding is an additional reassurance to the audience. Dogberry and his fellows are the most naturally befuddled characters, yet it is their basic goodwill that, in spite of almost insuperable barriers to communication, resolves the action. The play's interpretative problems are not essentially different from those of most stage works for which we have limited knowledge of the author's intentions. And they enhance rather than diminish its theatrical robustness. It withstands varied treatments and is a constant source of pleasure.

There is a legend that Shakespeare wrote *The Merry Wives of Windsor* rapidly, because Queen Elizabeth wanted to see "Sir John in love." A passage in Act Five alluding to the ceremony of the Feast of the Knights of the Garter clearly has topical reference, and the play almost certainly has some connection with special Garter ceremonies, but we cannot be sure in what year. 1597 has been suggested, but the play's relationship with the other Falstaff plays seems to require a later date. It was first published, in a bad text, in 1602; a better text appeared in the Folio. In spite of its superficial naturalism it has a strongly literary background. Several of the characters derive from Shakespeare's own plays about Henry IV; and though no clear source of the plot has been identified, it is closely related to the ribald tales of tricked lovers and husbands included in many contemporary collections.

Legends about the play's origin, and the fact that its central character is called Falstaff, have damaged its critical reputation. It might be more profitably approached as another of Shakespeare's experiments. It is untypical in various ways. It includes proportionally more prose than any other of his plays. It is his only comedy to have an English setting and to be closely related to contemporary life. In Master Ford, Shakespeare comes closer than anywhere else to writing "humours" comedy in the Jonsonian style. But Shakespeare could never commit himself to Jonson's antiromantic view of life. Ford is shamed out of his jealous humor and kneels to his wife for pardon. Falstaff also undergoes a corrective process of castigation leading to penitence. Shakespeare's essential romanticism shows itself too in the subplot of Anne Page and her suitors. The climax of the love plot comes in the verse passage in which Fenton, safely married, not merely defends his deception of Anne's parents but rebukes them for their previous opposition to the match and their willingness to have her married for money (V.v. 207–217).

The Merry Wives of Windsor does not belong to the mainstream of Shakespearian comedy but is recognizably Shakespearian. It is a neat, ingenious, witty comedy of situation. It has attributes of the corrective, satirical comedy that Jonson was making popular at the close of the century, but it also displays a strong moral bent and a romantic attitude to love and marriage. The style suits the matter, and much of the writing is delightful, even if it would not be at home in *Henry IV.* The characterization is partly by types, but the major roles offer excellent opportunities to their performers, and there are passages of subtly manipulated dialogue. Critics have patronized the play. Audiences never fail to enjoy it.

Pastoralism, derived from classical models, exerted an important influence on sixteenth-century literature. We have seen how some of Shakespeare's kings envied the shepherd his life attuned to the seasons and the natural processes. Elsewhere, too, Shakespeare plays with pastoral conventions. In *The Two Gentlemen of Verona* and *A Midsummer Night's Dream,* for example, the movement of lovers from their accustomed environment to a place apart assists their self-discovery. But it is in *As You Like It* that Shakespeare conducts his most searching examination of the pastoral ideal. The play, first published in 1623, is based on Thomas Lodge's *Rosalynde,* a prose romance printed in 1590 and reprinted in 1592, 1596, and 1598. Shakespeare's play of the book, written about 1600, is exceptionally literary in its origins, and he does not attempt to conceal its artificiality. He manipulates the relationship between story and dialogue, between the enactment of events and reflection upon the events, between characters as agents of the action and characters as talkers, to permit the introduction of many of the commonplace debating topics of his times: the relationship for instance between nature and fortune, nature and nurture, court and country. These topics are all associated with the pastoral tradition. Related to them is an idea that fascinated Shakespeare: that wisdom is a kind of folly, folly a potential source of wisdom. He seems to have felt that the effort to attain wisdom may result in an overearnestness that can lead to folly, and that the unguardedness of the subconscious, relaxed mind may, for all its dangers, bring the rewards of unsought illumination. He betrays a concern with the proper use of man's time on earth; and in this comedy in which the central character plays so elaborate, extended, and ultimately important a game, the idea of time, of its uses and abuses, is also, appropriately, pervasive.

Rosalind's game is directed toward the attainment of love, and attitudes to love are dominant among the play's concepts. The forest of Arden is inhabited by lovers, actual and potential. Silvius and Phebe are straight out of the Renaissance pastoral convention, unreal but touching, because in them Shakespeare isolates one aspect of love. Opposed to it is the earthy love affair of Touchstone and Audrey. Touchstone's attitude is partly a criticism of Silvius' but is itself criticized: being purely physical, it is, as he perceives himself, temporary. Subsuming both of these attitudes is that of Orlando and Rosalind. Orlando has attributes of the conventional lover. He hangs verses on trees, sighs out his soul in praise of his beloved. Yet his idealism is robust enough to withstand the mockery of Jaques, the professed cynic, whose criticism is seen to be destructive, joyless, self-absorbed, and without love.

The fullest character of the play, the one who embraces most attitudes within herself and resolves them into a rich synthesis of personality, is Rosalind. Aware of the humorous aspects of love, she knows its potency, too. Her awareness of the danger of folly becomes a self-awareness born of experience, her boyish disguise a means of simultaneously revealing and controlling her emotion. She bears secrets; her revelation that she is a woman is an inward as well as an outward resolution of the play's action. In an early scene Amiens congratulates Duke Senior on being able to "translate the stubbornness of fortune / Into so quiet and so sweet a style" (II.i. 19–20). The quality of human experience is determined partly by the character of the experiencer; Jaques will always be melancholy, but Rosalind and Orlando can win quietness and sweetness from adversity by an exercise of the imagination. To this extent, life can be as we like it.

As You Like It gains its impetus rather from the juxtaposition of opposed attitudes than from plot tension. In *Twelfth Night,* also written about 1600 and not published until 1623, Shakespeare returns to a tighter structure. Part of the plot is based on a story from Barnaby Rich's *Farewell to Military Profession* (1581), but Shakespeare idealizes its characters and heightens its romantic tone. The romance framework of separation, search, and reunion that he had already used in *The Comedy of Errors* is here more closely integrated into the action, and there is only one pair of twins to cause comic complications. As in *As You Like It,* love is a unifying motif, but it is often a wistful, frustrated, and sometimes nonsexual emotion. The play opens with Orsino's richly romantic expression of thwarted passion. Death overhangs the early scenes: the death of Olivia's brother, to whose memory she is dedicated, and the supposed death of Viola's brother. Olivia is jested out of her mourning, and Viola is more resilient, but passion continues to be thwarted, sometimes because those who declare it are lost in the fantasies of self-love. Olivia, wooed by Orsino, Sir Andrew, and Malvolio, responds to none of them. She also is thwarted, loving Viola in the belief that she is a man. Viola in her disguise can express her love for Orsino only obliquely. The lovers' folly generates comedy, of which Olivia's fool, Feste, makes much capital. From their first appearance together, an opposition is set up between Malvolio, the professed wise man, and Feste, the professional fool. The exposure of Malvolio is engineered by Maria and Sir Toby Belch, the upholder of the festive virtues of cakes and ale. Feste joins in, and the comedy deepens disturbingly as Malvolio remains incapable of seeing the truth. The play's most positive values are embodied in the enchanting Viola, and it is her reunion with her brother, celebrated in a moving antiphon (V.i. 218–249), that resolves the action. Now there are no obstacles to the union of Viola and Orsino, Olivia and Sebastian. For them, the shadows are dispelled; but Malvolio remains unregenerate, and Sir Toby's harshness to Sir Andrew sours our view of him. After the lovers' happiness, we are left with the wise but lonely Feste's song of the wind and the rain.

UNROMANTIC COMEDIES AND LATER TRAGEDIES

About 1600, Shakespeare's imagination turned in new directions. Two tragedies, *Julius Caesar* and *Hamlet,* may even have been written before *Twelfth Night.* An isolated elegy, "The Phoenix and the Turtle," dense, plangent, and probably of irrecoverable allegorical significance, appeared in Robert Chester's *Love's Martyr* in 1601. After that, there appears to be a period of uncertainty and experimentation before the full, confident achievement of the later tragedies.

All's Well That Ends Well, first printed in 1623, is usually dated 1602–1603 because of its links with *Measure for Measure,* which can more confidently be assigned to 1604. Since about 1900, these plays, along with *Troilus and Cressida,* have frequently been classed as "problem plays." Shakespeare based the main plot of *All's Well That Ends Well* on a story from Boccaccio's *Decameron,* which he probably read in the English translation in William Painter's *Palace of Pleasure* (1566–1567). He added important characters, notably the Countess; invented the subplot of Parolles; and elaborated both the story and the manner of its telling. In his hands the tale of a physician's daughter who healed a king and demanded as a reward the hand of a handsome, rich, and reluctant young nobleman be comes the vehicle for a discussion of many ideas about human life, especially the extent to which human virtue is innate or acquired. The subplot of the cowardly Parolles illumines the ideas cast up by the main plot, and the comedy of his exposure reflects upon the disgraceful behavior of the nobleman, Bertram. Boccaccio's story employs motifs of fairy tale and folk legend. In some ways Shakespeare enhances its romantic nature, adding, for example, the motif of apparent resurrection that recurs frequently in his work. But his treatment of the story is generally unromantic, producing a tension between the conventionality of some of its elements and the reality of the terms in which he presents them. The play's intellectual qualities, the unromantic nature of its despicable hero, and the fact that the heroine is obliged to behave in an unladylike manner to win him, have counted against its popularity; but it fascinates by its comic brilliance, its passages of tender and delicate emotional writing, and its deeply serious concern with the events and characters that it portrays.

Measure for Measure, too, betrays a tension between conventional plot elements and psychological verisimilitude. First printed in 1623, it is based on a two-part play, *Promos and Cassandra* (1578), by George Whetstone. In his first three acts Shakespeare involves us intimately in his characters, moral dilemmas. Claudio's sin of fornication is hardly more than a technical offense. It seems monstrous that he is condemned by Duke Vincentio's "outward-sainted" deputy, Angelo. Isabella's scenes of pleading with Angelo are both personally and intellectually involving, and his internal crisis as he discovers his susceptibility to sexual emotion moves us even while we deplore his duplicity. The scene (III.i) in which the Duke advises Claudio to be "absolute for death" and Claudio expresses his fear of death is a masterly demonstration of what Keats called Shakespeare's "negative capability" in its convincing expression of opposed attitudes.

After this point Shakespeare changes the focus. The duke, in his manipulations, becomes a surrogate playwright. Claudio's fate interests us, yet he appears once only and has a single, brief speech. Angelo becomes a subject of argument rather than an object of psychological exploration. In the final scene much is left to the interpreters. Isabella and the brother she had believed dead are given no words to speak on their reunion, nor does she make any verbal response to the Duke's two unexpected proposals of marriage. Yet the scene works up to an exciting climax as the

Duke tests Isabella's capacity to exercise mercy, and, as in *All's Well That Ends Well,* a silent moment of kneeling has great theatrical power. *Measure for Measure* is passionately and explicitly concerned with moral issues. Each of the "good" characters fails in some respect; none of the evil ones lacks some redeeming quality. Even Barnardine, the drunken, convicted murderer, is finally forgiven his "earthly faults." We are all, in the last analysis, "desperately mortal."

The problems of *Troilus and Cressida* differ from those of *All's Well That Ends Well* and *Measure for Measure.* We do not know how long it had been written before its entry in the Stationers' Register on 7 February 1603. The statement made then that it had been played at the Globe was repeated on the original title page of the 1609 quarto, but this page was withdrawn and an added, anonymous epistle described it as "a new play, never staled with the stage, never clapper-clawed with the palms of the vulgar, and passing full of the palm comical." In the Folio it was originally to have appeared among the tragedies, but, perhaps because of copyright difficulties, printing was delayed and it was finally placed between the histories and the tragedies.

This draws attention to problems about the play's genre. Its inspiration is partly classical, partly medieval. Shakespeare went to the first installment of Chapman's translation of Homer, published in 1598, and to Caxton, Lydgate, and Ovid, for the material relating to the siege of Troy; but the love story, which is a late accretion, derives largely from Chaucer's *Troilus and Criseyde,* and the underlying assumptions about the Greeks and Trojans are also generally medieval. The plot is partly historical: it deals with what was regarded as the first important event in the world's history. There is some comedy, largely satirical, in Shakespeare's handling of the story. The tone is in many ways tragic, yet no character achieves tragic stature. *Troilus and Cressida* stands alone, a uniquely exploratory work. It is in every way uncompromising. The language is difficult, the action frequently slow, the dialogue philosophical. Great characters of antiquity—Agamemnon, Achilles, Ajax, Hector—are portrayed as all too fallibly human. Helen, the cause of the Trojan War, is shown on her only appearance (III.i) as a silly sensualist. The most poignant figure is Troilus. Shakespeare makes us feel the intensity of his obsession with Cressida as keenly as his bitter disillusionment at her treachery. Yet we also see him, and the other characters, from outside, as through the wrong end of a telescope, distanced, diminished. Then "Love, friendship, charity" are seen as "subjects all / To envious and calumniating Time" (III.iii. 173–174). Agamemnon epitomizes part of the play's effect in his contrast between the "extant moment" and "what's past and what's to come," which is, he says, "strewed with husks / And formless ruin of oblivion" (IV.v. 166). Thersites, the professional fool, is deflating, reductive, savagely bitter, a railer rather than a jester. As he reduces war to its lowest level, so Pandarus reduces love. Pandarus' final, exhausted meditation breaks across the time barrier of the play, linking the past with the present and suggesting a vision of all between as a "formless ruin of oblivion." All that is left of the great events of Troy is a dying old pander, bequeathing his diseases to the audience.

LATER TRAGEDIES

A Swiss visitor to London, Thomas Platter, saw a play about Julius Caesar on 21 September 1599. Probably this was an early performance of Shakespeare's play, in which he turns again to politics. Drawing heavily on Thomas North's fine translation of Plutarch's *Lives of the Noble Grecians and Romans* (1579), he turns history into drama, unerringly finding the right style for the subject; the language is classical in its lucidity and eloquence. And he succeeds once again in relating the particular to the general. Characteristically, the first scene sounds a basic theme: the citizens "make holiday to see Caesar, and to rejoice in his triumph," yet the

Tribunes denigrate him, and their comments on Pompey, the last popular hero, suggest both the transitoriness of human glory and the fickleness of the mob, which will be much exploited later in the play. Caesar dominates the action even after his death, yet Cassius, Brutus, and Mark Antony are of no less interest. Brutus is one of Shakespeare's most problematic characters. He is "with himself at war" (I.ii. 46), and is easily seen as an adumbration of the later tragic heroes. Self-doubt, perhaps subconscious, is suggested by the rhetoric with which he dresses up the inglorious deed in noble but hollow words: "Let's be sacrificers, but not butchers, Caius" (II.i. 166). Soothing self-delusion contrasts with brutal reality as he talks of "waving our red weapons o'er our heads" crying " 'Peace, freedom, and liberty!' " (III.i. 110–111). What this leads to is the senseless and ferocious murder of Cinna the poet (III.iii).

The Romans were especially associated with rhetoric; it is also one of the dramatist's instruments. In this play Shakespeare examines its uses and abuses. With it Cassius seduces Brutus, and Brutus deceives himself and hopes to justify his actions. Caesar creates glory for himself by a rhetoric of action as well as words; and the Forum scene (III.ii) magnificently demonstrates the power of emotive speech to sway men, to lower a crowd into a mob, to overwhelm reason by passion. At its climax we take aesthetic pleasure in the rhetorical virtuosity with which Shakespeare's artistry endows Antony as he calmly, intellectually, manipulates the crowd, finally standing at the still center of the storm of his own creation. Words continue to be important: in the quarrel of Brutus and Cassius (IV.iii), in Antony's taunt that Brutus has tried to disguise his guilt with "good words" (V.i. 30), in the fact that false words cause Cassius' death (V.iii). Antony ends the play with fine words about Brutus, but are they true? Do we know Brutus better than Antony did? Does Shakespeare end with a totally affirmative statement, or an implied question?—with an endorsement of the verdict of history, or a hint that history has its own rhetoric, no more to be trusted than any other of the words of men?

With *Hamlet,* we may feel, Shakespeare's return to tragic territory is complete, yet some critics have classed this work, written and acted by 26 July 1602 (when it was entered on the Stationers' Register), as a problem play. Its rapid popularity is attested by the publication of a pirated, seriously corrupt text—the bad quarto—in 1603. A much better text, apparently based on Shakespeare's manuscript, appeared in the following year. This "good" quarto has about 230 lines that are not in the theatrically influenced First Folio text (1623), which however adds about 80 lines. Editors print a composite version. Shakespeare's source may have been a play, now lost and referred to as the Ur-*Hamlet,* known to have existed by 1589.

Hamlet is exceptionally long and ambitious. It is far-ranging in linguistic effect. Shakespeare's virtuosity enables him to create distinctive styles with which to individualize characters such as Claudius, Polonius, the Gravediggers, and Osric. The play offers a wide variety of theatrical entertainment, including such well-tried pleasures as a ghost, a play-within-the-play, a mad scene, a duel, and several deaths. Emotionally, too, the range is wide. This is Shakespeare's most humorous tragedy. Yet the comedy is never incidental. Polonius' verbal deviousness and Osric's affected circumlocutions, comic in themselves, are among the many barriers to honest communication that intensify Hamlet's tragic dilemma. The Gravediggers' phlegmatic humor is an essential element in Hamlet's contemplation of death. And Hamlet's own wit has both a princely elegance that adds to the sense of waste evoked by his destruction, and a savage intellectuality that defines his isolation from those around him and serves him as a weapon against hypocrisy and deception.

Hamlet's appeal derives from his youth, intelligence, charm, vulnerability, and, above all, his intellectual and emotional honesty. He is a raw nerve in the Danish court, disconcertingly liable to make the instinctive rather than the conditioned response. Though this cuts him off from those around him, it puts him into a position of peculiar intimacy with the audience. And in his soliloquies, Shakespeare shows us Hamlet's own raw nerves. Hamlet lacks a distinctive style, at least until the play's closing stages. This is a symptom of his inability to identify himself, to voice his emotions from within a defined personality. But it enables him to speak in a wonderful range of styles, reflecting the openness to experience that is an essential feature of his honesty. The language of his soliloquies presents us not with conclusions, but with the very processes of his mind. Never before had dramatic language so vividly revealed "the quick forge and working-house of thought" (*Henry V,* V Chorus. 23).

Hamlet's progress through the play is a dual exploration of outer and inner worlds. The ghost's command requires that he discover the truth about those who surround him; it leads also to intense self-questioning about his own attitudes to life and, especially, death. During this process he both undergoes and inflicts torments. He causes mental suffering to his mother and to Ophelia, for whose death he is indirectly responsible. He kills Polonius and engineers the deaths of Rosencrantz and Guildenstern. He arrives finally at the truth about the world around him. Whether he ultimately reaches a state of self-knowledge and acceptance is less certain. The new quietude that he demonstrates after his return from England suggests to some critics a fatalistic submission to worldly values; for others, it indicates rather a state of spiritual grace reflecting a full integration of his own personality along with an acknowledgment of human responsibility. Generations of readers and spectators share in Hamlet's self-questionings; it is partly because of his openness to disparate interpretation that he continues to fascinate.

Othello, given at court on 1 November 1604 and first published in 1622, must have been written in 1602 or 1603. Like *Romeo and Juliet,* it is based, not on history or legend, but on a contemporary fiction. Shakespeare here transforms a rather sordid tale from Giraldo Cinthio's *Hecatommitthi* (1565), which he seems to have read in Italian. Whereas *Hamlet* is discursive and amplificatory, *Othello* is swift, concise, and tautly constructed. Most of Shakespeare's tragic heroes are royal figures whose fate is inextricably bound up with their nations and whose suffering has a metaphysical dimension. Othello is a servant of the state, not a ruler. His play is in some senses a domestic tragedy, in which we are invited to concentrate on individual human beings rather than to see a connection between their fates and universal, elemental forces. All Shakespeare's tragedies show evil at work. Only in *Othello* is it concentrated in one, centrally placed intriguer. Iago is the playwright within the play. He controls the plot, makes it up as he goes along with improvisatory genius; and, also like the playwright, he retreats ultimately into silence. He is several times called a devil, and historians have seen him as a development of the stereotype of the Vice, an allegorical presentation of an abstract concept. On stage he is as much of a human being as any of the other characters.

In some of Shakespeare's plays we are frequently invited to see the stage action as emblematic of a larger dramatic conflict being played out on a universal stage. The significance of *Othello* resides more purely in the passions and fates of the human beings whom we see before us. But Shakespeare does not present the tale as a documentary imitation of reality. We are made conscious of paradox. Iago, who reveals his villainy to the audience, is "honest" to everyone in the play except Roderigo. Othello's physical blackness joins with the traditional symbolism of black and white as a fruitful source of irony and ambiguity. The language draws our attention to general concepts, and causes us to reflect on the varieties of human behavior. Iago is a rationalist. His characteristic language is a cynically reductive prose; he speaks of the act of love as a bestial coupling: "An old black ram / Is tupping your white ewe" (I.i. 89–90). Othello is a nobly credulous idealist. His "free and open nature" makes him think "men honest that but seem to be so" (I.iii. 393–394). His susceptibility to Iago's corruptive power is a concomitant of his virtue. For him, Shakespeare created a magniloquent verse style suggestive rather of imagination than of intellectuality. The contrast between these two, the way that Iago drags Othello down to his own level, and that Othello, too late, shakes himself clear of him, forms the central dramatic action. The universality of the play lies in our consciousness of Iago's plausibility and our sympathy with Othello's insecurities. Inside the most loving human relationship lie seeds that, once germinated, may destroy it. In Claudius' words:

> There lies within the very flame of love
> A kind of wick or snuff that will abate it.
> (*Hamlet,* IV.vii. 114–115)

In *King Lear,* Shakespeare compounded a story from legendary history with one from prose fiction. Holinshed tells briefly the tale of King Lear. Other versions (all ending happily) include a play, *King Leir,* written by 1594, which is one of Shakespeare's sources. Its publication in 1605 may have given him the impetus to write his play, first recorded in a court performance on 26 December 1606 and printed in 1608. His subplot of the earl of Gloucester derives from Sir Philip Sidney's *Arcadia* (1590). His interweaving of the two stories is crucial to his design. Lear and Gloucester are both faulty but not wicked. Lear has two evil daughters and a good one, Gloucester has an evil son and a good one. Each misjudges his offspring, favors but is turned against by the evil ones, wrongs the good one, suffers as a consequence, learns the truth, and dies. Gloucester's error and suffering are mainly physical. His evil son, Edmund, is a bastard, begotten in adultery. The climax of Gloucester's suffering comes when Lear's daughters, Goneril and Regan, put out his eyes. Lear's fault lies in his warped judgment, and his suffering is primarily mental; its climax is his madness after his daughters have cast him out into the storm. Other characters relate to this patterning. The Fool, physically frail, "labours to out-jest" Lear's "heart-struck injuries" (III.i. 16–17) and to bring him to an understanding of his situation by way of his mind, in snatches of song, witticisms, paradoxes, and parables. Kent, the other servant who remains faithful to Lear through the storm, is more practical, ministering rather to his physical needs. Edmund's sexuality, which in his adulterous relationship with both Goneril and Regan brings about his downfall, recalls his father's. Edgar, Gloucester's virtuous son, metamorphosed into Poor Tom, is of both physical and mental help to his father. The callous, skeptical rationality of Edmund, Goneril, and Regan is opposed to the imagination and sympathy of Edgar, the Fool, and Cordelia.

The employment of the two basic components of human life, the body and the mind, as a structural principle reflects the depth of Shakespeare's concern with fundamentals in this play. In his examination of the values by which men live, he stresses the pre-Christian setting of his story, avoiding any suggestion of religious dogma. His play explores the paradoxes of value. Those who are committed to the world and the flesh destroy themselves. They are deceived by false appearances; so, initially, are Gloucester and Lear. But these two come to "see better" (I.i. 157) when they trust the mind rather than the body. Nowhere is this more apparent than in Shakespeare's causing Gloucester's apprehension of the truth about his sons to follow immediately upon his blinding: "A man may see how this world goes with no eyes" (IV.vi. 150–151). Lear and Gloucester go through purgatory and commune with one another in the amazing scene on Dover cliff. Lear's cynical and disillusioned statements here are only one facet of the play. After this comes his return to sanity and his reconciliation with Cordelia, which is also a reconciliation with life. Nor is this negated by Cordelia's death. This relentlessly unsentimental play puts Lear through the greatest mental torment, but ultimately the man who had vowed never again to see Cordelia's face seeks desperately in her eyes for signs of life. He has learned that she is indeed "most rich, being poor; / Most choice, forsaken; and most lov'd, despis'd" (I.i. 250–251).

His final outpouring of love is unselfish; she can do nothing for him now. Her body is dead and useless, but the values for which she stood are those that endure.

Macbeth, written probably in 1606, is easily Shakespeare's shortest tragedy. Its topic was particularly relevant to the patron of his company, James I, and the only surviving text, of 1623, may have been specially written or adapted for court performance. Holinshed again provided the basic narrative, but, as in *King Lear,* Shakespeare treated it with much more freedom than in the English histories. To a greater extent even than in *King Lear,* he seems more interested in general ideas than in historical accuracy or particularity of characterization. Many of the characters are purely functional. Duncan is primarily a symbol of the values that Macbeth is to overthrow. He is counterbalanced by the equally generalized Weird Sisters. Even Banquo figures mainly as a measure of the norm from which Macbeth deviates. The witches, with their incantations, spells, and grotesque rituals, suggest evil as a universal force that can be tapped and channeled through human agents.

Like her counterparts in *King Lear,* Lady Macbeth, the play's principal human embodiment of evil, attempts to deny the powers of the imagination. A speech from *All's Well That Ends Well* epitomizes this aspect of *Macbeth.* "They say miracles are past," says Lafeu, "and we have our philosophical persons to make modern and familiar things supernatural and causeless. Hence is it that we make trifles of terrors, ensconcing ourselves into seeming knowledge when we should submit ourselves to an unknown fear" (II.iii. 1–6). Lady Macbeth seeks to reduce "supernatural and causeless"—inexplicable—things to the level of the "modern"—commonplace—"and familiar": "The sleeping and the dead/ Are but as pictures. . . . A little water clears us of this deed" (II.ii. 53–54, 67). This is the "seeming knowledge" that turns "terrors" into "trifles," and refuses to acknowledge the "unknown fear" of which Macbeth is so vividly conscious. His imaginative visions almost overwhelm his reason. Better for him if they had, for the play acts out the truth of Lafeu's statement. Lady Macbeth's rationalistic urgings of her husband are at odds with her own incantation "Come you spirits. . . ." (I.v. 37ff.), and when her reason breaks down, her self-assurance is seen to be only a "seeming knowledge" that gives way, too late, to the "unknown fear." Her sleepwalking scene, a soliloquy unheard even by its speaker, is a technically brilliant device to reveal the subconscious acknowledgment in her divided being of "things supernatural and causeless."

In his last three tragedies Shakespeare returns to more fully documented periods of history and, in two of them, to a more particularized presentation of it. The exception is *Timon of Athens,* a problematic play. Thematic resemblances to *King Lear* and *Coriolanus* along with stylistic evidence cause it generally to be dated 1606–1608, but the state of the text, first printed in 1623, is such that study of it can be only provisional. As it appears to have been printed from an uncompleted manuscript, it is exceptionally interesting to the student of Shakespeare's working methods. There are signs of the rapidity of composition with which he was credited by his contemporaries. He seems to have been anxious to lay down the groundwork, to evolve a shape and structure that could later have been filled in. He concentrates on the central role, which is long and taxing. Minor characters might have been developed later; there is uncertainty about some of their names, and there are many anomalies in the action. While some of the language, both verse and prose, is polished, other passages are obviously in draft, veering between verse and prose. There are strong lines of recurrent imagery that might later have been more subtly worked into the structure. The acts of eating and drinking, for instance, and the opposition between roots and gold take on heavily symbolic associations. As in *King Lear,* Shakespeare is concerned with the difference between "true need," which can be satisfied by roots, and superfluity, represented by banquets and gold.

We usually read the play in an edited version, in which some of the imperfections have been smoothed away. Much more tinkering is needed to create a performable text. The result is that this play is peculiarly open to interpretation, raising more questions than it answers. Its strongly schematic quality allies it more closely with *King Lear* and *Macbeth* than with *Coriolanus* and *Antony and Cleopatra.* It is based on Plutarch and treats Timon's story as a two-part structure: Timon in prosperity, followed by Timon in adversity. In the first part, the rich, lavish, magnanimous lord is contrasted with Apemantus, the cynic philosopher. As Timon learns that he has spent all he owned, his flatterers are revealed, in skillfully satirical episodes, as a "knot of mouth-friends" (III.vi. 89), and Apemantus is partly justified. An awkwardly unrelated scene, which might well have become the climax of a subplot, shows the Athenians' ingratitude to Alcibiades. The second part, as it stands, is virtually an interrupted soliloquy by Timon, in which he encounters those he had known in his former way of life. In his misanthropy induced by disillusionment he is as extravagant as he had previously been in his generosity. Now he resembles Apemantus, as a fine scene (IV.iii) between them shows, but Apemantus is a contented cynic, whereas Timon needs to give full emotional vent to his rejection of mankind. The appearance of his steward, Flavius, comes as a reminder of the possibility of love, loyalty, and friendship; and Timon himself accepts, though with difficulty, that he is mistaken in his wholesale denunciation of mankind. The final scenes, showing Timon's death and Alcibiades' successful campaign against Athens, are sketchy.

Timon of Athens is underdeveloped and inconclusive. Its tone is harsh and bitter, though other attitudes are present in Flavius and other servants, in Alcibiades, even in Timon's tirades, which suggest a desire to be reconciled with humanity by the very force with which he rejects it. The play has pungent invective, clever satire, a few passages of noble poetry, a clear if crude structure, and some profound revelations of humanity. We can only guess what it might have become if Shakespeare had completed it.

His remaining tragedies, *Coriolanus* and *Antony and Cleopatra,* both first published in 1623, are based closely on Plutarch and reflect Plutarch's concern with the idiosyncrasies and oddities of human character and with the way such characteristics shape national as well as human destinies. *Coriolanus* (probably written 1607–1608) tells a story of war and peace, love and hate. The broad framework is one of national warfare, epitomized in a personal conflict between Caius Marcius, later Coriolanus, and the Volscian leader, Tullus Aufidius. Their relationship is ambiguous; after Coriolanus has been banished from Rome, Aufidius welcomes him with "I . . . do contest / As hotly and as nobly with thy love / As ever in ambitious strength I did / Contend against thy valour" (IV.v. 109–113). Strife within Rome also resolves itself into a largely personal conflict, between Coriolanus and the two unscrupulous Tribunes. His arrogance, inseparable from his valor, brings about his banishment, so that from being the enemy within the state he becomes identified with the enemy outside it. He is at conflict, too, within his own family. His mother, Volumnia, eager for his fame, expresses her love for him in terms that might rather betoken hatred: "O, he is wounded, I thank the gods for't" (II.i. 114). Sharing his hatred of the commons, she yet advises him to dissemble with his nature to catch their votes, and so forces a conflict within Coriolanus himself. His efforts to play the part for which she casts him produce some comedy, but the issues of integrity and honor with which the play is concerned are focused in his ultimate refusal to do so, "Lest I surcease to honour mine own truth, / And by my body's action teach my mind / A most inherent baseness" (III.ii. 121–122). In his consequent banishment he has to pretend hatred of those he loves. When his family come to plead with him, he is forced into self-recognition: "I melt, and am not / Of stronger earth than others" (V.iii. 28–29). His mother insists again on the need for compromise, for, if he conquers Rome, he conquers her. He "holds her by the hand, silent" in a moment of submission that is also a moment of self-examination.

> O mother, mother!
> What have you done? Behold, the heavens
> do ope,
> The gods look down, and this unnatural
> scene
> They laugh at. O my mother, mother! O!
> You have won a happy victory to Rome;
> But for your son—believe it, O believe it!—
> Most dangerously you have with him
> prevail'd,
> If not most mortal to him. But let it come.
> (V.iv. 182–189)

Acknowledging that he can no longer maintain a godlike aloofness from natural emotion, he accepts the full burden of his humanity and also the inevitability of his death. "But let it come" is the equivalent in this play to Hamlet's "The readiness is all," and to "Ripeness is all" in *King Lear.* But it is the final paradox of the mother-son relationship in *Coriolanus* that Volumnia, in calling forth a full expression of her son's love, brings about his death. Thus closely are love and hate allied.

Coriolanus is a great achievement of the intellect and the historical imagination. Its characteristic style seems to be carved out of granite. *Antony and Cleopatra,* written about the same time (it was entered in the Stationers' Register on 20 May 1608), is less intellectual and even more imaginative. Few of Shakespeare's plays derive their greatness less from their design, more from their characterization and language. Its style is supple, relaxed, and sensuous. Cleopatra rivals Falstaff as Shakespeare's greatest feat of characterization, and her "infinite variety" is created largely by the flexibility and range of the language with which Shakespeare endows her. The scope of *Antony and Cleopatra* is vast. The action takes place over an area that seems particularly large because characters move so easily from one part of it to another, far distant. Empires are at stake; the play is peopled by their leaders. Nevertheless, much of the play's setting is domestic. Many scenes portray the home life of Egypt's queen, and Shakespeare's greatness as a dramatic writer shows itself particularly in a dialogue of nuance, which gives great significance to oblique statements, exclamations, pauses, and silences. So when Cleopatra is brought to comfort Antony after his "doting" withdrawal from battle:

> *Eros* Nay, gentle madam, to him!
> Comfort him.
> *Iras* Do, most dear Queen.
> *Charmian* Do? Why, what else?
> *Cleopatra* Let me sit down. O Juno!
> *Antony* No, no, no, no, no.
> *Eros* See you here, sir?
> *Antony* O, fie, fie, fie!
> *Charmian* Madam!
> *Iras* Madam, O good Empress!
> *Eros* Sir, sir!
> (III.ix. 25–34)

Or, in one of Shakespeare's most pregnant monosyllables:

> *Thyreus* He [Caesar] knows that you
> embrace not Antony
> As you did love, but as you
> fear'd him.
> *Cleopatra* O!
> (III.xiii. 56–57)

But when necessary Shakespeare writes to the very height of his eloquence. Language is intimately related to form, and so a double tragedy presents special problems. In Shakespeare's only other one, *Romeo and Juliet,* the hero and heroine at least die in the same scene; here, their deaths are necessarily separated, and Shakespeare averts anticlimax in the second, Cleopatra's, partly by introducing a new character—the Clown who carries the instrument of her death—partly by the richly symbolic nature of her conversation with him, and, above all, by the transcendent poetry of her closing speeches.

The tension between Egyptian and Roman values in *Antony and Cleopatra* is an aspect of Shakespeare's recurrent portrayal of the opposing claims of festivity and austerity, license and discipline, in plays such as *Twelfth*

Night and *1* and *2 Henry IV.* Style and imagery cause us to relate this conflict to the divergent claims of the imagination and the reason, and to man's sense of the potential glory of human achievement along with his awareness of the limitations imposed by mortality. So, as in *Julius Caesar* and *Troilus and Cressida,* we can both live in the moment and see it in relation to eternity. Antony is "the triple pillar of the world" and a "strumpet's fool" (I.i. 12–13); "Kingdoms are clay" (I.i. 35); "Royal Egypt" is "No more but e'en a woman . . ." (IV.xv. 71–73); and the instrument of Cleopatra's death is a worm. These extremes are shown not simply in opposition, but sometimes in double perspective, at other times, movingly, in dissolution from one to the other: Antony, dying, "cannot hold this visible shape" (IV.xiv. 14), "The crown o, th' earth doth melt" (IV.xv. 63). Ultimately Shakespeare seems to support the values of sensitivity and the imagination. In Falstaff he had done so covertly; here, he does so openly. Enobarbus learns the limitations of reason and regrets that he has followed its dictates; and Cleopatra's ultimate celebration of the flesh in the spirit creates a vision that may lack substance but is glorious while it lasts. No other tragic character except, perhaps, Wagner's Isolde, dies with such exaltation.

LATE SHAKESPEARE

We saw that Shakespeare's return to tragedy overlapped with his later experiments in comedy. Similarly, while he was writing his last tragedies his thoughts seem to have been turning again to comedy, though only, as we should expect, because he saw new possibilities in the form. Four of his late plays make up perhaps the most closely interrelated group among his output. All employ motifs of romance literature. Their plots include highly improbable and supernatural elements. They tell of highborn families and lovers separated by catastrophe, sometimes natural, sometimes humanly contrived. They span large areas of space and time, and involve leading characters in great suffering. Settings are remote. The presentation of character tends to the general and the ideal. Suffering is overcome, obstacles to reunion and reconciliation are removed, sometimes as a result of supernatural intervention, and harmony is restored.

All these characteristics can be found in Shakespeare's earlier comedies, but they are present in greater concentration in what are variously known as the Last Plays, the Romances, or the Late Romances. And these plays have more than superficial resemblances. Shakespeare was never one-track minded. Even plays that employ a relatively narrow focus, such as *Richard II* and *King Lear,* have a range of emotional impact. *Timon of Athens* shows the extremes of a man's experience but, as Apemantus says, little between them: "The middle of humanity thou never knewest, but the extremity of both ends" (IV.iii. 299–301). In his late plays Shakespeare shows a wish to encompass the extremes in a yoking of opposites that will confine a full range of human experience within the local and temporal limitations of a play, and will synthesize the disparate elements so as to allow each to exert its energy.

External influences have sometimes been adduced as an explanation of Shakespeare's change of direction. The increased use of spectacle in the late plays has been attributed both to the growing popularity of masques at court and to the acquisition by the King's Men of an indoor theater, the Blackfriars, which would offer increased opportunities for spectacular staging. Yet the company continued to use the Globe, and the late plays were performed there as well. The first, *Pericles,* presents almost as many problems as *Timon of Athens.* It may have been written before both the purchase of the Blackfriars and the composition of the last of the tragedies. It is based on the old story of Apollonius of Tyre, told by John Gower in his *Confessio Amantis* (1385–1393), and on the version of it in Laurence Twine's *The Pattern of Painful Adventures* (1576?). Shakespeare had already used the tale, in *The*

Comedy of Errors, and his attention may have been drawn to it again by the reissue of Twine's book in 1607. Like *Antony and Cleopatra, Pericles* was entered in the Stationers' Register on 20 May 1608 by Edward Blount, who, however, published neither. A prose romance by George Wilkins, *The Painful Adventures of Pericles, Prince of Tyre,* published in 1608, refers to the play on the title page and borrows from both it and Twine. *Pericles* was very popular on the stage, but the text published in 1609 is corrupt. It was reprinted five times by 1635, but Heminges and Condell omitted it from the First Folio, presumably because they knew how defective this text was and could not find a better. It is so badly garbled, especially in the first two acts, as to have raised doubts about its title-page ascription to Shakespeare, and some scholars believe that it was either his revision of another dramatist's work or a collaboration.

Editors of *Pericles,* as of *Timon of Athens,* smooth away some of its defects. If we read it with sympathy, we can imagine that the authentic play stood high among Shakespeare's achievements. The device of a presenter, the poet Gower, is used to frame and control the far-flung narrative; and the archaic style and naive tone of his choruses induce the proper mood for the reception of a tale of wonder. The initial stages of the action, in which Pericles gains a wife, Thaisa, are episodic; but it gains in concentration with the birth at sea of their daughter, Marina, and Thaisa's apparent death. Even in its damaged state, some of the verse associated with these events has a unique magic. Marina is a mystically ideal portrayal of the power of chastity, and her presence in a brothel, the inmates of which are sketched with truly Shakespearian immediacy, is one illustration of the play's use of extremes. As in all the romances, there is a strong sense that life is controlled by inscrutable, if ultimately beneficent, powers, symbolized by sea and storm. Thus, Marina laments:

> Ay me! poor maid,
> Born in a tempest, when my mother died,
> This world to me is like a lasting storm,
> Whirring me from my friends.
> (IV.i. 18–21)

Out of the tempest comes a calm of which music is the apt symbol. Thaisa, believed dead and committed to the waves, is revived to the sound of instruments, and Marina sings to her father to try to restore him from the coma into which grief has driven him. Their protracted reunion scene, masterly in its control, draws from Pericles' lines in which he expresses two recurrent ideas of these plays: the close relationship between the apparent extremes of pain and joy, and the capacity of the young to renew their parents' lives:

> O Helicanus, strike me, honour'd sir;
> Give me a gash, put me to present pain,
> Lest this great sea of joys rushing upon me
> O'erbear the shores of my mortality,
> And drown me with their sweetness. O,
> come hither,
> Thou that beget'st him that did thee beget;
> Thou that wast born at sea, buried at
> Tharsus,
> And found at sea again!
> (V.i. 189–196)

When Marina's identity is established, the music of the spheres induces in Pericles a vision of Diana leading to the revelation that Thaisa is alive and to the miraculously joyful outcome of the action.

Shakespeare appears to have followed *Pericles* with *Cymbeline,* composed probably 1609–1610 and first published in 1623, in which he implausibly yokes together Roman Britain and Renaissance Italy. The historical background is freely based on Holinshed, and the intrigue tale derives from Boccaccio. The play is peopled by antithetical characters: some, such as Imogen, Pisanio, Belarius, and those children of nature, Arviragus and Guiderius, are paragons of virtue; others, such as Cloten and the Queen, are "Too bad for bad report" (I.i. 17). Iachimo moves from outright villainy to penitence; Posthumus from virtue to debasement brought about by Iachimo's deception, and back to virtue again. Some of the characters seem the reverse of their true selves: the Queen conceals her villainy from most of those around her, Posthumus is made to believe that Imogen is false to him; some—Imogen, Cloten, Posthumus—are disguised for part of the action; others—Arviragus and Guiderius—are unaware of their own true identity. The plot is based on both national and personal opposition: Britain and Rome are at war; many of the characters are at enmity with one another. The design of some of the scenes stresses the falsity of appearance, as when Cloten's attendant lords comment upon him in ironical asides (I.ii), or the Queen's villainous plotting is framed by her instructions to her ladies about gathering flowers (I.v). The language, too, is frequently antithetical. The play's oppositions reach their climax in the scene (IV.ii) in which Imogen, disguised as a boy and believed to be dead as the result of the Queen's drugs, is mourned by the two young men who, unknown to any of them, are her brothers, and lain to rest beside the headless body of Cloten. She has said she values him less than the "meanest garment" of her husband, Posthumus; now he is dressed in Posthumus' clothes. The beauty of the verse in which Imogen is mourned and of the flowers with which the bodies are strewn is juxtaposed with the hideous spectacle of the headless corpse; and her waking speech, in which she identifies Cloten with Posthumus, is perhaps the most bizarre and daring in the whole of Shakespeare.

If this scene gives us both heaven and hell simultaneously, the final one gives us heaven alone. It is prepared for by the appearance of Jupiter to the sleeping Posthumus, which raises the action on to a plane of the ideal. The multiple denouements of the final scene, in which all disguises are removed, all identities made known, and all misunderstandings removed, strike with the wonder—and, unless tactfully performed, the implausibility—of the miraculous achievement of the impossible. In the play's closing lines, Cymbeline celebrates the resolution of discord into harmony:

> . . . Let
> A Roman and a British ensign wave
> Friendly together . . .
> . . . Never was a war did cease,
> Ere bloody hands were wash'd, with such a peace.

Cymbeline is a fantasy, an exercise in virtuosity, intricate in style and self-conscious in its artifice. In *The Winter's Tale,* which Simon Forman saw at the Globe on 15 May 1611 and which was probably written later than *Cymbeline,* Shakespeare engages more closely with reality. The story, based on a prose romance of the 1580's, Robert Greene's *Pandosto,* covers sixteen years and moves in space from the Sicilian court to the Bohemian countryside, and back to the court again. The central character, Leontes, king of Sicily, passes through extremes of emotion, from the near tragedy of his suffering, culminating in the death of his son and the apparent deaths of his wife and daughter, through the "saint-like sorrow" (V.i. 2) of his penitence to the rapture of the ending, in which he is reunited with those he had believed dead.

Shakespeare fully exploits the variety of theatrical entertainment inherent in this material. But whereas *Cymbeline* works largely through the juxtaposition of opposed elements, *The Winter's Tale* is notable rather for the transitions by which the movement between extremes is controlled. Leontes' obsessive sexual jealousy is vividly experienced, but the audience is partly distanced from it by Paulina's ironical attitude and by the grotesqueness of Leontes' language. The first movement of the play reaches a powerful climax in the trial of his queen, Hermione (III.ii). Shakespeare skillfully guides us into the idealized pastoralism of the middle section by presenting the terrible (and improbable) subsequent events—the abandonment of Leontes' infant daughter, Perdita, on the shore of Bohemia along with the deaths of Antigonus and the entire crew of the ship on which they traveled—through the eyes of the comically uninvolved Clown and with the assistance of the notorious bear (III.iii).

Long gaps of time are inconvenient to dramatists. Shakespeare solves the problem in *The Winter's Tale* by giving Time a prominent place in the play's structure of ideas. The opening scene includes a poetic evocation of childhood illusions of timelessness (I.i. 62–74); Time makes a personal appearance, as the Chorus (IV.i); Florizel's love speech magically suggests that Perdita's beauty and his love for her can suspend the passage of time (IV.iv. 134–143); the concluding episodes show time offering opportunities for repentance and redemption; and a sense of renewal is created by the fact that the son and daughter of the estranged kings bring about their parents' reconciliation by their marriage. Also prominent among the play's ideas is the antithesis, commonplace in the thought of the period, between art and nature. Their relationship is explicitly discussed in IV.iv, and a kind of art is apparent in the exercise of the will by which Leontes expresses his penitence and the lovers control their ardor.

These ideas merge in the final scene. Shakespeare departs from his source in keeping Hermione alive, and the daring stroke of making her pose as her own statue is symbolically appropriate as well as theatrically effective. Hermione's resurrection is a conquest over time. Self-control brings its rewards as art melts into nature and the stone becomes flesh. The play ends in the joy and wonder characteristic of romance, but they are counterpointed by our consciousness of the suffering out of which the miracle has emerged.

Shakespeare's last independently written play, *The Tempest,* published in 1623, was performed at court on 1 November 1611; probably he wrote it during that year. In its composition he drew on his reading of Ovid, Montaigne, and contemporary travel literature; but he wove the plot out of his own imagination, creating a fantasy that is his most overtly symbolic drama. We have no reason to believe that he knew he was coming to the end of his career, but it is easy to see this as an exceptionally personal play. In it he disciplines the sprawling material of romance by confining it within the limits of the neoclassical unities that he had employed only once before, in the early *Comedy of Errors.* Instead of following the events of the tale from beginning to end and place to place, he concentrates the action into a few hours and the locale into a few acres. We see only the end of the story; the earlier stages are recapitulated in Prospero's narration. This creates a tension between form and content that finds many correspondences in the action. Like Oberon, Duke Vincentio, and Iago before him, Prospero is a playwright within the play. He seeks to discipline his erring fellows and needs self-discipline to do so. His power, though magical, is limited. He can create visions, but they are easily destroyed: the masque vanishes into air at his recollection of Caliban's malice. Prospero can exercise moral influence, but only over those who are predisposed to receive it. Alonso and Ferdinand are better for their experiences, but Antonio and Sebastian remain unregenerate.

It is easy to see this as an allegory of the artist and his work. The masque can only fulfill its purpose of pleasing and instructing if it is received with sympathy. The artist needs a fit audience. *The Tempest* itself may be regarded as one of the glories of mankind or a load of wastepaper. To this extent it may properly be considered as an autobiographical document. But it is very much more. The compression of the plot necessitates a high degree of stylization. The resultant symbolic action and generalized characterization open the play to a wide range of interpretation. Though Prospero can be seen as an artist, he can be seen also as a father, a teacher, a scholar, a scientist, a magistrate, an explorer, a ruler, even a god. We can discuss the play in terms of the artist and his public; but it relates also to many of the concepts that we have found recurring in Shakespeare's work: art and nature, nature and fortune, the imagination and reason, justice and mercy, sin and retribution, guilt and repentance, right rule and rebellion, illusion and reality, self-deception and self-knowledge.

The Tempest resists clear-cut allegorical readings; this is a measure of its success. It is a supremely poetic drama, not just because it includes some of Shakespeare's greatest poetry, but because it speaks, as the greatest poetry does, on many levels, universally relevant and—if we can hear Ariel's music—universally effective.

SHAKESPEARE AND FLETCHER

Shakespeare's successor as leading dramatist for the King's Men was John Fletcher (1579–1625), known for his collaboration with Francis Beaumont (*ca.* 1584–1616), who gave up writing for the stage about 1613. At about this time, Fletcher appears to have begun to collaborate with Shakespeare. *Henry VIII,* published as the last of the Histories in the First Folio (1623), was in performance, possibly for the first time, at the Globe when the theater burned down on 29 June 1613. For a long time its attribution to Shakespeare was unquestioned, but in 1850 James Spedding propounded the theory that parts of it are by Fletcher, and many other scholars have followed him in this belief. Certainly in its overall layout it is unlike the history plays that Shakespeare had written during the 1590's, though in its elegiac tone, its generalized characterization, and the sense that it conveys of destiny working itself out through human life, it has something in common with his romances. It has less variety than most of Shakespeare's plays and presents a series of tableaux showing, as the Prologue says, "How . . . mightiness meets misery." We see the falls successively of Buckingham, Wolsey, and Queen Katherine, each of them eloquent in resignation. But the play works toward the birth of Anne Boleyn's child, and the last scene fulsomely celebrates not only the future Queen Elizabeth I, but also her successor, the patron of the King's Men.

> So shall she leave her blessedness to one—
> When heaven shall call her from this cloud
> of darkness—
> Who from the sacred ashes of her honour
> Shall star-like rise, as great in fame as she
> was,
> And so stand fix'd.
> (V.v. 43–47)

This speech is not generally attributed to Shakespeare.

Henry VIII has been successful in the theater. It offers several strong acting roles and great opportunities for spectacle, which have caused it to be performed particularly at times of national rejoicing, such as coronations. Some of its most effective passages, including Wolsey's well-known "Farewell, a long farewell, to all my greatness!" (III.ii. 351), are attributed to Fletcher. According to a Stationers' Register entry of 9 September 1653, Shakespeare and Fletcher collaborated on a play called *Cardenio,* now lost, which was given twice at court by the King's Men in the season 1613–1614. A manuscript of it may have lain beyond a play called *The Double Falsehood* by Lewis Theobald, one of Shakespeare's editors, which was acted at Drury Lane in 1727 and printed the following year. The last surviving play in which Shakespeare is believed to have had a hand is *The Two Noble Kinsmen,* a tragicomedy written at some time between February 1613 (the date of the performance of a masque by Francis Beaumont from which it borrows a dance) and 31 October 1614 (when Jonson's *Bartholomew Fair,* which contains an allusion to it, was first performed). It was omitted from the First Folio but appeared in 1634 as "written by the memorable worthies of their time, Mr John Fletcher, and Mr William Shakespeare, Gent." The passages generally attributed to Shakespeare make up about one-third of the play and are characteristic of his late verse style.

The works surveyed in the preceding pages have given Shakespeare his status as the greatest writer in English, perhaps in any language. Like most great artists, he built on foundations laid by other men. His genius was not primarily innovative, though, as we have seen, he constantly experimented with dramatic forms and techniques. The theatrical medium appears to have provided a necessary challenge that sometimes constrained him. In plays such as *The Comedy of Errors, As You Like It, Othello,* and *The Tempest* we feel an absolute matching of content and form. In others, such as *The Merchant of Venice, Hamlet, King Lear,* and *Cymbeline,* signs of struggle may be discerned. The teeming fullness of Shakespeare's creativity results sometimes in writing of convoluted, even bizarre, density and in structures that make exceptional demands in both complexity and length on theater audiences.

Yet his powers as an entertainer were such that his plays can appeal on many levels. The best of them are dramatic and linguistic structures of infinite complexity, which explore mankind's most fundamental concerns. Even in so brief a study as this we have seen something of his interest in government of both the individual and the state, in the moral pressures of society upon the individual, in the part played by reason and the imagination in human affairs, in the need for self-knowledge, in the relation between the past and present, and in the power of language. These are philosophical questions. Shakespeare uses the emblematic and metaphorical techniques of the poetic dramatist to body them forth with a wholly human particularity that is as recognizable today as it was to his first audiences.

THE PUBLICATION OF SHAKESPEARE'S WORKS

Shakespeare seems to have concerned himself with the printing of only two of his works, the poems *Venus and Adonis* (1593) and *The Rape of Lucrece* (1594). These volumes bear his only dedications, both to the earl of Southampton, and are carefully printed. As for the plays, Shakespeare apparently regarded performance as publication. The scripts belonged to the company, which in general was not anxious to release them for performance. But there was a market for printed plays, and several of Shakespeare's appeared first in corrupt texts that seem to have been assembled from memory by some of the actors who appeared in them. These are known as the "bad" quartos. Sometimes, however, printers were able to work from Shakespeare's own manuscripts, or transcripts of them. Texts produced from such authoritative sources are known, even when they are poorly printed, as "good" quartos. Altogether, nineteen of Shakespeare's plays appeared in separately printed editions in his own lifetime, and *Othello* followed in 1622. Some appeared only in bad texts, some only in good ones, and some in both. The Sonnets were printed in 1609 in a good text.

After Shakespeare died, his colleagues John Heminges and Henry Condell undertook a collected edition of his plays. They had at their disposal the printed quartos and a number of manuscripts, some of which had been annotated for theatrical use. They brought them together in the First Folio, which appeared in 1623, with the Droeshout engraving of Shakespeare, their dedication to the brother earls of Pembroke and Montgomery, their epistle "To the Great Variety of Readers," several commendatory poems including the well-known one by Ben Jonson, and a list of the "Principal Actors" in the plays. The Folio included eighteen plays not previously printed but omitted *Pericles* and *The Two Noble Kinsmen.*

No literary manuscript by Shakespeare survives, unless we accept the attribution to him of three pages of a collaborative play, *Sir Thomas More,* of uncertain date. Otherwise the early printed editions give us our only evidence of what Shakespeare wrote. Unfortunately, this evidence is often unreliable and conflicting. There are many misprints both in the quartos and in the Folio, some obvious, some only suspected. When a play survives in both quarto and Folio, there are often divergences that may be attributed to a variety of causes, including errors of transcription; printing errors; theatrical alterations, omissions, and additions; censorship; authorial revision; and so on. Even the Folio-only plays sometimes show signs of departing from the author's manuscript from which they must ultimately derive.

For a long time no systematic attempts were made to correct Shakespeare's texts. In reprints of the quartos, which went on appearing during the seventeenth century, sporadic corrections of obvious misprints were made, but these texts have no independent authority. Nor do the reprints of the Folio of 1632, 1663, and 1685. The second issue (1664) of the third Folio was the first to include *Pericles*; it also added six apocryphal plays.

Only in the eighteenth century was a start made on the process of correcting the early texts and presenting them in newly attractive and helpful ways. In 1709 the playwright Nicholas Rowe issued an edition, in six volumes, which was prefaced by the first formal biography and illustrated with engravings. It was based on the fourth Folio, with some consultation of quartos; but Rowe, like almost all subsequent editors, introduced modernizations of spelling and punctuation. His is the first edition to divide the plays systematically into acts and scenes, and to indicate locations for the scenes. He also made many necessary textual corrections. The process that Rowe began was continued and developed by many later editors with varying degrees of thoroughness and scholarship. For modern readers, editions from Rowe's to those of the mid-nineteenth century are of mainly historical interest; but it is worth remembering that during this period most of the standard emendations were made, and many explanatory annotations that are still current were first offered. Equally, many conventions of presentation were established, some of which continued to be adopted, often unthinkingly, by later editors. Rowe's successors included Alexander Pope (1723–1725); Lewis Theobald (1733); Sir Thomas Hanmer (1743–1744); William Warburton (1747); Samuel Johnson (1765), whose preface and notes put him among the great Shakespeare critics; Edward Capell (1767–1768); George Steevens (1773, 1778, 1785, 1793); and Edmond Malone (1790). Much of the scholarship of these editors was brought together in the second edition of Malone, completed by James Boswell the younger, published in 1823, and sometimes called the Third Variorum. (The First Variorum [1803] was Isaac Reed's, based on Steevens; the Second Variorum was an 1813 reprint of this.)

Of the many complete editions that appeared during the nineteenth century, the most important is the nine-volume Cambridge Shakespeare (1863–1866, revised 1891–1893), edited by W. G. Clark, J. Glover, and W. A. Wright. For many years this edition was the standard text, especially in the single-volume, Globe version of 1864. In 1871 appeared the first volume of the American New Variorum, a play-by-play edition edited originally by H. H. Furness, which is still in progress. W. J. Craig's Oxford edition dates from 1891, and the thirty-seven volumes of the original Arden edition were published from 1899 to 1924.

At the beginning of the twentieth century a revolution in textual studies greatly advanced understanding of the bases of Shakespeare's text and transformed attitudes to the editing of his works. A number of important editions have resulted. *The New Shakespeare* (1921–1966), edited by J. Dover Wilson and others, has valuable notes and other material but is textually eccentric. G. L. Kittredge's (1936, revised in 1970) has a reliable text and excellent notes. Peter Alexander's unannotated, collected edition (1951) is often used for reference, though it follows the line numbering of the Globe. Hardin Craig's annotated text (1951) has been popular in the United States. In 1951 a new Arden began to appear, a one-play-per-volume series with detailed annotation, which in general is now regarded as the standard edition for scholarly purposes. It is still incomplete. C. J. Sisson's one-volume edition (1954) has useful introductions and appendices. The Pelican (1956–1967) and Signet (1963–1968) lightly annotated paperback editions have been reprinted as hardback single volumes; the New Penguin (1967–) offers fuller annotation and more extended introductions. The Riverside edition (1974), under the general editorship of G. Blakemore Evans, has an overconservative text, but otherwise its wealth of ancillary material makes it the ideal desert-island Shakespeare.

There is no end to the editing of Shakespeare, partly because an infinite number of solutions can be offered to the problems posed by his text, partly because different methods of presentation and annotation are required for an everchanging readership, and a little because of advances in scholarship. No satisfactory old-spelling edition has appeared, but those wishing to read the texts as they were originally printed are well served by *The Norton Facsimile of the First Folio of Shakespeare,* prepared by Charlton Hinman (1968), and by the Shakespeare Quarto Facsimiles, edited by W. W. Greg and, later, Charlton Hinman (1939–).

SHAKESPEARE IN PERFORMANCE

We know little about performances of Shakespeare's plays during the years immediately following his death. Court performances are recorded, and it is clear that some, at least, of the plays remained in the regular repertory of the King's Men. The closing of the theaters in 1642, when Cromwell came to power, is the most decisive break in the history of the English stage. When they reopened, in 1660, conditions changed greatly. The new buildings resembled the closed, private theaters of the earlier period rather than the open, public ones. Women took over the boys' roles. Some of Shakespeare's plays, especially the romantic comedies, were not revived. Patents were given to only two companies, and the plays were distributed between them. Some, such as *Hamlet, Othello,* and *Julius Caesar,* continued to be performed in versions which, if abbreviated, were not substantially altered. Others were radically adapted both to suit the new conditions and to conform to changes in taste. Sir William Davenant (1606–1668), who boasted of being Shakespeare's natural son and who had written for the Caroline stage, led one of the new companies, for which he adapted *Macbeth* (1663) and combined parts of *Measure for Measure* and *Much Ado About Nothing* to make *The Law Against Lovers* (1662). He collaborated with the young John Dryden on an adaptation of *The Tempest* as *The Enchanted Isle* (1667; further revised as an opera by Thomas Shadwell, in 1673). Dryden himself adapted *Troilus and Cressida* (1679); Nahum Tate, *King Lear* (1681); and Colley Cibber, *Richard III* (1699). The *Macbeth* had singing, dancing, and flying witches; additional scenes for the women characters; and a moralistic dying speech for Macbeth. *The Enchanted Isle* added sisters for both Miranda and Caliban; balanced Ferdinand with Hippolito, who has never seen a woman; added a female sprite; and greatly increased the play's spectacular appeal. Tate introduced into *King Lear* a love affair between Edgar and Cordelia; omitted the Fool; and sent Lear, Gloucester, and Kent into peaceful retirement. Cibber greatly shortened *Richard III,* altered its structure, added passages from other plays, omitted important characters, and increased the relative length of Richard's role. All these authors rewrote and added speeches. Their adaptations, and others like them, are important because they kept the original plays off the stage, some of them well into the nineteenth century. Cibber's influence extends even as far as Sir Laurence Olivier's film (1955).

The greatest actor on the Restoration stage was Thomas Betterton (*ca.* 1635–1710), who played many of the principal Shakespearian roles, most notably Hamlet. No one of comparable stature emerged until David Garrick (1717–1778) made his sensational London debut in Cibber's *Richard III* in 1741. He excelled in roles as varied as Benedick, Richard III, Hamlet, Romeo, King Lear, and Macbeth. Though he restored Shakespeare's language in some passages of the adaptations, he made new versions of *The Taming of the Shrew* (as *Catharine and Petruchio,* 1756), *The Winter's Tale* (as *Florizel and Perdita,* 1756), and *Hamlet* (1772). His great admiration was largely instrumental in establishing the reverential attitude to Shakespeare as England's major classic author, and the Jubilee that Garrick organized at Stratford-upon-Avon in 1769 was the first large-scale celebration.

This attitude intensified during the Romantic period. Like Garrick, John Philip Kemble (1757–1823) was important as actor, manager, and, to a lesser extent, play reviser. He and his sister, Sarah Siddons (1755–1831), were classical performers: he, impressive as Hamlet, Brutus, and Coriolanus; she, as Volumnia, Constance, and, supremely, Lady Macbeth. Far different was Edmund Kean (1787–1833), volatile and electrifying as Shylock, Richard III, Hamlet, and Othello.

Objections to the standard adaptations were increasingly voiced, and among the earliest to put them into practice was William Charles Macready (1793–1873), who in 1838 restored Shakespeare's King Lear. But the performances of the greatest integrity since the early seventeenth century seem to be those of Samuel Phelps (1804–1878), the actor-manager who presented all but six of Shakespeare's plays at Sadler's Wells from 1844 to 1862. Increasingly during the nineteenth century attention was paid to visual effect. With Macready and Phelps it was controlled with discretion and taste, but Charles Kean (1811–1868), whose major productions were given at the Princess's from 1850 to 1859, sacrificed textual integrity and even theatrical excitement to pictorialism and archaeological verisimilitude. Sir Henry Irving (1838–1905) was a far finer actor as well as the successful manager of the Lyceum.

Reaction against the spectacular tradition began effectively with the work of William Poel (1852–1934), whose productions with the Elizabethan Stage Society (founded in 1894), though textually impure, attempted with some success to return to Elizabethan staging methods and so opened the way for performances in which better texts could be played without rearrangements necessitated by scene changing. He worked with Harley Granville Barker (1877–1946), whose productions at the Savoy from 1912 to 1914 showed that it was possible to combine textual integrity with scenic appeal.

The period between the two world wars included much experimentation, as in the modern-dress productions of Sir Barry Jackson (1879–1961), Sir Tyrone Guthrie (1900–1971), and others, though disciples of William Poel such as Robert Atkins (1886–1972), W. Bridges-Adams (1889–1965), and B. Iden-Payne (1881–1976) directed performances in a more traditional style. Gradually directors increased in importance, though Sir Donald Wolfit (1902–1968) continued the tradition of the actor-manager, and major players, including Dame Sybil Thorndike (1882–1976), Dame Edith Evans (1888–1976), Sir John Gielgud, and Sir Laurence (later Lord) Olivier, distinguished themselves in Shakespearian roles at the Old Vic, the Stratford Memorial Theatre, and elsewhere.

The dominance of the director increased still further after World War II, with the work of Peter Brook, Peter Hall, John Barton, and Trevor Nunn, all of whom have worked at what is now the Royal Shakespeare Theatre, Stratford-upon-Avon, which, since the closure of the Old Vic in 1963, has become the main center of Shakespearian production in England, although important performances have been given at the National Theatre and by many other companies.

Shakespeare belongs, of course, to far more than the English stage. Books by Charles Shattuck and Robert Speaight listed in the bibliography tell something of the story of his popularity in American and continental theaters. Annual festivals at Ashland, Oregon; Stratford, Connecticut; Stratford, Ontario; and in Central Park, New York City, present his work to the great American public. All over the world the plays are enjoyed in many languages, and through the media of radio, television, cinema, and the phonograph as well as the stage. Shakespeare's wooden O has become the great globe itself.

SHAKESPEARE'S CRITICS

Critical comment on Shakespeare by his contemporaries is limited to scattered remarks such as Francis Meres's empty eulogy, William Drummond of Hawthornden's reports of Ben Jonson's informal conversation, and the tributes printed in the First Folio. For a century or more after this, most comment is of a general nature, and much of it tells us more about the taste of the time than about Shakespeare. John Dryden wrote the first important criticism, mainly in the *Essay on the Dramatic Poetry of the Last Age* (1672), the preface to *Troilus and Cressida* (1679), his adaptation of Shakespeare's play, and the *Essay of Dramatic Poesy* (1688). Though he found that "the fury of his fancy often transported him beyond the bounds of judgement, either in coining of new words and phrases, or racking words which were in use, into the violence of a catachresis," he praised Shakespeare nobly as "the man who of all modern and, perhaps, ancient poets had the largest and most comprehensive soul." Thomas Rymer's notoriously destructive criticism of *Othello* comes in his *Short View of Tragedy* (1693).

During the eighteenth century, editions of the plays provided an outlet for opinion. Dryden's view that Shakespeare's greatness lies in his successful imitation of nature persisted. Alexander Pope, in his preface (1725), wrote, "His characters are so much nature herself that 'tis a sort of injury to call them by so distant a name as copies of her." Dr. Johnson, in his magisterial preface and in the pithy notes to his edition (1765), enumerated both Shakespeare's faults and his merits. He found Shakespeare's morality unsatisfying: "He sacrifices virtue to convenience, and is so much more careful to please than to instruct, that he seems to write without any moral purpose." But he also praised Shakespeare as "the poet that holds up to his readers a faithful mirror of manners and of life."

During the later part of the century there developed a fascination with Shakespeare's characters as independent creations, evinced in William Richardson's *Philosophical Analysis of Some of Shakespeare's Remarkable Characters* (1774) and Maurice Morgann's fine *Essay on the Dramatic Character of Sir John Falstaff* (1794), which is romantic in its imaginative identification with the character. Walter Whiter's *Specimen of a Commentary on Shakespeare* (1777) anticipates some of the imagery criticism of the twentieth century.

German interest developed early, and August Wilhelm Schlegel probably influenced Samuel Taylor Coleridge, whose detailed appreciations, seminal in their effect, have to be retrieved from a multitude of sources, including notebooks, marginalia, and other people's reports of his lectures. Coleridge encouraged a reverential submission to Shakespeare, finding that the plays have their own organic unity. William Hazlitt's eulogistic *Characters of Shakespear's Plays* (1817), based in part on his theater reviews, reveals a preoccupation with dramatic character that reflects the nature of performances in an age of great acting. Keen theatergoer though he was, Hazlitt shared some of the sentiments that Charles Lamb expressed in his essay "On the Tragedies of Shakespeare Considered With Reference to Their Fitness for Stage Representation" (1811), in which he argued that the plays suffer in performance. The mid-nineteenth century produced little distinguished Shakespeare criticism, but its later decades saw an increase in scholarly interest, which, along with the establishment of English studies as a university discipline, greatly increased the amount of serious writing on Shakespeare. Edward Dowden's *Shakspere: His Mind and Art* (1875) is a thoughtful study of Shakespeare's development that has had deserved popularity. Much of Bernard Shaw's brilliant, sometimes iconoclastic, criticism is found in the reviews of performances written for the *Saturday Review* from 1895 to 1898. Far different is A. C. Bradley's sensitive, scrupulous, philosophical study, *Shakespearean Tragedy* (1904), limited to *Hamlet, Othello, King Lear,* and *Macbeth,* which is in some respects a culmination of earlier interest in character portrayal.

A reaction against this is found in the work of E. E. Stoll and L. L. Schücking, both of whom sought a more objective approach, insisting that Shakespeare should be considered in the context of his life and the literary conventions of his age. Stoll, in his many writings, asserted the importance of poetry, and the primacy of plot over character. Harley Granville-Barker, in his series of prefaces to individual plays, published from 1927 to 1947, usefully discussed them in terms of the problems and opportunities with which they confront their performers.

In the 1930's the dominance of a school of criticism concerned with close verbal analysis precipitated language-based studies such as Caroline Spurgeon's pioneering *Shakespeare's Imagery and What It Tells Us* (1935), Wolfgang H. Clemen's *The Development of Shakespeare's Imagery* (1936, translated 1951), and the many books of G. Wilson Knight, a verbal critic of great subtlety who has added to our understanding of Shakespeare's symbolism and, more generally, of his imaginative processes. From among the critics of more recent years it is difficult to distinguish equally dominant figures. This may be because we lack historical perspective, but it also reflects the increasing fragmentation of critical approaches to Shakespeare. The bibliography appended to this essay lists important studies of the sources and of the literary and dramatic background by, among others, W. W. Lawrence, M. C. Bradbrook, Geoffrey Bullough, Kenneth Muir, Anne Righter, and Emrys Jones; of the historical background by Hardin Craig, Lily B. Campbell, and E. M. W. Tillyard; writings showing a particular concern with Shakespeare's social environment, by S. L. Bethell and Alfred Harbage; theatrically based studies by Arthur Colby Sprague, Nevill Coghill, John Russell Brown, Marvin Rosenberg, and Joseph G. Price; ones based on psychoanalytical procedures, by J. I. M. Stewart and Ernest Jones; others grounded in moral preoccupations, by Derek Traversi, L. C. Knights, and Arthur Sewell; some with an anthropological basis, by Northrop Frye, C. L. Barber, and John Holloway; and examples of close stylistic analysis by M. M. Mahood, Harry Levin, and Maurice Charney. Most of these critics, and others, are, to a greater or lesser degree, eclectic in their methods. Shakespeare continues to stimulate not merely professional diploma pieces but challenging criticism, because his works remain alive as an intellectual and imaginative force, constantly creating newly fruitful relationships between themselves and those who experience them whether in the theater or on the page. So long as they are enjoyed, there will be something new to be said about them.

Selected Bibliography

This bibliography is, necessarily, highly selective. Individual essays, which often contain good criticism, are omitted; they, along with other items, may be traced through the bibliographies listed in the opening section and through the annual bibliographies, critical surveys, and reviews in the Shakespeare periodicals. Reprints are not listed.

BIBLIOGRAPHIES

Jaggard, William, *Shakespeare Bibliography: A Dictionary of Every Known Issue of the Writings of Our National Poet and of Recorded Opinion Thereon in the English Language,* (Stratford-upon-Avon, 1911); Ebisch, W., and L. L. Schücking, *A Shakespeare Bibliography,* (Oxford, 1931), and *Supplement for the Years 1930–35,* (Oxford, 1937); Smith, Gordon Ross, *A Classified Shakespeare Bibliography, 1936–1958,* (University Park, Pa., 1963); Berman, Ronald S., *A Reader's Guide to Shakespeare's Plays,* (Chicago, 1965, rev., 1973); Stanley Wells, ed., *Shakespeare: Select Bibliographical Guides,* (Oxford, 1973); McManaway, James G., and Jeanne Addison Roberts, *A Selective Bibliography of Shakespeare,* (Charlottesville, Va., 1975).

COLLECTED EDITIONS

W. G. Clark, W. A. Wright, and J. Glover, eds., 9 vols. (London, 1863–1866; 2nd ed., 1867; 3rd ed., revised by Wright, 1891–1893), the Cambridge Shakespeare, on which the Globe (1864) was based; H. H. Furness, Jr., *et al.*, eds., (Philadelphia, 1871–1928; New York, 1929–1955), the New Variorum; C. F. Tucker Brooke, ed., *The Shakespeare Apocrypha,* (Oxford, 1918); J. Dover Wilson, Sir A. T. Quiller-Couch, *et al.*, eds., (Cambridge, 1921–1966), the New Shakespeare; G. L. Kittredge, ed., (Boston, 1936); W. W. Greg and Charlton Hinman, eds., *Shakespeare Quarto Facsimiles,* (London, 1939–1952; Oxford 1957–); Peter Alexander, ed., (London-Glasgow, 1957–); Hardin Craig, ed., (Chicago, 1951); U. Ellis-Fermor, Harold F. Brooks,

Harold Jenkins, and Brian Morris, eds., (London, 1951–), the new Arden; C. J. Sisson, ed. (London, 1954); Alfred Harbage, general ed., (Baltimore, 1956–1967; one-volume ed. [the Pelican], 1969); Sylvan Barnet, general ed., (New York, 1963–1968; one-volume ed. [the Signet], 1972); *Shakespeare's Poems . . . a Facsimile of the Earliest Editions,* (New Haven, 1964), with a preface by Louis M. Martz and Eugene M. Waith; T. J. B. Spencer, general ed., (Harmondsworth, 1967–), the New Penguin; Charlton Hinman, ed., *The First Folio of Shakespeare,* (New York, 1968), a facsimile; and G. Blakemore Evans, ed., (Boston, 1974, the Riverside).

TEXTUAL STUDIES

Pollard, A. W., *Shakespeare Folios and Quartos: A Study in the Bibliography of Shakespeare's Plays 1594–1685,* (London, 1909); Pollard, A. W., *Shakespeare's Fight With the Pirates and the Problems of the Transmission of His Text,* (London, 1917; 2nd ed., Cambridge, 1920); Greg, W. W., *The Editorial Problem in Shakespeare: A Survey of the Foundations of the Text,* (Oxford, 1943; rev., 1951–1954); Walker, Alice, *Textual Problems of the First Folio: "Richard III," "King Lear," "Troilus and Cressida," "2 Henry IV," "Othello,"* (Cambridge, 1933); Greg, W. W., *The Shakespeare First Folio: Its Bibliographical and Textual History,* (Oxford, 1955); Sisson, C. J., *New Readings in Shakespeare,* 2 vols. (Cambridge, 1956); Hinman, Charlton, *The Printing and Proof-Reading of the First Folio of Shakespeare,* 2 vols. (Oxford, 1963); Honigmann, E. A. J., *The Stability of Shakespeare's Text,* (London, 1965); and Bowers, Fredson, *On Editing Shakespeare and the Elizabethan Dramatists,* (Philadelphia, 1955; 2nd ed., Charlottesville, Va., 1966).

REFERENCE WORKS AND PERIODICALS

Shakespeare Jahrbuch, West, vols. 1–99 (Berlin, 1865–1963), vols. 100– (Heidelberg, 1964–); Abbott, E. A., *A Shakespearian Grammar,* (London, 1869; rev., 1871); Schmidt, Alexander, *Shakespeare-Lexicon,* 2 vols. (Berlin, 1874–1875; rev. by G. Sarrazin, 4th ed., Berlin, 1923); Onions, C. T., *A Shakespeare Glossary,* (Oxford, 1911); Stokes, F. G., *A Dictionary of the Characters and Proper Names in the Works of Shakespeare,* (London, 1924); Sugden, E. H., *A Topographical Dictionary to the Works of Shakespeare and His Fellow Dramatists,* (Manchester, 1925); Partridge, Eric, *Shakespeare's Bawdy: A Literary and Psychological Essay and a Comprehensive Glossary,* (London, 1947; rev., 1968); *Shakespeare Survey,* (Cambridge, 1948–); *Shakespeare Quarterly,* (New York, 1950–1972; Washington, D.C. 1972–); Thomson, W. H., *Shakespeare's Characters: A Historical Dictionary,* (Altrincham, 1951); Halliday, F. E., *A Shakespeare Companion 1550–1950,* (London, 1952), rev. as *A Shakespeare Companion 1564–1964,* (Harmondsworth, 1964); Kökeritz, Helge, *Shakespeare's Names: A Pronouncing Dictionary,* (New Haven, 1959); *Shakespeare Jahrbuch,* East (Weimar, 1965–); *Shakespeare Studies,* vols. 1–3 (Cincinnati, 1965–1967), vols. 4–7 (Dubuque, Iowa, 1968–1971), vol. 8 (Columbia, S.C., 1972–); Campbell, Oscar James, and Edward G. Quinn, *The Reader's Encyclopaedia of Shakespeare,* (New York, 1966); Seng, Peter J., *The Vocal Songs in the Plays of Shakespeare,* (Cambridge, Mass., 1967); Spevack, Marvin, *A Complete and Systematic Concordance to the Works of Shakespeare,* (Hildesheim, 1968–1970); Spevack, Marvin, *The Harvard Concordance to Shakespeare,* (Cambridge, Mass., 1973); Kenneth Muir and S. Schoenbaum, eds., *A New Companion to Shakespeare Studies,* (Cambridge, 1971); and Wells, Stanley, *Shakespeare: An Illustrated Dictionary,* (London-New York, 1978).

BIOGRAPHICAL STUDIES

Chambers, Sir Edmund K., *William Shakespeare: A Study of Facts and Problems,* 2 vols. (Oxford, 1930), abridged by Charles Williams as *A Short Life of Shakespeare With the Sources* (Oxford, 1933); Hotson, Leslie, *Shakespeare Versus Shallow,* (Boston, 1931); Wilson, J. Dover, *The Essential Shakespeare: A Biographical Adventure,* (Cambridge, 1932); Hotson, Leslie, *I, William Shakespeare,* (London 1937); Fripp, Edgar I., *Shakespeare, Man and Artist,* 2 vols. (Oxford, 1938); Baldwin, T. W., *William Shakespeare's Petty School,* (Urbana, Ill., 1943); Baldwin, T. W., *William Shakespeare's Small Latine and Lesse Greeke,* 2 vols. (Urbana, Ill., 1944); Hotson, Leslie, *Shakespeare's Sonnets Dated: and Other Essays,* (Oxford, 1949); Reese, M. M., *Shakespeare: His World and His Work,* (London, 1953); Muir, Kenneth, *Shakespeare as Collaborator,* (London, 1960); Bentley, Gerald Eades, *Shakespeare: A Biographical Handbook,* (New Haven, 1961); Eccles, Mark, *Shakespeare in Warwickshire,* (Madison, Wis., 1961); Quennell, Peter, *Shakespeare,* (London, 1963); Alexander, Peter, *Shakespeare,* (Oxford, 1964); Schoenbaum, S., *Shakespeare's Lives,* (Oxford, 1970); Schoenbaum, S., *Shakespeare: A Documentary Life,* (Oxford, 1975; compact ed., 1977); and Speaight, Robert, *Shakespeare: The Man and His Achievement,* (London, 1977).

REPUTATION AND HISTORY OF CRITICISM

Smith, D. Nichol, *Shakespeare in the Eighteenth Century,* (Oxford, 1928); Ralli, A., *A History of Shakespearian Criticism,* 2 vols. (Oxford, 1932); Munro, J., *The Shakespeare Allusion-Book,* 2 vols. (Oxford,

1932), rev. by Sir Edmund K. Chambers; Bentley, Gerald Eades, *Shakespeare and Jonson: Their Reputations in the Seventeenth Century Compared,* 2 vols. (Chicago, 1945); Marder, Louis, *His Exits and His Entrances: The Story of Shakespeare's Reputation,* (Philadelphia, 1963); Oswald Le Winter, ed., *Shakespeare in Europe,* (Cleveland, 1963); Harbage, Alfred, *Conceptions of Shakespeare,* (Cambridge, Mass., 1966); Eastman, Arthur M., *A Short History of Shakespearean Criticism,* (New York, 1968); and Brian Vickers, ed., *Shakespeare: The Critical Heritage,* vol. 1, 1623–1692 (London, 1974), vol. 2, 1693–1733 (London, 1974), vol. 3, 1733–1752 (London, 1975), vol. 4, 1753–1765 (London, 1976), in progress.

SOURCES, INFLUENCES, AND BACKGROUND STUDIES

Naylor, Edward W., *Shakespeare and Music,* (London, 1896; rev.. 1931); Madden, D. H., *The Diary of Master William Silence: A Study of Shakespeare and of Elizabethan Sport,* (London, 1897; rev., 1907); Sir Sidney Lee and C. T. Onions, eds., *Shakespeare's England: An Account of the Life and Manners of His Age,* 2 vols. (Oxford, 1916); Noble, Richmond, *Shakespeare's Use of Song,* (London, 1923; rev., 1931); Noble, Richmond, *Shakespeare's Biblical Knowledge and Use of the Book of Common Prayer,* (London, 1935); Linthicum, M. C., *Costume in the Drama of Shakespeare and His Contemporaries,* (Oxford, 1936); Craig, Hardin, *The Enchanted Glass: The Elizabethan Mind in Literature,* (Oxford, 1936); Curry, W. C., *Shakespeare's Philosophical Patterns,* (Baton Rouge, La., 1937); Tillyard, E. M. W., *The Elizabethan World Picture,* (London, 1943); Pettet, E. C., *Shakespeare and the Romance Tradition,* (London, 1949); Scott-Giles, C. W., *Shakespeare's Heraldry,* (London, 1950); Bamborough, J. B., *The Little World of Man,* (London, 1952); Thomson, J. A. K., *Shakespeare and the Classics,* (London, 1952); Wilson, F. P., *Marlowe and the Early Shakespeare,* (Oxford, 1953); Whitaker, Virgil K., *Shakespeare's Use of Learning,* (San Marino, Calif., 1953); Jorgensen, Paul A., *Shakespeare's Military World,* (Berkeley, Calif., 1956); Geoffrey Bullough, ed., *Narrative and Dramatic Sources of Shakespeare,* (London, 1957–1975); Briggs, K. M., *The Anatomy of Puck,* (London, 1959); Merchant, W. Moelwyn, *Shakespeare and the Artist,* (Oxford, 1959); Briggs, K. M., *Pale Hecate's Team,* (London, 1962); Sternfeld, F. W., *Music in Shakespearian Tragedy,* (London, 1963); Frye, R. M., *Shakespeare and Christian Doctrine,* (Princeton, N.J., 1963); Spencer, T. J. B., *Shakespeare's Plutarch,* (Harmondsworth, 1964); Hartnoll, Phyllis, *Shakespeare in Music,* (London, 1964); Falconer, A. F., *Shakespeare and the Sea,* (London, 1964); Keeton, George W., *Shakespeare's Legal and Political Background,* (London, 1967); Velz, John W., *Shakespeare and the Classical Tradition: A Critical Guide to Commentary,* (Minneapolis, 1968); T. J. B. Spencer, ed., *Elizabethan Love Stories,* (Harmondsworth, 1968); Richard Hosley, ed., *Shakespeare's Holinshed,* (New York, 1968); Gesner, Carol, *Shakespeare and the Greek Romance,* (Lexington, Ky., 1970); Milward, Peter C., *Shakespeare's Religious Background,* (London, 1973); Colman, E. A. C., *The Dramatic Use of Bawdy in Shakespeare,* (London, 1974); Muir, Kenneth, *Shakespeare's Sources,* (London, 1977); and Jones, Emrys, *The Origins of Shakespeare,* (Oxford, 1977).

LANGUAGE AND STYLE

Whiter, Walter, *A Specimen of a Commentary on Shakespeare,* (1794), edited by Alan Over and Mary Bell (London, 1967); Spurgeon, Caroline F. E., *Shakespeare's Imagery and What It Tells Us,* (Cambridge, 1935); Joseph, Sister Miriam, *Shakespeare and the Arts of Language,* (New York, 1947); Clemen, Wolfgang H., *The Development of Shakespeare's Imagery,* (London, 1951); Evans, B. Ifor, *The Language of Shakespeare's Plays,* (London, 1952); Hulme, Hilda M., *Explorations in Shakespeare's Language: Some Problems of Lexical Meaning in the Dramatic Text,* (London, 1962); Vickers, Brian, *The Artistry of Shakespeare's Prose,* (London, 1968); and Brook, G. L., *The Language of Shakespeare,* (London, 1976).

SHAKESPEARE'S THEATER

Chambers, Sir Edmund K., *The Elizabethan Stage,* 4 vols. (Oxford, 1923); Harbage, Alfred, *Shakespeare's Audience,* (New York, 1941); Smith, Irwin, *Shakespeare's Globe Playhouse: A Modern Reconstruction,* (New York, 1956); Hotson, Leslie, *Shakespeare's Wooden O,* (London, 1959); Joseph, Bertram, *Acting Shakespeare,* (London, 1960); Beckerman, Bernard, *Shakespeare at the Globe: 1599–1609,* (New York, 1962); Smith, Irwin, *Shakespeare's Blackfriars Playhouse: Its History and Design,* (New York, 1964); Styan, J. L., *Shakespeare's Stagecraft,* (Cambridge, 1967); Hodges, C. Walter, *The Globe Restored,* (London, 1953; 2nd ed., Oxford, 1968); and Gurr, Andrew, *The Shakespearian Stage, 1571–1642,* (Cambridge, 1970).

SHAKESPEARE IN THE POST-RESTORATION THEATER

Odell, George C. D., *Shakespeare—From Betterton to Irving,* 2 vols. (New York, 1920); Spencer, Hazelton, *Shakespeare Improved: The Restoration Versions in Quarto and on the Stage,* (Cambridge, Mass., 1927); Sprague, Arthur Colby, *Shakespeare and the Actors: The Stage Business in His Plays, 1660–1905,* (Cambridge, Mass., 1944); Hogan, C. B., *Shakespeare in the Theatre 1701–1800,* 2 vols. (Oxford, 1952–1957);

Sprague, Arthur Colby, *Shakespearian Players and Performances,* (Cambridge, Mass., 1953); Trewin, J. C., *Shakespeare on the English Stage 1900–1964,* (London, 1964); Knight, G. Wilson, *Shakespearian Production:With Especial Reference to the Tragedies,* (London, 1964); Christopher Spencer, ed., *Five Restoration Adaptations of Shakespeare,* (Urbana, Ill., 1965); Shattuck, Charles H., *The Shakespeare Promptbooks: A Descriptive Catalogue,* (Urbana, Ill., 1965); Brown, John Russell, *Shakespeare's Plays in Performance,* (London, 1966); Gámini Salgádo, ed., *Eyewitnesses of Shakespeare: First-Hand Accounts of Performances, 1590–1890,* (London, 1975); Shattuck, Charles H., *Shakespeare on the American Stage, From the Hallamsto Edwin Booth,* (Washington, D.C., 1976); Speaight, Robert, *Shakespeare on the Stage: An Illustrated History of Shakespearian Performance,* (London, 1973); Styan, J. L., *The Shakespeare Revolution,* (Cambridge, 1977); and Wells, Stanley, *Royal Shakespeare: Four Major Productions at Stratford-upon-Avon,* (Manchester, 1977).

GENERAL CRITICAL STUDIES

Hazlitt, William, *The Characters of Shakespear's Plays,* (London, 1817); Dowden, Edward, *Shakspere: A Critical Study of His Mind and Art,* (London, 1875); D. Nichol Smith, ed., *Eighteenth-Century Essays on Shakespeare,* (Glasgow, 1903; rev., Oxford, 1963); Bradley, A. C., *Oxford Lectures on Poetry,* (London, 1909); Schücking, L. L., *Character Problems in Shakespeare's Plays,* (London, 1922); Stoll, Elmer Edgar, *Shakespeare Studies, Historical and Comparative in Method,* (New York, 1927); Granville-Barker, Harley, *Prefaces to Shakespeare,* 5 vols. (London, 1927–1947); T. M. Raysor, ed., *Coleridge's Shakespearian Criticism,* 2 vols. (London, 1930; rev., London, 1960); Knight, G. Wilson, *The Wheel of Fire,* (Oxford, 1930; rev., London, 1949); Knight, G. Wilson, *The Imperial Theme,* (Oxford, 1931); Knight, G. Wilson, *The Shakespearian Tempest,* (Oxford, 1932); Stoll, Elmer Edgar, *Art and Artifice in Shakespeare: A Study in Dramatic Contrast and Illusion,* (Cambridge, 1933); Murry, J. Middleton, *Shakespeare,* (London, 1936); Stoll, Elmer Edgar, *Shakespeare's Young Lovers,* Oxford (1937); van Doren, Mark, *Shakespeare,* (London, 1939); Stoll, Elmer Edgar, *Shakespeare and Other Masters,* (Cambridge, Mass., 1940); Campbell, Oscar James, *Shakespeare's Satire,* (London, 1943); Bethell, S. L., *Shakespeare and the Popular Dramatic Tradition,* (London, 1944); Wilson, F. P., *Elizabethan and Jacobean,* (Oxford, 1945); Armstrong, E. A., *Shakespeare's Imagination: A Study of the Psychology of Association and Inspiration,* (London, 1946; rev., Gloucester, Mass., 1963); Harbage, Alfred, *As They Liked It: An Essay on Shakespeare and Morality,* (New York, 1947); Sitwell, Dame Edith, *A Notebook on William Shakespeare,* (London, 1948); Stewart, J. I. M., *Character and Motive in Shakespeare: Some Recent Appraisals Examined,* (London, 1949); Sewell, Arthur, *Character and Society in Shakespeare,* (Oxford, 1951); Goddard, Harold C., *The Meaning of Shakespeare,* 2 vols. (Chicago, 1951); Bradbrook, M. C., *Shakespeare and Elizabethan Poetry,* (London, 1951); Harbage, Alfred, *Shakespeare and the Rival Traditions,* (New York, 1952); Cruttwell, Patrick, *The Shakespearean Moment and Its Place in the Poetry of the Seventeenth Century,* (London, 1954); Knight, G. Wilson, *The Sovereign Flower,* (London, 1958); Knights, L. C., *Some Shakespearian Themes,* (London, 1959); Coleridge, Samuel Taylor, *Writings on Shakespeare,* edited by Terence Hawkes (New York, 1959), repr. as *Coleridge on Shakespeare,* (Harmondsworth, 1969); W. K. Wimsatt, ed., *Samuel Johnson on Shakespeare,* (New York, 1960), repr. as *Dr. Johnson on Shakespeare,* (Harmondsworth, 1969); Rossiter, A. P., *Angel With Horns: and Other Shakespeare Lectures,* (London, 1961); J. R. Brown and Bernard Harris, eds., *Early Shakespeare,* Stratford-upon-Avon Studies 3 (London, 1961); Righter, Anne, *Shakespeare and the Idea of the Play,* (London, 1962); Spencer, Theodore, *Shakespeare and the Nature of Man,* (Cambridge, Mass., 1962); Edwin Wilson, ed., *Shaw on Shakespeare,* (London, 1962); Schanzer, Ernest, *The Problem Plays of Shakespeare: A Study of "Julius Caesar," "Measure for Measure," "Antony and Cleopatra,"* (London, 1963); Kott, Jan, *Shakespeare Our Contemporary,* (London, 1964; rev., 1967); Coghill, Nevill, *Shakespeare's Professional Skills,* (London, 1964); North, Marion B., *Dualities in Shakespeare,* (Toronto, 1966); J. R. Brown and Bernard Harris, eds., *Later Shakespeare,* Stratford-upon-Avon Studies 8 (London, 1966); Hamilton, A. C., *The Early Shakespeare,* (San Marino, Calif., 1967); Rabkin, Norman, *Shakespeare and the Common Understanding,* (New York, 1967); Arthur Sherbo, ed., *Johnson on Shakespeare,* 2 vols. (New Haven, 1968), which are vols. VII and VIII of the Yale edition of Samuel Johnson; Edwards, Philip, *Shakespeare and the Confines of Art,* (London, 1968); Bradbrook, M. C., *Shakespeare the Craftsman,* (London, 1969); Wilson, F. P., *Shakespearian and Other Studies,* ed. Helen Gardner (Oxford, 1969); Jones, Emrys, *Scenic Form in Shakespeare,* (Oxford, 1971); Calderwood, J. L., *Shakespeare's Metadrama,* (Minneapolis, 1971); Goldman, Michael, *Shakespeare and the Energies of Drama,* (Princeton, 1972); Clemen, Wolfgang H., *Shakespeare's Dramatic Art,* (London, 1972); Muir, Kenneth, *Shakespeare the Professional and Related Studies,* (London, 1973); Weiss, Theodore, *The Breath of Clowns and Kings: Shakespeare's Early Comedies and Histories,* (New York, 1971); and Young, David P., *The Heart's Forest: A Study of Shakespeare's Pastoral Plays,* (New Haven, 1972).

CRITICAL STUDIES OF THE COMEDIES

Lawrence, W. W., *Shakespeare's Problem Comedies,* (New York, 1931); Yates, Frances, *A Study of "Love's Labour's Lost,"* (Cambridge, 1936); Campbell, Oscar James, *Comicall Satyre and Shakespeare's "Troilus and Cressida,"* (San Marino, Calif., 1938); Charlton, H. B., *Shakespearian Comedy,* (London, 1938); Gordon, George, *Shakespearian Comedy and Other Studies,* (London, 1944); Stevenson, David Lloyd, *The Love-Game Comedy,* (New York, 1946); Watkins, Ronald, *Moonlight at the Globe: An Essay in Shakespeare Production Based on Performance of "A Midsummer Night's Dream" at Harrow School,* (London, 1946); Knight, G. Wilson, *The Crown of Life: Essays in Interpretation of Shakespeare's Final Plays,* (Oxford, 1947); Bethell, S. L., *"The Winter's Tale": A Study,* (London, 1947); Tillyard, E. M. W., *Shakespeare's Last Plays,* (London, 1948); Tillyard, E. M. W., *Shakespeare's Problem Plays,* (London, 1950); Sen Gupta, S. C., *Shakespearian Comedy,* (London, 1950); Hotson, Leslie, *Shakespeare's Motley,* (London, 1952); Welsford, Enid, *The Fool: His Social and Literary History,* (London, 1953); Lascelles, Mary, *Shakespeare's "Measure for Measure,"* (London, 1953); Hotson, Leslie, *The First Night of "Twelfth Night,"* (New York, 1954); Traversi, Derek, *Shakespeare: The Last Phase,* (London, 1954); Goldsmith, R. H., *Wise Fools in Shakespeare,* (East Lansing, Mich., 1955; Liverpool, (1958); Brown, John Russell, *Shakespeare and His Comedies,* (London, 1957; rev., 1962); Barber, C. L., *Shakespeare's Festive Comedy: A Study of Dramatic Form and Its Relation to Social Custom,* (Princeton, 1959); Evans, Bertrand, *Shakespeare's Comedies,* (Oxford, 1960); Muir, Kenneth, *Last Periods of Shakespeare, Racine, and Ibsen,* (Liverpool, 1961); Green, William, *Shakespeare's "Merry Wives of Windsor,"* (Princeton, 1962); Grebanier, Bernard, *The Truth About Shylock,* (New York, 1962); Marsh, D. R. C., *The Recurring Miracle: A Study of "Cymbeline" and the Last Plays,* (Durban, 1964); Kimbrough, Robert, *Shakespeare's "Troilus and Cressida" and Its Setting,* (Cambridge, Mass., 1964); Frye, Northrop, *A Natural Perspective: The Development of Shakespearean Comedy and Romance,* (New York, 1965); Baldwin, T. W., *On the Compositional Genetics of "The Comedy of Errors,"* (Urbana, Ill., 1965); Hunter, R. G., *Shakespeare and the Comedy of Forgiveness,* (New York, 1965); Tillyard, E. M. W., *Shakespeare's Early Comedies,* (London, 1965); Stevenson, David Lloyd, *The Achievement of Shakespeare's "Measure for Measure,"* (New York, 1966); Phialas, Peter G., *Shakespeare's Romantic Comedies,* (Chapel Hill, N.C., 1966); Young, David P., *Something of Great Constancy: The Art of "A Midsummer Night's Dream,"* (New Haven, 1966); Nuttall, A. D., *Two Concepts of Allegory: A Study of Shakespeare's "The Tempest" and the Logic of Allegorical Expression,* (London, 1967); Price, Joseph G., *The Unfortunate Comedy: A Study of "All's Well That Ends Well" and Its Critics,* (Toronto, 1968); M. Bradbury and D. J. Palmer, eds., *Shakespearian Comedy,* Stratford-upon-Avon Studies 14 (London, 1972); Salingar, L. G., *Shakespeare and the Traditions of Comedy,* (Cambridge, 1974); and Leggatt, Alexander, *Shakespeare's Comedy of Love,* (London, 1974).

CRITICAL STUDIES OF THE ENGLISH HISTORY PLAYS

An Essay on the Dramatic Character of Sir John Falstaff, (1777), Morgann, Maurice, in his *Shakespearian Criticism,* ed. D. A. Fineman (Oxford, 1972); A. W. Pollard, ed., *Shakespeare's Hand in the Play of "Sir Thomas More,"* (Cambridge, 1923); Wilson, J. Dover, *The Fortunes of Falstaff,* (Cambridge, 1943); Tillyard, E. M. W., *Shakespeare's History Plays,* (London, 1944); Campbell, Lily B., *Shakespeare's "Histories": Mirrors of Elizabethan Policy,* (San Marino, Calif., 1947); Ribner, Irving, *The English History Play in the Age of Shakespeare,* (Princeton, 1957; rev., London, 1965); Reese, M. M., *The Cease of Majesty: A Study of Shakespeare's History Plays,* (London, 1961); Sprague, Arthur Colby, *Shakespeare's Histories: Plays for the Stage,* (London, 1964); Richmond, H. M., *Shakespeare's Political Plays,* (New York, 1967); Clemen, Wolfgang H., *A Commentary on Shakespeare's "Richard III,"* (London, 1968); Kelly, H. A., *Divine Providence in the England of Shakespeare's Histories,* (Cambridge, Mass., 1970); Riggs, David, *Shakespeare's Heroical Histories: "Henry VI" and Its Literary Tradition,* (Cambridge, Mass., 1971); Ornstein, Robert, *A Kingdom for a Stage: The Achievement of Shakespeare's History Plays,* (Cambridge, Mass., 1972); Prior, Moody E., *The Drama of Power: Studies in Shakespeare's History Plays,* (Evanston, Ill., 1973); and Berry, Edward I., *Patterns of Decay: Shakespeare's Early Histories,* (Charlottesville, Va., 1975).

CRITICAL STUDIES OF THE TRAGEDIES AND ROMAN PLAYS

Bradley, A. C., *Shakespearean Tragedy,* (London, 1904); MacCallum, M. W., *Shakespeare's Roman Plays and Their Background,* (London, 1910); Stoll, Elmer Edgar, *Hamlet: An Historical and Comparative Study,* (Minneapolis, 1919); Campbell, Lily B., *Shakespeare's Tragic Heroes: Slaves of Passion,* (Cambridge, 1930); Waldock, A. J. A., *Hamlet: A Study in Critical Method,* (Cambridge, 1931); Wilson, J. Dover, *What Happens in "Hamlet,"* Cambridge (1935); Heilman, Robert B., *This Great Stage: Image and Structure in "King Lear,"* (Baton Rouge, La., 1948); Charlton, H. B., *Shakespearian Tragedy,* (Cambridge, 1948); Jones, Ernest, *Hamlet and Oedipus,* (London, 1949); Danby, John F., *Shakespeare's Doctrine of Nature: A Study of*

"King Lear," (London, 1949); Paul, H. N., *The Royal Play of "Macbeth,"* (New York, 1950); Farnham, Willard, *Shakespeare's Tragic Frontier,* (Berkeley, Calif., 1950); James, D. G., *The Dream of Learning: An Essay on "The Advancement of Learning," "Hamlet,"* and *"King Lear,"* (Oxford, 1951). Alexander, Peter, *Hamlet, Father and Son,* (Oxford, 1955); Heilman, Robert B., *Magic in the Web: Action and Language in "Othello,"* (Lexington, Ky., 1956); Dickey, Franklin M., *Not Wisely but Too Well: Shakespeare's Love Tragedies,* (San Marino, Calif., 1957); Bonjour, Adrien, *The Structure of "Julius Caesar,"* (Liverpool, 1958); Spivack, Bernard, *Shakespeare and the Allegory of Evil: The History of a Metaphor in Relation to His Major Villains,* (New York, 1958); Wilson, H. S., *On the Design of Shakespearian Tragedy,* (Toronto, 1959); Levin, Harry, *The Question of Hamlet,* (New York, 1959); Knights, L. C., *An Approach to "Hamlet,"* (London, 1960); Ribner, Irving, *Patterns in Shakespearian Tragedy,* (New York, 1960); Rosenberg, Marvin, *The Masks of Othello: The Search for the Identity of Othello, Iago, and Desdemona by Three Centuries of Actors and Critics,* (Berkeley, Calif., 1961); Charney, Maurice, *Shakespeare's Roman Plays: The Function of Imagery in the Drama,* (Cambridge, Mass., 1961); Holloway, John, *The Story of the Night: Studies in Shakespeare's Major Tragedies,* (London, 1961); Weitz, Morris, *"Hamlet" and the Philosophy of Literary Criticism,* (Chicago, 1965); Mack, Maynard, *"King Lear" in Our Time,* (Berkeley, Calif., 1965); Elton, William R., *King Lear and the Gods,* (San Marino, Calif., 1966); Frye, Northrop, *Fools of Time: Studies in Shakespearean Tragedy,* (Toronto, 1967); Brooke, Nicholas, *Shakespeare's Early Tragedies,* (London, 1968); Bartholomeusz, Dennis, *Macbeth and the Players,* (Cambridge, 1969); Charney, Maurice, *Style in "Hamlet."* (Princeton, 1969); Brower, Reuben A., *Hero and Saint: Shakespeare and the Graeco-Roman Tradition,* (Oxford, 1971); Alexander, Nigel, *Poison, Play, and Duel: A Study in "Hamlet,"* (London, 1971); Rosenberg, Marvin, *The Masks of King Lear,* (Berkeley, Calif., 1972); Muir, Kenneth, *Shakespeare's Tragic Sequence,* (London, 1972); and Honigmann, E. A. J., *Shakespeare: Seven Tragedies: The Dramatist's Manipulation of Response,* (London, 1976).

CRITICAL STUDIES OF THE POEMS AND SONNETS

Hubler, Edward, *The Sense of Shakespeare's Sonnets,* (Princeton, 1952); Knight, G. Wilson, *The Mutual Flame: On Shakespeare's Sonnets and "The Phoenix and the Turtle,"* (London, 1955); Leishman, J. B., *Themes and Variations in Shakespeare's Sonnets,* (London, 1961); Stirling, Brents, *The Shakespeare Sonnet Order,* (Berkeley, Calif., 1968); Booth, Stephen, *An Essay on Shakespeare's Sonnets,* (New Haven, 1969); and Melchiori, Giorgio, *Shakespeare's Dramatic Meditations,* (Oxford, 1976).

RECORDINGS

The Marlowe Society of Cambridge, with professional players, has recorded the complete works under the direction of George Rylands in Dover Wilson's text for Argo. Most of the works have been recorded by professional players in G. B. Harrison's text on the Caedmon label. There are other recordings of individual plays and extracts that may be traced through the catalogs of the record companies.

PERCY BYSSHE SHELLEY
(1792–1822)

G. M. MATTHEWS

I

IT IS NO GOOD making up one's mind too hastily about Shelley. Contemporary reviewers called various of his works a "dish of carrion," "drivelling prose run mad," "the production of a fiend, and calculated for the entertainment of devils in hell." The Victorians thought his lyrics "absolutely perfect"; he was "the Divine" poet. Early twentieth-century critics could see at a glance that there was "no brain work" in Shelley's poetry; it was "antipathetic to the play of the critical mind." Generalizations about him have always differed wildly. To Charles Kingsley, Shelley was "utterly womanish"; to D. H. Lawrence, he was "transcendently male"; and the man whose friends thought him "full of life and fun" while they knew him, T. S. Eliot in 1933 found humorless and pedantic.

Shelley was no perfectibilist. He saw human society in terms of unending struggle, and controversy delighted him, so his work is understandably controversial. But most judgments of it have been impressionistic: rationalizations of instant liking or distaste. The hostile criticism of the 1930's plainly took no trouble to understand the material it was dismissing: that "Alastor," for instance, was not a form of the name "Alastair" but Greek for an avenging fury; that "The Indian Serenade" was Indian, and a serenade; that when a snake renewed its "winter weeds outworn" (in Shelley or in William Shakespeare), it was changing its skin, not raising a fresh crop of nettles. Only in the last fifty years, and chiefly by Americans, has it been shown how complex this deceptively fluent verse often is, and how patiently its symbolic language needs learning.

Poor texts are still a handicap, and there is still room for disagreement. In this language, for example, electricity or "lightning" pervades the physical, as love pervades the moral, world; the fire of sun and stars is the counterpart of the One, the Unity or Spirit that shapes the beauty of the world; and the changing forms of cloud and vapor represent the mutations of matter that "veil" or refract this brightness and resist its influences. Some of the vocabulary is Platonic, perhaps Neoplatonic; but the language is Shelley's. His "Intellectual Beauty" (a phrase from William Godwin and James Burnett, Lord Monboddo, not from Plato) may express itself in revolutionary action (as in the "Ode to Naples," 149–176) and in sexual intercourse (*as in Laon and Cythna*, 2650–2665).

What fascinated Shelley was not *being* but *process*; not John Keats's timeless urn or William Wordsworth's "permanent forms of nature," but the sun-awakened avalanche, the destroying and preserving wind, the "unpastured sea hungering for calm." So it is true that as a poet he never looked steadily at an object for long, and this elusiveness can be irritating to his readers. By a principle of indeterminacy he passed on to what the object was becoming, or to what caused it. But accurate knowledge was generally taken for granted as the starting point of his invention. He was a country boy; most of his life was spent out-of-doors; and he read a good deal about the workings of nature. In many ways he was a very exact poet—more exact and knowledgeable than some of his critics.

Shelley was also a versatile craftsman. Unlike Geoffrey Chaucer, or George Gordon, Lord Byron, he was not interested in the full scope of human activity, but only in the great problem of humanity's place in the universe and of the achievement of happiness. Can man, through self-conquest, master his own future? Shelley's poetry was the changing comment of his own life experience on this unvarying question. But the angle of the comment, the stylistic range, was very wide. He wrote well in many different "kinds": epic, epigram, pastoral elegy, political ballad, familiar epistle, tragedy, lyric, burlesque. He is best known as the poet of fiery imaginings:

> And the green lizard, and the golden snake,
> Like unimprisoned flames, out of their
> trance awake[1]
> (*Adonais*, 161–162)

The colors are heraldic, and oppressed creatures break like volcanic fire out of the "trance" of winter; yet as a physical picture every detail is vivid and apt. He could also write with a sensuous verbal relish not unlike Keats's:

> Blue thistles bloomed in cities; foodless
> toads
> Within voluptuous chambers panting
> crawled
> (*Prometheus Unbound*, I. 170–171)

Again a symbolic description, with a strong undertone of social criticism; yet again it recalls eyewitness accounts of Hiroshima a few months after atomic bombardment. Or his imagery could be plain and familiar: "like a flock of rooks at a farmer's gun"; "as bats at the wired window of a dairy"; "like field smells known in infancy."

1. All quotations are from G. M. Matthews, ed., Shelley: *Selected Poems and Prose* (Oxford, 1964).

One important quality in Shelley's later verse, expressing itself in both rhythm and tone, might be defined as witty play:

> Where light is, chameleons change
> Where love is not, Poets do:
> ("An Exhortation," 14–15)

This "power of entering thoroughly into the spirit of his own humour," as Shelley's cousin Thomas Medwin remembered it, not only informs long poems like "The Witch of Atlas" and the "Hymn to Mercury," but also can be recognized in the absorbed dramatic roles of lyrics such as "The Cloud" and "The Two Spirits." Until recently readers have been unwilling to notice this quality. When Francis Palgrave and Alfred, Lord Tennyson, put "The Invitation" into *The Golden Treasury* in 1861, they left out the playfully mocking middle passage, presumably because they thought it spoiled the serious idealism of the poem.

Shelley was not a particularly self-centered poet. Less than six percent of the poems in his *Collected Works* begin with the first-person pronoun, compared with more than fifteen percent of those in William Butler Yeats's; and only nineteen percent of his first lines contain "I," "me," "my," "mine," compared with nearly twenty-three percent of John Dryden's. The test is a rough one, of course, since the pronoun "I" does not necessarily mean the writer; but that is as true in Shelley as in Yeats or Dryden.

II

Percy Bysshe Shelley was born on 4 August 1792 at Field Place, near Horsham, Sussex. His father was the heir of an American-born adventurer who had twice married money, and who became a baronet in 1806. His family called him Bysshe, after his grandfather; his first wife called him Percy; and everyone else has simply called him Shelley.

As the indulged eldest son of a country gentleman and member of Parliament, Shelley became a fair horseman, an excellent shot, and a memorable practical joker; and by his early teens he was already romantically devoted to a pretty cousin, Harriet Grove. But in adolescence he could not take his conventional, rather dim-witted father seriously as an advocate of Whig ideals such as parliamentary reform, and sometimes mocked his shortcomings not only to friends but even—less openly—in letters to his father himself.

Shelley's uncompetitive home life had not fitted him for survival at Eton, where he was savagely ragged for his non-conformism. (He entered in 1804.) But though vulnerable, he was fearless; and it was probably at Eton that the self-commitment recorded in his dedication to *Laon and Cythna* was made:

> I will be wise,
> And just, and free, and mild, if in me lies
> Such power, for I grow weary to behold
> The selfish and the strong still tyrannize
> Without reproach or check.
> (31–35)

He would not learn what his "tyrants" taught, he decided, but would "Heap knowledge from forbidden mines of lore"—from science, for example (then outlawed at Eton), and the writings of Godwin and the French skeptics. His tyrants did succeed in teaching him Latin and Greek.

Just before Shelley entered University College, Oxford, in October 1810, the parents concerned broke off his friendship with Harriet Grove, alarmed at its effects on her beliefs, and she dutifully married the nephew of a clergyman. In the spring of 1811, Shelley was sent down from Oxford for circulating an unsigned leaflet, *The Necessity of Atheism,* written with his friend Thomas Jefferson Hogg, who shared the same fate.

The shock of these arbitrary acts confirmed Shelley's intellectual revulsion from Christianity. His reaction, in August 1811, was to elope with a sixteen-year-old friend of his sister's, Harriet Westbrook. This marriage failed, but not before it had inspired his first important poem. Even at twenty-one Shelley was a well-published author, with two prose thrillers to his discredit and two volumes of mainly sensational, "gothic" verse.

Queen Mab, never regularly published, was, ironically, the one popular success of Shelley's career. From 1821 on, it was frequently reprinted—more to the author's amusement than dismay—and became one of the most respected texts in the Radical working-class movement, "the Chartists' Bible."

There is much in it to deserve respect. The fairy title was camouflage to cover "long notes against Jesus Christ, & God the Father and the King & the Bishops & marriage & the Devil knows what," as Shelley later remembered them, so that *Queen Mab,* like all his political verse, was solidly buttressed by prose argument. But the poem has a plain, simple structure—a perspective of the past, present, and future conditions of mankind—and the writing, though modeled on the irregular verse of Robert Southey's *Thalaba the Destroyer* (1801), is hard and clear. Many features of *Queen Mab* have a continuous development throughout Shelley's subsequent work. Human society is always seen in a cosmic setting, and human history as inseparable from the history of stars and insects. From the vantage point to which Mab has carried her, the soul of Ianthe (Harriet) is shown

> The flood of ages combating below,
> The depth of the unbounded universe
> Above, and all around
> Nature's unchanging harmony.
> (II. 254-Z57)

The order of nature is unchanging, a "wilderness of harmony," but its constituent parts are "combating below" in a continual storm of change. Thus the ruined civilizations that Mab exhibits are not—as in many eighteenth-century poems—mere illustrations of human pride humbled by time; they are part of a process in which man is endlessly implicated with nature. Necessity, "mother of the world" and moving in it everywhere like the West Wind, rules this "Imperishable change / That renovates the world." Only man does not yet cooperate. "Matter, with all its transitory shapes, / Lies subjected and plastic at his feet"; but he cannot master it, not by reason of his supposed

evil nature, that apology
Which kings who rule, and cowards who
crouch, set up
For their unnumbered crimes
(IV. 76–78)

but because his false institutions and superstitions offend the natural law. "Nature rejects the monarch, not the man."

Yet life goes on aspiring, "like hungry and unresting flame," and must triumph in the end. Then the playthings of man's social childhood—thrones, cathedrals, prisons—will be abandoned, and man will take his place among his fellow creatures in the natural order:

. . . Man has lost
His terrible prerogative, and stands
An equal amidst equals . . .
(VIII. 225–227)

Men and women, too, will be equal, and thus truly free to love; the old quarrel between passion and reason will end once sexual relations are no longer distorted by commercial exploitation or venereal disease. And eventually the nightshade berries will outgrow their old habit of being poisonous, and the lions their customary fierceness.

Much of the egalitarianism of *Queen Mab,* its sun that shines as sweetly on cottage thatch as on the domes of palaces, was traditional. The style, too, was still eighteenth-century rather than romantic. Shelley did not find his way back to this sort of harsh clarity until the very different "Triumph of Life" a decade later.

For some three years after the writing of *Queen Mab,* Shelley's hectic life gave him little time for poetry; and the forms of direct action that he tried first—agitation in Ireland, land reclamation in Wales—resulted in prose tracts and manifestos rather than poems. Harriet's role as wife of a "committed" poet was hard to keep up, and the gap between their interests widened. In 1814, Shelley met Mary Godwin, daughter of Mary Wollstonecraft and the radical thinker William Godwin; and after a brief agony of indecision, they fled to Switzerland together, accompanied by Mary's stepsister Claire Clairmont.

The practical result of this second elopement was a year desperately spent in trying to raise credit on which to live and in dodging creditors. The strain made Shelley ill; he was told he was dying of consumption. Not until the summer of 1815, when his grandfather died, was there a reasonable subsistence for all concerned.

But in August, Shelley, now permanently addicted to boats, made a ten-day voyage up the Thames that mended his health and resulted in the first poem of his early maturity. *Alastor* is exploratory, a languidly beautiful product of convalescence. It is broadly in the eighteenth-century tradition of James Beattie's *The Minstrel,* that of moralizing on the way various experiences affect the sensibility of a young genius, but its landscapes are no longer diagrams thrown on a cosmic screen: they are symbolic, inseparable from the psychic and emotional states of the Poet passing through them.

The Greek title "Alastor," an avenging power, applies to the "self-centred seclusion" that tempts the Poet to waste his life in pursuing a dream lover of impossible perfection instead of making do with the love of his fellow beings. Was Shelley thinking mainly of himself? (He had given up direct political action, and a quiet country life certainly tempted him: a little later he was styling himself the "Hermit of Marlow.") Or Wordsworth? Or Coleridge? Short poems critical of both were included in the *Alastor* volume, but Shelley always took care that the minor poems in his collections matched the principal one. In any case, as the preface admits, his sympathies were on both sides; and the poem tends to romanticize what it was supposed to condemn.

Six weeks of the summer of 1816 were spent on the Lake of Geneva, near Lord Byron. The meeting was occasioned by Byron's liaison with Claire Clairmont; but the two poets liked each other, and their mutual literary admiration, at least, remained to the end. At this time Wordsworth's intuition in "Tintern Abbey" of

> A motion and a spirit, that impels
> All thinking things, all objects of all
> thought,
> And rolls through all things

was beginning to haunt Shelley's imagination. In "Mont Blanc," a poem the obscurity of which is partly due to technical clumsiness, the mountain embodies a secret Power, perhaps identical with Necessity, that, once acknowledged, could regenerate the world. In a companion "Hymn to Intellectual Beauty," reworked after his return home, Shelley celebrates "Intellectual Beauty" almost as the spiritual aspect of this immanent power, a radiance that invests Necessity with sympathy and loveliness, somewhat as Asia in *Prometheus Unbound* spiritualizes the inscrutable Demogorgon.

Back in England, the suicide of Fanny Imlay (Mary Shelley's half sister) on 9 October 1816 was swiftly followed by Harriet's suicide, in obscure circumstances; and early the following year the lord chancellor, John Scott, 1st earl of Eldon, ruled that Shelley was not fit to take care of Harriet's two children, although he had regularized his claim on them by marrying Mary. His friendships with Hogg, Thomas Love Peacock, and especially Leigh Hunt helped Shelley through these disastrous months. Hunt introduced him to John Keats, and the two young poets agreed each to complete a 4,000-line poem during the summer of 1817. Shelley's poem was *Laon and Cythna; or, The Revolution of the Golden City: A Vision of the Nineteenth Century,* a romance epic in Spenserian stanzas. Despite its Turkish setting, it was intended as a lesson to those supporters of the French Revolution who had been disillusioned by events since 1789. There is no easy optimism here (nor, indeed, anywhere else in Shelley's poems). Although the road to egalitarian objectives is always open, it leads through disappointment, bloody defeat, sacrifice, and death. To "break through the crust of those outworn opinions on which established institutions depend," Shelley made his revolutionary lovers brother and sister (the biological hazards not then being understood), and also stressed the bloodthirstiness of Christianity; but his publisher prevailed on him to modify these features, and to adopt a tactfully distancing title, *The Revolt of Islam.*

This poem has had very few to praise, and none to love it. Whereas the realism of its great prototype, *The Faerie Queene,* vitalizes the allegory, Shelley's symbolic treatment undermines the intended human interest. What stay in the mind are single images, as of the sunlit sea depths from which a diver "Passed like a spark sent up out of a burning oven," and single episodes, such as the opening duel between the eagle of darkness and the snake of light, the description of plague and famine in canto X, and Laone's hymn of hope during the "winter of the world" in canto IX, which anticipates the seasonal imagery of the "Ode to the West Wind."

Shelley was very depressed by the failure of *The Revolt of Islam,* still feeling, three years later, that its "date should have been longer than a day." This and the move to Italy in the spring of 1818—partly for the sunshine, partly to take Claire Clairmont's illegitimate daughter Allegra to her father, Byron—temporarily unsettled him. When he could "absolutely do nothing else" he translated Plato's *Symposium* and the *Cyclops* of Euripides. But August brought the stimulus of a reunion with Byron in Venice. Claire wanted to see her little girl again, and Shelley had gone alone to negotiate a meeting. He succeeded—but when his family joined him at the villa near Este that Byron had lent them, the long, hot journey from Leghorn proved too much for his own year-old daughter Clara. She died of dysentery soon after arrival.

Out of this loss came the "Lines Written Among the Euganean Hills," a minor masterpiece. From the highest point of the Colli Euganei, on the lower slopes of which the Shelleys were living, could be seen Padua and Venice to the east, the Alps to the north, and the Apennines to thc south. Islanded in space, making one October day an island in the flux of time, Shelley moves out of the storms of his own life to prophesy over the cities of the plain, enslaved and corrupted by foreign occupation, yet transfigured momentarily under the eternal sunlight. As usual he writes best when his private feelings dissolve into feeling for others; but even the "mariner" of the opening lines is not himself only, for the date is only a week from the anniversary of Fanny Imlay's suicide.

Just as individual lives are wrecked because love is willfully withheld until it is too late, so Venice and Padua face destruction because they lack the will to assert their ancient greatness. The line "Men must reap the things they sow" is bitterly ironical, for the harvests are being gathered—to supply the invader. The meter is that of John Milton's "L'Allegro," a favorite measure in the eighteenth century used, for instance, in John Dyer's Grongar Hill poems, and one with a flexibility that appealed to Shelley,

> And of living things each one,
> And my spirit which so long
> Darkened this swift stream of song,
> Interpenetrated lie
> By the glory of the sky:
> Be it love, light, harmony,
> Odour, or the soul of all
> Which from heaven like dew doth fall,
> Or the mind which feeds this verse
> Peopling the lone universe.
> (310–319)

There was reason for the new note of artistic assurance in this poem. Act I of *Prometheus Unbound* had just been finished.

Prometheus Unbound, Shelley's central poetic achievement, was composed over three widely spaced sessions that it will be necessary to treat as one. All but this first act was written during 1819: Acts II and III in the spring, at Rome, and Act IV in the autumn, at Leghorn and Florence. The "myth" of the poem is the great European humanist myth of the Titan who steals fire from the sun and teaches man all the arts and sciences, in defiance of an outraged deity. Shelley's version derives from that of Aeschylus' *Prometheus Bound* (and it is Aeschylus' Prometheus, not Shelley's, that is discussed in the preface); but he reminds readers of his great predecessor partly in order to underline the differences. *Prometheus Bound* was one play of a trilogy in which the hero eventually compromised with Jupiter; Shelley reorders the myth so that it will incorporate the knowledge gained in the struggle for human emancipation since the fifth century B.C.

Prometheus Unbound, as Shelley explained in the preface, was not a program of action, which could better be provided in prose tracts such as the "Essay on Christianity" and the "Philosophical View of Reform"; it was an "idealism"—an imaginative picture of "what ought to be, or may be"—meant to condition people's minds for the stupendous changes that society must undergo in becoming truly human. "Man must first dream the possible before he can do it." So even where the poem is closest to allegory, its characters cannot be translated exactly into moral or political terms, and different aspects of their significance are emphasized at different moments. Nor can the poem be summed up as a "drama in the mind"—or even in a universal Mind—although some of its actions are mental, such as Prometheus' renunciation of the curse, and his torture by the Furies, who represent his own temptations to despair.

At one level the poem mirrors the contemporary social order. Jupiter represents the ruling classes of Europe with their apparatus of repression and propaganda:

> Thrones, altars, judgement-seats, and
> prisons; wherein,
> And beside which, by wretched men were
> borne

Sceptres, tiaras, swords, and chains, and
tomes
Of reasoned wrong, glozed on by
ignorance. . . .
(III. iv. 164–167)

Freedom can come only when this entrenched order is overthrown from below. But from another viewpoint all these repressive institutions, and the prestige that makes them effective, exist because mankind installed them and tolerated them: they "were, for his will made or suffered them," and man is able to undo his own mistakes. Jupiter is in this sense the creation of Prometheus. This is why he is described at his fall as "sunk, withdrawn, covered, drunk up / By thirsty nothing"—a mere hole in social and moral space that Love fills up.

At the beginning of the drama, the position is deadlocked. To defy power keeps hope alive, yet defiance alone cannot either dislodge the old regime or create a new one. Necessity, the natural law, cannot operate as one day it must, until the right conditions are met; and one essential condition is that Prometheus should give up his adversary's vindictive attitude of mind. Milton's God in *Paradise Lost* had allowed Satan freedom to act, "That with reiterated crimes he might / Heap on himself damnation." But Prometheus learns through centuries of suffering to forgo revenge; then Asia (Love, his wife and natural counterpart) can be inducted willingly into the realm of Demogorgon. Thus Love, the law that governs the moral world, interacts with Necessity, the law that governs all other worlds, and the Hour of liberation is released.

The imaginative implications of this unusual "plot" are many-sided. Appropriately in a drama about Prometheus, Shelley made part of the action into a geophysical metaphor. The scientist James Hutton had recently explained how the earth recreated itself by periodic cycles of volcanic activity, and it was believed that eruptions were triggered by the entry of water from the sea. So when Asia and her sea sisters penetrate the mountain of Demogorgon, who is described as if he were made of molten lava, they activate an eruption out of which the old earth is reborn. As Sir Humphry Davy had observed of volcanoes in 1811, "The evil produced is transient; the good is permanent. The ashes which buried Pompeii have rendered a great country continually productive. The destruction is small and partial—the benefit great and general." Shelley constantly used volcanic imagery in his poetry. Christianity placed God in Heaven and the Devil in the Pit; but for Shelley evil was rained from above, while the ultimate source of power and energy was located below, at the center. So the earth produced "fountains," or springs, and breathed up exhalations; these might be mischievous, corrupted as earth was under Jupiter, but in origin they were the "wine of life," sources of inspiration, prophecy, and action.

The dramatic center of Act I is the confrontation between Prometheus and the Furies, who are brought by Mercury to force him into despair. The contrast between the mealy-mouthed, self-indulgence of Mercury and the tight-lipped, dismissive irony of Prometheus is very effective:

Mercury. Thou canst not count thy years
to come of pain?
Prometheus. They last while Jove must
reign; nor more, nor less
Do I desire or fear.
Mercury. Yet pause, and plunge
Into Eternity, where recorded time,
Even all that we imagine, age on age,
Seems but a point, and the reluctant mind
Flags wearily in its unending flight,
Till it sink, dizzy, blind, lost, shelterless;
Perchance it has not numbered the slow
years
Which thou must spend in torture,
unreprieved?
Prometheus. Perchance no thought can
count them, yet they pass.
Mercury. If thou might'st dwell among
the Gods the while
Lapped in voluptuous joy?
Prometheus. I would not quit
This bleak ravine, these unrepentant pains.
Mercury. Alas! I wonder at, yet pity thee.

> *Prometheus.* Pity the self-despising slaves of Heaven,
> Not me, within whose mind sits peace serene,
> As light in the sun, throned: how vain is talk!
> Call up the fiends.
> (I. 414–432)

To the Furies, Prometheus is curt and laconic:

> Pain is my element, as hate is thine;
> Ye rend me now: I care not.
> (I. 477–478)

And there is equal economy of language in a Fury's demoralizing summary of human impotence: even the greatest human figures

> . . . dare not devise good for man's estate,
> And yet they know not that they do not dare.
> The good want power, but to weep barren tears.
> The powerful goodness want: worse need for them.
> The wise want love, and those who love want wisdom;
> And all best things are thus confused to ill.
> (I. 623–628)

The wintry poetic language of the alpine first act matches the dramatic situation; the language of the second act, borrowing its scenery from the luxuriant area around Naples, opens with a burst of colors to match the revitalizing forces set in motion by Prometheus' change of heart. In one dialogue—virtually a monologue—Asia is inspired to speculate, to the limit of her own insight (and Shelley's), on the authorship of evil; but some of the most original writing in this act is lyrical. In the "Semichorus of Spirits," a key passage with its remarkable reconcilement of free will and determinism in the final stanza, the clogged movement, the intricate syntax, the images of vegetation, gloom, and moisture aptly suggest the dense forest surrounding the causal source of material life:

> Nor sun, nor moon, nor wind, nor rain
> Can pierce its interwoven bowers,
> Nor aught, save where some cloud of dew,
> Drifted along the earth-creeping breeze
> Between the trunks of the hoar trees,
> Hangs each a pearl in the pale flowers
> Of the green laurel, blown anew;
> . . .
> And the gloom divine is all around;
> And underneath is the mossy ground.
> (II. ii. 5–11; 22–23)

The "Voice in the Air, Singing" in celebration of Asia is at another extreme, for here Asia is to Demogorgon as spiritual light is to physical heat:

> Child of Light! thy limbs are burning
> Through the vest which seems to hide them,
> As the radiant lines of morning
> Through the clouds ere they divide them;
> And this atmosphere divinest
> Shrouds thee wheresoe'er thou shinest.
> (II. v. 54–59)

In Act III, after Jupiter has fallen, the gradual change to a new civilization is abridged for formal reasons; there seems to be little difference in things at first, but by the end the old idols are moldering ruins. And as in *Queen Mab,* not only is man reaching out into the deeps of space, but his morality is affecting the ecology of nature. The precision and quality of the lines in which the Spirit of the Earth rejoices over this development prove how seriously Shelley took it:

> All things had put their evil nature off:
> I cannot tell my joy, when o'er a lake
> Upon a drooping bough with nightshade twined,
> I saw two azure halcyons clinging downward
> And thinning one bright bunch of amber berries
> With quick long beaks, and in the deep there lay
> Those lovely forms imaged as in a sky. . . .
> (III. iv. 77–83)

Act IV, the lyrical "cosmic dance" added to the poem when it was already half-copied for the printer, is patchy, but fascinating, as Mary Shelley said, for its "abstruse and imaginative theories with regard to the Creation." The extraordinary song of the Moon to the Earth, which turns gravitation into a metaphor of sexual love, is an example of the unique kind of analogical vitality that Shelley could derive from physical science:

I, thy crystal paramour
Borne beside thee by a power
Like the polar Paradise,
Magnet-like, of lovers' eyes;
. . .
Sheltered by the warm embrace
Of thy soul, from hungry space. . . .
(IV. 463–466; 479–480)

The end of the act is, in effect, a proclamation by Demogorgon to his reclaimed empire, summarizing the central experience of the poem:

To defy Power, which seems omnipotent;
To love, and bear; to hope, till Hope creates
From its own wreck the thing it contemplates;
Neither to change, nor falter, nor repent;
This, like thy glory, Titan! is to be
Good, great and joyous, beautiful and free;
This is alone Life, Joy, Empire and Victory.
(IV. 572–578)

From Este, with *Prometheus* one-quarter finished, the Shelleys traveled south to winter in Naples, an obscure and unhappy period in which only the "Stanzas Written in Dejection" were completed. But it is probable that "Julian and Maddalo," though planned at Este, was mostly written between Acts I and II of *Prometheus*; if so, Shelley was already experimenting consciously in a very different, familiar style, and a "*sermo pedestris* way of treating human nature," in the middle of his lyrical drama. The successful parts are in fact its vivid descriptions of Venice and its imitations of "the actual way in which people talk with each other"—in this case Julian (Shelley) and Maddalo (Byron), on the shores and canals of Venice:

Of all that earth has been or yet may be,
All that vain men imagine or believe,
Or hope can paint or suffering may achieve,
We descanted, and I (for ever still
Is it not wise to make the best of ill?)
Argued against despondency, but pride
Made my companion take the darker side.
(43–49)

So Julian maintains, once more, that men are enslaved to evil because they make no effort to be otherwise; "it is our will / That thus enchains us to permitted ill." "You talk Utopia" Maddalo retorts; men are too weak ever to control their own destinies. And he supports his case by showing Julian someone whose reason has been destroyed by personal suffering. Perhaps the concept of this maniac derives from the madness of Torquato Tasso, and parts of his story from the private affairs of Shelley or Byron, but the episode as a whole is a "comment for the text of every heart." The poem ends with the argument still unsettled.

"Julian and Maddalo" subtitled "A Conversation" was a stylistic bridge between *Prometheus Unbound* and the "sad reality" of *The Cenci,* which Shelley wrote for the stage. All that he ironically called "mere poetry" was banished from the script, which was to be objective and lucid, "a delineation of passions which I had never participated in, in chaste language," and the principal part was angled toward a particular actress, Eliza O'Neill. But the true-life plot proved too unchaste for the theater management; Miss O'Neill could not be asked even to read it.

The heroine, Beatrice, is a mortal Prometheus who, because her oppressor is hateful, cannot help hating him, and answers rape with murder. Her conviction that a just God endorses her deed is so sustained and passionate that a puzzling dramatic tension is set up by "the restless and anatomizing casuistry with which men seek the justification of Beatrice, yet feel that she has done what needs justification." She is given other motives for her pose of innocence, including the fear of death. In the Old Vic production of 1959, Barbara Jefford spoke Beatrice's final words of the play, "Well, 'tis very well" with a stinging derision that epitomized the vitality and complexity of this remarkable heroine. *The Cenci* cannot properly be judged away from the theater, and in the theater it is powerful but defective. It is also memorably original. Except in the most trivial ways it is quite un-Shakespearean, in versification as in content.

Most of *The Cenci* was written near Leghorn. Mary Shelley had been grief-stricken by the death of their son William in June 1819; and the Shelleys had fled from Rome, now childless, to seek consolation from an old friend, Maria Gisborne, who had nursed Mary as a baby. Shelley did, of course, write private verses to express his feelings, but the two public poems composed during this unhappy summer were entirely objective. The second of these was "The Masque of Anarchy," a vigorous fusion of biblical prophecy, poetic vision, and street balladry:

> As I lay asleep in Italy
> There came a voice from over the Sea,
> And with great power it forth led me
> To walk in the Visions of Poesy.
> (1–4)

Asleep at his post of duty to others, Shelley meant. The news of the Peterloo massacre of 16 August, when a peaceful reform demonstration in Manchester was ridden down by drunken yeomanry, had reached him on 5 September; next day he told his publisher, "The torrent of my indignation has not yet done boiling in my veins"; and within three weeks a ballad of ninety-one stanzas was on its way to Leigh Hunt for publication. Again a poem was addressed to a popular audience, and again it was held back for fear of the consequences. Perhaps with reason, for although its appeal is to the advantages of passive resistance and (shrewdly) to "the old laws of England" the refrain "Ye are many—they are few" would hardly have tranquilized the frightened leaders of Lord Liverpool's government, nor would the opening stanzas, in which each leader is made to seem a mere "front" for the evil that inhabits him:

> I met Murder on the way—
> He had a mask like Castlereagh. . . .
> (5–6)

Murder wears the face of Lord Castlereagh (foreign secretary); Hypocrisy, that of Lord Sidmouth (home secretary and builder of churches for the starving poor); Fraud is a mock-up of Lord Eldon (a judge). Thus the title is a pun: "masque" pageant play, and "mask," disguise. Once more the constructive side of the poem takes the form of a prophetic vision, but the writing is forceful and concrete. "Freedom" is no abstract slogan: it means bread on a table, a home, and clothes.

Shelley's other political songs are less interesting than the long, incomplete prose essay "A Philosophical View of Reform," written soon after "The Masque of Anarchy." Its modest proposals to abolish the national debt, to disband the army, to make religious intolerance illegal, to extend the jury system and the franchise were not, of course, all that Shelley wanted, but only what he thought it possible to get. The long-range aspirations of his poetry always have somewhere behind them this sort of short-term prose practicality.

From this time on, with minor exceptions, Shelley gave up trying to reach a wide audience on subjects of topical concern, as he had earlier given up direct action. But one major poem, the "Ode to the West Wind," ends this period of passionate commitment. Shelley had just read an attack on *The Revolt of Islam* in the *Quarterly Review,* full of innuendo against the poet's private life and concluding, "Instead of relying on his own powers, he must feel and acknowledge his weakness, and pray for strength from above." Shelley takes this advice with ironic literalness: he acknowledges his weakness, and prays to the wind. The West Wind he invokes is the "breath of Autumn's being," the essence of seasonal change, one aspect of that universal Power operating at every level in all the elements, from the star-fretted sky to the weed on the seabed: the Power that destroys leaves and people of all colors but also resurrects them as children of another spring.

The reviewer (who had known Shelley at Eton) called him "unteachable in boyhood." If only he could be an unteachable boy again, or if the Wind would simply order him about, as it orders all inanimate things: wave, leaf, and cloud! So it does, for he too is subject to the universal Law; his own leaves are falling. But he is a man, not a leaf, and must use the Wind as well as serve it, just as Asia on her journey used as well as obeyed the "plume-uplifting wind" steaming from Demogorgon's mountain. He is a poet, and must give back music to the Wind; he is a prophet, and the Wind must trumpet his words abroad. Cause and effect interpenetrate to proclaim the same message of hope.

The ode is one of the great lyrics of the language, unique for its athletic swiftness within a tightly controlling form. Its imagery and diction, which a few critics have thought suspiciously beautiful, have turned out on closer inspection to be equally exact and subtle.

The day "West Wind" was begun in Florence was probably the day after *Peter Bell the Third* was finished, this last a shrewd joke at Wordsworth's expense, with much hard-hitting contemporary satire:

> Hell is a city much like London—
>   A populous and a smoky city;
> There are all sorts of people undone
> And there is little or no fun done;
>   Small justice shown, and still less pity.
>   (147–151)

There was also a literal "new birth" in November 1819. Percy Florence Shelley, who survived his father, owed his second name to the suggestion of a visiting friend, Sophia Stacey. Sophia flirted amicably with Shelley, sang to him, and was courted in a resourceful variety of poetic attitudes: with playful practicality in "Love's Philosophy," with oriental sensuality in "The Indian Serenade," and ethereally in "Thou art fair and few are fairer" (a lyric evidently once intended for Asia, but readdressed from a "nymph of air" to a "nymph of earth"). Perhaps the unclaimed flowers of "The Question" would have been Sophia's too, if she had stayed to accept them.

In January 1820, Shelley took his family to Pisa, where a small group of friends later began to gather: Edward Williams and Jane Johnson early the following year, he a young officer on half-pay, she a refugee from her real husband; and in 1822, Edward Trelawny, a supposed former privateer who was as devoted as his credentials were unreliable.

The severe winter in Florence, and perhaps Miss Stacey's departure, influenced Shelley's first poem of 1820, "The Sensitive Plant" (*Mimosa pudica*), a parable of man's precarious situation within nature. This was followed by the grandiloquent "Ode to Liberty," inspired by news of the revolution in Spain against Ferdinand VII. Perhaps some of the shorter poems of this spring were more successful within their limits. Shelley obviously enjoyed the challenge to his craftsmanship of commissioned work, and it was probably after writing what is known as the "Hymn of Apollo" which the sun god sings in the first person, for a verse play of his wife's that Shelley went on to write, in the same manner but just for fun, his dazzling meteorological nursery rhyme "The Cloud."

The other long poems written in 1820 are all light in tone, especially the accomplished (and funny) translation of Homer's "Hymn to Mercury." "The Witch of Atlas" is more serious than it seems, but is still a holiday poem. And early in July, Shelley wrote the verse letter that Maria Gisborne called "that delightful and laughable and exquisite description in verse of our house and Henry's workroom"—the poem generally entitled "Letter to Maria Gisborne," although it was sent to the family. It was not that he was especially lighthearted. What the playful tone represents is a new artistic maturity in Shelley, a sort of Mozartian wryness, compounded of sadness and self-mockery, that is characteristic of some of his best work from 1820 on.

The Gisbornes had gone to London, and Shelley was writing from the workroom of Maria's son Henry, who was a nautical engineer. It is a true letter to close friends, not a public poem, and its deceptively careless form gives the illusion of spontaneous informality. The spider and silkworm of the opening introduce several themes—"threads of friendship," "machinery," and "habitation"—that permeate the poem. These verses are not to catch readers, Shelley says; they are just an expendable way of making my friends remember me. What really counts is not the apparatus of constraint, but the ties of affection, natural beauty, and domesticity. Later the spider's meretricious web becomes equivalent to London, and the silkworm's mulberry tree to the peaceful environment of Italy (silk was the chief industrial product of Italy). All this with playful courtesy—for instance, in the recollection of how Maria Gisborne, who had cared for Shelley's wife as a baby, had nursed him also through his infancy in the Spanish language. Topics of every degree of seriousness grow effortlessly out of one another: torture, toy boats, tea, life after death, prostitution, mince pies; and the appropriate modulations of tone are managed with a happy confidence:

> You will see Coleridge, he who sits obscure
> In the exceeding lustre and the pure
> Intense irradiation of a mind
> Which, with its own internal lightning
> blind,
> Flags wearily through darkness and
> despair—
>
> . . .
>
> But we will have books, Spanish, Italian,
> Greek,
> And ask one week to make another week
> As like his father as I'm unlike mine,
> Which is not his fault, as you may divine.
> (202–206; 298–301)

There is throughout a concrete particularity—a sense of locality and of things—which is not often credited to Shelley:

> . . . a shabby stand
> Of hackney coaches, a brick house or wall
> Fencing some lordly court, white with the
> scrawl
> Of our unhappy politics . . .
> (265–268)

The poem is a triumph of graceful craftsmanship and civilized feeling.

A more intense but much narrower poem resulted from Shelley's celebration of a young Italian girl, Emilia Viviani, as the final embodiment of the Ideal Beauty he had been seeking all his life. In a way *Epipsychidion* ("a little soul beside a soul") is the most "typical" of all Shelley's works, an extreme concentration of a single element in his genius. But Keats would have called it "too smokeable"—too easy to smile at. When, eventually, Shelley found Emilia "a cloud instead of a Juno" he reacted against the poem too, and sent word to stop its further publication.

He was still under the spell of this platonic friendship when he wrote his best-known prose work, "A Defence of Poetry," unpublished until 1840. It was part of an answer to Thomas Love Peacock's half-serious argument that poetry in a utilitarian age was obsolescent, and his treatment is therefore very general. But his metaphors are generally used, as in Francis Bacon, not for mere eloquence but in order to make complex meanings intelligible ("the mind in creation is as a fading coal, which some invisible influence, like an inconstant wind, awakens to transitory brightness"); and some of the incidental discussions are of much interest: for example, the question why a great poem such as *Paradise Lost* will go on revealing new significances long after its social context, and even the religion that inspired it, have disintegrated. "Veil after veil may be undrawn, and the inmost naked beauty of the meaning never exposed." This is an important commentary on Shelley's own adaptations of myth.

News came in April 1821 of Keats's death in Rome. Shelley had not known him well; but he had seen from *Hyperion* that Keats was a major poet, and the supposed primary cause of his death—the *Quarterly Review* attack on

Endymion in 1818—roused him to fury. Yet *Adonais* is "a highly wrought *piece of art,*" for in this most complimentary of English elegies, Shelley purposely followed Keats's advice to "curb his magnanimity" (that is, his humanitarian zeal) and "be more of an artist." So it is statelier, more conscious of its own verbal substance, than many of Shelley's poems.

To counter the reviewers' dismissal of Keats as an illiterate Cockney, Shelley chose to honor him by adopting the graceful classical artifice of the pastoral elegy, as Edmund Spenser had mourned Sir Philip Sidney in *Astrophel,* and Milton his friend Edward King in "Lycidas." The classical pastoral transfers personal emotions and relationships to a more or less idealized country community; the shepherd with his pipe, living in close contact with nature, becomes a type of the poet, and the death of a shepherd-poet is lamented by his fellow shepherds and by nature itself. The convention derives from Theocritus and his Latin imitator Vergil; but Shelley's more immediate influences were Moschus' elegy on the Greek poet Bion, and Bion's own *Lament of Venus for Adonis,* lines from both of which he had translated. Thus *Adonais* belongs to a tradition extending from the Greek idyll to Matthew Arnold's "Thyrsis"—and even, in some respects, to T. S. Eliot's *The Waste Land.*

Keats had used the myth of Adonis, whose name suggested "Adonais," in his *Endymion.* He was a boy loved by the goddess Venus, but one day a boar killed him while he was hunting. He was permitted to return to life for half the year, spending the other half asleep in the underworld. This was a close fit: Keats was loved by immortal Poetry (Urania) and killed by a reviewer, yet in death he had rejoined the Spirit whose "plastic stress" shapes the beauty of the material world. Like Asia, Urania is composite. She is not Adonais' love but his mother, and she is imagined as being Milton's spiritual widow, with Adonais as their youngest offspring. This is because Shelley regarded the author of *Hyperion* as the poetic heir of Milton, who had adopted Urania as his single "heavenly born" Muse in *Paradise Lost*; so, after Milton's death, Keats was the "nursling of her widowhood." But at times she is also Venus Genetrix, goddess of love and organic life.

The almost unrelieved grief of the opening stanzas, expressed in imagery of cloud and vapor, is not to be dispelled by the return of spring, although

> The leprous corpse touched by this spirit
> tender
> Exhales itself in flowers of gentle breath;
> Like incarnations of the stars . . .
> (st. 20)

The flowers are earthly versions of the stars, radiating perfume instead of light. But for the dead man there is no renewal of life, as Moschus had said in his lament for Bion. Death is the price paid on earth for the colors of sky and field. Even Urania, undying mother of generation, cannot revive Adonais.

Adonais' own poetic imaginings lament him, and there are many references to Keats's poems: the "pale flower by some sad maiden cherished" is "Isabella"; Adonais is washed from a "lucid urn"; his spirit's sister is the nightingale; like his own Hyperion he could scale Heaven. His fellow poets lament him, too, mountain shepherds in honor of Endymion, who kept sheep on Mount Patmos; these include Byron, Thomas Moore, and Leigh Hunt. Shelley's own presence among them is often thought an embarrassment to the poem, and there is some evidence that he meant to omit these stanzas in a second edition. But the episode is not irrelevant; an obscure mourner, who identifies his fate with that of Adonais, asks: If the enemies of the imagination could not even discriminate between the extremes represented by Cain and Christ, what justice can be expected for any of us? Yet, in some sense at least, Adonais is with the "enduring" dead, like pure metal melted down and returned to the furnace, whereas the reviewer and his kind are ashes only:

> Thou canst not soar where he is sitting
> now—

Dust to the dust! but the pure spirit shall
flow
Back to the burning fountain whence it came,
A portion of the Eternal. . . .
(st. 38)

So the poem reaches its final affirmation, expressed in imagery of light and fire. Adonais has "awakened from the dream of life"—this life the flowers, arts, and cultures of which can only partially embody the Power working through them—and has become identified with that Power:

He is a portion of the loveliness
Which once he made more lovely he doth
bear
His part, while the one Spirit's plastic stress
Sweeps through the dull dense world,
compelling there
All new successions to the forms they wear;
Torturing the unwilling dross that checks
its flight
To its own likeness, as each mass may bear;
And bursting in its beauty and its might
From trees and beasts and men into the
Heavens' light.
(st. 43)

In death the white sunlight of Unity is no longer refracted into colors by the "dome" of the mundane. atmosphere. And that Unity, to attain which Shelley would almost accept a death like Keats's ("why shrink, my Heart?"), touches him in the act of writing his poem and authorizes its final daring paradoxes of grammar and metaphor:

That Light . . .

. . .

Which through the web of being blindly
wove
By man and beast and earth and air and sea,
Burns bright or dim, as each are mirrors of
The fire for which all thirst, now beams
on me,
Consuming the last clouds of cold
mortality.
(st. 54)

In the autumn Shelley completed *Hellas* ("Greece") in honor of the Greeks' insurrection against their Turkish overlords. It was written, like W. H. Auden's *Spain,* for the cause; and though it has some fine lyrical choruses, the blank verse tends to be strained. Shelley called it "a mere improvise."

Byron had moved to Pisa late in 1821, to write for *The Liberal,* which Leigh Hunt was coming from England to edit; and in March and April 1822, Shelley translated some scenes from Pedro Calderón de la Barca and from *Faust* for publication in the new journal. But he was again in a very unsettled state. He had already abandoned work on a new play, *Charles I.* Some of his uncertainty related to Edward and Jane Williams—especially Jane, whom he found increasingly attractive. As the months of 1822 passed, the eight lyrics he gave her came to form the best—indeed, the only—group of unequivocally personal love poems he ever wrote. For all their tact and delicacy, these poems have a new undertone of skepticism, almost earthiness:

. . . the sweet warmth of day
Was scattered o'er the twinkling bay;
And the fisher with his lamp
And spear, about the low rocks damp
Crept, and struck the fish who came
To worship the delusive flame.
(43–48)

These "Lines Written in the Bay of Lerici" were composed when the Williams and Shelley families were in joint occupation of Casa Magni, the only house available to them on that beautiful coast. Claire's little Allegra had died of fever, and it had been imperative to get her mother well away from Byron, whom she was bound to blame for this tragedy. In May, Shelley's new boat, the *Don Juan,* arrived; and the outward things of life seemed very favorable to him, for once:

> Williams is captain [he wrote], and we drive along this delightful bay in the evening wind, under the summer moon, until earth appears another world. Jane brings her guitar, and if

the past and the future could be obliterated, the present would content me so well that I could say with Faust to the passing moment, "Remain, thou, thou art so beautiful."[2] (letter to John Gisborne, 18 June 1822)

Inwardly it was otherwise. His poetry had failed, and the popular cause had been defeated over almost all of Europe. Four children he had loved were dead; his wife was ill and unhappy; and he was in love with someone unobtainable. In this complex of troubles he began "The Triumph of Life."

Shelley's last, unfinished, poem is difficult and enigmatic. Stylistically it is like a combination of "The Masque of Anarchy" and *Adonais*—that is, of directness and economy with a "highly wrought" verbal texture—but the literary influences behind it are no longer English or Greek, but Italian: Petrarch and Dante. Although most of the poem exists only in rough draft, the movement of the verse is so fluent that Shelley's technical mastery of the terza rima goes almost unnoticed. The homage of all creation to the sun, at the opening, is followed by a vision of the car of light, in front of which the young execute a frenzied erotic dance, until

One falls and then another in the path
Senseless, nor is the desolation single,

Yet ere I can say *where,* the chariot hath
Passed over them; nor other trace I find
But as of foam after the ocean s wrath

Is spent upon the desert shore.—Behind,
Old men and women foully disarrayed
Shake their grey hair in the insulting wind,

Limp in the dance and strain with limbs decayed
To reach the car of light which leaves them still
Far behind, and deeper in the shade.

But not the less with impotence of will
They wheel, though ghastly shadows interpose,
Round them and round each other, and fulfil

Their work, and to the dust whence they arose
Sink, and corruption veils them as they lie,
And frost in these performs what fire in those.
(159–175)

One fallen worshipper, Jean Jacques Rousseau, describes how the car seduced him from what seemed an early ideal, a "fair Shape" brighter than the sun, and then destroyed him as it had destroyed these others.

What is being repudiated in this poem? The "suicidal selfishness" of *Queen Mab,* the "loathsome mask" of *Prometheus Unbound,* all the moral and social targets of Shelley's earlier attacks? These, certainly; but some feel that earthly life is now being rejected altogether, that Rousseau's "fair Shape" was a double agent, a delusive embodiment of the true Ideal. The poem breaks off, and no one knows whether there would have been another side to this somber vision, or whether it was already almost complete.

Leigh Hunt's arrival must have interrupted the answer to that final question, "What is Life?" After a busy but happy reunion with him in Leghorn, Shelley and Williams sailed for home on 8 July; but on the way the boat was wrecked in a squall. Because of the quarantine laws, the bodies of Shelley and his friend were burned on the foreshore under Trelawny's supervision; and Shelley's ashes were interred in the Protestant cemetery in Rome on 21 January 1823, that "flame transformed to marble" that had been celebrated in *Adonais.* At about the same age of twenty-nine, Wordsworth, who considered Shelley "one of the best *artists* of us all," was just thinking of writing a preface to his *Lyrical Ballads.*

2. From F. L. Jones, ed., *The Letters of Percy Bysshe Shelley* (Oxford, 1964), vol. II, pp. 435–436.

Selected Bibliography

BIBLIOGRAPHY

Forman, H. B., *The Shelley Library,* (London, 1886) pt. I: "Shelley's Own Books, Pamphlets and Broadsides; Posthumous Separate Issues; and Post-humous Books Wholly or Mainly by Him," no pt. II was published; Sharp, W., *Life of Percy Bysshe Shelley,* (London, 1887) includes bibliography by J. P. Anderson, still useful for critical articles 1822–1887; *A Lexical Concordance to the Poetical Works of Shelley,* F. S. Ellis, comp. (London, 1892) repr. with app. by T. Saito, (Tokyo, 1963) based on H. B. Forman's 1882 ed. of the poems; Granniss, R., *A Descriptive Catalogue of the First Editions in Book Form of the Writings of Shelley,* (New York, 1923) with 30 plates; Wise, T. J., *A Shelley Library. A Catalogue of Printed Books, Manuscripts and Autograph Letters,* (London, 1924) privately printed, essentially vol. V of *The Ashley Library,* (London, 1924); deRicci, S., *A Bibliography of Shelley's Letters, Published and Unpublished,* (Paris, 1927) privately printed; *Keats-Shelley Journal,* (1952–) contains an annual bibliography; Patton, L., *The Shelley-Godwin Collection of Lord Abinger, Duke University Library Notes,* 27 (1953) 11–17; Taylor, C. H., *The Early Collected Editions of Shelley's Poems: A Study in the History and Transmission of the Printed Text,* (New Haven, Conn., 1958); *Shelley and His Circle 1773–1822,* K. N. Cameron, ed. (Cambridge, Mass.-London, 1961–) vols. I–II (1961); D. H. Reiman, ed., vols. III–IV (1970) vols. V–VI (1973); to be completed in about 8 vols.; *Keats, Shelley, Byron, Hunt and Their Circles: A Bibliography 1 July 1950–30 June 1962,* D. B. Green and D. E. G. Wilson, comps. (Lincoln, Nebr., 1964); Massey, I., *Posthumous Poems of Shelley: Mary Shelley's Fair Copy Book, Bodleian MS. Shelley Adds. d.9,* (Montreal, 1969); Dunbar, C., *A Bibliography of Shelley Studies: 1823–1950,* (Folkestone, 1976).

PRINCIPAL COLLECTED EDITIONS

The Poetical Works of Coleridge, Shelley, and Keats, (Paris, 1829) the Galignani ed., with a memoir by C. Redding; *The Poetical Works,* M. W. Shelley, ed. 4 vols. (London, 1839) *Queen Mab* printed with omissions; new rev. ed. in 1 vol., adding *Swellfoot, Peter Bell the Third* and *Queen Mab* complete, (London, 1839) [title page dated 1840]; *The Poetical Works, Including Various Additional Pieces from MS and Other Sources, the Text Carefully Revised, with Notes and a Memoir,* W. M. Rossetti, ed. 2 vols. (London, 1870) rev. ed., 3 vols. (1878); *The Poetical Works,* H. B. Forman, ed. 4 vols. (London, 1876–1877) new eds. in 2 vols. (London, 1882) with Mary Shelley's notes, and in 5 vols. (London, 1892) the Aldine ed.; *The Works in Prose and Verse,* H. B. Forman, ed. 8 vols. (London, 1880); *Complete Poetical Works,* G. E. Woodberry, ed. 4 vols. (Boston, 1892) (London, 1893) also in 1 vol. (Boston, 1901) the Cambridge Poets ed.; *Complete Poetical Works,* T. Hutchinson, ed. (London, 1904) with textual notes by Hutchinson, also published in Oxford Standard Authors ed. (London, 1905) with intro. by B. P. Kurtz, (New York, 1933) and without intro. (London, 1934) 2nd ed. (1970) the latter rev. by G. M. Matthews; *The Poetical Works,* A. H. Koszul, ed. 2 vols. (London, 1907) with intro. by Koszul, also rev. ed. with new intro., 2 vols. (London, 1953) in Everyman's Library, poems published in chronological order; *The Poems,* C. D. Locock, ed. 2 vols. (London, 1911) with intro. by A. Clutton-Brock, the only complete ed. with explanatory notes; *The Complete Works,* R. Ingpen and W. E. Peck, eds. 10 vols. (London, 1926–1930) repr. (New York, 1965) the Julian ed.; *Shelley's Prose,* D. L. Clark, ed. (Albuquerque, N.M., 1954) repr. with corrs. (1967) a usefully full collection, but very unreliable textually and in dating; *The Complete Poetical Works,* N. Rogers, ed. vol. I *1802–1813,* (Oxford, 1972) vol. II: *1814–1817* (Oxford, 1975) to be completed in 4 vols.

SELECTIONS

Select Letters, R. Garnett, ed. (London, 1882); *Essays and Letters,* E. Rhys, ed. (London, 1886); *Shelley's Literary and Philosophical Criticism,* J. Shawcross, ed. (London, 1909) with intro. by Shawcross; *Peacock's Four Ages of Poetry; Shelley's Defence of Poetry; Browning's Essay on Shelley,* H. F. B. Brett-Smith, ed. (London, 1921) expurgated ed. (1923); *Poetry and Prose, with Essays by Browning, Bagehot, Swinburne, and Reminiscences by Others,* A. M. D. Hughes, ed. (London, 1931); *Selected Poetry and Prose,* C. Baker, ed. (New York, 1951) the Modern Library ed.; *Selected Poetry, Prose and Letters,* A. S. B. Glover, ed. (London, 1951) the Nonesuch ed.; *My Best Mary: The Selected Letters of Mary W. Shelley,* M. Spark and D. Stanford, eds. (London, 1953) with intro. by the eds.; *Selected Poems,* E. Blunden, ed. (London, 1954) with a long intro. and notes; *Selected Poetry and Prose,* K. N. Cameron, ed. (New York, 1956); *Selected Poems,* J. Holloway, ed. (London, 1960) with intro. by Holloway; *Selections from Shelley's Poetry and Prose,* D. S. R. Welland, ed. (London, 1961); *Shelley: Selected Poems and Prose,* G. M. Matthews, ed. (Oxford, 1964) contains a new poem; *Selected Poetry and Prose,* H. Bloom, ed. (New York, 1966); *Shelley's Critical Prose,* B. R. McElderry, ed. (Lincoln, Nebr., 1966); *Alastor and Other Poems: Prometheus Unbound with Other Poems: Adonais,* P. Butter, ed. (London, 1970); *Political Writings Including "A Defence of Poetry,"* R. A. Duerksen, ed. (New York, 1970); *Selected Poetry,* N. Rogers, ed. (London, 1970) an Oxford Paperback; *Shelley's Poetry and Prose,* D. H. Reiman and S. B. Powers, eds. (New York, 1977) includes new texts and fifteen critical articles; *Selected Poems*, T. Webb, ed. (London, 1977) with new texts.

SEPARATE WORKS IN VERSE AND PROSE

Original Poetry by Victor and Cazire, [Shelley and his sister Elizabeth] (Worthing, 1810) photofacs. in S. J. Hooker, *Shelley, Trelawny and Henley*, (Worthing, 1950); *Posthumous Fragments of Margaret Nicholson, Being Poems Found Amongst the Papers of That Noted Female Who Attempted the Life of the King in 1786*, John Fitzvictor [P. B. Shelley], ed. (Oxford, 1810) also privately printed by H. B. Forman, (London, 1877); *Zastrozzi: A Romance*, (London, 1810) repr. in E. Chesser, *Shelleyand Zastrozzi: Self-Revelation of a Neurotic*, (London, 1965); *The Necessity of Atheism*, (Worthing, 1811) published anonymously by Shelley and T. J. Hogg, photofacs. in S. J. Hooker, *Shelley, Trelawny and Henley*, (Worthing, 1950); *St Irvyne or the Rosicrucian: A Romance, by a Gentleman of the University of Oxford*, (London, 1811; reiss., 1822); *An Address to the Irish People*, (Dublin, 1812); *Declaration of Rights*, (Dublin, 1812) an unsigned broadside, two copies are in the Public Record Office; *The Devils' Walk: A Ballad*, (Barnstaple [?], 1812) unsigned broadside, one copy in the Public Record Office and one at the University of Texas, Austin; *A Letter to Lord Ellenborough*, (London, 1812) privately printed, one copy in the Bodleian Library; *Proposals for an Association of . . . Philanthropists . . .*, (Dublin, 1812); *Queen Mab: A Philosophical Poem, with Notes*, (London, 1813) privately printed, many unauthorized eds. (1821–1857); *A Vindication of a Natural Diet, Being One in a Series of Notes to Queen Mab, a Philosophical Poem*, (London, 1813); *A Refutation of Deism, in a Dialogue*, (London, 1814) published anonymously; *Alastor: or The Spirit of Solitude, and Other Poems*, (London, 1816).

History of a Six Weeks' Tour Through a Part of France, Switzerland, Germany and Holland, (London, 1817) published anonymously by Percy and Mary Shelley; *A Proposal for Putting Reform to the Vote Throughout the Kingdom, by the Hermit of Marlow [Shelley]*, (London, 1817) facs. of the MS published by H. B. Forman, (London, 1887); *Laon and Cythna; or, The Revolution of the Golden City: A Vision of the Nineteenth Century in the Stanza of Spenser*, (London, 1818) suppressed, rev. and reiss. as *The Revolt of Islam: A Poem in Twelve Cantos*, (London, 1818) some copies dated 1817; *The Cenci: A Tragedy in Five Acts*, (Leghorn, 1819) 2nd ed. (London, 1821) repr. by G. E. Woodberry, (Boston, 1909) with bibliography; *Rosalind and Helen: A Modern Eclogue; with Other Poems*, (London, 1819); *Oedipus Tyrannus: or, Swellfoot the Tyrant: A Tragedy in Two Acts, Translatedfrom the Original Doric*, (London, 1820) this unsigned ed. was suppressed; *Prometheus Unbound: A Lyrical Drama in Four Acts, with Other Poems*, (London, 1820) the principal separate modern eds. are V. Scudder, ed. (Boston, 1892) R. Ackermann, ed. (Heidelberg, 1908) A. M. D. Hughes, ed. (Oxford, 1910) repr. (1957) L. J. Zillman, ed. (Seattle, 1959); (New Haven, Conn.-London, 1968); *Adonais: An Elegy on the Death of John Keats, Author of Endymion, Hyperion, etc.*, (Pisa, 1821) 2nd ed. (Cambridge, 1829) annotated ed. by W. M. Rossetti, (Oxford, 1890) was rev. by Rossetti and A. O. Prickard, (London, 1903) photofacs. in N. Douglas, ed. (London, 1927); *Epipsychidion: Verses Addressed to the Noble and Unfortunate Lady Emilia V—Now Imprisoned in the Convent of—*, (London, 1821) facs. ed. (Menston, 1970) this unsigned ed. was withdrawn; *Hellas: A Lyrical Drama*, (London, 1822).

POSTHUMOUS WORKS

Posthumous Poems, M. W. Shelley, ed. (London, 1824) this ed. was suppressed; *The Masque of Anarchy: A Poem Now First Published*, (London, 1832) with preface by L. Hunt, photofacs. of the "Wise," MS published by H. B. Forman, (London, 1887); *The Shelley Papers: Memoir by T. Medwin and Original Poems and Papers by Shelley*, (London, 1833) includes a spurious poem "To the Queen of My Heart"; *Essays, Letters from Abroad, etc.*, M. W. Shelley, ed. 2 vols. (London, 1840) includes "A Defence of Poetry"; *An Address to the People on the Death of Princess Charlotte, by the Hermit of Marlow*, (London: *ca.*, 1843) probably from a MS written *ca.* 1817 and now lost; *Shelley Memorials*, Lady J. Shelley and R. Garnett, eds. (London, 1859) includes "An Essay on Christianity"; *Relics of Shelley*, R. Garnett, ed. (London, 1862); *The Daemon of the World*, H. B. Forman, ed. (London, 1876) privately printed; *Notes on Sculptures in Rome and Florence, Together with a Lucianic Fragment and a Criticism on Peacock's Poem "Rhododaphne,"* H. B. Forman, ed. (London, 1879) privately printed; *The Wandering Jew*, B. Dobell, ed. (London, 1887); Locock, C. D., *An Examination of the Shelley Manuscripts in the Bodleian Library*, (Oxford, 1903); *Shelley's Poetry in the Bodleian Manuscripts*, A. H. Koszul, ed. (Oxford, 1910); "A Defence of Poetry," "Essay on Christianity," and fragments; *Note Books of Shelley, from the Originals in the Library of W. K. Bixby*, deciphered, transcribed, and edited by H. B. Forman, 3 vols. (Boston, 1911) privately printed; *A Philosophical View of Reform*, T. W. Rolleston, ed. (Oxford, 1920); W. E. Peck, ed. "An Unpublished Ballad by Shelley" ("Young Parson Richards"), (*Philological Quarterly* 5, 1926) 114–118; *The Shelley Notebook in the Harvard Library*, G. E. Woodberry, ed. (Cambridge, Mass., 1929) a photofacs., autograph ascriptions were corrected by H. Darbishire in (*Review of English Studies*, July 31, 1932) 352–354.

Verse and Prose from the Manuscripts of Shelley, J. C. E. Shelley-Rolls and R. Ingpen, eds. (London, 1934) privately printed; " 'Sadak the Wanderer': An Unknown Shelley Poem," D. Cook, ed., (*Times Literary Supplement* May 16, 1936) 424; *A Shelley Letter,* E. H. Blakeney, ed. (Winchester, 1936) Shelley's verse epistle to Feargus Graham (1811); Notopoulos, J. A., *The Platonism of Shelley,* (Durham, N.C., 1949) includes "Shelley's Translations from Plato: A Critical Edition," edited by the author, and unpublished material; G. M. Matthews, ed. "The Triumph of Life: A New Text," (*Studia Neophilologica* 32, 1960) 271–309; *The Esdaile Notebook: A Volume of Early Poems,* K. N. Cameron, ed. (New York, 1964) slightly rev. (London, 1964); Reiman, D. H., *Shelley's "The Triumph of Life": A Critical Study Based on a Text Newly Edited from the Bodleian MS,* (Urbana, Ill., 1965); *The Esdaile Poems,* N. Rogers, ed. (Oxford, 1966); Chernaik, J., "Shelley's 'To Constantia,'" (*Times Literary Supplement,* February 6, 1969) 140, a new text of "To Constantia Singing"; T. Webb, ed. "Shelley's 'Hymn to Venus': A New Text," (*Review of English Studies* n.s. 21, August 1970) 315–324; J. Chernaik and T. Burnett, eds. "The Byron and Shelley Notebooks in the Scrope Davies Find," (*Review of English Studies* 29, February 1978) 36–49.

LETTERS AND JOURNALS

Shelley and Mary, Lady J. Shelley and Sir P. F. Shelley, eds. 3 (or 4) vols. (London, 1882) privately printed; *The Letters,* R. Ingpen, comp. and ed. 2 vols. London (1909) new ed. adding five letters (London, 1912) rev. ed. (1914); *The Shelley Correspondence in the Bodleian Library,* R. H. Hill, ed. (Oxford, 1926) contains lists of MSS, letters, and relics; *Shelley's Lost Letters to Harriet,* L. Hotson, ed. (London, 1930) with intro. by Hotson; *After Shelley. The Letters of T. J. Hogg to Jane Williams,* S. Norman, ed. (Oxford, 1934); *Letters of Mary W. Shelley,* F. L. Jones, comp. and ed. 2 vols. (Norman, Okla., 1944); *Mary Shelley's Journal,* F. L. Jones, ed. (Norman, Okla., 1947); *New Shelley Letters,* W. S. Scott, ed. (London, 1948) letters by Shelley and members of his circle from the papers of T. J. Hogg; *Maria Gisborne and Edward E. Williams, Shelley's Friends: Their Journals and Letters,* F. L. Jones, ed. (Norman, Okla., 1951); *The Letters of Percy Bysshe Shelley,* F. L. Jones, ed. 2 vols. (Oxford, 1964); *The Journals of Claire Clairmont,* M. K. Stocking, ed. (Cambridge, Mass., 1968).

BIOGRAPHICAL AND CRITICAL STUDIES

Medwin, T., *Journal of the Conversations of Lord Byron,* (London, 1824) in E. J. Lovell, ed. (Princeton, N.J., 1966); Hunt, L., *Lord Byron and Some of His Contemporaries,* (London, 1828) also in J. E. Morpurgo, ed. (London, 1949) see also Hunt's *Autobiography,* 3 vols. (London, 1850); Bagehot, W., *Estimates of Some Englishmen and Scotchmen,* (London, 1858) repr. in his *Literary Studies* vol. I, R. B. Hutton, ed. (London, 1879); Hogg, T. J., *Life of Shelley,* 2 vols. (London, 1858) the MS of two further vols. has been lost; Peacock, T. L., "Memoirs of Shelley," (*Fraser's* magazine, June 1858–March 1862) in H. F. B. Brett-Smith, ed. (Oxford, 1909); Trelawny, E. J., *Recollections of the Last Days of Shelley and Byron,* (London, 1858) repr. (1906) (1952) rev. as *Records of Shelley, Byron and the Author,* 2 vols. (London, 1878) repr. (London, 1905) (New York, 1968); *Shelley Memorials,* Lady J. Shelley and R. Garnett, eds. (London, 1859); Hunt, T., "Shelley, by One Who Knew Him," (*Atlantic Monthly* 11, February 1863) 184–204; MacCarthy, D. F., *Shelley's Early Life, from Original Sources,* (London, 1872) Shelley's activities and publications in Ireland; Dowden, E., *Life of Shelley,* 2 vols. (London, 1886) the 1-vol. rev. and abr. version (1896) in H. Read, ed. (London, 1951); Arnold, M., *Essays in Criticism,* 2nd ser. (London, 1888) includes an essay on Shelley; Salt, H. S., *Shelley: Poet and Pioneer,* (London, 1896).

Yeats, W. B., *Ideas of Good and Evil,* (London, 1903) includes "The Philosophy of Shelley's Poetry," repr. in his *Essays and Introductions,* (London, 1961); Droop, A., *Die Belesenheit Shelleys,* (Weimar, 1906); Bates, E. S., *A Study of Shelley's Drama "The Cenci,"* (New York, 1908) repr. (1969); Bradley, A. C., *Oxford Lectures on Poetry,* (London, 1909) includes "Shelley's View of Poetry," (*Bulletin of the Keats-Shelley Memorial, Rome* vol. I, 1910) vol. II (1913) both repr. (1961) journal subsequently published yearly from vol. III (1950); Clutton-Brock, A., *Shelley: The Man and the Poet,* (London, 1910) rev. ed. (1923); Koszul, A. H., *La jeunesse de Shelley,* (Paris, 1910); Angeli, H. R., *Shelley and His Friends in Italy,* (London, 1911); Brailsford, H. N., *Shelley, Godwin and Their Circle,* (London, 1913) rev. ed. (Oxford, 1951); Ingpen, R., *Shelley in England: New Facts and Letters from the Shelley-Whitton Papers,* (London, 1917); de Madariaga, S., *Shelley and Calderón and Other Essays,* (London, 1920); Strong, A. T., *Three Studies in Shelley,* (Oxford, 1921); Campbell, O. W., *Shelley and the Unromantics,* (London, 1924); Blunden, E., *Shelley and Keats as They Struck Their Contemporaries,* (London, 1925); Solve, M. T., *Shelley: His Theory of Poetry,* (Chicago, 1927) repr. (New York, 1964).

Grabo, C. H., *A Newton Among Poets: Shelley's Use of Science in Prometheus Unbound,* (Chapel Hill, N.C., 1930); *The Life of Percy Bysshe Shelley as Comprised in the "Life of Shelley" by T. J. Hogg, "The Recollections of Shelley and Byron" by E. J. Trelawny, "Memoirs of Shelley" by T. L. Peacock,* 2 vols. (London, 1933) with intro, by H. Wolfe; Kurtz, B. P., *The Pursuit of Death: A Study of Shelley's Poetry,* (New York, 1933); Grabo, C. H., *Prometheus Unbound: An Interpretation,* (Chapel Hill, N.C., 1935); Grabo, C. H., *The Magic Plant: The Growth of Shelley's Thought,* (Chapel Hill, N.C., 1936); Read, H., *In Defence of*

Shelley and Other Essays, (London, 1936) rev. and repr. as *The True Voice of Feeling,* (London, 1953); Barnard, E., *Shelley's Religion,* (Minneapolis, 1937) repr. (New York, 1964); Grylls, R. G., *Mary Shelley: A Biography,* (Oxford, 1938); White, N. I., *The Unextinguished Hearth: Shelley and His Contemporary Critics,* (Durham, N.C., 1938) repr. (1968) a full collection of the early reviews of Shelley.

White, N. I., *Shelley,* 2 vols. (New York, 1940) rev. ed. (London, 1947) abr. to the 1-vol. *Portrait of Shelley,* (New York, 1945) the standard biography; Blunden, E., *Shelley: A Life Story,* (London, 1946); Barrell, J., *Shelley and the Thought of His Time,* (New Haven, Conn., 1947); Hughes, A. M. D., *The Nascent Mind of Shelley,* (Oxford, 1947); Baker, C., *Shelley's Major Poetry: The Fabric of a Vision,* (Princeton, N.J., 1948); James, D. G., *The Romantic Comedy,* (Oxford, 1948) has a section on *Prometheus Unbound;* Fogle, R. H., *The Imagery of Keats and Shelley,* (Chapel Hill, N.C., 1949); Notopoulos, J. A., *The Platonism of Shelley,* (Durham, N.C., 1949).

Cameron, K. N., *The Young Shelley: Genesis of a Radical,* (New York, 1950) (London, 1951) Shelley's life and work up to 1814; Butter, P. H., *Shelley's Idols of the Cave,* (Edinburgh, 1954); Norman, S., *Flight of the Skylark: The Development of Shelley's Reputation,* (Norman, Okla., 1954); Pulos, C. E., *The Deep Truth: A Study of Shelley's Scepticism,* (Lincoln, Nebr., 1954); Rogers, N., *Shelley at Work: A Critical Inquiry,* (Oxford, 1956) rev. ed. (Oxford, 1968); Bloom, H., *Shelley's Mythmaking,* (New Haven, Conn., 1959); Perkins, D., *The Quest for Permanence: The Symbolism of Wordsworth, Shelley and Keats,* (Cambridge, Mass., 1959); Wasserman, E. R., *The Subtler Language,* (Baltimore, 1959) essays on "Mont Blanc," "The Sensitive Plant" and *Adonais;* Wilson, M., *Shelley's Later Poetry: A Study of His Prophetic Imagination,* (New York, 1959).

King-Hele, D., *Shelley: His Thought and Work,* (London, 1960); Boas, L. S., *Harriet Shelley: Five Long Years,* (Oxford, 1962); Lemaitre, H., *Shelley, poète des éléments,* (Paris, 1962); *Shelley: A Collection of Critical Essays,* G. M. Ridenour, ed. (Englewood Cliffs, N.J., 1965); Wasserman, E. R., *Shelley's Prometheus Unbound; A Critical Reading,* (Baltimore, 1965); Wilkie, B., *Romantic Poets and Epic Tradition,* (Madison, Wis., 1965) on *The Revolt of Islam* as epic; Schulze, E. J., *Shelley's Theory of Poetry: A Reappraisal,* (The Hague, 1966); *Shelley,* R. B. Woodings, ed. (London, 1968) 17 critical essays (1943–1968), in the Modern Judgments series; Reiman, D. H., *Percy Bysshe Shelley,* (New York, 1969); Guinn, J. P., *Shelley's Political Thought,* The Hague (1969); McNiece, G., *Shelley and the Revolutionary Idea,* (Cambridge, Mass., 1969); Curran, S., *Shelley's "Cenci": Scorpions Ringed with Fire,* (Princeton, N.J., 1970); Wasserman, E. R., *Shelley: A Critical Reading,* (Baltimore, 1971); Chernaik, J., *The Lyrics of Shelley,* (Cleveland, Ohio, 1972) new texts of 25 lyrics, with full commentary; Cameron, K. N., *Shelley: The Golden Years,* (Cambridge, Mass., 1974); Holmes, R., *Shelley: The Pursuit,* (London, 1974) a full biography; *Shelley: The Critical Heritage,* J. E. Barcus, ed. (London, 1975); Carey, G., *Shelley,* (London, 1975); Curran, S., *Shelley's Annus Mirabilis: The Maturing of an Epic Vision,* (San Marino, Calif., 1975); Robinson, C. E., *Shelley and Byron: The Snake and Eagle Wreathed in Fight,* (Baltimore, 1976); Webb, T., *The Violet in the Crucible: Shelley and Translation,* (Oxford, 1976); Webb, T., *Shelley: A Voice Not Understood,* (Manchester, 1977); Brown, N., *Sexuality and Feminism in Shelley,* (Cambridge, Mass., 1979); Duffy, E., *Rousseau in England: The Context for Shelley's Critique of the Enlightenment,* (Berkeley, 1979) a study of "The Triumph of Life"; Murphy, J. V., *The Dark Angel: Gothic Elements in Shelley's Works,* (Lewisburg, Pa., 1979).

Sir Philip Sidney
(1554–1586)

KENNETH MUIR

When the news of Sir Philip Sidney's death reached England, there was an extraordinary demonstration of grief. He was mourned by ordinary people as a soldier who had died fighting for the Protestant cause. He was mourned by his friends and relations as the "light of his family," a man who had seemed destined for greatness as a statesman. He was mourned by scholars and writers as a generous patron, and by his fellow poets as one of the best, and certainly one of the most influential, poets of his time. Oxford and Cambridge published collections of Latin elegies; and Edmund Spenser, Fulke Greville, and others contributed to *Astrophel,* a volume of English elegies. Years later, Greville regarded his friendship with Sidney as his chief title to fame; and when Percy Shelley wrote *Adonais,* he could speak of his great ancestor as one of the "inheritors of unfulfilled renown":

> Sidney, as he fought
> And as he fell, and as he lived and loved,
> Sublimely mild, a spirit without spot.

It is difficult to consider Sidney merely as a man of letters, since his writing was only a spare-time occupation. He is the best English example of the Renaissance ideal: he was Jack of all trades and master of them all. Not that he was simply a gifted amateur; although he sometimes spoke of his writings as toys, this (as K. O. Myrick has shown) "is but an example of *sprezzatura,* the courtly grace which conceals a sober purpose and is, indeed, the mark of consummate artistry"; or, as Greville put it, "men commonly (to keep above their works) seem to make toys of the utmost they can do."

The Sidney family became prominent in the middle of the fifteenth century. William Sidney was knighted after Flodden Field and became tutor to Edward VI. Henry Sidney, his son, was Edward's companion; and by his marriage to Mary Dudley he became connected with some of the most powerful families in England. Three years later, on November 30, 1554, Philip Sidney was born at Penshurst in Kent, an estate given to William Sidney by Edward VI. He was named, by what proved to be a singular irony, after his godfather, King Philip of Spain.

Philip Sidney was educated at Shrewsbury School and Christ Church, Oxford. He left Oxford in 1571, without taking a degree, when the colleges were closed on account of the plague. He spent a short time at Cambridge and then completed his education by traveling on the Continent. He was in Paris at the time of the massacre on St. Bartholemew's Eve, 1572, an event that left an indelible mark on his mind; he proceeded to Frankfurt, Heidelberg, Vienna, Hungary, Italy, Poland, and Holland, improving his knowledge of languages, acquiring insight into foreign affairs, and making many friends, of whom the most important was Hubert Languet, who hoped that Queen Elizabeth would become the champion of Protestantism.

Sidney visited Ireland, where his father was lord deputy, with the earl of Essex, who hoped to arrange a marriage between his daughter,

Penelope, and Sidney; but it was not until Penelope had been married against her will to Lord Rich that Sidney fell in love with her. In 1577 he was sent on an embassy to congratulate Emperor Rudolph II on his succession, and he took the opportunity to travel widely, as he was still hoping for the formation of a Protestant League. On his return to court he wrote an appeal to the queen not to marry the duke of Anjou. Sidney never obtained an important post at court, and this may have been partly due to Elizabeth's resentment of his unsolicited advice. He became a member of Parliament in 1581, and he was knighted; but he was in debt and felt frustrated at not being allowed to exercise his talents as a statesman to the full. From the other frustration, of his unreturned love for Penelope, if we may assume that the frustration expressed in his sonnets had some basis in fact, he may have escaped by his marriage to Frances Walsingham in September 1583. He was involved in a scheme of colonization in the New World; and in 1585 the queen intervened to prevent him from sailing with Drake on an expedition to Spain. He left in November to take up the post of governor of Flushing. Nearly a year later, on October 2, 1586, he took part in a skirmish to prevent the relief of Zutphen. One horse was killed under him in the second charge. In the last charge he was struck in the thigh by a musketball, a wound he would have escaped if he had not thrown away his thighpieces on seeing that the lord marshal was not wearing his. As he was being carried off the field, he called for drink; but as he was putting the bottle to his lips, he noticed a dying soldier. "He delivered it to the poor man with these words, *Thy necessity is yet greater than mine*" (Greville). He was taken in a barge to Arnheim, where he was nursed by Lady Sidney; but it was soon obvious that his wound was fatal. He died on October 17, displaying singular courage and religious fortitude.

Some of Sidney's writings are of little importance. The metrical version of the Psalms, completed by his sister, the countess of Pembroke, perhaps with the help of other poets, is not worse than Milton's and was admired by Ruskin; but it is a work of piety rather than of poetry. The entertainment *The Lady of May,* performed before the queen, is a courtly trifle thought by some critics to have given Shakespeare a hint for the character of Holofernes in *Love's Labour's Lost.* His translation of part of Philippe de Mornay's *Vérité de la religion chrétienne* is admirably straightforward and lucid (it has, however, recently been argued that the translation was by Arthur Golding). His masterpieces are *The Countess of Pembroke's Arcadia, Astrophel and Stella,* a few lyrical poems, and *The Defence of Poesie* (or *Apologie for Poetry,* as one edition calls it).

The Defence was written in reply to Stephen Gosson's *School of Abuse* (1579), dedicated to Sidney, which attacked "poets, pipers, players, jesters, and such like caterpillars of a commonwealth." Poetry, Gosson argued, had been useful in the old days for celebrating "the notable exploits of worthy captains"; but modern poetry had a deplorable effect on the manners and morals of the age. The exact date of Sidney's reply is unknown. If the King James to whom Sidney refers was James VI of Scotland, four or five years must have elapsed before the *Defence* was completed; but it was, in any case, written before the first plays of Christopher Marlowe and Shakespeare were performed. Sidney could therefore say little in defense of the contemporary stage. The only modern play in which he could find anything to praise was *Gorboduc,* which had not been written for the popular stage; and even *Gorboduc,* "full of stately speeches and well-sounding phrases, climbing to the height of Seneca his style, and as full of notable morality which it doth most delightfully teach," violated the unities of time and place. Later readers have taken little delight in *Gorboduc,* but they have found plenty in Sidney's mocking description of plays written for the popular stage in which the unities were more grossly disregarded:

> But if it be so in *Gorboduc,* how much more in all the rest, where you shall have Asia of

> the one side and Affricke of the other, and so many other under kingdoms, that the player when he comes in must ever begin with telling where he is, or else the tale will not be conceived. Now you shall have three ladies walk to gather flowers, and then we must believe the stage to be a garden. By and by we hear news of shipwreck in the same place: then we are to blame if we accept it not for a rock. Upon the back of that comes out a hideous monster with fire and smoke, and then the miserable beholders are bound to take it for a cave: while in the mean time two armies fly in, represented with four swords and bucklers, and then what hard heart will not receive it for a pitched field?
>
> Now of time they are much more liberal. For ordinary it is that two young princes fall in love, after many traverses she is got with child, delivered of a fair boy; he is lost, groweth to a man, falleth in love, and is ready to get another child, and all this in two hours' space: which how absurd it is in sense, even sense may imagine, and art hath taught, and all ancient examples justified.

Shakespeare himself was to apologize for the representation of Agincourt by "four or five most vile and ragged foils"; and in *The Winter's Tale,* which might almost have been written to demonstrate how a great work of art could be made in defiance of the rules, he brings in Father Time to excuse just such a violation of the unities as Sidney satirizes.

Sidney's assumption that Seneca was the best model for tragedy was made by all Elizabethan critics, and the countess of Pembroke's circle of poets all attempted plays in the French Senecan manner. But, whatever the merits of Samuel Daniel's *Cleopatra* and Thomas Kyd's *Cornelia*—and poetically they are considerable—these plays were not intended for the stage. Sidney, we may be sure, would have delighted in *Hamlet* and *King Lear,* even though he objected to the mingling of kings and clowns.

Sidney was luckier with nondramatic poetry. He deplored the failure of the poets of his own age to equal the achievement of Chaucer in his *Troilus and Criseyde,* "of whom truly I know not whether to marvel more, either that he in that misty time could see so clearly, or that we in this clear age go so stumblingly after him." But he praises Henry Howard, earl of Surrey; and if he does not refer to Thomas Wyatt, we may suspect that he did not distinguish between the contributors to Tottel's *Songs and Sonnets,* in which Wyatt's and Surrey's lyrics had first appeared. He praises *The Mirror for Magistrates* and the book with which Spenser had just emerged as a fine poet, *The Shepheardes Calendar,* although, as he confesses, "that same framing of his style to an old rustic language, I dare not allow."

But the value of Sidney's essay, which was written before the golden age, does not depend on his criticism of his contemporaries. It depends, rather, on its tone and style, graceful, civilized, and urbane; on the fact that it contains the first real criticism in the language, unequaled before John Dryden; and on the easy mastery with which Sidney makes use of the ideas and methods of Julius Caesar Scaliger, Antonio Sebastiani Minturno, and Ludovico Castelvetro.

Like Horace, Sidney maintains that delightful teaching is the aim of poetry; and he argues that the poet is a more effective teacher than the philosopher because he is more concrete and gives pleasure as he teaches:

> The philosopher showeth you the way, he informeth you of the particularities, as well of the tediousness of the way, as of the pleasant lodging you shall have when your journey is ended, as of the many by-turnings that may divert you from your way. But this is to no man but to him that will read him, and read him with attentive studious painfulness, which constant desire, whosoever hath in him hath already passed half the hardness of the way. . . . The philosopher teaches those who are already taught.

The poet, on the other hand, entices the reader to listen and makes him swallow the pill of morality by coating it with sugar:

> For he doth not only show the way, but giveth so sweet a prospect into the way as will entice

any man to enter into it. Nay, he doth, as if your journey should lie through a fair vineyard, at the very first give you a cluster of grapes that, full of that taste, you may long to pass further. He beginneth not with obscure definitions, which must blur the margent with interpretations and load the memory with doubtfulness, but he cometh to you with words set in delightful proportion.

The historian is likewise inferior to the poet because he is "better acquainted with a thousand years ago than with the present age," because he is "curious for antiquities and inquisitive of novelties," and because he is "so tied, not to what should be, but to what is, to the particular truth of things, and not to the general reason of things." Poets, untrammeled by the literal facts of history, are able, by representing virtue and vice, to encourage their readers to cultivate the one and shun the other.

Sidney distinguishes between verse and poetry, as Shelley was later to do; and he shows that poetry can be written in prose. "There have been many most excellent poets that never versified," he tells us; and, he adds characteristically, "now swarm many versifiers that need never answer to the name of poets." Heliodorus wrote in prose, so it is plainly "not rhyming and versing that maketh a poet."

To the argument that Plato, the most poetical of philosophers, banished poets from his Republic, Sidney answers that "the poets of his time filled the world with wrong opinions of the Gods," that Plato was "banishing the abuse, not the thing," and that elsewhere he gave "divine commendation unto poetry." As for the charge that poetry is the mother of lies, Sidney shows that a poet is not lying, because he does not pretend that what he writes is literally true.

Although Sidney naturally stresses the didactic element in poetry, he was too fine a poet to believe that the inculcation of morality and virtue was its sole function. Nor, in spite of his justifiable strictures on his contemporaries, was his taste narrow. One of the most famous passages in the *Defence* is his shamefaced confession that he had enjoyed *Chevy Chase*:

> Certainly I must confess mine own barbarousness, I never heard the old song of Percy and Douglas, that I found not my heart moved more than with a trumpet; and yet is it sung but by some blind crowder,[1] with no rougher voice than rude style: which being so evil apparelled in the dust and cobwebs of that uncivil age, what would it work, trimmed in the gorgeous eloquence of Pindar?

The whole essay is written in a singularly attractive style, witty and persuasive, and modeled, as Myrick has argued, on a classical oration. Gosson was scorned for dedicating his attack on poetry to Sidney; but the reply is quite without personalities, and even its invective is tempered with good humor and moderation, as in the concluding curse:

> If you have so earth-creeping a mind that it cannot lift itself up to look to the sky of poetry, or rather, by a certain rustical disdain, will become such a Mome as to be a Momus of poetry; then, though I will not wish unto you the ass's ears of Midas, nor to be driven by a poet's verses as Bubonax was, to hang himself, not to be rhymed to death, as is said to be done in Ireland; yet thus much curse I must send you, in the behalf of all poets, that while you live, you live in love, and never get favour for lacking skill of a sonnet, and, when you die, your memory die from the earth for want of an epitaph.

The countess of Pembroke's Arcadia is the only English masterpiece that has been allowed to go out of print. It has never been included in a popular series of classics, and one must conclude that it is read now only by scholars. It has, indeed, a reputation for tediousness. T. S. Eliot, though writing in defense of the countess of Pembroke's circle, dismissed *Arcadia* as "a monument of dullness"; F. L. Lucas called it "a rigmarole of affected coxcombry and china shepherdesses"; Vir-

1. A fiddler.

ginia Woolf described her reactions as "half dreaming, half yawning." Dullness is the one fault that the general reader neither can nor should forgive. Yet for three generations the book was read by everyone interested in literature, and there were thirteen editions between 1590 and 1674. Its popularity was partly due, like that of Rupert Brooke's poetry, to the legend attaching to the author; but it was perused by dramatists in search of plots—with Shakespeare at their head—by those who loved romances, and by those who liked their moral lessons presented in a delightful form, by Charles I, and by John Milton, who spoke of it as a "vain, amatorious poem" while conceding its worth and wit.

If, therefore, the modern reader finds it tedious, it may be because he comes to it with the wrong expectations. The development of the novel since the early eighteenth century has conditioned our views of what prose fiction should be: we look for a plot embodying a theme, for subtle characterization, for criticism of society, and usually for realism. But Sidney was not attempting to write a novel; his book is set in an imaginary past, his characters are much less vital than those of the best Elizabethan and Jacobean dramatists, and his story is wildly improbable. We are bound to be disappointed if we ask of his masterpiece what it makes no attempt to provide.

Arcadia has been published in three versions. The short version, not published until 1926, was written first. Sidney described it in the dedication as "this idle work of mine," telling his sister, the countess, that it was not intended for publication:

> being but a trifle, and that triflingly handled. Your dear self can best witness the manner, being done in loose sheets of paper, most of it in your presence, the rest, by sheets, sent unto you, as fast as they were done.

This version (the old *Arcadia*, as it is called) is in five books or acts. In his last years Sidney began expanding and rewriting the work; and he had gotten halfway through the third book, without making any use of the original third book, when he died—or when he departed to take up his post as governor of Flushing. The first two books in the revised form are twice as long as those in the old *Arcadia.* This second version, divided into chapters probably by Fulke Greville, was published in 1590. Three years later the countess of Pembroke published the third version, which consists of the 1590 version without Greville's aids to the reader, but with the addition of the unexpanded concluding books. Some of the alterations in these books apparently were made by Sidney himself, or by his sister in accordance with his intentions; for others she may have been wholly responsible. Sidney had expressed a wish that the manuscript be destroyed, no doubt partly because the revision was incomplete.

The old *Arcadia* is a straightforward romance, with the events in approximately chronological order.[2] In the new *Arcadia*, Sidney remodeled the book under the influence of the *Æthiopian History* of Heliodorus and the *Diana* of Jorge de Montemayor. He deliberately upset the chronological sequence of events, interspersing the main plot with others. We know from *The Defence of Poesie* that Sidney regarded both Xenophon's *Cyropaedia* and Heliodorus' *Æthiopian History* as "absolute heroical poems, even though they were written in prose; and he rewrote *Arcadia* to convert it into a poem, mingling the heroic and the pastoral as Montemayor had done. Even in the old *Arcadia*, Sidney had followed

2. For those who have not read the book, the following summary of the old *Arcadia* may be helpful: Basilius, terrified by an oracle prophesying disgrace and disaster to his family, abdicates for the year to which the prophecy refers. The two heroes, Pyrocles and Musidorus, fall in love with Philoclea and Pamela, the two daughters of Basilius. Pyrocles disguises himself as a woman, and Musidorus as a shepherd. Both Basilius and Gynecia, his wife, fall in love with Pyrocles, Gynecia having penetrated his disguise; but he tricks them both so that they share a bed with each other instead of with him, thus fulfilling part of the prophecy. Pyrocles and Musidorus are accused of seducing the princesses and of conspiring with Gynecia to murder Basilius, who, having taken a love potion intended for Pyrocles, appears to be dead. The heroes are about to be executed when Basilius revives; they are thus able to marry the princesses.

Montemayor's example in interspersing verses in a predominantly prose narrative.

In the new *Arcadia* many other plots are interwoven with that of the original book: for instance, the story of Argalus and Parthenia, the story of the king of Paphlagonia and his two sons (used by Shakespeare for the subplot of *King Lear*), and the intrigues of Cecropia to obtain the throne for her son, Amphialus, and her cruel treatment of Philoclea and Pamela.

Sidney was confusing in his choice of names. Daiphantus is the name assumed by Pyrocles as well as a name given to Zelmane, the daughter of Plexirtus, and Zelmane is also a name used by Pyrocles.

Some critics have argued that Sidney spoiled the original *Arcadia* by his attempt to improve it. They admit the extraordinary ingenuity of the revised version, the "marvellous involution and complexity" (as S. L. Wolff calls it), a kind of jigsaw puzzle in which every piece is essential to the grand design of the whole; but they suggest that the book is made impossibly difficult by its complicated structure, that no one at a first reading can follow the various strands in the pattern, and that, as William Hazlitt put it, it is "one of the greatest monuments of the abuse of intellectual power on record." It has even been maintained that the style of the first version, less highly wrought than that of the revision, is for that very reason without the excessive ornament and preciosity that makes Sidney's later prose so difficult to read and so unhappy a model.

Elizabethan reading habits were different from ours, and there is no evidence that Sidney's contemporaries found *Arcadia* unnecessarily complicated. That all would not be clear at first reading is surely irrelevant to an estimate of the book's success. It would be reread and discussed, digested and savored; and the complications would be a source of added pleasure. The modern reader, if he wishes to appreciate the book, cannot skim through it as he would through a best seller. He must be prepared to read it more as he would a narrative poem or James Joyce's *Ulysses.* Nor, I think, can it be seriously maintained that the style of the old *Arcadia* is superior to that of the new. Although as early as 1588 Abraham Fraunce had used a manuscript of the old *Arcadia* to provide examples of figures of speech for his *Arcadian Rhetorike,* its style is rough and unpolished compared with that of the new *Arcadia.* Many passages, it is true, Sidney used again with only slight modifications; but others he polished and refined, and many of the finest passages in the revised version are completely new.

A typical comparison may be made of the passages in the two versions describing Pyrocles after he has been lectured by Musidorus for falling in love with Philoclea:

> These words spoken vehemently and proceeding from so dearly an esteemed friend as Musidorus did so pierce poor Pyrocles that his blushing cheeks did witness with him he rather could not help, than did not know his fault. Yet, desirous by degrees to bring his friend to a gentler consideration of him, and beginning with two or three broken sighs, answered to this purpose.
>
> Pyrocles' mind was all this while so fixed upon another devotion, that he no more attentively marked his friend's discourse than the child that hath leave to play marks the last part of his lesson; or the diligent pilot in a dangerous tempest doth attend the unskillful words of a passenger; yet the very sound having imprinted the general point of his speech in his heart, pierced without any mislike of so dearly an esteemed friend, and desirous by degrees to bring him to a gentler consideration of him, with a shamefast look (witnessing he rather could not help, than did not know his fault) answered him to this purpose.

The revised version is superior in several ways. Sidney has obviously improved the structure of the prose; he has added two useful psychological touches to the character of Pyrocles; and he has inserted two similes and a metaphor. These might be regarded as supererogatory in prose fiction; but they are desirable ornaments in a heroic poem, which the new *Arcadia* was intended to be.

How much Sidney's style was admired by his contemporaries can be seen not merely from numerous references to it but also from the way it was imitated. Robert Greene, for example, who had written in a euphuistic style in the 1580s, adopted the Arcadian style for his two best romances, *Menaphon* and *Pandosto.* Sidney had complained of the artificiality and monotony of euphuism; his own style employs a much wider range of rhetorical figures and avoids the exaggerated use of antithesis and alliteration, as well as the absurd similes, that make *Euphues* so tedious. His own similes and metaphors, though frequently farfetched, are never mechanical. He speaks, for example, of blood mingling with the sea in these terms: "their blood had (as it were) filled the wrinkles of the sea's visage." He describes a tree reflected in a stream: "It seemed she looked into it and dressed her green locks by that running river." He writes of "beds of flowers, which being under the trees, the trees were to them a pavilion, and they to the trees a mosaical floor." He speaks of a storm as winter's child, "so extreme and foul a storm, that never any winter (I think) brought forth a fouler child." Instead of saying that Queen Helen spoke, he says: "But when her breath (aweary to be closed up in woe) broke the prison of her fair lips."

A longer passage, describing Pamela at her embroidery, has been condemned for absurdity:

> For the flowers she had wrought carried such life in them that the cunningest painter might have learned of her needle: which with so pretty a manner made his careers to and fro through the cloth, as if the needle itself would have been loth to have gone fromward such a mistress, but that it hoped to return thenceward very quickly again: the cloth looking with many eyes upon her, and lovingly embracing the wounds she gave it: the sheers also were at hand to behead the silk that was grown too short. And if at any time she put her mouth to bite it off, it seemed, that where she had been long in making of a rose with her hand, she would in an instant make roses with her lips. . . .

The reader who does not enjoy this bravura piece is unlikely to appreciate *Arcadia* as a whole, for it is not only delightful in itself but also helps to create the total impression of one of the two heroines. G. K. Hunter has rightly observed that Sidney's similes are not, on the whole, concerned to make things more plain or even more vivid, but by comparing the less artificial to the more artificial, to stress the importance, the complexity, the significance of the world described. Each individual incident, every gesture, one might say, becomes universalized.

John Hoskins, in his *Directions for Speech and Style,* written in 1599, used *Arcadia* as his storehouse for figures of rhetoric; and, in commenting on the way Sidney "shunned usual phrases," he explained that "this of purpose did he write to keep his style from baseness." Virginia Woolf even suggested that "often the realism and vigour of the verse comes with a shock after the drowsy languor of the prose." But although Sidney was careful to keep his style from baseness in the heroic parts of *Arcadia,* he did this from a sense of literary decorum, as can be seen from the straightforward and direct prose he uses in passages of comic relief. In the heroic parts he was aiming at what Minturno advocated: "magnificent and sumptuous pomp of incidents and language."

This sumptuous pomp is not mainly a matter of vocabulary, though Sidney is fond of hyphenated epithets, but of using all the resources of rhetoric. Two of the commonest figures in *Arcadia* are antonomasia and periphrasis. Philoclea, for example, is called "the ornament of the Earth, the model of Heaven, the triumph of Nature, the light of Beauty, Queen of love"; and, instead of saying that the lambs bleated for their dams, Sidney tells us that "the pretty lambs with bleating oratory craved the dam's comfort." Hoskins gives several examples of this figure. Sidney calls a thresher "one of Ceres' servants"; and instead of "his name was known to high and low," he writes absurdly: "No prince could pretend height nor beggar lowness to bar him from the sounds thereof."

Many of the rhetorical figures consist of the repetition of words in different ways, the playing with them, and the departure from their natural order. Sometimes Sidney will end a sentence with a word taken from the beginning:

> The thoughts are but overflowings of the mind, and the tongue is but a servant of the thoughts.
>
> In shame there is no comfort, but to be beyond all bounds of shame.

At other times the word is repeated in the middle of the sentence, and in the following example the figure is underlined by alliteration:

> That sight increased their compassion, and their compassion called up their care.

Sometimes Sidney interrupts a sentence with a parenthesis, reinforcing the meaning or correcting it (that is, epanorthosis):

> In Thessalia I say there was (well I may say there was) a Prince.

Sometimes he uses oxymoron, as in the phrase "humane inhumanity"; and sometimes he plays with the meanings of words, as in the description of "a ship, or rather the carcass of the ship, or rather some few bones of the carcass."

These are only a few examples of the scores of different figures used by Sidney. The Arcadian style depends, not as euphuism does, on comparatively few overworked figures, but on the intensive use of a wide variety of figures; thus there is no danger of the reader's becoming tired of any particular one. It is a restless, brilliant, self-conscious prose, continually calling attention to itself as much as to the thing described and, it must be admitted, becoming intolerably affected in the hands of imitators without Sidney's comprehensive intelligence and high purpose.[3]

There are two qualities of Sidney's prose that have been appreciated by those who have been unable to enjoy its more obviously Elizabethan characteristics: its descriptive power and its rhythms. There had been great works of prose before the *Arcadia,* but Sidney was the first English writer to construct long and finely articulated sentences with a conscious but varied prose rhythm, the first, perhaps, to spend as much pains on the composition of prose as others spent on verse. On every page there are touches of beauty, visual and descriptive beauty and beauty of rhythm, often combined, as in the justly famous conclusion to a long sentence describing Arcadia:

> Here a shepherd's boy piping, as though he should never be old: there a young shepherdess knitting, and withal singing, and it seemed that her voice comforted her hands to work, and her hands kept time to her voice's music.

Another example, put into the mouth of the villainous Cecropia, has the same combination of qualities:

> Have you ever seen a pure rosewater kept in a crystal glass; how fine it looks, how sweet it smells, while that beautiful glass imprisons it? Break the prison, and let the water take his own course, doth it not embrace dust, and lose all his former sweetness and fairness? Truly so are we, if we have not the stay, rather than the restraint, of crystalline marriage.

3. Shakespeare seems to have been influenced by Sidney's style in the prose of *King Lear,* I, ii (presumably because he had been reading *Arcadia* for the Gloucester scenes); but his most notable exercise in the Arcadian style, reading like a parody of it and put into the mouth of an anonymous courtier, is in *The Winter's Tale,* V, ii:

> They seem'd almost, with staring on one another, to tear the cases of their eyes; there was speech in their dumbness, language in their very gesture; they looked as they had heard of a world ransom'd, or one destroy'd. A notable passion of wonder appeared in them; but the wisest beholder that knew no more but seeing could not say if th'importance were joy or sorrow—but in the extremity of the one it must needs be.

Sidney's art, however, was a means to an end. We have seen how he maintained that the function of poetry was to teach delightfully. Although some critics have supposed that Sidney taught by means of allegory, it is clear that, apart from a few allegorical touches, he avoided the method of his friend Spenser. What he was seeking was to create an imaginary world in which human actions and passions could be displayed, freed from the accidentals of the real world. The golden world created by the poet was, moreover, more beautiful than the brazen world in which we live. Nature, Sidney tells us:

> never set forth the earth in so rich tapestry as diverse poets have done, neither with so pleasant rivers, fruitful trees, sweet-smelling flowers, nor whatsoever else may make the too much loved earth more lovely: her world is brazen, the poets only deliver a golden.

The poet's method is to teach indirectly, by means of his story:

> He cometh to you with words set in delightful proportion . . . and with a tale forsooth he cometh unto you, with a tale which holdeth children from play and old men from the chimney-corner; and pretending no more, doth intend the winning of the mind from wickedness to virtue.

Like the ideal actor of whom Hamlet speaks, Sidney's purpose was "to show virtue his own feature, scorn her own image, and the very age and body of the time his form and pressure."

In some ways the old *Arcadia* is more directly didactic than the new. Sidney cut out the narrator's moralizing, often transferring it to one of the characters in the story. The debates, as Myrick shows, "have been subordinated to the action, and the aphorisms have been half concealed in dramatic narration." The teaching is to be found mainly in the examples of human beings, good and bad, in their actions and words. As Hoskins points out, "Men are described excellently in *Arcadia*. . . . But he that will truly set down a man in a figured story must first learn truly to set down an humour, a passion, a virtue, a vice, and therein keeping decent proportion add but names and knit together the accidents and encounters." Hoskins adds that "the perfect expressing of all qualities is learned out of Aristotle's ten books of moral philosophy" and that "the understanding of Aristotle's *Rhetoric* is the directest means of skill to describe, to move, to appease, or to prevent any motion whatsoever; whereunto whosoever can fit his speech shall be truly eloquent." It is significant that Sidney had translated the first two books of *Rhetoric,* which are concerned with the tasks of persuasion, an analysis of human motives and emotions, and a list of the various lines of argument available to different kinds of speakers. Hoskins' views are supported by Greville, who tells us that Sidney's

> purpose was to limn out such exact pictures of every posture in the mind, that any man being forced, in the strains of this life, to pass through any straits or latitudes of good or ill fortune, might (as in a glass) see how to set a good countenance upon all the discountenances of adversity, and a stay upon the exorbitant smilings of chance.

Although it was natural for Hoskins, writing on rhetoric, and for Greville, who in his old age sought in Sidney's works the qualities he aimed at in his own and who in his account of Sidney was belaboring the decadence of a later age, to stress the more purpose of *Arcadia,* they undoubtedly understood Sidney's intentions. It would be wrong, however, to suppose that the characters in *Arcadia* are mere exempla or that they are all plainly black or white. Cecropia has no redeeming characteristics, and Philanax and Pamela appear to be wholly admirable; but between these extremes there are many characters, weak and amiable, vain and brave, sinful but not vicious, who together provide a representative pageant of human nature. Basilius may be condemned for his foolishness, his credulity, and his attempted adultery; Gynecia may be held up as a bad example of passion usurping the place of reason; Amphialus may be a deluded egotist; but no one could pretend that these characters are wholly evil. The characters are revealed in their actions, and the reader is always guided in his response to what they do and say.

Even the heroes, Pyrocles and Musidorus, are not depicted as perfect; but it is interesting to notice that Sidney removed two flaws in their characters in the process of revision. In the old *Arcadia,* at the end of book III, the love of Pyrocles and Philoclea is consummated before matrimony. Sidney may well have felt, or have come to feel, that it was dangerous to depict Pyrocles succumbing to this temptation, especially since the author's comment is not disapproving:

> He gives me occasion to leave him in so happy a plight, lest my pen might seem to grudge at the due bliss of these poor lovers, whose loyalty had but small respite of their fiery agonies.

Musidorus, with less excuse, is so overcome by the beauty of Pamela as she lies asleep that he determines to ravish her; but he is prevented by the timely arrival of some bandits. Musidorus is an unlikely ravisher, and Sidney may have felt that the incident would make Musidorus' final happiness undeserved. There is no reason to suppose that the countess of Pembroke was responsible for altering these two passages; but, if she did, the alterations were probably in accordance with Sidney's known wishes.

Sidney's teaching in *Arcadia* covers the whole range of private and public morality. We see the operations of lust, pride, ambition, anger, and egotism, no less than those of love, friendship, courtesy, and valor. We see the evils of superstition, tyranny, and anarchy, as well as the value of magnanimity, justice, and good counsel. We see how rebellion is caused by bad government, how courtesy and injustice, love and egotism, can be embodied in a single character. Sidney was providing, among other things, a lesson to his aristocratic readers on their duties to the state as well as on questions of private behavior. He demonstrates the dangers of a weak monarchy and of factious nobles; he shows the evils of "policy"; and, on a different plane, he exemplifies the workings of divine providence.

Nor does Sidney convey these lessons merely by the presentation of appropriate incidents and the depicting of different types of character: scattered through *Arcadia* there are orations, letters, and set speeches that further illustrate his points. Early in book 1, for example, there is a letter written by Philanax to Basilius, urging him to follow wisdom and virtue and to ignore the oracle. Pyrocles, disguised as Zelmane, makes a "pacificatory oration" to the mutinous Arcadians. Pamela recites a prayer that Charles I borrowed for his private devotions. The evil Cecropia has three powerful speeches, one tempting Philoclea to marriage (III,5), one similarly addressed to Pamela (III,10), and one addressed to her son, urging him to rape Philoclea (III,17). It can be seen from the extract from the second of these that Sidney was quite prepared to give the devil his due, as Milton was to give some of his best poetry to Comus and Satan. Cecropia is endeavoring to combat Pamela's appeals to conscience by undermining her religion with Lucretian arguments:

> Dear niece, or rather, dear daughter (if my affection and wish might prevail therein), how much doth it increase (trow you?) the earnest desire I have of this blessed match, to see these virtues of yours knit fast with such zeal of devotion, indeed the best bond, which the most politic wits have found, to hold man's wit in well doing? For, as children must first by fear be induced to know that, which after (when they do know) they are most glad of: so are these bugbears of opinions brought by great clerks into the world, to serve as shewels to keep them from those faults, whereto else the vanity of the world and weakness of senses might pull them. But in you (niece) whose excellency is such, as it need not to be held up by the staff of vulgar opinions, I would not you should love virtue servilely, for fear of I know not what, which you see not: but even for the good effects of virtue which you see. Fear, and indeed, foolish fear

> and fearful ignorance, was the first inventor of those conceits. . . . Be wise, and that wisdom shall be a God unto thee; be contented, and that is thy heaven: for else to think that those powers (if there be any such) above, are moved either by the eloquence of our prayers, or in a chafe by the folly of our actions, carries as much reason as if flies should think, that men take great care which of them hums sweetest, and which of them flies nimblest.

Such a speech displays not merely Sidney's usual eloquence but also his capacity to put himself in the place of characters with whom he could have had little sympathy. It could be said of him, to adapt John Keats's remark, that he had as much delight in depicting a Cecropia as a Pamela.

It is true, in a sense, as Virginia Woolf said, that "in the *Arcadia,* as in some luminous globe, all the seeds of English fiction lie latent." Although, as we have seen, *Arcadia* is essentially a heroic poem rather than a novel, we can find in it foreshadowings of later novels. It was not an accident that Richardson christened his first heroine Pamela, though Sidney's Pamela is closer in character to Clarissa. But we do Sidney an injustice if we treat him as a forerunner, an imperfect experimenter in a form of literature that was yet to be invented. *Arcadia* is, indeed, closer to Elizabethan drama than to any kind of novel and closer still, despite his avoidance of allegory, to *The Faerie Queene.* Unfinished though it is, *Arcadia* is incomparably the greatest Elizabethan prose work, precisely because it was conceived as a poem. Peter Heylyn called it:

> a book which besides its excellent language, rare contrivances, and delectable stories, hath in it all the strains of Poesy, comprehendeth the universal art of speaking, and to them which can discern, and will observe, notable rules for demeanour both private and public.

We have seen that Sidney, in writing his *Defence of Poesie,* was somewhat embarrassed by the dearth of good poetry between the death of Chaucer and his own day. In spite of Wyatt, Surrey, and John Skelton in the first half of the century, there was a barren period between the death of Henry VIII (1547) and the accession of Elizabeth I (1558). Indeed, with the notable exception of Thomas Sackville's great "Induction," little memorable verse was written during the first twenty years of Elizabeth's reign. The transformation was brought about largely by Sidney, Spenser, and the poets associated with them. They determined to bring to English poetry the qualities of Pierre de Ronsard and Joachim Du Bellay, of Petrarch, of Ludovico Ariosto and Torquato Tasso, and to create a literature worthy to stand beside that of France and Italy.

At first both Spenser and Sidney wasted a great deal of time experimenting with classical meters. Almost all their work of this kind was lamentable, though Sidney did succeed in writing one poem in asclepiads that can still be read with pleasure:

> O sweet woods, the delight of solitariness!
> O how much I do like your solitariness!

Much more fruitful, however, were the verse experiments of other kinds scattered through *Arcadia.* They include examples of couplets, quatrains, six-line stanzas, madrigals, sonnets, double sestinas, canzone, and terza rima; and, although in some of these forms Sidney was a pioneer, they are all executed with remarkable skill. Some of the poems are suggested by the situations in *Arcadia*; others are detached eclogues; and in a few Sidney contrived to express more personal feeling (for instance, the lines beginning "The lad Philisides," written as a compliment to Penelope Devereux, and some stanzas about Hubert Languet). Their chief importance, however, lies in the fact that they are mostly poetic exercises, the means whereby Sidney taught himself to write. He and Spenser, by teaching themselves the craft of verse, not only made possible *Astrophel and Stella* and *The Faerie Queene* but also provided later poets with sure foundations on which to build.

The best poems in *Arcadia* are better than the worst sonnets in *Astrophel and Stella.* Sidney tells us in *The Defence of Poesie* that he had "slipped into the title of a poet," and here and there he displays the charm and mastery of his later work, as in the poem that begins "Lock up, fair lids, the treasure of my heart," or the famous "My true love hath my heart, and I have his."

Astrophel and Stella, Sidney's masterpiece, written while he was still in his twenties, was the first Elizabethan sonnet sequence interspersed with songs; it earned him the title English Petrarch. Some critics, indeed, have maintained that Sidney was not really in love with Penelope Devereux, that the sequence displays "detachment from the realities of ordinary passion," and that it was largely imitated from Continental models. But although we need not doubt that Sidney would not have written the sequence without the example of French and Italian sonneteers, none of the sonnets is merely a translation; the source hunters have been able to discover only a few examples of borrowing. There is, moreover, plenty of external evidence for identifying Stella with Penelope, besides the internal evidence of the sonnet in which Sidney puns on the name of her husband, Lord Rich. It may be mentioned, too, that this particular sonnet and stanzas from two of the interspersed songs were missing from the manuscripts that were first sent to the printing houses, possibly because they were regarded as too intimate for circulation, even among friends.

This does not mean, of course, that we can rely on the sonnets for biographical detail. Sidney was creating a work of art, even if he was also expressing his love. Although the poems doubtless reflect his real feelings, there is certainly an element of fiction, of dramatization. Some of the scenes may well be imaginary. The sonnet addressed to the River Thames may have been suggested by Petrarch's sonnets addressed to the Po and the Rhone (as Sir Sidney Lee believed) rather than by an actual incident. Even the feelings ascribed to Stella may have been invented. Stella was in love with Charles Blount before and after her forced marriage to Lord Rich; and it was this, rather than her "honor," that made her reject Sidney's advances. Sidney was not at liberty to tell the truth, even if the truth in this case had been as poetical as the fiction.

In *The Defence of Poesie* Sidney complains of the artificiality of much love poetry:

> But truly many of such writings, as come under the banner of unresistable love, if I were a mistress, would never persuade me they were in love: so coldly they apply fiery speeches, as men that had rather read lovers' writings, and so caught up certain swelling phrases.

It is clear that whatever the admixture of fiction in his own sonnets, he was determined at least to give the impression of a man deeply in love. In the very first sonnet—which probably was not written first—he makes the muse say to him: "Look in thy heart and write." In the third sonnet he dissociates himself from "dainty wits" and "Pindar's apes"—the imitators of Ronsard; and in Sonnet 28 he disclaims any allegorical intention. He writes, he tells us, "in pure simplicity." Shakespeare, similarly, was to contrast his own "true plain words" with the ornate rhetoric of his rival. It is arguable that this kind of protest is itself a rhetorical device, and it has been pointed out that poets of the Pléiade had forestalled his attack on those who imitate "poor Petrarch's long-deceased woes"; but the important thing is that Sidney, unlike many Elizabethan sonneteers, does convince us by his art of the reality of his love. The beauty proceeding from art appears to be what Keats called "the true voice of feeling."

Not all the sonnets are equally serious. They range from conventional compliments and lighthearted conceits to the overflow of powerful feelings and bitter self-questionings. Some read almost like parodies, and in some of the best there is an undertone of irony. Those critics who have complained of the artificiality of the sonnets perhaps have failed to recognize the varying seriousness to be found in them. The variety of mood is one of the means by which Sidney convinces us of the reality of the experience.

As an example of Sidney's complex irony we may take Sonnet 74, which follows a conventional sonnet about Cupid and a song in which Astrophel describes how he stole a kiss from Stella while she was asleep—a stock subject for more than a thousand years. In the sonnet, however, Sidney pretends that he has never been visited by the muses, that he is a "poor layman":

> And this I swear by blackest brook of hell,
> I am no pick-purse of another's wit.

As Richard B. Young has shown, Sidney, "assuming the pose of ingenuousness and simplicity he finds in his models, makes fun of it by protesting too much." Even this does not exhaust the irony, for the first eight lines of the sonnet, in which he protests that he is not a plagiarist, are a close imitation of Persius.

Another example of irony is found in the famous sonnet on the moon (No. 31), which is not, as some critics have assumed, written in a mood of unqualified self-pity:

> With how sad steps, O Moon, thou climb'st
> the skies,
> How silently, and with how wan a face!
> What, may it be, that even in heav'nly place
> That busy archer his sharp arrows tries?
> Sure if that long-with-love-acquainted eyes
> Can judge of love, thou feel'st a lover's case:
> I read it in thy looks; thy languish'd grace,
> To me that feel the like, thy state descries.
> Then ev'n of fellowship, O Moon, tell me
> Is constant love deem'd there but want of
> wit?
> Are beauties there as proud as here they be?
> Do they above love to be lov'd, and yet
> Those lovers scorn whom that love doth
> possess?
> Do they call virtue there ungratefulness?

The wan face and the languished grace of Diana in love with Endymion reflect on the half-pitiful and half-absurd figure of Astrophel; and in the sestet Sidney asks four questions. The first is aimed at those who regard his constancy as foolish; the next two are aimed at Stella, who, he implies, is the conventional proud beauty who despises the lover she deliberately attracts; and the last is aimed at himself for stigmatizing Stella's virtue, or chastity, as ingratitude.[4]

Thomas Nashe (in a preface to the first edition) described *Astrophel and Stella* as a "tragicomedy of love . . . performed by starlight . . . the argument cruel chastity; the prologue, Hope; the epilogue, Despair." This description is true as far as it goes, and the reference to starlight nicely hits off the climactic poem of the sequence; but the complexities and ironies that distinguish Sidney's sonnets from those of his many imitators are not brought out by Nashe's oversimplification.

The sequence exhibits three linked conflicts: that between reason and passion, between virtue and an adulterous love, in Astrophel's mind; the conflict in Stella's mind between sympathetic love and chastity; and the conflict between Astrophel and Stella, ending with his defeat. Many critics have contrasted the weakness and artificiality of the early sonnets with the impressiveness of the later ones; but it may well be that the sonnets were not composed in the order in which they were printed and that Sidney was varying his style to show the development of Astrophel's love, from the time when he "saw, and liked. . . . liked, but loved not" to the later stages, when love had become an all-absorbing passion. The conventional description of Stella's eyes (No. 7), the equally conventional description of her face (No. 9), and the dragging in of Cupid and Venus for the paying of mythological compliments (Nos. 8, 11, 13, 19) do not so much show Sidney's immaturity as a poet as Astrophel's immaturity as a lover. Shakespeare, in the same way, showed the element of unreality in Romeo's love for Rosaline, Juliet's predecessor, by the conventional conceits he employs.

4. Charles Lamb, John Drinkwater, and others have taken the last line to mean "Do they call ungratefulness there a virtue?" But this interpretation would make the line intolerably clumsy, more difficult to read, and less subtle.

The attempt to reconcile love and virtue begins early in the sequence, when, in Sonnet 4, Astrophel protests that Stella

> shrines in flesh so true a Deity
> That Virtue, thou thy self shalt be in love.

In the next sonnet (No. 5) he admits that the soul ought to govern the passions and that sexual love is a false idol, but he pleads that he cannot help loving Stella. He tells us (No. 16) that he has learned love right:

> As who by being poison'd doth poison know.

He laments the waste of his talents (No. 18) and admits the justice of a friend's criticism that his young mind is marred (No. 21), but he asks:

> Hath this world aught so fair as Stella is?

The conflict is intensified as the story comes to a climax. Sometimes Astrophel argues with himself, at other times he quotes what people say about him. When Stella confesses that she loves him platonically (No. 62), he prays:

> Dear, love me not, that ye may love me more.

His joy in her confession is soon changed to dissatisfaction with the platonic relationship she demands (Nos. 71, 72):

> But ah, Desire still cries: "Give me some food."

In the later sonnets the inner conflict is replaced by Astrophel's attempt to persuade Stella to surrender. He angers her by stealing a kiss (Second Song), but is afterward permitted to kiss her. He rides to her house, confident of success (Nos. 84, 85), only to find her adamant in her chastity. He presses his suit at night, after everyone else has gone to bed, and is met by a tender but firm refusal in what is perhaps the most exquisite of the songs:

> No, no, no, no, my dear, let be.

This is followed by the bitter reproaches of the Fifth Song, which is close in spirit to the litany, oddly excluded from *Astrophel and Stella,* that has been thought, less plausibly, to have been written on the occasion of Penelope Devereux's marriage:

> Ring out your bells, let mourning shows be spread,
> For Love is dead:
> All Love is dead, infected
> With plague of deep disdain:
> Worth, as nought worth rejected,
> And fair Faith scorn doth gain.
> From so ungrateful fancy,
> From such a female frenzie,
> From them that use men thus,
> Good Lord deliver us.

Astrophel recovers from his disappointment and again tries to persuade Stella to surrender, this time in a pastoral setting. Again she refuses him and makes explicit what had previously been implied:

> Tyrant Honour doth thus use thee,
> Stella's self might not refuse thee.

After this, Astrophel has to learn to live with his own despair, recognizing

> That in my woes for thee thou art my joy,
> And in my joys for thee my only annoy.

In two earlier sonnets, not included in *Astrophel and Stella* but providing a natural sequel, Sidney addresses Desire as

> Thou blind man's mark, thou fool's self-chosen snare,

and bids farewell to the "love, which reachest but to dust," so that he may embrace the love eternal.

This account of the central theme of *Astrophel and Stella* leaves out of consideration the extraordinary variety of mood in the sequence. Astrophel can be savage, as in his attack on Lord Rich (No. 24) or in his determination to cuckold him:

> Is it not evil that such a devil wants horns?

At other times he is able to smile at himself and to engage in conceits that are not meant to be taken seriously, as when, in reply to Stella's double "no," he professes to be delighted:

> For grammar says,—to grammar who says nay?
> That in one speech two negatives affirm!

The sonnets are firmly rooted in actuality, and we are given glimpses of the world outside—the designs of the Turks and the Poles, the campaign in Holland, intrigues in Scotland, the Irish question. There are no other Elizabethan sonnets—not even Shakespeare's—with such variety; and no others have such a coherent dramatic structure. The effect is obtained partly by the use of colloquial touches, the deliberate dissonances and the abrupt changes of mood that give the impression not of a poet with his singing robes about him, but of a man speaking to men or thinking aloud. "Sure, you say well," "O fools, or overwise," "What now, Sir Fool!"

> Guess we the cause? What, is it this? Fie, no.
> Or so? Much less. Flow then? Sure thus it is. . . .

> Come, let me write. And to what end? To ease
> A burthened heart.

> Let her go! Soft, but here she comes! Go to,
> Unkind, I love you not!

Sidney is using the sonnet form for dramatic monologue. These quotations are not taken from the best sonnets, but the effectiveness of the obvious masterpieces depends partly on their juxtaposition with the less "poetical" sonnets. That is why Sidney is a more important poet than he would seem to be from the anthologies. Even the great invocation to sleep gains from its context:

> Come Sleep, O Sleep, the certain knot of peace,
> The baiting place of wit, the balm of woe,
> The poor man's wealth, the prisoner's release,
> The indifferent judge between the high and low,
> With shield of proof, shield me from out the prease
> Of those fierce darts Despair at me doth throw;
> O make in me those civil wars to cease;
> I will good tribute pay if thou do so.
> Take thou of me smooth pillows, sweetest bed,
> A chamber deaf to noise, and blind to light,
> A rosy garland, and a weary head:
> And if these things, as being thine by right,
> Move not thy heavy grace, thou shalt in me
> Livelier than elsewhere Stella's image see.

The images are not particularly original, but they are fitted into the form of the sonnet with exquisite skill, so that there is no padding and no forcing. From the point of view of poetic artistry, it is one of Sidney's finest achievements. The nice variation of vowel sounds; the subtle alliteration of *p, l,* and *s* in the octave, binding the lines and quatrains together, yet interrupted in the sixth line (because of its content) by the hard dentals; the cross alliteration in the second line (*bwbw*)—these are some of the indications of the poet's craftsmanship. Samuel Daniel, perhaps, among Sidney's followers equaled this sonnet from the point of view of sound, and Michael Drayton, once or twice, in perfection of phrasing; but Sidney has stamped the lines with his own individuality, and they are part of a larger whole, being sandwiched between two other sonnets on insomnia.

There are a number of shorter poems worthy to stand beside the best sonnets in *Astrophel and Stella,* several of which are familiar to the general reader from their appearance in every anthology of Elizabethan lyrics. The best of all, written to an Italian tune, exhibits

Sidney's effortless mastery of a difficult stanza form:

The Nightingale, as soon as April bringeth
Unto her rested sense a perfect waking,
While late bare earth, proud of new clothing
springeth,
Sings out her woes, a thorn her song-book
making:
And mournfully bewailing,
Her throat in tunes expresseth
What grief her breast oppresseth,
For Tereus' force on her chaste will
prevailing.
O Philomela fair, O take some gladness,
That here is juster cause of plaintful
sadness:
Thine earth now springs, mine fadeth,
Thy thorn without, my thorn my heart
invadeth.

There is no doubt of Sidney's greatness. The admiration felt for him as a man by those who knew him has been echoed, with justice, by successive biographers. Fulke Greville, looking back on the idol of his youth, could say truly that "the greatness which he affected was built upon true worth; esteeming fame more than riches, and noble actions far above nobility itself." But Sidney, as I have tried to show, was great not only as a man but also as a writer, partly because his writings reflect the singular beauty of his personality and partly because of his achievement in three diverse literary fields. His *Defence of Poesie* is the first real English criticism; his *Astrophel and Stella* is one of the seminal works of the sixteenth century, more influential, because more imitable, than *The Faerie Queene*; and *Arcadia* is the first great masterpiece of Elizabethan prose, which might be more generally acknowledged as such if it were more readily accessible to the general reader. Sidney achieved all this in the space of ten years, in the interstices of a life devoted to many other things: to politics, diplomacy, tournaments, travel, translation, love, and war. Sir William Temple, at the end of the seventeenth century, declared that he esteemed Sidney as "both the greatest poet and noblest genius of any that have left writings behind them, and published in ours or any other modern language." The praise is excessive, but it is a notable tribute from a man writing in an age so different from Sidney's.

Selected Bibliography

BIBLIOGRAPHIES

Tannenbaum, S. A., *Sir Philip Sidney (Concise Bibliography)*, (New York, 1941); Poirier, M., *Sir Philip Sidney, le chevalier poète élisabéthain*, (Lille, 1948) with a list of relevant books.

COLLECTED EDITIONS

The Countesse of Pembrokes Arcadia. Now the Third Time Published with Sundry New Additions, (London, 1598; repr. 10 times before 1700), including *Certaine Sonets, Defence of Poesie, Astrophel and Stella, Her Most Excellent Majestie Walking in Wansteet Garden* ("The Lady of May"), published presumably with the authority of Sidney's executors and providing good texts everywhere, including the first correct text of *Astrophel and Stella, The Works in Prose, and Verse*, 14th ed. 3 vols. (London, 1724–1725); *Miscellaneous Works and Letters*, W. Gray, ed., (Oxford, 1829; repr. Boston, 1860) with life and notes, omitting *Arcadia* and *Psalms* but including political pamphlets and some letters; *The Complete Poems*, A. B. Grosart, ed., 2 vols. (London, 1873) in Fuller Worthies' Library; G. E. Woodbury, ed., *The Defence of Poesie: A Letter to Queen Elizabeth; A Defence of Leicester*, (Boston, 1908); *Poems*, J. Drinkwater, ed. (London, 1909); *The Complete Works*, A. Feuillerat, ed., 4 vols. (Cambridge, 1912–1926), the standard ed., with full collations (except in the case of the "old" *Arcadia*) but without notes, and sometimes spoiled by a bad choice of text, and including the translation doubtfully attributed to Sidney (and finished by Arthur Golding) of Philip de Mornay's *A Woorke Concerning the Trewnesse of the Christian Religion* (1587); *Silver Poets of the Sixteenth Century*, G. Bullett, ed. (London, 1947), including Wyatt, Surrey, Sidney, Walter Raleigh, and John Davies; *Poems*, W. A. Ringler, ed. (Oxford, 1962), the standard ed., in Oxford English Texts Series; *Selected Poetry and Prose*, T. W. Craik, ed. (London, 1965).

SEPARATE WORKS

The Countesse of Pembrokes Arcadia (London, 1590), facs. ed. by H. O. Sommer (London, 1891), Sidney's revision of the first three books of the "old" *Arcadia* (which remained in MS); *Syr P. S. His Astrophel and Stella . . . to the End of Which Are Added Sundry Other Rare Sonnets of Divers Noble Men and Gentlemen . . . for Thomas Newman* (London, 1591), with preface by Thomas Nashe, is an unauthorized and corrupt version, suppressed by Sidney's executors (the "Sundry Other Rare Sonnets" were stolen mainly from Samuel Daniel), repr. by Feuillerat, vol. II, without the "other rare sonnets," and in Sir Sidney Lee, ed., *Elizabethan Sonnets,* I (London, 1904); *Astrophel and Stella . . . for Mathew Lownes* London, 1591) follows the above; *Syr P. S. His Astrophel and Stella . . . for Thomas Newman* (London, 1591) omits the preface and "other rare sonnets," and improves the text—modern eds. by A. W. Pollard (London, 1888) and M. Wilson (London, 1931), text compiled, translated, and prefaced by M. Poirier (Paris, 1957); *The Countesse of Pembrokes Arcadia . . . Now Since the First Edition Augmented and Ended* (London, 1593), the revised version of the first three books, with the last two books of the "old" *Arcadia,* slightly changed, also available in a modernized text, with seventeenth-century completion and continuation, E. A. Baker, ed. (London, 1907); *The Defence of Poesie . . . for William Ponsonby,* (London, 1595) repr. by A. S. Cook (Boston, 1890), facs. ed. by Noel Douglas (London, 1928), the version authorized by Sidney's executors; *An Apologie for Poetry . . . for Henry Olney* (London, 1595), repr. by E. Arber (London, 1868), by E. S. Shuckburgh (Cambridge, 1891), by G. G. Smith in *Elizabethan Critical Essays,* I (London, 1904), by J. C. Collins (Oxford, 1907), by E. Rhys in *Prelude to Poetry* (London, 1927), by G. Shepherd (Edinburgh, 1965); "A Discourse of Syr Ph. S. to the Queenes Majesty Touching Hir Mariage with Monsieur" (written 1580), in *Scrinia Ceciliana* (London, 1663) and in A. Collins, ed., *Letters and Memorials of State,* I (London, 1746); "Defence of Robert Dudley, Earl of Leicester," written 1584 in A. Collins, ed., *Letters and Memorials of State, I; The Psalms of David, Begun by Sir P. Sidney and Finished by the Countess of Pembroke* (London, 1823) in *Select Early English Poets,* VIII (only the first forty-three sonnets are by Sidney), complete series repr. with comments in J. Ruskin, *Rock Honeycomb* (London, 1877), reiss. in Ruskin's *Works,* XXXI (London, 1907) and edited by J. C. A. Rathmell (New York, 1963); *The Correspondence of Sir Philip Sidney and Hubert Languet,* S. A. Pears, ed. (London, 1845), also edited by W. A. Bradley (Boston, 1912).

BIOGRAPHICAL AND CRITICAL STUDIES

Whetstone, G., *Sir Philip Sidney His Honorable Life, His Valiant Death,* and *True Virtues* (London, 1587), one of the many elegies on Sidney, containing valuable biographical material, especially about his death; Greville, F., *The Life of the Renowned Sir Philip Sidney* (London, 1652), repr. by N. Smith (Oxford, 1907), does not treat Sidney as a literary figure, but as a religious and political thinker; Zouch, T., *Memoirs of the Life and Writing of Sir Philip Sidney* (London, 1809); Bourne, H. R. F., *A Memoir of Sir Philip Sidney* (London, 1862), repr. as *Sir Philip Sidney, Type of English Chivalry* (London, 1891); Symonds, J. A., *Sir Philip Sidney* (London, 1886); Dobell, B., "New Light Upon Sir Philip Sidney's 'Arcadia,' " *Quarterly Review* 211 (1909) 74–100; Wolff, S. L., *The Greek Romance in Elizabethan Prose Fiction* (New York, 1912); Greenlaw, E. A., "Sidney's *Arcadia* as an Example of Elizabethan Allegory," *Anniversary Papers by Colleagues and Pupils of George Lyman Kittredge* (Boston, 1913) 327–337; Wallace, M. W., *The Life of Sir Philip Sidney,* (Cambridge, 1915); Scott, J. G., *Les sonnets élisabéthains* (Paris, 1929), the most complete listing of sources and traditions for the sonnet sequences, including *Astrophel and Stella;* Zandvoort, R. W., *Sidney's Arcadia, a Comparison Between the Two Versions* (Amsterdam, 1929), the basic work on this subject; Wilson, M., *Sir Philip Sidney* (London, 1931); Woolf, V., *The Common Reader: Second Series* (London, 1932), contains the essay "The Countesse of Pembroke's Arcadia,"; Myrick, K. O., *Sir Philip Sidney as a Literary Craftsman* (Cambridge, Mass., 1935), pioneer study of the art of Sidney's forms.

See also W. Ringler, "Master Drant's Rules," *Philological Quarterly,* 29 (1950), deleted passages from the "old" *Arcadia,* previously unprinted; and "Poems Attributed to Sir Philip Sidney," *Studies in Philology,* 47 (1950) 126–151; Crane, W. G., *Wit and Rhetoric in the Renaissance* (New York, 1938); Moffet, T., *Nobilis, or A View of the Life and Death of a Sidney,* edited and translated from the Latin by V. B. Heltzel and H. H. Hudson (San Marino, Calif., 1940); Dowlin, C. M., "Sidney and Other Men's Thought"; *Review of English Studies,* 20 (1944) 257–271; Spencer, T., "The Poetry of Sidney," *Journal of English Literary History,* 12 (1945), brilliant treatment of Sidney's poetic "sincerity"; Duhamel, P. A., "Sidney's *Arcadia* and Elizabethan Rhetoric," *Studies in Philology,* 45 (1948) 134–150; Danby, J. F., *Poets on Fortune's Hill: Studies in Sidney, Shakespeare, Beaumont and Fletcher,* (London, 1952), brilliant evocation of the moral ideals of the *Arcadia;* Buxton, J., *Sidney and the English Renaissance* (London, 1954), useful on Sidney's European connections; Tillyard, E. M. W., *The English Epic* (London, 1954); Boas, F. S., *Sir Philip Sidney, Representative Elizabethan* (London, 1955); Walker, D. P., "Ways of Dealing with Atheists: A Background of Pamela's Refutation of Cecropia," *Bibliothèque d'humanisme et renaissance,* 17 (1955) 252–277; Lever, J. L., *The Elizabethan Love Sonnet* (London, 1956); Yates, F. A., "Elizabethan Chivalry: The Romance of the Accession Day Tilts," *Journal of the*

Warburg and Courtauld Institutes, 20 (1957) 4–25; *Three Studies in the Renaissance: Sidney, Jonson, Milton,* R. B. Young et al., (New Haven, 1958), contains the essay "English Petrarke: A Study of Sidney's *Astrophel and Stella*"; Montgomery, R. L., *Symmetry and Sense: The Poetry of Sir Philip Sidney* (Austin, Tex., 1961); Van Dorsten, J. A., *Poets, Patrons and Professors* (London, 1962); Davis, W. R., and Lanham, R. A., *Sidney's Arcadia* (New Haven, 1965); Kalstone, D., *Sidney's Poetry* (Cambridge, Mass., 1965).

STEVIE SMITH
(1902–1971)

SUZANNE FOX

TWENTY YEARS AFTER her death, Stevie Smith remains as puzzling as a writer as she is endearing as a personality. As "Stevie," the literary spinster of Palmers Green, she is domestic, cozy, and classifiable; as "Stevie Smith," the poet, she is charming but elusive, as difficult to analyze as she is to categorize. Her life has been the subject of two full-length biographies as well as a play (Hugh Whitemore's *Stevie: A Play,* 1977) which was adapted into a popular film (*Stevie,* starring Glenda Jackson, 1978) while her work has been left relatively unexplored by the critical establishment. Many well-known contemporary writers have commented on her work, but all have done so briefly; both of the longer studies now in print are overviews, too general in scope to address her poetics in detail.

Stevie Smith herself created the skittish, companionable persona that has fed her posthumous popularity. For any writer, but for women writers particularly, the cultivation of such an eccentric mask both brings privilege and exacts a price. The roles that Smith played so enthusiastically—the dotty spinster, the childlike naïf, the impish witch—effectively released her from many of the personal and creative constrictions facing women writers of her generation. Yet they also have helped to abet what can only be called her poetic marginalization; Smith herself helped to manufacture the pickets that would be used to fence her out of the garden of serious poetry. Although the two women are dissimilar in personality, purpose, and magnitude of achievement, it is instructive to think in this regard of Emily Dickinson: another woman writer whose withdrawal from accepted sexual and maternal roles, deliberate eccentricity, and apparent childishness helped delay serious critical consideration of her work.

Even without the confusion engendered by the persona—one is almost tempted to say the product—that became "Stevie," Smith's poetic oeuvre would confound the critical expectations traditionally brought to bear upon and define serious poetry. Her output was bewilderingly large—more than a thousand poems as well as extensive work in prose. Many of the poems are brief—a couplet or one or two quatrains in length; many are undeniably slight in ambition and effect; many bear obvious relation to casual, "easy" genres such as nursery rhyme, song, or nonsense verse; many are humorous or offhand in tone. Smith insisted on singing, rather than respectably intoning, her poems at readings and on publishing them accompanied by her own drawings. This practice would seem to deny the self-sufficiency and seriousness of her poetic enterprise even if the drawings had, say, William Blake's visionary intensity rather than her own doodling, almost self-deprecating delicacy. Finally, her work displays little in the way of progression, either technically or thematically. The same strategies and subjects seen in her first book are found in her last, making it unhelpful to study her work through the familiar method of chronological development or improvement. In short, her individual poems and her oeuvre alike challenge Romantic and traditional assumptions that great poetry must be serious, pure, intense, painstakingly wrought, and difficult.

The issue here is neither to deny that such qualities can characterize great poetry nor to digress into the tempting but complex realm of critical parameters and expectations. Instead, it is simply to point out that the unconsidered application of these criteria has not served the study of Smith's particular gifts well. As Mark Storey writes, the critical establishment seems to have acknowledged her existence without accommodating her into the terms of its discourse (p. 42). Smith is widely praised, but too often the admiration seems bestowed despite her method rather than because of it. Her longer, most carefully composed, or most "serious" poems are singled out for note while her brief, humorous, or apparently offhand works are dismissed. Such an assessment finds her on her weakest ground and reinforces the very values she habitually rejected. In fact, serious consideration of Smith's oeuvre discloses a consistent resistance to this type of hierarchical ranking—a resistance she maintained even when that apostasy brought her decades of unwelcome critical obscurity.

The foundation of Smith's aesthetic is her deliberate persistence in scrambling the signals of poetic seriousness. Thematically as well as formally, her impulse is one of inclusion; she juxtaposes contradictory orders—silliness and despair, grandiosity and deflation, childishness and wisdom, enchantment and irony, irregularity and order, brevity and expansion, freedom and constraint, plain speech and mystery—until the falsity of such distinctions is revealed. Her work is so companionable, so unpretentious, so unfailingly lucid, that the profound anarchism inherent in this strategy goes unnoticed, leaving only an impression of originality and freshness along with a suspicion that the tidy boundaries of language have been gleefully transgressed. Smith's value in twentieth-century poetry is not her intermittent willingness to meet the aesthetic demands of the good or competent poem, but her boldness in stepping beyond them.

LIFE

Writers on Stevie Smith have often wondered how this dull, suburban spinster could create such a provocative, vividly unique body of work. In fact, though few readers would wish to live Smith's life, recent biographies suggest that it was not only sufficient but also bountiful in nurturing her particular gift. It fed her richly on the great hymns, ballads, and children's rhymes that informed her innately receptive ear; taught her the literary canon without exposing her to the academy's factionalism or self-consciousness; brought her into the heart of London literary life while offering her an escape from it; and provided what was, for her, the wholly necessary security of a fixed home, a familiar routine, and a trustworthy, undemanding, unvarying companion. Some of these advantages came to her by chance; others, by choice—Smith understood perfectly what supported her work and stuck to it even when it ran directly contrary to prevailing notions of creative imperatives. They are not by themselves enough to "explain" her originality, the fact that she wrote like no one else either then or since. But what artist's life, however dramatic or sophisticated, is like another's? The originality of her work is ultimately a function of the originality of her mind. Smith's mind, with its peculiar combination of rueful wit, moral and intellectual probity, verbal ingenuity, and sheer intelligence, would have been just as astonishingly sparkling in a salon in literary bohemia as it was immured in Palmers Green.

Stevie Smith was born Florence Margaret Smith on 20 September 1902, in the port of Hull. Called Peggy until her middle twenties, when a friend likened her to the popular jockey Steve Donoghue, she was the second daughter of Charles Ward Smith and Ethel Spear Smith. The Smith and the Spear families were solidly middle class, but by the time of Stevie's birth the family stability and fortunes had both begun to slip. The blame can be laid chiefly on Charles Ward Smith, whose lifelong desire to go to sea had been thwarted by a domineering mother. He took over his father's forwarding agency instead, but had little interest in the work. Slackly run, the firm began to founder; Smith's marriage seems to have been unsatisfactory as well, and in 1906 he left his wife and two children to work for the White Star Shipping Line. There was no legal separation, but Charles Smith never lived permanently with his wife and children again. Neither did he contribute to his family's tenuous livelihood, a failing that exacerbated Smith's later distaste for her father. He visited intermittently and sent brief, noncommittal postcards. Pompey, the autobiographical protagonist of Smith's *Novel on Yellow Paper,* remembers the words "Off to Valparaiso love Daddy" as the entire text of one of his cards and adds, "And a very profound impression of transiency they left upon me" (p. 76).[1] This experience of abandonment was the first of a series of childhood losses that affected Smith deeply.

In 1906, Mrs. Smith, her two daughters, and her sister Madge Spear moved to 1 Avondale Road, Palmers Green, the house in which Smith was to live for the rest of her life. Palmers Green, a suburb of London, was still primarily rural at the time the Smiths arrived. It offered Smith and her sister Molly fields, woods, and parkland to play in, an idyllic landscape given added spice by such suburban touches as a small railway station complete with poster advertisements. Smith loved Palmers Green even fifty years later, when it had grown crowded and shabby; she described it as an ideal setting for children and frequently memorialized it, only thinly disguised as Syler's or Bottle Green, in her essays and poems. The continuity, space, and unpretentious briskness the town offered were tremendously important to Smith, and she extolled her particular suburb's virtues even as she scathingly satirized the inanities of what she called the "suburban classes."

Smith's acclimatization to the new world of Palmers Green was interrupted almost immediately when she contracted a form of tuberculosis, at that time still impossible to treat quickly. With the exception of summer visits to the seaside with her family, she spent the next three years at the Yarrow Convalescent Home in Broadstairs, Kent. Her early days there were not unpleasant, but she became progressively lonelier and more homesick as her stay went on. She later attributed her first thoughts of suicide to this period, writing in *Novel on Yellow Paper* that her recognition at the age of eight that one could choose not to live was what made life bearable; in the same book she recommended, not entirely jokingly, that children be educated about the availability of suicide in order to "brace and fortify" them. Smith recovered and was able to leave the children's home at the age of nine, but chronic fatigue and a tendency to nervous strain were to remain constants throughout her life.

Smith returned from Broadstairs to Palmers Green to begin her formal education. The Palmers Green High School taught English literature and the classics intensively, with an emphasis on memorization that helped Smith further develop her storehouse of literary models and hone her acute poetic ear, a process that her family's attendance at Anglican worship, with its great hymns and liturgy, supported as well. Smith enjoyed this first school but was less happy at North London Collegiate, which succeeded it. During this period the Smith family held a stable if financially rather precarious place in the community of Palmers Green. Gradually, however, Ethel Smith's health began to decline. In 1919 she died of an extended and painful respiratory illness. The exhaustion and depression engendered by her mother's death, her relatively poor academic showing, and the family's lack of funds combined to steer Smith away from university training. Instead, she enrolled in a secretarial academy. Her first po-

1. Page references for the *Novel on Yellow Paper* are from the Virago Press edition first published in London in 1980.

sition after graduation was with an engineering firm. Within a year, however, she had found the job with the Pearson (later Newnes) publishing organization that she was to hold for thirty years.

By 1922, the basic patterns that Smith was to follow for most of her life were established. The house in Palmers Green; a quiet routine with Madge Spear, her "Lion Aunt," who became her lifetime companion until the aunt's death in 1968; her undemanding job at Newnes; intensive reading and writing; a cycle of lunches, dinners, and weekend visits with friends: these fixed points characterized most of Smith's life. Her routine was far from idyllic. Palmers Green was inconvenient and at times confining. Her job at Newnes was emotionally deadening and would prove financially inadequate. Even life with the Lion Aunt, who was stalwart, loving, protective, and, to Smith's mind, happily unliterary, had its strains. Yet clearly the fixity of her life satisfied a deep need, for Smith made few serious attempts to change it. She had romantic relationships of varying degrees of seriousness with one woman (whose name is not revealed) and several men, including Karl Eckinger and Eric Armitage (the "Karl" and "Freddy" of her novels and poems) and, reportedly, George Orwell. But by the time she was thirty, she seems to have acknowledged that marriage, children, and even serious romantic relationships were not for her. She preferred the more intermittent rhythms of friendship and was, according to contemporary accounts, a witty, scathing, entertaining, and at times demanding companion. She was gregarious and had a wide circle of friends, but the bond with her aunt formed the single long-term emotional commitment of her adult life.

Spurred in part by her embarrassment at not having attended university, Smith read voraciously during the 1920's. She kept a series of notebooks that list, comment on, and quote from her reading of the period, reading that broadened her knowledge through the addition of more modern and more varied works. These notebooks attest to the tremendous range of her reading, which included history, biography, theology, fiction, and literary criticism; they note works by authors including Euripides, Jean Racine, William Blake, Joseph Conrad, Edgar Allan Poe, D. H. Lawrence, Virginia Woolf, Franz Kafka, James Joyce, and lesser known writers of her period. The notebooks conclusively prove Smith's familiarity not just with classic literature but also with the literary trends of her own time, contradicting entirely the idea that she was either a naïf or a miraculous original without antecedents or influences. Many of the works she read during this period turn up later, their subjects adapted and their texts echoed, quoted, or parodied, in her poems and novels. The single area she appears to have avoided in her reading was contemporary poetry, which she seems to have feared imitating too closely.

Smith had begun writing verse while still at school but did not make her first sustained attempts at poetry until the mid-1920's. Her early poems display many of the hallmarks of her later style set within somewhat more timid and more derivative forms. She concealed her writing from most of her intimates for over a decade. In 1934 she sent a large group of poems—she was always a prolific writer—to the Curtis Brown literary agency, whose reader they bewildered and dismayed. A second group, sent to Chatto & Windus in 1935, received a more positive response. Ian Parsons, Smith's contact there, was unable to publish them but encouraged her to write a novel first in order to help establish her name.

Hesitant at first, Smith composed *Novel on Yellow Paper* during an intensely productive ten-week period in the fall of 1935. Despite revisions intended to make it more conventional in structure and punctuation, Chatto & Windus refused to publish the book. It was brought out by Jonathan Cape in September 1936. Its reviewers, who included some of the most prominent critics of the day, were not without their complaints, but virtually all recognized a new and original literary voice. This favorable response and the book's engaging, energetic, intimate tone—which seemed to suit its times perfectly—helped to make it a notable success. During this same period six of Smith's poems, including the strikingly insouciant "Freddy," were published by *The New Statesman.* By the beginning of 1937, Smith had decisively arrived, with force and fanfare, on the English literary scene. Perhaps the only negative voice was that of her employer, Newnes, which disliked her new notoriety and distrusted the increasingly idiosyncratic, childlike dress and persona she slowly began to adopt.

Smith's success created an immediate interest in her work—her reviews and essays as well as her poems. At the same time it dramatically expanded her circle of literary friends, contacts, and correspondents. She enjoyed and took advantage of the wider opportunities both changes afforded her. A highly social being, Smith welcomed the excitement and exposure to new ideas her friendships with prominent writers, editors, and critics brought to her life. The reassurance of success and the vein of creativity tapped by the composition of *Novel on Yellow Paper* yielded a steady stream of new work to meet the growing demand. Her poems appeared widely in periodicals, and her first collection of poetry, *A Good Time Was Had by All,* was published in 1937. A second book of poems, *Tender Only to One,* and a novel, *Over the Frontier,* both appeared in 1938. The response to the poetry was excellent, fueled by the recognition of the quirky uniqueness of her voice. *Over the Frontier* a far less effervescent production than *Novel on Yellow Paper,* was reviewed widely but to mixed notices by critics uncomfortable with its midstream switch from the familiar chatty narrative voice to an ominous, mysterious lyricism. Smith wrote a third novel, "Married to Death," in 1937 but abandoned the manuscript when a friend, the editor David Garnett, reluctantly declared it to be virtually unreadable.

By the early 1940's the war had helped to change the English national climate from gaiety to sobriety. Smith did volunteer work in London but, as always, refused both to ally herself with any political movement and to exaggerate the gloom of the times, since she found what she called "world-worrying" to be both prideful and self-aggrandizing. She began having difficulty publishing her work at this time—as several commentators have pointed out, its apparent lightness may have been considered unsuited to the somber wartime years. Smith's third volume of poetry, *Mother, What Is Man?,* did not appear until 1942, and *Harold's Leap* not until 1950. *The Holiday,* her final novel, was composed during the war but not published until 1949. She continued to write reviews, but her work was to stay out of fashion through the 1940's and much of the 1950's, an extended obscurity that affected her income, her confidence, and her sense of connection to a literary circle. In response to this frustration, as well as to those of chronic depression, a dreary job, and a tiring home life with her aging aunt, Smith attempted suicide in 1953. She was retired as a result and used her free time to write additional reviews and poetry. She received a pension from Newnes but her finances remained tenuous, as they had been for some time.

The André Deutsch organization rather reluctantly published *Not Waving But Drowning,* Smith's fifth collection of poems, in 1957. It received wider and more positive attention than her books of the 1940's and early 1950's, and marked the turn of the tide of both public taste and Smith's popularity. The 1960's were as generous with recognition as the previous years had been sparing. The decade saw the publication of her *Selected Poems* in England in 1962 and in America two years later; frequent appearances on BBC Radio; the acceptance of her work by leading periodicals in both England and America; widespread and favorable reviews of the *Selected Poems* (1962) and the subsequent *Frog Prince and Other Poems* (1966); recognition by peers including Robert Lowell, Phillip Larkin, and Sylvia Plath; and the honor of the Cholmondeley Award for Poetry in 1966. Smith reveled in these honors, which were especially welcome after the drought of so many years. Though they were physically draining, she also enjoyed her many opportunities to appear at the poetry readings and festivals that became hugely popular during this period. Her poetry, so often influenced by sung or spoken models, was ideal for performance. By all accounts she was a frail, eccentric, and captivating stage presence, a star who sang her poetry boldly in a high, oddly tuneless voice, outshone fellow readers who included some of the century's best-known poets, and was surprisingly popular with the young people in her audiences.

By 1969, when she was awarded the Queen's Gold Medal for Poetry (she believed she disconcerted the queen with her odd dress and chat about poetry and murder), Smith was a lively but increasingly fragile sixty-seven. Her beloved aunt had died in 1968 at the age of ninety-six, after a long period of invalidism, leaving Smith lonely and grief-stricken. Her sister, Molly, suffered a stroke in January 1969, requiring Smith to make frequent visits to Devon. Smith was at her sister's when, in the fall of 1970, she began experiencing dizziness and difficulties with speech. Her symptoms worsened quickly, and a biopsy revealed an inoperable brain tumor. She died on 7 March 1971. *Scorpion and Other Poems,* a posthumous collection, was published in 1972. It had as its final poem her second work titled "Come, Death," a work she had recited for visitors to her hospital room during her final illness.

> I feel ill. What can the matter be?
> I'd ask God to have pity on me,
> But I turn to the one I know, and say:
> Come, Death, and carry me away.
>
> Ah me, sweet Death, you are the only god
> Who comes as a servant when he is called,
>   you know,
> Listen then to this sound I make, it is sharp,
> Come Death. Do not be slow.

POETIC THEMES

Stevie Smith wrote a poetry of isolation in a determinedly social voice. Her poems are typically engaging in tone, direct in manner, and unpretentious in approach. Their slightness and eccentricity often mask the darkness of their vision, just as their diversity of subject and persona tend to obscure the relentless persistence with which she examined her few, central concerns. Smith's simple, apparently naive surfaces echo off of, collide with, underscore, mock, or are mocked by her stark themes of desolation, loneliness, and despair. This disjunction between content and manner explains, though it does not support, the frequent classification of this most "deathwards" of poets among the practitioners of light and children's verse.

In a recorded conversation with a friend, the writer and editor Kay Dick, Smith commented that "being alive is like being in enemy territory" (Dick, p. 45). Though uncharacteristically portentous in tone, this remark provides a useful key to her thematics. The sense of inhabiting an unfamiliar, even hostile domain; the necessity of remaining always wary; the feeling of being odd, incongruous, mysteriously misplaced: all are constants in her poetry. Her eye—and, even more intensely, her ear—has the wicked acuity of the eternal observer rather than the complacence of one at home; whether they misunderstand or are misunderstood, for Smith's characters all language seems a foreign language at times. Her comment prepares one, too, for the movement in her poetry, the frequency with which her characters find themselves traveling, seeking, wandering, departing or, even when at rest, restless.

In itself, this recognition of the human's innate alienation is not new. What distinguishes Smith from the many other modern writers who share it is her particularly rueful response. She is acutely aware of the essential comicality of incongruity, and she exploits it in both the form and the content of her poetry. She venerates a kind of sardonic stoicism that finds moral virtue in the simultaneous acknowledgment of and resistance to the yearning for consolation. She abhors sentimentality, exaggeration, and self-aggrandizement, whether born of love or of despair. Smith satirizes, teases, and debates the man-made tidinesses—Christianity, marriage, class and political groupings—that try to mask the essential isolation and confusion of life with a spurious order. Above all she welcomes Death as god, servant, friend, father, prince, and deliverer: the primal force, at once all-controlling and controllable, who ends life's exile and thus, paradoxically, makes it possible to live joyfully in that exile.

Smith's large oeuvre is as remarkable for the important genres it excludes as it is for those it encompasses. She wrote virtually no conventional love lyrics, little visually descriptive nature poetry. Instead she found her most natural voice in two modes: the poem of philosophical or moral speculation and the narrative. Her poems in the former category muse on religion, human and animal relationships, and the many passing subjects that caught Smith's attention: illegitimacy, river pollution, the validity of cheap editions of Walt Whitman. Some are brief and aphoristic, such as "From the Greek":

> To many men strange fates are given
> Beyond remission or recall
> But the worst fate of all (tra la)
> 's to have no fate at all (tra la).

Others, such as "This Is Disgraceful and Abominable," "Oh Christianity, Christianity," or "Pretty," are extended and conversational arguments. At their best their sustained attention to a topic yields rewards, but they always flirt with and often surrender to the dangers of polemicism. They become overly essayistic and declamatory: intelligent and sharply sarcastic, but without the necessary edge of irony.

Instead, Smith's most comfortable mode is that of monologue and narrative, genres she knew well from her extensive early reading. At the heart of her brief poetic stories are people; her *Collected Poems* (1975) has the air of a cocktail party given by an individual of large and diverse acquaintance: The crowds are lively, the personalities heterogeneous, and the chatter immensely. varied. She lifts characters from her own life; adapts historical figures from Hadrian to Cranmer; reworks mythical, legendary, or biblical beings such as Eve, Rapunzel, King Arthur, and Persephone. She invents a gallery of her own improbable characters, some handed simple, suburban names like Pauline, Elinor, and Amelia, others the fruit of a gleeful wordplay: the Romans Tenuous, Precarious, Hazardous, and Spurious, among others; the child killer, Malady Festing and her daughter Angel Boley; Lord Barrenstock and Lord Say-and-Seal; the commercial villains Profit and Batten; widowed Mrs. Courtly; and renegade Lady 'Rogue' Singleton. She writes often about children and almost as often about animals, from the Hound of Ulster to the lions that ate the Christian martyrs (whose contribution to the church she feels has been overlooked).

Smith presents all of her characters sparingly, without physical description, detailed characterization, or narrative resolution. Her monologues offer a chatty surface, but the stories themselves are truncated, mysterious, and oblique.

> I shall be glad to be silent, Mother, and hear
> you speak,
> You encourage me to tell too much, and my
> thoughts are weak,
> I shall keep them to myself for a time, and
> when I am older
> They will shine as a white worm shines
> under a green boulder.
> ("The White Thought")

> Standing alone on a fence in a spasm,
> I behold all life in a microcosm.
> Behind me unknown with a beckoning
> finger
> Is the house and well timbered park. I linger
> Uncertain yet whether I should enter, take
> possession,
> still the nuisance
> Of a huge ambition; and below me is the
> protesting
> face of my cousin.
> ("The Cousin")

Smith includes only what captures her imagination, that is, the alienation of her characters from themselves, others, their language, and their world. Their relationship to those around them is typically one of failed communion and missed connections; they are excessive or eccentric, wistfully or defiantly out of step, time, and tune. Virtually all share, in one way or another, the misfit, misunderstood loneliness, at once excruciating and comical, of "The Songster":

> Miss Pauncefort sang at the top of her voice
> (Sing tirry-lirry-lirry down the lane)
> And nobody knew what she sang about
> (Sing tirry-lirry-lirry all the same).

The poems' apparently offhand quality is deliberate. Casual, brief, or light-verse forms—nursery rhymes, nonsense stanzas, clerihew quatrains, songs—echo her characters' marginality. The childlike rhythms refract their painful subjects, functioning like prisms whose simple transparency makes visible a rainbow of distinct and complex colorations. Smith's songster (perhaps not incidentally, she performed her own poems by singing them) is savored by her creator, in the poem and in the drawing of a buxom, widemouthed, platter-hatted woman that accompanies it, as an undeniably comical figure. Yet her painful isolation and patent absurdity are heroic: She resists assimilation or, in this case, silence. The poem, like many of Smith's best, leaves the reader "on the fence in a spasm," hovering between pity and laughter, admiration and ridicule. The subtle indeterminacy of the parenthetical lines adds a characteristic element of ambiguity to Smith's habitually lucid literal surface.

Smith models many of her poems on children's literature, especially nursery rhymes and fairy tales. She writes often and unsentimentally about children, whom she finds powerful and anarchic rather than sweet. Her children are uncannily canny beings; the key to lack of innocence is perhaps their parents, who emerge again and again in Smith's oeuvre as misguided or malevolent figure—"But Murderous," "Mother," "Advice to Young Children," "A Mother's Hearse," "Little Boy Lost," and "Parents" are only a few examples. Whether scheming or indifferent, they fail to provide the nurturing necessary for helpless infants. Virtually all of her children are "cynical babes," as she says in "Infant," and, as she adds, not without cause. They have a premature prescience that both protects and isolates them.

> My mother was a romantic girl
> So she had to marry a man with his hair in
> curl
> Who subsequently became my unrespected
> papa,
> But that was a long time ago now.
> . . .
> I sat upright in my baby carriage
> And wished mama hadn't made such a
> foolish marriage.
> I tried to hide it, but it showed in my eyes
> unfortunately
> And a fortnight later papa ran away to sea.
>
> He used to come home on leave
> It was always the same
> I could not grieve
> But I think I was somewhat to blame.
> ("Papa Love Baby")

Here Smith juxtaposes the sentimentally simplistic family history with the sophisticated, even jaded voice of the child. In this world it is adulthood that is naive and foolish, overly susceptible to dreams of romance, and childhood that is ironic and detached. This deliberate self-distancing becomes the child's salvation from the uncertainty of the adult's insincere, arbitrary love. "The Orphan Reformed" is not "right" until she ceases "looking for parents and cover," until she realizes that "really she is better alone," until "when she cries, Father, Mother, it is only to please" rather than with the expectation of true love. "The Wanderer" uses echoes of the supernatural ballad to explore the same theme, though in a manner that allows the underlying longing to surface even as it is denied.

> Twas the voice of the Wanderer, I heard her
> exclaim,
> You have weaned me too soon, you must
> nurse me again,

She taps as she passes at each window pane,
Pray, does she not know that she taps in
vain?

Her voice flies away on the midnight wind,
But would she be happier if she were
within?
She is happier far where the night winds fall,
And there are no doors and no windows at
all.

Many of Smith's characters share this sense of premature weaning, this "Dream of Nourishment," to use the title of one of her poems. "I had a dream of nourishment / Against a breast," it begins, then continues, "But in my dream the breast withdrew." For Smith, surrender to the longing for nurture inevitably courts rejection, just as surrender to the yearning for home risks alienation. As the speaker of "Fairy Story" says, "I sang a song, he let me go, / But now I am home again there is nobody I know." It is safer to remain unloved and unrooted like the Wanderer or the narrator of "Lightly Bound," who says, "Do you suppose I shall stay when I can go so easily?" Smith habitually uses images of wind and air to describe the refuge chosen by these characters: the windy flight of the Wanderer, the elopement with the north wind of "Lightly Bound," the journeying and "rushing air" of "In My Dreams." Such flights are cold and isolating, but they are safe because they permit no false hopes, ask only for the freedom they can give themselves.

In my dreams I am always saying goodbye
and riding away,
Whither and why I know not nor do I care.
And the parting is sweet and the parting
over is sweeter,
And sweetest of all is the night and the
rushing air.

In my dreams they are always waving their
hands and saying goodbye,
And they give me the stirrup cup and I
smile as I drink,
I am glad the journey is set, I am glad I am
going,
I am glad, I am glad, that my friends don't
know what I think.
("In My Dreams")

Unlike so many other writers concerned with blighted love, Smith never overvalues the intimacy her characters fail to achieve. Alienation, for her, is in the nature of things, engendered both by love— ". . . if she were not so loving / She would not be so miserable," she writes in "Unpopular, Lonely and Loving"—and by the avoidance of love. The choice is not between intimacy and isolation but between an isolation masked by apparent closeness (and thus terrifying) and the less dangerous isolation of actual aloneness.

Isolation, in this sense, becomes a function of language. Like the narrator of "The After Thought," Smith's characters often find they cannot be heard: "What is that darling? You cannot hear me? / That's odd. I can hear you quite distinctly." Even when heard, they are frequently misunderstood. Language, the medium of intimacy, is almost always the medium of misperception as well.

I love little Heber
His coat is so warm
And if I don't speak to him
He'll do me no harm
But sit by my window
And stare in the street
And pull up a hassock for the comfort of
his feet.

I love little Heber
His eyes are so wide
And if I don't speak to him
He'll stay by my side.
But oh in this silence
I find but suspense:
I must speak have spoken have driven him
hence.
("Heber")

This variation on both nursery rhyme and Blake's "The Chimney Sweeper" is far more troubling and unsettled than its models. Heber appears as both human and animal, raising doubts about the potential for either response or understanding. The poem's indeterminate conclusion, straddling the future and the past, denies closure. Most important, perhaps, speech itself—more typically regarded as a bridge to intimacy—becomes a dangerous and alienating force, an action tabooed by a mysterious interdict. The text itself announces this: Afraid to speak, its persona takes refuge in the comforting patterning of regular stanzas and apparent lightness of nursery rhyme repetitions—they create a form of discourse that is childish enough to seem safe. Inevitably the freight of emotion is too heavy for this slight vehicle; the rigid self-control of the stanzas literally breaks down, spilling over into two desperately unwieldy final lines.

"Lady 'Rogue' Singleton," another poem about human relationships, pits two forms of language, rather than speech and silence, against one another:

> Come, wed me, Lady Singleton,
> And we will have a baby soon
> And we will live in Edmonton
> Where all the friendly people run.
>
> I could never make you happy, darling,
> Or give you the baby you want,
> would always very much rather, dear,
> Live in a tent.
>
> I am not a cold woman, Henry,
> But I do not feel for you,
> What I feel for the elephants and the
> miasmas
> And the general view.

The pedestrian regularity, stilted repetitions, and flat-footed rhymes of Henry's first-stanza proposal mimic the conventionality of his mind. Its invitation to marriage, baby, and suburban bliss debase the erotic passion of the love lyrics on which it is based in the same way its choices of diction—the specificity of "Edmonton," the banal "friendly"—do. In contrast, Lady Singleton is delicate, dangerous, and unpredictable. Her rhythmic boldness and its range of diction—from the flat, conversational "I am not a cold woman" to the vagueness of "miasmas"—make her words simple, memorable, and irreducible: It is as impossible to explain the symbolism of Lady Singleton's three "true loves" as it is to forget them. Yet underneath the humor Smith's typical seriousness can be glimpsed. Lady Singleton has forsaken the security of marriage without gaining any significant compensation except freedom from its stifling conventionality: the elephants, the miasmas, and the general view are at best indifferent, at worst threatening—in any case, they provide neither solace nor company.

Smith's most famous poem, "Not Waving But Drowning," plays with similar concerns. The lilting chime of "waving," "drowning," and "larking" is exactly its point: Not only do friends not understand, but language itself has gone awry—there is not enough linguistic difference between the terror of "drowning" and the childish play of "larking" to allow the narrator's peril to *be* understood. The betrayal is as much that of language as that of love.

> Nobody heard him, the dead man,
> But still he lay moaning:
> I was much further out than you thought
> And not waving but drowning.
>
> Poor chap, he always loved larking
> And now he's dead
> It must have been too cold for him his heart
> gave way,
> They said.
>
> Oh, no no no, it was too cold always
> (Still the dead one lay moaning)
> I was much too far out all my life
> And not waving but drowning.

So inadequate is the man's communication during his lifetime that he continues to "moan" after his supposed death, like a spirit doomed to search forever for the human connections that eluded him in life. Language itself is, for Smith, something that appears to be waving even as it is drowning; her speakers are seduced by its charms even as they are victimized by it.

Smith conducted a lifelong argument with Christianity, and many of her debates with it are voiced through her poems. In significant ways, Christianity was for Smith both a parent promising a spurious safety and a deeply unreliable construct of language. She and her personae long for the comfort, the fatherhood, the companionship of a God. Yet she distrusts the form in which this comfort is offered, the neat package of beliefs, rules, and dogmas. They offer a solace that denies what Smith believed to be the harsher, more random nature of reality; they are ultimately too tidy, too human, too convenient, and thus too dangerous to accept. Her conscience and her temperament lead her to insist on the "emptiness of an indifferent universe" (Barbera and McBrien, pp. 218–219) and to reject the wishful thinking that prefers spurious coziness. "Write that word right, say 'hope,' don't say 'belief,' " she wrote in her essay "The Necessity of Not Believing" (Barbera and McBrien, p. 218). We must learn to "be good without enchantment," she says in the conclusion of the long poem "How Do You See":

> I do not think we shall be able to bear it
> much longer the dishonesty
> Of clinging for comfort to beliefs we do not
> believe in,
> For comfort, and to be comfortably free of
> the fear
> Of diminishing good, as if truth were a
> convenience.
> I think if we do not learn quickly, and learn
> to teach children,
> To be good without enchantment, without
> the help
> Of beautiful painted fairy stories pretending
> to be true,
> Then I think it will be too much for us, the
> dishonesty,
> And, armed as we are now, we shall kill
> everybody,
> It will be too much for us, we shall kill
> everybody.

Again and again Smith's poems attack organized religion, particularly the Christian church. She found the concepts of sin and damnation cruel, even monstrous, and wondered how a God of love could condemn his own creatures, exiling man from the same grace he simultaneously created. She disliked the dominating, hectoring element so prominent in Christian doctrine. Above all, perhaps, Smith distrusted what she called its tidiness, the neatness of rules and hierarchies that she felt bore the "mark of our humanity" (Spalding, p. 235) far more than the mark of a god. "A god is Man's doll, you ass, / He makes him up like this on purpose. / He could have made him up worse. / He often has, in the past," she wrote in "Was He Married?" Yet Smith admitted that her feelings on God and religion fluctuated widely over time; she could never entirely discard the plentiful attractions of belief. In the end, as she said of Blake, though she herself "rows and grumbles at God and nags him . . . he cannot forget Him" (Spalding, p. 241). The intimacy and personalization of her verbs are both poignant and telling.

Paradoxically, the intensity of her feelings about Christianity weakens most of Smith's poems about it. They are among her most aggressively prosy and argumentative works, imbued with an insistent rationalism that precludes mystery. It is as though the lure of belief is so strong that she cannot afford to give in to its enchantment—in contrast with the works discussed earlier that embody enchantment even as they expose it. Far more successful are the poems that meditate on or invent Smith's own gods rather than allowing Christianity to constrain them. Among these "God the Eater" is notable and worth quoting in full.

> There is a god in whom I do not believe
> Yet to this god my love stretches,
> This god whom I do not believe in is
> My whole life, my life and I am his.
>
> Everything that I have of pleasure and pain
> (Of pain, of bitter pain and men's contempt)
> I give this god for him to feed upon
> As he is my whole life and I am his.
>
> When I am dead I hope that he will eat
> Everything I have been and have not been
> And crunch and feed upon it and grow fat
> Eating my life all up as it is his.

All of Smith's strengths are here. The voice of the poem is complex, at once seductive and disturbing. It is disenchanted, in the sense that it offers no easy escape, no placid, sentimental vision of godhead: This god feeds with relish on his flock rather than nurturing them. Yet the power, the attraction, of merging with a god (however ominous) is palpable within it. It is a poem that is at once highly controlled—note the regular stanzas—and thoroughly abandoned; the speaker submits herself entirely to her god, leaving the dangerous overtones of this submission unverbalized, to resonate within the reader. Unlike so many of the poems on Christianity, its "meaning" can neither be paraphrased nor reduced. It is unresolved, unresolvable, and thus haunting.

Ultimately, for Smith, death was the one truly satisfactory god. His very bleakness is his attraction: He makes no false promises, offers no neat orders. Smith again uses the imagery of air to denote the freedom from false shelter and confining structure that forms death's paradoxical appeal:

Why do I think of Death as a friend?
It is because he is a scatterer
He scatters the human frame
The nerviness and the great pain
Throws it on the fresh fresh air
And now it is nowhere
Only sweet Death does this
Sweet Death, kind Death,
Of all the gods you are best.
("Why Do I . . .")

Or, as she writes in "The Donkey," ". . . : at last, in Death's odder anarchy / Our pattern will be all broken up." "I aspire to be broken up," she concludes.

Unlike parents, lovers, spouses, friends, or even other gods, death is entirely reliable. "Your friends will not come tomorrow / As they did not come today / You must rely on yourself, they said," the poem "Company" states. Its speaker responds by invoking death: "Sweet Death it is only you I can Constrain for company." Confident in him as in no other, Smith and her personae engage in dialogue with death, sometimes wistfully, as in Scorpion's poignant "Scorpion so wishes to be gone, and at other times peremptorily. She believes that an awareness of the availability of suicide affords control over the potentially unbearable despair, exhaustion, or isolation her characters so often face. Yet, as she writes in *Novel on Yellow Paper,* "It is just as possible to be ignoble in self-slaying as in every other department of human activity" (p. 160). Death should not be chosen out of fear or self-pity, but earned by attempting to live life; awareness of the presence of death should be used to make life possible and to enrich the possibilities and awareness of the moment. Hers is, essentially, a Stoic's philosophy.

Yet a time may come when a poet or any
person
Having a long life behind him, pleasure and
sorrow,
But feeble now and expensive to his country
And on the point of no longer being able to
make a decision
May fancy Life comes to him with love and
says:
We are friends enough now for me to give
you death,
Then he may commit suicide, then
He may go.
("Exeat")

Ironically, perhaps, the only poems in which Smith abandons her insistent focus on disjunction and isolation are those about death. In this single relationship she found no strain, no abandonment, no conflicting or inadequate languages, no need to mask pain or longing in bravado or irony. In the end, though still as oblique and scrupulous as ever, Smith comes the closest to a love poetry of tenderness and reciprocation not to parents, children, lovers, or friends, but to death.

I have a friend
At the end
Of the world.
His name is a breath

Of fresh air.
He is dressed in
Grey chiffon. At least
I think it is chiffon.
It has a
Peculiar look, like smoke.

It wraps him round
It blows out of place
It conceals him
have not seen his face.

But I have seen his eyes, they are
As pretty and bright
As raindrops on black twigs
In March, and heard him say:

I am a breath
Of fresh air for you, a change
By and by.

. . .

But this friend
Whatever new names I give him
Is an old friend. He says:

Whatever names you give me
I am
A breath of fresh air,
A change for you.
("Black March")

POETIC FORM

A quick reading of Stevie Smith's best-known poems may suggest that she was unpracticed at conventional stanza and metrical structures, like a fledgling tennis player who knows the rules but cannot control her swing. Closer scrutiny proves Smith to be capable of, in fact skilled at, orthodox poetic practice. What begins to strike the reader instead are the arbitrary limitations the sport imposes. To continue the analogy, Smith's strategy is to flout those restrictions, acknowledging but breaking the rules and even mixing different games together. To read her work carefully is to become aware of the rigidity not just of traditional or metrical poetic structures but of most free verse as well.

Smith's is a highly referential poetry, rife with parodies, variations, and adaptations of other literature. She learned and loved the work of Tennyson, Browning, Milton, the seventeenth-century religious writers, Blake, Wordsworth, Coleridge, and many other poets. Borrowings from them, as well as from Shakespeare, Racine, fairy tales, the Bible, and the classics, abound in her poems. Sometimes these are accurate renderings, but more often they are fragmentary or twisted. The rhythms as well as the words of other literature are insistently heard. Smith writes capably and at times conventionally in a range of meters and uses traditional stanzaic patterns including heroic couplets, tercets, and a variety of quatrain forms. Her work is always reminding the reader of its highly traditional roots—in fact, it does so far more obviously than the work of many more overtly conventional poets.

Yet—and this is certainly the key to its popularity if also to its critical difficulty—it does not look, does not *sound,* like the canon on which it is modeled. One reason is suggested by the fact that Smith performed her work by singing rather than by reading it. She did not just read but memorized virtually all of the poets just mentioned—that is, she apprehended them by ear, not just by eye—and, equally important, was deeply familiar with Anglican hymns, old English and popular ballads, folk songs, nonsense and children's verse, and nursery rhymes. She was intensely aware of the rhythms of everyday speech, the music of ordinary language. The influence of these sung or spoken models is of tremendous importance to her work. Its heritage intersects—one might even say collides—with her borrowings from a more purely literary tradition. This deliberate conjunction of disparate modes, with its inclusion of the rhythms and formats of marginal or "low" discourses along with those of higher and more academic ones, helps to locate Smith's originality even as it helps explain her exclusion from the canon of "great" poetry. It also allows her to be simultaneously one of the most and one of the least literary of modern writers.

Informed by a broad knowledge of verse

structures but ultimately holding herself accountable to none, gifted with a perceptive, mimetic, and musical ear, Stevie Smith is a master of the poetic line. She works it with the virtuosity of a fisherman, flinging it out in a single extended cast, then reeling it in with uninterrupted fluidity. Read silently or spoken aloud, her lines declare themselves endlessly malleable, infinitely plastic. Her oeuvre encompasses everything from regular lines fit into formal stanzas—

Forgive me forgive me for here where I
stand
There is no friend beside me no lover at
hand
No footstep but mine in my desert of sand.
("Forgive Me, Forgive Me")

I shall be glad when there's an end
Of all the noise that doth offend
My soul. Still Night, don cloak, descend.
("Up and Down")

—to longer, almost prosy ones, apparently formless but underlain by the casual rhythms of colloquial speech.

And would people be so sympathetic if they
knew how the story went?
Best not put it to the test. Silence and tears
are convenient.
("Silence and Tears")

"It's the truth," Mrs Simpkins affirmed,
"there is no separation
There's a great reunion coming for which
this life's but a preparation."
("Mrs Simpkins")

Yet Smith's distinctiveness stems not so much from her ability to play in a variety of line lengths and meters as from her willingness to combine different modes—long lines with short, regular lines with irregular ones, fixed patterns with shifting structures-within the confines of a single work. She simultaneously establishes and rejects the contract of form; first embraces, then discards, a predictable pattern. Both strategies work by creating a norm, then interjecting one or more lines that are obviously too long, too awkward, or too unwieldy within its context. The dislocation of expectations is refreshing—and unsettling. It forces the reader to question the original patterning and to adapt to a new, more pluralistic text. Consistent with Smith's distaste for false orders and deceptive tidinesses—whether personal, religious, economic, or political—it accommodates a world of disjunctive realities even as it teases conventional assumptions about poetic unity. "Lady 'Rogue' Singleton" is typical of this strategy. So is "Pad, Pad," which shares its concern with failed love and its distinctive mix of popular, Latinate, and archaic diction:

I always remember your beautiful flowers
And the beautiful kimono you wore
When you sat on the couch
With that tigerish crouch
And told me you loved me no more.

What I cannot remember is how I felt when
you were unkind
All I know is, if you were unkind now I
should not mind.
Ah me, the power to feel exaggerated, angry
and sad
The years have taken from me. Softly I go
now, pad pad.

The poem's abandonment of the limerick form of its first stanza, with its inherent comicality and bravado, for the messier line and less controlled mode of the second verse is not just witty but entirely to the point, as is the break between voices. "Do Take Muriel Out" is radically different in effect but similar in strategy. Smith uses the simple, spare quatrains of the ballad—one of her favorite forms—as a foundation for its ominous narrative.

Do take Muriel out
She is looking so glum
Do take Muriel out
All her friends have gone.

The regularity begins to falter in the third stanza, though the rhyme and parallel structure are retained:

All her friends have gone
And she is alone
And she looks for them where they have
never been
And her peace is flown.

The intrusion of the long, loping line into the grimly neat stanzas prefigures the poem's startling end, which intensifies the impact of another irregular line with a deliberately blighted rhyme. The point of the variation, its chilling relevance, becomes clear with the recognition that the release from the etiquette of Muriel's stark, overly ordered existence can come only with the great anarchy of death:

Do take Muriel out
Although your name is Death
She will not complain
When you dance her over your blasted
heath.

Stevie Smith used rhyme extensively. End rhymes were, as Hermione Lee points out in her introduction to *Stevie Smith: A Selection,* "her most pronounced device for controlling the line" (p. 21), a fact that helps to explain the weakness of some of the unrhymed works scattered throughout her books. Not surprisingly, her use of rhyme flouts conventional expectations. Smith is not afraid of full, thumping rhymes, the kind that would be laughed out of a contemporary poetry workshop: "Your sins are red about your head / And many people wish you dead," for example, from "Lord Barrenstock"; but she also uses polysyllabic rhymes frequently: "introspective/reflective," "protocreation/imagination," "calculating/revolting," "ecstasy/artery." She rhymes English with Latin or French—for example, "Where speaking sub Specie humanitatis / Freddy and me can kiss" ("Freddy"). Even more frequently, and contrary to standard poetic practice, she rhymes on the unaccented last syllable of a polysyllabic word: "nightfall/radical," "estuary/Mary," "frequently/distinctly," "instant/confidante." Such rhymes fracture the normal spoken rhythm of her lines—one stumbles over them, trying to force both rhyme and stress to work naturally at the same time. The effect is to hammer home the artificiality, the "createdness," of the poetic construct.

Smith's frequent and masterful use of impure and slant rhymes gives her work a subtle, offbeat quality. Like the couples in her poetic narratives, the rhymes form pairs that are never quite compatible. The mismatching of her half rhymes reflects the misfitting within the poems. For example, from "Magna Est Veritas":

With my looks I am bound to look simple or
fast I would rather look simple
So I wear a tall hat on the back of my head
that is rather a temple
And I walk rather queerly and comb my
long hair
And people say, don't bother about her.

Similarly, in "The Orphan Reformed" the felicity of the rhyming stems from the fact that within the poem "for ever" and "Mother" rhyme as badly in concept as they do in sound; the same is true of "tedious" and "generous in "Child Rolandine":

But still she cries, Father, Mother
Must I be alone for ever?
Yes you must. Oh wicked orphan, oh
rebellion,
Must an orphan not be alone is that your
opinion?
("The Orphan Reformed")

Likely also, sang the Childe, my soul will
fry in hell
Because of this hatred, while in heaven my
employer does well
And why should he not, exacerbating
though he be but generous
Is it his fault I must work at a work that is
tedious?
Oh heaven sweet heaven keep my thoughts
in their night den
Do not let them by day be spoken.
But then she sang, Ah why not? tell all,
speak, speak,

Silence is vanity, speak for the whole truth's
sake.
("Childe Rolandine")

As in the "gone/alone" and "death/heath" from "Do Take Muriel Out," Smith's unusual rhymes are not always comical; often they work to unsettlingly beautiful—or beautifully unsettling—effect. Like that of her lines, Smith's manipulation of rhyme is tremendously versatile, capable of engendering a delicate, chilling, brittle, fragile, admonitory, haunting, or poignant effect. Whichever emotional resonance Smith chooses, her slant rhymes always subtly prevent resolution, keeping the poem, and the reader, gently off balance.

Thieves honor him. In the underworld he
rides carelessly.
Sometimes he rises into the air and flies
silently.
("The Ambassador")

Oh Man, Man, of all my animals dearest,
Do not come till I call, thou thou weariest
first.
("God and Man")

As with her line lengths, Smith's success with rhyme lies not only in the virtuosity of individual pairings but also in her willingness to establish regular schemes, only to abandon or transmute them. "So to Fatness Come" takes advantage of this freedom, moving from an unrhymed stanza to a series of rhymed couplets and then back, to intensify its deliberate, somber persistence.

Poor human race that must
Feed on pain, or choose another dish
And hunger worse.

. . .

I am thy friend. I wish
You to sup full of the dish
I give you and the drink,
And so to fatness come more than you
think
In health of opened heart, and know peace.
Grief spake these words to me in a dream.
I thought
He spoke no more than grace allowed
And no less than truth.

As many of the excerpts suggest, Smith's diction is tremendously rich and astonishingly varied. She mined the potential of varied vocabularies to the full, welcoming the anarchic energy released by allowing clashing idioms to meet. She savored the almost tangible textures of archaism, slang, cliché, the grand formulations of literature, the jargons of religion, science, and scholarship. Her characteristic strategy is to confront the highest of idioms—Latinate, archaic, biblical, or purely poetic language—with the lowest. The combination creates poetry that is very much the product of its own time, place, and class, yet finds a paradoxical freedom within its specificity of manner. Both "The River God" and "Magna Est Veritas," for example, mix the chatty, offhand locutions of suburban England —"plenty of go," "dear," "in a bit"—with direct and indirect echoes from the literary canon.

Hi yih, yippety-yap, merrily I flow,
O I may be an old foul river but I have
plenty of go.
Once there was a lady who was too bold
She bathed in me by the tall black cliff
where the water runs cold,
So I brought her down here
To be my beautiful dear.
Oh will she stay with me will she stay
This beautiful lady, or will she go away?
She lies in my beautiful deep river bed with
many a weed
To hold her, and many a waving reed.
("The River God")

I regard them as a contribution to almighty
Truth, magna est
veritas et praevalebit,
Agreeing with that Latin writer, Great is
Truth and will
prevail in a bit.
("Magna Est Veritas")

Where many modern poets have sought to reduce the elitism, artificiality, and distance of poetry by eliminating purely "poetic" diction entirely, Smith takes a different tack: By accommodating the most popular, the least pretentious of idioms, she is able to accommodate the grandest as well without sacrificing the colloquial, apparently spontaneous transparency of her surfaces. Her use of nonsense syllables like "tra la" or "yippety-yap"; her inclusion of contemporary slang and clichés; her love for simple, almost childlike words; her dismissal of all but essential punctuation; her use of companionable, engaging questions, appositions, invocations; and her heavy emphasis on the exclamations and qualifiers—"rather," "dear," "oh," "really," "well," "a bit," "quite"—that are usually excised from all discourse but everyday speech, help mask the sophistication of her subjects and models. When used without careful relation to content, these techniques can seem gimmicky or disingenuous. At her best, however, Smith is adept at using them simultaneously to deflate, intensify, and enliven the themes and models of her poems.

Technically, Smith remains distinctive for the confidence with which she discards conventional assumptions about poetic consistency, unity, and purity and for the boldness with which she brings together what has been kept apart. Her deliberate combinations of tight with loose forms, metrical with irregular lines, full with off rhymes, and high with low diction expand the sheer possibility within her work exponentially—the potential permutations are endless. Moreover, her aesthetic of combination keeps each poem open to change or adjustment at every moment in its progression: The establishment of one pattern never precludes another. The risk of Smith's strategy is dilution of effect, and there are poems in which she succumbs to this danger. More often, however, she reaps its rewards, obtaining for herself a poetic method that is uniquely adaptable, responsive, and *alive.*

NOVELS

In addition to a thousand or more poems, Stevie Smith wrote four novels, several short stories, a smattering of essays, and scores of reviews. Among her prose pieces the stories are charming but slight, without either great intensity of feeling or strength of technique. Smith's essays are by turns provocative and lyrical; her reviews—on works of technology, history, biography, and anthropology as well as fiction—intelligent, lucid, at once companionable and imbued with an authority essentially moral rather than literary. All of these brief prose works remain enjoyable to readers today, though few are of real literary importance. Instead, it is Smith's three published novels (a fourth was abandoned and the manuscript destroyed), written between 1936 and 1949, that stand out as her most significant prose achievement.

Smith's biographer Francis Spalding calls her *Novel on Yellow Paper* "a poet's book." This description fits all of Smith's novels well. They are books, written by a poet and studded with the author's poems, that are as much "about" their own extravagant, overweening language as any poem. They are also books that adopt the privilege, familiar from collections of poetry but rarer in extended fictions, of presenting truth as a series of disjunctive possibilities rather than as a single consistent reality. They offer a plethora of opinions on subjects from the philosophy of Boethius to the paintings of George Grosz at the same time they withhold a unified tonal, structural, or imagistic resolution. Their unfixed quality alternately enchants and unsettles, enlivens and baffles. The writer and editor David Garnett, commenting on the manuscript of Smith's abandoned novel "Married to Death," commented to her that "A book must have shape, bones, foundations. It ought to be built like a house. This is liquid, a flowing stream of words" (Spalding, p. 141). Smith's three published novels all share the fluidity Garnett identified, partaking of the speed, adaptability, and liveliness of liquid as well as of its often frustrating formlessness.

Smith's novels, which have often been likened to the equally eccentric, talkative *Tristram Shandy,* are almost entirely plotless. Their events occur in succession but not in response to one another; their narratives are propelled by the quicksilver dartings of a curious consciousness rather than by external causality. Smith makes little attempt to convey a sense of place or sustain a chronologically accurate narrative. Nor, though her characters are based so recognizably on her friends and acquaintances that libel was always a risk, did she attempt to create rounded or realistic characterizations. In her experimentalism Smith reflects the interest of the 1920's and 1930's in new and disjunctive fictional structures. She had certainly read Joyce's *Ulysses* and had commented on Virginia Woolf's *The Common Reader,* whose essays "Modern Fiction" and "The Russian Point of View" espouse the same fluidity she was to exploit, in her reading notebook. She was influenced by American fiction as well. She must have been familiar with Gertrude Stein, whose playful inversions and repetitions heavily influenced her novelistic rhythms. She admired Sinclair Lewis's novels *Arrowsmith* and *The Man Who Knew Coolidge*; the latter, like her novels, takes the form of a single extended monologue. She enjoyed the jazzy energy of Anita Loos and Dorothy Parker, from whom she picked up what she called "this sort of pseudo (for me) American accent" (Dick, p. 47), a brassiness of tone and a wisecracking approach, most evident in *Novel on Yellow Paper,* that she came to dislike quite heartily.

Smith's extended interior monologues attain neither Woolf's lyrical intensity nor Joyce's opulence of detail. Instead, as the critics of the time immediately recognized, the originality and freshness of her achievement lies in her voice: in her own words, the "talking voice that is so sweet, how hold you alive in captivity, how point you with commas, semi-colons, dashes, pauses and paragraphs?" (p. 39). The rhythm of this voice shifts slightly over time, from the skittish teasing of *Novel on Yellow Paper* to the dreamlike narrative of *Over the Frontier* and again to the melancholy introspection of *The Holiday.* Yet in all three novels it remains essentially similar and intensely distinctive. It is a swift, engaging voice, at oncc vigorous and sensitive, ruthlessly attentive and quickly distractible, pliable and brittle, honest and arch. It takes full advantage of the discontinuities of spoken conversation, yet at the same time is far more exaggerated and mannered. As does her poetry, it blends a potpourri of idioms that are rarely mixed, jumbling foreign words, archaisms, slang, and literary quotations and echoes together. Spoken through the ventriloquistic mouths of her protagonist/narrators Pompey Casmilus, in *Novel on Yellow Paper* and *Over the Frontier,* and Celia Phoze in *The Holiday,* this complex voice is both the novels' most memorable achievement and one of their greatest limitations.

Nowhere is this more true than in Smith's first book, *Novel on Yellow Paper.* This soliloquy, which loosely traces the progress of Pompey Casmilus' love affairs with Karl and Freddy in between interludes in her office, at her home, and among her friends, is the most entertaining of Smith's novels. Pompey is highly conscious of her audience, whom she flirts with, teases, provokes, admonishes, informs, questions, and, sometimes, rejects; her tone is by turns humorous, plaintive, cruel, and lyrical. Her address to the reader on the subject of her book is characteristic in its wit, its liveliness, its velocity, its slangy colloquiality, and its bravado:

> But first, Reader, I will give you a word of warning. This is a foot-off-the-ground novel that came by the left hand. And the thoughts come and go and sometimes they do not quite come and I do not pursue them to embarrass them with formality to pursue them into a harsh captivity. And if you are a foot-off-the-ground person I make no bones to say that is how you will write and only how you will write. And if you are a foot-on-the-ground person, this book will be for you a desert of weariness and exasperation. So put it down.

> Leave it alone. It was a mistake you made to get this book. You could not know. . . .
>
> Foot-on-the-ground person will have his grave grave doubts, and if he is also a smug-pug he will not keep his doubts to himself; he will say: It is not, and it cannot come to good. And I shall say, Yes it is and shall. And he will say: So you think you can do this, so you do, do you?
>
> *Yes I do, I do.*
>
> That is my final word to smug-pug. You all now have been warned. (pp. 38–40)

When, immediately after, Pompey says, "So now I will go back again to play with and pet for a moment this delicious idea . . . (p. 40), her verbs are entirely apt. She toys with and discards an astonishingly wide range of emphemera: ruthless portraits of people; disquisitions on books; childhood memories; previously unpublished poems (Pompey assures her readers that they "get the first look in"); folk and popular songs; discussions of the Christian church, marriage, death, and the education of children; a compendium of favorite quotations whose sources include Gibbon, overheard conversations, Henry Adams, and the *East African Courier*; retellings of the stories of *Phèdre* and *The Bacchae*—and more. The book's ability to accommodate the weight of this diversity, like a fairy-tale sack capacious enough to encompass an endless (and endlessly motley) assortment of objects, is due to the deftness of the narrator's conversational voice. The language of Pompey's soliloquy, if at times irritating, is also astonishingly tensile and elastic. Its velocity blurs the disparate elements of its own discourse into unity. It overtly rejects consistency and refuses to be responsible for the reader's need for resolution or explanations—a rejection made explicit in both the content and the style of the first words of the book:

> Beginning this book (not as they say "book" in our trade—they mean magazine), beginning this book, I should like if I may, I should like, if I may (that is the way Sir Phoebus writes), I should like then to say: Good- bye to all my friends, my beautiful and lovely friends.
>
> And for why?
>
> Read on, Reader, read on and work it out for yourself. (p. 9)

Despite the sassiness and effervescence that both charmed and exhausted contemporary readers, *Novel on Yellow Paper* is essentially a somber book, its gaiety born of desperation. In a 1957 letter to a friend, the critic Hans Häusermann, Smith wrote:

> How right you are about the nervousness of the writing, there is some dreadful fear that pursues always, and that has no form or substance . . . It *is* like the sea, sunny and bright (sometimes) on the surface and black and so cold seven miles down, and with such pressure the water lies. . . . So now you know why I don't want to write another novel. (Spalding, p. 180)

This pressure is evident in the book's insistent motion—Pompey seems unable to still her mind, yet even an incessant mental liveliness cannot protect her from the fear. In the midst of the bright chatter she relates her recognition of the falsity of adult love and her discovery of suicide at the age of eight, describes her pain at the agonizing death of her mother, shares a moment of anguish over her breakup with Freddy, and discovers a demon of horrific emptiness in a sea of ice cream wrappers.

> So round about Hythe and all through the streets of this little town, and up on the hills by the canal, there were pieces of paper, and there were cartons that had held ice cream and there were those little cardboard spoons that go with it. And there were newspapers and wrapping papers.
>
> There was every sort of paper there, only the devil was there too, and he was not wrapped up in paper. And I had this vision of the fiend, and he was looking like—well he was certainly not looking like that great angel Lucifer that was so fallen, so changed, but

> was still that great angel that raised impious war in heaven and battle proud. . . .
>
> No this was the fiend that is so. That is so. That is.
>
> Oh I went too far for my walk that evening and I was wishing my dear Freddy, my sweet boy Freddy, was there to bring me home, and hold my arm, and be so loving and giving, as he is so sweet. . . . (pp. 70–71)

It is characteristic that even in the midst of relating this uncanny and frightening vision, Pompey's tone shifts with great speed. From the flat, stark repetitions of fear she moves to grandiose literary echoes, wordplay (the clichéd "Oh I went too far . . ."), and sentimental posturings. She distracts herself from the peculiarly modern devil of meaninglessness with the less frightening, because more human, presence of Milton's Lucifer and the insipid charms of Freddy. And yet the shift is also Smith's backhanded way of acknowledging the exaggeration inherent in such visions—and thus their innate comicality. In her preface to the Virago edition of the novel (1980), Mary Gordon writes that Smith's work is always "balanced between terror and hilarity" (p. vii). In *Novel on Yellow Paper* the balance is not that of the scales, which settle into stasis, but that of the seesaw, liable at any moment to lurch from an unfixed airiness, with a thudding crunch, onto solid ground, from elation at the joyous plenitude of life to an intolerable despair.

Pompey's only immediate response to her terrific vision of the fiend, the painful "tearing inside" (p. 236) that she feels after breaking off with Freddy, her helplessness during her mother's death, or her inexplicable despair is to shift the subject. Yet she is not entirely without defenses against her own desolation. As it is in Smith's poetry, in *Novel on Yellow Paper* death is the presence that saves Pompey from unbearable despair. She meditates on it at length. One of the novel's most crucial passages is inspired by Pompey's childhood memory of a maid she knew at the convalescent home. The maid's affectionate actions were like those of Pompey's mother, yet the child Pompey perceived that underneath them lay not a steady love but an absence of feeling, a void "without depth or significance" (p. 156). This perception gives Pompey her first taste of real terror and her first intuition of the benevolence of death.

> It was a little early perhaps you see, to encounter the deceitfulness of outward similarity, and that perhaps is why this maid, who was so thoughtlessly and you would think harmlessly affectionate, terrified me first in such a way that I had never before been terrified, and touching my pride, sent my thoughts again toward death.
>
> And the thought of death, and I understood it so far that it is possible to die by falling off a high cliff, or out of a high window, the thought of this death was very consoling and very comforting to me. It was also a great source of strength, so that I came out of that experience very strong and very proud.
>
> (p. 156)

"Always the buoyant, ethereal and noble thought is in my mind: Death is my servant," Smith writes (p. 159). Later, she lectures with a parodic heartiness on the value of educating children about their power to avail themselves of death. The deliberately mocking tone and unsophisticated diction do not hide the urgency with which she insists on the relief afforded by death's accessibility.

> To brace and fortify the child who already is turning with fear and repugnance from the life he is born into, it is necessary to say: Things may easily become more than I choose to bear. . . . But that "choose" is a grand old burn-your-boats phrase that will put beef into the little one, and you see if it doesn't bring him to a ripe old age. If he doesn't in the end go off natural I shall be surprised. Well look here, I am not paid anything for this statement, but look here, here am I. See what it's done for me. I'm twice the girl I was that lay crying and waiting for death to come at that convalescent home. No, when I sat up and said: Death has got to come if I call him, I never called him and never have.
>
> (pp. 160–161)

Pompey's surname, Casmilus, underscores the centrality of death to the novel. Smith found the name in Lemprière's *Classical Dictionary,* where it was listed as one of the appellations used for the Greek god Hermes. (Actually, her edition misprinted Camilus, the correct name.) Hermes' character as trickster-messenger, a capricious and sometimes untrustworthy figure, is closely related to the quickly changing, often cruel Pompey. Even more important, his role as the conductor of souls to the underworld allowed Hermes to fly freely from life to death and back again. Like Hermes Camilus, Pompey holds dual citizenship in these realms. She is able to travel back and forth between them; in doing so, she makes the two realities one.

Not surprisingly, the novel ends with an image that brings together heroism and burlesque, veers from poignancy to absurdity, and bridges life and death. The tigress Flo, whose slapstick story concludes the book, completes its circle by balancing the image of the horse Kismet from the first page of the novel. Kismet, a "great eater," suggests the death hidden within the life force, the mingling of destructiveness with its motion, power, and appetite. Flo might be looked on as Kismet's mirror image, an exemplar of the vitality and courage necessary to embrace death.

> There was pity and incongruity in the death of the tigress Flo. Falling backwards into her pool at Whipsnade she lay there in a fit. The pool was drained and Flo, that mighty and unhappy creature, captured in what jungle darkness for what dishonourable destiny, was subjected to the indignity of artificial respiration. Yes, chaps, they worked Flo's legs backwards and forwards and sat on Flo's chest, and sooner them than me, you'll say, and sooner me than Flo, that couldn't understand and wasn't raised for these high jinks. Back came Flo's fled spirit and set her on uncertain pads. She looked, she lurched, and sensing some last, unnameable, not wholly apprehended, final outrage, she fell, she whimpered, clawed in vain, and died.
>
> (pp. 251–252)

The Holiday was Smith's favorite among her novels. In it she replaces Pompey Casmilus with Celia Phoze, who works in a government ministry. Like Pompey, Celia simultaneously savors and satirizes her London friends; labors at a dull job; writes, reads, and quotes poems; muses on a bewildering variety of subjects; and lives with a stalwart and affectionate aunt. Yet the voices of the two narrators differ, less because of an adjustment to Smith's characterization than because her own voice had changed over time. *The Holiday* finds her less energetic but also less self-conscious. A tone of melancholy passivity supersedes the air of arch skittishness. The novel accommodates more reflection and stronger physical descriptions; the schoolchildren in South Kensington, the park in Celia's suburb, the flat shore landscape of the holiday are effectively evoked. Like its predecessors, *The Holiday* is a structure built around emptiness and pain, but its surfaces are plainer, its design less baroque.

Though its first half is thickly populated with Celia's London colleagues, employers, and acquaintances, the key characters in *The Holiday* are few. Smith seems to have developed them in a series of complementary pairs, which include Celia's friend and colleague Tiny and his repugnant brother Clem; her aunt and her Uncle Heber, a vicar, in whose house she spends the holiday of the title; her mad cousin Tom, whom she fears yet considers marrying, and her cousin Casmilus or Caz, whom she loves and yet who is denied her by the suspicion that they share the same father.

This possibility can neither be proved nor disproved, leaving the cousins in a state of limbo Celia calls "eternally ridiculous and eternally unbearable" (p. 181).[2] The theme of incest is underscored by Smith's bestowal of Pompey's surname on Caz, a tactic that suggests a splitting of the previously single protagonist into a male and a female persona. Whatever her intentions, Smith has invested the unfulfillable yearning of the relationship

2. Page references for *The Holiday* are from the edition published by Virago Press in London in 1979.

of Celia and Caz with some of the power of the Platonic myth of creation, in which an androgynous whole is divided into halves that eternally long for reunification. Caz is, as he tells Celia, "the most flesh and blood" of any of her dreams (p. 149), and perhaps the most flesh and blood of Smith's novelistic males. Like all of her characters, he is roughly and rather vaguely sketched. Yet the interludes between the cousins have a tremendous power, particularly compared, say, with her distanced, satiric depictions of the relationship of Pompey and Freddy. Smith is never explicit, but the intensity of the thwarted physical passion between the cousins is undeniable—the language used to describe their meetings attains at times a stark simplicity rare among Smith's lively chatter.

> Caz now led me away and we went off together, treading the dark forest rides until we came to a patch of bracken and trod it down and lay down together, close together against the chilly night; where we lay for an hour.
> (p. 185).

The mingled poignancy and desperation of this central relationship helps suffuse *The Holiday* with its predominant sad, restless tone.

Smith wrote *The Holiday* during the early 1940's but was unable to find a publisher for it until 1949. To update it's setting to the postwar period, she revised it extensively before publication. There are oversights in her emendations—the most notable occurs in Chapter Nine, when an escaped German prisoner parachutes from a burning Hurricane. Yet Smith succeeds brilliantly in evoking "the trivial, the boring, the necessary, the inescapable" postwar period (p. 184), that era of "the war won, and the peace so far away" (p. 155), of which "it cannot be said that it is war, it cannot be said that it is peace, it can be said that it is post-war; this will probably go on for ten years" (p. 13).

The characters of *The Holiday,* though the panic and violence of war have passed, have taken with them its intensity, urgency, and energy. Celia admits that "there is something devilish about war, devilish exciting I mean U (p. 184). What is left in its wake is deprivation without the redemptive possibility of heroism. The novel depicts a peace that has left food still scarce, London in ruins, the staff of Celia's ministry still deciphering codes, and the British Empire beginning to dismantle itself. There is none of the ease or comfort of victory. "The peace goes badly, it goes very badly for us" (p. 7), Celia remarks, proceeding on her mundane daily rounds of "this work that is so bustling and so cosy" (p. 32) while wondering what, if anything, this work adds up to.

Early in the novel, Celia exclaims rebelliously, "Yes, certainly, it is the Devil of the Meridian, it is the devil of a middle situation that has us by the throat. . . . So that is how it is and we are rightly wretched. Courage, we should rather cry: Work in silence for the time to pass" (p. 53). The postwar period is a time of what can only be called middleness, against which no action but waiting is possible. Celia's inner life also reflects the difficulties of the "middle situation." She sees herself as dark and corrupt, yet longs for innocence. She cannot believe in Christianity, which "too much bears the human wish for something finished off and tidy" (p. 43), yet she is unable to relinquish it entirely; her ambivalence makes her life a painful exile—"If we are to be taken back, oh why were we sent out, why were we sent away from God?" she cries (p. 116). Celia finds herself, as well, in middle age, a phase of the life cycle dominated by an uncongenial "intellectuality." In contrast, she feels,

> . . . *instinctuality,* that brings with it so much glee, so much pleasure that cannot be told, so much of a vaunting mischievous humility, so much of a truly imperial meekness, runs with childhood and old age; and as I am by nature of this type of person, it is perhaps because I now run in these *middle* years that I am not enjoying it but must cast ever backwards to my childhood and forwards to my old age . . .

> The feeling of full enjoyment will flood in again, we must get through these middle years. (p. 124)

Perhaps most important, like her predecessor Pompey, Celia is poised irresolute between life and death. When asked by her cousin why, if she wants to die, she does not, she answers, "One part of us wants to die, I suppose, and the other part does not, and the two are always crying out against each other . . ." (p. 159). Humorously, Caz offers a metaphor that at once captures and deflates the sense of passive waiting, at once anticipatory and apprehensive, which characterizes the book.

> Life is like a railway station, said Caz, the train of birth brings us in, the train of death will carry us away, and meanwhile we are cooling our heels upon the platform and waiting for the connection, and stamping up and down the platform, and passing the time of day with the other people who are also waiting.
>
> . . . you are romantic about death. Yes, he said, the train of death that you are waiting for is an excursion train, yes, that is what it is: All aboard for a day in the country.
>
> (p. 155)

This lighthearted, ironic view is balanced by the death wish engendered by true despair. The first morning of Celia's holiday, she makes a serious suicide attempt and is saved only by her cousin's arrival.

> But now the earth's moisture, drawn in spirals round my knees, struck upward to my heart, and I was oppressed by such a sense of melancholy sweet sadness, of a tragedy of huge dimension but uncertain outline, of wrongs forgotten whose pain alone remains, that I cried out in fear and threw myself upon the ground. There is not one thing in life, I cried, to make it bearable.
>
> I decided to go for a swim . . . I swam straight out and turned on my back to let the current carry me down into the lake. Oh, God, I thought, we are not innocent, yet innocence is what one would wish for. The water was as cold as ice. I had a sleepy feeling that I was floating away from the Ministry, and the London parties, and Lopez, and the Indian problems, and going to have a fine long sleep and no dreams. (pp. 102–103)

The novel's postwar accidie and irresolvable relationships provide a dual focus for this despairing sadness, an emotion felt not just by the sensitive Celia but also by characters such as Tiny. All agree that it is a time of sadness, coldness, the time of a "black split heart." Yet though what Smith called a "loamish" sadness is dominant, the reader cannot ignore the joy, strain, volatility, euphoria, and terror the novel also evokes. The shifting play of emotion can become exaggerated in degree, yet entirely accurate to the swift fluidity of a sensitive—perhaps oversensitive consciousness. Celia, like Pompey, seems at times too vulnerable, too permeable, as though she lacks the protective membrane necessary to protect the psyche.

> This sadness cuts down again upon me, it is like death. And the bright appearance of the friends at the parties, makes it a terrible cut, like a deep sharp knife, that has cut deep, but not yet quite away.
>
> My teacup fell from my hand and I began to cry and scream, for there was such a pain in my heart as twisted my heart and muscles, so that I was bent backwards as though it was an overdose of strychnine. (p. 171)

The pain in such passages becomes almost excruciating, particularly when surrounded, as it so often is, by bright chatter or intellectual play.

Late in the book, Celia's Uncle Heber is quoted: "There is no answer, he says: You would not expect an answer? No, no, I say, feeling at once immensely lightened, I should not wish for an answer, and I smile at my Uncle and I say that I suppose an answer suffocates" (p. 145). *The Holiday* risks no such suffocation. Celia's affair with Caz neither ends nor is fulfilled; the volatility of her consciousness continues, fixing on neither life nor death, joy nor despair, as a point of stasis; the postwar middleness drags on. Celia searches for the source of her sadness, wondering, "Shall I ever be rid of this misery, is it papa's legacy, or my mama's, or is it the war, or is it the guilt of our social situation that is so base bottom bad?" (p. 42), yet she can find no answer. Significantly, the novel ends on a note of indeterminacy, with the ominous but unconfirmed suggestion that Celia's holiday may not end: that she may never go, or perhaps will not be welcomed, back to the ministry at which she worked before this respite. As in so many of Smith's poems, it has been made apparent that the only resolution, the only relief, the only true holiday is death.

Selected Bibliography

BIBLIOGRAPHY

Barbera, J., McBrien, W., and Bajan, H., *Stevie Smith: A Bibliography,* (London and Westport, Conn., 1987).

SELECTED AND COLLECTED WORKS

Selected Poems, (London, 1962, New York 1964); *The Collected Poems of Stevie Smith,* (London, 1975, New York 1976); *Me Again: The Uncollected Writings of Stevie Smith,* ed. by J. Barbera and W. McBrien (London, 1981, New York 1982); *Stevie Smith: A Selection,* ed. by H. Lee (London, 1983); *New Selected Poems,* (New York, 1988).

SEPARATE WORKS

Novel on Yellow Paper, (London, 1936, 1980, New York, 1937, 1982); *A Good Time Was Had by All,* (London, 1937); *Over the Frontier,* (London, 1938, New York, 1982); *Tender Only to One,* (London, 1938); *Mother, What Is Man?* (London, 1942); *The Holiday,* (London, 1949, New York, 1982); *Harold's Leap,* (London 1950); *Not Waving But Drowning,* (London, 1957); *Some Are More Human Than Others,* (London, 1958); *The Frog Prince and Other Poems,* (London, 1966); *The Best Beast,* (New York, 1969); *Scorpion and Other Poems,* (London, 1972).

INTRODUCTIONS

Cats in Colour, ed. and with intro. by Smith (London, 1959, New York, 1960); *The Batsford Book of Children's Verse,* ed. and with preface by Smith (London, 1970, repr. as *The Poet's Garden,* New York, 1970).

BIOGRAPHIES

Whitemore, H., *Stevie: A Play,* (London and New York, 1977); Barbera, J., and McBrien, W. *Stevie: A Biography of Stevie Smith,* (London, 1985, New York, 1987); Spalding, F., *Stevie Smith: A Critical Biography,* (London, 1988, New York 1989).

CRITICAL STUDIES

Dick, K., *Ivy & Stevie: Ivy Compton-Burnett and Stevie Smith,* (London, 1971, 1983); Enright, D. J., "Did Nobody Teach You? On Stevie Smith," *Encounter* 36, (June 1971, repr. in his *Man Is an Onion: Reviews and Essays,* London, 1972); Tatham, M., "That One Must Speak Lightly . . . A Study of Stevie Smith," *New Blackfriars* 53, (July 1972); Bedient, C., "Stevie Smith," in his *Eight Contemporary Poets* (London, 1974); Williams, J., "Much Further out Than You Thought," *Parnassus: Poetry in Review* 2, (Spring/Summer 1974); Heaney, S., "A Memorable Voice," *Irish Times,* (April 3, 1976, repr. in *Preoccupations: Selected Prose 1968–1978,* London, 1980); Wade, S., "Stevie Smith and the Untruth of Myth," *Agenda* 15, (Summer/Autumn 1977); Thaddeus, J., "Stevie Smith and the Gleeful Macabre," *Contemporary Poetry* 3, no. 4, (1978); Storey, M., "Why Stevie Smith Matters," *Critical Quarterly* 21, no. 2, (1979).

Ricks, C., "Stevie Smith," *Grand Street* 1, (Autumn 1981, rev. and repr. as "Stevie Smith: The Art of Sinking in Poetry," in his *The Force of Poetry,* Oxford, 1984); Oates, J. C., "A Child with a Cold, Cold Eye," New York Times Book Review (October 3, 1982); Rankin, A. C., *The Poetry of Stevie Smith: Little Girl Lost,* (Gerrards Cross, U.K., and Totowa, N.J., 1985); Pumphrey, M., "Play, Fantasy and Strange Laughter: Stevie Smith's Uncomfortable Poetry," *Critical Quarterly* 28, no. 3, (1986); Sternlicht, S., *Stevie Smith,* (Boston, 1990).

Stephen Spender

(1909–1995)

DAVID ADAMS LEEMING

STEPHEN SPENDER IS an enduring but neglected presence in the literary world of the twentieth century. Sometimes praised for great lyrical moments and original critical insights, he has just as often been scorned or simply passed over as the poet who wrote "I think continually of those who were truly great," but who never became great himself. Much of the treatment of Spender derives from the association of his career with that of his friend W. H. Auden.

The linking of Auden and Spender in the "Auden Group" or "Oxford School" was the inevitable result of several factors. As undergraduates at Oxford, they read their poems to each other, discussed literature and personal philosophies, and generally shared a variety of aesthetic, sexual, and political interests. The fact that Spender in 1928 printed small books of poems by himself *(Nine Experiments: Being Poems Written at the Age of Eighteen)* and by Auden on his own handpress added a Wordsworth-Coleridge note to their relationship. Later their common opposition to fascism in the context of the Spanish Civil War would draw them even closer together in the public mind. But most important, as "new poets" of the 1930's generation, publishing against a background of thc socio-political upheavals of their time, Auden and Spender, with Cecil Day Lewis and sometimes Louis MacNeice, were collectively drafted by the critics to fill the enormous gap left by the slaughter of the previous generation of young poets in World War I.

If the influence of Auden was dominant in the group it was because he was a more intellectual poet, more of a theoretician than the others. As Spender noted in a 1980 interview with *The Paris Review,* because Auden was "very conscious of his own mental superiority" he was perfectly willing to insist on his point of view. His influence is perhaps most evident in the group's tendency to make poetry out of the modern industrial landscape. In the early years Auden, following T. S. Eliot, insisted on this. What Auden added to Eliot's view was an attitude toward the social decline between the wars that was less gloomy, a younger generation's sense that the decline was not altogether a bad thing, that, in fact, it provided exciting material for poetry.

As far as Spender's career is concerned, Auden's dominance was to have both a beneficial and a detrimental effect. It seems clear that Auden, always eccentric, vocal, and somewhat imperative, imposed his views on his rather reticent and shy friend. To the very end of Auden's life Spender craved his approval and reserved for his somewhat older colleague the kind of slightly resentful adulation usually reserved for demanding mentors. In his *Journals 1939–1983* (1985), Spender is perfectly candid about his feelings: "To measure my attitude to Auden, it is that of a somewhat battered observer. Moreover when a friend forms an idea of one when both he and you are very young and retains the same attitude throughout one's life, one feels a bit resentful" (p. 356).

It is true that during the Oxford years Auden rightly prevailed upon Spender to curb his Romantic tendencies as a poet, but it is also true that the attachment to Auden placed Spender in the position of having to be constantly compared to a poet of entirely different sensibilities and talents. Thus it is commonplace that Spender is overshadowed by Auden. Compared to Auden, his detractors say, Spender is a minor writer, one whose personal vagueness and old-fashioned English awkwardness are mirrored by clumsy lines and imprecise thoughts. Spender himself, always self-effacing and shy, seems to join happily in the criticism: "My mind is not clear, my will is weak, I suffer from an excess of ideas and a weak sense of form," he wrote in *The Making of a Poem* in 1955 (1973 reprint, Westport, Conn., p. 49).

But to see him in Auden's light is to miss the point about Stephen Spender. While it can be useful to compare his poetry to Auden's as a means of differentiating the two poets and illustrating Spender's unique voice, it is just as important to avoid the commonplace by not evaluating Spender according to how well he lives up to Auden's understanding of the techniques and functions of poetry. As Spender stated in a 1970 interview in *The Review,* "For better or worse—probably for *my* worse—we are absolutely different kinds of writer. We really have very little in common" (p. 27). It seems fair to say that Auden was an intellectual poet influenced by the discoveries of psychoanalytical practice, while Spender, as he describes himself in his autobiography, *World Within World* (1951), was "an autobiographer restlessly searching for forms in which to express the stages of my development" (pp. 125–126).

The first thing that must be said of Spender is that the many facets of his career stand together as a coherent whole. He has been a poet in the broad sense of that word, a public presence following a vocation that has transcended his role as a writer of verse, a critic, a playwright, a novelist, a teacher, a journalist, and a recorder of significant moments with the great people of his day. By applying his considerable talents in each of these areas Spender has been faithful to a credo he articulated in 1937 when he wrote in *Fact* magazine, "the poet is essentially sensitive to the life of his time" (p. 18). Samuel Hynes in *The Auden Generation* suggests that Spender's attitude towards poetry is based on "a romantic notion of the artist, as a man with a superior morality and a higher responsibility" to reveal "the truth about historic public issues" (p. 105).

As a man not given, like Auden, to sharp wit, satire, or hard, self-contained images, Spender analyzes the public world by way of an often disarmingly honest and almost old-fashioned lyrical use of events in his own life. If that life is marked by ambiguity, by the scars resulting from a peculiarly English upper-middle-class, duty-bound background, by a naive innocence that cohabits with a tendency toward hedonism, and by a humility that borders at times on masochism, it serves well as a source for metaphors, and it provides the poetic voice that is Stephen Spender with a large capacity for spiritual and moral exploration that reminds us more of William Wordsworth, Wilfred Owen, and T. S. Eliot than it does of W. H. Auden. Spender is an artist of conscience, in the best sense a moralist, at once a confessional poet and a sociopolitical one translating and probing for significance in the events of his time.

As all aspects of Spender's literary and personal life are so closely intertwined, it seems best to consider his career in a biographical context, studying the verse, the criticism, the fiction, and the journalism as pieces in a larger "poem" that Spender has been composing since the 1920's.

EARLY LIFE AND WORK

Stephen Harold Spender was born in London on 28 February 1909. In his parents and his relationship with them we find seemingly clear sources for much of what was to become the struggle in Spender between the public life and the confessional mode. His father, Edward Harold Spender, was a well-known journalist and sometimes politician committed to the values of the Liberal Party as articulated by Lloyd George in what can now be seen as its dying days. An author of books on Byron, on mountaineering, on home rule, on Herbert Asquith, and on Lloyd George, he was the son of the Victorian novelist Mrs. J. K. Spender. Harold Spender's ideals were those of the upper-middle-class reformers who before World War I had optimistically believed in the possibility of preserving respectability and dignity and even the class system by applying the new scientific and unsuperstitious principles to old social wrongs. Desperately clinging to those ideals after the war, Harold Spender and men like him were fervent supporters of the League of Nations and free trade. But as Stephen Spender was to realize later, looking back at his childhood in his autobiography, *World Within World,* "the war had knocked the ballroom floor from under the middle-class English life. People resembled dancers suspended in mid-air yet miraculously able to pretend that they were still dancing" (p. 2). The result for the Spender children, Christine, Humphrey, Michael, and Stephen, and others of their class, was a childhood characterized by virtuous isolation in a world drifting into chaos and immorality: "My brothers and sisters and I were brought up in an atmosphere which I would describe as 'Puritan decadence' " (*World Within World,* p. 285). The mood was tragic; calamity loomed everywhere, as evident in "My Parents," first published in 1933 as "Parents," in the collection titled *Poems.*

> My parents kept me from children who
> were rough
> Who threw words like stones and wore torn
> clothes.
>
> . . .
>
> They were lithe, they sprang out behind
> hedges
> Like dogs to bark at my world. They threw
> mud
> While I looked the other way, pretending to
> smile.
> I longed to forgive them, but they never
> smiled.
> ("My Parents")[1]

Spender seems to have felt from an early age a mild aversion to his father, his ardently journalistic outlook, his commitment to public rather than personal needs. Harold Spender inhabited "a world of rhetorical situations" in which his son's having to play football was meant "to harden the tissues of my character."

> Old man, with hair made of newspaper
> cutting
> A public platform voice,
> Tail coat and top hat strutting
> Before your constituents' applause—
> ("The Public Son of a Public Man")

Yet Spender learned his father's lesson well to the extent that throughout his life he has found it necessary to turn to journalism, to public issues, even against the advice of men and women as important to him as T. S. Eliot and Virginia Woolf. He has done so out of a real moral commitment to a later version of his father's liberalism, but he has always done so with a tinge of regret for a quieter, more withdrawn life better suited to his Romantic sensibilities:

> O father, to a grave of fame I faithfully
> follow
> Yet I love the glance of fa-lure, tilted up,
> Like a gipsy's amber eyes that seem to
> swallow
> Sunset from the evening like a cup.
> ("The Public Son of a Public Man")

The dark mood of the Spender childhood was compounded by the semi-invalid state of Spender's mother, Violet Hilda (Schuster) Spender. One of the poet's earliest memories was of his mother's reaction to the childrens' playing trains in the nursery above her bed-

1. Unless otherwise noted, all poems quoted in this essay are from *Collected Poems 1928–1985* (London, 1985).

room by appearing "with a white face of Greek tragedy" and exclaiming "like Medea: 'I now know the sorrow of having borne children' " (*World Within World,* p. 3).

Still, Spender remembers his mother as being also "intelligent and sensitive," a delicate woman whose "painting, embroidery, and poetry had a sacred, unchallenged reputation among us" (p. 4). That reputation was justified when a book of her poetry was published posthumously in 1923. If she was understandably a moody woman, Violet Spender nevertheless provided her son with a set of aesthetic and personal values that could to some extent temper the public ones he inherited from his father.

Much of Spender's early childhood was distinctly colored by World War I. The family moved to Sheringham on the east coast during the war years, and some of Spender's earliest memories are of nearby military camps and Zeppelin raids and of the news that his mother's favorite brother, Alfred Schuster, had been killed on the front. War was to remain an important theme in the background that provided the setting for his life's work. Some of his best poetry was inspired by the Spanish Civil War and by World War II. War provided a dynamic context for the meeting of Spender's public and private sides and the result was an often subtle combination of deep compassion and bitter antiwar sentiments:

> The killed, filled with lead,
> On the helpless field
> May dream pious reasons
> Of Mercy, but alas
> They did what they did
> In their own high season.
> ("The War God")

Spender traces the beginning of his interest in verse and his prediliction for romanticism to a summer spent in Wordsworth country near Derwentwater in the Lake District of England. Stephen was nine years old. The extraordinarily beautiful countryside and his father's reading aloud of Wordsworth "fused" in his mind and "the seed of poetry was planted in me." The poems of Wordsworth conveyed "a sense of the sacred cloaked vocation of the poet" (*World Within World,* p. 79). Wordsworth remained a primary influence for Spender, a reminder that even public issues could be approached by way of nature and the inner self.

The Derwentwater summer was the happy prelude to several years of misery. In the fall he entered the Old School House Preparatory School of Gresham's School, Holt, and was immediately overcome by homesickness of such intensity as to preclude any kind of social or academic success. Spender wrote movingly of his school experience in *World Within World,* and he used it as the basis for his first novel, *The Backward Son* (1940), a rather terrifying representation of the kind of educational and class hypocrisy against which Spender would always stand. The principled, if somewhat naive and romantic child isolated in the world of the Old School House was, as Spender later recognized, a mask for the man he would become:

> The fact remains that I am and was the same person: when I was a child there were moments when I stood up within my whole life, as though it were a burning room, or as though I were rowing alone on a sea whose waves were filled with many small tongues of fire . . . (*World Within World,* p. 304)

The Old School House experience confirmed the young Stephen Spender in his sense of his own difference. By the time he moved on to a London day school, University College School in Hampstead, he had other immediate problems to confront and was better able to cope with that difference.

Violet Spender died when Stephen was twelve; Harold Spender died when he was seventeen. After their mother's death, the day-to-day care of the Spender children was left to a pair of old family servants, later joined by a companion for Christine, and at about the age of fifteen Stephen came under the important influence of his maternal grandmother, Hilda

(Weber) Schuster. Mrs. Schuster was above all a loving woman and one whose "view of life was entirely personal" (*World Within World*, p. 10). She provided her grandson with much-needed counterbalance to the public and rhetorical views of his father and the emotional distance of his mother. Like Stephen, Mrs. Schuster was an innocent; she encouraged her grandson in his appreciation of modern art and "advanced" ideas without any thought as to the "proper" interests of an upper-class English school boy. She also encouraged him in his writing of poetry. In short, she provided legitimacy to what his peers perhaps considered his oddities.

Spender had always known that his grandparents' origins were German, but it was not until he was about sixteen that he discovered that his grandfather, Ernest Joseph Schuster, had been a Jew. For Spender, always anxious to understand the sources of and the nature of his difference from others, this was an important and welcome discovery; it helped solidify his sense of virtuous isolation from the ordinary upper-class English ways epitomized by school life. He began to realize that he "had more in common with the sensitive, rather soft, inquisitive, interior Jewish boys, than with the aloof, hard, external English" (*World Within World* p. 12).

Before going off to the University College, Oxford, Spender was sent by his grandmother on a trip to the Continent. This was the beginning of what was to become a pattern. For most of his life Spender has lived almost as long a time abroad as in England. During and after his Oxford years he lived for extended periods in Germany. Later he taught and lectured regularly in the United States at the University of Cincinnati, the University of California at Berkeley, the University of Connecticut at Storrs, Northwestern University, the University of Florida at Gainsville, Wesleyan University, Cornell University, Loyola University, Emory University, and elsewhere. In later life he spent a great deal of every year at a home in the south of France. The effect of Spender's living abroad has been to make his writing singularly un-insular and cosmopolitan. His concerns have been international rather than national; his poetry has been composed in the context of a wide knowledge of European and American as well as English literature. If Wordsworth has been important to Spender, so have Rainer Maria Rilke and Robert Lowell. If British public policy has been a concern, so, for instance, has censorship in the third world or the status of indigenous Palestinian Jews in Israeli kibbutzim. Spender has traveled widely in most parts of the world, not as a tourist but as a poet driven by a need and a duty to concern himself with "the life of his time."

When, after his first European tour, he entered Oxford, Spender was appalled by what he considered to be the dominance of English public school attitudes there. He resisted and masked his own extreme shyness and insecurity by affecting pacifist and socialist points of view and by associating with other outsiders. Eventually he met and became friendly with Louis MacNeice, Christopher Isherwood, Isaiah Berlin, and Auden. These connections and his reading of modernists such as James Joyce, Virginia Woolf, Ernest Hemingway, Ezra Pound, Eliot, and D. H. Lawrence, changed his idea of what art was. He began to see that "unpoetic-seeming things were material for poetry," that anything created by humans must be seen to be symbolic of "an inner state of consciousness within them" (*World Within World*, p. 86). He took in Auden's remark that the most beautiful walk in Oxford was the one along the canal near the power plant. Joyce's *Ulysses* and Eliot's *The Waste Land*, especially, were proof that "modern life could be material for art."

> What excited me about the modern movement was the inclusion within new forms, of material which seemed ugly, anti-poetic and inhuman. . . . [Joyce and Eliot] showed me that modern life could be material for art, and that the poet, instead of having to set himself apart from his time, could create out of an acceptance of it. (*World Within World*, p. 86)

Furthermore, Joyce, Eliot, and Woolf opened up new sensibilities and demonstrated that the creative process itself could be the writer's subject. And D. H. Lawrence appealed to Spender's Romantic nature, pointing the way to a modernist approach to the depiction of deep emotion and nature. What Spender learned in his Oxford reading has remained with him throughout his career. His own writing has always been based on the understanding, learned from the great modernists, that "poetry was a use of language which revealed external actuality" of all sorts "as symbolic inner consciousness" (*World Within World,* pp. 86–87). Although he later turned away from such self-conscious use of the industrial landscape, in his early poem "The Pylons," for instance, Spender makes use of singularly unpoetic objects to symbolize, as the *The Waste Land* had done, the inner consciousness of a civilization that is in danger of losing its interconnected and personal center:

The secret of these hills was stone, and
 cottages
Of that stone made,
And crumbling roads
That turned on sudden hidden villages.

Now over these small hills, they have built
 the concrete
That trails black wire;
Pylons, those pillars
Bare like nude, giant girls that have no
 secret.

In the summer of 1929, at the invitation of a German Jew he had met at Oxford, Spender made the first of his many trips to Germany. In Hamburg, where his host lived, he was suddenly confronted with the "fusion of naked liberation with a kind of bitter pathos" that was characteristic of Weimar Germany. "Intoxicated" by the sense of abandonment so foreign to his English experience, he eagerly embraced, physically if not spiritually, the free love, the atonal music, the homosexuality, the nudism, the bare modernist art: "It was easy to be advanced. You had only to take off your clothes" (*World Within World,* p. 96ff).

The Hamburg summer and aspects of other trips to Germany are recorded in *The Temple,* an unveiled autobiographical novel begun in 1929 and finally revised and published in 1988. *The Temple* is most successful as a semi-historical document—a resource for those interested in the mores and attitudes of young Germans between the wars. And it conveys something of the attitudes of Spender and his friends—Auden and Isherwood appear in the book as the characters Simon Wilmot and William Bradshaw—towards English repressiveness during the same period. As Spender suggests in his introduction, in writing the novel he "had the sense of sending home to friends and colleagues dispatches from a front line in our joint war against censorship" (p. xi). But there was a sense, too, of something ominous in the new life of Weimar as depicted in *The Temple,* something Spender described also in a prophetic poem about his friendship with two Germans in the summer of 1929:

Our fathers' misery, their spirits' mystery,
The cynic's cruelty, weave this philosophy:
That the history of man, traced purely from
 dust,
Is lipping skulls on the revolving rim
Or war, us three each other's murderers—
 ("In 1929")

The voice that tells the German story in *World Within World,* in the poems of the period, and in *The Temple,* revels in the freedom of this very un-English experience, but it never loses its sense of poetic distance from the events being described. Here, too, in this seemingly liberated paradise Stephen Spender was somehow out of place, driven by his poetic vocation to see in the events he was describing the externalization of a national consciousness and, in this case, a national despair. The young men with whom the British poet frolicked were part of a generation "which had been born into war, starved in the blockade, stripped in the inflation—and which now, with no money and no beliefs and an extraordinary anonymous beauty, sprang like a breed of dragon's teeth waiting for its leader, into the center of Europe" (*World Within World,* p. 105).

POLITICS AND WAR

Spender never completed his Oxford studies. Determined to pursue a career as a writer, he followed Christopher Isherwood to Germany in 1930 and for the next three years lived at least half of the year there writing poetry and observing the rise of fascism in Berlin and Vienna. These years are described by Spender in *World Within World.* Somewhat older, more established in his commitment to writing, Isherwood was an important presence in Spender's life at the time. Most of all, he gave his friend confidence in his abilities as a poet. In spite of disagreements, Spender and Isherwood remained close friends until Isherwood's death in 1988.

It was in 1932, with the publication of an anthology of poetry called *New Signatures* (1932), edited by Michael Roberts, that Spender had his first taste of fame. Among the London literary circle Spender was already considered a poet as a result of his *Nine Experiments* and the 1930 publication by Basil Blackwell of *Twenty Poems,* a collection of his better undergraduate writing; but it was the *New Signatures* collection that solidified his association with Auden and Day Lewis in the minds of critics. It should be pointed out that Spender, Day Lewis, and Auden never met under the same roof until 1949, but in his introduction to the book, Roberts finds a means of creating a "school": "The writers in this book have learned to accept the fact that progress is illusory, and yet to believe that the game is worth playing; to believe that the alleviation of suffering is good even though it merely makes possible new sensitiveness and therefore new suffering" (p. 12).

It seems unlikely that Spender thought of progress as illusory. He was already interested in communism as a means of combatting fascism and soon he joined the Communist Party for a short time. The poets of *New Signatures* did have in common with each other and their older mentors, William Butler Yeats and Eliot, a sense of a society's death agony, and they shared a belief in the need for revolutionary change. They were torn between a distrust of polemical writing and a sense that in those days they had no choice but to go public against fascism. "Why should poetry be concerned with public affairs rather than with the private interests of the individual?" Spender asked in 1937. "The answer is that it is precisely within the consciousness of many separate individuals that the political struggle is taking place. . . . the central drama of our time . . . is the historic struggle as it effects the mind of the individual . . . ("Poetry," *Fact,* pp. 18–19).

The German years culminated for Spender with the 1933 publication of his *Poems* and with an enlarged version of the same book a year later. With this little volume Spender came into his own as a poet, and over the next twenty years produced some eleven books of verse, most notably *Vienna* (1934), *The Still Centre* (1939), *Ruins and Visions* (1942), and *The Edge of Being* (1949), before Faber printed his *Collected Poems 1928–1953* (1955). New poems came less frequently after the early 1950's, but there were a few volumes, including *Inscriptions* (1958) and *The Generous Days* (1969; enlg. ed. 1971), before a new large collection, *Selected Poems* (1964), and the comprehensive *Collected Poems 1928–1985* (1985).

It is especially in *Poems* that Spender takes up the Eliot-Auden challenge to bring the powers of verse to bear on the technology, the agony, the fragmentation, and the material tyranny of his time. His subjects are "The Pylons", "The Express", "Unemployed", "The Prisoners", "In Railway Halls":

> After the first powerful plain manifesto
> The black statement of pistons, without
> more fuss
> But gliding like a queen, she leaves the
> station.
> ("The Express")

In railway halls, on pavements near the
traffic,
They beg, their eyes made big by empty
staring
And only measuring Time, like the blank
clock.
("In Railway Halls")

However imprecise the imagery in these poems, the effect of a loss of values on the inner consciousness of a civilization and of immanent disaster is clearly if subtly expressed.

Vienna, the volume that followed *Poems,* was a continuation of Spender's commentary on the decline of the civilization of his time. This commentary depicted the brutal suppression in Austria of a socialist insurrection.

The Reichstag that the Nazis set on fire—
And then our party forbidden—
("Perhaps")

In *Vienna* Spender attempted, unsuccessfully, to relate this political and historical event to a love experience of his own: ". . . in a world where humanity was trampled on publicly, private affection was also undermined" (*World Within World,* p. 174.) The problem with the poetry of *Vienna* is, as Spender recognized, its failure to maintain the proper tension and, therefore, the proper relationship between the public and the personal. The tragic events of the rise of fascism are treated in self-conscious images rather than in poetry grounded in the poet's person: the poem fails to "attain a unity where the inner passion becomes inseparable from the outer one" (p. 174). Most readers, however, recognized the validity of Spender's attempt.

Poems and the publications that followed established Spender more fully in London literary society. The process of his acceptance had begun in 1929 when he met Eliot, who had read some of Spender's early Oxford verse and been impressed by it. Eliot remained Spender's friend and supporter and, as a director at Faber and Faber, he became his principle publisher. The meeting with Eliot may have been the beginning of what became one of Spender's major occupations in life, the cultivation of his relations with the famous. This never became a name-dropping activity as some have suggested. Given Spender's sense of the poet's role in society as an articulator of his time, it was natural that he should seek out others bent on the same goal.

I think continually of those who were truly
great.
Who, from the womb, remembered the
soul's history.
("The Truly Great")

Spender became close to the Bloomsbury group—particularly to the Woolfs—although his politics were considerably more radical than theirs. He knew E. M. Forster, Harold Nicolson, and Vita Sackville-West. He was introduced to Yeats in Lady Ottoline Morrell's living room, a meeting he describes amusingly in *World Within World,* remembering how badly the meeting went until Virginia Woolf was summoned by phone to save the day. He remembers Yeats explaining to Virginia Woolf that her novel, *The Waves,* could be understood in light of modern theories in physics and new discoveries in psychic research (*World Within World,* p. 149).

Spender's *World Within World* and *Journals 1939–1983* sparkle with such anecdotes. Few people can be said to have known and so acutely observed nearly all of the major figures in the arts from W. B. Yeats and Virginia Woolf to Allen Ginsberg and Margaret Drabble. He writes with characteristic humility in *World Within World,* "What can I feel but gratitude that l was taken into this great wave of the talent of my time? When l had bathed in it, I was imperceptibly changed" (p. 151).

CULTURAL STUDIES

Spender's interest in the literary overview, in the relationship between the artist and his or her time, became evident in his first major critical work, *The Destructive Element: A Study of Modern Writers and Beliefs,* published in 1935. The central figures here are particular Spender favorites—Henry James, Yeats, Eliot, and Lawrence—each of whom is evaluated in the context of the Conradian "destructive element," the loss of values and order in the fragmented modern wasteland. Does James's world foreshadow that wasteland? How is the poetry and prose of Eliot, Yeats, and Lawrence related to it? *The Destructive Element* is Spender's most Marxist work, focusing as it does on literature in the context of the collapse of capitalist-bourgeois civilization. Later he would reject its philosophical premise, but nevertheless it is a brilliant work, the first segment in a literary commentary that continues into the 1990's.

The Destructive Element began as a book on Henry James, a writer to whose revival Spender may be said to have contributed, and whether or not Marxist in origin, it contains serious insights into James's work in the context of his era. Spender suggests that James, faced with the destructive element, "retired more and more into the inventions of his own mind" (p. 47); it was history itself that was responsible for the Jamesian late style. The same history is seen to be the source of Yeats's "magical system," Eliot's religion, and Lawrence's sexual preoccupations. But if James and the others took refuge in the subjective world of their own individuality, in James's late works, at least, Spender saw "a profound indictment of our civilization." He wondered whether it was time now for a more social and objective form of art, for a Marxist confrontation with the destructive element.

In the mid 1930's Spender continued to search in a variety of formats for an understanding of his world. His first attempt at fiction, five short stories, was published in 1936 as *The Burning Cactus.* These stories are autobiographical in that their heroes are suffused with Spender's sensitivity and his sense of isolation in a fragmented world. In the long essay *Forward from Liberalism* (1937) Spender urged liberals to accept the methods of communism in the interest of defeating fascism. The Communist versus Fascist theme from a much less Marxist perspective is pursued in Spender's first attempt at drama, a verse tragedy titled *Trial of a Judge,* produced in London in 1938 at the Group Theatre. Here Spender, having been disillusioned by his experience in the Spanish Civil War, has his judge condemn both sides for their betrayal of essential human values of justice.

In *The Still Centre* Spender's sense of the disintegration of civilization achieves its highest articulation.

> At night I'm flooded by the future
> Incoming tide of the unharnessed war.
> ("The Uncreating Chaos")

The Still Centre contains some of Spender's most memorable poetry, particularly that which grew out of his experience in the Spanish Civil War in 1937. Spender had been sent to Spain by the Communist Party as a propagandist but soon found that the stretching of truth involved in that work was incompatible with his nature. He wrote an article for the *New Statesman* in April 1937 in which he denounced the tendency of propaganda to turn the war dead into heroes in order to justify abstract political ideologies. The civil war poetry, as Samuel Hynes suggests in *The Auden Generation,* is in the spirit of Wilfred Owen, a young poet of World War I. Spender's war poetry does not take sides. Like Owen's, it focuses on human suffering and conveys the poet's moral indignation. Perhaps most important, it takes its emotional power from a deep compassion conveyed by the poet's personal relation to his subject. In these poems Spender succeeds where in *Vienna* he had failed. The public and the personal serve each other. The dead boy in "Ultima Ratio Regum," for example, is strikingly real because we feel in the poet's treatment of him a consuming passion, a sense of loss that is based not only on the poet's moral concerns but on his physical longing:

> The guns spell money's ultimate reason
> In letters of lead on the Spring hillside.
> But the boy lying dead under the olive trees
> Was too young and too silly

To have been notable to their important eye.
He was a better target for a kiss.

In *The Still Centre,* as the title of the volume indicates and as A. K. Weatherhead suggests in *Stephen Spender and the Thirties,* Spender seems to be seeking "unity of being or an image of the integrated self" (p. 177).

He was frantically seeking unity of being in his personal life as well. In 1936, after several difficult relationships with both men and women, Spender married Inez Pearn, an Oxford student involved with the Spanish Aid Committee. The decision to marry was impulsive on both sides: "we both saw marriage as a solution of temporary problems," a means "to fill the emptiness of living alone" (*World Within World,* p. 187). The end of the marriage in 1939 coincided with the fall of Republican Spain, further disillusionment with communism, the Munich settlement, the German invasion of Czechoslovakia, and the terminal illness of Margaret Spender, his sister-in-law and confidante. For Spender this was a difficult period. It was in all likelihood the more serious nature of his sister-in-law's predicament that saved him from despair, that and necessarily distracting events involved in the beginning of World War II.

. . . to accept the worst
Is finally to revive
("Elegy for Margaret")

It was at this point, during the "phony war" of 1939, that Spender planned the literary cultural review *Horizon* with Cyril Connolly and Peter Watson. He was already on the board of John Lehmann's *New Writing,* but *Horizon* provided his first concentrated editorial experience. Although *Horizon* became in many ways Connolly's magazine, it remained an important social and cultural place in Spender's life until the death of Connolly in 1973. Spender's most significant piece for *Horizon* was "Rhineland Journal," an account of meetings with German intellectuals during his postwar service in Germany as a civilian member of the occupying forces with a commission to report on the attitudes of the intelligentsia. A 1946 book, *European Witness,* was an outgrowth of the *Horizon* article.

Horizon was evacuated to the Devon coast during the German Blitz of 1940. Spender felt frustrated at being away from London. He could watch air raids as they occurred in Plymouth, not far away:

A buzz, felt as ragged but unseen
Is chased by two Excaliburs of light
A thud. An instant gleams
Gold sequins shaken from a black-silk
screen.
("Air Raid Across the Bay at Plymouth")

After an unsuccessful term as a school teacher in Devon, Spender joined the National Fire Service in London. In 1940 France fell. The potential for despair was great.

Yet under wild seas
Of chafing despair
Love's need does not cease.
("The War God")

And in April 1941, Spender married Natasha Litvin, a concert pianist. The Spenders produced two children, Matthew and Elizabeth (Lizzie), both of whom have made careers in the arts.

The marriage and the continued association with *Horizon* colleagues, with new Hampstead friends such as Anna Freud and her brother, Ernst Freud, as well as with older friends—Eliot, E. M. Forster, Elizabeth Bowen, and others—made the war years more than bearable. There was not a great deal of time for writing, what with the constant tension of the bombing and his duties as a firefighter, but Spender still managed to produce several important works.

The autobiographical novel *The Backward Son,* about his boarding school years, appeared in 1940, and the first of several collections of earlier and some new poems, *Selected Poems,* was also published in 1940 by Faber and Faber and Random House. It immediately became the sourcebook for those who saw Spender as primarily a poet of the thirties. *Ruins and Visions* is a revision of *The Still Centre* with a few new poems. *Life and the Poet* (1942) is, in a sense, a formal rebuttal of Spender's more Marxist position in *The Destructive Element.* In this long essay he emphasizes, much as Henry James had done in "The Art of Fiction" (1884), the necessity of allowing the artist his freedom of subject and approach. A propagandist cannot be expected to represent reality faithfully. In 1943 Spender published, with William Sansom and James Gordon, *Jim Braidy: The Story of Britain's Firemen,* an outgrowth of his wartime job. Another work related to the war is *Citizens in War—and After* (1945). And in 1945 he began a subsidiary career as an art critic with his introduction and notes to a collection of ten Sandro Botticelli reproductions.

During the middle of the war Spender privately printed a small book of sonnets, *Spiritual Exercises (To Cecil Day Lewis)* (1943), a meditation on death in the context of war. *Spiritual Exercises* (revised as "Spiritual Explorations" in *Poems of Dedication*) is part of Spender's continuing search for personal identity in a world dominated by public realities. In their spirituality the poems of this collection rank among Spender's most Romantic poetry, but the imagery is modernistic, almost surrealistic, reminding us more of Eliot in the *Four Quartets* than of Wordsworth, as seen in this untitled first poem of the series:

> Revolving with the earth's rim through the night
> We conscious fragments, pulsing blood and breath,
> Each separate in the self, yet reunite
> For that dark journey to no place or date
> Where, naked beneath nakedness, beneath
> Our human generation, we await
> The multitudinous loneliness of death.

Immediately after the war Spender returned to Germany and soon after published *European Witness* (1946), a work based on that trip and one that reflects a renewed idealism, a hope for a new Europe based on the free interplay of ideas. If this is a naive work it is nevertheless reflective of the valid hope of an artist who is true to his mission as a sounding board for his era. But perhaps the most significant work of the early postwar period is the little volume called *Poems of Dedication* (1947), containing the sonnet series "Spiritual Explorations" and "Elegy for Margaret," a long poem in reaction to the death of Spender's sister-in-law on Christmas Day, 1945. This is arguably Spender's most ambitious poem. The emotions are profound, based as they are on Spender's spiritual intimacy with Margaret and his preoccupation with death. Yet the emotional content of the poem is communicated with a clarity that owes much to the sure use of the elegiac form, with its dependency on a nature imagery compatible with the poet's Romantic inclinations. Margaret's death is universalized, like that of Milton's elegiac hero Lycidas, in the imagery of death by drowning:

> Darling of our hearts, drowning
> In the thick night of ultimate sea

Her struggle with death is crystalized in the image of

> . . . a tree choked by ivy, rotted
> By yellow spreading fungus on the bark
> Out of a topmost branch
> A spray of leaves is seen

But images of nature veil the agony as well and make the emotion bearable:

> Poor child, you wear your summer dress
> And your shoes striped with gold
> As the earth wears a variegated cover
> Of grass and flowers
> Covering caverns of destruction over
> Where hollow deaths are told.

And in keeping with the pastoral tradition, this modern Adonis is celebrated by the forces of nature, who absorb her and by so doing give death a larger meaning that transcends individual sorrow:

Already you are beginning to become
Fallen tree-trunk with sun-burnished limbs
In an infinite landscape among tribal bones
Encircled by encoraching ritualistic stones.

Even the death agony finds concrete expression in terms of "a final act of love" in nature:

. . . the world-storm fruit
Sperm of tangling distress,
Mouth roaring in the wilderness,
Fingernail tearing at dry root.

And finally, the heroine of the elegy achieves her Adonis-like resurrection, not in terms of the classical or Christian year-spirit myths, but in terms—borrowed again from nature—expressive of the poet's own idealism in the face of a world he does not pretend to understand. To accept Margaret's death is to celebrate her life and in so doing to overcome death:

As she will live who, candle-lit,
Floats upon her final breath,
The ceiling of the frosty night
And her high room beneath,
Wearing not like destruction, but
Like a white dress, her death.

When Spender made his first trip to America, in 1947, he went as an established man of letters to join a faculty at Sarah Lawrence College that included such notables as Mary McCarthy, Robert Fitzgerald, Horace Gregory, Joseph Campbell, and Randall Jarrell. In the summer following the 1947–1948 academic year, the Spenders visited Christopher Isherwood in Los Angeles and Frieda Lawrence and the remnants of the D. H. Lawrence circle in Taos, New Mexico. Spender, driven by Leonard Bernstein, returned to the Lawrence ranch later in the summer and stayed there for six weeks writing his autobiography, *World Within World.* In deciding to write an autobiography, Spender seemed to be signaling, perhaps mostly to himself, that he had finally achieved a tangible identity, a fusing of his personal and public life.

World Within World is a classic among modern autobiographies, an extraordinarily honest and moving portrait of an ambivalent and introverted individual whose background, historical circumstances, and apparent vocation demanded that he seek a meaningful public identity. *World Within World* is the major source for information about Spender's life and thought to the 1950's. Later, with the publication of *Journals 1939–1983,* more is revealed about Spender's private thoughts from the early period on through into the mid 1980's.

After his stay in Taos, Spender continued to cultivate his American connections. Much of 1948 was spent on lecture tours and developing further acquaintance with American intellectuals. It was also the year in which he wrote an essay for *The God That Failed: Six Studies in Communism* (1950), a work in which Spender and other intellectuals renounced communism in a series of essays.

In 1949 Spender published *The Edge of Being,* for the most part a collection of World War II poems that are much less Romantic than his Spanish Civil War poems, much more grounded in the real and not necessarily heroic concerns of survivors of the London bombings:

Against an acrid cloud of dust, I saw
The houses kneel, revealed each in its abject
Prayer, my prayer as well: 'Oh God,
Spare me the lot that is my neighbour's.'
("Rejoice in the Abyss")

Spender in 1949 was not, as some have suggested, a poet whose technical ability was not equal to wider experience and new depth of thought. If there is no longer the old naïveté or the sweeping lyrical lines of the early poetry, there is a new hardness more in keeping with the postwar, McCarthy era through which Spender, then in his forties, was moving. Spender held to his view that the poet's role was to be "sensitive to the life of his time."

In keeping with that role, in 1953 Spender accepted a position as coeditor of a new journal called *Encounter.* He remained with the magazine until 1967, when he discovered that some of its funding came from the Central Intelligence Agency. In spite of this questionable and covert connection, *Encounter* remained during Spender's tenure a moderately anticommunist journal that published views from all sides of the political spectrum and served as a literary review as well.

Spender's position with *Encounter* tended to encourage him to address public issues. In 1952, for instance, he published *Learning Laughter,* a book on the plight of indigenous Palestinian Jewish children in the Israeli kibbutzim. He became active in movements in support of political and cultural freedom in general, most especially PEN and later the *Index on Censorship* of which he was a founder. He attended conferences on the major postwar issues. But Spender never lost the poet's need to internalize his public life, to bring it into conjunction with more personal feelings. In 1956 he attended a meeting in Venice of Soviet and Western intellectuals where ideological debates were dominated by Jean-Paul Sartre and Maurice Merleau-Ponty, a friend who many years later would be "translated" by Spender into verse:

> I walked with Merleau-Ponty by the lake.
> Upon his face, I saw his intellect.
> Energy of the sun-interweaving
> Waves, electric, danced on him. His eyes
> Smiled with their gay logic through
> Black coins flung down from leaves.
> ("One More New Botched Beginning")

Another creative result of the Venice conference for Spender was a satiric novella called *Engaged in Writing* (1958).

In the 1950's Spender continued to search for a public and personal significance that could replace the disintegration of values he had described in *The Destructive Element* during his Marxist years. In 1953 he published a sequel to that book, called *The Creative Element: A Study of Vision, Despair and Orthodoxy Among Some Modern Writers.* Spender writes in the introduction:

> The creative element is the individual vision of the writer who realizes in his work the decline of modern values while isolating his own individual values from the context of society. He never forgets the modern context, in fact he is always stating it, but he does so only to create the more forcibly the visions of his own isolation.

The Creative Element is a continuation of Spender's study of modernism. The Marxist idealism of *The Destructive Element* gives way in this study to a developing belief, already inherent in the early poetry, that the poet "must restore the lost connection between man-made objects and inner life" (p. 39), that there is a heroism in the visionary isolation of the great modernist writers—Yeats, Eliot, Rimbaud, Rilke, Lawrence—who have had to struggle against the destructive element that "was simply society itself" (p. 12). For these "visionaries" and for Stephen Spender at this stage, values, significance, and belief, are grounded in the act of creation, itself the only source of meaning.

In *The Making of a Poem* (1955) Spender collects his essays on Goethe, Auden, Dylan Thomas, and others, emphasizing the confessional tendency of English poetry, including his own, rooted, as he suggests it is, in repression and guilt. The title essay is a highly sensitive analysis of the connection between poetry and experience. It can be said to be itself a metaphor for what has been Spender's lifelong pilgrimage to establish the connections between the public and the private, between life and art.

Spender continued during the 1950's to write poetry, drama, and fiction, if somewhat sporadically, given his career in teaching and journalism. His *Collected Poems 1928–1953* appeared in 1955 with a few new poems added to ones already published. Several small volumes of verse, *Sirmione Peninsula* (1954), *I Sit at the Window* (1955), and *Inscriptions* (1958) also appeared. And Spender found time to adapt two plays for New York and London productions, Friedrich von Schiller's *Mary Stuart* (1959) and Frank Wedekind's *Lulu.*

The 1960's found Spender still wrestling in his critical writing with the question of modernism. *The Imagination in the Modern World* (1962) and *The Struggle of the Modern* (1963) grew out of lectures delivered at Northwestern University, the University of California, and the Library of Congress in Washington, D.C. In these books Spender continues to point to the characteristically modern splits between art and life and between the inner and outer life. He sees in modernism an attempt to heal the wounds by way of a creative juxtaposition of the past with the present. Joyce, Eliot, and Yeats, for instance, all use the mythic past to bring significance to the materialist present.

By the 1960's Stephen Spender had attained the stature of a major literary figure. He received the CBE (Commander of the British Empire) in 1962, and in 1965 he was named Poetry Consultant at the Library of Congress for the academic year. In 1966 he was invited to give the Clark Lectures at Cambridge University. These lectures, published as *Love-Hate Relations: A Study of Anglo-American Sensibilities* (1974), outline the general cultural and specifically literary relationship between Britain and America. His early focus is Henry James, always in his mind one of the "truly great," whose work was grounded in that relationship and who maintained European cultural and literary values while remaining sensitive to the realities that informed the new American independence from those values. Spender traces the American literary pilgrimage through an early dependence on Europe to a new sense of *patria* based on "the severance of the American future from the European past" (p. xviii). He discusses the contemporary American threat to the European past itself. If Americans were at first overwhelmed by their European past, they have now developed a chaotic culture that defies tradition and threatens in turn to Americanize Western culture. For Europeans, America itself has now become the destructive element that, because of its commitment to instant profit or gratification, to "self-involvement," threatens the effective operation of past traditions in the present reality. "Americans fear the European past; Europeans fear the American future" (p. 62). There are various reactions to Americanization. Some in England have retreated into a Georgian past as a means of maintaining "distance and sanity." In spite of his sympathy for the "studied provincialism" of the sort practiced in England by poet Philip Larkin, however, Spender seems unwilling to dismiss the more "orgiastic" approach of America altogether. He prefers the attitude of D. H. Lawrence, another of his heroes who recognized that he had much in common with writers like Walt Whitman and Herman Melville, but maintained "a hierarchy of values within the chaotic and vague concept of 'life' " (p. 318) that marks the works of these and other Americans.

America has always interested Spender, but unlike Isherwood and Auden he seems never to have been tempted by expatriation. In fact, in spite of his international outlook Spender is much more at ease in Philip Larkin's England than he is in Allen Ginsberg's America. It seems likely that it is his commitment to the idea of the artist as social chronicler that has led to his fascination with a nation that has in so many ways dominated his era.

Spender's preoccupation with America reached a high point in the 1960's. America during the time of the student revolution fascinated him in much the way that Germany had fascinated him thirty years earlier. The ideological struggles on the American campuses where he spent so much of his time "reminded me of ideological debates in my own youth" (*Journals,* p. 258), and he decided to write about them. But first he visited Paris, Berlin, and Prague to study the revolts there. The result of his study of young students in America and Europe was *The Year of the Young Rebels* (1969), a book generally acclaimed by critics as a sensitive and perceptive view of the subject. In *The Young Rebels* Spender wonders whether the students of the 1960's will be able to avoid the pitfalls of the students of the 1930's, who succumbed to such destructive ideologies as fascism and communism.

At the age of sixty, Spender was appointed Professor of English Literature at University College London, a position he held until his retirement in 1975. In 1971 he received the Queen's Gold Medal for Poetry for *The Generous Days,* an expanded version of a book of poems published under the same title in 1969. The poet of the Spanish Civil War poems who is at once confessional and sensitive to his time is still present in these poems, but, as Doris Eder has suggested, the poems in *The Generous Days* show "a new leanness . . . compressing more meaning into smaller compass" (p. 362). If the poet still seeks a means of closing the gaps between the public and the private, between poetry and life, between bodily needs and spiritual ones, he does so with a new efficiency that Auden himself, whom Spender visited whenever he was in New York in the 1960's and 1970's, could admire. In the title poem of *The Generous Days* Spender writes:

> His are the generous days that balance
> Spirit and body. Should he hear the trumpet
> Echoing through skies of ice-
> And lightning through his marrow-
> At once one with that cause, he'd throw
> Himself across some far, sad parapet,
> Spirit fly upwards from the sacrifice,
> Body immolated in the summons.

The 1970's were a productive decade. Aside from *Love-Hate Relations* and *The Generous Days,* Spender wrote *T. S. Eliot* (1975), a major critical overview, and an anecdotal collection of essays and journal entries titled *The Thirties and After: Poetry, Politics, and People (1933–1975)* (1978) in which the author shares his unique experience of at least two generations of culture.

This same period was also marked by the deaths of old associates and friends. Auden died in 1973 and Cyril Connolly in 1974. Spender published *Cyril Connolly: A Memoir* in 1978 and edited W. H. Auden*: A Tribute* in 1975. And he worked on a formal five part elegy to Auden in the spirit of Auden's "In Memory of W. B. Yeats." As his *Journals* make clear, Spender agonized for several years over what was to be one of his finest poems. He wanted it to be a poem that would satisfy Auden's technical standards. It was almost as if he feared Auden's disapproval:

> One among friends who stood above your
>   grave
> I cast a clod of earth from those heaped
>   there
> Down on the great brass-handled coffin lid.
> It rattled on the oak like a door knocker
> And at that second I saw your face beneath
> Wedged in an oblong shadow under ground.
> Flesh creased, eyes shut, jaw jutting
> And on the mouth a grin . . .

Spender was in his seventies when in 1981 he traveled for three weeks with his friend David Hockney, in China. *China Diary* (1982) contains paintings and photographs by Hockney and a text by Spender. He continued to teach in the United States, as recently as the fall of 1987 at the University of Connecticut in Storrs. In 1983 he completed for an Oxford production a reworking of the Theban plays by Sophocles. These were produced again for a tour of India in 1989.

In 1983 Stephen Spender was knighted by Queen Elizabeth II. As if to round off his career, he published *Journals 1939–1983* in 1983 and *Collected Poems 1928–1985* in 1985. And then in 1989 his novel *The Temple,* which he had begun in 1929, was published. In the early 1990's he was at work on another novel and several new poems. He continued, as well, to write for literary journals and to accept interviews.

Of the later works, the *Journals,* in addition to the *Collected Poems,* deserve special attention. They are an extraordinary record of a dialogue between art and life, of a poet's conscientious attempt to listen to the messages and to comprehend the patterns of his time. They are the story of the poet at work, absorbing the world around him, recording the words and actions of the "great." Spender's

Journals, his many works of literary and cultural criticism, and his works of drama and fiction are themselves ample evidence of his importance, and they must be included in any overall evaluation of his place in literary history, but when all is said, it is verse that has been the dominant medium in the long autobiographical poem that has been Stephen Spender's career, and it is on his verse that his reputation will most depend.

CONCLUSION

Representing fifty-six years of work, *Collected Poems 1928–1985* contains the best of Spender's poetry. The artist who emerges from this collection is not a passé 1930's poet but a major poet whose verse deserves serious reconsideration. To some extent such reconsideration has begun. Geoffrey Thurley in *The Ironic Harvest,* while still concentrating, as most critics have, on the early poems, makes the somewhat revolutionary claim that Spender was "Auden's superior as a poet . . . the most powerful English poet of his time" (p. 79). Others have reached similar conclusions. A. K. Weatherhead calls Spender "one of the purest lyrical talents of the century" (*A Library of Literary Criticism,* 1975, p. 496). For Thurley, Spender's verse is of a superior quality because it "strives more continuously than [Auden's] for a unifying context both transcending and undercutting the immediate perception" (p. 80). Spender's consciousness of his role as a poet involves a personal commitment that makes possible a moral depth that compensates for his lack of Auden's technical skill: "Both in rhythm and body of verse, Spender's poetry is more powerful and more deeply organized than Auden's" (Thurley, p. 80).

Whether or not one agrees entirely with Thurley, it can be said that he provides a starting point for an understanding of a Stephen Spender released from Auden's shadow. He isolates Spender's difference, suggesting that it is precisely to Spender's naïveté and his "clumsiness" that the particular power of his early poetry can be attributed. The naïveté is a mask for a "genuine innocence of eye (Thurley, p. 81) that gives his verse a peculiar freshness and the clumsiness is an effect of genuine searching resulting in a sense of moral depth. If Auden's precision and dexterity and his irony are missing, there is, instead, what an anonymous critic reviewing *Collected Poems* in the *Times Literary Supplement* called "a stumbling eloquence or a sweeping gesture suddenly arrested" (1955). The images may not fully succeed visually or be used in the early poetry as efficiently as they might be, but the thought is so felt as to be deeply moving. What we see is not so much the external world as the world of the inner consciousness reflected in the external. In this connection, Doris Eder points to the surrealistic aspect of Spender's imagery and reminds us of his interest in painting, pointing to an early poem, like "Not Palaces":

> Eye, gazelle, delicate wanderer,
> Drinker of horizon's fluid line;
> Ear that suspends on a chord
> The spirit drinking timelessness;

In lines like these, Eder sees Spender's "sensitive eye" as "a dilated pupil looking inward quite as much as it gazes on the outward scene" (p. 356). This quality and power to move is found throughout Spender's poetry, in such lines as these from the early poem "The Room Above the Square":

> The light in the window seemed perpetual
> When you stayed in the high room for me;
> It glowed above the trees through leaves
> Like my certainty.

And from "Grandparents," a later poem:

> We looked at Matthew's child, our
> granddaughter,
> Through the glass screen where eight babies
> Blazed like red candles on a table.
> Her crumpled face and hands were like
> Chrysalis and ferns unrolling.
> "Is our baby a genius?" he asked a nun.

We went to the Uffizi and he looked at
Italian primitives, and found
All their *bambini* ugly.
He started drawing Maro and her daughter
Nine hours after Saskia had been born.

It is important to note here, as has been suggested earlier, that some of the early naïveté and lyricism gives way in the later poetry to more concreteness. But in both stages, the poetry reveals the deep emotional reaction of the poet to what he sees so clearly in the physical world. In the early poem light serves as the symbol of a feeling that is "explained" by the abstraction, "my certainty." In the later poem the images themselves—babies that "blazed like red candles" and "her crumpled face and hands" like "Chrysalis and ferns unrolling"—reveal the emotion directly. The poet has become more efficient, but he is very much the same poet, the poet who understands his experience by making it objectively public in art. Whether the subject matter is war or the birth of a grandchild, we are always reading the autobiography of the man whose primary and consistent goal is to be "sensitive to the life of his time."

Spender was asked in the late 1980's to write an article on his beliefs. In "What I Believe" (*The London Review of Books,* 26 October 1989, pp. 24–25) he articulates the belief system that has been the basis for a long and distinguished career as a poetic voice for his era, a career that extends from the 1920's into the 1990's. It is a belief system based on intellect and the "hero worship" of true intellectuals: "The friends of my life-time whom I have most admired and loved, the books and paintings I love—people and masterpieces I compare myself with, much to my own disadvantage—exemplify for me what I most profoundly believe. I believe in intellect. . . ." Spender defines intellect not in the sense of the mental activity of "public figures who can be induced to sign manifestos," but in a Proustian sense, the work of the intellect being the idea, the act, or the object of art that reminds us of a significance beyond our comprehension that is the source of our being. The creators of such works are heroes, the "truly great."

Who, from the womb, remembered the
soul's history
Through corridors of light, where the hours
are suns,
Endless and singing. Whose lovely ambition
Was that their lips, still touched with fire,
Should tell of the Spirit, clothed from head
to foot in song.
And who hoarded from the Spring branches
The desires falling across their bodies like
blossoms.
("The Truly Great")

Selected Bibliography

BIBLIOGRAPHY

Kulkarni, H. B., *Stephen Spender, Works and Criticism: An Annotated Bibliography,* (New York, 1976).

COLLECTED WORKS

Selected Poems, (London, 1940); *Collected Poems 1928–1953,* (London, 1955); *Selected Poems,* (New York, 1964); *Collected Poems 1928–1985,* (London, 1985).

SEPARATE WORKS

Nine Experiments: Being Poems Written at the Age of Eighteen, privately printed (London, 1928)

Twenty Poems, (Oxford, 1930); *Perhaps,* privately printed (1933), poems; *Poems,* (London, 1933, rev. ed. 1934); *Poem,* privately printed (1934); *Vienna,* (London, 1934) poem; *At Night,* privately printed, (Cambridge, Eng., 1935), poem; *The Destructive Element: A Study of Modern Writers and Beliefs,* (London, 1935, pprbk. ed. Philadelphia, 1953); *The Burning Cactus,* (London, 1936, repr. 1955), short stories; "Poetry," in *Fact,* 4 (July 1937), essay; *Forward from Liberalism,* (London, 1937), political essays; *Trial of a Judge,* (London, 1938), five-act play; *Danton's Death,* (London, 1939), adaptation of play by Georg Büchner, trans. with G. Rees; *The New Realism: A Discussion,* (London, 1939), essay; *The Still Centre,* (London, 1939), poems.

The Backward Son, (London, 1940), novel. *Life and the Poet,* (London, 1942), essays; *Ruins and Visions,* (London, 1942), poems; *Jim Braidy: The Story of Britain's Firemen,* (London, 1943), with W. Sansom and J. Gordon; *Spiritual Exercises (To Cecil Day Lewis),* privately printed (London, 1943), sonnets; *Botticelli,* (London, 1945), introduction and notes on ten reproductions; *Citizens in War—and After,* (London, 1945), essays; *European Witness,* (London, 1946), essays; *Poetry Since 1939,* (London, 1946), literary criticism; *Poems of Dedication,* (London, 1947); *Returning to Vienna 1947: Nine Sketches By Stephen Spender,* (Paulet, Vt., 1947) poems; *The Edge of Being,* (London, 1949), poems.

World Within World: The Autobiography of Stephen Spender, (London, 1951); *Europe in Photographs,* (London, 1952) photographs with commentary; *Learning Laughter,* (London, 1952) travel essays; *Shelley,* (London, 1952) essay; *The Creative Element: A Study of Vision, Despair and Orthodoxy Among Some Modern Writers,* (London, 1953); *Sirmione Peninsula,* (London, 1954), poems; *I Sit at the Window,* (Baltimore, 1955), poem; *The Making of a Poem,* (London, 1955), essays on writing; *Engaged in Writing and The Fool and the Princess,* (London, 1958), satire; *Inscriptions,* (London, 1958) poems; *Mary Stuart,* (London, 1959) adaptation of play by Friedrich von Schiller.

The Imagination in the Modern World, (Washington, D.C., 1962), three lectures; *Rasputin's End,* (Milan, 1963), play, with N. Nabokov; *The Struggle of the Modern,* (London, 1963), essays on modern life, art, and literature; *Ghika: Paintings, Drawings, Sculptures,* (London, 1964) essays, with P. L. Fermor; *Chaos and Control in Poetry,* (Washington, D.C., 1966), lecture; *The Magic Flute, Retold by Stephen Spender,* (New York, 1966), children's story; *The Generous Days,* (Boston, 1969, enlg. ed., London, 1971), poems; *The year of the Young Rebels,* (London, 1969), essays on student rebellion.

Art Student, (London, 1970), poem; *Descartes,* (London, 1970), poem; *W. H. Auden: A Memorial Address,* (privately printed, 1973); *Love-Hate Relations: A Study of Anglo-American Sensibilities,* (London, 1974), essays on the relationship between English and American literature; *Eliot,* (London, 1975, repr. as *T. S. Eliot* New York, 1976); *Cyril Connolly: A Memoir,* (Edinburgh, 1978); *Henry Moore: Sculptures in Landscape,* (London, 1978), with G. Shakerley; *Recent Poems,* (London, 1978); *The Thirties and After: Poetry, Politics, and People (1933–1975),* (London, 1978), reminiscences and literary criticism; *America Observed,* (New York, 1979), with P. Hogarth; *Venice,* (London, 1979), with F. Roiter.

Letters to Christopher, ed. L. Bartlett (Santa Barbara, Calif., 1980), Spender's letters to Christopher Isherwood 1929–1939 and two 1930's journals; *China Diary,* (London, 1982), contains paintings and photographs by David Hockney and text by Spender; *Oedipus Trilogy,* (London, 1984), drama; *Journals 1939–1983,* J. Goldsmith, ed. (London, 1985); *Henry Moore: A Memorial Address,* (London, 1987); *The Temple,* (London, 1988), novel; "What I Believe," *The London Review of Books* (October 26, 1989), 24–25, article.

WORKS EDITED, TRANSLATED, OR CONTAINING CONTRIBUTIONS BY SPENDER

New Signatures, M. Roberts, ed. (London, 1932), an anthology of young poets; *The God That Failed: Six Studies in Communism,* R. Crossman, ed. (London, 1950), contains an essay by Spender; *Penguin Modern Poets 20,* (London, 1971), an anthology with J. Heath-Stubbs and F. T. Prince; Wedekind, Frank, *The Lulu Plays and Other Sex Tragedies,* translated by Spender (London, 1972); *W. H. Auden: A Tribute,* (New York, 1975), edited by Spender.

INTERVIEWS

P. Orr, ed. *The Poet Speaks: Interviews with Contemporary Poets,* (New York, 1966), pp. 239–244; "A Conversation with Stephen Spender: The Creative Process," in *English Record,* 18 (April 1968).

"A conversation with Stephen Spender," in *The Review,* 23 (London, 1970), 21–27; "A Conversation with Stephen Spender," in *American Poetry Review,* 6 no. 6 (1977); "The Art of Poetry XXV," in The Paris Review, 77 (Winter/Spring 1980); G. Plimpton, ed. *Writers at Work: The Paris Review Interviews,* sixth series (New York, 1984), 29–78.

BIOGRAPHICAL AND CRITICAL STUDIES

MacNiece, L., *Modern Poetry,* (Oxford, 1938, rev. ed. 1968); Rosenthal, M. L., *The Modern Poets,* (Oxford, 1965); Connors, J. J., *Poets and Politics: A Study of the Careers of C. Day Lewis, Stephen Spender and W. H. Auden in the 1930's,* (New Haven, Ct., 1967); Tolley, A. T., *The Early Published Poems of Stephen Spender: A Chronology,* (Ottawa, 1967); Stanford, Derek, *Stephen Spender, Louis MacNeice, Cecil Day Lewis: A Critical Essay,* (Grand Rapids, Mich., 1969); Kulkarni, H. B., *Stephen Spender: Poet in Crisis,* (Glasgow, 1970); Thurley, G. "A Kind of Scapegoat: A Retrospect on Stephen Spender," in *The Ironic Harvest: English Poetry in the Twentieth Century* (New York, 1974), 79–97; Weatherhead, A. Kingsley, *Stephen Spender and the Thirties,* (Lewisburg, Pa., 1975); Hynes, S., *The Auden Generation: Literature and Politics in England in the 1930s,* (London, 1976); Eder, D. L., "Stephen Spender," *The Dictionary of Literary Biography,* vol. 20 (New York, 1983) 351–365; *Thirties Poets: "The Auden Group",* R. Carter, ed. (London, 1984).

Edmund Spenser
(ca. 1552–1599)

ALASTAIR FOWLER

I

"SAGE HOMER, VIRGIL, Spenser laureate." Spenser is one of our few classics. For that very reason, although his status has never been very seriously threatened, ideas of him have changed. Different ages and critics have given very different accounts of his work. Up to the eighteenth century, his reputation depended far more than it would now on *The Shepherd's Calendar.* Spenser was consequently a pastoral and love poet: even in *The Faerie Queen* he was "Heroic Paramour of Faerie Land", to be compared with Ariosto or Petrarch. On the other hand he was also a learned poet, an English Virgil, edited, cited as a classical author, and widely imitated. This posed problems for neo-classically minded readers, who had a blindingly clear idea of exactly what a classic work ought to be. *The Faerie Queen* could easily seem a bit too "uncultivate" and Gothic. Their solution was to turn attention away from Spenser's design, which broke too many rules, to the serious moral content—or else to his descriptive pictorial art. *The Faerie Queen* became "an excellent piece of morality, policy, history"—or Mrs. Spence's "collection of pictures." The influential John Hughes completed this development by combining both approaches. He showed how Spenser could be valued both as an "imager of virtues and vices" and a "rough painter" ("The embellishments of description are rich and lavish . . . beyond comparison.") without looking to him for epic or romance coherence. Unfortunately Spenser's morality was largely embodied in allegory. If the neoclassical critics were prepared to accord this element a lowly but secure place, "allegories fulsome grow", and the romantic critics were inclined to jettison it altogether. For William Hazlitt the allegory was something that would not bite so long as one left it alone. Even the perceptive critic James Russell Lowell followed this approach, recommending *The Faerie Queen* to those who wished "to be rid of thought." Spenser's sensuous vividness has always remained, together perhaps with the dazzling ease of transitions, and a deeper, more elusive imaginativeness, closer to dream. However variously described and subject to misunderstanding, he has occupied a special place in our literature as a nourisher of other poets, work. He was Cowley's first introduction to poetry; Pope's "mistress"; Wordsworth's "inspiration"; and a model to Milton, Dryden, Thomson, Yeats, and countless others. By almost common consent he is one of our most "poetic" poets, so that he serves as a sounding board even for those of a very different temper: his words run softly even through the lines of T. S. Eliot.

Twentieth-century criticism has been better equipped historically to interpret the poetry that Spenser wrote. Sharing a common view of him as a great and serious poet, it has mostly been taken up with explaining. The explanation tends to be detailed: the picture-gallery view has given way to iconographical studies. The best modern criticism is technically remarkable; but it usually lacks the proportion achieved in the eighteenth century by John Upton, still Spenser's best reader. Perhaps in consequence some judicious critics, who would not quite deny the greatness of Spenser, have nevertheless thought his poetry too much in need of difficult explanation to be worth the effort for modern readers. They have renewed and reinforced Ben Jonson's objections to his poetic diction and the Augustan charges of structural faults; or fallen back on the position that "the wittiest poets have been all short" (Owen Felltham). Neocritical, in fact, is neoclassical writ small. Recently, however, critics have shown more interest in longer poems. At the same time, a better appreciation of Gothic interlace—interweaving of linear narratives—is allowing revaluation of Spenser's complex neo-Gothic form. Very early on, John Hughes and Richard Hurd guessed that Spenser's Gothic cathedral might have its own kind of unity. But the implications of that valuable analogy can only now be fully developed. Poetry such as Spenser's is too central to our literature to be really threatened by critical opinion; some of it is too profound even to need much conscious understanding. Still, it is as well, from time to time, to revise our notion of the achievement. Where are Spenser's excellences, for us? We are beginning to have more interest than our predecessors in his vision of the totality of human experience—a vision as wide, in its way, as Milton's, or Blake's, or Hugh MacDiarmid's. We should be more inclined to see him as pursuing the highest and most philosophical ends of poetry.

II

Not much is known about Spenser's life. He was born in London, his "most kindly nurse", probably in 1552. Although related to the noble Spencers of Warwickshire and Northamptonshire, his immediate family circumstances seem to have been poor. He was educated at Merchant Taylors, School, an outstanding new grammar school, which he attended for eight years from its foundation in 1561. There the curriculum included a great deal of Latin, some Greek (certainly Homer), and the Hebrew psalter. As in other grammar schools, the Latin would be not only classical but Renaissance: Erasmus, Vives, perhaps Mantuanus' pastorals or Palingenius' *Zodiacus vitae.* Exceptionally, the curriculum extended to music and possibly even to English. For the headmaster was an advanced educationalist, the great Richard Mulcaster. No doctrinaire humanist, Mulcaster had a strong and original mind, which he expressed in a fine though sometimes obscure style. The ideas developed in *Positions* and *The Elementary* are sometimes ahead of any that have even yet been realized; nevertheless, they are compatible with a deep sense of history. The latter gave Mulcaster a reverence for such fragile institutions as customs and languages. Thus, his classicism allowed for the possibility of different classical periods in modern literatures. He read Ariosto: he advocated regular teaching of the vernacular ("I honour Latin, but worship English"); he defended the education of women. Many of Mulcaster's ideas seem to find a later echo in Spenser's writing: not least the belief that literature and learning may form the character of the individual for the public good.

Together with Lancelot Andrewes, Spenser left school in 1569 for Pembroke Hall, Cambridge, where he was a sizar (an undergraduate receiving an allowance from the college to enable him to study), paying no fees but performing certain chores. The next four years were spent in completing the trivium begun at school—by reading rhetoric, logic, and philosophy; the three years after on the quadrivium—arithmetic, geometry, astronomy, and music. These studies centered on a small number of set authors, all classical. In 1573 Spenser proceeded B.A.; in 1576 M.A. At Cambridge an oral tradition then vigorously prevailed of lectures and public disputation. The level of learned eloquence was high, fitting an excessive number for the administrative offices available. (The size of the university was small by modern standards: about

1,800, of whom 250 were sizars.) Spenser's contemporaries included the much older Thomas Preston, author of *Cambyses*; the younger Abraham Fraunce, poet, rhetorician, literary theorist; and Gabriel Harvey.

Harvey, who was Spenser's senior by about three years, became a fellow of Pembroke Hall in 1570, praelector (or professor) of rhetoric in 1574. His *Ciceronianus* and *Rhetor* show him to have been a brilliant scholar and writer, surely possessing one of the sharpest minds of his time. And he was probably, as Virginia Woolf surmised, a brilliant talker. Yet his Cambridge career was erratic, and in the end unsuccessful. This may have been not altogether to his discredit: he had ideas progressive enough to provoke opposition—including Ramist reform in logic, and unsound "paradoxes" such as Copernicus' heliocentric hypothesis. But he was also arrogant, quarrelsome, tactless, vain, silly, and a misfit. The man who could write "Sometime my book is unto me a god / Sometime I throw it from me a rod" was too restless for mere scholarship. In another age he might have been a literary critic, or even a columnist. As it was, he went after preferment with the desperation of frustrated greatness, perpetually encouraging himself the while, in countless Machiavellian marginalia, to futile circumspections.

In spite (or perhaps because) of our knowing so many of his private thoughts, he remains a baffling figure. Most—like Nashe in their public quarrel, and perhaps Shakespeare, in Holofernes—have regarded him as a foolish pedant. He took himself seriously; so that others have tended not to. But it is not Harvey who seems pedantic when Spenser and he differ about quantity in English verse. His greater experience and wide reading enabled him to enlarge Spenser's tastes and perhaps to make him more contemporary, more European. Harvey came to recognize the quality of an early version of *The Faerie Queen,* although he preferred (rightly or wrongly) Spenser's lost "Comedies." But this advice was resisted. Spenser was well able to exert his own taste decisively, using a bet, for example, to press Harvey to read *Lazarillo de Tormes.* Their friendship, which mattered to both men, was reciprocal and not dependent.

How did Spenser regard Harvey? The sonnet he addressed to him from Dublin in 1586 seems comically inappropriate now: "happy above happiest men . . . sitting like a looker-on / Of this world's stage," wielding his "critic pen," careless of suspicion. But Harvey, who was not yet the failure of later years, nor demeaned by controversy with the unfair and clever Nashe, perhaps had still an outsider's early idealism. However that may be, this strange man also cherished ambitious hopes of following in the footsteps of Cheke and Smith, and of becoming great in the councils of the mighty. From 1576 he pursued the favor of Leicester and, from 1578, of Sidney. He was thus in a position to introduce Spenser to two of the greatest patrons of the age. And when Spenser's *Shepherd's Calendar* appeared anonymously in 1579, it bore a dedication to Sidney.

Although the Cambridge of Spenser's day was dominated by radical Puritans of Thomas Cartwright's stamp, Spenser emerged a moderate but fervent Protestant, with views comparable to those of Richard Hooker or gentle Archbishop Grindal (the Algrin of *The Shepherd's Calendar*). In 1578, after some time in the north, Spenser became secretary to Edward Young, the former master of Pembroke Hall. By October 5, 1579, however, he had entered the household of the earl of Leicester and was familiar with Leicester's nephew Sir Philip Sidney. Together with Sidney and Sir Edward Dyer he made the experiments in "artificial" or quantitative verse that are discussed and developed in the correspondence with Harvey, published in 1580 as *Three proper, and witty, familiar Letters.* (This spirited but unsuccessful attempt to capture in the vernacular the sophisticated obliquity of smart neo-Latin epistles got Gabriel Harvey into a great deal of trouble with the authorities.) Probably about the same time, Spenser was writing his "lost" works ("Epithalamion Thamesis," "The Court of Cupid," "Dreams," "Pageants," etc.), some of which may be early versions of parts of *The Faerie Queen.* Also in

1579 he married, almost certainly, Machabyas Childe, by whom he was to have two children, Sylvanus and Katherine.

Then, in 1580, Spenser went to Ireland as secretary to the new governor, Arthur Lord Grey. (The English were making another of their incoherent attempts to anglicize barbarous Ireland, partly by colonial settlement, partly by the sword.) Inexplicably this move has been represented as exile consequent on some disgrace (perhaps Spenser offended Leicester, as his *Virgil's Gnat* hints?). But humanistically trained men of letters expected and hoped to exercise their pens in administrative tasks. A career's success was gauged by the minor offices collected, and the estates. Spenser was clerk of faculties in the Court of Chancery (1581: a sinecure); commissioner for musters (1583); deputy to Lodowick Bryskett as clerk of the Council of Munster (1584); prebendary of Limerick Cathedral (1585: a sinecure); and justice of the County of Cork (1594). From 1582 he leased New Abbey near Dublin; in 1586 he was assigned, and in 1590 formally granted, the very large estate of Kilcolman (3,000 acres, or about 1,214 hectares). Kilcolman was Spenser's real and emotional home: its landscape finds reflection in many passages of his poetry. In fact, he should be regarded as one of our great Irish writers.

Even in Ireland, however, he still belonged to the literary milieu of the court. Lodowick Bryskett, whose dialogue *Discourse of Civil Life* (1583) has Spenser as one of its interlocutors, was a poet and former tutor of Sidney's. Ralegh visited his nearby estate in 1589. And manuscript circulation of Spenser's work is argued by Abraham Fraunce's ability to quote from *The Faerie Queen,* book 2, before its publication.

In 1589 and again in 1595 or 1596 Spenser made visits to London that occasioned flurries of publication, partly of old work revised: 1590, *The Faerie Queen,* part 1, and *Muiopotmos;* 1591, *Daphnaida and Complaints;* 1595, *Amoretti and Epithalamion* and *Colin Clout's Come Home Again;* 1596, *The Faerie Queen,* part 2 (books 4–6), *Prothalamion,* and *Four Hymns. The Faerie Queen* may never have been finished. Of the six missing books, only the Cantos of Mutability (published posthumously) remain.

The *Complaints* volume was suppressed, probably because Spenser had criticized William Cecil, lord Burghley, in *The Ruins of Time* and *Mother Hubberd's Tale.* Burghley was nevertheless included, although cautiously, among the sixteen nobles to whom *The Faerie Queen* was presented (it was dedicated to the queen herself). He seems not to have liked it. The queen, however, did. She paid Spenser the unique honor in 1591 of a life pension of £50 a year (a considerable sum—more than twice the rent for Kilcolman). In 1594 Spenser was remarried, to Elizabeth Boyle. He solemnized the wedding day, June 11, in *Amoretti and Epithalamion.* 1596 finds him celebrating with *Prothalamion* the spousals of the earl of Worcester's daughters at Essex House in London. The poem expresses "old woes," the loss of his patron Leicester, who had died in 1588, and his consequent friendlessness; but it also looks forward to the favor of a new patron, the earl of Essex. Spenser's successful career culminated with his nomination (as one "with good knowledge in learning and not unskilful or without experience in the service of the wars") to the post of high sheriff of Cork, on September 30, 1598. But within a month the rebels had overrun Munster and burned Kilcolman. Spenser returned to London with dispatches on Christmas Eve; and on January 13, 1599, he died. He was buried in Westminster Abbey, near Chaucer, at the expense of Essex, "his hearse being carried by poets, and mournful verses and poems thrown into his tomb." There was an early tradition that Spenser died in want; but it seems to have been without basis.

III

The Shepherd's Calendar (1579) was Spenser's first considerable published work. This fact is a little misleading, in that he already had behind him the lost works, not to speak of the schoolboy translation of Van der Noodt's Protestant emblem book. Spenser was early drawn to poetry, yet had a slow development as a poet. Traditionally, pastoral offered an unassuming mode that might be attempted in prelude to more ambitious flights. *The Shepherd's Calendar,* however, is far from being apprentice work. It shows a high sense of control, and yet an astonishing freedom in the treatment of genre. It is far from mere imitation or combination of Theocritus, Virgil, Mantuan, and Marot. Indeed, considered historically, its achievement is so considerable as to make it a watershed on any map of English verse.

Spenser enlarged the pastoral tradition in several ways. The Renaissance eclogues by Mantuan and Barclay had already treated moral or religious matters: pastoral could be microcosmic and satiric rather than idyllic. Spenser took up this option and invested in it heavily. The landscape that he makes a mirror of his shepherd's plight is "barren ground, whom winter's wrath hath wasted": a land suffering from adverse weather, wolves, and disease. In fact, it is real country. And he introduces many fresh images from nature, such as the oak's top "bald and wasted with worms" and the bee "working her formal rooms in waxen frame," besides many country phrases not previously heard in serious poetry.

Most creative of all is his approach to the structure. Instead of the usual collection of independent "eclogues" (the term anciently implied separateness) Spenser has made a single work, unified by the structural principle of the natural year, and of seasons that symbolize stages in human life. As Pope noted, "the addition he has made of a calendar to his eclogues is very beautiful." The calendrical form not only holds the eclogues together, but contributes to their special character of endless variety combined with complex, elusive order. It works multifariously: in the changing weather; in seasonal customs (April's flower gathering was the occupation for that month by the conventions of visual art); explicitly astronomical imagery (Sol appears in July, the month of his own sign Leo, "making his way between the Cup, / and golden Diadem"); and even in physical proportions (May is by far the longest eclogue, since the sun was known to stay longer in Gemini than in any other sign). Spenser also achieved controlled variety by varying the meter, all the way from rough alliterative lines to the gentle, grave stateliness of November's elegy for Dido:

> But now sike [such] happy cheer is turned to heavy chance,
> Such pleasance now displaced by dolour's dint:
> All music sleeps, where death doth lead the dance,
> And shepherds' wonted solace is extinct.
> The blue in black, the green in grey is tinct [tinged],
> The gaudy garlands deck her grave,
> The faded flowers her corse embrave.
> O heavy hearse,
> Mourn now my muse, now mourn with tears besprint [sprinkled].
> O careful verse.
> (November 103–112)

Inset songs and fables introduce further variation. Then there is the alternation of three modes or categories—"plaintive," "moral," and "recreative"—and the interweaving of three large subjects: love, poetry, and religious politics. The command with which genres are deployed makes for admiration, even where this is not accompanied with understanding or enjoyment. Everything seems in scale, and orchestrated, giving a sense of various modes of life in harmony. January's love complaint gives way to February's *débat* between youth and age, which encloses (and perhaps underlies too) the fable of an episcopal oak and a Puritan briar. March offers an exploit of Cupid; April, an inset ode in praise of Elizabeth, with some delicately Skeltonic flower poetry; and May, a beast fable and more controversy.

The poetic statement made on this complex instrument is itself complex. For one thing, the shepherds enact a roman à clef, to which the key has been lost. Algrin is Archbishop Grindal and Hobbinol Gabriel Harvey; but others remain unidentified, even with the help of fashionably elaborate annotation by "E. K." (himself unknown). Moreover, some of the roles are multivalent. Thus, besides being a persona for Spenser, Colin Clout is a highly idealized laureate (combining poetic names from Skelton and Marot). Tityrus is both Virgil and Chaucer. And Pan figures severally as Henry VIII, as the pope, and as Christ. Nevertheless, the topical allegory is probably not intricate; Spenser seems to have tended to political simplicity as much as to intellectual subtlety.

Nowhere is there more subtlety than in the poem's structural pattern. To begin with, it sets out two calendars: the astronomical, running from March to February, and the Christian, from January to December. Circularity is suggested by the linking of the January and December eclogues, each of which has the single speaker Colin. They are "proportionable" in the octave ratio of perfect harmony, one being exactly twice as long as the other. Then, the plaintive (*p*), the moral (*m*), and the recreative (*r*) eclogues are arranged, with their speakers, in interlocking symmetries. For example, January to June (corresponding astrologically to the six "lunar" signs) form the sequence *p/m/r/r/m/p.* Moreover, Colin's concluding motto in June, as E. K. notes, answers that in January. Thus, the first half of the *Calendar* also forms a circle, a subsidiary "world" which may be interpreted as the mundane world of natural life. It begins with Colin's "wilfully" breaking his pipe and ends with his giving up false love and the unworthy Rosalind. Within this world are conflicts between the old and the new (February: oak versus briar), or between worldly pleasure and censorious morality (May: Palinode versus Piers). June, however, makes the challenges to an earthly paradise explicit, leading to July's myth of the Fall, and fatal disorders in nature. Here, at the poem's center, stands a mountain, the high place of God: there is mention of Sinai, Olivet, and "mighty Pan" or Christ.

The *Calendar's* second half becomes increasingly dark, the secular idyll more and more plainly illusion. Art's solace now replaces that of nature. But the mirror of art, which itself mirrors nature, brings deeper disenchantments still. October questions the use of poetry and even the possibility of literary life. Its talk of war contradicts the olive coronal of April, the matching month (with sign in opposition) of the *Calendar's* first half. To lighten this gloom there emerges the theme of grace. In September, Diggon Davie repents; in December, Colin himself. Indeed, one might see the whole *Calendar* as a confession of Colin's developing religious consciousness: as his palinode or retraction from earlier secularity. But the poem is more inclusive, more Chaucerian perhaps, than this would suggest. It finds room, after all, for natural beauty, for the worldly Palinode, for the retired Hobbinol. And it is the reformer Piers who overstates his case. The *Calendar* leaves us, in the end, with a sense of manifold fictive worlds, all comprehended in Spenser's detached vision of mutability.

This marvelous intellectual structure unfortunately no longer quite succeeds as poetry. This is not merely because of its coterie aspects—these are no insuperable obstacle with Shakespeare's poems. The reasons have to do with certain critical theories, fashionable in Spenser's day, about the language of literature. Following ideas of Joachim Du Bellay and others, he believed that a classical English style could be based on Chaucer's language. Hence his interweaving of rustic expressions appropriate to pastoral, Chaucerian archaisms, and ancient poetic words ("grieslie," "moe," "astert"), together with contrastingly easy conventional epithets ("riper age," "doleful verse"), to form a lexical tapestry of great, perhaps even excessive, richness. Especially desirable were dialectal or pseudodialectal words, parts, or mere spelling variants that preserved Chaucer's, Gavin Douglas', and earlier forms ("swincke," "sayne"). This diction was not quite so experimental then as it has since come to look; but intensified as it was by archaic syntax and combined with a style of plain pithy statement, its effect must always have been singular enough. Jonson says that Spenser "writ no language." Spenser might appeal to Theocritus, precedent—and to the many poets who have followed his, rather than Jonson's, example. The smooth element of Spenser's diction has influenced poetic taste ever since. But some of his rougher innovations now seem as decisively wrongheaded as any in Wordsworth's *Lyrical Ballads*:

> My ragged ronts [bullocks] all shiver and shake,
> As doen high towers in an earthquake. . . .
> (February 5–6)

Another unfortunate theory concerned Chaucer's versification. At a time when the Chaucerian canon was uncertain, and accessible only in bad texts, his verse was universally held to be rough. It was imitated by such devices as the addition of final *-e.* Spenser's fashionably rough verse now seems almost as dated as that of his contemporaries. At best it is workmanlike. Above its shaggy lowliness, as above a rusticated ground story, rises the piano nobile of inset songs (April, August, November). Here, and in only a few other passages, the *Calendar* displays a liquid ease and subtlety of movement adequate to the brilliant rhetoric:

> Why do we longer live, (ah why live we so long)
> (November 73; cf. 81, 111)

Note how the *correctio,* or restatement, puts a different accent on "we" and "live," reinforcing the meaning yet also making a tenderly elegiac music. In such passages Spenser achieves a remarkably mellifluous flow. His special gift was for counterpointing a great many structures and textures: rhetorical, phonetic, metrical. So in

> The mantled meadows mourn,
> Their sundry colours turn.
> (November 128–129)

the lines are matched by their similar clause length, their words of equivalent syllables symmetrically distributed, their rhetorical parallelism, and their literal meaning; so that the switch from alliteration (monochromatic consonants) to assonance (monochromatic vowels) mimes the drab change of color. Spenser's later verse is full of such correspondences, in which form continuously accompanies sense in a ceremony of meaning. His smooth style, indeed, has so dominated taste that we take it for granted and hardly notice the first beginnings. These should not be exaggerated either. The *Calendar* is high art, certainly; but only locally higher than that of Sidney. Overall, it is the *Calendar's* ambitious encyclopedic content that bodes well, not its poetic language. It already shows a very special combination of complicated medieval structure with Renaissance hyperconsciousness about consistency. But it has attracted too much attention for the good of Spenser's modern reputation.

Spenser continued to write pastoral throughout his life. In 1591 *Astrophel. A Pastoral Elegy* appeared as the framing introduction to a volume of elegies on Sidney. Certainly later than 1586, and probably later than 1590, it is a finer work than most of *The Shepherd's Calendar,* although it has not usually been valued so highly. The first part (lines 1–216) relates, under the allegory of a boar hunt, Sidney's death from a wound received at the battle of Zutphen (1586). Astrophel is gored by one of "the brutish nation" (the Spanish oppressors); mourned by his widow; and metamorphosed into a flower. This part, while always felicitous, preserves so impersonal a tone as to seem now a shade pallid, a little too consciously Bionesque. It is another matter with the Lay of Clorinda. This part, exactly half as long as the first—the proportions of harmony—purports to give the mourning song of Sidney's sister Mary, countess of Pembroke. It is a deeply serious expression of grief, from which Milton learned for *Lycidas.* Who is the mourner to address? She can hope for comfort neither from men nor from gods ("From them comes good, from them comes also ill"), so that she addresses her complaint to herself:

> The woods, the hills, the rivers shall
> resound
> The mournful accent of my sorrow's
> ground.
> (lines 23–24)

The resonance of "ground" ("ground bass," "basis") is characteristic of the Lay's self-referring style, which can be poignant—as in "The fairest flower . . . Was Astrophel; that *was,* we all may rue." The resolution in this second part is deeper and darker: Clorinda reflects that when we grieve we may be self-regarding, "Mourning in others, our own miseries". Sidney is better where he is. If this part was by Mary herself, as some have suggested, she wrote a better poem than Spenser on this occasion.

In December 1591, from Kilcolman, Spenser dedicated to Sir Walter Ralegh *Colin Clout's Come Home Again,* a pastoral eclogue about a recent visit to court. This popular yet incompletely appreciated work is directly autobiographical, if not so literally as some have thought (it transports Gabriel Harvey, surely in wish-fulfillment, to Ireland). Its engaging method is that of general conversation, with no fewer than ten shepherds and shepherdesses interrupting and questioning Colin. These familiar exchanges establish a sense of Spenser's social and literary circle. They also, by their distancing or alienating effect, allow transitions through a wide range of tones, from the strangely exalted to the quietly humorous. The humor of Colin's account of his voyage is quite broad: the sea ("A world of waters heaped up on high"), ships ("Glued together with some subtle matter"), and mythologized admirals (Triton and Proteus) are consistently described as they might appear to an innocent, quite unironic shepherd's eye. Less obvious is the joke whereby the most extensive piece of alliteration—lines 25–26—comes in a speech of Hobbinol's. Harvey disliked this device.

Most good eclogues are deeper than they look; and this one, probably the longest and most complex in the language, is no exception. It has an elaborate symmetrical structure to reflect its various but carefully balanced moods. There is even an inset eclogue, an account of a previous conversation with Ralegh, "the Shepherd of the Ocean," in which the narrative's doubly reported status expresses the remoteness of a primitive river myth of sexual rivalry in the far past. The first half is divided between nature (the watery wilderness; wild Ireland) and art (epitomized by a catalogue of England's twelve chief poets). This passage, where Spenser authoritatively reviews his literary milieu and freely reveals his tastes, has an interest similar to that of, say, W. H. Auden's *Letter From Iceland.* Most praise goes to Daniel and Alabaster (both named), to Astrophel, Alcyon (Sir Arthur Gorges), and to the mysterious Aetion. The second half answers with a catalogue of twelve ladies, courteously praised, and a lofty encomium of the queen. Why then did Colin ever leave the court? His reply offsets the gallantry with a sharp attack on the court's incivility: "it is no sort of life" and all its glory is "but smoke, that fumeth soon away." Hobbinol speaks up for Leicester, giving a well-informed review of his patronage program; but Colin responds with renewed attacks, this time on the court's immorality.

All this has been seen as Spenser's ambivalence; and so in a way it may have been, in personal terms. But the poem's effect seems not so much ambiguous as poised. Peaceful England is excellent, by comparison with disordered Ireland: the court is frivolous, by comparison with true civility. More delicately poised still is Colin's balance of Rosalind's cruelty to him with the queen's to Ralegh (whose suffering carries conviction—"Ah my love's queen, and goddess of my life"). He even reconciles a near-blasphemous panegyric of Elizabeth with the elevation of another vassalage to a higher place within the poem's little world. Its sovereign center honors not the queen, but the courteous grace of an unnamed "maid" (probably Elizabeth

Throckmorton, later Lady Ralegh), to whom Spenser pays ardent homage:

> And I hers ever only, ever one:
> One ever I all vowed hers to be,
> One ever I, and other's never none.
> (lines 477–479, of 955)

"Ever one . . . one ever . . . one ever" is no mere decorative rhetoric of chiasmus[1] or anaphora[2] but mimes the iconographic attitude of the three Graces, one facing forward, two turned in outgoing. For the rest, the poem glances at several of the main interests of Spenser's mature work: cosmogonic myth; a metaphysic of "Beauty the burning lamp of heaven's light"; and a passionate theology of love, with a myth of the androgynous Venus. He condemns the court's lewdness not from a puritanical standpoint, but because it profanes the "mighty mysteries" of love, "that dread lord." The poem's range of feeling is immense; no work gives a better sense of the possibilities of eclogue.

IV

In *Amoretti and Epithalamion* (1595) Spenser lays aside the pastoral weeds of Colin Clout to sing in his own person, as the lover of Elizabeth Boyle. Considering his early reputation as a love poet, it is strange how few now think him one of the great sonneteers. The *Amoretti* can easily seem low-pressure work, lacking the dramatic intensity of Sidney's *Astrophel and Stella.* However, interest grows when one appreciates how far Spenser's quieter virtues and more deeply poetic qualities have been missed. Take *Amoretti* 18, for example, in which the lover complains that whereas "The rolling wheel. . . . The hardest steel in tract of time doth tear" and raindrops wear the "firmest flint" yet he cannot move his lady. Stock images of obduracy; but how originally and deceptively they are put to work. Is the lady really discouraging? If tears are "but water," then the proverb holds and she will yield: only if tears are contrasted with rain would she be unmoved. Similarly when she "turns herself to laughter," who now is "the rolling wheel" and who "doth still remain"? Again, what association have flint and steel together, but kindled fire? The poetic indirection here is quite unlike anything in the other sonneteers of Spenser's time.

And in deeper ways too he is unlike them. Indeed, he came late enough in the vogue—after a dozen other English "sonnet sequences"—to have something different to offer. Shakespeare responded to a similar challenge by writing sonnets that seem to be about friendship and jealousy. But Spenser's are not about passion at all, in the ordinary sense, but about a love that ends happily, in marriage: the British romantic love, mingling friendship with sexual desire, in praise of which he wrote at greater length in *The Faerie Queen.* The lover of the *Amoretti* (partly followed by the reader) gets to know Elizabeth Boyle well, forming a full personal relation with her. And a keenly intelligent, witty person she is—an Elizabeth Bennett rather than a Penelope Rich—with a firm, unmistakable character. Unlike the usual Petrarchist lady, who is a trigger of passion and little else, Elizabeth does not wound with Cupid's darts, but calms passion's storm (8), and, characterized herself by "goodly temperature" (13), frames and tempers her lover's feelings too. Even after they are mutually committed (84), we hear of her "too constant stiffness." This intense but tender courtship of a young girl by a middle-aged lover has the air of reality. (The general situation is probably autobiographical. In *Amoretti* 60, Spenser implies that he is forty; and Elizabeth in fact outlived him, to have children by a second marriage at dates that make it likely that she was at least fifteen years younger.) Their love is deep, but too serious, too responsible, for passion.

Nevertheless, Elizabeth must receive every tribute usually paid to a slavishly worshipped

1. A figure of speech in which the word order in one clause is inverted in another phrase soon after.

2. The repetition of a word or phrase at the beginning of successive clauses or verses.

sonneteer's goddess. In performing this contract Spenser shows an astonishing capacity to fulfill the forms of love complaint, and yet all the time to be free from them, above them—not so much through irony or travesty (although these are sometimes not far away) as through the direct, open refusal of conventional literary attitudes. To the latter, he prefers the more complex human comedy. Sometimes, it is true, he carries the Petrarchist commonplaces far enough towards absurdity to expose their false logic, as in 32: "What then remains but I to ashes burn . . .?" But more often the commonplaces—the fire and ice, the tyrant and captive, the storm and cruel tigress—are taken up with just a hint of distancing humor, a bantering tone or self-deprecating smile, to remind us that they belong to only one of the ways of wooing. The lover knows Elizabeth too well to think that she is really a tigress (in that way, at least). Not that the pains of love are merely acted, in a sense that would make them unreal. Indeed, where the idea of acting becomes most explicit, in the theatrical conceit of 54, the lady—who as unmoved spectator does not act—sits admonished; she is less than alive: "a senseless stone." Alternatively, the commonplaces may be taken up seriously but transformed. So it is with the erotic "blazon," or item-by-item portrait, which had generated much loose poetry, particularly in French and Italian. Spenser has extremely sensuous sonnets of this type, such as the complete blazon in 64. There are several on Elizabeth's eyes, hair, and breasts. In each case, however, the idea is elevated. In 76, her breasts are a "bower of bliss," *pome acerbe* ("unripe apples"), "like early fruit in May," between which the lover's frail thoughts dive "through amorous insight." But the very next sonnet shows the same apples in a dream, now ripe and "golden" laid out for a sacred feast. For they surpass even those that Hercules came by in the Hesperidean garden of chastity: "sweet fruit of pleasure brought from paradise / By love himself." It is the exalted desire of the *Song of Solomon.* Meanwhile, as he waits and woos, the lover is concerned to allay Elizabeth's anxiety about the loss of freedom that marriage would involve:

> The doubt which ye misdeem, fair love, is vain,
> That fondly fear to lose your liberty,
> When losing one, two liberties ye gain,
> And make him bond that bondage erst did fly.
> Sweet be the bands, the which true love doth tie,
> Without constraint or dread of any ill:
> The gentle bird feels no captivity
> Within her cage, but sings and feeds her fill.
> There pride dare not approach, nor discord spill [destroy]
> The league 'twixt them, that loyal love hath bound:
> But simple truth and mutual good will,
> Seeks with sweet peace to salve each other's wound:
> There faith doth fearless dwell in brazen tower,
> And spotless pleasure builds her sacred bower.
> (*Amoretti* 65)

There is a tenderness and reciprocity of feeling here that would be impossible to match anywhere else in the Renaissance sonnet.

Spenser could hardly have given such a love simple dramatic expression. Instead of Sidney's individually intense sonnets forming moments in a narrative, he has written what seems much more obviously a long stanzaic poem (as is expressed formally by linked rhyme schemes). This continuity between sonnets, allowing complex large-scale imagery and amplitude of thematic development, goes back beyond the Petrarchists to the prolonged meditations of Petrarch's *Rime* themselves. Like Petrarch (and like Shakespeare), Spenser uses a calendrical structure to suggest the variety and natural growth of emotion. Thus there are New Year and Easter sonnets, set in their appropriate numerological places. The contradictory feelings that some have seen as problematic or indicative of revision all belong to this "whole year's work," leading to the marriage day celebrated in *Epithalamion.* Like other Elizabethan "sonnet sequences," *Amoretti* is really part of a composite work, combining sonnets with other stanza forms. Linking it to *Epithalamion* are four "anacreontic odes," or sweet epigrams, which languish for the bliss of the wedding night. These serve as generic transition to the major ode that follows.

Amoretti may fascinate as an interesting departure from the usual sequence or as a shorter treatment of themes developed in *The Faerie Queen.* But *Epithalamion* is unique. Nothing shows Spenser's creativity better than this poem, which most agree to be the finest major ode in English, and to be surpassed in ancient literature—if at all—only by Pindar. Classical comparisons are inevitable, because Spenser here invented for English literature the humanist ceremonial mode that was to be so important for Michael Drayton, Robert Herrick, and others—and carried it at once to its greatest height. Like Catullus' *Carmina* 61, Spenser's poem moves in festal exaltation through the events of a wedding day. But its structure is very different, rising as it does through a crescendo of gathering voices and sounds and excitement to the roaring organs and public affirmation of the marriage service at the altar, in the central two stanzas or strophes; before the feasting, the public "bedding" of the bride, consummation, and soft recession into the silence and darkness of the night. Each stage is due and accepted:

> Now welcome night, thou night so long expected,
> That long day's labour dost at last defray,
> And all my cares, which cruel love collected,
> Hast summed in one, and cancelled for aye:
> Spread thy broad wing over my love and me,
> That no man may us see,
> And in thy sable mantle us enwrap,
> From fear of peril and foul horror free.
> Let no false treason seek us to entrap,
> Nor any dread disquiet once annoy
> The safety of our joy:
> But let the night be calm and quietsome,
> Without tempestuous storms or sad affray:
> Like as when Jove with fair Alcmena lay,
> When he begot the great Tirynthian groom:
> Or like as when he with thy self did lie,
> And begot Majesty.
> And let the maids and young men cease to sing:
> Ne let the woods them answer nor their echo ring.
> (stanza 18)

What audacity for a poet to dare to speak to the goddess Night about her lovemaking!—and yet how apt, at the juncture when he is about to become intimate with his own wife. Throughout, mythological imagery mingles with real, external with psychological. Indeed, the comprehensiveness takes in even negative feelings, such as dread of an "affray," and sexual fears of "Medusa's mazeful head." Spenser's robust yet sensitive personal address is unflinchingly inclusive, as he faces both day and unconscious night in the ritual of love. His ceremony remains reverent; yet it affirms nature and finds authenticity in the role of Jupiter, spouse of Night. These and other deep archetypes and powers are recognized and profoundly composed: the *Horae,* the *Gratiae,* the *amorini* of passion, Cynthia the chaste destroyer yet patroness of childbirth, and, in the one stanza, Juno foundress of marriage and female genius, together with Genius himself, god of pleasure and generation. As Spenser invokes them in turn, or turns from one wedding scene to another, he dwells on each in such a way that the stanzas acquire their own characters and modalities. They are like the dances of a suite. Now all is private communing with the "learned sisters"; now expectant bachelors wait for Hymen's torchlit masque to move off; now pristine garlanded "nymphs" make final arrangements. One stanza will be a blazon of Elizabeth's beauties admired by all ("lips like cherries charming men to bite"), the next a mysterious praise of her chaste inner character. The poem's movement through this variety is fluid but calm and firm and sure. It is as if everything had its inevitable place.

And so, in numerological terms, it had. The spatial disposition of *Epithalamion* mimes with extraordinary precision the astronomical events of the day that it celebrates. Thus the 24 stanzas represent its 24 hours, with night falling at the right point for Saint Barnabas' Day, the summer solstice, "the longest day in all the year." Then, after stanza 16, the refrain changes from positive to negative: "The woods no more shall answer, nor your echo ring." And the *canzone*-like stanzas consist of pentameters and occasional trimeters, with the long lines numbering just 365 to represent the days of the year, during which the sun completes its journey round the 24 sidereal hours. The ceremony of time has never been realized so fully as in this most musical of Spenser's poems. It is indeed an "endless monument" to the poignantly short time of his day. Yet before the end it has carried the torches of its masque up to join the "thousand torches flaming bright" in the temple of the gods. It aspires to commemorate an anticipated cosmic event, addition to the communion of saints, eventual "stellification."

Prothalamion (1596), written for an aristocratic betrothal, has similar ceremonial qualities and a form almost as highly wrought. It too is a masterpiece of occasional art in the grand mannerist style. But, in spite of autobiographical references to "old woes," it is more public, more philosophical, and harder at first to warm to. Only after prolonged consideration and the effort of attending to its closely overdetermined images does its profundity emerge. It not only sums up the whole river-epithalamium genre, but sings the mutability of the height of life.

Spenser wrote other short works, notably the medievalizing satire *Mother Hubberd's Tale* and the lofty Christian-Platonic *Hymns.* The former is not dull; but neither does it show Spenser to have been a great satirist. As for the *Hymns,* they challenge more attention, as a vastly ambitious undertaking, a poetic theology of love and generation. Their extreme difficulty (and the correspondingly glorious opportunity they offer to the commentator) is not their only interest for Spenserians. They cast much cloudy light on Spenser's unexpected, syncretistic thinking. But this is not enough to make them great poems. Whether their metaphysical puzzles yield to solution or remain attributed to blunders, the *Hymns* must be counted noble failures. When all is said and done (and much has still to be said, for the love poems particularly), the work in which Spenser chiefly lives is *The Faerie Queen.*

V

The Faerie Queen occupies a very special place in English literature. Yet far more would acknowledge its classic status than would count themselves among its readers. There are doubtless several reasons for this, some of which I mention below. One may be a misconception about the kind of work *The Faerie Queen* is. Another, closely related, may be the disablement inflicted by much reading of "probable report" novels, which seems to produce insensitivity to less novelistic sorts of fictive realism. A third may be its length. For my own part, I was fortunate enough to come upon the poem during a convalescence: I could read without interruption. But there are other ways of reading such a work, which were not unknown to the Elizabethans themselves. In his translation of *Orlando Furioso,* Sir John Harington gives directions "for the several tales,. where to begin and end, those that may conveniently be read single." Of course such a method will not give a very adequate idea of the work, unless it is complemented by reading *in extenso.* Much of the characteristic quality of *The Faerie Queen* depends on juxtaposition of stories and episodes of different kinds, on interrupted, interwoven narrative, on multiplication.

And this is perhaps the first point to take hold of: that it is a work of interlaced art. Suppose you are following the story of Belphoebe. You pick it up in book 2, canto 3, stanzas 21–42, a luscious ten-stanza description of the heroine, broken up by a comic encounter with Trompart and the upstart Braggadocchio. Belphoebe explains that true honor comes by hard work and is more likely to be found in the forest (or studying at home) than at court. But when she has fiercely rebuffed an improper advance, and fled, she makes no further appearance in book 2—nor in the next, until 3.5.57, where she cares for the wounded Timias. Her parentage and relation to Amoret are explained in the canto following, through the myth of Chrysogone. But then she disappears again until book 4, by which time several other stories have been woven into the fabric. If the reader loses track of these windings he should on no account despair: all is going according to plan; the sense of labyrinthine unsearchability is a desired effect. Some degree of incomprehension is as deliberate a feature in Spenser's art as it is in certain types of medieval romance, or in the visual interlace of the *Book of Kells.* The reader may follow the pattern again and again, and have the experience, as in life, of gradual understanding.

To enjoy Spenser's *entrelacement,* feel free, first, to reread. Second, attend closely to the distant connections (whether of resemblance, variation, or contrast) between widely separate parts of the poem. As in most interlaced narratives, such internal allusions carry a great deal of the content. Third, notice the transitions between stories and between episodes. It is often at these points of juncture that Spenser indicates the fictive status of the various milieus that are brought into relation, and implies a deeper import. So the beautiful description of achieved true honor, Belphoebe alone, confronts the farcical pretensions of Braggadocchio (a thin character) and his sycophant. And this scene is in turn followed by Guyon's adventures on quite a different scale—far more minutely psychological—as he overcomes a series of difficulties in the pursuit of honor. The formal relation of interlaced narrative strands can offer a pleasure of its own, like that of abstract art. But with Spenser the interruptions of the story generally also give reminders of further reality. The breaks in his tapestry disclose glimpses of windows that look out on larger, more complex worlds. When Artegall returning victorious encounters the Blatant Beast (5.12.37), the juncture of stories shows how military success and administrative success are not enough: there is also a social world, with reputation to be won or lost. In this sense, polyphonic narrative serves the deeper purpose of comprehensiveness, of inclusiveness, of Renaissance epic's aspiration to complete unity. It is not quite the same as *entrelacement* in the older romances.

At one time, *The Faerie Queen* used to be thought of as the last great medieval work in English—although it was also supposed to have been written without much access to medieval literature. Now the manner of its medievalism is more problematic. Many would agree that Spenser knew Malory, together with other late romances. And there can be no doubt at all of his respect for old traditions: of his deep passion for "old records from ancient times derived," and of his avidity, as greedy as Guyon's, for romantic antiquities—chronicles and armor and heraldry and ruins and hermitages. *Ancient*—or, even older, *auncient*—is indeed one of his favorite words, which he is capable of using twice in the same line: "Ancient Ogyges, even the ancientest." There is some justice in C. S. Lewis' view that Spenser was "the first of the romantic medievalists." Certainly the retrospective Gothic taste in literature was identified from the start, in Pope and Thomas Warton for example, with a taste for *The Faerie Queen.* It should not be forgotten, however, that Spenser's own medieval enthusiasm was also coupled with a rather sharp stylishness. We miss a great deal of what he was about unless we appreciate his sophisticated modernity too. Not that Spenser was ever a merely fashionable writer. But he wrote in part to overgo Ariosto, who had established a vogue for Gothic costume narrative. It might be more accurate to characterize *The Faerie Queen* as mannerist neo-Gothic, rather than medieval. This stylistic character is reflected in the form, which is not romance but romantic epic.

Epic was supposed to give a sense of life's totality. And each Renaissance epicist in turn aimed at further, fuller inclusiveness, both by reaching out to a progressively more diverse or encyclopedic content, and by subsuming, whether through allusion or other means, contents already enclosed in the poetic domain of previous epics. Thus the commentators taught that Virgil's *Aeneid* combined an *Odyssey* (books 1–6) with an *Iliad* (7–12). Moreover, Julius Caesar Scaliger and other literary theorists had developed the doctrine that epic contains a wide variety of inset smaller forms. Spenser gave a creative turn to this idea: anticipating Milton's *Paradise Lost,* he included several different epic and romance forms in *The Faerie Queen.* Ariostan epic—all scramble and bravura and surprise—is probably his principal Italian ingredient. But he also uses Tasso's larger scale, especially for elaborate set pieces with luxuriant detail, such as the Bower of Bliss. Then there are passages of obscure Boiardan epic, burlesque, and puns like Pulci's, and even a few static hieroglyphs reminiscent of Trissino's *L'Italia Liberata dai Goti.* Ancient epic is represented not only in its Virgilian form—complete with descents into hell, games, extended similes, and stylistic formulas of the sort that Ford Madox Ford called "marmoreal Latinisms" but also in its Ovidian form (metamorphoses and loves of the gods). And it would risk Polonius's folly to enumerate the other types, such as pastoral epic, meandering through the world of the *Aethiopica* and the *Arcadia*; allegorical quests distantly resembling Deguilleville's or Hawes's; and (in the Cantos of Mutability) a procession like the ones in Du Bartas's Christian epic of creation.

All this should not be taken to mean that Spenser merely pillaged biblical, classical, medieval, and Renaissance epics for source material. (His sources are a separate topic, which hardly lends itself to brief treatment, being so poorly understood. Some of the poetical sources are beyond doubt. But the informational sources may have been fewer and more compendious, murkier and less literary, than scholars have assumed.) Allusion would be a better term than borrowing. Spenser is the first great allusive poet in English. And his mastery of generic variation goes further than I have suggested. With never a hint of pastiche, he deploys different kinds, almost as a composer scores for different instruments, to render life's various modes. Spenser is not always superior in handling a particular form. Ariosto's adventures, for example, run more easily; although Spenser's come very close in such an episode as Timias, skirmish with the foresters (3.5), and in any case are carrying more weight. But in shading such adventures into writing of other kinds, in using his far wider generic palette, in mixture, Spenser shows fictive genius of a different order altogether.

VI

The detachment of *The Faerie Queen* from previous epics is reflected in its decisive formal individuation. Its meter, the "Spenserian stanza," that great legacy to Thomson and Shelley and Keats, contrives to be at once novel and traditional. By comparison with the brisk heroic stanza of Ariosto and Tasso, *ottava rima—a b a b a b c c*—the larger English stanza is spacious and unhurried; while its more intricately interlaced rhymes—*a b a b b c b c c*—further slow its pace (usually: exceptions include the sprightly cadence at 7.7.46) and knit it more closely together. The final alexandrine, which determines much of the effect of stateliness and weight, allows us to think not only of a nine-line stanza, but of an eight-line stanza rounded off: *a b a b b c b c* C—the ballade or *Monk's Tale* stanza, in fact, extended and transcended. Chaucer's stanza consists of two separate, symmetrical, couplet-linked halves: *a b a b / b c b c.* But the notional halves of the indivisible Spenserian stanza are united by its shared central line:

a b a b b
b c b c C.

An Elizabethan critic describing it—as Drayton described his own *Barons' Wars* stanza—might also have observed how it rests like a column on its hexameter base (six feet, a number of perfection), or how its rhymes occur two, three, and four times: the numbers grouped by Macrobius and others as forming the ratios of the fundamental musical concords.

> Right in the midst the goddess, self did
>   stand
> Upon an altar of some costly mass,
> Whose substance was uneath [difficult] to
>   understand:
> For neither precious stone, nor dureful brass,
> Nor shining gold, nor mouldering clay it was;
> But much more rare and precious to esteem,
> Pure in aspect, and like to crystal glass,
> Yet glass was not, if one did rightly deem,
> But being fair and brickle [brittle], likest
>   glass did seem.
>   (4.10.39)

The Spenserian stanza has been well compared to a wave falling on a beach: breaking, it runs to implement the full alexandrine mark and to give, where needed, a meditative lull. It "closeth not but with a full satisfaction to the ear for so long detention." It is the greatest of all stanzas.

The Italianate division into cantos tends to be taken for granted, but it was an innovation in English. Spenser offset it against a different division, of antique association, into books. Within each book, the cantos may vary greatly in representational mode. This is indeed the poem's most copious source of variety. It relies on formal variegation more than on multiplication of narrative incident.

This point calls for enlargement. The stanza just quoted, describing a mysterious altar of Venus, comes from a canto about Scudamour's entry into the Temple of Venus, a fully realized allegorical place in the manner of medieval dream vision. Book 4 in general treats friendship; but this canto initiates us into the very sanctum of the virtue, its inner nature, foundation, ideals, meaning. In the same way, each book has some such medullary or "core" canto, in which, usually, the champion of a virtue visits a place that symbolizes its essential character. Saint George, the patron of Holiness, visits the House of Holiness in 1.10; Guyon, the patron of Temperance, the castle of Alma in 2.9; and Artegall Mercilla's Court in 5.9. In such cantos the virtue is developed visually through an orderly procession, a pageant tableau, or its descriptive equivalent. It is a special symbolic mode that goes back to medieval vision allegories. Valuations of it now differ sharply, usually according to the critic's familiarity with its subtle conventions. But few would question that in the fiction of a Chaucer or a Colonna or a Spenser it can be a profoundly eloquent, although very oblique, form. The expressionist mysteriousness of the Garden of Adonis or the Temple of Venus is quite unlike almost anything in Ariosto; it is more like Colonna's enigmatic *Hypnerotomachia,* that strange work of sexual mysticism, whose psychological intuitions fascinated many writers and artists of the Renaissance. To explain some features of Spenser's symbolic places it may help to compare the material of Venus, altar with the rich shining substance of the Fountain of Will in the Bower of Bliss (2.12.60), or to know that in erotic poetry, glass might figure the female pudendum (as, for example, in *Greek Anthology* 5.36). But schematic interpretation of the Temple of Venus would be unthinkable. Too much is deeply implicit or indirectly conveyed for that. How is the brittle glass related to Ptolomae's glass tower of marital fidelity at 3.2.20? And Phidias, whose Paphian idol is introduced to amplify the greater beauty of this living god: does his wretched love for a mere image belong with the many unhappy loves about the altar? Again, why do the lovers outside the Temple sport their pleasures, while those within, and closest to the strange hermaphroditic goddess, suffer and complain? If Spenser invites such questions, he does not encourage quick answers.

The strange symbolic places stand out prominently, each like a *temenos* or sanctuary or *arcanum* set in the deep forest of romance. But they form one kind of episode only, one component of the Spenserian book. Another sort, coming in an early position, serves to join the adventures and to show the relations between the virtues that the knights strive for. Thus Saint George, patron of holiness, and Guyon, patron of temperance, meet and almost fight at 2.1.26; and Britomart (chaste love) shows herself superior to Guyon in a trial of strength at 3.1.6. Then there are early passages that announce the book's subjects by developing emblems of the virtues in their abstract or common acceptation: Saint George's encounter with Error in 1.2, Guyon's visit to Medina's castle of moderation in 2.1, Cambina's reconciliation of combatants in 4.3. These passages pose the books' topics in broad terms. The subjects thus stated undergo modification as well as expansion, however, so that the virtues of the early emblems are by no means identical with those realized in the "core cantos." The latter present insights reached only after the experience (that is, adventures) of attempting the virtue. As for the intervening adventures themselves, they superficially appear like Ariosto's. But in reality they also contribute a medieval (or medievalizing) element. They have a far more continuous moral sense than the adventures of most romances—even of many medieval romances. The Spenserian hero encounters obstacles to his virtue, or aspects of the opposing vice, which are thus analyzed into branches or subdivisions like those familiar from older moral works such as Frère Lorens' *Somme le Roi.* (Sometimes the categories are surprising and thought-provoking, as when Sansloy, a brother of Sansfoy and Sansjoy—developed characters in book 1—makes a perfunctory appearance in book 2 on the quite different scale of an aberration from Medina's golden mean.) Certain of the vices are explored fully enough to call for "places" of their own, such as the Cave of Mammon (2.7) or the House of Busirane (3.11–12). Finally, there are "digressive" episodes, such as the inset chronicle histories at the Castle of Alma and the river-god spousals of Thames and Medway, or the subplot adventures of Florimell, Marinell, and Belphoebe.

If some such repertoire of forms gives variety within a book, each book has, nevertheless, its own individual character. And each seems so distinct in emotional key as to compose with the others a sequence of complementary movements. The apocalyptic book 1 runs a vast gamut of spiritual extremities, from dark to light. But in book 2 we move to a world at once more schematically controlled and more sensuously vivid, with a tendency to frequent confrontations between its single (almost single-minded) hero and his many, minutely problematic emotions. Book 3's ardors are in the ordinary proportion of romance. Its characters disperse in ramifying adventures; but they are regathered by the centripetal tendency of book 4, through which accumulating groups of four friends (true or false) join by aggregation in a movement towards the great nuptial feast of Thames and Medway. Book 5 is Draconian in its severity. But book 6 is unbraced and vulnerable, its knights disarmed or dressed in shepherds' clothes. Throughout, the atmosphere alters in the interests of variety, and alters again for a balanced view of the wholeness of human experience.

Perhaps for the same reason, the emotional colorations change without any hard-edged divisions. They shade into one another with a subtlety and delicacy that is one of the chief marks of Spenser's art. He seems to achieve the effect partly by running stories and themes over to blur the divisions, by arranging trailers or anticipations of any change of mood, and by suturing in the overlaps with an astonishing fineness and obliquity. (Metrically this finds reflection in a system of liaison of rhyme between stanzas.) Thus, although *The Faerie Queen* is manneristically composite and complicated outwardly, as a reading experience it is not like that at all. Inwardly it moves with an almost baroque fluidity. Its wonderful transitions, for example, have none of the alienating abruptness of Ariosto's, which, as scholars have noted, go back to medieval formulas such as "Mes a tant laisse li contes a parler de . . . et retorne a . . ." ("Now I stop telling the story of . . . and return to . . ."). Instead we move by a smooth, imperceptible progression from episode to episode, mode to mode, with even the explicit junctures, where these occur, accomplishing more than a mere narrative cut-and-join.

Thus, 3. 6 begins with the geniture of Belphoebe and her twinship with Amoret—an inset Ovidian tale of Chrysogone provides the canto's first mythological treatment of generation, inside an *occupatio* (a pretended refusal to discuss):

It were a goodly story, to declare,
By what strange accident fair Chrysogone
Conceived these infants" and how them
 she bare,
(3.6.5)

The work then slides into a lost Cupid myth. This naturally leads to a burlesque quarrel between the distraught Venus and the at first censorious then relenting Diana, until their accord brings discovery of the twin births of Belphoebe and Amoret and arrangements for their separate fostering: a separation that implies an emotional polarity corresponding to that which exists between the traditionally opposed goddesses (3.6.11–28). Cupid has been found, divided or "unfolded" into two forms. Then an apparently casual transition takes us into the famous Garden of Adonis: "She brought her to her joyous Paradise, / Where most she wonces [stays], when she on earth does dwell." Besides introducing a second mythological treatment of generation, however, this stanza adds a psychological, individually sexual strand, by its personal confession:

Whether in Paphos, or Cytheron hill,
Or it in Gnidus be, I wot not well;
But well I wot by trial, that this same
All other pleasant places doth excel, . . .

In the Garden itself (30–50), the metaphysical, physical, and mythic elements interweave with formidable ease yet without ever seeming clever—suggesting, rather, Virgil's profundity of feeling and suggestion.

There wont fair Venus often to enjoy
Her dear Adonis' joyous company,
And reap sweet pleasure of the wanton boy;
There yet, some say, in secret he does lie,
Lappèd in flowers and precious spicery,
By her hid from the world, and from the
 skill
Of Stygian gods, which do her love envy;
But she her self, when ever that she will,
Possesseth him, and of his sweetness takes
 her fill.

And sooth it seems they say: for he may not
For ever die, and ever buried be
In baleful night, where all things are forgot;
All be he subject to mortality,
Yet is etern in mutability,
And by succession made perpetual,
Transformèd oft, and changèd diversely:
For him the father of all forms they call;
Therefore needs mote [must] he live, that
 living gives to all.
(3.6.46–47)

The Garden is where an individual participates, through the act of sex, in making new life; and where the relation of form and matter, of permanence and change, declares itself. It is a Christian-Platonic-Pythagorean vision of the soul's vocation in a world of accident. At the same time, the canto is full of Spenser's own characteristic bittersweet cheerful melancholy. Wicked Time destroys the Garden's goodly things; but the pity of that cannot make it other than a gloriously creative place. Time's scythe mows, but Venus can still "reap sweet pleasure." The canto began with explanation of Belphoebe's inherited qualities, which led, through the confrontation of Venus and Diana, to the Garden of Adonis. But Spenser leaves the Garden for the story of Belphoebe's vulnerable twin, Amoret (52–53), and then (by a more distant modulation) for that of the still more fearful Florimell. We have moved from Belphoebe almost to her opposite, with hardly a break.

VII

The movement of *The Faerie Queen* seems fluid and unpredictable, almost like human experience. To get this realistic effect it must avoid obvious regularities of the composite parts. Consequently order, although everywhere discoverable, is everywhere hidden. Thus, placement of the so-called core cantos varies from book to book: 1.10, 4.10, and 6.10, but 2.9 and 5.9. Yet the variation is not random either, since it follows a number symbolism (the core cantos in ninth place enshrine cardinal virtues, Temperance and Justice). Similarly, the contents of books broadly follow the sequence of the planetary week, with book 1, as the book of Sol, book 2 as Luna, and so forth. Truth (troth, faith), the subject of book 1, was a usual association or meaning of the sun; just as Una's lion attendant—the terrible aspect of truth—would have been recognized as Sol's astrological house. The planetary series is interrupted, however, when book 3 proves to be not a book of Mars but of his feminine and wiser counterpart Minerva (a cult image of Queen Elizabeth). The overall narrative pattern of yearly quests shows a similarly regular irregularity. Saint George's mission against the dragon and Guyon's against Acrasia lead us to expect one adventure per book. But books 3 and 4 have between them only one, Scudamour's. Again, most of the books feature the titular patron of a virtue, sent out from Gloriana's court. In book 3, however, it is Britomart, not Scudamour, who defeats Busirane and frees Amoret; while book 4 has two other heroes, Cambel and Triamond, who do not belong to Gloriana's order of knighthood. These variations can easily seem random and confused. But they turn out to be governed by a structural logic, related to Christian-Platonic or Neoplatonic concepts such as the Triad. The latter not only informs many groupings of characters—Sansfoy, Sansjoy, Sansloy, for example—but also a division, confirmed by the order of publication, into three-book parts.

Another structural pattern that runs throughout is the arrangement of thematic images in ascending sequence, from evil, through less evil (or mixed), to good. In book 6 the series is of human "garlands" ranging from the cannibals gathered round Serena, through the lusty shepherds and lovely lasses round Pastorella, to the "hundred naked maidens lily white, / All ranged in a ring" round the three Grace—who themselves encircle "another damsel" Spenser's own love. The theme makes connection through the common figure of a garland, whose oblatory meaning becomes explicit in the primitive ritual (6.8.39, 6.9.8, 6.10.12, and 6.10.14). In the same way bad Venuses taking pleasure at the Bower of Bliss and the House of Malecasta precede the good Venus enjoying the Garden of Adonis. And the pains of a cruel Cupid triumphing at the House of Busirane (3.11–12) goes before the painful sentence pronounced by the "wise" Cupid at 6.8.22–25. It is a law of Fairyland. The quests are always making gradual labyrinthine approaches, or ascents in Platonic fashion, from perverse and dark images towards the reality of virtues themselves. The virtues have to be composed, step by step, in a process of integration. It is a remarkably inclusive vision. At the Temple of Venus are held in concord not only love and hate, "brethren both of half the blood" (4.10.32), but Venus and Cupid, potentially, and the pleasure and pain of love.

It is Spenser's Christian Platonism, his conception of things as images of reality, that makes sense of dwelling on symbolic objects rather than on probable action. Certainly *The Faerie Queen* is pictorial in the extreme. When Joseph Spence read it to his aged mother she said that he "had been showing her a collection of pictures;" and Pope appreciatively concurred. Not all post-Victorian critics have cared for this picturesque quality. Some have felt quite superior to the naivete of speaking pictures. But we should remember that in the Renaissance—even partly in Ruskin's time—pictures spoke conceptually and articulately. Whether or not our ancestors were also in closer touch with the images of the unconscious, they demonstrably used a conscious and conventional iconographical language. The adventure of the champion of temperance is full of emblems of that virtue, such as the bridle or collar, which appears in the "gorgeous barbs" of Guyon's horse Brigador *(briglia d'oro),* in the bridle put on Occasion's tongue, and perhaps in the elaborately described "silken camus lily white" worn by Belphoebe (Latin *camus,* "bridle, collar"; English *camis,* "tunic"). Belphoebe also wore

> a golden baldric, which forelay
> Athwart her snowy breast, and did divide
> Her dainty paps; which like young fruit in May
> Now little gan to swell, and being tied
> Through her thin weed their places only signified.
> (2.3.29)

The half-exposed bosom regularly emblemized true honor, so that an Elizabethan reader was prepared in advance to recognize the values latent in Belphoebe's confrontation with Braggadocchio and Trompart.

Spenser does not always give explanatory labels to such relatively simple iconography. And even when he seems explicit, as with the cruel hag Occasion, the labeling abstraction by no means exhausts the image's meaning. Literature dominated iconography, rather than the reverse: Spenser was forming images not yet in any handbook. His figure was not Occasion in general (who would have been a young girl), but a very specific Occasion, incorporating such additional features as the lameness of Poena (slow retribution). Possibly Spenser himself could not have identified the composite figure much more fully, in other terms than he has actually used. He was exploring psychological depths: the springs of impatience, the penalties of guilt. His emblematic pictures and hieroglyphs were not, after all, merely quaint, but a means to self-discovery. Having only a smattering of the language of emblem, our best approach is to meditate on the scene as a whole and to take in details of mood and appearance. We need to feel Occasion's intemperate readiness to blame—perhaps to guess at the suggestion of self-punishing remorse in the cruelty of her son Furor—before we know how to bring iconography to bear.

In a fiction that uses images as its words in this way, language is apt to be of secondary importance, at least compared with an epic such as Paradise Lost. I do not mean that *The Faerie Queen* is carelessly or flatly written. Its style can reach intensity when a grand theme calls for it—as in the description of

> Death with most grim and grisly visage seen,
> Yet is he nought but parting of the breath;
> Ne ought to see, but like a shade to ween [suppose],
> Unbodièd, unsouled, unheard, unseen.
> (7.7.46)

And it varies with every change of mode—lyrical, narrative, descriptive. But much of the time it makes little conscious impression on the casual reader. Like the clean window glass that you do not notice so long as you focus on a distant object, the language of *The Faerie Queen* is usually transparent. Every now and them comes a more noticeable stanza, such as the intricately eloquent, densely patterned, much quoted description of the Cave of Sleep (1.1.41). But such "opaqueness" is unrepresentative of a narrative style that mostly effaces itself. This shaven manner of the narrative allegory contrasts with the richer sonority of description sustained in the "core" cantos. There, epiphanies stand out with the dense force of language of a major ode. The disparity is of course deliberate. For the discriminating reader, indeed, this balance of plane surfaces and enriched areas offers one of the main pleasures of the poem.

Not that the diction is neutral or colorless, even in the narrative allegory. It has too marked a medieval tinge for that. Still, the notorious archaisms are fewer and less frequent than critics suggest: many stanzas have none, and others have only the token *ne* or *eke* of the poem's soon-familiar idiolect. On the other hand, there is a good deal more sly wordplay than used to be recognized. Sometimes Spenser draws on proverbial lore, which may provide the basis of a whole episode, in the manner of Langland or Nashe or Brueghel. But more often the wit takes the form of what Hazlitt called "an allegorical play upon words": a punning ambiguity, that is, with one meaning in the story and the other in the allegory; as at 6.9.5, where Calidore, who brought the faults of the court with him in his courtly nature, inquires after the Blatant Beast, "If such a beast they saw, which he had thither brought." Altogether the language, which owes much in this to Gavin Douglas, brilliantly compounds the high-flown and the vernacular.

VIII

I have left until now the problems of the allegory, since these have been exaggerated into unnecessary stumbling blocks. Victorian and Georgian critics were predisposed against what they saw as didactic and mechanical "naïve allegory." But Spenser's poem would now be generally exonerated from these charges. If its moral seems in any sense too bare, it is not in the sense of being crude or obvious. Besides, there is now more feeling for what was a dominant form of literature in the Middle Ages, and at least one of the most prominent in the Renaissance. Spenser, however, wrote a special sort of allegory, whose characteristics should be distinguished. He himself called *The Faerie Queen* "a continued allegory, or dark conceit" and noticed "how doubtfully all allegories may be construed" (Letter to Ralegh).

Like much Elizabethan criticism, this calls for sympathetic interpretation. When he calls the allegory "continued," Spenser probably means that it is not merely local, but kept up by the author all through. In this his poem differs from, say, *Orlando Furioso.* Ariosto has occasional allegories, such as that of Logistilla; and he was freely *allegorized,* by such anti-intentionalists *de ses jours* as Fornari and Bononome. But Spenser wrote throughout what was meant allegorically or symbolically. Unlike the strange places and marvels of medieval romance (and, to a large extent, those in Ariosto), Spenser's are interpreted. In consequence they are brought into unity with the rest of the work. Thus, the improbably numerous foundlings in book 6 are not left as a matter of surprise and delightful wonder. Spenser makes it plain that the marvel, anything but arbitrary, is designed to explore various relations between natural inheritance and "nurture" (environmental influences). To the various structures of the *Orlando,* therefore, *The Faerie Queen* adds another, quite distinct.

Moreover, this extra strand is itself manifold. Unlike Bunyan's allegory (which has only one sphere of reference, the religious), Spenser's may be religious or moral or psychological or philosophical or political. Most often, perhaps, it is moral, setting out virtues and vices, or distinctions within virtues and vices, in the narrative mode by which ethics used to be understood. Lucifera and the Giant Orgoglio present different kinds of pride; the six knights of Malecasta six steps into lechery. Other figures, however, such as Pyrochles and Cymochles, or Elissa and Perissa, treat polarities of a more psychological order. In Shamefastness and Praisedesire, indeed, Spenser explores the springs of moral behavior in two contrasting temperamental dispositions. It is often observed, and rightly, that his psychological insights seldom issue in character studies. But we should recall that each book really studies a single "supercharacter" its hero, whose traits are the individual allegorical characters. (And the Letter to Ralegh hints that Arthur himself composes a superhero from the hero parts of individual books.) Regarded in this light, Spenser's poem is seen to analyze psychological experience in unusual depth. Even so, some of his greatest passages tend in another direction altogether, belonging to a philosophical allegory enacted either by abstract personifications (Mutability) or by mythological figures (Adonis).

There is also, particularly in book 5, a political allegory, which many have found repellent in its severity. The iron man Talus with his flail seems uncomfortably proleptic of the harshest modem riot police. What is one to think, in particular, of Spenser's attitude to Ireland? As a patriot, he worked for the English oppressors. Yet he hated violence and loved peace and justice. Such an attitude wins few friends now. It has even been asserted, by Yeats and others, that Spenser hated the Irish. The fact remains that in his prose *View of the Present State of Ireland* Spenser attempted what few British and American writers have emulated: to understand the Irish. It does not do to forget the magnitude of the disorders or the weakness of government in Spenser's time.

The allegory, of course, often has multiple implications. Indeed, the same character may have a political or topical, as well as a moral, meaning. Artegall, for example, combines Sovereign Power, Justice, and Maleness-in-generation (not portrayed as a superior role) with Leicester, Essex, Grey, and perhaps other historical figures. Similarly, Belphoebe represents Queen Elizabeth, but also Virginality. But in approaching these "antique praises unto present persons fit" we must not be tempted into looking for a key. Such figures represent insights into life; they should not be reduced to system, but responded to with a correspondingly personal intuition.

This is true of all Spenser's allegories. You cannot be too subtle in interpreting them; but you can easily be subtle in the wrong way. Alertness is everything. In the Cave of Mammon episode, Guyon's refraining from combat with golden Disdain (who resembles "an huge Giant") has attracted ingenious explanations: Guyon is learning that martial heroism is not enough, et cetera. But the alert reader will sense that the supercilious hero has blundered. Perhaps what prompts him is a remembered law of Fairyland, that Giants are for fighting (as witness Orgoglio, Argante, Ollyphant, Corflambo, the Giant with the Scales, Geryoneo, and others). Or perhaps he reflects that Mammon's advice to "abstain from perilous fight" is unlikely to be dependable. (Another law: evil figures give bad advice.) In any event, by not fighting, Guyon has gone disastrously wrong. His moral heroism has degenerated into mere aristocratic *sdegno*: he is literally reconciled to disdain; and he rejects the world because he feels superior to it. He may be doing the right thing, but for the wrong reason. A really wakeful reader will also see Spenser's joke, that all the time golden Disdain is really not aristocratic but a "villain." Such a point is a matter for the attention of the third ear. The laws of Fairyland are not those of deductive logic.

IX

No sooner has one drawn attention to the complicated manifold character of *The Faerie Queen* than the balance must be righted by affirming its simplicity. Mere formal complication seems almost irrelevant to Spenser's serious purpose: his sophisticated detachment from forms serves other than formal values. He uses any means that will illustrate the deepest truth of the matter. Hence his easy freedom with sources. Since he is more concerned with truth than with elegance or poetic success, great predecessors never intimidate him. He has had his own glimpse of life; and in the end it is for his unified vision that we read *The Faerie Queen.*

Spenser's reliance on chivalric values may appear to contradict what I have just written, and to make any very high seriousness impossible. How can we take seriously a knighthood that was already outgrown in the poet's own time—that he himself presents, indeed, in anachronistic terms? Well, a reinterpreted knighthood, offering ideals for courtiers and administrators, may have formed a part of Spenser's purpose. But it would be a mistake to think of this as merely an aspiration to some Indian summer of English chivalry. At the very least, the adventures are moral psychomachies. And their content is quite as much private as public. They continually press behind virtues to the growth of "the fresh bud of virtue," to the "sacred nursery / Of virtue" "deep within the mind," and even to "the root" of all virtue, in love (4 Proem 2). In Spenser, virtues, and especially symbols of virtue, are "secret" or "hidden" (1.11.36, 3.1.10, 2.8.20). We may conclude that the heroes, approaches to the "sacred virtue(s)" pursue quests of self-discovery. Moreover, the virtues themselves, when discovered, are numinous mysteries that may even be described as "resembling God" (5 Proem 10). In fine, the adventures go to form a greater self: to fashion a person.

At the deepest level, therefore, the poem's narrative paradigm must be discovery: the discovery that characterizes romance, rather than the conflict of epic. Of course there are many battles, and the frequency of revenge is conspicuous. But *The Faerie Queen* usually avoids any simple *enantiodromia* or war of contraries. Indeed, its most striking moral feature is reconciliation or transcendence of opposites. It pursues wholeness. Is it more antipapist or more Catholic? More devoted to pleasure or to virtue? Traditional or innovative? Such questions have only to be formulated for us to see their inappropriateness. Spenser combines the great antipodes—reason and emotion, sovereignty and equity, male and female—into a single larger world of integrated identity. Not a bad emblem of *The Faerie Queen* would be Dame Concord's tempering of the fearful siblings Love and Hate (4.10.32). Unquestionably such *coincidentia oppositorum,* or union of opposites, runs the danger of limitless abysses. Perhaps in consequence, it arouses disagreeable apprehensions in some. Indeed, dislike of *The Faerie Queen,* when it arises, may have much to do with this feature. To lovers of the poem, distaste for it seems incomprehensibly perverse—like a distaste for life. But (again like life) *The Faerie Queen* can be difficult, dark with shades of half-thought meanings. The Victorian critics may not have been far wrong in calling it dreamlike. Only, its dream analysis is more worthwhile than they cared to admit—and already expressed by Spenser in what is more alert meditation than languid fantasy.

One of the pervasive antinomies that *The Faerie Queen* attempts to combine is the one between order and change. That Spenser shared Mulcaster's and Camden's reverence for ancient tradition needs no argument. His feeling for the sanctity of civilized order finds continued and varied expression, in metaphysical celebrations, in happy ceremonies, and in praises of Queen Elizabeth, not to mention execrations of savagery and disordered license. Nevertheless, Spenser may also be the first English poet to have written favorably of change, in any sense even remotely like what we should now call historical. In the Cantos of Mutability, Nature dismisses, it is true, Dame Mutability's claim to cosmic supremacy. But she does so for a strange and subtle reason: namely, that all things indeed change, "But by their change their being do dilate [implement]." Mutability, which generations of poets had taken as a subject of complaint, was for Spenser something quite different: a creative process, almost a subject of encomium. Her witnesses form the grand procession of the parts of time that has offered inspiration to many subsequent poets, and that all would now concede to be a high point of Spenser's oeuvre. Moreover, it sums up a vision informing the entire poem, of nature in multifarious transformation.

> I well consider all that ye have said,
> And find that all things steadfastness do
> hate
> And changèd be: yet being rightly weighed
> They are not changed from their first estate;
> But by their change their being do dilate:
> And turning to themselves at length again"
> Do work their own perfection so by fate:
> Then over them change doth not rule and
> reign;
> But they reign over change" and do their
> states maintain.
>
> Cease therefore daughter further to aspire,
> And thee content thus to be ruled by me:
> For thy decay thou seek'st by thy desire;
> But time shall come that all shall changed
> be,
> And from thenceforth" none no more
> change shall see.
> So was the Titaness put down and whist
> [silenced],
> And Jove confirmed in his imperial see.
> Then was that whole assembly quite
> dismissed,

And Nature's self did vanish" whither no
man wist [knew].
(Cantos of Mutability, 7.58–59)

The Faerie Queen as a whole could be said to hymn creation in process, rather than created nature. It aspires to unifying change; and, by exploring far back into historical origins, ancient myths, causes of wrath, and the deepest relations of "cousin passions," it searches, beneath outward and partial metamorphoses, for the changes of heart that could release life's fullness.

The world of *The Faerie Queen* is never vague. It may seem unsearchably vast and uncertain in measurement; but it is emotionally sure and distinctive in atmosphere. This has something to do with the long epic similes, which, like Homer's, introduce ordinary domesticities, but which have also a crisp, concentrated particularity that is Spenser's own ("The watery southwind from the seaboard coast"). From time to time, too, precise sensible details come into the story itself. These would be striking but for their immediate rightness: Arthur's savage squire shook his oaken plant so sternly "That like an hazel wand, it quivered and quook"; Glauce "the drunken lamp down in the oil did steep."

In general, of course, Spenser's poem needs the unfeatured continuum of romance. This is usually, with him, a fortuitous Brocéliande-like forest, "a forest wide, / Whose hideous horror and sad trembling sound / Full grisly seemed." This dark verdure serves as an unassertive background, from which marvels stand out in highlight: a Rich Strand, perhaps, heaped with "the wealth of the east," or a castle with magical flames guarding its porch. But the symbolic environments themselves are as distinct as places of the mind can well be. They are varied decisively, with a sharp discrimination that will be inherited (at whatever removes) by Dickens and Stevenson, Borges and de la Mare. One of Spenser's forests or caves is not like another. Here the "surges hoar, / . . . 'gainst the craggy clifts did loudly roar"; there dolphins drew the chariot of sad Cymoent so smoothly "that their broad flaggy fins no foam did rear, / Ne bubbling roundel they behind them sent." (Spenser is almost always specific about weather, being the first English, although not the first British, poet to notice it much.) The House of Busirane, with, its grandeurs and longueurs; Malecasta's fun house; and the difficult but desirable Temple of Venus: these are all places we should recognize instantly. As in dream, the presence of place is intense:

That house's form within was rude and
strong,
Like an huge cave, hewn out of rocky clift,
From whose rough vault the rugged
breaches [fractures] hung,
Embossed with massy gold of glorious gift,
And with rich metal loaded every rift,
That heavy ruin they did seem to threat;
And over them Arachne high did lift
Her cunning web, and spread her subtle net,
Enwrapped in foul smoke and clouds more
black than jet.
(2.7.28)

Unlike the world of common dreams, however, Spenser's Fairyland combines emotional precision with intense lucidity. We breathe in it a purer air that imparts not only excitement to the intellect but vigor to all the faculties. Its impression is fresh; yet it has been formed by thought, long brooded, deeply meditated. Its places and landscapes are symbolic rather than allegorical in a schematic way. And if it is pondered sufficiently, it is discovered to have a profundity that justifies the stress in early criticism on Spenser's "deep conceit."

Such poetry has never been easy to locate on the map of Parnassus. *The Faerie Queen* contrasts, in this respect, with the work of the more fashionable Sidney, who can quite readily be related to the mannerist literary movement of his time. Spenser fits in nowhere. Neither classical nor romantic, neither medieval nor merely neo-Gothic, neither historical nor wholly imaginary, neither fanciful nor rationally intelligible, his visionary work awaits the understanding and the judgment of ages. It has already shown an astonishing capacity to speak to our own century. How inadequate, we are bound to think, and yet how splendid too, was the inscription put on Spenser's monument in Westminster Abbey, naming him "the prince of poets in his time."

Selected Bibliography

BIBLIOGRAPHIES, ETC.

Osgood, C. G., *A Concordance to the Poems,* (Washington, D.C., 1915) repr. (Gloucester, Mass., 1963); Whitman, C. H., *A Subject Index to the Poems,* (New Haven, 1918) repr. (New York, 1966); Carpenter, Frederic I., *A Reference Guide to Edmund Spenser,* (Chicago, 1923) with supplement by D. F. Atkinson (Baltimore, 1937) repr. (New York, 1967); Johnson, F. R., *A Critical Bibliography of the Works Printed Before 1700,* (Baltimore, 1933) repr. (London, 1966) (Folcroft, Pa., 1969); *Spenser Newsletter,* vols. 1–5, (University of Western Ontario, 1970–1974) vols. 5– , (University of Massachusetts, Amherst and Holyoke Community College, 1974–); Cummings, R. M., *Spenser: The Critical Heritage,* (London, 1971); McNeir, W. F., and Provost, F., *Edmund Spenser: An Annotated Bibliography 1937–1972,* (Pittsburgh, 1975).

COLLECTED WORKS

The Faerie Queen: The Shepherd's Calendar: Together With the Other Works of England's Arch-Poet, Edm. Spenser: Collected Into One Volume, and Carefully Corrected (1611 or 1617), folio eds. of the collected poetry, consisting of seven separate sections independently printed at various dates, each with two main states, issued as single vol. bearing the date 1611 or 1617; *The Works of That Famous English Poet, Mr Edmond Spenser,* (1679) the third folio but the first collected ed. of the poetry and prose, with glossary; J. Hughes, ed. *The Works of Mr. Edmund Spenser,* 6 vols. (1715) with glossary and essays; H. J. Todd, ed. *The Works,* 8 vols. (1805) a variorum ed., reviewed by Walter Scott, in *The Edinburgh Review* 7 (1805); R. E. N. Dodge, ed. *The Poetical Works,* (Boston, 1908) sparsely annotated; J. C. Smith and E. de Sélincourt, eds. *The Poetical Works,* 3 vols. (Oxford, 1909–1910) Oxford English Texts series, with textual and bibliographic notes J. C. Smith and E. de Sélincourt, eds. *The Poetical Works,* (London, 1912) Oxford Standard Authors ed., with textual notes, glossary, and critical intro. by E. de Sélincourt, contains the Spenser-Harvey letters, first printed as *Three proper, and witty, familiar Letters,* (1580); W. L. Renwick, ed. *The Complete Works of Edmund Spenser,* 4 vols. (London, 1928–1934) omits *The Faerie Queen,* but includes all the other poems; E. Greenlaw et al., eds. *The Works: A Variorum Edition,* 9 vols (Baltimore, 1932–1949) repr. with index vol. by C. G. Osgood (1957); and with A. C. Judson, *Life of Spenser,* in 11 vols. (1966).

SEPARATE WORKS IN VERSE

van der Noodt, S. J., *A Theatre for Worldlings,* (1569) containing "Epigrams" and "Sonnets" trans. by Spenser, rev. in *Complaints* (1591); *The Shepherd's Calendar. Containing Twelve Eclogues Proportionable to the Twelve Months,* (1579) repr. (1581, 1586, 1591, 1597) subsequently in the folio eds., and in 1653, with Latin trans., includes preface and glosses by "E. K." *The Faerie Queen,* (1590) containing books 1–3 and Letter to Ralegh; 2nd ed., rev. (1596); *Daphnaida. An Elegy Upon the Death of . . . Douglas Howard . . . Wife of Arthur Gorges,* (1591) repr. with the *Hymns* (1596); *Complaints. Containing Sundry Small Poems of the World's Vanity,* (1591) including *The Ruins of Time, The Tears of the Muses, Virgil's Gnat, Prosopopoia: or Mother Hubberd's Tale, Ruins of Rome: by Bellay, Muiopotmos: Or the Fate of the Butterfly, Visions of the World's Vanity, The Visions of Bellay,* and *The Visions of Petrarch; Colin Clout's Come Home Again,* (1595) containing the title poem, *Astrophel. A Pastoral Elegy Upon the Death of . . . Sidney* (including *The Doleful Lay of Clorinda* without a separate title, and other elegies, one by L[odovick] B[ryskett]; *Amoretti and Epithalamion,* (1595); *Prothalamion: Or: A Spousal Verse,* (1596); *Four Hymns,* (1596) containing *An Hymn in Honour of Love, An Hymn in Honour of Beauty, An Hymn of Heavenly Love,* and *An Hymn of Heavenly Beauty; The Second Part of the Faerie Queen,* (1596) containing books 4–6 (more copies printed than of the 1596 ed. of the first part), facs. of both parts of 1596 ed., G. Hough, ed. 2 vols. (London, 1976) folio ed. of *The Faerie Queen,* (1609) first to include the Cantos of Mutability; J. Upton, ed. *The Faerie Queen. A New Edition With a Glossary, and Notes Explanatory and Critical* 2 vols., (1758) a great and classic ed.; E. Welsford, ed. *Spenser: Four Hymns: Epithalamionm,* (Oxford, 1967); R. Beum, ed. *Epithalamion,* (Columbus, Ohio, 1968); A. C. Hamilton, ed. *The Faerie Queen,* (London, 1977) Longman Annotated Poets series; T. P. Roche, ed. *The Faerie Queen* (in press).

SELECTED VERSE

C. S. Lewis, with essay "Edmund Spenser 1552–1599," in G. B. Harrison, ed. *Major British Writers,* 2 vols. (New York, 1954) repr. in C. S. Lewis, *Studies in Medieval and Renaissance Literature,* (Cambridge, 1966); P. C. Bayley, ed. *Spenser: "The Faerie Queen,"* book 2 (London, 1965); R. Kellogg and O. Steele, eds. *Books 1 and 2 of "The Faerie Queen": The Mutability Cantos and Selections From the Minor Poetry,* (New York, 1965); P. C. Bayley, *Spenser: "The Faerie*

Queen," book 1 (London, 1966); A. C. Hamilton, ed. *Edmund Spenser: Selected Poetry,* (New York, 1966); Zitner, S. P., *The Mutability Cantos,* (London, 1968); A. K. Hieatt and C. Hieatt, eds. *Edmund Spenser: Selected Poetry,* (New York, 1970); D. Brooks-Davies, ed. *Edmund Spenser: "The Faerie Queen": A Selection,* (London, 1976).

CRITICAL AND BIOGRAPHICAL STUDIES

Warton, T., *Observations on "The Faerie Queen,"* (London, 1754) enl. (1762) 2nd ed. repr. (New York, 1968, 1969) (Farnborough, 1969); Hurd, R., *Letters on Chivalry and Romance,* (London, 1762) edited by E. J. Morley (1911); Hazlitt, W., *Lectures on the English Poets,* (London, 1818); Ruskin, J., *The Stones of Venice,* vol. II (London, 1853) chs. 7, 8; Ruskin, J., *Modern Painters,* vol. III (London, 1856) ch. 8; Lowell, James Russell, "Spenser," in *The Writings of James Russell Lowell,* IV (1892); Legouis, E., *Edmond Spenser,* (Paris, 1923) rev. ed. (Paris, 1956) English trans. (London, 1926); Renwick, W. L., *Edmund Spenser: An Essay on Renaissance Poetry,* (London, 1925) repr. (London, 1965); Henley, P., *Spenser in Ireland,* (Cork, 1928) repr. (New York, 1969); Hughes, M. Y., *Virgil and Spenser,* (Berkeley, Calif., 1929) repr. (Port Washington, N.Y., 1969); Jones, H. S. V., *A Spenser Handbook,* (New York, 1930) repr. (London, 1947); Greenlaw, E., *Studies in Spenser's Historical Allegory,* (Baltimore, 1932) repr. (New York, 1967); Lotspeich, H. G., *Classical Mythology in the Poetry of Edmund Spenser,* (Princeton, 1932) repr. (1965); Spens, J., *Spenser's Faerie Queen: An Interpretation,* (London, 1934) repr. (New York, 1967); T. M. Raysor, ed. *Coleridge's Miscellaneous Criticism,* (London, 1936); Lewis, C. S., *The Allegory of Love,* (London, 1936); Rathborne, I. E., *The Meaning of Spenser's Fairyland,* (New York, 1937) repr. (New York, 1965); Bennett, J. W., *The Evolution of "The Faerie Queen,"* (Chicago, 1942) repr. (New York, 1960); Whitaker, V. K., *The Religious Basis of Spenser's Thought,* (Stanford, Calif., 1950) repr. (New York, 1966); Smith, H., *Elizabethan Poetry: A Study in Convention, Meaning and Expression,* (Cambridge, Mass., 1952) repr. (Ann Arbor, 1968); Lewis, C. S., *English Literature in the Sixteenth Century Excluding Drama,* (Oxford, 1954); Arthos, J., *On the Poetry of Spenser and the Form of Romances,* (London, 1956) repr. (New York, 1970); Berger, H., *The Allegorical Temper. Vision and Reality in Book 2 of Spenser's "Faerie Queen,"* (New Haven, 1957) repr. (Hamden, Conn., 1967); Mueller, W. R., *Spenser's Critics: Changing Currents in Literary Taste,* (Syracuse, N.Y., 1959) criticism of *The Faerie Queen* from 1715 to 1949, with intro.; Coleridge, S. T., *Shakespearian Criticism,* T. M. Raysor, ed. 2 vols. (London, 1960); Hieatt, A. K., *Short Time's Endless Monument. The Symbolism of the Numbers in Edmund Spenser's "Epithalamion,"* (New York, 1960) repr. (Port Washington, N.Y., 1972); Ellrodt, R., *Neoplatonism in the Poetry of Spenser,* (Geneva, 1960) reviewed by C. S. Lewis, in Etudes anglaises, 14 (1961); Satterthwaite, A. W., *Spenser, Ronsard and Du Bellay,* (Princeton, 1960); Hamilton, A. C., *The Structure of Allegory in "The Faerie Queen,"* (Oxford, 1961); McLane, P. E., *Spenser's "Shepherd's Calendar": A Study in Elizabethan Allegory,* (Notre Dame, Ind., 1961); Hough, G., *A Preface to "The Faerie Queen,"* (London, 1962); Greene, T., *The Descent From Heaven: A Study in Epic Continuity,* (New Haven, 1963); Frye, N., *Fables of Identity: Studies in Poetic Mythology,* (New York, 1963); Nelson, W., *The Poetry of Edmund Spenser: A Study,* (New York, 1963); Roche, T. P., *The Kindly Flame: A Study of the Third and Fourth Books of Spenser's "Faerie Queen,"* (Princeton, 1964); Fowler, A., *Spenser and the Numbers of Time,* (London-New York, 1964); Giamatti, A. B., *The Earthly Paradise and the Renaissance Epic,* (Princeton, 1966); Lewis, C. S., *Spenser's Images of Life,* A. Fowler, ed. (Cambridge, 1967); Watson, E. A. F., *Spenser,* (London, 1967); Alpers, P. J., *The Poetry of "The Faerie Queen,"* (Princeton, 1967); Dunseath, T. K., *Spenser's Allegory of Justice in Book Five of "The Faerie Queen,"* (Princeton, 1968); Sale, R., *Reading Spenser: An Introduction to "The Faerie Queen,"* (New York, 1968); H. Maclean, ed. *Edmund Spenser's Poetry: Authoritative Texts; Criticism,* (New York, 1968) texts and selections from 1590 to 1963; Grandsen, K. W., *A Critical Commentary on Spenser's "Faerie Queen,"* (London, 1969); Aptekar, J., *Icons of Justice: Iconography and Thematic Imagery in Book 5 of "The Faerie Queen,"* (New York, 1969); Meyer, S., *An Interpretation of Edmund Spenser's "Colin Clout,"* (Notre Dame, Ind., 1969); Evans, M., *Spenser's Anatomy of Heroism: A Commentary on "The Faerie Queen,"* (Cambridge, 1970); Freeman, R., *"The Faerie Queen": A Companion for Readers,* (Berkeley, Calif., 1970); Bayley, P., *Edmund Spenser: Prince of Poets,* (London, 1971); Fletcher, A., *The Prophetic Moment: An Essay on Spenser,* (Chicago-London, 1971); Hankins, J. E., *Source and Meaning in Spenser's Allegory: A Study of "The Faerie Queen,"* (Oxford, 1971); Tonkin, H., *Spenser's Courteous Pastoral: Book Six of "The Faerie Queen,"* (Oxford, 1972); Bender, J. B., *Spenser and Literary Pictorialism,* (Princeton, 1972); Cullen, P., *Infernal Triad: The Flesh, the World, and the Devil in Spenser and Milton,* (Princeton, 1974); Fowler, A., *Conceitful Thought: The Interpretation of English Renaissance Poems,* (Edinburgh, 1975); Giamatti, A. B., *Play of Double Senses: Spenser's "Faerie Queen,"* (Englewood Cliffs, N.J., 1975); Hieatt, A. K., *Chaucer: Spenser: Milton: Mythopoeic Continuities and Transformations,* (Montreal-London, 1975); Rose, M., *Spenser's Art. A Companion to Book 1 of "The Faerie Queen,"* (Cambridge, Mass., 1975); MacCaffrey, I. G., *Spenser's Allegory: The Anatomy of Imagination,*

(Princeton, 1976); Nohrnberg, J., *The Analogy of "The Faerie Queen,"* (Princeton, 1976).

ARTICLES

W. R. Mueller and D. C. Allen, eds., *That Sovereign Light. Essays in Honor of Edmund Spenser 1552–1952,* (Baltimore, 1952) repr. (New York, 1967); Allen, D. C., "The March Eclogue of *The Shepherd's Calendar*" and "Muiopotmos," *Image and Meaning, Metaphoric Traditions in Renaissance Poetry* (Baltimore, 1960) rev. (1968); W. Nelson, ed. *Form and Convention in the Poetry of Edmund Spenser,* (New York, 1961) Selected Papers From the English Institute; H. Berger, ed. *Spenser: A Collection of Critical Essays,* (Englewood Cliffs, N.J., 1968); R. R. Elliott, ed. *The Prince of Poets: Essays on Edmund Spenser,* (New York, 1968); A. Fowler, ed. *Silent Poetry: Essays in Numerological Analysis,* (London-New York, 1970) contains M. Baybak *et al.* "Placement 'in the middest', in *The Faerie Queen*" and A. Dunlop "The Unity of Spenser's *Amoretti*"; Editors of the *Journal of English Literary History, Critical Essays on Spenser From ELH,* (Baltimore, 1970); Kermode, J. F., *Shakespeare, Spenser, Donne: Renaissance Essays,* (London-New York, 1971); A. C. Hamilton, ed. *Essential Articles for the Study of Edmund Spenser,* (Hamden, Conn., 1972); J. M. Kennedy and J. A. Reither, eds. *A Theatre for Spenserians: Papers of the International Spenser Colloquium, Fredericton 1969,* (Toronto, 1973); P. Bayley, ed. *Spenser: "The Faerie Queen,"* (London, 1977).

Wallace Stevens
(1879–1955)

WILLIAM YORK TINDALL

WALLACE STEVENS WAS an insurance man. That he was also a poet seems odd; for nowadays around here poets and businessmen seldom agree. Their agreement in one person, in Hartford, Connecticut, is so strange that some, trying to account for it, have guessed it less agreement than uneasy split.

Whether an uneasy or an agreeable composite, Stevens commonly kept his sides apart and, in Hartford, kept one dark. At home, tending his roses in the evening, or in the morning walking to his office on Asylum Street, he jotted poems down—but never on company time. Poetry was none of his business, which, as he announced in *Who's Who,* was "insurance." Few of his associates suspected his eccentricity. When told of it, a fellow insurance man of Hartford exclaimed: "What! Wally a poet?" At the door of the Hartford Canoe Club Stevens cautioned a literate luncheon guest: "We don't talk about poetry here." Talking of poetry in their groves, the literate were inclined to ignore insurance or else to dismiss it with wonder. "In any case, Stevens seems, like the sailor of "Sailing after Lunch," to have been

A most inappropriate man
In a most unpropitious place.

For Stevens himself it was not a question of "direct and total opposites" in conflict but of their happy, changing relationship. "It gives a man character as a poet," he said, "to have daily contact with a job." His ideal was the "all-round" or "many-sided" man—Benjamin Franklin, for example, man of affairs, philosopher, composer of words, and compositor. "Money," said Stevens, "is a kind of poetry," and it is a fact that both money and poetry are made. The man who can afford to buy pictures, he added, is a better judge of pictures than the man who can only talk about them. The ruler of Stevens' Platonic republic would be the man who could build bridges between all incompatibles: between theory and money, art and life, "fact and miracle." Indeed, such bridges connect two present worlds, one of which he liked to call "reality," the other "imagination," though both were real enough to him. Their consequent "interaction," becoming his theme, determined both the manner of his poems and their method. Interaction is his word for his peculiar virtue and the virtue of his poetry.

Mann's Tonio Kröger embodies the union of bourgeois and artist that Joyce's aesthetic Stephen may also have achieved after meeting Mr. Bloom, an advertising man. Tonio and Stephen had to leave home to present their union with it. No man, however, was less of an exile than Stevens. Let Henry James and T. S. Eliot run as they would to better shores, here Stevens took his stand or walked, here in Hartford, the heart of American reality, confronting it, a "poet striding among cigar stores." There was no evasion on Asylum Street; yet like any asylum his chosen place, absurd and disconcertingly real at once, was a place for fictions.

Many, noting his elegance, have thought his odd asylum a kind of ivory tower. If so, it was ivory tower in vacant lot. Stevens accepted this metaphor: "The romantic poet now-a-days," he said, ". . . happens to be one who still dwells in an ivory tower," but this tower has "an exceptional view of the public dump and the advertising signs of Snider's Catsup, Ivory Soap and Chevrolet Cars; he is the hermit who dwells with the sun and moon, but insists on taking a rotten newspaper." Among such hermits Stevens also counted Marianne Moore of Brooklyn and William Carlos Williams of Rutherford. For all three the ivory tower seems a less appropriate metaphor than "The Man on the Dump." There he sits on the garbage of the past, rejecting it yet intent upon "the the" or what is here and now, garbage and all. "The the" was always the central concern of Wallace Stevens whatever his elegant airs.

Whatever those finical French airs, he was very American, descended on one side from Whitman. It may be that the lilacs of "Last Looks at the Lilacs" are not such as once in dooryard bloomed; but

Lightly and lightly, O my land,
Move lightly through the air again,

the last lines of "Imago," are Whitman himself, and it is he who, at the beginning of "Like Decorations in a Nigger Cemetery," strides "shouting the things that are part of him," his beard a flame. "Ploughing on Sunday" is a joyous celebration of freedom and space that Whitman, living now, might have written. Not Presbyterian maybe, and certainly not British, this secular exuberance on Sunday is American; and so is the dance of those children in "Life Is Motion." The significant landscapes in which Stevens delighted are not unlike those that Whitman, barbarously blaring, once delighted in: Oklahoma, Tennessee, Jersey City, Pascagoula, Schuylkill, and Neversink. Even the statues with which we adorn public parks and plazas fascinated Stevens. "The American Sublime," on General Jackson's statue at the White House, may show sublimity coming down to "empty spirit and vacant space," but mockery and despair are attended by affection; for

. . . the panorama of despair
Cannot be the specialty
Of this ecstatic air.

No poet since Whitman has loved America more, or more ambiguously. Even that finical elegance in which Stevens departs from his good, gray master is a product of our land—like furniture of the Gilded Age or the prose of Henry James. Maybe "slovenly wilderness" and "nigger cemetery" call for such decoration.

That Stevens was singer and decorator of America is plain. That he was romantic, too, is another question, one that teased him continually. He found no final answer. Certainly his concern with the imagination is that of Coleridge and Baudelaire. Adding strangeness to beauty occupied Walter Pater no more than it was to occupy Stevens, whose irony and insistence upon personality are equally romantic. Yet he was no transcendentalist nor was he devoted to fragments of the past. Aware of mixture (as T. S. Eliot, amorous of classicism, was also aware), Stevens was uneasy. On the one hand the romantic belonged on the dump with other garbage of the past: Mozart's music, Plato's paradigm, and Aristotle's skeleton. On the other hand, both vital and exploratory, the romantic pleased. Sometimes he, Marianne Moore, and William Carlos Williams seemed romantic; sometimes everything romantic seemed "vapidest fake." The labels do not matter. But it is plain that Stevens, singing "the present, its hoo-hoo-hoo," partly conforms to the tradition he sometimes rejected. This would not be worth mentioning had he not worried so much about it. Enough that he was an American poet, singing the here and now.

More than curiously named landscape and strangely decorated park, America was social and political scene as well, seen, however, by "the man that is rich and right"—and Republican. Stevens, caught in the depression, was aware of the novels of the poor, the inordinate demands of workers, the picket lines around the auto works, the swarming of Polacks in Jersey City, and, above all, the menace of communism, bad business for businessmen. Regarding these aspects of a "leaden time" without sympathy or hope, he devoted "Owl's Clover" (an unfortunate, long thing, wisely excluded from *The Collected Poems*) to his fears for order and art. "Logical lunatics" of a "grubby faith," those Russians, dictating to artists, keep Shostakovich down. *Pravda* (that "damned rag") and the mass of men constitute "the pressure of reality" that poets must resist or evade. Without social, moral, or political obligation, the true poet refuses to confuse the values of life and art. Far from committed, still less *engagé,* he is true to himself alone and to pure form.

Stevens was a Republican, a Taft Republican, who thought Eisenhower a dangerous radical. It may be that few poets have occupied this position. But there is something austere, something fine and private—indeed, something heroic about it. All the romance of lost causes finds its happiest concentration here.

This extraordinary Republican was born in Reading, Pennsylvania, in 1879. Surrounded by farms, Reading is full of factories. There is a gallery of pictures there and an orchestra; and in the middle distance is the peak of Neversink:

> Unsnack your snood, madanna, for the stars
> Are shining on all brows of Neversink.

As suits one born near Neversink, Stevens was a Pennsylvania Dutchman—not German Dutch, he insisted, but Holland Dutch. Though Zeller, his mother's name, is German, Stevens is a Dutch name. (His father was a lawyer, a poet, a Presbyterian, and a Democrat.) An impressive Pennsylvania Dutchman, Stevens was "tall and of a port in air." Undemonstrative and shy, he was, nevertheless, among congenial people, genial.

Leaving Harvard without a degree in 1900, he went to the New York Law School. He was admitted to the bar in 1904, and in 1916 joined the legal department of the Hartford Accident and Indemnity Company, of which, in 1934, he became vice president. One daughter blessed his marriage to Elsie Kachel of Reading. Stevens did not keep a Cadillac. Indeed, he had no car; and the estate he left (in 1955) was small, considering his probable salary. But, more than most, he was in love with living and all good things: wine, pictures, and roses. An agent in Paris sent him the pictures.

To remain in America is what one expects of an American poet; but it may seem strange that one who was also the poet of lions in Sweden never visited Europe. He did go to Key West and Jersey City, but probably not to Tennessee, Tallapoosa, or Oklahoma. Voyaging around his chamber was enough for this mental traveler, and his office an adequate asylum. "I was the world in which I walked," says Hoon in his Palaz, his beard dripping ointment; and "what I saw," he adds, "came not but from myself."

The earliest verses of Stevens-Hoon, set down before the titivation of that beard, appeared in the *Harvard Advocate* before 1900. Of them, he said years later, "They give me the creeps." In New York, practicing law, he went around with William Carlos Williams, Marianne Moore, Alfred Kreymborg, and Carl Van Vechten. At this time, under the spell of Ezra Pound, who was intent on haiku, Noh, and Chinese décor, the Imagist movement was in full career. Free verse, accurate words, bright analogies, and eagerness to astound the conventional occupied Stevens and his Imagist companions, who also dared experiment beyond Imagist limits. From 1914 Stevens contributed to Harriet Monroe's *Poetry* and from 1915 to Kreymborg's *Others.* The two more or less Chinese or Japanese poetic plays that Stevens attempted around this time are "wrong as a divagation to Peking." Both lack, as he implied later on, the "terrible genius" a poetic play must have before it is more than a "literary relic." But the New York verses (now in *Opus Posthumous*) display the themes and manners that were to distinguish *Harmonium*:

> All over Minnesota,
> Cerise sopranos . . .

Such verses, as he observed in one of them, are "fecund in rapt curios." Yet this curious poet marked, sometimes, "the virtue of the common-place."

However conservative in politics, Stevens was daring in poetics. However bourgeois, he was out to outrage the bourgeoisie. Many of his poems, like Mencken's essays, seem designed to dismay high-toned old Christian women. His gaiety rebuked their stuffiness; his youth, persisting into middle age, rebuked the middle age of those who never had been young. Their suburb was full of white nightgowns. None was "purple with green rings."

Harmonium, a selection of these poems, appeared in 1923, when Stevens was forty-four. It attracted little notice; but *The Man with the Blue Guitar* (1937), *Transport to Summer* (1947), and other dazzling volumes established him as "virtuoso." He won prizes, among them the Bollingen and the Pulitzer; and universities bestowed honorary degrees. None of his books before *Collected Poems* (1954) enjoyed wide sale. But, as he said, he wrote for an "élite," by which he was judged one of America's finest poets—as he certainly is. To read his poems in the little reviews where they appeared made one, as he put it, "one of the gang." As for general readers: he was either too odd or too bare to read generally. Or too obscure: the secretary of the Ice Cream Manufacturers' Association, having come across "The Emperor of Ice-Cream," wrote to Stevens, asking if he was for ice cream or against it.

The Necessary Angel (1951) consists mostly of speeches on the nature of poetry delivered without inflection before academic audiences. Easier to read than to hear as he delivered them, these essays are dense, intricate, and unsystematic, filled with contradictions; and sometimes, disconcertingly, they are full of fun: "The accuracy of accurate letters," he begins, "is an accuracy with respect to the structure of reality." Surely he is speaking through the persona of the scholar and mocking him—mocking himself too and his audience. It is as if, addressing Weisheit, his rabbi, he said: "We'll give the weekend to wisdom." Passionately devoted to poetry, he was an amateur of ideas. Other essays or speeches appear in *Opus Posthumous* (1957). (Would not *Posthumum* or *Postumum* be more seemly?)

His poems are of two kinds: the one strange and imagistic, the other lean and discursive. Both are odd and both persist from start to end of his career. There is little real development in theme or method. Analogy and interaction remain his principles.

From start to finish there are manners, each from a persona or mask, at once expressive and defensive. Sometimes the mask is that of the dandy, sometimes of the magnifico, sometimes of the rabbi. These masks are absurd, but so is he who speaks through them, so those who listen, and so the nature of things. Behind each mask is the poet-insurance man, obsessed by ideas that excited him, and what excited him produced his poems. These poems unite mask, man, and idea in forms that consist of rhythm, sound, tone—of words, in short —and their interaction. To single one element out is a mistake, and the commonest mistake to take Stevens as a philosopher. To do that is to get more and more of the same thing, and a pretty elementary thing. Not philosophies, his poems are poems; but it is easier to say what poems say than what they are.

His themes are limited. Despite an insistence on personality, Stevens is rarely personal. However lyrical, he seldom deals with love. Over and over again, excited by those few ideas, he deals with imagination and fact or subject, object, and the nature of reality. You can write poems about anything if you can.

What strikes one on looking into *Harmonium* is an air of florid elegance. Plainly, Stevens has his mask of dandy on. In the later volumes, instead of gallant artifice, fastidious gaudiness, and "quirks of imagery," we commonly find the elegance of severity. The "final elegance," he says, is "plainly to propound."

Stevens was a burgher, and burgher as dandy is a burgherly phenomenon. His "Weeping Burgher," lamenting "sorry verities," finds consolation in "excess" and in the "strange malice" with which he distorts the world—distorts by imposing, composing, transfiguring, and decorating: "I come as belle design / Of foppish line." The Restoration fop, Regency Brummell, Aubrey Beardsley, Oscar Wilde in Piccadilly, and Whistler at 10 o'clock in Chelsea—all these were dandies and all decorators of something like a "nigger cemetery." Dandyism, a comment on the commonplace and the quotidian, reveals these by their opposites. Revealing time and place, reworking fact, dandies display "the unreal of what is real" and, conversely, the real of what is unreal.

Keeping things as they are in mind, the dandy of our time responds not only to bourgeois society but to the nature exposed by science. Unnatural decorations suit this black continuum. But dandyism is unsuitable, too, as the deportment of Fragonard, all right at Fontainebleau, would violate Asylum Street. At once inappropriate and appropriate, dandyism depends on the interaction of opposites.

Not only a mask, dandyism is a dress and a style. The poem is its style, says Stevens, the style is the poet, and a change of style is a change of subject. Adjusting ruffle and cravat in vacant lot or, better, on the dump, Stevens displays Stevens and dump and Stevens on dump. (*Chacun a son égout.*) Whatever his style, he was always a realist and never more than when most elegant.

He came by artifice naturally; but the postwar period brought it out. Despair drove young Edith Sitwell to erect a rococo façade. Ronald Firbank responded to the aftermath of war by the precious and the bizarre, and even young Aldous Huxley found the air of a decadent Roman congenial. All were terribly gay, as Dame Edith said, all were funny, all serious, and however decadent in appearance, all were full of life. Stevens was their American counterpart:

> Natives of poverty, children of malheur,
> The gaiety of language is our seigneur.

There is always a French air—something a little foreign—about English or American elegance.

Example: "Le Monocle de Mon Oncle," one of the most precious poems of *Harmonium.* This poem is a traditional dramatic monologue, but, falling untraditionally into twelve sections of eleven lines, it mimics the sonnet sequence it misses being. Lordly blank verse upholds tradition as irregular rhyme and half-rhyme violate it. Coherence depends on the manner and tone of a single speaker.

Unlike Prufrock, this French uncle has lived and is still alive. His monocle, elegant and aristocratic, keeps distance between himself and life and between himself and self, as with mocking eye he regards love, age, and loss. His monocle is mask and he enjoys wearing it. Yet, however jaunty his tone, his feelings are mixed. Debonair, he is a little sad.

He displays his complexity by odd juxtapositions: of feeling and tone, of manner and matter, of the extravagantly poetic with the blandly ironic. "Saltier well" and "basic slate" are of one verbal kind; "bravura," "clippered," and "Cupido" of another; and "damsel" of a third. As for matter: the hair of part III is of two kinds, elaborately arranged or naturally disordered. As classical Chinese and Japanese or the ladies of eighteenth-century Bath once studied hairy artifice, so from sleep a present or remembered girl comes disheveled. From a romantic "pool of pink" in part XI a frog booms "from his very belly odious chords."

Part XII, the triumph toward which the sequence moves and its justification, depends on the relationship of two birds and two rabbis, all four of distinct shades. Whether soaring aloft or fluttering down, pigeons are appropriate to sentiment, be they blue or white; but putting rabbis next to them is the unlikeliest thing in the world, particularly when the old rabbi is "rose." Uncle is both rabbis; but, when young, he should have been rose, not dark. When young, instead of observing, he should have pursued. Here, blue and white, dark and rose, passive and active are curiously mixed. Things mixed and missed and white fluttering things bring age and death to mind. But eleven meditations, at once moving and distant, have led to this.

From a concert of elements (tone, feeling, metaphor, diction), from agreements and disagreements among them, comes the effect: how it feels to be forty or, at least, how a dandy of forty feels. Maybe, however, the feeling and idea of elegance itself, exceeding such particulars, are the ultimate effect. We have looked at life through a monocle awhile.

The strangely assorted diction, a principal element, is accurate in the senses of careful and precise. "My dame," said Stevens, addressing his Muse, "sing for this person accurate songs." His words for such songs are "fastidious, immaculate," and "scrupulous." However precious, inappropriate, and affected in appearance, such songs, he said, are of an "exquisite propriety." Their gaiety, too, is a value, and, as he said in "Adagia" (*Opus Posthumous*), "Gaiety in poetry" is "a characteristic of diction."

At a time when poets were commonly descending to common speech the speech of Stevens was uncommon, "besprent" with archaisms, foreign intrusions, neologisms, and insolent hoo-hoos. Rejecting the logical positivists, lamenting those who, prejudiced against perfection, demand plain English for all occasions, Stevens announced that poems may require a "hierophantic phrase." For the poet there is no common speech. Consisting of the right words in the right places, poems sometimes call for the "gibberish of the vulgate," sometimes for a "lingua franca et jocundissima." Whatever the words, Anglo-Saxon or Latin, they must be exact. "'*Je tâche,*'" he quotes Jules Renard, "'*en restant exact, d'être poète.*'"

"Not British in sensibility," says Stevens in "Adagia," Americans find the British tradition "inappropriate." Not so the French tradition. "Ach, Mutter," says the Pennsylvania Dutch girl in "Explanation":

> This old, black dress
> I have been embroidering
> French flowers on it.

French embroidery on a commonplace dress—there is the habit of young Stevens, on familiar terms with French poets from Baudelaire to Valéry and Laforgue.

Though Stevens explains one of Baudelaire's poems, he seems to have preferred the master's prose: his essays on dandyism, artifice, imagination, and painting. "Supreme fiction" comes from Baudelaire's "plus haute fiction." Plainly "Esthétique du Mal" owes something to Baudelaire. To Laforgue Stevens may owe the nonchalance and jauntiness that attend his complaints about the "malady of the quotidian." From Paul Jean Toulet, a gentleman of letters, come the elegant *maximes* and *pensées* of "Like Decorations in a Nigger Cemetery":

> Serve the rouged fruits in early snow.
> They resemble a page of Toulet
> Read in the ruins of a new society,
> Furtively, by candle and out of need.

These poets and others contributed something, often no more than airs and hints, but the most formidable debt was to the Verlaine of *Fêtes galantes.*

Verlaine's bizarre poems embody a dandy's nostalgia in a bourgeois time and place for the faded artifice of Watteau and Fragonard, "*élégants*" both, according to Stevens, who admired their paintings as much as he admired. Verlaine's response to them. "Messieurs," says Verlaine, regard

> Le chevalier Atys, qui gratte
> Sa guitar, à Chloris l'ingrate.

The place is Versailles or Fontainebleau, the time "un soir équivoque d'automne." "Fardées," the ingénues trail "longues jupes" along the avenues of the park,

> Et la mandoline jase
> Parmi les frissons de brise.

These lines from "Mandoline" reappear in *The Necessary Angel.* However faded now, says Stevens in "Study of Images," the "terraces of mandolins" are "inextricably there." His cortège, his colloquy, his ingenue, his *fantoche,* and all his mandolines and guitars are Verlaine's. Even the Doctor of Geneva is Verlaine's "excellent docteur Bolonais" with variations. The ordinary women of Stevens' poem rise from the poverty of the quotidian, "from dry catarrhs, and to guitars" go visiting Verlaine's Versailles with its "lacquered loges," its "girandoles" and "civil fans." How explicit their coiffures there. That those women must return to the old catarrhs improves the elegance of their evening out. As death is the mother of beauty, so reality of elegance.

Young Verlaine was a Parnassian, but most of Stevens' Frenchmen were "Symbolists." Plainly in a French tradition, was Stevens in the Symbolist tradition? Attempts to answer this question raise others. Take "Lions in Sweden." These stone lions of Stockholm, allegorical images of bourgeois virtues (Fides, Justitia, Patientia), are suitable for savings banks. Absurd perhaps, yet somehow the soul hankers after such "sovereign images." If the fault of these lions is theirs, Stevens tells Swenson, "send them back / To Monsieur Dufy's Hamburg whence they came. / The vegetation still abounds with forms." This calls for explanation. Raoul Dufy illustrated Guillaume Apollinaire's *Le Bestiaire.* Hamburg, a supplier of zoological specimens, stands for bestiary here; and a bestiary is commonly allegorical. Yet Apollinaire, author of a bestiary, is in the Symbolist tradition, whatever that is; and vegetation abounding with forms suggests Baudelaire's "forest of symbols."

The essays are of little help. There Stevens sometimes prefers the image without meaning; yet he praises the significant images of Bunyan and La Fontaine. Sometimes he calls an emblem or a sign a symbol. By his prose you can prove anything you like. It is a fact that however much he loved analogy, he hated the Hermetic transcendentalism on which the Symbolists based their analogies. Of no more help, his poems abound in allegorical signs with definite meanings, in allegorical personifications, and in unassigned symbols. His recurrent blue and green, north and south, moon and sun are signs for imagination and fact, not symbols. Many of his creatures (woman, giant, and ephebe) are allegorical. Yet many, "not too exactly labelled," are symbols. And his poems as significant forms are as symbolic as any. Was he, then, a Symbolist or an allegorist? The question is unprofitable. Like any good poet he used the analogies he required and all the other means.

Less elegant than bizarre, "The Virgin Carrying a Lantern" is his closest approach to the Symbolist manner. This picture of bears, roses, Negress, and virgin finds parallel—not necessarily source—in Mallarmé's

> Une négresse par le démon secouée
> Veut gouter une enfant. . . .

An odd desire, but no odder than the situation here. Stevens praised the "clear enigmas" of Mallarmé. In Stevens' little scene the details, which have the clarity of dream, share dream's darkness despite that lantern. What are the virgin and her observer doing there? Why are there no bears among the roses? Like a metaphor of Stevens' magnifico, this situation "will not declare itself yet is certain as meaning." Evading analysis, "The Virgin Carrying a Lantern" is indefinitely suggestive. It is a picture —like something by Rousseau, *le douanier.* It is a strange experience, and its meaning, like that of a picture, is what it is. "A poem," says Stevens in "Adagia," "need not have a meaning and like most things in nature often does not have."

His most elegant poems are a little bizarre. This, too, is in the French tradition. "Le beau," said Baudelaire, "est toujours bizarre." The passion for clowns that Stevens shared with Laforgue, Verlaine, and Baudelaire adds an element of the grotesque, which, Stevens said, is part of things as they are.

"The Emperor of Ice-Cream" owes its effect to unions of the grotesque and the quotidian, seeming and being, compassion and fun. However grotesque, death and the wake are part of life. The image of ice cream concentrates these meanings. At once cold and agreeable, ordinary and festive, it is a symbol of life and death. Imperative mood and the finality of the final rhyme add as much to this strange composition as the commonplace details: last month's newspapers in the first stanza and, in the second, the dresser lacking three glass knobs, the horny feet.

> Call the roller of big cigars,
> The muscular one, and bid him whip
> In kitchen cups concupiscent curds.
> Let the wenches dawdle in such dress
> As they are used to wear, and let the boys
> Bring flowers in last month's newspapers.
> Let be be finale of seem.
> The only emperor is the emperor of ice-
> cream.

Emperor and ice cream, though not opposites, have the effect of opposites. The interaction of such elements, as we have noticed, is one of Stevens' constant means. Let "Analysis of a Theme" serve as example. The theme, stated in prose, is poetic and mad: "How happy I was the day I told the young Blandina of three-legged giraffes." The analysis, stated in verse, is prosaic and logical in spite of diction and metaphor at odds with the habit of prose. Juxtaposed, verse and prose, logic and madness, are reversed. The verse of the more or less prosaic analysis deals with grotesques from the unconscious. But this quiet verse suddenly explodes into Herr Gott, "ithy oonts, and long-haired plomets." As Herr Gott to Blandina so ithy oonts to those giraffes.

Putting two elements together results in a third thing, their radiance. In "The Ordinary Women," as we have seen, the effect comes from the contrast of catarrh and guitar, linked by sound. In "Floral Decorations for Bananas" the effect is from the contrast of blunt bananas, at home in jungles "oozing cantankerous gum," and eighteenth-century bijouterie. In "Cortège for Rosenbloom" heavy rhythm and insistent repetition support ritual action. A cortège is elegantly French and active. Poor Rosenbloom is ordinary, Germanic, and passive. The "finical carriers" bear him to the sky, as if poets transfiguring the commonplace, making "the intense poem of the strictest prose of Rosenbloom." But other possibilities crowd the grotesque ceremony. In "The Plot against the Giant" this giant replaces Rosenbloom and three aesthetic girls replace his carriers. The third girl will undo him by French sounds, "heavenly labials in a world of gutterals," and by a "curious puffing."

Even the titles, conflicting with texts sometimes, are little dramas. "Hymn from a Watermelon Pavilion" combines three incompatibles. Phrases too, like seventeenth-century "conceits," make concords of discords, "icy Élysée," for example, or "beau caboose." *Beau* is French, *caboose* American. Last car on the freight train, a caboose suggests bums and the dry, summer loneliness of sidings. The two words are united, yet divided, by dissonance. In conjunction with caboose, elegance (as Mrs. Alfred Uruguay says) "must struggle like the rest."

Perhaps the most splendid example of harmony and contrast is "Peter Quince at the Clavier." This imitation of symphonic form has four movements, each related to the others by theme and motif, each different from the others in rhythm and key. The first movement, quiet and meditative, is a thought process, logical in frame, yet consisting of two analogies to be elaborated: that of music and that of Susanna and her red-eyed elders. Odd rhymes and "pizzicati," interrupting sobriety at the end, promise another development. The second movement, an andante, reveals Susanna bathing in green water. A dramatic intrusion of cymbal and horn introduces the third movement, a scherzo. Elegant couplets and absurd rhymes suit tambourines and "simpering Byzantines." The last movement, returning to the meditative mode of the first, renders "on the clear viol of her memory" the composer's ruminations about body, death, and beauty. His composition is at once musical, logical, and brightly imagistic. Rhythm, curious diction and rhyme, the interaction of contrasting movements, and, above all, those two elaborated analogies produce the strange radiance.

Suggestive of music, maybe, the poem is not music. An approximation in shape and rhythm, it is as close to music as one whose genius was pictorial and meditative could get. In spite of title and many aural felicities, *Harmonium* appeals less to ear than to eye. Stevens, who thought himself *"chef d'orchestre,"* lacked the high musical abilities of Milton or T. S. Eliot. Music for Stevens was another analogy; and a harmonium, after all, is a little organ.

"Peter Quince" is an elegant picture, but the triumph of elegance in *Harmonium* is "Sea Surface Full of Clouds," another picture, which, like most of Stevens' elegantiae, is as suave as *Fêtes galantes* and as malign. The ostensible theme is his constant obsession: the relations between inner and outer, observer and object. His object here is clouds in the sky and their reflections in the water. Of their relationship the inconstant observer, confronting inconstant object, makes five things; for he finds five ways of looking at the thing. These are the parts of his poem, each different in feeling from the others, but each like the others in tone and structure.

Parallel structure, persisting through changes of inner and outer climate, is an important element. Each part begins with the "slopping" of the sea. In the second triplet of each part is a caesura separating the recurrent but changing analogy of chocolate and umbrella from the changing appearance of the sea. The third and fourth triplets pose a question. The fourth answers it in elegant French that varies according to its circumstances. In the quiet remainder of each part the tensions of "the tense machine" are relaxed. The poem begins and ends with a concert of opposites. At the beginning Stevens puts November next to tropical Tehuantepec. At the end the opposites of sea and sky, now transfigured, are one; and subject, at last, is one with object. Green and blue, his customary tags for nature and imagination, carry the sense, but other colors (yellow, mallow, and clownish motley) seem more important.

The telling elements of the form are chocolate and umbrella, the French refrain, the tone, and the insistent structure. Affected by these, the ostensible theme, becoming an element with the rest, yields to the real theme: a vision of suave civility or what it feels like to be civilized. The effect is like that of dinner at Le Pavillon with a bottle of Montrachet.

His poem "Montrachet-le-Jardin," which seems to have nothing to do with this great wine, has to do with its opposite. The bottle is empty. Good-bye, says Stevens, to the "bastard chateaux and smoky demoiselles" in which he once delighted. Now let facts fall "through nakedness to nakedness." Ascetic poems on emptiness, interacting with their bizarre companions, occur even in *Harmonium,* where one kind sets the other off. The bizarre, creating feelings in which ideas play a part, are florid; the ascetic, devoted to expressing ideas in which feelings play a part, are bare. In the later volumes austere poems outnumber the florid. "No turban walks across the lessened floors. . . . A fantastic effort has failed." If nabob at all, now, Stevens is "nabob of bones." Yet, however much the two kinds differ—the one concrete, the other more or less abstract, the one imagistic, the other more or less discursive—there is less difference than there seems. Each kind offers immediate experience, and each is elegant. The first has the elegance of abundance, the second the elegance of severity.

Of this second kind "The Snow Man" is the earliest expression. Unadorned, the poem sweeps in one sentence to a shocking finality. There are symphonic effects and descriptions, but no metaphor intervenes until the end, where the snow man, there by aid of the title, embodies the "mind of winter" and the reality on which this mind casts a cold eye. Not only this snow man but the entire poem is an analogy for these. "Nothing that is not there and the nothing that is" concentrates the austerities that have led to it. This concentration, at once felicitous and terrible, proves the capacity of naked discourse. Winter words for wintry matter, as elegant as any decoration, involve our feelings as directly as image can, and, like epigram or wit itself, involve our minds. And, as Stevens says, naked discourse can imply the images it lacks.

The nothingness embodied and revealed by this poem is not the same as the poverty of those ordinary women, who, though like John Donne's "ordinary nothings" in one sense, have catarrhs; and catarrhs are something. Like Eliot's "female smells," catarrhs, however unseemly, are not extraordinary. The nothingness the snow man sees makes ordinariness and customary elegance alike irrelevant. Under lacquered loge and girandole is a dark cellar, over them an empty attic, and poverty to right and left. The nothingness Stevens looks at in "The Snow Man" is that of mathematical abstraction, the universe of twentieth-century science, emptier and even more discouraging than Hardy's nineteenth-century universe. The nothingness Stevens looks at is emptier than the darkness and deprivation of sitting Eliot, at the end of whose negative way is a chorus of martyrs and virgins.

The realist must choose not only things as they are but things as they are not, "the dominant blank" that underlies "device." The bare poem is a steady look at "the the," such as it is and is not. But such looking has its pleasures, too. A bare things has its proper beauty. Autumn and winter with black branches in bleak light, all dapple gone, and, below these, even below the snow, the rock—such images, abounding in the later poems, are good, but plain statement is better: "Bare earth is best. Bare, bare."

Virtues of bareness are integrity, shape, and radiance. Autumn has its auroras and those of winter are flashier. As for nothingness, not only our fate, it is our climate. We are natives there. Its virtues are challenge and space for the constructions it invites. As the poem "makes meanings of the rock" so that "its barrenness becomes a thousand things," so genius, entering the emptiest nothing, will inform it and build towers. The poet's job is to create shapes in nothingness and of it. Elegance, no longer evasive, is the property of structures raised in the void with full awareness of their place. Such elegance is severe, but even the lacquered loge and the girandole are fictions, or things made, good as such and reminders of their surroundings.

Creation from nothing is God's power and the poet's—and that of any man. Hence aesthetics or the study of shapes and their making is the proper study. Writing poems about poems, Stevens was writing about mankind. This brings us to the jar in Tennessee, a strange bare thing in the middle of nowhere. "Anecdote of the Jar" is an anecdote of a jar, a shape made by man and placed by him in a "sloveniy wilderness." The theme is interaction: the effect of the round jar on its surroundings and of them on it. This artifact composes nature, but not entirely; for the slovenly place still sprawls. Wilderness of bird and bush makes jar stand out, gray and bare, "like nothing else in Tennessee." Jar and wilderness, art and nature, need each other. But, however serious this theme, the story of the jar is absurd.

The structure of this poem on structure is exemplary. Unrhymed couplets lead up to two end-stopped lines, set off by rhyme. This premature finality lends an air of unfinality to the end, another unrhymed couplet, which, however, by returning to "Tennessee" joins end to beginning, rounding things out. Internal rhymes and repetition, assuring coherence, emphasize the interacting contraries. "Round" and "ground," pointing central meanings out by sound, are confirmed by "around" and "surround." The climactic end-rhymes, "everywhere" and "bare," restate the conflict. "It made . . . to it," a chiasmus, provides a rhetorical shadow of interaction. The shape is tight and bare, the diction lean; but questions arise. Why Tennessee? Is the jar empty or full? The raising of questions is a virtue of shape.

Stevens wrote three long poems on aesthetics and several short ones, all longer, however, than his "Anecdote," the first great statement of the theme. Of the long poems "The Comedian as the Letter C" is the earliest and the least successful. Yet, fascinating as document, it is a comprehensive display of the things that teased him.

Crispin, the hero of "The Comedian," is a philosopher, poet, and clown—or so he is labeled—and, as his name implies, he is also valet and saint. Overtly, the poem is about his journey from Bordeaux to Carolina. Less like that of Candide than of Bunyan's Christian, this voyage is an allegorical "pilgrimage." Places and people are insistently significant. At journey's end, for example, Crispin, an abstraction, cultivates a garden and raises four allegorical daughters. Like any allegory, this "anecdote" is a "disguised pronunciamento . . . invented for its pith"—not doctrinal in form but in design." The end of Bunyan's Christian is a place in heaven. By no means transcendental, that of Stevens' Crispin is a place on earth. His quest is for an "aesthetic." Christian's pilgrimage is up moral hills and down moral valleys. Crispin's is an "up and down between two elements," imagination and fact or intelligence and soil, until he finds their point of balance. The poles between which he oscillates bear allegorical tags: moon and sun, north and south, blue and green. Their conflict and synthesis are dialectical. Controlling theme, Stevens' principle of interaction controls manner and method, too.

His style, the outstanding element, is rococo fustian, an elaborate clowning at odds with the serious matter. Not Crispin but his author is the clown, whose "portentous accents" are also at odds with the bareness that sometimes intrudes. Ambiguity vies with fustian to conceal the doctrine the poem seems designed to offer. "The words of things entangle and confuse," and so do things of words.

Nobody knows exactly what the title means. Is that "Comedian" the narrator or Crispin or both? And what of "the Letter C"? Does it imply denudation, abstraction, or simple abbreviation? Is it a small letter, as "miniscule" implies, or a capital? The third letter, does it suggest third class, like an academic grade, or does it refer to the third stage of a development? The last line, "So may the relation of each man be clipped," is no less ambiguous. In context, "relation" may mean story or relative, a daughter in this case. "Clipped" may mean cut short, as by the third fatal sister or by an offhand author, clipped out, as from a newspaper, or clipped as hair is. Crispin has "a barber's eye," his daughters have curls, and hair has figured throughout, as importantly as those coiffures of "Le Monocle." As for tone: the last line may be deflationary or triumphant. In one sense it dismisses the matter as no matter; in another it affirms the synthesis it includes. On the one hand, a daughter represents nature, her hairdo, artifice. On the other hand—but, as the narrator jauntily says, "So much for that."

In the first part of the poem there is reason for the precious style. "Silentious porpoises," whose mustachios seem "inscrutable hair in an inscrutable world," will do as reflections in a barber's eye; and, what is more to the point, they represent a "civil" European's attempt at evading the sea, the "quintessential fact" that doctors of Geneva and connoisseurs of jupes and salad-beds must face at last. Triton, an evasion from the past, is dead; but rococo elegance may still do as reality's opposite, working as well in the "green barbarism" of Yucatan, the sea's exotic equivalent.

This will do, but inkhorn inflation, though abating after arrival in middling Carolina, still persists. "Pampean dits" for songs of the Pampas are a little too much for there and then, as are "palankeens" for baby carriages. Such residues of former elegance may be what realists must struggle against. Out of them, anyway, a realist's plainness begins to emerge. Example: "For realists, what is is what should be." The docks of Carolina and the "quotidian" welcome such "sinewy nakedness." Yet, even at the beginning of the journey "Nota" and "Sed quaeritur," absurd apart from the medieval manuscripts where they belong, surround "man is the intelligence of his soil," a prosaic proposition.

Failing to follow the transformation of Crispin from traditional European to bare American, the style remains more "poetic" than prosaic. Though he achieves a kind of "harmony" or "liaison," the style does not. "Trinket pasticcio" exceeds "veracious page on page, exact," and "the florist asking aid from cabbages" asks in vain. In a context between the elegance of abundance and the elegance of severity, abundance wins. This, after all, is early Stevens. But maybe—and we are left with buts and maybes—pomposity is the narrator's comment on himself. Far from representing imagination in conflict with sense, the style represents fancy alone.

The story of Crispin is a portrait of the artist—as a young man. As we ask if Stephen is Joyce, so we ask if Crispin is Stevens. Naturally there are resemblances between author and hero in each case; but in each the hero, distanced by irony, is also a figure of fun. Like Stephen, Stevens' unheroic hero evolves an aesthetic. Mann's Tonio Kröger, whose aesthetic adjustment involves the contraries of north and south, blond and dark, offers an even closer parallel. But Stevens chose to write his novel in blank verse. Not prose, not quite poetry, this work of fancy and reason misses being the thing of words a poem must be. Perhaps the poet's "appointed power," like Crispin's own, was "unwielded through disdain." Unlike Crispin, perhaps, the poet preferred gloss to text.

"Illuminating, from a fancy gorged by apparition, plain and common things" was not enough for Stevens, older now. In "The Man with the Blue Guitar," his second long poem on aesthetics, he reviews the themes of the first, but with more assurance and greater success. A product of what we call the creative imagination, "The Blue Guitar" is poetry, we say. This composition is a suite of thirty-three short parts in four-beat couplets, sometimes rhymed, commonly uiirhymed. These parts are variations on a theme.

Bright, clear images strike one first, and after this an air of tidiness and the gaiety that Stevens prized. The last of these effects comes from imagery in part, an imagery both familiar and strange, and in part from quick rhythms, neat structure, and a diction that successfully combines exactness with ambiguity. Order plays a part and so does drama. Each of the parts is a little drama with its conflict, climax, and appeasement, a drama not only of ideas but of structure, rhythm, and tone. In the conflict between clarity and obscurity that serves as underplot, clarity, after many trials, triumphs, for the play is a comedy. Among the personae, subtly masked, are a marionette and a clown. Though sedentary, the man with the guitar is more of an actor than either.

The first part seems a debate between player and audience. Their preferences, plainly stated, state the theme of the suite: actuality and imaginative transformation. The rhyme of "are" with "guitar" concentrates both the agreement and the disagreement of these contenders, both of whom are right. Their contest reveals two aspects of art, one from the player's point of view, the other from the listeners'. But, as subsequent poems show, this debate is internal. The speaker's head is the stage. Structure, also embodying the drama, suits the sense it reinforces. The first couplet, broken and unrhymed, sets the scene. "The day was green" is at once strange and natural. Day's green, moreover, contends with blue instrument. Then two rhymed, end-stopped couplets stage the conflict. "Guitar" and "are" in the first become "are" and "guitar" in the second, a significant reversal. These stopped and interlinked couplets are the climax. Following this come four run-on lines, the first two unrhymed, creating a momentary suspense. The second two, echoing "guitar" and "are," are for the moment final.

The last part brings all conflicts to an end—as usual, in Stevens, by an agreement of opposites; for he had looked into Hegel. Here, Sunday over, we put up with "Monday's dirty light." Both Sunday and Monday know bread and stone. The bread of Sunday is the daily bread of the Lord's Prayer; that of Monday is daily bread. The stone, Peter's rock on Sunday, is bedrock on Monday or the world itself. The "wrangling of two dreams" that has occupied us through the suite is brought to an end not only by bread and stone, composite opposites, but by the final phrase, "The imagined pine, the imagined jay," played now and again on the guitar. Pine is green, jay blue. Both are actual, both imagined, and both, being projections of our minds, are dreams. Rhyme, the only one in this part, makes the union certain. But "That's it" in the second couplet proves this end a sudden illumination, passing rather than final. We have shared a process of thought with its excitement and immediacy.

Of parts between last and first, most are good. Take XXV, in which the artist as juggling clown twirls a world on his nose. In the second part, as shearsman or tailor, unable to perfect his world, he has faced Mallarmé's penultimate. Now he brings something round or, shouting in his robes and symbols, thinks he does. Meanwhile liquid cats and graying grass remind us of Bergson's flux—if not that of Heraclitus. Nose and world, this juggler implies, beating time with fat thumb, are out of time and change, eternal. He is bizarre; his actions are gay and a little saddening. We know as well as he that his control of things is a moment's illusion, as unstable as liquid cats. The world he twirls "this-a-way" (or even that) is his, but he is in another.

In XXX the player evolves an "old fantoche," Verlaine's marionette as well as something more. This thing, responding to the strings of "Oxidia, banal suburb," could be the audience or Stevens in Hartford. Oxidia owes its name to *accidia,* medieval torpor, and to modern oxide or the soots and crusts of "stacks above machines." Here, surveying a "cross-piece on a pole," this *fantoche* sees three things at once: an actual telephone pole, the crossed stick that regulates marionettes, and Christ on cross, the last confirmed by "Ecce." By triple vision Oxidia, emerging from itself, seems not only soot but seed.

Other parts of the suite concern the artist's relation to art and its relation to society. The tenth poem, about art and politics, is suitably imperative in mood. A dictator is coming, his party indicated by the redness of columns and by consignment of bourgeois documents to the dump. Should the guitar celebrate such redness or assert blue individuality against it? Though the answer is clear enough, ambiguities of syntax leave details uncertain. Who is "hooing the slick trombones," dictator or adversary? In XII "Tom-tom, c'est moi." No more than opening gambit, this proposition confuses the issue. A tom-tom, though primitive, is a musical instrument, hence artificial. Being French, "c'est moi" is civilized, but, being the self, "moi" is natural. Part XXIII ironically proposes "a few final solutions." But the duet between an undertaker and a voice in the clouds settles nothing although, seeming to unite the above and the below, their song involves "Dichtung und Wahrheit." If art, the speaker asks in XV, is a "'hoard of destructions,'" as Picasso says, does it depict or destroy society and self? The mood is interrogative. Nota: Stevens said he did not have Picasso's picture of the guitarist in mind. This picture (at the Chicago Art Institute) is generally blue, but the guitar is brown.

Interrogative or imperative, the parts of this suite solve none of the problems they raise. Poems, not dissertations, they question the nature of things. They feel things out. The ideas that excited Stevens may detain the reader. But, as Stevens reminds him in XXII, "Poetry is the subject of the poem." The "thinking of art" in VI is not thinking about art but art's radiant activity, for which the metaphor of thought is fitting. Radiantly embodying encounters, these poems make them "for a moment final." Structures, feelings, tones, ideas, and textures work together to this end. What poems say, we say, is but a part of what they are.

Excited again by these ideas, Stevens rearranged them in "Notes toward a Supreme Fiction." Again it is their arrangement that counts. The last poem of *The Collected Poems* is named "Not Ideas about the Thing but the Thing Itself." Of "Notes toward a Supreme Fiction," as of "The Man with the Blue Guitar," we could say, not ideas in the thing but the thing itself.

The title is important. "Notes toward," suggesting the penultimate again, is tentative. Toward a theory of a "Fiction" or toward in the sense of attempting the thing itself? To answer this question we must consider the meaning of fiction. "Poetry is the supreme fiction, madame," Stevens had told the high-toned old Christian woman of *Harmonium,* who would have found Baudelaire's religion as the highest fiction more to her taste, but only a little more. She would have thought a fiction something false or feigned, as, in one sense, it is. But the first meaning of fiction, as we know from its origin in Latin *fingere,* is something shaped, formed, or imagined. To Stevens a fiction meant a work of art, what Clive Bell called "significant form" or Ernst Cassirer "symbolic form." Through such forms we encounter reality and present it. Such forms or "fictive things," both radiant and disturbing, "wink most when widows wince." Aware of widows and his limitations, Stevens modestly proposes a preliminary draft of the great poem he will never write. Yet he thought this approximation his masterpiece.

The matter he chose to shape into a work of art is the work of art—or it seems so on first reading. Choice of subject reveals the poet's personality, said Stevens, and what is poetry but a transaction between a person and something else? The poet writes about what he must. The subject Stevens had to choose for his "Notes" is not so remote from our general interests as it seems. If the work of art is an arrangement of reality, he is writing about ways of accosting reality. The ostensible subject, however, is not the real one. Not the formulation of an aesthetic but the experience of trying to formulate it is the subject here: how it feels to think things out. "Not to impose," he says, but "to discover." When he wanted to announce his aesthetic he wrote an essay or made a speech. This poem is an essay only in the sense of being an attempt to fix the feeling and quality of an experience. Less rational than it seems, this poem is not philosophy; for nothing here approaches systematic thought. Rather, it is a meditation and a drama of thought in progress with all its hesitations, failures, and triumphs.

The dramatic meditation is divided into three parts of ten poems each. Each of these constituent poems consists of seven tercets or triplets. The development, like that of "The Comedian," is dialectical. This process, borrowed from philosophy, provides firm structure and adds philosophical flavor. Moreover, a structure of process suits a poem of process. This poem proceeds on two levels: that of idea and that of method and manner. The thesis, dealing with abstraction, is suitably bare—for the most part. The antithesis, dealing with time and change, is suitably concrete. The third part attempts a synthesis of these ideas, methods, and manners.

Dialectical opposition and union appealed to a poet whose working principle was interaction. Providing general structure, interaction controls the parts. Stevens gets his particular effects by surprising conjunctions of discourse and image, of the bare and the bizarre. The discursive austerity that claims our notice first in the first part proves to be an element working with its opposite. Discourse as neighbor of absurd concretion serves a nondiscursive end. Note the fruitful juxtaposition of the plainly discursive with the outrageously odd in the third poem of the first part. Into the soberly established climate of thought, an Arabian suddenly intrudes "with his damned hoobla-hoobla-hoobla-how." Such violent contrasts, useful for drama and fun, are there to create a third thing by cooperation, and what they create we feel. In the poem of "hoobla-how" there is a subsidiary interaction of serious matter with frivolous manner. "Two things of opposite natures seem to depend / On one another, as a man depends on a woman," Stevens says in the fourth poem of the second part. Marriage, in the third part, becomes his symbol of this interdependence.

Crispin, coming to terms with the soil, comes to see the virtues of a prose that "should wear a poem's guise at last." In the later poems, poetry often seems to wear the guise of prose. Increasingly fascinated by the bareness of reality, Stevens found bare prose a fitting instrument, Crispin's "fecund minimum." In "Notes," however, the poet of ice cream and the poet of barren rock are one. The two faces of elegance put on a single mask, that of the aesthetician in his chair, a mask less tragic than comic. "To have nothing to say and to say it in a tragic manner," says Stevens in "Adagia," "is not the same thing as to have something to say," or, he might have added, to say it with a sense of its absurdity.

An air of the prosaic, like the flavor of philosophy, was useful for this meditation, the commonest device of which is the proposition. Each of the three parts has a proposition for title; many of the constituent poems begin with a proposition; and most include one. Not a statement, a proposition is a gambit, something to be accepted or denied. Either true or false, it allows choice while embodying the interaction of possibilities. Whitehead, the philosopher of process, found propositions the cousins of symbols and like them in effect upon our feelings. Stevens in his "Notes" is the poet of process and proposition. "Life," he says in "Men Made Out of Words" (his poem on "castratos of moon-mash"), "consists of propositions about life." "It Must Be Abstract," a proposition, begins the process here. Beginning a poem with a metaphor, John Donne proceeds to elaborate it by logic. Beginning a poem with a proposition, Stevens proceeds to elaborate it by metaphor. Their procedures are not dissimilar.

In the first part of "Notes" Stevens tells his "ephebe" about the abstract and general elements of poetry. The "first idea" is no longer transcendental: "Phoebus is dead, ephebe." Even harder to define, the notion of "major man" (from Hobbes?) calls for particulars: The MacCullough must become MacCullough to be conceived. Both abstract and general ideas are fictions, imagined things. This conclusion is intuitive, for "truth depends on a walk around a lake." In structure the tenth poem is typical. Beginning, as if Cassirer, with a proposition ("The major abstraction is the idea of man . . ."), Stevens proceeds by qualification and description. The question that follows (and questions are forms as significant as propositions) is strange and, after so pedestrian an approach, surprising. An intruding rabbi sees all men in a bum with baggy pants, "Looking for what was, where it used to be." That this shining line, a triumph of economy, is the climax of the process and its final elegance is indicated by the concluding proposition.

> What rabbi, grown furious with human
>   wish,
> What chieftain, walking by himself, crying
> Most miserable, most victorious,
>
> Does not see these separate figures one by
>   one,
> And yet see only one, in his old coat,
> His slouching pantaloons, beyond the town,
>
> Looking for what was, where it used to be?
> Cloudless the morning. It is he. The man
> In that old coat, those sagging pantaloons,
>
> It is of him, ephebe, to make, to confect
> The final elegance, not to console
> Nor sanctify, but plainly to propound.

The particulars of part II, contending with the abstractions of part I, are fittingly concrete to illustrate the other element of poetry. Strange scenes and curious stories, such as Nanzia Nunzio's, prove metaphor the agent of imaginative "transformation."

For "It Must Give Pleasure," the proposition that announces the third part, Stevens has the authority of Aristotle and Horace. What pleases seems the fecund marriage of abstraction and metaphor in a fiction. That the marriage of the maiden Bawda (reality) to her great captain (the artist) occurs in Catawba is more than verbally pleasing; for Catawba is in Carolina, where Crispin found harmony of intelligence and soil. The no less allegorical "fat girl" of the final poem ("a more than natural figure") is not only the earth-mother ("my green, my fluent mundo") but a great composite, uniting earth and art. She also serves as Muse, the "dame" invoked in part I as directress of "accurate song."

Stevens had addressed his Muse reverently in "To the One of Fictive Music," a poem of *Harmonium.* The fat girl, more convincing and attractive than this predecessor, claims a place beside the "Sister of the Minotaur," his Muse in *The Necessary Angel.* Not altogether reverent, his attitude toward her here is as enigmatic as she is ambiguous. Is the Minotaur's sister a half-sister, Ariadne, let us say—a real woman in a myth? Or is she an unknown sister, half-woman and half-cow? In either case, for a poet of interacting opposites that is a good Muse. But back to the fat girl: she is also a "crystal," a transparent shape and product of a process. Not only the Muse, she embodies the fiction.

"Notes toward a Supreme Fiction" is a poem on the poem. Many poets have written poems on this—Yeats and Dylan Thomas among them; for creation, whether of world or poem, fascinates creators. Stevens devoted poem after poem to the poem and its parts: "Imago," "The Motive for Metaphor," "A Primitive like an Orb," and more. But little here that was not said in "Notes," and little here so shapely.

"Notes toward a Supreme Fiction" is a shape concerning shape or order. Never through with ideas of order, Stevens also devoted "Connoisseur of Chaos" to them. "The Idea of Order at Key West" introduces Ramon Fernandez. Though Stevens claimed he picked this name out of a hat, the context makes Fernandez seem the neoclassicist, whose "rage for order" was as notable as that of Henri Focillon, author of *The Life of Forms,* one of Stevens' favorites.

Painting was his other art. Convinced that painting and poetry are alike, that what is said of one applies to the other, Stevens devoted poems to the sister art. Some are imitations of painting, some commentaries on it, and some are both. "The Apostrophe to Vincentine," who is "figured" nude between monotonous earth and sky, may be composed of the sounds and senses of words; yet it is an early Matisse, as *fauve* as the work of the master. "The Bouquet" is at once a still life, a commentary on it, and a comment on the commentary. For "meta-men" this object in a jar becomes a "para-thing" or symbol, "the real made acute by an unreal." That both elements are impermanent is proved by a soldier dumping their arrangement on the floor.

"So-and-So Reclining on Her Couch" is a transaction between a painter and his model or, at least, between her and his idea of what he is doing. There she is on that couch, "reclining on her elbow." He calls this pleasing sight "Projection A"; for he holds with Kant the idea that we project what we see. So projected, she is an anonymous thing of curves, a "motionless gesture." But the mind connects her with other things that complicate Projection A with Projections B and C:

> If just above her head there hung,
> Suspended in air, the slightest crown
> Of Gothic prong and practick bright,
>
> The suspension, as in solid space,
> The suspending hand withdrawn, would be
> An invisible gesture. Let this be called
>
> Projection B. To get at the thing
> Without gestures is to get at it as
> Idea. She floats in the contention, the flux
>
> Between the thing as idea and
> The idea as thing. She is half who made her.
> This is the final Projection, C.
>
> The arrangement contains the desire of
> The artist. But one confides in what has no
> Concealed creator. One walks easily
>
> The unpainted shore, accepts the world
> As anything but sculpture. Good-bye
> Mrs. Pappadopoulos, and thanks.

Anonymous no more, the thing in itself, evading all projections, emerges, shockingly.

Speaking to his "ephebe," Stevens exchanges the mask of aesthetician for that of teacher. Going further in some poems, he puts the mask of lecturer on to deliver "academic discourse" in Havana or elsewhere. Of the "Three Academic Pieces" in *The Necessary Angel* one is in prose, two are in verse, and all were delivered from a lectern. The verse develops from the prose. Each piece concerns "resemblance, his current word for metaphor, central to reality and poetry alike.

The difference between his most poetic prose and his driest poetry emerges from a comparison of these parallel specimens. The prose is more or less sober and straightforward. The poetry, both dense and intense, has a "particular tingle" and a few "whirroos and scintillant sizzlings such as children like" to vex "the serious folds of majesty." Far more metaphorical than the prose, the poetry is brighter, odder, gayer, and, as he says in "Man Carrying Thing," "it resists the intelligence almost successfully." This resistance, occupying our minds, allows the rhythms, images, oddities, and the sounds of words to work upon our feelings. Discourse, transfigured, becomes "bright excellence."

"Someone Puts a Pineapple Together," the second of these three academic pieces, is in verse. "O juventes, O filii," the lecturer begins. Still the aesthetician, he proceeds to examine the object before him, a pineapple on the table, another still life. There it is, and here is what we make of it. Once a pineapple was enough without a scholar's "enlargings and pale arrondissements." Now it invites "false metaphor." (The lecturer lists twelve resemblances or exfoliations, duly numbered.) "How thick this gobbet is with overlays . . . the sum of its complications, seen/ And unseen." That his depreciation of metaphor is highly metaphorical is no more than academic humor demands. This excellent lecture, which is also one of Stevens' most joyous poems, was delivered at Harvard. With the same mask on, Stevens also addresses the Academy of Fine Ideas. "Messieurs . . ." he begins. What follows is what he calls "the intense poem of the strictest prose."

The mask of lecturer off, Stevens put on the mask of rabbi, a man who, whether dark or rose, is a philosopher; but a Hartford poet as rabbi is bizarre. Stevens put his mask on when, more than aesthetician, he confronted a wider reality; and above the mask he wore a hat. A philosopher's hat is square, as "aquiline pedants find," and part of the mind. The Doctor of Geneva wears a stovepipe hat, and the Pastor Caballero, a sombrero with sweeping brim, an image of a mind with bravura. Marianne Moore's "very big hat" in "The Prejudice against the Past" is that of a fastidious poet, whose poems are not to be confused with articles in *The Encyclopaedia Britannica.* Whether masked as philosopher or as hidalgo with guitar, Stevens had a hat on. The one he wore for "An Ordinary Evening in New Haven" was that of the rabbi from Hartford.

In this poem of thirty-one parts of six tercets each, New Haven serves as occasion and object. It is an autumn night there. Wind blows leaves and old newspapers about. Sitting in his hotel, at the window, or walking the streets, Stevens thinks about the nature of reality, or what he has always thought about: subject, object, and their uncertain relations. Reduced to this, his thinking seems monotonous; but, as he says, the imagination never touches the same thing twice in the same way. Another "search for reality," this poem is as new as sunrise or love. New thinking of old things is a theme as good for poets as sunrise or love—though less customary. The poem of New Haven is a fresh attempt to "conceive," a word, Stevens said, pointing to "A Pastoral Nun," that embodies his intention. Each of the "resemblances" with which his nun is concerned "matters only in that which it conceives." The poem of New Haven is an adventure in conceiving through proposition and metaphor.

Beginning with a proposition, the sixth part, descending immediately to metaphor, compares naked Alpha with hierophantic Omega. A is reality; O or Z is what the mind does with it. Alpha is always beginning; Omega, like Stevens' thought, "is refreshed at every end." In one sense Omega is the poem; in another, like New Haven itself, the poem is a union of A and Z, whose contention here is more exciting than what they stand for. Walking "the metaphysical streets of the physical town," Stevens conceives "a total double-thing," at once New Haven and its poem, which is "part of the res itself and not about it."

"Le Cimetière Marin" is the closest parallel. Here Valéry's thinker, sitting in a graveyard, thinks about the nature of reality, death, and life. He is commonly metaphorical. His occasional abstractions and references to philosophy are there, said Valéry, only to lend a flavor of philosophy to the thinking of this particular *moi.* Indeed, the matter of the poem is no more than something to fill a shape. Stevens, in his later years, is closer to the Valéry of "Le Cimetière" and "La Jeune Parque" than to any other poet.

The "pseudo-statements" of I. A. Richards and his "music of ideas," which Stevens quotes, apply to him. Not his statements but their composite shape is the point of his poem. A little odd and like nothing else in New Haven, it is another shape for the feeling of trying to know what one has tried to know again and again. Not only the feeling of an endless affair ("It can never be satisfied, the mind, never") but the feeling of facing time and death emerges from this shape.

Autumn leaves, bare branches, and all the intimations of the rock become more eloquent here than ruminations about subject and object. "The robins are la-bas." Gaiety, hardly here except for the "gaiety of exactness," is gone with those robins. Yet relics of old oddness remain and a few grotesques. Professor Eucalyptus, keeping his analytic eye on the object, seems a critic at Yale. The scholar whose "Segmenta" come from "Adagia" seems Stevens himself.

His arrangement of "the eye's plain version" and the mind's improvements, though visual on the whole, has a rhythm depending on the possibilities of the tercet, in which syntactical structure may violate prosodic structure freely in a kind of counterpoint. More flexible than couplet or quatrain, the tercet seems more shapely than blank verse. In the thirty-first poem, for example, this form, at once selfcontained and uncontained, permits a long syntactical sweep of five tercets and the suddenness of two short periods in the last.

"An Ordinary Evening" is what in "Of Modern Poetry" Stevens calls "the poem of the mind in the act of finding." "Metaphors of a Magnifico" in *Harmonium* proves this theme an old one. Trying to fix reality here, a metaphysician looks, comes to his limit, and begins again. Frustrated again, he is left with a white wall and the fruit trees. This little poem (in imagistic free verse) seems to do more economically and intensely what "An Ordinary Evening" does. The theme of the feeling of thinking is the same; but, another shape, this poem offers another conception. Stevens' poems of the same thing are never the same poem.

"Sunday Morning," in which blank verse of the civilest kind establishes the quality of the experience, is another early adventure of the mind in the act of finding. Here the thinker is a woman at breakfast on a sunny terrace while her neighbors are at church. Coffee, oranges, and "green freedom" are here and now; but she is troubled, like all of Stevens' metaphysicians, with thoughts of a conflicting opposite, in this case, heaven and the "holy hush of ancient sacrifice." The contention in her mind between life and death, present and past, earth and heaven is the structure of the poem.

"We live in an old chaos of the sun," where it is good to be alive; but this woman longs for some "imperishable bliss." Living wins by death's assistance, for life's beauty depends on death. Sinking like a tired bird into blackness is inevitable, but the "ambiguous undulations" of the descent redeem it:

> She hears, upon that water without sound,
> A voice that cries, "The tomb in Palestine
> Is not the porch of spirits lingering.
> It is the grave of Jesus, where he lay."
> We live in an old chaos of the sun,
> Or old dependency of day and night,
> Or island solitude, unsponsored, free,
> Of that wide water, inescapable.
>
> Deer walk upon our mountains, and the
> quail
> Whistle about us their spontaneous cries;
> Sweet berries ripen in the wilderness;
> And, in the isolation of the sky,
> At evening, casual flocks of pigeons make
> Ambiguous undulations as they sink,
> Downward to darkness, on extended wings.

Her thought has proceeded from complacency to awareness. Death and its "winter branch," before us here as in New Haven, are comfortably remote, and we are left with bright, green wings.

To enjoy the sun and bright wings without thought was the constant desire of thinking Stevens. Elegant rhetorician, poet of double vision, he longed to see things with a single eye, without monocle; and he longed in vain. But sometimes, like some of his thinkers, he approached success. His poems of the thing itself are among his brightest, whether announcements of his desire or its approximate achievements. In "The Sense of the Sleight-of-Hand Man" one's "grand flights," soulful "tootings," and "Sunday baths . . . occur as they occur." So clouds in a blue sky, so bluejays. To mate one's life with these one must be ignorant as the dawn. The wise man's difficulty is a subject of "Angel Surrounded by Paysans." This angel, without wing or aureole, comes for a moment and is gone:

> I am the necessary angel of earth,
> Since, in my sight, you see the earth again.

With angelic help in "Of Bright & Blue Birds & the Gala Sun" we see for a moment the gaiety of things as things, as if there were a "bright scienza" outside ourselves, "a gaiety that is being, not merely knowing." The roses of "Bouquet of Roses in Sunlight," exceeding the rhetorician's scope, are "too much as they are to be changed by metaphor." But for Lady Lowzen of Hydaspia by Howzen, fond of "feen masquerie" and of skimming the "real for its unreal"—for this lady "what is was other things." This was the trouble for Stevens, too, although "reality" is the last word of his *Collected Poems.*

"A Lot of People Bathing in a Stream," an all but pure celebration of being, has something of the green and golden glory of Dylan Thomas' "Fern Hill," without its nostalgia. Not here once, we are here now in "the sun-filled water, brightly leafed," in today's "yellow green and yellow blue . . . floating without a head," natural grotesques and companions of the comic sun. Here is all summer in a day, and here the fitting introduction to "Credences of Summer."

About the feeling of a summer's day, "Credences of Summer" is also about how hard it is to feel the day as it is, without mind's intervention, and to put the feeling down in words. The season is important. More or less indifferent to romantic spring, Stevens turned more and more to autumn, which, in spite of its auroras, brings final nothingness to mind. But summer, static and fully there, was his darling. What Byzantium was to Yeats, summer was to Stevens—with this difference: Yeats's timeless city was out of nature, but Stevens' summer fields are as natural as ultimate cold and more pleasing. Threatening autumn is the mother of summer's beauty. A major poem of *Transport to Summer,* "Credences of Summer," transporting us, fulfills the promise of the volume.

"Now," the first word, and recurrent "this" are his keys to thisness. "Let's see the very thing and nothing else." Recurrent "see" and "look" are keys to the visible. Look at the sun "in its essential barrenness" and set it down "without evasion by a single metaphor." In the first two of the ten parts of this poem, metaphorical Stevens approaches his ideal of plain words for essential things: "This is the barrenness of the fertile thing that can attain no more." But metaphor, intruding in the third part, remains to plague him. Summer becomes a tower ("green's green apogee"), a mountain, and a ruddy old man. In the sixth part, summer becomes the rock, green below and blue above. Not the hidden, chilly rock of winter, "the rock of summer" is visible, solid and majestic—"As if twelve princes sat before a king." The summer day in the fifth part becomes a vital youth, an ephebe, no doubt, and one of the boys of summer.

Such images, bastards of the mind, failing to embody the feeling that the poet intends, put it off. But plain description, faithful to the eye, brings it back. The fourth part, on a land too ripe for enigmas, too secure, makes us "accept what is as good. . . . The utmost must be good and is." Fields of hay, baked in the sun, recall Oley, a town near Reading. It may be that memory of youth gets between the poet and the view; but "Credences of Summer" plays memory against eye and metaphor against plain speech.

"It was difficult to sing in face of the object." This difficulty, replacing immediate summer, becomes the subject. Deep in the woods, in VII, poets try to sing of summer in the fields. Whereas the "concentered self," out of the woods, grips the object "in savage scrutiny," grips, subjugates, and proclaims "this hard prize." In VIII, a trumpet announces the visible by sound. This instrument, replacing the old guitar, may make the visible more than visible, but that is better than the invisible, which the mind of man, "grown venerable in the unreal," prefers. The bright cock on the bean pole in IX seems the poet in our time. Summer is over:

> The gardener's cat is dead, the gardener gone
> And last year's garden grows salacious
> weeds.

In this wasteland, the cock observes the decay of old arrangements with all their *douceurs* and *tristesses.* Soft and civil, this polished bird, now on the barest bean pole, once sat in a "suave bush." Their "complex" has fallen apart. Yet, considering the possibility of another order, not so soft and civil as his first, the old cock makes an ambiguous sound. Life was once "an old casino in a park." Once civil and polished in a suave bush, Stevens sits on his bean pole. Still cocky, he looks at the barrenness around him and does his best.

After this wintry interlude summer returns to the stage, observing its "huge decorum." The "personae of summer," playing their parts as an "inhuman author" directs, wear costumes of blue and yellow, red and green, the motley of the sun. Fat and roseate, these personae, as their name proclaims, were once masks. A persona of summer now, Stevens has no mask or hat on.

In "Thirteen Ways of Looking at a Blackbird," among the earliest of his variations on a theme, Stevens found, or perfected, what was to be his agreeable structure and accosted the strange relations of idea and things that were to be his care. "Looking at" in thirteen ways means not only seeing but conceiving and imagining or having ideas about. The thing looked at or the blackbird itself, a far from simple thing, may be a black bird of ill omen or the ordinary blackbird of Haddam and the other regions of Connecticut. Contrast, interferences of outer with inner or of inner with outer, their interpenetrations, and elegant economy attend the development of this suite from its likely origin in Pound's haiku or Williams' "red wheel barrow" to more important arrangements than the limits of Imagism allow. The fifth look, passing through the bird, is at poetry and the thirteenth, with its décor of night, snow, and cedar, at death. The "glass coach" in Connecticut, an artifice suitable for "bawds of euphony" or even for displaced insurance men, may be transparent; yet it casts a shadow that the troubled looker-out mistakes for substance.

Art, like that coach, may be a thing, a shadowing thing, but blackbirds are the thing, the thing that in his later years Stevens, coachless now, tried to look at, not through or around. Williams said: "No ideas but in things." For Joyce with his significant bathtub and Eliot with his Chinese jar things also are embodiments of ideas or, at least, objects that, within a traditional frame of reference, carry ideas. No less detained by bodies, Stevens found his idea of man in a man; "It Must Be Abstract" comes to mean It Must Be Concrete. But trying to see things without the interference of mind and its overlays, Stevens belongs less with Williams, Eliot, and Joyce than with later men, Beckett, for example, and Robbe-Grillet. Beckett said: "No symbols where none intended." Stevens said: "Not Ideas about the Thing but the Thing Itself." This echo of Williams goes beyond him. But Beckett, Robbe-Grillet, and Stevens, trying to see their bananas plain—bananas or blackbirds, who cares which?—saw something else; for however empty of meaning bananas are meant to be and are, they invite ideas as residents or neighbors. Desire for the meaningless particular—for the ultimate thisness—is always frustrated by a looking mind. The ultimate banana, interfered with, becomes penultimate, an object less possessed than desired; and desire, as Stevens knew, is "not to have" or "to have what is not." To desire is to have ideas about. It was desire for "the things of August" that kept Stevens from them.

Selected Bibliography

WORKS OF WALLACE STEVENS

POETICAL WORKS

Selected Poems, (London: Faber and Faber, 1953) Selected by Stevens.

The Collected Poems, (New York: Knopf, 1954).

Wallace Stevens, Mattino Domenicale de Altre Poesie, translated by Renato Poggioli (Torino: Giulio Einaudi, 1954). Selected poems with translations into Italian, and notes on the poems by Stevens.

Opus Posthumous, edited, with an introduction, by Samuel French Morse (New York: Knopf, 1957) Contains plays "Adagia," early, late, and rejected poems, and miscellaneous prose.

Poems by Wallace Stevens, selected, with an introduction, by Samuel French Morse (New York: Vintage (Knopf), 1959).

The Palm at the End of the Mind, (Hamden, Ct.: Shoe String Press, 1984).

LETTERS AND MISCELLANY

Letters of Wallace Stevens, edited by Holly Stevens (New York: Knopf, 1966).

Sur Plusieurs Beaux Sujets: Wallace Stevens' Commonplace Book, a Facsimile and Transcription, (Stanford, Calif.: Stanford Univ. Press, 1989).

BIBLIOGRAPHY

Morse, Samuel French, *Wallace Stevens, A Preliminary Checklist of His Published Writings: 1898–1954,* (New Haven: Yale University Library, 1954.

CRITICAL AND BIOGRAPHICAL STUDIES

Blackmur, R. P., *The Double Agent,* (New York: Arrow, 1935).

Borroff, Marie, ed., *Wallace Stevens: A Collection of Critical Essays,* (Englewood Cliffs, N.J.: Prentice-Hall, 1963).

Brown, Ashley, and Robert S. Haller eds., *The Achievement of Wallace Stevens,* (Philadelphia: Lippincott, 1962).

Bryer, Jackson R., and Joseph N. Riddel, *Wallace Stevens Checklist and Bibliography of Stevens Criticism,* (Denver, Colo.: Swallow Press, 1963).

Enck, John J., *Wallace Stevens: Images and Judgments,* (Carbondale: Southern Illinois University Press, 1964).

Fuchs, Daniel, *The Comic Spirit of Wallace Stevens,* (Durham, N.C.: Duke University Press, 1963).

Gregory, Horace, *A History of American Poetry, 1900–1940,* (New York: Harcourt Brace, 1946).

Kermode, Frank, *Wallace Stevens,* (Edinburgh: Oliver and Boyd, 1960).

Kreymborg, Alfred, *Troubadour, an Autobiography,* (New York: Boni and Liveright, 1925).

Monroe, Harriet, *A Poet's Life,* (New York: Macmillan, 1938).

Moore, Marianne, *Predilections,* (New York: Viking, 1955).

Morse, Samuel French, "The Native Element," *Kenyon Review,* 20: 446–65 (Summer 1958). Contains letters and comments by Stevens. Mr. Morse is preparing a biography.

O'Connor, William Van, *The Shaping Spirit, A Study of Wallace Stevens,* (Chicago: Regnery, 1950).

Pack, Robert, *Wallace Stevens, An Approach to His Poetry and Thought,* (New Brunswick, N.J.: Rutgers University Press, 1958).

Riddle, Joseph N., *The Clairvoyant Eye: The Poetry and Poetics of Wallace Stevens,* (Baton Rouge: Louisiana University Press, 1966).

Rosenfeld, Paul, *Men Seen,* (New York: MacVeagh, 1925).

Tate, Allen, *Sixty American Poets,* (Washington, D.C.: Library of Congress, 1945).

Taupin, René, *L'Influence du symbolisme français sur la poésie américaine (de 1910 à 1920),* (Paris: Champion, 1929).

Vendler, Helen H., *On Extended Wings: Wallace Stevens' Longer Poems,* (Cambridge, Mass.: Harvard University Press, 1969).

Walsh, Thomas F., *Concordance to the Poetry of Wallace Stevens,* (University Park: Pennsylvania State University Press, 1963).

Wells, Henry W., *Introduction to Wallace Stevens,* (Bloomington: Indiana University Press, 1964).

Williams, William Carlos, "Wallace Stevens," *Poetry,* 87: 234–39 (January 1956).

Winters, Yvor, *In Defense of Reason,* (Denver, Colo.: University of Denver Press, 1947).

SPECIAL ISSUES OF MAGAZINES

Harvard Advocate, vol. 127 (December 1940).

Historical Review of Berks County, (Reading, Pennsylvania, vol. 24, 1959).

Trinity Review, vol. 8 (May 1954).

Mark Strand

(b. 1934)

JEFFERY DONALDSON

Mark Strand's closing words in his 1994 book on the painter Edward Hopper may serve as a first word on the poet himself:

> In Hopper's paintings we can stare at the most familiar scenes and feel that they are essentially remote, even unknown. People look into space. They seem to be elsewhere, lost in a secrecy the paintings cannot disclose and we cannot guess at. It is as if we were spectators at an event we were unable to name. We feel the presence of what is hidden, of what surely exists but is not revealed.

Strand's poems reveal a world that, like Hopper's, is ostensibly remote, unfamiliar, and secretive. His poems pay witness to an elusive reality with their own otherworldly spaces. Strand is the vatic poet of our moment. His lyric prophecies and oracular visions establish him as a modern symbolist, an heir of Ralph Waldo Emerson and Wallace Stevens. At the same time, he has fashioned for himself a style of language and vision that is uniquely his own. The Mark Strand signature is widely recognized: a plain-style vocabulary and straightforward syntax; lyric and narrative elements that recall documentary or journalistic reportage; a meditative tone that suggests allegorical or surrealist intentions; an otherworldly and often humorous and ironic quality; allusions to and echoes of other poets and their work; and broad but spare landscapes, simple contrasts such as light and dark, single rooms, one or two characters, and one or two happenings. All these elements combine to suggest more abstract truths that precise details or historical particulars might obscure.

Strand's poetic world is essentially psychological. His poems are allegorical ruminations on the nature and condition of the self as it discovers its place in a world of lack, absence, and desire. Strand's province is the darker side of the human psyche, where we know ourselves as divided, anxious, vaguely culpable, and where we find ourselves both astonished and paralyzed by our simple being in the world, by the mere consciousness of our having selves. In "The One Song" (*Darker,* 1970), Strand articulates the weight that the most basic aspects of life can have on the psyche:

> I prefer to sit all day
> like a sack in a chair
> and to lie all night
> like a stone in my bed.
>
> When food comes
> I open my mouth.
> When sleep comes
> I close my eyes.

His poems give voice to that estranged self, and in so doing they form a mythology that invokes the modernist negations of opposition, fragmentation, dissociation, and erasure. The critic Harold Bloom referred to Strand as "a dark child of [Wallace] Stevens." Indeed, he shares with his avowed mentor an intense regard for imaginative vision and a penchant for representations of reality as stark and diminished. He is heir to the wintry and meditative clarities of mind that we associate with Stevens, whose late-Romantic perceptions of reality are accomplished by a series of subjective negations and self-effacements. In a century dominated by the ironic mode, Strand is one of our great ironists. He speaks for the *undermined* self, the self caught up in a compromising struggle for control over its own identity.

Revelations of the self as impoverished and limited are one motif in Strand's oeuvre. Another motif concerns the world of poetic vision and its embodiment in poetry. This motif is the reforming powers of the imaginative word. For Strand, encountering a poem is an experience of a particular nature. In "Slow Down for Poetry" (1991), he writes,

> The way poetry has of setting our internal houses in order, of formalizing emotions that are difficult to articulate, is one of the reasons we still depend on it in moments of crisis and during those times when it is important that we know in so many words what we are going through.

Poetry helps us to interpret and control experience and its effects. It gives us room. During the 1960s and 1970s, when conspicuously formal verse was treated with skepticism if not disdain, Strand was praised for a formal acuity and finish. Often stunning in its marriage of simplicity and invention, Strand's poetry reveals a great trust in the unique properties and functions of the poem as a poem. In the ghostly sleight of hand of his plain style, readers have long detected a fertile, self-reflexive interest in the mere fact of poetic speech and all that can be accomplished there. These then are Strand's two main motifs—the limited self, the imaginative word—and the poet has developed them so closely that much of the time they are harmonious.

Although Strand takes as his subject the restless and diminished self, its failings and its experiences of paralysis and guilt, his poems have little in common with the confessional school or any other of the dominantly self-centered poetic traditions. In the more explicitly autobiographical poetry of such poets as Robert Lowell, John Berryman, and Anne Sexton, expressions of personal crisis are legion. But Strand's poems are really only biographical in the sense that they express a mythologized self, a deeper and truer self that is at once elusive, immanent, and potential and part of a reality and condition that underlies our everyday existence. His poems are an expression not only of the lives we live, but also of a potential life. His instances of struggle and alienation are universal parables. In this consideration, Strand's work is connected to an Emersonian line that passes through Wallace Stevens to such poets as John Ashbery and W. S. Merwin. Like them, Strand celebrates not a mere descent into the ordinary and the particular, but a transformation of it into myth, into a vision of the commonplace as more deeply strange than we conventionally imagine. Readers, then, ought not to look here for biography in the usual sense: we learn little about what actually happened in Strand's life, whom he knew, what he did, or where he had been. The poems are very respectful of their maker's privacy. At the same time, it is clear that these poems arise from important experiences and thoughts about them. Personal memory, for example, may have inspired the meditations on childhood that appear in *The Story of Our Lives* (1973) and *The Late Hour* (1978), but what Strand finally brings to light is metamorphosis and translation.

Mark Strand was born in Summerside, Prince Edward Island, Canada, on April 11, 1934, but lived there only as an infant. His father, Robert Joseph Strand, was a man of great intuition and intelligence, but insecure means. He was an itinerant professional, a salesman, who held no less than twenty jobs in the first few years of his son's life. By the time Strand was a young man, he had lived in Halifax, Montreal, Philadelphia, Cleveland, New York City, Croton-on-Hudson, Colombia, Peru, and Mexico. Summers were spent with his aunt in Nova Scotia, at Seabright, at French Village, and at Hackett's Cove, places that later came together in the poet's mind as a mythologized vision of home. His parents were bookish, but intellectually insecure and somewhat emotionally aloof. They were charmed by their son's manifest artistic temperament—Strand's mother, Sonia Apter Strand, felt that she could see a painter in her son's eyes when he was only a year old. As Strand grew into what he calls an absent-minded adolescent, they encouraged his art with the hope that it would not detract him from a more stable professional career. Strand describes his youth as having been characterized both by a sense of responsibility for his parents' happiness and well-being and by a certain inward imaginative existence that was his private domain. The ideals and permanent values of the interior life served even then as an antidote to itinerancy and the precarious emotional environment in which he lived.

Strand entered college in the mid-1950s, though he never felt that he was cut out to be a good student in the conventional sense. He received his B.A. at Antioch College in 1957, having studied under Nolan Miller and read a good deal of poetry. He recalls being moved by the meditative quality of the poems of Wallace Stevens and by the technical authority of many of the poets included in *New Poets of England and America* (1957), an anthology edited by Donald Hall, Robert Pack, and Louis Simpson that he carried around with him at school.

It was as a painter that Strand first tried to develop his talents. He went to Yale in 1959 and studied painting under Joseph Albers. However, it was not long before he felt that he was not destined to be a successful visual artist, and so he turned his hand to poetry. In 1960, as a Fulbright scholar, he traveled to Italy to study nineteenth-century Italian poetry, and mct his first wife, Antonia Ratensky (a daughter, Jessica, was born to them). He returned to America and completed his M.A. in 1962 at the University of Iowa, where he then took a position as an instructor of English until 1965. It was there that he published his first book of poems, *Sleeping with One Eye Open*. Divorced from his first wife, in 1976 he married Julia Runsey Garretson, with whom he had a son, Thomas Summerfield.

In a certain sense, Strand's professional career resembles his father's. The thirty years following his first book brought much travel and many teaching positions. He taught at Yale, Harvard, Princeton, Brandeis, Columbia, Wesleyan, and the universities of Washington, Virginia, and California (Irvine), before settling for thirteen years at the University of Utah in Salt Lake City. He received many fellowships (including a Guggenheim and a Rockefeller) and prizes (including one from the National Institute of Arts and Letters), and was awarded a MacArthur Foundation fellowship in 1987. He was named Poet Laureate of the U.S. Library of Congress in 1990, and as of 1995 held a position in the Writing Seminars at Johns Hopkins University.

The characteristic features of Strand's poetry are in evidence in even his earliest poems. *Sleeping with One Eye Open* was published in 1964 in a limited edition of 250 copies. The title is significant and derives from the epigraph of the book, John Fletcher's "Let one Eye his watches keep / While the Other Eye doth sleep." The quotation points to the fine line between the states of waking and dreaming, the external objective world of reality and the internal subjective worlds of human consciousness. Poems like "The Whole Story" and "The Tunnel" play at the edges of the solipsistic universe where the real world beyond wavers like a mirage. In "The Whole Story," we begin with a traveler and a companion:

> I nudge you and say,
> "That's a fire. And what's more,
> We can't do anything about it,
> Because we're on this train, see?"
> You give me an odd look
> As though I had said too much.

But the nature of the supposed journey and the reason for the speaker's curious observation remain a mystery throughout the poem, and what little we do seem to understand at the beginning (that there is a traveler, a companion, a fire outside the window) is eroded. By the end, our sense of a solid reality, of reliable relations between truth and illusion, has been replaced with a sense that the world "out there," beyond the window, may or may not exist and that the traveler who seems to be riding through that oddly inaccessible landscape may or may not be alone.

The reader of Strand's poetry comes quickly to recognize that the reality we inhabit in the world of the poem makes for a very special case. In "The Tunnel," a man sees another man in front of his house, becomes anxious, and in various discreet ways tries to get him to leave. When he fails, he digs a tunnel out of the house:

> I come out in front of a house
> and stand there too tired to
> move or even speak, hoping
> someone will help me.
> I feel I'm being watched
> and sometimes I hear
> a man's voice,
> but nothing is done
> and I have been waiting for days.

Like most of Strand's environments, the environment of "The Tunnel" is made up of the most basic elements: the interior of a house and the property surrounding the house. There are two people, one inside and one outside. By the end of the poem, the man who feels watched and who attempts to escape seems to have taken the place of the man in front of the house who was watching. But he has gotten nowhere. He is watchful of himself and therefore divided (that is, both watching and watched), trapped in a circle from which he cannot tunnel free. The poem dramatizes a state of paranoid self-consciousness. Any feeling we might have had at the beginning of the poem that there is a real world out there beyond the window is gradually replaced by a feeling of paranoia and a restless desire to get away.

The narrative of a poem like this is clearly unfolding on a level different from everyday lived experience. The simplicity of the story underlines its function as symbolic allegory, for the more straightforwardly and nonchalantly the events are narrated (a man posting suicide notes on his window, tunneling out of his house), the more we are forced to conclude that they are part of an alternative reality where such things are possible, one that is stranger, less recognizable, than the one we believe we inhabit. Strand's readers have tried to characterize that alternative reality and have found it useful to think of his work in terms of a surrealist aesthetic, though we need to be very careful with how we use this term.

Surrealist artists try to express the alternative and liberating logic of the dream state, of the unconscious. They think of poems and paintings as gateways, the artist's job being to represent the dream state by an effective use of poetic narrative and image pattern, which would initiate artist and audience alike into secret, preconscious orders. Surrealism has evolved continually since its first inception in the 1920s in France, and there are many exponents. A neo-surrealist movement became popular in the United States in the 1960s—through such poets as James Wright, W. S. Merwin, Galway Kinnell, and Robert Bly (almost all of whom went on to other things). Their search for what Bly called the "deep image" spoke to a generation that pursued various mind-expanding, altered states as a challenge to the historical and political realities of the decade.

Strand has been numbered among the surrealists, though for him especially it is a slippery and rather inadequate term. His own surrealist influences are more painterly than literary. Critics have pointed to the presence of such artists as René Magritte in his early work, and Strand has declared an allegiance to some visual artists who skirt the edge of what we would consider surrealist art (such as Balthus and Edward Hopper). Some of the relevant influences among the writers he admires are Bruno Schulz, Franz Kafka, Italo Calvino, and particularly the Argentinian writer Jorge Luis Borges (whom he has translated). But

Strand would not identify these writers, or himself, as surrealist. Lance Olsen prefers the term "literary fantasy" when characterizing Strand's poetic universe. He argues that the poetry produces "a psychological state characterized by daydreaming, hallucination, and a disregard for 'consensus-reality' . . . a mode of consciousness that in the end expresses all the liberation and all the terror of the schizophrenic who can never find release from the fantasmagoria of his own mind." Olsen argues that Strand's poems seek to "overthrow 'reality' by generating . . . autistic worlds of phobia, oppression, entrapment, and guilt" and that "at most his poems maintain a fragile awareness of the external universe." Strand himself was reluctant to make rigid distinctions between what is realistically observed and what is imagined. He said to David Brooks in an interview, "To a certain extent, we all depend on free association, and we all use the suggestions that come from our unconscious." He preferred to speak instead of those works which seem to deal in a "twilight zone of experience."

If we see surrealism as based on a destructive principle (the undoing of a "consensus-reality") that promotes the apparent chaos and disorder of the unconscious, then Strand would make a poor candidate as one of its practitioners. His subjects are strictly determined by the law and condition of the reality they find themselves in. Whereas in conventional surrealism we often feel that subjects are liberated into a state where anything can happen, Strand's subjects experience their place in a finished order that is not theirs to control or influence.

If the poet's subjects are seen to have little control over their fate in these early poems, the poet himself certainly does exercise control. In *Sleeping with One Eye Open,* reality is not surreal, but it does give the impression of having been conspicuously put together or constructed. The poet's world appears to be made up of stage-craft:

> Someone is always carting
> The scenery off to the wings
> And I,
> Set free from all the places
> I have never really been,
> Move on beyond the curtains
> Of a closing night ...
>
> We take the props
> and fixtures of our days
> With us into the dark.

These scenes have less to do with the unconscious than with a painted and fabricated reality, a product of artifice. With the knowledge that all the world is a movable stage comes the experience of estrangement and detachment from all that is and the feeling that everything in this world is subject to the poet's sleight-of-hand transformations. Strand is testing his powers as the artificer of a poetic universe. As he says in "The Map," he offers

> A diagram
> Of how the world might look could we
> Maintain a lasting,
> Perfect distance from what is.

Strand's second book, *Reasons for Moving* (1968), introduced him to a much wider audience and secured his reputation as an important new poet of his generation. He preserved four poems from his first collection, including the title poem, "A Reason for Moving," here renamed "Keeping Things Whole."

In this poem, Strand describes an inescapable anxiety about the space he takes up in the world:

> We all have reasons
> for moving.
> I move
> to keep things whole.

There may be wholeness and plenitude, but that "field" is always outside of and beyond the poet, who experiences himself as an absence, a hole, within it. Strand puns on the last word of the poem. His impossible task—the word itself shows us this—is to take the "hole" out of the "whole," to reassert plenitude and identity by removing himself as the displacing figure of absence. Strand's identity is in a sense the negative expression of the Hebrew God's own name for himself as he revealed it to Moses: "I am that I am." For Strand, "Wherever I am / I am what is missing." Instead of being wholly at one with himself, Strand quietly suggests that he is a simple mirror ("I am / I am"), an expression of human doubleness, of our penchant for reflection and self-scrutiny.

It is with *Reasons for Moving,* Richard Howard argues, that Strand first narrates for himself Rimbaud's discovery that "je est un autre" ("'I' is an other"). Strand takes this doubleness as the essence of our humanity. We watch ourselves, and in watching we experience a strange alienation and detachment from who and where we are.

The style and narrative design of the poems are characterized by a direct, unembellished language. Richard Howard writes that most lines in *Reasons for Moving* "are coincident with the simplest declarative statements. . . . The generally short lines . . . construct a simple report of things seen with all the odd exactitude of a documentary film." Events are described, laid out, like simple objects on a table. They suggest still lifes even as they further the narrative, as in "The Accident":

> A train runs over me.
> . . . .
> [The engineer] wipes my forehead,
> . . . .
> He whispers in my ear
> . . . .
> He talks
> . . . .
> Back home he sits
> . . . .
> He sees me sprawled
> . . . .
> He rushes
> from the house
> . . . .
> He puts his head
> down next to mine
> . . . .
> I listen to the wind.

Many of the poems employ a species of primer-book syntax:

> The poems are gone.
> The light is dim.
> The dogs are on the basement stairs and
> coming up.

Sentences and lines are often coterminous, complete in themselves:

> I cannot sleep.
> I cannot stay awake.
> The shutters bang.
> The end of my life begins.

Strand's plain style lends his poems an apparent directness and urgency that would seem to argue an open, ingenuous, and strong moral intent. Wayne Dodd and Stanley Plumly talk about "the sense of a great transparency in the language," as though in his pared-down diction and syntax the poet were trying to get outside the poem's metaphorical evasions. Yet Strand is nothing if not a master stylist who understands the deeper rhetorical effect of working in primary colors. In their exaggerated simplicity, his poems suggest a self-consciousness about intentionality. Even the poem "The Babies," which directly solicits the reader, avoids conviction:

> Let us save the babies.
> Let us run downtown.
> The babies are screaming.
> . . . .
> Let us not wait for tomorrow.
> Let us drive into town
> and save the babies.
> . . . .
> Let us hurry.
> Let us save the babies.
> Let us try to save the babies.

Our sense of the poem's apparently earnest call-to-action is attenuated by the exaggerated simplicity of the refrain; it is as though the poem were bringing to our attention a strangeness in the appeal.

There is an underlying humor in much of Strand's work, and often his most tragic poems flirt with the absurd, leaving the reader in doubt as to the purpose and nature of the poem. His style, moreover, suggests the unreal tragedy of cartoon caricature: our attention is drawn away from what is happening to the rhetorical impact of the caricature itself. Strand's style demonstrates well the poetics of irony that is so dominant in our century: the further you go with an effect and the more pronounced it is, the more self-conscious, duplicitous, and tongue-in-cheek your content will appear. Strand's plain style, then, points in two directions. In the end-stopped lines one senses the cogency of the poem's logic, which appears complete and at one with itself. The resemblance to documentary reportage and the ordinary diction suggest an urgency and directness that seems incompatible with the typically evasive surfaces of poetic language. Yet these same features, in their extremity, suggest an element of self-parody that compromises their initial impact on the reader. The cogency, urgency, and directness are part of a larger ironic effect; they play the role of the straight man in the poem's attempt to mean something. Strand's poems—like the characters we find in them—often seem to be watching themselves function as poems. They are shy about their identity and manifest the same duplicity of self that is at the heart of Strand's concern.

With one eye turned toward metaphysical and psychological concerns, and the other toward the nature and function of poetic language, it is not surprising that Strand's poetry is quite removed from the contemporary fashions of politically and socially activist poetry. His work is more revelatory than prescriptive, more focused on revealing things as they are than on telling us how to live and what to do. A poem like "The Babies" parodies the very sense of social engagement that it appears to solicit. This effect is in keeping with Strand's use of poetic language. Though he learned much from Walt Whitman, Strand shows little taste for the Whitmanesque vision of the poet as someone who can address an entire nation about concerns of national identity and destiny. His conception of the poet's role and relationship to an audience is considerably more modest and self-effacing:

> I don't believe poetry is for everyone anymore than I believe roast pork is for everyone. Poetry is demanding. It takes a certain amount of getting used to, a period of initiation. Only those people who are willing to spend *time* with it really get anything out of it. . . . I think all you can do is address yourself to ideas and issues that you yourself are concerned about.

The history of Strand's development as a poet is the history of his reading. Regarding his early work, critics point to the importance of Theodore Roethke and Elizabeth Bishop for simplicity of manner, Richard Wilbur for elegance and form, the stories of Borges and the poetry of Carlos Drummond de Andrade for a sense of the fantastical and phantasmagoric. In *Darker* (1970), Strand revealed a new and strong interest in the eighteenth century English poet Christopher Smart (an interest that he shared with his contemporary plain stylist W. S. Merwin). Smart's long poem-journal *Jubilate Agno* (1758–1763) is a litany of prayers, meditations, and prophecies. Its long lines and high supplicatory tone, its invocation of myth and biblical history, its penchant for maxim and apothegm, its meandering and discontinuous narrative line, are all evident in the major poems of Strand's new book. Experimenting with Smart's manner and voice, Strand said to David Brooks, "was one of the ways in which I broke the tyranny of writing those pseudo-narratives that I was writing in *Reasons for Moving.*" He was ready for a change: "I wanted some kind of rhetorical accretive effect in my poetry, rather than the plain, narrative, reductive, pinched thing I had been doing."

Strand's lines have become longer, more spacious, and make their impression through repetition and refrain rather than through the concentrated chessboard rhetorical strategies of his earlier lyrics. "The New Poetry Handbook," by its very title, promises a new manner and style, one that suggests an axiomatic wisdom based on fixed principles. But the title again is ironic. In "Notes on the Craft of Poetry," Strand writes that he is very wary of any formalizing of the rules of poetic creation. The "Handbook," on one level, makes light of the rise of the creative writing workshop in American colleges and universities and of the notion that good writing can be taught. Strand's precepts are anything but commonplace and prescriptive, and they invoke exactly the sorts of mysteries that a "handbook" ought to be solving: "If a man lets his poems go naked / he shall fear death," and "If a man fears death, / he shall be saved by his poems."

The tone here is as representative for this volume as the envoi "Eating Poetry" was in *Reasons for Moving*. "Eating Poetry" invokes a detached, fantastical, and wholly literary world, one that is made of poems and the reading of poems. The poem suggests a potential menace in the extreme solipsism of the speaker: he says, "I romp with joy in the bookish dark," without showing much concern for the meaning and impact of his reckless abandon. But in this new envoi, Strand seems attentive to just these concerns of meaning and effect. His prescriptive handbook points to those mysteries that lie beyond the reach of the language in which they are embodied. The poem exists not to solve those mysteries, but to suggest their force. With its use of supposition and a repetitive cause-and-effect construction (if this, then that), "The New Poetry Handbook" would seem to argue that poems can have an actual effect, that there are real consequences for our actions as readers and writers. When we consider the potential that Strand's vision in this book has for highlighting our impotence in the contemporary world, and when we think of his own reluctance to claim a political and social advantage for his poems, this tacit expression of the supplicatory and conjuring powers of verse takes on a subversive meaning and authority of its own.

In *Darker* we also witness a change in focus. The poems are, for one, darker. Death is a conspicuous presence here, a good deal more so than in the earlier poems. Richard Howard writes that "Strand is both nervous and morbid, and a consideration of finality is his constant project." What Strand says in "My Life" is true of the book in general:

> I grow into my death.
> My life is small
> and getting smaller.

In "The Sleep," Strand lists the varieties of repose that we experience, and ends with the most intimate and personal:

> And there is the sleep that demands I lie down and be fitted to the dark that comes upon me like another skin in which I shall never be found, out of which I shall never appear.

Coupled with the awareness expressed throughout these poems that "The future is not what it used to be" ("The Way It Is") is a clearer vision of the self as existing, by its very nature, everywhere in chains. We are caught up in ourselves, in all senses of the word, self-absorbed, entangled, trapped. Behind many of these poems is a Chekhovian vision of a long row of days, each one the same, each one showing us the limits of who we are and who we may be. Strand summarizes such a life in "The Hill":

> One foot in front of the other. The hours
> pass.
> One foot in front of the other. The years pass.
> The colors of arrival fade.
> That is the way I do it.

In the best of moments, our impotence can be a kind of grim repose. Strand writes in "Coming to This,"

> Coming to this
> has its rewards: nothing is promised,
> nothing is taken away.
> We have no heart or saving grace,
> no place to go, no reason to remain.

But at other times he experiences our condition as a form of imprisonment. "The Remains," for example, suggests an identification between the self and a Möbius strip:

I empty myself of the names of others. I
  empty my pockets.
I empty my shoes and leave them beside the
  road. . . .
Time tells me what I am. I change and I am
  the same.
I empty myself of my life and my life
  remains.

The use of refrain and repetition, as in a continuous litany, represents our sense of coming and going back to the same facts and the same conditions. In "Giving Myself Up," Strand seems to "give up" on losing himself:

I give up my eyes which are glass eggs.
I give up my tongue.
I give up my mouth which is the constant
  dream of my tongue.
I give up my throat which is the sleeve of
  my voice.

Throughout *Darker*'s expressions of our general condition, we notice a heightened note of the personal and intimate, particularly in the third and last section of the book, "My Life by Somebody Else." Although there is no increased appetite in these poems for personal information or factual detail, there is something less allegorical, less fabular, about them. The events they attend to seem more immersed in the credible details of the ordinary world. Family, for example, makes an appearance in "'The Dreadful Has Already Happened'":

The relatives are leaning over, staring
  expectantly.
They moisten their lips with their tongues.
  I can feel
them urging me on. I hold the baby in the
  air.
Heaps of broken bottles glitter in the sun.

A small band is playing old fashioned
  marches.
My mother is keeping time by stamping her
  foot.
My father is kissing a woman who keeps
  waving
to somebody else. There are palm trees.

In *Darker* we begin to leave behind those poems that seem to remove or estrange us from our familiar world. More and more Strand will be staying closer to home, showing us what is most otherworldly about it.

Critics generally agree that Strand's next book marked a turning point. "The career of Mark Strand appears to have two distinct phases," Peter Stitt wrote in 1983. "In what we may call the later poems . . . Strand writes concretely of remembered places and people. In the early poems . . . the real world is held very much at arm's length." *The Story of Our Lives* (1973) is generally considered the first in this next stage, and though reviews of the book were somewhat mixed, there was no doubt in readers' minds that it represented a departure. Robert Miklitsch called it "one of the most original books of poetry to appear in years." Strand himself talked of it more as a transitional work. There is more evidence here of actual personal experience than we are accustomed to seeing in his poems.

"Elegy for My Father," for instance, resembles the earlier poems in its struggle on an existential level with experiences of loss and grief. At the same time, it conveys the feeling of a personal conversation. It is as though the poet were addressing his observations directly to his father:

Why are you going?
*Because nothing means much to me
  anymore.*
Why are you going?
I don't know. I have never known.
How long shall I wait for you?
*Do not wait for me. I am tired and I want
  to lie down.*
Are you tired and do you want to lie down?
Yes, I am tired and I want to lie down.

We don't get the feeling here that Strand is being more revealing or more personal to us, but rather that he is being more personal or open towards himself and his own memories and reflections, and that we are overhearing for a moment a quiet conversation that he is having with his own inner voices.

The title of the book is significant. Most of Strand's poems are stories of a sort, parables, exempla, lyrical vignettes, and cameos. *The Story of Our Lives* is the first book that offers a series of extended narratives. There are only eight poems in the book as a whole, and the four longer poems (including "Elegy for My Father") average eight pages in length. We may have previously encountered the characters whose stories are told—they feel self-conscious, limited, and unable to act or change who they are—but Strand goes much further than merely to recount, this time in longer stories, a litany of our inertias. *The Story of Our Lives* is also the first of Strand's works that seems to be looking hard for a window of opportunity and of transcendence. These poems not only tell stories about our lives, but also reveal our lives as being stories themselves. We have seen, even as early as *Sleeping with One Eye Open*, how Strand has an intuitive sense of our reality as constructed, fabricated, written. He has not until now, however, turned to the relations between living and storytelling in his search for a means of liberation and self-creation.

In the title poem, the characters find themselves living their lives as though they were writing and reading them. They have a simultaneous sense of freedom and imprisonment. They feel the power that their words have in a world of words:

> We sit beside each other on the couch,
> reading about the couch.
> We say it is ideal.
> It is ideal.

At the same time, they experience a curious separation from themselves, finding everything they do, as they do it, already written. They feel the weight of that text, the weight of being caught inescapably in a world of words. They are incapable of writing their lives beyond the writing that they must read. The book that they live is both their redemption and their curse. They read in the end:

> *The book would have to be written*
> *and would have to be read.*
> *They are the book and they are*
> *nothing else.*

"The Untelling" offers a similar story, but from the perspective of memory. A character recalls a scene from early childhood: a luminous moment at evening, a lake, a lawn, a child with his young cousins, uncles, and aunts stretched out on the grass, a woman "in a long yellow dress," a man running across the grounds holding a piece of paper (these are in fact transformed fragments of Strand's earliest memory). The poet sitting at his desk over a sheet of blank paper trying to recreate the reality of the scene. He tries out various versions, plying and manipulating the elements of his story, but finds something always missing, always vanishing ahead of his approach:

> It bothered him,
> as if too much had been said.
> He would have preferred
> the lake without a story,
> or no story and no lake.
> His pursuit was a form of evasion:
> the more he tried to uncover
> the more there was to conceal
> the less he understood.
> If he kept it up,
> he would lose everything.

What is required, then, is a curious kind of "untelling" that would communicate what cannot be spoken. That telling might be a poem like this one that untells, retells, erases, and recreates different versions of the vanishing past. But the poem's most lasting impression—which is also perhaps its most effective way of untelling its story—is its blurring of the boundaries between the real life of the storyteller and the imagined life of the story. The teller's life seems to become a version itself of what he has told even as he tells it. The self and the poem, the life written and the life lived, become deeply enmeshed, mutually limiting and liberating. "It is the act of telling itself," Robert Miklitsch writes, "the lost self cast into the form of the imagined self, into the world of the poem, that is meaning." The imagined self cast into the world of the poem: this double projection is how Strand's poems bring an element of open space and possibility to the lives that we imagine for ourselves.

The Late Hour and *The Monument* (both published in 1978) represent two alternative lines of development that issued from *The Story of Our Lives*. One development was in the direction of personal memory, the other was in the direction of literature, its function in our lives.

The Late Hour contains more of what we might call personal poems than any other of Strand's books. Though they are not autobiographical in the strict sense, there are poems entitled "My Son" (modeled after a poem by Carlos Drummond de Andrade) and "For Jessica, My Daughter." The section entitled "Poor North" contains a series of childhood reminiscences and reflections. These explore sensations of loss and desire, the vulnerability and impermanence of memory; they search for traces of memory in the lived moment, its simultaneous presence and absence there. In "Pot Roast," for example, Strand emphasizes the solidity of memory, and in "The Garden," its mercurial nature:

> And now
> I taste it again.
> The meat of memory.
> The meat of no change.
> I raise my fork in praise,
> and I eat.
> . . . . .
> Even as you lean over this page,
> late and alone, it shines; even now
> in the moment before it disappears.

These are lovely and quiet poems, recalling something of the still waters of childhood that they speak of. The poems are more open, relaxed, and approachable—Strand called them "less riddling" in his interview with Brooks—and in a sense sadder in their evocation of the luminous ordinariness of our lives. They are the signs of the deeper and more spacious elegiac cadences of his later poems.

Yet Strand had reservations about these poems. He said to Katharine Coles,

> I never felt that poems about my childhood and my family were my poems or poems I really wanted to write. They were poems that were generated by the atmosphere of American poetry at the time. Lots of poets I admired were writing about their childhoods. So I wanted to be a member of the childhood club. But I discovered I didn't have much of a gift for it.

The gift he pursued in *The Monument* was in an altogether different literary direction: translation.

Strand had been active as a translator throughout his career, but was particularly so in the 1970s, publishing *New Poetry of Mexico* (1970), *18 Poems from the Quechua* (1971), *The Owl's Insomnia, Poems by Rafael Alberti* (1973), *Souvenir of the Ancient World, Selected Poems of Carlos Drummond de Andrade* (1976), and *Another Republic: 17 European and South American Writers* (1976). The strong allegorical and otherworldly quality of the poems of Drummond de Andrade and the fiction of Borges played a significant role in his early development as a poet. But for Strand, the idea of translation itself was also important. Like the self that Strand wrote about—divided, self-conscious, both self and other—translations are in a sense texts that are not themselves: they are carried across from their original language into another state.

As translation means "to be borne across," to be translated, then, is to accomplish a kind of immortality, and this struggle for translation is the work of *The Monument*. Speaking to us of its desire to live beyond itself, the text calls out to the one who is projected into the future, the one who will make it into more than it is: "Tell me that my ugly tomb, my transcending gesture, my way into the next world, your world, my world made by you, you the future of me, my future, my features translated, tell me that it will improve." How fitting that many of the fifty-two untitled sections of the book include epigraphs and quotations and extended passages from other writers, which the present text variously seems to translate, measure up to, and weigh itself against. The work becomes a hall of mirrors, reflecting on itself as a text and on all the texts that lie within and beyond it.

The experiment of *The Monument* represents an important stage in Strand's development, for it suggests that the ideal or mythic self that we may imagine, the one that expresses who we are in the form of a possible life, is becoming increasingly defined by the aspirations, limits, and nature of the living text in which it is brought into being. In an interview with Grace Cavalieri, Strand revealed a personal stake in the significance and limitations of translation: "And so it's that I want to be translated—not just what I've written—but I want to be translated in such a way that I can live infinitely . . . I want not translation but continuous life."

Strand's *Selected Poems,* which appeared in 1980, included five new poems (including one of Strand's finest in the mode of transcendent reminiscence, "Shooting Whales"), but over nine years passed before the publication of Strand's next full book of poems, *The Continuous Life* (1990). For about five of those years, Strand felt that he was far away from poetry. The eighties were in part a period of retooling, but they were not by any means an inactive time.

For Strand, it was a decade of prose that saw the publication of three children's books, two books on art, and a volume of short stories. It is no negative comment on the works themselves if we see each of them as a continuation of the poetry by other means. Each work reinforces, in one way or another, our sense of what is central to Strand's poetic achievement. In *Mr. and Mrs. Baby and Other Stories* (1985), we recognize the journalistic, at times almost deadpan reportage, the elements of an otherworldly psychological allegory, and in particular the pervasive ironic and comic vision. The stories are a powerful indictment of materialism and consumerism in contemporary society. The children's book *Rembrandt Takes a Walk* (1986)–in which the Dutch painter "comes down" from his painting and accompanies a young boy in a walk through the city—reveals a continuing interest in the power of artistic vision to "descend" into our world, make itself manifest, and transform the conditions of our lives.

Strand, however, did not leave prose behind when he again began publishing books of poetry in the 1990s. He authored several fine essays, most notable of which are his "Fantasia on the Relations between Poetry and Photography" (1990) and his 1990 address as Poet Laureate to the Library of Congress, "Views of the Mysterious Hill: The Appearance of Parnassus in American Poetry" (published in 1991). One senses in essays such as these, and especially in his art criticism, that Strand is attempting in part to articulate the aspirations of his own art as he seeks to characterize the vision of those poets and artists he most admires.

Reviewers spoke enthusiastically of the Strand who reappeared in 1990 with *The Continuous Life.* Strand's voice had been enlarged somehow: his lines are roomier, more spacious, with more light and air in them; they reveal an expanded breadth of concern and vision. These poems are more holistic, more communal, more absorbed in the relations and struggles of everyday life. At the same time—and here once again is Strand's unique genius—the poems are more deeply immersed than ever before in the literature of the past. In an interview with Cavalieri, Strand spoke of "rereading . . . Virgil and Robert Fitzgerald's splendid translation, and rereading the *Iliad* and the *Odyssey*": "They had a lot to do with my newer poems." Armed with neoclassical voices and allusions, Strand returned to and freshened his great theme—the desire to translate ordinary life and experience into the continuous life of song.

He describes this desire in "The Idea":

For us, too, there was a wish to possess
Something beyond the world we knew,
beyond ourselves,
Beyond our power to imagine, something
nevertheless
In which we might see ourselves . . .

To those seeking themselves in what lies beyond them, Strand offers poetry. In *The Continuous Life* he has given his readers an extended opportunity to see themselves poetically. He has moved to embrace the ordinary in his poems, but not in such a way that our lives seem unreal there and falsely mimed in the distortions of art. Poetry for Strand is not a distortion of real life. Instead, it gives expression to a quality of permanence and repose that exists within real life. As his poetry comes closer to the ordinary, it shows more and more the poetry that is already a part of our days there.

Strand's publication in 1987 and 1994 of books of art criticism—individual studies of realist painters William Bailey and Edward Hopper—provides us with important clues to an understanding of the poetry he wrote during this period. Although Strand was himself trained as a painter, it was not until the appearance of these two books that readers had an opportunity to consider his craft in relation to his tastes and proclivities in the visual arts. Strand seems to be particularly drawn to those painters whose work evinces a tension between elements of ordinary narrative time (such as indications of age, season, movement, chronology) and tacit expressions of permanence in the particular moment portrayed. In *Hopper,* he writes, we find "two imperatives—the one that urges us to continue and the other that compels us to stay." And elsewhere: "Everything in this painting [*Ground Swell,* 1939] suggests an equilibrium has been reached between the depiction of passage and the more powerful accommodation of stillness." Many of Strand's favorite paintings seem to represent something of that equilibrium, where the passages of real time that we see represented in the moments of ordinary domestic routine seem to partake of the continuous life. He writes of a life that is both itself (ordinary, inexpressive, limited in time and space) and more than itself (representative, luminous, and permanent).

Many of Strand's 1990s poems seem to puzzle out the meaning of that crossing, that momentary accommodation of the infinite in our temporal lives.

Of course, poems too evoke the tension between time and timelessness: we have, on the one hand, the sequential time of word following word and, on the other, those elements of poetic language that seem to effect a kind of stillness or repose. Strand seems always conscious of the poem running out of time and pulling against its own tendency to come to an end. He often dramatizes that tension in the scenes and settings of *The Continuous Life,* perhaps no more so than in the title poem:

. . . Tell the children to come inside,
That your search goes on for something you
lost—a name,
A family album that fell from its own small
matter
Into another, a piece of the dark that might
have been yours,
You don't really know. Say that each of you
tries
To keep busy, learning to lean down close
and hear
The careless breathing of earth and feel its
available
Languor come over you, wave after wave,
sending
Small tremors of love through your brief,
Undeniable selves, into your days, and
beyond.

It is by giving witness ("Tell," "Say"), Strand suggests, that the tension can be transformed. All our experiences of time—the past, the present, the future, continuity, permanence, loss, return, repetition, motion and stillness, progression and repose—become authentic through recognition and invocation. We can become conduits of a sort and make ourselves available to what timeless energies might pass through us.

The potential powers of a poem are such that it might give expression to, and perhaps in some way realize, this transformation into continuous life. The neoclassical "Orpheus Alone" speaks for that potential. As a pre-Homeric mythic figure, Orpheus attests to the continuous life of poetry. The various forms and fictions in which he has appeared make him an ideal figure with which to investigate relations of desire and time. The songs of this classical Ur-poet could redeem the dead and charm god and beast alike. We associate his music with the powers of transformation, or metamorphosis, but Strand has turned to him not to claim these powers as his own, but to review them in the light of twentieth-century skepticism and disbelief.

In his contemporary guise, Orpheus is alone and his role in the world somewhat changed. He might once have been able to take up the broken world

> and put in its place the world
> As he wished it would be, urging its shape
> and measure
> Into speech of such newness that the world
> was swayed.

But that is a poem "which no one recalls anymore." Instead, the greatest poem comes into the world, not as a magical force with transformative powers of its own, but as the world itself, in all its manifestations of permanence and mutability, death and birth. The greatest poem

> Came into the world as the world, out of
> the unsayable,
> Invisible source of all longing to be; it came
> As things come that will perish, to be seen
> or heard
> A while, like the coating of frost or the
> movement
> Of wind, and then no more . . .
> . . . .
> . . . it came in a language
> Untouched by pity, in lines, lavish and dark,
> Where death is reborn and sent into the
> world as a gift,
> So the future, with no voice of its own, nor
> hope
> Of ever becoming more than it will be,
> might mourn.

If Orpheus' last poem changes the world, it changes it in such a way as to make it more of what it is, leaving its longings and perishables intact. The poem becomes transparent to the everyday world, and in so doing gives that world a voice of its own.

Dark Harbor: A Poem (1993)—divided into forty-five Roman-numeraled sections—is Strand's best book as of 1995. He wrote it very quickly, in a rush of creative energy, and in fact ended up publishing only about half of the poems that he had written. The poems do not form a narrative but circle around a set of themes or motifs. In *Dark Harbor,* Strand's engagement with the ordinary moments in our lives, and his transformation of them into myth, into islands of stillness and calm, is complete. Water is one of the dominant symbols in these poems, and even when there is no water mentioned or alluded to, we feel its presence, its influence as a metaphor of freedom and release. Section XIV has us at the edge of the everyday, floating just beyond the reach of its influence, as we prepare ourselves to depart into the myths we imagined we might live by:

> Why are so many of them crowded at the
> rail,
> With the ship still dozing in the harbor?
> And to whom are they waving? It has been
>
> Years since the stores in town were open,
> Years since the flag was raised in the little
> park,
> Since the cloud behind the nearby mountain
> moved.

The magic of these poems is that we find ourselves as readers already launched into something like the space these passengers seem to long for. Orpheus again is the poet's representative here, wandering quietly among nearly half of the poems in the book. It becomes clear to us that he is working in his accustomed place, halfway between this and a remoter world, and that once again he is trying to bring that more distant and timeless realm back to life.

For Orpheus, song is life; the journey out into the dark harbors of experience is also a journey out to the end of the poem, a journey to the end of singing. Strand's poems have always seemed conscious of their own closed spaces, but here they seem particularly so, as passages from I, XI, XXXII, and XXXVIII attest:

> . . . for the ash
> Of the body is worthless and goes only so
>   far
> . . . the particular way our voices
> Erased all signs of the sorrow that had been,
> Its violence, its terrible omens of the end?
>
> An understanding that remains unfinished,
>   unentire,
> Largely imperfect so long as it lasts
>
> A fragment, a piece of a larger intention,
>   that is all.

The note of lamentation or complaint in the phrases "goes only so far," "omens of the end," "so long as it lasts," and "that is all" makes it almost seem that, as the poem concludes, it cannot help but draw discreet attention to the fact of its own imminent extinction. Yet, by using something like picture windows on the interior walls of the dissipating structure, Strand also shows a way beyond it.

Strand's work in the 1990s is increasingly absorbed in echo and allusion. Few other poets writing in English today so constantly suggest to the reader the tug of other voices, that sense of the ear reaching after some half-remembered expression, line, or phrase. Listen, for example, to Strand's variation in section II of Richard Wilbur's "the heaviest nuns walk in a pure floating / Of dark habits": "everyone dreams of floating / Like angels in sweet-smelling habits." This sort of aural cue can be found everywhere in the book. Strand's echoes of Stevens and W. B. Yeats, of Ovid, Dante, and Milton, enlarge the poem within its own space. For Strand, the presence of other poets in a poem do not weight it down or burden it, but rather open it up. When we hear echoes of other poets that we cannot quite name, we have a feeling of entering into spaces we did not know existed. They are in a sense unreal spaces, invisible and remote, except for that feeling of the mind casting off, being drawn away toward an unsuspected voice. As we read toward an inevitable conclusion, we feel we are already elsewhere, already listening to a choir of voices that is not a part of time, in which each voice has its permanent place.

And so these poems deliver on the promise of their subject. Throughout *Dark Harbor*, we are witness to groups of lost souls wandering in circles, trying to rise above their own shadows and not being able to, having to leave but wanting to remain, setting out into their dark harbors while trying to wrest from that remoteness and melancholy a sense of liberation and permanence. But in Orpheus' song and journey, that dark harbor is already an afterworld. We find ourselves participating, feeling nostalgia for the simple places and affections of our days and recognizing the sting of regret for lost chances and things that we left unsaid. In section XLV, Orpheus sings,

> . . . there were many poets
> Wandering around who wished to be alive
>   again.
> They were ready to say the words they had
>   been unable to say—
>
> Words whose absence had been the silence
>   of love,
> Of pain, and even of pleasure.

As Orpheus sings, the sufferings of the underworld become the accomplishments of our own restless passage in time—our aimless wandering, our straining against the shades of ourselves. Just as the poems echo into unseen rooms, we feel the enlargements of that afterlife, break through to it as we depart. And yet we are still here, not on the fatal river Styx, but on a darkening harbor. Strand's orphic enchantments simply return us to where we are, and help us to long for the things that we have in this world as we pilot among them.

Strand is a poet of mystery and the unknown. In all their craft and evocation, the poems harbor their mysteries and allow us to suspend ourselves within them for a while as we look to understand the relations between lived experience and the mythic shapes we give to it in poetry. He began his career attempting to invoke those mysteries, in part, through a form of modernist psychological irony—trying to give the self away or make nothing of it in order to transcend its limitations. Now he has become heir apparent to Wallace Stevens' "interior paramour"—that dweller in the imagination—looking to find safe haven for that self in the beguiling inward spaces of the poem and struggling to understand what it might mean to dwell in them. Strand's concluding remarks on Edward Hopper began this essay. We might end with the poet's concluding remarks on the painter William Bailey; lines that certainly summarize the achievement of Mark Strand himself at the end of the twentieth century: "His reality transcends our common experience, it has no visible moment of inception. His paintings are grandiose and hieratic, self-contained, and secretive. . . . They present us with a version of timelessness, of things disposed to perfection."

Selected Bibliography

WORKS OF MARK STRAND

POETRY

Sleeping with One Eye Open. Iowa City: Stone Wall, 1964.

Reasons for Moving. New York: Atheneum, 1968.

Darker. New York: Atheneum, 1970.

The Story of Our Lives. New York: Atheneum, 1973.

The Late Hour. New York: Atheneum, 1978.

The Monument. New York: Ecco, 1978.

Selected Poems. New York: Atheneum, 1980; Knopf, 1990.

The Continuous Life. New York: Knopf, 1990.

Dark Harbor: A Poem. New York: Knopf, 1993.

PROSE

The Contemporary American Poets: American Poetry since 1940. Edited by Mark Strand. New York: New American Library, 1969.

Art of the Real: Nine American Figurative Painters. Edited and introduced by Mark Strand. New York: C. N. Potter, 1983.

Mr. and Mrs. Baby and Other Stories. New York: Knopf, 1985.

William Bailey. New York: Abrams, 1987.

The Golden Ecco Anthology: 100 Great Poems of the English Language. Edited by Mark Strand. Hopewell, N.J.: Ecco, 1994.

Hopper. Hopewell, N.J.: Ecco, 1994.

UNCOLLECTED PROSE

"Landscape and the Poetry of Self." *Prose,* 6: 169–183 (Spring 1973).

"Notes on the Craft of Poetry." In *Claims for Poetry.* Edited by Donald Hall. Ann Arbor: University of Michigan Press, 1982.

"Fantasia on the Relations between Poetry and Photography." *Grand Street,* 9: 96–107 (Winter 1990).

"Slow Down for Poetry." *New York Times Book Review,* September 15, 1991, pp. 1, 36–37.

"Views of the Mysterious Hill: The Appearance of Parnassus in American Poetry." *Gettysburg Review,* 4: 669–679 (Autumn 1991).

MANUSCRIPT PAPERS

Lilly Library, University of Indiana, Bloomington.

TRANSLATIONS

18 Poems from the Quechua. Cambridge, Mass.: H. Ferguson, 1971.

New Poetry of Mexico. Selected and annotated by Octavio Paz, Ali Chumacero, Jose Emilio Pacheco, and Homero Aridjis. Edited and with translations by Mark Strand. New York: Dutton, 1970.

The Owl's Insomnia. Poems by Rafael Alberti. New York: Atheneum, 1973.

Souvenir of the Ancient World: Selected Poems of Carlos Drummond de Andrade. New York: Antaeus, 1976.

Another Republic: 17 European and South American Writers. Edited by Charles Simic and Mark Strand. New York: Ecco, 1976.

Travelling in the Family: Selected Poems. By Carlos Drummond de Andrade. Edited by Thomas Colchie and Mark Strand, with additional translations by Elizabeth Bishop and Gregory Rabassa. New York: Random House, 1986.

BIOGRAPHICAL AND CRITICAL STUDIES

Angel, Ralph. "In the Shadow Theatre." Review of *The Monument. American Poetry Review,* 21: 49–50 (May/June 1992).

Armand, Octavio. "Writing as Erasure, the Poetry of Mark Strand." Translated by Carol Maier. In *Strand: A Profile.* Edited by Frank Graziano. Iowa City: Grilled Flowers, 1979. Pp. 49–63.

Benfey, Christopher. "The Enigma of Arrival." Review of *Dark Harbor: A Poem. New Republic,* March 8, 1993, pp. 34–37.

Bensko, John. "Reflexive Narration in Contemporary American Poetry: Some Examples from Mark Strand, John Ashbery, Norman Dubie, and Louis Simpson." *Journal of Narrative Technique,* 16: 81–96 (Spring 1986).

Berger, Charles. "Poetry Chronicle: Amy Clampitt, Louise Gluck, Mark Strand." Review of *The Continuous Life. Raritan,* 10: 119–133 (Winter 1991).

Bloom, Harold. "Dark and Radiant Peripheries: Mark Strand and A. R. Ammons." *Southern Review,* 8: 133–149 (January 1972).

Bradley, George. "Lush and Lean." Review of *The Continuous Life. Partisan Review,* 58: 562–565 (Summer 1991).

Brennan, Matthew. "Mark Strand's 'For Her.'" *Notes on Contemporary Literature,* 13: 11–12 (January 1983).

Brooks, David. "The Genuine Remains." In *Strand: A Profile.* Edited by Frank Graziano. Iowa City: Grilled Flowers, 1979. Pp. 67–75.

Cole, Henri. Review of *The Continuous Life. Poetry,* 158: 54–57 (April 1991).

Crenner, James. "Mark Strand: *Darker.*" *Seneca Review,* 2: 84–89 (April 1971).

Donaldson, Jeffery. "The Still Life of Mark Strand's Darkening Harbor." *Dalhousie Review,* 74: 110–124 (Spring 1994).

French, Roberts W. "Eating Poetry: The Poems of Mark Strand." *The Far Point,* 5: 61–66 (1970).

Graziano, Frank, ed. *Strand: A Profile.* Iowa City: Grilled Flowers, 1979.

Howard, Richard. "The Mirror Was Nothing without You." In his *Alone with America: Essays on the Art of Poetry in the United States since 1950.* Enlarged Edition. New York: Atheneum, 1980.

Jackson, Richard. "Charles Simic and Mark Strand: The Presence of Absence." *Contemporary Literature,* 21: 136–145 (1980).

Kirby, David. "The Nature of No One." *Times Literary Supplement,* September 15, 1978, p. 1009.

Kirby, David K. *Mark Strand and the Poet's Place in Contemporary Culture.* Columbia: University of Missouri Press, 1990.

McMichael, James. "Borges and Strand, Weak Henry, Philip Levine." *Southern Review,* 8: 213–224 (January 1972).

Miklitsch, Robert. "Beginnings and Endings: Mark Strand's "The Untelling." *Literary Review,* 21: 357–373 (Spring 1978).

Olsen, Lance. "The Country Nobody Visits: Varieties of Fantasy in Strand's Poetry." In *The Shape of the Fantastic: Selected Essays from the Seventh International Conference on the Fantastic in the Arts.* Edited by Olena H. Saciuk. New York: Greenwood, 1990. Pp. 3–8.

Stitt, Peter. "Stages of Reality: The Mind/Body Problem in Contemporary Poetry." *Georgia Review,* 37: 201–210 (Spring 1983).

INTERVIEWS

Bacchilega, Christina. "An Interview with Mark Strand." *Missouri Review,* 4: 51–64 (Summer 1981).

Brooks, David. "A Conversation with Mark Strand." *Ontario Review,* 8: 23–33 (Spring/Summer 1978).

Cavalieri, Grace. "Mark Strand: An Interview by Grace Cavalieri." *American Poetry Review,* 23: 39–41 (July/August 1994).

Coles, Katharine. "In the Presence of America: A Conversation with Mark Strand." *Weber Studies,* 9: 8–28 (Fall 1992).

Cooper, Philip. "The Waiting Dark: Talking to Mark Strand." *Hollins Critic,* 21: 1–7 (October 1984).

Dodd, Wayne, and Stanley Plumly. "A Conversation with Mark Strand." *Ohio Review,* 13: 54–71 (Winter 1972). Revised and reprinted in *American Poetry since 1960: Some Critical Perspectives.* Edited by Robert B. Shaw. Cheadle, Great Britain: Carcanet, 1973.

Graziano, Frank. "An Interview with Mark Strand." In *Strand: A Profile.* Edited by Frank Graziano. Iowa City: Grilled Flowers, 1979. Pp. 27–48.

Miller, Nolan. "The Education of a Poet: A Conversation between Mark Strand and Nolan Miller." In two parts. *Antioch Review,* 39: 106–118 (Winter 1981) and 39: 181–193 (Spring 1981).

Vine, Robert, and Robert von Hallberg. "A Conversation with Mark Strand." *Chicago Review,* 28: 130–140 (Spring 1977).

ALGERNON CHARLES SWINBURNE
(1837–1909)

IAN FLETCHER

I

SWINBURNE IS NOT a Victorian curiosity, but a highly original poet, an exhilarating metrist; his poetry explores unusual areas of experience, and his lyricism, at its best, is rich and haunting. Yet till very lately he was a notorious critical "case," a synonym almost for a literary disease. In his own lifetime, a German journalist could place him definitively as a "higher degenerate" one of the symptoms being the poet's love of repetition, "echolalia."

And if Swinburne's later fortunes were singular, so was his contemporary reception. His first volume was virtually ignored; his second made him famous; his third was attacked on all sides and the publisher cowed into withdrawing it. *Poems and Ballads* (1866) had violated that high Victorian decorum, the tacit assumption that poetry represented an extension of ethics by other means, its subject matter only what was well above the girdle. Swinburne's earlier lyrics are a breviary of Freudian insights. He gives voice to the dark underside of the Victorian psyche, writing of the aggressive, the cruel, even the demonic aspects of sexual love, and of the suppression or perversion of human instincts by social and religious tyrannies. And in *Atalanta in Calydon* (1865), that great dramatic poem, he arrives at the notion of "the death of the family," the contention that this institution is by nature oppressive and must be superseded by more flexible social forms. Swinburne surely intended to shock his public by anti-Christian gestures and erotic polemics, although such were certainly not the limits of his aims; yet his own succès de scandale engulfed him. Readers were dazzled or repulsed by the violent rhythms or topics of his verse.

Swinburne has also suffered from the familiar slump of reputation in the years succeeding an author's death—the fate of George Bernard Shaw offers an obvious parallel. And before his fortunes could recover he became involved in the diffused attack of the 1920's on Victorianism in general. They were further soured by the critical propaganda for an autonomous "modern" movement in poetry, which was conducted largely by the "modern" poets themselves. T. S. Eliot and Ezra Pound, for example, were understandably anxious to secure themselves an audience, and that meant displacing their immediate predecessors. As Harold Bloom puts it, the poet *creates* his predecessors (by constructing fictions of literary history), but "the relation of . . . the new poet to his predecessors cannot be cleansed of polemics or rivalry," and this rivalry stems from anxiety about poetic identity.

Such a strategy was intended to mask the fact that Eliot was himself a deeply romantic poet, and to suggest that his poetry had more in common with the seventeenth-century metaphysical poets, with their wit and wordplay, than with the allegedly decaying romanticism of the late nineteenth century (the French, Charles Baudelaire and the symbolists, were absolvable). This involved the creation of a canon: Eliot called it "the main stream." Eliot was to describe his early essays as "a by-product of my private poetry-workshop; or a prolongation of the thinking that went on to the formation of my own verse," and this late candor sanctioned the admission of some of the poets who had been formerly excluded from "the main stream." In America a race of literary journalists and "new," close-reading, and not infrequently neo-Christian, critics arose, and since it had already been agreed that word-play, complexity, and ambiguity were not to be found in Swinburne, he was largely absent from their searching analyses. In England, F. R. Leavis and his adepts had their version of literary history. The one great poet of the later Victorian period, greater than Alfred Lord Tennyson or Robert Browning, was Gerard Manley Hopkins, and had not Hopkins himself, with the clairvoyance of genius, said the last but one word on Swinburne: "a perfect style must be of its age. In virtue of this archaism and on other grounds [Swinburne] must rank with the medievalists," and did not Swinburne suffer also from the defect of having "no real understanding of rhythm"? Paradoxically Hopkins and Swinburne now appear as the most extreme of the Victorian poets, though extreme in radically different ways. But by a further paradox, Hopkins, response to the "pied" particularity of things extends that stroking in of details so frequent in Tennyson, Browning, and Dante Gabriel Rossetti. Hopkins is, indeed, as one critic has suggested, more Victorian than the Victorians in his inspired clutter of detail. Swinburne, however, moves toward music and symbolist dream in attempting to create a closed world, without objects, through language. This point was made in Eliot's casuistical defense of Swinburne:

> The poetry [of *Poems and Ballads*] is not morbid, it is not erotic, it is not destructive. These are adjectives which can be applied to the material, the human feelings, which in Swinburne's case do not exist. The morbidity is not ofhuman feeling but of language. Language in a healthy state presents the object, is so close to the object that the two are identified. (*The Sacred Wood*, p. 149)

For Eliot, Swinburne's verse is sui generis. But his description does not take account of its characteristic tension between *subject matter* and *surface*, which is the outcome of a moral horror different in quality but not in kind from that of Baudelaire, nor does it admit that word-play and complexity are to be encountered in Swinburne.

The comparison with Baudelaire is crucial, because of the French poet's influence. There are affinities: woman as emblem of the unattainable; the "quarrel with God"; the inversions of *Les Litanies de Satan*, recalling a common use of litanies of supplication, worship, and terror in contexts of disgust and revolt. There is a shared distrust of overt morality as falsifying experience, a shared awareness of ennui as the human condition. The distinctions, however, are sharp. Unlike Swinburne, Baudelaire possessed a gift for luminous concision, and his ennui is counterpointed by an energy that is by no means always frenetic. Baudelaire is also more aware of the tang and resonance of objects, and this enables him to correlate outer and inner landscapes. This particularly enriches his interpretations of the modern city, with its workmen, prostitutes, and the numerous lives momentarily and obliquely touching his consciousness. William Wordsworth had presented London as an infernal carnival in the sixth book of *The Prelude*. Baudelaire's Paris is infernal also, but Wordsworth's healing image of the blind beggar is replaced by the procession of seven old men through the dirty fog, who mysteriously embody the intimate nightmare of the outer world. To this nothing in Swinburne corresponds. If on one occasion at least he evokes an industrial landscape,[1] the human figures evade him. The great Italian poet Gabriele D'Annunzio was to be influenced by Swinburne and himself creates

1. Such nights as these in England, the small town
Chatters and scrawls its purpose out in brown,
Searing with steam the hill's dead naked shape;
By juts of hurt impatience, let's escape
Quick sighs of fire from chimnied engine-works.
(Unpublished fragment)

a largely linguistic world. Objects, though "things" in D'Annunzio's best work possess an intense sensual presence, as it were, momentary incarnations of some panic energy in nature. D'Annunzio too can marvelously use older forms and masters; but, unlike Swinburne, he has a huge vocabulary and can be the subtler metrist.

There is, of course, an indictment for his admirers to answer. If Swinburne radiates some of the signs of genius—energy, abundance, and a powerful literary identity—his range of subject seems slender. The metrical effects, surprising, stunning even at first, gradually dull the response by reliance on anapests and iambs; the initial effect of wildness is eventually tamed by patterns of expectation; unlike Baudelaire, Swinburne did not dislocate his meters, while his alliterations were continuous, brash, and self-indulgent. The poet has a harem of words to which he remains depressingly faithful: his vocabulary is often heavily biblical, with a manneristic profusion of God, hell, serpents, stings, rods, flames, and thunders, a surprising characteristic in one who was so determinedly a hammer of the Christians. Swinburne's muse is indeed a kind of inverted Balaam: he curses God in the tones of an Old Testament prophet out of a job, or one perhaps resisting the burdens of office. And the subjects of Swinburne's verse seem to melt into one subject. Whether he is exploring a pungent sadomasochistic psychology or the sea as mother figure; extolling the liberation of Italy as emblem of man's liberation from all tyrannies, religious or political; or sounding the bracing moral suasions of the Navy League: it makes little difference. The noxious rhythms, the vocabulary, blurred and generalized, persist, so that we can barely tell if we are meant to admire a battleship or a breast. A. E. Housman, one of Swinburne's best and wittiest critics, sums it up: "The sea, like babies and liberty, went into the sausage machine into which he crammed anything and everything, round goes the handle and out of the other end comes . . . noise." Housman admired some of the poems, but considered that

> there is no reason why they should begin where they do orend where they do; there is no reason why the middleshould be in the middle; there is hardly a reason why, having once begun, they should ever end at all; and it would bepossible to rearrange the stanzas which compose them inseveral different orders without lessening their coherencyor impairing their effect.

But Tennyson's comment has an equal aptness: "He is a reed through which all things blow into music."

The most serious charge against Swinburne is that his insights seem always to move toward the peripheral, the immature. His work resounds with echoes from his wide reading. Besides the Bible, there are the classics, Jacobean drama, the continental literatures, the border ballads. But literature fashioned out of other literature is finite. Swinburne was sometimes a deliberate, often highly accomplished pasticheur; he was also a clever parodist. His pastiche and his parody can be readily enjoyed, but what of involuntary parody? Too often the poetry he proffers as original reads like self-parody or self-echo. In displaying such "Alexandrian" symptoms, he is not, of course, alone. Much Victorian poetry is self-consciously literary, abstracted even from the more formalized gestures of Victorian communication. But there is no poet whose style is so deliberate a literary mosaic. Even when Swinburne seems to speak most directly and feelingly to his reader, as in this passage from "The Triumph of Time"' he feels in quotation marks:

> "What should such fellows as I do?" Nay,
> My part were worse if I chose to play;
> For the worst is this after all; if they knew
> me,
> Not a soul on earth would pity me.[2]
> (st. 3)

Understanding of one's state and acceptance of humiliation should not, incidentally, be confused with self-pity.

2. All quotations from the works are from *The Complete Works*, 20 vols. (London, 1925–1927).

II

Swinburne is one of England's relatively few upperclass poets. His father, younger son of Sir John Swinburne (the baronetcy went back to 1660), was to achieve the rank of admiral in the British navy; his mother was the fourth daughter of the third earl of Ashburnham. A cousin vividly describes Algernon's first appearance at Eton.

> . . . he stood there between his father and mother, with his wondering eyes fixed upon me! Under his arm he hugged his Bowdler's Shakespeare, a very precious treasure, bound in brown leather....He was strangely tiny. His limbs were small and delicate; and his sloping shoulders looked far too weak to carry his great head, the size of which was exaggerated by the tousled mass of red hair standing almost at right angles to it.[3]

His actual size seems to have been about five feet. The cousin softens this description by referring to Swinburne's voice as "exquisitely soft . . . with a rather sing-song intonation," evidently the vatic, romantic reading voice, which was common to Wordsworth (according to Tom Moore's journal), to Tennyson, and to William Butler Yeats—as the last two have been preserved on record. Other accounts speak of Swinburne's voice rising to an eldritch shrillness, of his dancing steps and continuous vivid movements.

Swinburne's bohemianism, republicanism, and war with God can be viewed as a patrician individualism. This would have seemed less odd two generations earlier, in the regency period. It was mid-Victorian middle-class evangelical values that intensified its provocative qualities. Swinburne located (like Yeats) some of his most deeply felt values under the aristocratic notions of courage, honor, and chivalry. Of his own courage, moral and physical, there can be no doubt: fearless on a horse, he was a passionate swimmer in dangerous seas. Undoubtedly his small size led to a compensatory need to prove himself "manly"—hence his stoical endurance of beatings at Eton, his drinking with the bunch, and his close association with vigorous male personalities.

Much of Swinburne's childhood was spent on the Isle of Wight and at his grandfather's family seat, Capheaton, in Northumberland, a county on the Scots border. Northumberland's bleak spaces, its wildness in sea and wind, its legends and traditional ballads strongly attracted him. Of these last, Swinburne made many imitations, capturing directness, dialect, brutality, and anonymous narrative qualities with assured skill. The softer landscapes of the Isle of Wight passed also into his work. Close to the Swinburne house on that island lived his mother's sister Lady Mary Gordon and her husband, Sir Henry, the admiral's first cousin. Their daughter, Mary Gordon, a tomboyish girl (like Swinburne she rode well), with some gift for literature, was the close companion of his earlier years, probably the central personality in his emotional life, and certainly a muse figure. The two were so closely interrelated that marriage would have been considered dangerous, and Swinburne's physical oddity must have constituted a warning eugenic emblem.

Algernon's wide and intense reading had been initiated by acquiring French and Italian from his mother, but he also read enthusiastically at Capheaton in his grandfather's large library, which contained many French works. His education continued at Eton, to which he was sent in 1849 at the age of twelve. He seems to have become difficult, and after four years left school for three years of private tutoring, going up to Benjamin Jowett's Balliol College, Oxford, in 1856. Swinburne was soon involved with a club called Old Mortality, whose later members were to include Walter Pater and J. A. Symonds.

In 1857 he encountered the manic exuberance of Rossetti, William Morris, and Edward Burne-Jones, who were busy with mural painting at the Oxford Union debating hall. The meeting was decisive in several ways. It confirmed Swinburne's devotion to literature and art. The imagery of the murals was Ar-

3. Edmund Grosse, *The Life of Algernon Charles Swinburne* (London, 1917), p. 319.

thurian, and Swinburne was soon composing Arthurian verse in the naive idiom of Morris' *The Defense of Guenevere* (1858). Like numerous undergraduate groups, Old Mortality then proceeded to a magazine, *Undergraduate Papers*, to which Swinburne with characteristic versatility contributed poetry, an essay on his favorite Elizabethan and Jacobean dramatists, and an amusing mock-review. Jowett, who liked his young men to get along (and on) in the world, tended to disapprove of Swinburne's dedication to poetry. In 1858 and 1859, Swinburne was busy with writing and revising his *Rosamond*, a distinctly Pre-Raphaelite closet play, achieving a second class in moderations, working at a prize poem on the life and death of Sir John Franklin, and experimenting with devout pastiches of Francis Beaumont and John Fletcher, full of their witty sexual perversities as well as his own flagellant fantasias. *Laugh and Lie Down* (1859) plays with the theme of homosexuality, and this was to be repeated in later work. Swinburne's sexual life has been much discussed, the conclusions veering between sadomasochism and homosexuality. Discounting natural tendencies to the homoerotic, latent or displayed in many men, one must distinguish that, to quote Matthew Arnold, from any "descent to the realm of immediate practice." Possibly Swinburne had a playful relationship of this order with Simeon Solomon (whose tastes were unequivocal), and he was undoubtedly attracted to physically strong men. He was fascinated by Theodore Watts-Dunton's seven-year-old nephew in later life and on happier terms with his mother than with his father. Both of his known relationships with women were inconclusive.

With Jowett, Swinburne's later relationship was affectionate enough, but it is probable that the master was involved in Swinburne's departure from Oxford in November 1860. The publication that year of two plays, *The Queen-Mother* and *Rosamond*, may have confirmed Jowett's dubieties. In the following year, Swinburne met a more dangerous mentor: Richard Monckton Milnes, politician, man about town, dim poet, and collector of erotica. It was Milnes who introduced to Swinburne another of his formative influences, the marquis de Sade. In 1862 Swinburne published poetry and criticism in the *Spectator*, including his pioneering article on Baudelaire. In London he acquired a reputation as a delphic talker, a genius. To an American observer he appeared as "a tropical bird, high-crested, long-beaked, quick-moving, with rapid utterance and screams of humour, quite unlike any English lark or nightingale." For a time he joined Rossetti in that bizarre ménage at 16 Cheyne Walk, with its menagerie and artists, models. The mythologizing of Rossetti and his associates was already beginning, but the story of Solomon and Swinburne sliding naked down the banisters and Rossetti roaring at them for disturbing his painting has at least a typical truth. Rossetti's relationship to Swinburne was partly that of master to disciple, and they shared memories of Rossetti's wife, Lizzie, who had committed suicide in 1862 and to whom Swinburne had been chivalrously devoted. In a friendly way, however, Rossetti soon indicated that he wished to terminate the cotenancy.

Between 1862 and 1865, Swinburne was perfecting *Poems and Ballads*. His main models were the meters of Greek poetry, Percy Bysshe Shelley, Baudelaire, William Blake, and a discovery that he probably owed to Rossetti and greeted with the same levity and admiration he accorded to the "divine" marquis. This was the doctor from Georgia in the American "old South," Thomas Holley Chivers, transcendentalist friend of Edgar Allan Poe, from whose poems those of Chivers are sometimes indistinguishable. Chivers' headlong meters are to be found in volumes of strange title, such as *Eonchs of Ruby* and *Nacoochee*. Very close to the note almost of burlesque in Swinburne's "Dolores":

> Cold eyelids that hide like a jewel
>   Hard eyes that grow soft for an hour;
> The heavy white limbs, and the cruel
>   Red mouth like a venomous flower;
> (st. 1)

is this from Chivers' "Lily Adair":

> Her eyes, lily-lidded, were azure,
> Cerulean, celestial, divine—
> Suffused with the soul-light of pleasure,
> Which drew all the soul out of mine.

even if Swinburne could barely emulate those languid rhyming vowels of the southern states.

In 1863 Swinburne completed *Chastelard*, the first part of a trilogy devoted to his admired Mary Stuart, though the play was not to be published for another two years. In the autumn of that year, he was staying with the Gordons on the Isle of Wight, helping Mary write her *Children of the Chapel*, a romance full of flagellation scenes, and at work on his masterpiece, *Atalanta in Calydon*. From the same year dates what is probably the finest of his lyrical pieces, "The Triumph of Time." It was now perhaps that Swinburne realized there was to be no intimate future with Mary, that he was condemned to being, as he put it in the words of Mary Stuart's rival, Elizabeth, "but barren stock." Mary Gordon was married two years later to a middle-aged military man, who lived in the north of Scotland. There were no meetings and no surviving letters for another twenty-five years. Already Swinburne had begun his brilliant study of Blake, concluded a version of his novel *Love's Cross Currents*, and proceeded some way with another novel, *Lesbia Brandon*, but he had also begun to drink excessively.

Of *The Queen-Mother* and *Rosamond*, two notices only have been traced, both unfavorable; but with the publication of *Atalanta in Calydon* in 1865, Swinburne achieved immediate fame. Milnes is supposed to have engineered a program for publicizing the book, made more attractive by Rossetti's subtle and original binding, with its asymmetrical Celtic and Greek decorative forms. The following year Swinburne published *Poems and Ballads* (the contents of which were mostly earlier than *Atalanta*). One or two reviewers defended Swinburne's outspokenness, but even John Morley, later a friend, who was free from the familiar Victorian notion that art should idealize the actual to promote public and domestic pieties, described the poet as "the libidinous laureate of a pack of satyrs" and asked "whether there is really nothing in woman worth singing about except 'quivering flanks' . . . 'splendid supple thighs' . . . 'stinging and biting'?" Rossetti, concerned that Swinburne was without normal sexual experience with women, paid Adah Isaacs Menken, burly, busty circus-rider and writer of Whitmanesque verse, the sum of ten pounds to seduce the poet. Menken was honest enough to return the money with a complaint that echoed Morley's: "I can't make him understand that biting's no use." However, a change of direction in Swinburne's art, though not in his life, soon occurred. Early in 1867 Swinburne had completed a longish political poem, *A Song of Italy*, and in that same year he had written his "Ode on the Insurrection at Candia." In the following year, he published "Siena" one of those poems that were to form his volume on the liberation of Italy, *Songs Before Sunrise*. An amusing, probably apocryphal story, told by Edmund Gosse, relates how a meeting of Swinburne's friends and associates, including Jowett, Karl Blind, and Giuseppe Mazzini, was convened to discuss "what could be done *with* and *for* Algernon." That there were meetings of family and friends we need not doubt. Swinburne was prepared to transfer his devotions to a lady as exacting as, but nobler than, Dolores, Our Lady of Pain. Or, as Edward Thomas puts it, "Freedom or Liberty was a safer object of worship than Man, because she could never be embodied, though too easily personified." Embodied, however, in the person of Mazzini, she was.

In 1868 appeared *William Blake*, Swinburne's greatest work in prose, in 1871 *Songs Before Sunrise*, and in 1874 his "double-length chronicle play" *Bothwell*; 1876 saw his second essay on Greek tragic poetry, *Erechtheus*, and 1878 the second series of *Poems and Ballads*, which comprised such cardinal pieces as his elegy on Baudelaire, "Ave Atque Vale," and "A Forsaken Garden." The last two were of all Swinburne's volumes the most indulgently reviewed.

Yet now, if we except *Tristram of Lyonesse*, published in 1882 but begun early in the 1870's, a dozen or so poems, and some criticism, his good work was finished, though he was to live for a further thirty-one years. In the 1870's the alcoholic collapses became more frequent. After each crisis Swinburne would rapidly recover in the family home, but on his return to his London rooms the cycle of crisis, collapse, and recovery would recommence. He was becoming lonely. The most serious separation was from Rossetti, whose feelings of guilt, followed by his unhappy affair with Jane Morris and the attacks on the "fleshliness" of his poetry, had finally brought him to attempted suicide. Rossetti's brother advised Swinburne not to approach his old friend and mentor. From 1872 to the time of Rossetti's death in April 1882, there was neither direct communication nor meeting. Increasingly Swinburne became dependent on the last of his father-figures, Theodore Watts (later Watts-Dunton), a solicitor with literary interests, who already had been usefully involved with Rossetti's affairs. In 1879, Watts was sanctioned by the Swinburne family to take Algernon into care: the poet was by then forty-two and for the next thirty years Watts acted as his guardian. Points can be made against Watts: he was probably jealous of Swinburne's old associates and tended to treat the poet as his own property. Swinburne clearly became dependent on him and made no attempt to break out of the suburban prison at The Pines, 2 Putney Hill. Watts also influenced Swinburne in the direction of conformism. The poet's moral tone improved; he foamed at Parnell when in earlier days he had pleaded for the Fenians; he sonorously slanged the Boers and rhapsodized over the jubilee of the Divine Victoria. Extravagantly loyal to friends, he had, however, exhibited moral inflexibility even before The Pines closed round him: in 1873, for example, when Simeon Solomon had been charged with an act of homosexual indecency, Swinburne's reaction had been one of panic-stricken prudery.

Each morning Swinburne would take a long, healthy walk across Putney to the Rose and Crown public house at Wimbledon, South West London, for his single bottle of beer, crooning a rune over every pram he encountered on the outward and return journeys. Indoors, on occasions of celebration, a little wine might be drunk: if the demon poetry had been domesticated, the demon drink had been tamed. Increasing deafness cut off Swinburne still more radically from the outer world, perhaps in the end even from the other inhabitants of The Pines. Inwardly he seems to have been happy; his old friends he may have lost; he had his books. In April of 1909, there came first influenza, then pneumonia, then death.

III

In 1876 when a new edition of *Poems and Ballads* was proposed, their author suggested to his publishers that some poems might be transferred to a volume of earlier work, including also *The Queen-Mother*, *Rosamond*, and various unpublished poems. His proposal, which was not taken up, would have clarified the central themes and tones of *Poems and Ballads*.

That earlier work mostly betrayed Pre-Raphaelite influence: Morris' juxtaposition of dream and violence, in Walter Pater's phrase "the desire of beauty quickened by the sense of death" and, more important, Rossetti's juxtaposition of realism and the supernatural. Rossetti, Jerome J. McGann has convincingly argued, deliberately manipulates Christian imagery in such a way as to exclude traditional responses. By emptying such imagery of its inherited content, Rossetti enables us to experience physical detail "in a new and wholly sensational way," and this relates to his belief in eros rather than agape; that is, in sexual affection exalted as the highest known value (though arguably Rossetti's final position involves, like Swinburne's, the sublimation of the self through art). In Rossetti's poem "The Woodspurge," perfect grief leaves the speaker simply with the irreducible: "The woodspurge has a cup of three." It reads like a failed emblem in the tradition of the seventeenth-century poem of meditation, in which all natural objects lead the mind to a Creator who is also immanent within creation. But here the flower is no easy symbol of Trinitarian hope; what remains to the speaker is "the enormous relevance of the flower's nonsymbolic fact. At that time and in that place the speaker gained a measure of relief from the simple act of observation . . . the poem hints at the mystery . . . in the mere fact of sensory observation." If we compare Rossetti's "The Woodspurge" with Swinburne's "Sundew," we may perceive some distinction between the two poets. Swinburne's poem opens:

> A little marsh-plant, yellow green,
> And pricked at lip with tender red.
> Tread close, and either way you tread
> Some faint black water jets between
> Lest you should bruise the curious head. . . .
> (st. 1)

and ends by rejecting the flower because it does not recall the woman whom the speaker loves. The sundew is actually carnivorous, its tentacles extended in a rosette of leaves. The appearance of precision here misleads, and there is no triumphant conclusion in the sufficiency of sensuous experience. Rossetti's attitude to the Christian associations he undercuts is in general decorous; similarly, Swinburne in "A Christmas Carol," suggested by one of Rossetti's drawings, captures all the solemn candor of the form. "The Two Knights" an early poem omitted from *Poems and Ballads*, altogether capitulates to "The Blessed Damozel," but "The Leper" interestingly marks the transition to Swinburne's personal style. This dramatic lyric, somewhat reminiscent of Morris' early manner, is spoken by a medieval clerk whose love has a masochistic tinge. He panders for the girl he hopelessly loves by bringing the knight she desires to her bedroom in secret. She thanks her "sweet friend" for preserving her from scandal. Then she becomes afflicted with leprosy. All, including

> . . . he inside whose grasp all night
> Her fervent body leapt or lay,
> Stained with sharp kisses red and white,
> Found her a plague to spurn away.
> (st. 17)

The clerk hides her in "wattled" house and tends her:

> Six months, and I sit still and hold
> In two cold palms her cold two feet.
> Her hair, half grey half ruined gold,
> Thrills me and burns me in kissing it.
> Love bites and stings me through, to see
> Her keen face made of sunken bones.
> Her worn-off eyelids madden me,
> That were shot through with purple once.
> (st. 26–27)

Baudelaire's "Une Charogne" is a source, though the tone is distinct. "The Leper" ends with a moral casuistry that echoes Browning's "Porphyria's Lover."

> It may be now she hath in sight
> Some better knowledge; still there clings
> The old question. Will not God do right?
> (st. 35)

The subdued metaphor throughout is "the body of love": communion. The speaker, searching still for total communion, empathizes happily: he is necrophiliac, sacrilegious, vampiristic. These are acts that violate taboo. Taboo's function is to expel the violence of the "sacred," those fierce experiences that unify the self with a higher ground of being and whose violence leads them to be proscribed by society. Taboo inspires both fear and religio-erotic fascination, even adoration. "Invading the sacred" through erotic desire, the Swinburnean hero, as Chris Snodgrass has pointed out, himself becomes a sanctified figure, and paradoxically by such erotic and "perverse" acts reconstitutes and makes once more immediately present the sacred "center." In "The Leper" Swinburne glimpsed the dialectic of "spiralling contraries": he was partly to realize that dialectic in his art, though not in his life.

Swinburne tops up the poem with a mock-source for this fictive tale in his best Renaissance French. Identity begins to be established here by parody and caricature, stylistic and iconographical, used by the poet to transcend his source: the hair, profuse sexual symbol among the Pre-Raphaelites, is not "dim" merely, as it becomes in Morris' "Old Love," but rancid, "half grey half ruined gold," while Pre-Raphaelite archaism is also mocked. Through such ironic mockery of his sources, Swinburne, like Donne, protects his tone from absurdity or bathos.

IV

Those early poems were probably written before the "moment of truth" between Swinburne and Mary Gordon; the cousins' situation certainly underlay the remainder. Mary and Algernon had shared a private world; part of their mythology was Mary's fictional role as Swinburne's younger brother at school, sympathetically involved in his experiences of flogging. The relationship was so independent of sexual distinction that the shock was more profound when it became apparent they must separate; Mary must marry. For this "fall" from a world of unity the family was directly responsible, and, behind the family, society, and the power, "God" which both expressed. This power, sensed only as cruelty and violation, had been responsible for the peculiarities of Swinburne's personality (and physique).

In his analysis of *Poems and Ballads*, Morse Peckham distinguishes between "self" and "personality" which "is simply something that is given . . . is, in a strange but true sense, entirely alien to oneself," and in Swinburne's case, with the capacity to humiliate the self. Personality is hell and can only be understood and accommodated to as far as possible. Swinburne's insights into his own psychology and his need to aestheticize the self, a transformation of concrete situation into artifice, result in peculiarities of style and negation of development. As Peckham puts it: "from the meaningless chaos of experiences, the self creates through art a world of order and value. Style offers a stance, an orientation, safely to experience that chaos . . . the selfhood of each poet of the past redeems the other as model. The artist can achieve impersonality, make a unique use of tradition which will give him an individuality or selfhood." In a late, self-conscious, Alexandrian or silver Latin age of culture, it is necessary, in Harold Bloom's phrase, "to become one with the redemptive imagination of the precursor." This is a dialectic not of imitation of external characteristics but of impersonation, parody, caricature sometimes of the precursor. Peckham describes Swinburne's style in *Poems and Ballads* as one of "non-expressive aesthetic"; that is to say, with a surface beauty that arrests penetration into the painful depths of content. This surface is won by Swinburne's control over the styles of many writers, and by numerous forms, including many modulations of rhymed stanzas, some distinctly unusual. It becomes fused by continuous usage of alliterations, assonances, patterns of repeated vowel noises, repeated syntactical patterns. That Swinburne intended this highly glazed reflexive surface, there can be no doubt. Often he strews epithets, simply for sound, as decor; tepid words such as "sweet" found four times in a single stanza of "A Ballad of Death," "sad," "pale," "fair," "bright," all contributing to the nonexpressive surface. Sometimes as many as four epithets (which may be internally rhymed) exhaust their substantive. Such are not emotional shorthand merely, but analogous rather to the many unaccented articles, conjunctions, and prepositions, which are designed to assure a glancing rapidity of reading. But the reader must be alert. "As bones of men under the deep sharp sea"; that second epithet is witty, not decorative. Criticism has justly observed that the diction of *Poems and Ballads* is rarely ornate. Dismissed as overlush and decadent, Swinburne is, on the contrary, according to John Rosenberg, the most *austere* among the greatly gifted poets of the nineteenth century:

> Oh yet would God this flesh of mine might be
> Where air might wash and long leaves cover me,
> Where tides of grass break into foam of flowers,
> Or where the winds' feet shine along the sea.
> ("Laus Veneris," st. 14)

A master of monosyllables; he is indeed "the supreme master in English of the bleak beauty of little words."

"The structure of the book," Swinburne himself commented, "has been as carefully considered and arranged as I could make it." And in a pamphlet defending himself against the reviewers, he wrote that

> the book is dramatic, many-faced, multifarious; and no utterance of enjoyment or despair, belief or unbelief, can properly be assumed as the assertion of its author's personal feeling or faith. (*Notes on Poems and Reviews*, para. 4)

This is not necessarily history. But we may believe that Swinburne made some attempt to distance the personal, and he was obviously familiar with Baudelaire's ordering of *Les Fleurs du Mal* into sections representing possible avenues of escape from a modern *accidie*. The effect of *Poems and Ballads*, however, is rather that of a continuous monologue that resounds through a number of masks.

Swinburne rationalized the "fall" in terms of his mentors Sade, Blake, and Baudelaire, and so furnished for the speaker of *Poems and Ballads* an intellectual program that has been brilliantly analyzed for us by Julian Baird. While Swinburne respected Sade as theologian, he was less impressed by Sade as artist. But even as theologian Swinburne probably considered Sade inferior to Blake, for Sade persisted in the Christian dualism that distinguished between body and spirit. According to him the body is fulfilled only in filth, misery, and cruelty, by means of which the individual consciousness is engulfed in unity with another. In spite of Sade's anti-Christian polemics, his was mere despairing mortification of the flesh, not pagan freedom. Blake, according to Swinburne's reading, realized that body and spirit were indivisible, "body" should never be "bruised to pleasure soul"; "above all gods of creation and division, [Blake] beheld by faith in a perfect man a supreme God." There was neither divine person nor divine thing but the human. But this insight needs to be won from a "fallen" world of custom and restraint in which Christian immanence has retracted, but nature's divinity is not admitted; rather, a transcendent and cruel creator is postulated. Against this "new" nature and this "new Nature's god," man must rebel and himself become God:

> God is man, and man God; as neither of himself the greater, so neither of himself the less: but as God is the unfallen part of man, man the fallen part of God, God must needs be (not more than man, but assuredly) more than the qualities of man. . . . The other "God" . . . who created the sexual and separate body of man did but cleave in twain the "divine humanity," which becoming reunited shall redeem man without price and without covenant and without law; . . . meantime, the Creator is a divine daemon, liable to error, subduable by and through this very created nature of his invention, which he for the present imprisons and torments. (*William Blake*, 1868 ed., pp. 155–156)

The ideal of *Poems and Ballads* is therefore a species of gnosticism. It institutes an attempt to transcend the dualism of spirit and matter and return to hermaphrodite unity, through a series of variations on the dominant theme of love, heterosexual, homosexual, oral-genital, and sado-masochistic, a dialogue between the poems themselves.

The volume opens with two imitations of early sixteenth-century court ballads, "A Ballad of Life" corresponding to a Blakean state of innocence, which "the poet-dreamer can appreciate as beautiful, but from which he is separated by intervening years and which he does not fully understand." "A Ballad of Death" represents Blake's state of experience, "a sorrowful waking state which takes full cognizance of the death of innocent physical love in a world which accepts laws for the flesh," (Baird). Both poems are addressed to Lucrezia Borgia: the first celebrates her as the divinity of matter,[4] the second laments her death "as a vesture with new dyes, / The body that was clothed with love of old." The allusion is to that notion of sacred and profane love, best known through Titian's famous painting, where sacred love has been-interpreted as the naked, profane love as the clothed, lady: shame comes with the "fall."[5] Lucrezia, in legend, had committed incest with father and brother, but here she is seen as representing purified nature, the love that must be distinguished behind the lineaments of lust. Emblem of unity, of Renaissance paganism, she becomes the first in a series of emblematic ladies, all of whom are judged in the light of the living Lucrezia. Figures such as Faustine and Dolores (no less than the "nightmare life-in-death" of Samuel Taylor Coleridge, and Shelley's Medusa) mark the reappearance in romantic poetry of those dazzling witches of romantic epic: Alcina, Acrasia, and Armida. The Swinburne female represents the familiar, paradoxical attempt to reconcile the romantic antinomies: pleasure-pain; mystery-knowledge; coition-death; and to preserve essence in a world of flickering phenomena. Essentially passive, she is both victim and victress: though the poet sacrifices himself to her, her gaze (like that of Yeats's ladies on unicorns, in "Meditations in Time of Civil War"), is turned inwards, in an act of self-worship that becomes masochistic precisely because she has taken herself as object. Swinburne uses other literary commonplaces, but always in a strictly personalized manner: the sexual, for example, as emblem of cosmic disorder. The varieties of love are symbolized by Venus as popular or heterosexual love, as homoerotic, as sapphic, and as Venus Anadyomene. In this last the sea is represented as sexual "Mother and lover" older than history, beyond family and society, with whom one can intensify identity and yet be, as with other lovers one cannot, totally mingled, and whose embraces are at once more fatal and sexually keen than those of others.

"A Ballad of Death" concludes with a journey and a return:

> . . . it may be
> That when thy feet return at evening
> Death shall come in with thee.

Even the proposed revision of the volume would not have assured that subtle placing and cogent unfolding of poem after poem in dialogue with one another that we find in the maturity of Yeats. Yet a broad narrative line can be traced in *Poems and Ballads*. The end of "A Ballad of Death" leads naturally on to "Laus Veneris." This poem relates the poet Tannhäuser's fruitless journey to Rome for absolution by the pope from the sin of his service to Venus under the Venusberg.[6] The pope refuses absolution and Tannhäuser returns to Venus. Originally a medieval legend, this tale had been retold several times in the nineteenth century, by Heinrich Heine, Ludwig Tieck, in Richard Wagner's opera (1849), and in Baudelaire's defense of the work twelve years later, while the subject became popular in England particularly in the fin de siècle.[7]

4. This is presumably the origin of Lucrezia's puzzling appearance as Madame Hulé in the thirtieth of Ezra Pound's *Cantos*.

5. See "Sacred and Profane Love," in E. Wind, *Pagan Mysteries in the Renaissance*, 2nd and rev. ed. (London, 1967), for the complex history of interpretation.

6. The mountain that became the refuge of Venus after the defeat of the pagan gods by Christianity. Burne-Jones's lost watercolor of 1861 on the topic probably influenced Swinburne. A larger version of the theme in oil of 1873–1878 has a Venus who was aptly described by a contemporary as "wan and death-like, eaten up and gnawn away by disappointment and desire." Its iridescent colors, "shot" reds and golds, also connect with Swinburne's imagery.

7. See, for example, John Davidson's "A New Ballad of Tannhäuser" in *New Ballads* (London-New York, 1897); Herbert E. Clarke's *Tannhäuser and Other Poems* (1896); Walter Pater's allusions in the unpublished portions of *Gaston deLatour* (1896); and Aubrey Beardsley's *Venus and Tannhäuser* (1896).

The medieval setting recalls Heine's theory that the pagan gods after the triumph of Christianity either enlisted in the new religion or became demons.

In Swinburne's poem, written in a stricter variation of the meter used by Edward Fitzgerald in his *Rubáiyát* (1859), we meet further literary commonplaces creatively distorted. The Venusberg, in its heat and aridity, resembles one of those false secondary gardens of Eden that are found in Renaissance epic. "The scented dusty daylight burns the air." Just as temptation *creates* Edmund Spenser's Bower of Bliss (though the reader remains informed by imagery no less than by comment that it *is* illusion, infernal not paradisal), so Tannhäuser recreates Venus as succuba, notwithstanding his choice of her in place of Christ. In Julian Baird's reading, the situation is that of "A Ballad of Life" inverted. In that poem the lover could distinguish the gold of love under the dusty overlayer of lust. For Tannhäuser, who believes in duality of body and spirit, love and lust remain the same, but individuated still. Thus as knight he believes in Christ, but as lover in Venus: here there is no epiphany of feminine purity, as in some versions of the Tannhäuser story. In the traditional false earthly paradise the lover sleeps, while the insatiate succuba wakes. Here Venus sleeps with the lineaments of satisfied desire; the only sign of life is "a purple speck / Wherein the pained blood falters and goes out." But Tannhäuser desires final death and judgment, associating Venus with the great harlot of Revelation.

For till the thunder in the trumpet be,
Soul may divide from body, but not we
  One from another; . . .

I seal myself upon thee with my might,
Abiding always out of all men's sight
  Until God loosen over sea and land
The thunder of the trumpets of the night.
  (st. 105–106)

This is the longing for confirmation of damnation experienced by the inverted Christian who cannot transcend what he hates and loves. The poem conforms also to the traditional romantic theme of the quest, and Tannhäuser's return journey mirrors the aesthetic pilgrim's penitential reversal.

Next in order there follows a fragment of dialogue between Phaedra and Hippolytus with choric interventions. If Tannhäuser remains strangely passive in love, Phaedra is aggressive, a woman obsessed with desire for her stepson, the victim of an unknown god who, like Death, cannot be appeased with gifts, or rather can only be appeased by the death of both Phaedra and Hippolytus. Phaedra's madness communicates itself through images bestiality. The mother-son relationship precisely inverts that in *Atalanta in Calydon*: Hippolytus sacrifices himself to the false "god" of custom and restraint. This is followed by three poems associated by Swinburne and bearing directly on the autobiographical situation.

In "The Triumph of Time," half allegory, half narrative, Swinburne speaks in his own voice. The poem is at once rapid in movement and long in proportion to its intellectual content, that length suggesting the processional rite of the "triumph" form as practiced by poets from Petrarch to Shelley. The theme is the conspiracy of fates, gods, and Time, again a love which is imaged sacramentally: "This wild new growth of the corn and vine"; but the speaker learns that communion will be impossible; he is alone. Time, in traditional mode, acts as both destroyer of his love and revealer of his true situation.

The hermaphrodite image of innocent primitive unity, two bodies and souls, is invoked:

Twain halves of a perfect heart, made fast
Soul to soul while the years fell past;
. . .
But now, you are twain, you are cloven
  apart;
Flesh of his flesh, but heart of my heart;
And deep in one is the bitter root,
  And sweet for one is the lifelong flower.
  (st. 6 and 13)

And so, to the marine Venus:

O fair green-girdled mother of mine,
Sea, that art clothed with the sun and the rain,
Thy sweet hard kisses are strong like wine,
Thy large embraces are keen like pain.
Save me and hide me with all thy waves,
Find me one grave of thy thousand graves,
Those pure cold populous graves of thine,
Wrought without hand in a world without stain.
(st. 34)

Late in the poem, to generalize the adolescent fantasy of dying for the loved one, Swinburne recalls the troubadour Rudel, who fell in love with the Princess of Tripoli, set out for her duchy, saw her, and died in her smile.

There lived a singer in France of old,
By the tideless dolorous midland sea.
In a land of sand and ruin and gold
There shone one woman, and none but she.

(The troubadours were viewed in the nineteenth century as the originators of romantic love.)

The second poem, "Les Noyades," presents a similar strategy; this is a rapid balladish version of an incident from the French Revolution that had been vividly reported by Thomas Carlyle. Carrier, an agent of the Revolution, is sent to suppress a revolt in Nantes. To dispose of the numerous prisoners he adopts a "final solution," having many supporters of the *ancien régime* placed on board ships on the Loire, which are then sunk: "daylight . . . witnesses Noyades: women and men are tied together, feet and feet, hands and hands; and flung in: this they call *Mariage Républicain*." In Swinburne, though nowhere else, Carrier appears as a destructive androgyne: "A queen of men, with helmeted hair." A young worker and a noble "maiden, wonderful, white" are bound together and the young man exults in this consummation through death. The speaker in the poem breaks away from the past into the present and imagines himself and his lost love being driven down from the Loire to the sea:

We should yield, go down, locked hands and feet,
Die, drown together, and breath catch breath;
(st. 19)

but the poem twists at the end:

But you would have felt my soul in a kiss,
. . .
And I would have given my soul for this
To burn for ever in burning hell.

The last poem of this trilogy, "A Leave-Taking," is ceremoniously controlled, but concludes with the same wish, dissolution in the sea. The theme of incest and sacrifice is pursued in "Itylus." "Anactoria," which follows, is a monologue of the Lesbian poet Sappho modeled on the tirades of Ovid's "Sappho to Phaon" and Alexander Pope's baroque "Eloisa to Abelard." The couplets often fall into an Augustan mode, in which the balanced phrases are underscored by alliteration:

Bade sink the spirit and the flesh aspire,
Pain animate the dust of dead desire,
(179–180)

Sappho's obsession with Anactoria's image is mimed in the recurring rhymes of some couplets that fracture Augustan decorum. Sappho represents the most frenetic example of the desire to restore primitive unity by means of a violent mingling with the beloved, but love turns to the wish to violate what is loved, as in the witty couplet that transforms sterile love into art:

Take thy limbs living, and new-mould with these
A lyre of many faultless agonies?
(139–140)

But art too is as sterile as love, its emblem for Anactoria. Sappho's hatred extends to "the mute melancholy lust of heaven" and God:

"Him would I reach, him smite, him desecrate." Finally, self-violation ensues, and Sappho hurls herself into the "insuperable" sea. "Anactoria" had touched on the failure of immortality through art; death and immortality are the themes of the "Hymn to Proserpine," a monologue spoken by a pagan at the close of the ancient world, who is caught between worlds.

In "Hermaphroditus" Swinburne exploits a Pre-Raphaelite derangement of a tradition, that of lyrics and sonnets closely related to the visual arts.[8] Like Rossetti, Swinburne does not use the genre merely to exalt art over nature, or to argue a hierarchy of arts, or make a "picturesque" attempt to reproduce visual effects in language. Rossetti, for example, invariably *interprets* the image, relating his poem to a particular work of art, considered as capturing "a moment's monument." "Hermaphroditus" is based on a statue in the Louvre with female breasts and male genitals, reclining on a couch in ambiguous posture. The literary source is Ovid's recounting of the tale of Salmacis and Hermaphroditus, who blend into one androgynous being in water. Rossetti had described picture and poem as bearing "the same relation to each other as beauty does in man and woman: the point of meeting where the two are identical is the supreme perfection." The "beauty" of the picture is reciprocated by the "identical"—if superficially dissimilar—"beauty" of the poem, resulting in an indivisible ideal unity, comparable only to the state of love. In Rossetti's sonnets for pictures of women, the metaphor is actualized as an encounter between observer-poet and portrait-beloved. Swinburne's own prose interpretation connects "Hermaphroditus" with art and the artist. Of his friend Simeon Solomon's painting *My Soul and I*, Swinburne wrote: "[It] contains both the idea of the separation of male and female qualities and their union as body and soul . . ." And of Solomon's iconography in general, "In almost all of these there is perceptible the same profound suggestion of . . . the identity of contraries." (Swinburne's "Erotion" originated in a picture of Solomon's.) The Pre-Raphaelite hermaphrodite stems from the male-female union of the epiphany of the woman soul to the young painter in Rossetti's "Hand and Soul."[9] Swinburne's response is poised between the optimism and pessimism that the hermaphrodite image generated in the nineteenth century:

> A strong desire begot on great despair,
> A great despair cast out by strong desire.
> (st. 1)

"Fragoletta" or "little strawberry" prolongs the same theme and is followed by two poems that introduce the tyrannies of the religion of law: "A Litany" presents an Old Testament God who speaks a threatening first antiphon and the human response slavishly echoes both syntax and rhyme. "Faustine" a tour de force of forty-one stanzas, pivoting on the proper name at the end of each, is another critical presentation of the fatal woman: the transformation of a contemporary into the Empress Faustine, beautiful and vicious in legend. Like all fatal women, continuously reincarnated, she becomes victim of men's images of her. In his notes Swinburne refers to her as "doomed as though by accident from the first to all evil and no good, through many ages and forms, but clad always in the same type of fleshly beauty." This is followed by another poem for a painting, "Before the Mirror," designed to accompany James MacNeil Whistler's *The Little White Girl*, which shows a girl in profile leaning on a mantelpiece while her reflection in three-quarter view in the mirror reveals a pensive, perhaps suffering expression. The elegy for Walter Savage Landor and the ode to one of Swinburne's constant heroes, Victor Hugo, celebrate two figures who championed private and public liberty and so extend the concept of freedom

8. The genre goes back to Homer's Shield of Achilles, the sixteenth book of the Greek Anthology, and to Renaissance "gallery" poems. Typically, Swinburne parodies Rossetti's sonnets for pictures.

9. Another source is Théophile Gautier's *Mademoiselle de Maupin* (Paris, 1835).

from the religious to the social and political plane. At this climactic stage of *Poems and Ballads* we encounter three closely interrelated poems: "Dolores," "The Garden of Proserpine," and "Hesperia."

"Dolores" is the most notorious poem of the volume, a lyric of frenzied negations devoted to the madonna of sado-masochism, a parody almost of the fatal woman theme: Medusa's or Lamia's head has become suspiciously similar to King Charles in *David Copperfield*. In "Faustine" "Les Noyades," or "Laus Veneris" we witness the transformation by guilt of woman from either past or present into *femme fatale*. In "Dolores" the image in itself is convoked. Each individual stanza is possessed by that rhythm of tumescence and detumescence that flows and ebbs through "Anactoria." His letters indicate that Swinburne sometimes considered "Dolores" as a "black" joke: "Thy skin changes country and color, / And shrivels or swells to a snake's." The poem ends with the promise that death will bring" the joys of thee seventy times seven, / Our Lady of Pain," regardless of any belief or blankness about immortality, hell, or heaven. The conclusion of "Anactoria" is parodied. The coda is exhaustion, but also purgation. In "The Garden of Proserpine," Thanatos, a severe Greek angel, is welcome after Eros in all his wilder shapes:

> Pale, beyond porch and portal,
> Crowned with calm leaves, she stands
> Who gathers all things mortal
> With cold immortal hands;
> . . .
> She waits for each and other,
> She waits for all men born;
> . . .
> From too much love of living,
> From hope and fear set free,
> We thank with brief thanksgiving
> Whatever Gods may be
> That no life lives for ever;
> That dead men rise up never;
> That even the weariest river
> Winds somewhere safe to sea.
> (st. 7, 8, and 11)

"Hesperia" alludes to that land in the west of the fortunate dead and pleasant memories, reigned over by Proserpine. The poem's rhythms contrast with its two predecessors by slow authority, as of sea music, the second short half of every first and third line finishing with an inflexing feminine rhyme, the breaking wave. After the feral interiors of "Dolores" and the windless void of Proserpine's garden, the reascent from the experiences recorded in the whole volume is marked now by memories of wind and the sea, of wild riding, and, associated with the healing presence of the Venus Anadyomene, of the one woman who underlay all images of loss, hatred, and compensation,

> Thee I behold as a bird borne in with the
> wind from the west,
> Straight from the sunset, across white
> waves whence rose as a daughter
> Venus thy mother, in years when the world
> was a water at rest.
> (10–12)

transfigured now synesthetically into a muse: "Thy silence as music, thy voice as an odour that fades in a flame." The speaker hopes that the loved woman will understand and pity, but not love; for love, he has proved, is "As the cross that a wild nun clasps till the edge of it bruises her bosom" (validating the comparison of "Anactoria" with "Eloisa and Abelard"). Dolores is transcended and the poem concludes with a memory of Swinburne's reckless horse-riding with Mary, creating a future of its own.

The two translated love songs that follow are of appropriate lightness; "Félise," a dramatic monologue, is spoken by a young man to a somewhat older woman, after a year's absence from one another. Swinburne commented that he had expressed their story "Plainly and 'cynically' enough! Last year I loved you Félise and you were puzzled, and didn't love me—quite." The poem affects the reader—as other diffused poems do not—as overelongated, though the young man is playing rather cruelly. The intention is to present a new "mask," one of control over the personality, but the drift into a familiar antitheism undercuts the objectivity. "Hendecasyllabics"—following "An Interlude" of spring—has art, winter, and endurance as its themes and, like its companion piece, "Sapphics," the stress on exercise indicates distance and control. "Sapphics" also "corrects" "Anactoria" in its ritual, chastened version of Sappho's death:

> By the grey sea-side, unassuaged, unheard of,
> Unbeloved, unseen in the ebb of twilight,
> Ghosts of outcast women return lamenting,
> Purged not in Lethe.
> (st. 19)

The loose progression of the volume is continued with the ballads whose subject foreshadows that of Swinburne's next major work, *Atalanta in Calydon*, in particular that of "The Bloody Son," a tale of fratricide and exile. The new work centers on the tyranny (and death) of the family.

V

To write a play in the style of the Greek tragic poets was not unusual in nineteenth-century England; but the form was often used to evade the realities of the contemporary scene. Swinburne, however, used it to confront, if obliquely, his own age. The principal sources for *Atalanta in Calydon* are Homer, Ovid's Metamorphoses, and the extant fragments of Euripides' *Meleager*. The legend runs: Althaea, Queen of Calydon, pregnant with her first child, Meleager, dreams that she has given birth to a firebrand. The three Fates attend his birth and prophesy that he will be strong and fortunate and will live as long as a brand, at that time in the fire. His mother plucks out the brand and guards it. While Meleager is away with Jason's Argonauts, his father, King Oeneus, sacrifices to all the gods but Artemis. In revenge Artemis stirs up various tribes to fight against the Calydonians, and becomes still more angry when Oeneus defeats his enemies. She then sends a wild boar to Calydon that ravages the land, killing many who attempt to hunt it down. Men come from all over Greece to try their hand at destroying this beast. With them comes Atalanta, a virgin, who is highly favored by Artemis. For Atalanta's sake Artemis allows the boar to be killed. Atalanta pierces the beast with her spear and then Meleager kills it, presenting its carcass to Atalanta, with whom he has fallen in love. Althaea's brothers, Toxeus and Plexippus, who have already grumbled hugely about Atalanta's presence on the hunt, attempt to take the spoil from her, but Meleager protects Atalanta and kills the pair of them. On hearing this Althaea in a frenzy of rage takes the brand and throws it into the fire. As the brand (clearly connected with sexual identity) is consumed, so Meleager wastes away and dies and his mother dies soon after him, broken with grief, though in Swinburne's play she suffers a "symbolic" death only.

Atalanta can be structurally related to the formal design of Greek tragedy: prologos, parodos, episode, stasimon, exodos. Of the three extant tragic poets, Swinburne apparently most admired Aeschylus; but to detect Aeschylus as model is difficult. Swinburne does not use the chorus to carry portions of the narrative, nor does he attempt any Aeschylean reconciliation of human and divine order. At the close of the *Oresteia*, moreover, the old goddesses, the Furies, are persuaded to yield by new patriarchal gods; in *Atalanta* the female principle triumphs, nominally Artemis, though there must be doubt as to her precise nature, while the symbolic destruction of Althaea qualifies the triumph. Some have proffered unconvincing Sophoclean readings of the play as asserting a "golden mean" that Althaea, Atalanta, and Meleager all violate: but this would deny the work any modern element and in any case this is a reading of Sophocles no competent commentator would now wish to maintain: those who advise moderation or *sophrosyne* (Ismene in the *Antigone*, Chrysothemis in the *Electra*) are shown to be morally inferior to the absolutists. Swinburne is closer to Euripides in sometimes using the chorus as lyrical refreshment or mirror of the action. The chorus beginning, "O that I now, I too were / By deep wells and water-floods" clearly recalls the famous chorus in the *Hippolytus*: "Would that I might hide in the secret hollows of the mountains" representing a similar moment of evasion. There is, however, no *deus ex machina* in *Atalanta*. More broadly, Swinburne's moral tone is often as mysterious as that of Euripides.[10]

The choric odes are not merely Greekish but often susceptible to precise Greek metrical analysis. Swinburne makes extensive use of what are now called the aeolic meters, whose nucleus is the choriamb: -uu-, with or without variables on either side. He was probably thinking of anapests rather than dactyls, perhaps unfortunately, since he considered that anapests were as natural in English as dactyls were alien.

In *Atalanta* the chorus sometimes gives a lyrical formulation to the inner feelings of the protagonists. They begin with the innocently hopeful "When the hounds of spring are on winter's traces" chanted at dawn: if light follows dark, spring, winter—the boar must surely be killed. This motif is counterpointed immediately by Althaea's assertion of a determined cycle of pain and pleasure to which men's lives are confined. But even in the opening chorus, the implication of such a cycle troubles the imagery: "scare / The wolf that follows, the fawn that flies," resolved by Althaea's "Night, a black hound, follows the white fawn day." Criticism has remarked a further structural element: the conflict between the dialectic public world of the iambic meter and the Dionysiac world of the choric. The chorus' exuberance dwindles finally to a curt, bleak utterance: the lords of life, whoever they may be, have a kingdom of "strong hands" reflecting on the pitiful manly strength of Meleager and the brothers (and perhaps on the pitiful diminutiveness of Swinburne himself).

10. Oddly enough, as Swinburne detested that "Zola of the fifth century."

This larger structural device is supported by iterative imagery. Swinburne has as usual been accused here of infatuation with certain words, but the repetitions are deliberate and regulated: night/day; spring/winter; male/female; flower/blossom/bud; hard/soft; and, at the play's onset, are invoked in the persons of Artemis and Apollo, moon and sun. Contrapuntal words that dominate are "fire" associated with Althaea, and "snow" and "whiteness" Atalanta's properties as surrogate of Artemis. But these images are not polarized merely; they are also ambiguous in the play's plural world. Fire is alluded to as purging disease—the boar is to be "consumed"; but fire also destroys life, Meleager's life. Atalanta is a snowy *rose*. In terms of character, Althaea is passionate and unforgiving; Atalanta, for all her desolating purity, is at the end still capable of pity.

> Hail thou: but I with heavy face and feet
> Turn homeward and am gone out of thine
> eyes.
> (2310–2311)

The simplest reading of the play is to isolate Althaea as agent in a *Sons and Lovers* situation. Swinburne was fascinated by matriarchal, aristocratic figures subtly controlling their families. Althaea is a tragic version of the ruthless antiromantic Lady Midhurst of *Love's Cross Currents*. But among Swinburne's aims in *Atalanta* was that of excluding the overtly modern and discursive. To achieve this he had to subdue the autobiographical and the amusement of attacking the Christian God under veil of complaint about the Greek pantheon. To be sure, Althaea and Meleager are pivotal figures: Althaea is both passionately and intensely stoical, distrustful of the gods. For her, life has "much to be endured and little to be enjoyed." One must be wary, attempt to sustain patterns of civility, kingdom, and family, our only refuge in a cruel world: the Victorian parallels are clear. Althaea belongs with those who practice restraint and distrust nature. Her husband, King Oeneus, plays an oddly muted part. A compromiser, past his best, he attempts to mediate with "soft obstetric hand" between Meleager and Althaea:

> Nor thee I praise, who art fain to undo
> things done:
> Nor thee, who art swift to esteem them
> overmuch.
> (627–628)

These well-meaning banalities are futile. Althaea's two brothers are presented rather as rugby club hearties, thrusting their virility at everyone. On Atalanta their genial comment is that the only justification for virgins is that their throats can be cut for purposes of sacrifice. Such beefy conservatism strongly contrasts with the intelligent conservatism of Althaea. Swinburne was not one of those arrogant radicals who assume that all reactionaries are by definition stupid.

Atalanta herself has all the passivity of the fatal woman: she does not tempt Meleager, though it is through her that Althaea and Artemis destroy him. Indeed, Althaea cooperates with Meleager in creating Atalanta's fatal woman aspect:

> She the strange woman, she the flower, the
> sword,
> Red from spilt blood, a mortal flower to
> men,
> Adorable, detestable—even she
> Saw with strange eyes and with strange lips
> rejoiced.
> (1692–1695)

Does Althaea detect some numinous tinge about Atalanta? She fears her because Atalanta is literally a stranger, a foreigner, outside the warm structure of family and kingdom but, more profoundly, strange as a virgin by vocation, one who lives in the white shadow of Artemis. Atalanta has evaded the roles that give woman social identity: she does not weave and breed as do other women: she hunts with men. But Althaea is also distrustful of romantic love as such; it is, by Greek tradition, a disaster; its strict correlative, pain, so the chorus chants: "For an evil blossom is born / Of sea-foam and the frothing of blood," alluding apparently to Aphrodite's birth (and Atalanta's effect on Meleager) but with dramatic irony defining Althaea: "For they knew thee for mother of love, / And knew thee not mother of death."

What of Meleager's attitudes? A plausible suggestion is that he anticipates the aestheticism so eloquently expressed in Pater's "Conclusion" to *Studies in the History of the Renaissance* (1873). Meleager too recognizes the inevitability of a pleasure-pain cycle, that life becomes more flame-like from the fact that "each man, dying' is earth and shadow; the nothing sinks into nothingness" to cite the fragment from Euripides' *Meleager* that Swinburne prefixed to his play. Meleager's response is that the individual must seize on the good moment before the cycle returns to pain. He embodies the Dionysiac reverberation of the opening chorus: not to lay hold of joy "on this short day of frost and sun" is "to sleep before evening." But that seizure precisely brings Meleager to sleep before evening; it is the dim Oeneus who survives. Yet Meleager chooses joy, love, and, it has been suggested, in Paterian mode, art. At the close of the Greek play that *Atalanta* most resembles, the *Hippolytus* of Euripides, as the virgin Artemis leaves the dying hero, he addresses her as a Madonna come to witness his *pietà*: "thou leavest me now, blessed virgin," but Artemis is void of power to ease his pain; she can say only that if gods could weep, she would. Hippolytus asks the human auditors to cover his face with his cloak that he may retain dignity in the last anguish. Atalanta, a mortal, though Artemis, double, can feel pity and more. Meleager asks her:

> But thou, dear, hide my body with thy veil,
> And with thy raiment cover foot and head,
> And stretch thyself upon me and touch
> hands
> With hands and lips with lips. . . .
> (2298–2301)

It is a traditional orgasm-as-death passage (very close to a similar passage in Torquato

Tasso's *Aminta*, but also to Wagner's *Tristan*). Meleager does not die alone; this is communion, a life-enhancing ritual moment; life measured not by length but intensity; life as the end of life, in this mime of the sexual act, a ghostly Eros. Pater is again relevant: "With this sense of the splendour of our experience and of its awful brevity, gathering all we are into one desperate effort to see and touch." Such insight brings Meleager joy and death. He forgives Althaea, recognizing that she can only act out the antinomies of her role:

> . . . thou too, queen,
> The source and end, the sower and the
> scythe,
> The rain that ripens and the drought that
> slays . . .
>
> . . .
>
> To make me and unmake me—thou, I say,
> Althaea, since my father's ploughshare,
> drawn
> Through fatal seedbed of a female field
> Furrowed thy body . . . I
>
> . . .
>
> Hail thee as holy and worship thee as just
> Who art unjust and unholy . . .
>
> . . .
>
> . . . me too thou hast loved, and I
> Thee; but this death was mixed with all
> my life,
> Mine end with my beginning.
> (2210–2212; 2214–2217; 2221–2222;
> 2237–2239)

Althaea in destroying Meleager destroys her role and herself: "I am severed from myself, my name is gone," and employs for the last time the image of fire: "My name that was a healing, it is changed, / My name is a consuming. / From this time . . . / My lips shall not unfasten till I die." So she has no words for Meleager's last speech. As L. Wymer observes, she suffers a death-in-life that epiphanizes her past life and role. Ironically she has become her own image of Atalanta: a stranger to herself and her son. The play, indeed, abounds with the words "division," "cleave": in Meleager's dying speech, for example, "I sprang and cleft the closure of thy womb."

The ancient form acts as challenge and discipline: Swinburne achieved in *Atalanta in Calydon* an effect paralleled by *Samson Agonistes*. In either case the poet, without violating the Greek norms, arrives at a highly personal tragic insight. Just as Milton's blindness gives acuity to his drama of temptation, so Swinburne's peculiar psychology enables him to realize the price that a weak-bodied aesthete must pay in a world without gods or personal immortality.

VI

Many nineteenth-century poets were deeply involved in romantic politics. Reacting from the Enlightenment and its instrument, the internationalist French Revolution, there emerged a nationalism of the "sacred soil," of ancestors "who stemmed with their own bodies" the invader. Nations were defined by wars of independence, first in Germany, then on that most sacred soil of all, the Greek. Byron's effort and death for Hellenism became profoundly symbolic. The "Young Ireland" group of poets and politicians and the Italian *Risorgimento* form part of this same vivid movement. The first phase of the *Risorgimento*, or "resurrection" associated with Swinburne's master Mazzini, was, however, strongly tinged with notions from the Enlightenment. But by the later 1860's, when Swinburne was composing most of his *Songs Before Sunrise*, the Italian struggle had mutated into a more narrow nationalism.

Songs Before Sunrise is Swinburne's celebration of the *Risorgimento* as it moved toward its climax in the loss by "Pius Iscariot" (so Swinburne called Pius IX) of the Patrimony of Peter to the kingdom of Italy. The models are Walt Whitman and Hugo's *Les Châtiments*. Swinburne's republican zeal can be detected as early as 1852, the date of his first surviving political poem. The strategy of *Songs Before Sunrise* is to appropriate the rhetoric of ecclesiastical tyranny, of typology also, to dignify Italy and republicanism. Despite the political reality, the *Risorgimento* is presented here as part of a world process, in which man creates himself God through aggregation to a perfect society: "Love, the beloved republic." These notions were widespread among "advanced" men of letters. As one of Swinburne's contemporaries put it:

> Every great poet of the last half century is loud in this demand for liberty of passion and liberty of action—freedomof the individual will. But if the individual be thus free, what guarantee is there that he will not injure his neighbour and reduce society to chaos? The answer is that love is the harmonizer of the passions, and that large idea of friendship—the universal brotherhood of democracy—the harmonizer of human action.[11]

Italy becomes Madonna, the people Christ; the republic, a Christ in the tomb. This rhetoric (its polemics have interesting connections with those of Blake) functions sometimes successfully, sometimes with results as grotesque as those of Richard Gashaw's deliberate confusions of spiritual and physical: in "Blessed Among Women" we learn that Italy is "four times blest, / At whose most holy breast / Four times a godlike soldier-savior hung."

The contents fall into three broad categories, the weakest celebrating topical events in the war for liberty. "The Ride from Milan" veers toward doggerel; the odes are tumid merely. But the quasi-philosophic poems such as "Genesis," "Mater Triumphalis," and "Hertha," which combine evolutionary themes with a mystical pantheism, are surprisingly impressive. "Hertha" for example, asserts the mother-creative principle against the false creator-god of Blake, who seeks to limit men, by imposing on them the identity of servants. Yet it is when all large abstractions melt into some sense of the sacred actualities of Italy, as in "Siena" (evoking St. Catherine of Siena's voluptuous trances of a vicarious suffering, no less than her public role as rebuker of great men and mentor of popes); or in the inevitable but still piercing comparison of Italy with Israel in bondage, "Super Flumina Babylonis" that Swinburne remains most moving. In "Christmas Antiphones," he appropriates the Christian form of the carol with a conspicuous success. And the rhythms are subtle still, as in this stylized grief, some peasant woman released by the wordless rocking of the body:

> Who is this that sits by the way, by the wild
> wayside,
> In a rent stained galment, the robe of a cast-
> off bride,
> In the dust, in the rainfall sitting, with
> soiled feet bare,
> With the night for a garment upon her, with
> torn wet hair?
> She is fairer of face than the daughters of
> men, and her eyes,
> Worn through with her tears are deep as the
> depth of skies.
> ("Mater Dolorosa," st. 1)

Swinburne perhaps had reservations about Mazzini's practical failure: his distrust of materialism (and so of material means). There is a curious episode in *Lesbia Brandon* involving Mazzini's surrogate, Attilio Mariani. Of Mariani we read that "even the sublime vanity of martyrs has its weak side," and on his death he bequeaths the hero two books, whose titles point to contradictions in Mazzini's personality: the memoirs of Felice Orsini and Stendhal's *La Chartreuse de Parme.*

VII

Few people think of Swinburne as the author of prose fiction, yet he published one striking novella, *Love's Cross Currents*, while two substantial fragments, *Lucretia Borgia: The Chronicle of Tebaldeo Tebaldei* and *Lesbia Brandon*, have since been edited from manuscript. There is also a short story, "Dead Love," in Morris' early manner; a considerable fragment of a novel in French, and two

11. John Todhunter, Reading University (England), MS 202/4/3/1.

shorter, highly amusing French burlesques: *La Fille du Policeman*, a tale, and an unfinished play, *La Soeur de la Reine*.

Written early in the 1860's, *Love's Cross Currents* appeared in serial (and abbreviated) form in 1877 under the pseudonym of Mrs. Horace Manners, possibly on account of its situations representing a refinement of those played out on the Isle of Wight between Swinburnes and Gordons. *Love's Cross Currents* offers us an aristocratic family group, complexly interrelated with violent emotions of hate and affinity, but with its members necessarily united against the bourgeois world. After a prologue detailing the web of relationships, the narrative is unfolded through letters in the manner made popular in the eighteenth century. The two principal figures are Lady Midhurst, now in her early sixties, ruthless, intelligent, patrician heir of the Enlightenment, and Mrs. Clara Radworth, in her later twenties, less intelligent, more passionate, married to a dull husband and impatient of the family game. These two ladies conduct a struggle over one of Lady Midhurst's grandchildren, Reginald Harewood (a character who bears some resemblance to the author). Reginald, responding to some not too veiled encouragement, has fallen in love with Clara. Lady Midhurst wishes to break up this relationship, partly because it threatens family stability, partly because she is fond of Reginald. That the affair is so far technically innocent is irrelevant: it may provoke a scandal. Moreover the role of lap-dog barely suits Redgie's style: it makes him much less amusing. Lady Midhurst's other problem is her granddaughter, Reginald's half-sister, who has married Clara's cousin, Lord Cheyne (with whom Clara has herself been in love). Amicia, a dim, glimmering creature of Pre-Raphaelite aspect, possibly echoes Rossetti's wife, Lizzie Siddall. She and Clara's brother, Frank, had once loved one another, meet again, have an affair. The plot becomes as tortuous as any Restoration comedy of intrigue and is drastically resolved. Lord Cheyne is drowned and Frank inherits the great house and title. Clara believes she has triumphed doubly over Lady Midhurst. But Lady Midhurst then discloses that Amicia is pregnant, actually by Frank, who, though all the family become aware of the child's true father, loses by his own precipitancy both house and title. A suavely bullying Lady Midhurst now dissolves her other problem by threatening to show Redgie some letters written by Clara when infatuated with a Frenchman. These will conflict with the image Clara has imposed on her admirer. Clara is forced to send Redgie about his business in cold terms.

Though the tone of *Love's Cross Currents* is French rather than English, its social ambiance is immediately convincing: Swinburne really knew those country houses. Finely characterized though Mrs. Radworth is, Lady Midhurst, with her tart brilliance, is among the most pungent characters in the Victorian novel, sustaining comparison with the Countess de Saldar, Mrs. Brookenham, or even Becky Sharp. Swinburne evokes her in rich phrase: "she worried him with dexterous feline mouth" (Lady Midhurst at the dinner table). A character in *Lesbia Brandon* (in which Lady Midhurst also appears) mistakenly opines that "she is nothing now but husks and fangs." Clara is equally overconfident and mistaken when she observes that Lady Midhurst has "fallen into a sort of hashed style, between a French *portière* and a Dickens nurse," for Lady Midhurst is always stylish, even when, after Cheyne's death, she gives her tepid granddaughter stoical advice. We may believe that Swinburne endorses every pagan word: "All slavishness, whether of body or spirit, leaves a taint where it touches. It is as bad to be servile to God as it is to be servile to man. Accept what you must accept, and obey where you must obey, but make no pretense of a free-will offering." More characteristic is the radiant malice in her dismissal of Clara, whom she not merely triumphs over by letter, but actually visits to enjoy the aesthetics of a visible defeat.

> To use her own style, she is *dead beat*, and quite safe; viciously resigned. . . . She would have me racked if shecould, no doubt, but received me smiling from the tips ofher teeth

> outwards, and with a soft dry pressure of the fingers. Not a hint of anything kept back. . . . I have no doubt she will set all her wits to work and punish him forher failure. She will hardly get up a serious affair again, or it might be a charity to throw her some small animal byway of lighter food. It would not surprise me if she fell to philanthropic labour, or took some devotional drug byway of stimulant. The *bureau d'amourettes* is a bankrupt concern, you see: her sensation-shop is closed for good. Iprophesy she will turn a decent worrying wife of thesimpler Anglican breed; home-keeping, sharp-edged,earnestly petty and drily energetic. Negro-worship now, or foreign missions, will be about her mark; perhaps too adash and sprinkle of religious feeling, with the chill just off; with a mild pinch of the old Platonic mixture now and thento flavour and leaven her dead lump of life. . . . Pity she had not more stock in hand to start with. (ch. 30)

The success of *Love's Cross Currents* owes much to the dry clarity enforced on it by the epistolary form: the "avenging buds of the birch" barely emerge, and Swinburne's perpetual awareness of the inbreeding subject is muted and comically modulated. He preserves all the immediacy of the novel in letters, though the range of characters is sufficient to evade the implausibilities inherent in the form that troubled the eighteenth-century practitioners. Among mid-Victorian fiction it remains unique: a welcome alternative to the prevailing idealism or didacticism; a relief from the heavy "aesthetic teaching" of a George Eliot.

Lesbia Brandon is a more ambitious work, but too fragmentary to grasp as a whole. Swinburne is inconsistent about dates, and dates are important here, while the family interrelationships have become still more dramatically intricate: Denham, the tutor, in himself an interesting creation, in love with Lady Wariston, after some years somewhat implausibly becomes her lover, and the aged, sadistic Linley (a male counterpart of Lady Midhurst without her affections) reveals that Denham is Lady Wariston's half-brother, a disclosure quite in the mode of contemporary, "sensation" novelists such as Mary Elizabeth Braddon. There is a distinct sense of *déjà vu*: this cerebral androgyne, this sadistic tutor, the sexual play of sister with pretty younger brother—all have been met before, expressed with more authority, in *Poems and Ballads*. But *Lesbia Brandon* reads well. Lady Midhurst makes a subordinate but vivid appearance; the lengthy fragment is full of a sharp and detailed eloquence of landscape and psychological casuistry: Linley with his "horrible delicacy of ear"; Denham, frustrated in his love, beating Lady Wariston's young brother with additional savagery because of the haunting difference between Herbert and his sister. Herbert's dream is a brilliant adolescent case study:

> He saw the star of Venus, white and flowerlike as he hadalways seen it, turn into a white rose and come down out of heaven, with a reddening centre that grew as it descended liker and liker a living mouth; but instead of desire he felt horror and sickness at the sight of it, and averted his lips with an effort to utter some prayer or exorcism; vainly, for the dreadful mouth only laughed, and came closer. And cheek or chin, eyebrow or eye, there was none; only this mouth. . . . (ch. 7)

Was Swinburne an important novelist *manqué*? Possibly the more objective form of the novel might have distanced the aggressively autobiographical had he persisted. Could he have achieved a *bildungsroman*? I incline to doubt it, though we must regret that the impossibility of an audience constrained him finally to abandon *Lesbia Brandon*, which is best regarded as the brilliant detritus of the poetry of the middle 1860's. When that poetry was written, there was little need for the novel, yet one would surely be content to exchange most of Swinburne's later verse for an achieved *Lesbia Brandon*.

VIII

That later verse can be summarily discussed. The second series of *Poems and Ballads* is a good miscellaneous volume: some pieces, such as "Ave Atque Vale" a dreamily eloquent memorial poem on Baudelaire whose theme reverses that of "Laus Veneris," were written in the middle 1860's. Another admirable poem, "A Forsaken Garden" has been well described as "symbolizing a total world beyond death and time realized through art alone": first of a kind of ideal autobiographical musing over those earlier years when Swinburne's emotional life had been most intense: "What lies before me is my past." In such a vein, he nearly always writes commandingly: "Thalassius" and "On the Cliffs" in later collections. This volume contains also a distinguished group of translations from François Villon, though Swinburne discreetly replaced certain lines by asterisks in his published version of "La Belle Heaulmière." His finest translation from Villon did not appear until 1964 in "The Ballad of Villon and Fat Madge," where the earthier and exuberantly comic aspects of Swinburne's genius, too often muted, are at last released:

> When all's made up she drops me a windy word,
> Bloat like a beetle, puffed and poisonous:
> Grins, thumps my pate, and calls me dickey-bird,
> And cuffs me with a fist that's ponderous.
> We sleep like logs, being drunken both of us;
> Then when we wake her womb begins to stir;
> To save her seed she gets me under her
> Wheezing and whining flat as planks are laid:
> And thus she spoils me as whoremonger
> Inside this brothel where we drive our trade.
> (*New Writings by Swinburne*, pp. 13–14)

The grimly wry and direct confessional note is brilliantly caught.

Four years later appeared the last major volume, *Tristram of Lyonesse and Other Poems.* In the title poem, Swinburne outdoes Tennyson's "Idylls of the Prince Consort" particularly "The Last Tournament" (1871), where Tristram and Iseult, as servants of Tennyson's cautionary tale against adultery, become coarse echoes of Launcelot and Guenevere: emblems of the autumnal moment of Arthur's court. By contrast, Swinburne presents them as guiltless, absolute for love, and wins a nice debating point by recounting how Modred is the fruit of Arthur's adultery with Morgause. Tennyson's presentation of Mark is nastily effective; Swinburne presents the King sympathetically, so intensifying the love-hate role of Iseult of Brittany. The architectonic of *Tristram of Lyonesse* depends on a cyclic rhythm of months and the larger rhythms of the sea acting out a tragic determinism. The repetition of certain words and phrases has been not inaptly compared with the leitmotifs of Wagner's luscious opera: "sea" "rose" "flame," "molten," "melting," and the image of unity through the four lips of the lovers becoming, at the close of the first canto, "one burning mouth" and "one silent mouth" at the last. Orgasm and death are associated, but with more tragic authority than in *Poems and Ballads.* The poem is too long: the third canto and the interspersed lyrics are mediocre, and the diction is not always satisfying. Still, despite all "languors and ardours" a strong and rapid narrative line remains; the meter acts like a funnel; the pace of the language carries one along and, for once, physical love is fulfillment. This prolonged hymn to erotic consummation remains the last irradiation of Swinburne's youth. From then on, though often skillful, Swinburne has increasingly less to say. Occasionally he hits on a new theme. It has been noted that he adds to the image of Pan so popular in the second half of the nineteenth century. In the three later poems devoted to the god, "A Nympholept," "Pan and Thalassius," and "The Palace of Pan," the goat-foot becomes ambiguous, close to Pater's presentation of Dionysus and Apollo. In Swinburne's version of him, Pan brings both terror and ecstasy, good and evil—so evading any sentimentalizing of nature. Recent criticism has with some justice pointed to the neglected achievements of Swinburne's later verse. It can hardly be denied that among the sad flux of the poetry after 1882 one can find impressive poems that have not been sufficiently remarked. "By the North Sea" for example, is one of the poet's most splendid offerings. Here, metrical brilliance is exercised in the evocation of a brooding underworld landscape that has only to be read once to haunt the memory.

IX

Most of the great English critics have been practicing poets; immediate examples comprise Ben Jonson, John Dryden, Samuel Johnson, Wordsworth, Coleridge, John Keats, Matthew Arnold, and Yeats. To this select group, Swinburne belongs, though important rather than great in his criticism. T. S. Eliot has aptly summarized its virtues: Swinburne had read widely and discriminatingly. And with the great critics, he has this in common: one senses that the whole European literary tradition is for him a continuous presence. His value judgments are firm and lasting. Eliot has pointed also to Swinburne's defects: his language, sometimes suggesting falsetto parody of his verse; hectic alliteration tangling with florid insult and rapture; his impatience with carrying through analysis; his refusal to focus rigorously on individual lines or images to make general points.

Such limitations partly rise from Swinburne's canons of criticism, which are both neoclassic and romantic. Neoclassic in that he believed in critical justice; in treating a work as a whole and in conversing with the reader by stating the pervasive general truth. This saves him from the disjunctive approach to Elizabethan drama of Charles Lamb and other earlier romantic critics, with their distillation of "specimens" and "beauties." Like Lamb, however, Swinburne is rarely aware that his texts are documents of the theater, created mostly under conditions of actual staging, not in some Parnassian airpump. In his later criticism particularly, Swinburne assumed the mannerism of Augustan prose with its pomp of periphrasis. His romantic aspect appears in an open-mindedness to originality, innovation, and difficulty. He was an enthusiast for George Chapman, Charlotte and Emily Brontë, Whitman—authors not precisely fashionable in the mid-nineteenth century. He was alert also to what was best (and worst) in his older and immediate contemporaries; but after 1879 he not merely failed to respond to younger contemporaries, he revoked some of his former generosities.

In the earlier criticism, he is sinuous in his sympathies. A devoted classicist, Swinburne found Shakespeare's *Troilus and Cressida* repulsive; he acutely senses that all the characters (with the possible exception of Ulysses) are flawed, even though he tends to identify Thersites' point of view with that of the author. Yet he can still refer to "this . . . mysterious and magnificent monster . . . one of the most admirable of all Shakespeare's works" at a time when few nineteenth-century critics could bring themselves even to discuss the play. In *A Study of Shakespeare* (1880), he takes a pioneering glance at the earlier quarto of *Hamlet*. About multiple authorship of the plays in the Shakespeare Folio, he is cautious: he finds that *Henry VIII* is Shakespeare's absolutely, and he refuses to enlarge the canon to admit the agreeable, anonymous *Edward III*, in a stylistic analysis of some length. His attacks on the New Shakespeare Society and on the yet wilder logic of certain German scholars are still funny and apposite. Himself an inspired amateur, Swinburne tended to have a low opinion of professional scholars. He knew as much, if not more than they, and the poetry was the thing. The oddity of his prose style often veils a luminous common sense about literary matters.

His dramatic criticism, is, however, less rewarding than his earlier essays on art and literature. The "Notes on Designs of the Old Masters at Florence" and the *Notes on the Royal Academy Exhibition, 1868*, with their lingering cadences and troubled images, influenced Pater (though Rossetti's prose is the archetype). Such evocations of works of art belong to a tradition of "impressionist" criticism that includes the aesthete and poisoner

T. G. Wainewright, William Hazlitt, and Théophile Gautier. In this tradition, impressions could be both subject and aesthetic object simultaneously. If we compare Swinburne's evocations of particular artifacts with those of Pater, we discover that, while both remain eloquent and suggestive, Pater more frequently intuits elements in the picture or the sculpture apparently not available from the historical record or within the limits of the observer's temperament.

Of the literary essays, we may note that on *Les Fleurs du Mal*, contributed in 1862 to the *Spectator*, in which Swinburne recognizes that "those who will look for them may find moralities in plenty behind every poem of M. Baudelaire." But in what is a very early though not simple-minded statement of the "art for art's sake" position in England, he urges that it is not the business of art to teach *directly*. If an artist is scrupulous in matters of art, his work will involve a corresponding moral scrupulousness. The *William Blake* essay contains the mature exposition of Swinburne's "art for art's sake" views. We may conclude with this quotation: "Art is not like fire or water, a good servant and a bad master; rather the reverse. . . . Handmaid of religion, exponent of duty, servant of fact, pioneer of morality, she cannot in any way become. . . . Her business is not to do good on other grounds, but do good on her own: all is well with her while she sticks fast to that."

Swinburne's essay on Byron begins by praising the third and fourth cantos of *Childe Harold*, but then sharply insists that the great Byron is only to be found in the satires, broadly the modern view. The polemical *Notes on Poems and Reviews* (1866) and *Under the Microscope* (1872), Swinburne's contribution to the "fleshly school" controversy around Rossetti, are written in the avowedly biased tradition of the pamphlet and still make trenchant reading.

His *William Blake* is not merely essential for an understanding of Swinburne's work in the 1860's; it remains one of the major documents of nineteenth-century criticism. An intensely difficult author is sympathetically and intelligently handled. Swinburne dismisses at once the widely held contemporary opinion that the obscurity of Blake's writing and the eccentricity of his opinions originate in his madness. Introducing a commentary on the prophetic books, Swinburne did not succeed, perhaps hardly wished to, in uncovering their dark mythological scheme. He was handicapped also by not being aware of the *Four Zoas*, which would have provided something of a key. But he does analyze searchingly such a work as *The Marriage of Heaven and Hell*, which he considered to be Blake's greatest. But the heart of the volume lies in the first two sections: the "Life and Designs" and the "Lyrical Poems." His Blake is of course made in Swinburne's image; as Harold Bloom puts it: "an uneasy blend of Rousseau and De Sade, at once somehow an heroic naturalist and an erotic rebel straining against even the limits of nature in his vitalism." Swinburne seizes on any opportunity to stress pagan joy in Blake and recounts the oral report that Blake had suggested the introduction of a second wife into his household. Failure to grasp that, for Blake, nature and imagination were antithetical lies at the heart of Swinburne's fruitful misunderstanding of Blake. For Swinburne the antinatural was generally limited to the anticonventional. Morality for him remains polarized with art for art's sake; there is no middle view, no alternative. As one critic observes, he is "hamstrung by the very puritan tradition he is trying to shake off." Consequently he anticipates Yeats in making a gnostic of Blake, a sexual (but not ascetic) antinomian, for whom the erotic is demonic illusion. As the extract already quoted shows, the demiurge who

> created the sexual and separate body of man did but cleave in twain "the divine humanity" . . . is a divine daemon, liable to error, subduable by and through this very created nature of his invention, which he for the present imprisons and torments. His law is the law of Moses, which according to the Manichean heresy Christ came to reverse as diabolic. (*William Blake*, 1868 ed., pp. 155–156)

It is perhaps less that Swinburne misunderstands than that he diminishes Blake by imprisoning him in this simple dualism of preference for desire and energy over reason and restraint. Swinburne brilliantly but falsely interprets *The Marriage of Heaven and Hell* as an inversion of accepted values, not sensing that the "spiralling contraries" of that mélange of prose and verse are both necessary. Missing the two meanings of "hell" in "The Marriage", he actually invents two meanings of "nature" in *Jerusalem* and *Milton*, because his neo-Sadian theology requires that. Wonderful book though it is, the *William Blake* could have been a different, perhaps better work if Swinburne had not as usual paused at the point of moving beyond a Blake necessary for himself. He recognizes, for example, that the *Songs of Innocence and of Experience* are counterpointed, but does not proceed with the insight; and after one piece of actual exegesis of the prophetic books that is now generally accepted, Swinburne hastily flinches, "Lest, however, we be found unawares on the side of those hapless angels and baboons, we will abstain with all due care from any not indispensable analysis." Yet what Yeats was to term "the great procession of symbols" was surely indispensable.

X

Swinburne was a pertinacious author of poetic dramas. For this activity, the nineteenth century was barely auspicious. To isolate any single cause is difficult: there was the evangelical assault on the play and the player and the tyranny of Shakespeare, while English prose drama was itself in eclipse (painfully recovering in the 1860's with the work of Tom Taylor and Thomas Robertson). The English scene, moreover, had been unusually barren of good dramatic criticism. Although there were actor-managers ready to encourage poets, Tennyson and Browning achieved no more than moderate success. But Shelley and Thomas Beddaes, who wrote for private reading rather than performance, were more successful—could at least challenge the later Jacobeans. Swinburne follows their practice (we noted how in his own dramatic criticism he took little account of stage conditions).

His two early plays, *The Queen-Mother* and *Rosamond*, reveal Jacobean influence crossed with Pre-Raphaelitism. In either case, a strong matriarch, queens Catherine and Eleanor, destroys other women. The character of Denise, maid-in-waiting and devoted mistress to Henry III of France, is a triumph. *The Queen-Mother* pivots on her role as the Queen's pawn in bringing on the King's involvement with the Bartholomew massacre and her reactions on realizing she has been misled. *Chastelard*, first of the Mary Stuart trilogy, is closely tuned with *Poems and Ballads*. Mary at once enjoys and detests her role as fatal woman; Chastelard himself is one who finds erotic consummation in death; but it is difficult for the reader to involve his emotions with either. The exposition is competent, the verse often striking, and the scene where Chastelard induces Mary to kiss him on the neck at the spot where he knows the axe will fall is luridly memorable. In *Bothwell* (1874) and *Mary Stuart* (1881), Swinburne perceptibly becomes more constrained by historical sources and more sympathetic to Mary, but in these plays her character is comparatively weakly projected. The later plays sometimes display routine skill in exploiting situation; but few of them now hold their interest. *The Sisters* (1892), however, has unusual qualities. Set ostensibly in 1816, it involves once more the close aristocratic world of *Love's Cross Currents* and is deeply autobiographical—the last reworking of the Mary Gordon story. The blank verse is relaxed:

Anne: April again, and not a word of war.
Last year, and not a year ago, it was
That we sat wondering when good news would come.

Mabel: And had not heard or learnt in lesson-books
If such a place there was as Waterloo.

. . .

Reginald: We are lucky. There's the old laboratory, made
It seems for our stage purpose, where you know
Sir Edward kept his chemicals and things—
Collections of the uncanniest odds and ends. . . .

(I.i; III.i)

That last epithet has a casual 1890's note. Swinburne should have realized that his general idiom was suitable for comedy or tragifarce, but not for tragedy. Anne, the jealous, murdering sister, deviates into high blank verse and the play reaches a faltering climax through a holocaust, which, although set in a nineteenth-century drawing room, is worthy of Jacobean tragedy.

XI

Swinburne discovered his poetic identity through the distinction between personality and "self" trapped within personality, in his case an absurd body, without access to women. His solution was to transmute concrete being into artifice by imitation, parody, and caricature. In other words, he tried to release identity by remolding the styles of the past into an integrity that was of the surface only, and thus to achieve selfhood with the aid of tradition. But the price was negation of development; the quest for unity of being was broken off at a stage of precarious balance. This disequilibrium begins with *Songs Before Sunrise,* where the self is unlocated, is operatically merely voice. Such failure of the redemptive imagination in the middle years has precedents in romantic poetry; in, for example, Wordsworth and Coleridge, though both these poets were able to transfer loss into triumph. But Wordsworth, however unlike Swinburne in most respects, furnishes a model of genius mutating into low-keyed talent. Swinburne found no means of living out a mythology, or rather the self-mythology he could live by proved self-defeating. As a consequence Swinburne was not able to take up history and nation into the self-drama. He belonged to a dying class; there was no idea or group with which he could fruitfully identify, and this explains the abstractions and inconsistencies of his political attitudes. The price of negating development was that his work finally became pure surface over void. Those strict forms of rondeau and sonnet by which he sought to chasten an imagined abundance merely emphasized poverty. Fixed at the level of tension between personality and self, Swinburne failed to arrive at a notion of antiself "filling up all that the self fell short in." As a consequence the self was never reborn. Had Swinburne correctly read *The Marriage of Heaven and Hell,* he would have grasped that the dialectic of poetic development lay through "spiralling contraries."

Selected Bibliography

BIBLIOGRAPHY

T. J. Wise, *A Bibliography of the Writings in Prose and Verse of A. C. Swinburne,* 2 vols, (London, 1919–1920); *The Ashley Library: A Catalogue of Printed Books, Manuscripts and Autograph Letters,* T. J. Wise, ed. 11 vols. (London, 1922–1936), vols. VI–X (1925–1930) contain Swinburne entries; *A Swinburne Library,* T. J. Wise (London, 1925), a repr. of vol. VI, privately printed, limited ed.; *Swinburne's Literary Career and Fame,* C. J. Hyder, (Durham, N.C., 1933); *An Enquiry Into the Nature of Certain Nineteenth-Century Pamphlets,* J. Carter and H. G. Pollard, (London, 1934), exposes Wise's forgeries of eds. of Swinburne, *Bibliographies of Twelve Victorian Authors,* T. G. Ehrsam, R. H. Deily and R. M. Smith, (New York, 1936). *Forging Ahead,* W. Partington, (New York, 1939), enl. ed. titled *Thomas J. Wise in the Original Cloth* (London, 1946); *The Firm of Charles Ottley, Landon & Co.: Footnote to An Enquiry,* J. Carter and H. G. Pollard, (London, 1948); *The Victorian Poets: A Guide to Research,* F. E. Faverty, ed. (Cambridge, Mass., 1956, rev. ed. 1968); Swinburne studies are discussed by C. K. Hyder, *Texas Quarterly,* Swinburne Manuscripts at Texas, W. B. Todd, P. 2 (Autumn 1959), essays by J. Carter, H. G. Pollard, and W. B. Todd; *Pre-Raphaelitism: A Bibliocritical Study*, E. Fredeman (Cambridge, Mass., 1965).

COLLECTED WORKS

The Poetical Works (New York, 1884). also includes some dramas, *The Queen-Mother, Rosamond, Chastelard, Atalanta in Calydon, Bothwell,* and *Erechtheus; The Poems*, 6 vols. (London, 1904); *The Tragedies*, 5 vols. (London, 1905); *Poems and Tragedies*, 2 vols. (Philadelphia, 1910); *The Golden Pine Edition*, 7 vols. (London, 1917–1925); *Collected Poetical Works*, 2 vols. (London, 1924); *The Complete Works*, 20 vols. (London, 1925–1927); the Bonchurch ed., vols. I–X contain the poetry and dramas; *The Swinburne Letters*, C. Y. Lang, ed. 6 vols. (New Haven, Conn., 1959–1962).

SELECTED WORKS

R. H. Stoddard, ed., *Selections* (New York, 1884); *Selections* (London, 1887); *Lyrical Poems*, W. Sharp, ed. (Leipzig, 1901), the Tauchnitz ed., *Dead Love and Other Inedited Pieces* (Portland, Me., 1901); W. M. Payne, ed., *Selected Poems* (Boston, 1905); *Selected Lyrical Poems* (New York, 1906); *Poems*, A. Beatty, ed. (New York, 1906); *Dramas*, A. Beatty, ed. (New York, 1909); selected by the ed.; *A Pilgrimage of Pleasure, Essays and Studies* (Boston, 1913), contains, "A Pilgrimage of Pleasure," "Dead Love," "Les Fleurs du Mal," "Charles Dickens," and some reviews, also a bibliography of the works of Swinburne by E. J. O'Brien; *Springtide of Life: Poems of Childhood*, E. Gosse, ed. (London, 1918); *Poems*, E. Rhys, ed. (New York, 1919); Modern Library ed., *Selections*, E. Gosse and T. J. Wise, eds. (London, 1919); *A Golden Book of Swinburne's Lyrics*, E. H. Blakeney, ed. (London, 1922); *The Triumph of Time and Other Poems*, G. S. Viereck, ed. (Girard, Kans., 1925); *Selections*, W. O. Raymond, ed. (New York, 1925); *Selections*, H. M. Burton, ed. (Cambridge, 1927); *Selected Poems*, H. Wolfe, ed. (London, 1928); *The Best of Swinburne*, C. K. Hyder and L. Chase, eds. (New York, 1937); *Selected Poems*, L. Binyon, ed. (London, 1939); World's Classics ed., *Poems and Prose*, R. Church, ed. (London, 1940); Everyman Library ed., *Selected Poems*, Treece, ed. (London, 1948); *Selected Poems*, H. Hare, ed. (London, 1950); *Selected Poems*, E. Shanks, ed. (London, 1950); *A Swinburne Anthology: Verse, Drama, Prose, Criticism*, K. Foss, ed. (London, 1955); *Swinburne: A Selection*, E. Sitwell, ed. (London, 1960); *Poems*, B. Dobré, ed. (London, 1961); *New Writings by Swinburne: A Medley of Poems, Critical Essays, Hoaxes and Burlesques*, C. V. Lang, ed. (Syracuse, 1964); *Selected Poetry and Prose*, J. D. Rosenberg, ed. (New York, 1968); *Poems and Ballads and Atalanta in Calydon*, M. Peckham, ed. (New York, 1970); *Swinburne as Critic*, C. K. Hyder (London-Boston, 1972).

SEPARATE WORKS

J. F. Waller, ed. "William Congreve," in *Imperial Dictionary of Universal Biography*, 3 vols. (London, 1857); repr. in, *Pericles and Other Studies*, (London, 1914); *Laugh and Lie Down*, (London, 1859); *The Queen-Mother, Rosamond: Two Plays*, (London, 1860); "Dead Love", in *Once a Week* (October 1862), short story repr. *ca.*1888 in a forced first ed. (1864; facs. ed. 1904); "The Sundew," in *Spectator* (July 26, 1862) a rev. version appears in, *Poems and Ballads* (London, 1866); "The Pilgrimage of Pleasure," M. Gordon, *Children of the Chapel*, (London, 1864), a morality play included as ch. 5 in *Atalanta in Calydon: A Tragedy* (London, 1865; facs. repr. Oxford, 1930); *Chastelard: A Tragedy* (London, 1865); *Poems and Ballads* (London, 1866), issued first by Moxon, then by Hotten; *Notes on Poems and Reviews* (London, 1866); Swinburne's reply to his critics, repr. in C. K. Hyder, ed., *Swinburne Replies*, (Syracuse, N.Y., 1966); "Preface," in *A Selection from the Works of Lord Byron*, (London, 1866), an excellent essay on Byron; "Cleopatra," in *Cornhill* (September 1866), poem written to illus. a drawing by F. Sandys (repr. ca. 1887 in a forged ed. dated 1866); *An Appeal to England* (London, 1867), verse, for clemency to the Fenian rebels, publ. simultaneously in the *Morning Star* (November 22, 1867) and as a broadside; "Regret," in *Fortnightly Review* (September 1867), verse, repr. in rev. form in *Poems and Ballads: Second Series*, (London, 1878); *A Song of Italy* (London, 1867); *William Blake: A Critical Essay* (London, 1868), seems to have been available in December 1867; *Notes on the Royal Academy Exhibition, 1868* (London, 1868), repr. with omissions in, *Essays and Studies*, (London, 1875); "Siena," in *Lippincott's* (June 1868), separately printed the same year in Philadelphia and London; "Introduction," in *Christabel and the Lyrical and Imaginative Poems of S. T. Coleridge* (London, 1869).

Ode on the Proclamation of the French Republic (London, 1870); "Tristram and Iseult: Prelude of an Unfinished Poem," in [J. Friswell, ed.], *Pleasure: A Holiday Book of Prose and Verse*, (London, 1871); rev. in, *Tristram of Lyonesse*, (London, 1882); *Songs Before Sunrise* (London, 1871); *Bothwell, Act One* (London, 1871), privately printed; *Under the Microscope* (London, 1872), a masterly, ironic prose pamphlet directed against the philistine critics of Rossetti and himself; [A. Lemerre, ed.]. *Le Tombeau de Théophile,Gautier* (Paris, 1873), poems by various authors on the death of Gautier, those by Swinburne in four languages, two in English, two in French, one in Latin, one in Greek. *Bothwell: A Tragedy* (London, 1874); "Introduction," *The Works of George Chapman* (London, 1874–1875), also separately printed the same year; *Songs of Two*

Nations (London, 1875); "The Devil's Due," in *Examiner* (December 11, 1875), published under the pseudonym "Thomas Maitland," a privately printed ed., dated 1875, appeared ca. 1896 and is probably forged; *Essays and Studies* (London, 1875); "Francis Beaumont" and "John Fletcher," in *Encyclopaedia Britannica*, (London, 1875); *Notes of an English Republican on the Muscovite Crusade* (London, 1876); "Introduction," in C. J. Wells, *Joseph and His Brethren: A Dramatic Poem* (London, 1876), I have suspected that Swinburne may have been more actively concerned with the revision; *Erechtheus: A Tragedy* (London, 1876); *Lesbia Brandon* (London, 1877), novel, only galley proofs printed, used by R. Hughes in his 1952 ed.; *A Note on Charlotte Brontë* (London, 1877); "William Congreve," in *Encyclopaedia Britannica*, (London, 1877); *Poems and Ballads: Second Series*, (London, 1878); *An Election* (London, 1879), verse, a lithographed pamphlet; "Frank Fane: A Ballad," in *Pearl*, 1 (1879), an unsigned contribution to an "underground" magazine.

Songs of the Springtides (London, 1880); *Specimens of Modern Poets: The Heptalogia, or The Seven Against Sense* (London, 1880), a vol. of parodies. *Studies in Song* (London, 1880); *A Study of Shakespeare* (London, 1880); *Mary Stuart: A Tragedy* (London, 1881); *Tristram of Lyonesse and Other Poems* (London, 1882); *A Century of Roundels* (London, 1883); the strict form adopted by Swinburne to chasten his fluency, an object not achieved; "Dolorida," in A. Moore, ed., *Walnuts and Wine*, (London, 1883); verses in French; "Introduction," *Les Cenci* (Paris, 1883); intro. in French to T. Dorian's trans. of Shelley's play "Christopher Marlowe," in *Encyclopaedia Britannica* (London, 1883); "Mary Queen of Scots," in *Encyclopaedia Britannica* (London, 1883); "Wordsworth and Byron," in *Nineteenth Century* (April–May 1884); *A Midsummer Holiday and Other Poems* (London, 1884); *Marino Faliero: A Tragedy* (London, 1885); *The Commonweal: A Song for Unionists* (London, 1886); repr. from the *Times* (London, July 1, 1886); *Miscellanies* (London, 1886); a collection of previously printed periodical and encyclopedia articles; *A Study of Victor Hugo* (London, 1886); "Introduction," in H. Ellis, ed., *Thomas Middleton* (London, 1887), The Mermaid ed., *A Word for the Navy* (London, 1887); verse, privately printed. *The Whippingham Papers* (London, 1888), privately printed, about half the vol. written by Swinburne; "Cyril Tourneur," in *Encyclopaedia Britannica*, (London, 1889); *A Study of Ben Jonson* (London, 1889); *Poems and Ballads: Third Series* (London, 1889); *The Ballad of Dead Men's Bay* (London, 1889); "A Logical Ballad of Home Rule," in *St. James's Gazette* (March 2, 1889).

A Sequence of Sonnets on the Death of Robert Browning (London, 1890); privately printed; "Preface," in R. Herrick, *The Hesperides and Noble Numbers* (London, 1891); the Muses' Library ed.; *Music: An Ode* (London, 1892); *The Sisters: A Tragedy* (London, 1892); *Grace Darling* (London, 1893), verse, privately printed; *Astrophel and Other Poems* (London, 1894); *Studies in Prose and Poetry* (London, 1894); *Robert Burns: A Poem* (Edinburgh, 1896), privately printed and pirated; *The Tale of Balen* (London, 1896), verse; "Introduction," in E. B. Browning, *Aurora Leigh* (London, 1898); *A Channel Passage* (London, 1899); *Rosamond, Queen of the Lombards: A Tragedy* (London, 1899); "Victor Hugo," in *Encyclopaedia Britannica*, (London, 1902); *Percy Bysshe Shelley* (Philadelphia, 1903), also publ. in, *Chambers Cyclopaedia of English Literature* (London, 1903); *A Channel Passage and Other Poems* (London, 1904), includes numerous poems previously published only in periodicals; *Love's Cross Currents: A Year's Letters* (London, 1905), novel, first published in installments in the *Tatler* (August 25 through December 29, 1877), pirated in an ed. from Portland, Me., 1901, and publ. in a fuller version in 1905. "Introduction," in *Pericles*, (London, 1907); vol. XIII Lee's ed. of Shakespeare (London, 1906–1909); *The Duke of Gandia* (London, 1908), drama, reads like an early work; *The Age of Shakespeare* (London, 1908); *M. Prudhomme at the International Exhibition* (London, 1909), privately printed; *Of Liberty and Loyalty* (London, 1909), privately printed; *The Saviour of Society* (London, 1909), verse, privately printed; *The Portrait* (London, 1909), verse, privately printed; *The Marriage of Monna Lisa* (London, 1909), privately printed; *The Chronicle of Queen Fredegond* (London, 1909), privately printed; *In the Twilight: A Poem* (London, 1909), privately printed; *Lord Scales: A Ballad by a Borderer* (London, 1909), privately printed; *Lord Soulis: A Ballad by a Borderer* (London, 1909), privately printed; *The Worm of Spindlestonheugh: A Ballad by a Borderer* (London, 1909), privately printed; *Border Ballads* (London, 1909), privately printed; contains Earl Robert Duries Dyke Westland Well, *"Ode to Mazzini,"* (London, 1909), privately printed; *Shakespeare* (London, 1909).

A Criminal Case: A Sketch (London, 1910), privately printed; *A Record of Friendship* (London, 1910), privately printed; Swinburne's account of his relationship with Rossetti and Lizzie Rossetti written in 1882 after Rossetti's death. *The Ballade of Truthful Charles and Other Poems* (London, 1910), privately printed; *Les Fleurs du Mal, and Other Studies* (London, 1913), privately printed; *Charles Dickens* (London, 1913), repr. in part from, "Quarterly Review," (July 1902). *A Study of Victor Hugo's, "Les Misérables,"* E. Gosse, ed. (London, 1914), privately printed, the first and fifth essays not by Swinburne; *Pericles and Other Studies* (London, 1914), privately printed;, reprs. *Pericles*, with essays and articles not separately published elsewhere; *Thomas Nabbes: A Critical Monograph* (London, 1914), privately printed; *Chris-*

topher Marlowe in Relation to Greene, Peele and Lodge (London, 1914), privately printed; *Théophile*, E. Gosse, ed. (London, 1915), privately printed; *Lady Maisie's Bairn, and Other Poems* (London, 1915), privately printed; *Poems from Villon, and Other Fragments* (London, 1916); *The Death of Sir John Franklin* (London, 1916), privately printed, an undergraduate poem; *The Triumph of Gloriana*, E. Gosse, ed. (London, 1916), privately printed; *Poetical Fragments* (London, 1916), privately printed; *A Vision of Bags*, E. Gosse, ed. (London, 1916), burlesque, privately printed; *Wearieswá: A Ballad* (London, 1917), privately printed; *The Posthumous Poems*, E. Gosse and T. J. Wise, eds. (London, 1917); *Rondeaux Parisiens* (London, 1917), privately printed; *The Italian Mother, and Other Poems* (London, 1918), privately printed; *The Ride from Milan, and Other Poems* (London, 1918), privately printed; *The Two Knights, and Other Poems* (London, 1918), privately printed; *A Lay of Lilies, and Other Poems* (London, 1918), privately printed; *Queen Yseult: A Poem in Six Cantos* (London, 1918), privately printed; *Undergraduate Sonnets* (London, 1918), privately printed; *Lancelot, The Death of Rudel, and Other Poems* (London, 1918), privately printed; *The Character and Opinions of Dr. Johnson* (London, 1918), privately printed; *Contemporaries of Shakespeare*, E. Gosse and T. J. Wise, eds. (London, 1919); *The Queen's Tragedy* (London, 1919), privately printed; *French Lyrics* (London, 1919), privately printed.

W. A. Maclnnes, ed., *Ballads of the English Border* (London, 1925), includes all known previously publ. and unpubl. ballads; *Swinburne's Hyperion, and Other Poems*, G. Lafourcade, ed. (London, 1928); *Lucretia Borgia: The Chronicle of Tebaldeo Tebaldei*, R. Hughes, ed. (London, 1942); C. K. Hyder, ed. "Swinburne: 'Changes of Aspect' and 'Short Notes'," *PMLA*, 58 (March 1943); *A Roundel of Retreat*, (Washington, D.C., 1950), privately printed, the imprint reading "London, Charles Ottley, Landon & Co., 1950," clearly a joke; *Pasiphaë: A Poem*, R. Hughes, ed. (London, 1950), an extremely interesting fragment dated approximately (1866); *Will Drew and Phil Crewe and Frank Fane by a Great English Literary Figure*, (1962), privately printed; *Le Prince Proletaire* (Bethesda, Md., 1963), privately printed; *The Influence of the Roman Censorship on the Morals of the People* (Brooklyn, 1964), privately printed; *New Writings by Swinburne*, C. Y. Lang, ed. (Syracuse, N.Y., 1964), includes some uncollected poems, the early burlesques, *La Soeur de la Reine, and La Fille du Policeman*, with extensive annotations; *Swinburne Replies*, C. K. Hyder, ed. (Syracuse, N.Y., 1966), repr., *Notes on Poems and Reviews, Under the Microscope, and the Dedicating Epistle to the Collection of 1899*, with an intro. and notes; *Shelley*, J. S. Mayfield, ed. (Worcester, Mass., 1973); *A Year's Letters*, F. J. Sypher, ed. (New York, 1974); reedited from British Library MS Ashley 5073 and MS in J. A. Symington Collection, Rutgers University Library; *Hide and Seek*, J. S. Mayfield, ed. (London, 1975), with notes, an early unpublished poem in the meter of Meredith's *Love in the Valley*, E. P. Schuldt, ed., "Some Unpublished Balliol Essays of A. C. Swinburne," in *Review of English Studies*, 27 (November 1976).

Letters from Swinburne have been published in the following issues of *Notes and Queries*: 19 (February 1972), 20 (February 1974), 21 (June 1974), 22 (October 1975), 23 (February 1976), 26 (August 1979), 27 (June 1980).

Note: There are numerous MSS extant. Particularly important are those in the Ashley collection in the British Museum.

BIOGRAPHICAL AND CRITICAL STUDIES

Baron Houghton [R. M. Milnes] "Swinburne's Atalanta in Calydon," in *Edinburgh Review*, 122:249 (July 1865); *Fortnightly Review*, Baron Houghton [R. M. Milnes], "Mr. Swinburne's *Chastelard*," 4:23 (April 15, 1866); *Poems and Ballads* in *Athenaeum*, R. W. Buchanan, review of, in *Athenaeum*, p. 2 (1866); *Fortnightly Review*, R. W. Buchanan, "Immortality in Authorship," 6:33 (September 15, 1866); *Saturday Review*, J. M. Morley, "Mr. Swinburne's New Poems," 22 (August 4, 1866); *Swinburne's Poems and Ballads: A Criticism*,W. M. Rossetti (London, 1866); *National Reformer*, J. Thomson, "The Swinburne Controversy," (December 23, 1866), repr. in his, *Satires and Profanities* (London, 1884); *William Blake*, in *Fortnightly Review*, M. D. Conway, review of, n.s. 3:14 (February 1, 1868); *Temple Bar*, A. Austin, "The Poetry of the Period: Mr. Swinburne," 26 (July 1869), repr. in his *The Poetry of the Period* (London, 1870).

R.W. Buchanan, *The Fleshly School of Poetry* (London, 1872); *Quarterly Review*, W. J. Courthorpe, "The Latest Development of Literary Poetry: Swinburne, Rossetti, Morris," 132:263 (January, 1872); *Nineteenth Century*, W. K. Clifford, "Cosmic Emotion," 2 (October 1877), repr. in his, *Lectures and Essays* (London, 1879); *Histoires lnsolites*,V. de l'Isle Adam (Paris, 1888), contains "Le Sadisme Anglais."

O. Wilde, review of *Poems and Ballads: Third Series*, in *Pall Mall Gazette*, p. 27 (June 1889), repr. in his *Reviews*, vol. 11 (London, 1910); *Modern Studies*, O. Elton, (London, 1907); *Algernon Charles Swinburne: A Critical Study*, E. Thomas (London, 1912); *Catalogue of the Library of Swinburne*, Sotheby, Wilkinson and Hodge (London, June 19–21, 1916); *The Life of Algemon Charles Swinburne*, E. Gosse (London, 1917), repr. in Bonchurch ed. vol. XIX; *The Boyhood of Swinburne*, M. C. J. Leith (London, 1917); *Fortnightly Review*, A. Symons, "Swinburne," n.s. 101:605 (May 1917); *Modern Language Review*, E. Gosse, "The First

Draft of Swinburne's Anactoria," 14 (July 1919), also privately printed, n.d., and repr. in his *Aspects and Impressions* (London, 1922).

T. S. Eliot, *The Sacred Wood*, (London, 1920), contains essays "Swinburne as Critic" and "Swinburne as Poet"; *The Home Life of Swinburne*, C. Watts-Dunton (London, 1922); *Revue Anglo-Américaine*, G. Lafourcade, "Swinburne et Baudelaire," 1 (February 1924); *Atalanta in Calydon*: "le manuscrit, les sources," G. Lafourcade, in "Revue Anglo-Américaine," 3 (October–December 1925); *A Study of Swinburne*, T. E. Welby (London, 1926); *Swinburne*, H. Nicolson, (London, 1926); *Modern Language Review*, G. Lafourcade, "Swinburne and Whitman," 22 (January 1927), rev. version in, *Revue Anglo-Americaine* 9 (October 1931); *La Jeunesse de Swinburne 1837–1876*, G. Lafourcade, 2 vols. (Paris, 1928); *PMLA*, C. K. Hyder, "*Laus Veneris* and the Tannhäuser Legend," 45 (December 1930); *La Carne, la Morte e il Diavolo nella Letteratura Romantica*, M. Praz (Florence, 1930), trans. as *The Romantic Agony* (Oxford, 1933), a pathography of romantic literature; *PMLA*, C. K. Hyder, "The Medieval Background in 'The Leper'," 46 (December 1931); *Swinburne's Literary Career and Fame*, C. K. Hyder (Durham, N.C., 1931); *Swinburne: A Literary Biography*, G. Lafourcade (London, 1932); *PMLA*, C. K. Hyder, "Swinburne and the Popular Ballad," 49 (March 1934); *Hippocrate*, G. Lafourcade, "L'Algolagnie et Swinburne," (March–April 1935); *Études Anglaises*, G. Lafourcade, "Le Triomphe du Temps: ou la réputation de Swinburne," 1 (March 1937; *PMLA*, R. C. Child, "Swinburne's Mature Standards of Criticism," 52 (September 1937).

R. Hughes, "Unpublished Swinburne," in *Life and Letters*, 56 (January 1948); *Studies in Philology*, C. Dahl, "Swinburne's Loyalty to the House of Stuart," 46 (July 1949); *PMLA*, J. A. Cassidy, "Robert Buchanan and the Fleshly Controversy," 67 (March 1952); *PMLA*, J. K. Robinson, "A Neglected Phase of the Aesthetic Movement: English Parnassianism," 68 (September 1953), relates Swinburne's experiments in Old French forms to similar work by Lang, Gosse, Dobson, etc.; *Swinburne's Boo*, J. S. Mayfield (Bethesda, Md., 1953), privately printed, repr. in, *English Miscellany*, 4 (Rome, 1953), separately bound and privately reiss. (Washington, D.C., 1954); *Yale University Library Gazette*, C. Y. Lang, "The First Chorus of *Atalanta*," 27 (January 1953); *The Critic's Alchemy*, R. Z. Temple (New York, 1953), on Swinburne as critic and interpreter of French literature; *Journal of Rutgers University Library*, C. Y. Lang, "Some Swinburne Manuscripts," 18 (Autumn 1954); *Harvard Library Bulletin*, A. W. Henry [Ehrenpreis], "A Reconstructed Swinburne Ballad," 12 (Autumn 1958); *Modern Language Review*, P. R. Baum, "The Fitzwilliam Manuscript of Swinburne's *Atalanta*, Verses 1,038–1,204," 54 (1959).

C. Y. Lang, "*Atalanta* in Manuscript," in *Yale University Library Gazette*, 37 (July 1962); *Swinburne's Theory of Poetry*, T. E. Connolly (Albany, N.Y., 1964); *The Crowns of Apollo: Swinburne's Principles of Literature and Art*, R. L. Peters, (Detroit, 1965); *Victorian Studies*, J. D. Rosenberg, "Swinburne," 11:2 (December 1967); *American Book Collector*, "A Rare Find," 17 (March 6, 1967), two missing pages of *Lesbia Brandon*; *Dalhousie Review*, R. E. Lougy, "Swinburne's Poetry" and "Twentieth-Century Criticism," 48 (Autumn 1968); *Queen's Quarterly*, K. McSweeney, "The Structure of Swinburne's *Tristram of Lyonesse*," 75:iv (Winter 1968); *Swinburne: A Critical Biography*, J. O. Fuller (London, 1968), useful, if somewhat highlighted; *PMLA*, R. L. Peters, "A. C. Swinburne's 'Hymn to Proserpine': The Work Sheets," 83 (October 1968).

C. K. Hyder, ed., *Swinnburne: The Critical Heritage*, (London, 1970), a useful anthology of views of Swinburne's work and personality up to the period before WW1; *Victorian Revolutionaries: Speculations on Some Heroes of a Culture Crisis*, M. Peckham (New York, 1970); *Victorian Poetry*, C. Y. Lang, ed. 9: i–ii (Spring–Summer 1971), a special issue devoted to Swinburne, contains some of the finest criticism to date, particularly essays by T. L. Wymar and R. Mathews on *Atalanta*, by J. Baird on "Swinburne, Sade and Blake," by D. A. Cook on "Anactoria," and by J. J. McGann on "Ave Atque Vale"; *Studies in English Literature*, K. McSweeney, "Swinburne's *Poems and Ballads* (1866)," 11 (Autumn 1971); *At the Pines: Swinburne and Watts-Dutton in Putney*, M. Panter-Downes (London-New York, 1971); *Swinburne's Poetics*, M. Raymond (The Hague, 1971); *Swinburne: An Experiment in Criticism*, J. J. McGann (Chicago, 1972); *Studies in Philology*, W. D. Jenkins, "Swinburne, Robert Buchanan, W. S. Gilbert," 79: iii (1972), suggests that reflections of Swinburne's sado-masochism appear in some of the choric passages in *Patience* and relates the character of Grosvenor in *Patience* to Buchanan; *Texas Studies in Literature*, B. F. Fisher IV, "Swinburne's *Tristram of Lyonesse* in Process," 14:3 (Fall 1972); *Victorian Studies*, J. O. Jordan, "The Sweet Face of Mothers: Psychological Pattems in *Atalanta in Calydon*," 11:2 (Summer 1973); *Swinhurneiana: A Gallimaufry of Bits and Pieces About Algernon Charles Swinburne*, J. S. Mayfield (Gaithersbury-London, 1974); *Swinburne: The Portrait of a Poet*, P. Henderson (London, 1974); *Victorian Poetry*, R. C. Murfin, "Athens Unbound: The Unity of Swinburne's *Erechtheus*," 12:3 (Autumn, 1974); *Notes and Queries*, J. Forces, "Two Flagellation Poems by Swinburne," 22 (October 1975), attributes to Swinburne two poems found in the pornographic periodical *Pearl*: "Frank Fane, a Ballad," and "Charlie Collingwood's Flogging"; *Aeolian Harps*, I. Frieke and D. C. Frieke, eds, "The Proserpine Figure in Swinburne's

Poems and Ballads I," (Bowling Green, Ohio, 1976); *English Language Notes*, D. C. Frick, "The Idea of Love in Swinburne's *The Sundew*," 13 (March 1976); *Victorian Poetry*, T. L. Meyers, "Shelley's Influence on *Atalanta in Calydon*," 14:2 (Summer 1976); *Victorian Poetry*, R. A. Greenberg, "Swinburne and the Re-Definition of Classical Myth," 14:3 (Autumn 1976); *A Pre-Raphaelite Circle*, R. Trevelyan (London, 1978), material on Swinburne's relations with the Trevelyan family; *Swinburne, Hardy, Lawrence and the Burden of Belief*, R. C. Murfin (Chicago, 1978); *English Literary History*, G. M. Ridenour, "Time and Eternity in Swinburne: Minute Particulars in Five Poems," 45 (Spring 1978); *Swinburne: A Study of Romantic Mythmaking*, D. G. Riede (Charlottesville, Va., 1978); *Swinburne: The Poet in His World*, D. Thomas (Oxford, 1979); *The Pre-Raphaelite Review*, J. W. Rosenbaum, "Of Hunts and Hunters: *Atalanta in Calydon*," 3 (November 1979).

A. H. Harrison, "Love Strong as Death and Valour Strong as Love: Swinburne and Courtly Love," in *Victorian Poetry*, 181 (Spring 1980); *Journal of Pre-Raphaelite Studies*, C. W. Morley, "Swinburne as Art Critic," 1:2 (May 1981); *Tennyson and Swinburne as Romantic Naturalists*, K. McSweeney (Toronto-London, 1981), a brave attempt to rehabilitate the later Swinburne; "The Poetry of Swinburne," in W. E. Buckler, *The Victorian Imagination* (Brighton, 1981).

ALFRED TENNYSON
(1809–1892)

BRIAN SOUTHAM

I

FOR MANY YEARS the prevailing image of Tennyson has been of one of the great corruptors of English poetry, of a writer with a style so meretricious and insidiously molding that he misshaped the taste of generations of readers and the practice of generations of poets. A succession of influential critics, from Matthew Arnold to F. R. Leavis (and their many disciples), have condemned Tennyson as a second-rater, as an artist of Tennysonian verse—polished, melodious, and decorative; and in this artistry marooned, isolated from the central vitality of English poetry, cut off from the resources of the living language as Keats, immediately before him, was not. In this perspective the creative effort of Yeats, Eliot, and Pound, at the beginning of the century, is seen as a disinfection of poetic language and style, a breaking away from the Tennysonian embrace and the foundation of the modern movement as a counterforce to the Victorian poetic: the old style characteristically escapist, weakly romantic, medievalizing, moralizing, sentimental, simple, and unsubtle in its thought and feeling, the new style characteristically intelligent, unromantic, subtle, and complex in its tones and irony, realistic in its approach to human experience, seeking not to escape but to confront.

Broadly, this is an acceptable theory of action and reaction. Tennyson's popular style was indeed swamping; it formed public taste and set a standard by which poetry was to be judged; and a great deal of his writing can be described as Tennysonian, the heavy hand against which the modern poets turned in protest, just as there was a widespread reaction against Victorianism in general. Tennyson suffered particularly as the representative Victorian poet. His rejection was part of a historical process. But the continuing prejudice against Tennyson is as indefensible as the romantics' rejection of Pope and Dryden. Difference is not inferiority. Although there is a good deal of Tennyson that is pompous, banal, grotesquely sentimental, and in many other ways laughably or unpleasantly Victorian, there is a sufficient body of his finest work to place him among the great poets of English literature. The refreshing challenge for anyone coming to Tennyson in the 1980's is precisely in this question, for there is no commonly accepted view of his achievement. Many critics see him as a minor poet of a minor period, of historical interest only. Others see him as an early symbolist poet, with modern affinities, a writer whose work repays the closest attention and responds to the kind of detailed analysis that we put to poetry of richness and complexity.[1]

Whatever we or posterity may decide on these questions, as a cultural and intellectual figure Tennyson occupies a unique position in

1. See particularly M. McLuhan, "Tennyson and Picturesque Poetry" (1951) and "Tennyson and the Romantic Epic" (1959); C. Brooks, *The Well-Wrought Urn* (1947); F. W. Bateson, *English Poetry* (1950); G. Hough, "Tears, Idle Tears" (1951); L. Spitzer, " 'Tears, Idle Tears' Again" (1952). All are reprinted in J. Killham, ed., *Critical Essays on the Poetry of Tennyson* (London, 1960).

English history. No writer has ever dominated his age so completely as Tennyson dominated Victorian England; no poet has ever been so completely a national poet. His writing entered the consciousness of the age. As Henry James said in 1875, his verse had become "part of the civilization of his day." To illustrate the true quality of faith, George Eliot quoted from the opening to *In Memoriam*; to discuss the capacities of women, she quoted from *The Princess.* Tennyson, she wrote in 1885, voiced "the struggles and the far reaching thoughts of this nineteenth century"; *In Memoriam* "enshrines the highest tendency of this age." Matthew Arnold prophesied that in a time of science and spiritual doubt, poetry would come to take the place of religion. How close the poetry of Tennyson came to fulfilling that prophecy we can judge from the words of the historian J. A. Froude:

> Your father in my estimate stands and will stand far away by the side of Shakespeare above all other English Poets, with this relative superiority even to Shakespeare, that he speaks the thoughts and speaks to the perplexities and misgivings of his own age.

Froude was writing to Hallam Tennyson in 1894, when the biographer-son was compiling the monumental *Memoir.* But this is something more than obituary homage; the comparison with Shakespeare was not mere lip service; nor was Froude a critical simpleton (as anyone can see from his discussion of Shakespeare in "The Science of History").[2] What he says here is an assertion of Tennyson's hold upon the Victorian mind.

Tennyson's domination of the later nineteenth century is partly to be explained by the prosaic fact of his longevity. His career extended over seventy-five years, from childhood until his death in 1892, and he was a known poet, through his published work, from 1830 onward. He began in the shadow of the great romantics and lived to be the older contemporary of Hardy and Yeats. He came to an open field. The earlier generation was dead: Keats in 1821, Shelley in 1822, Byron in 1824; Scott, turned novelist, in 1832; Coleridge, turned philosopher, in 1834. Only Wordsworth survived, the young Wordsworth dead, until 1850, when he was succeeded as poet laureate by Tennyson, the then supreme poet of *In Memoriam.* In these terms Tennyson opened a fresh, post-romantic period in English poetry, a period further defined by historical events, notably the Reform Bill of 1832, the first real step toward modern parliamentary democracy, and the accession of Queen Victoria in 1837. Victorian England developed an unmistakable character. Its sustaining dynamic was the idea of Progress—full-blooded material progress in the growth of industry and trade; social progress in concern for the poor; nervous political progress in the direction of responsible democracy; fearful scientific progress toward the facts of creation and evolution; moral progress, as it was seen, in the ideals of purity and of family life, of paternalism, motherhood, and domesticity; religious progress, again, as it was seen, in the pietism of the Anglican church. There was also a higher, more speculative ideal of progress arising out of the grandiose vision of man's nature and destiny formulated by Thomas Carlyle, the "thinker" of the century, in "Signs of the Times" (*Edinburgh Review,* June 1829):

> We have a faith in the imperishable dignity of man; in the high vocation to which throughout his earthly history, he had been appointed. . . . Doubtless this age also is advancing. Its very unrest, its ceaseless activity, its discontent contains matter of promise. Knowledge, education are opening the eyes of the humblest; are increasing the number of thinking minds without limit. This is as it should be; for not in turning back, not in resisting, but only in resolutely struggling forward, does our life consist.

Whether Tennyson read these words, we have no direct evidence. But only four years later, he was using this same cluster of ideas about man's "imperishable dignity" and the "un-

2. In *Short Studies of Creat Subjects* (London, 1867).

rest" and "ceaseless activity" of the age in the dramatic monologue "Ulysses," where the aged hero of Homer and Dante becomes a mouthpiece for the nineteenth century, rallying his shipmates with a Carlylean cry:

> One equal temper of heroic hearts,
> Made weak by time and fate, but strong in will
> To strive, to seek, to find, and not to yield.[3]
> (68–70)

In this poem, as in many others, Tennyson shows himself to be emphatically a modern poet, immersed in the circumstances of the age, its currents of thought and feeling, its way of life. Sometimes his involvement was in the line of duty. As poet laureate he was required to provide verses for the comings and goings of the royal family, and celebratory pieces for great events, such as the funeral of the duke of Wellington and the opening of the International Exhibition of 1862 (where he faced the technical problem of composing an ode suitable for a choir of four thousand). He met these demands with style and a sure sense of rhetoric and public verse.

Outside his official capacity Tennyson came to see himself as a kind of national watchdog. Early in 1852, for example, he thought that the government was not sufficiently alert to the threat of invasion from France. So he fired off a series of squibs to the press, calling on the ministers to wake up and rousing the country to arms. The archenemies were the "vile" Napoleon III and "bastard Christianity," his term for Roman Catholicism, to be opposed by the stout English virtues of traditional liberty and the strength of national character. In 1854–1855, sections of *Maud* were written against the "peace-at-any-price" party in the Crimean War; and other sections of the poem were directed against contemporary scandals—the adulteration of food, the condition of the poor in the industrial cities, the worship of money (then vilified as Mammonism). Later in the century, in "Politics," he encouraged the former prime minister, Gladstone, to take back the reins of government with a firm hand; this was in 1889, at the end of a troublesome decade which had seen the Irish home rule issue and the Reform Bill of 1884. Occasionally these poems rise above doggerel and survive for some quality of verse. "The Charge of the Light Brigade" is one such poem. It sprang from a report in the *Times* for 2 December 1854; was written, said Tennyson, "in a few minutes"; and appeared in the *Examiner* seven days later.

Tennyson was also determinedly up-to-date in his science and scholarship. The twentieth-century nightmare is the horror of the nuclear age. The nineteenth-century nightmare was the discovery of man's place in the universe, the discrediting of the biblical story of creation, the realization of man's animal origin. These were some of the questions that Tennyson faced in *In Memoriam,* bringing to his poetic task the latest state of scientific knowledge. Readers in the 1850's were reassured that their poet laureate was no warbling songster but a poet-philosopher whose trains of thought involved cold fact and hard speculation—the cataclysmic theory of creation and its refutation in Sir Charles Lyell's counter-theory of uniformitarian creation, the nebular hypothesis of the origin of the stars, the biological theory of mutability. What they read in Elegy CXXIII was not a string of poetic images but an account of the earth's past and future which they could substantiate in the textbooks of geology; reading in "Locksley Hall," in 1842, of the weighing of the sun, they would think of the astronomer Baily, who had been attempting that calculation since 1838.

In *In Memoriam* Tennyson set out to provide the nineteenth century with a moral interpretation of the universe, the meaning of life, and the nature of faith in a scientific world. In "Locksley Hall," he shows the impact of science and technology upon the imagination of contemporary man. The prospect of the future brings an uneasy excitement:

3. All quotations of poetry are from C. Ricks, ed., *The Poems of Tennyson* (London, 1969).

For I dipt into the future, far as human eye
 could see,
Saw the Vision of the world, and all the
 wonder that would be;

Saw the heavens fill with commerce,
 argosies of magic sails,
Pilots of the purple twilight, dropping down
 with costly bales;

Heard the heavens fill with shouting, and
 there rain'd a ghastly dew

From the nations' airy navies grappling in
 the central blue. . . .
 (119–124)

This is the lesson of history, of man morally incapable of controlling his inventions. But the pattern takes a new turn. War is quelled in "the Federation of the world," "the Parliament of man."

In *The Princess* the scientific-technological vision is domesticated, playfully, to a fete day in the Kentish countryside of the 1840's:

 and somewhat lower down
A man with knobs and wires and vials fired
A cannon: Echo answer'd in her sleep
From hollow fields: and here were telescopes
For azure views; and there a group of girls
In circle waited, whom the electric shock
Dislink'd with shrieks and laughter: round
 the lake
A little clock-work steamer paddling plied
And shook the lilies: perch'd about the
 knolls
A dozen angry models jetted steam:
A petty railway ran: a fire-balloon
Rose gem-like up before the dusky groves
And dropt a fairy parachute and past:
And there thro' twenty posts of telegraph
They flash'd a saucy message to and fro
Between the mimic stations; so that sport
Went hand in hand with Science,
 otherwhere
Pure sport: a herd of boys with clamour
 bowl'd
And stump'd the wicket; babies roll'd about
Like tumbled fruit in grass; and men and
 maids
Arranged a country dance, and flew thro'
 light
And shadow, while the twangling violin
Struck up with Soldier-laddie, and overhead
The broad ambrosial aisles of lofty lime
Made noise with bees and breeze from end
 to end.
 (prologue, 64–88)

This is Tennyson's social vision of midcentury life, in the mixing of the classes, the squire among his tenants and their families; in the mingling of the countryfolk with the workingmen of the nearby town. Past, present, and future join hands in the encounter between newfangled science and the world of country sports, songs, and dances. This is the Victorian holiday Arcadia of harmony between man and man, between man and his inventions, and, in the closing lines, of an attendant harmony in nature.

Tennyson's distinctive Victorianism is most clearly shown in a large group of descriptive-narrative poems which he called his "English Idyls."[4] He borrowed the term from the Greek idyll, a type of pastoral poem presenting a scene or event in country life. He knew the form well from his reading of Theocritus and the Latin imitation in Vergil. Nothing quite like it had ever existed in English poetry. Perhaps the closest equivalent was in Crabbe and Wordsworth, telling of "man's inhumanity to man," the harsh realities of country poverty and despotism, and of the human and spiritual values of life in simple communities close to nature. In Tennyson these realities and intuitions are Victorianized. Nature is picturesque, ruralized; man is domesticated, his spiritual and emotional life cozily bounded by the pieties of the cradle, the family hearth, and the parish church. Inhumanity, where it occurs, is often in the shape of the seducer or the oppressive snob. The scenes and stories are carried in poetry of extraordinary descriptive power, such as this passage from "The Gardener's Daughter":

4. Including "The Gardener's Daughter," "Audley Court," "Edwin Morris," "The Miller's Daughter," and many other poems.

Not wholly in the busy world, nor quite
Beyond it, blooms the garden that I love.
News from the humming city comes to it
In sound of funeral or of marriage bells;
And, sitting muffled in dark leaves, you hear
The windy clanging of the minster clock;
Although between it and the garden lies
A league of grass, wash'd by a slow broad
  stream,
That, stirr'd with languid pulses of the oar,
Waves all its lazy lilies, and creeps on,
Barge-laden, to three arches of a bridge
Crown'd with the minster-towers.
                The fields between
Are dewy-fresh, browsed by deep-udder'd
  kine,
And all about the large lime feathers low,
The lime a summer home of murmurous
  wings.
  (33–48)

Here language is pushed to its fullest expressive reach. The weight and density and richness of the water meadows and the "deep-udder'd kine" are carried toward and over us in the embracing onomatopoeia; it is a highly sensuous verbal gesture the effect of which we can compare with another kind of virtuosity in this delicate atmospheric image from "The Miller's Daughter":

I loved the brimming wave that swam
  Through quiet meadows round the mill,
The sleepy pool above the dam,
  The pool beneath it never still,
The meal-sacks on the whitened floor,
  The dark round of the dripping wheel,
The very air about the door
  Made misty with the floating meal.
  (97–104)

This stanza, like so many passages in Tennyson, can be read quite on its own as a beautiful vignette.

This style of pictorialism, applied to English country life and the English scene, was a feature of Tennyson's poetry that shaped nineteenth-century sensibility, although his own practice was shaped in turn—very directly so—in response to advice and criticism of individual poems. We can follow this process closely in the revisions he effected to certain pieces in the volumes of 1830 and 1833. When they were reprinted in *Poems* (1842), many were changed verbally and metrically, sometimes much for the worse, as with "The Miller's Daughter." The narrator is a man country-born and bred. In the 1833 version he is given a touching simplicity of style, a rustic quaintness of diction and phrasing. In the 1842 version this quality is lost. The language is decorated, poeticized; and the story of the fresh and innocent joy of first love is overlaid with what we come to recognize as a typically Victorian celebration of filial ties and domesticity. One such addition is the stanza in which the young man, a squire's son, seeks the consent of his widowed mother:

And slowly was my mother brought
  To yield consent to my desire:
She wished me happy, but she thought
  I might have looked a little higher;
And I was young—too young to wed:
  "Yet must I love her for your sake;
Go fetch your Alice here," she said:
  Her eyelid quivered as she spake.
  (137–144)

It is probably fair to say that an important side to Tennyson's Victorianism was his willingness to conform to popular taste, to write a style of poetry that was easily understood and enjoyed, both in its poetic technique and in themes and subject matter which fell within the popular notion of what poetry should be about. To a degree he was able to create and extend these limits by the force of his own writing. One excursion was into dialect poetry, rude eccentricity, perhaps, for a poet of such refined art. Whether the motive was experiment or a nostalgic return to the language of his Lincolnshire childhood (the thick twang of which he never lost) the poems themselves[5] are masterpieces of characterization and irony, Chaucerian in their gusto,

5. "Northern Farmer, Old Style" (written 1861), "Northern Farmer, New Style" (1865), "The Spinster Sweet-Arts" (1884), "The Church-warden and the Curate" (1890).

their wit, their observation, and their penetration of human nature. They are portraits that Browning would have envied and Dickens enjoyed.

Tennyson's major innovation was to bring to English poetry a very remarkable and sophisticated experience of classical literature, something quite apart from his English-Vergilianism, the characteristics of which are neatly itemized in his official tribute, "To Virgil," written in 1883. He refers there to some of the qualities he most admired in the Roman poet and which he tried to imitate in his own choice of subject matter and in the musicality of his diction: Vergil the "Landscape-lover," the "lord of language," of "many a golden phrase," "majestic in thy sadness," "Wielder of the stateliest measure ever moulded by the lips of man." Much of Tennyson's poetry is decoratively and melodiously Vergilian in these ways. But not his best and most interesting work. There the Vergilian element is often assimilated in a larger, more complex classical presence, to be manipulated as a device of style and meaning, as it is in Elegy IX of *In Memoriam,* where the classical-Augustan surface is a deliberate aestheticism, a contrived face of art, which is destroyed by the sudden breakthrough of emotion, the encroachment of grief. Sometimes the classical presence excludes Vergil altogether for the social tones, the ease, and urbanity of Horace; and the voice we hear again and again in many of the finest lyrics is the voice of Catullus—not Catullus imitated or merely alluded to, but received and controlled in Tennyson's experience, as it is in Elegy LIX, Tennyson's formal and nonetheless beautiful version of the famous song of Catullus, "Vivamus, mea Lesbia, atque amemus," a favorite among English poets (as we see in Marlowe's "The Passionate Shepherd to his Love," Jonson's "To Celia," Donne's "The Baite"):

O Sorrow, wilt thou live with me
  No casual mistress, but a wife,
  My bosom-friend and half of life;
As I confess it needs must be;

O Sorrow, wilt thou rule my blood,
  Be sometimes lovely like a bride,
  And put thy harsher moods aside,
If thou wilt have me wise and good.

My centred passion cannot move,
  Nor will it lessen from to-day;
  But I'll have leave at times to play
As with the creature of my love;

And set thee forth, for thou art mine,
  With so much hope for years to come,
  That, howsoe'er I know thee, some
Could hardly tell what name were thine.
(1–16)

Each poet has his distinctive version. Marlowe's shepherd sings a seductive account of the pleasures they will "prove" together. Jonson's lover is a logic-chopping seducer—love stolen is no sin, only stolen love discovered. Donne is seductive in metaphysical style, in paradoxical hyperbole. This witty and sophisticated tradition is the ironic context, part of the meaning of Tennyson's poem, which has its own internal wit, sad and sardonic, turning the not-a-mistress-but-a-wife joke through the tones of resignation, pleading, stoic fatalism, and fearful wonder as the poet woos Sorrow, the classical muse Melpomene.

The allusive subtlety and literary sophistication of this poem are new in nineteenth-century literature. Ezra Pound thought that he was the discoverer of Catullus for the modern world, the Latin poet he most admired and judged untranslatable. But would he have been quite so contemptuous of Tennyson if he had taken account of Elegy LIX, or "Frater Ave atque Vale," or "Prefatory Poem to my Brother's Sonnets," or "Hendecasyllabics," a brilliant pastiche of Catullus' favorite meter in which Tennyson slyly rebuked the reviewers for their inability to at tune to his poetic effects?

O you chorus of indolent reviewers,
Irresponsible, indolent reviewers,
Look, I come to the test, a tiny poem
All composed in a metre of Catullus,
All in quantity, careful of my motion,

Like the skater on ice that hardly bears him,
Lest I fall unawares before the people,
Waking laughter in indolent reviewers.
Should I flounder awhile without a tumble
Thro' this metrification of Catullus,
They should speak to me not without a
welcome,
All that chorus of indolent reviewers.
Hard, hard, hard is it, only not to tumble,
So fantastical is the dainty metre.
Wherefore slight me not wholly, nor believe
me
Too presumptuous, indolent reviewers.
O blatant Magazines, regard me rather—
Since I blush to belaud myself a moment—
As some rare little rose, a piece of inmost
Horticultural art, or half coquette-like
Maiden, not to be greeted unbenignly.

This is no more than a skit. But, playful as it is, it illustrates as well as any of the lyrics or any of the classical monologues—"Ulysses," "Tithonus," "Tiresias," or "Demeter and Persephone" —that Tennyson's essential classicism is in his view of the poem as a work of art, with form as its distinguishing characteristic. It is this concern that sets him apart from the romantic poets and from the beginnings of the modern movement.

II

Tennyson's poetry can be divided chronologically into three distinct groups: the poetry written before the death of Arthur Hallam in September 1833; the poetry written from the autumn of 1833 to the publication of *Maud* in 1855, including *The Princess* and *In Memoriam;* and the later writing, including his largest and most ambitious work, the *Idylls of the King,* the first section of which appeared in 1859 and which was virtually complete by 1872. Reading the works in this order, we can watch the poet's emergence from the imitative and derivative stage of his earliest childhood writing; and, in the late 1820's and early 1830's, the development of his own special kind of art poetry, the pictorializing treatment of scenes and situations and the highly expressive technique in the handling of language and verse form. The death of Arthur Hallam, his closest friend, in September 1833 was the immediate inspiration for his finest work in the 1830's and 1840's, leading to the collection of the elegies and their publication together in *In Memoriam* (1850). *Maud* marks a turning point in his career. It is a poem of great emotional violence and remarkable originality of form—as Tennyson described it, a lyric "Monodrama" —a strange work as original and unprecedented in English literature as *The Waste Land.* At the time the critics rejected *Maud* as a mistake, tainted by morbidity, a work of spasms. Thereafter Tennyson's creative drive was slackened, his fieriness burned out. A harsher, pessimistic note sounds increasingly in his public poetry, a disenchantment with materialism, a fear of overwhelming social and moral chaos following in the train of democracy, fear of contamination from the new freedoms in literature and art. In 1886, in "Locksley Hall Sixty Years After," he delivered his report on the state of Victorian civilization, a ranting diatribe against modern man and his creations: risen "from out the beast," to bestialism he is returning via atheism, radicalism, and the sewer realism of Zola. The idyllic serenity of pastoral England is blotted out by the canker of industrialism and its city-infernos of human degradation. All he could conjure against this was the countervision of the *Idylls,* an attempt to recreate the Arthurian story as a moral and spiritual allegory; and the series of historical plays—*Queen Mary, Harold, Becket,* and *The Foresters*—published between 1875 and 1892, in which he set out to portray periods of crisis in the struggle between right and might in what he called "the making of England." His ambition was to complement the history plays of Shakespeare. But Tennyson's grasp of drama and character was feeble, his sense of history incomplete; and his imagination and lyrical genius were never at home in these surroundings.[6]

6. G. W. Knight has argued strongly for the power of these plays in *The Golden Labyrinth* (London, 1962).

The poetry of Tennyson's middle and later years is unmistakably the work of an aging man, finally of an old man—world-weary, reflective, disillusioned, sometimes wise and humane, an ancient sage, sometimes peppery and intolerant, a castigating Timon, sometimes just silly. Yet from the 1830's onward until the end of his life, Tennyson's poetry reveals a curious lack of development. The language, imagery, form, and imaginative vision of the best of the later poetry are not essentially different from the best of the middle years, and this in turn from the best of the early poetry. There is not, for example, the line of radical development that we find in Yeats: the Tennysonianism of his earliest poetry and the Celtic Twilight of the 1880's and 1890's are followed by a purging sharpness and clarity which give way to the rich symbolism of the Byzantium poems, followed in turn by the Crazy Jane poetry and the masks and gnomism of the later 1930's. This development was partly a consequence of the literary situation. Whatever his own impulse toward change, Yeats had change thrust upon him by Eliot and Pound and by the twentieth-century demand for a new poetry, whereas Tennyson's public, by contrast, clung to the style and taste that the poet had himself created and which remained the poetic norm, at a popular level, until the end of the century. This historical, circumstantial explanation is of some value. But the inertia in Tennyson is more than stylistic; its center is in a strange recessive quality of his imagination which we come to recognize in his poetry in the recurrence of certain situations and moods around the experience of doubt, horror, isolation, and loss, of friends absent or dead, of loved ones yearned for, of scenes and events recalled from long ago.

This is naturally the poetry of old age—of "To the Rev. W. H. Brookfield" (1874), of "Vastness" and "To Mary Boyle" (1888), of "The Roses on the Terrace" and "Merlin and the Gleam" (1889), of "The Silent Voices" (1892). Yet this valetudinarian experience is also a feature of Tennyson's early poetry. Declarations of loneliness and deep melancholy are a phase of adolescence and a favorite stance of the Romantic Agony. But there is a note of genuine imaginative morbidity in "The Outcast," in "In Deep and Solemn Dreams," and in the "Ode to Memory," which date from 1826; and among the trivia of the *Poems* (1830 and 1833), the individual poetic voice sounds darkly in the "Mariana" poems, "Song," "The Kraken," "The Dying Swan," and "The Lady of Shalott," where the themes of death, abandonment, and isolation are so closely, sometimes obsessively, explored. So dramatically convincing is the note of depression and desperation in "The Two Voices" that critics have always accepted at face value the statement of Hallam Tennyson that the poem "was begun under the cloud" of his father's "overwhelming sorrow after the death of Arthur Hallam." In fact, the poem, then known as "Thoughts of a Suicide," was largely in existence by June 1833. Similar questions of style make it impossible to decide whether "Youth" and "From Sorrow Sorrow Yet Is Born," both written in 1833, date from before or after Hallam's death.

Insofar as there can be any clue to the peculiar cast of Tennyson's imaginative temper, it is probably in the renowned "black-bloodedness" of the family, a hereditary melancholia, and in the circumstances of his home life at Somersby. His father was neurotic and took to drink to escape the fits of depression which overwhelmed him increasingly into the 1820's and drove him to homicidal violence. Tennyson recalled how as a child he used to run from the rectory on such occasions, throwing himself down among the gravestones in the churchyard, praying for a release in death. We can only conjecture about the impact of these experiences upon his creative imagination. What Tennyson does discuss about his childhood is "the passion of the past," a phrase which he used to describe the inspiration for "Tears, Idle Tears," and it is this "passion" which provides our best understanding of the recessive quality of his imagination, of which the melancholic and morbid aspects are only a part:

> It is what I have always felt even from a boy, and what as a boy I called "the passion of the

> past". And it is so always with me now; it is the distance that charms me in the landscape, the picture and the past, and not the immediate today in which I move.

The poetic elaboration of this idea comes in "The Ancient Sage," written in 1885:

> Today? but what of yesterday? for oft
> On me, when boy, there came what then I called,
> Who knew no books and no philosophies,
> In my boy-phrase "The Passion of the Past".
> The first gray streak of earliest summer-dawn,
> The last long stripe of waning crimson gloom,
> As if the late and early were but one—
> A height, a broken grange, a grove, a flower
> Had murmurs "Lost and gone and lost and gone!"
> A breath, a whisper—some divine farewell—
> Desolate sweetness—far and faraway—
> What had he loved, what had he lost, the boy?
> I know not and i speak of what has been.
> (216–228)

Tennyson's "for oft" is a playful echo of the "For oft" that opens Wordsworth's remembered vision of the "golden daffodils." But there is no pretension to a mystical or philosophical interpretation, no move to penetrate the nature of the experience. He remains content to contemplate its reminders and images—of half-light, of solitariness, remoteness, and neglect—and to ascribe to them a strange evocative power, as of something loved and lost, which he cannot and will not explain. Three years later, in 1888, Tennyson wrote "Far—Far—Away," a poem which contemplates, with similar delicacy, the "strange charm" that these three words held for him since childhood, a charm inexpressible (he says) in poetry, its meaning only to be guessed at:

> What vague world-whisper, mystic pain or joy,
> Through those three words would haunt him when a boy,
> Far—far—away?
> (7–9)

In "Tears, Idle Tears," Tennyson defined "the passion of the past" more precisely: its origin and compelling force are located not in childhood but in the adult experience of unassuageable love:

> Dear as remember'd kisses after death,
> And sweet as those by hopeless fancy feign'd
> On lips that are for others; deep as love,
> Deep as first love, and wild with all regret;
> O Death in Life, the days that are no more.
> (16–20)

This poem was written in 1845, and "the days that are no more is almost certainly a reference to his years of friendship with Arthur Hallam, the "Death in Life" a reference to the years after Hallam's death.

The memory of Hallam remained a haunting, obsessive presence for the remainder of Tennyson's life, a focal point for all his sadness and passion, his feelings of yearning, desolation, and loss, the emotional experiences at the heart of his finest work. The Hallam origin can be surprising. For example, it is a recent discovery that the lyric "Oh! That 'Twere Possible," the nucleus around which *Maud* was built in 1854–1855, was first written, in a slightly shorter version, in the winter of 1833–1834. We can see in the opening stanzas that only a matter of weeks or months after his death, Hallam, in Tennyson's imagination, had already been transformed into a symbolic figure, here an androgynous lover:

> Oh! that 'twere possible,
> After long grief and pain,
> To find the arms of my true-love
> Round me once again!
> When I was wont to meet her
> In the silent woody places
> Of the land that gave me birth,
> We stood tranced in long embraces,
> Mixt with kisses sweeter, sweeter,
> Than any thing on earth.
> (1–10)

Hallam's death was a precipitating experience rather than an experience in itself. Tennyson's rhetoric of affection, sometimes strongly sexual, can be properly interpreted only if we understand that the Hallam of the poet's imagination was invested with many roles—wife, lover, consoler, savior, muse. In "Vastness," written almost sixty years later, Tennyson reviewed the history of man's existence, the unending succession of revolution and change—"what is all of it worth?"

> What the philosophies, all the sciences, poesy, varying voices of prayer?
> All that is noblest, all that is basest, all that is filthy with all that is fair?
>
> What is it all, if we all of us end but in being our own corpse-coffins at last,
> Swallow'd in Vastness, lost in Silence, drown'd in the deeps of a meaningless Past?
>
> What but a murmur of gnats in the gloom, or a moment's anger of bees in their hive?—
>
> . . .
>
> Peace, let it be! for I loved him, and love him for ever: the dead are not dead but alive.
> (31–36)

For Tennyson, so many years later, the simple affirmation of continuing love is offered as a sufficient and final answer; pathetically, we may think. It was the only answer he could give, a flat, assertive statement. His deepest experiences of Hallam are in the "dark house" sections of *In Memoriam* (VII, XCIX), in the "Valley of Cauteretz," most powerfully of all in "Cold and clear-cut face" in *Maud,* a single, sustained lyric sentence projecting the haunted mind, the psychological reality of a nightmare vision, unequaled in English literature from Shakespeare's Pericles to Eliot's *Marina*:

> Cold and clear-cut face, why come you so cruelly meek,
> Breaking a slumber in which all spleenful folly was drown'd,
> Pale with the golden beam of an eyelash dead on the cheek,
> Passionless, pale, cold face, star-sweet on a gloom profound;
> Womanlike, taking revenge too deep for a transient wrong
> Done but in thought to your beauty, and ever as pale as before
> Growing and fading and growing upon me without a sound,
> Luminous, gemlike, ghostlike, deathlike, half the night long
> Growing and fading and growing, till I could bear it no more,
> But arose, and all by myself in my own dark garden ground,
> Listening now to the tide in its broad-flung shipwrecking roar,
> Now to the scream of a madden'd beach dragg'd down by the wave,
> Walk'd in a wintry wind by a ghastly glimmer, and found
> The shining daffodil dead, and Orion low in his grave.
> (88–101)

III

On the evidence of Tennyson's early poetry, up to 1833, it would have been inconceivable to predict the emergence of a great national poet. The quality of imagination is introspective and withdrawn; the poems themselves, highly aesthetic. They announce a writer devoted to exploring language as the medium of art and the forms of poetry as the forms of art distancing and art stylization, with the single poem as an art object, shaped and constructed, to be admired for its formal qualities of shapeliness and poise. *Poems* (1830) also reveals a writer whose sense of his poetic identity is very uncertain. There is an extraordinary unevenness in the collection, with a number of laughable album verses (today's ladies' magazine doggerel), trivially sentimental. At Cambridge he was surrounded by a group of high-minded idealists, the Apostles, who believed (according to one of their members) that it was their mission "to enlighten the world upon things intellectual and spiritual" and "to interpret the oracles of transcendental wisdom to the world of Philistines." Hallam was the born leader, Tennyson the poetic spokesman; and it is easy to understand the kind of pressure to which he was subjected. A neat illustration of this is in "The Palace of Art," his first important discussion of the artist's outward responsibility, his duty toward society.

According to Tennyson himself, the poem was written in response to the challenging remark of a fellow Apostle—"Tennyson, we cannot live in Art." Tennyson's poetic answer is on this same level of platitude: of course, it tells us, we cannot live alone, away from mankind, within our own world of created beauty. The soul that tries to do this is tormented by its conscience and quits the art palace for the humility and down-to-earthness of a country cottage. The art/life question left Tennyson's imagination untouched. The formal argument of the poem exerts no apparent control over its structure, which is largely a succession of isolated pictorial images, projecting the soul's fantasies as individual scenes. Some of these are symbolic landscapes in miniature:

> One seemed all dark and red—a tract of sand,
> And some one pacing there alone,
> Who paced for ever in a glimmering land,
> Lit with a low large moon.
>
> . . .
>
> A still salt pool, locked in with bars of sand,
> Left on the shore; that hears all night
> The plunging seas draw backwards from the land
> Their moon-led waters white.
> (65–68; 249–252)

This is the neurotic vision of "Mariana," the psychological setting of "Mariana in the South," with the strange, uncanny horror of isolation and abandonment. But the poem's structure is elaborative, not defining; the images might have been continued endlessly; and Tennyson's real answer is implicit in the poem's failure—the artist cannot work by slogans, and imagination will have its say, whatever the artist intends.

His positive response to the art/life question is in "The Lady of Shalott," written, unsolicited, at about the same time, in 1831–1832. The allegory is simple and lucid. It stresses the "magic" of art, and its necessity. The "fairy" lady weaves the "magic" sights from her mirror into a "magic" tapestry. But at last she grows weary of mirror images. Her attention is seized by the brilliant figure of Sir Lancelot. She leaves the tapestry and the mirror to look at him directly. These objects break and she suffers the "curse." She surrenders herself to the swollen river and the stormy night and is carried down to Camelot singing into death. The meaning of this fable is clear. The artist has no choice. He follows his calling, and fate decides the rest. His moral stance is not dedication but submission. His artistic stance is reverence for the magic and mystery of his art. The artist is both the magician and the enchanted, the wielder of the magic power and its subject. The poem asserts this in the fable and in its own poetic magic—the power of its images, its insistent and subtly varied rhythms, its intricately shaped stanzas and patterned lines, its sharp pictorialism, its brilliance of detail. It effects the verbal illusion of a new art experience, of a Pre-Raphaelite tapestry-enamel finely and glowingly colored. It is Tennyson's "Kubla Khan," the creation of the possessed, visionary poet, working his spell of words with such insinuating memorability.

As a quality of poetry and of the poetic imagination, the "magic" of art was a familiar idea to the romantic poets and their critics. Matthew Arnold found "natural magic" to the highest degree in Shakespeare and Keats. The "something magic" Tennyson himself found in Keats belonged, he said, to "the innermost soul of poetry." In turn, Whitman was to find a magic in Tennyson, in his "finest verbalism," in his evocation of the "latent charm of mere words, cunning collocutions, and in the voice ringing them." To appeal to magic and the spell of words in the 1980's may seem like critical antiquarianism. But no amount of technical analysis of sound effects and rhythms can explain the mysterious process whereby certain kinds of poetry are able to engage us, as "The Lady of Shalott" has engaged generations of readers. Its effects are the effects of art. Its figures, scenes, and events are pictorialized. It is a story from the legendary past and, stylized picturesquely, is kept there. There is nothing familiar, no human motivation, nothing for the reader to identify with or to understand in terms of his own experience or any imaginable experience other than the experience of the artist and his art. Perhaps this very exclusiveness and concentration are the secrets of its power, its symbolism so compelling that the allegory and fable assume the universality of myth. Certainly the poem carries Tennyson's personal myth of the artist's isolation, his loneliness and vulnerability, his "magic" of creation, his surrender to its working, his fatalism, his submission to necessity, to Camelot's river of life, which is for him the dark river of dissolution.

The imaginative reality of these experiences became fact with the death of Arthur Hallam. This was the tragedy, according to Hallam Tennyson, which "for a while blotted out all joy from his life, and made him long for death." Tennyson's immediate grief was poured into "Speak to Me," "Hark! the Dog's Howl," "Whispers," "On a Mourner, "Oh! That 'Twere Possible," and the earliest of the elegies. These are subjective, emotional utterances, the private poetry of desolation and mourning. At the same time he was searching for ways in which to answer his private needs, to carry his personal vision, in poetry addressed outward to the public at large, thereby attempting to fulfill his Apostolic sense of duty within the resources and compulsions of his own poetic character.

His first invention was a special form of dramatic monologue or dramatic narrative, adapting some classical or legendary situation, reinterpreted obliquely in terms of his own predicament. This group includes "Ulysses," "Morte d'Arthur," "Tiresias," "Tithon" (and possibly "St. Simeon Stylites," which was completed by November 1833, but may have been commenced before Hallam's death). The first two poems carry a message for the age. The Carlylean aspect of "Ulysses" has been referred to earlier. For Tennyson personally, the poem was an act of survival. Written at a time of depression and annihilating grief it gave his feeling, he said, "about the need of going forward and braving the struggle of life." This resolve is echoed in Ulysses' rallying cry to his fellow adventurers:

> One equal temper of heroic hearts,
> Made weak by time and fate, but strong in will
> To strive, to seek, to find, and not to yield.
> (68–70)

But there is a discrepancy between this declared moral stance and the character of the poem itself, which is curiously unresolved and undetermined. Its rhythms are long and swelling, lyrical in their larger movement, its imagery expansive and dissolving:

> The long day wanes: the slow moon climbs: the deep
> Moans round with many voices. Come, my friends,
> 'Tis not too late to seek a newer world.
> Push off, and sitting well in order smite
> The sounding furrows; for my purpose holds
> To sail beyond the sunset, and the baths
> Of all the western stars, until I die.
> It may be that the gulfs will wash us down:
> It may be we shall touch the Happy Isles,
> And see the great Achilles, whom we knew.
> Tho' much is taken, much abides; and tho'
> We are not now that strength which in old days
> Moved earth and heaven; that which we are, we are;
> (55–67)

The one distinct objective is Achilles-Hallam, the comrade in arms who died at Troy. But this aim is far distant. The pervasive experience is the voyager's extinction into eternity, his glorious dissolution "beyond the sunset":

> Yet all experience is an arch wherethro'
> Gleams that untravell'd world, whose margin fades
> For ever and for ever when I move.
> . . .

And this gray spirit yearning in desire
To follow knowledge like a sinking star,
Beyond the utmost bound of human
thought.
(19–21; 30–32)

The discrepancy is between defiance and surrender, between the rousing moral and the poetic counter-pull, between the blunt, prosaic, robust good sense of Ulysses' final words and the large, vague, romantic mirage toward which he will endlessly sail, endlessly hopeful. The Homer-Dante Ulysses is Tennysonianized. The poem becomes a metaphor for the poet's own voyage of self-discovery. He knows what, responsibly, he should be doing, what moral sinews should be flexed. Yet his deepest need is not for exhortation or exercise but for consolation.

The allegorical circumstances of "Morte d'Arthur" are very exact. King Arthur-Arthur Hallam is dying; the Round Table-Apostolic brotherhood is breaking up; Sir Bedivere's questions are Tennyson's own. What is left in the world when the leader is gone? What hope remains when fellowship is destroyed? Arthur's answer is Tennyson's poetic rationalization:

The old order changeth, yielding place to
new,
And God fulfils Himself in many ways,
Lest one good custom should corrupt the
world.
. . .
Pray for my soul. More things are wrought
by prayer
Than this world dreams of. Wherefore, let
thy voice
Rise like a fountain for me night and day.
For what are men better than sheep or goats
That nourish a blind life within the brain,
If, knowing God, they lift not hands of
prayer
Both for themselves and those who call
them friend?
(240–242; 247–253)

In delivering these words Tennyson was addressing his contemporaries as well as seeking a shred of comfort for himself. In an age of intellectual doubt and oppressive materialism, what were to be the guiding values? To these questions "Morte d'Arthur" returns no precise answer, only a general sense of good advice in the air and a readiness to believe. Tennyson's own uncertainty, and his limited means of assuaging it, are sounded in Arthur's final, puzzled, consolatory farewell. The visionary promise of Avilion, in all its poetic beauty, is offered as the one substantial comfort:

But now farewell. I am going a long way
With these thou seest—if indeed I go—
(For all my mind is clouded with a doubt)
To the island-valley of Avilion;
Where falls not hail, or rain, or any snow,
Nor ever wind blows loudly; but it lies
Deep-meadow'd, happy, fair with orchard-
lawns
And bowery hollows crown'd with summer
sea,
Where I will heal me of my grievous wound.
(256–264)

The interest of these poems is their statement of dilemma and, equally, their acceptance of dilemma as a condition of experience. Tennyson acknowledges his need for inspiration, whether in the heroics of the Carlylean message or in the Christian-Stoic resignation of Arthurian pulpit oratory. Yet he was too good a poet, too faithful to his weaker, more pathetic self, to deny his need for consolation, for an un-Christian, unmoral, unrespectable escape into fantasy and myth, into the wan, wistful illusion of Hallam's immortality.

Whereas both "Ulysses" and "Morte d'Arthur" carried a prominent and acceptable public message, and duly appeared in the next collection, *Poems* (1842), the other two poems of this group were held back: "Tithon" until 1860, when it was published, in a revised and lengthened form, as "Tithonus," and "Tiresias," also revised, until 1885. They are not notably inferior poems, and Tennyson's reluctance to make them public in 1842 was almost certainly on account of their lack of a theme more positive than the burden of existence, the appeal of death, and, for Tiresias, the longing for ennoblement in the heroic realms of the afterlife. Possibly Tennyson judged these dramatizations to be too indulgent, too confessional; and his great imaginative effort in the later 1830's, in "Locksley Hall" (written 1837–1838) and *The Princess* (begun by 1839), until *In Memoriam* and *Maud,* was the attempt to write poetry more securely distanced, to create verse structures in which he could develop a more optimistic countervision to the dilemma of "Ulysses" and "Morte d'Arthur" and to the inert withdrawal of "Tithon" and "Tiresias." Tennyson's task was to reconcile his Apostolic sense of duty with his interior nature as the poet of Shalott; and the creative cost of this ambition is clearly marked in the poetry of these years.

During the 1840's, especially after the success of *Poems* (1842), Tennyson's friends and reviewers (sometimes, significantly, the same people) urged him to change course, to engage with one of the great subjects of modern life, something with a human touch. His answer was *The Princess,* published in 1847. Since 1839, possibly earlier, he had been interested in the idea of a poem on women's education, a topic then much in the air. This was to provide the core of the work. Tennyson enlarged on this social theme, taking in the high Victorian notion of womanhood, its proper rights and duties. At a more profound level he considered the false ambitions and delusive ideals that can lure woman along the unnatural path of sexual and intellectual solitude, and within this moral theme, he explored the emotional implications of such separation. Described in this way, *The Princess* is neat and schematic. But for all the poem's ideas, and its seriousness of theme, and, on occasion, its seriousness of treatment, it reveals Tennyson's uneasiness, his inability to dramatize a public theme which touched him so deeply. His recourse is to a mock archaic style, quaint and fanciful, an evasive playfulness, a deprecatory whimsicality.

The modern social picture in the prologue and the conclusion is playful and naively idyllic, unpretentiously so. The message is universal harmony—between the classes, the sexes, mankind and science and nature, and a harmony of all creation with "the Heaven of Heavens." But the assertion is rhetorical; the poem itself is grossly unharmonious—stylistically and imaginatively it remains, as it is subtitled, *A Medley.* In effect it merely serves as a showcase for some of the great lyrics—"Tears, Idle Tears," "Ask Me No More," "Now Sleeps the Crimson Petal."

Tennyson's most ambitious structure and most embracing countervision was achieved in the formation of *In Memoriam.* When he wrote the first elegies in the winter of 1833–1834, it was with no thought of publication or any larger design. But the poems in this common stanza form accumulated until, eventually, in the 1840's, Tennyson introduced narrative-chronological sections and arranged the poems sequentially, so that they recounted a spiritual biography: the first prostration of grief, the onset of religious doubt and hopelessness, checked by the intimation of a new and tempered faith, leading to a happy sense of God's purpose. The poem's crown is the epilogue, an epithalamium in which there is the fullest exposition of Tennyson's grand myth of consolation and comfort, involving Hallam, nature, and mankind in a triumphant single vision. He looks forward to the child of the marriage, destined to bring the human race one step closer to its highest state. The mood is serene and joyful, with the *Princess*-like harmonies of man, nature, and the universe beyond. Tennyson's prophetic myth is constructed from contemporary evolutionary thought adjusted to the romantic idealism of the age; and both these elements joined to his private fantasy of Hallam as forerunner of the "noble type," the link between later nineteenth-century man and his evolved form as "the crowning race."

The epilogue is a tour de force, a beautiful and suave conclusion to the poem's line of argument. But it has no more than a formal connection with the center of experience of the finest elegies, the poems that arise from Hallam. *In Memoriam* is a construct, an exploitation of the early elegies for the sake of Tennyson's ambition to deliver the great philosophical poem of the age and his need to ameliorate the Hallam experience, just as in *The Princess* the central core of emotion is separated off in the lyrics, contained in a Chinese-box extravaganza.

Tennyson's other recourse, in "Locksley Hall" and *Maud*, was not the escape from personality but its indulgence; not the measured, composed voice of the lyrical seer, nor the indirection of the virtuoso, with his "medley" of artful tones and styles, but the dense psychological and temperamental expression of confused or disordered minds, a thin ventriloquial disguise for the poet's own violence of feeling. Tennyson insisted that "Locksley Hall" was a "dramatic impersonation," not autobiography, a denial repeated more vehemently with *Maud.* But there are striking similarities in the circumstances of both heroes, with a common background story of tyrannical relations, frustrated love, and the power of money; and recent studies of these poems put it beyond doubt that Tennyson was writing out of his own bitterness and frustration in love, his poverty, and the feud with another, snobbishly superior, branch of the family.

Tennyson himself gave a very tepid account of "Locksley Hall": that it "represents young life, its good side, its deficiencies, and its yearnings"; and it was probably in this spirit that he included it in *Poems* (1842) as a young Victorian's view of the years ahead, of accelerating change and the promise of a new age of science and invention. What comes across, however, is not a representative point of view, not a neutrally Victorian response to the future, but the portrait of a disturbed mind, of someone dizzied and terrified by the vistas of change, yet cursing and rejecting the past embodied in the hall, whose name carries this symbolic, "locked" meaning:

> Howsoever these things be, a long farewell to Locksley Hall!
> Now for me the woods may wither, now for me the roof-tree fall.
> Comes a vapour from the margin, blackening over heath and holt,
> Cramming all the blast before it, in its breast a thunderbolt.
> Let it fall on Locksley Hall, with rain or hail, or fire or snow;
> For the mighty wind arises, roaring seaward, and I go.
> (189–194)

As in the opening section of *Maud,* we are faced here with an unaccountable violence, a fantasy of rejection and denial for which there is no explanation either in the circumstances of the poem or in the character of the speaker. We have the impression of something left unsaid or imperfectly rendered, of effect without cause. In *Maud,* Tennyson allowed himself greater license in the persona of a madman; artistically, a dangerous license, for verisimilitude could justify the fragmentation of experience, the disassociation of thought and feeling, the lurchings and incoherences and wildness of a mind out of control—ironically so, since the poem itself is an outstanding exhibition of lyrical virtuosity and technical command over a great range of feeling and tone, from the fine ironies of "She came to the village church" (I.viii) to the sensuous lyricism of "I have led her home" (I.xviii) and the intense psychological realism of "Cold and clear-cut face" (I.iii) and "I heard no sound" (I.xiv. 516–526). One would guess that these sections of the poem, together with "Come into the garden" and several others, belong to the Hallam experience (remembering that the poem's starting point was "Oh! that 'twere possible") and to Tennyson's positive emotional life of the 1830's. The sections of madness come from another part of his experience altogether, from his hurt and pain, from the bitterness and injury of those years, feelings which rankled and which he was unable to exploit creatively, other than in the madman's ravings:

> And the vitriol madness flushes up in the ruffian's head,
> Till the filthy by-lane rings to the yell of the trampled wife,
> And chalk and alum and plaster are sold to the poor for bread,

And the spint of murder works in the very
means of life,

And Sleep must lie down arm'd, for the
villainous centre-bits
Grind on the wakeful ear in the hush of the
moonless nights,
While another is cheating the sick of a few
last gasps, as he sits
To pestle a poison'd poison behind his
crimson lights.

When a Mammonite mother kills her babe
for a burial fee,
And Timour-Mammon grins on a pile of
children's bones,
Is it peace or war? better, war! loud war by
land and by sea,
War with a thousand battles, and shaking a
hundred thrones.
(I.i. 36–47)

Of course, this is not Tennyson in person. But in a strange sense it is. The images of horror are figments of a demented mind; yet they have a rational, external, historical existence. The adulteration of bread was a current scandal much written about in the period 1851–1855. The "Mammonite" mother was a horrible reality. Children had indeed been murdered for the sake of the "burial fee" of (pounds) 3 or (pounds) 4. It is impossible to judge where Tennyson's revulsion ends and the dramatic character of the madman begins. In those closing lines war is a symptomatic image of the hero's own divided, disruptive personality. Yet in the concluding sections of the poem, when the hero has emerged into sanity, war is presented as the ennobling cause, the great destiny which will raise and unify the nation:

For the peace, that I deem'd no peace, is
over and done,
And now by the side of the Black and the
Baltic deep,
And deathful-grinning mouths of the
fortress, flames
The blood-red blossom of war with a heart
of fire.
Let it flame or fade, and the war roll down
like a wind,
We have proved we have hearts in a cause,
we are noble still,
And myself have awaked, as it seems, to the
better mind;
It is better to fight for the good than to rail
at the ill;
I have felt with my native land, I am one
with my kind,
I embrace the purpose of God, and the doom
assign'd.
(III.iv-v. 50–59)

There is nothing remarkable in the fact of Tennyson's warmongering; it is exactly in character with his newspaper squibs of 1852; and he was an opponent of those who wanted peace in the Crimea. What is remarkable is the apparent ease and confidence with which this rousing finale is delivered, so alike in style and manner to the endings of *The Princess* and *In Memoriam,* but to what different harmonies! There the vision was idyllic and spiritual; here it is the glorification of war as a moral force, as the destiny to uplift society and assert the nation's strength, and to join the individual to this great common purpose. This is Tennyson's secular, propagandizing, energizing countervision, to ward off the Hallam experience, to deny the poet of Shalott, to fulfill the Apostolic mission. We must admire the synthesizing power of the verse in answering these complex demands; but we can only regret the imaginative necessity that drove Tennyson to seek a solution so unworthily and triumphantly expedient.

Maud was an act of catharsis. Whatever the personal and imaginative pressures that drove him to this strange, inventive creation, there was no return after this to the anguish and yearning for Hallam or to the powerful eroticism of the lyrics. The lyrical vein continues, much subdued, in poems of friendship—"To Mary Boyle," "To E. Fitzgerald," "To the Master of Balliol," "June Bracken and Heather," "The Roses on the Terrace." These Horatian lyrics are graceful, charming, and witty. But the impulse is low-powered. We see this too in the elegiac poems and the reminiscences of Hallam—"In the Garden at Swainston," *In Memoriam* XXXIX (written in 1868), "Prefatory Poem to my Brother's Sonnets," "Frater Ave atque Vale" —beautiful and moving tributes from which the anguish and poignance have gone.

For the public of the 1850's, *Maud* was an aberration. Tennyson redeemed himself, became once again the poet of *In Memoriam*—and, more than that, a modern Vergil, a great national poet—in the *Idylls of the King.* Tennyson regarded the story of Arthur as "the greatest of all poetical subjects" and Malory's version the best of the existing accounts, full of "very fine things but all strung together without Art." The Arthurian stories had fascinated him since childhood and he planned and hesitated for over twenty years, from about 1833 to the mid-1850's, before seriously embarking upon the poem entire, of which "Morte d'Arthur" had appeared as a separate piece in 1842. Eventually, the *Idylls* came out in four volumes between 1859 and 1885, when they were first collected and placed in their final order.

The "Art" which he applied to his sources, principally to Malory, was characteristically Tennysonian. The cycle of stories is drawn upon to provide the raw material for a group of pictorialized scenes and events, each one isolated and presented rather like a stage tableau, showing a step in the rise and fall of Arthurian society, from Arthur's "Coming" to his "Passing." The moral allegory is pronounced: this is what happens to the ideals of chivalry and Christian heroism—brotherhood degenerates into enmity, love into lust, honor into pride, courage into brutality, vision into delusion. This is the cost of man's all-too-human humanity.

Tennyson is successful in the *Idylls* where we would expect him to be—in the descriptive writing, in establishing atmosphere and mood and the reality of particular disturbed states of mind and feeling. His failure is in the treatment of the figures. On the one hand, he was unable to distance and stylize them allegorically, in the accomplished manner of Chaucer or Spenser; on the other hand, he was unable to bring them to life naturally and realistically (as he did successfully in the Lincolnshire poems); nor could he even manage the halfway dramatization that Wordsworth discovered as the perfect medium for his beggars, leech gatherers, shepherds, and other countryfolk who have both a symbolic and a natural role. It was not simply a technical deficiency but a failing in dramatic sense, which is really an absence of human sympathy. This comes across very sharply, for example, in the confrontation between Arthur and Guinevere. After listening to his wife's plea for forgiveness for her unfaithfulness with Lancelot, Arthur delivers a reprimand two hundred lines long, veering between his allegorical function as the conscience of society:

> Yet must I leave thee, woman, to thy shame.
> I hold that man the worst of public foes
> Who either for his own or children's sake,
> To save his blood from scandal, lets the wife
> Whom he knows false, abide and rule the house:
> ("Guinevere," 508–512)

and his part in the human drama:

> I cannot touch thy lips, they are not mine,
> But Lancelot's: nay, they never were the King's.
> I cannot take thy hand; that too is flesh,
> And in the flesh thou hast sinn'd; and mine own flesh,
> Here looking down on thine polluted, cries
> "I loathe thee":
> (548–553)

Arthur sounds no better than an outraged husband in a Victorian melodrama—shades of Mr. Collins! If we try to localize the problem, it is in Tennyson's decision to purify the legendary Arthur, to transform him into a being sent by God and returning to Him unsullied by his earthly passage. Tennyson was proud to point out this purification in a dedicatory poem "To the Queen," published in the 1872 edition, in which he underlined the fact that his Arthur was not Malory's "Touched by the adulterous finger of a time / That hovered between war and wantonness, / And crownings and dethronements, and later he inserted a line exactly describing Arthur's allegorical character: "Ideal manhood closed in real man."

To be precise, Tennyson's crucial act of censorship was to ignore the stories of Arthur's adulterous conception and of his unwitting incestuous relationship with his half sister, of which the offspring is Modred. These elements in the Arthurian story constitute the doom of the house, the cruel and tragic destiny, which any Greek dramatist would have lighted upon as a fable as strong and significant as that of Oedipus. Whether or not we judge this to be a fair analogy,[7] the *Idylls* face us squarely with the question of Tennyson's later achievement, its scope and limitations, its timelessness in placing the poet as a teller of old tales, its peculiar Victorianism in the adaptation of the tale and the style of its telling.

Selected Bibliography

BIBLIOGRAPHY

Detailed bibliographical information can also be found in the *New Cambridge Bibliography of English Literature* vol. III (Cambridge, 1969); Wise, T. J., *A Bibliography of the Writings of Alfred, Lord Tennyson,* (London, 1908) privately printed, the most detailed, analytical bibliography, includes Wise's forged eds.; F. E. Faverty, ed. *The Victorian Poets: A Guide to Research,* (Cambridge, Mass., 1956) rev. ed. (1968) contains a sound account of modern research and criticism by P. F. Baum, the latter contains an updated account by E. D. H. Johnson; Tennyson, C., and Fall, C., *Alfred Tennyson: An Annotated Bibliography,* (Athens, Ga., 1967) the only classified bibliography, useful but with many inexplicable omissions; A. E. Dyson, ed. *English Poetry: Select Bibliographies,* (Oxford, 1971) contains the best descriptive and critical bibliography of the works of Tennyson, comp. by J. D. Hunt.

7. Swinburne's discussion of this point in *Under the Microscope* (London, 1872) is the most sustained criticism of Tennyson as a poet reduced by his own notion of morality.

REFERENCE WORKS

Baker, A. E., *A Concordance to the Poetical and Dramatic Works of Alfred, Lord Tennyson,* (London, 1914) supp. (1931) reiss. (1966); Baker, A. E., *A Tennyson Dictionary,* (London, 1916); Marshall, G. O., *A Tennyson Handbook,* (New York, 1963).

COLLECTED WORKS

Poetical Works, 4 vols. (Leipzig, 1860); *Works,* 10 vols. (London, 1870) the Pocket Volume (Miniature) ed. augmented by one vol. in 1873 and two more in 1877; A. C. Loffelt, ed. *Complete Works,* (Rotterdam, 1871); *Works,* 6 vols. (London, 1872–1873) reiss. (1877) the Imperial Library ed.; *Works,* 12 vols. (London, 1874–1877) the Cabinet ed., augmented by an additional vol. (1881); *Works,* 7 vols. (London, 1874–1881) the Author's ed.; *Works,* (London, 1878) the Crown ed.; *Works,* (London, 1884) the Macmillan ed. often repr.; *Works,* (London, 1894) the standard complete one-vol. ed. of the poems and plays, also issued in the Oxford Standard Authors series as *Tennyson: Poems and Plays* (London, 1965); *Life and Works of Alfred, Lord Tennyson,* 12 vols. (London, 1898–1899) the Edition de Luxe, the "Life" by Hallam, second Baron Tennyson; Hallam, Lord Tennyson, ed., *Poems, Annotated by Alfred, Lord Tennyson,* 9 vols. (London, 1907–1908) the Eversley ed.; C. Ricks, ed. *The Poems of Tennyson,* (London, 1969) supersedes all previous "complete" eds. of the poetry, presenting all the known poems, published and unpublished, omitting only MS material still under restriction, has full textual, historical, and bibliographical notes and can properly be regarded as the basic document in any study of Tennyson.

SELECTED WORKS

F. T. Palgrave, ed. Lyrical Poems, (London, 1885) in the Golden Treasury series, important because Tennyson advised Palgrave on the selection; J. C. Collins, ed. *The Early Poems,* (London, 1900); H. J. C. Grierson, ed. *Poems,* (London, 1907); B. C. Mulliner, ed., *Shorter Poems and Lyrics 1833–42,* 2 vols. (Oxford, 1909); J. C. Thompson, ed. *Suppressed Poems, 1830–68,* (London, 1910); T. S. Eliot, ed. *Poems,* (Edinburgh, 1936); W. H. Auden, ed. *A Selection from the Poems,* (New York, 1944); D. Bush, ed. *Tennyson: Selected Poetry,* (New York, 1951); C. Tennyson, ed. *Poems,* (London, 1954); M. McLuhan, ed. *Selected Poetry,* (London, 1956); J. H. Buckley, ed. *Poems,* (Cambridge, Mass., 1958); B. C. Southam, ed. *Selected Poems,* (London, 1964) the only ed. apart from the complete one by Ricks to place the poems in order of composition and to attempt comprehensive historical and explanatory notes; D. Cecil, ed. *A Choice of Verse,*

(London, 1971); D. Cecil, ed. *In Memoriam, Maud and Other Poems,* (London, 1975) the Everyman ed.

SEPARATE WORKS

Poems by Two Brothers, (London-Louth, 1827) by Alfred and Charles, with three or four pieces by Frederick; 2nd ed., H. Tennyson, ed. (London, 1893); *Timbuctoo,* (Cambridge, 1829) *Prolusiones Academicae; Poems, Chiefly Lyrical* (London, 1830); *The Lover's Tale,* (London, 1833) 1st authorized ed., (London, 1879) the former was privately printed; *Poems,* (London, 1833); *Poems,* 2 vols. (London, 1842) contains many poems repr., and some rev., from *Poems* of 1830 and 1833; *The Princess: A Medley,* (London, 1847) rev. eds. (1850) (1851) (1853); *In Memoriam,* (London, 1850) an additional poem in the 4th ed. (London, 1851) and another inserted in 1870; *Ode on the Death of the Duke of Wellington,* (London, 1852) rev. ed. (1853); *Maud, and Other Poems,* (London, 1855) rev. eds. (1856) (1859); *Idylls of the King,* (London, 1859) enl. eds. (1862) (1869) (1872) (1885) early eds. consisted of "Enid," "Vivien," "Elaine," and "Guinevere"; *Enoch Arden, and Other Poems,* (London, 1864); *The Holy Grail, and Other Poems,* (London, 1870); *Gareth and Lynette,* (London, 1872); *Queen Mary: A Drama,* (London, 1875); *Harold: A Drama,* (London, 1877); *Ballads and Other Poems,* (London, 1880); *Becket,* (London, 1884) drama; *The Cup, and, The Falcon,* (London, 1884) dramas; *Tiresias, and Other Poems,* (London, 1885); *Locksley Hall Sixty Years After,* (London, 1886); *Demeter, and Other Poems,* (London, 1889); *The Death of Oenone, Akbar's Dream, and Other Poems,* (London, 1892); *The Foresters: Robin Hood and Maid Marian,* (London, 1892) drama; C. Tennyson, ed. *The Devil and the Lady,* (London, 1930); C. Tennyson, ed. *Unpublished Early Poems,* (London, 1931).

LETTERS

Tennyson, H., *Alfred Lord Tennyson: A Memoir,* 2 vols. (London, 1897) vol. I, ch. 10, contains letters 1842–1845, and vol. II, chs. 16 and 23, letters 1862–1864; F. A. Mumby, ed. *Letters of Literary Men,* (London, 1906) vol. II, pp. 561–567; L. Pierce, ed. *Alfred Lord Tennyson and William Kirby: Unpublished Correspondence,* (Toronto, 1929); M. J. Ellmann "Unpublished Letters of Tennyson," *Modern Language Notes,* 65 (1950).

BIOGRAPHICAL AND CRITICAL STUDIES

Some of the following articles are repr. in J. D. Jump, ed. *Tennyson: The Critical Heritage* (London, 1967) or in J. Killham, ed. *Critical Essays on the Poetry of Tennyson,* (London, 1960). They are referred to under the titles given in those publications. Hallamm, A. H., "Poems, Chiefly Lyrical, 1830," *Englishman's Magazine* 1 (August, 1831) an unsigned review, repr. in Jump, further discussed in M. McLuhan, "Tennyson and Picturesque Poetry," see below; Eliot, G., "Maud and Other Poems," (*Westminster Review,* October 1855); Bagehot, W., "Idylls of the King, 1859," *National Review* 9 (October 1859) an unsigned review, repr. in Jump; Arnold, M., *On Translating Homer: Last Words,* (London, 1862) includes a section on Tennyson's simplicity that is repr. in Jump; Taine, H., *Histoire de la littérature anglaise,* 4 vols. (Paris, 1863–1864) trans. by H. Van Laun into English, 2 vols. (London, 1871) contains the ch. "Poetry-Tennyson," repr. in Jump; W. Bagehot, "Wordsworth, Tennyson, and Browning: or Pure, Ornate and Grotesque Art in English Poetry," *National Review* n.s. 1 (November 1864) an unsigned article, repr. in Jump, contains a review of Tennyson's *Enoch Arden,* further discussed in Dodsworth, M., "Patterns of Morbidity: Repetition in Tennyson's Poetry," in I. Armstrong, ed. *The Major Victorian Poets,* see below; Simpson, R., "Mr. Tennyson's Poetry," (*North British Review,* January 1871); Swinburne, A. C., *Under the Microscope,* (London, 1872) includes comments on *Idylls of the King* that are repr. in Jump; H. James, "Tennyson's Drama," (*Galaxy,* September 1875); Swinburne, A. C., *Miscellanies,* (London, 1886) includes the essay "Tennyson and Musset," a reply to Taine (above), extracts repr. in Jump; Huttoh, R. H., *Literary Essays,* (London, 1888) contains the ch. "Tennyson," replying to Swinburne (above) and repr. in Jump; Tennyson, H., *Materials for a Life of A. T.,* 4 vols. (London, 1896) privately printed, basic source material for the author's later official biography; Tennyson, H., *Alfred Lord Tennyson: A Memoir,* 2 vols. (London, 1897).

Bradley, A. C., *A Commentary on Tennyson's "In Memoriam,"* (London, 1901) rev. eds. (1902) (1930); Lang, A., *Alfred Tennyson,* (London, 1901); Chesterton, G. K., and Garnett, R., *Tennyson,* (London, 1903); Ker, W. P., *Tennyson,* (Cambridge, 1909) the Leslie Stephen Lecture, Cambridge (November 11, 1909); Chesterton, G. K., *TheVictorian Age in Literature,* (London-New York, 1913); Bradley, A. C., *The Reaction Against Tennyson,* (London, 1917) English Association pamphlet no. 39; Nicholson, H., *Tennyson: Aspects of His Life, Character and Poetry,* (London, 1923) 2nd ed. (1925) the most popular and influential account, very readable and convincing as a psychological-literary portrait, but must be read with caution; Leavis, F. R., *New Bearings in English Poetry,* (London, 1932) rev. ed. (1950) together with his *Revaluation* and *The Common Pursuit* (below), contains this author's influential views; Eliot, T. S., *Essays Ancient and Modern,* (London, 1936) contains the essay "In Memoriam," which is repr. in Killham; Leavis, F. R., *Revaluation: Tradition and Development in En-*

glish Poetry, (London, 1936); Young, G. M., *Victorian England: Portrait of an Age,* (London, 1936); Bush, J. N. D., *Mythology and the Romantic Tradition in English Poetry,* (Cambridge Mass, 1937) Harvard Studies in English no. 18; C. C. Abbott, ed. *Further Letters of Gerard Manley Hopkins,* (London, 1938) includes a letter dated 10 September 1864 that discusses Tennyson's language and is repr. in Jump; Young, G. M., *The Age of Tennyson,* (London, 1939) the Warton Lecture on English Poetry, 1939, also printed in *Proceedings of the British Academy,* 35 (1939).

Paden, W. D., "Tennyson and the Reviewers, 1827–35," (*University of Kansas Publications, Humanistic Studies* 6, no. 4, 1940) 15–39; Paden, W. D., *Tennyson in Egypt: A Study of the Imagery in His Earlier Work,* (Lawrence, Kans., 1942); Brooks, C., *The Well-Wrought Urn,* (London, 1947) includes the ch. "The Motivation of Tennyson's Weeper," on "Tears, Idle Tears" which is repr. in Killham; Baum, P. F., *Tennyson Sixty Years After,* (Chapel Hill, N.C., 1948); Tennyson, C., *Alfred Tennyson,* (London, 1949) the standard biography, excellent both historically and interpretatively; Bateson, F. W., *English Poetry: A Critical Introduction,* (London, 1950) contains the ch. "Romantic Schizophrenia: Tennyson's 'Tears, Idle Tears' "; A. J. Carr, "Tennyson as a Modern Poet," *University of Toronto Quarterly* 19 (1950) repr. in Killham; Buckley, J. H., *The Victorian Temper: A Study in Literary Culture,* (Cambridge, Mass., 1951); Hough, G., "Tears, Idle Tears," (*Hopkins Review,* 1951) repr. in Killham; McLuhan, M., "Tennyson and Picturesque Poetry," *Essays in Criticism* 1 (January 1951) repr. in Killham, relates to Hallam's review (above); Johnson, E. D. H., *The Alien Vision of Victorian Poetry: Sources of the Poetic Imagination in Tennyson, Browning and Arnold,* (Princeton, N.J., 1952); Leavis, F. R., *The Common Pursuit,* (London, 1952); Shannon, E. F., *Tennyson and the Reviewers: A Study of His Literary Reputation and of the Influence of the Critics upon His Poetry, 1827–1851,* (Cambridge, Mass., 1952); Spitzer, L., " 'Tears, Idle Tears' Again," (*Hopkins Review,* 1952) repr. in Killham, a reply to Hough (above); Tennyson, C., *Six Tennyson Essays,* (London, 1954); Langbaum, R., *The Poetry of Experience: The Dramatic Monologue in Modern Literary Tradition,* (London, 1957); Robson, W. W., "The Dilemma of Tennyson," *The Listener* 13 (June 1957) repr. in Killham; B. Ford, ed. *The Pelican Guide to English Literature,* vol. VI (London, 1958) contains Mayhead, R., "The Poetry of Tennyson"; Killham, J., *Tennyson and the Princess: Reflections of an Age,* London (1958); McLuhan, M., "Tennyson and the Romantic Epic," in Killham, (London, 1960).

Buckley, J. H., *Tennyson: The Growth of a Poet,* Cambridge, Mass.-London (1960) an important biographical-historical study giving a detailed scholarly and critical account of Tennyson's development; J. Killham, ed. *Critical Essays on the Poetry of Tennyson,* (London, 1960) a representative collection of the best modern criticism, repr. studies by Eliot, T. S., Young, G. M., Brooks, C., McLuhan, M., Hough, G., Spitzer, L., Carr, A. J., Robson, W. W.; H. S. Davies, comp. *The Poets and Their Critics: Blake to Browning,* (London, 1962) gives extracts of adverse criticism of Tennyson; Knight, G. W., *The Golden Labyrinth: A Study of British Drama,* (London, 1962); Pitt, V., *Tennyson Laureate,* (London, 1962); Richardson, J., *The Pre-eminent Victorian: A Study of Tennyson,* (London, 1962); Rader, R. W., *Tennyson's Maud: The Biographical Genesis,* (Berkeley-Los Angeles, 1963) explores the significant relationship of the poet's private life and art; Steane, J. B., *Tennyson,* (London, 1966); J. D. Jump, ed. *Tennyson: The Critical Heritage,* (London, 1967) reprs. a selection of reviews, essays, and other comments for the period 1831–1891 and discusses the contemporary response and critical reception in an extensive intro., selections include criticism by A. Hallam (reviewing *Poems,* 1830) Bagehot, W., Arnold, M., Hopkins, G. M., Swinburne, A. C., Taine, H., Hutton, R. H., and many others; Ricks, C., "Tennyson's Methods of Composition," *Proceedings of the British Academy* 52 (1967); I. Armstrong, ed. *The Major Victorian Poets: Reconsiderations,* (London, 1969) includes essays by M. Dodsworth, B. Bergonzi, A. Sinfield, and A. S. Byatt; *Tennyson's "In Memoriam": A Casebook,* J. D. Hunt, ed. (London, 1970) a collection of documents and critical essays on the poem; Ricks, C., *Tennyson,* (London, 1972); D. J. Palmer, *Tennyson,* ed. (London, 1973); F. E. L. Priestley, ed. *Language and Structure in Tennyson's Poetry,* (London, 1973); Tennyson, C., and Dyson, H., *The Tennysons: Background to Genius,* (London, 1974); Kincaid, P., *Tennyson's Major Poems: The Comic and Ironic Patterns,* (New Haven, Conn., 1975); Culler, A. D., *The Poetry of Tennyson,* (New Haven, Conn., 1977); Henderson, P., *Tennyson: Poet and Prophet,* (London, 1978); Hagen, J. S., *Tennyson and His Publishers,* (London, 1979); Pattison, R., *Tennyson and Tradition,* (Cambridge, Mass., 1980); Martin, R. B., *Tennyson: The Unquiet Heart,* (London, 1980).

DYLAN THOMAS
(1914–1953)

LESLIE NORRIS

DYLAN THOMAS WAS born in Swansea, Wales on 27 October 1914. No examination of his work can ignore the importance of his birthplace. Even his death in New York in 1953 is less a simple fact than an allegory of how far from home the poet had traveled. From this distance in time it is very easy to see that all his work is based on an assumption that Swansea and its surrounding green county is the center of the world, that all the poet saw and said resulted from the relation of his experience to the small miles of Wales in which he grew up.

No poet of our time lived more in the eye of the world than Thomas. His early recognition—he was famous in the little community of modern poets when he was nineteen—the accounts of his bohemian life-style, the impact of his work on critics and on other poets, all made him a public figure. At the time it seemed that readers waited for the small collections he published every few years as if starved of poetry. As his fame spread, Thomas was regarded as the very type of the romantic poet, wild, dissolute, inspired. This was not the complete truth, but when he died in 1953, tragically and sensationally after a bout of drinking, it was as if Dionysus had died again.

That was a long time ago. We ought to be able to look more objectively at the verse, to see it as it is presented to us in the *Collected Poems* (1952), to realize that it is the whole life's work. It should be possible to decide how much of Thomas' poetry has stood up against insidious time and against changing fashion in verse. We should, moreover, realize that the man's prose has grown in importance since his death, that it is easier to see him as a more interesting figure, more complex and complete, developing marvelous gifts of narrative and humor, than as a poet dead before his time. It has long been acknowledged that Thomas was a conscious artist, well aware of what he was doing, industrious, serious, and dedicated. His letters to his friend Vernon Watkins, particularly the earlier ones, are clear proof of how seriously he took his craft. To read through the *Collected Poems* is to experience a continuous development and refining of Thomas' technical skills from the rather heavy iambic early verse through the conscious experiments of his middle period to the extraordinary mastery of his late poems. The truth is that Thomas was always an artist, not only aware of what he was doing but delighting in it. He would have agreed with William Butler Yeats that there is no art without toil.

He realized early that he could write, and he was serious about the possession of such a gift. His father, David John Thomas, was an English master at the local grammar school, a man of taste and intelligence, widely read. Although he came from a Welsh-speaking background, he made his home one in which English was the sole language and its literature valued above all others. A fine reader, he introduced his son to the great poets at an early age. His example, together with the splendid voice he passed on to Dylan, was to result in the extraordinary public readings that made Thomas' work familiar to many people who would normally not have been interested in poetry. D. J. Thomas came of a family famous in South Wales. His uncle, William Thomas, had been a prime mover in the Unitarian movement in western Wales and had been politically active in the unrest between landlords and tenants in the years after 1867. He was, moreover, a good poet in the Welsh language, using the bardic title of Gwilym Marles.

It was a proud inheritance, and D. J. Thomas paid tribute to Gwilym Marles when he gave his son the middle name of Marlais. Yet he tried to ensure that any trace of Welsh language influence was erased when he insisted his two children have elocution lessons. Thomas grew up without the distinctive Swansea accent. He spoke an English untouched by any regional tinge.

Similarly, he remained unaware of much of what was happening to his country outside his immediate experience. It was a bad time for Wales, and other young poets—a little older than Thomas, it is true—were aware of the despair of the miners, of ruinous unemployment, and wrote about these subjects. He seemed sublimely uninterested in politics. If he knew no Welsh, he had a traditional Welsh attitude toward poetry. It must be rich in sound, it must be beautifully crafted, it must be glorious and as far as possible immortal. He prepared himself to write such poetry. His verse had been influenced, too, by the great English poets particularly the romantics. The modern poets he read were those whose work his father possessed, Walter de la Mare, John Masefield, the Georgians. From his wide reading he had already mastered a formidable technique, but it was a technique quite unlike that of his contemporaries. David Daiches, in his essay on Thomas in *Dylan Thomas: A Collection of Critical Essays* writes: "No modern poet in English has had a keener sense of form or has handled stanza and verse-paragraphs—whether traditional or original—with more deliberate cunning." This is an indication of the individuality of Thomas' voice and his technique. Of all the poets of his generation, he alone seemed to have been uninfluenced by the work of T. S. Eliot, then preeminent in English poetry. For Thomas it was as if Eliot had never written. We know from his letters, however, that the younger poet was very well aware of Eliot's, work and it is possible that he wrote differently because he knew his own gifts well, realized that he would travel in other directions.

The unusual thing is that Thomas came to this knowledge while still very young. The *Collected Poems* of 1952, prepared by Thomas himself contains a total of ninety poems. When the poet's friend Dr. Daniel Jones published his edition of *The Poems* in 1971, he included many more poems; even so he was at pains to state that this was still a selection. Most of these additional poems were written while Thomas was yet a schoolboy but so were many of the poems Thomas selected for the collection he chose himself.

Between the years 1930 and 1934, that is between the ages of fifteen and nineteen, Thomas wrote "at least four times more poetry than in the remaining nineteen years of his life" (*The Poems,* introduction, p. xvi) according to Dr. Jones. Thomas' published *Notebooks* offer convincing evidence of his astonishing early industry, as well as showing how this wealth of early work was revised, sometimes only very slightly revised, to become the poems from which the poet formed his successive books. Although he did write new poems for each new book, a surprising number were rescued from the poems of his adolescence.

It is obvious then that the majority of the poems remain the work of a very young man, a provincial young man untouched by London literary society or the discipline of a university. In a sense, despite the influence of his father, Thomas was an autodidact unaware of the very latest in poetical fashions. He had trained himself in the orthodox metrical forms of English verse and was far away from the current new poets, W. H. Auden, Stephen Spender, and C. Day-Lewis. Working almost alone in Swansea—for he did not meet Watkins, perhaps the most helpful of his friends until after the publication of *Eighteen Poems* in 1934—his most interesting subject matter was himself. So that when he began to publish, both his matter and his manner, traditional though they were, seemed astonishingly new and very exciting.

Certainly *Eighteen Poems* was received with unusual attention. "I was in London with him," wrote Glyn Jones in *The Dragon Has Two Tongues* (p. 183) "soon after his book appeared . . . and it was a delight to me to witness the excitement with which the book and its author were received." Jones had very early recognized the unique quality of the poetry and remains one of the most acute and objective of Thomas admirers.

It is as well to consider here, since we have stressed that much of Thomas' verse is orthodox and traditional, just what was unique in the work of the new arrival. First there is the important influence of Thomas environment. Hard though D. J. Thomas fought to give his son the sense of an English language culture, the boy was exposed every day of his formative years to an atmosphere very largely based on Welsh values and mores. He would have heard the language even, since it was more commonly spoken in Swansea during his boyhood than it is today, and in the country districts to the west of the town it was very largely the first language. This means that the English Thomas heard in the streets and classrooms, even that he would use when with his friends, was in a sense a transitional language, its syntax and its rhythms very slightly askew when compared to the language of Englishmen. The poet's usage thus acquires a kind of exotic strangeness and power, adding to his awareness of language—in Thomas' case an obsession with language that might have been the most obvious facet of his poetry. "I wanted to write poetry in the beginning," wrote Thomas in 1951, in reply to a students questions "because I had fallen in love with words" (*Modern Poets on Modern Poetry,* p. 195). He was never to fall out of love with them.

And if his language was exotically rich and musical when we think of the thin, political, poetry popular at the time, then its form too was unusual, again for what we might think of as Welsh reasons. Welsh poetry is complex and difficult in form, its poets skilled in the craft to a high degree, the traditional meters demanding long training. I do not suggest that Thomas knew very much about the forms of Welsh language poetry, despite efforts by a few critics to show a deliberate use of some of the constructions, but he grew up in a community in which formal poetry—the belief that poems must be well made—was universal. This is a not an unusual circumstance among poets from Celtic countries. "Irish poets learn your trade / Sing whatever is well mate" ("Under Ben Bulben" V) admonished Yeats. Certainly Scottish, Irish, and Welsh poets seem for these reasons to use poetic form and language sufficiently unlike that of their English contemporaries to make their work recognizably Celtic. It is not entirely fanciful to suggest that Thomas' mastery of intricate forms had something to to with his nationality and his background.

So his work was significantly novel in both word and form. It is true that there were poets writing at that time who were influenced by the current interest in surrealism; despite superficial similarities—the use of striking imagery is an example—Thomas' extreme control is enough to show that he has no place in such a group. Nor was his adolescent interest in himself, and in particular in his own sexuality, a common subject for verse in 1934. This was a period in which many young writers were greatly concerned with social and political themes. In prose and verse many of them were trying to analyze the causes of great political upheaval in Europe, and to warn about the war that they saw as inevitable. Thomas seemed untouched by this concern just as he was not influenced by savage unemployment and poverty in his own country. And if these young people, some of whom were to go on to fight in the Spanish Civil War in a few years time, seemed to represent that call for individual and political freedom which had been so potent a charge in the early nineteenth century to poets like William Blake and William Wordsworth to Percy Shelley and Lord Byron, then Thomas perhaps represented the viewpoint of even younger poets who had not outgrown the natural interest in self shown not only in budding lyrical poets but in all normal adolescents. We have to remember just how young Thomas was at this time and to recall moreover just how much younger he had been when he had written the work in *Eighteen Poems.* Whatever the reasons, young poets found his work exciting and in a sense liberating. His work influenced that of poets in England and America to an extraordinary extent, as a reading of almost any anthology of poetry of the time will show. In retrospect it seems that he changed the direction of contemporary English poetry with his first book, although its real virtues were not always recognized.

In addition to all these factors, Thomas came of families long settled in the Swansea and Carmarthenshire areas. He had a familiar age-old environment of sea and shore and surrounding hills in which to place his work. His very provincialism, far from being a handicap, gave him safety and strength. His is a recognizable country. His advantages were formidable.

All this is more easily seen from a reading of *The Collected Poems* than from a study of the work in his first book alone. The poems in *Eighteen Poems,* though are still exciting enough to help us understand some of the furor they caused in the small world of poets and a few of them remain among the best that Thomas ever wrote.

An old poet has told me how, when he was an undergraduate, he and his friends would walk the streets chanting the poems of Algernon Charles Swinburne, and a similar, almost mesmeric, incantatory quality is felt when one reads these early poems of Thomas. I, as a boy of thirteen, read "The force that through the green fuse drives the flower" in an anthology and could not believe that it was a poem. It seemed like something alive and physical, too vital for the page to contain. It could well be that such an immediate effect, a feeling that the words contained something beyond meaning and appealing with enormous power to the senses, is not only the first quality of Thomas' early verse, but its most permanent quality still to be felt. Yet there was, too, a certain confidence in the statement of the poetry, something in addition to the music and the mystery, which persuaded many of us that Thomas was saying something important. How strong some of the opening lines still seem: "I see the boys of summer in their ruin"; "A process in the weather of the heart / Turns damp to try"; "Where once the waters of your face / Spun to my screws." The poetry was obscure, but with a peculiar kind of obscurity. John Bayley has pointed out ("Chains and the Poet," *New Critical Essays,* p. 57) that we were hearing once again "the Bards voice" and that even if the words seem obscure the message is very simple. "Thomas," wrote Bayley, "was the first great and evident talent of the modern movement . . . to concentrate on what it felt like to be himself to make his poetry the feeling of his being."

But no poet can be entirely absorbed in self. We know from the evidence of his friends in the Swansea of his youth that Thomas was observant, fond of company, funny. His later stories and broadcasts demonstrate very clearly that little went by his keen and tolerant eye, so it is fair to assume that his adolescent concern with himself was abnormal only in that it formed the matter for much of his poetry that he was very much aware of the external world and his place in it. Like other intelligent young people he was concerned with the great imponderables, time, sex, life, religion. His poetry could be said to attempt to balance such forces within himself and in the world in which he lived.

That effort is serious and arduous. Early critics who felt that Thomas worked thoughtlessly and without effort saw neither the skill for so young a man nor the struggle throughout poem after poem to find a conclusion that satisfied his doubts. He certainly knew what he was doing. In many of his poems he uses man as a microcosm and himself as a mirror of the huge and inexplicable world in order to assert some order over chaos. It is not mere rhetoric that he intends (nor, it seems to me, did he ever intent mere rhetoric) when he ends a superbly serious poem, "If I were tickled by the rub of love," with a simple declaration—"Man be my metaphor." It is a truth he remained loyal to throughout his career. If we remember this, some of the difficulties of the work in *Eighteen Poems* seem less perplexing when we read:

Light breaks where no sun shines;
Where no sea runs, the waters of the heart
Push in their tides;
("Light breaks where no sun shines")

or even more illuminating these lines from the same poem:

Dawn breaks behind the eyes;
From poles of skull and toe the windy blood
Slides like a sea.
(13–15)

It is not, however simply that Thomas saw himself as the world or the world as himself; he saw himself as being subject to the same forces as the world and his effort is to understand those forces and to see how they affect him. Much of his poetry then is a journey in self-discovery. Those strong confident lines are also paths of doubt and uncertainty and the poem was successful only when he had successfully negotiated a way to a conclusion the poem had found for him. Much of the supposed obscurity of the early poetry is the result of the division between the confidence of the technique and the uncertainty—more correctly the innocence—of the thought. But we can certainly understand more readily now just why these poems use so many images of blood and body. They are not merely images, they form the subject matter of Thomas first public utterances.

And when the poem works it is very successful. Such an example would be "The force that through the green fuse drives the flower" in which everything combines to produce a remarkable unity. Here Thomas makes his complete identification with the natural world even more apparent than in other poems. It is not merely an identification with the external world that Thomas understands; it is an interrelationship so firm that its very statement is the poem. The poem opens with something that is almost a definition of the life force, in that the poet shows us how it affects both the flower representative of external life and himself:

The force that through the green fuse drives
the flower
Drives my green age; that blasts the roots of
trees
Is my destroyer.

He shows us then his place in the natural world. It is precisely that of every other living thing subject to growth and decay. He links his youth to that of the flower by his use of the common adjective "green"; he anticipates the hardening of age by aligning himself with "the roots of trees." But he does not understand the force he is considering; in fact he is unable to explain to the rose marred by winter that he is subject to the same fate:

And I am dumb to tell the crooked rose
My youth is bent by the same wintry fever.
(4–5)

The next two stanzas follow a repetitive pattern insisting not only on the poets relationship with the natural world and its laws—

The force that drives the water through the
rocks
Drives my red blood;

but on his inability to explain the nature of relentless time of inevitable decay. He is "dumb" for these purposes; not only is he unable to explain to the dying rose the reason for its death he is identically powerless to explain it to himself:

And I am dumb to mouth unto my veins
How at the mountain spring the same
mouth sucks.
(9–10)

Water and blood the springing liquids of external and internal worlds both are ruled by the same inexplicable forces.

Paradoxically, it is the realization of his inability to do more than recognize the intricate rclations of natural things ruled by time to be unable to explain any more than this which gives power and assurance to the poem qualities reinforced by the relentless drive of the rhythm by the repetition of the formal pattern and by the separated coupled with which he ends the poem. This last piece of virtuosity also brings out clearly the hidden pun the poet intends when he uses "dumb" to describe his helplessness. In it he ironically accuses himself of being stupid when he fails to persuade the dead lover of the universality of death:

> And I am dumb to tell the lovers tomb
> How at my sheet goes the same crooked
> worm.
> (21–22)

All in all, this is a most subtle and engaging poem well worth lengthy study. Even in small matters, as in the manner the poem is rounded off by the final image of the "crooked" worm echoing that of the "crooked" rose—and both possibly, reminding us of William Blakes "sick rose"—the poem is the work of a young man of great ability, writing at the top of his form.

It is this topic of death and decay that is most frequently examined in the first poems, and the universality of the subject in some measure helps to disguise the extreme introspection of much of the work. Yet it is clear that in all these poems, Thomas is firmly at the center of his world, relying almost entirely on his own sense perceptions. He is hardly ever objective in the ordinary meaning of the word, his thought and his emotion seeming to be an amalgam of these qualities, almost a new and highly individual power. His poems arise as he tells us straight out of his senses—"I see the boys of summer"—and we are tempted to think that without that first sight the boys would not have existed at all, nor the poem either. As it is they can go on living in thoughtless and careless folly blind to their certain ruin:

> I see the boys of summer in their ruin
> Lay the gold tithings barren,
> Setting no store by harvest freeze the soils;
> There in their heat the winter floods
> Of frozen loves they fetch their girls,
> And drown the cargoed apples in their tides.

But not all the first poems can be so classified. "Especially when the October wind" is made more recognizably from the visible world in and about Swansea (and is probably the first of several poems written in succeeding October months when the poet celebrated his birthday) and by some process of relation, from the act of writing poems. "Where once the waters of your face" also seems a more direct and external poem than most. What difficulties exist in the reading of this poem ease when it is realized that we are listening to a boat (or perhaps the owner of a boat) speaking to the ghost of a water that has dried up.

> Where once the waters of your face
> Spun to my screws, your dry ghost blows,
> The dead turns up its eye;

Here, too, we are given such a wealth of sea and tidal images that we are reminded that Thomas lived most of his life by the sea was increasingly influenced by seascape in his work. It is in this poem that we find the poet perhaps for the first time offering some measure of protection against time and dissolution, even if it is to a dry pool:

> There shall be corals in your beds,
> There shall be serpents in your tides,
> Till all our sea-faiths die.
> (22–24)

I have suggested that despite the energy and strength of the rhythms of these poems, they are sometimes less than sensitive, sometimes monotonous and heavy, and I believe this to be true. Yet the best, and the best made (for these are nearly always identical with Thomas), are free of this charge, and an examination of his rhymes would show how cleverly he avoids any suggestion of monotony here. His use of half-rhyme and false rhyme, easily to be seen in the lines already quoted, will show how successful he was. Admirable, too, is his strict search for accuracy; one can only be delighted by the combination of "dry" and "ghost", for instance, in "Where once the waters of your face."

All this meant that Thomas had established at once an easily recognized style and a highly individual voice, strange, exciting, and genuinely poetic. The poems to be found in *Twenty-five Poems* (1936) support and confirm the nature of his gifts, although there are some that seem simpler and more direct and a few that suggest a sadder and less convinced poet. Examples of the first kind are "This bread I break," "Ears in the turrets hear," "The hand that signed the paper," "Should lanterns shine," "I have longed to move away," and "And death shall have no dominion." They form no small proportion of the work, and while a few of them are new, some are poems that Thomas had rejected for his first collection and revised for this later publication. The poems of melancholy can be represented by the beautiful "Out of the sighs" with its wavering cadences, its slow melody:

Out of the sighs a little comes,
But not of grief, for I have knocked down
 that
Before the agony; the spirit grows,
Forgets and cries;
A little comes, is tasted and found good;
All could not disappoint;
There must, be praised, some certainty
If not of loving well, then not,
And that is true after perpetual defeat.

Perhaps not sufficient attention has been paid to this poem, one of the few pieces that contains none of the famous Thomas images, indeed hardly any images at all yet no other poet could have written it.

There are more typical poems, some of them going over old ground looking once again at the apparent division of flesh and soul, exhibiting the presence of death in the newborn:

I, in my intricate image, stride on two levels
Forged in man's minerals, the brassy orator
Laying my ghost in metal,
The scales of this twin world treat on the
 double,
My half ghost in armour hold hard in
 death's corridor
To my man-iron sidle.

Beginning with doom in the bulb the spring
 unravels. . . .
 ("I, in my intricate image")

And there are a few poems so frankly obscure ("Now," "How soon the servant sun,") that they are almost jokes. I do not pretend to understand them at all.

But the most important and substantial work of this period are the ten religious stanzas called "Altarwise by owl-light." Written between December 1935 and the summer of 1936, these poems, or rather this poem (since I agree with Dr. Jones that this is a single poem with ten sonnet-like stanzas [*The Poems*, p. 262]), is something of a watershed in Thomas' work. It is his longest piece up to this time and also the most compressed and the most highly metaphorical. It has been the subject of controversy and explication since it first appeared as a whole in 1936, and opinion has ranged from outright dismissal to prolonged and complex analysis such as that by Elder Olson (*The Poetry of Dylan Thomas*, pp. 63–87). Experts are even divided about how it should be read, some of them (for example Marshall W. Stearns, "Unsex the Skeleton," *Transformation* 3, 1946) convinced that it is a series of separate sonnets despite Thomas' own statement that "this poem is a particular incident in a particular adventure" (*Sunday Times*, September 1936). Obscure it certainly is, compressed it certainly is. Afterwards, as if he had gone as far as he wished in those directions, Thomas verse became more free, its music more varied and lyrical.

"We were both religious poets," wrote Watkins (*Letters to Vernon Watkins*, p. 17), and there is enough proof of this statement throughout the work of both poets to sustain this assertion. In Thomas' case we have the example of his early poem, "Before I knocked" in which he speaks for the Christchild even before His birth:

> Before I knocked and flesh let enter,
> With liquid hands tapped on the womb,
> I who was shapeless as the water
> That shaped the Jordan near my home
> Was brother to Mnetha's daughter
> And sister to the fathering worm.

And there are references to his continued absorption with religion right up to the final statement of his prefatory note to *The Collected Poems.* "These poems, with all their crudities, doubts, and confusions are written for the love of Man and in praise of God."

Thomas was twenty-one when he wrote "Altar-wise by owl-light." It represents a remarkably sustained and unified effort by the young poet. The poem came quickly to him, when one considers its density and complexity, but it is in no way an easy poem and remains one of the most challenging for the reader. Dr. Jones suggests that we should think of it as "absolute" poetry and that "comprehension is irrelevant" (*The Poems,* p. 263). Its difficulty he considers akin to that of a Bach fugue, and certainly the intricate weaving of images and the stern control of the sonnet form give this opinion some credence. But the poem is also made of words and possesses the properties of meaning.

What seems evident is that Thomas has taken for his subject the biblical themes of divine redemption and the reality of human sacrifice in an attempt to reconcile them. He has not confined his resources, his imagery, his information to the material of the Old and New Testaments; the poem is made of all his concerns and part of its difficulty is the wide range of Thomas' curious and personal learning and our difficulty in relating its disparate elements.

Each of the fourteen-line stanzas is organized into an octet and a sestet, the rhymes regular in pattern but not in sound, Thomas using the half-rhymes common with him:

> Altarwise by owl-light in the half-way house
> The gentleman lay graveward with his furies;
> Abaddon in the hangnail cracked from Adam,
> And from his fork, a dog among the fairies,
> The atlas-eater with a jaw for news,
> Bit out the mandrake with to-morrow's
> scream.

This is Thomas' version of the Nativity. It is no traditional Christmas scene, full of radiance and the light of promise. Christ's mortality is recognized as early as line 2. He is not surrounded by angels, but by furies. He is descended from Adam so already aware of sin. Abaddon is an unlikely figure here; he is the Angel of the Bottomless Pit, so the Christchild born at dusk or owl-light is in dangerous and cast-out company from the time of his birth. His half-way house is already one of dreadful omen.

The second stanza continues the story, so it is possible to see that Thomas, wrestling with words and meaning, was on a journey of understanding as profound as any he had yet made. The child whose birth we attended in the first stanza is growing up:

> Death is all metaphors shape in one history;
> The child that sucketh long is shooting up

—but we are told again of death toward the end of this stanza:

> Hairs of your head, then said the hollow
> agent,
> Are but the roots of nettles and of feathers

It is, too, a precise and horrible prophecy that Death ("the hollow agent," a skull) gives, since we are reminded that Christ will wear on his head a crown of thorns, or nettles.

I cannot pretend that it is other than very difficult to trace Thomas' thought through these extraordinarily powerful stanzas, but some of them treat the theme more directly than others. One such is the eighth stanza, which states its message with urgency:

This was the crucifixion on the mountain,
Time's nerve in vinegar the gallow grave
As tarred with blood as the bright thorns
  I wept;
The world's my wound, God's Mary in her
  grief,
Bent like three trees and bird-papped
  through her shift,
With pins for teardrops is the long wound's
  woman.

There is little of the extreme difficulty here of some of the other stanzas, since Thomas has followed closely the Gospel accounts of the Crucifixion. The images are those we would expect and at the same time reinforce and interrelate with each other: for example, Christ's tears are as savage as the thorns he wears, Mary's are as sharp and hard as pins. In her grief, Mary is bowed with that invisible weight exactly as the three trees are bent with the weight of three men. The stanza ends with Christ's statement that he is there to heal the world:

I, by the tree of thieves, all glory's sawbones,
Unsex the skeleton this mountain minute,
And by this blowclock witness of the sun
Suffer the heaven's children through my
  heartbeat.

He first unsexes "the skeleton" of Death, and then, as the blowclock witness (which I take to be a seeding dandelion, something to be found everywhere and whose seeds are carried everywhere by the wind, a symbol of delicate and silent power), measures that eclipse of the sun which accompanied the execution; Christ suffers "the heaven's children" through his "heartbeat." This is quite explicit. His suffering allows us into heaven; as his heart stops, we, "the heavens children" are promised immortality.

This stanza is for me, perhaps because it is the easiest to read, the high point of the poem. Stanza nine is extremely difficult and does not seem to continue, as the first eight do, a retelling and examination of events. But the final stanza, puzzling as it is in its confused syntax and images, ends on a note of hope, a prayer almost, in which Thomas asks that the garden, essentially the garden of Eden, which he has imagined sunken beneath the sea, shall rise again and, holding Adam's tree and Christ's tree allow the serpent to build "a nest of mercies" in "the rude, red tree," the blood-stained tree upon which Christ died.

This was the last poem in *Twenty-five Poems.* After this, Thomas was never again as fertile a poet. He was at this time living in dire poverty, newly married—he married Caitlin MacNamara in October 1937—and despite the marvelous reception given to *Twenty-five Poems,* the book made little money. He began to work on the autobiographical stories later collected in *The Portrait of the Artist as a Young Dog* (1940), in the hope that these would be more successful financially; but first he put together a volume of seven stories and sixteen new poems, called *The Map of Love.* This was a beautiful book, the stories a selection from Thomas' early prose and the poems including some most exciting work, all proving an even greater technical virtuosity, a number—for example, "After the funeral"—destined to be among his most famous. But ill-luck of the most unhappy kind attended the appearance of this book. Coming out at the end of August 1939 it was overwhelmed by the outbreak of World War II. Neither this nor *The World I Breathe,* a sizable collection of his poetry and prose that appeared in December of the same year and was his first American volume, did very much to relieve his financial straits.

The poems in *The Map of Love* do, however, mark a departure. Much more varied in theme and in style, they form a most interesting group. Still completely personal, they demonstrate a much greater interest in the external world. There are still poems that aroused the conservative critics to anger—particularly the opening poem "Because the pleasure-bird whistles"—and there are fine poems of the sort we have met before, like the splendid sonnet "When all my five and country senses see," but through them all there runs like a slender narrative thread a suggestion that the poet is no longer alone. "We lying by seasand" begins a poem of recognition that the poet cannot disturb the ravages of time, but it is also a poem of tender resignation, allowing that "wishes breed not" and that the poet and his companion should watch "yellow until the golden weather / Breaks." We are in fact being given a map of love. "If my head hurt a hair's foot" is a poem in which his unborn child speaks to its mother and the mother responds. "Twenty-four years"—another of the poems for his own birthday—is a celebration of his journey toward death ("sewing a shroud for a journey") and of his responsibilities as husband and father:

> Dressed to die the sensual strut begun,
> With my red veins full of money,
> In the final direction of the elementary town
> I advance for as long as forever is.
> (6–9)

It seems that the poet has new directions to explore as well as a new viewpoint for his perennial themes. His love, too, extends outside his immediate concerns. The aunt with whom he had spent much time when a child, on the farm he was to immortalize in "Fern Hill," had died and he made for her the passionate elegy, "After the funeral."

The original version of this poem was written on 10 February 1933, a few days after his aunts death. Five years were to pass before Thomas went back to the poem and transformed it into the deeply felt elegy we now have. He is bitter and angry at what he feels to be an insufficient sorrow among the mourners, calling their conventional sadness

> . . . mule praises brays,
> Windshake of sailshaped ears, muffle-toed tap
> Tap happily of one peg in the thick
> Graves foot, blinds down the lids . . .
> (1–4)

But he moves through his memories of the living Ann Jones into a noble eloquence, assuming for her a position as "Ann's bard on a raised hearth," calling all

> The seas to service that her wood-tongued virtue
> Babble like a bellbuoy over the hymning heads
> Bow down the walls of the ferned and foxy woods
> That her love sing and swing through a brown chapel.
> (22–25)

And he offers her his continual service of love and eloquence until the dead return to life:

> . . . until
> The stuffed lung of the fox twitch and cry Love
> And the strutting fern lay seeds on the black sill.
> (38–40)

It is in these poems that we see for the first time a poet who is part of the outside world, offering as a partial solution to all the puzzles of life his personal love. In "After the funeral" for instance, we are shown a most careful ordering of the imagery, all the properties being those in and about the farm, the "stale fern," "the stuffed fox," the woods behind the house. Dr. Jones has told us that Thomas was not a ready observer of the world of nature, but that "if observation was directly relevant to his central interests, and only in that case, he could observe, and where the relevance was great, his observation could be keen" (*My Friend Dylan Thomas,* p. 56). The force of this remark can be appreciated when we remember that the flower in "The force that through the green fuse" remains an unnamed flower, but that in "After the funeral" a wealth of observed images are identified and ordered into powerful use. This ability was to be used more and more often, reinforcing Thomas' great auditory gifts. Thomas' changed status as a husband gave to him a wider range of subject and a greater involvement with other people.

This was part of a process that led to the comparative clarity and luminosity of the later poems. For a variety of reasons, possibly related to Thomas' work as a film-script writer and to the lack, until he removed to the

Boathouse, Laugharne, in 1949 of a settled home, fewer poems were written. These years saw the growth of his reputation as a reader of poetry, not only his own. In February 1946 he published *Deaths and Entrances,* a tiny volume in size but great in achievement and influence. Here were such anthology pieces as "The Hunchback in the Park," which drew on his childhood memories of Cwmdonkin Park; the few war poems included in his work; two long narrative poems, "A Winter's Tale" and "Ballad of the Long-legged Bait"; poems of superb virtuosity like "There was a Saviour," in which a complex rhyme scheme is incredibly maintained; and amid a whole galaxy of wonderful things, "Poem in October" and "Fern Hill."

It has been fashionable to think that Thomas' early work is superior to these later poems. That must be mistaken opinion. That they are different in many respects, while retaining Thomas highly individual style, is fairly obvious. The main reason for this difference is one that the poems in *Deaths and Entrances* reflects. Previous to these poems, Thomas had been busily adapting the work contained in his early notebooks that series of exercise books now in the Lockwood Memorial Library in Buffalo. For seven years these books had held the material for his poetry, but in the spring of 1941 he sold them to a London dealer in rare books and manuscripts. "It would be hard" wrote Constantine FitzGibbon "to imagine a more significant gesture on Dylan's part a greater renunciation of his past than this. Those notebooks were his youth, those notebooks were his poems, those notebooks were Dylan the young poet. . . . The boy-poet, the Rimbaud of Cwmdonkin Drive, had ceased to exist (*The Life of Dylan Thomas,* p. 247)." What we have from this time on are the poems of the mature poet. They demonstrate his presence in wartime London, prey to "many married London's estranging grief," and his growing concern with other sufferers ("The conversation of prayer," "A refusal to mourn," "Ceremony after a fire raid"). Among such resonant elegies, the most personal is probably the best known, the touching poem to his father, "Do not go gentle into that good night." For many of his admirers, the new clarity of these poems, the recognizable scenes of his meditations, were increasing virtues.

By almost any standards the poems in *Deaths and Entrances* are remarkable. They display technical virtuosity of dazzling proportions, ranging from the strict villanelle in which Thomas contained his love for his father in "Do not go gentle," through the odelike forms of "Into her Lying Down Head" and "Unluckily for a Death"; the revived medieval patterns of "Vision and Prayer"; the invented stanza of "A Winter's Tale"; and the relatively simple shapes of "The Hunchback in the Park" and "In my Craft or Sullen Art." As a demonstration of the poet's craft they are almost unique, and Thomas himself suggests the importance of his skill when he places "craft" before "art":

> In my craft or sullen art
> Exercised in the still night
> When only the moon rages
> And the lovers lie abed
> With all their griefs in their arms,
> I labour by singing light
> Not for ambition or bread
> Or the strut and trade of charms
> On the ivory stage
> But for the common wages
> Of their most secret heart.

And surely there cannot be a more complete statement of the poet's calling than that, nor a more complete refutation of any possibility of Thomas' lack of utter seriousness as an artist. Here he even tells us that he writes now for an audience, even though such people may not be aware of his existence. The young poet who sang himself only is certainly gone.

There are however two poems that are personal, not from the absorbed, fascinated examination of self that had characterized the young poet, but poems filled with a piercing melancholy because time has taken away the innocence of childhood. They are "Poem in October" and "Fern Hill."

These famous poems have much in common. Their structure is similar; the verse stanza in each is complex, formal, and invented by Thomas. The difficulty of such forms must have been most challenging, yet Thomas succeeded in making them lyrical, musical, their intricacy and complexity never obtrusive but necessary to the unity of the poetry. To read them aloud is almost to have to sing them. "Poem in October" has seven stanzas, each of ten lines. The lines are syllabic; that is, Thomas, as he had been doing for some time, did not write them in regular rhythmic patterns but adopted the method of counting the syllables, so that the first line in every stanza has nine syllables, the second line twelve syllables, the third nine the fourth three, and so on. The rhyme scheme is both unusual and far from obvious. Thomas is using a convention that can be seen in other poems of this period, in "There was a Saviour," for example. He rhymes the vowels only—in our example he rhymes "saviour" with "radium." In "Poem in October" the rhymes are not quite as easily recognized yet they are there and tactfully hold together the verse stanzas despite the variety of line lengths and the strength and dance of the rhythms. We can see that "heaven" in line 1 rhymes with "heron" in line three "beckon" in line 5 and "second" in line 9. Similarly "wood," "rook," and "foot" share the same quality of vowel sound as do "shore" and "forth." One can easily identify this technique in the other stanzas.

The poem is one of that series of October poems in which Thomas celebrates his birthday; others have already been noted. Here he is not so much celebratory as apprehensive, looking back from the anniversary of his "thirtieth year to heaven" to earlier birthdays, those of his innocence when he

> . . . saw in the turning so clearly a child's
> Forgotten mornings when he walked with
>   his mother
>   Through the parables
>   Of sun light
> And the legends of the green chapels
>   (4–50)

What he sees is "the true joy of the long dead child" who was himself. His final lines express the hope that his "hearts truth" may "Still be sung / On this high hill / In a years turning."

The poem is unashamedly nostalgic, something that has caused some critics to minimize its importance; yet it is also beautiful and perfectly written. It is possible that Thomas idealizes the innocence of childhood, creating a brief moment of visionary happiness in which "a boy . . . whispered the truth of his joy / To the trees and the stones and the fish in the tide." But this is a startling achievement, and he has offered us the vision in highly sophisticated verse, from an adult point of view, and in the hope that he can retain such perfection of truth in the future. Imperfect though his life may have been, his aim is both the perfection of his art and, through it, a vision of perfection.

"Fern Hill" seems to me an even better poem. "Poem in October" includes merely a glimpse of the child's heaven; here he makes heaven as the boy knew it palpable and visible for us. Like the children in Blake's *Songs of Innocence,* the child Dylan on his aunt's farm, in a country world flawless and shining and without enemies, plays in ignorance that he is a prisoner of time:

> . . . nothing I cared, at my sky blue trades,
>   that time allows
> In all his tuneful turning, so few and such
>   morning songs,
>   Before the children green and golden
>   Follow him out of grace
>   (42–45)

The poem is much more than a paean of regret for times past and lost. Sensuous, opulent in language, rich in imagery and music, it paradoxically mourns the passing of an innocent vision that has made a heaven from a poor hill farm in rough country, something possible only for a child who loves the place, and even while mourning its passing re-creates that very heaven, its brilliance of color, the music of its smoke, its magical horses and foxes.

Thomas knows that he has made Eden once again: "So it must have been after the birth of the simple light / In the first spinning place." To lose such a condition, and to know one has lost it, is an appalling plight. It was Thomas' strength and his fate that he never lost such knowledge, that he kept the child's vision and the man's knowledge. His poem possesses both. He has made both his innocence and his sense of loss clear for all of us as long as his language remains.

There are not many poems after this. Whatever the reasons, Thomas wrote few poems in the last years of his life. He includes in his *Collected Poems* only six more poems, if we count the prologue written specially for that volume. Among them are two that few of his admirers would wish to be without, "Poem on His Birthday" and "Over Sir John's Hill." Both reflect the landscape about his house on the shore—"his house on stilts"—at Laugharne; both are calmer more resigned. It is tempting to see in them some foreknowledge of the poet's death:

> And freely he goes lost
> In the unknown famous light of great
> And fabulous dear God.
> ("Poem on His Birthday" 46–48)

and to suggest that his frequent references to God mean that he has made his peace and no longer fears time, that he possesses some consolation. But it seems to me that these are probably the more mature manifestations of his old obsessions: death, religion, the inevitability of time. If he had some peace, it was as he says in his "Authors Prologue," a poor peace.

> In my seashaken house
> On a breakneck of rocks . . .
> At poor peace I sing
> To you strangers. . . .
> (4–5; 23–24)

His "true joy" remains what it always was, that his "ark sings in the sun."

Although poems were few in his later years, he was not idle. Apart from his reading tours and his broadcasts, he continued to write prose, and he was a superb prose writer. His letters are joyous documents his telegrams even. Having left his shirts in Dr. Jones's house, he sent his friend a wire that read, "For Pete's sake send my shirts, Love Pete" (*My Friend Dylan Thomas*, p. 114). Prose was the medium in which he found an outlet for his narrative skill, for his humor, for all the sides of his life for which poetry—and it will be remembered that for him poetry was used only for the most serious and profound and mysterious work—was not possible. He had a great deal to offer. He was a born teller of tales.

From the very beginning of his career he knew this. He thought of himself as a writer of poems and stories. This is how he describes himself in a letter, written when he was nineteen, to Glyn Jones: "You ask me to tell you about myself, but my life is so uneventful it is not worth recording. I am a writer of poems and stories" (*The Dragon Has Two Tongues*, p. 172). His life did not remain uneventful, but he was to remain a writer of poems and stories. He had contributed stories as well as poems to *The Swansea Grammar School Magazine.* In an appendix to *The Collected Stories* (1984), the editor, Walford Davies, includes three of these schoolboy pieces, the earliest having appeared in the school magazine in April 1931. There is plenty of evidence that Thomas considered poems and stories equal products of his talent, drawing no distinctions between them, knowing they came from the same source. The magazine he hoped to found and edit, on which he spent some time in the effort to promote it, was to be called *Prose and Verse.* It never appeared, but it is noteworthy that he allows prose to appear first in its title. And Glyn Jones and other friends have told us that when they visited him at his parent's house he was as eager to read his stories to them as he was his poems. They were, indeed very like his poems.

If we read "The Tree," or any of the stories that eventually appeared in *The Map of Love,* it is evident that they possess the same obsessive imagery, are written in the same heightened rhythms, deal very largely with the same interior world as the poems of that period. It is true that, since they are narratives, Thomas had to pay more attention to the observable world; but it remains largely a place of dreams, the details not very clearly the result of observation; nor do the events of the story necessarily proceed from each other with the force of the inevitable. But they have the same sensuous power as the poems, and their very texture is exciting to discover.

> Rising from the house that faced the Jarvis hills in the long distance, there was a tower for the day-birds to build in and for the owls to fly around at night. From the village the light in the tower window shone like a glow-worm through the panes; but the room under the sparrows' nests were rarely lit. ("The Tree" *Collected Stores,* p. 5)

When Thomas first went to London in November 1934, he had already published stories in the magazines. Arriving in Soho, he found his poetry and prose equally admired. In "Where Tawe Flows," one of the autobiographical stories yet to be written and which would be included in *Portrait of the Artist as a Young Dog,* Thomas remembers this period: "Young Mr Thomas was at the moment without employment, but it was understood that he would soon be leaving for London to make a career in Chelsea as a free-lance journalist; he was penniless and hoped in a vague way to live on women."

But all this was in the future. And if the appearance of his first book of poems in December 1934 meant there was to be a comparative neglect of his prose Thomas was not aware of it. He continued to write his stories to sent them to editors. From the room off the Fulham Road he shared with his Swansea friend Fred Janes and where "for yards around" there was "nothing but poems, poems, poems, butter, eggs, mashed potatoes, mashed among my stories and Janes's canvases," he wrote with pride of the stories that had been accepted by various periodicals. He was a teller of stories all his life.

They were not, however, collected into a volume as the poems were and when *Eighteen Poems* was followed by *Twenty-five Poems,* Thomas was firmly established as a poet not a prose writer. He tried to persuade Richard Church, his editor at Dents to publish a collection of stories, but Church refused judging the work obscene. This opinion was shared by the printers, who refused to set the stories for another publisher a little later. It was not until 1939 that a representative sample of Thomas stories appeared in book form, when seven were included with the poems of *The Map of Love.* In December of the same year *The World I Breathe,* a collection of the poems of the first three books and three stories in addition to those in *The Map of Love* was published in America. At last the early prose, or those stories which were considered suitable, had found a home.

Thomas, too, had found a home. He and Caitlin had moved into a small house in Laugharne, the little seaside town in Carmarthenshire that was to be his home for much of the rest of his life. They were very poor, and Thomas set about earning money by writing a different kind of story altogether. Glyn Jones recalls that in the summer of 1938 he mentioned to Caitlin Thomas that he was engaged on a volume of stories about childhood: "She seemed very surprised and told me that Dylan had already started doing the same thing. His were the autobiographical stories which in 1940 appeared as *Portrait of the Artist as a Young Dog*" (*The Dragon Has Two Tongues,* p. 191). The new stories were direct uncomplicated evocations of the Swansea in which Thomas had grown up. They were not at all dreamlike; instead they revealed a most observant eye for the oddities of behavior, and an ear for the eccentricities within patterns of ordinary speech, that allowed Thomas to create credible and individual characters for the men, women, and children who people his stories. And while Thomas had written these stories—there were ten of them—at great speed and in the hope that they would be more commercial than his previous narratives, they also proved that this was the medium he could use for all his skills as a commentator on the world in which he lived, for his sense of fun, for his understanding of the small inevitable tragedies that fill ordinary lives.

Just as he had learned his trade as a poet from his reading of the great poets, particularly those of the nineteenth century, so he had served his willing time with the short-story writers. Among other authors, he knew the work of D. H. Lawrence, H. E. Bates, and Liam O'Flaherty; he had read James Joyce's *Dubliners*; he was an admiring student of Charles Dickens. Among Welsh writers he had a particular interest in the work of Caradoc Evans, whose stories had already used a Welsh background with success. With Glyn Jones he had visited the older man in 1936. They had driven north to Aberystwyth, the two young men wearing each other's hats, to speak to "the great Caradoc Evans," as Thomas called him in a story included in *The Portrait of the Artist as a Young Dog.* There is no direct influence of the Cardiganshire writer's work on Thomas, but he is probably important as someone whose example may have inspired the poet to write about Swansea and its people.

Again Thomas had been living unprotected in the world for a number of years, his eye and his wits sharpened, his naturally alert senses alive to what was about him. He had already abandoned in many ways the interior universe of his early work and, as we have seen in his poems, was ready to create a world more related to that in which he lived. Above all, he had become a great storyteller, famous (as he almost said himself) about the bars. He realized that there were great areas of his ability and his personality that he would never use for lyric poetry, but he could use them in his stories. From this time on, the difference between his poetry and prose was marked.

Thomas believed that poetry is a solemn art, and he was a serious poet, dedicating his life to the service of his muse, restricting his themes to a few great and inevitable subjects. There is a great deal of word-play in his verse, of ecstatic delight in the combination of opulent sounds and highly exact, unusual meaning, in the presence in his lines of serious puns, but there is no room for laughter. Yet he was also a brilliantly funny man, and it is in the ten stories we are considering that a comic Thomas made his appearance. The stories, united in that they have as a central character "young Mr Thomas," move from the innocence of the first three stories ("The Peaches," "A Visit to Grandpa's," "Patricia, Edith, and Arnold"), through two splendid stories of his school days (in one of which, "The Fight," we meet Dr. Daniel Jones as a boy), to a more complex and jaunty person, Thomas as a cub reporter, his cigarette worn in admiring imitation of the old reporter he accompanies through the public houses of the town ("Old Garbo"). We see him as a haunter of deserted winter beaches as a young man about to leave the town for London. It is with this portrait of himself that Thomas takes as decisive a leave of his younger self as he did with his sale of his notebooks.

The stories are full of wonderful talk, something in which Thomas himself excelled. We hear and recognize the characters as they preach from the back of a cart:

> I sat on the hay and stared at Gwilym preaching, and heard his voice rise and crack and sink to a whisper and break into singing and Welsh and ring triumphantly and be wilt and meek. The sun through a hole shone on his praying shoulders and he said: "O God, Thou art everywhere all the time, in the dew of the morning, in the frost of the evening, in the field and the town, in the preacher and the sinner, in the sparrow and the big buzzard." ("The Peaches," *Collected Stories,* p. 128)

They are irreverent to school teachers, joke and wisecrack their way to the shore, stare in sadness and despair at the sea. A great mimic Thomas realized his exceptional narrative skills in these stories: his sense of place, his fine ear for speech, and his love, appreciative and unjudging, for the people he creates.

These are the qualities that make him a fine writer as distinct from a fine poet, and they are the qualities that helped to make him generally popular. Had he not written his stories he would have been a lesser, and a less interesting figure.

Portrait of the Artist as a Young Dog is a title that pays clear tribute to Joyce, but it is not Joyce's *Portrait of the Artist as a Young Man* that one is reminded of when reading Thomas book. Rather the stories are clearly of the same type as those in Joyce's *Dubliners,* and Thomas is surely telling us this. Both books are set in provincial cities, both relate the important small events in unimportant lives and make them important. Stylistically, however, they are very different. Thomas himself denied that there was any Joycean influence on his work:

> I cannot say that I have been "influenced" by Joyce, whom I enormously admire and whose "Ulysses," and earlier stories, I have read a great deal. . . . As you know, the name given to innumerable portrait paintings by their artists is, "Portrait of the Artist as a Young Man." . . . I myself made a bit of doggish fun at the painting title and intended no possible reference to Joyce. ("Notes on the Art of Poetry," *Texas Quarterly,* Winter 1961)

Be that as it may, it is certain that "the bit of doggish fun" is his own. Although Thomas' title is said to have been the suggestion of Richard Hughes, the distinguished author of *A High Wind in Jamaica* and other fine work, Thomas had almost used it years before when he wrote, in 1933, to his friend Trevor Hughes. In that letter Dylan had advised his friend to "dive into the sea of yourself like a young dog." In his own stories, Thomas had taken his own advice and dived into the sea of his childhood and youth.

Portrait was published in 1940 the last of Thomas books to appear until the war was over. He was—after a short period in which things looked very uncertain—working fairly regularly as a writer of film scripts and a broadcaster his own writing pushed aside somewhat. He was, however, working intermittently on a novel, and was sending parts of it to London publishers, without success. This was the comic novel, just as autobiographical as his stories, eventually called *Adventures in the Skin Trade.* It was never completed and was published posthumously in 1955.

Despite its late public appearance—an extract had been published in *Folios of New Writing* in 1941—most of it seems to have been written in the summer of 1941. Its hero, Samuel Bennet, seems to be none other than the young Mr. Thomas of the *Portrait* and he continues where that young man left off, departing from Swansea by the very train that Thomas himself left home in "to make a career in Chelsea as a free-lance journalist." Vernon Watkins, who wrote an interesting foreword to the novel when it eventually appeared, thought that it remained unfinished because of the impact of the war, particularly of the air raids on London, on what he called Thomas' "essentially tragic vision," but he also thought that Thomas mistrusted his own facility. Certainly Thomas was able to write this sort of prose very quickly, but I feel that there may well have been other reasons for the failure to continue the adventures of Samuel Bennet. The novel is loosely structured as picaresque and moves forward in an arbitrary and rather casual manner. Thomas, that deliberate artist, must have felt very dubious about it; it is impossible to see, for example, any serious reason for it to end anywhere, or indeed to continue. It is funny and inventive, with passages of brilliant slapstick, but Thomas may simply have come to the end of what he had to say. He was, moreover, not a natural novelist; he was a natural short-story writer; the novel was too long for him. The very nature of his talent, selective, concentrated, meant that he was not at home with the novel, a form into which one can pack almost anything. And while Thomas recognized his kinship with Dickens when he called *Adventures in the Skin Trade* "a mixture of Oliver Twist, Little Dorrit, Kafka, Beachcomber, and 3-adjectives-a-penny belly-churning Thomas," it was Dickens' energy and humor that he was acknowledging, the furious poetry. Thomas never actually put his novel away entirely. As late as 1953 the year of his death he was still suggesting that he might continue it.

For all practical purposes the novel was abandoned when Thomas went to London to work, and the demands on his time from then on resulted in there remaining only seven short narratives from this last period of his life, and six of the seven were written for broadcasting. It is ironic that his great popular reputation may rest on one or two of these and on *Under Milk Wood,* his "play for voices." It is also understandable, for they are entirely memorable pieces, bringing us the whole man, his warmth, the wide range of his humor, his pathos, his brilliant images, his incredible memory for the days and places of his childhood, his moving sadness for what had gone forever, and even enough magic to remind us that he was a great poet.

The first of these late pieces "Quite Early One Morning," reads like a first draft of *Under Milk Wood,* for it deals with the dreams of a small sleeping town in the early morning, where Captain Tiny Evans, a trial Captain Cat, sleeps and dreams of "a rainbow of flying fishes." But it is "A Child's Christmas in Wales" that everyone knows. All over the world in the days immediately before Christmas we can hear from schools and houses the poets voice rebuilding for us an impossible and utterly satisfying Christmas. Compounded of two similar stories, "Memories of Christmas" and "Conversation about Christmas," this was first published in *Harper's Bazaar* as "A Child's Memories of Christmas in Wales" in December 1950. It is a rich confection as rich with gifts as any Christmas can hope to be, its snow untouched, its parties warm and musical packed as a pudding with fruit and brandy. Dickens is not far away, but there are unforgettable Thomas moments too, like that when "with dog-disturbing whistle and sugar fags I would scour the swatched town for the news of the little world and find always a dead bird by the white Post Office or the deserted swings; perhaps a robin, all but one of his fires out" (*The Collected Stories,* p. 300).

"The Followers" is a ghost story of the most cunning and surprising sort. On a wet night, so beautifully realized that we must believe it, two bored young men, almost penniless, but bravely keeping up appearances, one with a gallant cap, the other with a rolled umbrella and an attempted mustache, follow an ordinary girl home through the soaked, domestic streets. In such a world, so solid and convincing, ghosts should not happen, and it is all the more credible and terrifying when they do—and also funny. Thomas has learned how to select and create his detail; he has looked hard and lovingly at his world.

"The Followers" is the only one of these late narratives not written for broadcasting and perhaps the only one that does not have the sound of Thomas' unique voice in it as a result. Certainly the uproarious events of "A Story" were made for him alone to tell, and the very structure of the sentences as they lie on the page seems to carry with them the mans own telling:

> But there he was, always, a steaming hulk of an uncle, his braces straining like hawsers. . . . As he ate the house grew smaller; he billowed out over the furniture, the loud check meadow of his waistcoat littered, as though after a picnic, with cigarette ends, peelings, cabbage stalks, birds' bones, gravy. (*The Collected Stories,* p. 337)

Reading again these short narratives, as personal as any he wrote as a young man, it is impossible not to regret the loss of the work he might have written and to wonder in what direction Thomas might have moved. We have not considered yet *Under Milk Wood,* the play for radio that was successively broadcast, adapted for the stage and filmed. This might suggest that Thomas would have turned more and more to the stag for his work. His death put an end to the projected opera libretto he was to write for Igor Stravinsky, but we know he was enormously excited by the prospect. *Under Milk Wood* was first performed, in almost its final form, in New York only weeks before Thomas died there. He was working on it even during its performance, sending altered and additional lines to the actors as they read, and Thomas continued to tinker with it almost to his death.

Yet it is astonishly complete and unified, its cast of daft characters amiably dependent one on the other, the laws of its self-contained community thoroughly justifiable in the terms of that community. It cannot be said to have a plot. Its events are those of a single day in a small sea town in South Wales, Laugharne maybe, with echoes of New Quay, in Dyfed, where Thomas also lived. Raymond Williams has distinguished "three kinds of writing" in the play, "narrative dialogue song," an observation that helps to define the simplicity of its structure and to point the subtlety of the writing. The unity of the play, its corresponding and related oppositions, of darkness to light, of public chorus to individual musing, of song to prose, of innocence to innocent guilt—these make it remarkable. In it suggests Williams, "Thomas wrote his adequate epilogue, his uproarious and singing lament" ("Dylan Thomas's Play for Voices" in Dylan Thomas, C. B. Cox ed., p. 98).

There are always difficulties in measuring the stature of a poet. It seems to me that Thomas wrote enough remarkable poetry to justify our calling him great. There are poems that have enriched our literature and his work has influenced a whole generation of poets. He changed the direction of English language poetry, his example being just as powerful in America as in Britain; nor were they always poets younger than himself who followed his lead. His life may well seem chaotic and without direction, yet it was purposeful and direct when we think of his one aim, to wait for his poems and to write them to the very best of his ability. All his working life he "laboured by singing light" to refine and perfect his skill; he was a great craftsman. For nearly a year he worked on the "Authors Prologue" to his *Collected Poems,* refusing to allow the book to go forward until he had completed to his satisfaction the almost impossibly difficult task of writing a poem of one hundred and two lines, in which line 102 rhymes with line 1, line 101 with line 2, and so on until they meet in a couplet at the heart of the poem. My belief is that the poetry is as remarkable as the technical ability. And there may be another test of greatness, perhaps one that is more important than the opinion of any critic. On 1 March 1982, when the ceremony for the dedication of the poet's memorial stone took place in Westminster Abbey the great hall was full. People stood in the aisles at the pediments of pillars, wherever there was a foot of room. Hundreds stood outside in the rain unable to hear a word of the proceedings. Ordinary people as well as the great and famous had come to pay their respects, many years after his death to the poet. "He was loyal to the poem," said Theodore Roethke (*Encounter,* January 1954, p. 11) "he was one of the great ones." And the people had come to agree with that judgment, to affirm that poetry was necessary for the language and to honor the man who had proved it for them. That may well be greatness.

Selected Bibliography

SEPARATE WORKS

Eighteen Poems, (London, 1934); *Twenty-five Poems,* (London, 1936); *The Map of Love,* (London, 1939); *The World I Breathe,* Norfolk Conn. (1939); *Portrait of the Artist as a Young Dog,* (Norfolk Conn. and London, 1940); *New Poems,* (Norfolk Conn., 1943); *Deaths and Entrances,* (London, 1946); *Selected Writings of Dylan Thomas,* (New York, 1946); *In Country Sleep and Other Poems,* (New York, 1952); *Collected Poems 1934–1952,* (London, 1952); *Under Milk Wood,* (London, 1954); *Quite Early One Morning,* (London, 1954); *A Prospect of the Sea,* (London, 1955); *Letters to Vernon Watkins,* (London, 1957); "Notes on the Art of Poetry," *Texas Quarterly,* (Winter 1961); *The Notebooks of Dylan Thomas,* (New York, 1967) ed. by R. Maud also pub. as *Poet in the Making* (London, 1968); *The Poems,* (London, 1971) ed. by D. Jones; *The Death of the King's Canary,* (London, 1976) with J. Davenport; *The Collected Stories,* (London, 1984) ed. by W. Davies.

BIOGRAPHICAL AND CRITICAL WORKS

Treece, H., *Dylan Thomas, "Dog Among the Fairies,"* (London, 1949); Olsen, E., *The Poetry of Dylan Thomas,* (Chicago, 1954); Brinnin, J. M., *Dylan Thomas in America,* (Boston, 1955); Thomas, C., *Leftover Life to Kill,* (Boston and London, 1957); *Dylan Thomas: The Legend and the Poet,* E. W. Tedlock ed. (London, 1960); Kleinmann, H. H., *The Religious Sonnets of Dylan Thomas,* (Berkley, Calif., 1963, New York 1979); FitzGibbon, C., *The Life of Dylan Thomas,* Boston and London (1965); *Dylan Thomas: A Collection of Critical Essays,* C. B. Cox ed. (New York, 1966) includes essay by D. Daiches; *Modern Poets on Modern Poetry,* J. Scully ed. (London, 1966); Jones, G., *The Dragon Has Two Tongues,* (London, 1968); Maud, R., *Dylan Thomas in Print,* (Pittsburgh, Pa., 1970); Davies, W., *Dylan Thomas,* (Cardiff, 1972); *Dylan Thomas: New Critical Essays,* W. Davies ed. (London, 1972); Kidder, R. M., *Dylan Thomas: The Country of the Spirit,* Princeton N. J. (1973); Kirshner, R. B. Jr., *Dylan Thomas, The Poet and His Critics,* (Chicago, 1976); Jones, D., *My Friend Dylan Thomas,* (London, 1977); Ferris, P., *The Life of Dylan Thomas,* (London, 1977); Ackerman, J., *Welsh Dylan,* (Cardiff, 1979); Thomas, C., *Caitlin,* (London, 1986) with G. Tremlett.

WALT WHITMAN
(1819–1892)

TENNEY NATHANSON

WALT WHITMAN MAY be America's most uneven great poet. There is general consensus that *Leaves of Grass*, Whitman's gradually accreting collected poems, is better in its early incarnations than in its late ones. But from the beginning, Whitman could be maddeningly inconsistent. His prodigious variety is by no means always a defect. By turns highfalutin and slangy, abstract and quirkily concrete, the idiom of his early editions shows an unusual range that is one of Whitman's greatest strengths: his often brilliant idiomatic variety registers a potentially daunting range of mid-nineteenth century American life, which he sometimes appears content simply to celebrate. But the stylistic melange of Whitman's poetry is not always so successful or so convincingly accounted for. From its first publication, *Leaves of Grass* was by turns pithy and vague, incisive and baggy. Whitman is often trite and bombastic, effects characteristically associated with his notorious though sometimes brilliant "catalogs" or extended lists. In "Salut au Monde!" (1856) the poet is determined to "see" all the races and nationalities that people the earth. This perhaps laudable project leaves him badly overextended. Whitman's imagination cannot keep pace with his determination, and the resultant catalogs display an air of distraction, as if the poet had had time to do no more than quickly fill in the blanks, deploying the first thing that came to mind, which frequently was cliché:

> I see vapors exhaling from unexplored
>   countries,
> I see the savage types, the bow and arrow, the
>   poison'd splint, the fetich, and the obi.
> I see African and Asiatic towns,
> I see Algiers, Tripoli, Derne, Mogodore,
>   Timbuctoo, Monrovia,
> I see the swarms of Pekin, Canton, Benares,
>   Dehli, Calcutta, Tokio,
> I see the Kruman in his hut, and the
>   Dahoman and Ashantee-man in their huts,
> I see the Turk smoking opium in Aleppo,
> I see the picturesque crowds at the fairs of
>   Khiva and those of Herat,
> I see Teheran, I see Muscat and Medina and
>   the intervening sands, I see the caravans
>   toiling onward

There is material even in relatively weak passages like this one that will repay attention: the biblical parallelism; the obsessive fascination with place names, in whose sounds the audience is invited to revel; the implication that the poet, who is supposedly omniscient, may be omnipresent as well. Yet few would wish the poem longer than it is. Composed mostly of lengthy catalogs like the one from which the lines above are excerpted, "Salut au Monde!" continues on for 226 lines, some twelve pages. The poet himself, as he nears the finish line, seems slightly dazed by his prodigious effort:

> My spirit has pass'd in compassion and
>   determination around the whole earth,
> I have look'd for equals and lovers and
>   found them ready for me in all lands,
> I think some divine rapport has equalized
>   me with them.

If the reader too emerges glassy-eyed, this stupor is not necessarily a sign of the poet's failure, as this state resembles meditative absorption, a condition Whitman might well have wished to produce.

But stretches like this hardly characterize Whitman at his finest. Just as he keeps his eye on unlikely detail in his strongest descriptive passages, so is his diction capable of unexpected idiomatic swerves, which serve to alter in dramatic ways the enunciatory situation, the public and oratorical or intimately conversational scene the audience is invited to imagine. Whitman is often at his brilliant best in short passages in which the poem's audience is talked to directly and personally, and talked to, moreover, in circumstances intriguingly difficult to pin down. In the early editions of *Leaves of Grass*, the audience, fuddled or made restive by one of Whitman's long lists, is regularly pulled up short by brief passages of a very different order. Addressed directly to the audience, these passages seem ambiguously sacramental or seductive, and the eerie way they seem to focus on the reader can both delight and discomfit. So in his 1855 masterpiece "Song of Myself" Whitman modulates his direct address from teasing questions to a characteristically disconcerting pair of assertions. The poet directs his attention intently to his audience:

> Do you guess I have some intricate purpose?
> Well I have . . . for the April rain has, and
> the mica on the side of a rock has.
> Do you take it I would astonish?
> Does the daylight astonish? or the early
> redstart twittering through the woods?
> Do I astonish more than they?
>
> This hour I tell things in confidence,
> I might not tell everybody but I will tell you.

Whitman's closing suggestion that he is talking to his audience in the here and now is not one which will likely be taken literally. In one sense it amounts to a kind of joke, trading on the contrast between the text that is literally being read and the whispering voice that invites each member of the poet's audience to imagine that he or she is being addressed, out of all the book's readers, alone. Yet the joke is a serious one, and the illusion it fosters is crucial to the imaginative economy of *Leaves of Grass*. Whitman said on more than one occasion that as a poet he "intended to throw together for American use, a gigantic embryo or skeleton of Personality, fit for the West, for native models." Yet the self that stands so magnificently at the center of his poetry is not merely a reflection of his times, a democratic identity finding its way in mid-nineteenth-century America—though it is surely that in part. In passages such as the one quoted above, which abound in the first two editions of *Leaves of Grass*, the poet seems able to single out for special intimacy the "you" to whom he whispers; he seems to speak to that special "you" right now. The outlook is simultaneously panoramic and local, public and intimate; it is as if the shared public space were being transformed into the place of a private communion. The self who could initiate such a transaction would be more than just a representative instance of nineteenth-century democratic identity. The transformative encounter Whitman claims to initiate indeed suggests something sacramental: a presence rises up as if by magic, whenever these words are repeated, deflecting linear time into the cycle of eternal return, extended space into the sacred spot defined by this manifestation.

The epiphany repeatedly enacted in Whitman's poems is erotic as well as religious. The presence that makes itself manifest is a desiring body as well as a transcendent spirit, as the lines immediately preceding those quoted above from "Song of Myself" make clear:

> This is the press of a bashful hand . . . . this
> is the float and odor of hair,
> This is the touch of my lips to yours . . . .
> this is the murmur of yearning,
> This is the far-off depth and height
> reflecting my own face,
> This is the thoughtful merge of myself and
> the outlet again.

Each repetition of the word "this" seems to suggest an act of pointing. The effect might seem to be unfortunately comic: Whitman declares a presence and, to prove it, points to a collection of body parts that turn out not to be there. But there is an upside to this gesture: pointing to a presence the reader cannot quite see, Whitman conjures up a body that seems elusive and fluid: "I effuse my flesh in eddies and drift it in lacy jags," the poet declares near the end of "Song of Myself." This liquid quality, which is seen throughout much of *Leaves of Grass*, is made to seem deliciously sexual. At the same time, however, such an elusive form may suggest a sacramental, barely material presence. The erotic and the religious are consistently confounded in Whitman's early editions.

These lines may also suggest that a presence is just now putting on flesh, just now becoming incarnate as these words are spoken. Perhaps the words themselves are generating the presence, the magical body. "And God said let there be light, and there was light." And Whitman said let there be Walt, becoming, as it were, the Word incarnate. Both Whitman's poems and his essays on language recur repeatedly to this sense of shamanistic speech, of performative utterance (language that does something, that makes something true) that is magical and not merely conventional. "I now pronounce you man and wife," says the minister, not describing a marriage but performing one. Whitman wants to go the minister one better:

> It avails not, time nor place—distance
> avails not,
> I am with you, you men and women of a
> generation, or ever so many generations
> hence,
> I project myself, also I return—I am with
> you, and know how it is.

If they work, these lines from the important 1856 poem "Crossing Brooklyn Ferry" make something seem to happen, not just in the symbolic, social realm governed by custom, but in the actual physical world shaped by literal action—or magic.

EARLY YEARS

Whitman was born on May 13, 1819, in West Hills, Long Island. Buffeted by the economic instability of the period, his family moved numerous times during his childhood and adolescence, shuttling at irregular intervals from house to house in Brooklyn, and between Brooklyn and various other parts of Long Island. Walt's father, Walter Whitman Sr., was a carpenter, housebuilder, and sometime minor real estate speculator, who never quite found his way in the emerging entrepreneurial culture of early nineteenth-century America. Long Island, where the Whitman family had settled as far back as the early seventeenth century, was somewhat less susceptible to boom and bust than the rapidly expanding, bustling but economically precarious world of Brooklyn. Yet this place of partial retreat was by no means a stable haven for the Whitman family. Walt's father sold the last of the family holdings in West Hills in 1836. Walt left school and entered the printing trades as an apprentice at the age of twelve and thereafter shuttled among the thriving metropolis of Manhattan, the still somewhat rural but giddily growing city of Brooklyn, and various family homes on Long Island.

Whitman was the second of nine children, and while his younger brothers thrived the fates of many of his other siblings were grim. There were important countervailing sources of stability and strength within the family, however. In later years Whitman consistently described his mother, Louisa, to whom he was devoted, as the crucial figure in his life and a key influence on the values registered in *Leaves of Grass*. He spoke especially of her Quaker heritage. In his youth Whitman heard the radical Quaker leader Elias Hicks preach, and in his mind Hicks's inner-light theology dovetailed with the democratic radicalism that was the poet's crucial intellectual heritage from his father. Yet in the 1820s and 1830s, as this artisanal world progressively disappeared, such idealized portraits of the trades were matched by radical proposals for reform among the emergent working class; such relatively mild schemes as advocacy of mass public education vied with calls for redistribution of property and other radical measures. Walter Whitman knew the Revolutionary-era radical Tom Paine, and reform meetings and reform literature were part of Walt's upbringing. Like his father, he was also well read in the "freethinking" literature of France's revolutionary enlightenment.

Whitman entered the printing trade as an apprentice in 1831 and trained as a compositor, but soon began writing and editing copy. In 1842 he took over briefly as editor of the *Aurora*, a Manhattan daily, and in 1846 he became editor of the Brooklyn *Daily Eagle*. In the course of an active career in journalism that lasted well into the late 1850s, Whitman worked for countless papers as both writer and editor. Despite occasional charges of on-the-job loafing (training for his subsequent profession, perhaps), he enjoyed a career whose bumpiness was far from peculiar. Whitman lost his position as editor of the *Daily Eagle* in 1848, when the paper returned to the more conservative Democratic fold; Whitman, a more radical Democrat and Free-soiler, was left in the lurch.

The crucial issue that divided the New York Democratic party, like the rest of the nation, in the 1840s and 1850s was slavery, which intertwined in sometimes tricky ways with labor issues. Like Lincoln until 1863, Whitman resisted the abolitionist position, except for brief periods of waffling, arguing that attaining the goal of immediately freeing southern slaves was not worth endangering the survival of the union; like many, he believed that slavery would gradually disappear in the course of anticipated social, economic, and moral developments. Like Lincoln, he favored repatriation—sending those slaves who were freed back to Africa. But like much of New York labor culture and many northern reformers, he was a "free-soiler," staunchly opposing the introduction of slavery into the western territories and arguing that these should be admitted to the union only as "Free [labor] states." Whitman believed that the country was caught in a moral quagmire that party politics only exacerbated. Increasingly, he looked to populist energies as the best possible source for a moral and cultural, if not immediately political, national renewal. Undoubtedly he understood *Leaves of Grass*, at least in part, as contributing to this populist trend.

Whitman's demotic leanings were personal as well as political. His newspaper work and his recreational urban cruising—activities that tended to blend into one another—helped fuel the emerging poet's street-level populism. Whether covering stories or sauntering the city for pleasure, Whitman reveled in the surging and unregulated street life of Brooklyn and Manhattan. He seems to have been drawn particularly to working-class men. He loved to ride the city omnibuses and engage the drivers in talk; anticipating his later Civil War hospital visits, he used to frequent hospital wards to chat with injured or sick drivers. Whitman also admired, and wrote approvingly of, the working-class street culture of the tough-nut "Bowery B'hoys" and (with more ambivalence) the early urban "gang" culture of New York's "roughs" and "loafers."

When the spectacular Crystal Palace exhibition, a massive World's Fair, opened in Manhattan in 1853, Whitman became an enthusiastic and inveterate visitor. He trolled the crowds as well as the exhibits, mingling, meeting people, talking. Yet there is a haunted quality to the notes he made about these encounters, just as there is to a notebook entry he made somewhat later, probably in the late 1850s, adjuring himself to keep up his social researches:

> Talk to everybody everywhere—try it on—keep it up—*real* talk—no airs—real questions—no one will be offended—or if any-one is, that will teach the offender just as any one else

Here Whitman encourages himself to try on, as a salutary exercise, the role of hearty democratic comrade he elsewhere invites readers to imagine as naturally his. The diarist who reminds himself to engage in "*real* talk" (the emphasis is Whitman's) is not simply a happy conversationalist; rather, he appears intent on acquiring a skill, almost like someone striving to learn a foreign language. Although the passage focuses on what might be called professional research (it appears among notes Whitman made for a projected, never-completed book on the American language), it nonetheless sounds rather like an attempt to overcome inveterate personal isolation.

The running record Whitman kept of his Crystal Palace cruising has something of the same quality:

> Bill Guess—aged 22. A thoughtless, strong, generous animal nature, fond of direct pleasures, eating, drinking, women, fun etc. . . . Was with me in the Crystal Palace.
>
> Peter ——— ———, large, strong-boned young fellow, driver. Should weigh 180. Free and candid to me the very first time he saw me.

Whitman kept similar records through the 1850s:

> Johny (round faced—in Dunbar's and engine house—full eyes) and liquid
>
> John Kiernan (loafer young saucy looking pretty goodlooking.)

Such passages seem poignant: they read like memorials of unfulfilled desire, marking intimacy as a briefly glimpsed possibility. They might be regarded instead as a sort of brag sheet, a tally of conquests, which is how the critic Charley Shively reads them, citing notebook passages that seem to point to consummated assignations in the early 1860s, during the Civil War:

> William somewhat feminine [. . .] told me he had never been in a fight and did not drink at all gone in 2nd N.Y. Lt Artillery deserted, returned to it slept with me Sept 3d

The contemporary meaning of the poet's phrases is not always clear to the late-twentieth-century reader: the term "slept with" does not necessarily have a sexual meaning. This is particularly the case with what would now be categorized as homosexual relations. The very term "homosexual" did not come into use until the end of the nineteenth century. Until then, social historians have demonstrated, sexual acts were not linked to the notion of some essential or dominant sexual "orientation." It is apparently also the case that same-sex displays of physical affection, and same-sex sentimental attachments, were quite common and were regarded as entirely "normal." It is fairly certain that Whitman in later years had long-term sexual relationships, and formed deep emotional bonds, with men who later went on to marry. Whether his notebooks of the 1850s and 1860s are tallies of sexual assignations, rather than notations of casual meetings or "sentimental" but not overtly sexual intimacies, tinged with Whitman's own longing, is less certain.

The notebooks do not make mention of the sort of sustained erotic and affectional intimacy that Whitman apparently achieved in later years. Shively notes that "while there is considerable evidence of Whitman's homosexual liaisons as early as 1836, there were no lovers until [Fred] Vaughan [in the late 1850s]"—that is, no sustained love relationships so far as is known. Whitman's biographer, Justin Kaplan, in a similar vein, remarks on Whitman's "chronically objectless affections." "The completeness of object-erosion in him is striking," Quentin Anderson likewise notes of the Whitman of the 1850s.

Such judgments about Whitman's private life in the pre–Civil War years are admittedly somewhat conjectural. Toward the end of his career, Whitman assiduously pruned his massive personal archives, removing or revising many items that failed to jibe with the portrait of the "good gray poet" (his friend William O'Connor's brilliant polemical phrase) he was preparing for posterity. The 1850s in particular exist primarily as an extended blank in this revised record. Like the written archive, the photographic one is problematic but suggestive. The critic Ed Folsom notes the astonishing fact that, while Whitman preserved an elaborately plotted collection of personal photographs (a kind of iconography in progress), there currently exists no picture taken of Whitman before the Civil War in which he is seen with another person. Later pictures display him—sometimes in "marriage" poses—with lovers. It is possible that this oddity is the result of Whitman's archival tinkering. Yet the notebooks and photographic record suggest a personal impasse that the poetry tends to confirm: neither the 1855 nor 1856 editions of *Leaves of Grass* offers us even the hint of a particular intimacy, or even, for all their focus on the "self," of Whitman in anything like intimate biographical detail—the poet's self is insistently generic.

To read Whitman's poetry simply as a kind of versified political platform or populist social vision is thus to risk thinning out the work. Whitman's poems are in important respects also an imaginative grappling—sometimes triumphant, sometimes comic, sometimes desperate or forlorn—with intimate needs and desires. The poet figure who can be viewed as the guarantor of a demotic social ideal or the solution to a political impasse serves also to assuage needs of a less public or universal order.

LEAVES OF GRASS (1855)

There is still pretty general agreement that when *Leaves of Grass* first appeared in 1855 it marked a spectacular breakthrough for Whitman, as well as for American poetry. Ralph Waldo Emerson, for one, went on record immediately and resoundingly. Whitman, still largely unknown in national literary circles, had the temerity to send a copy of his cottage-industry first edition to the preeminent American man of letters, and Emerson responded:

> Dear Sir,
>
> I am not blind to the worth of the wonderful gift of "Leaves of Grass." I find it the most extraordinary piece of wit & wisdom that America has yet contributed. I am very happy in reading it, as great power makes us happy. . . . I greet you at the beginning of a great career, which yet must have had a long foreground somewhere, for such a start.

This generous appreciation suffered an ungenerous fate. Whitman, well-schooled in the hucksterism of the New York newspaper world, had few qualms about recycling Emerson's personal letter in unauthorized forms, brandishing this and other excerpts from it as advertising copy for his book. Emerson, who was outraged, nevertheless generally continued to champion Whitman's work.

The mysterious "foreground" Emerson mentions has tantalized several Whitman critics and biographers. What is there, in Whitman's prior writings, that might anticipate the ungainly genius of his mature work? In most important senses, not much. His earlier poetry fits conspicuously into the category of juvenilia: published in newspapers and periodicals, his efforts are stilted exercises in rhyme and rhythm-making; their thematic burden, generally melancholy, is entirely conventional. In light of his mature career, Whitman's early attempts at fiction writing—several published short stories, as well as the commissioned temperance novel *Franklin Evans*, which sold some twenty thousand copies—are interesting as antecedents but not much more. Characterized by a lurid and violent undercurrent of the macabre despite their moralizing armature, they anticipate several of the sexual and familial anxieties explored more compellingly in *Leaves of Grass*.

In the absence of a visible and sustained apprenticeship leading clearly toward the sorts of expressive, social, and sexual values evident in *Leaves of Grass*, critics long tended to recur to one or another illuminationist model to account for Whitman's achievement. Whitman (who claimed he could "go negative" and stop the flow of his thoughts when he wanted) was a mystic whose ecstatic experiences transformed him from hack to genius; or he underwent a spectacular sexual initiation that changed him forever. This may be so. On the other hand, the breakthroughs that help make *Leaves of Grass* a revolutionary and exciting work are in part anticipated by short notebook passages, most likely dating from the late 1840s. These passages register not only erotic and visionary excitement, but also the political turmoil that engaged Whitman in his public and professional life. They also include several brief attempts to concoct a mythic poetic persona capable of subsuming the sectional, racial, and class conflicts provoked by the issue of slavery.

The dangers of invoking one or another illuminationist hypothesis to account for *Leaves of Grass* thus include the tendency to read the poems in a single register only (sexual *or* mystical) and, perhaps more important, the temptation to regard them as the retailing of an already fully achieved personal breakthrough—rather than as an ongoing, sometimes perilous grappling with a complex of recalcitrant issues, both personal and political, that through his peculiar genius for language Whitman struggled to resolve. Several of Whitman's notebook entries seem to be testing the resources of a new sort of poetic idiom and a new sort of poetic line; they move haltingly toward the sorts of verbal textures that define the early editions of *Leaves of Grass*, breaking through the limits of iambic pentameter into longer, more loosely and irregularly measured lines aware of both American vernacular speech and prophetically cadenced biblical idiom, two limits between which the language of Whitman's poems often seems to play.

The 1855 edition as a whole violated decorum in a number of roughly congruent ways. It had a title on the cover and a title page inside, but no author's name on either. The copyright, however, belonged to "Walter Whitman," and in one of the poems the speaker refers to himself as "Walt Whitman... one of the roughs." Unlike later editions, the 1855 volume included no poem titles, no section numbers dividing the longer pieces into more manageable units, or absolutely clear demarcations indicating where one poem ended and another began. Designed by Whitman and hand set, partly by Whitman himself, it was published in an edition of 795 copies by the small firm of Rome Brothers and distributed by Fowler and Wells. Seeming partly austere and partly casual in its disregard of the proprieties, the volume's very appearance mirrors the strange mix of demotic and prophetic traditions already noted in Whitman's style: its appearance, like its apparently authorless condition, places it ambiguously as an anonymous casual production or a sacred text.

The mythic, annealing persona tried on in the notebooks turns up in several of the printed poems, perhaps most conspicuously in the piece subsequently known as "Song of the Answerer":

> Every existence has its idiom . . . . every thing has an idiom and tongue;
> He resolves all tongues into his own, and bestows it upon men
> . . .
> One part does not counteract another part. . . . He is the joiner . . . he sees how they join.
>
> He says indifferently and alike, How are you friend? to the President at his levee,
> And he says Good day my brother, to Cudge that hoes in the sugarfield;
> And both understand him and know that his speech is right.

This transcendental ward heeler, a fantasized instrument of political consensus, grapples elsewhere in the poem with more recalcitrant obstacles to democratic fulfillment. He must not simply consult, but transform his constituency by (re)-embodying them:

> The insulter, the prostitute, the angry person, the beggar, see themselves in the ways of him . . . . he strangely transmutes them,
> They are not vile any more . . . . they hardly know themselves, they are so grown.

Toward the beginning of the poem, this remaking is made to seem magical, the "answerer" cast less as statesman than as shaman:

> Him all wait for . . . . him all yield up to
> . . . . his word is decisive and final,
> Him they accept . . . . in him lave . . . . in
> him perceive themselves as amid light,
> Him they immerse, and he immerses them.

Here the poet's word—or is it his body?—becomes a kind of transfiguring baptismal fluid: poetry does not reveal the solution to political problems through some special insight; it makes it happen, magically, or aspires to. Claiming to activate an extreme power, these lines intervene in an imagined political or social crisis that is presented as correspondingly extreme. Yet they do more. The poet's ductile body itself may be a quirky figure for the solution to a political impasse, but that can also seem pretty delicious. Might polymorphous sexuality serve as a figure for political resolution? Or as a literal political strategy? Or is it the other way round, the poem's political agenda serving primarily as respectable cover for a more urgent substratum of erotic fantasy and visionary erotic fulfillment?

It is worth noting, in this regard, that the space these bodies occupy is tricky to map: "Him they immerse and he immerses them." This ductile, illogical space in which we are inside what is inside us is the imaginative space of much of the poetry of Whitman's early editions. This does not mean that he had a deep-seated desire to return to the womb. But for powerful personal as well as urgent public reasons his work is haunted by images of division and self-division, separation, isolation, and fragmentation. And the poetry, where it is most like a shamanistic spell cast against these terrors, tends to conjure up a delicious (or stifling) fluid space in which bodies and selves mingle and blur. This polymorphous space is significantly regressive—it conjures up fleeting and partial visions of how, supposedly, the infant experiences body and world. This regression need not be a defect: "strong memory," often in the form of infantile or childhood material, frequently serves to figure utopian content; and sexual and political fulfillment not uncommonly figure, or enable, each other. In such highly charged and unstable terrain, it is probably unwise to read in one direction only: to regard visionary erotic material in *Leaves of Grass* as always simply an elaborate metaphor for political possibility—or the reverse.

"A Song for Occupations" and "I Sing the Body Electric" both make extensive use of Whitman's catalog technique: the former is largely a listing of the tools employed in various occupations; the latter, among other things, is a spectacularly extended list of big and small body parts. Both lists seem curiously poised between passive appreciation and apotropaic litany, an incantation intended to ward off something. The lists of gadgets, for example, might be celebrations of the glorious accouterments of industry; attempts to memorialize (or magically preserve) the tools of the workplace before mechanization sweeps them away along with the small artisan workshop; or desperate efforts to conjure away their dispiriting solidity, to redeem an increasingly cluttered world of things that threatens to control us. The poem, like much of Whitman's work composed during this period, accordingly seems to hover ambivalently amid reportage, didactic political intervention, and shamanistic spell. "I Sing the Body Electric" ranges among a similar variety of speech acts, ambivalently exploring the political and social control of the body, the eroticization of public and social space.

"SONG OF MYSELF"

The volatile mixture of public and private concerns, political and sexual material, utopian content and regressive fantasy that characterizes Whitman's best work is managed with spectacular success in "Song of Myself." The poem as a whole is the sometimes buoyant, sometimes anguished, and ultimately unresolved attempt to turn these various preoccupations into facets of a single mystery, or vision. This tolerance for irresolution—or to figure it differently, Whitman's ability in "Song of Myself" to keep a lot of balls in the air at once, without dropping too many or fretting too much when one happens to fall—is similar to Keats's poetics of "Negative Capability," that is, the capability "of being in uncertainties, Mysteries, doubts, without any irritable reaching after fact & reason."

But as the critic Richard Chase points out, the resultant maddeningly open-ended poem is also crucially modern or modernist: nervous attempts to extract a neat plot or orderly pattern of development are bound to founder when negotiating Whitman's plotless epic, which profoundly engages and only partly resists the confusing, decentered, or polycentric, space of modernity; the critic needs to exercise some of the negative capability the poem displays. "Song of Myself" is loosely structured around a number of recurrent but by no means constant preoccupations; the relations among these foci of attention are likewise variable. A list of what might be called the poem's social concerns should include the following: American vastness as challenge or threat, danger or instigation; the panoramic variety of American life as auguring disunion or as enabling the resiliency of what would now be called multiculturalism; political turmoil and its ambiguous relation to populist upheaval; urbanization and modernization, and the breakup of closed communities that accompanies them, as potentially both alienating and liberating. To these concerns we should add the preoccupation with American nature as a healing force. If the poem also ponders the relation of the individual to such vast agents, it tends to do so by considering the force and fate of thc body, especially the sexual body. To what extent is the body the medium through which social demands or social anxieties are internalized; conversely, to what extent might sexuality model or unleash an anarchic energy that challenges such constructions, or an agglomerative urge that can anneal social space?

If Whitman's language is sometimes the imagistic medium that cannily records social and sexual landscapes, it often aspires to a performative or shamanistic power to redeem what it names. The poet's own presence and body, likewise, are characteristically lent a power of sacramental or sexually based transfiguration. Such shamanistic urges toward redemption or control tend to assume one of two characteristic forms, in "Song of Myself" as well as in other major poems of Whitman's first two editions. The poet's word in his catalogs exercises a centripetal pull on what it names, sliding objects toward a sacred space or center ultimately indistinguishable from the poet's own presence. This presence, in the poet's apostrophes, tends to effuse outward, in a centrifugal movement that conveys a diffused and redemptive body. This imaginative pattern is repeated, in rather more schematic form, in such other major pre—Civil War poems as in "Crossing Brooklyn Ferry" (and "Salut au Monde!"). But part of the peculiar difficulty of "Song of Myself"—and a source of the poem's greatness—is Whitman's tendency, in this poem as in no other, to gum up the shamanistic works. The poem is virtually unique in Whitman's oeuvre in its willingness to include, at unexpected junctures, material that seems to call into question the poem's own overarching aims; "Song of Myself" slides toward delicate comedy or pathos as Whitman registers a vast variety of competing energies and claims that delay or disrupt the poet's project.

Though the poem does not begin with one, the extended list or catalog is a conspicuous feature of "Song of Myself." What is now known as section 15 of the poem begins:

> The pure contralto sings in the organloft,
> The carpenter dresses his plank . . . . the
> tongue of his foreplane whistles its wild
> ascending lisp,
> The married and unmarried children ride
> home to their thanksgiving dinner,
> The pilot seizes the king-pin, he heaves
> down with a strong arm,

Sixty lines later, the proceedings are still in progress:

> Patriarchs sit at supper with sons and
> grandsons and great grandsons around
> them,
> In walls of adobe, in canvass tents, rest
> hunters and trappers after their day's
> sport.

It is difficult to know how to attend to such extended litanies, just as it is difficult to characterize what they are up to; Whitman's catalogs have occasioned a great deal of critical disagreement. It is clear that they are not imaginatively situated in any single scene or locale. The prodigious expansion of attention that characterizes such passages might be understood as an enacting of American populism (everything matters), and as the faithful, celebratory recording of the staggering variety of American life (merely listing its wonders is enough). Likewise the tendency to parallelism (most lines cued with an initial repetition, here the word "the") can be taken as encoding democratic values (one man, one vote; one person, one line). Yet the catalog's conclusion implies a more complex and ambivalent agenda:

> And these one and all tend inward to me,
> and I tend outward to them,
> And such as it is to be of these more or less
> I am.

The second of these lines is the more modest (especially that "more or less"): stopping short of claiming one identity with all he records, the poet here settles for partial identification. The word "tend," in the prior line, might be read as similarly modest: a tendency need not be fully realized or universal. Yet the movement traced in this line is one that is imaginatively crucial to Whitman's work: things move in toward the poet, while the poet flows outward to meet and characteristically subsume them. The line also possesses a possibly disconcerting performative force: "these one and all tend inward to me," I make it happen, by saying so. The preceding catalog may likewise function as performative, or as a sort of shamanistic spell: not simply celebrating what is, but by imaginatively transfiguring it, the poet's naming would bring into being a world of other selves and an American space worthy of such celebration. If the vast panorama of American life and the doings of so many other selves, perhaps, provoke anxiety as well as pleasure—threatening to reduce the poet, as it were, to only a single mote in the prodigious array—the poem would thus be the private, but socially resonant, cure for the very anxieties it records.

A number of features of Whitman's list can be understood as contributing to the redemptive spell the poet weaves. There is the very extent of the litany; coupled with insistent patterning, this stretching of attention tends to produce a blurry receptivity, which suggests both the trancelike experience of ritual and the fluid space in which objects mingle that ritual might produce. The catalog's parallelism can likewise suggest shamanistic spell as much as democratic paean: if populist-minded readers are reminded of "one man, one vote," others might remember the substitution drills for learning foreign languages. Once the grammatical pattern is established, anything at all can be slotted into it. As the passage progresses, this insistently repeated operation increasingly suggests the substitutability of whatever is subjected to it. Everything is made to inhabit the same space or same position ("these one and all tend inward to me"), into which the poet's spell entrances it. The distended and difficult world of objects is gathered up into a ritual space and imaginatively controlled.

Similarly, time in Whitman's catalog is registered less as a series of discrete instants separated by intervals than as a collapsible continuum in which every moment can be superimposed on every other one: the linear time of profane historical change and action, as it were, turns into the cyclical time of the sacred. All Whitman's verbs in the catalog hover ambiguously between the "continuous" versus the "simple" present. To say that "the pure contralto sings in the organloft" might mean that she is doing so right now (dynamic), or it might mean that she habitually or repeatedly does so (stative). In context, this ambiguity works to collapse the simple and the continuous present, suggesting an odd sort of time in which all present actions are varieties of recurrent processes; what happens now is simply an instance of what happens forever. If things were truly so, the world would be less vertiginously complicated, more manageable; if the poet's word makes it so, he manages the world, for himself and for everyone.

While looking at Whitman's catalog technique, a brief glance ahead will show how some catalogs in other poems vary the techniques displayed in this passage from "Song of Myself," pressuring perception more forcefully toward the ritual contours described. A brief excerpt from an extended catalog in "Crossing Brooklyn Ferry" can serve as an example:

> I too saw the reflection of the summer-sky
>   in the water
>
> . . .
>
> Looked toward the lower bay to notice the
>   arriving ships,
> Saw their approach, saw aboard those that
>   were near me,
> Saw the white sails of schooners and sloops,
>   saw the ships at anchor,
> The sailors at work in the rigging or out
>   astride the spars,
> The round masts, the swinging motion of
>   the hulls, the slender serpentine
>   pennants,
> The large and small steamers in motion, the
>   pilots in their pilot-houses,
> The white wake left by the passage, the
>   quick tremulous whirl of the wheels

As this passage progresses, grammatical structure gets progressively attenuated, suggesting a world in which independent being and doing grow increasingly vestigial. The "I" of the first line is the subject of a massively distended sentence (there is no period until after six additional long lines): a world full of multiple agents is thus transformed into a more manageable one, in which everything becomes the object of the poet's organizing perception. That perception ("I too saw") is the only action to which the passage accords grammatical weight. Moving forward through the passage, the repeated verb "saw" is also omitted. Having dropped verb as well as grammatical subject, there are simply ten long object phrases, parallel instances of what the speaker "saw." This is a substitution drill with a vengeance: everything the speaker names drops into an identical grammatical space, another parallel instance of what the poet "saw." Here vision becomes visionary and the one who sees becomes a seer. And what, we may ask, are all these substitutable, superimposed people and objects doing? As the passage renders them, other acts have lost the initiatory power of finite verbs. Rendered by participles and verbals, what might well have been actions have instead become diffuse, continuous processes (the swinging, the whirl); no longer initiated by independent persons or things, they seem instead to flow through the entire scene, like manifestations of a single suffusing impulse which the poet's word traces, or propels. Such grammatical shamanism is a crucial attribute of several poems in Whitman's early editions.

In "Song of Myself" not only do things tend inward to the poet, as in Whitman's characteristic catalogs, the poet also tends outward to them. This flowing outward of a diffuse, transfiguring presence is often suggested most strongly in those moments where the poet addresses his audience directly, seeming to hover as a vaporous body conveyed on the accents of the poet's voice. One such moment constitutes the poem's beginning:

> I celebrate myself,
> And what I assume you shall assume,
> For every atom belonging to me as good
>   belongs to you.

Whitman's "you" here is ambiguous, being simultaneously intimate and universal; the poet thus seems to flow outward (on the voice that announces his presence) in all directions at once, a godlike emanation. Since what is we are promised are the very atoms that make him up, the audience "assumes" what the poet assumes not simply in the sense of believing what he believes, but in the stranger one of putting on his disseminating body as its own. Political prospect (we are one because we share the same beliefs) jostles for imaginative priority with a more archaic transaction here (I have turned you into myself, or floated myself out to flow inside you). The complex of social and personal aspirations and anxieties that might motivate such an imaginative confounding is surely resistant to any single, neat formulation, whether couched in terms of politics or psychology.

The quirkier Whitman's depictions of the poet's presence, the more resistant they will be to didactic reduction. "Song of Myself" abounds in such peculiar formulations, many of them outlandishly sexual. In one passage, whatever the poet comes into erotic contact with becomes in effect part of him; yet he brushes up against some unlikely partners, his own sexual ebullience suggesting the sexuality of all he comes across. The confounding of self and other here, and of eros and nature, is truly wild:

> If I worship any particular thing it shall be
> some of the spread of my own body;
> Translucent mould of me it shall be you,
> Shades ledges and rests, firm masculine
> coulter, it shall be you,
> Whatever goes to the tilth of me it shall be
> you,
>
> . . .
>
> You sweaty brooks and dews it shall be you,
> Winds whose soft-tickling genitals rub
> against me it shall be you,
> Broad muscular fields, branches of liveoak,
> loving lounger in my winding paths, it
> shall be you,
> Hands I have taken, face I have kissed,
> mortal I have ever touched, it shall be
> you.

Elsewhere, the poet makes love to futurity in a consummation at once outrageously cosmic, comic, and tender:

> By my life-lumps! becoming already a
> creator!
> Putting myself here and now to the
> ambushed womb of the shadows!

Just as the tone in these passages can change abruptly or glide almost undetectably from one register to another, so too these proclamations of the poet's godlike powers seem to shuffle unpredictably among gigantesque ambition, megalomanic euphoria, sexual bravado, and comic or wistful irony. The poet who could write them was surely a remarkable writer. Yet they suggest an odd mix of jaunty self-confidence, lurking anxiety, compensatory boasting, and lingering pathos that, in combination, make both the significance of these passages and the personal and cultural work they perform elusive. Such tolerance for irresolution, for Keatsian "negative capability," surfaces frequently in the poem as irony, whether wistful or ebullient, pathos-filled or playful. One moment of high comedy shows the absorptive body of the poet's innards as cluttered up with objects, while his hide is plastered with the stuff that apparently could not be taken inside him:

> I find I incorporate gneiss and coal and long-
> threaded moss and fruits and grains and
> esculent roots,
> And am stucco'd with quadrupeds and birds
> all over.

Likewise the catalogs, which tend to enucleate what they name, in "Song of Myself" frequently encounter the sort of recalcitrant peculiarity that resists such assimilation. Unlikely metaphor, typically, suggests the sort of quiddity that will stick in the shaman's craw: "Where the alligator in his tough pimples sleeps by the bayou"; "Where the ground-shark's fin cuts like a black chip out of the water."

Such moments perhaps suggest good humor more than self-doubt. It is as if Whitman, discovering his imaginative powers in this great early poem, took pleasure both in exercising them and in holding back—in letting things be, from time to time, rather than subjecting them right away to the newfound verbal and imaginative resources of his homemade ritual.

LEAVES OF GRASS (1856)

The thorny issue of the status and possible meaning of such ritual powers seems to have preoccupied Whitman even before the first edition of *Leaves of Grass* went to press. The 1855 preface (composed just before the volume was published) strenuously insists on the national provenance and function of the ensuing poetry; the poetry itself, as the critic John Kinnaird points out, mentions the United States far less often than the preface does. In keeping with Whitman's populist and largely anti-institutional sympathies, the preface, like "Song of the Answerer," casts the poet in the role of cultural healer, reconciling threatening differences which the president and political parties have been unable to absorb into the body politic of the United States: "Their Presidents shall not be their common referee so much as their poets shall. . . . [The poet] is the arbiter of the diverse and he is the key. He is the equalizer of his age and land." Yet this political function, the solid and respectable public ground on which the volume is presumably being placed, blurs into the shamanistic role we found in the overdetermined universe of the poems.

In the 1856 edition of *Leaves of Grass*, large chunks of the preface turn up virtually unedited in the poem "By Blue Ontario's Shore." That this recycled material seems different in its new context is largely the result of the change of genre; the change nevertheless turns out to be symptomatic. In the ostensibly expository context of the preface, Whitman's manically distended sentences, with their agrammatical ellipses in place of more standard punctuation, deflect even hortatory pronouncements toward exuberant, comic excess. Set as poetry, by contrast, it is the hortatory insistence that comes through.

The 1856 edition of *Leaves of Grass* is not without its fine moments, and fine poems. But on the whole it lacks the unpredictable idiomatic and imaginative suppleness of its predecessor. In the new pieces Whitman composed, the poet's powers tend to be proclaimed more solemnly and less jauntily, and their exercise is more unremitting. Resistance and the doubt it can occasion tend to provoke, not wistful self-deprecation or outlandish comic bravado, but anxious insistence or momentary despair. This shift, which characterizes to a lesser extent the poems Whitman composed for the important 1860 edition as well, likely has several causes. In the mid to late 1850s, the political landscape of the country darkened as war loomed closer. Whitman's passional life, from the little we know of it during this period, seems also to have been intense but dark. *Leaves of Grass*, likewise, failed to fare as well as its author had hoped. In later years, Whitman wildly exaggerated both the success and the utter neglect of the 1855 edition, as occasion dictated. On the whole, however, despite Emerson's glowing acknowledgment, *Leaves of Grass* was probably more notorious for its sexual explicitness than admired for its poetic qualities, and it enjoyed neither the notoriety nor the admiration that would have propelled Whitman into the sort of national prominence to which he aspired.

The insistent quality of "By Blue Ontario's Shore" is evident as well in several of the other twenty-odd poems Whitman composed for the 1856 volume. It mars not only the minor "Salut au Monde!" but also the more important "Song of the Open Road," a poem whose declarations of American open-endedness and faith in adventurous wandering are belied rather than exemplified by the poem's relatively monochromatic diction and sometimes hectoring tone, as well as by a kind of programmatic tightening up of the digressive and meandering style of "Song of Myself"; the poem claims to revel in the glories of unexpected by-roads but in fact explores few of them.

The most important new poem of the 1856 edition is undoubtedly "Crossing Brooklyn Ferry," which recapitulates the crucial transactions of "Song of Myself" in a condensed and more consistently lyrical manner. Missing are the digressions, idiomatic shiftiness, and abrupt tonal variations that make the earlier poem such a challenge and triumph. Though a lesser achievement, "Crossing Brooklyn Ferry" is without doubt one of Whitman's most important poems, offering perhaps the best brief introduction to the imaginative universe of his crucial first two editions.

Missing, too, from "Crossing Brooklyn Ferry" is the giddy shifting of scenes and perspectives at work in "Song of Myself." Here the single locale of New York's East River where the ferry crossed between Manhattan and Brooklyn provides Whitman with an ideal site for enacting his characteristic vision of erotic and social blending: as several critics have pointed out, the river, the forms drifting on it, and the haze overhead proved especially congenial to Whitman's purposes, allowing the poet to enact what he elsewhere calls "the merge" without seeming to do violence to the objects of things his ritual acts upon. On this limited scene and in a comparatively compact performance, Whitman works his characteristic verbal ritual in an almost schematic fashion. Yet his typical ambivalence is also evident. On the one hand, from the outset the poem proclaims itself a celebration of the contemporary scene, which despite its welter of activity and sense of evanescence is declared to be the harbinger of eternity. On the other hand, the bulk of the poem works the sort of transformative shamanistic spell on this scene typical of Whitman's 1855 and 1856 poems. A convincing case might be made that it is only this imaginatively transfigured scene that Whitman's poem celebrates, and that the very urgency and scope of the transformation bespeaks an intense discomfort with the harbor world and the American conditions that this world typifies: the anonymity and "rushing and raging" activity, as Whitman calls it in a newspaper piece he earlier wrote on the ferries, of a great American city caught up in the throes of industrial development and breakneck urban growth.

The traces of Whitman's transformative project are evident in the poem's bizarre but effective, and altogether typical, temporal scheme, which stands out sharply. Beginning in the present tense, much of the poem is couched in the past. But it turns out that these two tenses refer to the same time span, the one in which the poem's speaker rides the ferry in what we might call the poem's "profane" present moment. The vantage he speaks the bulk of the poem from, and from which the time spent aboard the ferry may be said to be superseded, is not so much an imagined future moment as the eternal one of sacred time, in which ritual events repeat themselves and "now" becomes forever. Few of Whitman's poems evoke the poet's floating omnipresence so powerfully or insistently, and few declare so clearly the centripetal effects on profane time and space that this figure supposedly exerts:

> What is it, then, between us?
> What is the count of the scores or hundreds
> of years between us?
>
> Whatever it is, it avails not—distance avails
> not, and place avails not.
>
> Closer yet I approach you,
> What thought you have of me now, I had as
> much of you—I laid in my stores in
> advance,
> I consider'd long and seriously of you before
> you were born.
>
> Who was to know what should come home
> to me?
> Who knows but I am enjoying this?
> Who knows but I am as good as looking at
> you now, for all you cannot see me?

The second of these passages owes its difficulty to the presence of both profane and sacred time: sliding into the past tense to describe the initially profane moment in which, supposedly standing aboard the ferry in 1856, he throws his voice to his audience (the present tense of the poem's opening) and using the present tense to refer to the future moment in which that audience will receive his word. He also proclaims the sacred "now" of his manifestation, a paradoxically eternal moment that conjoins the first two times and collapses the distance between them. The poem's catalogs work a complementary magic on both space and time: while the poet's addresses evoke his effusing, centrifugal presence, his catalogs seem to collapse objects inward and lever them into the same sort of "eternal moment" as his proclamations of presence generate.

In one sense, the shaman's advent, proclaimed when Whitman addresses the reader, seems to lift both the poet himself and those who hear him out of anonymous, treacherous public space, conveying the audience to a redeemed realm that is also deliciously intimate:

> What is more subtle than this which ties
> me to the woman or man that looks in
> my face?
> Which fuses me into you now, and pours
> my meaning into you?
>
> We understand, then, do we not?
> What I promised without mentioning it,
> have you not accepted?
> What the study could not teach—what the
> preaching could not accomplish is
> accomplished, is it not?
> What the push of reading could not start is
> started by me personally, is it not?

Yet such imagined encounters can seem confining rather than liberating, and as oppressively abstract despite their air of private communion. Whitman's play with mode here—his proclamation of a personal presence, supposedly attested to and conveyed by the voice these lines want to make his audience thinks it hears, and his concomitant dismissal of reading—is a tenuous sleight of hand that can end up working either way. The poet claims to single "you" out from public space and usher you into a protected realm of magical intimacy; but the text of Whitman's book offers this salvation simultaneously to everyone, in a transaction every bit as abstract and anonymous as the public space from which it aspires to save us.

Since social conflicts and contradictions are as intractable as they are—and since imaginative writers grow up inside the cultures whose problems they often claim to solve—this double reverse is neither surprising nor wholly disabling. It is certainly not a sign that Whitman was not a good poet or a culturally resonant imaginative thinker. According to the critic Quentin Anderson, the peculiar bind here is indeed one Whitman shares with several other major American authors, including his contemporaries Thoreau and, most notably, Emerson. Their gigantesque claims of an inclusive and total power, which supposedly allowed them to achieve visionary possession of a world they thereby transfigured, are in Anderson's account a desperate defense against an inclusive social predicament they end up mirroring rather than solving.

Whitman, that is, despite his political commitments, is in the imaginative universe of the poems of 1855 and 1856 ultimately less concerned with political action than with a kind of visionary or magical transformation of the self and its objects, which ought to be available to a inclusive act of possession and transfiguration. The unlimited scope of this imagined transfiguration suggests, according to Anderson, at one and the same time: the sweeping nature of the transformation wrought by the emergent capitalist economy on antebellum America; the absence of noncapitalist social structures sufficiently well established and powerful to provide an effective counterforce to this change; the anxiety such a total transformation of the social scene provoked in individuals set adrift in the essentially anonymous and unmoored space defined by the impersonal laws of economic exchange; the desperate though seemingly triumphant status of an act of imaginative resistance that relied on the powers of the single self; and the peculiarly abstract or generic status of this self (Walt as shaman, devoid, in the poems, of personal history), an abstraction that, ironically, reproduces the very anonymity this figure has been designed to cure, so that his transformative acts replicate the impersonality of the law of exchange his advent supposedly supersedes.

One virtue of this account is that it lets us see the personal predicaments that helped shape *Leaves of Grass* as symptomatic in a cultural and not merely personal sense, as revelatory rather than merely idiosyncratic or disqualifying. The evidently unmoored quality of Whitman's personal life through the mid 1850s, that is, presents an extreme version of an increasingly common condition: in Whitman's case private sources of isolation dovetailed with contributing conditions which were shared and public, resulting, in *Leaves of Grass*, in an imaginative landscape at once intensely personal and socially resonant. Likewise Whitman's imaginative solutions, both in what they proclaim and in what they avoid, in their blindness as well as their insight, turn out to be an extreme version of a common cultural pattern.

LEAVES OF GRASS (1860)

Surprisingly, the wholesale transformations of social and psychic space that characterize the 1855 and 1856 editions of *Leaves of Grass* turn out to be pretty much confined to this extraordinarily productive phase of Whitman's career. By the time Whitman published the third edition of *Leaves of Grass* in 1860, this intensely imagined universe had very nearly dissolved. The 1860 edition no longer centers on the figure of the poet as shaman; nor is language deployed so as to display or enact its supposed performative power to transfigure social and personal space. In part, public events were overtaking Whitman's redemptive project.

In the 1860 edition of *Leaves of Grass* shamanistic magic is superseded not only by a darkened mood appropriate to the times, but also by many moments of great tenderness, and by a feeling of emotional reconciliation rather than cataclysm. Such feelings, for the most part, surface in the poet's extended meditations on homosexual love. It has been argued, on occasion, that this turn to the world of intimate relations is itself a symptom of political malaise: Whitman writes about personal life, because he despairs of public life. Yet this surely accords political events too singular a role in the evolution of Whitman's career, and thus to risk reducing him to what the poet Wallace Stevens later called, not in reference to Whitman, "the lunatic of one idea." Though the hard evidence that remains in the aftermath of Whitman's assiduous archival prunings is somewhat scanty, Whitman biographers tend to concur that sometime before publishing his 1860 edition he had fallen in love and experienced a period of intense and apparently reciprocated romantic attachment. The most likely candidate is Fred Vaughan; like Whitman's other most serious partners he was a younger working-class man to whom Whitman was a mentor and quasi father-figure as well as a lover. Along with the changing course of American history, perhaps, this experience and the changed sense of personal possibility it seems to have inaugurated were responsible for the shifting contours of Whitman's poetry.

This love experience almost undoubtedly provided the crucial personal impetus for Whitman's "Calamus" sequence, one of the great achievements of the 1860 edition of *Leaves of Grass*. Oddly, despite their quality and their volatile subject matter, Whitman's "Calamus" poems pretty much escaped notice when they were published. The ire that might have been directed to them fell instead on the companion Children of Adam sequence, Whitman's labored attempt to do for heterosexuality what he had already done for homosexuality in the "Calamus" poems. Emerson, still in Whitman's corner despite the purloined letter, apparently argued long and hard with the poet, during a walk in Boston Common, that the Children of Adam sequence had to be excised or expurgated, so that *Leaves of Grass* could make its way without the already weighty indecency albatross continuing to hang around its neck. As it turned out, Emerson proved both right and wrong: while several reviews were vituperative, others praised Whitman for an essentially "healthy" or "natural" view of sex. On the whole the sequence's notoriety probably helped sales more than it hurt them, keeping Whitman in the public eye. Thayer and Eldridge, Whitman's abolitionist Boston-based publishers, wrote the poet that their initial printing of a thousand copies had virtually sold out; unfortunately, their plans for a second run never materialized, as the firm went bankrupt in 1861. In retrospect it is hard to get very excited about the poems that stirred up this fuss: healthy-minded to a fault, they are certainly not prurient by present standards. Poetically, they are entirely unexceptionable, and curiously abstract or abstracted. The poet has a hard time working up credible enthusiasm for heterosexual intercourse; intended eroticism tends to collapse quickly into eugenicist cheerleading.

By contrast the "Calamus" sequence is intensely imagined and felt. Where the forced enthusiasm of Children of Adam produces frenetic or hectoring rhetoric, the tone in "Calamus" is both resonant and mobile. The poems glide between tenderness and poignancy, longing and regret, solemnity that is understated rather than overblown and erotic bravura tinged with wistfulness or self-deprecating humor. An early and shorter version of the sequence, called "Live-Oak with Moss," is more clearly narrative and presumably autobiographical than "Calamus" in its entirety, telling the story of the growth and then the decline and death of a love affair. Yet the public claims and concerns of "Calamus," which some critics see as merely an attempt to distance the sequence from these autobiographical intensities, are present in the earlier series as well. In one respect, then, "Calamus" rewrites the demotic populism of the 1855 and 1856 editions by tying it more clearly, perhaps even exclusively, to what we now call homosexuality. Whitman tended to use the phrenological term "adhesiveness" for both same-sex romantic passion and, more generally, friendship. As this term indicated, they had the power, in Whitman's view to knit the nation together as laws and politicians could not. Yet the sequence, published as war loomed nearer, seems to imagine these ties as enduring cataclysm rather than preventing it; part of the sequence's complex resonance derives from its insistent stepping aside from public space, its imagining of a kind of adhesive or homosexual shadow republic out of which the meaning of America might eventually be reconfigured, its promise reinvented and fulfilled beyond whatever disaster sectional strife would bring.

If the series escaped the notoriety that descended on Children of Adam, it is probably due not only to its political, even nationalist, strands, but also to the borderline relation it establishes between accepted traditions of same-sex friendship and homosexual love. Writing in an era before the notion of homosexuality as a distinct sexual orientation existed, Whitman both appeals to the aboveboard tradition of same-sex romantic friendship and slides it discreetly toward a range of overtly sexual expression and behavior less accepted and less openly discussed. One result of this blurring is that Whitman manages, in "Calamus," simultaneously to proclaim the political and cultural value of widespread homosociality and more furtively to celebrate (and strengthen) the rituals of an emergent community of what we would now call homosexuals. In effect, he establishes discreetly, for his era, a sort of "homosexual continuum," in some ways anticipating Adrienne Rich's later recent overt proclamation of the crucial social and political role played by a "lesbian continuum" in women's history and women's lives.

Yet at the same time "Calamus" enacts a tentative gay coming out, it acts as Whitman's coming into culture. If the 1855 and 1856 editions stage the poet as a shaman who stands above culture to transfigure and redeem it, the "Calamus" sequence envisions the personal and communal rituals, at once erotic and social, that might place him more firmly within culture, imagining gay history as America's secret history. This shift away from the huge imaginative claims of 1855 and 1856 can be criticized by characterizing the scope of Whitman's ambitions here as smaller than heretofore; but it can be praised by calling their scale more human. (Thoreau, apparently a bit unnerved upon meeting Whitman in 1855, noted that the poet "occasionally suggests something a little more than human.")

Whitman's own response to this shift in his life and work seems in effect to have been divided between these two hypothetical reactions. Among the 1860 edition's other major poems are "Out of the Cradle Endlessly Rocking" and "As I Ebb'd with the Ocean of Life." While the first celebrates the discovery or affirmation of human scale, the second explores the anxiety and near despair provoked by a shedding of the shamanistic stance of the earlier work and the psychological advantages that it provided. The latter poem has become the more widely praised. "Out of the Cradle," once much admired for the economy and consistency of its compressed system of symbols, has come to look a little dogmatically neat. Detailing an awakening to love and personal loss as the origin of his poetic calling, the poem's speaker recounts the genesis of the art of the 1860 "Calamus" sequence rather than the poems of 1855 and 1856. Telling a story in which love is cut short by death, Whitman both dramatically heightens the poem's situation and registers a fundamentally human recognition. Yet this heightening may be partly obfuscatory and melodramatic—obscuring Whitman's own loss of Fred Vaughan, who had not died but had simply moved out.

By contrast the extreme anxiety and bitterness of "As I Ebb'd with the Ocean of Life" seem wholly earned. The poem is an agonized appraisal of an apparent vanishing of powers, both personal and poetic. They are, as detailed in the poem, powers that seem very much like those of the shaman of 1855 and 1856. The diminished poet confronts an opposing self who might be the shaman: "I musing late in the autumn day, gazing off southward,/ Alone, held by the eternal self of me that threatens to get the better of me, and stifle me." Further on, this earlier, grandly aspiring poet figure is bitterly excoriated as a preposterous sham:

> Oppress'd with myself that I have dared to
> open my mouth,
> Aware now, that, amid all the blab whose
> echoes recoil upon me, I have not once
> had the least idea who or what I am.

As he gazes down at the rows of sediment while he walks the Long Island beach, the poem's diminished speaker enumerates a catalog gone bust, naming a world of lifeless forms not gathered and reanimated by the poet's power, but dispersed and irretrievable:

> Fascinated, my eyes, reverting from the
> south, dropped to follow those slender
> windrows,
> Chaff, straw, splinters of wood, weeds, and
> the sea-gluten,
> Scum, scales from shining rocks, leaves of
> salt-lettuce, left by the tide.

The poet no longer capable of redeeming this detritus is now reduced to imagining himself part of it:

> I, too, but signify at the utmost a little
> wash'd-up drift,
> A few sands and dead leaves to gather,
> Gather, and merge myself as part of the
> sands and drift.

The poem is complex in its bitterness; "the merge," earlier Whitman's favorite name for the transfiguring process the poet was said to help propel, is bitterly echoed as the poet merges with "the sands and drifts." Turning partly against the grand claims of Whitman's earlier editions, now seen as pretensions, it also ambivalently mocks the self who has failed to fulfill them. Yet whether the poem blames the figure of the shaman or the lover who has foolishly bartered away his sacramental vocation for a personal happiness that turned out to be elusive, the poem confronts the resultant anxiety and despair unflinchingly. In ensuing years Whitman apparently went on to find a personal happiness as well as a public fame that had hitherto eluded him; yet "As I Ebb'd with the Ocean of Life" may be the last great poem he ever wrote.

POST-1860 POETRY

If the last is an arguable judgment, it is a fairly common one. Once praised fairly frequently, if by no means universally, for their supposed polish and imaginative consistency or their supposedly Hegelian doctrinal clarity, most of the poems Whitman added to *Leaves of Grass* after 1860 have for some time been widely dismissed as minor work. Their once-vaunted smoothness of idiom criticized as a retreat to gentility; their nicely manageable symbol systems judged as plodding; and their availability to neat doctrinal paraphrase seen as the sign of an imaginatively exhausted poet's lapse into not especially profound cogitation or tireless but tiring exposition. This severe judgment has been mitigated somewhat by the leveling tendencies of new historicist literary criticism and cultural studies, for both of which the socially symptomatic status of the poem or the cultural work it performs may outweigh other concerns. On the whole, however, the later poetry is not as well regarded and less frequently read and written about than the earlier work.

Since Whitman, as early as the 1860 edition, began to tinker with the ordering of the ever-expanding list of poems that made up *Leaves of Grass*, arranging them in various thematic "cluster" schemes rather than chronologically, the general falling off of intensity and quality in the later work can be difficult to discern from a quick perusal of the so-called "deathbed" edition (essentially the edition of 1881). A look at the three-volume *Variorum*, which arranges the poems by date of first appearance in *Leaves of Grass*, is therefore a useful exercise.

The poems first published in 1865 as a separate volume, *Drum-Taps*, display a shift of focus and scope that is altogether understandable: no longer the poet of mythic transfigurations in which present pleasure and anxiety are rewritten under the sign of utopian prospect, Whitman becomes first the cheerleader of the war effort and then the haunted but accepting chronicler of its costs and the typically quiet heroism with which these were borne. The bombast of the first strain is more than made up for by the understated dignity of the latter one; Whitman, much moved, commits himself to a modest and minor poetry of chronicle, eschewing both epic and the earlier visionary mode of his greatest work. *Sequel to Drum-Taps*, oddly dated 1865–1866, prints eighteen new poems, most memorably Whitman's elegy for Lincoln, "When Lilacs Last in the Dooryard Bloom'd," an undoubtedly important poem most resembling, perhaps, "Out of the Cradle" among Whitman's earlier works. Like the earlier poem, this one is both heartfelt and occasionally purple. Almost uniformly somber in tone, it shares with the earlier poem the exalted diction and sustained decorum appropriate to commemoration. Its public provenance and function likewise virtually necessitate the imaginative compression that a limited and consistently manipulated system of symbols can give. (As in "Out of the Cradle," Whitman gives birds pride of place.)

As with the tendency to oversimplify the powerfully overdetermined imaginative contours of the triumphant early editions of *Leaves of Grass*, it is necessary to be on guard against the temptation to posit some single cause for the sustained decline of Whitman's poetry. Age and illness are assuredly important factors. Beginning in the 1860s Whitman sustained a number of strokes from which he never fully recovered. For a poet who made such grand claims for the body and reconfigured America in his poems as the agglomerating space an extravagantly polymorphous sexuality suggests, such difficulties must have been especially disabling. Increasing artistic caution, an eye increasingly trained on fame and thus surreptitiously glancing at propriety, also surely played a part. At the same time, the Civil War affected Whitman so intensely that the poetry of myth and possibility seems to have given way to the less ambitious poetry of chronicle. By contrast the Gilded Age appears to have thoroughly discomfited him as a writer. The world of industrial and social rationalization that grew out of the Civil War's massive mobilization of the American citizenry and economy was one to which he responded ambivalently, but not poetically. His later poetry seems often to fly as high above American space, and as close to some timeless empyrean as possible, an ascent for which his earthy talents and intense if ambivalent immersion in American social and political life left him ill-suited.

By contrast, his poetic imagination had been deeply and perhaps irrevocably engaged by the pre–Civil War period, the decades in which American capital and attendant social organizations emerged from the precapitalist artisanal and social forms that Whitman's strongest poetry evokes, and the passing of which it marks. Perhaps as important as all this, however, are Whitman's own changed circumstances: his emergence from a largely rootless condition into public fame, a domestic life in which he both lived once more among family and hosted a growing circle of friends who were also admirers, disciples, and acolytes; and a passional life apparently marked by sustained if stormy intimacies. It may seem odd that such settling in should have proved detrimental to his poetry. But it may well have been the case. Perhaps rootlessness—provoking as it did the peculiar combination of open-ended possibility, grandiosity, poignant self-doubt, and largely compensatory comic bravado that characterizes the early editions of *Leaves of Grass*—was as important a stimulant to Whitman's imagination as quirky erotic material and populist turbulence.

LATER YEARS

If the new poetry Whitman produced in the years after 1860 grew less intense and interesting, his life assuredly did not. His brother George, who had enlisted in the Union army in 1861, was wounded in late 1862 during the debacle at Fredricksburg. Whitman traveled south to Virginia to tend to him; returning to Washington for an indeterminate period, he ended up staying for the duration of the war and well beyond. What drew him, powerfully enough to be called mesmerically, were the war hospitals. Beginning as an unofficial visitor, Whitman became an unpaid "delegate" of the Christian Commission, a kind of volunteer companion and nurse to wounded and dying soldiers. By the time the war ended, Whitman had made some six hundred visits to army hospitals, several of these lasting for days at a time. He brought special items of food and other small gifts to those in his care, wrote letters and read to them, stayed to soothe and to talk, and often to kiss and embrace. In a consummation at once horrific and wondrous, Whitman seems to have found among this community of the wounded an unlikely fulfillment, at one and the same time, of the heroic populism *Leaves of Grass* had promulgated, the homosocial republic imagined in "Calamus," and, to some degree at least, the passionate intimacy he had begun to experience in the late 1850s. Whitman's attachment to some of these young men was extremely intense, a feeling that seems at least in part to have been reciprocated in more than one instance.

Yet the intense and turbulent world of the war hospitals was partly offset for Whitman, during his Washington years, by the growing stability he came to enjoy. He was appointed to a government clerkship in the Office of Indian Affairs early in 1865. When he was fired later that same year as part of a supposed moral purge engineered by the new secretary of the interior, James Harlan (who had supposedly read Whitman's working copy of *Leaves of Grass* while ransacking the poet's desk), that turned out to be a piece of great good fortune too. Before the ruckus had cleared Whitman had been transferred to a better job in the Attorney General's office. More important, his abolitionist friend William O'Connor came to Whitman's defense. O'Connor was a brilliant and spirited polemicist, and his invective—originally planned as a letter of protest to be delivered to Harlan but published instead as a privately printed pamphlet, *The Good Gray Poet*—stirred up a storm and played an important role in changing the footing on which Whitman's reputation was based. O'Connor argued that the work of this supposedly notoriously prurient poet was in fact surpassingly moral.

After Whitman moved to Camden, in declining health in 1873 (he lived first with his brother George and later in a small house of his own on Mickle Street, which is now maintained as a sort of Whitman museum), his circle of friends and admirers widened, coming to include, among others, the Canadian alienist Richard Maurice Bucke, who also wrote a book on Whitman. But the welter of feverish activity on Mickle Street was increasingly matched by burgeoning interest in centers of cultural power, in England as well as in the United States. A selection of Whitman's poems published in England in 1868, edited by William Michael Rossetti, secured his reputation in England, and in subsequent years Whitman's rising stock in America was to some degree sustained by the backwash from England. Famous visitors, both English and American, trooped to Camden, and the American press took note. By the time he died, following a lingering last illness, on March 26, 1892, in Camden, he was a public figure and person of letters of general renown if of disputed stature.

This burgeoning of both public attention and devoted attendance by an inner circle of acolytes seems to have been matched by a brightening of Whitman's intimate life. Beginning with the former Confederate soldier and streetcar conductor Peter Doyle, several younger men—mostly working class—seem to have reciprocated Whitman's affections and entered into sustained and intense intimacies with him.

PROSE WORKS

Whitman's most important work during this long period was done not in poetry but in prose—not as utopian myth-making but as memoir, or as frequently cogent social criticism essentially untinged by the exuberant imaginative excess characteristic of the early editions of *Leaves of Grass*. *Specimen Days*, published in 1882, is an odd but often affecting conglomeration of writings from several occasions, part diary or daybook and part episodic memoir of Whitman's Civil War experiences.

Democratic Vistas, combining essays written in 1867 and 1868 and published in pamphlet form in 1871, is probably the most significant piece of writing Whitman did during the last thirty years of his life. Responding to Thomas Carlyle's scathing attack on democracy in "Shooting Niagara; and After?" (1867), Whitman both admits the force of Carlyle's criticisms, indeed offering his own bill of particulars, and turns his indictment into the occasion for a renewed declaration of faith in American democracy. Part cogent denunciation of the unchecked triumph of greed and commercialism in the Gilded Age, the essay is also a striking instance of what Sacvan Bercovitch calls the American jeremiad, a culturally pervasive pattern of castigation and call for recommitment that helps both to instigate and to limit the scope of reform in United States political and cultural debate. Both a paean to American individualism and a critique of it, the essay ponders the ways in which polis and person may be mutually reenforcing rather than at loggerheads. Perhaps not surprisingly, Whitman finds his answer in culture, in a double sense: literature, or cultural production, is both to grow out of and knit together American culture in the broader meaning of that term. Culture's crucial function is to encourage a superb, redeemed individualism.

Some politically oriented criticism of Whitman's work has ably drawn out the ways in which his imaginative vision of a transfigured America ironically extols as virtues and resources some of the very habits and strategies that, in hindsight, can be seen to have exacerbated the problems they were called on to cure. Yet such limitations certainly do not vitiate, though they may qualify, the achievement of *Leaves of Grass*—notably its utopian hopes and energies and the peculiar, mobile, and nearly always eroticized imaginative constellations that sometimes support but often remain irreducible to the book's political ambitions. If Whitman is our most uneven great poet, he is also arguably our greatest uneven one. That at least has been the judgment of countless twentieth-century poets, major as well as minor, for whom Whitman has been a crucial resource despite his notoriously slack stretches. While each poet undoubtedly has his or her own Whitman, it is probably safe to say that it is the poet of the first three editions who has proved to be a crucial challenge or enabling instigation. And if it is in a way a joke to call the poems of this period peculiarly timeless, the joke is peculiarly Whitmanian, and serious. We can end with it:

> Whoever you are, now I place my hand upon
> you, that you be my poem,
> I whisper with my lips close to your ear,
> I have loved many women and men, but I
> love none better than you.

Selected Bibliography

WORKS OF WALT WHITMAN

POETRY

Leaves of Grass. Brooklyn, 1855. (Printed by Rome Brothers.)

Leaves of Grass. Brooklyn: [Fowler & Wells], 1856.

Leaves of Grass. Boston: Thayer and Eldridge, 1860.

Drum-Taps. New York, 1865.

Leaves of Grass. New York, 1866. (W. E. Chapin, Printer. This is the so-called 1867 edition.)

Leaves of Grass. Washington, D.C., 1871. (Printed by J. S. Redfield, New York.)

Leaves of Grass. Boston: James R. Osgood, 1881–1882. (Copyright is 1881. Modern Whitman editors regard this as the final edition of *Leaves of Grass*. The plates from this edition were used for all later printings, including the so-called "death-bed edition" of 1891–1892. Various annexed poems were appended to *Leaves of Grass* proper in subsequent printings.)

PROSE WORKS

Democratic Vistas. Washington, D.C., 1871.

Specimen Days and Collect. Philadelphia: Rees Welsh, 1882.

FACSIMILES AND REPRINTS

Leaves of Grass: The First (1855) Edition. Edited by Malcolm Cowley. New York: Viking, 1959.

Leaves of Grass: Facsimile of the First Edition of Leaves of Grass, Published by Whitman in Brooklyn in 1855. New York: Eakins Press, 1966.

Leaves of Grass: Facsimile of 1856 Edition. With an introduction by Gay Wilson Allen. Norwood, Pa.: Norwood Editions, 1976.

Leaves of Grass: Facsimile Edition of the 1860 Text. With an introduction by Roy Harvey Pearce. Ithaca, N.Y.: Cornell University Press, 1961.

COLLECTIONS

The Complete Writings of Walt Whitman. Edited by Richard Maurice Bucke, Thomas B. Harned, and Horace L. Traubel. 10 vols. New York: Putnam, 1902.

The Uncollected Poetry and Prose of Walt Whitman. Edited by Emory Holloway. 2 vols. Garden City, N.Y.: Doubleday, Page, 1921.

The Poetry and Prose of Walt Whitman. Edited by Louis Untermeyer. New York: Simon & Schuster, 1949.

Whitman's Manuscripts: Leaves of Grass *(1860): A Parallel Text*. Edited by Fredson Bowers. Chicago: University of Chicago Press, 1955.

The Collected Writings of Walt Whitman. Edited by Gay Wilson Allen and Sculley Bradley. 22 vols. to date. New York: New York University Press, 1961–. (Among the volumes in the New York University edition are the following: *The Correspondence*. Edited by Edwin Haviland Miller. 6 vols. 1961–1977. *The Early Poems and the Fiction*. Edited by Thomas L. Brasher. 1963. *Prose Works 1892*. 2 vols. Edited by Floyd Stovall. 1963–1964. [Volume I is *Specimen Days*.] *Leaves of Grass: Comprehensive Reader's Edition*. Edited by Harold W. Blodgett and Sculley Bradley. 1965. *Daybooks and Notebooks*. Edited by William White. 3 vols. 1978. *Leaves of Grass: A Textual Variorum of the Printed Poems*. Edited by Sculley Bradley et al. 3 vols. 1980. *Notebooks and Unpublished Prose Manuscripts*. Edited by Edward F. Grier. 6 vols. 1984.)

WALT WHITMAN

BIBLIOGRAPHIES AND CONCORDANCE

Eby, Edwin Harold. *A Concordance of Walt Whitman's* Leaves of Grass *and Selected Prose Writings*. Seattle: University of Washington Press, 1954.

Myerson, Joel. *Walt Whitman: A Descriptive Bibliography*. Pittsburgh: University of Pittsburgh Press, 1993.

CRITICAL AND BIOGRAPHICAL STUDIES

Allen, Gay Wilson. *The New Walt Whitman Handbook*. New York: New York University Press, 1975.

———. *The Solitary Singer: A Critical Biography of Walt Whitman*. New York: New York University Press, 1967.

Anderson, Quentin. *The Imperial Self: An Essay in American Literary and Cultural History*. New York: Knopf, 1971.

———. *Making Americans: An Essay on Individualism and Money*. New York: Harcourt, 1992.

———. "Whitman's New Man." In *Walt Whitman's Autograph Revision of the Analysis of* Leaves of Grass *(For Dr. R. M. Bucke's Walt Whitman)*. Text notes by Stephen Railton. New York: New York University Press, 1974.

Asselineau, Roger. *The Evolution of Walt Whitman*. 2 vols. Cambridge, Mass.: Harvard University Press, 1960–1962.

Burroughs, John. *Notes on Walt Whitman as Poet and Person*. New York: American News Co., 1867.

Chase, Richard. *Walt Whitman Reconsidered*. New York: William Sloane Associates, 1955.

Erkkila, Betsy. *Whitman the Political Poet*. New York: Oxford University Press, 1989.

Erkkila, Betsy, and Jay Grossman, eds. *Breaking Bounds: Whitman and American Cultural Studies*. New York: Oxford University Press, 1996.

Folsom, Ed. "Whitman's Calamus Photographs." In *Breaking Bounds*. Edited by Betsy Erkkila and Jay Grossman. New York: Oxford University Press, 1996.

Hollis, C. Carroll. *Language and Style in* Leaves of Grass. Baton Rouge: Louisiana State University Press, 1983.

Kaplan, Justin. *Walt Whitman, A Life*. New York: Simon & Schuster, 1980.

Kinnaird, John. "*Leaves of Grass* and the American Paradox." *Partisan Review* 25: 380–405 (1958). Revised and reprinted in *Whitman: A Collection of Critical Essays*. Edited by Roy Harvey Pearce. Englewood Cliffs, N.J.: Prentice-Hall, 1962.

Larson, Kerry C. *Whitman's Drama of Consensus*. Chicago: University of Chicago Press, 1988.

Lawrence, D. H. *Studies in Classic American Literature*. New York: T. Seltzer, 1923; New York: Viking, 1961.

Matthiessen, F. O. *American Renaissance: Art and Expression in the Age of Emerson and Whitman*. New York: Oxford University Press, 1941.

Miller, Edwin Haviland. *Walt Whitman's Poetry: A Psychological Journey*. New York: New York University Press, 1968.

Miller, James E., Jr. *A Critical Guide to* Leaves of Grass. Chicago: University of Chicago Press, 1957.

Moon, Michael. *Disseminating Whitman: Revision and Corporeality in* Leaves of Grass. Cambridge, Mass.: Harvard University Press, 1991.

Nathanson, Tenney. *Whitman's Presence: Body, Voice, and Writing in* Leaves of Grass. New York: New York University Press, 1992.

O'Connor, William Douglas. *The Good Gray Poet: A Vindication*. New York: Bunce and Huntington, 1866.

Pease, Donald E. "Blake, Crane, Whitman, and Modernism: A Poetics of Pure Possibility." *PMLA* 96: 64–85 (1981).

———. *Visionary Compacts: American Renaissance Writings in Cultural Context*. Madison: University of Wisconsin Press, 1987.

Reynolds, David S. *Walt Whitman's America: A Cultural Biography*. New York: Knopf, 1995.

Shively, Charley, ed. *Calamus Lovers: Walt Whitman's Working-Class Camerados*. San Francisco: Gay Sunshine, 1987.

Thomas, M. Wynn. *The Lunar Light of Whitman's Poetry*. Cambridge, Mass.: Harvard University Press, 1987.

Traubel, Horace. *With Walt Whitman in Camden*. 6 vols. [Various places and various publishers], 1908–1983.

Warren, James Perrin. *Walt Whitman's Language Experiment*. University Park: Pennsylvania State University Press, 1990.

Zweig, Paul. *Walt Whitman: The Making of the Poet*. New York: Basic Books, 1984.

Richard Wilbur
(b. 1921)

PETER SACKS

Richard wilbur's place among preeminent contemporary American poets is uncontested. And yet, despite broad confirmations (the poet laureateship, the Pulitzer and Bollingen prizes, among many other awards), this place has been somewhat more narrowly delimited than it should have been. This study will therefore attempt to augment the standard perception of Wilbur as the quintessentially refined New Critical poet whose musical and metaphorical wizardry has conjured some of the most dazzling yet suavely balanced and self-reconciliatory lyric poems of our time. During a mid century less given to contained forms of serious affirmation than to a barbarous history and its irregular songs of hurt or counterprovocation, Wilbur's, art has been identified as fair-minded and masterful, a white magic devoted more to restorative and celebratory acts than to the darker perturbations of the agonized or the wild at heart. Wilbur has been regarded by some as lacking a "saving vulgarity"—too much Prospero, too little Caliban. While recognizing a degree of accuracy in that definition, one should also be alive to what challenges even the most admiring of its terms. Not only should one see how elements of Wilbur's later work have cracked the definition that had crystallized around his first two or three books; one should read the early work itself as having addressed more powerful incongruities than those which (primarily New Critical) readers saw as having been so gracefully resolved.

Slightly younger than the first generation of poets whose work began to be published during or after World War II—John Berryman, Randall Jarrell, Elizabeth Bishop, and Robert Lowell were born between 1911 and 1919—Wilbur is one of a larger group born during the 1920's: among them are Howard Nemerov, Anthony Hecht, Louis Simpson, Denise Levertov, James Dickey, Donald Justice, James Merrill, W. D. Snodgrass, Allen Ginsberg, A. R. Ammons, James Wright, John Ashbery, W. S. Merwin, Galway Kinnell, Philip Levine, John Hollander, and Adrienne Rich. Of all these postwar writers, he has hewn most closely and consistently to the grain of one of the most dominant kinds of poetry to emerge in the wake of the earlier modernists. Wilbur wrote in "On My Own Work" (1966, collected in *Responses: Prose Pieces 1953–1976*):

> Most American poets of my generation were taught to admire the English Metaphysical poets of the seventeenth century and such contemporary masters of irony as John Crowe Ransom. We were led by our teachers and by the critics whom we read to feel that the most adequate and convincing poetry is that which accommodates mixed feelings, clashing ideas, and incongruous images. Poetry could not be honest, we thought, unless it began by acknowledging the full discordancy of modern life and consciousness. I still believe that to be a true view of poetry.

Wilbur was referring to the tenets of New Criticism, developed after T. S. Eliot by such theorists and practitioners as I. A. Richards,

John Crowe Ransom, Alan Tate, Robert Penn Warren, and Cleanth Brooks. Less revolutionary than the modernists, the New Critics shrank from what they viewed as certain excesses in the ambitions of modernism, associated as these were with the harsh polarities of totalitarianism and chaos. More interested in forms of provisional restabilization rather than of further ground breaking or system building, New Critics also were initially skeptical about the modernist long poem, as well as about the poet's use of grand cultural or political designs. Hence they held a preference for brief, tense, formally balanced lyrics that stressed the artifice of textual autonomy and inner symmetries rather than overt biographical or historical referents. If the latter were evoked, they appeared less in their own "right" than as elements in a rhetorical composition; and if there were potentially dramatic or dynamic forces at work, these were carefully wrought into the counterpoise of art: Wilbur said in his "The Genie in the Bottle" (published in John Ciardi's *Mid-Century American Poets*):

> The use of strict poetic forms, traditional or invented, is like the use of framing and composition in painting: both serve to limit the work of art, and to declare its artificiality: they say, "This is not the world, but a pattern imposed upon the world or found in it; this is a partial and provisional attempt to establish relations between things."

There had, of course, been other schools of postwar American poetry, one of the most notable being that derived from Ezra Pound, William Carlos Williams (whom Wilbur has consistently admired), and Charles Olson. And, following the late 1950's, most of Wilbur's initially like-minded contemporaries broke from the enclosures of New Criticism toward more open poetic forms, or toward the admission (in some cases confession) of apparently less artificial and less controllable material, whether autobiographical, historical, mythic, or surreal. Against these departures, Wilbur's career appears less volatile; and the equable tone of his work has reinforced the appearance of stable consistency, as if the entire oeuvre were itself a New Critical poem. Yet beneath its composed surfaces, Wilbur's poetry has, despite great coherence, developed and altered considerably. And in many respects these developments have underscored the least tractable (and most valuable) features of the earlier work—features that, like the subsequent developments, have seldom been fully measured either by Wilbur's few detractors or by many of his insightful admirers. By exploring the entire range of his work one can hope to gain a better sense not only of the superb array of "bottles," to use his metaphor for craft and container, but also of the often dark and uncanny genie moving within and between them.

Richard Wilbur was born in New York City on March 1, 1921. His mother, Helen Purdy Wilbur, "came of a Baltimore family with a tradition of newspaper-editing"—hence Wilbur's inherited commonsensical allegiance to pragmatic, communicative language, an allegiance that would long outlast his editorship of *The Amherst Student*; his father, Lawrence L. Wilbur, was a portrait painter—hence Wilbur's "busy eye" and painterly sense of composition. In an autobiographical sketch (1974, in *Conversations with* Richard Wilbur), Wilbur told his interviewer, Philip Dacey:

> I am not yet feeble enough to be interested in genealogy, but it may as well be said that I am of the 11th generation from Samuel Wildbore, and am descended from settlers of Massachusetts and Rhode Island. The fact does not seem definitive to me. . . . In a time of ethnic and racial self-consciousness, it is of no particular advantage to a writer that he belongs to the Anglo-Saxon minority, which is now felt to lack decided characteristics, and about which, significantly, no jokes are told. Robert Lowell is the only writer of recent years to make much use of such ancestry, and it is by and large people of other provenance who now claim to represent some version of "the American experience."

Beyond Wilbur's blend of modesty and assurance, the statement points to his lack of the ancestral or ethnic agons by which many American poets most readily weld their private psyches to that of the nation. This accounts for the relative absence of inflation in Wilbur's work—the language and tone are those of a biographically reticent New Englander, whose half-rueful centrality neutralizes the means for various self-amplifications while also depriving him of the outsider's (or, in Lowell's case, rebellious insider's) leverage on which much poetry has depended for its contestatory weight or edge.

In addition, one may perceive an ancestral element in Wilbur's apparent impartiality and ethnically unburdened buoyancy as a poet, as well as in his uninflected access to the standard English that has flowed with deliberate clarity since Tudor times, passing through such poets as Robert Herrick and John Dryden, eventually to reach A. E. Housman and Philip Larkin. To this, Wilbur has brought his own exuberant inventiveness, as well as a leaven of American usage, cross-grained with the semantic wit of one who knows how to evoke the Latin or Romance echoes still layering so many English words:

> In those lapped roars
> And souring resonance he heard as well
> Hoarse trains that highball down the world's
>   ravines . . . sick thrills
> Of transit and forsaking.

The result is a wide-ranging play of vocabulary, but one that seems to move outward from a core of plainness, just as many of Wilbur's lyrics themselves—for all the acts of persuasion in their rhetoric and form—seem to issue from a serenely centered voice, free of bias or special pleading. Indeed, the resulting freedom of the reader, the absence of obvious solicitations, may be the most difficult of gifts to receive. When reading lyric poems, we are more accustomed to being led by prosecution or defense than to hearing the more evenhanded accents of a judge or expert witness, seemingly impartial, however urgently engaged: while admiring its "brilliant negative," Wilbur's poem "Cottage Street, 1953" regards and, indeed, judges Sylvia Plath's work as "helpless and unjust." In a postwar culture unnerved by continuing abuses of power, we often withhold assent from poems that (however outraged) do not patently and with immediate pathos situate themselves in the unbalanced field of force where power, justice, or centrality itself is a matter of dispute.

Moving to what was still rural New Jersey in 1923, Wilbur's family settled "at modest rental in a pre-Revolutionary stone house on the estate of an English millionaire." (This and subsequent recollections can be found in *Conversations.*) On these "four-hundred-odd acres in North Caldwell. . . . transformed into the Platonic idea of an English gentleman's farm," Wilbur absorbed the "decent, attractive, civilized" temper of this "spontaneous English colony": "all was tea, bowls, tennis, Episcopalianism, gardening, music, and bridge, with agriculture and commerce in the middle distance and background." There, invigorating this gently mocked gentility, he developed his abiding regard for the natural world—"it comes natural to me to use, in particular, botanical materials"—especially where a mild wildness abuts or partially submits to forms of cultivation. A similar, contrastive vigor characterized his "riding the rails and hitchhiking all over America" during vacations from Amherst; and it marks his poetry's sensitivity to what evades even the most ingenious of forms.

At Amherst (1938–1942) Wilbur found a "superior English department," at that time riding the high tide of New Criticism. "Converted . . . to disciplined reading," he became inclined toward what for some time promised to be a career as a literary scholar and critic. Although he had published a few poems while still an undergraduate, the jarring motive for becoming a poet in earnest came after graduation. Shortly after marrying Charlotte Hayes Ward in June 1942, Wilbur joined the 36th Infantry Division and served at Monte Cassino at Anzio, in the invasion of southern France, and on through the Siegfried Line. Wilbur has spoken (1975) of his wartime experience in ways that connect it directly to his writing:

> I began to write rather constantly once I got abroad in the service. It was one of the few things one could do, under what were chiefly boring circumstances, to keep sane. . . . I think it was a question of confusion, or a desire to make order of confusion, to give words to one's fears and uncertainties and so tame them a little. . . . You have to have some experience of danger, lostness and mess. The bottom has to fall out of your thoughts periodically before you feel the need to be clear and orderly in words.

The above statement deepens our reading of Wilbur's early and subsequent work, as does his account of his reading experience during the war—especially his reading of Edgar Allan Poe (along with James Joyce, Dylan Thomas, Gerard Manley Hopkins, and Alfred Lord Tennyson):

> I can remember that during one long week in which I scarcely got out of my foxhole at Monte Cassino, I read that whole paperback of Poe. For the first time I began to have a sense that there was something besides spookery in Poe, that there might be some kind of allegorical depth to his fiction. . . . Perhaps it was because under circumstances where one did very little save sleep and wake, one's attention was drawn to all of the semistates which lie between full waking and deep slumber. I began to perceive that in Poe's fiction some effort was being made to represent the stages or stations of the mind.

We will soon measure the extent of Wilbur's self-described "public quarrel with the aesthetics of Edgar Allan Poe." But it is worth recognizing how many of Wilbur's own poems cross and recross the semistates along the borders of sleep and wakefulness (among them "Clearness," "The Pardon," "Merlin Enthralled," "Marginalia," "Love Calls Us to the Things of This World," "Walking to Sleep," and "In Limbo"), as well as how many of them take for their deeper subjects the "stages or stations of the mind."

In the light of these reflections on fear, boredom, and loss, as well as on the disorientation and attempted reordering of the world and the mind, we can now turn to Wilbur's first collection. While at war he was sending poems home to his wife and a few friends; after his return to graduate school at Harvard the poems were brought to the attention of the publishers Reynal Hitchcock, who published them with some newer work as *The Beautiful Changes* (1947).

Several features of Wilbur's first book were immediately praised by Louise Bogan:

> He has a remarkable variety of interest and mood, and he can contemplate his subjects without nervousness, explore them with care, and then let them drop at the exact moment that the organization of a poem is complete. This ease of pace, this seemingly effortless advance to a resolute conclusion, is rare at his age; the young usually yield to tempting inflation and elaboration.

Equally striking is the extraordinary freshness with which Wilbur re-perceives his world. This is partly a matter of tone and music, but for the moment let us notice the salient devices of simile and metaphor, and ask what makes Wilbur's use of them so distinctive. First, some early examples: Slicing open a potato is "like breaching a strangely refreshing tomb" ("Potato"); "The snow came down last night like moths / Burned on the moon" ("First Snow in Alsace"); ". . . twilight / Glides like a giant bass" ("The Peace of Cities"); "Then your love looked as simple and entire / As that picked pear you tossed me" ("June Light"). In each case the comparison creates something new, and the shock of that creation does much to provide the energy of Wilbur's poetry. But, unlike many metaphorists, Wilbur channels and ramifies that energy onward through the poem—by maintaining a modulated speaking voice and by integrating the comparison into larger currents of syntax, cadence, or stanzaic form. The effects and possible motives for this are several, and it is worth dwelling on them for a moment, because they lie near the heart of Wilbur's entire work.

Certainly the shock of refreshment is prolonged and shaped—becoming more a wave than an explosion; but beyond the pleasing athletic dexterity and vitality of this shaping, Wilbur is extending another effect of the metaphor itself: the sense of connectedness. Since one of his "motives for metaphor" is the creation of relatedness (Wilbur has spoken of the religious element in this enterprise), it is no coincidence that his comparisons are seldom left to shine alone but are invariably woven into a larger verbal scheme. This larger scheme is also that of a courteous conversationalist (perhaps a social analogue and instrument for the poem's creations of cooperative relatedness), whose interest is in keeping the discourse moving fluently along rather than stopping its flow with some arresting brilliance. In both these regards, Wilbur may be drawing on his admiration for seventeenth-century prose—and it is this, as much as his flair for compound description and allegory, that lies at the root of his early affinity with Marianne Moore. A virtuoso syntactician, careful to draw otherwise unassimilable curiosities of fact or figure into an unflappable conversational pursuit, Moore praised such authors as Donne, Francis Bacon, and Thomas Browne in the following terms: "Suggesting conversation and strengthened by etymology there is a kind of effortless compactness which precludes ornateness, a 'fearful felicity,' in which like the pig in the churn, imagination seems to provide its own propulsiveness."

The propulsiveness and fluency with which Wilbur integrates his metaphors may have yet further motives, at which the word "fearful" could hint. Indeed, the early poem "Objects" ends with the speaker self-described as "fearfully free." Bearing in mind that much of his early poetry emerged from the war, one notices that Wilbur's comparisons often register an estrangement that is as threatening as it is thrilling: the potato as tomb, the twilight as predator; even the lovely pear becomes "more fatal fleshed." In "First Snow in Alsace," the opening line ("The snow came down last night like moths") is pleasantly poetic; but the discomforting enjambment and extension of the simile to "Burned on the moon" brings an abrupt and mortal change. Characteristically, Wilbur moves beyond a possible fixation on this strangeness, pausing only for a caesural semicolon before calmly resuming, "it fell till dawn, / Covered the town with simple cloths." Like the syntax, the simplicity absorbs and recovers from the strangeness, even as the metaphoric play has now eased onward from burned moths to simple cloths. Similarly, the poetic form crystallizes quietly into the first of a series of interlaced stanzas of terza rima. In such ways the poem rehearses the experience of uncovering and recovering from the shock of estrangement.

Estrangement of a violent kind is clearly at the thematic core of the poem, which continues thus:

> shellbursts scattered and deranged,
> Entangled railings, crevassed lawn.
>
> As if it did not know they'd changed,
> Snow smoothly clasps the roofs of homes
> Fear-gutted, trustless and estranged.

"Deranged," "changed," "estranged": from the first, Wilbur's readers should have measured the toll in this persistant rhyme. (The later poem "Praise in Summer" again rhymes "derange" and "strange," and variants of "strange" recur in numerous others.) Clearly the brio of perceived resemblance has its disjunctive underside—comparison as crisis, not just delight—and the composures of phrasing and rhyme have compensatory as well as celebratory designs. Indeed, Wilbur's achievement makes these oppositions almost indistinguishable.

Continuing "First Snow in Alsace," one cannot think now of snow without also envisioning burned moths, wrecked homes, and such scenes of death as the poem goes on to describe: "beyond the town a mile / Or two, this snowfall fills the eyes / Of soldiers dead a little while." While calm, the hush is also that of desolation. And although the apparently amenable diction of "a mile / Or two" or "a little while" may lessen the horror, it renders such diction either limited or yet more menacing—as if a half-echo of Robert Frost's "Stopping by Woods on a Snowy Evening" were introduced only to make the familiar voice of Frost himself now seem either naively inadequate to this foreign enormity or still more disquieting from within its provinciality. Yes, "frost makes marvelous designs," as the poem goes on to concede; but Wilbur weighs such marvels of natural design against the ghastly mess or yet more hideous design of war. Wilbur's line may thus evoke the darker and more pertinent Frost of "Design," which also rhymed "cloth" with a victim "moth" as part of its remorseless etching of "death and blight." However deftly en passant, Wilbur may thus have relayed both the genial and the vigilant nature of his inheritance from Frost—who has remained one of his principal influences.

In the same vein, Wilbur concludes by measuring the self-warming innocence of youth ("Ten first-snows back in thought . . . [the night guard] was the first to see the snow") against the chill of the dead, or of soldiers aged by the experience of last things. How much is a residual innocence now worth? The question has no obvious answer. On the one hand, boyish boastings of priority are ironized by subsequent warfare, and may even involve the competitive impulses that lead to war. On the other, such warmth and recollected freshness of perception, however marred, may revive an otherwise lethal freezing of the night guard's sensibility. Without it, the eyes of the survivors may be as snow-blinded as those of the dead.

"First Snow" ends, noteworthily, by representing the consciousness of a night guard. Having noticed that the refreshing power of Wilbur's similitudes is inseparable from a perception of threatening otherness and change, like that of war, we may now add that his alertness is likewise inextricable from a kind of vigilance. In fact, several poems in Wilbur's first book adopt overt or implied attitudes of guardedness. "Objects" enjoins us to "Guard and gild what's common," while the soldiers of "Mined Country" must unlearn their trust in the natural world so as to guard against concealed land mines. Like the homes in Alsace, "trustless and estranged," these pastures and woods, as well as the men "Stepping with care and listening / Hard for hid metal's cry," are

> so mixed up
> With earliest trusts, you have to pick back
> Far past all you have learned, to go
> Disinherit the dumb child.

Part of the trust fund lost to estrangement is thus an innocent infancy, as well as an early pastoral language. History's invasion of pastoral is an old story, going back past Edmund Spenser to Virgil; but the invasion and suffering are always renewed, as is the demand for an appropriate language to be used by those who guard the flocks: "Shepherds must learn a new language; this / Isn't going to be quickly solved." In many ways this threatening necessity, balanced by an implied originality, serves as a manifesto for a young poet breaking or guarding the ground of his own career. And while Wilbur's poetry will track man's historical or conceptual violations of the natural world, it will also guard against quick poetic solutions. Like many poems to come, "Mined Country" proposes a recovered wildness rather than an inner or outer region mined by our impositions:

> Tell him to trust things alike and never to
>   stop
> Emptying things, but not let them lack
> Love in some manner restored; to be
> Sure the whole world's wild.

As "in some manner" betrays, however, the restoration of wildness is a paradoxical goal, compromised by the manners of language as much as by the necessary technology of a mine detector—a latter-day shepherd's crook. For Wilbur, whose brilliant mind and manners always shape the very wildness they would restore or praise, this further problem, too, will not be "quickly solved." It remains one of the most fascinating elements of his entire career.

This sensitivity to wildness suggests yet another motive for the distinctive fluency with which Wilbur tends to surpass even the most inspired of his comparisons. To the accommodated recognition of strangeness, and to the ductility of civil address, we can add Wilbur's skepticism about imposing upon or deludedly trying to apprehend a "wild" reality that evades even the most ingenious of our figures. "Objects" speaks of "a net which catches nothing," and it urges us to "forget / Uses and prices and names; have objects speak." The net recurs in "An Event," where Wilbur supersedes one simile for flocking birds ("As if a cast of grain leapt back to the hand") with another ("They roll / Like a drunken fingerprint across the sky!")—only to reject that last superb comparison:

> Or so I give their image to my soul
> Until, as if refusing to be caught
> In any singular vision of my eye
> Or in the nets and cages of my thought,
>
> They tower up, shatter, and madden space
> With their divergences, are each alone
> Swallowed from sight, and leave me in this
> place
> Shaping images to make them stay: . . .

Even the refutation of his figures of speech requires yet further metaphors (nets, cages, tower, madden, swallowed), as if to confess that language itself, particularly its figurative element, is unavoidably mined with that which it would sweep clear. And so the vigilance spoken of earlier extends as much to Wilbur's craft and medium as to his subjects—even when the subject is that very need for vigilance. One way to measure the course of Wilbur's development—extending to as late a poem as "Lying"—is to follow the deepening skepticism of that vigilance, associated as it is with more than merely epistemological concerns.

Wilbur's "Praise in Summer" confronts the distortion that inheres in any refreshing use of metaphor—but here it suggests something like a compulsion in the poet's malpractice:

> And then I wondered why this mad *instead*
> Perverts our praise to uncreation, why
> Such savor's in this wrenching things awry.
> Does sense so stale that it must needs
> derange
> The world to know it? . . .

The sonnet is bound by such urgent words as "must needs," "mad," and "awry" ("Mined Country" had worried that "Some scheme's gone awry"); "perverts" and "wrenching" dramatize the turning of figuration. Clearly, such rhetoric admits more than a decorative compunction for its abuses. But if we expect a purgative return to literal truths, the poem concludes:

> To a praiseful eye
> Should it not be enough of fresh and strange
> That trees grow green, and moles can course
> in clay,
> And sparrows sweep the ceiling of our day?

Not only is the question rhetorical, its rhetoricity is stressed by the return to metaphoric play within the final line. The question answers itself by the very language with which it has been posed.

With a deepened sense of Wilbur's necessary rather than merely willed estrangements, we should turn back to several other early poems that portray the estranger himself. "Water Walker" is the most remarkable of these. Here the very means of self-portrayal is inherently metaphorical and estranging, since the speaker's self is presented only via the multiple figures of the caddis fly and of the apostle Saul/Paul—each of which is subject to metamorphosis. Like the fly and the convert, the poet may be condemned (by a force somewhere between biological and spiritual necessity) to exist in a state of betweenness, waterborne yet in flight, a convert Roman preaching to Greeks, an uneasy foreigner who, like metaphor or poetic language itself, keeps crossing the borderline of his own otherness, "Always alike and unlike." To the radically converted survivor of war, the world will obviously seem other than what it was. To such a survivor who is also a poet, a maker of metaphoric conversions, his own identity will have become that of a "Stranger to both" sides of the several divisions between literal and figurative, or familiar and unfamiliar, worlds. Unable to dwell in a world whose otherness he has noted *and* augmented, he discovers "Heaven and hell in the poise / Betwixt 'inhabit' and 'know' "—a discovery that evokes ultimate judgment. And, as the poem concludes, "justice" is somehow the heart of the matter:

> Who learns
> How hid the trick is of justice, cannot go
> home, nor can leave,
> But the dilemma, cherished, tyrannical,
> While he despairs and burns
>
> Da capo da capo returns.

Those lines serve a writ on Wilbur's entire career—its musically recapitulated cherishing of a need to do justice to the changing world. The need is tyrannical, and the poet is its main victim and disciple, repeatedly compelled to a task that can have no resolution. The presence of tyranny confirms that Wilbur's estrangements were suffered rather than merely administered, and it sharpens the "dilemma" noticed in the poet's testing of his own words. While such a perception moves beyond New Critical claims of poetic resolution, it also points to how many of Wilbur's other poems wrestle with the very matter of justice—a justice often directed beyond the supposed limits of the poem. Thus "On the Eyes of an SS Officer" both diagnoses the self-blinding injustice of fanatics and calls down an actual judgment on the worst of such would-be purifiers: "I ask my makeshift God of this / My opulent bric-a-brac earth to damn his eyes."

Similarly, other poems adjudicate between the possessiveness of a collector and the work of a painter like Pieter de Hooch, whose way of doing justice to "A Dutch Courtyard" makes the scene immune to consumption; or between the narrowly honor-bound Percy or Hal and the roundly life-affirming Falstaff ("Up, Jack"); or between the "small strict shape" of the costumed performing dancer and her unmeshed return to "a little wilderness of flesh" ("L'Etoile"). Meanwhile, to forestall his own errors of perceptual judgment, Wilbur conjures the baffling and fluent variegations of a sycamore so that his eye "will never know the dry disease / Of thinking things no more than what he sees" ("Poplar, Sycamore").

In each case, Wilbur's fidelity is to a world beyond strict apprehension or even comprehension. The book's first poem, "Cicadas" (called "Cigales" in *The Beautiful Changes*), celebrates a "thin uncomprehended song [that] springs healing questions into binding air." Like that song, although far from thin, Wilbur's own poems reserve a teasing element—either of incomprehensible music or of contradiction—that pledges the world which "darts without the word." As we now recognize, that pledge marks a restless fidelity to what changes. Like the visions of Paul, this "troubles" us by enforcing a loss of the familiar world or self, and by pointing to our own mortality. One cannot embrace change without also accepting mortal loss; and it is this mature renunciation, deeper than its aesthetic or conceptual counterparts, that gives Wilbur's work its early and lasting depth, as well as its unusual balance of calm and celebration. This is what allows him to "choose / To welcome love in the lively wasting sun" ("Sunlight Is Imagination"), and to write the extraordinary philosophical love poem that titles and concludes the book. "The Beautiful Changes" meditates on how beauty (and, by implication, poetic metaphor) alters, both reflexively and as an agent that quickens us to see things as yet more strangely other than they once appeared—less our own, and yet by loss released to that mysterious stirring beyond recognition or selfhood that lies at the heart of wonder:

One wading a Fall meadow finds on all sides
The Queen Anne's Lace lying like lilies
On water; it glides
So from the walker, it turns
Dry grass to a lake, as the slightest shade of
  you
Valleys my mind in fabulous blue Lucernes.

The beautiful changes as a forest is changed
By a chameleon's tuning his skin to it;
As a mantis, arranged
On a green leaf, grows
Into it, makes the leaf leafier, and proves
Any greenness is deeper than anyone
  knows.

Your hands hold roses always in a way that
  says
They are not only yours; the beautiful
  changes
In such kind ways,
Wishing ever to sunder
Things and things' selves for a second
  finding, to lose
For a moment all that it touches back to
  wonder.

The Beautiful Changes appeared while Wilbur was studying English literature at Harvard Graduate School. After studying for a year on the G.I. Bill, and receiving an M.A. degree (1947), he began three years as a junior fellow at Harvard's Society of Fellows. During this time he continued his study of Poe—a study that yielded ground-breaking essays and lectures on Poe's work. While marking the limits of Poe's exclusionary poetry ("with few exceptions . . . what brilliance they have is like that of a Fourth of July rocket destroying itself in the void"), Wilbur reveals the allegories of otherworldly disengagement that work like "undercurrents" through the fiction. A true poet-critic, he applies a far from disinterested edge to these studies of such works as "Ligeia," *The Narrative of Arthur Gordon Pym,* and the detective stories. As in a Poe narrative, where (according to Wilbur's insight) two characters may represent divergent parts of a single soul, Wilbur draws critically close to his subject in order to clarify and perhaps exorcise Poe's remorseless drive for dematerialization. Although fascinated by Poe's dream exploration of shifting borders of consciousness, and by his "estranging" spirituality, Wilbur makes of Poe a "road not taken"—one that covers similar psychic territory but leads in a direction whose very oppositeness dramatizes Wilbur's intended celebration of the "things of this world." That celebration becomes one of the main objects of Wilbur's second collection of poems, *Ceremony and Other Poems* (1950).

If Poe sought the absolute and the timeless, the poems of *Ceremony* necessarily embrace the temporal world. Even more intensely than had been true of his earlier registry of change, Wilbur's espousal of incarnate, material existence ("A World Without Objects Is a Sensible Emptiness") commits him to "a most material loss" and to a "lament for grace's early term" ("Lament"). And whereas a chief element and agent of estrangement in *The Beautiful Changes* had been war, it is now time and a more general sense of mortality that (in "The Beautiful Changes") "sunder[s] / Things and things' selves for a second finding"—if, indeed, such recoveries are possible.

This last doubt troubles such poems as "The Pardon" and "The Death of a Toad." In the former, the speaker is haunted by the dog whose death he had once evaded ("I could not forgive the sad or strange / In beast or man"). Now the dog returns, if not for redemption ("I dreamt the past was never past redeeming: / But whether this was false or honest dreaming"), then for an acknowledgment that would humbly extend the limits of kindness to encompass the strangeness of death ("I beg death's pardon now. And mourn the dead.") Similarly—as Randall Jarrell failed to see—"The Death of a Toad" incriminates its own idealizing compensations ("ebullient seas . . . Amphibia's emperies") with a final, unflinching regard for what is lost. If "A World Without Objects" deliberately blurs its poetic lampshine in "the steam of beasts," these two poems about dead beasts modulate such "light incarnate" from the glowing "fierce and mortal green" of "The Pardon" to the "haggard daylight" of "The Death of a Toad."

Wilbur's prismatic images or phrases thus render something more than poetic luminosity itself. And the ceremonies suggested by the volume's title are often designed to humble the human and the poetic will—partly by urging it to tend the mortal rather than the mental flower ("La Rose des Vents"), and partly by warning it against solipsism ("The Terrace") or the infernal insistence on autonomy ("A Problem from Milton"). These and other poems caution against versions of a "Thüle of the mind's worst vanity" ("Clearness"); as in "Grasse: The Olive Trees," they point out the dangers and futilities of attempting to possess or to bring near any idealized state of paradise, be it Eden ("Castles and Distances"), or a purchased love ("Marchéaux Oiseaux"), or a realized, rather than a projected, linguistic sufficiency ("Games Two").

It would be wrong, however, to suppose that Wilbur's sense of limits and of renunciations leads to an inertly resigned poetry. The opposite is true, for various reasons. By exploiting the genre of argument or meditational debate, several poems give free rein to an impulse of spirit, imagination, or desire before checking that impulse by exposing its futility or cost. The poems thus not only enjoy a measure of dramatic complexity and dynamism; they also actually exercise rather than suppress the drives they seek to curb. Or perhaps it would be more accurate to say that Wilbur's poems redirect their spiritual, quest-like energies into their celebrations of the given world. This world is consequently perceived with an unusual vibrancy that inheres as much in the mobility and the textures of Wilbur's subjects as in the embodiments of such qualities in his craft. Both world and poem come to share an interanimating "scintillant embrace," in which the network of mind, senses, and language seems to mesh with the reticulated vitality of its objects. Three examples follow, from "A Glance from the Bridge," "Conjuration," and "Part of a Letter":

> [Gulls] rise and braid their glidings, white
> and spare,
> Or sweep the hemmed-in river up and
> down,
> Making a litheness in the barriered air, . . .
>
> Backtrack of sea, the baywater goes; flats
> Bubble in sunlight, running with
> herringbone streams;
> Sea-lettuce lies in oily mats
> On sand mislaid; stranded
> Are slug, stone, and shell, as dreams
> Drain into morning shine, and the cheat is
> ended.
>
> Easy as cove-water rustles its pebbles and
> shells
> In the slosh, spread, seethe, and the back-
> sliding
> Wallop and tuck of the wave, and just that
> cheerful,
> Tables and earth were riding
>
> Back and forth in the minting shades of the
> trees.

Such writing is clearly buoyed by an intense participatory relish; and despite Wilbur's caution that "never noun / Found what it named," his poems constantly exceed mere acts of denomination. Perhaps not since Gerard Manley Hopkins (but here without a sacrificial drive) has a poet so brilliantly and empathetically deployed the more than denotative resources of lyric poetry to celebrate the "ingenerate grain" of the world.

In this participatory sense, whereby unnatural artifice accentuates the stress and play of natural energy, Wilbur's title poem declares that "ceremony never did conceal, / Save to the silly eye, which all allows, / How much we are the woods we wander in." This poem (on a painting by Bazille) self-reflexively concludes:

> What's lightly hid is deepest understood,
> And when with social smile and formal
> dress
> She teaches leaves to curtsy and quadrille,
> I think there are most tigers in the wood.

Imagining tigers, the mind's eye recalls the "striped blouse" of the painted woman; but instead of assimilating the animals to artifice and fashion, it detects how artifice and fashion reveal their own and the woman's element of wildness. "We are the woods we wander in" recovers the old association of woods with wilds, and of "wood" with human wildness (the lovers in *A Midsummer Night's Dream* became "wood within the wood").

Thus, at the heart of human artifice Wilbur stresses a hunting restlessness, a quality that inhabits the sculptured figures in one of *Ceremony's* finest poems, "Giacometti." Rejecting inert stone statues that freeze the human image and the human will, Wilbur honors Giacometti's art for its mobility, its truth to moments when "we ourselves are strange / To what we were," its portrayal of a stripped-down pilgrim, anonymous and "unspeakably alone." This fully present but radically incomplete "starless walker, who cannot guess / His will" becomes Wilbur's Everyman, "in whose guise we make / Our grim departures now, walking to find / What railleries of rock, what palisades?" Like his wood wanderer or his earlier water walker or night guard, Wilbur's anonymous pilgrim may be one of the most uneasy but most authentic figures for his own poetic vocation and career. Beneath the "formal dress" of his work we may imagine "the single form we can assume," a roughened, shuffling creature "made / Of infinite farewells," a migrant figure "pruned of every gesture, saving only / The habit of coming and going."

The genie of Wilbur's career certainly seems to have been "walking, walking" during the years following the publication of *Ceremony.* Despite his position as Briggs-Copeland assistant professor of English composition at Harvard (1950–1955), Wilbur spent long periods away from Cambridge, first as a Guggenheim Fellow in New Mexico (1952–1953), then as a Prix de Rome Fellow in Italy (1954–1955), before accepting an appointment as associate professor at Wellesley College (1955–1957), from which he moved again to become a professor of English at Wesleyan University (1957–1977). These years also brought further departures as a writer—an early attempt to write a verse drama, a highly successful verse translation of Molière's *The Misanthrope,* the award-winning short story "A Game of Catch," the compilation *A Bestiary* (poems and prose, illustrated by Alexander Calder), and a sequence of lyrics for a Broadway version of Voltaire's *Candide* in collaboration with Lillian Hellman and Leonard Bernstein. At the same time, Wilbur continued to write lyric poetry, publishing his third collection, *Things of This World,* in 1956.

Although the poems of *Things of This World* have much in common with Wilbur's earlier work, they move with greater freedom and authority, and the elegant build of his poems now seems to have taken on further muscle and robustness. Certain themes have gained in cogency and range of application, while the manner of their presentation has become both more relaxed and more high-spirited. One such theme, emphasized by the title, is the poet's continuing devotion to "things of this world"; and the signature poem, "Love Calls Us to the Things of This World," suggests how strongly that devotion now defines the poet's very "calling":

> The eyes open to a cry of pulleys,
> And spirited from sleep, the astounded soul
> Hangs for a moment bodiless and simple
> As false dawn.
>   Outside the open window
> The morning air is all awash with angels.
>   Some are in bed-sheets, some are in
>   blouses,
> Some are in smocks: but truly there they
>   are.
> Now they are rising together in calm swells
> Of halcyon feeling, filling whatever they
>   wear
> With the-deep joy of their impersonal
>   breathing;
>
>   Now they are flying in place, conveying
> The terrible speed of their omnipresence,
>   moving
> And staying like white water; and now of a
>   sudden
> They swoon down into so rapt a quiet

That nobody seems to be there.
                                        The soul shrinks

   From all that it is about to remember,
From the punctual rape of every blessed day,
And cries,
      "Oh, let there be nothing on earth but
      laundry,
Nothing but rosy hands in the rising steam
And clear dances done in the sight of
   heaven."

   Yet, as the sun acknowledges
With a warm look the world's hunks and
   colors,
The soul descends once more in bitter love
To accept the waking body, saying now
In a changed voice as the man yawns and
   rises,

   "Bring them down from their ruddy
      gallows;
Let there be clean linen for the backs of
   thieves;
Let lovers go fresh and sweet to be undone,
And the heaviest nuns walk in a pure
   floating
Of dark habits,
                    keeping their difficult balance."

With an exuberant play of high and low diction, direct speech, and variously indented lines of differing length, Wilbur gives fresh, accessible force to the old debate of body and soul—here capturing the moments of transition through which the soul chooses to acknowledge both the waking body and the world. Crossing Poe's territory in reverse, the poem turns from sleep and the shapings of pure spirit, to embrace the "hunks and colors" of daily life; but even its initial phantasm of angels inhabits such ordinary stuff as laundry—indeed, depends on laundry for its manifestation. Wilbur himself admits, "I don't really want to have much truck with angels who aren't in the laundry, who aren't involved in the everyday world. It's a poem against dissociated and abstracted spirituality."

While the intention of the poem is clearly expressed, its theme is not merely argued in the abstract but, rather, exemplified by its own "embodiment" within both a narrated action (the story of an awakening) and a dramatized turn of direct speech. Whereas the beautifully entranced fantasia of angels ends with the suspicion that "nobody seems to be there," the poem itself ends within the presence of a direct speaker: the embodied soul, whose "changed voice" marks its journey from a momentary shrinkage to a full acceptance of incarnation. The laundry may now serve as a garment for the body, rather than only as a fabric for angels or the "angelic imagination." And the final stanza ("Bring them down . . . Let there be . . .") leads the descendental impulse home with nothing less than a redemptive and creative authority. Saving the laundry (and angels) from the gallows, and hence rejecting any notion that martyrdom must be the price of spirituality, the soul also uses the language of divine creative fiat as it brings a world into being—a balanced world occupied not only by thieves and heavy nuns but also by the continuing possibility of finding angels in the wash.

A descendental impulse invigorates many other poems in *Things of This World.* Most literally, there is the slow downward dance of "Piazza de Spagna, Early Morning"—a poem that moves from a "sleepy pirouette" to a "called-for falling glide and whirl," as if this were again a figure of vocation; or the "down again" speaker in "A Voice from Under the Table"; or the brilliantly registered descents of water in "A Baroque Wall-Fountain in the Villa Sciarra." Blending description and debate, this last poem sets the "saecular ecstasy" of an earthly "faunmenage" against the vertical "water-saints" outside St. Peter's. The poem's life is in the engaged virtuosity of its water portraits:

Sweet water brims a cockle and braids down

                    Past spattered mosses, breaks
On the tipped edge of a second shell, and
   fills
   The massive third below. It spills
In threads then from the scalloped rim, and
   makes

A scrim or summery tent
For a faun-menage and their familiar goose.
Happy in all that ragged, loose
Collapse of water, its effortless descent

. . . .

Before St. Peter's—the main jet
Struggling aloft until it seems at rest

In the act of rising, until
The very wish of water is reversed,
That heaviness borne up to burst
In a clear, high, cavorting head, to fill

With blaze, and then in gauze
Delays, in a gnatlike shimmering, in a fine
Illumined version of itself, decline,
And patter on the stones its own applause?

Although Wilbur prefers the fauns "at rest in fullness of desire / For what is given," his conclusion points to the residual spirituality of this preference; for the baroque sculpture figures a perfectly fulfilled unfulfillment from which we ourselves remain separate, and to which we can at best aspire with Franciscan devotion—a "dreamt land / Toward which all hungers leap, all pleasures pass.

In addition to being called down to the things of this world, we are thus committed to a "humble insatiety," a state explored with growing frequency in Wilbur's work. Whether in the drunken phrases of "A Voice from Under the Table" ("The end of thirst exceeds experience . . . Well I am down again, but not yet out. / O sweet frustrations, I shall be back for more"), or in the thoughtful essay on Emily Dickinson's "Sumptuous Destitution" (1959), Wilbur urges that privation may be our paradoxically enriching fate.

> The creature of appetite (whether insect or human) pursues satisfaction, and strives to possess the object in itself; it cannot imagine the vaster economy of desire, in which the pain of abstinence is justified by moments of infinite joy, and the object is spiritually possessed, not merely for itself, but more truly as an index of the All.

Wilbur's metaphorical unifications may thus be not only an imitation of the world's own single braid but also an expressive procedure and product of "the vaster economy of desire" that unifies things by virtue of its "profound perspective." Perhaps another name for this is love—the love that calls us to the things of this world, that relishes the light incarnate or the play of falling water, that moves Bruna Sandoval "For love and in all weathers" to keep the church of San Ysidro ("A Plain Song for Comadre"), and that enables the poet's eye to perceive angel feathers in the stained suds of Bruna's scrub water. Such love is at the far-from-complacent center of Wilbur's work, whose very intricate craft, no less than its metaphorical leaps, may well be the sign of its strenuous desire.

Desire can be kept sharp only by its perpetual defeat. Hence a deepening of Wilbur's early stress on the related insufficiency of language itself. Even metaphor must fail to apprehend its object, as in "Mind" or "An Event"—the challenge being to keep that failure a "graceful error." So, too, the mind should never relinquish its own dreaming, for it is precisely the "vain attempt" of imagination and metaphor that provides one of the "cross-purposes" by which "the world is dreamt." The cautionary fable "Merlin Enthralled" exposes the impoverished world of fact that survives after the enchanter's power is gone; and it is from "the blue unbroken reveries / Of the building dead" that even such an admittedly pragmatic structure as a railway station may arise ("For the New Railway Station in Rome"). Clearly, if love calls us to the things of this world, the answer to that call is what we make of such things—and therefore what we add to them:

> "What is our praise or pride
> But to imagine excellence, and try to make
> it?
> What does it say over the door of Heaven
> But *homo fecit*?"

It is at this high pitch of wit and confidence, with a strongly reinforced faith in the purpose and craft of his vocation—even to the point of supposing the fabrication of heaven—that Wilbur concludes his third book.

Things of This World received the National Book Award, the Pulitzer Prize, and the Edna St. Vincent Millay Memorial Prize. In 1957, *Poems 1943–1956* was published in London by Faber and Faber, and Wilbur was elected to the National Institute of Arts and Letters. While a professor of English at Wesleyan, he became general editor of the Laurel Poetry Series, was elected chancellor of the Academy of American Poets, and visited the Soviet Union as a cultural representative of the United States. In short, the years between Wilbur's third and fourth books of poetry—*Advice to a Prophet and Other Poems* appeared in 1961—brought not only great recognition but also a broadening of Wilbur's cultural presence as a poet. And the effects of this appear in the new poems. Almost half of them are spoken by a communal "we," and many of them assume the authority of deliberate instruction (as "advice" suggests). In some respects, Wilbur's poetic stance has thus widened to include a more social basis while also moving from states of responsiveness to exercises of responsibility. To be sure, Wilbur remains very much a lyric poet; but it is worth noticing his achievement of a socially tempered lyricism (marked by a more direct conversational style, greatly reinforced by his work in verse drama), and his unusual reclamation of the lyric's potential for a discreet and valuable didacticism.

These achievements were especially rare in American poetry after the late 1950's. Just as the descendental impulse in *Things of This World* (an impulse shared by many writers of the time, particularly after Lowell's *Life Studies*) was unfashionably braced by Wilbur's dramatic spiritual impulse and affirmative demeanor, so the personal accents of Wilbur's lyric speech paradoxically stand out through their supple inclusions of social address and by their potentially communal as well as communicable nature. During a decade in which lyric poetry became either increasingly introverted and private, on the one hand, or a socially oriented toward objectivism, myth, or "deep image," on the other, Wilbur's work thus attained a distinction that should not be overlooked. This socially tempered (often first person plural) lyricism, and a regained capacity for lyric didacticism, should be counted among Wilbur's contributions to the poetry of his time.

Confirming the importance of verse drama to Wilbur's development of a more immediate conversational address, *Advice to a Prophet* includes an excerpt from Molière's *Tartuffe* (a segment that nicely negotiates the demands of rhymed couplets and of rapid dialogue). The volume opens with a debate in direct speech, "Two Voices in a Meadow," matched later by "The Aspen and the Stream." In the former, an apparent divergence between the floating milkweed and the unmoving stone is mediated by their shared (and symmetrically phrased) submission to their own natures, and thereby to their place in a shared scheme both of nature and of divinity. Emblematic of Wilbur's new work, this debate both sharpens dramatically assertive individual voices ("As casual as cowdung / Under the crib of God, / I lie where chance would have me, / Up to the ears in sod"), *and* sketches the "yield[ing]" of such voices to a greater common design.

"Advice to a Prophet" focuses precisely on communicative strategy, here the attuning of prophetic utterance to its audience. Maintaining a dramatic intensity, the poem is spoken not by the isolated prophet but, rather, by one of the civic community ("When you come, as you soon must, to the streets of our city"). This crucial strategic move suggests an important element of Wilbur's own evolving stance—here designed to mediate, as if from within the social sphere, between the isolated knowledge or sensibility of the prophet and the communal need of a society.

The need for this kind of mediating (rather than "mad-eyed") speaker is urgently historical—as is the content of his speech, which is also personal, since it focuses on how we may affectively (hence effectively) be made to experience the abstract threat of nuclear war. This public lyric is therefore designed to enhance our fear and our belief, to make our emotions capable of registering what otherwise leaves us dangerously numb. And the emphasis pursues a distinctly lyric turn from the obvious facts to a more subjective, indeed poetic, truth regarding our dependence on the natural world for images of our best selves. To threaten nature is to threaten the mirror and language by which we figure forth our courage, our love, and our spiritual identity:

> Ask us, prophet, how we shall call
> Our natures forth when that live tongue is
> all
> Dispelled, that glass obscured or broken
>
> In which we have said the rose of our love
> and the clean
> Horse of our courage, in which beheld
> The singing locust of the soul unshelled,
> And all we mean or wish to mean.

Countering several forms of dangerous isolation, "Advice to a Prophet" thus reforges links between the citizen and the prophet, the human and the natural world, as well as between a personal and a historical domain. It is an integrative poem against selfishness—or, rather, a poem that reveals how even self-interest requires the safeguarding of otherness. In this respect the poem advances Wilbur's thematic and stylistic concerns; and several other poems in *Advice to a Prophet* similarly set examples of interdependence and cooperation against kinds of blind selfishness.

"The Undead" is one such poem, a portrait of demonic vampires whose possessive fear of life and loss has dispossessed them of both selfhood and vitality, leaving them in the condition of mere predators forever isolated from their prey. But the poem's didactic intent, well balanced by the vivid and amusing gothicism of its vampire lore, goes beyond condemnation. By calling on our sympathy, it seeks to avoid our potentially self-isolating or predatory attitude toward the undead. We must go beyond merely using them for our own edification:

> Nevertheless, their pain is real,
> And requires our pity. Think how sad it
> must be
> To thirst always for a scorned elixir,
> The salt quotidian blood
>
> Which, if mistrusted, has no savor;
> To prey on life forever and not possess it,
> As rock-hollows, tide after tide,
> Glassily strand the sea.

The sympathy of this appeal is intriguing, particularly when viewed alongside other poems in which Wilbur points to the inherent "insatiety" of both language and human desire—their inability to possess their objects. ("The Undead" appeared in *The New Yorker* just two months after "Ballade for the Duke of Orléans," whose refrain varies the line "*I die of thirst, here at the fountain-side.*") Perhaps the demons of "The Undead" are uneasily close to those of poetry itself, even while the poem explores the very danger that Wilbur's current development seeks to avoid. Not unlike earlier rebuttals of abstract spirituality, "The Undead" summons in order to acknowledge as well as to exorcise. If its stylizations, rhetoric, and voice make a dominant element of the lyric poem inherently self-isolating and self-regarding (whether as New Critical icon or as confessional cry), Wilbur's strength is to point the lyric away from the dangers of "utter self-concern."

Once noticed, the positive motif of self-yielding emerges in such diverse poems as "October Maples, Portland," "A Fire-Truck," "The Aspen and the Stream," the inventively parabolic "Shame," and the haunting "Fall in Corrales." The communal speaker of the last comes to "Stand in the wind and, bowing to this time, / Practise the candor of our bones." Beyond the play of bone whiteness and truth, Wilbur speaks of a more-than-intellectual practice—a submission not just to forces beyond us but also to other than merely rational powers or susceptibilities within the self. This may lead to the uncanny or surreal underworlds glimpsed in "Stop," "Junk," and "A Hole in the Floor" (the last quoted below):

For God's sake, what am I after?
Some treasure, or tiny garden?
Or that untrodden place,
The house's very soul,
Where time has stored our footbeats
And the long skein of our voices?

Not these, but the buried strangeness
Which nourishes the known:
That spring from which the floor-lamp
Drinks now a wilder bloom,
Inflaming the damask love-seat
And the whole dangerous room.

Here Wilbur returns to that domain of estrangement noticed since his earliest work. This is the idiosyncratic vision, however adjusted between the singular "I" and the "long skein of our voices," that lurks as a crucial presence below what might otherwise have been the too secure floorboards of Wilbur's poetry. Beneath either domesticity or sociability, this nourishing genie also bewilders, inflames, and endangers. In its curious light, we may now recognize how even the carefully public "Advice to a Prophet" depends on reckoning the right degree of strangeness in order to conjure "an undreamt thing." And (despite the book's conclusion with the communal and reconciliatory "A Christmas Hymn") no reading of *Advice to a Prophet,* or of Wilbur's increasingly complex work at large, can afford to slight this haunting and nearly unassimilable element—hushed and resistant in "Another Voice," hideously threatening in "Someone Talking to Himself":

Off in the fathomless dark
Beyond the verge of love
I saw blind fishes move,
And under a stone shelf
Rode the recusant shark—
Cold, waiting, himself.

The commingling of a direct, instructive address with an element of strangeness or psychological exploration marks the title poem and several others in *Walking to Sleep* (1969). And Wilbur's experimental widening of his own repertoire beyond the New Critical lyric argument-poem now extends to several narrative works, including "The Agent," a disturbing story in blank verse. So, too, he further diversifies his own voice by means of almost a dozen translations, each of which displays Wilbur's characteristic humility, fidelity, and virtuosity as a translator while also allowing him to write in a manner sometimes very different from his own.

Clearly, Wilbur's talent is restlessly continuing to test and extend itself. Matching or driving these changes, there is also a deepening of vision. *Walking to Sleep* not only ranges more widely to encompass the perspectives of geology, astronomy, and myth; such rangings frequently respond to various intensified states of alarm—fear, insomnia, anxiety. Although still generally affirmative, this is a more troubled book, and Wilbur's capacity for cheer or comfort preserves itself only by the most arduous endeavor.

The opening poem, "The Lilacs," warns of what will come. Set in the insistent, alliterative pattern of Old English verse, but with the lines broken, like the lilacs,

. . . stark, spindly,
                    and in staggered file,
Like walking wounded
                    from the dead of winter

the poem dwells with great violence on the lilacs' return to blossom:

Out of present pain
                    and from past terror
Their bullet-shaped buds
                    came quick and bursting,
As if they aimed
                    to be open with us!

What is fascinating here is not only the emphatic torment and near-military threat but also the gathering focus on the act of disclosure. As the poem continues, it suggests a reference both to a return to poetry (underscored by the poem's placement) and to the way Wilbur's poems themselves may ask to be read. In this regard, "Lilacs" may be both an act of reopening and a manifesto, especially to those readers whose superficial response to Wilbur's elegance or reticence has prevented them from recognizing how such effects not only may derive from but also may essentialize or transfigure states of unease, silence, or perceived mortality:

These lacquered leaves
where the light paddles
And the big blooms
buzzing among them
Have kept their counsel,
conveying nothing
Of their mortal message,
unless one should measure
The depth and dumbness
of death's kingdom
By the pure power
of this perfume.

We may ask why Wilbur's admission of torment or threat has deepened in this new book. The second poem, "On the Marginal Way," offers one significant answer: It is "the time's fright within me which distracts / Least fancies into violence." Accounting for a sudden fall into fantasies of holocaustal violence (he is viewing boulders strewn along a beach), the speaker implies an era of both nuclear threat and intensifying conventional warfare that must have revived his own memories of mass violence ("The Agent" returns to World War II). This is the decade of Hecht's *The Hard Hours* and Lowell's *For the Union Dead*; and Wilbur soon wrote "A Miltonic Sonnet" to castigate President Lyndon Johnson for the crassness and brutal imperialism that were imposing their "cattle-brand" on the American psyche as much as upon the victimized small nations.

As one might expect, Wilbur attempts to press back against "the time's fright within me." Apart from the rather uncharacteristic political satire of "A Miltonic Sonnet," his strategy involves a vigorous turn to a world beyond either the individual self or the human domain. Thus "On the Marginal Way" moves to "take cover in the facts," although this means turning away from a fantasy based on historical fact ("Auschwitz' final kill") to a different order of fact—the actual rocks on the beach, and their geological history. By a dramatic lengthening of perspective beyond that of human history, Wilbur reaches a vision of creation by which to offset the nightmare of human destruction, and in which to resituate and renew our human origins. The strewn boulders now seem "Comely as Eve and Adam, near a sea / Transfigured by the sun's return"; and this regenerative news may now counterpoise the "tidings of some dirty war." Pointedly, this perspective requires the kind of imaginative self-yielding noticed in *Advice to a Prophet.* Now the intent has become more purgatorial, and its earnest perfection and joy are carefully framed by prayer:

Though, high above the shore
On someone's porch, spread wings of
newsprint flap
The tidings of some dirty war,
It is a perfect day: the waters clap
Their hands and kindle, and the gull in
flight
Loses himself at moments, white in white,

And like a breaking thought
Joy for a moment floods into the mind,
Blurting that all things shall be brought
To the full state and stature of their kind,
By what has found the manhood of this
stone.
May that vast motive wash and wash our
own.

In addition to internalized historical fear, there is an increasingly intimate attention in Wilbur's new work to threats of aging and death, on both a personal and a planetary scale. And here again, Wilbur's resistant equilibrium depends on a depth of perspective that "takes cover" in the facts of botanical or astronomical time. In this way his work expands to the far-reaching movements of "Fern-Beds in Hampshire Country," "In the Field," "Seed Leaves," and "Under Cygnus" while also doing justice to the intimate losses and fears of "For Dudley" and "Running."

"I am part of that great going, / Though I stroll now, and am watchful." These lines, from the third section of "Running" ("Dodwells Road"), with their echo of Hardy's "The Going" and their matured version of Wilbur's own original vigilance, characterize much of Wilbur's work from this time forward. They introduce a somber meditation on inevitable exhaustions and losses, from which Wilbur shakes free only by turning once again with a benedictory offering to the world beyond him and to the generation that will survive him. The direct, colloquial language—Wilbur now grafting his dramatic skills onto the heart of the lyric—is part of that urgent breakthrough:

> But why in the hell spoil it?
> I make a clean gift of my young running
> To the two boys who break into view. . . .

"Walking to Sleep" is by no means directly autobiographical. Instructing an insomniac on the art of falling asleep, the speaker refers more to his addressee than to himself; and his own position is the purportedly impersonal and controlled stance of the teacher. Yet the poem's psychological focus gives it an introverted cast, while the speaker's generously elaborated knowledge—complete with the kinds of fear and watchfulness found in adjacent poems—does seem to derive from personal experience. The instructional stance, like the poem's wit and expatiatory largess, may itself be a compensation, a version and attempted self-application of the suggested cure. Perhaps this instructor is speaking to himself.

The lesson is couched in a suave and ample blank verse, which promotes the careful relaxation, the fluent transitions, and the sense of surfeit conducive to sleep. And yet, despite its humor, the poem is shot through with images of violence and horror, sleep being at one point wooed as the "kind assassin [who] will draw a bead / And blow your brains out." We are still within the region of "On the Marginal Way," but the angle of presentation has grown more inwardly acute and the fears more persecutory—to the point of near-paranoia. One is trapped in the remorseless self-gaze of the insomniac; there is no easy access to the "cover" of external fact. Rather, the path to sleep must lead to an uncovering of "your dearest horror," for only by bringing such horrors to consciousness can the mind undo the defensiveness that keeps it awake. The poem cannot end without leading its supposed addressee to the "crossroads and its laden gallows tree," where he must "lift your gaze and stare your brother down, / Though the swart crows have pecked his sockets hollow." Though he craves sleep, perhaps this is what the insomniac most fears: to hang suspended, eyeless, dead to the world.

For a poet as wakeful and visually observant as Wilbur (we may think back to the night guard of "First Snow in Alsace," whose open eyes oppose the snow-filled eyes of the dead), this figure might be especially haunting. Horribly twinned to the insomniac, he might indeed be a demon relative of the dark genie that haunts and perhaps even motivates Wilbur's generally bright work. Inseparable from Wilbur's celebratory "wit and wakefulness," the unease of this far-from-calm agent may thus be fathomed moving not only throughout "Walking to Sleep" but also beneath the composed surface of the poem's destination—"a pool / On whose calm face all images whatever / Lay clear, unfathomed, taken as they came."

In another formal departure, "The Agent" extends Wilbur's mastery of blank verse to a narrative about an American agent dropped behind enemy lines during World War II. Sent to prepare the destruction of a European town, he carries out his mission with deft professionalism. The story is told with unfussed and vivid detail; but what gives the poem its luster, and its menace, is the complex way in which the apparent detachment of the third-person narrative nevertheless allows the entire event to unfold from the agent's point of view. Hence the distance between agent and narrator is reduced—a reduction intensified by the portrait of the agent's near-poetic gifts: his linguistic skill attuned to dialectal nuance, his finely honed senses, his creative ability to forge a self (as Wilbur now forges the identity of the agent). This is not to suggest that the poem is a self-portrait but, rather, to explore what investment Wilbur might have had in writing this unique narrative.

In a crucial phrase, the agent is said to "savor and betray." Since few would question Wilbur's savoring fidelities, perhaps the agent fascinates by his antithetical nature—he is the faithful poet's nightmare. But what if there were a yet more intimate fascination? What if Wilbur were still haunted by his early insight that even the most faithful celebration, if cast in a poetry as rich in metaphor as his own, betrays its literal subject? "Praise in Summer" had asked "why this mad *instead* / Perverts our praise to uncreation, why / Such savor's in this wrenching things awry." How is that "uncreation" different from destruction?—a question Wallace Stevens also faced. Is Wilbur wrestling, however obliquely, with the demon that accuses those writers who most strongly savor this world, but who have nevertheless crossed what Seamus Heaney has called "the frontier of writing"? In a similar vein, we may read more intimately into the poem's final portrait not only of betrayal ("a pure impostor / Faithless to everything") but also of the agent's irremediable exile between worlds (recall the early "Water Walker") and his self-punitive fantasy of execution by his own side. However literally remote from Wilbur, the agent's work and fate thus take on a minatory fascination—one that marks "The Mind-Reader," just as versions of its enmeshments exercise the canny and uncanny "Lying."

Walking to Sleep includes a section of translations; and while the task of translation may provoke its own anxieties about fidelity and betrayal, Wilbur's versions of poems by Jorge Luis Borges, Andrei Voznesensky, François Villon, and others are scrupulously faithful without sacrificing an equivalent fluency or formal rigor within his own language. Unlike Lowell's "Imitations," Wilbur's translations follow his preference elsewhere for honoring a world beyond the ego, as well as for tempering his private voice to accommodate a shareable speech. Still, his selections are motivated; and it is probably that the feverish surreality of Voznesensky and the earthy valedictions of Villon will allow Wilbur both to speak in ways that his own more equable and decorous temperament seldom allows, and to continue to stretch the limits of his own work.

Wilbur has said of his translations of Molière and Racine, "It can help you to broaden your expressive range. . . . Translating drama involves impersonation, the imitation of attitudes and emotions. There's undoubtedly some transference from such practice to one's own work; more of oneself becomes articulate." Broadening his expressive range, Wilbur's continuing translations of Molière have further sharpened the dramatic as well as the social edge of his own lyrics, while also providing a vehicle for his comedic war against rigidities of all kinds. These prize-winning and popular works (*The Misanthrope, Tartuffe, Candide, The Learned Ladies*) are among the few successful verse dramas to be performed in our time. Accompanied by Wilbur's illuminating prefaces, they have much to tell us of both the original dramatist and the translator.

The 1970's brought Wilbur further acclaim: several poetry awards, honorary degrees, the presidency and then successive chancellorships of the American Academy of Arts and Letters. Such recognition increased through the 1980's, culminating in his appointment as second poet laureate of the United States. Yet his work shows no sign of resting on such laurels, either in theme or in method. On the contrary, *The Mind-Reader* (1976) includes the unprecedented long dramatic monologue of the title poem, as well as several works of a newly autobiographical nature—the mordant narrative in quatrains ("Piccola Commedia"), poems addressed to members of his family ("The Writer" and "A Wedding Toast"), a haiku on sleeplessness ("Sleepless at Crown Point"), and the poem "In Limbo," which brings a more private urgency to Wilbur's fascination with states of disorientation, self-loss, imposture, homeless borderings between the worlds of sleeping and waking, spirit and flesh. With such innovations, Wilbur follows the example of the trees in "A Black Birch in Winter":

> New wood, new life, new compass, greater girth,
> And this is all their wisdom and their art—
> To grow, stretch, crack, and not yet come apart.

No matter how autobiographical, Wilbur's poems never approximate the confessional verse of many of his contemporaries. Avoiding the unprotected immediacies of Lowell, Berryman, or Plath (he explicitly distances himself from Plath, however sympathetically, in "Cottage Street, 1953"), he joins such masters of oblique or mediated disclosure as Elizabeth Bishop, James Merrill, and Anthony Hecht. While poems like "Walking to Sleep," "The Agent," and "The Mind-Reader" objectify certain issues that interest him, the exact nature and degree of that interest cannot be narrowly specified. At least three advantages result: a rewarding complexity, a portrayal of traits or dilemmas shared by persons other than the poet, and a certain largess and buoyancy in the independent detailing and mood of the work. Even when penetrating psychological depths, Wilbur's commitment is always to a world "Not governed by me only."

"The Mind-Reader" is one of Wilbur's most suave and beguiling works—although such qualities, associated with his own charms as a poet, are now ironically displayed as part of the dubious wares of a somewhat seedy and perhaps alcoholic telepathist. In an effortlessly sinuous blank verse, so caressing and flexible that it seems to be telepathically attuned to the listener's mind, the speaker confesses the origins and practice of his work. He opens with a mesmerizing fugue on the subject of loss:

> Some things are truly lost. Think of a sun-hat
> Laid for the moment on a parapet
> While three young women—one, perhaps, in mourning—
> Talk in the crenellate shade. A slight wind plucks
> And budges it; it scuffs to the edge and cartwheels
> Into a giant view of some description:
> Haggard escarpments, if you like, plunge down
> Through mica shimmer to a moss of pines
> Amidst which, here or there, a half-seen river
> Lobs up a blink of light. The sun-hat falls,
> With what free flirts and stoops you can imagine,
> Down through that reeling vista or another,
> Unseen by any, even by you or me.
> It is as when a pipe-wrench, catapulted
> From the jounced back of a pick-up truck, dives headlong
> Into a bushy culvert; or a book
> Whose reader is asleep, garbling the story,
> Glides from beneath a steamer chair and yields
> Its flurried pages to the printless sea.

This luxuriously ravishing passage, whose every amenability is a carefully manipulated solicitation, binds the listener to a doubly motivated account: the speaker is in love with such losses, and these "truly lost" objects contrastively introduce those which his powers *can* retrieve. By an irony that is surely relevant to the poet, the most uncanny and, hence, powerful aspect of the mind reader's gift is precisely what disempowers and entraps him. It is this terrible dispossession, even more than the subsequent confessions of occasional charlatanism, that make Wilbur's poem one of the most arresting among other typically postmodern ironizations of the ancient topos of inspiration:

> I tell you this
> Because you know that I have the gift, the burden.
> Whether or not I put my mind to it,
> The world usurps me ceaselessly; my sixth
> And never-resting sense is a cheap room
> Black with the anger of insomnia,
> Whose wall-boards vibrate with the mutters, plaints,
> And flushings of the race.

"Black with the anger of insomnia." Hence, as in "Walking to Sleep," a longing for release—figured as the place where "the book is drowned." And, like Prospero requesting that his audience's "indulgence set me free," the speaker solicits (telepathically of course—"Ah, you have read my mind") another mezzo-litro to bring him closer to oblivion. This last ploy shrewdly extends the speaker's self-subversions to the reader: if the mind reader is the victim of his compulsions, are we (who have now come to share a version of his gift: to obey his solicitations, and to support his habit) any less addicted in our listenings? If the mind reader is a figure for the tyrannical aspects of a poet's genie, what kind of grip does he have on our own need for uncanny retrievals and prophecies? If habitual readers of poetry are any less addicted than the poets, it may be only a matter of degree. The closing words of this "studious" drinker are "Grazie, professore."

"The Writer" also attends to a painfully compelled travail; and by a characteristic self-revision (itself evincing the kind of work he describes), Wilbur surpasses his metaphor-wish that his daughter have a "lucky passage" in the craft of her art. Recalling a trapped starling that had battered itself "humped and bloody" before managing to escape through a window, he acknowledges, "It is always a matter, my darling, / Of life or death, as I had forgotten. I wish / What I wished you before, but harder." The blend of tact, patience, and passion is typically Wilbur's, as is the arduously engaged spiritual dimension of the poem, linked as it is to the writer's quest: "our spirits rose" on seeing the bird "clearing the sill of the world."

New and Collected Poems (1988) breaks yet further ground. It does so in at least three directions. First, there is the adventurous experiment "On Freedom's Ground," a cantata in celebration of the Statue of Liberty. Here Wilbur's gift for writing a communal lyric utterance tests itself against the challenges of a musical setting and the hazards of potential simplicity or sentimentality. The poem succeeds by its formal versatility, its graceful (and democratic) interweaving of ceremonial and colloquial language, and its related modulations among retrospect, praise, critique, mourning, and continuing aspiration.

A second departure, "Lying," takes Wilbur's blank verse into the realm of the meditative essay while furthering his long and frank exploration of some of the more troubling motives and premises of poetry's ineradicably fictive nature. Since the early "Praise in Summer," the issue has teased or haunted a number of poems; now it reaches its most rewarding trial, crossed as it is with Wilbur's equally challenging fascination with fidelity. The poem ends with the paradoxical proof that even the great images of fidelity, like that of Roland, are the work of fiction, or have been shaped by the benign infidelity of the image maker. Whether lying to enliven a dead party—a resurrective act, depending on its own genetic fiat (of an unseen bird)—or resorting to lies about art's tempering of brutality (Chiron teaching Achilles the art of the lyre), or fabricating the scene of our own origins and fall, poetry has always been an uncanny and ungrounded trick of deception. At times the duplicity of words, exaggerated as it is by the medium of poetry itself, would seem to be the original double agent, the liar in the lyre, the faker in the inscription *homo fecit* over the door of heaven.

Finally, Wilbur broaches a new response to the pressures of time and mortality. Several new poems continue to celebrate acts of self-yielding, but do so now with a consistent stress on the generative nature of such acts. The figures of the milkweed and the aspen had offered early versions of this; but now—as if against the threat or limit of individual mortality—Wilbur offers images of finite creatures giving up their bound identities, thereby prolonging or transforming their life force into further incarnations. A dominant new figure is that of dissemination. In "All That Is":

> Under some clipped euonymus, a mush-
> room,
> Bred of an old and deep mycelium
> As hidden as the webwork of thc world,
> Strews on the shifty night-wind, rising now,
> A cast of spores as many as the stars.

Hence a different mode of release: instead of the escape into oblivion, an invigorating dispersal toward new life and to a renewed weaving of the webs of creation and of language—this poem is largely an ode to crossword puzzles, which, like poems, provide a "rite of finitude" by which to conjure and braid a world beyond the puzzle.

The disseminative image of strewn spores matches that of the "loose change" in "Icarium Mare," or the "sifting" of the fire bush in "Alatus," or of the shadblow in "Shad-Time," where once again the links are made to the mind and to an art associated with poetry:

> The shadblow's white racemes
> Burst here or there at random, scaled with red,
> As when the spitting fuse of dreams
> Lights in a vacant head,
>
> Or as the Thracian strings,
> Descending past the bedrock's muted staves,
> Picked out the signatures of things
> Even in death's own caves.

"Rites of finitude" would be a good term for Wilbur's poems, provided that one recognizes both their air of spontaneous improvisation and their homage to what lies infinitely beyond them. Despite their maturity, these late poems are in many ways his most youthful, charged with the joyful and rejuvenating participation in a more-than-finite life force. With an astonishing litheness that marks their "wide-deploying motives of delight," these poems seem to imitate the transformative fluencies of a subject that "Instant by instant chooses to / Affirm itself and flow."

Just as such affirmations go beyond the finite self, so they require a more than cognitive or merely aesthetic faculty and motive. Wilbur seems to have found a way to suggest a combination of physical thrust and intuitive surmise. In the brilliant, death-tinged "Alatus," he writes:

> See how the fire-bush, circled
> By a crimson verge
> Of its own sifting,
> Bristles aloft its every
> Naked stem, lifting
>
> Beyond the faint sun,
> Toward the hid pulse of things, its
> Winged skeleton.

Such resurrective bristling thus comes as much from the bone as from the mind. Or from the deepest region of the mind, beneath intellection. Giving up certainty, being caught into a more than individual identity—this is the "rite / Or masque, or long charade / Where we, like these, / Had blundered into grand / Identities" ("Leaving"). Just as it is the true catch in "Trolling for Blues," where the bluefish breaks free from its first metaphoric identity to pull the fisherman toward a revision of his own:

> He is a type of coolest intellect,
>
> Or is so to the mind's blue eye until
> He strikes and runs unseen beneath the rip,
> Yanking imagination back and down
> Past recognition to the unlit deep
> Of the glass sponges, of chiasmodon,
>
> Of the old darkness of Devonian dream,
> Phase of a meditation not our own,
> That long mêlée where selves were not, that life
> Merciless, painless, sleepless, unaware,
> From which, in time, unthinkably we rose.

In their own striking and running to the long melee past recognition, and in their bringing of language itself into a disseminating flow of vitality—as if the words themselves were racemes, spores, or strewn stars—Wilbur's most recent poems thus seem to challenge any confident definition of the limits and artificiality of poetry. They may be rites of finitude, but the enactment of their rituals summons or joins for a moment something unlimited and wild. And if there must remain a border between their closed (because manifest) identities and the unassimilable multiplicity of life beyond them, that border works more as a lure than as an aesthetic device. Along with his darker genie, it is this bright margin and lure that will no doubt keep drawing Wilbur to his remarkably joyful and unappeased pursuit. As he asks in "Hamlen Brook":

How shall I drink all this?

Joy's trick is to supply
Dry lips with what can cool and slake,
Leaving them dumbstruck also with an ache
Nothing can satisfy.

Selected Bibliography

WORKS OF RICHARD WILBUR

POETRY

The Beautiful Changes and Other Poems, (New York: Reynal & Hitchcock, 1947).

Ceremony and Other Poems, (New York: Harcourt, Brace, 1950).

Things of This World, (London: Harcourt, Brace, 1956).

Poems 1943–1956, (London: Faber & Faber, 1957).

Advice to a Prophet and Other Poems, (New York: Harcourt, Brace & World, 1961).

Loudmouse, (New York: Crowell-Collier, 1963).

The Poems of Richard Wilbur, (New York: Harcourt, Brace & World, 1963).

Walking to Sleep: New Poems and Translations, (New York: Harcourt Brace Jovanovich, 1969).

Digging for China: A Poem, (Garden City, N.Y.: Doubleday, 1970).

Opposites, (New York: Harcourt Brace Jovanovich, 1973).

Seed Leaves: Homage to R. F., (Boston: David Godine, 1974).

The Mind-Reader: New Poems, (New York: Harcourt Brace Jovanovich, 1976).

Seven Poems, (Omaha: Abattoir Editions, 1981).

New and Collected Poems, (San Diego: Harcourt Brace Jovanovich, 1988).

PROSE

Responses: Prose Pieces 1953–1976, (New York: Harcourt Brace Jovanovich, 1976).

Elizabeth Bishop: A Memorial Tribute, (New York: Albondocani Press, 1982).

"Advice from the Muse," (Deerfield, Conn.: The Deerfield Press, 1981).

TRANSLATED WORKS

The Misanthrope, by Molière (New York: Harcourt, Brace, 1955).

Candide, by Voltaire Translated with others (New York: Random House, 1957).

Tartuffe, by Molière (New York: Harcourt, Brace and World, 1963).

The School for Wives, by Molière (New York: Harcourt Brace Jovanovich, 1971).

The Learned Ladies, by Molière (New York: Harcourt Brace Jovanovich, 1978).

Molière: Four Comedies, (New York: Harcourt Brace Jovanovich, 1982).

The Whale and Other Uncollected Translations, (Brockport, N.Y.: BOA Editions, 1982).

Phaedra, by Racine (San Diego: Harcourt Brace Jovanovich, 1986).

MANUSCRIPT PAPERS

Apart from some early manuscripts in the Poetry Collection, Lockwood Memorial Library, State University of New York at Buffalo, the primary archive of Wilbur's papers is in the Robert Frost Library, Amherst College. This extensive collection includes poetry, translations and adaptations, and miscellaneous papers.

BIBLIOGRAPHY

Field, John P., *Richard Wilbur: A Bibliographical Checklist,* (Kent, Ohio: Kent State University Press, 1971). Lists both primary and secondary works.

BIOGRAPHICAL AND CRITICAL STUDIES

BOOKS

Conversations with Richard Wilbur, Butts, William, ed. (Jackson: University Press of Mississippi, 1990). An indispensable collection of interviews (1962–1988) with a biographical chronology.

Hill, Donald L., *Richard Wilbur,* (New York: Twayne, 1967).

Contemporary American Poetry, Poulin, A., Jr., ed. 2nd ed. (Boston: Houghton Mifflin, 1975). Pp. 391–405

Richard Wilbur's Creation, Salinger, Wendy, ed. (Ann Arbor: University of Michigan Press, 1983). A collection of reviews and essays that includes a bibliography of secondary works.

Wallace, Robert, *Writing Poems,* (Boston: Little, Brown, 1982) 302–309.

ARTICLES

Bogan, Louise, "Verse," *The New Yorker,* (November 15, 1947). Pp. 130, 133–134.

Ciardi, John, "Our Most Melodic Poet," *The Saturday Review,* (August 18, 1956). Pp. 18–19.

Farrell, John P., "The Beautiful Changes in Richard Wilbur's Poetry," *Contemporary Literature* 12: 74–87 (Winter 1971).

Hall, Donald, "Claims on the Poet," *Poetry* 88: 398–403 (September 1956).

Hecht, Anthony, "The Motions of the Mind," *Times Literary Supplement* no. 3923: 602 (May 20, 1977).

Hecht, Anthony, "Master of Metaphor," *The New Republic,* (May 16, 1988). Pp. 25, 27–30, 32.

Jarrell, Randall, "A View of Three Poets," *Partisan Review* 18: 691–700 (November–December 1951).

Jarrell, Randall, "Fifty Years of American Poetry," *Prairie Schooner* 37: 1–27 (Spring 1963).

Jensen, Ejner J., "Encounters with Experience: The Poems of Richard Wilbur," *New England Review* 2: 594–613 (Summer 1980).

Leithauser, Brad, "Reconsideration: Richard Wilbur. America's Master of Formal Verse," *The New Republic,* (March 24, 1982). Pp. 28–31.

McClatchy, J. D., "Dialects of the Tribe," *Poetry* 130: 41–53 (April 1977). Includes a review of Wilbur's *Mind-Reader.*

Mills, Ralph J., Jr., "The Lyricism of Richard Wilbur," *Modern Age* 6: 436–440 (Fall 1962).

Nemerov, Howard, "What Was Modern Poetry? Three Lectures," in his *Figures of Thought: Speculations on the Meaning of Poetry and Other Essays* (Boston: David Godine, 1978). See Lecture 3 "What Will Suffice," pp. 183–198.

Oliver, Raymond, "Verse Translation and Richard Wilbur," *The Southern Review* Baton Rouge 11: 318–330 (April 1975).

Sayre, Robert F., "A Case for Richard Wilbur as a Nature Poet," *Moderna Spraak* 61: 114–122 (1967).

Taylor, Henry, "Two Worlds Taken as They Come: Richard Wilbur's 'Walking to Sleep'," *The Hollins Critic* 6: 1–12 (July 1969).

Weatherhead, A. K., "Richard Wilbur: Poetry of Things," *ELH* 35: 606–617 (1968).

William Carlos Williams
(1883–1963)

JOHN MALCOLM BRINNIN

Among the poets of his own illustrious generation, William Carlos Williams was the man on the margin, the incorrigible maverick, the embattled messiah. During the years when T. S. Eliot, Ezra Pound, Wallace Stevens, Marianne Moore, and E. E. Cummings were departing from traditional English practice in ways that stamped the character of American poetry in the twentieth century, Williams quite by himself was trying to impart to poetry a new substance and a violent new orientation. Something in his blood that was not in theirs had already made him the more congenial fellow of strangers who, unknown to him, were shaping in the rickety garrets of Montmartre the artifacts and totems of a new era. In secret alliance with little known painters, he nevertheless became famous along with his literary contemporaries and still tends to be indiscriminately categorized with them in the annals of poetry. But as modern poetry consolidates its academic position and ceases to challenge the young and adventurous, the singularity of Williams' contribution is being discovered, rediscovered, and put to uses that presage the most striking development in American poetry since J. Alfred Prufrock rolled the bottoms of his trousers and listened to the mermaids.

From the moment of his first adult recognition of himself as a poet, Williams built his career on opposition—opposition to every form of poetry that depends on meter or rhyme or any other device that, to his mind, served only to falsify the experience it would transcribe—opposition to every kind of thinking that orders itself in generalities rather than submits to the hazards of unwieldy particulars. He continually put forth theories that sounded like sweeping new programs for the whole art of poetry but which turned out to be merely new formulations of the private practice of William Carlos Williams. He railed against T. S. Eliot as though he were disaster incarnate, and against the scholars who explicated Eliot as though they were members of some nefarious academic cabal. His poetic disciples included from time to time such younger masters as Theodore Roethke and Robert Lowell, as well as a whole rag, tag, and bobtail succession of meagerly talented iconoclasts who thought that by assuming his freedom they might somehow inherit his integrity. In either case, Williams greeted them all with the zeal of a salvationist embracing new converts. In pursuit of the antagonisms that kept him young through a creative span of more than fifty years, he fumed, proclaimed, and shook his head with an air of nettled divinity. But while his theories indicate that, as critic and prophet, he was often narrow in outlook, preoccupied with repetitions of the obvious, old-fashioned in his persistent "newness," his poems unequivocally excuse and justify all his talk. As an aesthetic achievement in itself, the body of his work cannot be accorded less than major status. As an influence upon the development of a native American idiom, it stands beside, and will probably loom above, the celebrated contributions of Ezra Pound and T. S. Eliot.

The quest to which Williams addressed himself as early as 1912 is essentially the same as that to which his attention was turned five decades later: What is the measurable factor in language that will replace metrics as a basis for poetic composition? An apparently simple and exclusively technical point of inquiry, this question nevertheless involved for Williams the whole meaning of poetry. Since he believed that experience does not objectively exist until it is embodied in language, the nature of that language—its ability to convey actuality without distorting it through the crippling biases of "literary" means—is all-important. Far more by example than by precept, Williams demonstrated that there are moments and phases of experience that, by an economy of means so strict as to defy analysis, can be lifted from the meaningless flux of actuality into reality and significance. When this happens, all the ways and means that remain tangled and unresolved in his pronouncements are quite simply and convincingly documented in his poems.

The primary concerns of Williams—too clearly the applications of naive good sense and native intelligence to be canonized—were constant: to devise the poetic structure that would formalize experience without deforming it; to let the beat of speech determine the measure; to rinse the language of ornament and encrustation; to be scrupulously selective but to allow for accident and impingement. Philosophy and metaphysics to Williams had no place and no meaning apart from the structures by which they were expressed or could be deduced. "No ideas but in things," he said, and he believed that the poet's business is "not to talk in vague categories but to write particularly as a physician works, upon a patient, upon the thing before him, in the particular to discover the universal." *Discovery* is a key word in anything he undertakes—discovery of the relationship between actuality and the mind confronting it, discovery of the language that would in turn make that discovery "true" and communicable. Where his contemporaries adapted or rechanneled old forms of poetry, Williams, ignoring the shapes in which poetry had been cast, sought always to rediscover poetry itself. And yet his dismissal of entrenched forms of English poetry—his lifelong crusade against the iambic pentameter, for instance, and his endlessly burning scorn for the sonnet—should not blind his readers to the fact that his searchings and his concerns were exclusively directed toward formal solutions. Where other poets achieved a homespun celebrity by exploiting regional or "Americanese" subject matter, Williams pursued a far more difficult and less rewarding path. Taking his native scene as much for granted as the view from his office window, he used his gifts of perception to reconstitute it freshly. He resisted the antiquarian charms of folklore and the chauvinist pleasures of Americana to search for the rhythm in the American grain, the timeless in the momentary, the universal in the immediate and local. He thus escaped the sort of provincialism that might guarantee him a place in the academies and joined an international company of geniuses whose astonishing innovations in literature and the plastic arts parallel the twentieth century's great discoveries in physics.

William Carlos Williams was born on September 17, 1883, in Rutherford, New Jersey. His father was of pure English ancestry; his mother's family, settled on various islands of the Caribbean, contained elements of French, Spanish, and Jewish cultures. With his younger brother, Edward, Williams went to public schools in his home town, attended the Unitarian church, of which his father was a staunch pillar, and, when he was fourteen, went with his family to Europe for two years. There he attended the Château de Lancy near Geneva and, later, the Lycée Condorcet in Paris. Upon the family's return to the United States, he was sent to Horace Mann High School in New York City, to which he commuted daily by streetcar and Hudson River ferryboat. When he had decided on a career in medicine, he took the entrance examinations and, since in those years it was still possible to enter medical school without a degree, was admitted to the University of Pennsylvania Medical School. In Philadelphia his interest in poetry led him into acquaintance with the poets Ezra Pound and H. D. (Hilda Doolittle), and the painter Charles Demuth, all of whom became his lifelong friends.

After his graduation in 1906, he interned at the old French Hospital in New York City and later at the Nursery and Child's Hospital. His first poems, published at his own expense, appeared in 1909, and shortly afterwards he went abroad again, to Leipzig where he did postgraduate work in pediatrics. In Europe he renewed his friendship with Ezra Pound and through him was introduced to the literary life of prewar London and, on more than one occasion, to William Butler Yeats. After a brief period of travel in Italy and Spain, he returned to Rutherford to marry a local girl, Florence Herman, the "Flossie" of his poems, and to begin the practice of medicine. He became the father of two boys, William and Paul, during the next few years and when he bought the big old house at 9 Ridge Road his lifetime residence was established. A very active pediatrician with a wide practice among the industrial population of the region, Williams continued to be a deeply committed poet and a literary man happily caught up in the various cliques, publishing ventures, and general creative ferment that charged Greenwich Village in the years of World War I and after.

In 1924 he went to Europe with his wife for six months, a period of dazzling introductions and exhausting participation in the expatriate life of the movers and shakers of the American "lost generation" and their French counterparts. Ezra Pound was again his cicerone, along with the young publisher Robert McAlmon, and through them Williams associated with such people as Hemingway, Gertrude Stein, Sylvia Beach, Kay Boyle, Man Ray, George Antheil, and such members of the French literati as Valéry Larbaud and Philippe Soupault. In 1927 he made another European visit when he and his wife escorted their sons to school in Switzerland. He wrote a novel, *A Voyage to Pagany,* based on these visits, and in the course of it recorded his response to Paris: "Where *la France*? he cried within himself, as if expecting to see some symbolic image of joy rise from the ground and stride forward carrying flowers in her hand triumphantly. . . . Paris as a serious city, the beloved of men; Paris that releases what there is in men—the frivolity that means a knife cut through self-deception."

A prolific writer, Williams continued in the following years to apportion his talents among prose—short stories, essays, novels, an autobiography—poetry, and plays and, seemingly unaffected by constant professional demands and intrusions, to publish volumes eventually counted by the score. Turning over his medical practice to his son William in the middle 1950's, he devoted himself wholly to writing, with frequent appearances at colleges and universities to lecture and to read his poems. In 1949 he received an appointment to the Chair of Poetry at the Library of Congress. But this was withdrawn before he could assume his duties in Washington, partly because of accusations concerned with his supposed leftist sympathies, partly because of his old association with Ezra Pound who by then was committed to a psychiatric hospital after having been returned to America to stand trial as a traitor and propagandist for Italian fascism. In the same year he suffered the first of a series of strokes that eventually made him a semi-invalid. But in spite of consequent periods of difficulty with his vision and his speech, he continued to live a vigorous creative life and to travel in the United States and, on two occasions, to the Caribbean. He died at the age of seventy-nine, on March 4, 1963. Two months later he was posthumously awarded the Pulitzer Prize and the Gold Medal for Poetry of the National Institute of Arts and Letters.

While he always had the great admiration of many of his contemporaries, some of whom were highly influential in the literary world, general recognition came slowly to Williams. When it did come, however, he was the recipient of many awards, honorary degrees, and extensive critical appraisals—honors that merely certified in a public way the distinction for which he had been recognized by independent readers, by critics, and, even anti-academic Williams himself had finally to admit, by the many members of the teaching profession who for years sympathetically expounded his cause and promoted his reputation.

Keats was the first influence in Williams' career forceful enough to induce imitation; Whitman was the second. By the time he came to know Ezra Pound (during his freshman year at medical school), he had already completed a bulky manuscript of "studied Keatsian sonnets," an imitation of *Endymion,* and eighteen copybooks full of "quick spontaneous poems" whose free forms were derived from *Leaves of Grass,* which he didn't really like except for "Song of Myself." "Before meeting Ezra Pound," Williams said, "is like B.C. and A.D.," even though Pound showed notably little enthusiasm for the poems Williams offered for criticism. Pound's influence on Williams seems to have been mainly the communication of an attitude—an aesthete's concern for the primacy of art and a craftsman's concern for poetry as direct as speech and for lean, fresh expression at all costs, even at the cost of clarity. In other ways Pound influenced Williams by directing him to books that had formed Pound's own taste, and by praising Williams for his commendable independence, his "opacity" which he considered an un-American virtue, his refusal to cultivate "the magazine touch" and to accede to the demands of editors. Under Pound's influence and other stimuli, Williams was soon ready to close the door on the "studied elegance of Keats on one hand" and "the raw vigor of Whitman on the other." Keats had begun to seem intolerably archaic and Whitman, he came to feel, had foundered on an abstract idea of freedom, "an idea lethal to all order, particularly to that order which has to do with the poem" and had consequently "resorted to a loose sort of language with no discipline about it of any sort." Casting off his mentors, Williams continued to listen to Pound and to rummage through *Palgrave's Golden Treasury,* studying the models of the past, yet certain in his own mind that "If poetry had to be written, I had to do it my own way."

Many of his very early poems are almost indistinguishable from some of Pound's written during the same period. Both poets tended to write short aphoristic pieces studded with classical names and colored by an assumed mood of Alexandrian weariness. Frequently they adopted a courtly tone—sometimes daintily romantic, sometimes bluffly mocking—in poems addressing real or imaginary ladies; and in other poems they spoke with a roguish forthrightness, as though they were heroes out of some picaresque novel rather than modern men attempting to cut through the lacy conventions of parlor poesy. But within a very short time neither poet sounded like the other. Pound kept his wryness, his astringent understatement, his satire, and his cantankerousness. Williams maintained his capacity for surprise, his determination to meet life head-on; his naiveté remained fresh, his subject matter homely, his speech underlined for emphasis and riddled with punctuation marks.

The reformist movement known as Imagism had cleared the air at this period and its emphasis on direct apprehension of natural things and minor social phenomena was attractive to a man who had already foreseen that his best poetic strategy would be simply the deft, uncalculated transcription of what he saw and felt. Williams later looked upon his Imagist phase as a passing and tangential involvement, yet no other American poet—with perhaps the exception of H. D.—has written so many poems that can serve as models illustrating the Imagist canon. Concretion, exactitude, observation without comment, vulgar subject matter, common speech, homely details glittering with a mineral clarity—Williams exhibits them all and achieves over and over again that complexity of emotion within an instant of time that was the goal of the true Imagist. The tenets of Imagism gave him a sanction, and the loosely constituted Imagist "school" afforded him his first association with a group of poets consciously trying to find an idiom to oppose the stale metrics and mellifluous rhythms of the popular Georgian poets. But he soon became impatient with the limitations on structure that Imagism imposed. He believed that a focus on concrete imagery was a necessary step toward the rehabilitation of the poem, yet he felt that Imagism "lost its place finally because as a form it completely lacked structural necessity. The image served for everything so that the structure, a weaker and weaker free verse, degenerated into a condition very nearly resembling that of the sonnet."

Imagism was never for American poets quite the doctrinaire thing it was for a small group of English poets, notably those under the aegis of T. E. Hulme, its unofficial philosopher. Imagism nevertheless provided a healthy climate for a man of Williams' persuasions and a mode of expression in which his nervous sort of poetic shorthand seemed less idiosyncratic. He perhaps contributed to the movement as much as he learned from it, and helped to make it the crucible in which many talents far different from his own were refined. In any case, the spare hard smack of Imagist language is a note that echoes throughout his career. On poetry that had become muddy and stagnant, Imagism acted like an agent that clarifies a solution without seriously changing its chemical structure. While it undoubtedly helped Williams to define his own peculiar language, it did not serve his greater need for a broader and more viable sense of structure, a means of moving on from the miniature, Japanese-y organization of the typical Imagist poem. At the very time of his strongest Imagist affinities, a more important and longer lasting influence was already working in his poetic bloodstream. This influence came from the plastic arts—the American paintings from Philadelphia's "Black Gang" and from New York that foreshadowed a revolution in taste and subject matter, the Parisian paintings that pointed to a revolution in technique established by Impressionism and strengthened by the related developments of Fauvism, Cubism, and the various splinter movements to which the latter gave rise. "As I look back," Williams wrote decades later, "I think it was the French painters rather than the writers who influenced us, and their influence was very great. They created an atmosphere of release, color release, release from stereotyped forms, trite subjects." The impact of painting on many of Williams' poems dates from 1913, the year of the famous Armory Show which opened for Americans a broad window on the blocked-in landscapes of Cézanne, the swabbed-on colors and visual rhythms of Matisse, the constructions of Picasso. Meanwhile, he was swiftly evolving the technique which, once he had it wholly in his control, would make it register as uniquely as a signature.

When he dispensed with measure by count, with the assured music of rhyme and metrics that can buoy a poet's natural cadences, Williams had to depend completely on the simple rightness of his eye and ear. The success of any one of his poems came to depend on its movement, its line-to-line tensions, the tightrope-walking progress of an idea. In a typical Williams poem a notion is introduced, then sent off on a balancing act that involves interruptions, sudden twists and turns, moments of jeopardy when the wire goes slack, brief shifts of weight, tripping steps and sudden stops, and, finally, rest and poise. When this sense of performance is most alive in Williams, his poems give the illusion of the mind in the process of thinking. The reader has no sense of emotion recollected in tranquillity, but rather of emotion as a process—a living document of experience rather than a delayed report of experience. But when this sense of performance is least alive, he fails to keep the delicate relationship between actuality and reality on which the success of the poem depends and the result is a note instead of a composition. The poem then becomes an item of marginalia, something picked up and dropped by the poet as easily as it is scanned and discarded by the reader.

One of the earliest poems bearing the unmistakable Williams signature is "Le Médecin Malgré Lui." Here he steps away from Pound and drops the little stances and postures that gave many of his early poems a naively transparent literary gloss. The French title is perhaps a concession to "poetic" orientation, and "my Lady Happiness" is a prettier phrase than any the poet would soon care to entertain. Otherwise the poem consists of the homely, nervous lines that are already his stock in trade:

LE MÉDECIN MALGRÉ LUI

Oh I suppose I should
wash the walls of my office
polish the rust from
my instruments and keep them
definitely in order
build shelves in the laboratory
empty out the old stains
clean the bottles
and refill them, buy
another lens, put
my journals on edge instead of
letting them lie flat
in heaps—then begin
ten years back and
gradually
read them to date
cataloguing important
articles for ready reference.
I suppose I should
read the new books.
If to this I added
a bill at the tailor's
and at the cleaner's
grew a decent beard
and cultivated a look
of importance—
Who can tell? I might be
a credit to my Lady Happiness
and never think anything
but a white thought!

When he had found his way to this free speech with its rough prose measure, Williams was on his own. Forty years later he would be ready to come to a complicated long poem, epical in dimension and intention, but until then his technique, in spite of various dispositions of measure, is remarkably all of a piece. Unlike the poet whose lifework is clearly segmented in periods, Williams wrote poems in the 1960's, as he had in every other decade of his career, very much like those he wrote in 1914. One cannot study him with the expectation of tracing gradual changes in structure and diction that signify successive methods. He did not so much develop a technique as he exploited a general attitude which determinedly avoided the repetitions on which technique is based. "What Williams sees he sees in a flash," wrote Kenneth Burke. "[He] is the master of the glimpse. A line of his . . . will throw the reader into unexpected intimacy with his subject, like pushing open a door into some foreign face. . . . It would be mere idleness to give his *ars poetica* in more presumptuous terms. The process is simply this: There is the eye, and there is the thing upon which the eye alights; while the relationship existing between the two is the poem."

Consequently, Williams' technical development was largely a matter of canny dispositions of language within a limitless area; his philosophical development mainly a matter of the representation of ideas elaborating the view of life with which he began. His technique per se remained comparatively static, allowing for intensification and extension but not for complication. The philosophy reflected Williams' zealous involvement in his personal poetic mission and, to a lesser extent, in the life of his times—occasionally in overt concern with politics, economics, and the global dilemmas of the nuclear age, but mostly as the effects of contemporary history were manifest in purely local instances. Just as his technique inhibited development, his philosophy precluded systematization. Since immediately present sensation was the only thing he wholly trusted, the work produced by such impetus was necessarily an index of feeling rather than a register of thought. "A work of art," Williams once wrote, "is important only as evidence, in its structure, of a new world which it has been created to affirm. . . . A life that is here and now is timeless. That is the universal I am seeking: to embody that in a work of art, a new world that is always 'real.' " Since he conceived the poem "as a field of action, at what pitch the battle is today and what may come of it," one does not look toward Williams for considered conclusions and summations. In catching the tilt and shine of his observations, however, and by participating in his endless forays into the immediate, one can deduce attitudes and convictions. These give little substance to a philosophical position normally embodied in statements and tenets. Instead they reveal a pragmatic vision continually energized by action and reaction.

In the years just before World War I, Williams' associates were just as often painters as they were writers. In the New York studio of Walter Arensberg he met Marcel Duchamp, whose "Nude Descending a Staircase" became the *cause célèbre* of an era, and there he saw the new works from Paris that were to rechannel the course of American painting. "I bumped through these periods like a yokel," he said, "narrow-eyed, feeling my own inadequacies, but burning with the lust to write." His conviction that American poetry had to be new, that it had to find a way to cast off the heavy pall of gentility and servile provincialism, to find the means to use the advance that Whitman presaged but, according to Williams, did not develop, was passionate. In the new paintings, not only those from Montmartre and Montparnasse, but those by such Americans as Charles Sheeler, Marsden Hartley, and Stuart Davis who had already absorbed the spirit of Paris, Williams sensed a spirit that promised to generate a method. "Here was my chance," he wrote, "that was all I knew. There had been a break somewhere, we were streaming through, each thinking his own thoughts, driving his own designs toward his self's objectives. Whether the Armory Show in painting did it or whether that also was no more than a facet—the poetic line, the way the image was to lie on the page was our immediate concern. For myself all that implied, in the materials, respecting the place I knew best, was finding a local assertion—to my everlasting relief." When Williams came to make his "local assertion," it was phrased in modes suggesting he had borrowed from two kinds of painting, both of which were importantly represented in the Armory Show.

One was the native product of what was popularly known as the "Ash Can" school—the group of artists who brought into the forefront unsentimentalized versions of the ugly vitality of American city life. In scores of poems, Williams catches the same hitherto neglected fragments of observation as those with which the painters were dealing, letting his figures and his city-scapes speak for themselves, unencumbered by academic notions of design or the rehearsed pathos of the genre painter or poet.

The other kind of painting to which Williams responded with instinctual shocks of recognition was the Parisian import in which the preeminent thing was stress on new forms, new apprehensions and constructions of reality. Mainly this was Cubism which, in all of its forms, placed emphasis upon construction rather than upon representation. As a technique it offered Williams that release for which he was always searching and he borrowed it and used it with such easy authority that he might have invented it. One of the poems that best illustrates his use of Cubist techniques is the following:

ST. FRANCIS EINSTEIN OF THE
DAFFODILS

On the first visit of Professor Einstein
to the United States in the spring of 1921.

"Sweet land"
at last!
out of the sea—
the Venusremembering wavelets
rippling with laughter—
freedom
for the daffodils!
—in a tearing wind
that shakes
the tufted orchards—
Einstein, tall as a violet
in the lattice-arbor corner

is tall as
a blossomy peartree

O Samos, Samos
dead and buried. Lesbia
a black cat in the freshturned
garden. All dead.
All flesh they sung
is rotten
Sing of it no longer—
Side by side young and old
take the sun together-
maples, green and red
yellowbells
and the vermilion quinceflower
together—

The peartree
with foetid blossoms
sways its high topbranches
with contrary motions
and there are both pinkflowered
and coralflowered peachtrees
in the bare chickenyard
of the old negro
with white hair who hides
poisoned fish-heads
here and there
where stray cats find them—
find them

Spring days
swift and mutable
winds blowing four ways
hot and cold
shaking the flowers—
Now the northeast wind
moving in fogs leaves the grass
cold and dripping. The night
is dark. But in the night
the southeast wind approaches
The owner of the orchard
lies in bed
with open windows
and throws off his covers
one by one.

Discussing the content, but not the technique, of the poem, Williams made this comment: "It is always spring time for the mind when great discoveries are made. Is not Einstein, at the same time, saintly in the purity of his scientific imagining? And if a saint it seems to me that the thorough logic which St. Francis saw as sparrows or donkeys, equally to be loved with whatever other living aspect of the world, would apply equally to Einstein's arrival in the United States a number of years ago to celebrate the event in the season's shapes and colors of that moment." This indicates the theme and general feeling, yet the real difficulty of the poem lies in the tenuous conjunctions and loose order of its images and allusions. A place must be found for each of these things: Einstein, St. Francis of Assisi, a black cat named Lesbia, a pear tree, peach trees, an old Negro who sets cat-traps, and a man who can't sleep. The challenge of discerning a logical order in a sequence so disparate is modified only when the reader becomes aware that the poem has been conceived in terms of a kind of painting in which all of these things must be apprehended at a glance.

The elements of the poem are necessarily presented in a series—in time. But their relationships to one another are perceived only when they are viewed simultaneously—in space. As the Cubist painter adds the dimension of time to his composition—enabling him to present in one picture not only the observed surface of a table, for instance, but its undersides, legs, and many possible angular views of it—Williams adds the dimension of space, thereby establishing a panoramic surface on which everything can be seen at once. Einstein and St. Francis, whose lives were separated by hundreds of years, become one composite agent of discovery in an actual springtime that is also the springtime of the mind. A tag—"Sweet land"—from the hymn "America," immediately superimposed upon "the Venusremembering wavelets," produces a montage: America and all the brave clichés of its anthem mingle intimately with Botticelli's "The Birth of Venus"—a figure from the classical past borne shoreward like Einstein, but on a great scallop shell instead of on an ocean liner. When these central evocations have set the historical time and imaginative space in which the poem is composed, its other elements become relevant to them. Samos, another reminder of the classical past, is "dead and buried"; Lesbia survives—only as a namesake—in the figure of the black cat that scavenges in the blossoming season and presumably meets her death in the course of her pursuit. "The old negro," involved in everything without knowing it, causes the cat's death simply by pursuing, like her, a set way of existence. The little conflict of hunger and survival, dispassionately regarded in terms of history, is really a deadly backyard drama, enacted within the flowering orchards of a man who feels the season's change—not only a change in the weather but a nameless change in the conditions of his life made inevitable by the discoveries of Einstein, the saint-scientist. Throwing off his blankets, he makes his meek, entirely human adjustment to warmer weather and a new life. The devious logic of the poem is merely a thread and a new life. The devious logic of the poem is merely a thread on which its visual sequence is strung. The meaning of the poem lies in simultaneity—the comprehension in an instant of tenuously related elements which, on the flat surface of a canvas, could be taken in at a glance.

Of the many painters whose works have influenced Williams—from the realist Americans like George Luks, Robert Henri, and John Sloan through the Parisian Cubists, the surrealists, and on to "action" painters like Jackson Pollock—the one with whom he has the clearest technical and thematic affinities is the American Edward Hopper. Williams never mentions Hopper in his essays and memoirs, and seems curiously unaware of a contemporary whose career parallels his own. Yet a joint exhibition featuring their paintings and poems would present a view of experience remarkably cohesive in substance and attitude. Many of Williams' poems might be anecdotes drawn from the particular seam of American life Hopper records on canvas; many of Hopper's paintings might be visual realizations of a mood, a situation, or a figure from the poetic documentation of Williams. Both men listen to the human pulse that beats beneath urban squalor, both are moved by the pathetic self-sufficiency of lives eked out in the isolation of steel and stone, and both detect the muted beauty that lurks in the tawdry, vulgar, even in the grotesque. Hopper's paintings are as free of "painterly" techniques as photographs, yet they are emotionally charged in ways no photograph could match. Like Williams' poems, they say what they have to say in a glimpse, leaving the observer to provide the human frame and, within his capacities, to feel the human resonance. Their successes are of the same nature; pigment or words convey the illusion of actuality passing into art without deformation. Their failures are also similar: actuality is merely recorded, without the accompaniment of that aesthetic benison that makes an observed fact part of an imposed vision. Williams' incorrigible zest for life as a going concern, the way in which, as Randall Jarrell remarked, he "spins willingly on the wheel of things," and his indiscriminate acceptance of its heinous injustices and incongruities tend to separate him from Hopper, whose temperament is far more selective. But on nearly all other grounds, painter and poet, through the greater part of their respective careers, share a proximity that is unique in American art.

One of the shortest, and perhaps the most famous, of Williams' poems is "The Red Wheelbarrow." Since it has long been recognized as a staunch contribution to modern poetry, and can now be accommodated without strain among many other similar poems by Williams and by others, a contemporary reader can gain a sense of its original impact only by putting himself in the position of the reader of some forty years ago. Then, most poetry, American as well as English, was comfortably couched in Georgian nostalgias, measured in lines that ticked off rhymes at predictable intervals, and furnished with the dainty figurations that certified the license of its authors. Confronted by an odd-looking book from obscurely private publisher, what was the cultivated reader to make of these sixteen words that might just somehow have fallen from the typesetter's font?

THE RED WHEELBARROW

so much depends
upon

a red wheel
barrow

glazed with rain
water

beside the white
chickens

About similar poems of Williams', Hugh Kenner remarked, "If you are obliged to *talk* about poetry of this kind, your only recourse is to provide it with a theoretical scaffolding. Of such an enterprise, it may be noted that the function of theory is to make the cautious mind feel that the poems so located exist by some right, and after that to disappear." Against the temptation to let the little poem stand in its own realized moment, there is also the temptation to ask, What possibly "happens" in his poem to make it so durable? Because it is, after all, a composition and not a typographical accident, the poem, like others of its kind, *can* be talked about as long as the talk is an account of a response and not an attempt to grind it fine in the mills of a system. First: "so much depends . . . This deliberately vague but enormously suggestive phrase leads the reader to expect, at least, a subject open to contrary possibilities and, at most (*what* is contingent upon *what*?), some relaxation of the little thrust of tension the phrase sets up. Except for the slight metaphorical lift of the word "glazed," what the reader gets is flat actuality, ignoring his rising expectation and answering in its own disinterested and incontrovertible terms. The movement of the poem is in the nature of a reversal: a yearning toward what might or could be is quietly checked by the homely beauty of what *is*.

While his subjects include almost anything that would normally come within the purview of a busy physician on his rounds, Williams' whole and very ample theme is himself—a feeling man who charges the commonplace with his own uncommon ardors and who makes of his relations with the ordinary an idyll and a romance. By isolating details, magnifying them, or cinematically "freezing" them, he gives to the average and quotidian a significance that would otherwise go unnoticed. By imposing his own *joie de vivre* on the life within his house, on his street, and across the breadth of his home town, he makes lyrics out of circumstances that would often seem more ripe for the sociological casebook or for the chilling satire of a Daumier etching. The following poem is an instance of Williams in his role as the poet of domesticity:

DANSE RUSSE

If when my wife is sleeping
and the baby and Kathleen
are sleeping
and the sun is a flame-white disc
in silken mists
above shining trees,—
if I in my north room
dance naked, grotesquely
before my mirror
waving my shirt round my head
and singing softly to myself:

"I am lonely, lonely,
I was born to be lonely,
I am best so!"
If I admire my arms, my face,
my shoulders, flanks, buttocks
against the yellow drawn shades,—

Who shall say I am not
the happy genius of my household?

In moments of pure observation he takes scenes that anyone might witness a hundred times without a thought and invests them with a pathos that is as real as it is intangible. In "The Lonely Street," which might be a poet's transcription of a typical subject of Edward Hopper, words merely annotate a situation that must, for the most part, be inferred. Since Williams comes clean, so to speak, without a frame and without any tradition but his own, much of his work demands unusually close participation on the part of the reader: the poet provides a picture, sets a mood with gravity and economy, but the meaning of the poem is heard only in its reverberations.

THE LONELY STREET

School is over. It is too hot
to walk at ease. At ease
in light frocks they walk the streets
to while the time away.
They have grown tall. They hold
pink flames in their right hands.
In white from head to foot,
with sidelong, idle look—
in yellow, floating stuff,
black sash and stockings—
touching their avid mouths
with pink sugar on a stick—
like a carnation each holds in her hand—
they mount the lonely street.

In the simplicity and starkness of his recordings of an observed action or a figure, Williams throws away many of the conventional advantages of poetry as a form of expression and thereby takes chances few poets are willing to hazard. Other poets depend largely on craft, maneuver, and all the learned strategies of an art with a long history. Williams depends on little more than the feeling that can be evoked, or conveyed, by a spontaneous sequence of words arranged in a manner meant to echo the artlessness of ordinary speech. When he succeeds, the result is an impact and a surprise, a sudden, sometimes shocked awareness on the part of the reader that affirms the reality of what he records. In a poem such as the following, the separating distance between an event and its report falls away; reality and its poetic apprehension are joined in a compatibility that seems absolute.

COMPLETE DESTRUCTION

It was an icy day.
We buried the cat,
then took her box
and set match to it
in the back yard.
Those fleas that escaped
earth and fire
died by the cold.

But there are frequent occasions in the body of Williams' work where his exclusive dependence on the sort of poetic shorthand that might catch actuality *in situ* leads him into banality and even into the overweening poetic fancy he most abhors. In a passage from his autobiography, he pinpoints the occasion of a particular poem: "Once on a hot July day coming back exhausted from the Post Graduate Clinic, I dropped in as I sometimes did at Marsden's [Hartley] studio on Fifteenth Street for a talk, a little drink maybe and to see what he was doing. As I approached his number I heard a great clatter of bells and the roar of a fire engine passing the end of the street down Ninth Avenue. I turned just in time to see a golden figure 5 on a red background flash by. The impression was so sudden and forceful that I took a piece of paper out of my pocket and wrote a short poem about it." Here it is:

THE GREAT FIGURE

Among the rain
and lights
I saw the figure 5
in gold
on a red
firetruck
moving
tense
unheeded
to gong clangs
siren howls
and wheels rumbling
through the dark city.

Clearly a case where Williams' material remains quite where he found it, this poem neither heightens the prose account nor extends the perception it reports. The poetic version, in fact, muddies the simplicity of the prose statement, "just in time to see a golden figure 5 on a red background flash by." The attempt to give significance to an observation that had no significance beyond the fact that he made it leads Williams into sophomoric poetic straining. The possibility that the figure 5, or any other figure, on a fire engine might be "tense" is absurd; the statement that it is "unheeded" is, in the testimony of the poem itself, patently false. After these sentimentalities, the spuriously ominous note of "wheels rumbling / through the dark city" is as phony as a tumbrel in Times Square.

Alternation of happy accident and bad chance is necessarily the lot of any poet, no matter how great his talent, who is a personality gifted with a knack more than he is a craftsman pledged to a profession. Because of his preoccupation with finding the measure that would dictate the form and the demonstrated dexterity with which he pursued it, and because of the great number of his poems that exist without the support of convention, Williams was not quite either. He was a phenomenon: a master whose precepts, dutifully followed, led almost always to disaster; a poet whose example, on the other hand, had tonic effect on a generation of poets not remotely like him. When Williams wrote criticism, he often unconsciously parodied the academic lingo he officially deplored, and when he gave advice, he tended to ignore the personal temperament and private circumstance that made his own working methods special. He admitted, for instance, that "I didn't go in for long lines because of my nervous nature," and that, from his beginnings as a poet, he felt he was "*not* English," and that rhyme and other means of organizing a poem seemed to him intolerably restrictive. Consequently, when he came to use his personal limitations as the basis of a general program, he was guilty of an exclusiveness his nature otherwise seemed to deny. Many modern poets are able to compose a long line in an equilibrium of spirit as well as of metrics, and many have found the old devices of poetry flexible, capable of entirely new variations, and more advantageous than obstructive. As a practicing physician, continually working long hours day and night, Williams usually had to write in moments stolen between appointments, in snatches and fragments, on prescription blanks sometimes, or any other writing surface at hand. This necessity should not be discounted as a very large factor in his particular development. The wonder is that so many hurried notations and seized moments should have become part of the permanent record of a career and a poetic era.

The only "official" program with which Williams was identified was the one that went by the name of Objectivism. This was a term devised to give emphasis to certain notions he and others shared with Gertrude Stein about the literal and structural qualities of "words being words," and came to signify a short-lived movement confined to himself, the poet Louis Zukofsky who was a disciple of Ezra Pound's, Charles Reznikoff, and George Oppen. Together these men organized and financed the Objectivist Press from which, in a short career, issued a handful of books including Williams' *Collected Poems.* In Williams' own words, Objectivist theory was this:

"We had had 'Imagism' . . . which ran quickly out. That, though it had been useful in ridding the field of verbiage, had no formal necessity implicit in it. It had already dribbled off into so called 'free verse' which, as we saw, was a misnomer. There is no such thing as free verse! Verse is measure of some sort. 'Free verse' was without measure and needed none for its projected objectifications. Thus the poem had run down and became formally non extant.

"But, we argued, the poem, like every other form of art, is an object, an object that in itself formally presents its case and its meaning by the very form it assumes. Therefore, being an object, it should be so treated and controlled—but not as in the past. For past objects have about them past necessities—like the sonnet—which have conditioned them and from which as a form itself, they cannot be freed.

"The poem being an object (like a symphony or cubist painting) it must be the purpose of the poet to make of his words a new form: to invent, that is, an object consonant with his day. This was what we wished to imply by Objectivism, an antidote, in a sense, to the bare image haphazardly presented in loose verse."

Most poets who reach an artistic maturity as advanced as Williams' define for themselves an area in which poems inspired by new experience and the surprise encounters of everyday existence quite naturally find a place. If they do not come to a settled view of life, they at least are marked by attitudes that color their thinking and lend a consistent tone to its expression. These poets achieve a style of language that identifies them as surely as the clothes they wear. When their individual interests are repeated and developed in the course of many poems, their predilections, like their uses of language, tend to fall into patterns. Once a pattern has become clear, its rhythms obvious and its figures familiar, it takes on the character of a territory staked out and settled. The poet's authority there is both natural and appropriate: he has found a local habitation and created a world of such distinctive character that any sensitive reader knows at once just what territory he has ventured. The worlds of Frost and Stevens and Cummings can be recognized at the threshold; and while, in each case, objects that loom beyond may vary enormously, they are always harmonious with their settings and obedient to laws of sensibility that are seldom relaxed.

In the case of Williams, the sense of a large controlling spirit, on the one hand, and of an essentially homogeneous landscape, on the other hand, is comparatively minor. He maintained a refreshing ability to surprise himself as often as he was surprised by what he met, but since the element of chance was the liveliest agent in his purview, Williams' vision remained expectant and unsettled. Where other poets tend to dwell in wonder, Williams, refusing to stay put, made wonder the vehicle on which he rode. His creative life depended upon his being alive to contingencies; and since these recurred with a relentlessness that kept him always newly addressed to his task, he gave the appearance of a man forever trying to transmute base metals into gold or to reinvent the umbrella. He never gave up the attempt to capture the thing that cannot be captured, to do the work that is never done. Unlike the master craftsman who apportions his energies with an inherent sense of economy, Williams spent his with profligacy. Since he was less interested in arriving anywhere than he was in maintaining the journey at a high pitch of movement and purposiveness, his career had the quality of a vector that continually points a direction that needs no goal.

Tracking Williams' progress is a remarkably brief operation. When he had broken with the poets of the past and those of his contemporaries whose disposition, he felt, was to make accommodation rather than revolution, he had taken the one stride within which all his lesser steps are subsumed. The progress is begun and ended almost at once; there remains the development. Technically speaking, Williams' creative life can be conveniently viewed in at least five distinct phases. Beginning as an imitator of nineteenth-century forms inherited from the romantics, particularly Keats, but including also small persistent echoes of Browning, he moves on toward a Whitmanesque free verse somewhat incongruously modified by the classic stances and *fin de siècle* sophistications that crop up in the early work of Ezra Pound. Imagism later provides a salubrious climate for his hard clear transcriptions of natural, urban, and domestic life, and for the pithy short forms into which his poetic thought characteristically falls. But through each of these phases he is searching for the measure that will afford him greater freedom and, at the same time, tighter control—a measure replacing the strict count of metrics that will open to him, and all the other poets of the new age, a means of getting through to the American idiom that is recognized as a cultural fact but persists as a poetic anomaly. This search takes on the obsessive power of a mystique for Williams and through many variations in free form he eventually comes to the notion of the "variable foot," his name for a vague entity meant to delineate a unit of language that might carry into formal expression the tilt and accent of natural speech. In a letter to Richard Eberhart in 1954, Williams explains:

> "I have never been one to write by rule, even by my own rules. Let's begin with the rule of counted syllables, in which all poems have been written hitherto. That has become tiresome to my ear.
>
> "Finally, the stated syllables, as in the best of present-day free verse, have become entirely divorced from the beat, that is the measure. The musical pace proceeds without them.
>
> "Therefore the measure, that is to say, the count, having got rid of the words, which held it down, is returned to the *music.*
>
> "The words, having been freed, have been allowed to run all over the map, 'free' as we have mistakenly thought. This has amounted to no more (in Whitman and others) than no discipline at all.
>
> "But if we keep in mind the *tune* which the lines (not necessarily the words) make in our ears, we are ready to proceed.
>
> "By measure I mean musical pace. Now, with music in our ears the words need only be taught to keep as distinguished an order, as chosen a character, as regular, according to the music, as in the best of prose.
>
> "By its *music* shall the best of modern verse be known and the *resources* of the music. The refinement of the poem, its subtlety, is not to be known by the elevation of the words but—the words don't so much matter—by the resources of the *music.*
>
> "To give you an example from my own work—not that I know anything about what I have myself written:
>
> (count):—not that I ever count when writing but, at best, the lines must be capable of being counted, that is to say, *measured*—(believe it or not).—At that I may, half consciously, even count the measure under my breath as I write.—
>
> (approximate example)
>
> (1) The smell of the heat is boxwood
>   (2)when rousing us
>   (3) a movement of the air
> (4) stirs our thoughts
>   (5) that had no life in them
>   (6) to a life, a life in which
>
> (or)
>
> (1) Mother of God! Our Lady!
>   (2) the heart
>   (3) is an unruly master:
> (4) Forgive us our sins
>   (5)as we
>   (6) forgive.
> (7) those who have sinned against
>
> "Count a single beat to each numeral. You may not agree with my ear, but that is the way I count the line. Over the whole poem it gives a pattern to the meter that can be felt as a new measure. It gives resources to the ear which result in a language which we hear spoken about us every day."

As an explanation, and an attempted demonstration of the "variable foot" as meticulous as any Williams made, this account nevertheless gives a reader or critic little more than a statement of intention. Williams anticipates the difficulty when he says, "You may not agree with my ear, but that is the way I count the line." His count is arbitrary, applied to lines that may ring with an authentic music in his ears, but which are apt to register with an entirely different measure, and consequently a different music, on the ears of anyone else. The way in which one hears naturally determines the way one writes, but the enormous variability in the capacity to hear, plus all the intricacies of selection that set one hearer apart from another, gives Williams' theory so much latitude that it becomes all but useless for analysis or for emulation. That this method worked for him is indisputable. But if it is to work for anyone else, its pretensions as theory and method must be put aside in favor of the unique pragmatic ingenuity which gives his poetry its character.

There are distinguishing aspects of American speech on many levels—regional, societal, occupational, cultural; the phonetic emphases that Americans make in the thousands of phrases they use in their everyday exchanges—shorthand expressions that signify a mood or an attitude—are distinctively different from British usage as well as from general literary or journalistic usage; the poet who can hear these streamlined expressions, who can catch the relationship between a thought and the gesture of words that carries it, should find a way to use them. When Williams does not try to make a limiting formula of a spontaneous practice, his explanation of the way he works is succinct and clarifying: ". . . in some of my work all I have to do is to transcribe the language when hot and feelingly spoken. For when it is charged with emotion it has a tendency to be rhythmic, lowdown, inherent in the place where it is being used. And that is, to me, the origin of form, the origin of measure. The rhythmic beat of charged language." Poets other than Williams have used such moments of charged vernacular speech, sometimes as embellishments or variations on formal passages, sometimes in verse somewhat freely conceived as a nice succession of cadences, but also at times within the strictures of iambic or trochaic meter. Williams must be credited with knowing the source and strength of his own endeavors, but when he attempts to fit them into a formula, he appears unnecessarily determined to predicate a system and to offer it as generally applicable when, actually, it is based on practices congenial only to himself.

In his final phase, Williams carries forward his innovations and expands their range in several individual volumes of lyrics and in one of the longest poems of modern times, *Paterson.* The lyrics, more subdued and mellow in feeling than most of the earlier poems, are technically as free but handled with notably more consistency and assurance as Williams exploits his congenial personal discovery, the "variable foot." In *Paterson,* recapitulating the adventure of his poetic and personal history, Williams tests the adequacy of his techniques in the light of the special demands of epic expression.

As an epic, *Paterson* shares with a number of other modern poems the fact that its structure, suggested partly by an available cultural situation, is nevertheless mostly the device of an author who, in despair, creates what he has failed to inherit—a body of myth, a roster of dramatis personae, a religious sanction. The official facades of democracy and Christianity cannot disguise the fact that the contemporary world is characterized more by disparity than by unity. Consequently, the poet is denied the advantage of a homogeneous community where the deeds of religious and political heroes reflect common ideals. While it is likely that he knows his heritage better than most people, the poet who wants to write an epic today tends to ignore the possibilities still available to him in the legends of Christianity and the annals of democracy, and to look for, or to make, some over-all structure that may includea spects of both but which does not pretend wholly to represent either. Usually this structure takes the form of a "model of confusion" that reflects the contradictions implicit in a society that is at once intensely self-conscious and self-deceptive. All but the thinnest line of narrative is dispensed with. In its place the poet offers a polyhedral view of experience, forcing the reader to witness as a fact the historical and spiritual dislocation that not only provides the poem with its theme but suggests its shape.

Readers familiar with the mythical structures of Joyce's *Ulysses* and *Finnegans Wake,* Eliot's *The Waste Land,* or Hart Crane's *The Bridge* will discern in *Paterson* methods with which they are already acquainted, and a few that belong uniquely to Williams. The theme of his epic is, almost inevitably, another drainatized statement of his long quest for the language that will record actuality with the natural force of actuality—"the redeeming language by which a man's premature death . . . might have been prevented." As he moved gradually toward the undertaking of a long poem, Williams knew that his theme was set and understood that he was challenged to find a symbolical situation—some tangible equivalent of a myth built like a coral formation, cell by cell, through the cultural phases of a people or a nation—that might embody his theme locally and yet allow for its universal application. In a half-conscious, almost subliminal way, Williams had for many years been aware of just such a reticulum of ideas and had in fact used some of these ideas in poems where landscape is treated as a kind of emotional topography. Persistently ambitious to write a long poem, he continued to lack any clear notion of its architecture. As a saint's spiritual exercises prepare him for revelation, Williams' long poetic life had prepared him to recognize at once the idea that would serve him. When suddenly it came, it was set down as a modest three lines first appearing in a pamphlet of poems, *The Broken Span,* published in 1941:

> A man like a city and a woman like a
> flower—who are in love. Two
> women. Three women. Innumerable
> women, each like a flower. But only
> one man—like a city.

From this kernel—"A man like a city"—the whole poem flowered.

But, first, there was the question of *what* city. "Like what baby when I decided to write about babies," said Williams. "The problem of the poetics I knew depended upon finding a specific city, one that I knew, so I searched for a city. New York? It couldn't be New York, not anything as big as a metropolis. Rutherford wasn't a city. Passaic wouldn't do. I'd known about Paterson, even written about it . . . Suddenly it dawned on me I had a find. I began my investigations. Paterson had a history, an important colonial history. It had, besides, a river—the Passaic, and the Falls. I may have been influenced by James Joyce who had made Dublin the hero of his book. . . . But I forgot about Joyce and fell in love with my city. The Falls were spectacular; the river was a symbol handed to me. I began to write the beginning, about the stream above the Falls. I read everything I could gather, finding fascinating documentary evidence in a volume published by the Historical Society of Paterson. Here were all the facts I could ask for, details exploited by no one. This was my river and I was going to use it. I had grown up on its banks, seen the filth that polluted it, even dead horses. . . . I took the river as it followed its course down to the sea; all I had to do was follow it and I had a poem."

The virtue of Williams' idea was its viability. As soon as he had begun to give it full expression he found that everything was interactive and relevant: history from local archives gave identity to a population in general and to one man in particular; the mutations of geology gave spaciousness to a concept and recognizable silhouettes to giant figures; the composite City-Man was a hero of many parts, each of which caught and objectified some facet of truth about the other; the sweep of actuality—a Babel of speech and brute action—resounded like the Falls, overheard but not interpreted; like existence into time, the Passaic River flowed every day, eternally, toward the ocean.

An extended meditation on an idea that cannot be reduced to a statement, the poem makes a continuous graph-like recording of a process of discovery and affirmation, flux and stasis, permanence and mutability. In a vast collocation of fragments—a sort of mosaic of the contents of consciousness—poetry is interspersed with long and short passages of prose. Over these the poet's imagination moves like a flame sporadically burning, fed by the debris of old letters personal and anonymous, old journals, newspaper reports, advertisements, and passages from historical documents. In certain of these the language is inchoate, flat, choked with sentiment or cloyingly prettified by flourishes of fine writing. In others, the prose account serves to introduce matters that underline, counterpoint, or in some way vary the central theme. These interpolations serve for *Paterson* as Eliot's appended annotations served for *The Waste Land* and as Hart Crane's marginal commentaries served for *The Bridge.* What in another poem would be regarded as addenda, or the dross of the author's investigations, become in *Paterson* an essential part of the process of the poem.

The dramatis personae consists of scores of characters who drift in and out of its five books, a few whose problems are persistent, many who make one brief contribution, then disappear, and one all-embracing figure, the Man-City, Paterson, Dr. Paterson, Noah Faitoute Paterson who is, first, William Carlos Williams and all the factors of environment, heritage, and history of which he is composed. In his mythological role, he is a geological giant who lies sleeping on his right side on the bank of the Passaic River with the noise of the great Falls tumbling in his ear, facing the recumbent figure of another geological giant, Garrett Mountain, his female counterpart. The river flows between them, a stream of consciousness, a stream of language which, at the spillway of the Great Falls, speaks in torrential dialects which the poet must unravel, must comb "into straight lines / from that rafter of a rock's / lip."

Having conceived *Paterson* as a poem primordially involved in history and, at the same time, overwhelmed by the thousand voices of immediacy, Williams arrived at two distinct methods of dealing with his materials: a method of contrast and a method of dispersion. In the former he follows one of the devices used in *The Waste Land* and, to a lesser extent, in *The Bridge.* The present is compared with the past in terms of spiritual grace and spiritual vulgarity; pastoral charm and urban tawdriness; the human capacity for awe and its debasement to an appetite for sensation. This is all familiar, amounting to something like a concession on Williams' part to the academically certifiable poetry to which he normally gives no quarter. The second of his methods, dispersion, finds him quite in character and on his own. Truth lies in the search for truth, he seems to say; the energy with which the mind deals with experience is the thing, and not the little conclusions about experience that the mind might sort out. In this method he gives up any pretension toward the intellectual's drive to fuse and unify. Differing from poets who seek, like Eliot, the recovery of the wholeness that religious faith once made possible, or those, like Crane, who seek a recovery of faith in the generative power of love, Williams seeks the key to that awareness that would make all life transcendent. This pursuit leads him away from dependence on the consolations of philosophy and into the belief that, as the physicist unlocks the structure of matter, the poet may find the measure that identifies the human.

In the method he adopts he is characteristically closer to the painters than he is to the poets, especially to those comparatively recent American artists known as "action" painters. Williams' goal, like theirs, is the release of energy rather than the reassembling of familiar counters; he strives for a poem that will, in its own process, answer the question it continually poses. Like the abstractionist painter who gives up identifiable shapes and forms for visual rhythms, Williams dispenses with poetic modes that might unify his poem, hopeful that incursions of indiscriminate subject matter may find their place in his overall design. His aim is similar to that of the painter who expects that his rhythmic emphases will find their functional place in the over-all "writing" that covers his canvas. The massed dispersions of a late Jackson Pollock—energies flowing from and ordered by one consciousness—are duplicated in the thrusts and charges by which Williams creates a field of action. The achievement in both cases is a styleless style in which energy and force take precedence over organization and the graceful disposition of subject matter.

Release of energy in *Paterson* is both a theme and a technique. As a technique it operates continually; as an explicit theme it occurs sporadically throughout the poem, and most importantly in *Book III,* in relation to the figure of Marie Curie who, with her husband Pierre, discovered radium in 1898. In an early typescript of *Paterson,* Williams notes the ways in which a lecture on atomic fission suggested to him how the antennae of the poet and the yardstick of the scientist work on the same subject: "The lecture on uranium (Curie), the splitting of the atom (first time explained to *me*) has a literary meaning . . . in the splitting of the foot . . . (sprung meter of Hopkins) and consequently is connected thereby to human life or death. . . . Three discoveries here: 1. radium. 2. poet's discovery of modern idiom. 3. political scientist's discovery of a cure for economic ills." In her book *The Metamorphic Tradition in Modern Poetry,* Sister M. Bernetta Quinn further delineates these concepts as they are used in *Paterson*:

"The analogy between the poet's business and the physicist's is treated at length. Madame Curie's discovery—and by implication the poet's also—being compared to that of Columbus. Both Madame Curie and Paterson were seeking the radiant gist, the luminous stain:

A dissonance
in the valence of Uranium
led to the discovery

Where dissonance
(if you are interested)
leads to discovery

"Through the experience of twentieth-century scientists like the Curies, a man's old dream of transmuting the elements . . . has indeed come true. . . . Basic to such metamorphoses is the conversion of mass into energy, as predicted by Einstein, whose work revised the traditional concept of the indestructibility of matter to the present law of conservation of mass and energy. Because of physical research in this direction, scientists can now go through the Mendeleev molecular weight table, explicitly referred to by Williams, changing one element into another—for instance, mercury to gold—by capturing into a nucleus such extra particles as protons, neutrons, deuterons, and alpha particles. Another aspect of artificial transmutation is the splitting of the uranium 235 atom. Man-made devices, such as the cyclotron, can today achieve a metamorphosis which will set up chain reactions of incredible power.

"By the inevitable laws of nature itself, uranium transmutes into radium and finally to the stable substance of lead: 'Uranium (bound to be lead) / throws out the fire.' The important part of this process, however, is not the lead, its conclusion, but the enormous forces for good or evil which the giving off of radioactive emanations (Gamma rays) means for the human race. All these implications Williams weaves into his poem."

The idea of *Paterson* is superb, clearly equal in its dimensions to the other celebrated modern poems based on myth structures, elastically appropriate to Williams' temperament and practice, and charged heroically with purpose. But the idea on which this and any other epic is based is, unfortunately, merely the abstract, the blueprint, and the non-poet can devise an impressive one as easily as the poet. The enormous accommodation provided for in a method of dispersion gives *Paterson* an all-of-a-piece consistently on an intellectual level, but on an emotive level the poem is vastly uneven and at times hopelessly fragmented. Like Joyce in some of the most clotted arcana of *Finnegans Wake,* Williams appears to be guilty of a fetishism of the very instrument he has taken great pains to perfect. An obsession with freedom has resulted in anarchy; the poem becomes more accident than design. Moments of brilliance are succeeded by stretches of dullness and the whole work seems clogged in its own machinery. These failures would not seem so great if the successful parts of the poem were not so luminous. *Book I* is the paragon. Here idea and illustration are electrically related; prose informs the poetry and poetry enhances the prose; the vertical plane of the past and the horizontal plane of the present intersect in bursts of illumination. Everything strikes fire from everything else and the effect is that of a crystalline substance that can be turned endlessly, facet by facet catching the points of light that shed a radiance.

But where, in *Book I,* the idea serves to polarize all the materials in its field, in successive books the materials refuse to respond to any magnet and often lie curiously inert. The structure consequently begins to seem hammered together and rickety. When the energy of the idea holds things together, the result is a miraculous appositeness that extends to the most disparate conjunctions of material. When the energy flags, however, waywardness takes over and the will tries desperately to do the work of the imagination. Randall Jarrell, who felt that the term Organization of Irrelevance might describe Williams' type of structure, posed questions that may occur to other readers who have ventured into the interior of *Paterson*: "Such organization is *ex post facto* organization: if something is somewhere, one can always find Some Good Reason for its being there, but if it had not been there would one reader have missed it? if it had been put somewhere else, would one reader have guessed where it should have 'really' gone?" According to Jarrell, Williams was not able to resist the dangerous license that his structure permitted and was guilty of a crippling arbitrariness. "Sometimes these anecdotes, political remarks, random comments seem to be where they are for one reason: because Dr. Williams chose—happened to choose—for them to be there. One is reminded of that other world in which Milton found Chance 'sole arbiter.' "

Nearly ten years after *Paterson* had been published as a completed poem in four books, Williams added a fifth book in the nature of an afterword or coda. Included in this book were sections published as single lyrics, or under the title "Work in Progress," in his *Desert Music* and *Journey to Love. Book V,* more relaxed in tone than the rest of the poem and more consistent in its employment of the loose "step down" measure of the "variable foot," recovers some of the magic of the best sections of the earlier books. Here, from the vantage point of old age and the height of achievement, the poet looks back and down upon his life and his poems. Two themes are woven through his meditation: (1) the endurance of art as an immortal seam of reality and (2) the Virgin and the Whore—the female principle, existing beyond the discriminations of morality, that ensures the continuity of the race of man. In this last book, the methods of contrast and dispersion are somewhat relaxed in favor of a sense of quietly unifying reflection. Speaking more clearly in his own person than in the terms of his multi-faceted projection, Dr. Paterson, Williams recounts his involvements in art and his involvements in love. Together they make affirmations of what he always believed and what he instinctively knew. As *Paterson* begins with a question, it ends with an answer.

This is the question:

"Rigor of beauty is the quest. But how will
you find beauty when it is locked in the
mind past all remonstrance?"

This is the answer:

The measure intervenes, to measure is all
we know,
a choice among the measures . . .

the measured dance

"unless the scent of a rose
startle us anew"

Equally laughable
is to assume to know nothing, a
chess game
Massively, "materially", compounded!
Yo ho! ta ho!

We know nothing and can know nothing
but

the dance, to dance to a measure
contrapuntally,
Satyrically, the tragic foot.

The question poses the grand attempt; the winning of wisdom, the answer suggests, involves not the comfort of conclusion but the discovery of a means.

Selected Bibliography

WORKS OF WILLIAM CARLOS WILLIAMS

Poems, (Rutherford, N.J.: Privately printed, 1909).

The Tempers, (London: Elkins Mathews, 1913).

Al Que Quiere!, (Boston: Four Seas Co., 1917).

Kora in Hell: Improvisations, (Boston: Four Seas Co., 1920).

Sour Grapes, (Boston: Four Seas Co., 1921).

Spring and All, (Dijon: Contact Publishing Co., 1923).

Go Go, (New York: Monroe Wheeler, 1923).

The Cod Head, (San Francisco: Harvest Press, 1932).

Collected Poems 1921–1931, (New York: Objective Press, 1934).

An Early Martyr and Other Poems, (New York: Alcestis Press, 1935).

Adam & Eve & The City, (Peru, Vt.: Alcestis Press, 1936).

The Complete Collected Poems of William Carlos Williams 1906–1938, (Norfolk, Conn.: New Directions, 1938).

The Broken Span, (Norfolk, Conn.: New Directions, 1941).

The Wedge, (Cummington, Mass.: Cummington Press, 1944).

Paterson, Book One, (New York: New Directions, 1946).

The Clouds, (Aurora, N.Y. and Cummington, Mass.: Wells College Press and Cummington Press, 1948).

The Pink Church, (Columbus, Ohio: Golden Goose Press, 1949).

Selected Poems, (New York: New Directions, 1949).

Paterson, Book Two, (New York: New Directions, 1948).

Paterson, Book Three, (New York: New Directions, 1949).

The Collected Later Poems, (New York: New Directions, 1950).

The Collected Earlier Poems, (New York: New Directions, 1951).

Paterson,Book Four, (New York: New Directions, 1951).

The Desert Music and Other Poems, (New York: Random House, 1954).

Journey to Love, (New York: Random House, 1955).

"The Lost Poems of William Carlos Williams or The Past Recaptured," in *New Directions 16* (New York: New Directions, 1957) 3–45.

Paterson, Book Five, (New York: New Directions, 1958).

Pictures from Brueghel and Other Poems, (Norfolk, Conn.: New Directions, 1962). Includes *The Desert Music* and *Journey to Love*.

Paterson, (Norfolk, Conn.: New Directions, 1963).

The Collected Later Poems of William Carlos Williams, (Norfolk, Conn.: New Directions, 1963).

The Selected Poems of Williams Carlos Williams, with an Introduction by Randall Jarrell (Norfolk, Conn.: New Directions, 1963).

Autobiography of William Carlos Williams, (New York: New Directions, 1967).

BIBLIOGRAPHIES

Engels, John, *Checklist of William Carlos Williams*, (Columbus, Ohio: Charles E. Merrill, 1969).

Heal, Edith, ed., *I Wanted to Write a Poem*, (Boston: Beacon Press, 1958).

Wallace, Emily M., *A Bibliography of William Carlos Williams*, (Middletown, Conn.: Wesleyan University Press, 1968).

White, William, "William Carlos Williams: Bibliography Review with Addenda," *American Book Collector* 19, vii: 9–12 (1969).

CRITICAL AND BIOGRAPHICAL STUDIES

Blackmur, R. P., *Form and Value in Modern Poetry*, (New York: Doubleday, 1957).

———, *Language as Gesture*, (London: Allen and Unwin, 1954).

Breslin, James E., *William Carlos Williams: An American Artist*, (New York: Oxford University Press, 1970).

Burke, Kenneth, "The Methods of Williams Carlos Williams," *Dial* 82: 94–98 (February 1927).

Cambon, Glauco, *The Inclusive Flame: Studies in American Poetry*, (Bloomington: Indiana University Press, 1963).

Ciardi, John, "Epic of a Place," *Saturday Review* 41: 37–39 (October 11, 1958).

Coffman, Stanley K., *Imagism: A Chapter for the History of Modern Poetry*, (Norman: University of Oklahoma, 1951).

Conarroe, Joel O., "A Local Price: The Poetry of *Paterson*," *PMLA* 84: 547–58 (May 1969).

Cook, Albert, "Modern Verse: Diffusion as a Principle of Composition," *Kenyon Review* 21: 208–12 (Spring 1959).

Deutsch, Babette, *Poetry in Our Time*, (New York: Holt, 1952).

Dijkstra, Abraham, "William Carlos Williams and Painting: The Hieroglyphics of a New Speech," Unpublished dissertation. (University of California Berkeley, 1967).

Donoghue, Denis, "For a Redeeming Language," *Twentieth Century* 163: 532–42 (June 1958).

Ellmann, Richard, "William Carlos Williams: The Doctor in Search of Himself," *Kenyon Review* 14: 510–12 (Summer 1952).

Engels, John, *Guide to William Carlos Williams*, (Columbus, Ohio: Charles E. Merrill, 1969).

Garrigue, Jean, "America Revisited," *Poetry* 90: 174–78 (June 1958).

Guimond, James, *The Art of William Carlos Williams: A Discovery and Possession of America*, (Urbana: University of Illinois Press, 1968).

Hoffman, Frederick J., "Williams and His Muse," *Poetry* 84: 23–27 (April 1954).

Honig, Edwin, "City of Man," *Poetry* 69: 277–84 (February 1947).

Hoskins, Katherine, "Sweating Out a Birthright," *Nation* 185: 226–27 (October 5, 1957).

Jarrell, Randall, "A View of Three Poets," *Partisan Review* 18: 691–700 (November–December 1951).

———, *Poetry and the Age,* (New York: Vintage [Knopf], 1955).

Kenner, Hugh, "To Measure Is All We Know," *Poetry* 94: 127–32 (May 1959).

Koch, Vivienne, *William Carlos Williams,* (Norfolk, Conn.: New Directions, 1950).

———, "William Carlos Williams: The Man and the Poet," *Kenyon Review* 14: 502–10 (Summer 1952).

———, "Williams: The Social Mask," *Poetry* 80: 89–93 (May 1952).

Lechlitner, Ruth, "The Poetry of William Carlos Williams," *Poetry* 54: 326–35 (September 1939).

Lowell, Robert, "Paterson II," *Nation* 166: 692–94 (June 19, 1948).

———, "William Carlos Williams," *Hudson Review* 14: 530–36 (Winter 1961–62).

Miller, J. Hillis, ed., *William Carlos Williams: A Collection of Critical Essays,* (Englewood Cliffs, N.J.: Prentice-Hall, 1966).

Moore, Marianne, "A Poet of the Quattrocento," *Dial* 82: 213–15 (March 1927).

———, "Things Others Never Notice," *Poetry* 44: 103–06 (May 1934).

Morgan, Frederick, "William Carlos Williams: Imagery, Rhythm, Form," *Sewanee Review* 55: 675–90 (1947).

Paul, Sherman, *The Music of Survival: A Biography of a Poem by William Carlos Williams,* (Urbana: University of Illinois Press, 1968).

Peterson, Walter S., *An Approach to Paterson,* (New Haven, Conn.: Yale University Press, 1967).

Pound, Ezra, "Dr. Williams' Position," *Dial* 75: 395–404 (November 1928).

———, *Polite Essays,* (London: Faber and Faber, 1937).

Quinn, Sister M. Bernetta, *The Metamorphic Tradition in Modern Poetry,* (New Brunswick, N.J.: Rutgers University Press, 1955).

Rosenfeld, Paul, *Port of New York,* (New York: Harcourt, Brace, 1924).

Rosenthal, M. L., "Salvo for William Carlos Williams," *Nation* 186: 497, 500 (May 31, 1958).

———, *The Modern Poets: A Critical Introduction,* (New York: Oxford University Press, 1960).

Shapiro, Karl, *In Defense of Ignorance,* (New York: Random House, 1960).

Taupin, René, *L'Influence de symbolisme français sur la poésie américaine (de 1910 à 1920),* (Paris: Champion, 1929).

Thirlwall, John C., "William Carlos Williams' 'Paterson'," *New Directions 17* (New York: New Directions, 1961) 252–310.

Wagner, Linda Welshimer, *The Poems of William Carlos Williams,* (Middletown, Conn.: Wesleyan University Press, 1963).

Weatherhead, A. Kingsley, *The Edge of the Image,* (Seattle: University of Washington Press, 1967).

Weaver, Mike, *William Carlos Williams. The American Background,* (London: Cambridge University Press, 1971).

Wilson, T. C., "The Example of Dr. Williams," *Poetry* 48: 105–07 (May 1936).

Winters, Yvor, *Primitivism and Decadence in Contemporary Poetry,* (New York: Arrow, 1937).

SPECIAL ISSUES OF MAGAZINES

Briarcliff Quarterly, vol. 3 (October, 1936). Contains articles, letters, and comments on Williams by various hands.

Massachusetts Review, vol. 3, no. 2 (Winter 1962). Contains "A Gathering for William Carlos Williams," pp. 277–344 with contributions by Clinton J. Atkinson, Carlos Baker, Cid Corman, H. E. F. Donohue, Raymond A. Kennedy, Hugh Kenner, David Leviten, Gosta Peterson, Seldon Rodman, Charles Sheler, Mary Ellen Solt, John Thirlwall, Gail Turnbull, and Louis Zukofsky.

Perspective, vol. 6, no. 4 (Autumn–Winter 1953). Contains articles by Robert Beum, Gary Davenport, Sanford Edelstein, Hugh Kenner, Ralph Nash, and George Zabriskie.

Western Review, vol. 17, no. 4 (Summer 1953). Contains "American Letters: A Symposium," which is an article by Russell Roth followed by comments by Elizabeth Hardwick, Robert B. Heilman, and William Van O'Connor.

WILLIAM WORDSWORTH
(1770–1850)

F. R. WATSON

LIFE

IN HIS GREAT autobiographical poem, *The Prelude,* Wordsworth tells the story of his early years; but it is important to remember that the truth was more complex than the poem suggests. *The Prelude,* like all poems, selects its own imaginative material from the experience on which it is based; and many of Wordsworth's poems are founded on his own life and his interpretation of it. To understand his poetry fully, we need to know something of Wordsworth's life, in more detail than we do with other poets whose imaginations are not so intricately connected to their own experience.

William Wordsworth was born at Cockermouth, Cumberland, on 7 April 1770, the second child of John and Ann Wordsworth. John Wordsworth was an attorney, the "agent" of Sir James Lowther, for whom he acted in legal and political matters. The Wordsworth children were born in a substantial house in Cockermouth, where the family lived until 1778; but in March of that year Ann Wordsworth died, and the family was split up. William's beloved sister Dorothy (born 25 December 1771) was sent to live at Halifax with her mother's cousin, and the boys were sent to school at Hawkshead. Fortunately they were well educated there and well cared for: they lived in a cottage with an old lady named Ann Tyson, who took in school boarders and who seems to have given them the right amount of affection and freedom. The impression conveyed by *The Prelude* is one of extraordinary energy and activity, but also of normality; he played games, both indoor and outdoor, with a natural exuberance and enthusiasm.

On 30 December 1783, when William was thirteen, his father died; years later he remembered the boyish anticipation of going home for the Christmas holidays and the sadness that followed. The house at Cockermouth had to be given up, and from then on the boys spent their holidays either with their uncle at Whitehaven or, more frequently, at Penrith with their maternal grandparents, the Cooksons, and their uncle, Christopher Crackanthorpe Cookson. There the boys were patronized and made to feel dependent, and William was rebellious: it is clear that his childhood was by no means as uniformly happy as *The Prelude* suggests, and it is of Hawkshead and not Penrith that the poet writes when he looks back to the happiness of the early years.

In October 1787, the young Wordsworth left the Lake District for the first time, to become an undergraduate at St. John's College, Cambridge. Although there were other boys from Hawkshead there, and he was in many ways contented, he was also uneasy in his mind and restless; just how restless may be seen from the marvelous fourth book of *The Prelude* when he describes the joy of returning to Hawkshead for his first summer vacation. The most spectacular evidence of his unease came two years later, in the long vacation of 1790, when he and his friend Robert Jones undertook a strenuous walking tour through

France and Switzerland. By then he had given up any intention of getting an honors degree, and his leaving Cambridge at a time when he might have been preparing for examinations was a snub to the academic life. The tour itself, which gave rise to *Descriptive Sketches* and later to the sixth book of *The Prelude,* was one of the great imaginative experiences of Wordsworth's life.

It was followed by an unsettled period: after graduating from Cambridge without honors in January 1791, he lived in London for some months before spending the summer in Wales, revisiting Cambridge, and then leaving for France in November.

His motive for visiting France was probably to learn the language: the results were very different. First, in a country that was experiencing a revolution he received his early political education, partly from his own observation and partly from his friendship with Michel de Beaupuy. Beaupuy was an unusual man, an army officer who was isolated from his fellow officers as a consequence of his revolutionary sympathies. Beaupuy's politics were simple and humane: he was against corruption and poverty, and looked forward to a time when men would live in liberty and brotherhood and the world would be a better place. Second, Wordsworth met Annette Vallon, the daughter of a deceased surgeon of Blois; they became lovers, and she became pregnant.

Thus, in a little over a year, Wordsworth had experienced a remarkable political and sexual awakening. Moreover, it was a time of great events: during his time in France the attack on the Tuileries, the September massacres, the abolition of the monarchy, and the split between the moderate Girondins (some of whom Wordsworth knew) and the Jacobins heralded the trial and execution of the king (21 January 1793) and the Terror. By late December 1792, however, Wordsworth had returned to England; his child, Anne-Caroline, was born and baptized on 15 December.

The following year, 1793, was of considerable importance to Wordsworth in several ways. In the first place, it saw the first publication of any of Wordsworth's poems: *An Evening Walk* and *Descriptive Sketches* appeared on 29 January. Three days later, France declared war on England, and England responded by declaring war on France on 11 February. Wordsworth's response, as he tells us in *The Prelude,* was painfully confused: his natural patriotism conflicted with his hope for the Revolution, and he must also have been disturbed by the separation from Annette and the child. Some of his anger is found in the "Letter to the Bishop of Llandaff," an unpublished reply to a sermon on *The Wisdom and Goodness of God in Having Made Both Rich and Poor*: the bishop's appendix to the sermon criticized the French and complacently preferred the British constitution and British justice. Wordsworth's reply demonstrates his impatience with what he called "the baleful influence of aristocracy and nobility upon human happiness and virtue" (p. 46) and his use of a classic argument for the revolutionary use of force:

> . . . a time of revolution is not the season of true Liberty. Alas! the obstinacy & perversion of men is such that she is too often obliged to borrow the very arms of despotism to overthrow him, and in order to reign in peace must establish herself by violence.[1] (1.33)

The "Letter" shows clearly Wordsworth's hatred of inherited rank and wealth, of rich clergy, and of the British system of justice (from which he and his brothers and sisters had suffered: after the death of their father, Lowther, now Lord Lonsdale, refused to pay for the work that he had done, and a long and inconclusive lawsuit followed).

It was at this moment that a friend, William Calvert, proposed a tour of the west of England, traveling in a small cart called a "whiskey": they began on the Isle of Wight, where Wordsworth's anger was probably further inflamed by the sight of the English fleet

1. All prose quotations are from W. J. B. Owen and J. W. Smyser, eds., *The Prose Works of William Wordsworth,* 3 vols. (Oxford, 1974). References are to volume and page numbers.

preparing for war. From there they set out across Salisbury Plain: an accident occurred to the whiskey, and Calvert took the horse, leaving Wordsworth to walk. Salisbury Plain was a desolate part of the country, and his solitude must have seemed to the young poet to be emblematic of his isolation and lonely frustration: he walked northward, past Stonehenge, having frightening visions (*The Prelude,* book XII, 1805 text) of ancient Britons engaged in savage war and human sacrifice. From there he traveled northwest, to Tintern Abbey and up the Wye valley to his friend Robert Jones in north Wales. The journey was remembered by him with a peculiar vividness: fifty years later he told Isabella Fenwick that it "left on my mind imaginative impressions the force of which I have felt to this day" (*Poetical Works,* I.330).[2] From it came experiences that represent two seminal themes of Wordsworth's poetry: his King Lear-like awareness of the houseless poverty of the outcasts of society, and his vivid appreciation of the beauty of a scene like that a few miles above Tintern Abbey. Meanwhile we may gain some insight into the kind of young man he appeared to be, if we realize that a tinker (who later became Peter Bell in the poem of that name) thought he might be a murderer. He had no doubt been sleeping rough and probably looked unkempt and farouche.

To the following months and years belong a variety of experiences, but none so significant as this remarkable journey on foot. Later in 1793, Wordsworth probably revisited France in secret, supposedly fleeing from Paris when his life was in danger; in 1794 he spent a happy few weeks with his sister Dorothy at Keswick; later in the year he stayed with a friend, Raisley Calvert (brother of William), being his companion during a terminal illness. Calvert died in January 1795, leaving Wordsworth a legacy that enabled him to live independently though simply. He returned to London, where he furthered his acquaintance with the radical political philosopher William Godwin, and in September he accepted the offer of a house in Dorset called Racedown (between Crewkerne and Lyme Regis) from some Bristol friends. There he and Dorothy settled down, and he began to recover from the upheavals of the previous years. He wrote much of the second version of a poem on the Salisbury Plain experience and a verse drama, *The Borderers*; though the main benefit of these years was a steady growth in the belief in his own powers. This was given a powerful boost by the developing acquaintance with Samuel Taylor Coleridge, whom Wordsworth had first met in 1794 and subsequently corresponded with. Coleridge visited Racedown in June 1797, leaping over a gate and bounding across a field in his eagerness to arrive. They read their poems to each other, with mutual delight; by mid-July, after Coleridge had brought William and Dorothy back with him to Nether Stowey (in North Somerset), they had moved into Alfoxden House nearby. There followed a year of buoyant spirits and happy activity, walking, writing, and preparing the *Lyrical Ballads* (1798). The final poem, "Lines Composed a Few Miles Above Tintern Abbey," was added in July after a short walking tour with Dorothy, in which they revisited the landscape that Wordsworth had seen in 1793; its confident tone of sustained and assured thankfulness indicates Wordsworth's joy at finding his imagination working at full stretch after the troublesome years that followed his return from France.

Throughout these years, it is difficult to overemphasize the importance of Dorothy Wordsworth's love and care: she continued to have faith in her brother and his poetry, and her vivid appreciation of nature (recorded in her journals) was an inspiration to both Wordsworth and Coleridge. The three left for Germany in September 1798, in the same month that saw the appearance of *Lyrical Ballads.* The plan was to settle near a university town, learn German, and attend lectures. They split up, to avoid speaking English all the time, and the Wordsworths settled in Goslar, during an unusually severe winter:

2. *The Poetical Works of William Wordsworth,* revised edition by E. de Selincourt and H. Darbishire, 5 vols. (Oxford, 1952–1959).

deprived of books and company, William began to write again, composing some of the "Lucy" poems and the first parts of what was later to be book I of *The Prelude.* They left Goslar in February 1799, and after a short walking tour in Germany returned to England in the spring. In December 1799, they finally came to rest in the Lake District, in the cottage at Grasmere that is now called Dove Cottage. Except for occasional short periods or visits, Wordsworth lived in the Lake District for the rest of his life, at first at Grasmere and (after 1813) at Rydal, the next village.

The first years at Grasmere were years of great happiness, for Wordsworth seems to have felt a very deep sense of homecoming (which is expressed in "Home at Grasmere," a poem that remained unpublished at his death). In October 1802 he married Mary Hutchinson, after a brief visit to France to see Annette and the nine-year-old Anne-Caroline; he had known Mary Hutchinson and her family since childhood and stayed with them at their farm at Sockburn-on-Tees after returning from Germany. Meanwhile, Coleridge had settled at Keswick, thirteen miles away, though he was unhappy with his wife and often in poor spirits. He left Keswick for Malta in January 1804, and although the friends met again, there was never the same creative interchange and intimacy that had taken place in 1797–1798. Before leaving, however, Coleridge had introduced Wordsworth to Sir George Beaumont, a wealthy patron and connoisseur, who became a benefactor and friend until his death in 1827: it was to Beaumont that Wordsworth turned for support during the greatest crisis of his adult life, the death of his brother John at sea in February 1805.

The death of John Wordsworth, followed by the growth of the friendship with Sir George and Lady Beaumont, herald the later years of Wordsworth's life. They were, perhaps inevitably, less exciting than before: in 1813 he became distributor of stamps for Westmorland, a post that carried with it a commission on the sale of stamps, which amounted to some (pounds) 400 a year, although clerks and other officials had to be paid out of this. Nevertheless, the post marked a significant change in Wordsworth's status and way of life; similarly, the friendship with Beaumont was with a man who was, unlike Coleridge, conventional and conservative in every way. We can only speculate on the reasons why Wordsworth wrote so little good poetry after 1807; but his increasingly respectable life, and the loss of Coleridge's stimulus, may have been partly responsible.

Apart from some Scottish and Continental tours, Wordsworth remained at Rydal Mount from 1813 to his death on 23 April 1850. In his later years, he was revered and honored: the University of Durham gave him an honorary degree in 1838, and Oxford followed in 1839; in 1843, on the death of Southey, he became poet laureate. His later years were clouded by the protracted illness of his sister, Dorothy, and by the death of his beloved daughter Dora in 1847; but he had the satisfaction of seeing his poems grow in popularity, and his fame spread through the English-speaking world. His faith that his poetry "must sooner or later work its way into the hearts and minds of the people"[3] had been fully justified.

EARLY POEMS

In 1843, Wordsworth said that "no change has taken place in my manner for the last forty-five years." This dates Wordsworth's mature style at 1798, with the publication of *Lyrical Ballads,* and suggests that in the earlier poems he had failed to find his own individual voice. At first sight this seems to be the case: *An Evening Walk* and *Descriptive Sketches* (1793) are written in heroic couplets and contain many borrowings and influences from eighteenth-century poets; while another major poem of these years, the Salisbury Plain poem (in two versions), is written in Spenserian stanzas, another popular eighteenth-

3. Mary Moorman, *William Wordsworth: A Biography,* vol. II: *The Later Years 1803–1850* (Oxford, 1965), p. 544.

century form. In other respects, too, they seem conventional, with titles, diction, and description following the eighteenth-century patterns. They were later revised extensively by Wordsworth, and they are best read in the 1793 text, which is printed in many editions. There the reader can see the dominance of the contemporary style:

> —Then Quiet led me up the huddling rill,
> Bright'ning with water-breaks the sombrous gill;
> To where, while thick above the branches close,
> In dark-brown bason its wild waves repose,
> Inverted shrubs, and moss of darkest green,
> Cling from the rocks, with pale wood-weeds between;
> Save that, atop, the subtle sunbeams shine,
> On wither'd briars that o'er the craggs recline;
> Sole light admitted here, a small cascade,
> Illumes with sparkling foam the twilight shade.
> Beyond, along the visto of the brook,
> Where antique roots its bustling path o'erlook,
> The eye reposes on a secret bridge
> Half grey, half shagg'd with ivy to its ridge.
> (*An Evening Walk,* 71–84)

Here the reader notices immediately the personification of "Quiet," the use of words like "sombrous, "illumes," and "visto," the use of inversion, with a latinate postponement of the main verb, and the use of a Latin participial construction, "Sole light admitted here," to make an adjectival phrase. All these disappear in later versions, which suggests that Wordsworth himself came to regard them as blemishes on the poem. Yet the early poetry is not so unoriginal as it looks. It was *Descriptive Sketches* that first drew Coleridge's attention to Wordsworth, as he tells us in *Biographia Literaria*:

> In the form, style, and manner of the whole poem, and in the structure of the particular lines and periods, there is an harshness and acerbity connected and combined with words and images all a-glow, which might recall those products of the vegetable world, where gorgeous blossoms rise out of the hard and thorny rind and shell, within which the rich fruit was elaborating. The language was not only peculiar and strong, but at times knotty and contorted, as by its own impatient strength; while the novelty and struggling crowd of images, acting in conjunction with the difficulties of the style, demanded always a greater closeness of attention, than poetry, (at all events, than descriptive poetry) has a right to claim.[4] (I.56)

What Coleridge is describing here is a kind of individual voice, powerful and original, which he had detected: and it is true that the verse is full of energy, bursting out of the heroic couplets as a child outgrows its clothes. The subject matter, too, seems too big for the form of these poems: *An Evening Walk,* for instance, is principally about a landscape seen during the course of an afternoon, but it also contains a section in the middle that describes a destitute mother and her starving children. Similarly, *Descriptive Sketches,* which is about Wordsworth's tour of the Alps in 1790, contains a great diversity of material including descriptions of the mountain scenery, reflections on the lot of the Swiss and of mankind in general, and a prophecy of liberty. Both poems look two ways, in fact, to nature and to man, and in this we can see the beginnings of Wordsworth's continuous later concern with the interaction of the two. In these early poems they exist side by side, uncomfortably juxtaposed; in the later poetry there is a creative interaction, so that Wordsworth can portray himself.

> On Man, on Nature, and on Human Life,
> Musing in solitude. . . .
> (preface to *The Excursion,* 1–2)

The introduction of man and human life here is not just a tautology: Wordsworth surveys man, and nature, but also the larger significance that arises from the interaction be-

4. All references to *Biographia Literaria* are to the J. Shawcross edition (Oxford, 1907).

tween the two, between man and the world around him; he is to investigate the nature and purpose of human life, its good and evil, its joy and sorrow. These things are latent in *An Evening Walk* and *Descriptive Sketches*: both are filled with images of the beauty and sublimity of nature, but they are also conscious that mankind, besides having such enjoyments, often has to suffer hardship and misery.

Descriptive Sketches, which was written during Wordsworth's residence in France in 1792, contains a good deal of explicit political suggestion. The "Salisbury Plain" poems carry this further. They are different versions of the same poem, which ends up in the *Poetical Works,* somewhat toned down, as "Guilt and Sorrow," though part of it was published in the *Lyrical Ballads* under the title of "The Female Vagrant." The first Salisbury Plain poem draws its inspiration from Wordsworth's solitary wanderings in 1793 and his angry state of mind at the time: the first version ends with an impassioned plea for revolution and a new order:

> Heroes of Truth pursue your march, uptear
> Th'Oppressor's dungeon from its deepest
> base;
> High o'er the towers of Pride undaunted rear
> Resistless in your might the herculean mace
> Of Reason; let foul Error's monster race
> Dragged from their dens start at the light
> with pain
> And die; pursue your toils, till not a trace
> Be left on earth of Superstition's reign,
> Save that eternal pile which frowns on
> Sarum's plain.
> (541–549)

The story of the poem concerns a good-hearted sailor (the first stanzas of the second version show him helping an aged soldier) who has been forced into the navy by a press-gang and dismissed without reward. In his anger he robs and kills a traveler, and now wanders homeless across the plain. In a ruined building he meets a woman, the female vagrant, who relates her story: her father was forced to leave his home by a rapacious landowner, and her husband joined the army to provide for the family; they followed the army to America, where the husband and children all died; and the woman was then shipped back to England. On the following morning the sailor and the vagrant continue their journey, pacifying an angry father who is beating his child, until they meet a dying woman, who turns out to be the sailor's wife; her death affects the sailor so deeply that he gives himself up to justice and is hanged.

In the later published version, entitled "Guilt and Sorrow," the sailor is deemed to have suffered enough; in the earlier (second) version, Wordsworth drives home the message of the poem with a remorseless and fixed anger. The female vagrant is one victim of a society that allows the rich to deprive the poor of their livelihood, and in which there is no alternative to poverty but enlistment in the army. The poor and helpless, however benevolent and well disposed, are cast out to fend for themselves, while old soldiers and sailors are thrown on the scrap heap. The sailor is an example of a man who is driven to desperation by the treatment he has received; even more bitter, perhaps, is the way in which at the end, he is surrounded by complacent people who bring him to justice; like the judge in Camus's *L'Etranger,* they make no attempt to understand him. After his death, as he swings in chains on a gibbet, a fair is set up beneath, in a final macabre touch. Meanwhile, the housewife who cares for the dying woman in her last hours stands out as a type of the Good Samaritan, and we are also allowed to see the deep humanity of the sailor and the female vagrant. The sustained anger of the poem is matched only by the poet's admiration for those who can preserve their natural benevolence and kindness in the face of such adversity.

In the years following 1793 this relationship between individual behavior and the creation of the good society was clearly much in Wordsworth's mind, particularly in view of the later course of the French Revolution. The motives of the Revolution had been so good, and its outcome so disastrous (especially,

Wordsworth thought, under Robespierre), that some explanation was desirable. This Wordsworth attempted to supply in *The Borderers,* the other major work of these years. The complicated plot of this tragedy in verse is conducted to a point at which a good man, Marmaduke, is persuaded to leave an old blind man to die in a bleak wasteland; Marmaduke has been deceived by Oswald, who had committed a similar crime many years before, after being manipulated by others. Marmaduke's motives are correct; he is a benevolent man who ends the play in remorse and penitence. Oswald, on the other hand, is driven by his crime to renounce remorse, to see in himself a terrible freedom from normal principles of benevolence and restraint. This is the freedom that he urges upon Marmaduke, and it was such a freedom that Wordsworth saw a man like Robespierre exercising. "Let us suppose, says Wordsworth, describing Oswald in the preface of *The Borderers,* "a young man of great intellectual powers, yet without any solid principles of genuine benevolence" (*Prose Works,* I.76). His action shows "the dangerous use which may be made of reason when a man has committed a great crime" (*ibid.,* p. 79). The note to *The Borderers* connects this clearly with the experience in France, for Wordsworth writes that "sin and crime are apt to start from their very opposite qualities," and that he had seen this "while the revolution was rapidly advancing to its extreme of wickedness" (*Poetical Works,* I.342).

When Coleridge heard Wordsworth read *The Borderers* he described it as "absolutely wonderful" (*Poetical Works,* I.344); he praised the work for its "*profound* touches of the human heart," seeing in it what later critics have come to recognize as a primary interest of Wordsworth's, the concern with the human heart, traditionally the seat of the affections and the organ of shared feeling between man and man. The concern for the human heart, and for what Wordsworth describes in the preface as "the primary laws of our nature," is brilliantly expressed in *Lyrical Ballads.* In *The Borderers* it is tangled up with a complicated plot and an undramatic scenario; in *Lyrical Ballads* it is produced in a marvelous series of spare, taut narrative poems, interwoven with concrete expressions of Wordsworth's own belief and ending with the triumphant "Tintern Abbey."

LYRICAL BALLADS

Coleridge described Wordsworth's part in *Lyrical Ballads* in his *Biographia Literaria.* While his own energies were to be directed toward the supernatural, Wordsworth

> was to propose to himself as his object, to give the charm of novelty to things of every day, and to excite a feeling analogous to the supernatural, by awakening the mind's attention from the lethargy of custom, and directing it to the loveliness and the wonders of the world before us; an inexhaustible treasure, but for which, in consequence of the film of familiarity and selfish solicitude we have eyes, yet see not, ears that hear not, and hearts that neither feel nor understand. (II.6)

It will be seen that Wordsworth's role was to present the ordinary so that the reader would see it with new eyes; as he said himself about "The Thorn": "Cannot I by some invention do as much to make this Thorn permanently an impressive object as the storm has made it to my eyes at this moment?" (*Poetical Works,* II.511). The result is that *Lyrical Ballads* contains many poems that are concerned with simple people in ordinary surroundings, who have problems that are common, sometimes universal: old age, poverty, pregnancy and betrayal, cold, bereavement. Their stories are narrated in a style that is simple and direct, influenced by the street ballads in its dramatic abruptness. This style has sometimes been seen as unsuccessful, as Wordsworth's theory running away with his practice, yet its awkward simplicity is often peculiarly effective. Wordsworth writes a poetry the texture of which allows no escape, which is perhaps why it has been disliked: the lines shock the reader into a recognition of the suffering and the happiness of his fellow human beings, and there is no delicate transfusion of life into art, but, rather, a direct rendering of life into something more tactless and immediate than art. In its spirit it resembles Marianne Moore's poem "Poetry":

> I, too, dislike it: there are things that are
> important
> beyond all this fiddle.

And yet, paradoxically, Wordsworth's is a highly functioning poetic art, in the sense described by Marianne Moore in her last verse:

> . . . if you demand on the one hand,
> the raw material of poetry in
> all its rawness and
> that which is on the other hand
> genuine, then you are interested in
> poetry.

Wordsworth certainly presents the raw material in all its rawness, in a way that, for many, commands respect; if he leaves himself open to the jeers of the cynic or the skeptic, this is a price he is willing to pay, for the greatest poets have always been vulnerable in this way. So we have Simon Lee's thick ankles, and the little pond in "The Thorn," which is three feet long and two feet wide, and poor Betty in "The Idiot Boy," "in a sad distemper." Not only is there a distinct rawness in these lines, but there is also "that which is on the other hand/genuine," the respect for the figures who appear in the poems, a respect that comes from love. Wordsworth is well aware of the danger of becoming a voyeur of human suffering: in "The Thorn," for instance, he introduces just such a figure, a retired sea captain who has too little to occupy his time, so that he becomes endlessly curious about his neighbors, and especially about the plight of one of them. We are presented, therefore, with a poem that is at once a narrative and a dramatic monologue; other examples of the sophistication of Wordsworth's art are found in "The Idiot Boy," where the diction creates its own rhetorical and rhythmical patterns, and "Simon Lee," where the colloquial simplicities of the earlier verses give way to a final quotation that requires the reader to think, sharply and suddenly, to penetrate beneath the conventional complaint of man's ingratitude to something more profound and more pathetic.

It is this respect for his fellow creatures, and this craft, that are the distinguishing marks of *Lyrical Ballads*: they are poems that challenge our very ideas about the nature of poetry and that also confound our expectations in other ways. If we accommodate ourselves to the rhetoric of "The Idiot Boy," we are surprised by the ritual game of "Expostulation and Reply" and "The Tables Turned," in which Matthew and William play out a game of statement and counterstatement. If we become accustomed to the simplicity of the ballad style, both in narrative poems and in reflective ones, we are surprised by the majestic reflections of "Lines Composed a Few Miles Above Tintern Abbey." This final poem, the last in the 1798 collection, is written in the eighteenth-century meditative blank-verse style, but with such individuality, originality, and organization as to make it a fitting conclusion to the volume; it should be seen not as the one success in a curious collection but as the open statement of what is explicit or implicit in so many of the other poems, a wonderful openness to feeling and experience. In the preface to *Lyrical Ballads*, published in the second edition (1800), Wordsworth writes of the poet that he is

> a man speaking to men: a man, it is true, endowed with more lively sensibility, more enthusiasm and tenderness, who has a greater knowledge of human nature, and a more comprehensive soul, than are supposed to be common among mankind; a man pleased with his own passions and volitions, and who rejoices more than other men in the spirit of life that is in him; delighting to contemplate similar volitions and passions as manifested in the goings-on of the Universe, and habitually impelled to create them where he does not find them. (*Poetical Works*, II.393)

The importance of this definition is not only in its splendid statement of a shared humanity between the poet and others; it is also concerned with the character of the poet as enthusiast, who is able to express his joy at being alive and finding himself in a world that is full of the same kind of passion and life. To be thus aware of the joy of the world is to be aware also of its variety and complexity, its pain as well as its joy; and Wordsworth is a great tragic poet as well as one who celebrates the happiness of man. He sees the pain of old age, the miseries of poverty, the tragicomedy of idiocy. The extraordinary feature of *Lyrical Ballads* is that they carry everywhere the evidence of the poet's love for life, for his fellow human beings, for those who are oppressed by society, for his sister, for the natural world around him. This energetic love of life is, in Wordsworth's eyes, evidence of a full humanity; in the preface he describes a poet as "singing a song in which all human beings join with him" (*Poetical Works,* II.396).

The fundamental conception of the poet as human being, sharing in the joys and sorrows of all mankind with a more than common enthusiasm, has tended to become obscured in the preface by Wordsworth's statements about poetic language. The principal object of *Lyrical Ballads* was, he said,

> to choose incidents and situations from common life, and to relate or describe them, throughout, as far as was possible in a selection of language really used by men, and, at the same time, to throw over them a certain colouring of imagination. whereby ordinary things should be presented to the mind in an unusual aspect. . . . (*ibid.,* II.386)

The phrase "a selection of language really used by men," and a similar one from the first paragraph, "a selection of the real language of men in a state of vivid sensation," have caused many problems to critics of Wordsworth, from Coleridge onward, who have wanted to know what is meant by "a selection" or by "real" language; other difficulties have been posed by those who have solemnly taken Wordsworth to task for what follows:

> Humble and rustic life was generally chosen, because, in that condition, the essential passions of the heart find a better soil in which they can attain their maturity, are less under restraint, and speak a plainer and more emphatic language; because in that condition of life our elementary feelings co-exist in a state of greater simplicity, and consequently, may be more accurately contemplated, and more forcibly communicated; because the manners of rural life germinate from those elementary feelings, and, from the necessary character of rural occupations, are more easily comprehended, and are more durable; and, lastly, because in that condition the passions of men are incorporated with the beautiful and permanent forms of nature. (*ibid.,* II.386–387)

We may disagree with Wordsworth about the need to choose humble and rustic life (although there are clear sociological indications that he may have been right), but his motives are clear and creditable: they are concerned with "the essential patterns of the heart," "elementary feelings," and "the passions of men" which are "incorporated with the beautiful and permanent forms of nature." His theory of language (partly set out in the appendix to the preface) is that primitive poets, although using a language of extraordinary occasions, spoke a language "which, though unusual, was still the language of men." In the course of time, the unusual became mistaken for the reality, so that diction became "daily more and more corrupt, thrusting out of sight the plain humanities of nature by a motley masquerade of tricks, quaintnesses, hieroglyphics, and enigmas" (*Poetical Works,* II.406). It is clear that Wordsworth was attempting to return to what he saw as a correct simplicity and directness, and that the choice of humble and rustic life, together with a predilection for ordinary language, is connected with this. The poetic results show how unprejudiced Wordsworth was about the matter, and how the actual language of his poetry varied according to the needs of the poem in question: thc language of "Simon Lee" is very different from that of "We Are Seven," and the impassioned blank verse of "Tintern Abbey" is very different from the austere simplicities of "Michael." In every case the aim is to provide "little falsehood of description" and ideas "expressed in language fitted to their respective importance." So we have the hymnlike utterances of "To My Sister":

And from the blessed power that rolls
About, below, above,
We'll frame the measure of our souls:
They shall be tuned to love.
(33–36)

or the nursery rhyme cadences of "We Are Seven":

I met a little cottage Girl,
She was eight years old, she said;
Her hair was thick with many a curl
That clustered round her head.
(5–8)

The deliberate simplicity of this latter verse is characteristic of some of the shorter poems in *Lyrical Ballads*: critics have often found them naive and oversimple, but Wordsworth was not stupid and clearly had a specific effect in mind, an effect that may not seem as mature or complex as "Tintern Abbey" but that has an equal importance for an understanding of Wordsworth. He is a poet who is capable of writing with an amazing directness and hard sense, yet he is also capable of writing a poetry that has deeper and more elusive meanings.

As an example of the first kind, we may take "Simon Lee." It is a poem that underwent a number of changes after its first publication in 1798, but for convenience I shall take the version that appears in the Oxford Standard Authors edition, by Hutchinson. There the poem begins with a description of Simon Lee as a young man:

In the sweet shire of Cardigan,
Not far from pleasant Ivor-hall
An old Man dwells, a little man,—
'Tis said he once was tall.
Full five-and-thirty years he lived
A running huntsman merry;
And still the centre of his cheek
Is red as a ripe cherry.
(1–8)

Here the jingle of the rhythm, and the feminine rhyme at the end, encourage a curious jauntiness, an attention such as one gives to a straightforward, cheerful, and undemanding narrative: such a register is even clearer in the 1798 version of the second four lines:

Of years he has upon his back
No doubt, a burthen weighty;
He says he is three score and ten,
But others say he's eighty.

where the random guessing about Simon's age suggests the trivial and simple. In the reworked version of the poem, the first three verses, describing Simon in the past, continue this mood. They describe him as a huntsman in his prime, running, hallooing, and pushing himself to the limit of his endurance. Then comes the change, heralded by a phrase borrowed from Wordsworth's favorite, John Milton:

But, oh the heavy change!—bereft
Of health, strength, friends, and kindred,
see!
(25–26)

The same deliberate simplicity is carried on in the following stanzas, which describe the aged and feeble man: it is as though a primitive painter had produced a diptych entitled "Youth" and "Age." Now the reader is given the facts with a hard matter-of-factness:

And he is lean and he is sick;
His body, dwindled and awry,
Rests upon ankles swoln and thick;
His legs are thin and dry.
(33–36)

After this, however, comes a surprise, as the poet himself enters the poem, with a direct address to the reader:

My gentle Reader, I perceive
How patiently you've waited,
And now I fear that you expect
Some tale will be related.

O Reader! had you in your mind
Such stores as silent thought can bring,
O gentle Reader! you would find
A tale in every thing.
What more I have to say is short,
And you must kindly take it:
It is no tale; but, should you think,
Perhaps a tale you'll make it.
(61–72)

Here the style seems to be the same, with the same insistent meter and feminine rhyme; the idea behind these lines, too, seems to be of the same order of simplicity as the earlier descriptive passages, and the continual addressing of the reader has a jocular effect. But beneath the simple words, especially "tale" and "think," there lie considerable reverberations. The point of these verses, which contain the central analysis of how to consider Simon Lee and others like him, is that they emphasize the fact that Simon Lee *is*: he is a sad spectacle, an old man past his prime, living on in poverty and unable to perform the simplest task. There is ample matter for the feeling heart to consider here, and there will be no tale, for there should be none: we are contemplating old age, and there will be no escape into a story to take our minds off it. There is, as the poem's subtitle tells us, "an incident," but that is all: however, if we *think*, we can make much of that incident, that is, if we have hearts that feel, eyes that perceive, and minds that understand; if, in other words, we *think* about the plight of the elderly, we shall find a deep significance in the trivial incident that follows. It is a significance that is simple because it is universal, containing within itself the awareness of human life as brief, transitory, and often painful. So although it is no story, it contains a deep and inescapable truth:

It is no tale; but, should you think,
Perhaps a tale you'll make it.

The poem is given a final twist, as the traditional complaint against ingratitude is exploited to make something even more pathetic:

—I've heard of hearts unkind, kind deeds
With coldness still returning;
Alas! the gratitude of men
Hath oftener left me mourning.
(93–96)

There are times, it appears, when gratitude is actually worse than ingratitude: from the simplicity of the earlier verses the reader is now faced with a paradox, for the poet grieves more for the pathetic condition of Simon Lee (which makes him weep for the simplest kind of help) than for the usual ingratitude.

If "Simon Lee" moves from simplicity to a sudden complexity, surprising the reader by its final turn, the movement of "Tintern Abbey" is much more deliberate, and the poem modulates with consummate skill between different registers of simplicity and complexity. It is a poem that moves between the outer world of nature and the inner world of the mind in a way that beautifully suggests the interaction between the two. There is not space enough here to provide a full examination of the poem, but the way in which its reflective moments alternate with descriptions of the actual landscape is a feature that stands out, although it is most subtly and sensitively accomplished. The poem begins with the river Wye, bounded by its steep and lofty banks, with the pastoral farms and hedgerows, and the quiet sky; at the end the poem comes to rest in the same landscape, with a sense of having gone out and returned that is artistically very satisfying. Between the beginning and end, intertwining with the descriptions of landscape, is the exploration of the poet's mind and heart, and his expressions of confidence and love for his sister and the influence of nature upon her. The poem witnesses to his own experience and his trust that the same blessing will be hers.

The poem is dated "July 13 1798," and records a visit to the Wye some five years after the memorable walk of 1793. It records the effect of the landscape on the poet's mind as he remembered it, an effect that is both moral and mystical. The movement of the verse here is characteristic of a certain kind of Wordsworthian blank verse, which begins with a fairly straightforward idea, which it then expands; this leads to a further idea, or a further development, as one moment, or one insight, gives rise to another. The paragraph rises and falls, only to rise higher; the first statements of an idea are taken up and expanded a few lines later ("that blessed mood, . . . that serene and blessed mood"); moments of insight that the reader thinks have been described are suddenly taken up again:

. . . These beauteous forms,
Through a long absence, have not been to me
As is a landscape to a blind man's eye:
But oft, in lonely rooms, and 'mid the din
Of towns and cities, I have owed to them,
In hours of weariness, sensations sweet,
Felt in the blood, and felt along the heart;
And passing even into my purer mind,
With tranquil restoration:—feelings too
Of unremembered pleasure: such, perhaps,
As have no slight or trivial influence
On that best portion of a good man's life,
His little, nameless, unremembered acts
Of kindness and of love. Nor less, I trust,
To them I may have owed another gift,
Of aspect more sublime; that blessed mood,
In which the burthen of the mystery,
In which the heavy and the weary weight
Of all this unintelligible world,
Is lightened:—that serene and blessed mood,
In which the affections gently lead us on,—
Until, the breath of this corporeal frame
And even the motion of our human blood
Almost suspended, we are laid asleep
In body, and become a living soul:
While with an eye made quiet by the power
Of harmony, and the deep power of joy,
We see into the life of things.
(22–49)

The same process is found in the great central passage describing the loss and gain of Wordsworth's imaginative development: if he has lost the dizzy rapture of his first coming to the Wye valley, he has gained a maturity that allows him both to learn and to feel. In this passage the second verb echoes the first, heralding a stronger and more assured statement of an inspiration ("For I have learned. . . . And I have felt"). The central section is in three parts, rising, declaiming, and descending, with the middle part ("a sense sublime . . .") containing a great enveloping conception of the whole of nature as interfused with spirit and movement, with a life that is found in the mind of man and in the external world:

. . . For I have learned
To look on nature, not as in the hour
Of thoughtless youth; but hearing oftentimes
The still, sad music of humanity,
Nor harsh nor grating, though of ample power
To chasten and subdue. And I have felt
A presence that disturbs me with the joy
Of elevated thoughts; a sense sublime
Of something far more deeply interfused,
Whose dwelling is the light of setting suns,
And the round ocean and the living air,
And the blue sky, and in the mind of man:
A motion and a spirit, that impels
All thinking things, all objects of all thought,
And rolls through all things. . . .
(88–102)

It is tempting to see the impassioned blank verse of "Tintern Abbey" as the true voice of Wordsworth, regarding "Simon Lee" or "We Are Seven" as unfortunate applications of a theory of simple language. This is the theory of Wordsworth as the poet of "two voices," which takes its name from J. K. Stephen's parody of Wordsworth's own sonnet:

Two voices are there: one is of the deep;
It learns the storm-cloud's thunderous melody,
Now roars, now murmurs with the changing sea,
Now bird-like pipes, now closes soft in sleep:
And one is of an old half-witted sheep
Which bleats articulate monotony,

And indicates that two and one are three,
That grass is green, lakes damp, and
mountains steep:
And, Wordsworth, both are thine. . . .

This is a sensible and witty view to take, but it ignores so much of the idiosyncrasy that makes Wordsworth himself and no other: it neglects to observe the way in which Wordsworth clung tenaciously to the very lines that seem most ludicrous to modern readers. When his friend Henry Crabb Robinson told Wordsworth that he did not dare to read these lines aloud, the poet replied, "They ought to be liked." For us to write them off is to make Wordsworth into our own poet, the poet of "Tintern Abbey" and the other meditative or narrative blank verse poems. We would be truer to the spirit of the poet himself if we took *Lyrical Ballads* as a whole and observed it with the spirit that Wordsworth himself had in a letter he wrote in 1802. A young correspondent, John Wilson, had written to him, praising *Lyrical Ballads* but querying the suitability of "The Idiot Boy," which he thought not so likely to please. Wordsworth's reply (7 June 1802) was "please whom? or what?"

> I answer, human nature, as it has been and ever will be. But where are we to find the best measure of this? I answer, from within; by stripping our own hearts naked, and by looking out of ourselves towards men who lead the simplest lives most according to nature men who have never known false refinements, wayward and artificial desires, false criticisms, effeminate habits of thinking and feeling, or who, having known these things, have outgrown them.[5]

And if this is the ideal, the poet is to point to it by leading men toward the good, rather than by reflecting the wishes and feelings of the majority of men:

> You have given me praise for having reflected faithfully in my poems the feelings of human nature. I would fain hope that I have done so. But a great Poet ought to do more than this he ought to a certain degree to rectify men's feelings, to give them new compositions of feeling, to render their feelings more sane pure and permanent. In short, more consonant to nature, that is, to eternal nature, and the great moving spirit of things. He ought to travel before men occasionally as well as at their sides. (*ibid.*)

5. From E. de Selincourt, ed., *Letters of William and Dorothy Wordsworth, The Early Years, 1787–1805,* revised by C. L. Shaver (London, 1967). p. 355.

THE PRELUDE

The first attempts at *The Prelude* are found in a small notebook, known as MS.JJ, which Wordsworth used in Germany during the autumn of 1798. By 1799 a two-part *Prelude* of nearly 1,000 lines was complete; this became an almost completed five-book poem, taking the account through the Cambridge years and into the dedication to poetry that is now in book IV. In 1804 and 1805 Wordsworth added the later books on London, the French Revolution, his despair at its outcome and at the war, and his developing confidence in himself as a poet through the help of Dorothy and Coleridge. The result is the 1805 text, which is the complete poem in thirteen books; this was revised and altered later, with the tenth book divided into two, so that the first publication of the poem in 1850 contained fourteen books. The 1850 text is in some ways more polished, and it contains some fine observations; but the 1805 text (which will be used here) is usually preferred for its freshness and its revelation of Wordsworth's mind at this time.

The Prelude is an extraordinary poem, both in conception and execution, principally because it is epic, history, and autobiography. It is a poem about a single person, a child growing up in the Lake District in the 1770's and 1780's and a young man experiencing the university and the French Revolution; yet it is also much more than this. It contains wonderfully vivid descriptions of the experiences of childhood, but they are contained and given significance by the structure and form of the poem. Basically the poem's experience is one of loss and gain: the loss of the intense childhood experiences and a corresponding gain in maturity and insight. But that experience of loss and gain is set in an epic pattern. In *Paradise Lost,* Milton had written a new kind of epic, as the opening to his book IX shows; Wordsworth, too, is writing a new kind of epic, challenging the traditional concepts of what heroic action consists of. In book III he claims that childhood itself is heroic:

> . . . Of genius, power
> Creation and divinity itself
> I have been speaking, for my theme has been
> What passed within me. Not of outward things
> Done visibly for other minds, words, signs,
> Symbols or actions, but of my own heart
> Have I been speaking, and my youthful mind.
> O Heavens! how awful is the might of souls,
> And what they do within themselves while yet
> The yoke of earth is new to them, the world
> Nothing but a wild field where they were sown.
> This is, in truth, heroic argument,
> And genuine prowess, which I wished to touch
> With hand however weak, but in the main
> It lies far hidden from the reach of words.
> (III.171–185)

The suggestion that the poem's subject is "Not of outward things" recalls Milton's determination not to write about wars and battles,

> . . . the better fortitude
> Of Patience and Heroic Martyrdom
> Unsung. . . .
> (*Paradise Lost,* IX.31–33)

Wordsworth carries Milton's innovation a stage further, with an epic treatment of material that is traditionally not associated with the epic; in so doing he claims an epic significance for the growth of a mind, and particularly (as in this case) the growth of a poet's mind. That he had *Paradise Lost* in mind is suggested by an echo at the very beginning of *The Prelude,* where Wordsworth writes

> The earth is all before me—with a heart
> Joyous, nor scared at its own liberty,
> I look about, and should the guide I chuse
> Be nothing better than a wandering cloud,
> I cannot miss my way. . . .
> (I.15–19)

This takes up the final image of *Paradise Lost,* when Adam and Eve leave Paradise:

> The World was all before them, where to choose
> Thir place of rest, and Providence thir guide
> (XII.646–647)

Where *Paradise Lost* ends, *The Prelude* begins: Milton shows us Adam and Eve at the beginning of human history, faced with the choice of free will and guided by the providence of God; Wordsworth shows us a man in time, able to choose and confident of his ability to use his freedom. In *The Prelude* liberty has replaced the theologians' conception of free will, and the wandering cloud has replaced the workings of Divine Providence: Wordsworth is writing his epic on his own terms of natural goodness and human freedom. What the child does with that freedom is the subject of the early books of *The Prelude*; how the young man survives the pressure of events and retains his imaginative power is the continuation. The whole conception is daring: it is, said Wordsworth, "a thing unprecedented in literary history that a man should talk so much about himself" (letter to Sir George Beaumont, 1 May 1805). He is, in effect, writing an individual *Paradise Lost,* a poem that sees the life of an obscure country boy in the northwest of England as its own kind of significant progress, its own kind of movement from innocence to experience, from paradise to the world outside. Wordsworth makes the reference to *Paradise Lost* clear in a passage of Miltonic pastiche in *The Prelude* (VIII.119–143), a long paragraph of exotic vocabulary and latinate syntax including a description of Gehol's gardens "for delight / of the Tartarian Dynasty composed" and the Great Wall of China, "that mighty Wall, not fabulous, / (China's stupendous mound!)."

Immediately afterward, Wordsworth swings into his own comparison:

But lovelier far than this the paradise
Where I was reared, in Nature's primitive gifts
Favored no less, and more to every sense
Delicious, seeing that the sun and sky,
The elements, and seasons in their change,
Do find their dearest fellow-labourer there
The heart of man—a district on all sides
The fragrance breathing of humanity,
Man free, man working for himself, with choice
Of time, and place, and object; by his wants,
His comforts, native occupations, cares,
Conducted on to individual ends
Or social, and still followed by a train,
Unwooed, unthought-of even: simplicity,
And beauty, and inevitable grace.
(VIII.144–158)

The curious sliding movement of the syntax here is not very common in Wordsworth; but although the elements occur in apposition, they allow a characteristic accumulation of different effects, so that paradise appeals to the senses and to the heart of man, and is a place that encourages the best side of man: man free to work as he wishes and to live in harmony with himself and his fellow men. The sense of living as a member of a community is very important in *The Prelude*: it underlies the happiness of the early years and the early enthusiasms of the French Revolution, while the lack of an organic community was one of the features of London. It is described by Wordsworth at the beginning of book VII in one of those homely observations that he does so well:

. . . Above all, one thought
Baffled my understanding, how men lived
Even next-door neighbours, as we say, yet still
Strangers, and knowing not each other's names.
(VII.117–120)

The Prelude describes this vital sense of a community in a number of ways. The child himself is part of it and knows his school friends, the villagers, and the landscape with a delighted familiarity. There are many instances of this, but perhaps the most vivid is the opening of book IV, where Wordsworth describes the feelings of a university student coming home for the long vacation. He bounds down the hill, shouting for the old ferryman, who greets him; he walks on a few miles to Hawkshead, where he sees the familiar church; he is welcomed, with tears of joy, by Ann Tyson and walks around the village with her, greeting everybody. He sees the old rooms, the old garden, the boxed-in stream; he takes his place at the well-loved table and sleeps in his accustomed bed. The whole first section of book IV is a most beautiful re-creation of the emotions of coming home to a well-known landscape and a well-loved community; it looks back, of course, to the scenes of books I and II, especially to the passages that describe the children playing together, skating, or playing cards with the battered and dirty pack (the cards themselves cherished like old soldiers), or rowing or riding. It looks forward, too, to the hopes for the French Revolution as the beginning of the new Jerusalem:

For, born in a poor district, and which yet
Retaineth more of ancient homeliness,
Manners erect, and frank simplicity,
Than any other nook of English land,
It was my fortune scarcely to have seen
Through the whole tenor of my schoolday time
The face of one, who, whether boy or man,
Was vested with attention or respect
Through claims of wealth or blood; . . .
. . .
. . . It could not be
But that one tutored thus, who had been formed
To thought and moral feeling in the way

This story hath described, should look with
awe
Upon the faculties of man, receive
Gladly the highest promises, and hail
As best the government of equal rights
And individual worth. . . .
(IX.217–226; 242–249)

The Prelude, then, is an epic that deals with the loss of paradise; it is Wordsworth's childhood seen as myth, in that he has constructed around his own experience a reading of events that corresponds to the paradise myth. We know that he was not happy at Penrith, and we can only guess at the effect of his mother's death when he was eight and his father's when he was thirteen. Both of these are referred to in *The Prelude,* but not until books V and XI respectively, and there is nothing in the early books to suggest unhappiness and bereavement. There is fear, but that is accepted—indeed, welcomed—as part of the educative ministry of nature:

Fair seed-time had my soul, and I grew up
Fostered alike by beauty and by fear
(I.305–306)

But the individual development through beauty and fear is supported by the sense that the individual is part of the community. He can be himself, but he can also be one of a number, as the skating episode shows. The pronouns shift from singular to plural in a way that conveys the mixture of individual impression and communal feeling:

. . . All shod with steel
We hissed along the polished ice in games
Confederate, imitative of the chace
And woodland pleasures, the resounding
horn,
The pack loud bellowing, and the hunted
hare.
So through the darkness and the cold we
flew,
And not a voice was idle. With the din,
Meanwhile, the precipices rang aloud;
The leafless trees and every icy crag
Tinkled like iron; while the distant hills
Into the tumult sent an alien sound
Of melancholy, not unnoticed; while the
stars,
Eastward, were sparkling clear, and in the
west
The orange sky of evening died away.

Not seldom from the uproar I retired
Into a silent bay, or sportively
Glanced sideway, leaving the tumultuous
throng,
To cut across the image of a star
That gleamed upon the ice. And oftentimes
When we had given our bodies to the wind,
And all the shadowy banks on either side
Came sweeping through the darkness,
spinning still
The rapid line of motion, then at once
Have I, reclining back upon my heels,
Stopped short—yet still the solitary cliffs
Wheeled by me, even as if the earth had
rolled
With visible motion her diurnal round.
Behind me did they stretch in solemn train,
Feebler and feebler, and I stood and watched
Till all was tranquil as a dreamless sleep.
(I.460–489)

In this brilliant passage, with its wonderful recreation of the movement and sound of skating, and of a Lake District winter twilight, the child is sharing in the experience and in the delight of the game with the others. Yet he is also able to retire "into a silent bay," and to perceive the way the earth seems to move, at a sudden stop. Like the poet of the preface to *Lyrical Ballads,* he is a child speaking to (or for) children, yet also a child endowed with more lively sensibility, rejoicing more than others in the spirit of life that is in him. The joyful energy of this passage is one of its most obvious characteristics, tempered as it is with a solemn awareness of the beauty and majesty of the earth. *The Prelude* as a whole is a striking combination of these qualities of individual energy and delight, with an equally important sense that the mind of the poet is, in many ways, a representative mind. It is aware, as we have seen, of the importance of the community; and the poem is also concerned with a major historical event, the

French Revolution, an event of which the hopes and disappointments dominated the romantic movement. In the books on France, Wordsworth is recording the fact that he was present at the Revolution's various stages: when he first landed in France, on 13 July 1790, he and Robert Jones saw "benevolence and blessedness / Spread like a fragrance everywhere, like Spring" (VI.368–369). He had the enthusiasm and optimism of youth:

> Bliss was it in that dawn to be alive,
> But to be young was very heaven! . . .
> (X.692–693)

and this optimism was based upon observations, upon conversations with Beaupuy, upon a direct experience of a nation struggling to find its new liberty. In book X, Wordsworth relates, with a painful authenticity, how he was torn in sympathy when prayers for an English victory were offered in church, and how his attitudes to the Revolution changed as the French became "oppressors in their turn" (X.791). He describes how he studied the problem relentlessly,

> . . . endlessly perplexed
> With impulse, motive, right and wrong, the ground
> Of moral obligation—what the rule,
> And what the sanction—till, demanding proof,
> And seeking it in every thing, I lost
> All feeling of conviction, and, in fine,
> Sick, wearied out with contrarieties,
> Yielded up moral questions in despair. . . .
> (X.893–900)

Book X of *The Prelude* is a most impressive record of a sensitive mind in confrontation with the great political events of the day: not only the French Revolution and the war, but the campaign for the abolition of the slave trade (X.202–226). He saw revolution become madness, and the rise and fall of Robespierre, with all the intense involvement of a contemporary; he remembered exactly where he was when he heard of the death of Robespierre, crossing Ulverston sands after visiting the grave of his beloved schoolmaster, William Taylor, at Cartmel. The scene (X.466–566), with the smooth sands of the Leven estuary in the foreground and the Lake District mountains in the background, is one of the most vividly pictorialized in *The Prelude*; the moment when the passing traveler told him that Robespierre was dead is sharpened by the poet's awareness of his surroundings and his feelings. It is no accident, of course, that the death of Robespierre is told to Wordsworth just after he had been thinking of the death of Taylor: the one famous and tyrannical, the other obscure and benevolent. In ways such as this, *The Prelude* is a record of what it was like to live through those years, to be a child at Hawkshead, a young man at Cambridge, a spectator in London, and an enthusiast in France.

Above all, however, these roles or stages were seen by Wordsworth in *The Prelude* as part of the growth of a poet's mind (the poem's alternative title). And if the poem is about the paradise myth, with the child growing up in the good community, and about history, with the child and young man responding to historical and social conditions around him, it is also about the development of a very special and very gifted man. Once again, it is possible to see Wordsworth referring back to Milton, who saw the role of the poet as a prophet or inspired teacher. In *Il Penseroso* the poet longs for the learning and wisdom of old age:

> Till old experience do attain
> To something like Prophetic strain.
> (173–174)

and in *Paradise Lost* he remembers other figures who have suffered the same fate as himself, the loss of sight—

> So were I equal'd with them in renown,
> Blind *Thamyris* and blind *Maeonides*,
> And *Tiresias* and *Phineus* Prophets old.
> (III.34–36)

Wordsworth, too, uses the word "Prophet"; and in some ways the whole of *The Prelude* can be seen as moving toward the final paragraph, in which he sees himself and Coleridge as engaged in the teaching of mankind:

Prophets of Nature, we to them will speak
A lasting inspiration, sanctified
By reason and by truth; what we have loved
Others will love, and we may teach them
how:
Instruct them how the mind of man
becomes
A thousand times more beautiful than the
earth
On which he dwells, above this frame of
things
(Which, 'mid all revolutions in the hopes
And fears of men, doth still remain
unchanged)
In beauty exalted, as it is itself
Of substance and of fabric more divine.
(XIII.442–452)

It is toward this end, with the poet as a responsible member of society and an inspired teacher, that so much of *The Prelude* has been moving. The range of experience that contributes to this is considerable, including the childhood episodes, education, books, and the sublime experiences that remain in the memory long after they have passed. Wordsworth calls them "spots of time" in a crucial passage:

There are in our existence spots of time,
Which with distinct preeminence retain
A renovating virtue, whence, depressed
By false opinion and contentious thought,
Or aught of heavier or more deadly weight
In trivial occupations and the round
Of ordinary intercourse, our minds
Are nourished and invisibly repaired—
A virtue, by which pleasure is enhanced,
That penetrates, enables us to mount
When high, more high, and lifts us up when
fallen.
(XI.257–267)

Such moments, he goes on to say, are "scattered everywhere" (XI.274), though they may be most conspicuous in childhood; he gives an example of two episodes that are vividly remembered, being lost and finding himself beneath a murderer's gibbet, and waiting for the horses to take him home just before his father's death. In both cases there is a mysterious intensity about the episode, a moment of perception that remains with extraordinary sharpness. In the first, the child, regaining the path, sees

A naked pool that lay beneath the hills,
The beacon on the summit, and more near,
A girl who bore a pitcher on her head
And seemed with difficult steps to force her
way
Against the blowing wind. . . .
(XI.303–307)

The poet recalls how he later revisited the spot and remembered the earlier occasion:

. . . So feeling comes in aid
Of feeling, and diversity of strength
Attends us, if but once we have been strong.
(XI.325–327)

We recognize this as one of Wordsworth's complex states, in which "feeling comes in aid / Of feeling." He is not clear exactly why the force of the episode is so great, but he knows that it is: the greatness of man is mysterious and deep, and it is by the exploration of such episodes that we come to understand and acknowledge it. As a child, the poet was lost; as an adult, looking back, he now says:

I am lost, but see
In simple childhood something of the base
On which thy greatness stands—but this I
feel,
That from thyself it is that thou must give,
Else never canst receive. . . .
(XI.329–333)

The sentiment is reminiscent of Coleridge's "we receive but what we give" (from the "Letter to Sara Hutchinson"), and it indicates something of the interacting relationship between the mind and the external world that was so important to both poets. In their most confident moments, both poets felt a great union between man and nature, a profound interaction, or what Wordsworth describes as a "consummation" between the human mind and the natural world. Sometimes this comes at unexpected moments, as it does in the second "spot of time" in book XI. This describes the poet and his brothers waiting for the horses to take them home at Christmastime: through the misty day he waited beside a stone wall, with a single sheep and a hawthorn tree for company (it is remarkable how often single trees or lonely people and animals occur in Wordsworth). He had been so impatient to get home, the poet records, and then ten days later his father died; he saw himself tritely as punished for his impatience, though clearly this is not the point of the passage. The long wait in the mist and rain, the strange company of sheep and tree (in his impatience he had left his brothers further down the pass), these constituents of the moment remained with him as a testimony to his imaginative grasp of a situation:

> And afterwards the wind and sleety rain,
> And all the business of the elements,
> The single sheep, and the one blasted tree,
> And the bleak music of that old stone wall,
> The noise of wood and water, and the mist
> Which on the line of each of those two
> roads
> Advanced in such indisputable shapes—
> All these were spectacles and sounds to
> which
> I often would repair, and thence would
> drink
> As at a fountain. . . .
> (XI.375–384)

In this description we notice not only the emphasis on the particular objects (the wind, the rain, the single sheep, the blasted tree) but an emphasis on what Wordsworth elsewhere calls the "goings-on" of the physical world. He animates the dreariness with unobtrusive life: "all the business of the elements," "the bleak music of that old stone wall," "The noise of wood and water," the mist that "Advanced in such indisputable shapes," all these suggest a mind that goes out to the universe and responds to what it is doing—a mind that apprehends the "business," hears the "music," and sees the shapes of the mist. Wordsworth is here celebrating not the power of nature, but the power of the imagination and the memory.

The same can be said of two other great passages in *The Prelude* that are concerned with the growth of the inspired prophet-poet. The first is the crossing of the Alps section in book VI (494 and following). Once again, as in the "spots of time" moments of book XI, there is a loss of direction, a momentary sense of failure, an unfulfilled expectation; as in those "spots of time," the failure and loss, the mistaken hope, are suddenly transformed into an awareness of the power of the imagination. In book VI, it is addressed directly, in a startling apostrophe that erupts into the verse:

> Imagination!—lifting up itself
> Before the eye and progress of my song
> Like an unfathered vapour, here that power,
> In all the might of its endowments, came
> Athwart me. I was lost as in a cloud,
> Halted without a struggle to break through,
> And now, recovering, to my soul I say
> 'I recognize thy glory'. In such strength
> Of usurpation, in such visitings
> Of awful promise, when the light of sense
> Goes out in flashes that have shewn to us
> The invisible world, doth greatness make
> abode,
> There harbours whether we be young or old.
> Our destiny, our nature, and our home,
> Is with infinitude—and only there;
> With hope it is, hope that can never die,
> Effort, and expectation, and desire,
> And something evermore about to be.
> (VI.525–542)

Here the imagination itself is like a vapor or mist; the poet seems overcome by it, lost in it as he was on the Alpine path. But he suddenly sees the power of the imagination, not in the fact but in the promise, not in the material world but in the glimpse of something higher and beyond. As he sees this he becomes aware of the sheer power of an imagination that can so transcend its material circumstances as to become conscious of its activity. Similarly, in the "climbing of Snowdon" passage from the final book of *The Prelude,* the poet describes a night climb from Bethgelert through the mist, until suddenly he and his companions came out of the mist into the moonlight. They found themselves surrounded by a sea of mist, out of which the Welsh hills lifted their peaks and over which the moon looked down "in single glory." So strong is the impression of the mist as a sea that Wordsworth has to describe it as moving eventually

> Into the sea, the real sea. . . .
> (XIII.49)

The fact that Wordsworth has to describe it as "the real sea" is a testimony of how powerful his imagination has become. Before, the real world existed, and the imagination erupted from it; now the imagination seems to be supreme, and the real world has to be admitted. Between the mountain and the shore is a chasm, a fracture in the mist:

> A deep and gloomy breathing-place through which
> Mounted the roar of waters, torrents, streams
> Innumerable, roaring with one voice.
> (XIII.57–59)

The stupendous natural vision is one that Wordsworth sees as an emblem of the power of the mind; only with such a powerful landscape can he begin to say what the mind is capable of doing:

> . . . it appeared to me
> The perfect image of a mighty mind,
> Of one that feeds upon infinity,
> That is exalted by an under-presence,
> The sense of God, or whatsoe'er is dim
> Or vast in its own being—above all,
> One function of such mind had Nature there
> Exhibited by putting forth, and that
> With circumstance most awful and sublime:
> That domination which she oftentimes
> Exerts upon the outward face of things,
> So moulds them, and endues, abstracts, combines,
> Or by abrupt and unhabitual influence
> Doth make one object so impress itself
> Upon all others, and pervades them so,
> That even the grossest minds must see and hear,
> And cannot chuse but feel. . . .
> (XIII.68–84)

The imaginative minds are ever on the watch, building up greatness from the least suggestion, or from failure, or from ordinary expectations that have come to grief. This, the poet concludes, "this alone is genuine liberty" (XIII.122); the ability of the mind to transcend its surroundings, to become aware, even when it is least expected, of the strength of the imagination. For often it surprises, and surprise is a favorite idea of Wordsworth's. Moments come upon the imagination with strange suddenness: as the child rows a stolen boat out from the shore at Patterdale, he is astonished and terrified to see the mountain coming after him; as the child who is hooting to the owls (V.389 and following) fails to get a response, he is suddenly aware of something else:

> Then sometimes in that silence, while he hung
> Listening, a gentle shock of mild surprize
> Has carried far into his heart the voice
> Of mountain torrents; or the visible scene
> Would enter unawares into his mind
> With all its solemn imagery, its rocks,
> Its woods, and that uncertain heaven, received
> Into the bosom of the steady lake.
> (V.406–413)

Here the mind receives, but it receives because it is a mind that can give. The boy of Winander hooting to the owls is contrasted throughout book V with the fact-getting, well-behaved, unnatural child; the boy, who died young, was one of those with whom Wordsworth played:

> A race of real children, not too wise,
> Too learned, or too good, but wanton, fresh,

And bandied up and down by love and hate;
Fierce, moody, patient, venturous, modest, shy,
Mad at their sports like withered leaves in winds;
Though doing wrong and suffering, and full oft
Bending beneath our life's mysterious weight
Of pain and fear, yet still in happiness
Not yielding to the happiest upon earth.
(V.436–444)

And so, as so often with Wordsworth, the greatest sublimity is linked with the celebration of the ordinary; and to pursue the development of the prophet-poet, and the great creative imagination, is to be reminded that they are rooted in an ordinary childhood. It is all wonderfully simple, yet wonderfully mysterious and profound:

Oh mystery of man, from what a depth
Proceed thy honours! I am lost, but see
In simple childhood something of the base
On which thy greatness stands— . . .
(XI.328–331)

and the greatness of *The Prelude* is that it does succeed in testifying to the power of the imagination while being firmly rooted in human experience.

SHORTER POEMS AFTER 1798

The sheer ordinariness that is an essential part of Wordsworth is continued in the poems written after *Lyrical Ballads*; yet it is an ordinariness transformed, as in *The Prelude,* by an imaginative balance that seems to achieve just the right adjustment between the subject matter and its transformation.

In the "Lucy" poems, for instance, most of which were written in Germany during the winter of 1798–1799, Wordsworth writes of the death of a young girl who is an embodiment of all the natural forces of simplicity and grace. In one poem she is a "flower" and "sportive as the fawn"; she lives in the poet's memory as an ideal figure who has died while she is still in a fresh and youthful state of communion with nature. In the greatest of these poems, "A Slumber Did My Spirit Seal," she is first an ideal, almost spiritual creature and then a dead girl; yet even then she is reunited with nature in a way that seems appropriate and that turns her death into a fitting reunion with the world of which she was a part. She is both girl and nature form, shaped and molded by a force outside her; the poet sees her for a time, and loves her, only to lose her. Thus the "Lucy" poems are both elegies for a loved one and something more, a perception of an ideal and an indication of the transience of natural innocence. In his description of *Lyrical Ballads* in *Biographia Literaria,* Coleridge wrote of "the two cardinal points of poetry":

> . . . the power of exciting the sympathy of the reader by a faithful adherence to the truth of nature, and the power of giving the interest of novelty by the modifying colors of imagination. (II.5)

This is a remarkable insight into the working of Wordsworth's shorter poems: they are true to nature, that is, to a visible and recognizable external world, and yet that world is given a significance that it normally lacks. The significance is given to it by the perceiving mind, which allows the thing or person to be seen more vividly and yet as something more than its material self. So the sheepfold in "Michael" remains a sheepfold but becomes a symbol of all the unfulfilled hopes of the shepherd's life, and of more than that: it is a symbol and not an allegorical representation of something. So it has a life of its own: it exists in the eye of the passerby as he walks up the path beside Green-head Ghyll, and it has a history that sums up the whole life and fate of Michael and his family. They are simple, frugal people, who prefer to remain on the land rather than sell it to pay off the indemnity; Michael's work is with the elements, among the fields and hills, and be is summoned to work by the winds. His feelings, too, are elementary passions of the kind that Wordsworth saw as existing among rustic folk: his tenderness for his son and his love of the land on which he has worked all his life. The laying of the cornerstone of the sheepfold, done by Luke at his request, is an act of faith and hope: the sheepfold becomes a covenant between the father and the son but also, in its way, an act of defiance against the destructiveness of the monetary and city world. Michael and Luke are forced to separate, and Luke comes to grief: Michael continues to go to the sheepfold, but he is unable to finish it, although he continues to work at it. The celebrated line

> And never lifted up a single stone
> (466)

has tended to make the reader forget that in fact Michael did continue to work at the sheepfold for seven years after Luke's downfall. Michael is a man of determination and perseverance; his life has been one of industrious labor, and the downfall of Luke does not alter this. But he has no heart to continue at times when the grief is too great; the sheepfold is an emblem of his purpose in life, the construction of something that will survive for Luke, as he hoped that the patrimonial fields would pass to him. Instead, in the city, Luke

> . . . gave himself
> To evil courses: ignominy and shame
> Fell on him, so that he was driven at last
> To seek a hiding-place beyond the seas.
> (444–447)

In this poem, the sheepfold and the cottage are the foreground, and the city is far away; Luke's downfall is portrayed with a brisk absence of detail, whereas Michael's speeches are recorded verbatim. It is a masterly use of perspective to emphasize the quality of life and the destruction that comes into it from outside; as we know from *The Prelude,* Wordsworth had a particular admiration for shepherds, and "Michael" is a narrative poem that records the way in which the shepherd and his wife seem hardly to understand other ways. They are touchingly naive about Luke's departure, and presumably about life and conditions in the city; yet their naiveté is associated throughout with love. Michael loves the land and has an abiding love for Luke. He promises the boy that

> ". . . whatever fate
> Befall thee, I shall love thee to the last,
> And bear thy memory with me to the grave."
> (415–417)

So too, after the brief account of Luke's fall, comes the resounding line

> There is a comfort in the strength of love;
> (448)

which indicates the contrary movements of love and despair that exist within Michael: he is a man who has experienced a lifetime of love, in his work and its surroundings, in the domestic happiness of his frugal home, in his land, and in the tenderness of his relationship with his son. When the last of these is broken the others remain; as so often in Wordsworth, the figures who are bereft of human relationships retain a strange and lonely dignity that comes from an affinity with nature. Michael is deeply moving because he represents every aging father with an only child in whom his hopes are centered; he is also awesome in his ability to go on loving. He is a man for whom the reader feels not tragic pity and fear but a mixture of pity and admiration.

The same is true of other solitaries in Wordsworth, most notably the leech-gatherer in "Resolution and Independence." If "Michael" is written in an austere and stately blank verse (for although the meter is the same, the language is quite different from the impassioned diction of "Tintern Abbey"), "Resolution and Independence" is written in stanza form, with a peculiar and very effective diction. It is metrically very formal, with an alexandrine at the end of each stanza, and the diction is often archaic, with a biblical cadence and rhythm:

> Motionless as a cloud the old Man stood,
> That heareth not the loud winds when they call;
> And moveth all together, if it move at all.
> (75–77)

The use of subjunctives ("if it move") and the older forms of the verb (heareth, moveth) are linked with rhythms that echo biblical ones ("consider the lilies of the field, how they grow": "That heareth not the loud winds when they call"). The result is a poem that describes an encounter with a poor old man in formal and stately terms, so that the old man himself is given dignity. In Dorothy Wordsworth's journal, he appears as "an old man almost double":

> He had on a coat, thrown over his shoulders, above his waistcoat and coat. Under this he carried a bundle, and had an apron on and a night-cap. . . . His trade was to gather leeches, but now leeches are scarce, and he had not strength for it. He lived by begging. . . . (3 October 1800)

When Wordsworth wrote "Resolution and Independence" some eighteen months later (in the productive spring of 1802), any of these details that might make the old man seem ludicrous were carefully removed. He enters the poem now at a moment when the poet is gloomily contemplating his own future: it is a brilliant fresh morning after rain, yet the poet feels uncertain about the fate of fellow poets and his own failure to provide; like the grasshopper in the fable, his whole life has been lived "in pleasant thought, / As if life's business were a summer mood" (36–37). Instead of being made to regret this by the hard-working ant, however, he meets the leech-gatherer, whose appearance is preceded by words such as "grace":

> Now, whether it were by peculiar grace,
> A leading from above, a something given,
> Yet it befell that, in this lonely place,
> When I with these untoward thoughts had striven,
> Beside a pool bare to the eye of heaven
> I saw a Man before me unawares:
> The oldest man he seemed that ever wore grey hairs.
> (50–56)

The great simplicities of Wordsworth's poetry appear to wonderful effect in a line like "I saw a Man . . . ," especially as Wordsworth goes on to qualify this:

> As a huge stone is sometimes seen to lie
> Couched on the bald top of an eminence;
> Wonder to all who do the same espy,
> By what means it could thither come, and whence;
> So that it seems a thing endued with sense:
> Like a sea-beast crawled forth, that on a shelf
> Of rock or sand reposeth, there to sun itself. . . .
> (57–63)

Here the old man is likened to a stone and to a strange sea beast; or, to complicate the process, he could be said to be likened to a stone that itself is like a sea beast. Either way, here is a strange combination of inanimate and animate, as though the old man is half immobile and insensate, and half strangely alive. It is interesting, too, to see how the rhythm of the line unobtrusively emphasizes the strangeness of the old man. He is like a stone "Couched on the bald top of an eminence," where the words "bald top" give two strong syllables in the middle of the line. Without the word "bald," the line would be regularly dactylic, with three feet:

```
 /      x  x   /  x x  /  x  x
Couched on the top of an eminence
```

With "bald," it becomes strangely out of joint, especially when followed by the trochaic "Wonder" in the following line. But Wordsworth unerringly brings the reader back to the reality in the following line:

> Such seemed this Man, . . .

which echoes "I saw a Man" and allows all the strangeness of the earlier verse to be clamped between the two occurrences of "Man." The man's humanity is asserted, even, it might be said, his basic humanity: he is Man, old and unaccommodated, and the poet's meeting with him has something of the meeting of the sophisticated with the elementary or primitive. The old man's physical condition is miserable: he is bent double with age, and like the stone *cum* sea beast, he seems "not all alive nor dead." Yet he returns a courteous answer to the poet's greeting, and replies to his inquiry "what are you doing?" The poet describes him thus:

> Ere he replied, a flash of mild surprise
> Broke from the sable orbs of his yet-vivid
> eyes.
>
> His words came feebly, from a feeble chest,
> But each in solemn order followed each,
> With something of a lofty utterance drest—
> (90–94)

The understated skill of Wordsworth's verse is brilliantly demonstrated here, in the contrast between the rhetorical and poetic language of the first two and the last two lines here, and the strong simplicity of the middle line. In the first two lines the diction ("sable orbs," "yet-vivid eyes") might have come from Milton; so might the image of words following each other dressed in their lofty utterance. In the center is the line full of effort, with the repetition of "feebly, . . . feeble," the alliteration of which suggests a difficulty in breathing or speaking freely. The contrast embodies the whole sense of strangeness that is found within the poem, the coexistence of an internal state that does not match the external conditions. The poet is miserable on a beautiful morning; the decrepit man is firm in his courage and his optimism. As he describes his condition to the poet (and it is noticeable that in this version he is no longer begging) the poet becomes curiously abstracted; it is as though the individual situation becomes lost in its wider implications.

> The old Man still stood talking by my side;
> But now his voice to me was like a stream
> Scarce heard; nor word from word could I
> divide;
> And the whole body of the Man did seem
> Like one whom I had met with in a dream;
> Or like a man from some far region sent,
> To give me human strength, by apt
> admonishment.
> (106–112)

The idea of the old man as having been sent "from some far region" links up with the earlier description of him as "a something given"; he seems to be both natural and in some way supernatural. He comes to bring the poet human strength, yet in the last verse the poet turns to God:

> "God," said I, "be my help and stay secure;
> I'll think of the Leech-gatherer on the lonely
> moor!"
> (139–140)

The leech-gatherer seems to stand for something, or rather to be something, above and beyond the customary experience and certainly above the worldly cares of the poet. It would be a great mistake to see him as an allegory of some kind of religious presence, but he is clearly an indication of something outside the poet, a strength and a resolution that contrasts forcibly with the poet's own failure to keep a serene mind. The leech-gatherer, in fact, embodies qualities that Wordsworth signally admired: an independence and a serenity that freed him from financial and other worldly responsibilities; this liberty is, for Wordsworth, a true freedom from anxiety, and it is connected with other freedoms that he celebrates in his poetry.

Politically, a love of freedom made him a supporter of the French Revolution, and later a fervent patriot; in social terms he admired societies like the one he had known in his youth, where men seemed to be independent and not bound together in a master-slave relationship; and in personal terms, he sought a freedom from anxiety, a freedom that does not seek to avoid misfortune but that comes from having the resources to bear it. Meanwhile, the relationship between this ideal freedom and the actual world of man continues to exercise Wordsworth; the ideal world is found in many forms, especially associated with nature and childhood, and the poet's delight in it is found in many of the poems written in these years, especially in the spring of 1802. Many of these poems, "The Tinker," "To a Butterfly," "Among All Lovely Things My Love Had Been," "To the Small Celandine," celebrate happiness and freedom, while others are aware of the forces that destroy these things. "The Sailor's Mother" is one, and the "Ode. Intimations of Immortality from Recollections of Early Childhood" is another. The great Ode, as it is sometimes called, balances a marvelous recapturing of the child's innocence and closeness to nature with an awareness of the later perception of an adult; the poet laments the inevitable process of growing into adulthood, embraced so enthusiastically by the child who acts grown-up parts, and yet the Ode is informed by a mature and responsible understanding that this process is necessary. A Neoplatonic sense of a reality elsewhere is joined to the memory of the child's experience, and through it our life on earth is seen to be an absence from a home in God. Yet the life on earth has its own precious moments, and not only in childhood:

> The thought of our past years in me doth
>   breed
>   Perpetual benediction. . . .
>   (137–138)

The benediction comes not just from the memory of delight and liberty, but from something more elusive and profound:

> . . . those obstinate questionings
> Of sense and outward things,
> Fallings from us, vanishings;
> Blank misgivings of a Creature
> Moving about in worlds not realised,
> High instincts before which our mortal
>   Nature
> Did tremble like a guilty Thing surprised.
>   . . .
>   (145–151)

With this praise for the mysterious and marvelous, there is another source of comfort, in the strength that the adult gains through contemplating life in all its confusion and limitations:

> In the primal sympathy
> Which having been must ever be;
> In the soothing thoughts that spring
> Out of human suffering;
> In the faith that looks through death,
> In years that bring the philosophic mind.
>   (185–190)

The great Ode is a key poem in the understanding of the complexity of Wordsworth's beliefs. It contains, without fracturing into different pieces, the joy in childhood and liberty, the unity of this with the rejoicing natural world, and the sense, too, of the mature understanding of the role of man in the created world. The child is a prophet; the man can only remember, and understand, but his view of life involves an accommodation with things as they are that is a gain to compensate for the loss of the childhood vision.

Wordsworth's belief in the faith that looks through death was tested to the uttermost in February 1805, when his favorite brother, John, was drowned at sea. In his grief the poet turned to a favorite subject, the daisy, the "unassuming Common-place / Of Nature," which he saw as sleeping and waking upon the sailor's grave; even here there is a comfort from the simple things of nature. But in a greater poem, "Elegiac Stanzas, Suggested by a Picture of Peele Castle, in a Storm, Painted by Sir George Beaumont," Wordsworth chronicled a change. He had stayed near Peele Castle in fine weather, in 1794; now he saw Beaumont's picture, which showed it in a very different condition: a ruined tower beaten by the waves (the painting also contained a ship going down offshore, which would have reminded Wordsworth of his brother's death). The stormy sea he now sees as the true reflector of the condition of life, and the idea of a world governed by fine weather has disappeared:

A power is gone, which nothing can restore;
A deep distress hath humanised my Soul.
(35–36)

As so often with Wordsworth, loss is turned into gain, and he sees himself as becoming more human and less likely to idealize in his bereavement. Certainly his poetry, from this time on, becomes less elusive and imaginative: even "Peele Castle" has an allegorical construction that is uncomfortably schematic—fine weather contrasted with bad weather, the castle standing against the storms of life, the sense of a "before" and "after" scene. It is saved by its austere diction and its stern sense of mourning tempered by hope:

Farewell, farewell the heart that lives alone,
Housed in a dream, at distance from the
Kind!
Such happiness, wherever it be known,
Is to be pitied; for 'tis surely blind.

But welcome fortitude, and patient cheer,
And frequent sights of what is to be borne!
Such sights, or worse, as are before me
here.—
Not without hope we suffer and we mourn.
(53–60)

SONNETS, THE EXCURSION, AND LATER POEMS

The "Elegiac Stanzas," "Resolution and Independence," the "Immortality Ode," and many of Wordsworth's best-known shorter poems (such as "The Solitary Reaper" and "I Wandered Lonely as a Cloud") were published in *Poems, in Two Volumes* in 1807. This volume also contains some of Wordsworth's finest sonnets, a form in which he delighted. Once again his great master was Milton, and both poets use the same Italianate form, reveling in its compression and the artistic demands of its rhyme scheme. "Nuns fret not at their convent's narrow room," wrote Wordsworth, and be seems to have relished the discipline required to produce a good sonnet. Among the sonnets are some of the best patriotic poetry ever written, which links a love of England with qualities of spiritual nobility, as in "Milton! thou shouldst be living at this hour." The arresting first line is a feature of Wordsworth's sonnets: "Earth has not anything to show more fair" is perhaps the best-known example, but there are others, such as "Once did She hold the gorgeous east in fee" (another sonnet on a political subject, the extinction of the Venetian republic by Napoleon) and "It is a beauteous evening, calm and free." In this last example, the sonnet continues with a literally breathtaking image

The holy time is quiet as a Nun
Breathless with adoration; . . .
(2–3)

and then, as so often, Wordsworth anchors the image in straightforward natural description—

. . . the broad sun
Is sinking down in its tranquillity;
(3–4)

—only to invite the imagination to work again by the use of figurative language:

The gentleness of heaven broods o'er the
Sea:
Listen! the mighty Being is awake,
And doth with his eternal motion make
A sound like thunder—everlastingly.
(5–8)

It is not clear to whom the word "Listen!" is addressed. Its introduction here gives it a general sense, as though anyone on a calm evening might, by listening, hear the workings of a mighty Being. But it then acquires a particular meaning, as Wordsworth turns to address his French daughter:

> Dear Child! dear Girl! that walkest with me here,
> If thou appear untouched by solemn thought,
> Thy nature is not therefore less divine:
> Thou liest in Abraham's bosom all the year;
> And worshipp'st at the Temple's inner shrine,
> God being with thee when we know it not.
> (9–14)

There is a very delicate change of mood here, from the impersonal to the personal, with an equalizing movement from the ordinary to the sacred. A further balancing is found between the tender and the reflective as the poet notes the distance between the child's unconscious communion with heaven and her conscious ordinariness. The difference between the child's apparent state, walking on the sands with a mind "untouched by solemn thought," and her actual state is underlined by the biblical formality of the last lines, which apply to the child in a mysterious and remote, yet authoritative way. Yet throughout the grand reflections is the memory of "Dear Child! dear Girl!," the outburst of genuine feeling that is so much a part of Wordsworth's poetry.

Not all the sonnets are successful: some are plainly tedious, and others are mistakenly pretentious. The long series of *Ecclesiastical Sonnets,* written at the suggestion of Sir George Beaumont, has the air of a dull exercise. At their best, however, the sonnets have the same kind of forceful austerity that Wordsworth admired in Milton, and the characteristic blend of homely tenderness and lofty sentiment.

In the later sonnets something of the magic goes out of Wordsworth's poetry. It is difficult to say what it is, but the ideas that seemed so powerful now become commonplace. The same can be said of *The Excursion* (1814), with the exception of book I, and that is better read in its earlier version as "The Ruined Cottage" (written 1797–1798). There it is a moving story of the decline of a family and the ruin of their lives and hopes by sickness and economic recession (in some respects a return to the preoccupations of the Salisbury Plain poems). In *The Excursion* it is still very fine, though to some tastes the Christian conclusion is false and trite. The central figure of Margaret, the last human tenant of the ruined cottage (last human tenant as opposed to the natural creatures who later take up their abode there), is drawn with a sustained economy and gravity: she is

> . . . a Woman of a steady mind
> Tender and deep in her excess of love;
> (I.513–514)

while her husband is "Frugal, affectionate, sober, and withal / keenly industrious." A succession of calamities (bad harvests, war, and illness), however, causes him to lose his work and sense of purpose, and he finally leaves to join the army. Margaret has to part with her elder child to a kind farmer; the younger child dies; and she is left alone, waiting for the return that never comes. Her love and loyalty prevent her from leaving the cottage, and from having any other hope in life; her continued disappointment leads to her sickness and death.

Her story is told by a central figure in *The Excursion,* the Wanderer (in the earliest version, the Pedlar), who is one of those ideal Wordsworth characters who has given up a regular and settled employment for something that is freer and more haphazard. He has no interest in what Wordsworth called "getting and spending"; he is a traveling and solitary man, who possesses a tranquil and steady mind. The result is that his energies are not directed to his own problems:

> . . . and, by nature tuned
> And constant disposition of his thoughts
> To sympathy with man, he was alive
> To all that was enjoyed where'er he went,
> And all that was endured; for, in himself

Happy, and quiet in his cheerfulness,
He had no painful pressure from without
That made him turn aside from
wretchedness
With coward fears. He could *afford* to suffer
With those whom he saw suffer. . . .
(I.362–371)

The Wanderer is an ideal figure, who is contrasted in the poem with the Solitary, a man who has experienced the hopes and miseries of the French Revolution, and whose personal sufferings have made him misanthropic. A third character, the Pastor, is perhaps the most important of all: he dominates the latter part of the poem with his practical Christian wisdom, and the final book ends with a delightful scene of the Pastor and his family. This forms an obvious contrast to the first book of the poem: from the ruined family to the happy and prosperous one is a journey that involves a full acceptance and understanding of human misery, together with an ability to remain optimistic and benevolent. Both the Wanderer, in his solitude and peripatetic life, and the Pastor, who stands for the settled family life, are able to bring comfort to others and remain at peace with themselves.

The Excursion is thus an extended illustration of different ways of approaching the central problems of human life—the failure of hopes, the loss of loved ones, the doubtful consolations of religion. In its counseling of orthodox Christian belief, *The Excursion* looks toward the work of the later Wordsworth, and indeed the poet's orthodoxy may be one reason why his later poetry is not informed by the same intense conviction as the earlier poetry that expresses his sense of natural power. It is this awareness of the power of natural life and its relation to the mind of man that Wordsworth conveys so well: it is a power beside which the preoccupation of man with material things seems idle, and it is a power whose essential optimism is a counterbalance to the very real suffering and misery of men. If men were to behave with this power as their guide, there would be less misery, for human unhappiness often comes from a failure of society to provide properly for its members. Instead, there would be

. . . a better time,
More wise desires, and simpler manners. . . .
(103–104)

These lines come from the preface to *The Excursion,* originally part of a longer poem entitled "Home at Grasmere." In it we see a summary of many of Wordsworth's most deeply held beliefs. As so often, Milton is in the background as Wordsworth thinks of the earthly paradise. He knows that he (like Milton visiting Hell) will have to travel

. . . near the tribes
And fellowships of men, and see ill sights
Of madding passions mutually inflamed;
Must hear Humanity in fields and groves
Pipe solitary anguish; or must hang
Brooding above the fierce confederate storm
Of sorrow, barricadoed evermore
Within the walls of cities— . . .
(73–80)

But he also intends to celebrate the beauties of paradise, not just as a concept or an idea, but as an actual possibility:

. . . Paradise, and groves
Elysian, Fortunate Fields—like those of old
Sought in the Atlantic Main—why should
they be
A history only of departed things,
Or a mere fiction of what never was?
For the discerning intellect of Man,
When wedded to this goodly universe
In love and holy passion, shall find these
A simple produce of the common day.
(47–55)

The last beautiful line, with its utter simplicity (and the language really used by men), emphasizes the way in which Wordsworth regarded the universe that he found all around him. It was a world that contained its full share of human misery, but that had the power of being transformed by the human mind. In that process, the poet had his full part to play, and that is why Wordsworth always thought of himself as a teacher. The poet as he described him in the preface to *Lyrical Ballads* is many things, but above all

> He is the rock of defence for human nature; an upholder and preserver, carrying everywhere with him relationship and love. (*Poetical Works,* II.396)

Selected Bibliography

BIBLIOGRAPHY

Cooper, L., *A Condordance to the Poems of William Wordsworth,* (London, 1911); Wise, T. J., *A Bibliography of the Writings in Prose and Verse of William Wordsworth,* (London, 1916); Wise, T. J., *Two Lake Poets: A Catalogue of Printed Books, Manuscripts etc., by Wordsworth and Coleridge,* (London, 1927); Logan, J. V., *Wordsworthian Criticism: A Guide and Bibliography,* (Columbus, Ohio, 1947); *Catalogue of the Library at Dove Cottage,* (London, 1948); G. H. Henley, comp., *The Cornell Wordsworth Collection,* (London, 1957); Henley, E. F., and D. H. Stam, *Wordsworthian Criticism 1945–1964: An Annotated Bibliography,* (New York, 1965); Stam, D. H., *Wordsworthian Criticism 1964–1973: An Annotated Bibliography, Including Additions to Wordsworthian Criticism 1945–1964,* (New York, 1974).

COLLECTED WORKS

Poems, Including Lyrical Ballads, 2 vols. (London, 1915) the first collected ed.; *Miscellaneous Poems,* 4 vols. (London, 1820–1827), 5 vols. (London, 1832), 6 vols. (London, 1836–1846), 7 vols. (London, 1849–1850); *The Poems,* (London, 1845); *The Poetical Works,* 6 vols. (London, 1857), with I. Fenwick's notes; T. Hutchinson, ed., *The Poetical Works,* (London, 1895), rev. by E. de Selincourt (London, 1950), The Oxford Standard Authors series, also in Oxford Paperback (London, 1969); E. de Selincourt and H. Darbishire, eds., *The Poetical Works,* 5 vols. (Oxford, 1940–1949, rev. ed., 1952–1959); W. J. B. Owen and J. W. Smyser, eds.,*The Prose Works of William Wordsworth,* 3 vols. (Oxford, 1974); J. O. Hayden, ed., *William Wordsworth: The Poems,* 2 vols. (Harmondsworth, 1977), does not include *The Prelude;* S. Parrish, ed., *The Cornell Wordsworth,* (Ithaca, N.Y.-Hassocks, Sussex, 1975–); S. Gill, ed., *The Salisbury Plain Poems,* (1975); S. Parrish, ed., *The Prelude, 1798–99,* (1977); B. Darlington, ed., *Home at Grasmere,* (1977); J. Butler, ed., *The Ruined Cottage and The Pedlar,* (1979).

SELECTED WORKS

M. Arnold, ed., *Poems of Wordsworth,* (London, 1879); T. Hutchinson, ed., *Poems in Two Volumes,* (London, 1897), from the original ed. of 1807, edited by H. Darbishire (London, 1914), and rev. ed. (London, 1952); J. Butt, ed., *Wordsworth, Selected Poetry and Prose,* (London, 1964); G. H. Hartman, ed., *William Wordsworth: Selected Poetry and Prose,* (New York, 1969); R. S. Thomas, ed., *A Choice of Wordsworth's Verse,* (London, 1971); W. J. B. Owen, ed., *Wordsworth's Literary Criticism,* (London, 1974); W. Davies, ed., *Wiliam Wordsworth: Selected Poems,* (London, 1975).

SEPARATE WORKS

An Evening Walk, (London, 1793), verse; *Descriptive Sketches,* (London, 1793), verse; *Lyrical Ballads, with a Few Other Poems,* (Bristol, 1798), also in R. L. Brett and A. R. Jones, eds. (London, 1965), W. J. B. Owen, ed. (London, 1967), and Scolar Press facs. ed. (London, 1971); *Lyrical Ballads, with Other Poems,* 2 vols. (London, 1800), also in D. Roper, ed. *Lyrical Ballads, 1805* (London, 1968); *Poems, in Two Volumes,* (London, 1807), also in H. Darbishire, ed. (London, 1914); *Concerning the Relations of Great Britain, Spain, and Portugal to Each Other, and to the Common Enemy at This Crisis, and Specifically as Affected by the Convention of Cintra* (London, 1809), prose; *The Excursion, Being a Portion of "The Recluse",* (London, 1814), verse; *The White Doe of Rylstone,* (London, 1815), verse, also in Scolar Press facs. ed. (London, 1971); *Thanksgiving Ode, 18 January 1816,* (London, 1816); *Peter Bell, a Tale in Verse,* (London, 1819); *The Waggoner,* (London, 1819), verse; *The River Duddon, a Series of Sonnets,* (London, 1820); *Memorials of a Tour on the Continent,* (London, 1822), verse; *Ecclesiastical Sketches,* (London, 1822), verse; *A Description of the Scenery of the Lakes in the North of England; Originally Published with Select Views in Cumberland, Westmorland, etc., by the Rev. J. Wilkinson* (London, 1822), prose; *Yarrow Revisited, and Other Poems,* (London, 1835); *A Guide Through the District of the Lakes in the North of England,* (London, 1835), prose, also in E. de Selincourt, ed. (London, 1906); *The Sonnets of William Wordsworth,* (London, 1838); *Poems Chiefly of Early and Late Years; Including the Borderers a Tragedy,* (London, 1842); *Ode on the Installation of His Royal Highness Prince Albert as Chancellor of the University of Cambridge,* (London, 1847); *The Prelude or Growth of a Poet's Mind; An Autobiograpical Poem,* (London, 1850)—the standard ed. is that of E. de Selincourt, edited from the MSS with intro. and notes (London, 1926), rev. by H. Darbishire, Oxford English Texts (London, 1959); 1805 text, E. de Selincourt ed., rev. by S. Gill (London, 1970); 1805 and 1850 texts, J. C. Maxwell, ed. (Harmondsworth, 1971); 1799,

1805, and 1850 texts J. Wordsworth M. H. Abrams, and S. Gill, eds. (New York, 1979); *Journals of Dorothy Wordsworth,* E. de Selincourt, ed. 2 vols. (London, 1941) also M. Moorman, ed. (London, 1971).

LETTERS

W. Knight, ed., *Letters of the Wordsworth Family,* 3 vols. (London, 1907); L. N. Broughton, ed., *Wordsworth and Reed: The Poet's Correspondence with His American Editor: 1836–50,* (London, 1933); E. de Selincourt, ed., *Letters of William and Dorothy Wordsworth,* 6 vols. (Oxford, 1935–1939), rev. ed. in progress: *The Early Years, 1787–1805* rev. by C. L. Shaver (London, 1967), *The Middle Years, Part 1, 1806–1811* rev. by M. Moorman (London, 1969), *The Middle Years, Part 2, 1812–1820* rev. by M. Moorman and A. G. Hill (London, 1970), *The Later Years, Part 1, 1821–1828* A. G. Hill, ed. (London, 1978); L. N. Broughton, ed., *Some Letters of the Wordsworth Family,* (Ithaca, N.Y., 1942); P. Wayne, ed., *Letters of William Wordsworth,* (London, 1954), in the World's Classic ed.; M. E. Burton, ed., *The Letters of Mary Wordsworth, 1800–1855,* (Oxford, 1958); C. H. Ketcham, ed., *The Letters of John Wordsworth,* (Ithaca, N.Y., 1969).

BIOGRAPHICAL AND CRITICAL STUDIES

Coleridge, S. T., *Biographia Literaria,* (London, 1817)—there is a valuable modern ed., J. Shawcross, ed. (Oxford, 1907), also G. Watson, ed. (London, 1971); Hazlitt, W., *Lectures on the English Poets,* (London, 1818); Landor, W. S., *Imaginary Conversations of Literary Men and Statesmen,* vol. I (London, 1824); Hazlitt, W., *The Spirit of the Age,* (London, 1825); De Quincy, T., "Literary and Lake Reminiscences," *Tait's* magazine (1834, 1839) —see also D. Masson, ed. *Collected Writings of De Quincey* (London, 1889–1890); Cottle, J., *Early Recollections,* (London, 1837); Ruskin, J., *Modern Painters,* (London, 1840–1860); Wordsworth, C., *Memoirs of William Wordsworth,* 2 vols. (London, 1851); Wilson, J., *Recreations of Christopher North,* vol. II (London, 1854); W. Knight, ed., *Transactions of the Wordsworth Society,* (1882–1887); Arnold, M., *Essays in Criticism,* 2nd ser. (London, 1888); Rawnsley, H. D., *Literary Associations of the Lakes,* (London, 1894); Legouis, E, *La jeunesse de William Wordsworth,* (Paris, 1896), trans. by J. W. Matthews as *The Early Life of of William Wordsworth* (London, 1897); Pater, W., *Appreciations,* (London, 1899).

Raleigh, W., *Wordsworth,* (London, 1903); Bradley, A. C., *English Poetry and German Philosophy in the Age of Wordsworth,* (London, 1909); Bradley, A. C., *Oxford Lectures on Poetry,* (London, 1909); E. J. Morley, ed., *Blake, Coleridge, Wordsworth, etc.: Selections from the Remains of Henry Crabb Robinson,* (London, 1922); Legouis, E., *William Wordsworth and Annette Vallon,* (London, 1922); Garrod, H. W., *Wordsworth: Lectures and Essays,* (London, 1923); Read, H., *Wordsworth,* (London, 1930, rev. ed., 1948); de Selincourt, E., *Dorothy Wordsworth: A Biography,* (London, 1933); Burra, P., *Wordsworth,* (London, 1936); E. L. Griggs, ed., *Wordsworth and Coleridge: Studies in Honour of George McLean Harper,* (Princeton, N.J., 1939); Wilson, J. D., *Leslie Stephen and Matthew Arnold as Critics of Wordsworth,* (London, 1939); Meyer, G. W., *Wordsworth's Formative Years,* (Ann Arbor, Mich., 1943); Smith, J. C., *A Study of Wordsworth,* (London, 1944); Stallknecht, N. P., *Strange Seas of Thought: Studies in Wordsworth's Philosophy of Man and Nature,* (Durham, N.C., 1945); de Selincourt, E., *Wordsworthian and Other Studies,* (London, 1947); Nicholson, N., *Wordsworth: An Introduction and a Selection,* (London, 1949);

Darbishire, H., *The Poet Wordsworth,* (London, 1950)—Clark Lectures (1949), Oxford Paperback (1966); *Wordsworth at Cambridge: A Record of the Commemoration Held at St. John's College, Cambridge,* (London, 1950),—contains a detailed survey of Wordsworth portraits; G. T. Dunklin, ed., *Wordsworth: Centenary Studies,* (Princeton, N.J., 1950); Abercrombie, L., *The Art of Wordsworth,* (London, 1952); Margoliouth, H. M., *Wordsworth and Coleridge,* (London, 1953); Jones, J., *The Egotistical Sublime: A History of Wordsworth's Imagination,* (London, 1954); Bateson, F. W., *Wordsworth: A Re-Interpretation,* (London, 1954, rev. ed., 1956); Moorman, M., *William Wordsworth: A Biography,* 2 vols. (Oxford, 1957–1965), reprinted in Oxford Paperback London (1968); Schneider, B. R., *Wordsworth's Cambridge Education,* (London, 1957); K. Coburn, ed., *The Notebooks of Samuel Taylor Coleridge,* 2 vols. (London, 1957); Todd, F. M., *Politics and the Poet: A Study of Wordsworth,* (London, 1957); Z. S. Fink, ed., *The Early Wordsworthian Milieu,* (London, 1958)—a notebook of Christopher Wordsworth, with a few entries by William Wordsworth; Ferry, D., *The Limits of Mortality: An Essay on Wordsworth's Major Poems,* (Middletown, Conn., 1959); Blanshard, F., *Portraits of Wordsworth,* (London, 1959);

Danby, J. F., *The Simple Wordsworth: Studies in the Poems, 1797–1807,* (London, 1960); Clark, C. C., *Romantic Paradox: An Essay on the Poetry of Wordsworth,* (London, 1963); Lindenberger, H., *On Wordsworth's Prelude,* (London, 1963); Danby, J. F., *William Wordsworth: The Prelude and Other Poems,* (London, 1963); Perkins, D., *Wordsworth and the Poetry of Sincerity,* (Cambridge, Mass., 1964); Hartman, G. H., *Wordsworth's Poetry, 1787–1814,* (New Haven, Conn., 1964), contains a good critical bibliography; King, A., *Wordsworth and the Artist's Vision,* (London, 1966); Salvesen, C., *The Landscape of Memory,* (London, 1966); Groom, G. B., *The Unity of Wordsworth's Poetry,* (London, 1966); Reed, M. L., *Wordsworth: The Chronology of the Early Years 1770–1779,*

(London-Cambridge, Mass., 1967); Rader, M, *Wordsworth. A Philosophical Approach,* (Oxford, 1967); Halliday, F. E., *Wordsworth and His World,* (London, 1969), with 140 illustrations; Durrant, G., *William Wordsworth,* (London, 1969), Cambridge British Authors paperback; Woodring, C., *Wordsworth,* (Cambridge, Mass., 1968); Wordsworth, J., *The Music of Humanity: A Critical Study of Wordsworth's "Ruined Cottage" Incorporating Texts from a Manuscript of 1799–1800,* (London, 1969); Heffernan, J. A. W., *Wordsworth's Theory of Poetry: The Transforming Imagination,* (Ithaca, N.Y., 1969); Wordsworth, J., *William Wordsworth: 1770–1969,* (London, 1969), British Academy Chatterton Lecture.

Wesling, D., *Wordsworth and the Adequacy of Landscape,* (London, 1970); Durrant, G., *Wordsworth and the Great System,* (London, 1970); Watson, J. R., *Picturesque Landscape and English Romantic Poetry,* (London, 1970); Byatt, A. S., *Wordsworth and Coleridge in Their Time,* (London, 1970); Heath, W., *Wordsworth and Coleridge,* (Oxford, 1970); Prickett, S., *Coleridge and Wordsworth: The Poetry of Growth,* (Cambridge, 1970); J. Wordsworth, ed., *Bicentenary Wordsworth Studies in Memory of John Alban Finch,* (Ithaca, N.Y., 1971); Garber, F., *Wordsworth and the Poetry of Encounter,* (Urbana, Ill., 1971); Thomas, G. K., *Wordsworth's Dirge and Promise,* (Lincoln, Nebr., 1971); Curtis, J. R., *Wordsworth's Experiments with Tradition,* (Ithaca, N.Y., 1971); Noyes, R., *William Wordsworth,* (New York, 1971); Onorato, R. J., *The Character of the Poet,* (Princeton, N.J., 1971); G. McMaster, ed., *William Wordsworth,* (Harmondsworth, 1972), Penguin Critical Anthology; A. R. Jones and W. Tydeman, eds., *Wordsworth, Lyrical Ballads,* (London, 1972), a casebook; W. J. Harvey and R. Gravil, eds., *Wordsworth, The Prelude,* (London, 1972), a casebook; Sharrock, R., *The Figure in a Landscape: Wordsworth's Early Poetry,* (London, 1972), British Academy Warton Lecture; Parrish, S. M., *The Art of the Lyrical Ballads,* (Cambridge, Mass., 1973); Sheats, P. D., *The Making of Wordsworth's Poetry,* (Cambridge, Mass., 1973); Grob, A., *The Philosophic Mind,* (Columbus, Ohio, 1973); Wlecke, A. O., *Wordsworth and the Sublime,* (Berkeley, 1973); M. H. Abrams, ed., *Wordsworth, a Collection of Critical Essays,* (Englewood Cliffs, N.J., 1973); Johnson, L. M., *Wordsworth and the Sonnet,* (Copenhagen, 1973); McConnell, F. D., *The Confessional Imagination,* (Baltimore, 1974); Reed, M. L., *Wordsworth: The Chronology of the Middle Years, 1800–1815,* (Cambridge, Mass., 1975); Brantley, R. E., *Wordsworth's "Natural Methodism",* (New Haven, Conn., 1975); Stelzig, E. L., *All Shades of Consciousness: Wordsworth's Poetry and the Self in Time,* (The Hague, 1975); Prickett, S., *Wordsworth and Coleridge: The Lyrical Ballads,* (London, 1975); Jacobus, M., *Tradition and Experiment in Wordsworth's Lyrical Ballads (1798),* (Oxford, 1976); Jordan, J. E., *Why the Lyrical Ballads?,* (Berkeley, 1976); Ferguson, F., *Wordsworth: Language as Counter-Spirit,* (New Haven, Conn., 1977); Beer, J., *Wordsworth and the Human Heart,* (London, 1977).

WILLIAM BUTLER YEATS

(1865–1939)

G. S. FRASER

I

FOR JUST OVER ten years before he died in a hotel in the south of France, at the beginning of 1939, William Butler Yeats had been universally recognized by his peers as the greatest poet of this century writing in the English language. The recognition dated from the publication in 1928 of his finest volume, *The Tower.* In June of 1939 he would have been seventy-four. He had been writing verses since his teens and had been a poet of some reputation since his twenties. Since the turn of the century, he would probably have been mentioned by any critic in a list of the four or five most distinguished English poets, and in any consideration of Irish poetry he would have headed the list. He had won the Nobel Prize for literature in 1923, he had done more than any other man to bring about the birth of the Irish theater, and he had sat in the senate of the Irish Free State. Yet every critic knows that these public honors are never the full measure of a poet's reputation. At regular intervals during his long life, shrewd critics had been convinced that Yeats was finished. To George Moore, in the Edwardian decade, it seemed that all Yeats's best poems had been inspired by his hopeless love for Maud Gonne; this love was never to find physical fulfillment, and Moore thought that Yeats's lyrical gift would wither, like cut flowers in a glass. To the young T. S. Eliot, in the early Georgian era, Yeats seemed not much more than an interesting survival from the 1890's. The young Ezra Pound, sending some of Yeats's poems to an American magazine, took it upon himself to polish and improve them. The young John Middleton Murry, one of the best poetry critics of his period, dismissed *The Wild Swans at Coole,* which came out in 1917, as the work of a used-up aesthete. The interesting generation of writers who came to Oxford after World War I thought little of Yeats. "Surely," wrote T. E. Lawrence to Pound, "Yeats is no good?" Robert Graves, in the *Pamphlet Against Anthologies,* which he wrote with Laura Riding, made jovial hay of "The Lake Isle of Innisfree." Thus, though Yeats had never been neglected, the full recognition of his greatness, like its full flowering, came very tardily.

To many critics it seemed that Yeats, wonderful as his gifts were, did not live wholly in the real world. Thus I. A. Richards, in *Science and Poetry* (1925), commenting on Yeats's interest in magic, wrote:

> Now he turns to a world of symbolic phantasmagoria about which he is desperately uncertain. He is uncertain because he has adopted as a technique of inspiration the use of trance, of dissociated phases of consciousness, and the revelations given in these dissociated states are unsufficiently connected with normal experience.

Quoting this comment, T. S. Eliot, in *After Strange Gods,* had even more severe things to say as late as 1934:

> Mr. Yeats's "supernatural world" was the wrong supernatural world. It was not a world

> of spiritual significance, not a world of real Good and Evil, of holiness and sin, but a highly sophisticated lower mythology summoned, like a physician, to supply the fading pulse of poetry with some transient stimulant so that the dying patient may utter his last words.

The centrally important critical problem about Yeats becomes clear if we contrast these passages with the noble tribute that Eliot paid to Yeats on his death:

> There are some poets whose poems can be considered more or less in isolation, for experience and delight. There are others whose poetry, though giving equally experience and delight, has a larger historical importance. Yeats was one of the latter. He was one of the few whose history was the history of our own time, who are part of the consciousness of our age, which cannot be understood without them.[1]

How are these pertinent strictures to be reconciled with this deserved praise? In what sense was the mental history of Yeats, which from a superficial point of view was so odd and eccentric, more profoundly "the history of our own time"? Was Eliot, feeling that every truly great poet must in some sense be representative of his time, and feeling intuitively sure of Yeats's major qualities, merely making a formal claim that Yeats must be representative? Or can Yeats's representative quality be illustrated in detail?

Since the first edition of this essay was published, a great deal of scholarly work has been done, by critics such as Frank Kermode, on Yeats's sources in the 1890's and what might be called the English symbolist tradition, one deriving from William Blake and the Pre-Raphaelites rather than from Stéphane Mallarmé. F. A. C. Wilson has also written interestingly on Yeats's debts to neo-Platonic and oriental mystical ideas, and Giorgio Melchiori on his use of themes suggested by Renaissance painting. The tendency of all this criticism has been to stress the fact that, in an informal way, Yeats was an extremely learned man and to stress also his lifelong interest in the supernatural. His correspondence with Sturge Moore reveals him as an amateur metaphysician of considerable ingenuity and eloquence. But though the above writers have very much deepened my own understanding in detail of Yeats, I remain convinced that his greatness as a poet lies in his realism, in his humanity, in his power to use fantasy and abstruse speculation as metaphors for, or means of exploring, the human situation; it lies at the pole of what Yeats himself called "self" or "heart," at the pole of the "mire and blood" of human veins, rather than at the pole of what he called "soul," or dreams of an abstract eternity. He had enough earthy strength and sap to be able to digest into true poetry a great deal of what Lord Castlereagh called "sublime mysticism and nonsense." What the poems record is the continuous conflict between the claims of a prophetic wisdom, a sense of insulation against the terrors of history, and, on the other hand, the claims, rewards, and pains of the moment.

II

When I. A. Richards, in *Science and Poetry,* suggested that a poet like Yeats, who took ghosts and fairies seriously, could hardly have anything quite centrally significant to say to the modern mind, he was making a crude but sensible point. The main debate of that mind, in England, since the 1880's, has been between an orthodox religious and an orthodox scientific attitude. Yeats was neither orthodoxly religious nor orthodoxly scientific; he had his own science, which was an occult one, and his own religion, or "sophisticated lower mythology," and in prose he sometimes reconciles them at the level of magic. In his better poetry, on the other hand, he often quietly jettisons both of them. The scientific attitude leads, in practice, to a kind of demo-

1. See Eliot's "The Poetry of W. B. Yeats" in *Purpose,* XII (1940), reprinted in *On Poetry and Poets* (London, 1957).

cratic humanitarianism. Yeats believed in aristocracy and, though his humane and fastidious temperament made him recoil from violence, he often allowed himself to romanticize violence when it was safely set in a mythological past. The modern Christian attitude tends to lead to a preoccupation with sin. From this, Yeats was quite free. In the last ten years of Yeats's life, these two contrasting attitudes were well represented in England by the work of W. H. Auden and Eliot. Auden, in the 1930's, was a kind of liberal semi-Marxist, profoundly but not always obviously affected by a Christian upbringing; Eliot was a Christian conservative, profoundly but not always obviously affected, particularly in his concern with social questions, by a liberal upbringing. These two poets, in fact, had much more in common with each other than either had with Yeats. Yet Auden, like Eliot, nobly saluted Yeats's passing:

Earth, receive an honoured guest:
William Yeats is laid to rest.
Let the Irish vessel lie
Emptied of its poetry. . . .
("In Memory of W. B. Yeats,")[2]

In saluting Yeats, neither Auden nor Eliot can have been merely saluting a great artist in verse. Given the deep seriousness of their critical attitudes, both must have found in Yeats's work a kind of wisdom, even though that expressed itself through ideas and gestures of which they disapproved. Yeats was as firmly set against Auden's attitude of the 1930's, which he symbolically described as "Moscow," as against Eliot's, which he symbolically described as "Rome." Just as he was never a political democrat, never at all sympathetic with the

levelling, rancorous, rational sort of mind
That never looked out of the eye of a saint
Or out of a drunkard's eye,

so he was very much farther, also, from any traditional Christian attitudes than many scientifically minded agnostics are. What may be called his morality was neither that of a diluted and imperfect Christianity nor that of a progressive humanitarianism. It could be better described as a morality of "style." It very much resembled (given that Yeats had a more genial and generous temperament) the morality of Nietzsche. Yeats's instinctive sympathies were with the strong and proud, not with the weak and humble; with the brilliant rather than the stupid, with the exceptional rather than the average. They were not, however, like those of Nietzsche, with the oppressor rather than the oppressed. Yet, as an Irish nationalist, Yeats identified himself with the liberal wing of the Protestant Ascendancy, with those like Jonathan Swift and Henry Grattan, "who gave though free to refuse," rather than with the masses of the Irish people. Yeats's frank admiration for such qualities as strength, beauty, recklessness, a dominating spirit, a "proper pride" set him against the obvious superficial currents of our age. If he does indeed have the central representativeness that Eliot claims for him, one reason may be that this aristocratic or "natural" morality—which is the morality of schoolboys, of film fans, of soldiers, a morality based on the instinctive admiration we feel for those who excel us—is more firmly rooted in us than we think, and that when we find it nobly expressed we instinctively respond to it. More broadly, for all our preoccupation today with "security," we still have hankerings after the heroic.

III

The case for Yeats's representativeness, however, has never been properly argued. The mere exposition of the meaning of many of Yeats's poems, as related to his personal history, to his social background, and to his philosophical opinions, is in itself such a complicated task that very little that can properly be called "criticism" of his poems—criticism in the sense of concrete evaluation, of dis-

2. In *Collected Shorter Poems, 1930–1944* (London, 1950).

tancing and placing—has been written. Maud Gonne and Mme. Blavatsky and the Abbey Theatre and Irish politics and the esoteric symbolism of *A Vision* tend to bulk so large in accounts of Yeats that they crowd out any consideration of his diction, his rhythms, his way of constructing a poem, the coherence and sensitivity of his responses. What John Wain wittily calls "the Gypsy Petulengro approach"—the painstaking exposition, with diagrams, of what Yeats meant by gyres and cones and "phases of the moon"—becomes so absorbing in itself that mere literary criticism no doubt seems dull by comparison. This sketch is not primarily concerned with Yeats as a magician or a mystic. Margaret Rudd may be perfectly right when, in her book about Yeats, she says that he is a rather inferior mystic if we compare him with Blake. What is also true is that the Blake of the prophetic books is a rather inferior artist if we compare him with Yeats—these have to be approached, as even Yeats's book of occult philosophy, *A Vision,* need not be, with a primarily extraliterary interest. And Yeats's prose poem *Per Amica Silentia Lunae,* a preliminary account of some parts of *A Vision,* needs no apology; it is an accomplished, even a moving, artifact in its own right. But we should remember a wise remark by his wife, George: "Willie," she is reported to have said, "you are a great poet, but you are no saint." The great poet is our subject. He was, of course, no saint; but we may make out a case in passing that he had many of the virtues of Aristotle's "magnanimous man" or of the *honnête homme* of the French seventeenth century. His representativeness for our own age does, as I have suggested, largely depend on the fact that he both possessed and praised what we think of as archaic virtues. He was the last quite wholehearted spokesman of the aristocratic idea.

IV

Yeats came from the outer fringe of the Irish Protestant Ascendancy, from a rather better family than George Bernard Shaw's, and perhaps from not quite such a good family as Oscar Wilde's. He spent his childhood between London and Ireland, and though in Ireland his family counted as minor gentry, in London, insofar as London bothers about such things, they probably counted as shabby-genteel bohemians. Yeats's father, J. B. Yeats, was a talented but unsuccessful painter who wrote brilliant letters and had a genius for friendship. As a painter he was influenced by the Pre-Raphaelites, and he handed down to his son the idea of a "religion of beauty" and a romantic taste in art and literature that even in Yeats's youth was a slightly old-fashioned one. There are certain great writers of the type of Henrik Ibsen whom the young Yeats could never absorb; to the end of his days his attitude toward the French painters Edgar Degas and Claude Monet was rather like that of Sir Alfred Munnings toward Pablo Picasso.[3] J. B. Yeats was also influenced in his ideas by the agnostic rationalism of Thomas Huxley and John Tyndall, and this in turn effected a change in his art to a naturalist impressionist portraiture. Against such beliefs and aesthetic practices the young Yeats violently reacted.

As a boy, Yeats was dreamy and backward, fond of long solitary walks. To his dying day, he never learned to spell properly, and diffidence about his scholarship prevented him from going to Trinity College, Dublin. This lack of a formal education is important in Yeats's development. He read very widely but never systematically. He was bad at languages; insofar as the French symbolist movement influenced him at all, it was through translations made by his friend Arthur Symons, and when in later life he said that he had "almost forgotten his Hebrew," he meant that at one period, for some occult purpose, he had memorized a few words of that language. Even for himself, the map of what he knew and did not know can never have had

3. Munnings was a member of the Royal Academy and a painter of horses in the naturalist manner. He was intensely conservative and unsympathetic to the avant-garde work by Picasso.

very firm outlines. Like many poets, he probably learned much from conversations with others, and, indeed, all his life he subjected himself to mentors, sometimes younger men than himself, who supplied the deficiencies in his stock of philosophy, connoisseurship, stagecraft, or mystical experience: Lionel Johnson, Charles Ricketts, John Synge, Gordon Craig, T. Sturge Moore.

The young Yeats began writing verses very early. This early work shows much vividness of imagery, but it was some time before Yeats learned to write in regular stanzas or even to make all his lines scan. The first drafts of his poems, to the end, often show a surprising technical hesitancy—a trite choice of words, a flat shaping of the line; the poems were perfected by a habit, early acquired, of endlessly patient revision. The young Yeats was lucky in that his father encouraged him to go on with his poetry and even actively discouraged him from tying himself down to the drudgery of regular newspaper work. Yeats, however, soon became a fluent freelance journalist, chiefly on topics of Irish folklore. By his early twenties, he had begun to make a reputation. In London, he became one of a group of minor poets, among them Symons, Johnson, and Ernest Dowson, whom today we tend to dismiss as "decadents."

This label has been attached to them partly because of their sense of the incurable materialism and philistinism of their own age, and of their self-created myth of themselves as doomed artists, and partly because of their almost exclusive devotion to their art. All of them—Lionel Johnson, Ernest Dowson, John Davidson, Arthur Symons, Aubrey Beardsley—had unhappy lives; most died young. A number were converts to Catholicism, and for them the possibility, ever present in their minds, of being damned gave not a relish but a momentousness to sin. Yeats's early poems are full of melancholy and falling rhythms, but have little to say about sin. The young Irishman was not haunted by the fear of damnation. He was chaste and temperate—the greatest love of his life, for Maud Gonne, was probably a chaste one, and his failure to win her did not drive him to prostitutes or to drink. In the middle 1890's he met a beautiful and talented woman, an unhappily married cousin of Lionel Johnson's, Olivia Shakespear, and for a short period they found happiness in their love affair. But before long, Maud Gonne appeared in London, asking for his help, and Olivia, sensing a divided loyalty, brought her affair with Yeats to an end. This renewed misery might well have brought him to the same end as the poets of "the tragic generation," had he not been rescued by the maternal kindness of Lady Gregory at the end of the decade. Shy and dreamy though Yeats was, he also was fundamentally a masterful man. Maud Gonne, dragging him at her heels on nationalist agitations, soon found that he was a natural orator and could easily dominate committees. His religion, far more than that of his companions, was genuinely a religion of poetry. Reacting against agnostic rationalism, he had not reacted in the direction of orthodoxy:

> I was unlike others of my generation in one thing only. I am very religious, and deprived by Huxley and Tyndall of the simple-minded religion of my childhood, I had made a new religion, almost an infallible church of poetic tradition, of a fardel of stories, and of personages and of emotions, inseparable from their first expression, passed on from generation to generation by poets and painters with some help from philosophers and theologians. (*The Trembling of the Veil,* 1926 ed., pp. 142–143)

How far, one wonders, was he right about himself? Was he really "very religious"? We wonder both about the word "fardel" with its dandified air and about the word "stories," which shrugs off the question of whether the stories are true. The attitude is aesthetic rather than ethical or religious; in a sophisticated way the young Yeats is playing a child's game of Let's Pretend. There are late poems of his, such as "Among School Children," that do express an authentically religious attitude, one of mystical acceptance of a world experienced as contradictory; but the genuinely religious attitude that is often to be found in Yeats's poetry has little to do with—even tugs against-the pseudoreligious notions. It is not a playing with fantasies but a response to the whole. The very fact that the young man could so easily concoct a "new religion" for himself—out of Irish folklore and Blake and Mme. Blavatsky and anything that came handy—is evidence of a rather unreligious nature; evidence of a blithe and irresponsible temperament, that of a young man sure of his genius, and unconvicted of sin. The note of the 1890's, the genuinely religious note that is not to be found in Yeats's early poems, is that of Lionel Johnson's "The Dark Angel":

Dark Angel, with thine aching lust!
  Of two defeats, of two despairs:
Less dread, a change to drifting dust,
  Than thine eternity of cares.

Yeats's early religion, if it was properly a religion at all, was one without anguish or dread.

The charm of much of Yeats's early poetry is thus slightly equivocal—dreamy and melancholy, passive and self-indulgent, as indeed from this account of his poetical religion we might expect it to be. Robert Graves's attack on "The Lake Isle of Innisfree" is, in fact, an attack on a poet for not being properly awake. In the poem "A Faery Song" from Yeats's volume of 1892, *The Countess Cathleen and Various Legends and Lyrics,* a modern reader is embarrassed by the monotonous doleful music, by the yearning that seems neither to have nor to seek for an object:

We who are old, old and gay,
O so old!
Thousands of years, thousands of years
If all were told:

Give to these children, new from the world,
Silence and love;
And the long dew-dropping hours of the
  night,
And the stars above. . . .
  (1–8)

Even throughout the 1890s, however, there was a constant, slow, hidden growth in another direction. In *The Wind Among the Reeds,* the volume of 1899, the diction does indeed seem on the surface as formal and faded, the cadences as mechanically "beautiful," as ever; and the symbolism also, increasingly intricate but not increasingly vivid,

  a coat
Covered with embroideries,

hangs now like a rich, worn tapestry between the poet and the hard stone walls of the world. But the yearning had now an object, Maud Gonne. The individual words clutch more at particular objects. There is a movement toward active feeling, positive grasp:

I became a man, a hater of the wind,
Knowing one, out of all things, alone, that
  his head
May not lie on the breast or his lips on the
  hair
Of the woman that he loves, until he dies;
Although the rushes and the fowl of the air
Cry of his love with their pitiful cries.
  ("He Thinks of His Past Greatness
    When a Part of the Constellations
    of Heaven")

Yeats, at some time after 1909, changed the "dreamy Celtic" dying fall of the last two lines to an arrogant rhetorical question:

O beast of the wilderness, bird of the air,
Must I endure your amorous cries?

The poem had enough latent strength to stand the change.

We should look, in the early poems, for that latent strength. Their weary, withdrawn note is a kind of protective coloring that Yeats had taken from his friends of the 1890's. (He was often, throughout his life, ready to imitate admiringly his minor, but never his major, contemporaries. A natural leader, he liked to disguise himself as a follower, even of small men.) There is, of course, a paradox here. Yeats made himself a major poet, starting with the equipment and apparently the tastes of a good minor one—with a chaste but excessively "poetic" diction, with exquisite but trite cadences, with a tendency to use symbols in a way that was decorative and even fussy rather than deeply exploratory, with a narrow and rather willfully sad range of moods, always just on the verge of the literary pose or the stock response. He started, also, without much grasp of the outer world; his early poems rarely make us see anything; we can weave our own daydreams round them, which is another matter. And though he acquired unique rank among his contemporaries as a visionary poet, it is probable that the merely *visible* world left him, to the last, rather cold. Usually he evokes it for us by a kind of trick, not describing the thing but reminding us of our feelings about it:

> A sycamore and lime-tree lost in night
> Although that western cloud is luminous
> . . .
> Back turned upon the brightness of the sun
> And all the sensuality of the shade. . . .
> ("Coole Park," 3–4; 30–31)

We remember our feelings about staring toward a fading distance at sunset, about sharp contrasts in a garden of light and shade. We ourselves, most of the time, *make* Yeats's physical world for him. We believe in it, because we believe in Yeats, rather as we believe in a painted Elsinore when Hamlet is talking. We can, in fact, think perhaps most fruitfully of Yeats's poems as speeches made by him at crucial moments in a long noble drama. No poet lends himself so little to the cold-blooded examination of his poems as isolated objects; no poet gains more from being read as a whole, with a full knowledge of his life. Yeats, as he grows older, acts out, with growing assurance and spontaneity, the difficult part of himself. The acting in the end, having gone through the stages of lyrical mime and heroic and satirical tirade, becomes almost naturalistic.

V

The Edwardian decade saw the masterful side of Yeats's nature coming to the surface. By 1908, when the first collected edition of his works came out, he had made a reputation not only as a poet and a dramatist, but as the man who had put the Abbey Theatre on its feet, who kept it going, and who had bravely defended Synge against local prejudice. Through Lady Gregory, who had become his patron, Yeats was now accepted by that "big house" society of which, in his childhood, he had only touched the fringes. He was becoming self-conscious about his ancestry. Some of the younger men in Dublin, and some older contemporaries like George Moore, thought him conceited and arrogant; but nobody any longer thought him a mere shy, ineffectual dreamer. He had resigned himself to unfulfilled love and found public activity a distraction. Maud Gonne had made an unfortunate marriage, and though she was separated from her husband she had become a Roman Catholic, so there was no prospect of her divorcing her husband and marrying Yeats. He and she, in any case, were becoming estranged in a deeper sense. She felt that the Abbey Theatre had tempted Yeats away from the national cause. She would have liked cheaper seats and plays that were straight nationalistic propaganda. Maude Gonne remained the central figure in his poetry, a muse figure; but her presence in so many of his first lyrics should not deflect us from stressing that women played an important role as friends, even as muse figures: his wife, the young dancer Margaret Ruddock, Dorothy Wellesley (the duchess of Wellington), Lady Gregory, and, perhaps supremely, Olivia Shakespear. Their closeness survived the unhappiness of their affair in the 1890's and continued to the end of her life, a year before his own death; and it was to her that he wrote his warmest and most eloquent letters. She is also the subject of one of his most beautiful poems, "After Long Silence." Both Olivia and Lady Gregory are more sympathetic and more intelligent figures than

Maude Gonne, and it is one of the achievements of later criticism that their roles in his life and art have emerged more clearly.

World War I, apart from the deaths of friends like Major Robert Gregory, hardly touched Yeats emotionally. But the Easter Rebellion of 1916, which took him by surprise (he was not in the confidence of any of the more extreme nationalists), made him regret his growing aloofness from the Irish cause. He remained a very moderate nationalist—he felt that England might still "keep faith"—and indeed the troubles of 1916 and after gave him a vivid sense of how violence can in a short time destroy values that it had taken the law centuries to build up:

> We had fed the heart on fantasies,
> The heart's grown brutal from the fare;
> More substance in our enmities
> Than in our love; O honey-bees
> Come build in the empty house of the stare.
> ("The Stare's Nest by My Window," st. 4)

Yet he felt himself more profoundly identified with the Irish people than he had been for many years.

Yeats's long romance with Maud Gonne had meanwhile ended in a kind of comic fantasy. Her husband, one of the rebels of 1916, had been shot. Yeats felt he ought to ask her to marry him again but was probably relieved when she refused. At the same time, he fell in love with her beautiful adopted daughter, who, as a young girl, had been half in love with him. The adopted daughter could not make up her mind. Yeats gave her a date by which to do so, and when her final decision was against marrying him, he suddenly married another young lady, George Hyde-Lees. Not unnaturally, after such a complication of emotions, he was in a state of depression and anxiety after his marriage—even if there had not been the business of Maud Gonne and her daughter, he was a man in his fifties, weighed down by anxiety for his country and married, after an unusually chaste bachelor existence, to somebody much younger than himself. It was partly to distract him that Mrs. Yeats started the experiments in automatic writing that ultimately gave him the material for *A Vision.* In judging Yeats's occult philosophy, we should always ask ourselves how far, at a fundamental level, he himself took it seriously; and how far it was a necessary plaything for a powerful and distressed creative mind.

VI

Many critics agree that it is on the volumes published in the last twenty years of his life, from *The Wild Swans at Coole* of 1917 to the posthumous *Last Poems and Two Plays* of 1939, that Yeats's future fame will mainly rest. The sharpening and hardening of his attitudes, the development of the tough, complex, and ironical later style can in fact be traced farther back, to the significantly named *Responsibilities* of 1914. There is even a hint of the new style in "Adam's Curse," from a volume of 1903, *In the Seven Woods*:

> I said, "It's certain there is no fine thing
> Since Adam's fall but needs much labouring.
> There have been lovers who thought love
> should be
> So much compounded of high courtesy
> That they would sigh and quote with
> learned looks
> Precedents out of beautiful old books;
> Yet now it seems an idle trade enough."

It can, however, be agreed that there is a remarkable new maturity, a new "realism," in the work of Yeats's last twenty years; and this can be traced to several sources.

Yeats was now writing as a married man, a man with a house and children of his own, more rooted in everyday life than he had previously been. He was writing also as a man who had seen the dream of his youth, Irish independence, come true; and who was becoming aware of certain ironies, for him tragic ironies, involved in its coming true. His own personal dream had been of a free Ireland that would be a kind of replica, without the tensions or troubles, without the injustice to the majority, of the Ireland of Grattan's Parliament.[4] He wanted to go back to the eighteenth century rather than on into the twentieth. He hoped that the "big houses" would survive, that the Protestant Ascendancy would still, because of their wealth, their wit, and their manners, constitute a dominant group. He thought of the local grandees patronizing poets and the peasants touching their hats. He was romantically innocent about politics. He found, of course, that what had come into existence was not a Protestant-dominated aristocratic republic but a Roman Catholic farmers' democracy; and the farmers did not want to touch their hats to anybody. Some of the "big houses" were burned in the troubles, others were deserted because they cost too much to keep up and because they, like even the nationalistic aristocracy, had outlived their social function. Yeats had hoped that Dublin, as the capital of a free Ireland, would become a great cultural center; he saw the "blind, bitter town" becoming more rather than less provincial. The Dublin city fathers gave the freedom of the city to a retired Tammany boss, a Mr. Croker, but rejected the suggestion of Oliver St. John Gogarty that they should also give it to Yeats. Sean O'Casey's tragic masterpiece, *The Plough and the Stars*, aroused as passionate an opposition from the Abbey Theatre audience as Synge's *Playboy of the Western World* had done. Yeats's growing bitterness comes out as early as *The Wild Swans at Coole* in one of his most powerfully sustained shorter poems, "The Fisherman":

> All day I'd looked in the face
> What I had hoped 'twould be
> To write for my own race
> And the reality;
> The living men that I hate,
> The dead man that I loved,
> The craven man in his seat,
> The insolent unreproved,
> And no knave brought to book
> Who has won a drunken cheer,
> The witty man and his joke
> Aimed at the commonest ear,
> The clever man who cries
> The catch-cries of the clown,
> The beating down of the wise
> And great Art beaten down.
> (9–24)

Yeats, in this new Ireland, was not, in spite of the prestige that the Nobel Prize brought him, a centrally representative figure. He became a senator, but found himself allied in the senate, a little unromantically, with rich bankers and brewers; a speech that he made protesting, on behalf of the religious minority, against a proposal to make divorce illegal made him unpopular. The esoteric philosophy of *A Vision* is partly to be understood, as we have suggested already, in terms of Yeats's need for distraction. We should not take that book more seriously than Yeats did. He had a long philosophical correspondence with Sturge Moore about hallucinatory cats and other visions of that sort. Are they real beings to which we have access only at privileged moments? Yeats would have liked to think so. Or are they, on the other hand, hallucinations? It is interesting that in this correspondence he never refers to either the "facts" or

4. Until 1780, the Irish Parliament could reject or accept, but not amend, laws relating to Irish matters passed by the British Parliament. Irish patriots like Henry Flood and Henry Grattan took advantage of the American Revolutionary War (which involved war with France) to claim and secure legislative independence for the Irish Parliament. The Volunteer Movement, a kind of unofficial defense militia ostensibly raised to resist invasion, was, in fact used to put moral pressure on the viceregal government. The viceroy and his staff, however, retained practical control of Irish affairs by offering honors and sinecures to the progovernment parliamentary majority. The new Parliament did not represent the Roman Catholic masses of the people, or even their wealthier elements. Thus the short period of Irish parliamentary independence—or really, of independence for the Protestant Ascendancy—ended in the bloody troubles of 1798 and a little later in the union, secured partly by lavish bribery, of the Irish with the imperial Parliament. Nevertheless, the short period of Grattan's Parliament was marked both by splendid oratory and by a gay and brilliant social life in Dublin, and was thus often remembered nostalgically in the nineteenth century by Irishmen who saw Dublin, both socially and culturally, becoming more and more of a provincial city.

the "arguments" of *A Vision* as having any relevant authority. He explicitly states elsewhere that it is not very profitable to discuss the theories of *A Vision* in terms of "belief." Many of the ideas in the book, like that of eternal recurrence, are not new; they can be found in the Italian philosopher Giovanni Vico, and in Nietzsche. Yeats, after he had written the first draft of *A Vision,* also found them in Oswald Spengler. Their truth or otherwise cannot be discussed here. They provided props for Yeats's attitude to life, which was becoming a kind of tragic stoicism. He saw life as tragic and felt that it could be acted out with the style of a tragedy. We can embrace our destiny joyfully: "Hamlet and Lear are gay."

It should be particularly noticed, however, that Yeats's attitude toward the supernatural was a profoundly ambiguous one. He wanted, from a world beyond ours, in contrasting moods, two apparently quite contradictory kinds of assurance: one, that we are in fact bound, as the Buddhists tell us we are, to the "great wheel of existence" and shall reappear upon this stage in various roles again and again; the other that, as the Buddhists also tell us, we can escape ultimately from the "great wheel"—not to nonbeing, a concept that never attracted Yeats, but to some kind of timeless perfection. He was not sure (as perhaps no Western man who studies Eastern thought ever is) that he really wanted to escape from the wheel. Thus, in the face of his "symbolic phantasmagoria," he retains the freedom of inconsistency. His images of a Byzantine heaven in which he would be transformed into a golden bird (the artist becoming an eternal work of art) symbolize his desire to escape from the disorder, the irony, the failure of life; but so also other symbols—as when he says he would like to live again, even in a "foul ditch," as a "blind man battering blind men"—stand for a craving for life at any level, the "lust and rage" of which he speaks in his *Last Poems,* that grew stronger in him as he grew older. Often he hated life for not being perfection. Sometimes, also, he feared perfection for not being life.

VII

Yeats's early love poems are dreamily erotic, but those addressed to Olivia Shakespear, particularly through the use of hair imagery, possess a shadowy sexuality. Some of his later poems are so harshly sexual that they cease, in effect, to be erotic:

From pleasure of the bed,
Dull as a worm,
His rod and its butting head
Limp as a worm,
His spirit that has fled
Blind as a worm.
("The Chambermaid's Second Song")

A glandular operation that Yeats underwent in his last years no doubt accentuated this tendency, but it was already there. It is best considered, however, as part of a more general tendency in his later poems toward self-questioning, self-stripping:

These masterful images because complete
Grew in pure mind, but out of what began?
A mound of refuse or the sweepings of a
street,
Old kettles, old bottles, and a broken can,
Old iron, old bones, old rags, that raving
slut
Who keeps the till. Now that my ladder's
gone
I must lie down where all the ladders start
In the foul rag-and-bone shop of the heart.
("The Circus Animals' Desertion," st. 5)

The man who wrote that stanza also wrote:

We were the last romantics—chose for
theme
Traditional sanctity and loveliness. . . .
("Coole Park and Ballylee," st. 6)

Anybody who wants to get the full range of Yeats must be able to respond to both kinds of statement—must be able to accept the tautness of a great poet's terrible sincerity. In that stanza from "The Circus Animals' Desertion," Yeats has become aware that the symbols of his poetry have a Freudian meaning of which for most of his life he has been unconscious. But we should notice also that this stanza, which bids farewell to the symbolist method, is a triumphant example of it; for we know what the poet is saying here, but we cannot say it in our own words. A merely clinical interpretation will not work. Is, for instance, "that raving slut/Who keeps the till" the Freudian censor—is the money she will give us in return for old rubbish a release of libido? Are the "old iron, old bones, old rags" and the "mound of refuse" symbols for the Freudian analerotic hoarding instinct? Is the "foul rag-and-bone shop of the heart" merely the sexual imagination, with its accumulated scraps of lustful memory? Quite obviously not, and quite obviously what Yeats is saying here is something more general and profound. There is something basically blind, grasping, insensate in all of us; something that hoards rubbish, that shuts doors, that hides away from the light. We climb up, but we never wholly get away. All is still under our feet, in the cellarage. And the "heart" is what grasps and is insensate but also what loves and suffers, and the "ladders"—the ways upward and outward to the free air and the life of the spirit—do start there. And when we have said all this, of course, the stanza still retains, as all great symbolist poetry does, its eternal residue of mysterious suggestiveness.

The bare honesty of such poems, even more than the rich, dark mysteriousness of "Byzantium" or "The Statues," may partly account for Yeats's hold on the young. In his last volume he asks himself more frankly than most poets have done whether he may not have done as much harm as good:

> Did that play of mine send out
> Certain men the English shot?

Yet he can still strike a last attitude:

> *Cast a cold eye*
> *On life, on death.*
> *Horseman, pass by!*
> ("Under Ben Bulben")

He would not, like Rainer Maria Rilke (these lines were written out of irritation with Rilke), accept death as a final dark consummation. He would not accept life itself uncritically. And in the last thing he was working on, *The Death of Cuchulain,* the harlot (an eternal harlot, who has slept with "Conall, Cuchulain, Usna's boys") speaks of polarities and antinomies, of disgust and delight in physical love, of dread and delight in battle; speaks also of the Irish patriots of 1916, who were always in Yeats's heart, delighting in what they dreaded; speaks of gods and heroes whom we seem to embody, or who seem to stand behind us, in the crucial moments of our lives:

> That there are still some living
> That do my limbs unclothe,
> But that the flesh my flesh has gripped
> I both adore and loathe.
> *(Pipe and drum music)*
> Are those things that men adore and loathe
> Their sole reality?
> What stood in the Post Office
> With Pearse and Connolly?
> What comes out of the mountain
> When men first shed their blood?
> Who thought Cuchulain till it seemed
> He stood where they had stood?

VII

Yeats felt that there was a tension between his life and his poetry. He thought sometimes of the poem as a kind of antipersonality that the poet builds up to compensate for or conceal personal weakness, of the poem as a mask." This idea has something in common with Ezra Pound's idea of the poem as a persona. Pound is a poet who, according to one of his most appreciative but also harshest critics, Percy Wyndham Lewis, has no "personality" of his own worth speaking of; he can function only by pretending to be somebody else, a Provencal troubadour or a Chinese sage. Yeats's masks in poetry are not of this sort; even in his earliest work his own personality—or at least an important aspect of it, the "poetic" aspect—seems to me to come over. Similarly, no doubt, at meetings of the Rhymers' Club in the 1890's, Yeats, fundamentally a very shy and diffident young man, put on a suitable "literary dandy" or perhaps sometimes a "dreamy Celt" personality. As Yeats's poetry matures, one of the things that happens is not so much that it becomes more personal, less of a mask, as that he gets more of his personality into it. He gets in things like irony, humor, arrogant irascibility, the coaxing manners of the professional Irish conversationalist, which in the 1890's he would probably have considered "antipoetic"; he gets in more of the prosaic detail of life, transformed by a poetic apprehension of it.

We might compare the generalized evocation of Maud Gonne, from "Fallen Majesty" in *Responsibilities,*

. . . A crowd
Will gather, and not know it walks the very street
Whereon a thing once walked that seemed a burning cloud,
(6–8)

with the prose bareness of a line and a half from "Beautiful Lofty Things," in *Last Poems*:

. . . Maud Gonne at Howth Station waiting a train,
Pallas Athene in that straight back and arrogant head. . . .
(10–11)

That line and a half evokes Maud Gonne, her setting, her bearing, her character (Pallas Athene, the goddess of wisdom, was severe and virginal). The more conventionally poetic phrase about "a burning cloud" tells us much about Yeats's feeling but does not evoke any image of a woman at all.

Often the force of the later poetry comes largely from this directness, like that of speech:

Before a woman's portrait suddenly I stand,
Beautiful and gentle in her Venetian way,
I met her all but fifty years ago
For twenty minutes in some studio.

. . .

And here's John Synge himself, that rooted man,
"Forgetting human words," a grave deep face. . . .
("The Municipal Gallery Revisited," st. 4 and 7)

Does the imagination dwell the most
Upon a woman won or woman lost?
If on the lost, admit you turned aside
From a great labyrinth out of pride,
Cowardice, some silly over-subtle thought
Or anything called conscience once;
And that if memory recur, the sun's
Under eclipse and the moon blotted out.
(The Tower)

There is no rhetoric in these passages; only in the latter of them any figures of speech, and these so commonplace (a human relationship as a labyrinth, the sense of loss seeming to blot out the sun and moon) that they could occur unaffectedly in ordinary conversation. Common turns of speech are also sometimes exploited for irony. In *The Tower* we are told the story of Mrs. French (it is in Sir Jonah Barrington's *Memoirs* of 1833) and how a footman at dinner one day clipped off the ears of a farmer who was behaving boorishly and brought them to her in a little covered dish. It is with a delighted shock that we meet the lady again, in a summary of the characters in the poems, as

Mrs. French,
Gifted with so fine an ear. . . .

Critics who have discussed to the verge of tedium Yeats's more obscure occult fancies might have discussed with more advantage this strong simplicity of his later style. Behind the strength is honesty of statement. The lines quoted above,

Does the imagination dwell the most . . .

express a complex of feelings that most of us have experienced but that few of us have the courage to put on record: a complex of feelings that might be called remorse or compunction. Yeats speaks for what he calls, in a poem addressed to Friedrich von Hütgel, the "unchristened heart"; but with a dignity and passion that make it very unlikely that his words should ever cause scandal to Christians.

Yet if there were only pride and pagan courage and high art, only contempt for "this filthy modern tide," only the obstinate "lust and rage" of a "wild, wicked old man" in Yeats, should we turn to him as we do, not only for distraction, not only for stimulus, but for wisdom and consolation? We look in poetry for love. All great poets are more profoundly capable of love than common men, and they may be terrifyingly more capable of hate too. Yeats's capacity for hate distressed even close friends of his, like the duchess of Wellington. It was there to the last, as in the poem "A Bronze Head":

> Or else I thought her supernatural;
> As though a sterner eye looked through her
> eye
> On this foul world in its decline and fall;
> On gangling stocks grown great, great stocks
> run dry,
> Ancestral pearls all pitched into a sty,
> Heroic reverie mocked by clown and knave,
> And wondered what was left for massacre to
> save.
> (st.4)

But he could hate like that *because* he could love. And the touchstones that I would choose from his poetry, to persuade an unsympathetic reader to reconsider it, all speak of love. I would choose these stanzas from "A Prayer for My Daughter":

> An intellectual hatred is the worst,
> So let her think opinions are accursed.
> Have I not seen the loveliest woman born
> Out of the mouth of Plenty's horn,
> Because of her opinionated mind
> Barter that horn and every good
> By quiet natures understood
> For an old bellows full of angry wind?
>
> Considering that, all hatred driven hence,
> The soul recovers radical innocence
> And learns that it is self-delighting,
> Self-appeasing, self-affrighting,
> And that its own sweet will is Heaven's
> will;
> She can, though every face should scowl
> And every windy quarter howl
> Or every bellows burst, be happy still.
> (st. 8–9)

I would choose a line or two from the gentle minor elegy "In Memory of Eva Gore-Booth and Con Markiewicz":

> Dear shadows, now you know it all,
> All the folly of a fight
> With a common wrong or right.
> The innocent and the beautiful
> Have no enemy but time. . . .
> (21–25)

I would choose the magnificent two last stanzas of "Among School Children":

> Both nuns and mothers worship images,
> But those the candles light are not as those
> That animate a mother's reveries,
> But keep a marble or a bronze repose.
> And yet they too break hearts—O Presences
> That passion, piety or affection knows,
> And that all heavenly glory symbolise—
> O self-mockery of man's enterprise;
>
> Labour is blossoming or dancing where
> The body is not bruised to pleasure soul,
> Nor beauty born out of its own despair,
> Nor blear-eyed wisdom out of midnight oil.
> O chestnut-tree, great-rooted blossomer,
> Are you the leaf, the blossom, or the bole?
> O body swayed to music, O brightening
> glance,
> How can we know the dancer from the
> dance?

And (though Yeats is not on the whole a poet of striking single lines, of lines that impress us out of their setting) I might choose a line and a half from "Nineteen Hundred and Nineteen":

Man is in love and loves what vanishes,
What more is there to say? . . .
(st.6)

Throughout his career, Yeats was a continuous reviser of his earlier work; and the student, when he quotes the work, needs to be careful that he is not basing his arguments on a text of 1908 or of the 1920's. This process is one of "making himself new." Essentially Yeats's poems are dramatic lyrics, and each of his volumes after *Responsibilities* (1914) consists of poems placed very carefully not in order of composition but in a cogent dramatic order, an unfolding, one poem commenting on its predecessor or its successor, amplifying or deflating. Each volume in turn leads on to its successor. So, for example, the last poem in *The Wild Swans at Coole,* "The Double Vision of Michael Robartes," with its figure of the dancer, is caught up in the little poem of the ensuing volume, *Michael Robartes and the Dancer* (1920).

I believe Yeats's poetry to be the centrally important part of his work. His work as a playwright is more difficult to assess.

IX

Yeats's approach is distinct from that of his contemporaries in the Irish dramatic revival. Theirs was to develop, first in the work of Synge and later in that of O'Casey, toward a drama of regional naturalism. Yeats on the other hand remained throughout his life the visionary of the movement, the one who aimed at a marriage of poetry and drama to be achieved by quite different methods. From the very beginning he took a vigorous and practical part in the artistic and technical development of the Irish theater, as well as in the day-to-day problems of administration, production, and experiment. He was by no means a Tennyson patronized by an Irving, but rather a combination of poet and man of the theater who created an integral dramatic form that was entirely new to his age. What distinguishes him from his dramatic contemporaries is his rejection of representation, a dramatic convention that had come to be accepted without question, because in Britain, at least, playwriting had for so long been overshadowed and dominated by the art of fiction. Yeats turned away not only from the large theater, with its sophisticated apparatus of illusion, and from the realistic conventions of performance, gesture, and details of staging and spectacle, but also from other conventions concerning dramatic composition:

> One dogma of the printed criticism is that if a play does not contain definite character, its constitution is not strong enough for the stage, and that the dramatic moment is always the contest of character with character. . . . when we go back a few centuries and enter the great periods of drama, character grows less and sometimes disappears. ("The Tragic Theatre," in the *Mask* [Florence], October 1910)

He sought, as he wrote elsewhere, "a deeper reality than any that can be reached by observation, for it is the reality of the imagination and comes from the withdrawal of the poet's mind into itself, not from the effort to see and record." His conception of the drama aimed at uncovering "not character, but those deeper forms of which character is merely a lineament."

Within these chosen limits, Yeats was to experiment for over thirty years to express his vision in dramatic form, first with the Irish Literary Theatre, then later with the Abbey; and his plays reveal a skill in the handling of his medium that increased slowly but unmistakably. In his early verse plays, such as *The Shadowy Waters* (1900), his aim is the realization of a vision of the transcendental. Next, in *Cathleen ni Houlihan* (1902)—the most popular of all his pieces—and *The Pot of Broth,* both written in collaboration with Lady Gregory, he begins to develop fluency in colloquial prose dialogue, coming down, as he put it, from the high window of dramatic verse. He returns to blank verse in a number of plays pitched in a more heroic key, notably *On Baile's Strand* (1903), centered on the episode of King Cuchulain's unwitting killing of his son, and *Deirdre* (1907), the tragic legend that was also dramatized by Synge. It is characteristic of Yeats's *Deirdre* that he contracts the action within a far smaller radius than that of Synge. Preparation is minimal and the attention of the audience is focused as soon as possible on the climax of love and death, the final tableau of queen, lover, and aged king, which constitutes the moment of insight of the play.

Yeats takes an even more radical step away from conventional dramaturgy in his *Four Plays for Dancers* (1921), which were shaped by the traditions of the Japanese Noh theater. "I wanted to create for myself an unpopular theatre," he wrote, and in these short pieces he strives to pare away still more rigorously what he regards as inessentials.

> All imaginative art remains at a distance, and this distance must be firmly held against a pushing world. . . . Our unimaginative arts are content to set a piece of the world as we know it in a place by itself, to put their photographs, as it were, in a plush or plain frame, but the arts which interest me, while seeming to separate from the world and us a group of figures, images, symbols, enable us to pass for a few moments into a deep of the mind that had hitherto been too subtle for our habitation. . . . (introduction to *Certain Noble Plays of Japan,* 1916)

The action in each of the four plays is framed by the presence throughout of masked musicians, who serve as prologue, chorus, and orchestra, and the plays mark a further stage in Yeats's perennial dramatic aim, to isolate particular moments of insight with the maximum of intensity.

The toughening and hardening of attitudes in Yeats's later years referred to in section VI of this essay—the replacing of music by fire, as B. Rajan has aptly put it—and its effect upon Yeats's poetic composition is paralleled by the continual effort to refine and purify his dramatic writing. Toward the end of his life his mastery of dramatic verse and dramatic prose became completely integrated, and his two finest pieces for the stage, albeit minor in scale, offer us an example of each: *Purgatory* (1939), a study of the imprisonment of people in themselves and in their heredity, is in verse; *The Words upon the Window Pane* (1934) is a histrionic tour de force in which the last days of Swift are described through the mouth of a spiritualistic medium in a state of trance.

X

Yeats wrote very delightful prose, and his reminiscences of the 1890's, in particular, are a primary document for a fascinating period. He was an erratic literary critic. His introduction to *The Oxford Book of Modern Verse, 1892–1935,* like his selection of poems in that book, is strikingly odd and eccentric; but it has the wit and charm of everything he wrote, and here and there, among statements that seem quite absurd, it has extremely penetrating paragraphs—particularly, perhaps, about his friend Ezra Pound, whose qualities and weaknesses no subsequent critic has estimated so justly. But it was into his poetry that he put himself most completely. The poetry, however, is better poetry because he gave himself to so many other things. His patriotism, his public spirit, his capacity for staunch friendship and passionate love all enrich it. The sense, which grew so strong in him in later life, that every victory he had worked for implied a defeat of something he perhaps cared about more, lends almost all his later work a pose of complex irony. The characteristics that some of his contemporaries disliked, such as his arrogance or "proper pride," are in his poems, too. Yet all true poets are fundamentally humble. Yeats was humble before the mystery of life. He never took either himself or his systems quite so seriously as some of his disciples have done. He was the last great poet in the English romantic tradition; and the only poet in that tradition, except Byron, with a genuine sense of humor and gift of wit. The true man, with the modesty and the generosity that underlay all his poses, comes out in the letters to Sturge Moore. Yeats writes about the Nobel Prize:

> Yes, it will be a great help to me in several ways. Here especially it will help. I will find it easier to get the Government to listen to me on artistic things. I look upon it as a recognition of the Free State, and of Irish literature, and it is a very great help. People here are grateful because I have won them this recognition, and that is the distinction I want. If I thought it a tribute to my own capacity alone, I, being a very social man, would be far less pleased. (23 November 1923)

All great poets tend to overawe us. They speak with "something above a mortal mouth." And they need their solitude to withdraw into. But it is as a lover, as a friend, and as a patriot, as "a very social man," that Yeats would like us to remember him. It is his broad and deep humanity that provides the substance of his art.

XI

The first edition of this essay was published in 1954 and revised in Yeats's centenary year, 1965. How does Yeats's reputation now stand, and what light have scholarship and criticism thrown on his work since it was first printed? Only one critic, Professor Yvor Winters, has made a full-scale attack on Yeats's reputation (there has also been a skirmishing raid by Robert Graves). Professor Winters' case is that Yeats more or less invented his "romantic Ireland," that his philosophy is private and incoherent, that his images, however vivid, correspond to no clear structure of thought, that he overdramatizes and appeals to those in search of "easy emotions," and that he does not really write "pure poetry" in the tradition of the French symbolists. Professor Winters' attack is beautifully written and argued, but the brief answer is that he is wrong about Ireland—"Easter 1916" is one of the most "realistic" political poems in our language, and Yeats had a very thorough and complete understanding of Irish character and history—and that the rest of his attack is doctrinaire, an attack on Yeats for not being a kind of poet he did not set out to be.

Nevertheless, Professor Winters has put his finger on something, for it is a certain theatrical quality in Yeats, a certain occasional overeasy dramatization of certain stock attitudes, that has worried recent critics. Most contemporary critics would admit, for instance, that "Under Ben Bulben," however gallant as a deathbed gesture, is a little too stagy to be wholly satisfactory as a poem. In a lecture at Sligo in the 1960's, Professor Donald Davie suggested that the peak of Yeats's achievement lay in several late midperiod poems, like "A Prayer for My Daughter," which have a certain classical poise and balance that represent the survival in Yeats's milieu and temperament of Irish eighteenth-century decorum. The most interesting recent criticism, like that of T. Parkinson and J. Stallworthy, has made use of the variorum edition and the manuscript drafts to re-create for us Yeats's agonizingly slow, almost Flaubertian methods of composition. Yeats's first drafts, sometimes in prose, are always clear as outline sketches but remarkably hesitant and sometimes clumsy in rhythm and diction; the "grand style" was forged not easily or naturally, but with blood, sweat, and tears.

The labor that lay behind Yeats's style is perhaps one reason why, like another great, laborious poet, Milton, he has been a dangerous influence on subsequent poets. Direct imitation of him reads always like parody or pastiche; Irish poetry went through a dull period after his death and, in the work of Thomas Kinsella, Richard Murphy, and John Montague, has recently achieved a new liveliness largely by dint of resisting the temptation to overdramatize in a Yeatsian fasion. On the other hand, both Yeats's critical writings and his plays now seem much more important to his admirers than they did when I wrote the first version of this essay. We are perhaps moving away from an age of practical criticism to one of critical theorizing, and there are those who claim that as an aesthetic or philosophical critic Yeats is as important as T. S. Eliot is in the opposite field of direct scrutiny of texts. Yeats's plays have still, at least for Englishmen and Americans, to be practically tested on the stage; but Professor Peter Ure has made very high claims for Yeats's skill and readiness to experiment as a practicing playwright, and F. A. C. Wilson has emphasized the importance of the plays for the study of Yeats's "philosophy."

More recent criticism has also tended to suggest that while Yeats renewed his energies continuously throughout his career as poet, the commonly accepted notion that he somehow became a different, a finer, poet after 1908 has been overstressed. The earlier poems, particularly *The Wanderings of Oisin,* have attracted more admiration, and a number of the poems of the middle period appear to suffer from a certain dryness; the note is forced. *The Tower* now appears as the summit of the poet's achievement, although he continued to write masterly works. More attention has been directed to the prose works, and not simply as commentary on the poems. Argument continues as to the precise nature of Yeats's commitment to Irish politics, though we are perhaps less censorious about his alignment with bankers in the senate and his brief involvement with the Fascist General O'Duffy's Blueshirts in the 1930's.

It might be thought that the general currents of creative literature in the last ten years—the vogue of Brecht and Beckett in drama, for instance, and the vogue in poetry for low-toned or deliberately informal verse like that of Philip Larkin or Robert Lowell—as well as the tendency in all the arts toward a suspicion of the "high style" and toward the undermining of traditional standards of dignity and decorum, would have told against Yeats. I have heard T. R. Henn claim that modern undergraduates, democratic, humanitarian, anti-aristocratic, scientifically minded, practical, down-to-earth, peace-loving, are bound sooner or later to react violently against Yeats; but as a teacher of poetry to the young I have not yet come up against this hostility to Yeats. I think also that Henn perhaps underestimates the degree to which Yeats was himself, in some broad sense, a liberal; hating the violence and barbarism of the Irish troubles, stating in "Easter 1916" that "England may keep faith," and taking a firm stand in the Irish senate against the censorship and divorce laws. I find more sanity and realism about political and social affairs in Yeats than most critics have found; I think his reaction against images of violence more important than his dallying with them.

He was a poet who in his own way made as rich a use of "the tradition" as Pound or Eliot did in their ways; he could use both Donne and Spenser; there are elements in his poetry of broadsheet ballad style, Augustan formality, the self-exploration of the great romantics, Walter Pater's aestheticism and the world-weariness of the 1890's, French Symbolist mystification (as well as Blake's naked sense of symbolic mystery). He could think poetically in both emblems and abstractions. He incorporates the tradition in a new and personal way, as all great poets do. The antithetical movement of his mind, on the other hand, with its perpetual clashes against itself and its occasional precarious resolutions, is specifically modern. He combines in a strange way the virtues of two great, utterly opposite writers whom he admired: Landor's proud care for "perfection of the work"; Balzac's bursting unpredictableness (the *Autobiographies* are a great Balzacian novel). His whole oeuvre is a world, a world with elements in it of jumble, failure, pose, provinciality, but "changed, changed utterly" by his art, till "a terrible beauty is born."

Selected Bibliography

Titles marked with an asterisk are those of books originally printed and published in limited editions by the Dun Emer (later the Cuala) Press, Dublin, founded by the poet's sisters. Yeats's texts were all republished in later editions and collections.

BIBLIOGRAPHY

Roth, W. M., *A Catalogue of English and American First Editions of W. B. Yeats,* (New Haven, Conn., 1939); Wade, A., *A Bibliography of the Writing of W. B. Yeats,* (London, 1951); rev. ed. with index (1958) the definitive bibliography, incorporates valuable material contributed by P. S. O'Hegarty to the *Dublin* magazine (1939–1940) and includes full particulars of Yeats's contributions to books and periodicals, and a complete catalog of Cuala Press publications. Most of Yeats's poems were originally published in periodicals.

COLLECTED WORKS

Collected Works in Verse and Prose, 8 vols. (Stratford-on-Avon, 1908); *Plays for an Irish Theatre,* (London, 1913) contains *Deirdre, The Green Helmet, On Baile's Strand, The King's Threshold, The Shadowy Waters, The Hour-Glass, Cathleen ni Houlihan; Later Poems,* (London, 1922) vol. I of the new *Collected Edition of the Works; Plays in Prose and Verse,* (London, 1922) vol. II of the new *Collected Edition of the Works* contains *Cathleen ni Houlihan, The Pot of Broth, The Hour-Glass, The King's Threshold, On Baile's Strand, The Shadowy Waters, The Unicorn from the Stars* in colaboration with Lady Gregory *The Green Helmet The Player Queen, Notes and Music; Plays and Controversies,* (London, 1923) vol. III of the new *Collected Edition of the Works* contains *"The Irish Dramatic Movement"* and the following plays: *The Countess Cathleen, The Land of Heart's Desire, At the Hawk's Well, The Only Jealousy of Emer, The Dreaming of the Bones,* and *Calvary; Essays,* (London, 1924) vol. IV of the new *Collected Edition of the Works; Early Poems and Stores,* (London, 1925) vol. V of the new *Collected Edition of the Works; Autobiographies,* (London, 1926) vol. VI of the new *Collected Edition of the Works* contains *Reveries over Childhood and Youth* and *The Trembling of the Veil,* new ed., (1955) see below; *Poems,* (London, 1927) the preface states that this ed. "contains what is, I hope, the final text of the poems of my youth."

The Collected Poems of W. B. Yeats, (London, 1933), rev. and enl. ed. (1950); *The Collected Plays of W. B. Yeats,* (London, 1934), 2nd ed. (1952); *Nine One Act Plays,* (London, 1937) contains *The Land of Heart's Desire, Cathleen ni Houlihan, The Hour-Glass, The Pot of Broth, On Baile's Strand, Deirdre, The Green Helmet, The Shadowy Waters, The Words upon the Window Pane; Poems,* 2 vols. (London, 1949) described as "the definitive edition" and lim. to 375 signed copies; *Autobiographies,* (London, 1955) a new and enl. ed., the first of four vols. of Yeats's collected prose works, the others being *Mythologies, Essays and Introductions,* and *Explorations,* see below; P. Allt and R. K. Alspach, ed. *The Variorum Edition of the Poems,* (New York, 1957); *Mythologies,* (London, 1959); R. Pearce, ed. *The Senate Speeches of W. B. Yeats,* (London, 1960); *Essays and Introductions,* (London, 1961); *Explorations,* (London, 1961); R. K. Alspach, ed. *The Variorum Edition of the Plays,* (London, 1966).

SELECTED WORKS

A. N. Jeffares, ed. *Selected Poetry,* (London, 1962); A. N. Jeffares, ed. *Selected Prose,* (London, 1964); A. N. Jeffares, ed. *Selected Criticism,* (London, 1964); A. N. Jeffares, ed. *Selected Plays,* (London, 1964); J. P. Frayne, ed. *Uncollected Prose by W. B. Yeats: First Reviews and Articles, 1886–1896,* (London, 1970); J. P. Frayne and C. Johnson, eds. *Uncollected Prose by W. B. Yeats: Reviews, Articles and Other Miscellaneous Prose, 1897–1939,* (New York, 1976).

LETTERS

Letters to the New Island, H. Reynolds, ed. (Cambridge, Mass., 1934) letters; *Letters on Poetry to Dorothy Wellesley,* D. Wellesley, ed. (London, 1940), K. Raine, ed., paperback ed. (London, 1964); C. Bax, ed. *Florence Farr, Bernard Shaw and Yeats: Letters,* (Dublin, 1941); R. McHugh, ed. *Letters to Katherine Tynan,* (Dublin, 1953); U. Bridge, ed. *Yeats and T. Sturge Moore: Their Correspondence 1901–1937;* A. Wade, ed. *Some Letters from W. B. Yeats to John O'Leary and His Sister from Originals in the Berg Collection,* (New York, 1953) a lim. ed. published by the New York Public Library; A. Wade, ed. *Letters,* (London, 1954) the fullest collection of Yeats's letters likely to be published, ed. with scholarly care by his bibliographer; R. McHugh, ed. *Ah, Sweet Dancer: W. B. Yeats and Margaret Ruddock. A Correspondence,* (London-Basingstoke, 1970).

SEPARATE WORKS

American issues or eds., published more or less concurrently with the English, and successive reprs. of combinations of separate works are not as a general rule included in this section. *Mosada, a Dramatic Poem,* (Dublin, 1886) first printed in *Dublin University Review* (June 1886) 100 copies of this pamphlet ed. printed; *The Wanderings of Oisin,* (London, 1889) verse; *John Sherman and Dhoya,* (London, 1891) stories, under the pseudonym of Ganconagh, no. 10 of the Pseudonym Library; *The Countess Cathleen and Various Legends and Lyrics,* (London, 1892) verse, the verse drama *The Countess Cathleen* later rev. and published separately, (1912); *The Celtic Twilight, Men and Women, Dhouls and Faeries,* (London, 1893) rev. ed. (1903) verse, essays, stories; *The Land of Heart's Desire,* (London, 1894) drama; *Poems,* (London, 1895), rev. eds. (1899), (1901) verse; *The Secret Rose,* (London, 1897) stories; *The Wind Among the Reeds,* (London, 1899) verse;

The Shadowy Waters, (London, 1900) verse; *Cathleen ni Houlihan,* (London, 1902) drama; *Ideas of Good and Evil,* (London, 1903) essays; **In the Seven Woods,* (London, 1903) verse, includes the verse play *On Baile's Strand*; *The Hour-Glass: A Morality,* (New York, 1904) drama, first published in the *North American Review,* (September 1903), 12 offprints made for copyright purposes by Heinemann Ltd., London; *The King's Threshold,* (New York, 1904) drama, 100 copies only, printed for private circulation, repr. in vol. V of Abbey Theatre series (Dublin, 1905); **Stories of Red Hanrahan,* (Dublin, 1904) stories; *Poems, 1899–1905,* (London, 1906); *Deirdre,* (London, 1907) drama; **Discoveries,* (Dublin, 1907) essays; **The Green Helmet and Other Poems,* (Dublin, 1910), *The Green Helmet,* a "heroic farce," separately printed at the Shakespeare Head Press (London, 1911); **Synge and the Ireland of His Time,* (Dublin, 1911) with a note concerning a walk through Connemara with Yeats by J. B. Yeats; *The Cutting of an Agate,* (New York, 1912; London, 1919) essays; *Stories of Red Hanrahan: The Secret Rose: Rosa Alchemica,* (London-Stratford-on Avon, 1913; New York, 1914) stories; **Responsibilities,* (Dublin, 1914; London, 1916) verse and a play; **Reveries over Childhood and Youth,* (Dublin, 1915; London, 1916) autobiography; **The Wild Swans at Coole,* (Dublin, 1917; London, 1919) verse and a play; *Per Amica Silentia Lunae,* (London, 1918) essays; **Two Plays for Dancing,* (Dublin, 1919) contains *The Dreaming of the Bones* and *The Only Jealousy of Emer.*

**Michael Robartes and the Dancer,* (Dublin, 1920) verse; *Four Plays for Dancers,* (London, 1921) contains *At the Hawk's Well, The Only Jealousy of Emer, The Dreaming of the Bones, Calvary*; **Four Years: Reminiscences, 1887–1891,* (Dublin, 1921) autobiography; **Seven Poems and a Fragment,* (Dublin, 1922); *The Trembling of the Veil,* (London, 1922) autobiography, subscribers' ed. of 1,000 copies; "Speeches," in Parliamentary Debates Official Report, vols. I–X (Dublin, 1923); **The Cat and the Moon and Certain Poems,* (Dublin, 1924) drama and verse; *A Vision,* (London, 1925) subscribers' ed. of 600 copies, rev. with additions (London, 1937), reiss. with corrections (London, 1962); *Autobiographies,* (London, 1926); **Estrangement: Being Some Fifty Thoughts from a Diary Kept in the Year 1909,* (Dublin, 1926) autobiography; **October Blast,* (Dublin, 1927) verse; *The Tower,* (London, 1928) verse; *Sophocles' "King Oedipus": A Version for the Modern Stage,* (London, 1928); **The Death of Synge and Other Passages from an Old Diary,* (Dublin, 1928) diary; **A Packet for Ezra Pound,* (Dublin, 1929) verse, an ed. of only 60 signed copies for sale; *The Land of Heart's Desire [and] The Countess Cathleen,* (London, 1929) drama.

Stories of Michael Robartes and His Friends, (Dublin, 1931) stories and a play, includes the play *The Resurrection*; **Words for Music Perhaps, and Other Poems,* (Dublin, 1932) incorporated in *The Winding Stair and Other Poems* (London, 1933); *The Winding Stair and Other Poems,* (London, 1933), much enl. ed. of *The Winding Stair* (London, 1929) and incorporating the contents of *Words for Music Perhaps . . .* ; *The Words upon the Window Pane,* (London, 1934) drama; *Wheels and Butterflies,* (London, 1934) contains *The Words upon the Window Pane, Fighting the Waves, The Resurrection, The Cat and the Moon*; *The King of the Great Clock Tower: Commentaries and Poems,* (London, 1934) verse; *A Full Moon in March,* (London, 1935) drama and verse, contains *A Full Moon in March,*and *The King of the Great Clock Tower*; **Dramatis Personae,* (Dublin, 1935; London, 1936) autobiography; *Modern Poetry,* (London, 1936) lecture, Broadcast National Lectures, no. 18; **Essays 1931–1936,* (Dublin, 1937); *The Herne's Egg,* (London, 1938) drama, published in America as *The Herne's Egg and Other Plays* (New York, 1938); **New Poems,* (Dublin, 1938); *The Autobiography of William Butler Yeats,* (New York, 1938) autobiography, contains *Reveries over Childhood and Youth The Trembling of the Veil,* and *Dramatis Personae*; **Last Poems and Two Plays,* (Dublin, 1939; London, 1940) contains *The Death of Cuchulain Purgatory*; **On the Boiler,* (Dublin, 1939) essays and verse; **If I Were Four and Twenty: Swedenborg, Mediums and the Desolate Places,* (Dublin, 1940) essays; **Pages from a Diary Written in Nineteen Hundred and Thirty,* (Dublin, 1944) diary; D. R. Clark and G. Mayhew, eds. *A Tower of Polished Black Stones: Early Versions of the Shadowy Waters,* (Dublin, 1971); W. H. O'Donnell, ed. *The Speckled Bird,* (New York, 1976); *A Critical Edition of Yeats's "A Vision",* G. M. Harper and W. K. Hood, eds. (London-Basingstoke, 1978); *The Secret Rose: Stories by W. B. Yeats. A Variorum Edition,* P. Marcus, W. Gould, and M. J. Sidnell, eds. (Ithaca, N.Y., London, 1981).

EDITED WORKS AND INTRODUCTIONS

W. B. Yeats, ed. *Fairy and Folk Tales of the Irish Peasantry,* (London, 1888); Carleton, W., *Stories from Carleton,* (London, 1889); intro. by Yeats; W. B. Yeats, comp. *Representative Irish Names,* 2 vols. (London, 1890) intro. and notes by Yeats; W. B. Yeats, ed. *Irish Fairy Tales,* (London, 1892) intro. by Yeats; W. B. Yeats, ed. *The Works of William Balke,* 3 vols. (London, 1893) lim ed. of 500 copies; W. B. Yeats, ed. *The Poems of Williams Blake,* (London, New York, 1893, 1905) in Muses' Library series; *A Book of Irish Verse,* (London, 1895) rev. ed. (1900) selected from modern writers with intro. and notes by Yeats; Horton, W. T., *A Book of Images,* (London, 1898) intro. by Yeats; W. B. Yeats, ed. *Beltaine. The Organ of the Irish Literary Theatre,* (Dublin, 1899–1900) 3 issues; W. B. Yeats, ed. *Samhain,* (Dublin, 1901–1908) ed. for the Irish Literary Threatre from 1901 to 1908; Lady Gregory, ed. *Cuchulain of Muirthemme,* (London, 1902) preface by Yeats; *Johnson, L., *Twenty-one Poems,* (Dublin, 1904) selected by Yeats; D. Hyde, trans. *The Love Songs of Connacht,* (Dublin, 1904) preface by Yeats; Lady Gregory ed. *Gods and Fighting Men,* (London, 1904) preface by Yeats; *Allingham, William, *Sixteen Poems,* (Dublin, 1905) selected by Yeats; Synge, J. M., *The Well of the Saints,* (London, 1905) intro. by Yeats; *Poems of Spenser,* (Edinburgh, 1906) selected and with intro. by Yeats, in Golden Poets series; *Eglinton, J., *Some Essays and Passages,* (Dublin, 1905) selected by Yeats; W. B. Yeats, ed. *The Arrow,* (London, 1906–1907) 3 issues; *Tynan, K., *Twenty-one Poems,* (Dublin, 1907) selected by Yeats; *W. B. Yeats and L. Johnson, eds. *Poetry and Ireland,* (Dublin, 1908) essays; *A Broadside,* *W. B. Yeats, ed. (Dublin, 1908); *Synge, J. M., *Poems and Translations,* (Dublin, 1909) intro. by Yeats.

*Synge, J. M., *Deirdre of the Sorrows,* (Dublin, 1910) intro. by Yeats; **Selections from the Writings of Lord Dunsany,* (Dublin, 1912) intro. by Yeats; *Tagore, R., *The Post Office,* (Dublin, 1914) a play with intro. by Yeats; *Fenellosa, E. F., *Certain Noble Plays of Japan,* (Dublin, 1916) intro. by Yeats; Tagore, R., *Gitanjali,* (London, 1919) intro. by Yeats; *The Complete Works, Oscar Wilde,* (New York, 1923) vol. III intro. by Yeats; *Yeats, J. B., *Early Memories,* (Dublin, 1923) preface by Yeats; *Gogarty, O., *An Offering of Swans,* (Dublin, 1923) preface by Yeats; de Lisle Adam, V., *Axel,* H. P. R. Finberg, trans. (London, 1925) preface by Yeats; A Ussher, trans. *The Midnight Court and the Adventures of a Luckless Fellow,* (London, 1926) intro. by Yeats; *Gogarty, O., *Wild Apples,* (Dublin, 1929) preface by Yeats; Hone, J. M., *Bishop Berkeley,* (London, 1931) intro. by Yeats; Swami, Shri Purohit, *An Indian Monk,* (London, 1932) intro. by Yeats; Hamsa, Bhagwan Shri, *The Holy Mountain,* Shri Purohit Swami, trans. (London, 1934) intro. by Yeats; Wellesley, D., *Selected Poems of Dorothy Wellesley,* (London, 1936) intro. by Yeats; *The Oxford Book of Modern Verse, 1892–1935,* (London, 1936) chosen and with intro. by Yeats; Ruddock, M., *The Lemon Tree,* (London, 1937) intro. by Yeats; *The Ten Principal Upanishads,* (London, 1937) put into English by Shri Purohit Swami and Yeats; Gogarty, O., *Others to Adorn,* (London, 1938) preface by Yeats; Shri Purohit Swami, trans. *Aphorisms of Yoga,* (London, 1938) with intro. by Yeats.

BIOGRAPHICAL AND CRITICAL STUDIES

Krans, H. S., *William Butler Yeats and the Irish Literary Revival,* (London, 1904) Contemporary Men of Letters series; Reid, F., *W. B. Yeats: A Critical Study,* (London, 1915); Gurd, P., *The Early Poetry of William Butler Yeats: The Poet in Contemporary Ireland,* (Lancaster, Pa., 1916); Hone, J. M., *William Butler Yeats:* (London, 1916).

Pollock, J. H., *William Butler Yeats,* (London, 1935); O'Donnell, J. P., *Sailing to Byzantium: A Study in the Development of the Later Style and Symbolism in the Poetry of William Butler Yeats,* (Cambridge, Mass., 1939); *The Arrow,* W. B. Yeats Commemoration Number (Summer 1939); Eliot, T. S., "The Poetry of W. B. Yeats," in *Purpose, III–IV, XII* (London, 1940) the first Annual Yeats Lecture delivered in the Abbey Theatre, Dublin (June 30, 1940), repr. in *On Poetry and Poets* (London, 1957);

L. S. Gwynn, ed. *ScatteringBranches: Tributes to the Memory of W. B. Yeats,* (Dublin, 1940); *Masefield, J., *Some Memories of W. B. Yeats,* (Dublin, 1940); MacNeice, L., *The Poetry of W. B. Yeats,* (London, 1941); Hone, J. M., *W. B. Yeats 1865–1939,* (London, 1942), rev. ed. (1965) the standard biography; Menon, V. K. N., *The Development of William Butler Yeats,* (London, 1942); Ure, P., *Towards a Mythology: Studies in the Poetry of W. B. Yeats,* (Liverpool, 1946); Stauffer, D. A., *The Golden Nightingale: Essays on Some Principles of Poetry in the Lyrics of W. B. Yeats,* (New York, 1949); Ellmann, R., *Yeats: The Man and the Masks,* (London, 1949) paperback ed. (1961); Jeffares, A. N., *W. B. Yeats, Man and Poet,* (London, 1949), rev. ed. and paperback ed. (1962);

J. Hall and M. Steinmann, eds. *The Permanence of Yeats: Selected Criticism,* (New York, 1950); Henn, T. R., *The Lonely Tower: Studies in the Poetry of W. B. Yeats,* (London, 1950), rev. ed. (1965); Parkinson, T., *W. B. Yeats, Self-Critic: A Study of His Early Verse,* (Berkeley-Los Angeles, 1951); Koch, V., *W. B. Yeats: The Tragic Phase. A Study of the Last Poems,* (London, 1951); Ussher, A., *Three Great Irishmen: Shaw, Yeats, Joyce,* (London, 1952); Rudd, M. E., *Divided Image: A Study of William Blake and W. B. Yeats,* (London, 1953); Ellmann, R., *The Identity of Yeats,* (London, 1954) paperback ed. (1964); Moore, V., *The Unicorn: W. B. Yeats's Search for Reality,* (New York, 1954); Saul, G. B., *Prolegomena to the Study of Yeats's Poems,* (Philadelphia, 1957); Kermode, F., *Romantic Image,* London (1957), paperback ed. (1961); Wilson, F. A. C., *W. B. Yeats and Tradition,* (London, 1958); Donoghue, D., *The Third Voice: Modern British and American Verse Drama,* (London, 1959);

Winters, Y., *The Poetry of W. B. Yeats,* (Denver, Colo., 1960); *The Whole Mystery of Art: Pattern into Poetry in the Work of W. B. Yeats,* (New York, London, 1960); Stock, A. C., *W. B. Yeats: His Poetry and Thought,* (London, 1961) paperback ed. (1964); Gordon, D. J., *W. B. Yeats: Images of a Poet. Catalogue of the Yeats Exhibition at Whitworth Art Gallery, University of Manchester,* (Manchester, 1961) with contributions from I. Fletcher, F. Kermode and R. Skelton; Gordon, D. J., *W. B. Yeats: Images of a Poet,* (Manchester, 1961); Kain, R. M., *Dublin in the Age of W. B. Yeats and James Joyce,* (London, 1962); Stallworthy, J., *Between the Lines: Yeats's Poetry in the Making,* (Oxford, 1963); Ure, P., *Yeats,* (Edinburgh, 1963); Ure, P., *Yeats the Playwright: A Commentary on Character and Design in the Major Plays,* (London, 1963); J. Unterecker, ed. *Yeats: A Collection of Critical Essays,* (New York, London, 1963); Vendler, H., *Yeats's "Vision" and the Later Plays,* (Cambridge, Mass., London, 1963); Parrish, S. M., *A Concordance to the Plays,* (Ithaca, N.Y., 1963); Engelberg, E. *The Vast Design: Patterns in W. B. Yeats's Aesthetic,* (Toronto, 1964); Parkinson, T., *W. B. Yeats: The Later Poetry,* (Berkeley, Los Angeles, 1964); A. N. Jeffares and K. G. W. Cross, eds. *In Excited Reverie. A Centenary Tribute to William Butler Yeats 1865–1939,* (London, 1965); Skelton, R., and Saddlerneyer, A., *The World of W. B. Yeats. Essays in Perspective. A Symposium and Catalogue,* (London, 1965); E. Malins, ed. *The Dolmen Press Yeats Centenary Papers,* (Dublin, 1965–); *Yeats Centenary Papers,* L. Miller, ed. (London, 1965–); Bradford, C., *Yeats at Work,* (Carbondale, Edwardsville, Ill, 1965); Clark, D. R., *Yeats and the Theatre of Desolate Anarchy,* (Dublin, 1965); Nathan, L. E., *The Tragic Drama of W. B. Yeats,* (London, 1965); Rajan, B., *W. B. Yeats: A Critical Introduction,* (New York, London, 1965); Salvadori, C., *Yeats and Castiglione: Poet and Courtier,* (Dublin, 1965); D. Donoghue and J. R. Mulryne, eds. *An Honoured Guest. New Essays on W. B. Yeats,* (London, 1966); D. E. S. Maxwell and S. B. Bushrui, eds. *W. B. Yeats, 1865–1965. Centenary Essays on the Art of W. B. Yeats,* (Ibadan, 1966); Bushrui, S. B., *Yeats's Verse Plays: The Revisions 1900–1910,* (London, 1966); Whitaker, T. R., *Yeats's Dialogue with History: "Swan and Shadow",* (Chapel Hill, N.C., 1965); Hoffman, D., *Barbarous Knowledge: Myth in the Poetry of Yeats's, Graves and Muir,* (London, 1967); *Yeats's Last Poems: A Casebook,* J. Stallworthy, ed. (New York, Oxford, 1968); Ellmann, R., *Eminent Domain: Yeats Among Wilde, Joyce, Pound, Eliot and Auden,* (New York, London, 1967); Ronsley, J., *Yeats's Autobiography: Life as a Symbolic Pattern,* (Cambridge, Mass., London, 1968); Jeffares, A. N., *A Commentary on the Collected Poems of W. B. Yeats,* (London, 1968; Stanford, 1969); Beum, R., *The Poetic Art of W. B. Yeats,* (New York, 1969); Grossmann, A. R., *Poetic Knowledge in the Early Years,* (Charlottesville, Va., 1969); Stallworthy, J., *Vision and Revision in Yeats's Last Poems,* (London, 1969).

Bloom, H., *Yeats,* (New York, London, 1970); Marcus, P. L., *Yeats and the Beginning of the Irish Renaissance,* (Ithaca, N.Y., London, 1970); Moore, J. R., *Masks of Love and Death: Yeats as Dramatist,* (London, 1971); Albright, D. R., *The Myth Against Myth,* (London, 1972); E. Domville, ed. *A Concordance to the Plays of W. B. Yeats,* (Ithaca, N.Y., 1972); Brown, M., *The Politics of Irish Literature from Thomas Davis to W. B. Yeats,* (London, 1973); Harper, G., *Yeats's Golden Dawn,* (London, 1974); Harris, D. A., *Yeats: Coole Park and Ballylee,* (Baltimore, London, 1974); Skene, R., *The Cuchulain Plays of W. B. Yeats,* (London, 1974); Ure, P., *Yeats and Anglo-Irish Literature,* C. J. Rawson, ed. (Liverpool, 1974); G. Harper, ed. *Yeats and the Occult,* (London, 1975); Jeffares, A. N., and Knowland, A. S., *A Commentary on the Collected Plays of W. B. Yeats,* (London, 1975); Johnson, J., *Florence Farr: Bernard Shaw's "New Woman",* (Gerrards Cross, 1975); Murphy, W. M., *Yeats's Early Poetry: The Quest for Reconciliation,* (London, 1975); O'Driscoll, R., and Reynolds, L., *Yeats and the Theatre,* (Niagara Falls, N.Y., 1975); Young, D., and Hulme, C., *Out of Ireland: A Reading of Yeats's Poetry,* (London 1975); Eddins, D., *Yeats: The Nineteenth Century Matrix,* (University, Ala., 1976); Flannery, J. W., *W. B. Yeats and the Idea of a Theatre: The Early Abbey Theatre in Theory,* (London, 1976); Taylor, R., *The Drama of W. B. Yeats: Irish Myth and the Japanese Noh,* (New Haven, Conn., London, 1976); Tuohy, F., *Yeats,* (London, 1976); Jeffares, A. N., *W. B. Yeats: The Critical Heritage,* (London, 1977); Miller, L., *The Noble Drama of W. B. Yeats,* (London, 1977); Flannery, J. W., *Yeats and Magic: The Earlier Works,* (London, 1978); Murphy, W. M., *The Life of J. B. Yeats: Prodigal Father,* (Ithaca, N.Y., 1978); Parkin, A., *The Dramatic Imagination of W. B. Yeats,* (London, 1978); Rosenthal, M. L., *Yeats, Pound and Eliot: Sailing into the Unknown,* (London, 1978); Reid, B. L., *W. B. Yeats: The Lyric of Tragedy,* (London, 1978); Lynch, A., *Yeats: The Poetics of the Self,* (Chicago, 1978).

Thuente, M. H., *Yeats and Irish Folklore,* (Iowa City, 1980); Cullingford, E., *Yeats, Ireland and Fascism,* (London, 1981); W. H. Pritchard, ed. *W. B. Yeats: A Critical Anthology,* (Harmondsworth, 1982).

Acknowledgments

JOHN ASHBERY Excerpts from "A Wave," "As One Put Drunk into the Packet-Boat," "At North Farm," "Down by the Station, Early in the Morning," "Fantasia," "Litany," "Paradoxes and Oxymorons," "The Pursuit of Happiness," "Scheherazade," "Syringa," "Tapestry," and "Worsening Situation," from *Selected Poems* by John Ashbery. Copyright © 1973, 1974, 1975, 1979, 1980, 1981, 1983, 1984 by John Ashbery. Reprinted by permission of Viking Penguin, a division of Penguin Books USA Inc., and Carcanet Press, Ltd. Excerpts from "Self-Portrait in a Convex Mirror," copyright © 1974 by John Ashbery, from *Self-Portrait in a Convex Mirror* by John Ashbery; and excerpt from "The Ice Storm," from *April Galleons* by John Ashbery. Copyright © 1984, 1985, 1986, 1987 by John Ashbery. Used by permission of Viking Penguin, a division of Penguin Books USA Inc. and from *Selected Poems* by John Ashbery by permission of Carcanet Press, Ltd. Excerpts from "The Instruction Manual," "The Painter," "Some Trees," and "Two Scenes" from *Some Trees*. Copyright © 1956 by John Ashbery. Excerpts from "Decoy," "Farm Implements and Rutabagas in a Landscape," "Fragment," "Soonest Mended," from *The Double Dream of Spring*. Copyright © 1970, 1969, 1967, 1966 by John Ashbery. Excerpts from "Clepsydra" and "The Skaters" from *Rivers & Mountains*. Copyright © 1962 by John Ashbery. Reprinted by permission of Georges Borchardt, Inc. for the author, and Carcanet Press, Ltd. Excerpts from "A Last World" and "Europe." Copyright © 1962 by John Ashbery. Reprinted from *The Tennis Court Oath* by permission of University Press of New England. Excerpt of interview from "John Ashbery (1976)," by Richard Kostelanetz, in *The Old Poetries and the New* (University of Michigan, 1981), by permission of the author (P.O. Box 444, Prince Street, New York, NY 10012-0008), copyright © 1976, 1981 by Richard Kostelanetz. Quote by John Ashbery from "John Ashbery" by A. Poulin, Jr. from a prose transcription of a videotape interview in October, 1969, sponsored by the Brockport Writers Forum, Department of English, State University College, Brockport, N.Y. 14420. All rights reserved, State University of New York. Reprinted by permission of A. Poulin, Jr., and John Ashbery.

W. H. AUDEN From *W. H. Auden: Collected Poems*, edited by Edward Mendelson. Copyright © 1976 by Edward Mendelson, William Meredith, and Monroe K. Spears, Executors of the Estate of W. H. Auden. Reprinted by permission of Random House, Inc. Permission also given by Faber and Faber Ltd. Extracts from *The English Auden: Poems, Essays and Dramatic Writings 1927–1939* by W. H. Auden reprinted by permission of Faber and Faber Ltd.

JOHN BERRYMAN From *Short Poems: The Dispossessed*, copyright 1948 John Berryman; *His Thoughts Made Pockets & the Plane Buckt*, copyright © 1958 John Berryman; *Formal Elegy*, copyright © 1964 John Berryman; *Berryman's Sonnets*, copyright 1952, copyright © 1967 John Berryman; *Homage to Mistress Bradstreet*, copyright © 1956 John Berryman; *His Toy, His Dream His Rest*, copyright © 1964, 1965, 1966, 1967, 1968 John Berryman, by permission of Farrar, Straus & Giroux and Faber and Faber Ltd. From "The Lovers" and "The Imaginary Jew," first published *The Kenyon Review*, by permission of Mrs. Berryman.

ELIZABETH BISHOP From *The Complete Poems*, copyright © 1936, 1937, 1944, 1946, 1947, 1948, 1949, 1956, 1960,1962, 1969 by Elizabeth Bishop, with permission of Farrar, Straus & Giroux, Inc., copyright renewed © 1971, 1973, 1974, 1976 by Elizabeth Bishop; from *Questions of Travel*, copyright © 1953, by Elizabeth Bishop; from *Geography III*. Copyright © 1972, 1976 by Elizabeth Bishop. Reprinted with the permission of Farrar, Straus & Giroux, Inc.; from a review by Selden Rodman and a review by Richard Eberhart in the *New York Times*, copyright 1946, 1955 by The New York Times Company, reprinted with permission; from a review by Lisel Mueller in *Poetry*, copyright © 1966, by permission of *Poetry*; from an interview by Ashley Brown, copyright © 1966 by Washington and Lee University, reprinted from *Shenandoah: The Washington and Lee University Review*, with the permission of the Editor.

E. E. CUMMINGS "nonsun blob a," copyright 1944 E. E. Cummings; copyright 1972 Nancy Andrews. Reprinted from E. E. Cummings, *Poems 1923–1954*, by permission of Harcourt Brace Jovanovich, Inc. and MacGibbon & Kee, Granada Publishing Limited. "mortals," copyright 1940 E. E. Cummings; copyright 1968 Marion Morehouse Cummings. Reprinted from *Poems 1923–1954* by permission of Harcourt Brace Jovanovich, Inc. and MacGibbon & Kee, Granada Publishing Limited. "1 (a," from *95 Poems*, copyright © 1958 E. E. Cummings. Reprinted by permission of Harcourt Brace Jovanovich, Inc. and MacGibbon & Kee, Granada Publishing Limited.

ACKNOWLEDGMENTS

EMILY DICKINSON From *The Complete Poems of Emily Dickinson*, edited by Thomas H. Johnson. Copyright 1914, 1929, 1935, 1942 by Martha Dickinson Bianchi; © renewed 1957, 1963 by Mary L. Hampson. By permission of Little, Brown and Company. And reprinted by permission of the publishers and the Trustees of Amherst College from *The Poems of Emily Dickinson*, Thomas H. Johnson, ed., Cambridge, Mass.: The Belknap Press of Harvard University Press, Copyright 1951, © 1955, 1979, 1983 by the President and Fellows of Harvard College. Quotations from letters of Emily Dickinson reprinted by permission of the publishers from *The Letters of Emily Dickinson*, edited by Thomas H. Johnson, Cambridge, Mass.: The Belknap Press of Harvard University Press, Copyright © 1955, 1986 by the President and Fellows of Harvard College.

T. S. ELIOT Excerpts from *Collected Poems 1909–1961*, *Four Quartets*, and *The Waste Land: A Facsimile and Transcript of the Original Drafts*, all by T. S. Eliot, are reprinted by permission of Harcourt Brace Jovanovich, Inc.; copyright 1936 by Harcourt Brace Jovanovich, Inc.; copyright 1943, © 1963, 1964 by T. S. Eliot; renewed 1971 by Esme Valerie Eliot, copyright © 1971 by Valerie Eliot. Extracts from *Collected Poems 1909–1962* by T. S. Eliot and seven lines from *The Waste Land: A Facsimile and Transcript* edited by Valerie Eliot. Reprinted by permission of Faber and Faber Ltd.

ROBERT FROST Excerpts from "Auspex," "Once by the Pacific," "Home Burial," "Design," "The Tuft of Flowers," "Mowing," "The Wood-Pile," "Mending Wall," "Birches," "Iris by Night," "Stopping by Woods on a Snowy Evening," "On a Tree Fallen across the Road," "Acquainted with the Night," and "Questioning Faces." From *The Poetry of Robert Frost*, edited by Edward Connery Lathem. Copyright 1936, 1944, 1951, 1956, 1958, 1960, 1962 by Robert Frost, © 1964, 1967 by Lesley Frost Ballantine, copyright 1916, 1923, 1928, 1930, 1934, 1939, © 1969 by Henry Holt & Co., Inc. Reprinted by permission of Henry Holt & Co., Inc.

ALLEN GINSBERG From *Sad Dust Glories*, by permission of Allen Ginsberg. From *The Gates of Wrath, Rhymed Poems: 1948–1952 by Allen Ginsberg*, 1972, by permission of Allen Ginsberg. From *Empty Mirror, Early Poems by Allen Ginsberg*, copyright © 1961 Allen Ginsberg, published by Corinth Books/Totem Press. From "Notes for *Howl and Other Poems*," in *The New American Poetry*, edited by Donald Allen. Copyright © 1960 by Donald M. Allen. Reprinted by permission of Grove Press, Inc. From *As Ever: Collected Correspondence with Neal Cassady, 1974*, copyright by Creative Arts Book Company for Allen Ginsberg and Carolyn Cassady 1977. From *Writers at Work: The Paris Review Interviews, 3rd series*. Edited by George Plimpton. Copyright © 1967 by The Paris Review, Inc. Reprinted by permission of Viking Penguin Inc. From *Howl and Other Poems*. Copyright © 1956, 1959 by Allen Ginsberg. Reprinted by permission of City Lights Books. From *Kaddish and Other Poems: 1958–1960*. Copyright © 1961 by Allen Ginsberg. Reprinted by permission of City Lights Books. From *Reality Sandwiches: 1953–1960*. Copyright © 1963, 1966 by Allen Ginsberg. Reprinted by permission of City Lights Books. From *Planet News: 1961–1967*. Copyright © 1968 by Allen Ginsberg. Reprinted by permission of City Lights Books. From *Fall of America: Poems of These States: 1965–1971*. Copyright © 1972 by Allen Ginsberg. Reprinted by permission of City Lights Books.

SEAMUS HEANEY Excerpts from "At a Potato Digging," "Death of a Naturalist," "Digging," "Diviner," and "Water Fall" from *Death of a Naturalist* and from *Poems, 1965–1975*; excerpts from "Bogland," "The Forge," "Gone," "Rite of Spring," "Shoreline," and "Undine," from *Door Into the Dark* and *Poems, 1965–1975*; excerpts from "A New Song" and "The Tollund Man" from *Wintering Out* and *Poems, 1965–1975*; excerpts from "Exposure," "The Grauballe Man," "Hercules and Antaeus," "Punishment," and "Whatever You Say Say Nothing," from *North* and *Poems, 1965–1975*; copyright © 1980 by Seamus Heaney. Excerpts from "Casualty," "Elegy," and "Glanamore Sonnets" from *Fieldwork*, copyright © 1979 by Seamus Heaney. Excerpts from "Clearances," "From the Frontier of Writing," "Hailstones," "The Haw Lantern," "The Land of the Unspoken," "The Mud Vision," and "Parable Island," from *The Haw Lantern*, copyright © 1987 by Seamus Heaney. Excerpts from "The Cleric," "The First Flight," "Sandstone Keepsake," and "Station Island," from *Station Island*, copyright © 1989 by Seamus Heaney. Reprinted by permission of Farrar Straus and Giroux, Inc., and Faber and Faber Ltd.

LANGSTON HUGHES Excerpt from *The Big Sea* by Langston Hughes. Copyright © 1940 by Langston Hughes. Renewal copyright © 1968 by Arna Bontemps and George Houston Bass. Reprinted by permission of Hill and Wang, a division of Farrar, Straus and Giroux, Inc.

TED HUGHES Selected lines of poetry from the following: *New Selected Poems* by Ted Hughes. Copyright © 1982 by Ted Hughes. *Crow: The Life and Songs of the Crow* by Ted Hughes. Copyright © 1971 by Ted Hughes. *Moortown* by Ted Hughes. Copyright © 1979 by Ted Hughes. *Gaudete* by Ted Hughes. Copyright © 1977 by Ted Hughes. *The Hawk in the Rain* by Ted Hughes. Copyright © 1956, 1957 by Ted Hughes. *River: New Poems* by Ted Hughes. Copyright © 1983 by Ted Hughes. All selections reprinted by permission of Harper and Row, Publishers, Inc. Reprinted by permission of Faber & Faber Ltd. Selections from *The Tiger's Bones and*

Other Plays for Children by Ted Hughes. Copyright © 1973 by Ted Hughes. From "Bride and Groom" from *Cave Birds: An Alchemical Cave Drama* by Ted Hughes. Copyright © 1978 by Ted Hughes. Reprinted by permission of Viking Penguin, Inc. *The Tiger's Bones and Other Plays for Children* published originally in the U.K. as *The Coming of the Kings* by Ted Hughes. Copyright © 1970 by Ted Hughes. Selections reprinted by permission of Faber & Faber, Ltd. Selections from *Season Songs* by Ted Hughes. Copyright © 1976 by Ted Hughes. Reprinted by permission of Viking Penguin, Inc. *All Around the Year* (Published by John Murray) by Ted Hughes. Copyright © 1979 by Ted Hughes. *Remains of Elmet* by Ted Hughes. Copyright © 1979 by Ted Hughes. *Wodwo* by Ted Hughes. Copyright © 1967 by Ted Hughes. *Lupercal* by Ted Hughes. Copyright © 1960 by Ted Hughes. Reprinted by permission of Faber & Faber, Ltd.

ROBINSON JEFFERS Acknowledgment is made to Random House, Inc. for permission to quote from the following copyrighted works of Robinson Jeffers: *Selected Poetry of Robinson Jeffers* and *The Beginnings and the End*, both by Robinson Jeffers. From "Hungerfield," "The Inhumanist," "Credo," "Mal Paso Bridge," "Dear Judas," "Tower Beyond Tragedy." Copyright by Robinson Jeffers. Reprinted by permission of Jeffers Literary Properties.

GALWAY KINNELL "Another Night in the Ruins," "The Bear," "How Many Nights," "The Last River," and "Vapor Trail Reflected in the Frog Pond" from *Body Rags* by Galway Kinnell. Copyright © 1965, 1966, 1967 by Galway Kinnell. Excerpts from "The Hen Flower," "Lastness," "Little Sleep's-Head Harouting Hair in the Moonlight," "The Shoes of Wandering," and "Under the Maud Moon" from *The Book of Nightmares* by Galway Kinnell. Copyright © 1971 by Galway Kinnell. Excerpts from "The Feast" *from First Poems 1946–1954* in *Selected Poems* by Galway Kinnell. Copyright © 1982 by Galway Kinnell. Excerpts from "The Apple," "Blackberry Eating," "52 Oswald Street," "Flying Home," "The Last Hiding Place of Snow," "The Sadness of Brothers," "The Still Time," and "There are Things I tell to No one" from *Mortal Acts, Mortal Words* by Galway Kinnell. Copyright © 1980 by Galway Kinnell. Excerpts from "The Frog Pond," "The Past," and "The Waking" from *The Past* by Galway Kinnell. Copyright © 1985 by Galway Kinnell. Reprinted by permission of Houghton Mifflin Co. Excerpts from "The River That Is East," from *Flower Herding on Mount Monadnock* by Galway Kinnell. Copyright © 1984 by Galway Kinnell. Excerpts from "The Avenue Bearing the Initials of Christ into the World," and "Freedom, New Hampshire" from *What A Kingdom It Was* by Galway Kinnell. Copyright © 1960 by Galway Kinnell. Copyright © 1988 by Galway Kinnell. Reprinted by permission of Houghton Mifflin Co. and Andrew Deutsch, Ltd. Excerpt of interview with Galway Kinnell by Louis Smith Brady from *New York Woman* Magazine. Copyright 1990 by New York Woman Magazine. Excerpt from "Approaching Home Ground: Galway Kinnell's *Mortal Acts, Mortal Words*" by Lorrie Goldensohn, *Massachusetts Review*, Summer 1984. Reprinted from *The Massachusetts Review*, © 1985 The Massachusetts Review, Inc. Excerpts of interviews with Galway Kinnell by Wayne Dodd and Stanley Plumly in *The Ohio Review*, Fall 1972. Reprinted by permission of Wayne Dodd, Stanley Plumly, and The Ohio Review. Excerpt from "Galway Kinnell" by Charles G. Bell in *Contemporary Poets*, 3rd Edition, edited by James Vinson. Reprinted by permission of St. Martin's Press, Inc. Excerpts from interview with Galway Kinnell by A. Poulin, Jr., and Stan S. Rubin; and excerpt of interview with Galway Kinnell by William Heyen and Gregory Fitz Gerald from a prose transcription of a videotape interview in October, 1969, sponsored by the Brockport Writers Forum, Department of English, State University College, Brockport, N.Y. 14420. All rights reserved, State University of New York. Excerpt from "A Winter Daybreak Above Vence" from *This Journey* by James Wright. Copyright © 1980 by Anne Wright, Executrix of the Estate of James Wright. Reprinted by permission of Random House, Inc.

DENISE LEVERTOV Excerpt from "Midnight Gladness" from *A Door in the Hive*. Copyright © 1984, 1987, 1989 by Denise Levertov. Excerpt from "Variations on a Theme by Rilke" from *Breathing the Water*. Copyright © 1984, 1985, 1986, 1987 by Denise Levertov. Excerpts from "Mass for the Day of St. Thomas Didymus" from *Candles in Babylon*. Copyright © 1978, 1979, 1980, 1981, 1982 by Denise Levertov. Excerpts from "Christmas, 1944," "The Dogwood," "Jackson Square," "To the Snake," and "With Eyes at the Back of our Heads" from *Collected Earlier Poems 1940–1960*. Copyright © 1958, 1959, 1960, 1961, 1979 by Denise Levertov. "To the Reader" and excerpts from "The Altar in the Street," "Eros at Temple Stream," "The Jacob's Ladder," "The Olga Poems," "A Place to Live," and "To Stay Alive" from *Collected Poems 1968–1972*. Copyright © 1958, 1959, 1960, 1961, 1962, 1963, 1964, 1965, 1966 by Denise Levertov. Reprinted by permission of New Directions Publishing Corporation.

ROBERT LOWELL From "The Drunken Fisherman," *Lord Weary's Castle*, copyright 1946 Robert Lowell, by permission of Harcourt Brace Jovanovich, Inc. and Faber and Faber Ltd. From *Poems 1938–1949*, by permission of Faber and Faber Ltd. From *Life Studies*, copyright © 1956, 1959 Robert Lowell; *For the Union Dead*, copyright © 1956, 1960, 1961, 1962, 1963, 1964 Robert Lowell; *Near the Ocean*, copyright © 1963, 1965, 1966, 1967 Robert Lowell; *Notebook*, revised edition, copyright © 1967, 1968, 1969, 1970 Robert Lowell; by permission of Farrar, Straus & Giroux, Inc. and Faber and Faber Ltd.

CLAUDE McKAY Excerpts from "Mulatto," "A Midnight Woman to the Bobby," "Cycle Manuscript," "In Bondage," and "Outcast" from *Selected Poems of Claude McKay*, Harcourt Brace Jovanovich. Copyright 1928, 1970. By kind permission of Hope McKay Virtue.

JAMES MERRILL Excerpts from "Days of 1964," "Dream About Clothes," "The Emerald," and "Up and Down," from *Braving the Elements*; excerpt from "Lost in Translation" from *Divine Comedies*; excerpts from "Another August," "The Friend of the Fourth Decade," and "Mornings in a New House," from *The Fire Screen*; excerpt from a poem beginning "The message hardly needs . . . ," from *Mirabell: Books of Number*; excerpt from "The Thousand and Second Night," from *Nights and Days*; excerpt from a poem beginning "Giving up its whole . . . " from *Scripts for the Pageant*; excerpt from a poem beginning "We were not tough- . . . " from *The Changing Light at Sandover*; excerpts from "Fire Poem," "Scenes of Childhood," "A Tenancy," and "An Urban Convalescence," from *Water Street*. Reprinted by permission of James Merrill. Excerpt from a poem beginning "Humbly our old poets . . . " from *The Inner Room* by James Merrill. Copyright © 1988 by James Merrill. Reprinted by permission of Alfred A. Knopf, Inc.

W. S. MERWIN Excerpts from "The Approaches," "Elegy," "Homeland," "In the Time of the Blossoms," "Lackawanna," and "Presidents" from *The Carrier of Ladders*. Copyright © 1967, 1968, 1969, 1970 by W. S. Merwin. Excerpts from "East of the Sun and West of the Moon" and "Fable" from *The Dancing Bears*. Copyright © 1954, 1975 by W. S. Merwin. Excerpt from "The Portland Going Out" from *The Drunk in the Furnace*. Copyright © 1956, 1957, 1958, 1959, 1960, 1975 by W. S. Merwin. Excerpts from "The Animals" and "The Hydra" from *The Lice*. Copyright © 1963, 1964, 1965, 1966, 1967 by W. S. Merwin. Excerpts from "Anabasis (II)" and "A Poem for Dorothy" from *A Mask for Janus*. Copyright © 1952, 1975 by W. S. Merwin. Excerpts from "The Crossroads of the World, etc.," "The Man Who Writes Ants," and "Recognition" from *The Moving Target*. Copyright © 1960, 1961, 1962, 1963 by W. S. Merwin. Excerpts from "Berryman," "A Pause by the Water," and "Talking" from *Opening the Hand*. Copyright © 1983 by W. S. Merwin. Excerpt from "The Silence Before Harvest" from *Writings to an Unfinished Accompaniment*. Copyright © 1969, 1970, 1971, 1972, 1973 by W. S. Merwin. Reprinted by permission of Georges Borchardt Inc. for the author. Excerpts from "The Archaic Maker," "Losing a Language," "Night Above the Avenue," "Sight," "The Solstice," "Summer '82," "Term," and "West Wall," from *The Rain in the Trees*. By W. S. Merwin. Copyright © 1988 by W. S. Merwin. Reprinted by permission of Alfred A. Knopf, Inc. Quote from Ezra Pound in postcard to W. S. Merwin. Copyright © 1991 by the Ezra Pound Literary Property Trust.

EDNA ST. VINCENT MILLAY All quotations from Edna St. Vincent Millay's poetry and letters are reprinted by permission of Elizabeth Barnett, Literary Executor for the Estate of Edna St. Vincent Millay/Norma Millay Ellis.

MARIANNE MOORE Excerpts from "To Military Progress," "The Fish," "England," "New York," and "Marriage," copyright 1935 by Marianne Moore, renewed 1963 by Marianne Moore and T. S. Eliot; excerpt from "Virginia Britannia," copyright 1941 and renewed 1969 by Marianne Moore. Reprinted with permission of Macmillan Publishing Company and Faber and Faber Ltd from *Collected Poems* by Marianne Moore. Excerpts from *The Complete Prose of Marianne Moore* by Marianne Moore. Copyright © Clive E. Driver, Literary Executor of the Estate of Marianne C. Moore, 1959, 1960, 1961, 1962, 1963, 1964, 1965, 1986. Introduction copyright © Patricia C. Willis, 1986. Copyright © Marianne Moore, 1941, 1942, 1944, 1946, 1948, 1955, 1958, 1959, 1960, 1961, 1962, 1963, 1964, 1965, 1966, 1967, 1968. Copyright renewed Marianne Moore, 1969, 1970, 1972. Copyright renewed Lawrence E. Brinn, 1974, 1976. Copyright renewed Lawrence E. Brinn and Louise Crane, 1983, 1985, 1986. All rights reserved. Reprinted by permission of Viking Penguin, a division of Penguin Books USA, Inc. Excerpt from T. S. Eliot, reprinted by permission of Mrs. Valerie Eliot and Faber and Faber Ltd from *Dial* LXXV.6 (December 1923). Excerpt from "Efforts of Affection: A Memoir of Marianne Moore" from *The Complete Prose* by Elizabeth Bishop. Copyright © 1984 by Alice Methfessel. Reprinted by permission of Farrar, Straus and Giroux, Inc. Excerpts from Louise Bogan, *A Poet's Alphabet* and *What the Woman Lived*, reprinted by permission of Ruth Limmer. All rights reserved. Quotations from *The Selected Letters of Ezra Pound 1907–1941*, edited by D. D. Paige (Copyright 1950 by Ezra Pound) and from *Selected Essays of William Carlos Williams* (Copyright 1931 by William Carlos Williams) are used by permission of New Directions Publishing Corporation. Photo caption from "Remarkable American Women: 1776–1976" in *Life*, 1976, Special Issue. *Life* Magazine (Time Warner).

SYLVIA PLATH From "Female Author," "Winter Landscape, with Rooks," "Pursuit," "Electra on Azalea Path," "In Plaster," "Blackberrying," "The Bee Meeting," "The Swarm," "Ariel," "Nick and the Candlestick," "Tulips," (Copyright © 1962 by Ted Hughes), "The Moon and the Yew Tree" (Copyright © 1963 by Ted Hughes), "Daddy" (Copyright © 1963 by Ted Hughes), "Lady Lazarus," (Copyright © 1963 by Ted Hughes) from *The Collected Poems of Sylvia Plath*, edited by Ted Hughes. Copyright © 1981 by Ted Hughes. Reprinted by permission of Harper & Row, Publishers, Inc. and Olwyn Hughes. Excerpts from "The Thin People," "All the Dead Dears," "This Disquieting Muses," "Full Fathom Five," "The

Beekeeper's Daughter," "The Colossus," and "The Stones." Copyright © 1960, 1961, 1962, 1967 by Sylvia Plath. Reprinted from *The Colossus and Other Poems* by Sylvia Plath, by permission of Alfred A. Knopf, Inc. and Olwyn Hughes.

POETS OF WORLD WAR II **Henry Reed:** From *A Map of Verona*. Reprinted by kind permission of the author and Jonathan Cape Ltd. **Gavin Ewart:** The Editor gratefully thanks Hutchinson Publishers for kind permission to reproduce material from the following poems—"Officers Mess," "Sonnet, 1940," and "When a Beau Goes In." From Gavin Ewart's *The Collected Ewart 1933–1980*. **Vernon Scannell:** From *New and Collected Poems 1950–1980* by Vernon Scannell. Originally published by Robson Books Ltd. Reprinted by permission of the publisher. **John Bayliss:** From *Not Without Glory*. Reprinted by permission of the Woburn Press. **George Fraser:** Reprinted from George Fraser's *Return to Oasis*, published by Shepheard-Walwyn Ltd. 1980, by permission of Mrs. George Fraser. **Hamish Henderson:** From *Elegies for the Dead in Cyrenaica*. Reprinted by kind permission of the author. **Norman Cameron:** From *Collected Poems*. Reprinted by kind permission of the Literary Estate of Norman Cameron and the Hogarth Press. **John Manifold:** "Ration Party" and "The Sirens." From *Collected Verse* (1978). Reprinted by courtesy of the University of Queensland Press. **Roy Campbell:** From *Collected Poems*. Reprinted by permission of Teresa Campbell. **Roy Fuller:** From *Collected Poems 1936–1961*, copyright © 1962, by Roy Fuller. Reprinted by permission of Dufour Editions Inc., Chester Springs, Pennsylvania, and by André Deutsch Ltd., London. **Edward Lowbury:** From *Time for Sale* (1961). Reprinted by kind permission of the author. **Bernard Gutteridge:** From *The Traveller's Eye*. Reprinted by permission of Routledge and Kegan Paul, London and Boston. **Alan Ross:** From *Poems 1942–1967*. Reprinted by kind permission of the author. **Charles Causley:** From *Collected Poems 1951–1975* by Charles Causley. Copyright © 1951, 1953, 1957, 1961, 1968, 1969, 1970, 1975. Reprinted by permission of David R. Godine, Publisher, Boston. **Sidney Keyes:** From *The Collected Poems of Sidney Keyes*, published by Routledge and Kegan Paul Ltd., London and Boston. Reprinted by permission of the publisher. **Keith Douglas:** From *The Complete Poems of Keith Douglas*, edited by Desmond Graham. Copyright © Marie J. Douglas 1978. Reprinted by permission of Oxford University Press. **Alun Lewis:** From the works *In the Green Tree*, *Raiders Dawn*, and *Ha! Ha! Among the Trumpets* by Alun Lewis. Reprinted by permission of Allen and Unwin Ltd.

EZRA POUND From *Personae*, copyright 1926 Ezra Pound; from *The Cantos of Ezra Pound*, copyright 1934, 1937, 1940, 1948, 1956 Ezra Pound; from *Women of Trachis*, copyright © 1957 Ezra Pound; from *Guide to Kulchur*, all rights reserved, copyright © 1970 Ezra Pound, by permission of New Directions Publishing Corporation and Faber and Faber Ltd.

ADRIENNE RICH The lines from "Aunt Jennifer's Tigers," "Storm Warnings," "Snapshots of a Daughter-in-Law," "Necessities of Life," "Leaflets," "Tear Gas," "Planetarium," "The Burning of Paper Instead of Children," "From an Old House in America," "Twenty-One Love Poems," "Power," "Phantasia for Elvira Shatayov," and "Transcendental Etude" are reprinted from *The Fact of a Doorframe: Poems Selected and New, 1950–1984*, by Adrienne Rich, by permission of the author and W. W. Norton & Company, Inc. Copyright © 1984 by Adrienne Rich. Copyright © 1975, 1978 by W. W. Norton & Company, Inc. Copyright © 1981 by Adrienne Rich. The lines from "Turning the Wheel," "The Spirit of the Place," and "For Memory" are reprinted from *A Wild Patience Has Taken Me This Far: Poems, 1978–1981*, by Adrienne Rich, by permission of the author and W. W. Norton & Company, Inc. Copyright © 1981 by Adrienne Rich. The lines from "Contradictions: Tracking Poems" and "North American Time" are reprinted from *Your Native Land, Your Life: Poems* by Adrienne Rich, by permission of the author and W. W. Norton & Company, Inc. Copyright © 1986 by Adrienne Rich. The excerpts from "Notes Toward a Politics of Location" are reprinted from *Blood, Bread, and Poetry: Selected Prose, 1979–1985*, by Adrienne Rich, by permission of the author and W. W. Norton & Company, Inc. Copyright © 1986 by Adrienne Rich. And reprinted by permission of Virago Press, Ltd., London. The lines from "Living Memory," "Turning," and "Divisions of Labor" are reprinted from *Time's Power: Poems, 1985–1988*, by Adrienne Rich, by permission of the author and W. W. Norton & Company, Inc. Copyright © 1989 by Adrienne Rich.

EDWIN ARLINGTON ROBINSON From *Collected Poems*, by Edwin Arlington Robinson, copyright 1916 Edwin Arlington Robinson, renewal copyright 1944 Ruth Nivison; copyright 1920 Edwin Arlington Robinson, renewal copyright 1948 Ruth Nivison; copyright 1929 Edwin Arlington Robinson, renewal copyright © 1957 Ruth Nivison and Barbara R. Holt, by permission of The Macmillan Company.

THEODORE ROETHKE "The Feud," copyright 1935 Theodore Roethke; "The Heron," copyright 1937 Theodore Roethke; "The Light Comes Brighter," copyright 1938 Theodore Roethke; "Open House," copyright 1941 Theodore Roethke; "The Return," copyright 1946 Modern Poetry Association, Inc.; "The Lost Son," copyright 1947 Theodore Roethke; "Cuttings (later)," copyright 1948 Theodore Roethke; "Orchids," copyright 1948 Theodore Roethke; "I Cry, Love! Love!," "Praise to the End," and "Where Knock is Open Wide," copyright 1950 Theodore Roethke; "Bring the Day" and "O Lull Me,

Lull Me," copyright 1951 Theodore Roethke; "Frau Bauman, Frau Schmidt, and Frau Schwartze," copyright 1952 Theodore Roethke; "Four for Sir John Davies," copyright 1952 by The Atlantic Monthly Company; "Meditations of an Old Woman" and "Words for the Wind," copyright © 1955 Theodore Roethke; "The Dying Man," copyright © The Atlantic Monthly Company; "Meditation at Oyster River," copyright © 1960 Beatrice Roethke as administratrix of the estate of Theodore Roethke; "The Tree, The Bird," copyright © 1961 Beatrice Roethke as administratrix of the estate of Theodore Roethke; "Wish for a Young Wife" and "Infirmity," copyright © 1963 Beatrice Roethke as administratrix of the estate of Theodore Roethke. All poems appear in the *Collected Poems of Theodore Roethke*. Reprinted by permission of Doubleday & Company, Inc. and Faber and Faber Ltd. "Once More, the Round," by Theodore Roethke, copyright © 1963 Hearst Corporation, by permission of *Harper's Bazaar*. "The Minimal," by Theodore Roethke, copyright 1942 Heart Magazines, Inc., by permission of *Harper's Bazaar*. "Roethke's Last Poems," by Ralph J. Mills, Jr., Poetry, copyright © 1964 The Modern Poetry Association, by permission of *Poetry*.

CARL SANDBURG From *Smoke and Steel*, by Carl Sandburg, "Wistful" and lines from "Pencils," copyright 1920 Harcourt Brace Jovanovich, Inc., copyright 1948 Carl Sandburg, by permission of Harcourt Brace Jovanovich, Inc. from "To a Contemporary Bunkshooter," "Mamie," "The Shovel Man," and *Chicago Poems*, by Carl Sandburg, copyright 1916 Holt, Rinehart and Winston, Inc., copyright 1944 Carl Sandburg, by permission of Harcourt Brace Jovanovich, Inc. from "Prairie," "Handfuls," "Loam," "A Million Young Workmen 1915," and "The Four Brothers," *Cornhuskers*, by Carl Sandburg, copyright 1918 Carl Sandburg, copyright 1946 Holt, Rinehart and Winston, Inc., by permission of Holt, Rinehart and Winston, Inc.

DELMORE SCHWARTZ From *The Last and Lost Poems of Delmore Schwartz*, edited by Robert Phillips, by permission of the publisher, Vanguard Press, Inc. Copyright © 1979 by Kenneth Schwartz. From Delmore Schwartz, *Vaudeville for a Princess*. Copyright 1950 by New Directions. Reprinted by permission of New Directions. From Delmore Schwartz, *Shenandoah*. Copyright 1941 by New Directions. Reprinted by permission of New Directions. From Delmore Schwartz, *Selected Poems: Summer Knowledge*. Copyright 1938 by New Directions. Reprinted by permission of New Directions. Random lines of poetry from "I am Cherry Alive" and "Darkling Summer, Ominous Dusk, Rumorous Rain," copyright © 1958 by Delmore Schwartz, "A Little Morning Music," copyright © 1959 by The New Yorker Magazine, Inc., "Seurat's Sunday Afternoon Along the Seine," copyright © 1959 by Delmore Schwartz, all appear in the *book Summer Knowledge: New and Selected Poems: 1938–1958* by Delmore Schwartz. Reprinted by permission of Doubleday & Company, Inc.

ANNE SEXTON Excerpts from "The Double Image," "Her Kind," "You, Dr. Martin," and "For John . . . " in *To Bedlam and Part Way Back* by Anne Sexton. Copyright © 1960 by Anne Sexton. Excerpts from "The Fortress" in *All My Pretty Ones* by Anne Sexton. Copyright © 1962 by Anne Sexton. Excerpts from "Little Girl, My String Bean, My Lovely Woman," "Live," and "Cripples and Other Stories" in *Live or Die* by Anne Sexton. Copyright © 1966 by Anne Sexton. Excerpts from "The Gold Key," "The White Snake," "Rumpelstiltskin," "Rapunzel," and "Sleeping Beauty" in *Transformations* by Anne Sexton. Copyright © 1971 by Anne Sexton. Excerpts and short phrases from "The Death of the Fathers" in *The Book of Folly* by Anne Sexton. Copyright © 1972 by Anne Sexton. Excerpts from "The Death Baby" and "Rats Live On No Evil Star" in *The Death Notebooks* by Anne Sexton. Copyright © 1974 by Anne Sexton. Excerpts from "Rowing," "The Rowing Endeth," and "Is It True?" in *The Awful Rowing Toward God* by Anne Sexton. Copyright © 1975 by Loring Conant, Jr., Executor of the Estate of Anne Sexton. Excerpt from "Food" in *45 Mercy Street* by Anne Sexton. Copyright © 1976 by Linda Gray Sexton and Loring Conant, Jr. Excerpts from *Anne Sexton: A Self-Portrait in Letters* edited by Linda Gray Sexton and Lois Ames. Copyright © 1977 by Linda Gray Sexton and Loring Conant, Jr., Executors of the Will of Anne Sexton. Reprinted by permission of Houghton Mifflin Company.

STEVIE SMITH "Come, Death," "The Cousin," "From the Greek," "God the Eater," "Heber," "In My Dreams," "Lady 'Rogue' Singleton," "Me Again," "Not Waving But Drowning," "Pad, Pad," "The Songster," "The White Thought," "Why Do I . . . ," and excerpts from "The After Thought," "The Ambassador," "Black March," "Childe Rolandine," "The Company," "Do Take Muriel Out," "The Donkey," "Dream of Nourishment," "Exeat," "Fairy Story," "Forgive Me, Forgive Me," "Freddy," "God and Man," "How Do You See," "Lightly Bound," "Lord Barrenstock," "Magna Est Veritas," "Mrs. Simpkins," "The Orphan Reformed," "Papa Love Baby," "The River God," "Scorpion," "Silence and Tears," "So to Fatness Come," "Up and Down," "Unpopular, Lonely, and Loving," "The Wanderer," and "Was He Married?" from *Collected Poems of Stevie Smith*. Copyright © 1972 by Stevie Smith. Reprinted by permission of New Directions Publishing Corporation, Agents for the Estate of Stevie Smith. Excerpt of 1957 letter to Hans Houserman reprinted by permission of New Directions Publishing Corporation, Agents for the Estate of Stevie Smith.

STEPHEN SPENDER Excerpts from "Air Raid Across the Bay at Plymouth," "Auden's Funeral," "Elegy to Margaret," "The Express," "The Generous Days," "In

1929," "In Railway Halls," "My Parents," "Not Palaces," "One More Botched Beginning," "Perhaps," "The Public Son of a Public Man," "The Pylons," "Rejoice in the Abyss," "The Room above the Square," "Spiritual Exercises," "The Truly Great," "The War God," "What I Believe," "Ultima Ratio Regum," and "The Uncreating Chaos" from *Collected Poems 1928–1985* by Stephen Spender. Copyright 1934, 1940, 1942 and renewed 1961, 1962, 1968, 1970, and 1986 by Stephen Spender. Reprinted by permission of Random House, Inc. and Faber and Faber Ltd.

MARK STRAND Excerpt from *Dark Harbor: A Poem* by Mark Strand. Copyright © 1993 by Mark Strand. Reprinted by permission of Alfred A. Knopf, Inc. Excerpt from *The Continuous Life* by Mark Strand. Copyright © 1990 by Mark Strand. Reprinted by permission of Alfred A. Knopf, Inc. Excerpt from *Darker*, Atheneum, 1980. Excerpt from *Reason for Moving*, Atheneum, 1968. Excerpt from *The Late Hour*, Atheneum, 1978. Except from *The Story of Our Lives*, Atheneum, 1973.

DYLAN THOMAS Excerpts from Dylan Thomas, *The Poems of Dylan Thomas*. Copyright 1938, 1939 by New Directions Publishing Corporation. Copyright 1945 by the Trustees for the Copyrights of Dylan Thomas. Copyright 1952, 1953 by Dylan Thomas. "Poem in October" was first published in *Poetry*. Reprinted by permission of New Directions Publishing Corporation. Also with kind permission of David Higham Associates. Published by J. M. Dent.

RICHARD WILBUR Excerpts from "Advice to a Prophet," "A Hole in the Floor," "Someone Talking to Himself," and "The Undead," in *Advice to a Prophet and Other Poems*, copyright © 1961 and renewed 1989 by Richard Wilbur; excerpts from "The Mind-Reader" in *The Mind-Reader: New Poems*, copyright © 1976 by Richard Wilbur; excerpts from "The Lilacs" in *Walking to Sleep*, copyright © 1963 by Richard Wilbur; excerpts from "On the Marginal Way" in *Walking to Sleep*, copyright © 1956 by Richard Wilbur; reprinted by permission of Harcourt Brace Jovanovich, Inc. and Faber and Faber Ltd. Excerpts from "Beautiful Changes," "First Snow in Alsace," "Mind Country," "Praise in Summer," and "Water Walker" in *The Beautiful Changes and Other Poems*, copyright 1947 and renewed 1975 by Richard Wilbur; excerpts from "Ceremony," "Conjuration," "A Glance from the Bridge," and "Part of a Letter," in *Ceremony and Other Poems*, copyright 1950 and renewed 1978 by Richard Wilbur; excerpts from "Alatus," "All that Is," "Hamlen Brook," "Shad-Time," and "Trolling for Blues" in *New and Collected Poems*, copyright © 1988 by Richard Wilbur; excerpts from "A Baroque Wall-fountain in the Villa Sciarra" in *Things of This World*, copyright 1955 and renewed 1983 by Richard Wilbur; excerpts from "An Event" and "Love Calls Us to the Things of This World" in *Things of This World*, copyright © 1956 and renewed 1984 by Richard Wilbur. Reprinted by permission of Harcourt Brace Jovanovich, Inc.

Original Publication Information

The essays in these volumes were originally published in other Scribner reference works, as indicated below. The articles drawn from *British Writers* Volumes 1–7 and Supplement I were edited by Ian Scott-Kilvert and were originally published in the British Council's pamphlet series. The articles drawn from *American Writers* Volumes 1–4 were originally published in the University of Minnesota Press's pamphlet series. They were edited for publication by Scribners by Leonard Unger, who also edited the original articles, specially commissioned by Scribners, in Supplement I. *American Writers* Supplements II, III, IV, and Retrospective Supplement I were edited by A. Walton Litz. *Modern American Women Writers* was edited by Elaine Showalter. *African American Writers* was edited by Valerie Smith, and *European Writers: The Middle Ages and the Renaissance* was edited by William T. H. Jackson.

POET	SOURCE
Arnold, Matthew	British Writers, Volume 5
Ashbery, John	American Writers, Supplement III, Part 1
Auden, W. H.	British Writers, Volume 7
Beowulf and Anglo-Saxon Poetry	European Writers: The Middle Ages and the Renaissance, Volume 1
Berryman, John	American Writers, Volume 1
Bishop, Elizabeth	American Writers, Supplement I, Part 1
Blake, William	British Writers, Volume 3
Browning, Elizabeth Barrett	British Writers, Volume 4
Browning, Robert	British Writers, Volume 4
Bryant, William Cullen	American Writers, Supplement I, Part 1
Burns, Robert	British Writers, Volume 3
Byron, Lord	British Writers, Volume 4
Cavalier Poets	British Writers, Volume 2
Chaucer, Geoffrey	British Writers, Volume 1
Coleridge, Samuel Taylor	British Writers, Volume 4
Cummings, E. E.	American Writers, Volume 1
Dickinson, Emily	Modern American Women Writers
Donne, John	British Writers, Volume 1
Eliot, T. S.	British Writers, Volume 7
Frost, Robert	American Writers, Retrospective Supplement
Ginsberg, Allen	American Writers, Supplement II, Part 1
Gray, Thomas	British Writers, Volume 3
Heaney, Seamus	British Writers, Supplement II
Hopkins, Gerard Manley	British Writers, Volume 5
Housman, A. E.	British Writers, Volume 6
Hughes, Langston	African American Writers
Hughes, Ted	British Writers, Supplement I

ORIGINAL PUBLICATION INFORMATION

POET	SOURCE
Jarrell, Randall	American Writers, Volume 2
Jeffers, Robinson	American Writers, Supplement II, Part 2
Keats, John	British Writers, Volume 4
Kinnell, Galway	American Writers, Supplement III, Part 1
Kumin, Maxine	American Writers, Supplement IV, Part 2
Levertov, Denise	American Writers, Supplement III, Part 1
Longfellow, Henry Wadsworth	American Writers, Volume 2
Lowell, Robert	American Writers, Volume 2
McKay, Claude	African American Writers
MacLeish, Archibald	American Writers, Volume 3
Merrill, James	American Writers, Supplement III, Part 1
Merwin, W. S.	American Writers, Supplement III, Part 1
Metaphysical Poets	British Writers, Volume 2
Millay, Edna St. Vincent	Modern American Women Writers
Milton, John	British Writers, Volume 2
Moore, Marianne	Modern American Women Writers
Plath, Sylvia	Modern American Women Writers
Poe, Edgar Allan	American Writers, Volume 3
Poets of World War I	British Writers, Volume 6
Poets of World War II	British Writers, Volume 7
Pope, Alexander	British Writers, Volume 3
Pound, Ezra	American Writers, Volume 3
Restoration Court Poets	British Writers, Volume 2
Rich, Adrienne	Modern American Women Writers
Robinson, Edward Arlington	American Writers, Volume 3
Roethke, Theodore	American Writers, Volume 3
Sandburg, Carl	American Writers, Volume 3
Schwartz, Delmore	American Writers, Supplement II, Part 2
Sexton, Anne	Modern American Women Writers
Shakespeare, William	British Writers, Volume 1
Shelley, Percy Bysshe	British Writers, Volume 4
Sidney, Sir Philip	British Writers, Volume 1
Smith, Stevie	British Writers, Supplement II
Spender, Stephen	British Writers, Supplement II
Spenser, Edmund	British Writers, Volume 1
Stevens, Wallace	American Writers, Volume 4
Strand, Mark	American Writers, Supplement IV, Part 2
Swinburne, Algernon Charles	British Writers, Volume 5
Tennyson, Alfred Lord	British Writers, Volume 4
Thomas, Dylan	British Writers, Supplement I
Whitman, Walt	American Writers, Retrospective Supplement
Wilbur, Richard	American Writers, Supplement III, Part 2
Williams, William Carlos	American Writers, Volume 4
Wordsworth, William	British Writers, Volume 4
Yeats, William Butler	British Writers, Volume 6

Index

Page numbers in **boldface** refer to the main entry on a subject.

B

C

D

INDEX

H

O

P

Q

INDEX

INDEX

U

V